W9-BVF-774

CANADIAN EDITION

ORGANIZATIONAL THEORY, DESIGN, AND CHANGE

GARETH R. JONES
Texas A&M University

ALBERT J. MILLS
Saint Mary's University

TERRANCE G. WEATHERBEE
Acadia University

JEAN HELMS MILLS
Saint Mary's University

Toronto

Library and Archives Canada Cataloguing in Publication

Organizational theory, design, and change / Gareth R. Jones ... [et al.]. — Canadian ed.

Includes index.
ISBN 0-13-124522-8

1. Organizational behaviour—Textbooks. 2. Organizational behaviour—Case studies. I. Jones, Gareth R.
HD58.7.O74 2005 302.3'5 C2005-903083-6

ISBN 0-13-124522-8

Vice-President, Editorial Director: Michael J. Young
Acquisitions Editor: Karen Elliott
Executive Marketing Manager: Cas Shields
Developmental Editor: Paul Donnelly
Production Editor: Cheryl Jackson
Copy Editor: Valerie Adams
Proofreader: Ron Jacques
Production Coordinator: Patricia Ciardullo
Page Layout: Carolyn E. Sebestyen
Cover and Interior Design: Michelle Bellemare
Cover Image: Getty Images/Phil Boorman

1 2 3 4 5 10 09 08 07 06

Printed and bound in Canada

For Nicholas and Julia *(GRJ)*

For the Sobey PhD Class of 2000
who influenced the culture of the programme *(AJM)*

For Marion, Riley, and Corwin—
your patience, my possibilities *(TGW)*

For Christopher Helms *(JHM)*

Brief Contents

PART I THE ORGANIZATION AND ITS ENVIRONMENT 1

CHAPTER 1 Organizations and Organizational Effectiveness 1

CHAPTER 2 Organizational Stakeholders, Management, and Ethics 34

CHAPTER 3 Managing in a Changing Global Environment 68

PART II ORGANIZATIONAL DESIGN 106

CHAPTER 4 Basic Challenges of Organizational Design 106

CHAPTER 5 Designing Organizational Structure: Coordination, Communication, and Control 143

CHAPTER 6 Designing Organizational Structure: Specialization and Coordination 176

CHAPTER 7 Creating and Managing Organizational Culture 213

CHAPTER 8 Organizational Design and Strategy in a Changing Global Environment 252

CHAPTER 9 Organizational Design, Competencies, and Technology 291

PART III ORGANIZATIONAL CHANGE 330

CHAPTER 10 Types and Forms of Organizational Change 330

CHAPTER 11 Organizational Transformations: Birth, Growth, Decline, and Death 372

CHAPTER 12 Decision Making, Learning, Knowledge Management, and Information Technology 407

CHAPTER 13 Innovation, Intrapreneurship, and Creativity 446

CHAPTER 14 Managing Conflict, Power, and Politics 478

CASE STUDIES 512

COMPANY INDEX 583

NAME INDEX 587

SUBJECT INDEX 589

Contents

PART I THE ORGANIZATION AND ITS ENVIRONMENT 1

Chapter 1 Organizations and Organizational Effectiveness 1

What Is an Organization? 1

How Does an Organization Create Value? 3

FOCUS ON NEW INFORMATION TECHNOLOGY
Amazon.com, Part 1 3

Why Do Organizations Exist? 6

Organizational Theory, Design, and Change 8

Organizational Structure 8

Organizational Culture 9

Organizational Design and Change 10

ORGANIZATIONAL INSIGHT 1.1
Political Change and Organizational Functions 11

ORGANIZATIONAL INSIGHT 1.2
Structure and Culture Changes at Ontario Power Generation 12

ORGANIZATIONAL INSIGHT 1.3
Opposite Organizing Approaches at Apple and Dell Computer 13

The Importance of Organizational Design and Change 15

The Consequences of Poor Organizational Design 17

ORGANIZATIONAL INSIGHT 1.4
Redesigning AOL–Time Warner 18

How Do Managers Measure Organizational Effectiveness? 19

The External Resource Approach: Control 20

The Internal Systems Approach: Innovation 20

ORGANIZATIONAL INSIGHT 1.5
Burntsand's Innovative Ways of Increasing Efficiency for Its Clients 21

The Technical Approach: Efficiency 21

ORGANIZATIONAL INSIGHT 1.6
Burntsand Expands and Then Retracts in the Name of Efficiency 22

Measuring Effectiveness: Organizational Goals 22

The Plan of This Book 24

Organizational Design 26

Organizational Change 26

SUMMARY 27

DISCUSSION QUESTIONS 28

ORGANIZATIONAL THEORY IN ACTION 28

CASE FOR ANALYSIS 31

REFERENCES 32

Chapter 2 Organizational Stakeholders, Management, and Ethics 34

Organizational Stakeholders 34
Inside Stakeholders 35
ORGANIZATIONAL INSIGHT 2.1
The Increasing Power of Institutional Investors 36
Outside Stakeholders 37
ORGANIZATIONAL INSIGHT 2.2
The Canadian Broadcasting Corporation and Its Customers 38

Organizational Effectiveness: Satisfying Stakeholders' Goals and Interests 41
Competing Goals 42
Allocating Rewards 43

Senior Management and Organizational Authority 44
The Chief Executive Officer 46
The Top-Management Team 47
Other Managers 48

An Agency Theory Perspective 48
The Moral Hazard Problem 48
Solving the Agency Problem 49

Managers, Employees, and Organizational Ethics 50
Sources of Organizational Ethics 52
ORGANIZATIONAL INSIGHT 2.3
The Use of Animals in Cosmetics Testing 53
ORGANIZATIONAL INSIGHT 2.4
Is It Right to Use Child Labour? 54
Why Do Ethical Rules Develop? 55
Why Does Unethical Behaviour Occur? 57
ORGANIZATIONAL INSIGHT 2.5
Conflicting Interests in Health Care 57

Creating an Ethical Organization 59
Designing an Ethical Structure and Control System 60
Creating an Ethical Culture 60
Supporting the Interests of Stakeholder Groups 61
SUMMARY 61
DISCUSSION QUESTIONS 62
ORGANIZATIONAL THEORY IN ACTION 62
CASE FOR ANALYSIS 64
REFERENCES 66

Chapter 3 Managing in a Changing Global Environment 68

What Is the Organizational Environment? 68
The Specific Environment 70
The General Environment 72

ORGANIZATIONAL INSIGHT 3.1
The Royal Bank of Canada: A Global Misstep 73

Sources of Uncertainty in the Organizational Environment 74

ORGANIZATIONAL INSIGHT 3.2
GE's Managers Stumble in Hungary 75

MANAGERIAL IMPLICATIONS
Analyzing the Environment 77

FOCUS ON NEW INFORMATION TECHNOLOGY
Amazon.com, Part 2 78

Resource Dependence Theory 78

Interorganizational Strategies for Managing Resource Dependencies 79

ORGANIZATIONAL INSIGHT 3.3
Mighty Microsoft 80

Strategies for Managing Symbiotic Resource Interdependencies 81

Developing a Good Reputation 81

Co-optation 82

Strategic Alliances 83

Long-Term Contracts 83

ORGANIZATIONAL INSIGHT 3.4
Ballard Power Systems: Navigating the Future 84

Merger and Takeover 88

Strategies for Managing Competitive Resource Interdependencies 88

Collusion and Cartels 88

Third-Party Linkage Mechanisms 89

Strategic Alliances 90

Merger and Takeover 90

MANAGERIAL IMPLICATIONS
Resource Dependence Theory 91

Transaction Cost Theory 92

Sources of Transaction Costs 92

Transaction Costs and Linkage Mechanisms 93

Bureaucratic Costs 94

Using Transaction Cost Theory to Choose an Interorganizational Strategy 95

ORGANIZATIONAL INSIGHT 3.5
A Web of Linkages at Magna 95

ORGANIZATIONAL INSIGHT 3.6
Li & Fung's Global Supply Chain Management 98

SUMMARY 99
DISCUSSION QUESTIONS 99
ORGANIZATIONAL THEORY IN ACTION 100
CASE FOR ANALYSIS 102
REFERENCES 103

PART II ORGANIZATIONAL DESIGN 106

Chapter 4 Basic Challenges of Organizational Design 106

Differentiation 106

ORGANIZATIONAL INSIGHT 4.1
B.A.R. and Grille Restaurant 107

Organizational Roles 108

Subunits: Functions and Divisions 110

Differentiation at the B.A.R. and Grille 111

Vertical and Horizontal Differentiation 112

Organizational Design Challenges 113

MANAGERIAL IMPLICATIONS
Differentiation 114

Balancing Differentiation and Integration 114

Integration and Integrating Mechanisms 115

ORGANIZATIONAL INSIGHT 4.2
Magna International: Structuring with Teams 118

Differentiation versus Integration 119

Balancing Centralization and Decentralization 120

Centralization versus Decentralization of Authority 120

ORGANIZATIONAL INSIGHT 4.3
Centralize or Decentralize: Adopting a Customer-Centric Approach to Structure at Nortel 122

Balancing Standardization and Mutual Adjustment 123

Formalization: Written Rules 124

Socialization: Understood Norms 124

Standardization versus Mutual Adjustment 125

FOCUS ON NEW INFORMATION TECHNOLOGY
Amazon.com, Part 3 126

MANAGERIAL IMPLICATIONS
The Design Challenges 127

Mechanistic and Organic Organizational Structures 127

Mechanistic Structures 127

Organic Structures 128

ORGANIZATIONAL INSIGHT 4.4
Sony's Magic Touch 129

The Contingency Approach to Organizational Design 130

Lawrence and Lorsch on Differentiation, Integration, and the Environment 131

Burns and Stalker on Organic versus Mechanistic Structures and the Environment 133

ORGANIZATIONAL INSIGHT 4.5
McDonald's Changing Environment 134

ORGANIZATIONAL INSIGHT 4.6
Wal-Mart's Race to the Top 135

SUMMARY 136
DISCUSSION QUESTIONS 137
ORGANIZATIONAL THEORY IN ACTION 137
CASE FOR ANALYSIS 139
REFERENCES 141

Chapter 5 Designing Organizational Structure: Coordination, Communication, and Control 143

Authority: How and Why Vertical Differentiation Occurs 143
The Emergence of the Hierarchy 144
Size and Height Limitations 144
Problems with Tall Hierarchies 147

ORGANIZATIONAL INSIGHT 5.1
A Flat Organizational Structure at Eagle Builds Trust 148

The Parkinson's Law Problem 149
The Ideal Number of Hierarchical Levels: The Minimum Chain of Command 149
Span of Control 150

ORGANIZATIONAL INSIGHT 5.2
Using the Hierarchy to Promote Creativity at EMI 151

Control: Factors Affecting the Shape of the Hierarchy 153
Horizontal Differentiation 153
Centralization 155

ORGANIZATIONAL INSIGHT 5.3
Union Pacific Decentralizes 156

Standardization 157

MANAGERIAL IMPLICATIONS
Authority and Control 157

The Principles of Bureaucracy 158

ORGANIZATIONAL INSIGHT 5.4
Never Underestimate the Power of Rules 162

The Advantages of Bureaucracy 163
Management by Objectives 164

The Influence of the Informal Organization 165

ORGANIZATIONAL INSIGHT 5.5
Wildcat Strikes in the Gypsum Plant 166

MANAGERIAL IMPLICATIONS
Using Bureaucracy to Benefit the Organization 167

IT, Empowerment, and Self-Managed Teams 167
SUMMARY 169
DISCUSSION QUESTIONS 170
ORGANIZATIONAL THEORY IN ACTION 170
CASE FOR ANALYSIS 172
REFERENCES 173

Chapter 6 Designing Organizational Structure: Specialization and Coordination 176

Functional Structure 176

FOCUS ON NEW INFORMATION TECHNOLOGY
Amazon.com, Part 4 178

Advantages of a Functional Structure 178

Control Problems in a Functional Structure 179

Solving Control Problems with a Functional Structure 180

From Functional Structure to Divisional Structure 180

MANAGERIAL IMPLICATIONS
Functional Structure 181

Moving to a Divisional Structure 183

Divisional Structure I: Three Kinds of Product Structure 183

Product Division Structure 184

Multidivisional Structure 185

ORGANIZATIONAL INSIGHT 6.1
Creating GM's Multidivisional Structure 188

ORGANIZATIONAL INSIGHT 6.2
Centralizing BMO's IT for Efficiency and Effectiveness 190

ORGANIZATIONAL INSIGHT 6.3
Iacocca Pioneers Chrysler's Team Structure 195

Divisional Structure II: Geographic Structure 196

Divisional Structure III: Market Structure 197

ORGANIZATIONAL INSIGHT 6.4
Wal-Mart Goes National, Then Global 198

People and Changing Structures 198

ORGANIZATIONAL INSIGHT 6.5
Re-engineering the Market at Nova Scotia Power 199

MANAGERIAL IMPLICATIONS
Changing Organizational Structure 200

Matrix Structure 201

Advantages of a Matrix Structure 201

Disadvantages of a Matrix Structure 203

The Multidivisional Matrix Structure 204

Network Structure and the Boundaryless Organization 205

Advantages of Network Structures 205

Disadvantages of Network Structures 206

The Boundaryless Organization 207

SUMMARY 207

DISCUSSION QUESTIONS 208

ORGANIZATIONAL THEORY IN ACTION 208

CASE FOR ANALYSIS 210

REFERENCES 211

Chapter 7 Creating and Managing Organizational Culture 213

What Is Organizational Culture? 213

ORGANIZATIONAL INSIGHT 7.1
How Global Culture Affects Organizational Culture 216

ORGANIZATIONAL INSIGHT 7.2
Mergers and Cultures 218

How Is an Organization's Culture Transmitted to Its Members? 220

Socialization and Socialization Tactics 220

Stories, Ceremonies, and Organizational Language 223

ORGANIZATIONAL INSIGHT 7.3
Creating and Managing Organizational Culture at Superior Propane 224

ORGANIZATIONAL INSIGHT 7.4
siteROCK's Military Management Culture 226

MANAGERIAL IMPLICATIONS
Analyzing Organizational Culture 227

Where Does Organizational Culture Come From? 227

Characteristics of People Within the Organization 227

ORGANIZATIONAL INSIGHT 7.5
Procter & Gamble's Culture Is Hard to Change 229

Organizational Ethics 230

ORGANIZATIONAL INSIGHT 7.6
Suncor's President Instrumental in Creating an Ethical "Green Culture" 232

Property Rights 233

ORGANIZATIONAL INSIGHT 7.7
A Clash of Two Cultures 234

ORGANIZATIONAL INSIGHT 7.8
Bimba Changes Its Property Rights System 236

Organizational Structure 238

Can Organizational Culture Be Managed? 239

MANAGERIAL IMPLICATIONS
Designing Organizational Culture 240

Social Responsibility 241

Approaches to Social Responsibility 241

Why Be Socially Responsible? 242

ORGANIZATIONAL INSIGHT 7.9
Social Responsibility Evident at Husky Injection Molding Systems Ltd. 243

SUMMARY 244

DISCUSSION QUESTIONS 245

ORGANIZATIONAL THEORY IN ACTION 245

CASE FOR ANALYSIS 247

REFERENCES 248

Chapter 8 Organizational Design and Strategy in a Changing Global Environment 252

Strategy and the Environment 252
Sources of Core Competencies 253
Global Expansion and Core Competencies 255
Four Levels of Strategy 256

Functional-Level Strategy 258
Strategies to Lower Costs or Differentiate Products 258
Functional-Level Strategy and Structure 260
Functional-Level Strategy and Culture 262

MANAGERIAL IMPLICATIONS
Functional-Level Strategy 263

Business-Level Strategy 264
Strategies to Lower Costs or Differentiate Products 264
Focus Strategy 265
Business-Level Strategy and Structure 265

FOCUS ON NEW INFORMATION TECHNOLOGY
Amazon.com, Part 5 266

Business-Level Strategy and Culture 269

ORGANIZATIONAL INSIGHT 8.1
Bombardier Restructures 270

ORGANIZATIONAL INSIGHT 8.2
How Culture Derailed the Merger Between AHP and Monsanto 271

MANAGERIAL IMPLICATIONS
Business-Level Strategy 272

Corporate-Level Strategy 272
Vertical Integration 272
Related Diversification 274
Unrelated Diversification 274
Corporate-Level Strategy and Structure 275

ORGANIZATIONAL INSIGHT 8.3
Hitachi Ltd. 277

Corporate-Level Strategy and Culture 277

MANAGERIAL IMPLICATIONS
Corporate-Level Strategy 279

Implementing Strategy Across Countries 279
Implementing a Multidomestic Strategy 280
Implementing International Strategy 282
Implementing Global Strategy 283
Implementing Transnational Strategy 283

SUMMARY 285
DISCUSSION QUESTIONS 285
ORGANIZATIONAL THEORY IN ACTION 286
CASE FOR ANALYSIS 288
REFERENCES 289

Chapter 9 Organizational Design, Competencies, and Technology 291

What Is Technology? 291

ORGANIZATIONAL INSIGHT 9.1
Progressive Manufacture at Ford 292

Technology and Organizational Effectiveness 294

Technical Complexity: The Theory of Joan Woodward 295

ORGANIZATIONAL INSIGHT 9.2
Evolving with Technology at EllisDon Construction 296

Small-Batch and Unit Technology 297
Large-Batch and Mass-Production Technology 298
Continuous-Process Technology 299
Technical Complexity and Organizational Structure 300
The Technological Imperative 302

Routine Tasks and Complex Tasks: The Theory of Charles Perrow 303
Task Variability and Task Analyzability 303
Four Types of Technology 304
Routine Technology and Organizational Structure 306
Nonroutine Technology and Organizational Structure 307

Task Interdependence: The Theory of James D. Thompson 308
Mediating Technology and Pooled Interdependence 309
Long-Linked Technology and Sequential Interdependence 310
Intensive Technology and Reciprocal Interdependence 312

ORGANIZATIONAL INSIGHT 9.3
Scheduling Effectiveness with AD OPT Technology 312

ORGANIZATIONAL INSIGHT 9.4
A New Approach at Hewlett-Packard 314

MANAGERIAL IMPLICATIONS
Analyzing Technology 315

From Mass Production to Advanced Manufacturing Technology 315

Advanced Manufacturing Technology: Innovations in Materials Technology 318
Computer-Aided Design 318
Computer-Aided Materials Management 319
Just-in-Time Inventory Systems 319
Flexible Manufacturing Technology and Computer-Integrated Manufacturing 321

ORGANIZATIONAL INSIGHT 9.5
Motorola's Factory of the Future 322

SUMMARY 323
DISCUSSION QUESTIONS 324
ORGANIZATIONAL THEORY IN ACTION 324
CASE FOR ANALYSIS 327
REFERENCES 328

PART III ORGANIZATIONAL CHANGE 330

Chapter 10 Types and Forms of Organizational Change 330

What Is Organizational Change? 330

Targets of Change 331

Forces for and Resistance to Organizational Change 332

Forces for Change 333

Resistances to Change 334

ORGANIZATIONAL INSIGHT 10.1
Nike, Reebok, Adidas, and the Sweatshops 335

Organization-Level Resistance to Change 335

Group-Level Resistance to Change 336

ORGANIZATIONAL INSIGHT 10.2
Genocide in Rwanda: A Monumental Failure of Organization 337

Individual-Level Resistance to Change 337

Lewin's Force-Field Theory of Change 338

MANAGERIAL IMPLICATIONS
Forces for and Resistances to Change 339

Evolutionary and Revolutionary Change in Organizations 339

Developments in Evolutionary Change 340

Sociotechnical Systems Theory 340

Total Quality Management 341

ORGANIZATIONAL INSIGHT 10.3
Citibank Uses TQM to Increase Customer Loyalty 342

ORGANIZATIONAL INSIGHT 10.4
The Total Quality Management of Ontario Hospitals 343

Flexible Workers and Flexible Work Teams 344

ORGANIZATIONAL INSIGHT 10.5
Flexible Work Teams at Globe 346

Developments in Revolutionary Change 346

Re-engineering 346

ORGANIZATIONAL INSIGHT 10.6
GM and Toyota Give Plant a New Lease on Life 347

ORGANIZATIONAL INSIGHT 10.7
How to Stay on Top in the Greeting Card Business 350

Restructuring 351

Innovation 352

ORGANIZATIONAL INSIGHT 10.8
Organizational Changes at Stelco 353

Managing Change: Action Research 353

Diagnosing the Organization 354

Determining the Desired Future State 355

Implementing Action 355

Evaluating the Action 357

Institutionalizing Action Research 357

MANAGERIAL IMPLICATIONS
Designing a Plan for Change 358

Organizational Development 358

OD Techniques to Deal with Resistance to Change 359

ORGANIZATIONAL INSIGHT 10.9
Competitive Advantage: Achieving Change Through Empowering Work Groups 360

OD Techniques to Promote Change 361

Making Sense of Organizational Change 364

SUMMARY 364
DISCUSSION QUESTIONS 365
ORGANIZATIONAL THEORY IN ACTION 365
CASE FOR ANALYSIS 367
REFERENCES 368

Chapter 11 Organizational Transformations: Birth, Growth, Decline, and Death 372

The Organizational Life Cycle 372

Organizational Birth 373

Developing a Plan for a New Business 374

A Population Ecology Model of Organizational Birth 376

ORGANIZATIONAL INSIGHT 11.1
The Rise and Fall of Salter Street Films 377

Number of Births 378
Survival Strategies 379
The Process of Natural Selection 380

The Institutional Theory of Organizational Growth 382

ORGANIZATIONAL INSIGHT 11.2
The YMCA's Response to Global Changes 383

FOCUS ON NEW INFORMATION TECHNOLOGY
Amazon.com, Part 6 384

Organizational Isomorphism 385
Disadvantages of Isomorphism 386

Greiner's Model of Organizational Growth 386

Stage 1: Growth Through Creativity 387
Stage 2: Growth Through Direction 388
Stage 3: Growth Through Delegation 389

ORGANIZATIONAL INSIGHT 11.3
The Membertou First Nation: Regenerating a Community through Corporatization 390

Stage 4: Growth Through Coordination 391
Stage 5: Growth Through Collaboration 392

MANAGERIAL IMPLICATIONS
Organizational Birth and Growth 392

Organizational Decline and Death 393

Organizational Inertia 393

Changes in the Environment 395
Weitzel and Jonsson's Model of Organizational Decline 396
ORGANIZATIONAL INSIGHT 11.4
General Dynamics Goes from Weakness to Strength 397
MANAGERIAL IMPLICATIONS
Organizational Decline 399
SUMMARY 399
DISCUSSION QUESTIONS 400
ORGANIZATIONAL THEORY IN ACTION 401
CASE FOR ANALYSIS 402
REFERENCES 403

Chapter 12 Decision Making, Learning, Knowledge Management, and Information Technology 407

Organizational Decision Making 407

Models of Organizational Decision Making 408
The Rational Model 409
The Carnegie Model 410
The Incrementalist Model 412
The Unstructured Model 412
ORGANIZATIONAL INSIGHT 12.1
Should GE Make or Buy Washing Machines? 413
The Garbage Can Model 414

The Nature of Organizational Learning 415
ORGANIZATIONAL INSIGHT 12.2
Microsoft Is Not All-Seeing After All 416
Types of Organizational Learning 417
Levels of Organizational Learning 417

Knowledge Management and Information Technology 421
ORGANIZATIONAL INSIGHT 12.3
Developing Knowledge Management Capability at Telus 422

Factors Affecting Organizational Learning 424
Organizational Learning and Cognitive Structures 425
Types of Cognitive Biases 425
Cognitive Dissonance 426
Illusion of Control 426
Frequency and Representativeness 427
Projection and Ego-Defensiveness 428
Escalation of Commitment 428
ORGANIZATIONAL INSIGHT 12.4
Mistakes and More Mistakes at the E-grocers 429

Improving Decision Making and Learning 430
Strategies for Organizational Learning 431
Utilizing Game Theory 432
Nature of the Top-Management Team 434

Devil's Advocacy and Dialectical Inquiry 435
Collateral Organizational Structure 436

MANAGERIAL IMPLICATIONS
Decision Making and Learning 437

SUMMARY 437
DISCUSSION QUESTIONS 438
ORGANIZATIONAL THEORY IN ACTION 438
CASE FOR ANALYSIS 441
REFERENCES 443

Chapter 13 Innovation, Intrapreneurship, and Creativity 446

Innovation and Technological Change 446
The Product Life Cycle 449

ORGANIZATIONAL INSIGHT 13.1
Innovation at The Gap 451

Innovation, Intrapreneurship, and Creativity 451

ORGANIZATIONAL INSIGHT 13.2
The WestJet Experience 452

ORGANIZATIONAL INSIGHT 13.3
Running Room 453

Managing the Innovation Process 455

Project Management 455
Stage-Gate Development Funnel 458
Using Cross-Functional Teams and a Product Team Structure 459
Team Leadership 461

ORGANIZATIONAL INSIGHT 13.4
Championing the Mustang 462

Skunk Works and New Venture Divisions 462
Joint Ventures 463

ORGANIZATIONAL INSIGHT 13.5
Too Much Innovation at Lucent 464

ORGANIZATIONAL INSIGHT 13.6
Tembec's "Company of People" Joining with Others in Successful Ventures 465

Creating a Culture for Innovation 465

ORGANIZATIONAL INSIGHT 13.7
Innovation at Mountain Equipment Co-operative 467

MANAGERIAL IMPLICATIONS
Innovation 469

Innovation and Information Technology 469
Innovation and Information Synergies 470
IT and Organizational Structure and Culture 471

FOCUS ON NEW INFORMATION TECHNOLOGY
Amazon.com, Part 7 471

SUMMARY 472
DISCUSSION QUESTIONS 473

ORGANIZATIONAL THEORY IN ACTION 473
CASE FOR ANALYSIS 475
REFERENCES 476

Chapter 14 Managing Conflict, Power, and Politics 478

What Is Organizational Conflict? 478

Pondy's Model of Organizational Conflict 481
Stage 1: Latent Conflict 482

ORGANIZATIONAL INSIGHT 14.1
Conflict Causes Slow Change at Kodak 483

ORGANIZATIONAL INSIGHT 14.2
Conflict Closes up Shop at Shermag Plant but Resolution Brings New Hope 484

ORGANIZATIONAL INSIGHT 14.3
How Rewards Produced Conflict at CS First Boston 485

Stage 2: Perceived Conflict 486
Stage 3: Felt Conflict 486
Stage 4: Manifest Conflict 487
Stage 5: Conflict Aftermath 487

ORGANIZATIONAL INSIGHT 14.4
The Trouble with Hollinger International 488

Managing Conflict: Conflict Resolution Strategies 488
Acting at the Level of Structure 489
Acting at the Level of Attitudes and Individuals 490

MANAGERIAL IMPLICATIONS
Conflict 491

What Is Organizational Power? 491

Sources of Organizational Power 492
Authority 492
Control over Resources 494
Control over Information 495
Nonsubstitutability 496
Centrality 496
Control over Uncertainty 496
Unobtrusive Power: Controlling the Premises of Decision Making 497
Knowledge and Discourse 497

Using Power: Organizational Politics 497
Tactics for Playing Politics 498

ORGANIZATIONAL INSIGHT 14.5
Power Struggles and Corporate Greed at WorldCom 500

ORGANIZATIONAL INSIGHT 14.6
Those in Power at Nortel Bring on Serious Troubles for Powerless Employees 501

Bringing in an Outside Expert 502
The Costs and Benefits of Organizational Politics 502

MANAGERIAL IMPLICATIONS
Power and Politics 504

SUMMARY 504
DISCUSSION QUESTIONS 505
ORGANIZATIONAL THEORY IN ACTION 506
CASE FOR ANALYSIS 508
REFERENCES 509

CASE STUDIES 512

Case 1: The Problem and "I": Some Reflections on Problems, Perception, Action, and Wisdom 512

Case 2: Groupe Noel 520

Case 3: Norton's Department Stores 522

Case 4: Southam Newspaper Group: Equalizing Employment Equity 529

Case 5: Lightco: The Case of the Serial Changers 539

Case 6: The Westray Mine Explosion 544

Case 7: Three Roads to Innovation 553

Case 8: Southwest Airlines 556

Case 9: Philips NV 561

Case 10: "Ramrod" Stockwell 564

Case 11: Rondell Data Corporation 567

Case 12: Oliver Davis's Entrepreneurial Success Story: No Lost Clients, No Employee Terminations, No Debt 576

COMPANY INDEX 583

NAME INDEX 587

SUBJECT INDEX 589

Preface

This Canadian edition of *Organizational Theory, Design, and Change* has retained the basic structure of the current U.S. edition. In particular we have retained and strengthened the focus on business ethics that was introduced in the wake of high-profile business scandals involving Enron, Tyco, WorldCom, and Arthur Andersen. All of these scandals had a profound effect on the Canadian business environment. Arthur Andersen LLP (Canada), for example, stopped practising public accounting in June of 2002, and most of the partners and staff joined Deloitte & Touche LLP. To ensure that Canadian capital markets are safer for investors, the federal government moved to tighten up regulations and established integrated market enforcement teams—consisting of RCMP corporate crime officers and provincial securities regulators—to monitor the business environment and bring to justice serious capital market fraud. We have continued to deal with business ethics as an important issue that runs through every major area of organizational theory. Thus, we include a section on ethics ("The Ethical Dimension") in each chapter so that students can consider ethical decisions in context.

We have also added two new related sections that encourage students to review the operations of selected companies ("Company Profiles") and to consider alternative ways of viewing organizations ("Alternative Perspectives"). The Company Profiles section encourages students to revisit companies that we have highlighted and compare current performance to that at the time of publication. This is to make students aware of the changing environment in which companies operate and the changing context in which decisions are made. In the process, students can examine how top managers maintain an ethical business stance in the face of changing socioeconomic demands. Ethical concerns are also strengthened in the Alternative Perspectives section where students are encouraged to weigh business decisions against the needs and concerns of employees, local communities, and the broader social interest.

The other new changes to the Canadian edition are the inclusion of over 40 new Organizational Insights of Canadian organizations. Many of these insights replace previous U.S. Organizational Insights. However, in keeping with the Canadian perspective in a North American context, we have included a strong balance of U.S.- and Canadian-owned or -based companies as insights and as exemplars throughout the chapters. We have also included a balanced number of Canadian cases and a new section of exercises. Canadian insights, cases, and examples have been chosen to reflect local and regional realities and include a number of small companies, French-Canadian and Quebec-based organizations, not-for-profit organizations, large and small family firms, and government agencies. The end-of-text Canadian cases also reflect the new focus on alternative perspectives.

ORGANIZATION OF THE CANADIAN EDITION

The Canadian edition closely follows the structure of its predecessor, the U.S. fourth edition, and provides greater focus on what an organization is, which stakeholders it serves, and how an organization is constructed to satisfy stakeholder needs—that is, the design of its organizational structure.

In Part II of the book we lay out the central design challenges facing an organization if it is to successfully create value for its stakeholders and achieve a competitive advantage that will allow it to thrive. This is followed by a discussion of the way contingency factors affect organizational design; the challenges organizations face in designing their organizational structures to improve their effectiveness is the focus of this analysis. By the end of Part II students will have a clear account of the main components of organizational structure and culture. The way in which the environment affects organizations, and the way organizations can manage the environment through their strategies and structures are clearly outlined. Parts I and II demonstrate the lessons of organizational design and what happens to organizations that do not get it right.

Part III presents much expanded coverage on the issue of organizational change processes. Our intent has been to show the many types and forms of change, and the many issues and problems that surround change. While each chapter contains additional material on change, it also allows the instructor to take the analysis of change in any way he or she chooses. For example, Chapter 10 describes six types of revolutionary and evolutionary change, and has a section on organizational development and action research. Chapter 10 provides a platform for a take-off into a module on restructuring and re-engineering. Chapter 11 on the organizational life cycle contains new material on the entrepreneurial task of developing a business plan, and the instructor could choose to make this an important learning theme for the student by way of an ongoing project. Chapter 12 contains new material on information technology, knowledge management, and game theory. The instructor could make the development of competency-enhancing skills through IT a major course theme. Chapter 13 contains new material on promoting creativity and intrapreneurship, also by the use of advanced information technologies. It also contains new material on project management that could provide a springboard for the instructor who wishes, for example, to incorporate Microsoft's planning software into the course and to make project management a major theme. Finally, Chapter 14 completes this analysis of organizational processes by examining the interrelated issues of conflict, power, and politics. The way in which these processes affect organizational change and development is a major focus of this final chapter.

COVERAGE OF SPECIAL IMPORTANCE

- Detailed coverage of the stakeholder approach to organizations and the implications of this approach for organizational effectiveness.
- Explanations of the most recent developments in organizational structure, such as the product team structure, outsourcing, and network organizations.
- An in-depth look at organizational culture that accounts for the origins of culture and its relationship to organizational effectiveness.
- Discussion of the recent literature on interorganizational linkage mechanisms, and an account of the role of resource dependence theory and transaction cost theory in explaining why organizations choose different types of linkage mechanisms.
- An integrated account of the strategy–structure relationship and coverage of international strategy and structure and global organizational design.
- An analysis of developments in information technology that is integrated in the traditional concepts used in organizational theory.
- A detailed discussion of transaction cost theory.

A FOCUS ON MANAGEMENT

The managerial implications of organizational design and change are clearly articulated for the needs of students. Each chapter has one or more managerial summaries, in which the practical implications of organizational theories and concepts are clearly outlined. In addition, each chapter has several "Organizational Insight" boxes in which the experiences of a real company are tied to the chapter material to highlight the implications of the material. Each chapter has two closing cases that allow a hands-on analysis by students.

A FOCUS ON ORGANIZATIONAL DEVELOPMENTS AND CHANGE

In each chapter we encourage students to use up-to-date sources—through the library, media, and the Internet—to track and reflect on companies that we have highlighted throughout the text. This is designed to encourage students to think about the problems of structure and design in the socio-political context in which organizations operate.

A CRITICAL EXAMINATION OF THE APPLICATION OF ORGANIZATION THEORY

In each chapter we encourage students to reflect on the outcome of organizational structure, design, and strategy on employees, customers, the local community, and other stakeholders, as well as organizational outcomes of performance, efficiency, and profitability.

LEARNING FEATURES AND SUPPORT MATERIAL

Each chapter ends with a section entitled "Organizational Theory in Action," which includes the following hands-on learning exercises/assignments:

- "Practising Organizational Theory," which is an experiential exercise designed to give students hands-on experience doing organizational theory. Each exercise takes about 20 minutes of class time. The exercises have been class tested and they work very well. Further details on how to use them are found in the Instructor's Manual.
- An "Ethical Dimension" feature, where students individually or in groups can debate the ethical dilemmas that confront managers during the process of organizational design and change.
- A "Making the Connection" feature, where students collect examples of companies to illustrate organizational design and change issues.
- A short closing "Case for Analysis" with questions, which provides an opportunity for a short class discussion of a chapter-related theme.
- An ongoing "Analyzing the Organization" feature, where students select an organization to study and then complete chapter assignments that lead to an organizational theory analysis and a written case study of their organization. This case study is then presented to the class at the end of the semester. Complete details concerning the use of this and the other learning features are in the Instructor's Manual.

In addition to these hands-on learning exercises, we have kept or refined the other learning features that appeared in earlier editions:

- Cases. At the end of the book are 12 cases to be used in conjunction with the book's chapters to enrich students' understanding of organizational theory concepts. We have added a number of Canadian cases to the existing U.S. cases. The cases should *not* be used for student write-ups; their value is in the in-class discussion they generate. We have written detailed instructor notes for these cases to show how we use these cases in our own courses in organizational theory. These notes are found in the Instructor's Manual.

- "Organizational Insight" boxes directly related to core chapter concepts.
- "Managerial Implications" sections that provide students with lessons from organizational theory.
- Detailed end-of-chapter summaries to facilitate learning.
- Discussion questions with detailed answers in the Instructor's Manual.
- A Case Development Exercise is included in the Instructor's Manual. It is a detailed, step-by-step outline to help students develop an in-class case. This allows students to research emerging issues, choose a relevant organization for study, and provides them with insights into case analysis.
- A Test Item File, which contains a detailed and comprehensive set of at least 60 multiple-choice questions and 15 true/false questions together with three short-answer and essay questions for each chapter. This is available on the Instructor's Resource CD-ROM.
- An Instructor's Manual, which details how the features in the text can be integrated with the chapter content and cases. This includes Teaching Objectives, Chapter Summaries, Outlines, Discussion Questions and Answers, Organizational Theory in Action, Cases for Analysis, Analyzing the Organization and Teaching Suggestions, and Ethical Dimensions. It also includes detailed case notes for each of the Case Studies. This is available on the Instructor's Resource CD-ROM.

ACKNOWLEDGMENTS

Developing this Canadian edition has been the work of a veritable army of people. Our thanks begin with Gareth Jones for providing a well-structured and clearly thought-out text to work with. Next we are grateful to James Bosma of Pearson for suggesting that we take on this task and to Karen Elliott for continued support. Paul Donnelly, our developmental editor, has done sterling work by editing out all our bad bits and keeping us on track. Margaret McKee, Ellen Rudderham-Gaudet, and Scott MacMillan are three hard-working Ph.D. students who took on the task of researching and writing up most of the new insights and end-of-chapter cases that give the book much of its Canadian feel. We are also grateful to the reviewers and colleagues who provided us with detailed feedback on the chapters—in particular, Kelly Dye and Jim Grant.

REVIEWERS OF THE CANADIAN EDITION

Kamel Argheyd, Concordia University
Celeste Brotheridge, University of Regina
Ali Dastmalchian, University of Victoria
Robert Gephart, University of Alberta
David Hannah, Simon Fraser University
Shaista Khilji, Carleton University
John Kyle, University of Victoria
Richard Roy, University College of the Cariboo
Mary Runte, University of Lethbridge
Frank Safayeni, University of Waterloo
Sudhir Saha, Memorial University of Newfoundland
Conor Vibert, Acadia University
Jeff Young, Mount Saint Vincent University

Organizations and Organizational Effectiveness

CHAPTER 1

Learning Objectives

Most organizations exist in changing, often uncertain, environments and continually confront new challenges and problems. Managers must find solutions to these challenges and problems if organizations are to survive, prosper, and perform effectively.

After studying this chapter you should be able to:

1. Explain why organizations exist and the purposes they serve.
2. Describe the relationship between organizational theory and organizational design and change, and differentiate between organizational structure and culture.
3. Understand how managers can utilize the principles of organizational theory to design and change their organizations to increase organizational effectiveness.
4. Identify the three principal ways in which managers assess and measure organizational effectiveness.
5. Appreciate the way in which several contingency factors influence the design of organizations.

WHAT IS AN ORGANIZATION?

In Canada people have an awareness of the contribution of organizations to the well-being of its citizens. That is because public ownership of key services is a vital part of the economic and political life of the country and approximately one in five of all employees works for one of the levels of government.[1] This is particularly true of health, welfare, and education, which are predominantly government services in Canada. Despite this general interest in organizational outcomes, we Canadians tend to take organizations for granted. Although we routinely enjoy the goods and services that organizations provide, we rarely bother to wonder how these goods and services are produced. We may pick up our mail, click on the Internet, take a bus into town, and switch on our television set, without giving a second thought to how or why these organizations go about their business. Most often, we think about organizations only when they fail us in some way—for example, when we can't get to work in time because the city has not ploughed the streets of snow, when we have to wait several months for an operation, or when our Internet service is unavailable. When such things happen, we wonder why the city did not anticipate the extent of the snowfall and the number of plough operators it would have to hire, or why our health system does not hire enough doctors and nurses, or why Internet services don't insist on higher quality hardware and bug-free software from their suppliers.

Most people have a casual attitude toward organizations because organizations are *intangible*. Even though most people in the world today are born, work, and die in organizations, nobody has ever seen or touched an organization. We see the products or services that an organization provides, and sometimes we see the people whom the organization employs as, for example, when we go into a Kinko's store or doctor's office. But the reason an organization, such as Kinko's, is motivated to provide goods and services, and the way it controls and influences its members so that it can provide them, are not apparent to most people outside the organization. Nevertheless, grouping people and other resources to produce goods and services is the essence of organizing and of what an organization does.[2]

Organization
A tool used by people to coordinate their actions to obtain something they desire or value.

An **organization** is a tool used by people to coordinate their actions to obtain something they desire or value—that is, to achieve their goals. People who desire political change establish political parties, such as the Conservative Party, the Liberal Party, or the New Democratic Party. Employees who want to protect and promote their workplace interests form trade unions (e.g., the Canadian Auto Workers). People who value sports develop teams, such as the Edmonton Oilers, the Saskatchewan Rough Riders, or the Toronto Blue Jays. People who desire spiritual or emotional support create churches, social service organizations, or charities. And, of course, people whose ultimate aim is to make money create any number of companies, from banks (e.g., Bank of Montreal), manufacturing (e.g., Magna International Inc.) and service (e.g., WestJet Airlines Ltd.) companies, to coffee houses (e.g., Second Cup) and hamburger restaurants (e.g., McDonald's). An organization is a response to and a means of satisfying some human need. New organizations are spawned when new technologies become available and new needs are discovered, and organizations die or are transformed when the needs they satisfied are no longer important or have been replaced by other needs. In recent years a number of Canadian companies, such as Eaton's, Canadian Airlines, Sydney Steel, and Dylex, have gone out of business in the face of changing customer needs and competition.

Who creates the organizations that arise to satisfy people's needs? Sometimes an individual or a few people believe they possess the necessary skills and knowledge and set up an organization to produce goods and services. In this way organizations like Swiss Chalet, Sympatico, and WestJet Airlines are created. Sometimes it is the energies and commitment of dedicated political actors that lead to the establishment of a new government program, such as the Atlantic Canada Opportunities Agency (ACOA). Sometimes several people form a group to respond to a perceived need by creating an organization. People with a lot of money may invest jointly to build a vacation resort. A group of people with similar beliefs may form a community action group (e.g., Greenpeace) or a service club (e.g., Rotary Club). In general, **entrepreneurship** is the term used to describe the process by which people recognize opportunities to satisfy needs and then gather and use resources to meet those needs.[3]

Entrepreneurship
The process by which people recognize opportunities to satisfy needs, and then gather and use resources to meet those needs.

In recent years, political and economic realities have greatly influenced the development and growth of organizations. Response to the global economy has encouraged many organizations throughout North America to restructure the way they do business. In Canada, for instance, we have witnessed the privatization of a number of government-owned companies over the past two decades, including Air

Canada, Ontario Power Generation, and Nova Scotia Power. These companies, like any other, must contend with the challenges of a competitive environment and provide valuable insights into the political and economic realities of doing business in Canada.

Another formidable influence has been the emergence of new information technology (IT). Today, many new organizations, particularly those experiencing the fastest growth, are producing IT-related goods and services. The increasing use of new media and technologies such as the Internet are revolutionizing the way all organizations operate. This book examines this crucial issue by focusing on one company that has achieved explosive growth, Amazon.com. In nine chapters of this book the story of this company is used to illustrate the many ways in which the new information technology revolution is affecting the way organizations operate and create value today. We begin this analysis below by examining why and how Amazon.com was founded.[4] (See Focus on New Information Technology.)

How Does an Organization Create Value?

The way in which an organization creates value is depicted in Figure 1-1. Value creation takes place at three stages: input, conversion, and output. Each stage is affected by the environment in which the organization operates.

FOCUS ON NEW INFORMATION TECHNOLOGY

Amazon.com, Part 1

In 1994, Jeffrey Bezos, a computer science and electrical engineering graduate from Princeton University, was growing weary of working for a Wall Street investment bank. With his computer science background prompting him, he saw an entrepreneurial opportunity in the fact that usage of the Internet was growing at over 2300 percent a year as more and more people were becoming aware of its information advantages.

Searching for an opportunity to exploit his skills in the new electronic, virtual marketplace, he decided that the book-selling market would be a good place to invest his personal resources. Deciding to make a break, he packed up his belongings and drove to the West Coast, deciding en route that Seattle, Washington, a new Mecca for high-tech software developers and the hometown of Starbuck's coffee shops, would be an ideal place to begin his venture.

What was his vision for his new venture? To build an online bookstore that would be customer-friendly, easy to navigate, and would offer the broadest possible selection of books. Bezos's mission? "To use the Internet to offer products that would educate, inform and inspire."[5] Bezos realized that compared to a real "bricks and mortar" bookstore, an online bookstore would be able to offer a much larger and more diverse selection of books. Moreover, online customers would be able to search easily for any book in print on a computerized, online catalogue, browse different subject areas, read reviews of books, and even ask other shoppers for online recommendations—something most people would hesitate to do in a regular bookstore.

With a handful of employees and operating from his garage in Seattle, Bezos launched his venture on line in July 1995 with US$7 million in borrowed capital. Word of his venture spread like wildfire across the Internet and book sales quickly picked up as satisfied customers spread the good word. Within weeks Bezos was forced to relocate to new larger premises and to hire new employees as book sales soared. Bezos's new venture seemed to be poised for success.

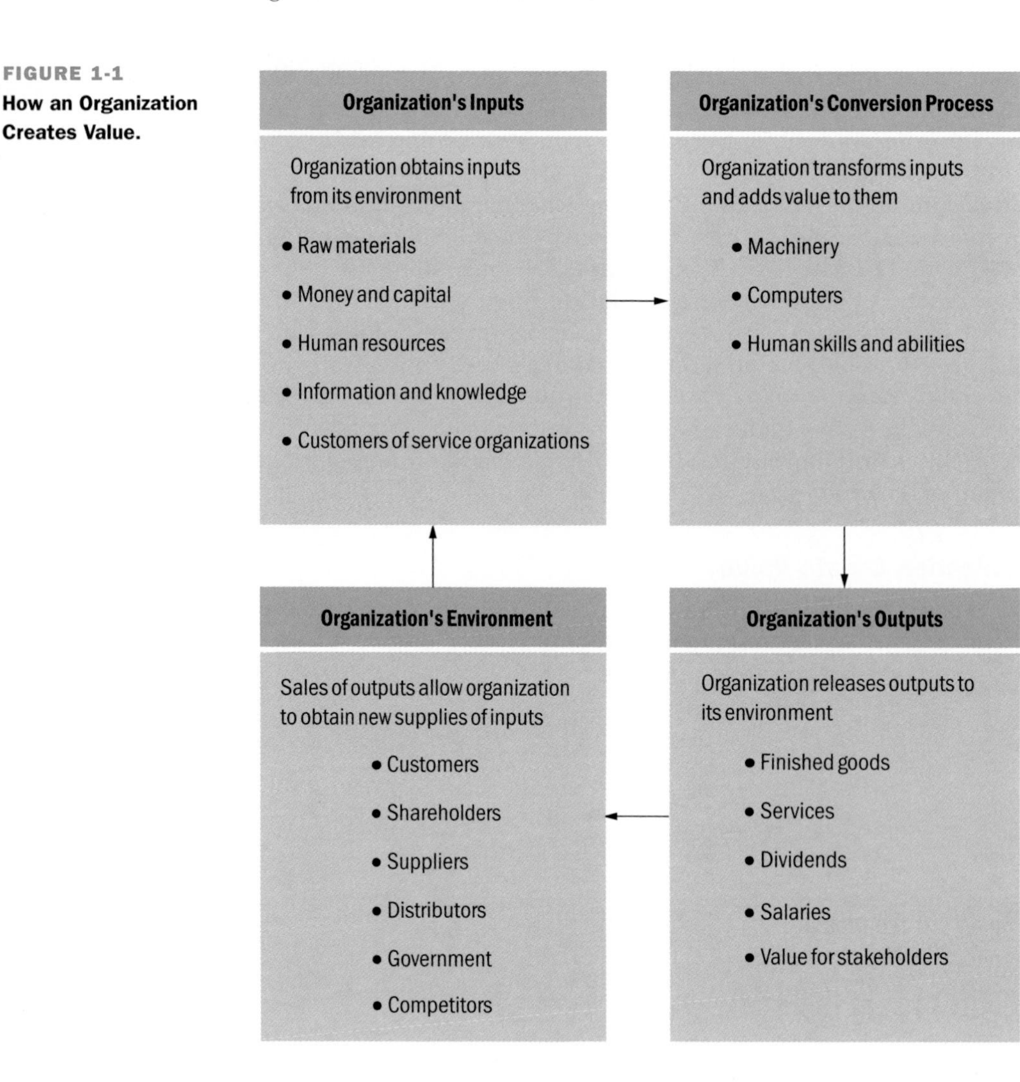

FIGURE 1-1
How an Organization Creates Value.

Inputs include human resources, information and knowledge, raw materials, and money and capital. The way an organization chooses and obtains from its environment the inputs it needs to produce goods and services determines how much value the organization creates at the input stage. For example, Jeff Bezos chose to make the design of the Amazon.com Web site as simple and user-friendly as he possibly could, and only recruited people who could provide high-quality, customer-friendly service that would most appeal to his Internet customers. If he had made poor choices and customers had not liked Amazon.com's Web site or customer service, his company would not have been successful.

The way the organization uses human resources and technology to transform inputs into outputs determines how much value is created at the conversion stage. The amount of value the organization creates is a function of the quality of its skills, including its ability to learn from and respond to the environment. For example, Jeff Bezos had to decide how best to sell and market his products to attract customers. His answer was to offer wide choice, low prices, and to ship books quickly to customers. His skill at these activities created the value that customers saw in his concept.

The result of the conversion process is an output of finished goods and services that the organization releases to its environment, where they are purchased and used by customers to satisfy their needs—such as delivered books. The organization uses the money earned from the sale of its output to obtain new supplies of inputs, and the cycle begins again. An organization that continues to satisfy people's needs will be able to obtain increasing amounts of resources over time and will be able to create more and more value as it adds to its stock of skills and capabilities.[6] Amazon.com has grown from strength to strength because satisfied customers have provided the revenues it needs to improve its skills and expand its operations.

A value creation model can be used to describe the activities of most kinds of organizations. Manufacturing companies, such as Magna International, General Motors, and IBM, take from the environment component parts, skilled or semiskilled labour, and technical knowledge and at the conversion stage create value by using their manufacturing skills to organize and assemble those inputs into outputs, such as cars and computers. Service organizations, such as Air Canada, McDonald's, Amazon.com, the Salvation Army, and your family doctor, interact directly with customers or clients, who are the "inputs" to their operations. Travellers who purchase a flight from Air Canada, hungry people who go to McDonald's for a meal, needy families who go to the Salvation Army for assistance, and sick people who go to a doctor for a cure are all "inputs." In the conversion stage, service organizations create value by applying their skills to yield an output: prompt arrival, satisfied hunger, a cared-for family, or a cured patient. Figure 1-2 is a simplified model of how McDonald's creates value.

McDonald's inputs: Obtained from its environment

- Raw materials (ground beef, sandwich buns, potatoes, milk-shake mix, etc.)
- Human resources (cooks, clean-up crew, order takers, managers)
- Information and knowledge (training, knowledge of fast-food industry)
- Money and capital (shareholders' investments)
- Customers

McDonald's conversion process: Tranforms inputs and adds value to them

- Machinery (grills, toasters, fry-o-lators, milk-shake machines)
- Computers (computerized cash registers, ordering systems, inventory tracking)
- Human skills and abilities (personnel trained in sandwich preparation, ordering, potato frying, overseeing the whole operation)

McDonald's outputs: Released to its environment

- Fast and cheap food
- Satisfied customers
- Satisfied shareholders

McDonald's environment: Sale of outputs to customers

- Satisfied customers
- Potential customers
- Suppliers of meat, potatoes, milk-shake mix
- Population from which to choose employees
- Government health regulations
- Competitors (Kentucky Fried Chicken, Burger King, Taco Bell)

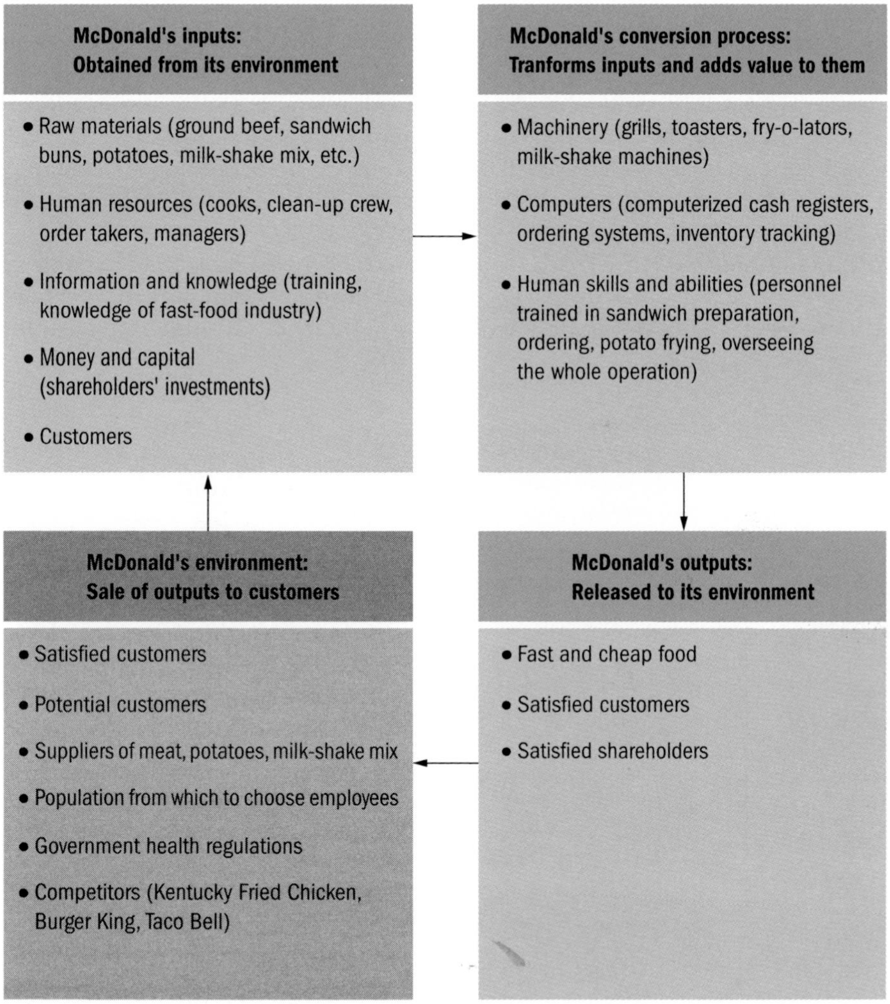

FIGURE 1-2
How McDonald's Creates Value.

Why Do Organizations Exist?

The production of goods and services most often takes place in an organizational setting because people working together to produce goods and services usually can create more value than people working separately. Figure 1-3 summarizes five reasons for the existence of organizations.

To Increase Specialization and the Division of Labour People who work in organizations may become more productive and efficient at what they do than people who work alone. For many kinds of productive work, the use of an organization allows the development of specialization and a division of labour. The collective nature of organizations allows individuals to focus on a narrow area of expertise; this allows them to become more skilled or specialized at what they do. For example, engineers working in the engineering design department of a large car manufacturer like GM or Toyota might specialize in improving the design of carburetors or other engine components. An engineer working for a small car manufacturer might be responsible for designing the whole engine. Because the engineer in the small company must do many more things than the engineer in the large company, the degree of specialization in the small company is lower; there is less chance of discovering what makes for a great carburetor and thus creating more value for someone who desires high speed.

Economies of scale
Cost savings that result when goods and services are produced in large volume on automated production lines.

Economies of scope
Cost savings that result when an organization is able to use underutilized resources more effectively because they can be shared across different products or tasks.

To Use Large-Scale Technology Organizations are able to take advantage of the economies of scale and scope that result from the use of modern automated and computerized technology. **Economies of scale** are cost savings that result when goods and services are produced in large volume on automated production lines. **Economies of scope** are cost savings that result when an organization is able to use underutilized resources more effectively because they can be shared across several different products or tasks. Economies of scope (as well as of scale) can be achieved, for example, when it is possible to design an automated production line to produce several different types of products simultaneously.

Toyota and Honda were the first automakers to design assembly lines capable of producing three models of a car instead of just one. Ford and DaimlerChrysler have followed suit and have achieved impressive gains in efficiency. Multimodel assembly

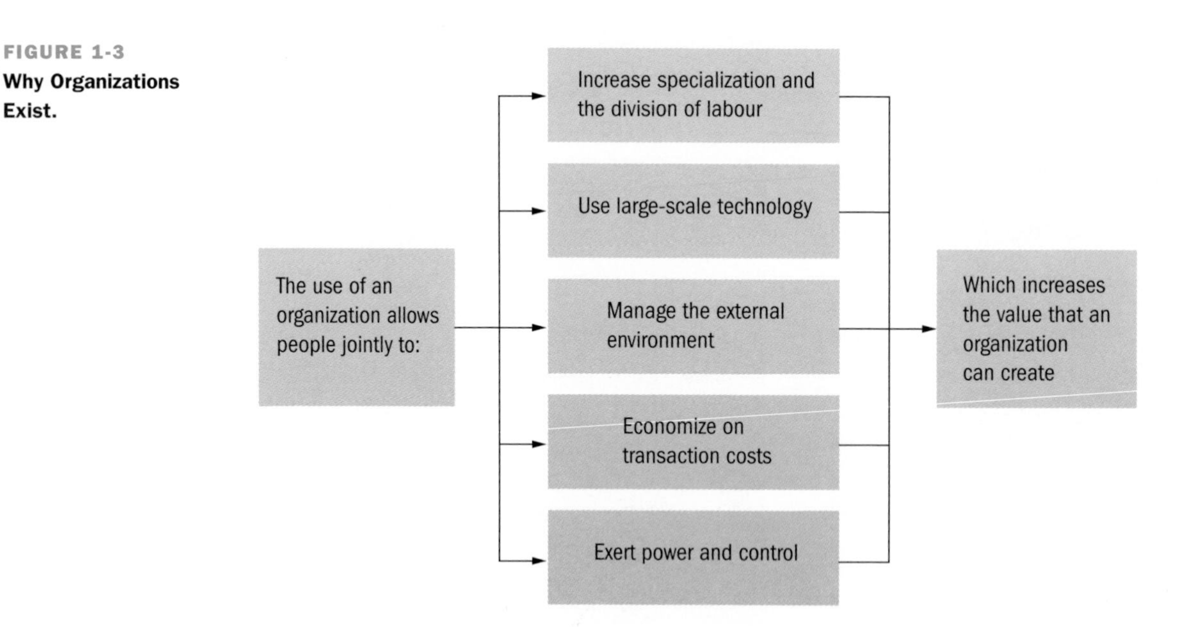

FIGURE 1-3
Why Organizations Exist.

lines give car companies lower manufacturing costs and greater flexibility to change quickly from one model to another to meet customer needs.

To Manage the External Environment Pressures from the environment in which organizations operate also make organizations the favoured mode for organizing productive resources. In some cases government may step in and control the environment through the establishment of an organization with exclusive legal rights of operation over a specified area of business. This was the case with the establishment of Trans-Canada Air Lines and its successor Air Canada. The airline developed with exclusive rights of operation over many interprovincial and international routes. An organization's environment includes not only political, economic, and social factors but also the sources from which the organization obtains inputs and the marketplace into which it releases outputs. Managing complex environments is a task beyond the abilities of most individuals, but an organization has the resources to develop specialists to anticipate or attempt to influence the many demands from the environment. This specialization allows the organization to create more value for the organization, its members, and its customers. Huge companies like Bombardier, Bell Canada, and Ford have whole departments of corporate executives who are responsible for monitoring, responding to, and attempting to manage the external environment, but those activities are just as important for small organizations. Although local stores and restaurants do not have whole departments to scan the environment, their owners and managers need to spot emerging trends and changes so that they can respond to changing customer needs; otherwise they will not survive. Jeff Bezos did this by scanning the business environment. Louis Comeau (the CEO of Nova Scotia Power) did this by scanning the political environment.

To Economize on Transaction Costs When people cooperate to produce goods and services, certain problems arise. As they learn what to do and how to work with others to perform a task effectively, people jointly have to decide who will do which tasks (the division of labour), who will get paid what amounts, and how to decide if each worker is doing his or her share of the work. The costs associated with negotiating, monitoring, and governing exchanges between people to solve these kinds of transaction difficulties are called **transaction costs**. Organizations' ability to control the exchanges between people reduces the transaction costs associated with these exchanges. Suppose Intel bought the services of its scientists on a daily basis and thousands of scientists had to spend time every day discussing what to do and who should work with whom. Such a system would be very costly and would waste valuable time and money. The structure and coordination imposed by the Intel organization, however, lets managers hire scientists on a long-term basis, assign them to specific tasks and work teams, and gives Intel the right to monitor their performance. The resulting stability reduces transaction costs and increases productivity.

Transaction costs
The costs associated with negotiating, monitoring, and governing exchanges between people.

To Exert Power and Control Organizations can exert great pressure on individuals to conform to task and production requirements in order to increase production efficiency.[7] To get a job done efficiently, it is important for people to come to work in a predictable fashion, to behave in the interests of the organization, and to accept the authority of the organization and its managers. All these requirements make production less costly and more efficient but put a burden on individuals who must conform to organizational requirements. When individuals work for themselves, they need to address only their own needs. When they work for an organization, however, they must pay attention to the organization's needs as well as their own. Organizations can discipline or fire workers who fail to conform and can reward good performance with promotion and increased rewards. Because employment, promotion, and increased rewards are important and often scarce, organizations can use them to exert power over individuals.

Over the years, the ability of organizational management to exert power over employees has led to the development of unions and employment protection laws. In Canada, more than three in every ten employed persons belongs to a trade union (compared to just over one in eight in the United States).[8] Although the degree of employment protection legislation in Canada is one of the lowest among member nations of the Organisation for Economic Co-operation and Development (OECD), it is three times that of the United States.[9]

Taken together, these five factors help to explain why often more value can be created when people work together, coordinating their actions in an organized setting, than when they work alone. Over time, the stability created by an organization provides a setting in which the organization and its members can increase their skills and capabilities, and the ability of the organization to create value increases by leaps and bounds. In the last 10 years, for example, Microsoft has grown to become the biggest and most powerful software company in the world because Bill Gates, its founder, created an organizational setting in which people are given freedom to develop their skills and capabilities to create valuable new products. In contrast, in the last 10 years other software companies like WordPerfect, Lotus, and Novell experienced huge problems because they have not been able to create innovative software at a price that customers will pay. Why does Microsoft's organization allow Microsoft to create more and more value while these other organizations have actually reduced the value they can create? Before we can answer this question, we need to take a close look at organizational theory, design, and change.

ORGANIZATIONAL THEORY, DESIGN, AND CHANGE

Organizational theory The study of how organizations function and how they affect and are affected by the environment in which they operate.

Organizational theory is the study of how organizations function and how they affect and are affected by the environment in which they operate. In this book, we examine the principles that underlie the design, operation, change, and redesign of organizations to maintain and increase their effectiveness. Understanding how organizations operate, however, is only the first step in learning how to control and change organizations so that they can effectively create wealth and resources. Thus the second aim of this book is to equip you with the conceptual tools to influence organizational situations in which you find yourself. The lessons of organizational design and change are as important at the level of first-line supervisor as they are at the level of chief executive officer, in small or large organizations, and in settings as diverse as the not-for-profit organization, the government agency, or the assembly line of a manufacturing company.

People and managers knowledgeable about organizational design and change are able to analyze the structure and culture of the organization for which they work (or which they wish to help, such as a charity or church), diagnose problems, and make adjustments that help the organization to achieve its goals. Figure 1-4 outlines the relationship among organizational theory, structure, culture, design, and change.

Organizational structure The formal system of task and authority relationships that control how people coordinate their actions and use resources to achieve organizational goals.

Organizational Structure

Once a group of people has established an organization to accomplish collective goals, organizational structure evolves to increase the effectiveness of the organization's control of the activities necessary to achieve its goals. **Organizational structure** is the formal system of task and authority relationships that control how people coordinate their actions and use resources to achieve organizational goals.[10] The principal pur-

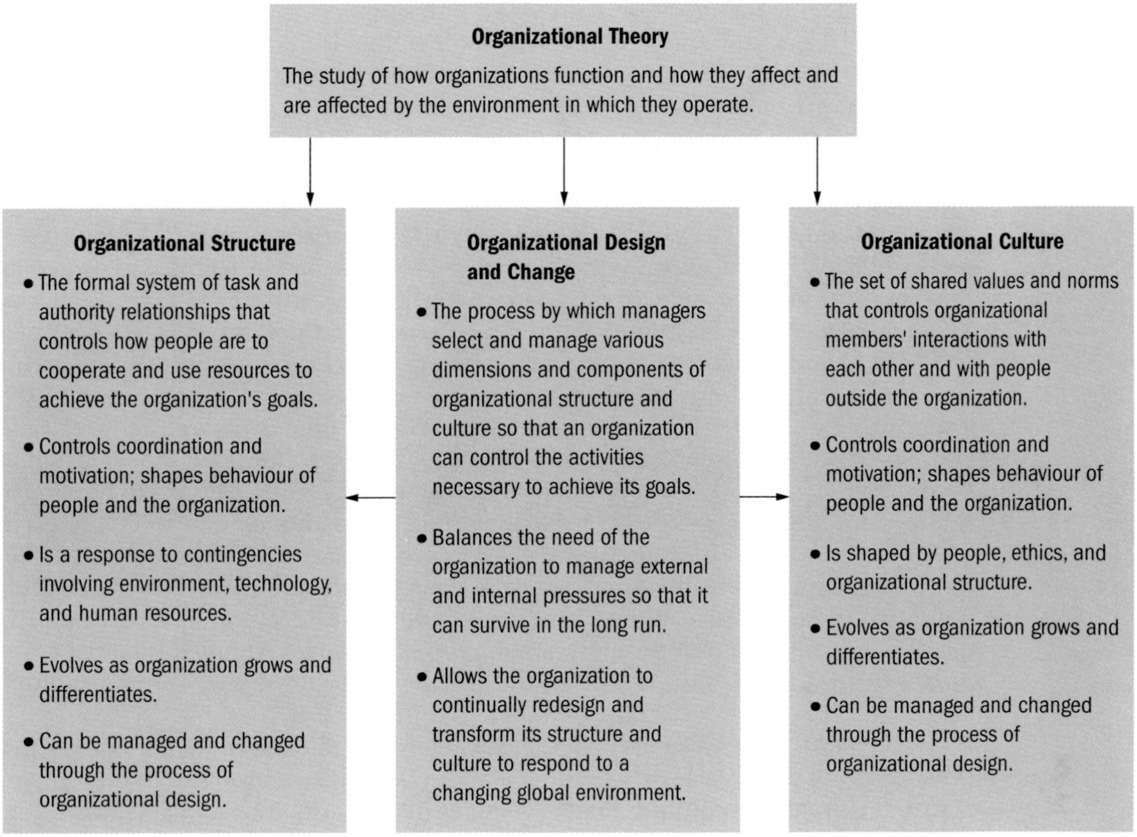

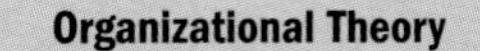
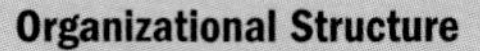

FIGURE 1-4
The Relationship Among Organizational Theory and Organizational Structure, Culture, and Design, and Change.

pose of organizational structure is one of control: to control the way people coordinate their actions to achieve organizational goals and to control the means used to motivate people to achieve these goals. At Microsoft, for example, the control problems facing Bill Gates were how to coordinate scientists' activities to make the best use of their talents, and how to reward scientists when they developed innovative products. Gates's solution was to place scientists in small, self-contained teams and to reward them with stock in Microsoft based on team performance. As we shall see shortly, the problem facing Louis Comeau when he took over as CEO of Nova Scotia Power was how to bring all divisions of the diverse company together to create a common set of values. Comeau's solution was to introduce a far-reaching culture change.

For any organization, an appropriate structure is one that facilitates effective responses to problems of coordination and motivation—problems that can arise for any number of environmental, technological, or human reasons.[11] As organizations grow and differentiate, the structure likewise evolves. Organizational structure can be managed through the process of organizational design and change.

Organizational culture
The set of shared values and norms that guides organizational members' interactions with each other and with suppliers, customers, and other people outside the organization.

Organizational Culture

At the same time that organizational structure is evolving, so is organizational culture. **Organizational culture** is the set of shared values and norms that guide organizational members' interactions with each other and with suppliers, customers, and other people outside the organization. An organization's culture is shaped by the people inside the organization, by the ethics of the organization, by employee employment rights, and by the type of structure used by the organization. Like organizational structure, organizational culture shapes and controls behaviour within the organization. It influences how people respond to a situation and how they interpret the environment surrounding the organization. At Nova Scotia Power, Louis Comeau created a set of values aimed at uniting the efforts of employees and management in a common goal of service efficiency. With a focus on valuing employees, Comeau attempted to overcome existing divisions between managers and workers that stood in the way of valuing customers. With a focus on valuing customers, Comeau defined the core business and provided a superordinate goal for its achievement. (See Organizational Insight 1.1.)

The cultures of organizations that provide essentially the same goods and services can be very different. For example, Coca-Cola and PepsiCo are the two largest and most successful companies in the soft-drink industry.[12] Because they sell similar products and face similar environments, we might expect their cultures to be similar. But they are not. Coca-Cola takes pride in its long-term commitment to employees; its loyal managers, many of whom spend their entire careers with the organization; and its cautious and cooperative approach to planning. By contrast, PepsiCo has a highly political and competitive culture in which conflicts over decision making cause frequent disputes, and often turnover, among top managers. Like organizational structure, organizational culture evolves and can be managed through organizational design and change.

At Ontario Power Generation, the change from a publicly owned monopoly to a privately owned business in a highly competitive industry brought about a major restructuring that required major changes in the organization's culture (see Organizational Insight 1.2).

Organizational Design and Change

Organizational design
The process by which managers select and manage aspects of structure and culture so that an organization can control the activities necessary to achieve its goals.

Organizational design is the process by which managers select and manage aspects of structure and culture so that an organization can control the activities necessary to achieve its goals. Organizational structure and culture are the *means* the organization uses to achieve its goals; organizational design is about how and why various means are chosen. An organization's behaviour is the result of its design and the principles behind its operation. It is a task that requires managers to strike a balance between external pressures from the organization's environment and internal pressures from, for example, its choice of technology. Looking outward, the design can cause organizational members to view and respond to the environment in different ways. Looking inward, an organization's design puts pressure on work groups and individuals to behave in certain ways. Achieving the proper balance helps to ensure that the organization will survive in the long run. The theories, concepts, and techniques covered in this book are intended to provide you with working models that you can use to analyze organizational situations and to propose and implement suitable solutions to change an organization and increase its effectiveness.

Organizations like Corel and Geac Computer, which operate in the high-tech computer industry, need to be flexible and capable of quick responses to their rivals' competitive moves, and they need to be innovative in developing new technology. At the same time, such organizations must have stable task relationships that allow their members to work together to create value, solve problems, and accomplish organizational objectives. In contrast, organizations like Inco and Alcan, which produce sheet steel and aluminum, face relatively stable environments in which customer needs are

ORGANIZATIONAL INSIGHT 1.1

Political Change and Organizational Functions

Nova Scotia Power (NSP) has been in operation in one form or another for the past 100 years. Today it is a subsidiary of the diversified energy and services company Emera Inc., but in 1992 it was a Crown corporation. When Louis Comeau was appointed company president in 1983, NSP suffered from low morale and bad customer relations. As a Crown corporation, it occupied a near monopoly in the field of electricity generation and supply. Steadily increasing electricity rates had served to make the company unpopular with customers throughout the province. The problem for the government of the day was that customers were also voters, and dissatisfaction with NSP was a factor in people's voting intentions. As a political appointee, Louis Comeau, a former Progressive Conservative Member of Parliament, was given the task of restructuring NSP to make it more acceptable to customers and employees alike.

In 1987, Comeau commissioned an attitudes survey of all employees. The survey confirmed the worst—that management was perceived as lacking in empathy, having an inability to communicate effectively, unresponsive to media criticism, aloof and uncaring to employees and customers alike, lacking in leadership skills, offering no feedback, and placing more emphasis on the job than on the employee.[13] Comeau's response was to restructure the company around a set of four core values that would serve as the focus of a company-wide culture change. Consultants were hired and management and employees went through a series of training sessions that emphasized that NSP was a company that valued its customers, employees, the province, and the environment.

In the meantime, the government at the time was already developing plans to sell off the company to private interests, and in 1992 NSP was privatized. Louis Comeau stayed on as president but now faced new restructuring issues as he sought to position the company to meet the demands of shareholders and to compete in a competitive and uncertain market. Searching for new business—rather than political—solutions, Comeau turned to business process re-engineering consultants who now instituted a new series of training sessions for employees and managers alike. Initially 400 jobs were eliminated and 250 were cut the following year. Employees were now expected to be multiskilled, as several jobs, previously done by different people, were either cut or merged into one multitasked position done by one person.

more predictable and technology changes more slowly. Consequently, their organizational design choices are likely to reflect the need for a structure and culture that reduce production costs rather than a structure and culture that promote flexibility. In Chapters 4, 5, 6, and 7 we discuss the organizational structures and cultures that managers can design to help ensure their organizations' survival.

Organizational change is the process by which organizations move from their present state to some desired future state to increase their effectiveness. The goal of organizational change is to find new or improved ways of using resources and capabilities to increase an organization's ability to create value, and hence its performance.[14] Once again, organizational structure and culture are a principal means or fulcrum managers use to change the organization so it can achieve its future desired state.

Organizational change
The process by which organizations redesign their structures and cultures to move from their present state to some desired future state to increase their effectiveness.

ORGANIZATIONAL INSIGHT 1.2

Structure and Culture Changes at Ontario Power Generation[15]

Ontario Power Generation (OPG) is a privately owned company generating and providing electricity primarily to Ontario but also to peripheral markets. Its principal goal is to become a leading provider of energy in North America while maintaining a reputation for conducting operations in a safe, transparent, and environmentally responsible way. The company's focus is currently on competitive strategies involving, in particular, its valuable generation assets.

The incorporation of OPG in 1998 and its ongoing restructuring challenges have been greatly influenced by the restructuring of the electricity industry itself. Internationally, the United Kingdom, continental Europe, Australia, New Zealand, some of South America, and many parts of United States and Canada have moved away from government-owned and -operated electricity supply monopolies towards more competitive market models. Until April 1999, Ontario Hydro was a vertically integrated electricity utility and the only supplier of electricity for most consumers in Ontario. When Ontario's electricity market opened up, OPG acquired employees, assets, rights, and obligations of the former government-owned Ontario Hydro, and was positioned to become a player in a newly formed competitive electricity market.

The conversion of a monopoly venture to a privatized structure and culture is a huge change. For OPG, meeting this challenge involved shifting the attitudes of employees to fit new realities. The company inherited Ontario Hydro's former culture of just "keeping the lights on," in which corporate, fiscal, or competitive considerations were minimal. OPG has needed to make major changes to build a culture focused more on fiscal requirements and less on the former service priority. OPG has made strides towards this end by changing its compensation structure and initiating various strategies to have its organizational members think and act in the company's long-term best interests.

Changing attitudes demanded attention to the bottom line from everyone at all levels of the organization. A new employee compensation structure reinforced this emphasis by linking potential annual bonuses to the company's financial performance (the company uses a formula based on a key financial measurement: earnings before interest, taxation, depreciation, and amortization). This structural change would not suffice on its own without an educational indoctrination as well, which in the case of OPG, has its particular challenges. OPG needs to effectively reach its members. Employees are situated widely from the central operating area of Toronto to the distant posts of generating stations in rural Ontario. Furthermore, OPG also needs to consider employees' educational backgrounds, which range from high school graduates right through to Ph.D.s in nuclear physics. But the most difficult challenge of all, in this case, was to change the cultural mindsets that had typically neglected the importance of profit margins in a privatized company.

OPG's finance department, in partnership with the public affairs department and a private consulting company, undertook the task to educate the workforce. The team chose to use videos to effectively rally the troops and change the corporation's historical service focus to one with employees more interested in following the financial performance of the company. To this end, the company uses quarterly videos to assist management team members to promote an open corporate culture receptive to the company's transition to a competitive market. OPG believes that developing this kind of culture, in which the workforce is well informed about the company's financial performance and requirements, will be key to the company's future success.

Organizational design and change are thus highly interrelated. Indeed, organizational change can be understood as the process of organizational redesign and transformation. As we discuss in later chapters, as organizations grow their structure and culture are constantly evolving, changing and becoming more complex. A large organization faces a different set of design and redesign problems than a small organization because its structure and culture are different from a small organization's. Managers—in both the private and public sector—need to recognize that their initial design choices will have important ramifications in the future as their organizations grow; indeed, it has been argued that initial choices are an important determinant of differences in long-run performance. For example, consider the difference in the way Steve Jobs and Michael Dell created the structures and cultures of the organizations they founded. (See Organizational Insight 1.3.)

ORGANIZATIONAL INSIGHT 1.3

Opposite Organizing Approaches at Apple and Dell Computer

In 1976, Steven P. Jobs sold his Volkswagen van and his partner Steven Wozniak sold his two programmable calculators and they invested the US$1350 proceeds to build a computer circuit board in Jobs's garage. So popular was the circuit board, which was eventually developed into the Apple II computer, that in 1977, they incorporated their new business as Apple Computer. By 1985 the company had sales of almost US$2 billion.[16] In 1984, Michael Dell took US$1000 of his savings and used it to establish a national mail-order computer company, the Dell Computer Corp. At the beginning, Dell worked with three employees around a table assembling low-cost personal computers, which were sold by telephone to customers around the United States. By 1993 his company had achieved sales of over US$2 billion a year.[17]

In 1985, Steve Jobs was forced out of the company he helped to found. Michael Dell, however, never lost control of his company, which today is the largest and most profitable maker of PCs in the world. Apple continues to struggle for profitability. Why did Steve Jobs lose control while Michael Dell did not? Jobs's and Dell's different approaches to organizing are a large part of the reason.

When Apple was founded, Steve Jobs announced that he had little interest in being responsible for the day-to-day management of his company, and experienced managers from other companies were recruited to oversee Apple's operations. However, as Apple grew, Jobs desired more power and began to demand more control over the company. In 1981, he became chairman of the board and began to intervene actively in the company's day-to-day operations; for example, Jobs started many new project teams to develop new models of personal computers. As his power and reputation increased, Jobs adopted an arbitrary and overbearing style toward members of the different project teams, often playing favourites. His actions led to a high level of competition between the different teams, many misunderstandings, and much distrust among team members.[18]

His divisive management style brought Jobs into conflict with John Sculley, Apple's CEO and the person formally responsible for managing the company.

Increasingly, Jobs began to compete with Sculley for control of the company. This caused major problems. First, employees had no clear picture of who was leading the company—Jobs (the chairman) or Sculley (the CEO). Second, both executives were so busy competing for control of Apple that neither had the time or energy to ensure it was using its resources efficiently. For example, little attention was paid to evaluating the performance of the different project teams. No budget was in place to curb their research and development (R&D) spending. Apple's costs started to soar, its profits fell, and the organization started to disintegrate. Apple's board of directors, realizing that Jobs's management style was leading to poor company performance, demanded that he resign as chairman. He left the company in 1985.

At Dell Computer, Michael Dell adopted a very different approach to managing his company. Like Jobs, Dell assumed the position of chairman and established many project teams to develop new kinds of PCs. Dell, however, developed a participative management approach, involved employees in decision making, and fostered a spirit of comradeship and cooperation among team members to encourage top performance. His management style engendered intense loyalty from his employees, who liked his hands-on approach and his close attention to managing his company.[19] For example, Dell was careful to watch the teams' progress closely. When a project seemed not to be working out or was costing too much, he would quickly end it and transfer engineers to other projects. He was very conscious of the need to control costs.

As his company grew, Dell, like Jobs, realized the need to recruit expert managers to help him manage his company. He hired experienced executives from companies like EDS and IBM and decentralized control of its functional operations like production and marketing to them. Unlike Jobs, Dell recognized that he could not be personally responsible for managing all of his company's activities, and he never tried to compete with his managers, recognizing their expertise and his limitations. Dell's organizing approach fostered a different kind of company culture, where people cooperate to improve its performance, and as noted above it has become the industry leader.[20]

In 1997, after Apple's profits continued to decline, the board of directors suggested to Jobs that he take control over the company again and become its CEO. In control of the company once again, he put the organizing skills he had subsequently developed as the founder of other companies such as NEXT and Pixar to good use. Understanding that what a company needs is a clear hierarchy of authority and task responsibilities, he energized and motivated employees to develop the next generation of Apple computers that would allow the company to survive. He established a clear structure of teams and team leadership to allow programmers to work together to develop the new computer. He delegated considerable authority to these team leaders, but he also established strict timetables and challenging "stretch goals" for these teams to achieve.

By all accounts, however, Jobs still makes enormous demands of his employees, constantly challenging their ideas and demanding superhuman efforts. Jobs has revitalized Apple and created a new culture that has speeded product development and allowed the organization to survive; however, its performance still lags behind Dell, and its ability to survive is still in doubt.[21]

As the example of Steven Jobs and Michael Dell illustrates, people who start new organizations may lack the kinds of skills, knowledge, and ability to manage an organization's structure and culture effectively. However, both these CEOs did develop that ability over time. An understanding of the principles behind organizational design and change speeds this process and deepens appreciation for the many subtle technical and social processes that determine how organizations operate.

The Importance of Organizational Design and Change

Because of increased global competitive pressures and because of the increasing use of advanced information technology (IT), organizational design has become one of management's top priorities. This has been particularly the case with Crown corporations, such as Nova Scotia Power, Ontario Power Generation, and Air Canada, that have been privatized and now have to contend with competitive rather than political pressures. Today, as never before, managers are searching for new and better ways to coordinate and motivate their employees to increase the value their organizations can create. There are several specific reasons why designing an organization's structure and culture, and changing them to increase its effectiveness, are such important tasks. Organizational design and change have important implications for a company's ability to deal with contingencies, achieve a competitive advantage, effectively manage diversity, and increase its efficiency and ability to innovate.

Contingency
An event that might occur and must be planned for.

Dealing with Contingencies A **contingency** is an event that might occur and must be planned for, such as a changing environment or a competitor like Amazon.com that decides to use new technology in an innovative way. The design of an organization determines how effectively an organization responds to various factors in its environment and obtains scarce resources. For example, an organization's ability to attract skilled employees, loyal customers, or government contracts is a function of the degree to which it can control those three environmental factors.

An organization can design its structure in many ways to increase control over its environment. An organization might change employee task relationships so that employees are more aware of the environment, or it might change the way the organization relates to other organizations by establishing new contracts or joint ventures. For example, when Microsoft wanted to attract new customers for its Windows 98 and later XP software, it recruited large numbers of customer service representatives and created a new department to allow them to better meet customers' needs. The strategy was very successful, and the Windows platform is used on over 95 percent of all PCs globally.

As pressures from competitors, consumers, and governments increase, the environment facing all organizations is becoming increasingly complex and difficult to respond to, and more effective types of structure and culture are continually being developed and tried. We discuss how the changing nature of the environment affects organizations in Chapter 3 and how organizations can influence and control their environments in Chapter 8.

One part of the organizational environment that is becoming more important and more complex is the global environment. Increasingly, Canadian companies like McCain Foods, Bombardier Inc., and Nortel Networks Corp. are under pressure to expand their global presence and produce and sell more of their products in markets overseas to reduce costs, increase efficiency, and survive. Organizational design is important in a global context because to become a global competitor, a company often needs to create a new structure and culture. Chapter 8 also looks at the structures and cultures that a company can adopt as it engages in different kinds of global activities.

Changing technology is another contingency to which organizations must respond. Today, the emergence of the Internet and advanced information technology (IT) as an important new medium through which organizations manage relationships with their employees, customers, and suppliers is fundamentally changing the design of organizational structure and has led to a huge round of organizational change as organizations have redesigned their structures to make most effective use of IT. We will examine the effects of IT on organizational design and change in almost all the chapters of this book, but particularly in Chapter 12.

Competitive advantage The ability of one company to outperform another because its managers are able to create more value from the resources at their disposal.

Core competencies Managers' skills and abilities in value-creating activities.

Strategy The specific pattern of decisions and actions that managers take to use core competencies to achieve a competitive advantage and outperform competitors.

Gaining Competitive Advantage Increasingly, organizations are discovering that organizational design, change, and redesign are a source of sustained competitive advantage. **Competitive advantage** is the ability of one company to outperform another because its managers are able to create more value from the resources at their disposal. Competitive advantage springs from **core competencies**, managers' skills and abilities in value-creation activities such as manufacturing, research and development (R&D), managing new technology, or organizational design and change. Core competencies allow a company to develop a strategy to outperform competitors and produce better products, or produce the same products but at a lower cost. **Strategy** is the specific pattern of decisions and actions that managers take to use core competencies to achieve a competitive advantage and outperform competitors.

The *way* managers design and change organizational structure is an important determinant of how much value the organization creates because this affects how it implements strategy. Many sources of competitive advantage, such as skills in research and development that result in novel product features or state-of-the-art technology, evaporate because they are relatively easy for competitors to imitate. It is much more difficult to imitate good organizational design and carefully managed change that brings into being a successful organizational structure and culture. Such imitation is difficult because structure and culture are embedded in the way people in an organization interact and coordinate their actions to get a job done. Moreover, because successful structures and cultures form early, as at Dell and Apple Computer, and take a long time to establish and develop, companies that possess them can have a long-term competitive advantage.

An organization's strategy is always changing in response to changes in the environment; organizational design must be a continuously evolving managerial activity if managers are to stay one step ahead of the competition. There is never a single optimal or "perfect" design to fit an organization's needs. Managers must constantly evaluate how well their organization's structure and culture work, and they should change and redesign them on an ongoing basis to improve them. In Chapter 8 we consider how organizations create value by means of their strategy.

Managing Diversity Since the Abella Commission's *Report on Equality in Employment* in 1984, and the subsequent legislation in 1986,[22] Canadian companies have been required to pay attention to their employment practices in regard to women, Aboriginal people, disabled persons, and visible minorities. The Abella Commission found that it was not so much the attitudes of individuals that created discriminatory practices but more so the organizational processes, structures, and systems that were in place. Thus, the Commission argued, workplace inequities should be viewed as the result of "systemic discrimination" that needs to be addressed by far-reaching cultural and structural changes at work. Such changes can lead to a reduction in workplace inequities and contribute to the quality of organizational decision making. For example, it can be argued that effective decision making is a function of the diversity of the viewpoints that get considered and of the kind of analysis that takes place. An organization needs to design a structure to make optimal use of the talents of a diverse workforce and to develop cultural values that encourage people to work together. An organization's structure and culture determine how effectively managers are able to coordinate and motivate workers.

Promoting Efficiency, Speed, and Innovation Organizations exist to produce goods and services that people value. The better organizations function, the more value, in the form of more or better goods and services, they create. Historically, the capacity of organizations to create value has increased enormously as organizations have introduced better ways of producing and distributing goods and services. Earlier, we discussed the importance of the division of labour and the use of modern technology in reducing costs, speeding work processes and increasing efficiency. The design and use of new and more efficient organizational structures is equally important. In today's global environment, for example, competition from countries with low labour costs is pressuring companies all over the world to become more efficient in order to reduce costs or increase quality.

The ability of companies to compete successfully in today's competitive environment is increasingly a function of how well they innovate and how quickly they can introduce new technologies. Organizational design plays an important role in innovation. For example, the way an organization's structure links people in different specializations, such as research and marketing, determines how fast the organization can introduce new products. Similarly, an organization's culture can affect people's desire to be innovative. A culture that is based on entrepreneurial norms and values is more likely to encourage innovation than is a culture that is conservative and bureaucratic because entrepreneurial values encourage people to learn how to respond and adapt to a changing situation.

Organizational design involves a constant search for new or better ways of coordinating and motivating employees. Different structures and cultures cause employees to behave in different ways. We consider structures that encourage efficiency and innovation in Chapters 4, 5, and 6 and cultures that do so in Chapter 7.

The Consequences of Poor Organizational Design

Many management teams fail to understand the important effects organizational design and change can have on their company's performance and effectiveness. Although behaviour is controlled by organizational structure and culture, managers are often unaware of the many factors that affect this relationship, paying scant attention to the way employees behave and their role in the organization—until something happens.

Air Canada, Nortel, Bombardier, Sears, and Kodak have all experienced enormous problems in the last decade adjusting to the reality of modern global competition and have seen their sales and profits fall dramatically. In response, they have dramatically reduced their workforces, reduced the number of services or products they make, and even reduced their investment in research and development. Why did the performance of these blue-chip companies deteriorate to such a degree? One reason is that they lost control of their organizational structures and cultures. They became so big and bureaucratic that their managers and employees were unable to change and adapt to changing conditions.

The consequence of poor organizational design or lack of attention to organizational design is the decline of the organization. Talented employees leave to take positions in strong, growing companies. Resources become harder and harder to acquire, and the whole process of value creation slows down. Neglecting organizational design until crisis threatens forces managers to make changes in organizational structure and culture that derail the company's strategy. In the 1990s, one major development at large companies has been the appointment of chief operating officers (COOs), who have become responsible for overseeing organizational structure and culture. COOs create and oversee teams of experienced senior managers who are responsible for organizational design and for orchestrating not only small and incremental but also organization-wide changes in strategy, structure, and culture. One person who was charged with just such a task was Bob Pittman, who was put in charge of the huge AOL–Time Warner merger. (See Organizational Insight 1.4.)

ORGANIZATIONAL INSIGHT 1.4

Redesigning AOL–Time Warner

When America Online and Time Warner joined to form the US$97 billion global entertainment media and information technology giant, AOL–Time Warner, Bob Pittman was put in charge of managing the organizational design and change process.[23] Pittman's task? To find the best way efficiently and effectively to combine the people and resources of both companies to create more products and services, such as Internet TV and video on demand, for customers and hence increase profits. Pittman's challenge was to find a way to get all the company's managers not just to focus on their own particular task and role, but to think about ways to make better use of the company's extensive resources organization wide. For example, Pittman needed to get the managers of *Time* magazine to think about how they could use AOL's Internet presence to increase the circulation and advertising revenues of their magazine. And he needed to get AOL managers to think about how best to expand their service into Time Warner's cable networks, as well as to get cable customers to sign up for AOL Internet service. Pittman was put in charge of this vital task because of his past successes at managing organization-wide change at AOL when it was buying many small dot-com companies and expanding its range of product offerings. Pittman is renowned for his diplomacy and his ability to get what he wants done by persuasion rather than command and to forge a team among managers from different parts of an organization, making collaboration, rather than competition, the basic value in AOL's culture. At the same time, Pittman's success had been due to concern for the bottom line—managing costs. His rise through the AOL hierarchy was achieved partly because he has great operational skills and recognizes ways to design and change structure to cut costs and speed new products to market. Pittman did this by decentralizing authority to managers and by establishing challenging targets for each manager and for each part of the company. One target was to increase annual revenues by 12 to 15 percent and realize more than US$1 billion in cost savings in the first year. To achieve these ambitious targets, Pittman set revenue and cost saving targets for his top managers to achieve; they in turn set targets for their subordinates to achieve; and so on down the organization.

Pittman also put in place a huge coordination effort that involved thousands of managers from different parts of the company coming together in weekly meetings to discuss, decide, and envision how they could create valuable new products or service that customers would want.[24] Countless meetings began to take place among managers from different parts of and from all levels in the organization to decide what course of action or goals to set for the new company.[25] One immediate obstacle he faced was that the previously separated companies had very different structures and cultures. The old Time Warner had been very hierarchical in nature, it was bureaucratic, and decision making was slow. At AOL, on the other hand, managers were used to the fast-changing environment of the Internet and the IT industry. They were used to making decisions in teams and to making them quickly. Pittman, who was from AOL, decided that the AOL organizing model was the one that would be most successful in the new company. He created teams of AOL and Time Warner managers but made AOL managers responsible for taking the lead, developing an organizational culture that would bring new products to market quickly.

As it happened, all of Pittman's huge efforts to change the company were not enough after the huge implosion of dot-com companies' share price, and the recession of the early 2000s. The collapsing value of AOL stock led AOL–Time Warner's board to side with old Time Warner executives, and a power struggle took place in which Pittman and most other senior AOL executives lost their leading role as old Time Warner executives reassumed control of the company.[26] In July 2002 the company announced that Pittman was leaving AOL Time Warner, and by early 2003 the company announced a US$45.5 billion loss in the previous quarter.

HOW DO MANAGERS MEASURE ORGANIZATIONAL EFFECTIVENESS?

Because managers are responsible for utilizing organizational resources in a way that maximizes an organization's ability to create value, it is important to understand how they evaluate organizational performance. Researchers analyzing what CEOs and managers do have pointed to control, innovation, and efficiency as the three most important processes managers use to assess and measure how effective they, and their organizations, are at creating value.[27]

In this context, *control* means having a strong influence over the external environment and having the ability to attract resources and customers. *Innovation* means developing an organization's skills and capabilities so that the organization can discover new products and processes. It also means designing and creating new organizational structures and cultures that enhance a company's ability to change, adapt, and improve the way it functions.[28] *Efficiency* means developing modern production facilities using new information technologies that can produce and distribute a company's products in a timely and cost-effective manner. It also means introducing techniques like Internet-based information systems, total quality management, and just-in-time inventory systems (discussed in Chapter 9) to improve productivity.

To evaluate the effectiveness with which an organization confronts each of these three challenges, managers can take one of three approaches (see Table 1-1). An organization is effective if it can (1) secure scarce and valued skills and resources from outside the organization (external resource approach); (2) creatively coordinate resources with employee skills to innovate products and adapt to changing customer needs (internal systems approach); and (3) efficiently convert skills and resources into finished goods and services (technical approach).

Table 1-1

APPROACHES TO MEASURING ORGANIZATIONAL EFFECTIVENESS

Approach	Description	Goals to Set to Measure Effectiveness
External resource approach	Evaluates the organization's ability to secure, manage, and control scarce and valued skills and resources	• Lower costs of inputs • Obtain high-quality inputs of raw materials and employees • Increase market share • Increase stock price • Gain support of stakeholders such as government or environmentalists
Internal systems approach	Evaluates the organization's ability to be innovative and function quickly and responsively	• Cut decision-making time • Increase rate of product innovation • Increase coordination and motivation of employees • Reduce conflict • Reduce time to market
Technical approach	Evaluates the organization's ability to convert skills and resources into goods and services efficiently	• Increase product quality • Reduce number of defects • Reduce production costs • Improve customer service • Reduce delivery time to customer

The External Resource Approach: Control

External resource approach A method managers use to evaluate how effectively an organization manages and controls its external environment.

The **external resource approach** allows managers to evaluate how effectively an organization manages and controls its external environment. For example, the organization's ability to influence stakeholders' perceptions in its favour and to receive a positive evaluation by external stakeholders is very important to managers and the organization's survival.[29] Similarly, an organization's ability to utilize its environment and to secure scarce and valuable resources is another indication of its control over the environment.[30]

To measure the effectiveness of their control over the environment, managers use indicators such as stock price, profitability, and return on investment, which compare the performance of their organization with the performance of other organizations.[31] Top managers watch the price of their company's stock very closely because of the impact it has on shareholder expectations. Similarly, in their attempt to attract customers and gauge the performance of their organization, managers gather information on the quality of their company's products as compared to their competitors' products.

Top management's ability to perceive and respond to changes in the environment or to initiate change and be first to take advantage of a new opportunity is another indicator of an organization's ability to influence and control its environment. For instance, the ability and willingness of the Roots Company to manage its environment by seizing any chance to use its reputation and brand name to develop new products that exploit market opportunities are well known. Similarly, Bill Gates has stated that his goal is to be at the forefront of software development in order to maintain Microsoft's competitive advantage in new product development. By their competitive attitude, these companies signify that they intend to stay in control of their environment so that they can continue to obtain scarce and valued resources such as customers and markets. Managers know that the organization's aggressiveness, entrepreneurial nature, and reputation are all criteria by which stakeholders (especially shareholders) judge how well a company's management is controlling its environment. One company that has had mixed fortunes in managing its environment and understanding the changing needs of its customers is Burntsand. (See Organizational Insights 1.5 and 1.6.)

The Internal Systems Approach: Innovation

Internal systems approach A method that allows managers to evaluate how effectively an organization functions and operates.

The **internal systems approach** allows managers to evaluate how effectively an organization functions and operates. To be effective, an organization needs a structure and a culture that foster adaptability and quick responses to changing conditions in the environment. The organization also needs to be flexible so that it can speed up decision making and rapidly create products and services. Measures of an organization's capacity for innovation include the length of time needed to make a decision, the amount of time needed to get new products to market, and the amount of time spent coordinating the activities of different departments.[32] These factors can often be measured objectively. For example, one year after the H-P–Compaq merger, the new H-P announced that its redesigned decision-making system had allowed it to speed the rate at which it could bring new products to market.

Improvements to internal systems that influence employee coordination or motivation have a direct impact on an organization's ability to respond to its environment. The reduction in product development time will allow H-P to match Japanese companies like Hitachi, which have always enjoyed short development cycles because of their extensive use of product teams in the development process. In turn, H-P's improved ability to get a product to market is likely to make the company attractive to new customers and may bring about an increase in shareholder returns.

ORGANIZATIONAL INSIGHT 1.5

Burntsand's Innovative Ways of Increasing Efficiency for Its Clients[33]

Burntsand is a business consulting and technology services company headquartered in Toronto, with operations throughout North America. It designs and implements information technology strategies to develop competitive advantages for its business clients. Burntsand was established in 1996 to focus on delivering innovative, cost-effective solutions on time and on budget. Although the company is relatively new on the scene, it has advanced in its success to become one of the best e-business solutions providers by internalizing strategy, technical, and creative services to maximize the use and effectiveness of current solutions and new technologies.

An important part of Burntsand's success and in turn what it sells to clients to improve their effectiveness is based on the "Burntsand Tool Set." The tool set is a combination of many integrated technologies that centralize, organize, and optimize business functions. Burntsand supplies its employees with these tools to give them effective and efficient access to knowledge so that they can subsequently use this benefit to help create competitive advantages for their customers.

The UpFront™ methodology is one of the main tools from Burntsand's Tool Set. It is a process that organizes a business vision into a series of manageable phases. Electronically, each project phase is organized into a set of synchronized, parallel workflows that contains all of the requirements and resources needed to complete each phase and workflow. A complementary component of the UpFront™ tool is an online customer satisfaction measurement tool. Project stakeholders can provide research, feedback, and satisfaction input to the appropriate individuals at all levels of the business process to ensure optimal project delivery. The UpFront™ tool is used in every client project. Burntsand also uses it internally to ensure success in its own e-business ventures.

The Technical Approach: Efficiency

The **technical approach** allows managers to evaluate how efficiently an organization can convert some fixed amount of organizational skills and resources into finished goods and services. Technical effectiveness is measured in terms of productivity and efficiency (the ratio of outputs to inputs).[34] Thus, for example, an increase in the number of units produced without the use of additional labour indicates a gain in productivity, and so does a reduction in the cost of labour or materials required to produce each unit of output.

Technical approach
A method managers use to evaluate how efficiently an organization can convert some fixed amount of organizational resources into finished goods and services.

Productivity measures are objective measures of the effectiveness of an organization's production operations. Thus it is common for production line managers to measure productivity at all stages of the production process and for them to be rewarded for reducing costs. In service organizations, where no tangible good is produced, line managers use productivity measures such as amount of sales per employee or the ratio of goods sold to goods returned to judge employee productivity. For most work activities, no matter how complex, there is a way to measure productivity or performance. In many settings the inducements offered to both employees and managers are closely linked to productivity measures, and it is important to select the right measures to

ORGANIZATIONAL INSIGHT 1.6

Burntsand Expands and Then Retracts in the Name of Efficiency[35]

In 2002, Burntsand pursued and was awarded a contract to provide a Web-based case, document, and workflow management solution for Public Works and Government Services Canada. The project had been valued at more than $1.7 million that would provide revenue over an approximate three-year period. The supply arrangement was expected to be a strong source of new business for Burntsand, whereby the Canada government was beginning its widely publicized strategy to invest significantly into having government information and services online to create greater access and new efficiencies. Burntsand subsequently expanded its business presence in Canada and United States from seven to eight client-based offices. This strategic redirection may very well have been the key for Burntsand to sustain effectiveness and efficiency for financial stability in a softening IT industry.

With downturns in the IT market segment, Burntsand has needed to endure economic operational challenges. Pursuing government projects did not prove to be an effective strategy for the company's defence in this regard. With the many uncertainties associated with federal government contracts and because the investment in this market area was slow to provide a reasonable rate of return, Burntsand reconsidered its priorities and focus. Less than two years after the company won the initial government contract, Burntsand announced that it was taking strategic action to rationalize its business in order to focus its effort and leverage key capabilities. An important part of this rationalization was to exit the governmental market segment and return to focusing on its stronger and longer standing business relations with technology partners. In this process it would also be simplifying its geographical representation and related management and administration structures—it closed its government office in Ottawa and also did some shuffling of administrative structures in the remaining offices.

evaluate effectiveness.[36] Employee attitude and motivation and a desire to cooperate are also important factors influencing productivity and efficiency.[37] The importance of continuously improving efficiency is very clear in Burntsand's attempt to deal with changing environmental pressures, as profiled in Organizational Insight 1.6 above.

Measuring Effectiveness: Organizational Goals

Managers create goals that they use to assess how well the organization is performing. Two types of goals used to evaluate organizational effectiveness are official goals and operative goals. **Official goals** are guiding principles that the organization formally states in its annual report and in other public documents. Usually these goals lay out the **mission** of the organization—they explain why the organization exists and what it should be doing. Official goals include being a leading producer of a product, demonstrating an overriding concern for public safety, and so forth. Official goals are meant to legitimize the organization and its activities, to allow it to obtain resources and the support of its stakeholders.[38] Consider the way the mission and goals of both Amazon.com (see Table 1-2) and Nova Scotia Power (see Table 1-3) have changed during the past 20 years as its managers have changed their business to better manage their environment.

Official goals
Guiding principles that the organization formally states in its annual report and in other public documents.

Mission
Goals that explain why the organization exists and what it should be doing.

Table 1-2

AMAZON.COM'S MISSION AND GOALS, 1995–2003

Where We Started

Amazon.com opened its virtual doors in July 1995 with a mission to use the Internet to transform book buying into the fastest, easiest, and most enjoyable shopping experience possible. While our customer base and product offerings have grown considerably since our early days, we still maintain our founding commitment to customer satisfaction and the delivery of an educational and inspiring shopping experience.

Where We Are Today

Today, Amazon.com is the place to find and discover anything you want to buy on line. We're very proud that millions of people in more than 220 countries have made us the leading online shopping site. We have Earth's Biggest Selection of products, including free electronic greeting cards, online auctions, and millions of books, CDs, videos, DVDs, toys and games, electronics, kitchenware, computers, and more.

Table 1-3

NOVA SCOTIA POWER'S MISSION AND GOALS, 1988–1995

The Culture Change (1988–1992)

Prior to the appointment of Louis Comeau in 1983, Nova Scotia Power did not have an explicit mission. When Comeau introduced culture change in 1988, a mission was developed and carefully spelled out. The mission embodied the new and clearer goals of making service a priority and providing that service in an efficient, courteous, and cost-effective manner; respecting the environment; recognizing employee contributions through timely feedback, fair and equitable rewards, opportunities, and compensation; and being a good corporate citizen that is a leader in the energy sector.[39]

The Re-engineering Years (1992–1995)

Once Nova Scotia Power was a privatized company, Comeau made changes in the goals and mission to emphasize a single primary goal of creating greater value for the customer in the delivery of electricity. Now the emphasis was on teamwork, keeping the competition at bay, focusing on the customer, and increasing value for the shareholders.

Operative goals are specific long- and short-term goals that guide managers and employees as they perform the work of the organization. The goals listed in Table 1-1 (p. 19) are operative goals that managers can use to evaluate organizational effectiveness. Managers can use operative goals to measure how well they are managing the environment. Is market share increasing or decreasing? Is the cost of inputs rising or falling? Similarly, they can measure how well the organization is functioning by measuring how long it takes to make a decision or how great conflict is between organizational members. Finally, they can measure how efficient they are by creating operative goals that allow them to "benchmark" themselves against their competitors—that is, compare their competitors' cost and quality achievements with their own. Numerous Canadian companies—including Magna International, Maple Leaf Foods, and CIBC—use benchmarking. For example, IBM Canada was able to turn around its flagging fortunes through benchmarking. In the early 1990s, when the company was experiencing serious customer dissatisfaction, it set out to measure itself against its leading competitors, focusing on "clear market segmentation, process re-engineering, best

Operative goals
Specific long- and short-term goals that guide managers and employees as they perform the work of the organization.

customer value, development of highly skilled teams, and enablement (empowerment) of staff."[40] This led to an extensive restructuring that included cutting various layers of management and establishing small operating units. Changes were also made to the corporate culture through encouraging risk-taking behaviour. Within five years of its benchmarking program, the company was reporting increased customer satisfaction and $10 billion in revenue.

An organization may be effective in one area but not in others.[41] For example, when Les Boutiques San Francisco Inc. first opened its doors in Montreal in 1994 it quickly became known for its innovative boutique shopping experience, with special rooms for nursing mothers, free shoeshines, and live music. Its innovative style led to quick success with the opening of several other boutiques. Within six years it had expanded into other retail ventures, with eight different banners, including the Les Ailes de la Mode department store chain. However, the new ventures stretched the company beyond its core competencies, and by August 2002 it faced a net loss of close to $44 million in a period of less than a year. To stave off future losses, the company appointed a chief restructuring officer who promptly cut 585 jobs in the clothing store chain, and sold off 58 of the company's specialty stores, with the loss of a further 577 jobs. At least one business consultant contends that the reason for Les Boutiques' serious difficulties was not so much a retail problem as a business executive problem.[42] The company overestimated the size of the market, moved too rapidly into different areas of the market, and expanded too rapidly outside Quebec, where these products had been geared to a specific market. In the end it had to rely on a dramatic restructuring to stay in business.

Managers must be careful to develop goals that measure effectiveness in all three dimensions: control, innovation, and efficiency. Moreover, companies must be careful to align their official and operative goals and eliminate any conflict between them. For example, senior management at Les Boutiques experienced initial growth through innovation but lost their way as they moved into environments that they were less certain of. Subsequent layoffs were much more severe than they would have been if managers had been following the official goals they claimed to believe in. When managers create a set of goals to measure organizational effectiveness, they must make sure that official goals and operative goals work together to enhance effectiveness.

The Plan of This Book

To understand how to manage organizational design and change, it is first necessary to understand how organizations affect, and are affected by, their environments. Then the principles of organizational design and change that managers use to improve the match or fit of an organization with its environment can be better understood. To facilitate this learning process, the chapters in this book are organized such that each builds upon the ones that have come before. Figure 1-5 shows how the various chapters fit together and provides a model of the components involved in organizational design and change.

After the scandals at Enron, Arthur Andersen, WorldCom, and Adelphia, it is more important than ever before that a clear link is made between ethics and organizational effectiveness because managers are responsible for protecting organizational resources and using them effectively. Chapter 2 examines the roles top managers perform in an organization, examines the claims and obligations of different organizational stakeholder groups, and examines the many ethical issues managers face in dealing with the claims of these different groups.

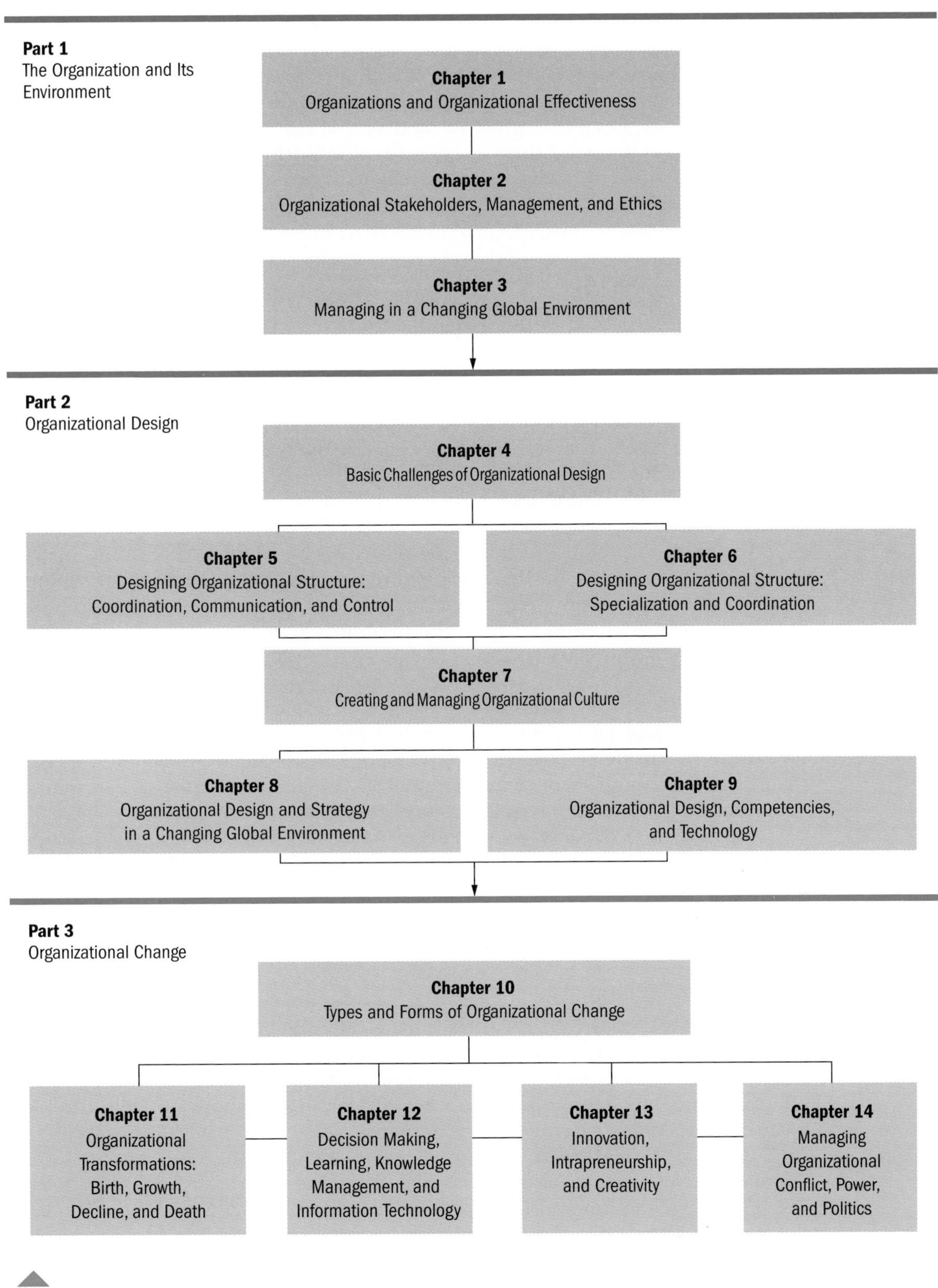

FIGURE 1-5
Components of Organizational Theory, Design, and Change.

The environment in which an organization operates is a principal source of uncertainty. If customers withdraw their support, if suppliers withhold inputs, if a global recession occurs, considerable uncertainty is created. Thus the organization must design its structure to manage adequately the contingencies it faces in the external environment. Chapter 3 presents models that reveal why the environment is a source of uncertainty and theories about how and why organizations act to meet uncertainties in the environment. Resource dependence theory examines how organizations attempt to gain control over scarce resources. Transaction cost theory examines how organizations manage environmental relations to reduce transaction costs.

Organizational Design

Organizational design is complicated by the contingencies that must be considered as an organization makes its design choices. Several types of contingency—the organization's environment (including government intervention and policy decisions), its strategy, technology, and internal processes that develop in an organization over time—cause uncertainty and influence an organization's choice of structure and culture. Throughout the rest of this book we analyze the sources of this uncertainty and how organizations manage it. We also discuss how organizations can go about the process of changing and redesigning their structures and cultures as contingencies change and lead managers to develop new goals and strategies for their organizations.

Chapters 4 through 7 examine the principles on which organizations operate and the choices available for designing and redesigning their structures and cultures to match the environment. As these chapters show, the same basic organizational problems occur in all work settings, and the purpose of organizational design is to develop an organizational structure and culture that will respond effectively to these challenges.

Chapter 8 discusses organizations' attempts to manage their environment by using their structures and strategies to improve their fit with their environments. We discuss how organizations develop functional, business, and corporate strategies to increase their control over and share of scarce resources. We also discuss the global strategies managers can adopt as they expand and work to increase their presence overseas.

Organizations produce goods and services. The competencies they develop to produce goods and services, and the uncertainty associated with different production methods or technologies, are major factors in the design of an organization. In Chapter 9 some theories that describe different competencies and technologies, and that explain the way in which they affect organizational structure and culture, are discussed.

Organizational Change

The third part of this book deals with the many different but related issues involved in changing and redesigning organizations to improve their effectiveness. It also highlights the way the need to foster innovation, utilize new information technologies effectively and, in general, speed the rate at which organizations can adjust to their environments has been changing organizations.

Chapter 10 examines the nature of organizational change and outlines several important different kinds of organizational change processes, such as restructuring, re-engineering, and innovation management. It also provides a model that explains the many different kinds of issues that must be confronted if managers are to succeed in their efforts to achieve a better fit with the environment.

When organizations are created and set in motion, various internal processes occur. As organizations grow and mature, many of them experience a predictable series of organizing crises, and as they attempt to change their strategies and structures, they confront similar problems. Chapter 11 presents a life cycle model of organizations and charts the typical problems they confront as they grow, mature, and decline.

Chapter 12 discusses organizational learning and decision making, and relates these processes to the use of information technologies to show the many ways in which IT is changing organizations. First, the ways in which managers make decisions is examined. Then the increasingly important question of why managers make mistakes, both strategically and ethically, is examined. Ways in which managers can avoid these mistakes and speed the level of organizational learning to improve the quality of decision making is then examined. Finally, we look at how new innovations in information technology, including the Internet, have been affecting organizations and changing organizational structure and culture.

Chapter 13 looks at the related issues of innovation and project management in organizations. Project management focuses on how project managers can utilize various techniques to speed and promote the development of new and improved goods and services. How to foster innovation and manage research and development is a pressing problem, particularly for organizations competing globally.

Finally, Chapter 14 covers problems of politics and conflict that arise as managers attempt to change and redesign organizational structure and culture. This chapter highlights the complex social and organizational processes that must be managed if an organization is to be able to manage the change process successfully and increase its effectiveness.

SUMMARY

We have examined what organizations are, why they exist, the purpose of organizational theory, design and change, and the different ways in which they can be evaluated. Organizations play a vital role in increasing the wealth of a society, and the purpose of managing organizational design and change is to enhance their ability to create value and thus organizational effectiveness. Chapter 1 has made the following main points:

1. An organization is a tool used by people to coordinate their actions to obtain something they desire or value—to achieve their goals.
2. Organizations are value-creation systems that take inputs from the environment and use skills and knowledge to transform these inputs into finished goods and services.
3. The use of an organization allows people jointly to increase specialization and the division of labour, use large-scale technology, manage the external environment, economize on transaction costs, and exert power and control—all of which increase the value that the organization can create.
4. Organizational theory is the study of how organizations function and how they affect and are affected by the environment in which they operate.
5. Organizational structure is the formal system of task and authority relationships that control how people coordinate their actions and use resources to achieve an organization's goals.
6. Organizational culture is the set of shared values and norms that control organizational members' interactions with each other and with suppliers, customers, and other people outside the organization.
7. Organizational design is the process by which managers select and manage aspects of structure and culture so that an organization can control the activities necessary to achieve its goals. Organizational design has important implications for a company's competitive

advantage, its ability to deal with contingencies and manage diversity, its efficiency, its ability to generate new goods and services, its control of the environment, its coordination and motivation of employees, and its development and implementation of strategy.

8. Organizational change is the process by which organizations redesign and transform their structures and cultures to move from their present state to some desired future state to increase their effectiveness. The goal of organizational change is to find new or improved ways of using resources and capabilities to increase an organization's ability to create value and hence performance.
9. Managers can use three approaches to evaluate organizational effectiveness: the external resource approach, the internal systems approach, and the technical approach. Each approach is associated with a set of criteria that can be used to measure effectiveness and a set of organizational goals.

DISCUSSION QUESTIONS

1. How do organizations create value? What is the role of entrepreneurship in this process?
2. What is the relationship among organizational theory, design, change, and organizational structure and culture?
3. What is organizational effectiveness? Discuss three approaches to evaluating effectiveness and the problems associated with each approach.
4. Draw up a list of effectiveness goals that you would use to measure the performance of (a) a fast-food restaurant and (b) a school of business.
5. Discuss the difference between a Crown corporation and a shareholding company in facing issues of control, innovation, and efficiency.

ORGANIZATIONAL THEORY IN ACTION

Practising Organizational Theory: Open Systems Dynamics

Form groups of three to five people and discuss the following scenario:

Think of an organization you are all familiar with, such as a Crown corporation, a local restaurant, store, or bank. Once you have chosen an organization, model it from an open systems perspective. For example, identify its input, conversion, and output processes.

1. Identify the specific forces in the environment that have the greatest opportunity to help or hurt this organization's ability to obtain resources and dispose of its goods or services.
2. Using the three views of effectiveness discussed in the chapter, discuss which specific measures are most useful to managers in evaluating this organization's effectiveness.

Making the Connection #1

At the end of every chapter you will find an exercise that requires you to search newspapers or magazines for an example of a real company that is dealing with some of the issues, concepts, challenges, questions, and problems discussed in the chapter.

Find an example of a company that is seeking to improve its effectiveness in some way. What dimension of effectiveness (control, innovation, or efficiency) is it seeking to improve? What changes is it making to address the issue?

The Ethical Dimension #1

An ethical exercise is present in every chapter to help you understand the many ways in which organizations can help or harm the people and groups in their environments, especially when they are managed in ways that are unethical. This exercise can be done alone or in a small group.

Think of some examples of ways in which a hospital, and the doctors and nurses who work within it, could act unethically toward patients. Also, think about behaviours that demonstrate that a hospital has high ethical standards.

1. List examples of these ethical and unethical behaviours.
2. How do these behaviours relate to the attempts of doctors and nurses to increase organizational effectiveness in the ways discussed in the chapter? Or, to attempts to pursue their own self-interest?

Analyzing the Organization: Design Module #1

To give you insight into the way real-world organizations work, at the end of every chapter there is an organizational design module for which you must collect and analyze information about an organization that you will select now and study all semester. You will write up the information you collect into a report to be presented to the class at the end of the semester.

Suppose you select Rogers Wireless Communications Inc. You will collect the information specified in each organizational design module, present and summarize your findings on Rogers for your class, and then produce a written report. Your instructor will provide the details of what will be required of you—for example, how long the presentation or report should be and whether you will work in a group or by yourself to complete the assignment. By the end of the semester, by completing each module, you will have a clear picture of how organizations operate and how they deal with problems and contingencies they face.

There are two approaches to selecting an organization. One is to choose a well-known organization about which a lot has been written. Large companies like IBM, Apple Computer, and Air Canada receive extensive coverage in business periodicals such as *Fortune*, *Business Week*, and *Canadian Business*. Every year, for example, the *Financial Post* publishes a list of the 500 largest corporations in Canada. If you choose a company on the *Financial Post*'s list, you can be sure that considerable information is published about it.

The best sources of information are business periodicals like *Canadian Business*, *Fortune*, *Business Week*, and *Forbes;* news magazines like *Time* and *Newsweek;* the *Financial Post*, the *National Post*, the *Globe and Mail*, the *Wall Street Journal*, and other newspapers. *F&S Predicasts*, *Value Line Investment Survey*, *Moody's Manuals on Investment*, and many other publications summarize articles written about a particular company. In addition, you should check industry and trade publications.

Finally, you should take advantage of the Internet and explore the World Wide Web to find information on your company. Most large companies have detailed Web sites that provide a considerable amount of information. You can find these web sites using a search engine such as Yahoo or Google and then download the information you need.

If you consult these sources, you will obtain a lot of information that you can use to complete the design modules. You may not get all the specific information you need, but you will have enough to answer many of the design module questions.

The second approach to selecting an organization is to choose one located in your city or town—for example, a large department store, manufacturing company, hotel, or nonprofit organization (such as a hospital or school) where you or somebody you know works. You could contact the owners or managers of the organization and ask whether they would be willing to talk to you about the way they operate and how they design and manage their company.

Each approach to selecting a company has advantages and disadvantages. The advantage of selecting a local company and doing your own information gathering is that in face-to-face interviews you can ask for detailed information that may be unavailable from published sources. You will gain an especially rich picture of the way a company operates by doing your research personally. The problem is that the local organization you choose has to be big enough to offer you insight into the way organizations work. In general, it should employ at least 20 people and have at least three levels in its hierarchy.

If you use written sources to study a very large organization, you will get a lot of interesting information that relates to organizational theory, because the organization is large and complex and is confronting many of the problems discussed in this book. But you may not be able to obtain all the detailed information you want.

Whichever selection approach you use, be sure that you have access to enough interesting information to complete the majority of the organizational design modules. One module, for example, asks about the international or global dimension of your organization's strategy and structure. If you pick a local company that does not have an international dimension, you will be unable to complete that assignment. However, to compensate for this lack of information, you might have very detailed information about the company's structure or product lines. The issue is to make sure that you can gain access to enough information to write an interesting report.

ASSIGNMENT

Choose a company to study, and answer the following questions about it.

1. What is the name of the organization? Give a short account of the history of the company. Describe the way it has grown and developed.
2. What does the organization do? What goods and services does it produce/provide? What kind of value does it create? If the company has an annual report, what does the report describe as the company's organizational mission?
3. Draw a model of the way the organization creates value. Briefly describe its inputs, throughputs, outputs, and environment.
4. Do an initial analysis of the organization's major problems or issues. What challenges confront the organization today—for example, in its efforts to attract customers, to lower costs, to increase operating efficiency? How does its organizational design relate to these problems?
5. Read its annual report and determine which kinds of goals, standards, or targets the organization is using to evaluate performance. How well is the organization doing when judged by the criteria of control, innovation, and efficiency?

Company Profiles #1*

Choose one or more of the organizations (e.g., companies, government agencies, or nonprofit organizations) that are profiled in this chapter. Do an Internet search to get up-to-date information on each organization you have selected, and answer the following questions.

1. What does the new information tell you about the organization's current effectiveness?
2. How does the information compare with the earlier information provided in the text and what does that tell you about organizations (e.g., does the organization appear to be more or less effective than before, and how do you explain this)?

Alternative Perspectives #1

This book approaches the topic of organization theory from a mainstream perspective. This approach is also sometimes referred to as functionalist (Burrell and Morgan, 1979) or managerialist (Mills, Simmons, and Helms Mills, 2005) because it views organizational theory from the manager's perspective.

What topics and points of interest are more likely to be included in the study of organizational theory if it was viewed from one or other of the following perspectives: actionalist, radical, feminist, racio-ethnic, and postmodernist.

To answer this question, read:

Mills, A. J., Simmons, T., and Helms Mills, J. 2005. Chapter 1: Developing a Critical Approach to Organizational Study. In *Reading Organization Theory: A Critical Approach to the Study of Organizational Behaviour and Structure.* 3rd ed. Toronto: Garamond Press.

Reading List

Burrell, G., and Morgan, G. 1979. *Sociological Paradigms and Organizational Analysis.* London: Heinneman.

Hatch, M. J. 1997. *Organization Theory: Modern Symbolic and Postmodern Perspectives.* Oxford: Oxford University Press.

Wilson, F. 2003. *Organizational Behaviour and Gender.* Aldershot: Ashgate.

* The authors would like to receive information from student groups and instructors on any companies where there have been dramatic changes to the information published in this text. We would be happy to publish the best of these changes in a subsequent edition, where we will focus on changing company profiles.

CASE FOR ANALYSIS

Organizational Structure Transformations at Cymat Corp.[43]

When Cymat of Mississauga, Ontario, incorporated in 1990, the company was specializing in the production of lightweight aluminum packaging and enclosures for the telecommunications and pharmaceutical industries. Through various acquisitions, partnerships, and R&D advancements, Cymat's steady growth and changing focus over the years have subsequently resulted in various transformations in its organizational structure. In particular, by 1995, Cymat had begun to change significantly when it established important connections with European companies and had acquired exclusive North American licensing rights to manufacture and sell Stabilized Aluminum Foam (SAF), an innovative material and technological industry advancement. In 2000, Cymat reorganized to focus exclusively on commercializing this technology. The company appointed new leaders to direct a changing structure that reflected an emphasis on research and development.

Just one year later, Cymat made major changes again when it merged and acquired further SAF technology and licensing through its relationship with Norsk Hydro. Norsk Hydro was a European company well situated in the industry with connections to countries such as Hungary, Brazil, Japan, Russia, and South Korea. Norsk Hydro became a significant shareholder in Cymat and joined Cymat's board of directors as part of this transaction. Cymat then gained worldwide manufacturing and marketing rights to advance the company even further. Consequently, the rapid growth and costs of research and development meant increasing reported losses. It was at this point, in 2001, that Cymat raised $17.25 million by listing shares on the Toronto Stock Exchange (under the symbol CYM).

Two years later, Cymat announced new shifts to the company's organizational structure. There appeared to be no departures or additions to the company's executive team, but corporate roles and responsibilities shifted to reflect changing priorities. Michael Liik, Cymat's chairman and CEO, explained the new structuring:

> The purpose behind the moves is to streamline operations by better aligning commercial and technical development activities, and to bring a higher level of focus to the finance and administrative side of the business. Cymat has grown rapidly, and we believe that with these and other changes to our leadership structure, we are well equipped to manage growth going forward and pursue the many global opportunities for our technology.

It would seem that Cymat is an organization of relatively constant change. As partnerships evolve, financial reserves and requirements fluctuate, and research and development initiatives provide innovative derivatives of their core technology (now known as Cymat SmartMetal™), Cymat engages in ongoing structure changes. The two founding tenets of Cymat, partnering and technology development, have greatly influenced the company's direction. The applicable nature of Cymat's core technology has meant forming partnerships and marketing its intellectual property and technology with many diverse companies. For example, recently, Cymat has joined up with PSA Peugeot Citroën, Europe's second-largest car manufacturer. The company has also formed a collaborative relationship with Dynatec to combine technologies and expertise in the underground mining environment. Indeed, it appears that Cymat is realizing its goal to commercialize its proprietary aluminum foam technology in as many markets as possible, as evidenced by its rapid growth and ever-changing structure.

DISCUSSION QUESTIONS

1. What different milestone events resulted in changes in Cymat's organizational structure?
2. What types of problems have also influenced structural changes at Cymat?

REFERENCES

1. Statistics Canada, Annual Estimates of Employment, Earnings, and Hours, 1997, *dsp-psd.communication.gc.ca.qe2a-proxy.mun.ca/Collection-R/Statcan/72F0002XIB/72F0002XIB-e.html.*
2. A. W. Gouldner, "Organizational Analysis," in R. K. Merton, ed., *Sociology Today* (New York: Basic Books, 1959); A. Etzioni, *Comparative Analysis of Complex Organizations* (New York: Free Press, 1961).
3. I. M. Kirzner, *Competition and Entrepreneurship* (Chicago: University of Chicago Press, 1973).
4. *www.amazon.com*, 2002.
5. *www.amazon.com*, "About Amazon.com," 2002.
6. P. M. Blau, "A Formal Theory of Differentiation in Organizations," *American Sociological Review*, 1970, vol. 35, pp. 201–218; D. S. Pugh and D. J. Hickson, "The Comparative Study of Organizations," in G. Salaman and K. Thompson, eds., *People and Organizations* (London: Penguin, 1977), pp. 43–55.
7. P. M. Blau, *Exchange and Power in Social Life* (New York: Wiley, 1964); P. M. Blau and W. R. Scott, *Formal Organizations* (San Francisco: Chandler, 1962).
8. Statistics Canada, Annual Report 2002, *www.statcan.ca/English*, 1 May 2005; Labor Demographics Report for 2001 (Orono, ME: Bureau of Labor Education, University of Maine), p. 1.
9. Job Quality.ca, *www.jobquality.ca/indicator_e/security002.stm*, 2001.
10. C. I. Barnard, *The Functions of the Executive* (Cambridge, MA: Harvard University Press, 1948); A. Etzioni, *Modern Organizations* (Englewood Cliffs, NJ: Prentice Hall, 1964).
11. P. R. Lawrence and J. W. Lorsch, *Organization and Environment* (Boston: Graduate School of Business Administration, Harvard University, 1967); W. R. Scott, *Organizations: Rational, Natural, and Open Systems* (Englewood Cliffs, NJ: Prentice Hall, 1981).
12. *www.cocacola.com*, 2002; *www.pepsico*, 2002.
13. J. Helms Mills, *Making Sense of Organizational Change* (Routledge: London, 2003).
14. M. Beer, *Organizational Change and Development* (Santa Monica, CA: Goodyear, 1980); J. I. Porras and R. C. Silvers, "Organization Development and Transformation," *Annual Review of Psychology*, 1991, vol. 42, pp. 51–78.
15. Organizational Insight by Ellen Rudderham-Gaudet, based on the following sources: About Ontario Power Generation, 2004, "Putting Our Energy to Good Use," retrieved 30 March 2004 from *www.opg.com/about/overview.asp*; Ontario Power Generation, 2002, "Annual Information Form for the Year Ended December 31, 2002," *www.opg.com/ir/Sedar/2002%20AIF.pdf*, 2 April 2004; M. Goulding and T. Pendlebury, "Corporate 'News Show' Introduces the Bottom Line to Staff," *Canadian HR Reporter*, 2002, vol. 15, p. 16.
16. M. Moritz, *The Little Kingdom: The Private Story of Apple Computer* (New York: Morrow, 1984).
17. S. Anderson Forest and C. Arnst, "The Education of Michael Dell," *Business Week*, 1993, March 22, pp. 82–88.
18. R. Cringely, *Accidental Empires* (New York: Harper Business, 1994).
19. D. McGraw, "The Kid Bytes Back," *U.S. News and World Report*, 12 December 1994, pp. 70–71.
20. *www.dell.com*, 2002.
21. *www.apple.com*, 2002.
22. R. S. Abella, *Equity in Employment: A Royal Commission Report* (Ottawa: Ministry of Supply and Services Canada, 1984).
23. *www.aol-timewarner.com*, 2001.
24. Ibid.
25. S. Prasso, "AOL Time Warner's Power Towers," *Business Week*, 11 June 2001, p. 43.
26. *www.timewarneraol.com*, 2002.
27. L. Galambos, "What Have CEO's Been Doing?" *Journal of Economic History*, 1988, vol. 18, pp. 243–258.
28. Ibid., p. 253.
29. J. P. Campbell, "On the Nature of Organizational Effectiveness," in P. S. Goodman, J. M. Pennings, & Associates, eds., *New Perspectives on Organizational Effectiveness*, pp. 13–55 (San Francisco: Jossey-Bass, 1977).
30. F. Friedlander and H. Pickle, "Components of Effectiveness in Small Organizations," *Administrative Science Quarterly*, 1968, vol. 13, pp. 289–304; R. H. Miles, *Macro Organizational Behavior* (New York: Goodyear Press, 1980).
31. Campbell, "On the Nature of Organizational Effectiveness."
32. Campbell, "On the Nature of Organizational Effectiveness."
33. Organizational Insight by Ellen Rudderham-Gaudet, based on the following sources: Burntsand, "Who We Are," *www.burntsand.ca/who_we_are/default.asp*, 14 April 2004; Burntsand, "How We Do It,"

www.burntsand.ca/how_we_do_it/the_burntsand_toolset.asp, 15 April 2004.

34. J. D. Thompson, *Organizations in Action* (New York: McGraw Hill, 1967).
35. Insight by Ellen Rudderham-Gaudet, based on the following sources: "Toronto Integrator Wins Fed Contract," *Channel Business,* 2002, vol. 15, p. 12; "Burntsand Takes Steps to Focus Its Business and Leverage Key Capabilities," *Canada NewsWire,* 4 December 2003, p. 13; Burntsand, 2004, "News and Events," *www.burntsand.com/news_events/default.asp,* 28 April 2004.
36. R. M. Steers, *Organizational Effectiveness: A Behavioral View* (Santa Monica, CA: Goodyear, 1977).
37. D. E. Bowen and G. R. Jones, "Transaction Cost Analysis of Customer Service Organization Exchange," *Academy of Management Review,* 1986, vol. 11, pp. 428–441.
38. T. M. Jones, "Instrumental Stakeholder Theory: A Synthesis of Ethics and Economics," *Academy of Management Review,* 1995, vol. 20, pp. 404–437.
39. J. Helms Mills, *Making Sense of Organizational Change* (Routledge: London, 2003).
40. Campbell, "On the Nature of Organizational Effectiveness," pp. 43–53; R. E. Quinn and J. Rohrbaugh, "A Spatial Model of Effectiveness Criteria: Towards a Competing Values Approach to Organizational Analysis," *Management Science,* 1983, 29, pp. 33–51.
41. *epe.lac-bac.gc.ca/100/201/301/tbs-sct/tb_manual-ef/Pubs_pol/opepubs/TB_O/10QG5-7E.html,* 24 May 2005.
42. Ibid.
43. Case by Ellen Rudderham-Gaudet, based on the following sources: About Cymat, "History," *www.cymat.com/Cymat_Information.htm,* 11 July 2004; Composite/Plastic Newsletter, "Cymat Loss Widens on Commercialization and R&D Expenses," retrieved 4 July 2004 from *http://composite.about.com/library/PR/2001/blcymat2.htm;* "Cymat Announces New Organizational Structure," *Canada NewsWire,* 30 May 2003, p. 1; *Cymat Says Newsletter,* Winter 2003, *www.cymat.com/winter2003nl/from_ceo.html,* 11 July 2004.

Organizational Stakeholders, Management, and Ethics

CHAPTER 2

Learning Objectives

Business and service organizations exist to create valued goods and services that people need or desire. Organizations may have either a profit or nonprofit orientation for the creation of these goods or services. But who decides which particular goods and services an organization should provide, and how do you divide the value that an organization creates among different groups of people such as management, employees, customers, shareholders, and other stakeholders? If people primarily behave self-interestedly, what mechanisms or procedures govern the way an organization uses its resources, and what is to stop the different groups within the organization from trying to maximize their own share of the value created, possibly at the detriment or expense of others? At a time when the issue of corporate ethics and management dishonesty and greed has come under intense scrutiny, these questions must be addressed before the issue of designing an organization to increase its effectiveness can be investigated.

After studying this chapter you should be able to:

1. Identify the various stakeholder groups and their interests or claims on an organization, its activities, and its created value.
2. Understand the choices and problems inherent in apportioning and distributing the value an organization creates.
3. Appreciate who has authority and responsibility within an organization, and distinguish between different levels of management.
4. Describe the agency problem that exists in all authority relationships and the various mechanisms, such as the board of directors and stock options, that can be used to align managerial behaviour with organizational goals or to help control illegal and unethical managerial behaviour.
5. Discuss the vital role played by ethics in organizations.

ORGANIZATIONAL STAKEHOLDERS

Stakeholders
People, groups or other organizations who have an interest, claim, or stake in an organization, in what it does, and in how well it performs.

Organizations exist because of their ability to create valued goods and services which yield acceptable outcomes for various groups of **stakeholders**, people who have an interest, claim, or stake in the organization, in what it does, and in how well it performs.[1] In general, stakeholders are motivated to participate in an organization if they receive inducements that exceed the value of the contributions they are required to make.[2] **Inducements** are rewards such as money, power, the support of beliefs or values, and organizational status. **Contributions** are the skills, knowledge, and expertise that organizations require of their members during task performance.

Inducements
Rewards such as money, power, personal accomplishment, and organizational status.

Contributions
The skills, knowledge, and expertise that organizations require of their members during task performance.

There are two main groups of organizational stakeholders: inside stakeholders and outside stakeholders. The inducements and contributions of each group are summarized in Table 2-1.[3]

Inside Stakeholders

Inside stakeholders are people who are closest to an organization and have the strongest or most direct claim on organizational resources: shareholders, managerial employees, and nonmanagerial employees.

Shareholders Shareholders are the owners of the organization, and, as such, their claim on organizational resources is often considered superior to the claims of other inside stakeholders. The shareholders' contribution to the organization is to invest money in it by buying the organization's shares or stock. The shareholders' inducement to invest is the prospective money they can earn on their investment in the form of dividends and increases in the price of the stock they have purchased. Investment in stock is risky, however, because there is no guarantee of a return. Shareholders who do not believe that the inducement (the possible return on their investment) is enough to warrant their contribution (the money they have invested) sell their shares and withdraw their support from the organization. As the following example illustrates, more and more shareholders are relying on large institutional investment companies to protect their interests and to increase their collective power to influence the activities of organizations. (See Organizational Insight 2.1.)

Managerial Employees Managers are the employees who are responsible for coordinating organizational resources and ensuring that an organization's goals are successfully met. Senior managers are responsible for investing shareholder money in various

Table 2-1

INDUCEMENTS AND CONTRIBUTIONS OF ORGANIZATIONAL STAKEHOLDERS

Stakeholder	Contribution to the Organization	Inducement to Contribute
Inside		
Shareholders	Money and capital	Dividends and stock appreciation
Managers	Skills and expertise	Salaries, bonuses, status, and power
Workforce	Skills and expertise	Wages, bonuses, stable employment, and promotion
Outside		
Customers	Revenue from purchase of goods and services	Quality and price of goods and services
Suppliers	High-quality inputs	Revenue from purchase of inputs
Government	Rules governing good business practice	Fair and free competition
Unions	Free and fair collective bargaining	Equitable share of inducements
Community	Social and economic infrastructure	Revenue, taxes, employment, quality of life, and concern for the environment
General public	Customer loyalty and reputation	National pride

ORGANIZATIONAL INSIGHT 2.1

The Increasing Power of Institutional Investors[4]

The high-profile corporate scandals of WorldCom, Enron, Adelphia, Global Crossing, and others in the United States, and Nortel Networks in Canada have sparked significant discussion in investor, government, media, and academic circles about the need for change to corporate governance standards and practice.

The United States government has opted for a regulative approach. On July 8, 2002, U.S. President George W. Bush introduced the Sarbanes-Oxley Act, which is intended to make corporate executives and their audit firms more accountable and responsible to shareholders. Canadian politicians are facing pressure to introduce similar legislation and are studying various options. In the meantime, though, one very important stakeholder group—institutional investors—is using its power to influence the governance practices of Canadian companies.

The Canadian Coalition for Good Governance (CCGG) is a group comprised of some 33 institutional investors. Between them, CCGG members manage $500 billion in assets. The Ontario Teachers Pension Plan and OMERS are among the CCGG's biggest members, managing the pension plan assets of Ontario's 252 000 public school teachers and 342 000 municipal government employees.

The CCGG formed in the spring of 2003 with an objective to jointly promote good governance practices and increased organizational performance in publicly traded Canadian companies. In very specific terms, the CCGG wants corporate boards to achieve a delicate balance between giving their management teams the freedom and incentive to pursue performance goals, while at the same time ensuring there are appropriate financial, legal, and ethical control systems in place. The group describes its approach as being able to "walk softly and carry a big stick." By that, the CCGG means it does much of its work behind the scenes—away from the media spotlight.

Using their own in-house financial analysts, institutional investors closely monitor and assess the financial performance and governance practices of the firms whose shares they own. Because of the size of their investments in many Canadian public companies—and because of the negative impact they'd have on these share prices if they sold them suddenly—institutional investors also command a lot of attention. If they have a concern, they are more likely to be able to meet with company executives and directors to discuss the issue and possible resolutions. Until the CCGG was formed, such exchanges were occurring between institutional investors and individual companies, but now the efforts are more coordinated and will most likely have greater impact. If desired improvements aren't forthcoming, the CCGG and its members have said they will use "the stick"—that is, they will speak publicly about their concerns. They may even go so far as to use their shareholder voting power to effect change.

The group is also working to raise the overall general awareness and understanding of corporate governance issues, making speeches before professional associations, business conferences, and educational forms. The CCGG is using the media and its own Web site to make people aware of the state of corporate governance in Canada and promotes governance standards and best practices. It is also publishing data collected by other groups, such as the Rotman School of Management's "report card" on Canadian governance practices.

What impact will the CCGG have? It's hard to say, since the group is still in its infancy. The CCGG has set a big task for itself in trying to align the interests of boards and management with those of shareholders, but it is an extremely important one. And with its financial clout, the CCGG will be a force difficult to ignore.

resources in order to maximize the future value of goods and services. Managers are, in effect, the agents or employees of shareholders and are appointed indirectly by shareholders through an organization's governance structure, such as a board of directors, to manage the organization's business.

Managers' contributions are the skills they use to direct the organization's response to pressures from within and outside the organization. For example, a manager's skills at opening up global markets, identifying new product markets, or solving transaction-cost and technological problems can greatly facilitate the achievement of the organization's goals.

Various types of rewards induce managers to perform their activities well: monetary compensation (in the form of salaries, bonuses, and stock options) and the psychological satisfaction they may get from accomplishing their work, from controlling the corporation, through exercising power, or even when taking risks with other people's money. Managers who do not believe that the inducements meet or exceed the level of their contributions are likely to withdraw their support by either reducing their contributions or through leaving the organization.

Nonmanagerial Employees An organization's workforce consists of nonmanagerial employees. These members of the workforce have responsibilities and duties (usually outlined in a job description) that they are responsible for performing. An employee's contribution to the organization is the performance of his or her duties and responsibilities. How well an employee performs is, in some measure, within the employee's control. An employee's motivation to perform well relates to the rewards and punishments that the organization uses to influence job performance. Like managerial employees, other employees who do not feel that the inducements meet or exceed their contributions are likely to withdraw their support for the organization by reducing their contributions or the level of their performance, or by leaving the organization.

Outside Stakeholders

Outside stakeholders are people who do not own the organization (such as shareholders), are not employed by it, but do have some interest in it or its activities. Customers, suppliers, the government, trade and other unions, local communities, special interest groups, and the general public are all outside stakeholders.

Customers Customers are usually an organization's largest outside stakeholder group. Customers are induced to select a product or service (and thus an organization) from potentially many alternative products or services. They usually do this through an estimation of what they are getting relative to what they have to pay. The money they pay for the product or service represents their contribution to the organization and reflects the value they feel they receive from the organization. As long as the organization produces a product or service whose price is equal to or less than the value customers feel they are getting, they will continue to buy the product or service and support the organization.[5] If customers refuse to pay the price the organization is asking, they usually will withdraw their support, and the organization loses a vital stakeholder. The broadcast services of the Canadian Broadcasting Corporation are an example of the challenges involved in meeting consumer needs. (See Organizational Insight 2.2.)

Suppliers Suppliers, another important outside stakeholder group, contribute to the organization by providing reliable raw materials, component parts, or other services that allow the organization to reduce uncertainty in its technical or production operations, thus allowing for cost efficiencies. Suppliers therefore can have a direct effect on the organization's efficiency and an indirect effect on its ability to attract customers.

ORGANIZATIONAL INSIGHT 2.2

The Canadian Broadcasting Corporation and Its Customers[6]

In 1936, an act of parliament created the Canadian Broadcasting Corporation (CBC), Canada's national public broadcaster. The CBC currently operates under the 1991 Broadcasting Act and is accountable to the Canadian parliament. According to the Broadcasting Act, the CBC must "provide radio and television services incorporating a wide range of programming that informs, enlightens and entertains" and that is "predominantly and distinctively Canadian." The Broadcasting Act also directs the CBC to meet the various needs of the diverse regions of Canada. The CBC has a mandate to service the varied needs of its customers.

The CBC broadcasts through 104 CBC/Radio-Canada stations, 1190 CBC Radio-Canada rebroadcasters, 19 private affiliates, and 272 affiliated or community rebroadcasters. While operations of the CBC generate some additional funding through advertising revenue, it is funded primarily by the federal government. The CBC is in a unique situation and faces challenges that most companies do not have, as the CBC has continually evolved since its inception and it is accountable to a number of stakeholders. Its mandate is from the government, but its audience is its customers. It must balance financial viability against its obligations under the Broadcasting Act.

This has historically been a difficult balancing act for the CBC. To meet its regional and Canadian content mandate, it must offer programs that may actually run at a financial loss, which therefore threatens long-term financial viability. CBC television is undergoing changes that will decrease programming or eliminate entire stations for reasons of cost control. Most local supper-hour news shows will be eliminated in favour of a national news broadcast supplemented by short local inserts. Additionally, over 500 jobs will be lost to downsizing.

However, at the same time the CBC tries to make itself fiscally responsible and financially viable it also faces added pressures. A decision in January 2004 by the Canadian Radio-television and Telecommunications Commission (CRTC) made expanded regional coverage a condition of CBC-TV's licence. This decision was met with anger by Robert Rabinovitch, the CBC president. He believes that the CRTC's demands are not reasonable and that they are not letting the CBC manage itself.

"Can the CBC be Canadian and public and still be popular and relevant?" asks Bill Brioux of the *Toronto Sun*. "How long can the best newscast in the land get hammered night after night by the likes of *Law & Order, CSI, ER* and *The Osbournes*? It's a brutally competitive TV world out there, with new networks and alternatives to TV springing up all the time. Still, CBC is driving some of its own viewers away by paying more attention to mandate than to the market." Customers vote with their eyes and their eyes are turning elsewhere. The problems of the CBC are also compounded by the fact that its operations and its role in preserving Canadian culture remains an ongoing political issue.

An organization that has high-quality inputs can make high-quality products or deliver high-quality services and attract more customers. In turn, as demand for its products or services increases, the organization demands greater quantities of high-quality inputs or services from its suppliers.

For example, one of the reasons why Japanese cars remain so popular in North America is that they still require fewer repairs than the average North American–made vehicle. This reliability is a result of the use of component parts that meet stringent quality control standards. In addition, Japanese parts suppliers are constantly improving their efficiency.[7] The close relationship between the large Japanese automakers and their suppliers is a stakeholder relationship that pays long-term dividends for both parties. Car manufacturers in Canada and the U.S. have realized this and over the last decade have attempted to replicate and improve upon the Japanese model and are rapidly improving the quality and reliability of their products.

Government Historically, various governments have had a major influence upon both the markets and the operating environment of Canadian business. This involvement has been both proscriptive and prescriptive in nature. As business operates within, and contributes to, our society, governments have several claims on an organization. While it wants companies to compete in a fair manner and obey the rules of free competition, it also wants companies to obey agreed-upon rules and laws concerning the payment and treatment of employees, workers' health and workplace safety, nondiscriminatory hiring practices, and other social and economic issues. Besides the purely legal aspects of business operations, governments often receive a mandate from the voting public concerning particular issues reflecting broader social concerns. The subsequent involvement of governments and their treatment of these issues may involve or affect business organizations and business conduct in various ways.

Whether it is a new regulation designed to improve accountability through changes to corporate reporting and audit procedures, legislation concerning environmental protection and guidelines for hazardous waste management, or quotas on the harvesting of natural resources, governments may enact various legislation originating at the federal, provincial, or municipal level. In this fashion, government is an organizational stakeholder, and the government makes a contribution to the other organizational stakeholders by standardizing regulations so that no one company or group of companies can obtain an unfair competitive advantage in the market. Governments also serve as mechanisms to introduce needed changes and facilitate economic growth, all while protecting and preserving our society as a whole. Consequently, governments control many of the rules of business practice and have the power to punish any company that breaks these rules.

For example, the major corporate scandals in the U.S. of the last several years have caused both provincial and federal governments to become increasingly attentive to the public's concern over corporate governance and organizational ethics. Both these levels of government are actively working with public interest groups and industry representatives to address these growing ethical and legal concerns. In the absence of a national regulatory body (such as the U.S. Securities Exchange Commission), provincial trade ministers are working together in an attempt to develop a national standard for the regulation of publicly traded companies. It is hoped that regulations and standards developed by this process will help ensure that Canadians may avoid similar circumstances in business and organizational conduct in this country.

In addition to market and legislative governance, another result of the Canadian federated system of government has been a broader economic concern with nation building. This has led to the historical evolution of agencies within the federal government whose role is to assist in regional economic development. While these agencies have no direct legislative role, they are designed to facilitate economic development in a number of ways. Agencies and departments such as the Atlantic Canada Opportunities Agency, the Business Development Bank of Canada, Canada Economic Development for Quebec Regions, or the Western Economic Diversification Canada may assist through market studies and analysis, seed or developmental financing for startups, or other general forms of business assistance.[8]

Within Canada, more than many other Western nations including the U.S., government plays a major role in the protection of not only shareholder interests, but also the interest of direct and indirect stakeholders. The Canadian governments, at various levels, have historically developed a responsibility to the public to oversee or mandate changes to business practice in order to protect social interests—areas of practice that historically have been left to market forces and business practices—such as governance and oversight, environmental concerns, and the enforcement protection of evolving social standards such as nondiscriminatory practices against same-sex couples.

Unionized Employees The relationship between a trade or other union and an organization can be one of conflict or cooperation. The nature of the relationship has a direct effect on the productivity and effectiveness of the organization, the union membership, and even other stakeholders. Cooperation between managers and the union can lead to positive long-term outcomes if both parties agree on an equitable division of the gains from an improvement in a company's fortunes. Managers and the union might agree, for example, to share the gains from cost savings due to productivity improvements that resulted from a flexible work schedule. However, the management–union relationship may also be antagonistic because unions' demands for increased benefits may conflict directly with shareholders' demands for greater company profits and thus greater returns on their investments. Or management may not be treating unionized members in accordance with the level of their contribution to the organization.

Disagreement between management and unions may also adversely impact both internal and external organizational stakeholders. In 2004, the unionized employees of the telecommunications company Aliant went on an extended strike lasting from April through September. During this time, customers could not order new services (e.g., get new phones installed) and they saw reduced customer service, so many switched to alternative phone service providers. Aliant's stock price dropped significantly, adversely affecting corporate investors through stock-value loss. Unionized employees had to survive on strike pay—an amount well below that they would normally make on the job. Management had to take up the slack and work overtime for the business to continue to operate. At times, the stress and tension between management and the union led to confrontations. Even after the strike action was resolved, the whole organization was affected by the tension between management and the unionized employees arising from the bitter feelings and emotions resulting from the strike.

Strikes in one organization may also affect other organizations or other stakeholders. For example, beyond the negative impact upon hockey fans, the lockout of the NHL players by the team owners in 2004 also negatively affected employees at the Canadian Broadcasting Company. Those employees who would normally have produced these televised games were laid off because there were no games to broadcast. Concession stand employees and other arena and stadium workers whose wages are directly associated with hockey games at the stadium were also affected—either laid off or having their hours reduced during the lockout. Other stakeholders were also indirectly affected, such as sports restaurants that saw a drop in clientele. On the other hand, local hockey leagues and the junior leagues saw an increase in attendance at their games.

Local Communities Local communities also have a stake in the performance of organizations because employment, housing, and the general economic well-being of a community are strongly affected by the success or failure of local businesses. This is of particular importance in Canada due to the unique nature of the Canadian geography and demographics. Unlike the United States, Canada has many smaller businesses and industries that are regionally based. This has important implications; for example, Ottawa's economy is closely tied to the organizational performance of Nortel and Windsor's to those of the automakers. Many of Canada's regional communities may have only one or two major businesses or industries that they rely upon for much of their economic activity.

While community dependency upon single organizations is changing across Canada, there are still many communities that are integrally tied to the economic fortunes of local business. When businesses shift focus or effort to keep themselves competitive in the rapidly globalizing environment, to open new markets, to create advantage through knowledge management initiatives, or to move away from a resource-based to a knowledge- or service-based focus, the surrounding community is affected. For example, when business increases its use of technology, whether for manufacturing, information processing, or service delivery, it changes the skill sets it needs in employees. This may make local college or university programs outdated or obsolete, thus affecting the educational and employment prospects of the next working generation in the community. If the community cannot adapt itself to these new needs, the business may have to close plants or offices and move to a community that can meet these needs. When this happens, jobs, salaries, and wages are removed from the community, which can have a devastating impact to the community as a whole.

Special Interest Groups and the General Public Canada's public also wants its corporations and other businesses to act in a socially responsible way so that corporations generally refrain or are constrained from taking any actions that may injure or impose unreasonable or unjust costs on other stakeholders. As Canada's social culture evolves, people become more aware of how business activity impacts the environment and social issues. Beyond elections and government mandates, many of these issues become particularly important to different subelements of the broader public or what are referred to as special interest groups. These groups may represent those with particular environmental concerns; for example, groups have lobbied to move shipping transit lanes in the Bay of Fundy to reduce ship collisions with whale populations.[9] Groups may also be motivated by concern for those with disabilities by sponsoring initiatives to make workplaces more accessible to those with mobility impairments. While many of these special interest groups start out small, they may grow in size and influence as the issues they raise become concerns for the general public.

ORGANIZATIONAL EFFECTIVENESS: SATISFYING STAKEHOLDERS' GOALS AND INTERESTS

An organization is used simultaneously by different groups of stakeholders to each accomplish or further their own goals. It is the collective contributions of all stakeholders that are needed for an organization to be viable and to accomplish its mission of producing valued goods and services. Each stakeholder group is motivated to contribute to the organization by its own set of goals, and each group evaluates the effectiveness of the organization by judging how well it meets the group's specific goals.[10]

Shareholders evaluate an organization by the return they receive on their investment; customers, by the reliability and value of its products relative to their price; and managers and employees, by their salaries, stock options, conditions of employment, and career prospects. Often these goals conflict, and stakeholder groups must bargain over the appropriate balance between the inducements that they should receive and the contributions that they should make. For this reason, organizations are often regarded as alliances or coalitions of stakeholder groups that directly (and indirectly) bargain with each other and use their power and influence to alter the balance of inducements and contributions in their favour.[11] An organization is viable as long as a dominant coalition of stakeholders has control over sufficient inducements so that it can obtain the contributions it needs from other stakeholder groups. However, when stakeholders refuse to participate, the organization is placed into peril. In the United States, the spectacular collapse of Enron and WorldCom occurred when their illegal actions became public and their stakeholders refused to contribute: Shareholders sold their stock, banks refused to lend money, and debtors called in their loans.

There is no reason to assume, however, that all stakeholders will be equally satisfied with the balance between inducements and contributions. Indeed, the implications of the coalition view of organizations are that some stakeholder groups have priority over others. To be effective, however, an organization must at least minimally satisfy the interests of all the groups that have a stake in the organization.[12] The claims of each group must be addressed; otherwise, a group might withdraw its support and injure the future performance of the organization, such as when banks refuse to lend a company money, or a group of employees goes out on strike. When all stakeholder interests are minimally satisfied, the relative power of a stakeholder group to control the distribution of inducements determines how the organization will attempt to satisfy different stakeholder goals and what criteria stakeholders will use to judge the organization's effectiveness.

Problems that an organization faces as it tries to win stakeholders' approval include choosing which stakeholder goals to satisfy, deciding how to allocate organizational rewards to different stakeholder groups, and balancing short-term and long-term goals.

Competing Goals

Organizations exist to satisfy stakeholders' goals, but who decides which goals to strive for and which goals are most important? An organization's choice of goals often has economic, political, and social implications. In most countries that have a capitalistic economy, it has been taken for granted that shareholders, the owners of the organization's accumulated wealth or capital—its machines, buildings, land, and goodwill—have first claim on the value created by the organization. According to this view, the job of managers is to maximize shareholder wealth, and the best way to do this is to maximize the organization's return on investment.

Is maximizing shareholder wealth always management's primary goal? According to one argument, it is not. When shareholders delegate to managers the right to coordinate and use organizational skills and resources, a divorce of ownership and control occurs.[13] Although in theory managers are the employees of shareholders, in practice managers' control over organizational resources gives them real control over the corporation even though the shareholders are actually the owners. A result of this dichotomy (real versus espoused control) is that managers may follow goals that promote their own interests but not the interests of shareholders.[14]

An attempt to maximize shareholder wealth, for example, may involve taking risks into uncharted territory and making investments in R&D that may bear fruit only in the long term, as new inventions and discoveries generate new products and hence new revenues. Managers, however, may prefer to maximize short-term profits because that is the goal on which they are evaluated by their peers and by market analysts who do not take the long-term view.[15]

Another view is that managers prefer a quiet life in which risks are small, and that they have no incentive to be entrepreneurial because they control their own salaries. Moreover, because managers' salaries are closely correlated with organizational size and growth, managers may prefer to pursue these goals even though they are only loosely associated with profitability and return on shareholders' investment.

As these examples suggest, the goals of managers and shareholders may compete, and because managers are in the organizational driver's seat, shareholder goals are not the ones most likely to be followed. But even when there is no competition between different stakeholders over whose goals should be followed, selecting goals that will enhance an organization's chances of survival and future prosperity is no easy task.

Suppose managers decide that the primary goal is to maximize shareholder wealth. What should be done to achieve this goal? Should managers try to increase efficiency and reduce costs to improve profitability? Should they increase the organization's ability to influence its outside stakeholders and perhaps become a global company? Should they invest all organizational resources in new R&D projects that will increase its competencies? An organization could take any of these actions to achieve the goal of maximizing shareholder wealth.

As you can see, there are no easy rules to follow. In many ways, being effective means making more right choices than wrong choices. One thing is certain, however: An organization that does not pay attention to its stakeholders and does not attempt at least minimally to satisfy their interests will lose legitimacy in their eyes and be doomed to failure. The importance of using organizational ethics to avoid this outcome is taken up at the end of the chapter.

Allocating Rewards

Another major problem that an organization has to face is how to allocate the rewards it gains as a result of being effective. How should an organization allocate inducements among various stakeholder groups? An organization needs to minimally satisfy the expectation of each group. But when rewards are more than enough to meet each group's minimum need, how should the "extra" rewards be allocated? How much should the workforce or managers receive relative to shareholders? What determines the appropriate reward for managers? Most people answer that managerial rewards should be determined by the organization's effectiveness. But this answer raises another question: What are the best indicators of effectiveness on which to base managerial rewards? Short-term profit? Long-term wealth maximization? Organizational growth? The choice of different criteria leads to different answers to the question. Indeed, in the 1980s a CEO's average salary was about 40 times greater than the average worker; by 2002 the CEO's salary was *400* times greater! Can this kind of huge increase be justified? More and more, given the many examples of corporate greed, analysts are saying no, and some have called for an across-the-board decrease in CEO salaries and other remuneration mechanisms.

The same kinds of consideration are true for other organizational members. What are the appropriate rewards for a middle manager who invents a new process that earns the organization millions of dollars a year, or for the workforce as a whole when the company is making record profits? Should they be given short-term bonuses, or should the organization guarantee long-term or lifetime employment as the ultimate inducement for good performance? Similarly, should shareholders receive dividends, or should all profits be invested in the organization to increase its skills and resources? How various organizational and personal goals or rewards are balanced against the interests of other organizational stakeholders can be a daunting and challenging task.

The allocation of rewards, or inducements, is an important component of organizational effectiveness because the inducements offered to stakeholders now determine their motivation—that is, the form and level of their contributions—in the future. Stakeholders' future investment decisions depend on the return they expect from their investments, whether the returns are in the form of dividends, stock options, bonuses, or wages. It is in this context that the role of top managers and the board of directors become important, because they are the stakeholder groups which possess the power that determines how much reward or inducements each group—including themselves—will ultimately receive. This is an important function of management with critical implications for the organization and its stakeholders. When carried out equitably, most organizational employees and stakeholders benefit. When carried out inequitably (whether for reason of incompetence, greed, or otherwise), there can be serious financial and social consequences for the organization and stakeholders alike. As the employees and shareholders of collapsed firms such as Enron (who lost all the value of their pensions and shares) found out, directors and top managers often do not perform this role well.

SENIOR MANAGEMENT AND ORGANIZATIONAL AUTHORITY

Since senior management is the stakeholder group that has the primary responsibility for setting company goals and objectives, and for allocating organizational resources to achieve these objectives, it is useful to take a closer look at top managers. Who are they, what roles and functions do they perform, and how do managers cooperate to run a company's business?

Authority
The power to hold people accountable for their actions and to make decisions concerning the use of organizational resources.

Authority is the power to hold people accountable for their actions and to influence directly what they do and how they do it. The stakeholder group with ultimate authority over the use of a corporation's resources is shareholders. Legally, they own the company and exercise control over it through their representatives, the board of directors. Through the board, shareholders delegate to managers the legal authority and responsibility to use the organization's resources to create value and to meet goals (see Figure 2-1). Accepting this authority and responsibility from shareholders and the board of directors makes corporate managers accountable for the way they use resources and for how much value the organization creates.

The board of directors monitors corporate managers' activities and rewards corporate managers who pursue activities that satisfy stakeholder goals. The board has the legal authority to hire, fire, and discipline corporate management. The chair of the board of directors is the principal representative of the shareholders and, as such, has the most authority in an organization. Through the executive committee, which consists of the organization's most important directors and top managers, the chair has the responsibility for monitoring and evaluating the way corporate managers use organizational resources. The position of the chair and the other directors is one of trusteeship: They act as trustees to protect the interests of shareholders and other stakeholders. The salary committee sets the salaries and terms of employment for corporate managers.

There are two kinds of directors: *inside* directors and *outside* directors. Inside directors are directors who also hold offices in a company's formal hierarchy; they are full-time employees of the corporation. Outside directors are not employees of the company; many are professional directors who hold positions on the boards of many companies, or are executives of other companies who sit on other companies' boards. The goal of having outside directors is to bring objectivity to a company's decision making, and to balance the power of inside directors, who obviously side with an orga-

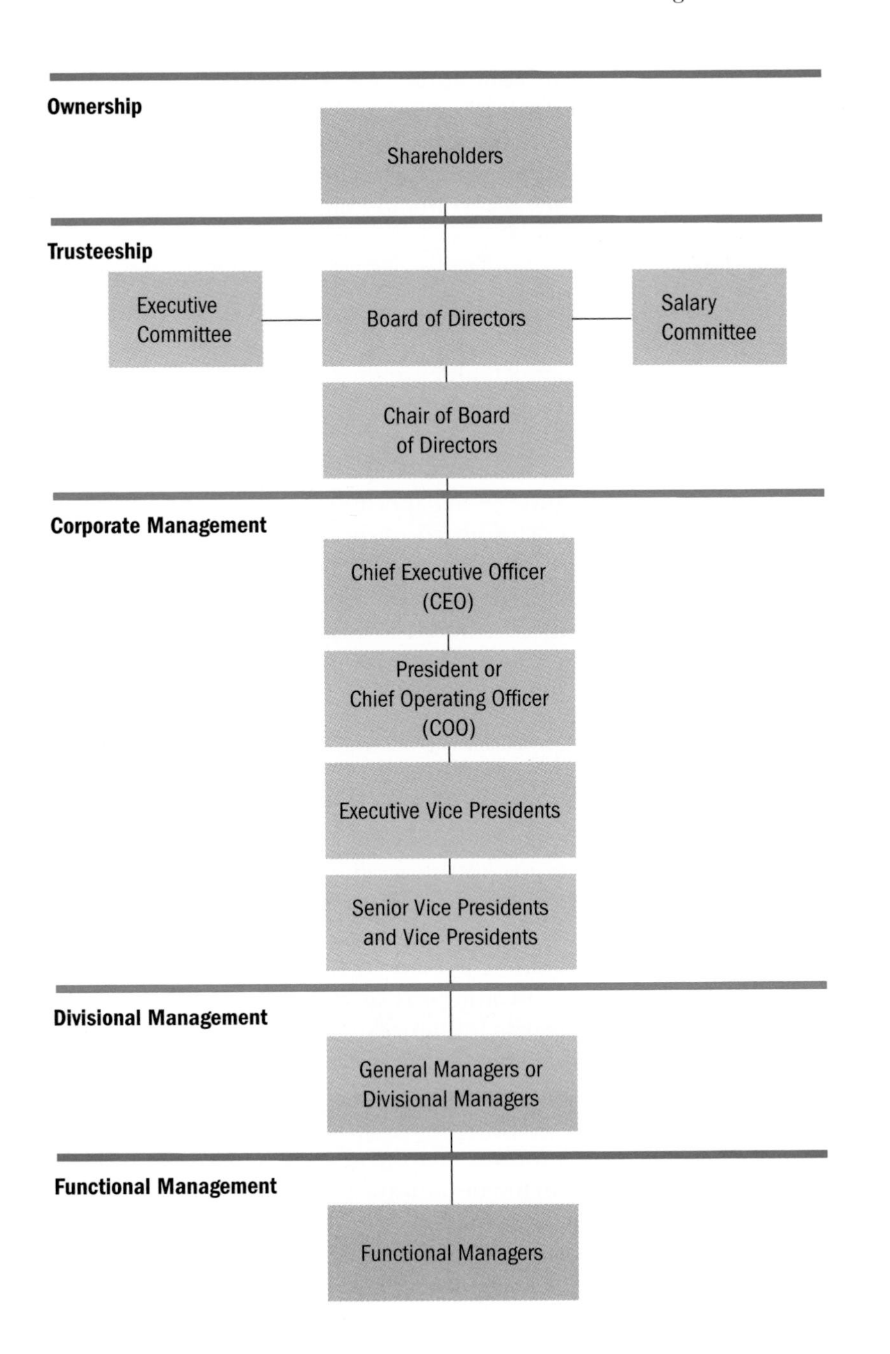

FIGURE 2-1
The Top-Management Hierarchy.
This chart shows the ranking of the positions in the hierarchy, not necessarily the typical reporting relationships.

nization's management. In practice, however, boards tend to be dominated by inside directors because these people have access to the most information about the company, and can use that information to influence decision making in management's favour. Moreover, many outside directors tend to be passive, and serve as a rubber stamp for management's decisions. It has been claimed that many of the problems that arose in the Enron debacle and similar cases were the result of passive directors, appointed by the CEO, who failed to exercise adequate supervision. Directors of some companies have been sued for their failure to do so.[16]

Corporate-level management is the inside stakeholder group that has ultimate responsibility for setting company goals and objectives, for allocating organizational

Chain of command
The system of hierarchical reporting relationships in an organization.

Hierarchy
A classification of people according to authority and rank.

resources to achieve objectives, and for designing the organization's structure. Who are the corporate managers? What exactly do they do, and what roles do they play? Figure 2-1 shows the typical hierarchy of management titles and the **chain of command**, that is, the system of reporting relationships of a large corporation. A **hierarchy** is a vertical ordering of organizational roles according to their relative authority.

The Chief Executive Officer

The chief executive officer (CEO) is the person ultimately responsible for setting organizational strategy and policy. Even though the CEO reports to the chair of the board (who has the most legal authority), in a real sense the CEO is the most powerful person in the corporation because he or she controls the allocation of resources needed by others in the organization. The CEO also has authority and considerable influence in the allocation of rewards to management and other employees within the company. The combination of resource and reward allocation can give the CEO considerable power within the organization. The board of directors gives the CEO the power to set the organization's strategy and use its resources to create value. Often the same person is *both* CEO and chair of the board. A person who occupies both positions wields considerable power and directly links the board to corporate management.

How does a CEO actually affect the way an organization operates? A CEO can influence organizational effectiveness and decision making in five principal ways:[17]

1. *The CEO is responsible for setting the organization's goals and designing its structure.* The CEO allocates authority and task responsibilities so that resources are coordinated and motivated to achieve organizational goals. Different organizational structures promote different methods of coordinating and motivating resources.
2. *The CEO selects key executives to occupy the topmost levels of the managerial hierarchy.* This sort of staffing is a vital part of the CEO's job because the quality of decision making is directly affected by the abilities of the organization's top managers. The CEO of General Electric, for example, personally selects and promotes GE's 100 top managers and approves the promotions of 600 other executives.[18] By choosing key personnel, the CEO heavily influences the values, norms, and culture that emerge in the organization. The culture determines the way organization members approach problems and make decisions: Are they entrepreneurial or are they conservative?
3. *The CEO determines top management's rewards and incentives.* The CEO influences the motivation of top managers to pursue organizational goals effectively.
4. *The CEO controls the allocation of scarce resources such as money and decision-making power among the organization's functional areas or business divisions.* This control gives the CEO enormous power to influence the direction of the organization's future value creation activities—the kinds of products the company will make, the markets in which it will compete, and so on. Henry Ford III won back the CEO's job at Ford after its former CEO, Jacques Nasser, came under criticism after spending tens of billions on countless global projects that had done little to increase the company's profitability. Similarly, Apple's Steve Jobs was returned to the company to repair the harm of its previous CEO for similar reasons. Both Jobs's and Ford's managerial philosophy is that managers must prove their projects will make money before they will allow organizational resources to be committed.
5. *The CEO's actions and reputation have a major impact on inside and outside stakeholders' views of the organization and affect the organization's ability to attract resources from its environment.* A CEO's personality and charisma can influence an organization's ability to obtain money from banks and shareholders and influence cus-

tomers' desire to buy a company's products. So can a reputation for honesty and integrity and a track record of making sound, ethical business decisions.

The ability to influence organizational decision making and managerial behaviour gives the CEO enormous power to directly influence organizational effectiveness. This power is also indirect, for CEOs influence decision making through the people they appoint or the organizational structure or culture they create and leave behind them as their legacy. Thus the top-management team that the CEO creates is critical not only to the organization's success now, but in the future.

The Top-Management Team

After the chair and CEO, the chief operating officer (COO), who is next in line for the CEO's job, or president, who may or may not be the CEO's successor, is the next most important executive. The COO or president reports directly to the CEO, and together they share the principal responsibility for managing the business. In most organizations, a division of labour takes place at the top between these two roles. Normally, the CEO has primary responsibility for managing the organization's relationship with external stakeholders and for planning the long-term strategic objectives of the organization as a whole and all its business divisions. The COO or president has primary responsibility for managing the organization's internal operations to make sure that they conform to the organization's strategic objectives. In a large company, the COO may also oversee the organization's most important business divisions.

At the next level of top management are the executive vice presidents. People with this title have responsibility for overseeing and managing a company's most significant line and staff responsibilities. A **line role** is held by managers who have direct responsibility for the production of goods and services. An executive vice president, for example, might have overall responsibility for overseeing the performance of all 200 of a company's chemical divisions or all of a company's international divisions. A **staff role** is held by managers who are in charge of a specific organizational function such as sales or R&D. For example, the executive vice president for finance manages an organization's overall financial activities, and the executive vice president for R&D oversees a company's research operations. Staff roles are advisory only; they have no direct production responsibilities, but their occupants possess enormous influence on decision making.

Line role
Managers who have direct responsibility for the production of goods and services.

Staff role
Managers who are in charge of a specific organizational function such as sales or R&D.

The CEO, COO, and the executive vice presidents are at the top of an organization's power structure. Collectively, managers in these positions form a company's senior- or **top-management team**, the group of managers who report to the CEO and COO and help the CEO set the company's strategy and its long-term goals and objectives.[19] All the members of the top-management team are **corporate managers**, whose responsibility is to set strategy for the corporation as a whole.

Top-management team
A group of managers who report to the CEO and COO and help the CEO set the company's strategy and its long-term goals and objectives.

Corporate managers
The members of the top-management team whose responsibility is to set strategy for the corporation as a whole.

The way the CEO handles the top-management team and appoints people to it is a vital part of the CEO's job. When, for example, the CEO appoints the COO, he or she is sending a clear signal to the top-management team about the kinds of issues and events that are of most importance to the organization. Often, for example, an organization will pick a new CEO, or appoint a COO who has the functional and managerial background that can deal with the most pressing issues facing a corporation. Many companies are carefully selecting a successor to the CEO to develop a long-term orientation, and obviously appointment to the top-management team is the first step in this process of developing the future CEO.[20] More and more, the composition of the top-management team is becoming one of the main priorities of the CEO and of a company's board of directors.

Other Managers

At the next level of management are a company's senior vice presidents and vice presidents, senior corporate-level managers in both line and staff functions. Large companies such as Maple Leaf Foods Inc., TransCanada, Nortel, CanWest, and Molson may have hundreds or more corporate-level managers. Also, at this level are those managers who head one of a company's many operating companies or divisions and who are known as general managers. In practice, general managers of the divisions commonly have the title of CEO of their divisions because they have direct line responsibility for their division's performance and normally report to the corporate CEO or COO. However, they set policy only for the division they head, not for the whole corporation, and are **divisional managers**, not corporate managers.

Divisional managers Managers who set policy only for the division they head.

An organization or a division of an organization may have functional managers with titles such as marketing manager or production manager. **Functional managers** are responsible for developing the functional skills and capabilities that collectively provide the core competencies that give the organization its competitive advantage. Each division, for example, has a set of functional managers who report to the general or divisional manager.

Functional managers Managers who are responsible for developing the functional skills and capabilities that collectively provide the core competencies that give the organization its competitive advantage.

AN AGENCY THEORY PERSPECTIVE

Agency theory offers a useful way of understanding the complex authority relationship between top management and the board of directors. An agency relation arises whenever one person (the principal) delegates decision-making authority or control over resources to another (the agent). Starting at the top of a company's hierarchy of authority, shareholders are the principals; top management are their agents, appointed by shareholders to utilize organizational resources most effectively. The average shareholder, for example, has no in-depth knowledge of a particular industry or how to run a company. They appoint experts in the industry—managers—to perform this work for them. However, in delegating authority to managers an **agency problem**—a problem in determining managerial accountability—arises. This is because if you employ an expert manager, by definition that person must know more than you; how then can you question the decisions of the expert and the way managers are running the company? Moreover, the results of managers' performance can be evaluated only after considerable time has elapsed. Consequently, it is very difficult to hold managers accountable for what they do. Most often shareholders don't until it is too late, when it becomes obvious (usually after the fact) that the company has lost profitability, market share, or customer loyalty. In delegating authority, to a large extent shareholders reduce their ability to influence managerial decision making.

Agency problem A problem in determining managerial accountability, which arises when delegating authority to managers.

The issue is that shareholders or principals are at an information disadvantage as compared to top managers. It is very difficult for them to judge the effectiveness of a top-management team's actions, especially as this can only be judged over several years. Moreover, as noted earlier, there may be a divergence in the goals and interests of managers and shareholders. Managers may prefer to pursue courses of action that lead to short-term profits, or short-term control over the market, while shareholders might prefer actions that lead to long-term profitability, such as increased efficiency and long-term innovation.

The Moral Hazard Problem

When these two conditions exist and a principal finds it (1) very difficult to evaluate how well the agent has performed because the agent possess an information advantage, and (2) the agent has an incentive to pursue goals and objectives that are different from the principal's, a moral hazard problem exists. Here, agents have the opportunity and incentive to pursue their own interests. For example, in 2002 the French conglomerate Vivendi came under attack because its CEO had made many acquisitions, which had not led to increased innovation, efficiency, or higher profits. Shareholders felt Vivendi's top-management team was pursuing the wrong strategies to make the company profitable. Shareholders felt its top managers were avoiding confronting the hard issues. They demanded a change in top management to change (1) the direction and goals of the company and (2) to give them more information so that they could overcome their information disadvantage. In short, they wanted more control over the affairs of the corporation to overcome the agency problem. They won when the CEO and top-management team resigned and many of its businesses were put up for sale.[21]

Solving the Agency Problem

In agency theory, the central issue is to overcome the agency problem by using **governance mechanisms**, or forms of control that align the interests of principal and agent so that both parties have the incentive to work together to maximize organizational effectiveness. There are many different kinds of governance mechanisms.

Governance mechanisms The forms of control that align the interests of principal and agent so that both parties have the incentive to work together to maximize organizational effectiveness.

First, the principal role of the board of directors is to monitor top managers' activities, question their decision making and strategies, and to intervene when necessary. Some have argued for a clear separation between the role of CEO and chair to curb the CEO's power, arguing that the huge increase in CEO pay is evidence of the need to prevent abuses of power. Another vital task here is to reinforce and develop the organization's code of ethics, as discussed later.

The next step in solving the agency problem is to find the right set of incentives to align the interests of managers and shareholders. Recall that it is very difficult for shareholders to monitor and evaluate the effectiveness of managers' behaviours because the results of their behaviours can often be seen only after several years have elapsed. Thus, basing rewards on behaviours is often not an effective alignment strategy. The most effective way of aligning interests between management and shareholders is to make managers' rewards contingent on the outcomes of their actions, that is, making the rewards dependant upon some measure of organizational performance. There are several ways of doing this, each of which has advantages and disadvantages.

Stock-Based Compensation Schemes **Stock-based compensation schemes** are one way of achieving this objective. Here, managers receive a large part of their monetary reward in the form of stocks or stock options that are linked to the company's performance. If the company does well, then the value of their stock options and monetary compensation is much enhanced. Effectively, interests are aligned because managers become shareholders. This strategy has been used in various companies like Bombardier, Nortel, GM, and IBM, where traditionally top managers had very low stock ownership in the corporation. The board of directors insisted that top managers purchase stock in the companies, and awarded stock options as a means of increasing top managers' stake in the company's long-term performance.

Stock-based compensation schemes Monetary rewards in the form of stocks or stock options that are linked to the company's performance.

Promotion Tournaments and Career Paths Incentives can also take other forms. One way of linking rewards to performance over the long term is by developing organizational career paths that allow managers to rise to the top of the organization. The power of the CEO role is something that many top managers aspire to, and a board of directors, by demoting some top executives and promoting or hiring new ones, often from the outside, can send a clear signal to top managers about what kinds of behaviours would be rewarded in the future. All organizations have "promotion tournaments" where executives compete for limited promotion opportunities by displaying their superior skills and competencies. By directly linking promotion to performance, the board of directors can send out a clear signal about future managerial behaviours that would lead to promotion—and make managers focus on long-term, not short-term, objectives.

The reward from promotion to the top is not just the long-term monetary package that goes with promotion, but also the opportunity to exercise power over resources, and the prestige, status, and intrinsic satisfaction that accompany the journey to the top of the organization.

Another alternative is to blend reward mechanisms. For example, one component would consist of salary, one component would be a quarterly or year-end bonus calculated upon short-term market gains, and a final component would be a stock option mechanism for the longer two-to three-year term. A mixed reward structure attempts to more fully balance managerial and shareholder goals in both the short and longer terms.

While there are no obvious immediate solutions to the agency issues raised, there is work being done to develop new and more effective ways for governance of organizations. The financial scandals involving CEOs, top management, and accounting firms over the last few years have given rise to new government initiatives and renewed consumer interest in regulating the behaviours of CEOs and top management.[22] The public is also calling for more transparency in CEO salary and bonus information, and new controls on how corporate governance structures, such as boards of directors or governors, are set up.

MANAGERS, EMPLOYEES, AND ORGANIZATIONAL ETHICS

Ethics
Moral principles or beliefs about what is right or wrong.

A very important mechanism of corporate governance, and one that has become increasingly important for a board of directors to emphasize after the recent corporate scandals, is to reinforce an organization's code of ethics, and to insist managers use these ethics to guide their decision making. **Ethics** are moral principles or beliefs about what is right or wrong. These beliefs guide individuals in their dealings with other individuals and groups (stakeholders) and provide a basis for deciding whether a particular decision or behaviour is right and proper.[23] Ethics help people determine moral responses to situations in which the best course of action is unclear. Ethics guide managers and employees in their decisions about what to do in various situations. Ethics also help managers decide how best to respond to the interests of various organizational stakeholders, particularly in light of the often competing interests.

As we discussed earlier, in guiding a company's business, both its dealings with outside and inside stakeholders, top managers are constantly making choices about what is the right or appropriate way to deal with these stakeholders. For example, a company might wonder whether it should give advance notice to its employees and middle managers about impending layoffs or plant closings, or whether it should issue a recall of its cars because of a known defect that may cause harm or injury to passengers; or whether it should allow its managers to pay bribes to government officials in foreign countries where corruption is the accepted way of doing business. In all these situations managers are in a difficult situation because they have to balance their interests, and the interests of the "organization," against the interests of other stakeholder groups. Essentially, they have to decide how to apportion the "helps and harms" that arise from an organization's actions between stakeholder groups. Sometimes, making a decision is easy because some obvious standard, value, or norm of behaviour applies. In other cases, managers have trouble deciding what to do and experience an ethical dilemma when weighing or comparing the competing claims or rights of various stakeholder groups.[24]

Philosophers have debated for centuries about the specific criteria that should be used to determine whether decisions are ethical or unethical. Three models of what determines whether a decision is ethical—the utilitarian, moral rights, and justice models—are summarized in Table 2-2.[25]

Table 2-2

UTILITARIAN, MORAL RIGHTS, AND JUSTICE MODELS OF ETHICS

Utilitarian model.
An ethical decision is a decision that produces the greatest good for the greatest number of people.

Managerial implications.
Managers should compare and contrast alternative courses of action based on the benefits and costs of these alternatives for different organizational stakeholder groups. They should choose the course of action that provides the most benefits to stakeholders. For example, managers should locate a new manufacturing plant at the place that will most benefit its stakeholders.

Problems for managers.
How do managers decide on the relative importance of each stakeholder group? How are managers to measure precisely the benefits and harms to each stakeholder group? For example, how do managers choose between the interests of shareholders, workers, and customers?

Moral rights model.
An ethical decision is a decision that best maintains and protects the fundamental rights and privileges of the people affected by it. For example, ethical decisions protect people's rights to freedom, life and safety, privacy, free speech, and freedom of conscience.

Managerial implications.
Managers should compare and contrast alternative courses of action based on the effect of these alternatives on stakeholders' rights. They should choose the course of action that best protects stakeholders' rights. For example, decisions that would involve significant harm to the safety or health of employees or customers are unethical.

Problems for managers.
If a decision will protect the rights of some stakeholders and hurt the rights of others, how do managers choose which stakeholder rights to protect? For example, in deciding whether it is ethical to snoop on an employee, does an employee's right to privacy outweigh an organization's right to protect its property or the safety of other employees?

Justice model.
An ethical decision is a decision that distributes benefits and harms among stakeholders in a fair, equitable, or impartial way.

Managerial implications.
Managers should compare and contrast alternative courses of action based on the degree to which the action will promote a fair distribution of outcomes. For example, employees who are similar in their level of skill, performance, or responsibility should receive the same kind of pay. The allocation of outcomes should not be based on arbitrary differences such as gender, race, or religion.

Problems for managers.
Managers must learn not to discriminate against people because of observable differences in their appearance or behaviour. Managers must also learn how to use fair procedures to determine how to distribute outcomes to organizational members. For example, managers must not give people they like bigger raises than they give to people they do not like or bend the rules to help their favourites.

In theory, each model offers a different and complementary way of determining whether a decision or behaviour is ethical, and all three models should be used to sort out the ethics of a particular course of action. Ethical issues, however, are seldom clear cut, and the interests of different stakeholders are often conflicting, so it is frequently extremely difficult for a decision maker to use these models to ascertain the most ethical course of action. For this reason many experts on ethics propose this practical guide to determine whether a decision or behaviour is ethical.[26] A decision is probably acceptable on ethical grounds if a manager can answer "yes" to each of these questions:

1. Does my decision fall within the accepted values or standards that typically apply in the organizational environment?
2. Am I willing to see the decision communicated to all stakeholders affected by it—for example, by having it reported in newspapers or on television?
3. Would the people with whom I have a significant personal relationship, such as family members, friends, or even managers in other organizations, approve of the decision?

From a management perspective, an ethical decision is a decision that reasonable or typical stakeholders would find acceptable because it aids stakeholders, the organization, or society. By contrast, an unethical decision is a decision a manager would prefer to disguise or hide from other people because it enables a company or a particular individual to gain at the expense of society or other stakeholders. How ethical problems arise, and how different companies respond to them, is profiled in Organizational Insight 2.3.

Ethical rules develop over time through negotiation, compromise, and bargaining among stakeholders. Ethical rules also can evolve from outright conflict and competition between different stakeholder groups where the ability of one group to impose its solution on another group decides which ethical rules will be followed. For example, employees might exert moral pressure on management to improve their working conditions or to give them warning of possible layoffs. Shareholders might demand that top management not invest their capital in countries that practise racism, or that employ children in factories under conditions close to slavery.[27] Over time, many ethical rules and values are codified into the law of a society, and from that point on, unethical behaviour becomes illegal behaviour. Individuals and organizations are required to obey these legal rules and can be punished for not doing so.

Sources of Organizational Ethics

In order to understand the nature of an organization's ethical values, it is useful to discuss the sources of ethics. There are three principal sources of ethical values that influence organizational ethics: (1) societal, (2) group or professional, and (3) individual.

Societal Ethics One important determinant of organizational ethics is societal ethics. Societal ethics are codified in a society's legal system, in its customs and practices, and in the unwritten norms and values that people use to interact with each other. Many ethical norms and values are followed automatically by people in a society because people have internalized society's values and made them part of their own. These internalized norms and values, in turn, reinforce what is taken as custom and practice in a society in people's dealings with one another. For example, ethics concerning the human rights of individuals are the result of decisions made by members of a society about how they want to be treated by others. The Canadian Charter of Rights and Freedoms is an example of the codification of social values. Ethics governing the use of bribery and corruption, or the general standards of doing business in a society, are

ORGANIZATIONAL INSIGHT 2.3

The Use of Animals in Cosmetics Testing

Along with other large cosmetics companies, Gillette, the well-known maker of razors and shaving-related products, has come under increasing attack for its use of animals in product testing to determine the safety and long-term effects of new product formulations. Gillette's managers have received hundreds of letters from angry adults and children who object to the use of animals in cosmetics testing because they regard such testing as cruel and unethical. Managers at several other companies have tried to avoid this ethical issue, but Gillette's managers have approached the problem head on. Gillette's ethical stance is that the health of people is more important than the health of animals and no other reliable method that would be accepted by a court of law exists to test the properties of new formulations. Thus, if the company is to protect the interests of its shareholders, employees, and customers and develop new, safe products that consumers want to buy, it must conduct animal testing.

Gillette's managers respond to each letter protesting this policy, and often even telephone children at home to explain their ethical position.[28] They emphasize that they use animals only when necessary, and they discuss their ethical position with their critics. Other cosmetics companies, such as The Body Shop, do not test their products on animals, however, and their managers are equally willing to explain their ethical stance to the general public: They think animal testing is unethical. However, even though The Body Shop does not directly test its products on animals, some of the ingredients in its products have been tested on animals by Gillette and other companies to ensure their safety.

Clearly, the ethics of animal testing is a difficult issue, as are most other ethical questions. The view of the typical stakeholder at present seems to be that animal testing is an acceptable practice as long as it can be justified in terms of benefits to people. At the same time, most stakeholders believe such testing should minimize the harm done to animals and be used only when necessary.

the result of decisions made and enforced by people deciding what is appropriate in a society. These standards differ from one society to another, and ethical values accepted in Canada may be similar to those of other countries such as the United States or the United Kingdom, but may not accepted in many other countries. One issue of particular ethical concern on a global level is whether it is ethical to use child labour, as profiled in Organizational Insight 2.4.

When societal ethics are codified into law, and then judged by the ethical standards of a society, all illegal behaviour may be regarded as unethical behaviour. An organization, its managers, and employees are legally required to follow all the laws of a society, and to behave toward individuals and stakeholders according to these laws. It is one of top management's main responsibilities to ensure that managers and employees throughout the organization are obeying the law, for top managers can be held accountable in certain situations for the performance of their subordinates. However, not all organizations behave according to the law. The typical kinds of crimes committed by these organizations are not only illegal: They may be also regarded as unethical to the extent they harm other stakeholder groups.

ORGANIZATIONAL INSIGHT 2.4

Is It Right to Use Child Labour?

In recent years, the number of Canadian companies that buy their inputs from low-cost foreign suppliers has been growing, and concern about the ethics associated with employing young children in factories has been increasing. In many developing or transition economies children as young as age six work long hours in deplorable conditions to make rugs and carpets for export to Western countries. Children in poor countries throughout Africa, Asia, and South America work in similar conditions. Is it ethical to employ children in factories, and should companies buy or sell products made by these children?

Many Canadian retailers source their clothing and other products from low-cost foreign suppliers. Managers in these companies have had to take their own ethical stance on issues such as child labour practices in other countries. Managers in Wal-Mart, Sears, Marks Work Wearhouse and the Hudson's Bay Company have developed and adopted voluntary codes of practice in this regard. The Retail Council of Canada, the Canadian Apparel Manufactures, and the Canadian Shoe Manufacturers are all actively engaged in promoting a "fair trade practices" philosophy in business through initiatives such as the formation of Canadian Retailers Advancing Responsible Trade (CRART).[29] The Hudson's Bay Company has a well-developed code of social responsibility that it uses to guide managerial and corporate decisions when choosing suppliers. The company will not deal with suppliers that engage in forced labour, child labour practices, or that do not treat their employees fairly in terms of wages, hours of work, overtime, and safe working conditions. The Hudson's Bay Company uses third-party compliance audits to ensure that its foreign business partners and suppliers adhere to the company's policies in this regard.[30] This type of socially responsible corporate behaviour is a growing trend in business in Canada and elsewhere.

Apparently, however, retailers differ widely in the way they choose to enforce this policy. Wal-Mart and some other companies take a tough stance and immediately sever links with suppliers who break their rule. But it has been estimated, for example, that more than 300 000 children under age 14 are being employed in garment factories in Guatemala, a popular low-cost location for clothing manufacturers that supply the North American market.[31] These children frequently work more than 60 hours a week and often are paid less than US$2.80 a day, the minimum wage in Guatemala. If organizations are to be true to their ethical stance on this troubling issue, they cannot ignore the fact that they are buying clothing or other products made by children, and they must do more to regulate the conditions under which these children work.

However, the opinions about the ethics of dealing with foreign firms and social issues such as child labour vary widely around the world. For example, Robert Reich, an economist and former secretary of labour in the United States for the first Clinton administration, believes that the practice is totally reprehensible and should be outlawed on a global level. Another view, championed in business circles by *The Economist* magazine, is that, while nobody wants to see children employed in factories, citizens of rich countries need to recognize that in poor countries children are often a family's only breadwinners. Thus, denying children employment would cause whole families to suffer, and one wrong (child labour) might produce a greater wrong (poverty). Instead, *The Economist* favours regulating the conditions under which children are employed and hope that over time, as poor countries become richer, the need for child employment will disappear.

Professional Ethics Professional ethics are the moral rules and values that a group of people uses to control the way they perform a task or use resources. For example, medical ethics influence the way that doctors and nurses are expected to perform their tasks and how they treat and deal with their patients. Doctors are expected not to perform unnecessary medical procedures, to exercise due diligence, and to act in the patient's interest, not in their own. Scientific and technical researchers are expected to behave ethically in preparing and presenting their results in order to ensure the validity of their conclusions. As with society, most professional groups can enforce the ethics of their profession. For example, doctors and lawyers can be disbarred should they break the rules and put their own interests first.

In an organization, there are many groups of employees whose behaviour is governed by professional ethics, such as lawyers, researchers, and accountants. These cause them to follow certain principles in deciding how to act in the organization. People internalize the rules and values of their profession, just as they do those of society, and they follow these principles automatically in deciding how to behave.

Individual Ethics Individual ethics are the personal and moral standards used by individuals to structure their interactions with other people. Based upon these ethics, a person may or may not perform certain actions or make certain decisions. Many behaviours that one person may find unethical another person may find ethical. If those behaviours are not illegal, individuals may agree to disagree about their ethical beliefs or they may try to impose those beliefs on other people, and try to make their ethical beliefs the law. If personal ethics conflict with law, a person may be subject to legal sanction. Many personal ethics follow society's ethics and have their origin in law. Personal ethics are also the result of a person's upbringing and may stem from family, friends, membership in a church, or other significant social institutions. Personal ethics influence how a person will act in an organization. For example, managers' behaviour toward other managers and toward subordinates will depend on the personal values and beliefs they individually hold as a result of their upbringing, their education, and their experience.

These three sources of ethics collectively influence the ethics that develop inside an organization, or organizational ethics, which may be defined as the rules or standards used by an organization and its members in their dealings with other stakeholders groups. Each organization has a set of ethics; some of these are unique to an organization and are an important aspect of its culture, a topic discussed in detail in Chapter 7. However, many ethical rules go beyond the boundaries of any individual company. Companies, collectively, are expected to follow the ethical practices and legal rules of society because of the advantages that are produced for a society and its members when its organizations and institutions behave ethically.

Why Do Ethical Rules Develop?

One of the most important reasons why ethical rules governing action develop is to slow down or temper the pursuit of self-interest. One of the best ways of understanding the self-interest issue is to discuss the "tragedy of the commons" problem. When common land (i.e., land owned by everyone) exists, it is rational for every person to maximize his or her use of it because it is a free resource. So all will graze their cattle on the land to promote their individual interests. But if everybody does this, what happens to the land itself, the common resource? The answer is that it is often destroyed by overuse as erosion from overgrazing leaves it defenceless to the effects of wind and rain and makes the land useless. Thus the rational pursuit of individual self-interest results in a collective disaster. The same is true in many other organized situations: Left to their own devices, people will often pursue their own goals at the expense of collective goals.

Ethical laws and rules emerge to control self-interested behaviour by individuals and organizations that threatens society's collective interests. For example, the reason why laws establishing what is good or appropriate business practice develop is because they are designed to provide benefits or protection to most everybody. Free and fair competition among organizations is only possible when rules and standards exist that constrain the self-interested actions that people can take in a certain situation. As a businessperson, it is ethical for Dave to compete with a rival and maybe drive that person out of business if he does so by legal means such as by producing a cheaper, better, or more reliable product. However, it is not ethical for Dave to deliberately lie or give false information concerning his rival's products, or through other unethical or illegal means. Competition by quality or price generally results in increased value for the consumer; competition by force results in monopoly and hurts the customer and the public interest. This is not to say that nobody gets hurt—the rival Dave forces out of business gets hurt—but the harm he does against the rival has to be weighed against the gain to consumers and to Dave himself.

Ethical issues are inherently complex ones where the problem is to distribute the helps and harms between different stakeholders. The issue is to try to act as people of goodwill and to try to follow the moral principles that seem to produce the most good. Ethical rules and moral codes develop to increase the value that can be produced by people when they interact with each other in order to protect and benefit everyone involved. Without these rules, free and fair competition often degenerates into conflict and warfare, and everybody loses. Another way of putting this is to say that ethical rules reduce the costs people have to bear to decide what is right or appropriate. Following an ethical rule avoids expending time and effort in deciding what is the right thing to do. In other words, ethical rules reduce *transaction costs* between people, that is, the costs of monitoring, negotiating, and enforcing agreements with other people. Transaction costs can be enormous when strangers meet to engage in business. For example, how do you trust the other person to behave ethically when you don't know that person? It is here again that the power of ethics in establishing the rules to be followed is so important. For if you can rely on the other person to follow the rules, you do not need to expend effort in monitoring the other person. Monitoring wastes time and effort and is largely unproductive. So, when people share common ethics this helps to reduce transaction costs.

Behaviour that follows accepted ethical rules confers a *reputation effect* on an individual or an organization that also reduces transaction costs. If an organization over time is known for engaging in illegal acts, how will people view that organization? Most likely with suspicion and hostility. However, suppose an organization always follows the rules and is known for its ethical business practices over and above strict legal requirements. It will have gained a reputation and this is valuable because people will want to deal with it. Unethical organizations over time are therefore penalized as people refuse to deal with them so that there are constraints on organizations beyond those of the law.

Reputation effects also help explain why managers and employees who work in organizations also follow ethical rules. Suppose an organization behaves unethically; what will be the position of its employees? To outsiders, employees come to be branded with the same reputation as the unethical organization because they are assumed to have performed according to its code of ethics. Even if the organization's unethical behaviour was the product of a few self-seeking individuals, this will affect and harm all employees. For example, in Japan in the stock crash of the 1990s many brokerage firms went bankrupt with irate clients suing these firms for disguising the real risks associated with investment in the inflated stock market. Employees of these firms found it very difficult to obtain jobs in other organizations because they were branded with the "shame" of having worked for these companies. Thus employees have an incentive for their firm to behave ethically because their fortunes are tied up with those of the organization. An organization's ill reputation will hurt its own employees as well. This is true at Arthur Andersen, Enron, and other disgraced companies whose employees are suffering from their companies' bad reputations.[32]

One intangible reward that comes from behaving ethically is feeling good about one's behaviour, and enjoying the good conscience that comes with doing so. Success by stealth and deceit does not provide the same intangible reward as success from behaving ethically because it is not a fair test of ability or personal qualities. Personal reputation is the outcome of behaving ethically, and the esteem or respect of one's peers has always been a reward that people desire.

In sum, acting ethically promotes the good of a society, and the well-being of its members. More value is created in societies where people follow ethical rules, and where criminal and unethical behaviour are prevented by law and by custom and practice from emerging. Nevertheless, individuals and organizations do perform unethical and illegal acts.

Why Does Unethical Behaviour Occur?

While there are good reasons for individuals and organizations to behave ethically, there are also many reasons why unethical behaviour takes place at the individual, group, or organizational levels. For a multilayered example, see Organizational Insight 2.5.

ORGANIZATIONAL INSIGHT 2.5

Conflicting Interests in Health Care[33]

In Canada, medical care is delivered in an environment that consists of a complex web of relationships between various users, providers, and other stakeholders. These include patients, doctors, insurance companies, pharmaceutical companies, and different levels of government. Consequently, a relational web of considerations exists between and across the stakeholders, particularly in light of the complex federal and provincial mechanisms in place for the public funding and distribution of drugs and other pharmaceuticals. It is quite common for pharmaceutical companies to lobby provincial governments in order to get their drugs covered by provincial health plans.

Once certain drugs are approved, patients have access to them and to the treatment regimes using them. This advances the sales of these drugs. While most pharmaceutical companies operate above board, some controversy surrounds incidents involving pharmaceutical companies and the manner in which they represent the benefits of their drugs to doctors or to patients. Doctors may be enticed by free samples of new pharmaceuticals, or by free meals and entertainment, or even by free trips sponsored and paid for by drug companies. One firm, the Boehringer Ingelheim Company, offered expensive vacation trips to Jamaica for doctors and their spouses—all without charge. In return for the "free" vacation, the doctors had simply to agree to attend several company seminars designed to educate them on the benefits of some of the firm's new arthritis drugs.

The pharmaceutical companies argue that this practice helps educate the medical community about the latest and best medicines available and thus contributes to the health-care capacity available to patients. Others, however, argue that offering free enticements to doctors within a publicly funded health-care system appears as a blatant effort to sway or influence opinions and choices in the pursuit of profits.

In Canada there is an increasing trend for drug companies to specifically target and lobby patients indirectly through their trusted health advocacy groups. The ethical challenge is that if patient groups are funded by a company that has an interest in having their drugs covered by provincial health funding, then the advocacy group's neutrality may be placed in question because almost every high-profile disease advocacy group relies on the financial backing of the drug industry.

Perhaps it is somewhat less known that doctors themselves have directly lobbied provincial governments on behalf of various pharmaceutical companies. This type of relationship also raises serious concerns about conflicts of interest among stakeholders. For an example of this type of conflict, consider the case of Fabry's disease, an inheritable condition affecting the body's ability to process and store fat.

Individuals with Fabry's disease are prone to pain, disfigurement, and early death due to heart attack or stroke. In Lunenburg, Nova Scotia, there was a small group of individuals who suffered from this condition. Recently, university-based research resulted in a drug that would greatly improve the quality of life for these patients through amelioration of many of the worst symptoms. Initially, the drug was supplied without cost to these patients by one of two pharmaceutical companies that had begun to produce the drug. However, once initial treatments had begun, and once the patients had enjoyed the benefits of the drug, the company warned patients that payment was required to continue receiving this life-enhancing drug. At a price tag of about $250 000 per year per patient, this cost was far beyond the patients' ability to manage and they turned to the health-care system for help. This meant that as the system, the doctors, drug companies, provincial governments, and insurance companies tried to decide if, how, when, and by whom the drugs would be paid for, the patients' health was placed in jeopardy. The patients could not afford to pay, the insurance companies did not want to pay, and the provincial government was unsure whether the public system could or should bear this great a cost in times of fiscal restraint. While the various stakeholders tried to resolve the issue, the patients waited.

Perhaps it is situations such as these that motivate doctors to lobby the government in order to spare patient suffering—to help desperate patients get the drug they obviously could not afford on their own. On the other hand, perhaps the pharmaceutical companies should not have offered free drugs to these patients without warning them of the future costs. What is evident is that stakeholder relationships are complex, that less-than-ethical practices in pursuit of stakeholder interest may arise, and that these usually come at the expense of the interests of other stakeholders.

Personal Ethics In theory, people learn ethical principles and moral codes as they mature as individuals in a society. Ethics are obtained from such sources as family and friends, churches, education, and professional training, and from organizations of all kinds. From these, people learn to differentiate what is considered right from wrong in a society or in a social group. However, suppose you are the son or daughter of a criminal, or an enormously wealthy family, and your upbringing and education takes place in such a context. You may come to believe that it is ethical to do anything and perform any act, up to and including murder, if it benefits your family's interests. These are the ethics you have learned. These are obviously not the ethics of the wider society and as such are subject to sanction by society if and when they are broken. Similarly, managers in an organization may come to believe that any actions that promote or protect the organization, or any one group of organizational stakeholders, are more important than consideration of the impacts on others, or for the potential harms that may be done to others.

Self-Interest We normally confront ethical issues when we are weighing our personal interests against the effects of our actions on others. Suppose you know that you will get a promotion to vice president of your company if you can secure a $100 million contract, but you know that to get the contract you must bribe the contract-giver with $1 million. What would you do? On one hand, your career and future seems to be assured by performing this act, and what harm would it do? Bribery is common anyway, and if you don't pay the $1 million, you can be sure that somebody else will. So what do you do? Research seems to suggest that people who realize they have most at stake in a career sense or a monetary sense are the ones most likely to act unethically. Similarly it has been shown that organizations that are doing badly in an economic sense and are struggling to survive are the ones most likely to commit unethical and illegal acts such as collusion, price fixing, or bribery.

Outside Pressure It has been found in many studies that the likelihood of a person's engaging in unethical or criminal behaviour is much greater when outside pressure exists for that person to do so. In Sears, for example, top managers' desires to increase performance led them to create a reward system that had the intentional or unintentional effect of making employees act unethically and overcharge consumers. Top managers can feel themselves to be under similar pressures from shareholders if company performance is deteriorating, and under the threat of losing their jobs they may engage in unethical behaviours to satisfy shareholders.

If all these pressures work in the same direction, we can easily understand how unethical organizational cultures, such as those of Enron, WorldCom, and Arthur Andersen, can develop as managers bought into unethical acts and a generalized climate of "the end justifies the means" permeated these organizations. The organization becomes more defensive as organization members pull together to disguise their unethical actions and to protect one another from prosecution.

The temptation for organizations collectively to engage in unethical and illegal anticompetitive behaviour is very great. Industry competitors can see quite clearly the advantages to acting together to raise prices because of the extra profits they will earn. The harm they inflict is much more difficult to see because their customers may number in the millions, and since each customer is perceived to be affected in such a small way, from the perspective of the organization they are hardly hurt at all. However, if every company in every industry behaved this way, and they all tried to extract money from their customers, customers would suffer severe harm.

The true social costs of various forms of unethical behaviour may be very hard to measure in the short term, but they can be easily seen over the long run in the form of mismanaged organizations that commit harm to employees, customers, and stakeholders of all types.

CREATING AN ETHICAL ORGANIZATION

In what ways can ethical behaviour be promoted so that, at the very least, organizational members resist the temptation to engage in illegal or unethical acts that promote personal or organizational interests at the expense of society's interests? Ultimately, an organization is ethical if the people inside it are ethical. How can people judge if they are making ethical decisions and thus acting ethically? The first way is to use the rule discussed earlier concerning a person's willingness to have his or her action or decision shared with other people.

Beyond personal considerations, an organization can encourage people to act ethically by putting in place incentives for ethical behaviour and disincentives to punish those who behave unethically. Because the board and top managers have the ultimate responsibility for setting policy, they can help establish the ethical culture or climate of the organization. There are many ways in which they can influence organizational ethics and an ethical climate. For example, a manager or board member outlining a company's position on business ethics acts as a figurehead and personifies the organization's ethical position. As a leader, a manager can promote moral values that result in the specific ethical rules and norms that people use to make decisions. Employees contribute to the ethical climate by their own decisions and actions. This also helps develop social norms of behaviour that reinforce good ethics in the workplace. Outside the organization, as a liaison or spokesperson, a manager can inform prospective customers and other stakeholders about the organization's ethical values and demonstrate those values through behaviour toward stakeholders—such as by being honest and acknowledging errors. A manager can also help align other employees' incentives to reinforce ethical behaviour and can develop rules and norms that state the organization's ethical position. Finally, a manager should make decisions to allocate organizational resources and pursue policies based on the organization's ethical position with due regard for other stakeholders and the public at large.

Designing an Ethical Structure and Control System

Ethics influence the choice of the structure and culture that coordinate resources and motivate employees.[34] Managers can design an organizational structure that reduces the incentives for people to behave unethically. The creation of authority relationships and rules that promote ethical behaviour and punish unethical acts, for example, will encourage members to behave in a socially responsible way.

Whistle-blowing occurs when an employee informs an outside person or agency, such as a government agency, a newspaper, or television reporter, about an organization's (its managers') illegal or immoral behaviour. Employees typically become whistle-blowers when they feel powerless to prevent an organization from committing an unethical act or when they fear retribution from the company if they voice their concerns. However, an organization can take steps to make whistle-blowing an acceptable and rewarded activity.[35] Procedures that allow subordinates access to upper-level managers to voice concerns about unethical organizational behaviour can be set up. The position of ethics officer can be established to investigate claims of unethical behaviour, and ethics committees can make formal ethical judgments. Ten percent of Fortune 500 companies have ethics officers who are responsible for keeping employees informed about organizational ethics, for training employees, and for investigating breaches of ethical conduct. While most stated organizational ethical values flow down from the top of the organization, they are strengthened or weakened by the design of the organizational structure and how individuals within the organization are rewarded.

Creating an Ethical Culture

The values, rules, and norms that define an organization's ethical position are part of its culture. The behaviour of top managers strongly influences organizational culture.

An ethical culture is most likely to emerge if top managers are ethical, and an unethical culture can become an ethical one if the top-management team is changed. But neither culture nor structure can make an organization ethical if its top managers or other employees do not behave ethically. The creation of an ethical organizational culture requires commitment at all levels of an organization, from the most senior to the most junior employee.[36]

Supporting the Interests of Stakeholder Groups

Shareholders are the owners of an organization. Through the board of directors they have the power to hire and fire top management and thus in theory can discipline managers who engage in unethical behaviour. Shareholders want higher profits, but do they want them to be gained by unethical behaviour? In general, the answer is no, because unethical behaviour will make a company a riskier investment and may bring harm to others. If an organization behaves unethically and brings harm to others, it may damage its reputation, or suffer the consequences of the behaviour (e.g., lawsuits or fines). Once the organization's reputation is damaged, the value of its shares may fall below the value of shares offered by similar organizations that do behave ethically. In addition, many shareholders do not want to hold stock in companies that engage in socially questionable activities, and other stakeholders may pressure the organization, shareholders, customers, or governments to hold the organization, or specific persons within it, accountable.

Pressure from outside stakeholders can also promote ethical organizational behaviour.[37] The government and its agencies, industry councils and regulatory bodies, consumers, and consumer watchdog groups all play a role in establishing the ethical rules that organizations should follow when doing business. Outside regulation sets the rules of competition and, as noted earlier, plays an important part in creating and sustaining ethics in society.

SUMMARY

Organizations are embedded in a complex social context that is driven by the needs and desires of its stakeholders. The interests of all stakeholders have to be considered when designing an organizational structure and culture that promotes effectiveness and curtails the ability of managers and employees to use organizational resources for their own ends or which damages the interests of other stakeholders. Creating an ethical culture, and making sure organizational members use ethical rules in their decision making, is a vital task for all those who have authority over organizational resources. The chapter has made the following main points:

1. Organizations exist because of their ability to create value and acceptable outcomes for stakeholders. The two main groups of stakeholders are inside stakeholders and outside stakeholders. Effective organizations satisfy, at least minimally, the interests of all stakeholder groups.
2. Problems that an organization faces as it tries to win stakeholders' approval include choosing which stakeholder goals to satisfy, deciding how to allocate organizational rewards to different stakeholder groups, and balancing short- and long-term goals.
3. Shareholders delegate authority to managers to use organizational resources effectively. The CEO, COO, and top-management team have ultimate responsibility for the use of those resources effectively.
4. The agency problem and moral hazard arise when shareholders delegate authority to man-

agers, and governance mechanisms must be created to align the interests of shareholders and managers to ensure managers behave in the interests of all stakeholders.

5. Ethics are the moral values, beliefs, and rules that establish the right or appropriate ways in which one person or stakeholder group should interact and deal with another. Organizational ethics are a product of societal, professional, and individual ethics.

6. The board of directors and top managers can create an ethical organization by designing an ethical structure and control system, creating an ethical culture, and supporting the interests of stakeholder groups.

DISCUSSION QUESTIONS

1. Give some examples of how the interests of different stakeholder groups may conflict.
2. What is the role of the top-management team?
3. What is the agency problem? What steps can be taken to solve it?
4. Why is it important for managers and organizations to behave ethically?
5. Ask a manager to describe an instance of ethical behaviour that he or she observed, and an instance of unethical behaviour. What caused these behaviours, and what were the outcomes?
6. Search business magazines such as *Canadian Business*, *Fortune*, or *Business Week* for an example of ethical or unethical behaviour, and use the material in this chapter to analyze it.

ORGANIZATIONAL THEORY IN ACTION

Practising Organizational Theory

Form groups of three to five people, and appoint one group member as the spokesperson who will communicate your findings to the class when called on by the instructor. Then discuss the following scenario.

You are the managers of the functions of a large chain of supermarkets, and you have been charged with the responsibility for developing a code of ethics to guide the members of your organization in their dealings with stakeholders. To guide you in creating the ethical code, do the following:

1. Discuss the various kinds of ethical dilemmas that supermarket employees—checkers, pharmacists, stockers, butchers—may encounter in their dealings with stakeholders such as customers or suppliers.
2. Identify a specific behaviour that the kinds of employees mentioned in item 1 might exhibit, and characterize it as ethical or unethical.
3. Based on this discussion, identify three standards or values that you will incorporate into the supermarket's ethical code to help determine whether a behaviour is ethical or unethical.

Making the Connection #2

Identify an organization whose managers have been involved in unethical actions toward one or more stakeholder groups or who have pursued their own self-interest at the expense of other stakeholders. What did they do? Who was harmed? What was the outcome of the incident?

The Ethical Dimension #2

Think about the last time that a person treated you unethically or you observed someone else being treated unethically, and then answer these questions.

1. What was the issue? Why do you think that person acted unethically?

2. What prompted him or her to behave in an unethical fashion?
3. Was the decision maker aware that he or she was acting unethically?
4. What was the outcome?

Analyzing the Organization: Design Module #2

In this module you will identify your organization's major stakeholders, analyze the top management structure, investigate its code of ethics, and try to uncover its ethical stance.

ASSIGNMENT

1. Draw a stakeholder map that identifies your organization's major stakeholder groups. What kind of conflicts between its stakeholder groups would you expect to occur the most?
2. Using information on the company's Web site, draw a picture of its hierarchy of authority. Try to identify the members of the top-management team. Is the CEO also the chair of the board of directors?
3. Does the company have divisional managers? What functional managers seem to be most important to the organization in achieving a competitive advantage? What is the functional background of the top-management team?
4. Does the organization have a published code of ethics or ethical stance? What kinds of issues does it raise in this statement?
5. Search for information about your organization concerning the ethical or unethical behaviour of its managers. What does this tell you about its ethical stance?

Company Profiles #2*

Choose one or more of the organizations (e.g., companies, government agencies, or nonprofit organizations) that are profiled in this chapter. Do an Internet search to get up-to-date information on each organization you have selected, and answer the following questions.

1. What does the new information tell you about the organization's current ethical behaviour?
2. How does the information compare with the earlier information provided in the text and what does that tell you about organizations (e.g., does the organization appear to be judged more or less ethical than before, and how do you explain this)?

Alternative Perspectives #2

Critical and mainstream organizational theorists alike are paying increased attention to the concept of "stakeholding," including new theorization concerning both internal and external stakeholders and their relationships with the organization. Historically, shareholders were viewed as the primary organizational stakeholders, and monetary returns to the shareholder held primacy. However, given the recent spate of ethical issues, fraudulent behaviours, and various detrimental impacts that organizational actions have had on society and the environment, a broader, more inclusive focus is now developing. Read one or more of the following readings and list the advantages and disadvantages of having more or less, direct and indirect, relations with stakeholders. In small groups, discuss whether it is possible for organizations to achieve their "for-profit" mandate as well as remain ethically responsible to their various stakeholders.

Reading List

Driscoll, C. and Starik, M. 2004. The Primordial Stakeholder: Advancing the Conceptual Consideration of Stakeholder Status for the Natural Environment. *Journal of Business Ethics,* 49(1): 55–73.

Guild, W. L. 2002. Relative Importance of Stakeholders: Analysing Speech Acts in a Layoff. *Journal of Organizational Behaviour.* 23(7): 837–852.

Gull, G. A and Doh, J. 2004. The "Transmutation" of the Organization: Toward a More Spiritual Workplace. *Journal of Management Inquiry.* 13(2): 28–40.

Jones, T. M. and Wicks, A. C. 1999. Convergent Stakeholder Theory. *Academy of Management Review.* 24(2): 206–221.

Mattingly, J. E. 2004. Redefining the Corporation: Stakeholder Management and Organizational Wealth. *The Academy of Management Review.* 29(3): 520–524.

* The authors would like to receive information from student groups and instructors on any companies where there have been dramatic changes to the information published in this text. We would be happy to publish the best of these changes in a subsequent edition, where we will focus on changing company profiles.

O'Connell, L., Betz, M.L, Shepard, J. M., Hendry, J. and Stephens, C. U. 2005. An Organizational Field Approach to Corporate Rationality: The Role of Stakeholder Activism. *Business Ethics Quarterly*. 15(1): 93–111.

Rose, C. 2004. Stakeholder Orientation vs. Shareholder Value—A Matter of Contractual Failures. *European Journal of Law and Economics*. 18(1): 77–97.

Unerman, J. and Bennett, M. 2004. Increased Stakeholder Dialogue and the Internet: Towards Greater Corporate Accountability or Reinforcing Capitalist Hegemony? *Accounting, Organizations and Society*. 29(7): 685–707.

Veser, M. 2004. The Influence of Culture on Stakeholder Management: Social Policy Implementation in Multinational Corporations. *Business and Society*. 43(4): 426–436.

CASE FOR ANALYSIS

Banking on a Culture of Ethics: Restoring the Reputation of the CIBC[38]

Just what is a corporate reputation worth these days? If you ask the Canadian Imperial Bank of Commerce (CIBC) that question, you'd likely hear it's worth millions—at least $50 million anyway. That's the amount CIBC announced it's spending to introduce new ethics training and a whistle-blowers hotline within the bank. The programs are part of an US$80 million agreement struck by CIBC with Canadian and U.S. regulators over the role played by the bank in contributing to the collapse of energy trader Enron. But, there was another ethical scandal involving company's employees that is also to be addressed by the new programs. Let's look at the company more closely.

CIBC was established as a retail bank in 1867—the same year Canada became a nation. In 2003, with assets totalling $277 billion, CIBC's 37 000 employees served more than 9 million personal banking and business customers around the world via its electronic and branch banking network. A publicly owned company with shares trading on both the Toronto and New York Stock Exchanges, CIBC had a very profitable 2003. Its share price had increased 57 percent over the year, and the company announced all-time record profits of $2.1 billion. It should have been hailed as an extremely good year for the company, but less positive news about the company also appeared in the media during the year.

The first scandal to make the headlines was news of CIBC's involvement in the demise of Enron. Investigations into the collapse of the energy giant revealed that six banks—identified as the company's Tier 1 banks—helped Enron through a series of financial transactions to wrongfully record on its financial statements at least US$1 billion in profits and US$9 billion in cash flow, and to understate its debt by some US$11 billion. In exchange for helping the company, the banks and investment firms received healthy fees and commissions. CIBC is reported to have earned some US$24 million from its dealing with Enron from 1998 to 2001.

The second blow to CIBC's reputation came with the news that a senior executive from its investment-banking group had been arrested on charges of fraud related to a U.S. mutual fund scandal. The former CIBC executive was charged with defrauding two U.S. mutual funds of more than US$2 million through illegal trading and deceptive timing of market transactions. If convicted, the individual could face 25 years in prison and a lifetime ban on working in the industry. And more bad news could still come, since the bank and several other employees are still being investigated as part of the case.

With all the negative publicity, CIBC needed to act. One of its first steps was to announce the departure of the executive who had overseen the groups involved in the Enron and mutual fund scandals. Shortly thereafter, CIBC announced a $50 million investment in governance and reputational risk programs.

The money was earmarked for a number of initiatives. A big focus was on providing support for the employees of CIBC so that the company could meet its stated goal of having "everyone doing the right thing—always." Online training, focusing on legal risk and reputational issues, was announced for the bank's entire workforce. An ethics hotline was also introduced to provide employees with a vehicle to safely report ethical concerns. CIBC's telephone-based program would be operated by an independent third party and its toll-free number managed by specially trained staff at a call centre operating 24 hours a day, seven days a week. Details of employee concerns would be relayed confidentially and anonymously by the third party to company officials.

Other funds were allocated for process-related concerns. For example, a thorough review of the bank's procedures for approving financial transactions was announced, and new procedures and protocols were said to be forthcoming. And, CIBC executives have openly been speaking about the problems and the steps being taken to address them. John Hunkin, the CEO, acknowledged, "We stumbled where it counts... in trust and reputation." He added, "Our reputation is at the core of everything we do . . . . We see this investment as critical to CIBC's success."

Wayne Fox, the CIBC executive in charge of risk management, has also been speaking out about the company's experiences. He commented that CIBC has historically made the "management of risk, reputation, compliance, and financial reporting a top priority" and yet, as he pointed out, "that we have accomplished so much and yet stumbled so publicly with recent events like Enron is meaningful" for moving CIBC forward. In Fox's view, what is necessary to address problems of this nature is a "culture of governance." He believes that CIBC already has a strong foundation for such a culture with its existing governance rules, processes, and procedures—many of them considered best practices—and that there isn't a need for "an emergency, wholesale overhaul." Instead, Fox suggests that it is critical to make sure employees understand that this objective is not "just another flavour of the month" and that they have an important role to play in ensuring "doing the right things always" is the company standard. So Fox and the rest of the CIBC management team are actively communicating that there's a "zero tolerance for misconduct."

So far, Fox is positive about the message being heard: " . . . our people are responding. They're learning this, believing this and acting accordingly every day. Their belief and actions, in hand with CIBC's knowledge, desire and tools, are causing our governance culture to flourish and strengthening our ability to do the right thing, always."

DISCUSSION QUESTIONS

1. Why is corporate reputation important to any company? Is it of any greater concern to the stakeholders of a financial institution than another type of firm? Is there any relationship between the type of good or service a firm produces, its customers, and whether it needs to emphasize a culture of ethics?
2. What do you think of CIBC's approach? Do you think the bank is right to focus on development of a governance culture? Will the steps CIBC has announced help develop such a culture? Will CIBC be more or less ethical than before?
3. Are there any other actions that CIBC, or a similar firm in similar circumstances, could take? Whose interests are being served when a firm engages in a "program of ethics"?

REFERENCES

1. T. Donaldson and L. E. Preston, "The Stakeholder Theory of the Corporation: Concepts, Evidence, and Implications," *Academy of Management Review,* 1995, vol. 20, pp. 65–91.
2. J. G. March and H. Simon, *Organizations* (New York: Wiley, 1958).
3. Ibid.; J. A. Pearce, "The Company Mission as a Strategic Tool," *Sloan Management Review,* Spring 1982, pp. 15–24.
4. Organizational Insight by Margaret McKee, based on the following sources: Sarbanes-Oxley, H.R. 3763 Corporate and Auditing Accountability, Responsibility and Transparency Act of 2002," U.S. *House of Representatives,* 2002; M. Bevilacqua, Remarks by Secretary of State (International Financial Institutions) to Toronto Board of Trade, *www.fin.gc.ca/news02/*, 2002; CanadaNewswire, "Corporate Governance Issues Having a Greater Impact in Canada's Boardrooms, According to Canadian Coalition for Good Governance," *www.newswire.ca,* 2004; *www.otpp.com,* 2004; *www.omers.com, 2004*; CCGG, "Working to Improve Corporate Governance in Canada," *Canadian Coalition for Good Governance—Inaugural Report,* 2004; Q. Conklin, and F. Lesage, "Ethics and Competency: The Market Forces Boards to Take a Longer View," *Ivey Business Journal,* Nov./Dec. 2002, vol. 67, pp. 3–8.
5. C. W. L. Hill and G. R. Jones, *Strategic Management: An Integrated Approach,* 7th ed. (Boston: Houghton Mifflin, 2003).
6. Organizational Insight by Scott MacMillan, based on the following sources: B. Brioux, "10 Ways to Fix the CBC," *Toronto Sun,* 19 November 2002; *www.cbc.ca,* 2004; CBC/Radio Canada Annual Report 2002–2003, *www.cbc.radio-canada.ca,* 2003; C. Cobb, "Radical TV Plan Will Pit CRTC against Public Broadcaster," *Ottawa Citizen,* 16 April 2000, p. B4; Canadian Media Guild, "CBC: Corporation Creating a 'Shared Services Organization'," *www.cmg.ca,* 2004.
7. J. P. Womack, D. T. Jones, D. Roos, and D. Sammons Carpenter, *The Machine That Changed the World* (New York: Macmillan, 1990).
8. *www.canada.gc.ca,* 2004.
9. S. Richer, "Shipping News Buoys the Right Whale," *Globe and Mail,* 27 September 2004, A1.
10. R. F. Zammuto, "A Comparison of Multiple Constituency Models of Organizational Effectiveness," *Academy of Management Review,* 1984, vol. 9, pp. 606–616; K. S. Cameron, "Critical Questions in Assessing Organizational Effectiveness," *Organizational Dynamics,* 1989, vol. 9, pp. 66–80.
11. R. M. Cyert and J. G. March, *A Behavioural Theory of the Firm* (Englewood Cliffs, NJ: Prentice Hall, 1963).
12. R. H. Miles, *Macro Organizational Behaviour* (Santa Monica, CA: Goodyear, 1980), p. 375.
13. A. A. Berle and G. C. Means, *The Modern Corporation and Private Property* (New York: Commerce Clearing House, 1932).
14. Hill and Jones, *Strategic Management,* Ch. 2.
15. G. R. Jones and J. E. Butler, "Managing Internal Corporate Entrepreneurship: An Agency Perspective," *Journal of Management,* 1994, vol. 18, 733–749.
16. W. Zeller, "The Fall of Enron," *Business Week,* 17 December 2001, pp. 30–40.
17. A. K. Gupta, "Contingency Perspectives on Strategic Leadership," in D. C. Hambrick, ed., *The Executive Effect: Concepts and Methods for Studying Top Managers* (Greenwich, CT: JAI Press, 1988), pp. 147–178.
18. Ibid., p. 155.
19. D. C. Ancona, "Top-Management Teams: Preparing for the Revolution," in J. S. Carroll, ed., *Applied Social Psychology in Organizational Settings* (Hillsdale, NJ: Lawrence Erlbaum Associates, 1990), pp. 99–128.
20. R. F. Vancil, *Passing the Baton* (Boston: Harvard Business School Press, 1987).
21. *www.vivendi.com,* 2002.
22. W. Dabrowski, "Key Issues For Governance, Rules," *National Post,* 20 October 2004, B1.
23. T. L. Beauchamp and N. E. Bowie, eds., *Ethical Theory and Business* (Englewood Cliffs, NJ: Prentice Hall, 1979); A. MacIntyre, *After Virtue* (South Bend, IN: University of Notre Dame Press, 1981).
24. R. E. Goodin, "How to Determine Who Should Get What," *Ethics* (July 1975): 310–321.
25. T. M. Jones, "Ethical Decision Making by Individuals in Organizations: An Issue Contingent Model," *Academy of Management Journal,* 1991, vol. 16: 366–395; G. F. Cavanaugh, D. J. Moberg, and M. Velasquez, "The Ethics of Organizational Politics," *Academy of Management Review,* 1981, vol. 6: 363–374.
26. L. K. Trevino, "Ethical Decision Making in Organizations: A Person–Situation Interactionist

Model," *Academy of Management Review*, 1986, vol. 11: 601–617; W. H. Shaw and V. Barry, *Moral Issues in Business*, 6th ed. (Belmont, CA: Wadsworth, 1995).

27. W. H. Shaw and V. Barry, *op. cit.*
28. B. Carton, "Gillette Faces Wrath of Children in Testing on Rats and Rabbits," *Wall Street Journal*, 5 September 1995, A1.
29. *www.retailcouncil.org.*
30. *www.hbc.com.*
31. B. Ortega, "Broken Rules: Conduct Codes Garner Goodwill for Retailers But Violations Go On," *Wall Street Journal*, 3 July 1995, A1, A4.
32. "Why Honesty Is the Best Policy," *The Economist*, 9 March 2002, p. 23.
33. Organizational Insight by Ellen Rudderham-Gaudet, based on the following sources: CTV, *W-FIVE*, "Just Say No," first broadcast 17 May 2002, *www.ctv.ca*, 2004; E. Johnson, "Promoting Drugs through Patient Advocacy Groups," CBC Marketplace, first broadcast 14 November 2000; CBC News Broadcast, *The National*, 20 September 2004.
34. P. E. Murphy, "Implementing Business Ethics," *Journal of Business Ethics*, 1988, vol. 7, pp. 907–915.
35. J. B. Dozier and M. P. Miceli, "Potential Predictors of Whistle-Blowing: A Prosocial Behaviour Perspective," *Academy of Management Review*, 1985, vol. 10, pp. 823–836; J. P. Near and M. P. Miceli, "Retaliation Against Whistle-Blowers: Predictors and Effects," *Journal of Applied Psychology*, 1986, vol. 71, pp. 137–145.
36. J. A. Byrne, "The Best-Laid Ethics Programs...," *Business Week*, 9 March 1992, pp. 67–69.
37. D. Collins, "Organizational Harm, Legal Consequences and Stakeholder Retaliation," *Journal of Business Ethics*, 1988, vol. 8, pp. 1–13.
38. Case by Margaret McKee, based on the following sources: R. Ferguson, "CIBC Sets Up Ethics Hotline for Staff," *Toronto Star*, 24 February 2004, *www.tnwinc.com*, 2004; *www.cibc.com*, 2004; B. MacLean and P. Elkind, "Partners in Crime," *Wall Street Week with Fortune*, *www.pbs.org*, 2003; N. Carr "Amid U.S. Scandal, McCaughey Succeeds Kassie as CIBC World Markets CEO," 5 February 2004, *http://money.canoe.ca*, 2004; W. Fox "Developing a Governance Culture," *The Western Corporate Governance Forum*, 29 March 2004, p. 3; R. Ferguson "CIBC Sets Up Ethics Hotline for Staff," *Toronto Star*, 24 February 2004, *www.tnwinc.com*, 2004; J. Gray, "Saving CIBC—Shareholders Don't Seem to Mind That the Bank Has Stumbled," *Canadian Business*, 1 March 2004, p. 9.

Managing in a Changing Global Environment

CHAPTER 3

Learning Objectives

An organization's environment is the complex network of changing forces that affect the way it operates. The environment is a major contingency for which an organization must plan and to which it must adapt. Furthermore, it is a source of uncertainty that an organization must try to control or regulate. This chapter examines the external forces that make managing in a global environment an uncertain, complex process.

After reading this chapter you should be able to:

1. List the forces in an organization's specific and general environment that give rise to opportunities and threats.
2. Identify why uncertainty exists in the environment.
3. Describe how and why an organization seeks to adapt to and control these forces to reduce uncertainty.
4. Understand how resource dependence theory and transaction cost theory explain why organizations choose different kinds of interorganizational strategies to manage their environments to gain the resources they need to achieve their goals and create value for their stakeholders.

WHAT IS THE ORGANIZATIONAL ENVIRONMENT?

Environment
The set of forces surrounding an organization that have the potential to affect the way it operates and its access to scarce resources.

The **environment** is the set of forces surrounding an organization that have the potential to affect the way it operates and its access to scarce resources. Scarce resources include the raw materials and skilled workers the organization needs to produce goods and services; the information it needs to improve its technology or decide on its competitive strategy; and the support of outside stakeholders, such as the customers who buy its goods and services, and the banks and financial institutions that supply the capital that sustains it. Forces in the environment that affect an organization's ability to secure these scarce resources include competition from rivals for customers; rapid changes in technology, which might erode an organization's competitive advantage; and an increase in the price of important inputs, which raises the organization's costs.

Canadian business has a deep history that is rooted in global trade. In fact, the very origins of Canada as a modern nation stem from the European search for new resources to satisfy the growing urbanization of France, England, and Spain in the

1400s.[1] From the arrival of the European fishing fleets off the Grand Banks of Newfoundland to harvest the rich fishing grounds, to the westward continental treks for trade in furs with the peoples of the First Nations, Canada's economy has been focused abroad. In the early part of the 20th century, Canadian business slowly transitioned away from its historical focus on natural resources and entered global trade in resources, manufacturing, and services.[2] That trend has continued until today. As a member of the G8 (the most industrialized nations of the world), Canada's economy and business acumen rank among the top in the world. Whether doing business in the U.S., Mexico, or Europe, or the Pacific Rim nations, Canada's business remains committed to the global marketplace.

An organization attempts to manage the forces in its environment to obtain the resources necessary to produce goods and services for customers and clients (see Figure 3-1). The term **organizational domain** refers to the particular range of goods and services that the organization produces, and the customers and other stakeholders whom it serves.[3] An organization establishes its domain by deciding which customers it is going to serve and then deciding how to manage the forces in its environment to maximize its ability to secure needed resources. To obtain inputs, for example, an organization has to decide which suppliers to deal with from the range of possible suppliers and how to manage its relationships with its chosen suppliers. To obtain money, an organization has to decide which bank to deal with and how to manage its relationship with the bank so that the bank will be inclined to authorize a loan.

Organizational domain The particular range of goods and services that the organization produces and the customers and other stakeholders whom it serves.

An organization attempts to structure its transactions with the environment to protect and enlarge its domain so that it can increase its ability to create value for customers, shareholders, employees, and other stakeholders. For example, Gerber

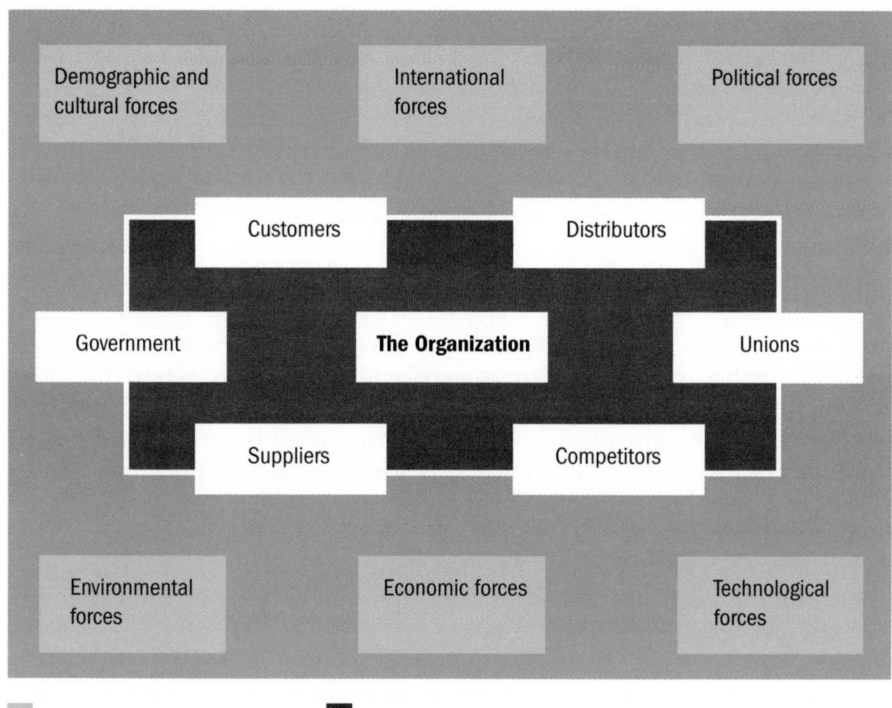

FIGURE 3-1
The Organizational Environment.
In the specific environment are forces that directly affect an organization's ability to obtain resources. In the general environment are forces that shape the specific environments of all organizations.

Products' domain is a wide range of baby foods and other baby-related products (clothing, diapers, pacifiers) that the company makes to satisfy the needs of babies and their families.[4] Gerber structures transactions with its environment—that is, with suppliers, bankers, customers, and other stakeholders—to obtain the resources it needs to protect and enlarge its domain.

One major way in which an organization can enlarge and protect its domain is to expand internationally. Global expansion allows an organization to seek new opportunities and new markets in order to exploit its core competencies and to create more value for stakeholders. Before discussing the specific ways in which organizations manage their environment to protect and enlarge their domain, we must understand in detail which forces in the environment affect organizations. The concepts of specific environment and general environment provide a useful basis for analysis.[5]

The Specific Environment

Specific environment The forces from outside stakeholder groups that directly affect an organization's ability to secure resources.

The **specific environment** consists of forces from outside stakeholder groups that directly affect an organization's ability to secure resources.[6] Customers, distributors, unions, competitors, suppliers, and the government are all important outside stakeholders who can influence and pressure organizations to act in certain ways (see Figure 3-1).

For baby-food maker Gerber, competitors, such as Beech-Nut and H. J. Heinz, are an important force that affects the organization's ability to attract resources: customer revenue. Competition makes resources scarce and valuable because the greater the competition for resources, the more difficult they are to obtain. Competitors can be domestic or international. Each type has different implications for a company's ability to obtain resources.

In Canada, Sony, Toyota, Philips, Mercedes-Benz, and other overseas companies compete with both North American and overseas companies for consumers. Abroad, Canadian companies face competition from organizations both inside and outside the countries in which they operate. The European divisions of General Motors and Ford, for example, compete not only with European car companies such as Fiat, Peugeot, and BMW, but with Japanese companies such as Toyota and Honda. Indeed, during the 1990s, Japanese car companies operating in Europe established plants with the capacity to produce 450 000 new cars a year and thus threaten the prosperity of European makers such as Volkswagen, Renault, Fiat, and Volvo.

Changes in the number and types of customers and changes in customer tastes are another force that affects an organization. An organization must have a strategy to manage its relationships with customers and attract their support, and the strategy must change over time as customer needs change. Gerber has an international reputation based on its high standards of purity, quality, and caring. However, in the 1990s, increasing demands from customers for additive-free, organic baby food led it to change the formulation of some of its food products. In the global environment, satisfying customer needs presents new challenges because customers differ from country to country. For example, customers in Europe—unlike Canadians—typically do not like their cereal sweetened, so Kellogg and General Mills modify their products to suit local European tastes. An organization must be willing and able to tailor or customize its products to suit the tastes and preferences of different consumers if it expects to attract their business.

Besides responding to the needs of customers, organizations must decide how to manage relationships with suppliers and distributors to obtain access to the resources they provide. An organization has to make many choices concerning how to manage these exchanges in order to secure most effectively a stable supply of inputs or dispose of its products in a timely manner. For example, should Gerber buy or make its inputs? Should it raise cattle and chickens and vegetables and fruits? Should it make glass jars? Or should it buy all of these inputs from suppliers? The purity of baby foods is a vital issue; can input suppliers be trusted to ensure product quality? What is the best way for Gerber to distribute its products to ensure their quality? Should Gerber own its own fleet of vehicles and sell directly to retail stores, or should it use wholesalers to distribute its products?

In the global environment, supplies of inputs can be obtained not just from domestic sources but from any country in the world. If companies do not explore opportunities to lower the cost of their inputs by locating abroad or by buying from overseas suppliers, they know that their overseas competitors will do so and will hurt their competitive advantage.

The challenges associated with distributing and marketing products increase in the global environment. Because the tastes of customers vary from country to country, many advertising and marketing campaigns are country specific, and many products are customized to overseas customers' preferences. Moreover, in Japan and some other countries, domestic producers tightly control distribution systems, and that arrangement makes it very hard for companies to enter the market and sell their products. Global distribution also becomes difficult when an organization's products are complex and customers need a lot of information to operate or use them successfully. All of these factors mean that an organization has to consider carefully how to handle the global distribution of its products to attract and retain customer support. Should the organization handle overseas sales and distribution itself? Should it sell to a wholesaler in the overseas market? Should it enter into a strategic alliance with an organization in a particular country and allow that company to market and distribute its products? Organizations operating in many countries must weigh all these options.

Other outside stakeholders include the government, unions, and consumer interest groups. Various government agencies are interested in Gerber's policies concerning equal employment opportunity, food preparation and content, and health and safety standards, and these agencies pressure the organization to make sure it follows legal rules. Unions pressure Gerber to secure favourable wages and benefits, and to protect the jobs of their members who work for Gerber. Consumer interest groups seek to prevent Gerber from reducing the quality of its foods.

An organization that establishes global operations has to forge a working relationship with its new workforce and develop relationships with any unions that represent its new employees. If a Japanese manufacturer opens a new plant in a foreign country such as Canada or the U.S., the Japanese management team has to understand the expectations of these workers—that is, their attitudes toward pay, seniority, and other conditions of employment. A global organization has to adapt its management style to fit the workforce's style, and workers also have to modify their expectations.

Finally, each country has its own system of government and its own laws and regulations that govern the conduct of business. Any company that enters a new country must learn to conform to the host country's institutional and legal system. Sometimes, as in the European Community (EC), the rules governing business conduct are standardized across several countries. Increasingly, companies competing globally are complaining about the protection that host governments offer to domestic companies. Often, domestic competitors lobby their home governments to combat what is seen as "unfair" global competition. The decades-old softwood lumber dispute between Canada and the U.S. is one example. U.S. domestic firms continue to pressure their government for protection from what U.S. firms see as unfair trade. U.S. domestic firms argue that Canadian softwood lumber producers are subsidized unfairly. On several occasions, the U.S. government has responded with trade tariffs on Canadian softwood so as to raise the cost of imported lumber and make domestic lumber more price-competitive within the U.S. marketplace. This form of protectionism is one challenge that firms face when entering the global market.

An organization must engage in transactions with each of the forces in its specific environment if it is to obtain the resources it requires to survive and to protect and enhance its domain. Over time, the size and scope of its domain will change as those transactions change. For example, an organization that decides to expand its domain to satisfy the needs of new customers by producing new kinds of products in new countries will encounter new sets of forces and may need to engage in a different set of transactions with the environment to gain resources. See Organizational Insight 3.1 for how the Royal Bank of Canada experienced the challenges of operating in a global environment firsthand.

The General Environment

General environment The forces that shape the specific environment and affect the ability of all organizations in a particular environment to obtain resources.

The **general environment** consists of forces that shape the specific environment and affect the ability of all organizations in a particular environment to obtain resources (see Figure 3-1, p. 69). *Economic forces,* such as interest rates, the state of the economy, and the unemployment rate, determine the level of demand for products and the price of inputs. National differences in interest rates, exchange rates, wage levels, gross domestic product, and per capita income have a dramatic effect on the way organizations operate internationally. Generally, organizations attempt to obtain their inputs or to manufacture their products in the country with the lowest labour or raw-materials costs. Obviously, an overseas competitor based in a country with low wages has a competitive advantage that may be crucial in the battle for the price-conscious Canadian consumer. Many North American companies are forced to move their operations abroad to compete with the low-cost operations of overseas manufacturers. Levi Strauss, for example, moved jeans production from the United States to Mexico and the Dominican Republic to reduce production costs. (Chapter 8 looks specifically at how an organization manages global expansion).

Technological forces, such as the development of new production techniques and new information-processing equipment, influence many aspects of organizations' operations. The use of computerized manufacturing technology can increase productivity. Similarly, investment in advanced research and development activities influences how organizations interact with each other and how they design their structures. (The role of technology is examined further in Chapter 9).

The international transfer of technology has important implications for an organization's competitive advantage. Organizations must be able to learn about and have access to technological developments abroad that might provide a low-cost or differentiation advantage. Traditionally, the trend in technology transfer as been from North America outward. Many Canadian and American companies have been slow to take advantage of overseas technological developments.

The willingness and ability of any company competing in the global marketplace to learn from its overseas competitors are becoming increasingly important. Such technological learning allows an organization to develop its core competencies and apply them around the world to create value, as Amazon.com has done.

Political and environmental forces influence government policy toward organizations and their stakeholders. For example, laws that favour particular business interests, such as a tariff on imported cars, influence organizations' customers and competitors. Pressure from environmentalists, such as pressure to reduce air pollution or a

ORGANIZATIONAL INSIGHT 3.1

The Royal Bank of Canada: A Global Misstep[7]

Ask people in Canada and they will tell you they are more than familiar with the Royal Bank of Canada (RBC). Founded in Halifax in 1875, today the RBC has over 1300 branches and 4100 banking machines, making it a very visible Canadian financial institution. It's also a very large one. In bank rankings, RBC typically places first or second in terms of the common metrics for evaluating bank operations, whether that's by scope of product offering, number of customer accounts, or purely in terms of customer assets under management. What many Canadians may not be aware of is that RBC also has a large international presence as well, with offices in more than 30 countries. With its operations in Canada, the Unites States, the Caribbean and other parts of the world, RBC reports that it serves "more than 12 million personal, business and public sector clients."[8] The company's shares also trade on two stock exchanges, the Toronto Stock Exchange (TSX) and the New York Stock Exchange (NYSE).

As you might imagine, operating in these different jurisdictions brings with it a special set of challenges. Let's consider the very basic issue of meeting the regulatory reporting requirements for the two stock exchanges. With the introduction of the Sarbanes Oxley Act in the U.S. in July of 2002, the reporting requirements for NYSE-listed firms became a lot more stringent. This new legislation was introduced by U.S. President George W. Bush to make corporate executives and their audit firms more accountable and responsible to shareholders. With the rash of corporate scandals, few have questioned the need for such legislation, but for organizations it has introduced new management challenges. RBC's chief financial officer, Peter Currie, came face to face with this issue in September 2003.

Currie learned that a seemingly innocent $200 000 consulting assignment for an RBC subsidiary undertaken by its appointed auditors, Price Waterhouse Coopers (PWC), had violated U.S. regulations around auditor independence.[9] While the amount is minuscule for a company that spends $3.5 billion a year on the purchase of goods and services,[10] the discovery triggered a number of actions, including the resignation of PWC as RBC's auditors and the introduction of a new review process for any work assignments involving the bank's outside auditors. In speaking about the incident, Currie commented, "We can say this is silly and it's overkill but it's the law of the land in the largest and most vibrant capital market in the world. So we deal with it—we have no choice."

desire to decrease the level of solid waste, affect organizations' production costs. Environmentally friendly product design and packaging may alter organizations' relationships with competitors, customers, and suppliers. New engines introduced by Toyota and Honda in 2002 result in virtually no pollution and meet and exceed some of North America's most stringent clean air requirements. Globally, countries that do little to protect the environment see an influx of companies that take advantage of lax regulations to set up low-cost operations there. The result can be increased pollution and mounting environmental problems.

Demographic, cultural, and social forces—such as the age, education, lifestyle, norms, values, and customs of a nation's people—shape organizations' customers, managers, and employees. The demand for baby products, for example, is linked to national birth rates and age distributions. Demographic, cultural, and social forces are important sources of uncertainty in a global environment because they directly affect the tastes and needs of a nation's consumers. Cultural and social values affect a country's attitudes toward both domestic and overseas products and companies. Customers in France and Italy, for example, generally prefer domestically produced cars even though overseas products may be superior in quality and value.

A company establishing operations in a country overseas must be attuned to the host country's business methods and practices. Countries differ in how they do business and in the nature of their business institutions. They also differ in their attitudes toward union–management relationships, their work habits, in their ethical standards, and in their accounting and financial practices. In some countries bribery and corruption are acceptable practices. In Japan, the law supports organizations in their attempt to protect their market and distribution systems against the entry of overseas competitors. Antitrust sentiment is far weaker in Japan and South Korea than in many other countries. That attitude enables domestic Japanese and Korean companies to collude to keep overseas rivals out of their respective markets. The story of GE's experiences in Hungary illustrates these issues. (See Organizational Insight 3.2.)

As the example of GE and Tungsram illustrates, managers who want to take advantage of the opportunities created by changing global political, legal, social, and economic forces face a major challenge. If an organization manages the forces in its general and specific environments effectively, so that it obtains the resources it needs, its domain will grow as it attracts new customers and produces more goods and services. If an organization manages the forces in its general and specific environments poorly, stakeholders will withhold their support, the organization will not obtain scarce resources, and the organization's domain may shrink. Eventually, unless it can find a better way to manage its environment, the organization may cease to exist.

Sources of Uncertainty in the Organizational Environment

An organization likes to have a steady and abundant supply of resources so that it can easily manage its domain and satisfy its stakeholders. All the forces discussed above, however, cause uncertainty for organizations and make it more difficult for managers to control the flow of resources they need to protect and enlarge their organizational domains. The set of forces that cause these problems can be looked at in another way: in terms of how they cause uncertainty because they affect the complexity, dynamism, and richness of the environment. As these forces cause the environment to become more complex, less stable, and poorer, the level of uncertainty increases (see Figure 3-2).

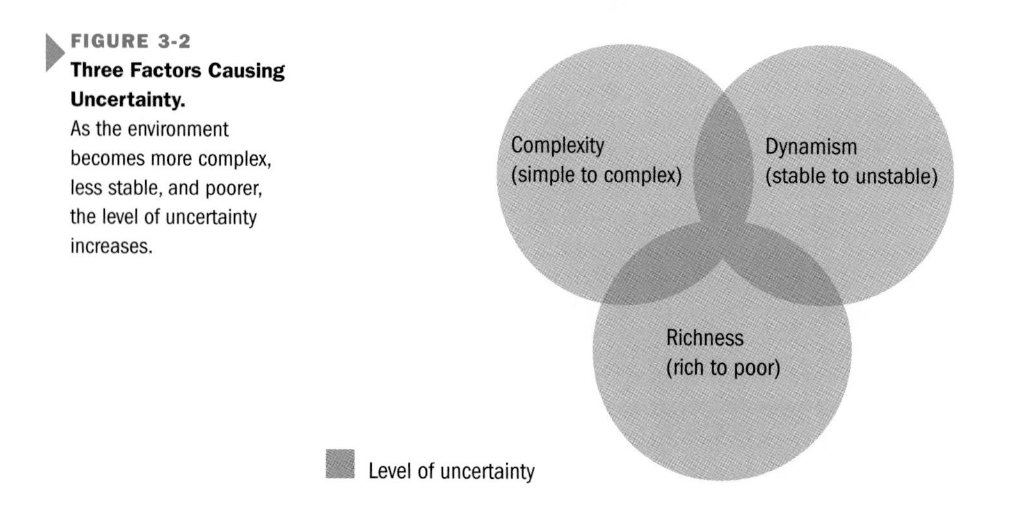

FIGURE 3-2
Three Factors Causing Uncertainty.
As the environment becomes more complex, less stable, and poorer, the level of uncertainty increases.

ORGANIZATIONAL INSIGHT 3.2

GE's Managers Stumble in Hungary

Seeking to expand globally, General Electric (GE) agreed to acquire 51 percent of Tungsram, a maker of lighting products and widely regarded as one of Hungary's best companies, at a cost of US$150 million. GE was attracted to Tungsram because of Hungary's low wage rates and the possibility of using the company as a base from which to export lighting products to Western Europe. At the time, many analysts believed that GE would show other Western companies how to turn organizations once run by communist party officials into capitalist money-makers. GE transferred some of its best managers to Tungsram and waited for the miracle to happen. It took a long time, for several reasons.

One problem resulted from major misunderstandings between the GE managers and the Hungarian workers. The GE managers complained that the Hungarians were lazy; the Hungarians thought the managers were pushy. GE's management system depends on extensive communication between workers and managers, a practice uncommon in the previously communist country. Changing behaviour at Tungsram proved to be difficult. The GE personnel wanted strong sales and marketing functions that would pamper customers; in Hungary's former planned economy, these were unnecessary. In addition, Hungarians expected GE to deliver Western-style wages; but GE came to Hungary to take advantage of the country's low-wage structure.[11]

As Tungsram's losses mounted, GE learned what happens when grand expectations collide with the grim reality of inefficiency and indifference toward customers and quality. Looking back, GE managers admit that, because of differences in basic attitudes between countries, they had underestimated the difficulties they would face in turning Tungsram around. To improve performance, GE laid off half of Tungsram's employees, including two out of every three managers. It invested over US$1 billion in a new plant and equipment and in retraining the remaining employees and managers to help them learn the work attitudes and behaviours that a company needs to survive in a competitive global environment. In the 2000s its Hungarian operations have become some of the most efficient in Europe. The plant exports its light bulb all over the European Economic Community.

Environmental Complexity **Environmental complexity** is a function of the strength, number, and interconnectedness of the specific and general forces that an organization has to manage.[12] The greater the number, and the greater the differences between them, the more complex and uncertain is the environment and the more difficult to predict and control. Ford, for example, used to obtain inputs from over 3000 different suppliers. To reduce the uncertainty associated with dealing with so many suppliers, Ford embarked on a program to reduce their number and thus reduce the complexity of its environment. Now Ford deals with fewer than 500 suppliers; acquiring the information needed to manage its relationships with them is much easier than acquiring information to facilitate dealings with ten times that number. Complexity also increases when a company produces different products for different groups of customers. For example, if a company like McDonald's suddenly decided to enter the insurance and banking businesses, it would need a massive infusion of information to reduce the uncertainty surrounding the new transactions.

Environmental complexity The strength, number, and interconnectedness of the specific and general forces that an organization has to manage.

Complexity can increase greatly when specific and general forces in the environment become interconnected—that is, when they begin to interact and their effect on the organization becomes unpredictable.[13] The more interconnected the forces in an organization's specific and general environments are, the more uncertainty the organization faces. Suppose a major breakthrough in car-making technology makes existing factories obsolete. This general force will cause the price of a car manufacturer's stock (like Ford's) to fluctuate wildly and will send financial markets into turmoil. Car manufacturers will be unsure how the breakthrough will affect their business, competition between rivals will increase (a specific force), and both management and the unions will be uncertain of the effect this will have on jobs and the future of the organization. If customers then stop buying cars (another specific force) until new models made with the new technology come out, the result may be layoffs and further decreases in the price of car company stocks.

The more complex an organization's environment, the greater the uncertainty about that environment. Predicting and controlling the flow of resources becomes extremely difficult, and problems associated with managing transactions with the environment increase.

Environmental dynamism
The degree to which forces in the specific and general environments change quickly over time and thus contribute to the uncertainty an organization faces.

Environmental Dynamism **Environmental dynamism** is a function of how much and how quickly forces in the specific and general environments change over time and thus contribute to the uncertainty an organization faces.[14] An environment is *stable* if forces affect the supply of resources in a predictable way. An environment is *unstable and dynamic* if an organization cannot predict the way in which the forces will change over time. If technology, for example, is changing as rapidly as it does in the computer industry, the environment is very dynamic. An organization in a dynamic, unstable environment will seek ways to make the environment more predictable and thereby lessen the organization's uncertainty about its environment. Later in the chapter, we discuss strategies for managing potentially dynamic parts of the environment, including long-term contracts and vertical integration.

Today, the existence of huge new global markets for companies to enter, and the possibility of gaining access to new global resources and new global core competencies, provide opportunities for an organization to enlarge its domain and create more value for its stakeholders. However, global expansion makes the environment more uncertain and difficult to predict and control. As companies compete both at home and abroad, the environment becomes increasingly complex (there are greater numbers of forces to be managed, and the forces are interconnected) and increasingly dynamic (the forces change rapidly).

Environmental richness
The amount of resources available to support an organization's domain.

Environmental Richness **Environmental richness** is a function of the amount of resources available to support an organization's domain.[15] In rich environments, necessary resources are plentiful and uncertainty is low because organizations need not compete for resources. Oil companies in Alberta, for example, have a large pool of experienced management and skilled technicians from which to draw their labour force. In contrast, in technically poor environments, such as the Maritime provinces, these types of resources are scarce and uncertainty is high because organizations have to compete for those scarce resources.

Environments may be resource poor for two reasons: (1) The organization is located in a resource-poor country or in a resource-poor region of a country; and (2) there is a high level of competition, and organizations are fighting over a limited supply of available resources.[16] In poor environments, organizations have to battle to attract customers or to obtain the best inputs or the latest technology. The end result of these battles is greater uncertainty for the organization. The poorer the environment, the more difficult the problems organizations face in managing resource transactions. In an environment that is poor, unstable, and complex, resources are especially hard to obtain and organizations face the greatest uncertainty. By contrast, in a rich, stable, and simple environment, resources are easy to come by and uncertainty is low.

Airline companies, such as Air Canada, American, Continental, and Delta, are currently experiencing a highly uncertain environment. New, low-cost airlines such as WestJet are entering the industry, which has increased the level of industry competition. The environment has become poorer as airlines fight for customers (a resource) and are forced to offer lower prices to attract them. The airlines' environment is complex because competing airlines (part of each airline's specific environment) are very interconnected: If one airline reduces prices, they all reduce prices to protect their domains, and these actions further increase uncertainty. Finally, the price of oil, the threat of overseas competition, and the state of the economy are all interconnected in the airlines' environment and change over time, making it difficult to predict or plan for contingencies.

In contrast, the environment of the pharmaceutical industry is relatively certain. Merck, Bristol-Myers-Squibb, Upjohn, and other large companies that invent drugs receive patents and are the sole providers of their respective new drugs for 20 years. The patent-owning company can charge a high price for its drug because it faces no competition and customers have no option but to buy the drug from the original manufacturer. Organizations in the pharmaceutical industry exist in a stable, rich environment: Competition is low, and no change occurs until patents expire. Throughout the rest of this chapter, we discuss in more detail the strategies that organizations pursue to manage their environments. First, however, it is useful to examine the nature of the environment that confronted Jeff Bezos after he founded Amazon.com.[17] (See Focus on New Information Technology.)

MANAGERIAL IMPLICATIONS

Analyzing the Environment

1. Managers at all levels and in all functions should periodically analyze the organizational environment and identify sources of uncertainty.
2. To manage transactions with the organizational environment effectively, managers should chart the forces in the organization's specific and general environments, noting (a) the number of forces that will affect the organization, (b) the pattern of interconnectedness or linkages between these forces, (c) how rapidly these forces change, and (d) the extent and nature of competition, which affects how rich or poor the environment is.
3. Taking that analysis, managers should plan how to deal with contingencies. Designing interorganizational strategies to control and secure access to scarce and valuable resources in the environment in which they operate is the first stage in this process.

FOCUS ON NEW INFORMATION TECHNOLOGY

Amazon.com, Part 2

The book distribution and book selling industry was changed forever in July 1995 when Jeff Bezos brought virtual bookseller Amazon.com online. His new company changed the whole nature of the environment. Previously, book publishers had sold their books either indirectly to book wholesalers who supplied small bookstores or directly to larger book chains like Barnes & Noble, Borders, Chapters, or Indigo, or to book-of-the month clubs. There were so many book publishers and so many booksellers that the industry was relatively stable, with both large and small bookstores enjoying a comfortable niche in the market. In this relatively stable, simple, rich environment, uncertainty was low and all companies enjoyed good revenues and profits.

Amazon.com's electronic approach both to buying and selling books changed all this. First, since it was able to offer customers quick access to all of the over 1.5 million books in print and it discounted the prices of its books, this led to a higher level of industry competition and made the industry environment poorer. Second, since it also negotiated directly with the large book publishers over price and supply because it wanted to get books quickly to its customers, this led to an increase in the complexity of the environment: all players—book publishers, wholesalers, stores, and customers—became more closely linked. Third, as a result of these factors, and continuing changes in information technology, the environment became more unstable and resources harder to secure.

What have been the results of the increase in uncertainty in the environment these changes have brought? First, these changes directly threatened the prosperity of small bookstores, many of which have closed their doors and left the business because they can't compete with online bookstores. Second, the larger booksellers like Barnes & Noble, Borders, and Indigo-Chapters have started their own online bookstores to compete with Amazon.com. Third, Amazon.com and the other online bookstores have been engaged in a price war. The prices of books have been further discounted, resulting in an even more competitive and uncertain environment.

IT is not specialized to any one country or world region. Access to the Internet and the World Wide Web means that an online company can sell to customers around the world, providing of course that its products are suitable or can be customized to the needs of overseas competitors. Jeff Bezos was quick to realize that his U.S.-based Amazon.com IT could be profitably customized and transferred to other countries to sell books. However, his ability to enter new markets was limited by one major factor: Amazon.com offers its customers the biggest selection of books written in the English language; he had to find overseas customers who could read English. Where to locate then?

An obvious first choice would be the United Kingdom, since its population speaks English, then other English-speaking nations such as Canada, Australia, New Zealand, India, and Germany. Germany? Of probably of any nation in the world, Germany has the highest proportion of English-as-a-second-language speakers because English is taught in all its high schools.

So far, Bezos has replicated its value-creation functions and customized its IT for four nations: In the United Kingdom it bought the company Bookpages, installed its proprietary technology and renamed it Amazon.co.uk in 1996. In Germany, it acquired a new online venture ABC Bücherdienst/Telebuch.de and created Amazon.de in 1998.[18] Amazon.com also entered the French, Austrian, and Japanese markets specifically with a national online presence, and is offering Spanish-speaking access through its international site. This pattern can be expected to be repeated as Amazon.com targets other nations and linguistic groups.

RESOURCE DEPENDENCE THEORY

Organizations are dependent on their environment for the resources they need to survive and grow. The supply of resources, however, is dependent on the complexity, dynamism, and richness of the environment. If an environment becomes poorer because important customers are lost or new competitors enter the market, resources are likely to become scarce and more valuable, and uncertainty is likely to increase. Organizations attempt to manage their transactions with the environment to ensure access to the resources on which they depend. They want their access to resources to be as predictable as possible because predictability simplifies the managing of their domain and promotes survival.

According to **resource dependence theory**, the goal of an organization is to minimize its dependence on other organizations for the supply of scarce resources in its environment and to find ways of influencing them to make resources available.[19] Thus an organization must simultaneously manage two aspects of its resource dependence: (1) It has to exert influence over other organizations so that it can obtain resources, and (2) it must respond to the needs and demands of the other organizations in its environment.[20]

Resource dependence theory
A theory that argues that the goal of an organization is to minimize its dependence on other organizations for the supply of scarce resources in its environment and to find ways of influencing them to make resources available.

The strength of one organization's dependence on another for a particular resource is a function of two factors. One factor is how vital the resource is to the organization's survival. Scarce and valuable inputs (such as component parts and raw materials) and resources (such as customers and distribution outlets) are very important to an organization's survival.[21] The other factor is the extent to which the resource is controlled by other organizations.

The personal computer industry illustrates the operation of both factors. Personal computer manufacturers such as Compaq, Gateway, and Dell are dependent on organizations such as Intel that supply memory chips and integrated circuits. Some, like Apple and IBM who do not sell online (Dell and Gateway are the online leaders), are also dependent on chains of computer stores and other retail stores that stock their products, and on school systems and corporate customers that buy large quantities of their products. When there are few suppliers of a resource such as integrated circuits, or few organizations that distribute and sell a product, companies become very dependent on the organizations that do exist. Intel, for example, makes many of the most advanced microchips and thus has a lot of power over computer makers who need its fastest chips to compete successfully. The greater the dependence of one organization on another, the more power the latter has over the former, and the more it can threaten or exploit the dependent organization if it wishes to do so.

To manage their resource dependence and control their access to scarce resources, organizations develop various strategies.[22] Just as nations attempt to craft an international policy to increase their ability to influence world affairs, so organizations try to find ways of increasing their influence over their environment. Microsoft offers a good example of the management of the environment to control resource dependence. (See Organizational Insight 3.3.)

INTERORGANIZATIONAL STRATEGIES FOR MANAGING RESOURCE DEPENDENCIES

As the Microsoft example shows, the flow of resources among organizations is uncertain and problematic. To reduce uncertainty, an organization needs to devise interorganizational strategies to manage the resource interdependencies in its specific and general environment. Managing these interdependencies allows an organization to protect and enlarge its domain. In the specific environment, an organization needs to manage its relationships with forces such as suppliers, unions, and consumer interest groups. If they restrict access to resources, they can increase uncertainty.

In the specific environment, two basic types of interdependencies cause uncertainty: symbiotic and competitive.[23] Interdependencies are symbiotic when the outputs

ORGANIZATIONAL INSIGHT 3.3

Mighty Microsoft

Microsoft dominates the operating systems market and is attempting to build its market share in the Internet, videogame, handheld, graphics, and local-area networking markets as well.[24] Many companies are dependent on Microsoft, but Microsoft is not dependent on them. Microsoft produces not only all kinds of software products but also the hardware—mouse and CD-ROM products, for example—that backs up its software. Moreover, if it wants to enter a lucrative new market niche quickly, it often takes over the dominant software company in that niche. In 1998, competitors accused Microsoft of using its dominant industry position to harm rivals and gain power over suppliers and other companies that rely on it, and in 1999 the U.S government sued Microsoft in court, arguing it to be a monopolist. Competitors believe Microsoft has an unfair advantage because it controls the development of basic computer operating systems, such as Windows 98 and XP, which in turn determine how well software applications work. In effect, Microsoft controls the input that other companies require—its widely used operating system. Rival software developers believe that Microsoft's expertise in operating systems gives Microsoft software designers an unfair opportunity to make Microsoft products run better than theirs. Adobe Systems, which makes software typefaces, thinks that Microsoft's Windows operating system was designed to print Microsoft's typefaces at twice the speed of Adobe's, and Adobe's sales suffered. Logitech Inc. complained that Microsoft's refusal to allow it to package Windows with its mouse made it difficult for Logitech to offer customers a competitive product. Netscape complained that Microsoft forced users of Windows 98 to use Microsoft's Web browser rather than Netscape's. In 2001, Kodak complained that users of its imaging software were switched to Microsoft's imaging software when they tried to use it.

These accusations and similar ones led to legal action in 2001, and Microsoft was found guilty of anticompetitive practices and forced to pay hundreds of millions of dollars in restitution. Microsoft, however, continued expanding its domain and in 2002 it introduced new software such as Windows XP and PocketPC for handheld devices that critics think will just propel it to leadership in these segments of the software market.[25] In 2004 Microsoft was found guilty of anticompetitive practices by the courts of the European Union, and is now involved in appeal processes concerning the ruling.[26] Microsoft's power to control resources has been so great that some analysts have suggested that Microsoft be broken up into a number of smaller companies, or it should be prevented from taking over any more. It, however, claims it has done nothing wrong.[27]

Symbiotic interdependencies Interdependencies that exist between an organization and its suppliers and distributors.

Competitive interdependencies Interdependencies that exist among organizations that compete for scarce inputs and outputs.

of one organization are inputs for another; thus **symbiotic interdependencies** generally exist between an organization and its suppliers and distributors. Intel and computer makers like Compaq and Dell have a symbiotic interdependency. **Competitive interdependencies** exist among organizations that compete for scarce inputs and outputs.[28] Compaq and Dell are in competition for customers for their computers and for inputs such as Intel's latest microchips.

Organizations can use various linkage mechanisms to control symbiotic and competitive interdependencies.[29] The use of these mechanisms, however, requires the actions and decisions of the linked organizations to be coordinated. This need for coordination reduces each organization's freedom to act independently and perhaps in its own best interests. Suppose that Compaq, to protect its future supply of chips, signs a contract with Intel agreeing to use only Intel chips. But then a new chip manufacturer comes along with a less expensive chip. The contract with Intel obliges Compaq to pay Intel's higher prices even though doing so is not in Compaq's best interests.

Whenever an organization involves itself in an interorganizational linkage, it must balance its need to reduce resource dependence against the loss in autonomy or freedom of choice that will result from the linkage.[30] In general, *an organization aims to choose the interorganizational strategy that offers the most reduction in uncertainty for the least loss of control.*[31]

In the next sections, we examine the interorganizational strategies that organizations can use to manage symbiotic interdependencies and competitive interdependencies. A linkage is formal when two or more organizations agree to coordinate their interdependencies directly in order to reduce uncertainty. The more *formal* a linkage is, the greater are both the direct coordination and the likelihood that coordination is based on an explicit, written agreement or involves some common ownership between organizations. The more *informal* a linkage is, the more indirect or loose is the method of coordination and the more likely is the coordination to be based on an implicit or unspoken agreement.

STRATEGIES FOR MANAGING SYMBIOTIC RESOURCE INTERDEPENDENCIES

To manage symbiotic interdependencies, organizations have a range of strategies from which to choose. Figure 3-3 indicates the relative degree of formality of four strategies. The more formal a strategy is, the greater is the prescribed area of cooperation between organizations.

Developing a Good Reputation

The least formal, least direct way to manage symbiotic interdependencies with suppliers and customers is to develop a **reputation**, a state in which an organization is held in high regard and trusted by other parties because of its fair and honest business practices. For example, paying bills on time and providing high-quality goods and services lead to a good reputation and trust on the part of suppliers and customers. If a car repair shop has a reputation for excellent repair work and fair prices for parts and labour, customers will return to the shop whenever their cars need servicing, and the organization will be managing its linkages with customers successfully.

Reputation
A state in which an organization is held in high regard and trusted by other parties because of its fair and honest business practices.

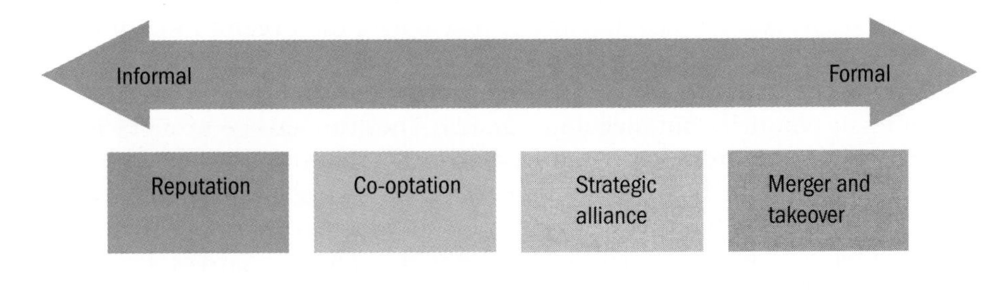

FIGURE 3-3
Interorganizational Strategies for Managing Symbiotic Interdependencies.
Symbiotic interdependencies generally exist between an organization and its suppliers and distributors. The more formal a strategy is, the greater the cooperation between organizations.

Federal Express (or FedEx) uses trust and reputation as a key method for linkage management of its customers. When companies arrange for the movement and delivery of material or documents, they know that FedEx will do everything possible to make deliveries on time and will monitor the delivery process at every step of the way. FedEx's commitment to its customers and its high quality of service hinges largely on its reputation.

Reputation and trust are probably the most common linkage mechanisms for managing symbiotic interdependencies. Over the long run, companies that behave dishonestly are likely to be unsuccessful; thus organizations as a group tend to become more honest over time.[32] Acting honestly, however, does not rule out active bargaining and negotiating over the price and quality of inputs and outputs. Every organization wants to strike the deal that best suits it and therefore attempts to negotiate terms in its favour.

Co-optation

Co-optation
A strategy that manages symbiotic interdependencies by neutralizing problematic forces in the specific environment.

Co-optation is a strategy that manages symbiotic interdependencies by neutralizing problematic forces in the specific environment.[33] An organization that wants to bring opponents over to its side gives them a stake in or claim on what it does and tries to satisfy their interests.

A common way to co-opt problematic forces such as customers, suppliers, or other important outside stakeholders is to bring them within the organization and, in effect, make them inside stakeholders. If some stakeholder group does not like the way things are being done, an organization co-opts the group by giving it a role in changing the way things are. Quite often, real estate developers who are interested in developing housing or industrial projects in urban areas will consult with the surrounding community, or with local community groups and representatives. This is done for several reasons. First, involving the local community members in the development process facilitates their awareness and understanding of the development project and reduces the likelihood that the community will raise objections. Many development projects get stalled when the local community mobilizes and raises objections with the media or local politicians. Second, by seeking input and advice from the community, the community itself becomes a partner or stakeholder in the project and may offer suggestions that benefit both the community and the development itself. For example, the local community members will be more aware of the traffic conditions within the area, and may have sound recommendations on how to best manage the increase for the least disturbance. Alternatively, they may suggest the incorporation of parkland, green spaces, or playgrounds.

All kinds of organizations use this strategy. Local schools, for example, attempt to co-opt parents by inviting them to become members of school boards or by establishing teacher–parent committees. In such an exchange, the organization gives up some control but usually gains more than it loses.

Outsiders can be brought inside an organization through bribery, a practice widespread in many countries but illegal in Canada. They can also be brought inside through the use of an **interlocking directorate**—a linkage that results when a director from one company sits on the board of another company. An organization that uses an interlocking directorate as a linkage mechanism invites members of powerful and significant stakeholder groups in its specific environment to sit on its board of directors.[34] An organization might invite the financial institution from which it borrows most of its money to send someone to sit on the organization's board of directors. Outside directors interact with an organization's top-management team, ensuring supplies of scarce capital, exchanging information, and strengthening ties between organizations.

Interlocking directorate
A linkage that results when a director from one company sits on the board of another company.

Strategic Alliances

Strategic alliances are becoming an increasingly common mechanism for managing symbiotic (and competitive) interdependencies between companies inside one country or between countries. A strategic alliance is an agreement that commits two or more companies to share their resources to develop joint new business opportunities.

Many Canadian retail outlets are allying themselves with specific banks in order to provide ATM and other banking and financial services within their stores. In this form of alliance, the store customer benefits from increased convenience, the retailers benefit from creating an environment that provides opportunity for increased customer purchases, and the banks benefit from the increased use of their ATMs and services.

In 2002 Dell and Microsoft formed a strategic alliance to bring high-performance InfiniBand technology to the next-generation business servers. InfiniBand provides significantly higher data performance for high-density servers, storage, and other network devices. Together, Dell and Microsoft are working on the hardware and software components essential for a complete InfiniBand solution for business customers. Similarly, Ballard Power Systems is using strategic alliances to solve several major challenges (see Organizational Insight 3.4.).

There are several types of strategic alliance. Figure 3-4 indicates the relative degree of formality of long-term contracts, networks, minority ownership, and joint ventures. The more formal an arrangement, the stronger and more prescribed the linkage and the tighter the control of the joint activities. In general, as uncertainty increases, organizations choose a more formal alliance to protect their access to resources.

Long-Term Contracts

At the informal end of the continuum shown in Figure 3-4 are alliances spelled out in long-term contracts between two or more organizations. The purpose of these contracts is usually to reduce costs by sharing resources or by sharing the risk of research and development, marketing, construction, and other activities. Contracts are the least formal type of alliance because no ties link the organizations apart from the agreement set forth in the contract. For example, to reduce financial risk, Bechtel Corporation and Willbros Group Inc., two leading multinational construction companies, agreed to pool their resources to construct a US$850 million oil pipeline in the Caspian Sea.[35] J. B. Hunt Transport, a trucking company, formed an alliance with Santa Fe Pacific Corporation, a railroad company. Santa Fe agreed to carry Hunt's trailers across the United States on railroad cars. At the end of the trip, the trains were met by Hunt's trucks, which transported the trailers to their final destination. This arrangement lowered Hunt's costs while increasing Santa Fe's revenues.

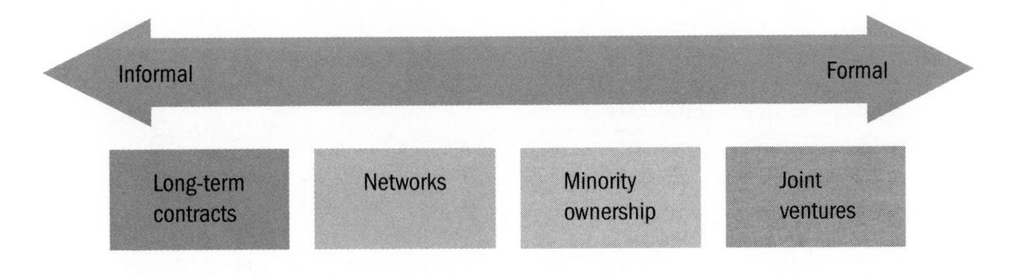

FIGURE 3-4
Types of Strategic Alliance.
Companies linked by a strategic alliance share resources to develop joint new business opportunities. The more formal an alliance, the stronger the link between allied organizations.

ORGANIZATIONAL INSIGHT 3.4

Ballard Power Systems: Navigating the Future[36]

The research and development costs associated with a new product, especially a leading-edge product, can be astronomically high. Just ask Ballard Power Systems of Burnaby, B.C., a company that's been working since 1983 to develop, manufacture, and market hydrogen fuel cells.

These revolutionary fuel cells are being adapted to power automobiles, buses, and other vehicles, as well as to power portable generators. The cells use hydrogen as their energy source—which is in abundant supply and creates zero emissions. With concerns over global warming and declining world oil reserves, these two features alone make hydrogen fuel cells very attractive to investors and consumers alike. But so far all this good news hasn't translated into profits for the company.

Now fine-tuning its fifth generation of fuel cells, Ballard Power Systems hasn't made a profit since its inception and, at its 2003 annual meeting of shareholders, company spokespeople predicted it wouldn't make a profit until 2007. One factor that will be key to Ballard's future profitability is commercialization—that is, wide-scale incorporation of its fuel cells into existing products and a way to refuel the cells. So how can a company like Ballard Power Systems accelerate the commercialization process? One answer is strategic alliances.

Not surprisingly, there are many companies interested in Ballard's fuel cell technology. The automotive industry in particular has been watching the developments in the field, and Ballard has already supplied fuel cells to Honda, Mitsubishi, Nissan, and Volkswagen. Several big-name automakers have chosen a slightly different route and have forged strategic alliances with Ballard to work together to explore ways to incorporate fuel technology in their vehicles. These alliances are critical to Ballard and its long-term success, but its partners also stand to gain.

Take, for example, the agreement (aptly named the "Vehicular Alliance") announced in 2004 by Ballard Power Systems, DaimlerChrysler AG, and Ford Motor Company. DaimlerChrysler has been working with Ballard since the early 1990s and was the first automaker to form a major alliance with the company. Ford joined the alliance in 1998. With their 2004 agreement, the partners have clearly delineated their individual areas of expertise.

Ballard is to focus on refining and enhancing its fuel cell technology, specifically the heart of the fuel cell engine. Ford and DaimlerChrysler are focusing on the challenge of effectively integrating the new power source into their existing vehicles. Ballard's partners are also providing much needed financing—in the form of $58 million in engineering revenues. They're also helping to lower the company's operational risk by agreeing to allow Ballard to be its exclusive supplier of fuel cell technology until 2021 and actively helping to build the Ballard fuel cell brand. The automakers stand to gain as well through a $55 million equity position in Ballard Power Systems.

So, will this spell success for Ballard Power Systems in its bid for widespread commercialization of its revolutionary fuel cells? It's too early to tell but, as Dennis Campbell, Ballard's president and chief executive officer, said shortly after the agreement was signed, "This transaction reduces Ballard's risk and increases our focus. It reduces our risk in financial terms, in operational terms, and in terms of commercialization." In a business environment where risk management is key, Ballard's latest strategic alliance seems likely to help make its goal of providing high-quality, low-cost fuel-cell products to the mass market more of a reality.

Contracts can be oral or written, casual, shared, or implicit. The CEOs or top managers of two companies might agree over lunch to meet regularly to share information and ideas on some business activity, such as standardizing computer systems or changing customer needs. Some organizations, in contrast, develop written contracts to specify procedures for sharing resources or information and for using the benefits that result from such agreements. Kellogg Company, the breakfast cereal manufacturer, enters into written contracts with the farmers who supply the corn and rice it needs. Kellogg agrees to pay a certain price for their produce regardless of the market rate prevailing when the produce is harvested. Both parties gain because a major source of unpredictability (fluctuations in corn and rice prices) is eliminated from their environments.

Networks A **network** or network structure is a cluster of different organizations whose actions are coordinated by contracts and agreements rather than through a formal hierarchy of authority. Members of a network work closely to support and complement one another's activities. The alliance resulting from a network is more formal than the alliance resulting from a contract, because more ties link member organizations and there is greater formal coordination of activities.[37] Nike and other organizations establish networks to build long-term relationships with suppliers, distributors, and customers while keeping the core organization from becoming too large or too bureaucratic.

Network
A cluster of different organizations whose actions are coordinated by contracts and agreements rather than through a formal hierarchy of authority.

The goal of the organization that created the network is to share its R&D skills with its partners and have them use those skills to become more efficient and help it to reduce its costs or increase quality. For example, AT&T created a network organization and linked its partners so that it could produce answering machines at low cost. AT&T electronically sends designs for new component parts and assembly instructions for new products to its network partners, who coordinate their activities to produce the components in the desired quantities and then ship them to the final assembly point.[38]

Minority Ownership A more formal alliance emerges when organizations buy a minority ownership stake in each other. Ownership is a more formal linkage than contracts and network relationships. Minority ownership makes organizations extremely interdependent, and that interdependence forges strong cooperative bonds.

The Japanese system of keiretsu shows how minority ownership networks operate. **Keiretsu** is a group of organizations, each of which owns shares in the other organizations in the group, and all of which work together to further the group's interests. Japanese companies employ two basic forms of keiretsu. Capital keiretsu are used to manage input and output linkages. Financial keiretsu are used to manage linkages among many diverse companies and usually have at their centre a large bank.[39]

Keiretsu
A group of organizations, each of which owns shares in the other organizations in the group, that work together to further the group's interests.

A particularly good example of the way a capital keiretsu network can benefit all the companies in it, but particularly the dominant ones, comes from the Japanese auto industry.[40] Toyota is one of the most profitable car companies in the world. Its vehicles are consistently ranked among the most reliable, and the company enjoys strong customer support. Interdependencies with its customers are not problematic because Toyota has a good reputation among them. One of the reasons for this good reputation is the way Toyota controls its input interdependencies.

Because a car's reliability depends on the quality of its inputs, managing this crucial linkage is important. To control its inputs, Toyota owns a minority stake, often as much as 49 percent, in most of the companies that supply its components. Because of these formal ownership ties, Toyota can exercise strong control over the prices that suppliers charge and over the quality of their products. An even more important result of this formal alliance, however, is that it allows Toyota and its suppliers to work together to improve product quality and reliability.

Toyota is not afraid to share proprietary information with its suppliers because of its ownership stake. As a result, suppliers participate in the car design process, and their participation can lead to the discovery of new ways to improve the quality and reduce the cost of components. Both Toyota and the suppliers share in the benefits that accrue from this close cooperation, and over time, this alliance has given Toyota a competitive advantage. In turn, this competitive advantage translates into control over important environmental interdependencies. Note also that Toyota's position as a shareholder in its suppliers' businesses means that there is no reason for Toyota to exploit them ruthlessly and depress their profits. All partners benefit from the sharing of activities. These close linkages paid off once again when Toyota introduced the latest model of the Camry sedan. By taking advantage of the skills in its network, Toyota was able to engineer US$1700 in cost savings in the new model and to introduce it at a price below that of the old model.

A financial keiretsu, dominated by a large bank, functions like a giant interlocking directorate. The dominant members of the financial keiretsu, which is composed of diverse companies, sit on the board of directors of the bank and often on the boards of each other's companies. The companies are linked by substantial long-term stockholdings, most of which are managed by the bank at the centre of the keiretsu. Member companies are able to trade proprietary information and knowledge that benefits them collectively. Indeed, one of the benefits that comes from a financial keiretsu is the way businesses can transfer and exchange managers to strengthen the network.

Figure 3-5 shows the Fuyo keiretsu, which centres on Fuji Bank. Its members include Nissan, NKK, Hitachi, and Canon. The directors of Fuji Bank link all the largest and most significant keiretsu members. Each large member company has its own set of satellite companies. For example, Nissan has a minority ownership stake in many of the suppliers that provide inputs for its auto operations.

Joint venture
A strategic alliance among two or more organizations that agree to jointly establish and share the ownership of a new business.

Joint Venture A **joint venture** is a strategic alliance among two or more organizations that agree to jointly establish and share the ownership of a new business.[41] Joint ventures are the most formal of the strategic alliances because the participants are bound by a formal legal agreement that spells out their rights and responsibilities. For example, Company A and Company B agree to set up a new organization, Company C, and then jointly design its organizational structure and select its top-management team (see Figure 3-6). Both Company A and Company B send executives to manage Company C, and they also provide the resources Company C needs to grow and prosper. Participants in a joint venture often pool their distinctive competencies. One, for example, might supply expert knowledge on efficient production techniques, and the other might supply some R&D skills. The pooling of skills in a new venture increases the value that can be produced.

The shared ownership of a joint venture reduces the problems of managing complex interorganizational relationships that might arise if the basis of the strategic alliance were simply a long-term contract. Moreover, the newly created organization (Company C in Figure 3-6) is free to develop the structure that best suits its needs, and the problems of managing interdependencies with the parent companies are reduced. A joint venture may allow the founding companies (Company A and Company B) to stay small and entrepreneurial.

In sum, organizations use informal and formal strategic alliances to manage symbiotic resource interdependencies. The degree of formality increases as environmental uncertainty increases.

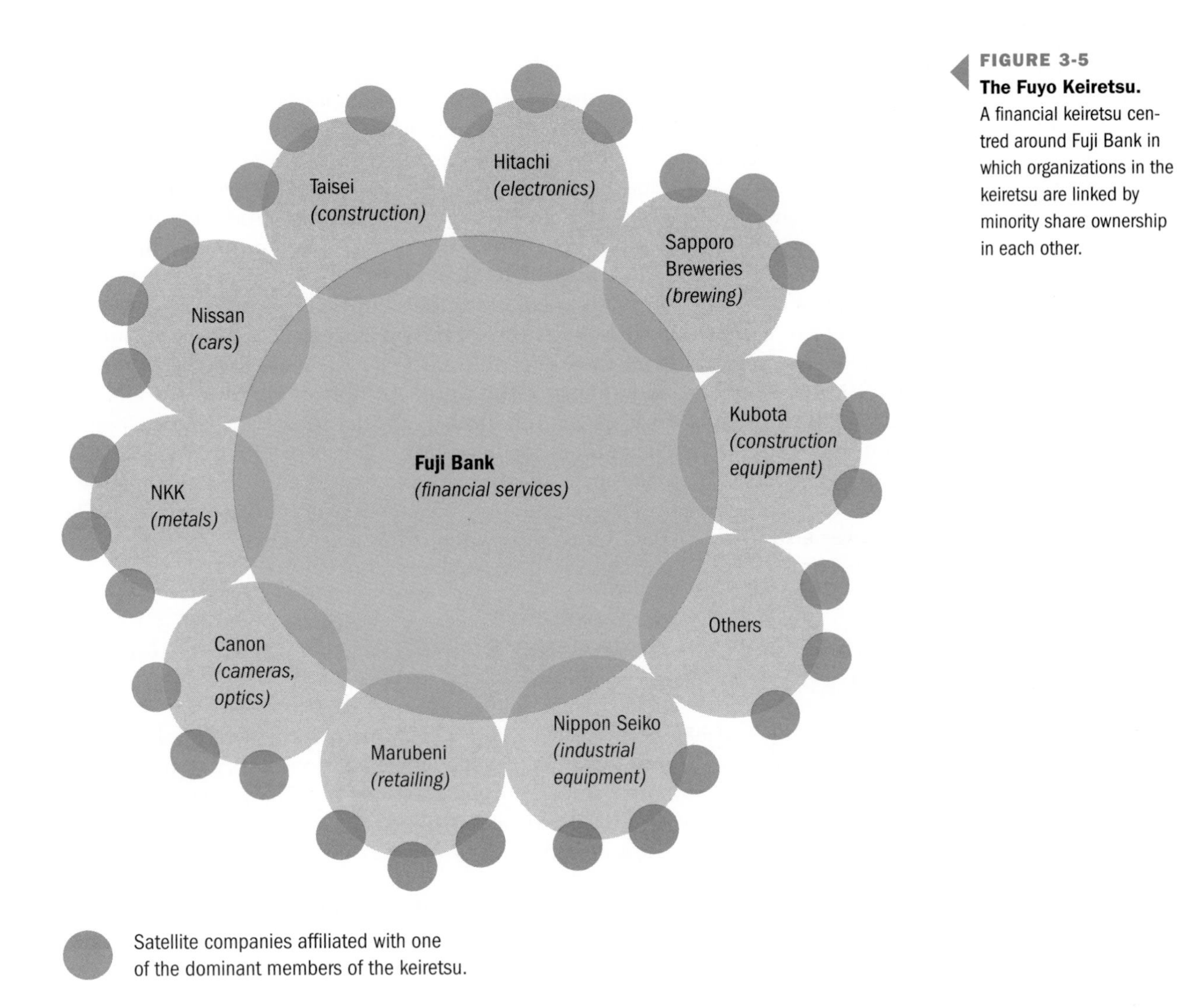

FIGURE 3-5
The Fuyo Keiretsu.
A financial keiretsu centred around Fuji Bank in which organizations in the keiretsu are linked by minority share ownership in each other.

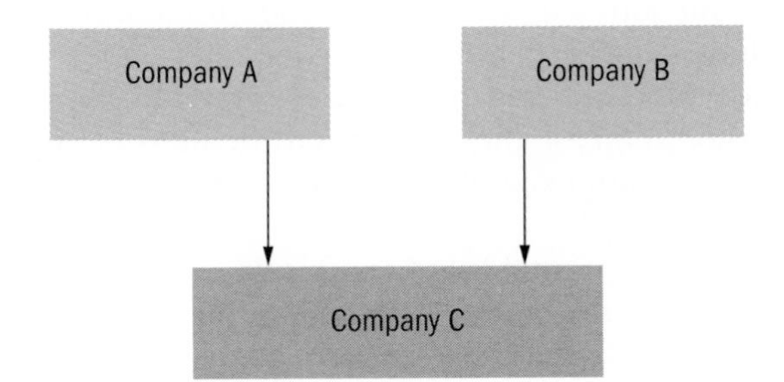

FIGURE 3-6
Joint Venture Formation.
Two separate organizations pool resources to create a third organization. A formal legal document specifies the terms of this type of strategic alliance.

Merger and Takeover

The most formal strategy (see Figure 3-4, p. 83) for managing symbiotic (and competitive) resource interdependencies is to merge with or take over a supplier or distributor. As a result of a merger or a takeover, resource exchanges occur *within* one organization rather than *between* organizations, and an organization can no longer be held hostage by a powerful supplier (that might demand a high price for its products) or by a powerful customer (that might try to drive down the price it pays for a company's products).[42] For example, Irving Oil, a major Canadian producer of refined petroleum products, owns several refineries, many retail gas outlets, and its own transportation firm. Thus Irving can control the costs of delivery of the product to the consumer. Similarly, McDonald's owns vast ranches in Brazil, where it rears, at a low cost, cattle for hamburger. Alcoa owns or manages most of the world's supply of aluminum ore and has effectively controlled the world aluminum industry for decades. Ford Motor Company, owner of Hertz Rent-a-Car, has a ready-made customer for its products.

An organization that takes over another company normally incurs great expense and faces the problems of managing the new business. Thus an organization is likely to take over a supplier or distributor only when it has a very great need to control a crucial resource or manage an important interdependency.

STRATEGIES FOR MANAGING COMPETITIVE RESOURCE INTERDEPENDENCIES

Organizations do not like competition. Competition threatens the supply of scarce resources and increases the uncertainty of the specific environment. Intense competition can threaten the very survival of an organization as product prices fall to attract fickle customers and the environment becomes poorer and poorer. For example, when cable companies started introducing both Internet and phone services, they began to compete with telephone companies. The entry of these new players increased the level of competition, which forced the providers of phone and Internet services to compete largely on price. For some companies, revenue rose and for others revenue dropped. The stronger the competition, the greater the number of companies that go bankrupt.[43] Ultimately, an organizational environment consists of a handful of the strongest survivors competing head to head for resources.

Organizations use a variety of techniques to directly manipulate the environment to reduce the uncertainty of their competitive interdependent activities.[44] Figure 3-7 indicates the relative formality of four strategies. The more formal a strategy, the more explicit the attempt to coordinate competitor's activities. Some of these strategies are illegal, but unethical organizations use them to gain an edge.

Collusion and Cartels

Collusion
A secret agreement among competitors to share information for a deceitful or illegal purpose.

Cartel
An association of firms that explicitly agree to coordinate their activities.

Collusion is a secret agreement among competitors to share information for a deceitful or illegal purpose. Organizations collude in order to reduce the competitive uncertainty they experience. A **cartel** is an association of firms that explicitly agree to coordinate their activities.[45] Cartels and collusion increase the stability and richness of an organization's environment and reduce the complexity of relations among competitors. Both of these strategies are illegal in Canada.

Competitors in an industry can collude by establishing industry standards.[46] Industry standards function like rules of conduct and may tell competitors, for example, what prices they should charge, what their product specifications should be, or what a product's profit markup should be. Industry standards may result from price leadership.

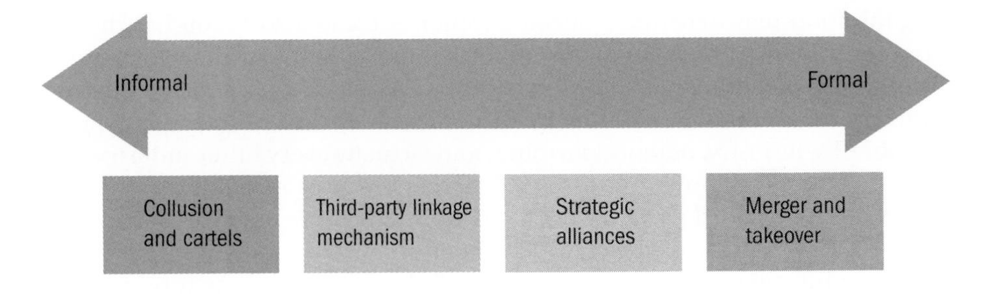

FIGURE 3-7 Interorganizational Strategies for Managing Competitive Interdependencies. Competitive interdependencies exist between an organization and its rivals. The more formal a strategy, the more explicit the attempt to coordinate competitors' activities.

The dominant organization is likely to be the price leader. It sets the prices for its products, and then the weaker organizations charge prices that conform to the price leader's. In this way, industry prices are fixed. Organizations can always make more profit if they collectively coordinate their activities than if they compete. Price fixing enables competitors to maintain artificially high prices and prevent destructive price competition. Customers lose because the prices that are established may be artificially high.

In North America today, price leadership is occurring in the market for large trucks. Import duties on large trucks keep out overseas trucks that otherwise would be less expensive than domestically made trucks. Behind this protective wall, GM and Ford indirectly coordinate their prices to keep the prices of large trucks artificially high. It has been estimated that 35 percent of the cost of a large North American truck is profit, compared with 10–15 percent for a sedan.[47] So high is the markup that when Toyota introduced its large truck it paid the 25 percent import duty in the United States and still made a 10–15 percent profit.

Organizations can also collude and form a cartel without formal written agreement by signalling their intentions to each other by public announcements about their future strategy. For example, they can announce price increases that they are contemplating and see whether their rivals will match those increases. In Canada, an example of how competition may be stifled by this type of behaviour is the way in which the market for petroleum products, particularly gas for cars, is sold at the pump. There are so few independent gas retailers in most regions of the country that often there may be only one or two retail suppliers in any area. Because the retail outlets are owned and supplied by large national retailers, price competition is limited.

Organizations in an industry can try to discipline organizations that break informal competitive industry rules. Some large companies have a reputation for ruthlessly going after competitors who break their industry's informal pricing rules. American Airlines has been accused of reducing prices below the level of its price-cutting rivals and keeping them there to deliberately punish weaker price-cutting firms. Back in the 1970s, the large airlines jointly conspired to drive a price-cutting small firm—Britain's Laker Airlines—out of business so that they could keep prices high.

Third-Party Linkage Mechanisms

A more formal but still indirect way for competing organizations to coordinate their activities is through a **third-party linkage mechanism**—a regulatory body that allows organizations to share information and regulate the way they compete.[48] An example is a trade association, an organization that represents companies in the same industry and enables competitors to meet, share information, and informally make agreements that allow them to monitor one another's activities.[49] This interaction reduces the fear

Third-party linkage mechanism A regulatory body that allows organizations to share information and regulate the way they compete.

that one organization may deceive or outwit another. A trade association has the collective resources (obtained from member organizations) to lobby strongly for government policies that protect the interests of its industry. We saw earlier how the pharmaceutical industry uses its powerful lobby to fend off attempts to reduce the price of drugs. The cable TV industry, defence, farming, and virtually every other industry seek to protect their own interests and increase their access to scarce resources.

Other examples of third-party linkage mechanisms include agencies such as the stock markets, a nation's central bank, and any other organization that is set up to regulate competitive interdependencies. Third-party linkage mechanisms provide rules and standards that stabilize industry competition and thus increase the richness of the environment. They reduce the complexity of the environment because they regulate the interactions of organizations. And by increasing the flow of information, they enable organizations to react more easily to change or to the dynamism of the environment. In short, third-party linkage mechanisms provide a way for competing organizations to manage resource interdependencies and reduce uncertainty. Organizations that use a third-party linkage mechanism co-opt themselves and jointly receive the benefits of the coordination that they obtain from the third-party linkage mechanism. For example, Microelectronics and Computer Corporation, an applied R&D cooperative funded by industry members such as Intel and Motorola, was set up to improve research in semiconductors. This organization channels the results of its research to its funding members. After three years, the funding members can license the results to other companies in the industry.[50] Japan is the model for such third-party linkage mechanisms. Its Ministry of International Trade and Industry (MITI) has a long history of promoting industry cooperation among domestic rivals to foster joint technical developments that allow Japanese companies to dominate the global marketplace.

Strategic Alliances

Strategic alliances can be used to manage not only symbiotic interdependencies, but competitive interdependencies.[51] Competitors can cooperate and form a joint venture to develop common technology that will save them all a lot of money, even though they may be in competition for customers when their final products hit the market. Apple Computer and IBM, for example, formed a long-term joint venture to share the costs of developing a common microchip that will make their machines compatible, even though they will be competitors in the personal computer market. Both Ford and Mazda have benefited from a strategic alliance (Ford owns a 25 percent stake in Mazda). Ford gained detailed knowledge of Japanese production techniques, and Mazda and Ford jointly cooperated to produce vehicles in the same U.S. plant. Although the kinds of joint ventures just described are not anticompetitive, organizations sometimes use joint ventures to deter new entrants or harm existing competitors. Philips and Bang & Olufsen, two leading consumer electronics companies, signed an agreement to share their production and design skills, respectively, to compete with Japanese giants Sony and Panasonic.[52] Organizations can also form a joint venture to develop a new technology that they can then protect from other rivals by obtaining and defending patents. The use of strategic alliances to manage competitive interdependencies is limited only by the imagination of rival companies.

Merger and Takeover

The ultimate weapon in an organization's arsenal for managing problematic competitive (and symbiotic) interdependencies is merger with, or takeover of, a competing organization.[53] Mergers and takeovers can improve a company's competitive position by allowing the company to strengthen and enlarge its domain and increase its ability to produce a wider range of products to better serve more customers. This is one of the organizational goals behind the Molson and Coors merger. Merging these two brewing giants will create a new firm that will have access to even larger customer segments, and with their combined resources will be more able to compete in the increasingly globalized marketplace.[54]

Many organizations might like to use merger to become a monopoly, the sole player in the marketplace. Fortunately for consumers, and for organizations themselves, monopolies are illegal in Canada, the United States, and most other developed countries, and if organizations become too strong and dominant, they are prevented by antitrust law from taking over other companies. An organization that is too dominant is itself the whole competitive environment and has virtually no need to manage organization–environment relations.[55] Nevertheless, cartels, collusion, and other anti-competitive practices can ultimately be bad for the organizations themselves. In the long run, as a result of changes in technology, cheap sources of labour, changes in government policy, and so forth, new entrants will be able to enter the industry, and existing companies that have reduced competition among themselves will then find themselves ineffective competitors. Protected from competition in an environment where uncertainty has been low, these monopoly-like organizations will become bureaucratic and unable to meet the challenges of a rapidly changing environment. GM, IBM, and Xerox are organizations that controlled their competitive environments for a very long time and suffered greatly when the environment changed and allowed more agile overseas and domestic competitors to enter and beat the established companies at their own game.

MANAGERIAL IMPLICATIONS

Resource Dependence Theory

1. To maintain an adequate supply of scarce resources, study each resource transaction individually in order to decide how to manage it.
2. Study the benefits and costs associated with an interorganizational strategy before using it.
3. To maximize the organization's freedom of action, always prefer an informal to a formal linkage mechanism. Use a more formal mechanism only when the uncertainty of the situation warrants it.
4. When entering into strategic alliances with other organizations, be careful to identify the purpose of the alliance and future problems that might arise between organizations, in order to decide whether an informal or a formal linkage mechanism is most appropriate. Once again, choose an informal rather than a formal alliance whenever possible.
5. Use transaction cost theory (see below) to identify the benefits and costs associated with the use of different linkage mechanisms to manage particular interdependencies.

TRANSACTION COST THEORY

Transaction costs
The costs of negotiating, monitoring, and governing exchanges between people.

Transaction cost theory
A theory that states that the goal of an organization is to minimize the costs of exchanging resources in the environment and the costs of managing exchanges inside the organization.

In Chapter 1, we defined **transaction costs** as the costs of negotiating, monitoring, and governing exchanges between people. Whenever people work together, there are costs—transaction costs—associated with controlling their activities.[56] Transaction costs also arise when organizations exchange resources or information. Organizations interact with other organizations to get the resources they require, and they have to control those symbiotic and competitive interdependencies. According to resource dependence theory, organizations attempt to gain control of resources and minimize their dependence on other organizations. According to **transaction cost theory**, the goal of the organization is to minimize the costs of exchanging resources in the environment and the costs of managing exchanges inside the organization.[57] Every dollar or hour of a manager's time spent in negotiating or monitoring exchanges with other organizations, or with managers inside one organization, is a dollar or hour that is not being used to create value. Organizations try to minimize transaction costs and bureaucratic costs because they siphon off productive capacity. Organizations try to find mechanisms that make interorganizational transactions relatively more efficient.

Health care provides a dramatic example of how transaction costs (i.e., the costs associated with billing, claims, and other documentation handling) lie at the heart of pressing organizational issues. Much of the debate in Canada surrounding the issue of private versus for-profit health care focuses on these costs (rather than the direct cost of health care itself). The debate centres on whether these costs will be lower if privatized health care is implemented. The debate itself does not centre on the direct care costs—such as the cost of a blood test—but on the costs of processing the blood test and informing the patient of the blood test results, while adhering to various health regulations.[58]

Sources of Transaction Costs

Transaction costs result from a combination of human and environmental factors.[59] (See Figure 3-8.)

Environmental Uncertainty and Bounded Rationality The environment is characterized by considerable uncertainty and complexity. People, however, have only a limited ability to process information and to understand the environment surrounding them.[60] Because of this limited ability, or bounded rationality, the higher the level of uncertainty in an environment, the greater the difficulty of managing transactions between organizations.

Suppose Organization A wants to license a technology developed by Organization B. The two organizations could sign a contract. Considerable uncer-

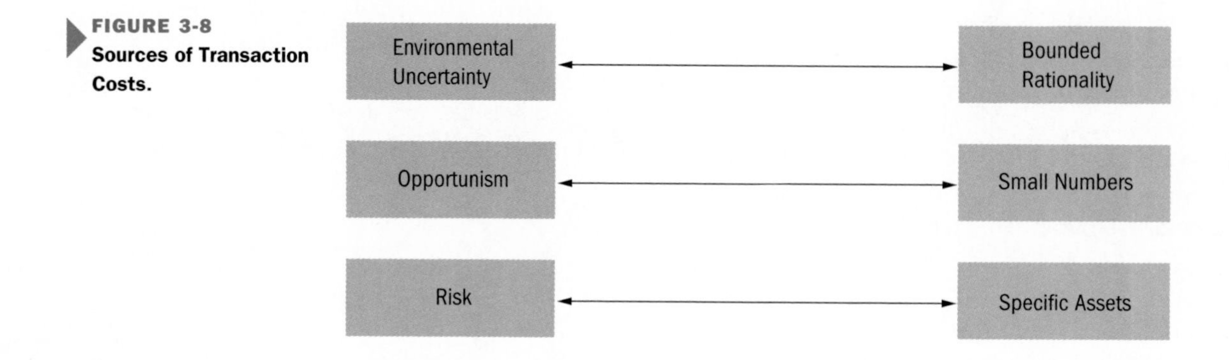

FIGURE 3-8
Sources of Transaction Costs.

tainty, however, would surround this contract. For example, Organization B might want to find new ways of using the technology to make new products for itself. Given bounded rationality, it would be difficult and prohibitively expensive to try to write a contract that not only protected Organization B, which developed the technology, but also spelled out how the two organizations might jointly share in the future benefits from the technology. In this situation, the developing company (Organization B) might prefer to proceed alone and not exchange resources with Organization A, even though it knows it could create more value by engaging in the exchange. Thus, because of bounded rationality and the high transaction costs of drawing up a contract, potential value that could have been created is lost. Environmental uncertainty may make the cost of negotiating, monitoring, and governing agreements so high that organizations resort to more formal linkage mechanisms—such as strategic alliances, minority ownership, or even mergers—to lower transaction costs.

Opportunism and Small Numbers Most people and organizations behave honestly and reputably most of the time, but some always behave opportunistically—that is, they cheat or otherwise attempt to exploit other forces or stakeholders in the environment.[61] For example, an organization contracts for component parts of a particular quality. To reduce costs and save money, the supplier deliberately substitutes inferior materials but bills for the more expensive, higher quality parts. Individuals, too, act opportunistically: Managers pad their expense reports or exploit customers by manufacturing inferior products.

When an organization is dependent on one supplier or on a small number of trading partners, the potential for opportunism is great. The organization has no choice but to transact business with the supplier, and the supplier, knowing this, might choose to supply inferior inputs to reduce costs and increase profit. When the prospect for opportunism is high because of the small number of suppliers to which an organization can go for resources, the organization has to expend resources to negotiate, monitor, and enforce agreements with its suppliers to protect itself. For example, the Canadian government has several agencies that are designed to protect itself from being exploited by various contractors that it deals with, whether these are suppliers of services, office furniture, or military equipment.[62]

Risk and Specific Assets **Specific assets** are investments—in skills, machinery, knowledge, and information—that create value in one particular exchange relationship but have no value in any other exchange relationship. A company that invests $100 million in a machine that makes microchips for IBM machines only has made a very specific investment in a very specific asset. An organization's decision to invest money to develop specific assets for a specific relationship with another organization in its environment involves a high level of risk. Once the investment is made, the organization is locked into it. If the other party tries to exploit the relationship by saying, for example, "We will not buy your product unless you sell it to us for $10 less per unit than you're charging now," the organization is in a very difficult situation. This tactic is akin to blackmail.

Specific assets
Investments—in skills, machinery, knowledge, and information—that create value in one particular exchange relationship but have no value in any other exchange relationship.

An organization that sees any prospect of being trapped or blackmailed will judge the investment in specific assets to be too risky. The transaction costs associated with the investment become too high, and value that could have been created is lost.[63]

Transaction Costs and Linkage Mechanisms

Organizations base their choice of interorganizational linkage mechanisms on the level of transaction costs involved in an exchange relationship. Transaction costs are low when these conditions exist:

1. Organizations are exchanging nonspecific goods and services.
2. Uncertainty is low.
3. There are many possible exchange partners.

In these environmental conditions, it is easy for organizations to negotiate and monitor interorganizational behaviour. Thus, in a low-transaction-cost environment, organizations can use relatively informal linkage mechanisms, such as reputation and unwritten, word-of-mouth contracts.

Transaction costs increase when these conditions exist:

1. Organizations begin to exchange more specific goods and services.
2. Uncertainty increases.
3. The number of possible exchange partners falls.

In this kind of environment, an organization will begin to feel that it cannot afford to trust other organizations, and it will start to monitor and use more formal linkages, such as long-term contracts, to govern its exchanges. Contracts, however, cannot cover every situation that might arise. If something unexpected happens, what will the other party to the exchange do? It has a perfect right to act in the way that most benefits itself, even though its actions are harmful to the other organization.

How does an organization act in a high-transaction-cost situation? According to transaction cost theory, an organization should choose a more formal linkage mechanism to manage exchanges as transaction costs increase. The more formal the mechanism used, the more control organizations have over each other's behaviour. Formal mechanisms include strategic alliances (joint ventures), merger, and takeover, all of which internalize the transaction and its cost. In a joint venture, two organizations establish a third organization to handle their joint transactions. Establishing a new entity that both organizations own equally reduces each organization's incentives to cheat the other and provides incentives for them to do things (e.g., invest in specific assets) that will create value for them both. With mergers, the same arguments hold because one organization now owns the other.

From a transaction cost perspective, the movement from less formal to more formal linkage mechanisms (see Figures 3-3, 3-4, and 3-7, pp. 81, 83, and 89) occurs because of an organization's need to reduce the transaction costs of its exchanges with other organizations. Formal mechanisms minimize the transaction costs associated with reducing uncertainty, opportunism, and risk.

Bureaucratic Costs

If formal linkage mechanisms are such an efficient way to minimize the transaction costs of exchanges with the environment, why do organizations not use these mechanisms all the time? Why do they ever use an informal linkage mechanism such as a contract if a joint venture or a merger gives them better control of their environment? The answer is that bringing the transactions inside the organization minimizes but does not eliminate the costs of managing transactions.[64] Managers must still negotiate, monitor, and govern exchanges between people inside the organization. Internal transaction costs are called *bureaucratic* costs to distinguish them from the transaction costs of exchanges between organizations in the environment.[65] We saw in Chapter 2 how difficult communication and integration between functions and divisions are. Now we see that integration and communication are not only difficult to achieve but cost money, because managers have to spend their time in meetings rather than creating value.[66] Thus managing an organization's structure is a complex and expensive problem that becomes much more expensive and complex as the organization grows—as GM and IBM have discovered.

Using Transaction Cost Theory to Choose an Interorganizational Strategy

Transaction cost theory can help managers choose an interorganizational strategy by enabling them to weigh the savings in transaction costs achieved from using a particular linkage mechanism against the bureaucratic costs of operating the linkage mechanism.[67] Because transaction cost theory brings into focus the costs associated with different linkage mechanisms to reduce uncertainty, it is able to make better predictions than is resource dependence theory about why and when a company will choose a certain interorganizational strategy. Managers deciding which strategy to pursue must take the following steps:

1. Locate the sources of transaction costs that may affect an exchange relationship and decide how high the transaction costs are likely to be.
2. Estimate the transaction cost savings from using different linkage mechanisms.
3. Estimate the bureaucratic costs of operating the linkage mechanism.
4. Choose the linkage mechanism that gives the most transaction cost savings at the lowest bureaucratic cost.

The success of Magna, one of the world's premier automotive parts and assembly suppliers exemplifies how linkage mechanisms may be utilized to reduce the transaction costs for buyers. Magna uses a combination of personal and technological ties to facilitate the interorganizational exchanges necessary for both Magna and its automotive partners to remain competitive and successful.[68] (See Organizational Insight 3.5.)

The implication of a transaction cost view is that a formal linkage mechanism should be used only when transaction costs are high enough to demand it. An organization should take over and merge with its suppliers or distributors, for example, only if the saving in transaction costs outweighs the costs of managing the new acquisition.[70] Otherwise, like Magna and its customers, the organization should rely on less formal mechanisms, such as strategic alliances and long-term contracts, to handle exchange relationships. The relatively informal linkage mechanisms avoid the need for an orga-

ORGANIZATIONAL INSIGHT 3.5

A Web of Linkages at Magna

Magna is a global supplier of automotive systems and components for the world's largest automobile manufacturers, including DaimlerChrysler, General Motors, Ford, BMW, Volkswagen, and others. Magna lies at the centre of a network of linkages that permits its customers to significantly reduce the transaction costs associated with supplying their needed assemblies. Through offering a broad range of comprehensive systems and total module packages, Magna is able to minimize the costs that automakers incur in the sourcing of these many systems. Magna has also taken steps to reduce these costs even further through the support and participation in a major business-to-business Internet exchange for the automotive industry—Covisint. Magna has been so successful at designing and supplying systems that its competencies in these areas have allowed the company to spin off many separate firms to operate in the same environment.[69]

nization to incur bureaucratic costs. Three linkage mechanisms that enable organizations to avoid bureaucratic costs while still minimizing transaction costs are keiretsu, franchising, and outsourcing.

Keiretsu The Japanese system of keiretsu can be seen as a mechanism for achieving the benefits of a formal linkage mechanism without incurring its costs.[71] The policy of owning a minority stake in its suppliers' companies gives Toyota substantial control over the exchange relationship and allows it to avoid problems of opportunism and uncertainty with its suppliers. Toyota also avoids the bureaucratic costs of actually owning and managing its suppliers. Indeed, keiretsu was developed to provide the benefits of full ownership without the costs.

In contrast, GM has full ownership of more suppliers than does any other car manufacturer and pays more for its inputs than the other car companies pay for theirs. Critics charge that these high costs arise because GM's internal suppliers are in a protected situation. GM is a captive buyer, so its supplying divisions have no incentive to be efficient and thus behave opportunistically.[72]

What should GM do? One course of action would be to divest its inefficient suppliers and then establish strategic alliances or long-term contracts with them to encourage them to lower their costs and increase their efficiency. If they cannot improve their cost or quality, GM would form new alliances with new suppliers. GM has been trying to do exactly that; in 1999 it spun off its Delco electronic parts subsidiary into an independent operating company.[73] GM is trying to obtain the benefits that Toyota has achieved from its strategy of minority ownership. Conversely, if GM were experiencing problems with obtaining the benefits from a strategic alliance (if, for example, its partner were acting opportunistically), it should move to a more formal linkage mechanism and buy and merge with its suppliers. GM is not in this situation, however. Its problem is finding the combination of ownership, strategic alliances, and long-term contracts that will minimize its input costs, which are still about US$1000 higher per car than the input costs of Japanese car manufacturers.

Franchising A franchise is a business that is authorized to sell a company's products in a certain area. The franchiser sells the right to use its resources (e.g., its name or operating system) to a person or group (the franchisee) in return for a flat fee or a share of the profits. Normally, the franchiser provides the inputs used by the franchisee, who deals directly with the customer. The relationship between franchiser and franchisee is symbiotic. The transaction cost approach offers an interesting insight into why interorganizational strategies such as franchising emerge.[74]

Consider the operational differences between McDonald's and Burger King. A very large proportion of McDonald's restaurants are owned by franchisees, but most Burger King restaurants are owned by the company. Why doesn't McDonald's own its restaurants? Why is McDonald's willing to make its franchisees millionaires instead of enriching its shareholders? From a transaction cost point of view, the answer lies in the bureaucratic costs that McDonald's would incur if it managed its own restaurants.

The single biggest challenge for a restaurant is to maintain the quality of its food. If McDonald's employed managers in company-owned restaurants, would those managers have the same incentive to maintain as high a quality of customer service as franchisees, who directly benefit from high performance? McDonald's believes that if it owned and operated all its restaurants—that is, if it used a formal linkage mechanism—the bureaucratic costs incurred to maintain the quality and consistency of the restaurants would exceed any extra value the organization and its shareholders would obtain from ownership. Thus McDonald's generally owns only those restaurants that are located in big cities or near highways. In big cities, it can spread the costs of employing a management team over many restaurants and reduce bureaucratic costs. On major highways, McDonald's believes, franchisees realize that they are unlikely to see the same travellers ever again and have no incentive to maintain standards.

The same issue arises on the output side when an organization is choosing how to distribute its products. Should an organization own its distribution outlets? Should it sell directly to customers? Should it sell only to franchised dealers? Again the answer depends on the transaction cost problems the organization can expect in dealing with the needs of its customers. Generally, the more complex products are and the more information customers need about how they work or how to repair them, the greater the likelihood that organizations have formal hierarchical control over their distributors and franchisees or own their own distribution outlets.[75]

Cars are typically sold through franchised dealers because of the need to provide customers with reliable car repair. Also, because cars are complicated products and customers need a lot of information before they buy one, it is effective for manufacturers to have some control over their distributors. Thus car manufacturers have considerable control over their dealerships and monitor and enforce the service that dealerships give to customers. Toyota, for example, closely monitors the number of customer complaints against a dealership. If the number of complaints gets too high, it punishes the dealership by restricting its supply of new cars. As a result, dealers have strong incentives to give customers good service. In contrast, the transaction costs involved in handling simple products like clothes or food are low. Thus few clothing or food companies choose to use formal linkages to control the distribution of their products. Less formal mechanisms such as contracts with wholesalers or with retail stores become the preferred distribution strategy.

Outsourcing Another strategy for managing interdependencies is outsourcing. **Outsourcing** is moving a value creation activity that was performed inside an organization to outside, where it is done by another company—for example, hiring a company to manage a company's computer network or to distribute its products instead of performing the activity itself. Increasingly, organizations are turning to specialized companies to manage their information processing needs. Eastman Kodak and IBM, for example, have set up divisions that supply this specialized service to companies in their environments.

Outsourcing
The process of moving a value creation activity that was performed inside an organization to outside, where it is done by another company.

What prompts an organization to outsource a function is the same calculation that determines whether an organization makes or buys inputs. Does the extra value that the organization obtains from performing its own marketing or information processing exceed the extra bureaucratic costs of managing such functions? If the answer is yes, the organization develops its own function. If it is no, the organization outsources the activity.[76] This decision is likely to change over time. Perhaps in 2001 it was best to have an information-processing department inside the organization. By 2006, however, specialized organizations may be able to process information more cheaply, and then it will pay to outsource that function. Outsourcing within networks, such as the one established by Nike, is another example of how outsourcing helps hold down the bureaucratic costs of managing exchanges inside an organization. Global supply chain management offers another example of how companies can reduce transaction costs and avoid bureaucratic costs, as illustrated in Organizational Insight 3.6.

In summary, a transaction cost approach sheds light on why and how organizations choose different linkage mechanisms to manage their interdependencies. It improves our ability to understand the process that organizations use to manage their environments to enhance their chances for growth and survival. Solutions exist for managing uncertain resource exchanges and organizational interdependencies.

These solutions range from less formal mechanisms like contracts to more formal mechanisms like ownership. The best mechanism for an organization is one that minimizes transaction and bureaucratic costs.

ORGANIZATIONAL INSIGHT 3.6

Li & Fung's Global Supply Chain Management

Finding the overseas suppliers that offer the lowest-priced and highest-quality products is an important task facing the managers of global organizations. Since these suppliers are located in thousands of cities in many countries around the world, finding them is a difficult business. Often, global companies use the services of overseas intermediaries or brokers, located near these suppliers, to find the one that best meets their input requirements. Li & Fung, now run by brothers Victor and William Fung, is one such broker that has helped hundreds of global companies to locate suitable overseas suppliers, especially suppliers in mainland China.[77]

In 2001, however, managing global companies' supply chains became a more complicated task. To reduce costs, overseas suppliers were increasingly specializing in just one part of the task of producing a product. For example, in the past, a major retail company might have negotiated with an overseas supplier to manufacture 1 million units of some particular shirt at a certain cost per unit. But with specialization, a retailer might find it can reduce the costs of producing the shirt even further by splitting apart the operations involved in producing the shirt and having different overseas suppliers, often in different countries, perform each operation. For example, to get the lowest cost per unit, rather than just negotiate with an overseas supplier over the price of making a particular shirt, retailers might first negotiate with a yarn manufacturer in Vietnam to make the yarn; then ship the yarn to a Chinese supplier to weave it into cloth; and then ship to several different factories in Malaysia and the Philippines to cut the cloth and sew the shirts. Then, another overseas company might take responsibility for packaging and shipping the shirts to wherever in the world they are required. Because a major retail company may have thousands of different clothing products under production, and these change all the time, the problems of managing such a supply chain to get the full cost savings from global expansion are clear.

Li & Fung has capitalized on this opportunity. Realizing that many global companies do not have the time or expertise to find such specialized low-price suppliers, they moved quickly to provide such a service. Li & Fung employs 3600 agents who travel across 37 countries to find new suppliers and inspect existing suppliers to find new ways to help their global clients get lower prices or higher quality products. Global companies are happy to outsource their supply chain management to Li & Fung because they realize significant cost savings. Even though they pay a hefty fee to Li & Fung, they avoid the costs of employing their own agents. As the complexity of supply chain management continues to increase, more and more companies like Li & Fung are appearing.

SUMMARY

Managing the organizational environment is a crucial task for an organization. The first step is identifying sources of uncertainty and examining the sources of complexity, how rapidly it is changing, and how rich or poor it is. An organization then needs to evaluate the benefits and costs of different interorganizational strategies and choose the one that best allows it to secure valuable resources. Resource dependence theory weighs the benefit of securing scarce resources against the cost of a loss of autonomy. Transaction cost theory weighs the benefit of reducing transaction costs against the cost of increasing bureaucratic costs. An organization must examine the whole array of its exchanges with its environment in order to devise the combination of linkage mechanisms that will maximize its ability to create value. Chapter 3 has made the following main points:

1. The organizational environment is the set of forces in the changing global environment that affect the way an organization operates and its ability to gain access to scarce resources.
2. The organizational domain is the range of goods and services that the organization produces and the clients that it serves in the countries in which it operates. An organization devises interorganizational strategies to protect and enlarge its domain.
3. The specific environment consists of forces that most directly affect an organization's ability to secure resources. The general environment consists of forces that shape the specific environments of all organizations.
4. Uncertainty in the environment is a function of the complexity, dynamism, and richness of the environment.
5. Resource dependence theory argues that the goal of an organization is to minimize its dependence on other organizations for the supply of scarce resources and to find ways of influencing them to make resources available.
6. Organizations have to manage two kinds of resource interdependencies: symbiotic interdependencies with suppliers and customers and competitive interdependencies with rivals.
7. The main interorganizational strategies for managing symbiotic relationships are the development of a good reputation, co-optation, strategic alliances, and merger and takeover. The main interorganizational strategies for managing competitive relationships are collusion and cartels, third-party linkage mechanisms, strategic alliances, and merger and takeover.
8. Transaction costs are the costs of negotiating, monitoring, and governing exchanges between people and organizations. There are three sources of transaction costs: (a) the combination of uncertainty and bounded rationality, (b) opportunism and small numbers, and (c) specific assets and risk.
9. Transaction cost theory argues that the goal of organizations is to minimize the costs of exchanging resources in the environment and the costs of managing exchanges inside the organization. Organizations try to choose interorganizational strategies that minimize transaction costs and bureaucratic costs.
10. Interorganizational linkage mechanisms range from informal types such as contracts and reputation to formal types such as strategic alliances and ownership strategies such as merger and takeover.

DISCUSSION QUESTIONS

1. Pick an organization, such as a local travel agency or supermarket. Describe its organizational domain; then draw a map of the forces in its general and specific environments that affect the way it operates.

2. What are the major sources of uncertainty in an environment? Discuss how these sources of uncertainty affect a small biotechnology company and a large carmaker.
3. According to resource dependence theory, what motivates organizations to form interorganizational linkages? What is the advantage of strategic alliances as a way of exchanging resources?
4. According to transaction cost theory, what motivates organizations to form interorganizational linkages? Under what conditions would a company prefer a more formal linkage mechanism to a less formal one?
5. What interorganizational strategies might work most successfully as a company expands globally? Why?

ORGANIZATIONAL THEORY IN ACTION

Practising Organizational Theory: Protecting Your Domain

Break up into groups of three to five people and discuss the following scenario:

You are a group of entrepreneurs who have recently launched a new kind of root beer, made from exotic herbs and spices, that has quickly obtained a loyal following in a major western city. Inspired by your success, you have decided that you would like to increase production of your root beer to serve a wider geographical area, with the eventual goal of serving all of Canada and the United States.

The problem you have is deciding the best way to secure your domain and manage the environment as you grow. On one hand, both the ingredients in your root beer and your method of making it are secret, so that you have to protect it from potential imitators at all costs—large soft drink companies will quickly copy it if they have a chance. On the other hand, you lack the funds for quick expansion, and finding a partner who can help you grow quickly and establish a brand name reputation would be an enormous advantage.

1. Analyze the pros and cons of each of the types of strategic alliances (long-term contracts, networks, minority ownership, and joint ventures) as your means of managing the environment.
2. Based on this analysis, which one would you choose to maximize your chance of securing a stable niche in the soft drink market?

Making the Connection #3

Find an example of a company that is using a specific interorganizational strategy, such as a joint venture or a long-term contract. What linkage mechanism is it using? Use resource dependence theory or transaction cost theory to explain why the organization might have chosen that type of mechanism.

The Ethical Dimension #3

In their search to reduce costs, many global companies are buying products from suppliers in overseas countries, which are made in sweatshops by women and children who work long hours for a few dollars a day. As we saw in Chapter 2 (see Organizational Insight 2.4, p. 54), there are complex arguments surrounding this issue. However, from an ethical perspective discuss:

1. When and under what conditions it is right for companies to buy their inputs from suppliers that employ women and children as sweatshop labour?
2. What kinds of interorganizational strategies could Canadian companies use to enforce any ethical codes they develop?

Analyzing the Organization: Design Module #3

This module and the modules in the next two chapters allow you to analyze the environment of your organization and to understand how the organization tries to manage its environment to control and obtain the resources it needs to protect its domain.

ASSIGNMENT

1. Draw a chart of your organization's domain. List the organization's products and customers and the forces in the specific and general environments that have an effect on it. Which are

the most important forces that the organization has to deal with?

2. Analyze the effect of the forces on the complexity, dynamism, and richness of the environment. From this analysis, how would you characterize the level of uncertainty in your organization's environment?
3. Draw a chart of the main interorganizational linkage mechanisms (e.g., long-term contracts, strategic alliances, mergers) that your organization uses to manage its symbiotic resource interdependencies. Using resource dependence theory and transaction cost theory, discuss why the organization chose to manage its interdependencies in this way. Do you think the organization has selected the most appropriate linkage mechanisms? Why or why not?
4. Draw a chart of the main interorganizational linkage mechanisms (e.g., collusion, third-party linkage mechanisms, strategic alliances) that your organization uses to manage its competitive resource interdependencies. Using resource dependence theory or transaction cost theory, discuss why the organization chose to manage its interdependencies in this way. Do you think the organization has selected the most appropriate linkage mechanisms? Why or why not?
5. In view of the analysis you have just made, do you think your organization is doing a good or a not-so-good job of managing its environment? What recommendations would you make to improve its ability to obtain resources?

Company Profiles #3*

Choose one or more of the organizations (e.g., companies, government agencies, or nonprofit organizations) that are profiled in this chapter. Do an Internet search to get up-to-date information on each organization you have selected, and answer the following questions:

1. What does the new information tell you about the organization's current ability to operate effectively in a global environment?
2. How does the information compare with the earlier information provided in the text and what does that tell you about organizations (e.g., does the organization appear to be more or less effectively involved in the global environment than before, and how do you explain this)?

Alternative Perspectives #3

Critical, postmodern, and postcolonial approaches to organizational theory are increasingly focusing on the effects and impacts of the globalization of the world's economy and the firm's place within it. While globalization is most often touted as "positive" (e.g., advancing the free-market concept, with the economic, political, and social benefits it brings to developing economies), if we read the discourse of globalization at a deeper level, we can discover the less positive and outright negative effects. It can be argued that the benefits of economic globalization are only possible if one accepts the political and social ideology that comes with them. This largely means that globalization is dominated by North American and Western European thought.

Read one or more of the following readings and list five ways that globalization can have a negative impact and five ways that it can have a positive impact. In small groups, discuss whether it is possible to gain economically through globalization without losing politically, socially, or culturally.

Reading List

Brady, D. 2004. Making Sweatshops: The Globalization of the US Apparel Industry, *Work and Occupations.* 31(2): 277–288.

Clegg, S. R. 1999. Globalizing the Intelligent Organization: Learning Organizations, Smart Workers (Not So) Clever Countries and the Sociological Imagination, *Management Learning.* 30(3): 259–280.

Dessing, M. 2004. Sweatshops: The Theory of the Firm Revisited. *Journal of Economic Studies.* 31(5/6): 549–579.

Guillen, M. F. 2001. Is Globalization Civilizing, Destructive or Feeble? A Critique of Five Key Debates in the Social Science Literature. *Annual Review of Sociology.* 27: 235–260.

* The authors would like to receive information from student groups and instructors on any companies where there have been dramatic changes to the information published in this text. We would be happy to publish the best of these changes in a subsequent edition, where we will focus on changing company profiles.

Jones, M. 2003. *Globalization and Organization(s) of Exclusion in Advanced Capitalism.* In R. Westwood and S.R. Clegg, eds., *Debating Organizations: Point-Counterpoint in Organization Studies* (pp. 252–270). Oxford: Blackwell.

Klein, N. 2000. *No Space, No Choice, No Jobs, No Logo: Taking Aim at the Brand Bullies.* New York: Picador.

Markoff, J. 1996. *Waves of Democracy: Social Movements and Political Change.* Thousand Oaks, CA: Pine Forge.

Osland, J. S. 2003. Broadening the Debate: the Pros and Cons of Globalization. *Journal of Management Inquiry,* 12(2): 137–154.

Wood, A. 1994. *North-South Trade, Employment and Inequality.* Oxford: Clarendon.

CASE FOR ANALYSIS

Change for McCain Foods Limited[78]

McCain Foods Limited was founded in January 1957 by several brothers—Harrison, Wallace, Andrew, and Robert McCain—in Florenceville, a small town in northern New Brunswick. The company's main product at that time was frozen French fries. As the company grew, it expanded the product line into other frozen foods, including green vegetables, mixed vegetables, desserts, pizza, juices and other beverages, oven meals, entrées, and other food products.

In its first year of operations, McCain Foods had 30 employees and overall sales of $152 678. This family-owned company grew steadily over the decades to become one of the largest companies in Canada, playing a major role in the regional and national food industry and the Canadian economy. Despite its size and global operations, McCain Foods only recently entered the U.S. market, in 1997, when it purchased Ore-Ida and Anchor Food Products. Today the company has over 20 000 employees, revenues of $6 billion, and 55 processing facilities and plants located on six continents. The company now sells its products in over 100 countries, and currently produces more than one-third of the world's total French fries.

McCain Foods, led by its new chief executive officer, Dale Morrison, is responding to several global challenges in order to move the company forward. Morrison notes that "the world is changing and we need to market to that changing world. The change has happened pretty quickly, and I think all companies need to move with the speed of a cheetah on this." Morrison's overall strategy involves global expansion and the creation of culture change for new product development. To further its global strategy, McCain Foods is now planning to expand operations by opening additional plants in China, Russia, and India. Supporting the globalizing strategy are internal efforts that concentrate on culture change within the organization. Morrison wants to balance the efficiencies of a large company with standardized routines, operations, and employee training and development, with a more decentralized structural approach for supporting the employees in their work.

One complicating environmental factor is a change in global eating habits and trends as obesity becomes recognized as a major health problem. Awareness of this issue has led many to decrease their consumption of carbohydrates and trans fatty acids, thus affecting many companies in the food industry. In response to this threat, McCain Foods plans to reposition itself as a more healthy choice. The company is planning to produce a healthier product by eliminating hydrogenated oils from its products, and repositioning its French fry products as a healthier food choice. Similarly, McCain Foods is listening to its customers' concerns regarding the use of genetically modified foods in world markets, and tailoring its offerings accordingly.

DISCUSSION QUESTIONS

1. Is McCain Foods managing its environment strategically? Is it simply reacting to pressures and consumer demands?
2. McCain Foods is not the only firm that deals in food products or services that is facing the challenges of an increasingly health-conscious market. How are other organizations managing the challenge? How do these mechanisms compare to McCain?

REFERENCES

1. W. T. Easterbrook and H. G. T. Aitken, *Canadian Economic History* (Toronto: MacMillan, 1956).
2. D. McCalla, *An Introduction to the Nineteenth Century Business World,* in T. Troves ed., *Essays in Canadian Business History* (Toronto: McClelland and Stewart, 1984), pp. 13–23.
3. J. D. Thompson, *Organizations in Action* (New York: McGraw-Hill, 1967).
4. *www.gerber.com,* 2002.
5. R. H. Hall, *Organizations: Structure and Process* (Englewood Cliffs, NJ: Prentice Hall, 1972).
6. R. H. Miles, *Macro Organizational Behaviour* (Santa Monica, CA: Goodyear, 1980).
7. Organizational Insight by Margaret Mckee, based on the following sources: *www.rbc.com;* Sarbanes-Oxley, H.R. 3763 Corporate and Auditing Accountability, Responsibility and Transparency Act of 2002, U.S. House of Representatives, 2002; G. Pitts, "New Rules Alter Role of Finance Officers: Canada's CFO of the Year Says Job Has Evolved and Widened," *The Globe and Mail Report on Business,* 29 September 2003, B55.
8. *www.rbc.com/aboutus/index.html,* 30 September 2004.
9. Pitts, "New Rules Alter Role of Finance Officers."
10. *www.rbc.com/aboutus/fastfacts.html,* 30 September 2004.
11. J. Perez, "GE Finds Tough Going in Hungary," *New York Times,* 25 July 1994, C1, C3.
12. J. Child, "Organizational Structure, Environment, and Performance: The Role of Strategic Choice," *Sociology,* 1972, vol. 6, pp. 1–22; G. G. Dess and D. W. Beard, "Dimensions of Organizational Task Environments," *Administrative Science Quarterly,* 1984, vol. 29, pp. 52–73.
13. F. E. Emery and E. L. Trist, "The Causal Texture of Organizational Environments," *Human Relations,* 1965, vol. 18, pp. 21–32.
14. H. Aldrich, *Organizations and Environments* (Englewood Cliffs, NJ: Prentice Hall, 1979).
15. W. H. Starbuck, "Organizations and Their Environments," in M. D. Dunnette, ed., *Handbook of Industrial Psychology* (Chicago: Rand McNally, 1976), pp. 1069–1123; Dess and Beard, "Dimensions of Organizational Task Environments."
16. Aldrich, *Organizations and Environments.*
17. *www.amazon.com,* 2002.
18. Ibid.
19. J. Pfeffer and G. R. Salancik, *The External Control of Organizations* (New York: Harper and Row, 1978).
20. Pfeffer, *Organizations and Organizational Theory,* p. 193.
21. Pfeffer and Salancik, *The External Control of Organizations,* pp. 45–46.
22. D. Miller and J. Shamsie, "The Resource-Based View of the Firm in Two Environments: The Hollywood Film Studios from 1936–1965," *Academy of Management Journal,* 1996, vol. 39, pp. 519–543.
23. Pfeffer and Salancik, *The External Control of Organizations,* p. 114.
24. *www.microsoft.com,* 2002.
25. C. W. L. Hill and G. R. Jones, *Strategic Management,* 7th ed., Chapter 7 (Boston: Houghton Mifflin, 2003).
26. C. L. Webb "Microsoft to Europe: Don't Be Cruel," 1 October 2004, *Washington Post, www.washingtonpost.com,* 2004.
27. K. Rebello and M. Lewyn, "Did Microsoft Shut the Windows on Competitors?" *Business Week,* 28 September 1992, pp. 32–33.
28. H. R. Greve, "Patterns of Competition: The Diffusion of Market Position in Radio Broadcasting," *Administrative Science Quarterly,* 1996, vol. 41, pp. 29–60.

29. J. M. Pennings, "Strategically Interdependent Organizations," in J. Nystrom and W. Starbuck, eds., *Handbook of Organizational Design* (New York: Oxford University Press, 1981), pp. 433–455.
30. J. Galaskeiwicz, "Interorganizational Relations," *Annual Review of Sociology,* 1985, vol. 11, pp. 281–304.
31. G. R. Jones and M. W. Pustay, "Interorganizational Coordination in the Airline Industry, 1925–1938: A Transaction Cost Approach," *Journal of Management,* 1988, vol. 14, pp. 529–546.
32. C. W. L. Hill, "Cooperation, Opportunism, and the Invisible Hand," *Academy of Management Review,* 1990, vol. 15, pp. 500–513.
33. P. Selznick, *TVA and the Grassroots* (New York: Harper and Row, 1949).
34. J. Pfeffer, "Size and Composition of Corporate Boards of Directors," *Administrative Science Quarterly,* 1972, vol. 17, pp. 218–228; R. D. Burt, "Co-optive Corporate Actor Networks: A Reconsideration of Interlocking Directorates Involving American Manufacturing," *Administrative Science Quarterly,* 1980, vol. 25, pp. 557–581.
35. "Bechtel, Willbros to Build Pipeline at Caspian Sea," *Wall Street Journal,* 26 October 1992, p. A3.
36. Organizational Insight by Margaret McKee, based on the following sources: *www.ballard.com,* 2004; N. Carr, "Ballard Selling German Vehicle Fuel Cell Business to DaimlerChrysler, Ford," *Canadian Press NewsWire,* 8 July 2004; P. Verburg, "Why Don't We Do It in the Road? Drive Fuel-Cell-Powered Cars, That Is," *Canadian Business,* 2004, vol. 76, p. 19; J. Crosse, "Fuel Cells—Today and Tomorrow—2004 Management Briefing: Alliances and Partnerships," Just-Auto, Bromsgrove, April 2004. p. 13.
37. W. W. Powell, K. W. Kogut, and L. Smith-Deorr, "Interorganizational Collaboration and the Locus of Innovation: Networks of Learning in Biotechnology," *Administrative Science Quarterly,* 1996, vol. 41, pp. 116–145.
38. R. Miles and C. Snow, "Causes of Failure in Network Organizations," *California Management Review,* 1992, vol. 4, pp. 13–32.
39. M. Aoki, *Information, Incentives, and Bargaining in the Japanese Economy* (New York: Cambridge University Press, 1988).
40. D. Roos, D. T. Jones, and J. P. Womack, *The Machine That Changed the World* (New York: Macmillan, 1990).
41. B. Kogut, "Joint Ventures: Theoretical and Empirical Perspectives," *Strategic Management Journal,* 1988, vol. 9, pp. 319–333.
42. J. Pfeffer, "Merger as a Response to Organizational Interdependence," *Administrative Science Quarterly,* 1972, vol. 17, pp. 382–394.
43. F. M. Scherer, *Industrial Market Structure and Economic Performance,* 2nd ed. (Boston: Houghton Mifflin, 1980).
44. A. Phillips, "A Theory of Interfirm Competition," *Quarterly Journal of Economics,* 1960, vol. 74, pp. 602–613; J. K. Benson, "The Interorganizational Network as a Political Economy," *Administrative Science Quarterly,* 1975, vol. 20, pp. 229–250.
45. D. W. Carlton and J. M. Perloff, *Modern Industrial Organization* (Glenview, IL: Scott, Foresman, 1990).
46. K. G. Provan, J. M. Beyer, and C. Kruytbosch, "Environmental Linkages and Power in Resource Dependence Relations Between Organizations," *Administrative Science Quarterly,* 1980, vol. 25, pp. 200–225.
47. "Why Networks May Fail," *The Economist,* 10 October 1992, p. 73.
48. H. Leblebichi and G. R. Salancik, "Stability in Interorganizational Exchanges: Rule-making Processes in the Chicago Board of Trade," *Administrative Science Quarterly,* 1982, vol. 27, pp. 227–242; A. Phillips, "A Theory of Interfirm Organization."
49. M. Olson, *The Logic of Collective Action* (Cambridge, MA: Harvard University Press, 1965).
50. A. Allison, "Computer Vendors Consolidate Resources," *Mini-Micro Systems,* 19 June 1992, pp. 54–57.
51. B. Kogut, "Joint Ventures: Theoretical and Empirical Perspectives," *Strategic Management Journal,* 1988, vol. 9, pp. 319–332.
52. *www.phillips.com,* 2002.
53. Scherer, *Industrial Market Structure and Economic Performance.*
54. *www.molsoncoors.com,* 2004.
55. J. Cook, "When 2 + 2 = 5," *Forbes,* 8 June 1992, pp. 128–129.
56. A. Alchian and H. Demsetz, "Production, Information Costs, and Economic Organization," *American Economic Review,* 1972, vol. 62, pp. 777–795.
57. O. E. Williamson, *Markets and Hierarchies* (New York: The Free Press, 1975); O. E. Williamson, "The Governance of Contractual Relationships," *Journal of Law and Economics,* 1979, vol. 22, pp. 232–261.
58. Commission on the Future of Health Care in Canada, "Final Report: Building on Values: The Future of Health Care in Canada," *www.hc-sc.gc.ca,* 2004.

59. Williamson, *Markets and Hierarchies.*

60. H. A. Simon, *Models of Man* (New York: Wiley, 1957).

61. Williamson, *Markets and Hierarchies.*

62. Office of the Auditor General of Canada, *www.oag-bvg.gc.ca*, 2004.

63. B. Klein, R. Crawford, and A. Alchian, "Vertical Integration: Appropriable Rents and the Competitive Contracting Process," *Journal of Law and Economics*, 1978, vol. 21, pp. 297–326.

64. R. H. Coase, "The Nature of the Firm," *Economica* N.S., 1937, 4, pp. 386–405.

65. G. R. Jones, "Transaction Costs, Property Rights, and Organizational Culture: An Exchange Perspective," *Administrative Science Quarterly*, 1983, vol. 28, pp. 454–467.

66. R. A. D'Aveni and D. J. Ravenscraft, "Economies of Integration Versus Bureaucracy Costs: Does Vertical Integration Improve Performance?" *Academy of Management Journal*, 1994, vol. 37, pp. 1167–1206.

67. G. R. Jones and C. W. L. Hill, "Transaction Cost Analysis of Strategy–Structure Choice," *Strategic Management Journal*, 1988, vol. 9, pp. 159–172.

68. *www.magna.com*, 2004.

69. Ibid.

70. G. Walker and D. Weber, "A Transaction Cost Approach to Make or Buy Decisions," *Administrative Science Quarterly*, 1984, vol. 29, pp. 373–391.

71. J. F. Hennart, "A Transaction Cost Theory of Equity Joint Ventures," *Strategic Management Journal*, 1988, vol. 9, pp. 361–374.

72. K. G. Provan and S. J. Skinner, "Interorganizational Dependence and Control as Predictors of Opportunism in Dealer–Supplier Relations," *Academy of Management Journal*, 1989, vol. 32, pp. 202–212.

73. *www.gm.com*, press release, 1998.

74. S. A. Shane, "Hybrid Organizational Arrangements and Their Implications for Firm Growth and Survival: A Study of New Franchisors," *Academy of Management Journal*, 1996, vol. 39, pp. 216–234.

75. D. E. Bowen and G. R. Jones, "Transaction Cost Analysis of Service Organization–Customer Exchange," *Academy of Management Review*, 1986, vol. 11, pp. 428–441.

76. E. Anderson and D. C. Schmittlein, "Integration of the Sales Force: An Empirical Examination," *Rand Journal of Economics*, 1984, vol. 26, pp. 65–79.

77. "Business: Link in the Global Chain," *The Economist*, 2 June 2001, pp. 62–63.

78. Case by Scott MacMillan, based upon the following sources: CBC News, "In Review," *www.tv.cbc.ca*, 2004; *www.mccain.com*, 2004; C. Morris, "French Fry King Dies," *Canadian Press*, *http://cnews.canoe.ca*, 2004; D. Mcmurdry, "Frying the Competition: McCain CEO Howard Mann Hopes to Continue Taking a Bite out of the International Food Market," *Canadian Business*, 2001, vol. 74, p. 17; G. Pitts, "McCain Boss Picks Up Pace of Global French Fry Assault," *Globe and Mail*, 14 June 2004, p. B1; T. Watson and K. Libin "The Countdown Continues: A French-Fry Empire and a Truly Inspired Bean-Counter Make the Top 75." *Canadian Business*, 2003, vol. 76, pp. 89–90.

Basic Challenges of Organizational Design

CHAPTER 4

Learning Objectives

If an organization is to remain effective as it changes and grows with its environment, managers must continuously evaluate the way their organizations are designed: for example, the way work is divided among people and departments, and the way its human, financial, and physical resources are employed, expended, and accounted for. Organizational design involves difficult choices about how to manage—that is, coordinate organizational tasks and motivate the people who perform them—to maximize an organization's ability to achieve its goals and create value. This chapter examines the challenges of designing an organizational structure so that it achieves stakeholder objectives.

After studying this chapter you should be able to:

1. Describe the four basic organizational design challenges confronting managers, consultants, and those interested in organizational design.
2. Discuss the way in which these challenges are often interdependent and how they must be addressed simultaneously if a high-performing organizational structure is to be created.
3. Distinguish among the design choices that underlie the creation of either a mechanistic or an organic structure.
4. Recognize how to use contingency theory to design a structure that fits an organization's environment.

DIFFERENTIATION

Design Challenge 1 People in this organization take on new tasks as the need arises and it's very unclear who is responsible for what, and who is supposed to report to whom. This makes it difficult to know on whom to call when the need arises and difficult to coordinate people's activities so they work together as a team.

Differentiation
The process by which an organization allocates people and resources to organizational tasks and establishes the task and authority relationships that allow the organization to achieve its goals.

As organizations grow, managers must decide how to control and coordinate the activities that are required for the organization to create value. The principal design challenge is how to manage differentiation to achieve organizational goals. **Differentiation** is the process by which an organization allocates people and resources to organizational tasks and establishes the task and authority relationships that allow the organization to achieve its goals.[1] In short, it is the process of establishing and controlling the **division of labour**, or degree of specialization, in the organization.

Division of labour The process of establishing and controlling the degree of specialization in the organization.

An easy way to examine why differentiation occurs and why it poses a design challenge is to examine an organization and chart the problems it faces as it attempts to achieve its goals (see Figure 4-1). In a *simple* organization, differentiation is low because the division of labour is low. Typically, one person or a few people perform all organizational tasks, so there are few challenges associated with coordinating who does what, for whom, and when. With growth, however, comes increasing complexity. In a *complex* organization, both the variety of the division of labour and level of differentiation are high. The story of how the B.A.R. and Grille restaurant grew illustrates the problems and challenges that organizational design must address. As the B.A.R. and Grille changed, its owners had to find new ways to coordinate and control the activities necessary to meet their goal of providing customers with a satisfying dining experience. (See Organizational Insight 4.1.)

ORGANIZATIONAL INSIGHT 4.1

B.A.R. and Grille Restaurant

In 1998, Bob and Amanda Richards (hence B.A.R.) trained as chefs and obtained the capital they needed to open their own restaurant, the B.A.R. and Grille, a 1950s-style restaurant specializing in hamburgers, hot dogs, French fries, fresh fruit pies, and fountain drinks. At the beginning, with the help of one additional person hired to be a waiter, Bob and Amanda took turns cooking and waiting on tables (see Figure 4-1A). The venture was wildly successful. The combination of good food, served in a "Happy Days" atmosphere, appealed to customers, who swamped the restaurant at lunchtime and every night.

This success soon saw Bob and Amanda overloaded. They worked from dawn to midnight to cope with all the jobs that needed to be done: buying supplies, preparing the food, maintaining the property, taking in money, and figuring the accounts. It was soon clear that there was not enough time for Bob and Amanda to accomplish all of these separate tasks themselves. It was also clear that the success was largely dependent on both Bob and Amanda being in the kitchen and that they needed additional help. They hired waiters, waiter-assistants, and other kitchen help to wash the mountains of dishes. The staff worked in shifts, and by the end of the third month of operations Bob and Amanda were employing 22 people on a full- or part-time basis (Figure 4-1B).

With 22 staff members to oversee, the Richardses now faced a new challenge. Because both of them were working in the kitchen, they had little time to oversee what was happening in the dining room. The waiters, in effect, were running the restaurant. Bob and Amanda had lost contact with the customers and no longer received their comments about the food and service. They realized that to make sure their standards of customer service were being met, one of them needed to take control of the dining room and supervise the waiters and waiter-assistants while the other took control of the kitchen activities. Amanda took over the dining room, and she and Bob hired two chefs to replace her in the kitchen. Bob oversaw the kitchen and continued to cook. The business continued to do well, so they increased the size of the dining room and hired additional waiters and waiter-assistants (Figure 4-1C).

It soon became clear that Bob and Amanda needed to employ further additional people to take over specific tasks because they no longer had the time, skills, or energy to handle them personally. To control the payment system, they employed full-time cashiers. To cope with customers' demands for alcoholic drinks, they hired a lawyer, got a liquor licence, and employed full-time bartenders. To obtain restaurant supplies and manage restaurant services such as cleaning and equipment maintenance, they employed a restaurant manager. The manager was also responsible for overseeing the restaurant on days when the owners took a well-deserved break. By the end of its first year of operation, the B.A.R. and Grille had 50 full- and part-time employees, and the owners were seeking new avenues for expansion (Figure 4-1D).

Eager to use their newly acquired skills to create yet more value, the Richardses began to search for ideas for a new restaurant. Within 18 months they opened a waffle and pancake restaurant, and a year later they opened a pizza restaurant. With this growth, Bob and Amanda left their jobs in the B.A.R. and Grille. They hired shift managers to manage each restaurant, and they spent their time managing central support functions such as purchasing, marketing, and accounting, training new chefs, and developing menu and marketing plans (Figure 4-1E). To ensure that service and quality were uniformly excellent at all three restaurants, they developed written rules and procedures that told chefs, waiters, and other employees what was expected of them—for example, how to prepare and present food and how to behave with customers. After five years of operation, they employed over 150 people full- or part-time in their three restaurants, and their sales volume was over $2 million a year.

The basic design challenge facing the owners of the B.A.R. and Grille was managing the increasing complexity of the organization's activities. At first, Bob and Amanda performed all the major organizational tasks themselves, and the division of labour was low. As the volume of business grew, the owners needed to increase the division of labour and decide which people would do which jobs. In other words, they had to differentiate the organization and allocate people and resources to the additional organizational tasks required to meet the growing demand.

Organizational Roles

Organizational role
The set of task-related behaviours required of a person by his or her position in an organization.

The basic building blocks of differentiation are organizational roles (see Figure 4-2). An **organizational role** is a set of task-related behaviours required of a person by his or her position in an organization.[2] For example, the organizational role of a B.A.R. and Grille waiter is to provide customers with quick, courteous service to enhance their dining experience. A chef's role is to provide customers with high-quality, appetizing, cooked-to-order meals. A person who is given a role with identifiable tasks and responsibilities can understand what he or she must do to contribute to the organization in an effective fashion and to be held accountable for the resources used to accomplish the duties of that position. Bob and Amanda held the waiter responsible for satisfying customers, the restaurant's crucial stakeholder group. The chef was accountable for providing high-quality meals to customers consistently and speedily.

As the division of labour increases in an organization, and as complexity rises, there is an increasing requirement to coordinate the various activities taking place

A. Bob and Amanda, the owners, cook and wait tables as needed. They employ one additional waiter.
(3 individuals in the organization)

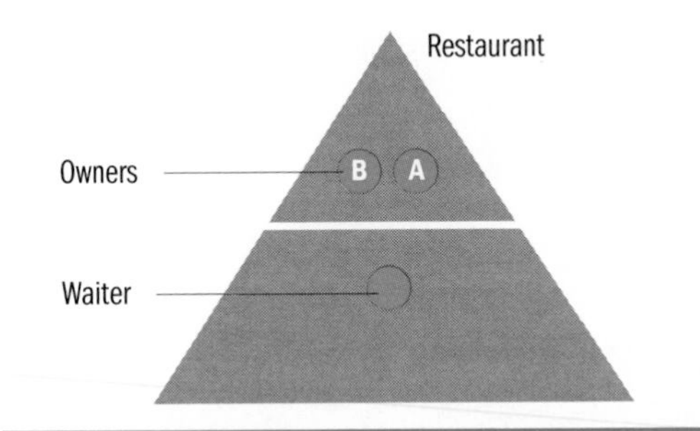

B. Bob and Amanda work in the kitchen full-time. They hire waiters, busboys, and kitchen staff.
(22 individuals in the organization)

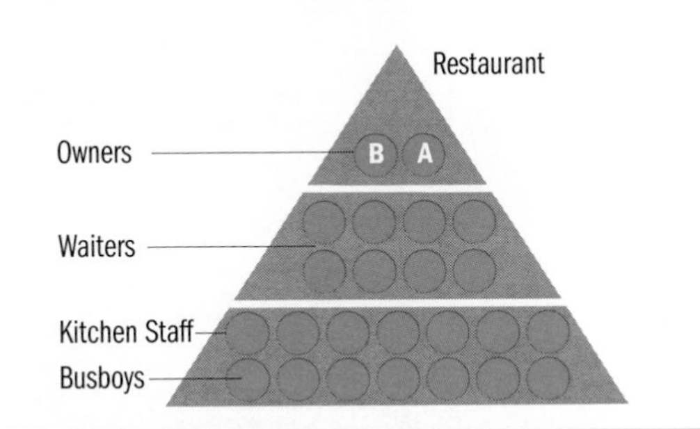

C. Unable to manage both the kitchen and the dining room, they divide tasks into two functions, kitchen and dining room, and specialize. Bob runs the kitchen, and Amanda runs the dining room. They also add more staff.
(29 individuals in the organization)

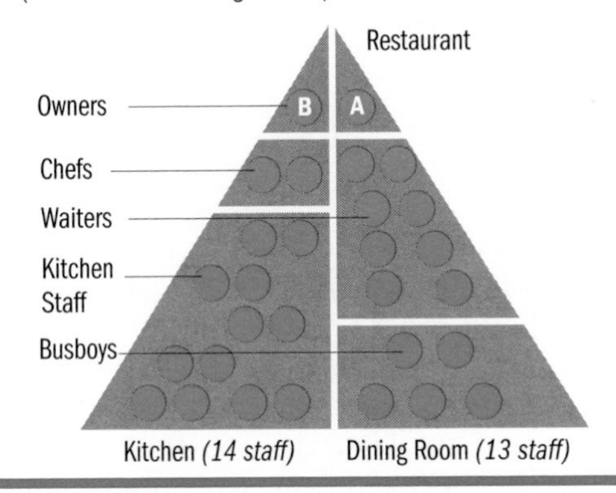

D. The business continues to prosper. Bob and Amanda create new tasks and functions and hire people to manage the functions.
(52 individuals in the organization)

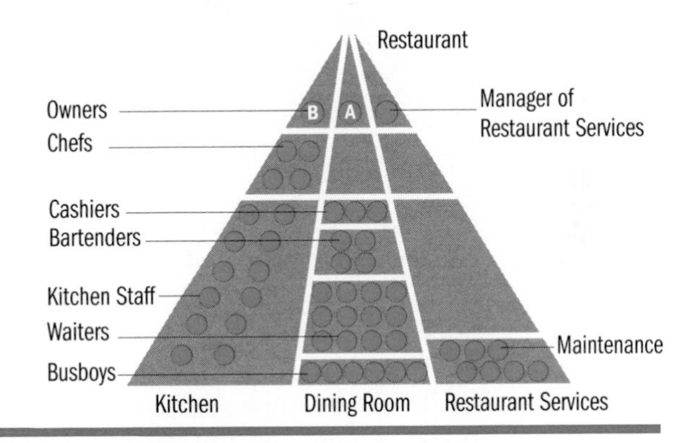

E. The Richardses see new opportunities to apply their core competences in new restaurant ventures. They open new restaurants, put support functions like purchasing and marketing under their direct control, and hire shift managers to manage the kitchen and dining room in each restaurant.
(150 individuals in the organization)

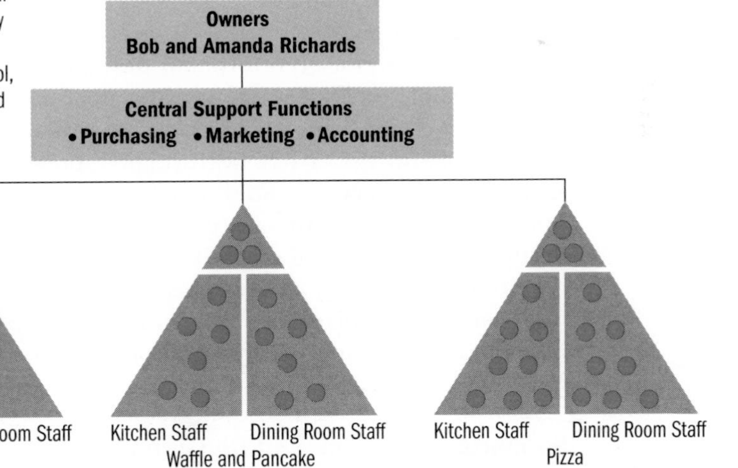

FIGURE 4-1
Design Challenge.
Differentiation at the B.A.R. and Grille.

FIGURE 4-2
Building Blocks of Differentiation.

Organization
Division
Function
Role

within the organization. Generally, there comes a point where people are needed to coordinate the work of other people. Usually these individuals are managers and they specialize in some roles and then hire additional people to specialize in others. Specialization allows people to develop their individual abilities and knowledge, which are the ultimate source of an organization's core competencies. At the B.A.R. and Grille, for example, the owners identified various tasks to be done, such as cooking, bookkeeping, and purchasing, and hired people with the appropriate abilities, skills, and knowledge to do them.

Organizational structure is based on a system of interlocking roles, and the relationship of one role to another is defined by task-related behaviours. Some roles require people to oversee the behaviour of others: Shift managers at the B.A.R. and Grille oversee the waiters and waiter-assistants. A person who holds another person accountable for his or her performance possesses authority over the other person. **Authority** is the power to hold people accountable for their actions and to make decisions concerning the use of organizational resources.[3] The differentiation of an organization into individual organizational roles results in authority and responsibility requirements for each role in the system. When an individual clearly understands the responsibilities of his or her role and what a superior can require of a person in that role, the result within the organization is **control**—the ability to coordinate and motivate people to work in the organization's interests.

Authority
The power to hold people accountable for their actions and to make decisions concerning the use of organizational resources.

Control
The ability to coordinate and motivate people to work in the organization's interests.

Subunits: Functions and Divisions

In most organizations, people with similar and related roles are grouped into a subunit. The main subunits that develop in organizations are usually oriented along functions (or departments) and divisions. A **function** is a subunit composed of a group of people, working together, who possess similar skills or use the same kind of knowledge, tools, or techniques to perform their jobs. For example, in the B.A.R. and Grille, chefs are grouped together as the kitchen function, and waiters are grouped together

Function
A subunit composed of a group of people, working together, who possess similar skills or use the same kind of knowledge, tools, or techniques to perform their jobs.

as the dining room function. A **division** is a subunit that consists of a collection of functions or departments that share responsibility for producing a particular good or service. Take another look at Figure 4-1E. Each restaurant is a division composed of just two functions—dining room and kitchen—which are responsible for the restaurant's activities. Large companies like General Electric, Bombardier, Siemens, and Procter & Gamble may have dozens of separate divisions, each one responsible for producing a particular product. Procter & Gamble faces the problem of how to organize these divisions on a global level so the company could create the most value, an issue discussed in detail in Chapter 8.

Division
A subunit that consists of a collection of functions or departments that share responsibility for producing a particular good or service.

The number of different functions and divisions that an organization possesses is a measure of the organization's complexity—its degree of differentiation. Differentiation into functions and divisions increases an organization's coordination and control over its activities and allows the organization to accomplish its tasks more effectively.

As organizations grow in size, they usually differentiate into five different kinds of functions.[4] **Support functions** facilitate an organization's control of its relations with its environment and its stakeholders. Support functions include *purchasing,* to handle the acquisition of inputs; *sales and marketing,* to handle the disposal of outputs; and *public relations and legal affairs,* to respond to the needs of outside stakeholders. Bob and Amanda Richards hired a manager to oversee purchasing for all three restaurants and an accountant to manage the books and a lawyer for legal affairs (see Figure 4-1E).

Support functions
Functions that facilitate an organization's control of its relations with its environment and its stakeholders.

Production functions allow the organization to produce the product or service itself. The main focus of these functions is to manage and improve the efficiency of an organization's conversion processes so that more value is created at less cost. Production functions include *production operations, production control,* and *quality control.* At Ford, the production operations department controls the manufacturing process; production control decides on the most efficient way to produce cars at the lowest cost; and quality control monitors product quality.

Production functions
Functions that manage and improve the efficiency of an organization's conversion processes so that more value is created.

Maintenance functions enable an organization to keep its departments in operation. Maintenance functions include *personnel,* to recruit and train workers and improve skills; *engineering,* to repair broken machinery; and *janitorial services,* to keep the work environment safe and healthy—conditions that are very important to a restaurant like the B.A.R. and Grille.

Maintenance functions
Functions that enable an organization to keep its departments in operation.

Adaptive functions allow an organization to adjust to changes in the environment. Adaptive functions include *research and development, market research,* and *long-range planning,* which allow an organization to learn from and attempt to manage its environment and thus increase its core competencies. At the B.A.R. and Grille, developing new menu choices to keep up with customers' changing tastes is an important adaptive activity.

Adaptive functions
Functions that allow an organization to adjust to changes in the environment.

Managerial functions facilitate the coordination and control of activities within and among departments. Managers at different organizational levels direct the *acquisition of, investment in, and control of resources* to improve the organization's ability to create value. Top management, for example, is responsible for formulating strategy and establishing the policies the organization uses to control its environment. Middle managers are responsible for managing the organization's resources to meet its operative goals. Lower-level managers oversee and direct the day-to-day organizational activities of the workforce.

Managerial functions
Functions that facilitate the coordination and control of activities within and among departments.

Differentiation at the B.A.R. and Grille

In the B.A.R. and Grille, the level of differentiation at first was minimal. The owners, with the help of one other person, did all the work and completed all the organizational tasks required. But with unexpected success came the need to further differentiate activities into separate organizational roles and functions, with Bob managing the kitchen and Amanda the dining room. As the restaurant continued to grow, Bob and Amanda were confronted with the need to develop skills and capabilities in the five functional areas. For the support role they hired a restaurant services manager to take charge of purchasing supplies and local advertising. To handle the production role, they increased the division of labour in the kitchen and dining room. They hired cleaning staff, cashiers, and an external accountant for maintenance tasks. They themselves handled the adaptive role of ensuring that the organization served customer needs. Finally, Bob and Amanda took on the managerial role of establishing the pattern of task and functional relationships that most effectively accomplished the restaurant's overall task of serving customers good food. Collectively, the five functions constituted the B.A.R. and Grille and gave it the ability to create value.

As soon as the owners decided to open new kinds of restaurants and expand the size of their organization, they faced the challenge of differentiating into divisions, to control the operation of three restaurants simultaneously. The organization grew to three divisions, each of which made use of support functions centralized at the top of the organization (see Figure 4-1E). In large organizations each division is likely to have its own set of the five basic functions and is, thus, a *self-contained division.*

As we discussed in Chapter 1, functional skills and abilities are the source of an organization's *core competencies,* the set of unique skills and capabilities that give an organization a competitive advantage.[5] An organization's competitive advantage may lie in any or all of an organization's functions. An organization could have superior low-cost production, exceptional managerial talent, or a leading research and development department.[6] A core competency of the B.A.R. and Grille was the way Bob and Amanda took control of the differentiation of their restaurant and increased its ability to attract customers who appreciated the good food and good service they received. In short, they created a core competency that gave their restaurant a competitive advantage over other restaurants. In turn, this competitive advantage gave them access to resources that allowed them to expand by opening new restaurants.

Vertical and Horizontal Differentiation

Figure 4-3 shows the organizational chart that emerged in the B.A.R. and Grille as differentiation unfolded. An organizational chart is a drawing that shows the end result of organizational differentiation. Each box on the chart represents a role or function in the organization. Each role has a vertical and a horizontal dimension.

The organizational chart *vertically* differentiates organizational roles in terms of the authority that goes with each role. A classification of people according to authority and rank is called a **hierarchy**. Roles at the top of an organization's hierarchy possess more authority and responsibility than do roles farther down in the hierarchy; each lower role is under the control or supervision of a higher one. Managers designing an organization have to make decisions about how much vertical differentiation to have in the organization—that is, how many levels should there be from top to bottom. To maintain control over the various functions in the restaurant, for example, Bob and Amanda realized that they needed to create the role of restaurant manager. Because the restaurant manager would report to them and would supervise lower-level employees, this new role added a level to the hierarchy. **Vertical differentiation** refers to the way an organization designs its hierarchy of authority and creates reporting relationships to link organizational roles and subunits.[7] Vertical differentiation establishes the distribution of authority between levels to give the organization more control over its activities and increase its ability to create value.

Hierarchy
A classification of people according to authority and rank.

Vertical differentiation
The way an organization designs its hierarchy of authority and creates reporting relationships to link organizational roles and subunits.

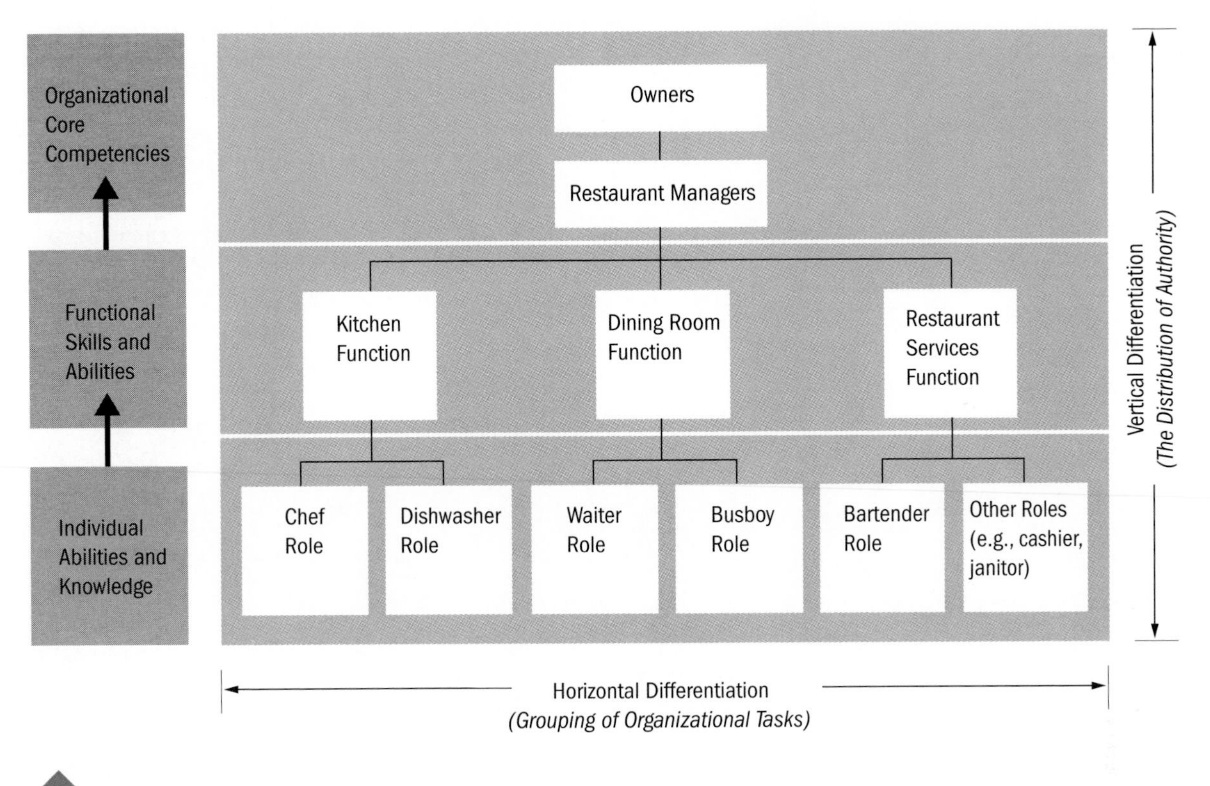

FIGURE 4-3
Organizational Chart of the B.A.R. and Grille.

The organizational chart *horizontally* differentiates roles according to main task responsibilities. For example, when Bob and Amanda realized that a more complex division of tasks would increase restaurant effectiveness, they created new organizational roles—such as restaurant manager, cashier, bartender, and busboy—and grouped these roles into functions. **Horizontal differentiation** refers to the way an organization groups organizational tasks into roles and roles into subunits (functions and divisions).[8] Horizontal differentiation establishes the division of labour, which enables people in the organization to become more specialized and productive and increases the organization's ability to create value.

Horizontal differentiation The way an organization groups organizational tasks into roles and roles into subunits (functions and divisions).

Organizational Design Challenges

We have seen that the principal design challenge facing an organization is to choose the levels of vertical and horizontal differentiation that allow the organization to coordinate and control its activities in order to achieve its goals. In Chapters 5 and 6 we examine further some principles that guide these choices.

In the remainder of Chapter 4 we look at three more design challenges that confront managers attempting to create a structure that will maximize their organization's effectiveness (see Figure 4-4). The first of the three is how to link and coordinate organizational activities. The second is determining who will make decisions. The third is deciding which types of mechanisms are best suited to controlling specific employee tasks and roles. The choices managers make as they grapple with all three challenges determine how effectively their organization works.

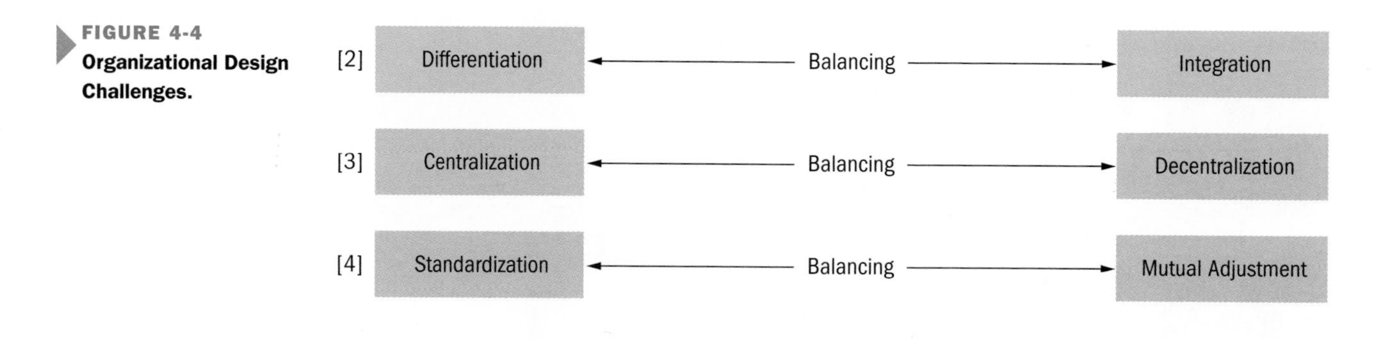

FIGURE 4-4
Organizational Design Challenges.

MANAGERIAL IMPLICATIONS

Differentiation

1. No matter what your position in an organization is, draw an organizational chart so that you can identify the distribution of authority and the division of labour.
2. No matter how few or how many people you work with or supervise, analyze each person's role and the relationships among roles to make sure that the division of labour is best for the task being performed. If it is not, redefine role relationships and responsibilities.
3. If you supervise more than one function or department, analyze relationships among departments to make sure that the division of labour best suits the organization's mission: the creation of value for stakeholders.

BALANCING DIFFERENTIATION AND INTEGRATION

Design Challenge 2 We can't get people to communicate and coordinate in this organization. Specifying tasks and roles is supposed to help coordinate the work process, but here it builds barriers between people and functions.

Subunit orientation
A tendency to view one's role in the organization strictly from the perspective of the time frame, goals, and interpersonal orientations of one's subunit.

Horizontal differentiation is supposed to enable people to specialize and thus become more productive. However, companies have often found that specialization limits communication between subunits and prevents them from learning from one another. As a result of horizontal differentiation, the members of different functions or divisions develop a **subunit orientation**—a tendency to view one's role in the organization strictly from the perspective of the time frame, goals, and interpersonal orientations of one's subunit.[9] For example, the production department is most concerned with reducing costs and increasing quality; thus it tends to have a short-term outlook because cost and quality are production goals that must be met daily. In research and development, on the other hand, innovations to the production process may take years to come to fruition; thus R&D people usually have a longer-term outlook. When different functions see things differently, communication is impeded and coordination becomes difficult, if not impossible.

To avoid the communication problems that can arise from increased horizontal differentiation, organizations try to find new or better ways to integrate functions—that is, to promote cooperation, coordination, and communication among separate subunits. Xerox uses its computer systems to find new ways for different functions to share databases, memos, and reports. Increasingly, companies are using electronic means of communication, like e-mail and teleconferencing, to bring different functions together. For example, buyers at Wal-Mart's home office use television linkups to show each store individually the appropriate way to display products for sale.

Integration and Integrating Mechanisms

How to facilitate communication and coordination among subunits is a major challenge for managers. One reason for problems on this front is that the development of subunit orientations makes communication difficult and complex. Another reason for lack of coordination and communication is that managers often fail to use the appropriate mechanisms to integrate organizational subunits. **Integration** is the process of coordinating various tasks, functions, and divisions so that they work together, not at cross-purposes. Table 4-1 lists seven integrating mechanisms that managers can use as their organization's level of differentiation increases.[10] The simplest mechanism is a hierarchy of authority; the most complex is a department created specifically to coordinate the activities of diverse functions or divisions. The table includes examples of how a company like Johnson & Johnson might use all seven types of integration mechanisms as it goes about managing one major product line—disposable diapers. We will examine each mechanism separately.

Integration
The process of coordinating various tasks, functions, and divisions so that they work together and not at cross-purposes.

Hierarchy of Authority The simplest integrating device is an organization's hierarchy of authority, which differentiates people by how much authority they have. Because the hierarchy dictates who reports to whom, it coordinates various organizational roles. Managers must carefully divide and allocate authority within a function and between one function and others to promote coordination. For example, at Becton Dickinson, a high-tech medical instrument maker, the marketing and engineering departments were frequently squabbling over product specifications. Marketing argued that the company's products needed more features to please customers. Engineering wanted to simplify product design to reduce costs.[11] The two departments could not resolve their differences because the head of marketing reported to the head of engineering. To resolve this conflict, Becton Dickinson reorganized its hierarchy so that both marketing and engineering reported to the head of the Instrument Product Division. The head of the division was an impartial third party who had the authority to listen to both managers' cases and make the decision that was best for the organization as a whole.

Direct Contact Direct contact between people in different subunits is an integrating mechanism that is more complex than a hierarchy of authority. The principal problem with integration across functions is that a manager in one function has no authority over a manager in another. Nor does one manager have authority over the employee of another. Only the CEO or somebody else above the functional level has power to intervene if two functions come into conflict. Consequently, establishing personal relationships between people at all levels in different functions is an important step in overcoming the problems that arise because people (or groups, or departments) have different subunit orientations. Managers from different functions who have opportunities for direct contact with each other can work together to solve common problems.

Table 4-1

TYPES AND EXAMPLES OF INTEGRATING MECHANISMS

Integration Mechanism (in order of increasing complexity)	Description	Example (e.g., in Johnson & Johnson)
Hierarchy of authority	A ranking of employees integrates by specifying who reports to whom.	Salesperson reports to Diaper Division sales manager.
Direct contact	Managers meet face-to-face to coordinate activities.	Diaper Division sales and manufacturing managers meet to discuss scheduling.
Liaison role	A specific manager is given responsibility for coordinating with managers from other subunits on behalf of his or her subunit.	A person from each of J&J's production, marketing, and research and development departments is given responsibility for coordinating with the other departments.
Task force	Managers meet in temporary committees to coordinate cross-functional activities.	A committee is formed to find new ways to recycle diapers.
Team	Managers meet regularly in permanent committees to coordinate activities.	A permanent J&J committee is established to promote new-product development in the Diaper Division.
Integrating role	A new role is established to coordinate the activities of two or more functions or divisions.	One manager takes responsibility for coordinating Diaper and Baby Soap divisions to enhance their marketing activities.
Integrating department	A new department is created to coordinate the activities of functions or divisions.	A team of managers is created to take responsibility for coordinating J&J's centralization program to allow divisions to share skills and resources.

If disputes still arise, however, it is important for both parties to be able to appeal to a common superior who is not far removed from the scene of the problem.

Liaison Roles When the need for communication among subunits increases, one member or a few members from a subunit are likely to have responsibility for coordinating with other subunits. The people who hold these connecting, or liaison, roles are able to develop in-depth relations with people in other subunits. This interaction helps overcome barriers between subunits. Over time, as the people in liaison roles learn to cooperate, they can become increasingly flexible in accommodating other subunits' requests. Figure 4-5A illustrates a liaison role.

Task force
A temporary committee set up to handle a specific problem.

Task Forces As an organization increases in size and complexity, more than two subunits may need to work together to solve common problems. Increasing an organization's ability to serve its customers effectively, for example, may require input from production, marketing, engineering, and research and development. The solution commonly takes the form of a **task force**, a temporary committee set up to handle a

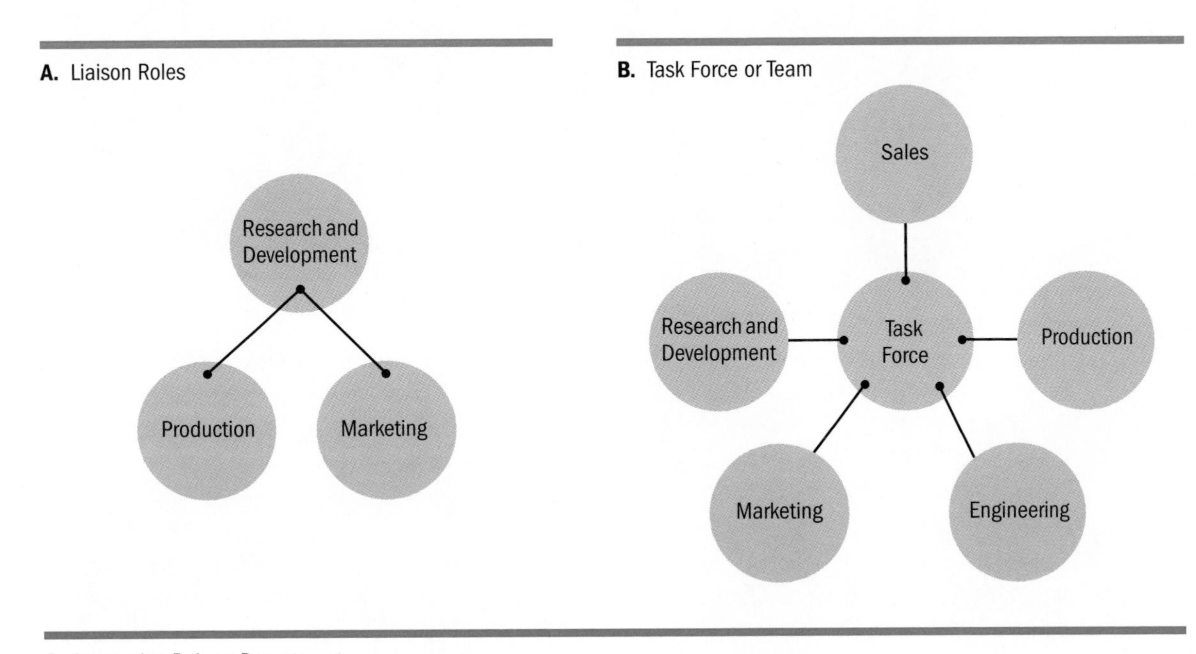

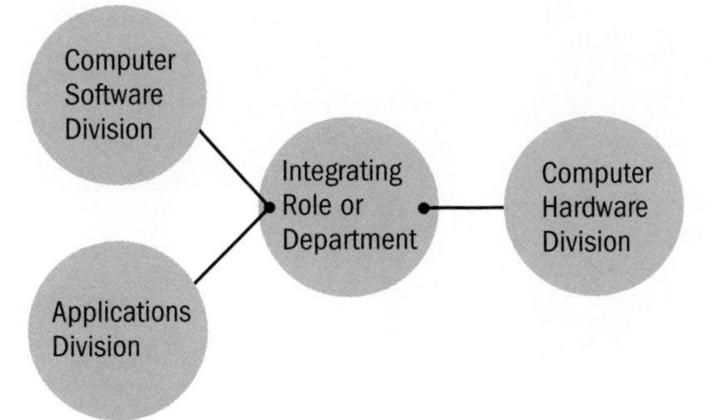

• Indicates managers with responsibility for integration between subunits.

FIGURE 4-5
Integrating Mechanisms.

specific problem (Figure 4-5B). One person from each function joins a task force, which meets until it finds a solution to the problem. Task force members are responsible for taking the solution back to their functional groups for group input and approval. To increase the effectiveness of task forces, a senior manager from outside all the functions involved usually chairs the meetings.

Teams When the issue a task force is dealing with becomes an ongoing strategic or administrative issue, the task force becomes permanent. A *team* is a permanent task force or committee. Most companies, for example, now have product development and customer contact teams to respond to the threat of increased competition in a global market. Such teams, once a rarity, are now a vital part of most successful organizations. For example, Magna uses teams at all levels of its structure to great benefit. (See Organizational Insight 4.2.)

ORGANIZATIONAL INSIGHT 4.2

Magna International: Structuring with Teams[12]

From its humble beginnings as a one-man tool shop with sales of $13 000 in 1957, Magna International has grown to a firm that employs more than 75 000 people in some 260 facilities located in 22 countries around the world. In 2003, the company's sales topped the $15 billion mark and it is now considered one of the most diversified automotive suppliers in the world. Magna-designed and -built components, systems, and modules can be found in millions of cars around the world sold by General Motors, Ford, Toyota, and Volkswagen, just to name a few. What may surprise people is that Magna also assembles vehicles from start to finish, including such well-known models as the Chrysler Jeep Grand Cherokee, the Mercedes G-class offroad vehicle, the Saab 9-3, and the BMW X3.

But just how did a little Canadian start-up company grow to be such a significant player in the highly competitive international automotive industry? Part of the answer lies in the way Magna founder Frank Stronach has structured the company.

A quick look at the corporate structure of Magna International Inc. reveals that it's a company with a number of highly specialized business groups (see Figure 4-6). These groups, of which there were ten in 2004, report upward to an executive strategy committee. Each group is then subdivided into individual divisions that are set up to operate as independent profit centres. Magna management believes this decentralized structure—which it identifies as one of its key operating principles—prevents bureaucracy and helps the company stay in close touch with its end customer. This close contact is intended to help the company remain more responsive and able to adjust to changing industry needs.

Magna's founder also believes its structure helps promote an entrepreneurial spirit within the organization. As the company's Web site outlines it, "the long-established strategy of spinning out certain automotive systems groups is the best way to preserve and continually renew Magna's entrepreneurial culture—a culture which gives its employees equity ownership in their places of business, fosters individual initiative and involvement, and ensures that Magna's operations remain lean, flexible and customer-focused. This dynamic corporate culture is the cornerstone of Magna's success."

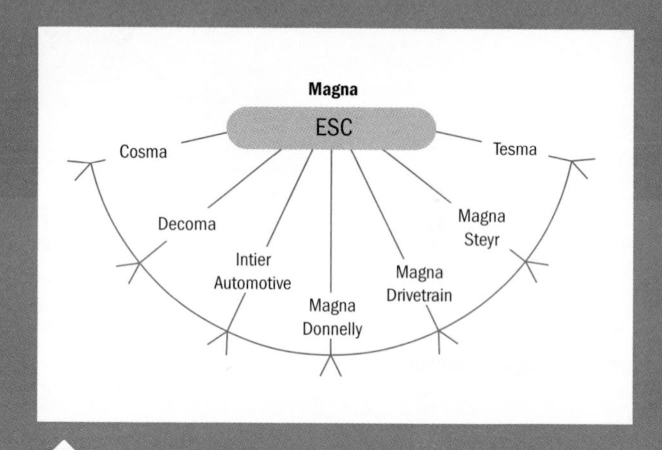

FIGURE 4.6
Global Structure of Magna International.

Source: http://www.magnaint.com/magnaWeb.nsf/webpages/Magna+Worldwide+-+Global+Structure?OpenDocument

Approximately 70 percent of a manager's time is spent in committee meetings.[13] Teams provide the opportunity for the face-to-face contact and continual adjustment that managers need to deal effectively with ongoing complex issues. As they set up teams, managers face the challenge of creating a committee system that gives them effective control over organizational activities. Very often teams are ineffective because the problems facing the organization change but team membership remains unchanged. People often fight to stay on a committee even when their services are no longer needed. Membership on a team gives a person power in the organization, but this power does not necessarily promote organizational goals. At Whirlpool, the appliance maker, CEO David Whitwam established hundreds of mini-management teams throughout the company to bring about change, improve quality control, and streamline production. Whitwam's goal? To use teams to change patterns of authority and decision making to increase interaction and promote creativity among managers.[14]

Integrating Roles or Departments As organizations become large and complex, communication barriers between functions and divisions are likely to increase. Managers in different product divisions, for example, may never meet one another. In organizations that employ many thousands of people, coordinating subunits becomes especially difficult. One way to overcome these barriers is to create integrating roles that coordinate subunits. An **integrating role** is a full-time position established specifically to improve communication between divisions. (A liaison role, by contrast, is part of a person's full-time job.) Figure 4-5C shows an integrating role that might exist in a large computer company like Compaq or Apple.

Integrating role
A full-time position established specifically to improve communication between divisions.

The purpose of an integrating role is to promote the sharing of information and knowledge to enhance organizational goals such as innovation and product development, increased flexibility, and heightened customer service. People in integrating roles are often senior managers who have decided to give up authority in a specific function and focus on integration. They often chair task forces and teams and report directly to top management or even the CEO.

When a company has many employees in integrating roles, it creates an integrating department, which coordinates the activities of subunits. Du Pont, the chemical company, has a department that employs over 200 people in integrating roles. In general, the more complex and highly differentiated an organization is, the more complex are the integration mechanisms needed to overcome communication and coordination barriers between functions and divisions.

Differentiation versus Integration

The design issue facing managers is to establish a level of integration that matches the organization's level of differentiation. Managers must achieve an appropriate balance between differentiation and integration. A highly complex organization that is highly differentiated needs a high level of integration to effectively coordinate its activities. By contrast, an organization that has a relatively simple, clearly defined role structure normally needs to use only simple integrating mechanisms. Its managers may find that the hierarchy of authority provides all the coordination and control they need to achieve organizational goals.

At all costs, managers need to be sure they do not differentiate or integrate their organization too much. Differentiation and integration are both expensive in terms of the number of managers employed and the amount of managerial time spent on coordinating organizational activities. For example, every hour that managers and employees spend on committees that are not really needed costs the organization thousands of dollars because the managers and employees are not being put to their most productive use.

Managers facing the challenge of deciding how and how much to differentiate and integrate must do two things: (1) carefully guide the process of differentiation so that it develops the core competencies that give the organization a competitive advantage; and (2) carefully integrate the organization by choosing appropriate integrating mechanisms that allow subunits to cooperate and that build up the organization's core competencies.[15]

BALANCING CENTRALIZATION AND DECENTRALIZATION

> Design Challenge 3 People in this organization don't take responsibility or risks. They are always looking to the boss for direction and supervision. As a result, decision making is slow and cumbersome, and we miss out on a lot of opportunities to create value or do things better.

In discussing vertical differentiation, we noted that establishing a hierarchy of authority is supposed to improve the way an organization functions because the hierarchy defines the area of each person's authority within the organization and this permits people to understand and be held accountable for their actions. Many companies, however, complain that when a hierarchy of authority exists, people are constantly looking to their superiors for directions.[16] When something new or unusual occurs, they prefer to let it pass, or they pass it on to their superior rather than assume responsibility and take the risk of dealing with it. As responsibility seeking and risk taking behaviours decline, so does organizational performance because the organization may not exploit new opportunities for using its core competencies. When nobody is willing to take responsibility, decision making becomes slow and the organization becomes inflexible—that is, unable to change and adapt to new developments.

At Levi Strauss, for example, workers often told former CEO Roger Sant that they felt they couldn't do something because "*They* wouldn't like it." When asked who "they" were, workers had a hard time saying; nevertheless, the workers felt that they did not have the authority or responsibility to initiate changes. Sant started a "Theybusters" campaign to renegotiate authority and responsibility relationships so that workers and managers could take on new responsibilities.[17] The solution involved decentralizing authority so that employees at low levels in the hierarchy had authority to decide on issues within their control. The issues of how much to centralize or decentralize the authority to make decisions offers a basic design challenge for all organizations.

Centralization versus Decentralization of Authority

Authority gives one person the power to hold other people accountable for their actions and the right to make decisions about the use of organizational resources that they will be held accountable for.

As we saw in the B.A.R. and Grille example, vertical differentiation involves choices about how to distribute authority. But even when a hierarchy of authority exists, the problem of how much decision-making authority to delegate to each level must be resolved.

It is possible to design an organization in which managers at the top of the hierarchy have all power to make important decisions. Subordinates take orders from the top, are accountable for how well they obey those orders, and have no authority to initiate new actions or use resources for other purposes that they may believe are important. When the authority to make important decisions is retained solely by managers at the top of the hierarchy, authority is said to be highly **centralized**.[18] By contrast, when the authority to make important decisions about organizational resources and to initiate new projects is delegated to managers at all levels in the hierarchy, authority is highly **decentralized**.

Centralized
Organizational setup whereby the authority to make important decisions is retained by managers at the top of the hierarchy.

Decentralized
An organizational setup whereby the authority to make important decisions about organizational resources and to initiate new projects is delegated to managers at all levels in the hierarchy.

Each alternative has certain advantages and disadvantages. The advantage of centralization is that it lets top managers coordinate organizational activities and keep the organization focused on its goals. Centralization becomes a problem, however, when top managers become overloaded and so involved in operational decision making about day-to-day resource issues (such as hiring people and obtaining inputs) that they have no time for long-term strategic decision making about future organizational activities (such as deciding on the best strategy to compete globally).

The advantage of decentralization is that it promotes flexibility and responsiveness by allowing lower-level managers or employees to make on-the-spot decisions. Managers remain accountable for their actions but have the opportunity to assume greater responsibilities and take potentially successful risks. Also, when authority is decentralized, managers can make important decisions that allow them to demonstrate their personal skills and competencies and may be more motivated to perform well for the organization. The downside of decentralization is that if so much authority is delegated that managers at all levels can make their own decisions, planning and coordination become very difficult and the company may lose control of its decision-making process. Organizational Insight 4.3 looks at the centralization issue at Nortel Networks.

So is it best to centralize or decentralize authority? It actually depends on the situation, as the following two examples illustrate. In 1998, the United Way was suffering from a public perception that it was spending too much of the donations it received on itself and not enough for the needy people it was set up to serve. The solution? It called in management consultants who recommended that the best way to save money and increase efficiency was to reduce the number of local organizations, and centralize many business functions such as data processing, marketing, and wealthy donor programs. However, many local organizations then became concerned that they would receive a smaller share of donations. To date the United Way is still working out the right balance between centralization and decentralization.[19]

To reduce disposal costs and save money, managers at a waste-management plant decided to deliberately turn off the plant's pollution-monitoring equipment. Soon after this decision was made, a container of chemicals exploded, and the company's managers were also accused of mislabelling up to a hundred barrels of hazardous waste to avoid disposal costs. Although top managers blamed local management for these problems and denied any knowledge of the situation, the decentralized management style of the company was blamed for the problems. According to former company managers, top managers took no interest in the plant's operations and put local management under intense pressure to reduce costs. The combination of decentralized control and bottom-line pressure led to the problems that occurred. The plant's top managers claimed that the organization's attitude was "Don't tell us what's going on; just keep turning out the profit."[20]

As these examples suggest, the design challenge for managers is to decide on the correct balance between centralization and decentralization of decision making in an organization. If authority is too decentralized, managers have so much freedom that they can pursue their own functional goals and objectives at the expense of the organization's. On the other hand, if authority is too centralized and top management makes all important organizational decisions, managers lower down in the hierarchy

ORGANIZATIONAL INSIGHT 4.3

Centralize or Decentralize: Adopting a Customer-Centric Approach to Structure at Nortel[21]

The past few years have been difficult ones for Nortel Networks. Once an acknowledged Canadian giant on the international telecommunications scene, sales of its networking equipment topped $30 billion in 2000 and the company boasted 95 000 employees worldwide. Nortel weathered the global collapse of the telecom market but that required slashing its workforce by some 65 000. Shortly thereafter, the company was hit with back-to-back financial reporting scandals, leading to the eventual dismissal of several of its most senior executives, including the chief financial officer, corporate controller, and president and CEO. As a result of the scandals, the company was required to reissue three years of financial statements. In February of 2005, it released its 2003 statements, revealing it had made a profit of $434 million, down from the $732 million it had initially reported, thereby significantly reducing the bonus amounts to be awarded to senior executives.

When companies are faced with such crises and want to try to engineer a comeback, one common strategy is to restructure the organization. In Nortel's case, that meant taking a close look at the organization's existing configuration, determining what needed to be changed and developing a new operating structure.

On August 19, 2004, Nortel's new president and CEO, Bill Owens, announced a more centralized configuration, saying the company's "streamlined organizational structure" would "improve alignment with enterprise and carrier customers." Essentially, what Nortel did was to collapse its four business units into two larger groups. The company's wireline, wireless, and optical businesses—the three lines of business that service the carrier companies such as Bell Canada, Verizon, and MCI that allow customers to connect to telecommunications networks—were combined into the carrier networks business unit. The fourth unit, enterprise, remained a stand-alone operation, providing large corporate or institutional customers, such as banks, hospitals, and universities, with their own networking solutions.

The move to consolidate the carrier businesses is seen by some as a reflection of Nortel's realization that while it was segmenting the company based on technology, its customers were not. Many customers perceived Nortel as one organization capable of supplying a variety of telecommunications solutions to meet their needs, and they wanted one primary point of contact within the organization. By reorganizing itself into business units reflective of customer needs and setting up employee teams to service its customer accounts, Nortel is making its structure more customer-focused. Its new structure also seems to more accurately reflect the evolution of the telecom industry into one that is geared to developing customer solutions that work across all types of networks and with any kind of communications device.

So, the new structure is said to make more sense from a customer perspective and also in terms of the future prospects for the industry. There are anticipated company benefits as well, with Nortel saying it expects its new "carrier-focused structure" will help streamline internal operations, reduce redundancies, and ultimately lower costs. The centralized corporate strategy and corporate marketing functions, which were created at the same time, are being positioned as a move that will also help the company look at the customer marketplace more holistically. With the marketing and strategy functions operating at the overall company level, Nortel can look at its businesses overall and identify where the best opportunities exist for growth and profitability.

become afraid to make new moves and lack the freedom to respond to problems as they arise in their own groups and departments. The ideal situation is a balance between centralization and decentralization of authority so that middle and lower managers who are at the scene of the action are allowed to make important decisions, and top managers' primary responsibility becomes managing long-term strategic decision making. The result is a good balance between long-term strategy making and short-term flexibility and innovation as lower-level managers respond quickly to problems and changes in the environment as they occur.

Why were the Levi Strauss managers so reluctant to take on new responsibilities and assume extra authority? A previous management team had centralized authority so that it could retain day-to-day control over important decision making. The company's performance suffered, however, because in spending all their time on day-to-day operations, top managers lost sight of changing customer needs and evolving trends in the clothing industry. The new management team that took over in the 1990s recognized the need to delegate authority for operational decision making to lower-level managers so that top management could concentrate on long-term strategic decision making. Consequently, top management decentralized authority until they believed they had achieved the correct balance.

As noted earlier, the way managers and employees behave in an organization is often a direct result of decisions made about how the organization is to operate. Managers who want to discourage risk taking and to maximize control over subordinates' performance centralize authority. Managers who want to encourage risk taking and innovation decentralize authority. In the armed forces, for example, the senior commanders generally wish to restrict the degree of initiative permissible for lower-level officers. This is necessary, for the armed forces often function in a dangerous and complex environment in which effective coordination of organizational operations is essential. If initiatives at lower levels are not carefully controlled, the interdependence of operations could be lost, and coordination of activities could suffer, thus exposing various elements in the organization to unacceptable levels of danger with little chance of operational success. Consequently, the armed forces have a highly centralized decision-making system that operates by strict rules and with a well-defined hierarchy of authority. By contrast, high-tech companies generally decentralize authority because decentralization encourages creativity of design, product innovation, and entrepreneurial risk taking.

Decisions about how to distribute decision-making authority in an organization usually change as the organization changes—that is, as it grows and differentiates itself. How to balance authority is not a design decision that can be made once and forgotten; it must be made on an ongoing basis and is one part of the managerial task. We examine this issue in more detail in Chapters 5 and 6.

BALANCING STANDARDIZATION AND MUTUAL ADJUSTMENT

Design Challenge 4 People in this organization pay too much attention to the rules. Whenever I need somebody to satisfy an unusual customer request or need real quick service from another function, I can't get it because no one is willing to bend or break the rules.

Written rules and standard operating procedures (SOPs) and unwritten values and norms help to coordinate or control behaviour and activities in organizations. They specify how an employee is to perform his or her organizational role, and they set forth the tasks and responsibilities associated with that role. Many companies, however, complain that employees tend to follow written and unwritten guidelines too rigidly instead of adapting them to the needs of a particular situation. Strictly following rules may stifle innovation; rules specifying how decisions are to be made leave no room for creativity and imaginative responses to unusual circumstances. As a result, decision making becomes inflexible, innovation is stifled, and organizational performance suffers.

IBM, for example, was traditionally a company respected for being close to its customers and responsive to their needs. But as IBM grew, it standardized responses to customers' requests, and its sales force was instructed to sell certain kinds of machines to certain kinds of customers, regardless of what the customer needed.[22] Standardizing operations had become more important than giving customers what they wanted. Moreover, internal communication among IBM's divisions and functions was increasingly conducted in accordance with formal rules rather than by relatively informal direct contact. These rigid patterns of communication slowed product development and ultimately resulted in dissatisfied customers.

The challenge facing all organizations, large and small, is to design a structure that achieves the right balance between standardization and mutual adjustment. **Standardization** is conformity to specific models or examples—defined by sets of rules and norms—that are considered proper in a given situation. Standardized decision-making and coordination procedures make people's actions predictable in certain circumstances.[23] **Mutual adjustment** is the process through which people use their judgment rather than standardized rules to address problems, guide decision making, and promote coordination. The right balance makes some actions predictable so that basic organizational tasks and goals are achieved, yet it gives employees the freedom to behave flexibly so that they can respond to new and changing situations creatively.

Standardization
Conformity to specific models or examples—defined by sets of rules and norms—that are considered proper in a given situation.

Mutual adjustment
The compromise that emerges when decision making and coordination are evolutionary processes and people use their judgment rather than standardized rules to address a problem.

Formalization
The use of written rules and procedures to standardize operations.

Formalization: Written Rules

Formalization is the use of written rules and procedures to standardize operations.[24] In an organization in which formalization and standardization are extensive—for example, the military, a hospital, or FedEx—everything is done "by the book." There is no room for mutual adjustment; rules specify how people are to perform their roles and how decisions are to be made, and employees are accountable for following the rules. Moreover, most employees have little or no authority to break the rules. A high level of formalization typically follows from centralization of authority. A low level of formalization implies that coordination is the product of mutual adjustment among people across organizational functions and that decision making is a dynamic process in which employees apply their skills and abilities to respond to change and solve problems. Mutual adjustment typically follows from decentralization of authority because employees must have the authority to commit the organization to certain actions when they make decisions.

In the 1990s IBM began fostering mutual adjustment to increase the flexibility of its decision making.[25] In five years, IBM underwent four major structural reorganizations designed to make the organization less formalized and more decentralized. IBM has used information technology (IT) to promote its new decentralized global strategy and is performing at a higher level than previously.

Rules
Formal, written statements that specify the appropriate means for reaching desired goals.

Socialization: Understood Norms

Rules are formal, written statements that specify the appropriate means for reaching desired goals. As people follow rules, they behave in accordance with certain specified principles. **Norms** are standards or styles of behaviour that are considered typical for a group of people. People follow a norm because it is a generally agreed-upon standard for behaviour. Many norms arise informally as people work together over time. In some organizations it is the norm that people take an hour and a quarter for lunch, despite a formally specified one-hour lunch break. Over time, norms become part of peoples' way of viewing and responding to a particular situation. They reflect the "taken-for-granted" nature of "how we do things around here."

Norms
Standards or styles of behaviour that are considered acceptable or typical for a group of people.

Although many organizational norms—such as always behaving courteously to customers and leaving the work area clean—promote organizational effectiveness, many others do not. Studies have shown that groups of managers or employees can develop norms that actually reduce performance. Several studies have found that workers can directly control the pace or speed at which work is performed by imposing informal sanctions on workers who break the informal norms governing behaviour in a work group. A worker who works too quickly (above group productivity norms) is called a "ratebuster," and a worker who works too slowly (below group norms) is called a "chiseller."[26] Having established a group norm, workers actively enforce it by physically and emotionally punishing violators.

This process occurs at all levels in the organization. Suppose a group of middle managers has adopted the norm of not rocking the organizational boat. A new manager who enters the picture will soon learn from the others that rocking the boat doesn't pay, or the other managers will find ways to punish the new person for violating the norm and trying to rock the boat—even if a little shaking up is what the organization really needs. Even a new manager who is relatively high in the hierarchy often has great difficulty in changing the informal norms of the organization.

The taken-for-granted way in which norms affect behaviour has another consequence for organizational effectiveness. We noted in the Levi Strauss example that even when an organization changes formal work rules, the behaviour of people does not necessarily change as quickly. Why is behaviour rigid when rules change? The reason is that rules may be internalized and become part of a person's psychological makeup so that external rules become internalized norms. When this happens, it is very difficult for people to break a familiar rule and follow a new rule. They slip back into the old way of behaving—their old work habits. Consider, for example, how difficult it is to keep new resolutions and break bad habits.[27]

Paradoxically, an organization often wants members to change and adopt a particular set of corporate norms and values. IBM and Intel, for example, cultivate technical and professional norms and values as a means of coordinating and standardizing the behaviour of highly skilled organizational members. However, once norms are established, they may be very difficult to change. And when the organization wants to pursue new goals and foster new norms, people find it difficult to alter their behaviour. There is no easy solution to this problem. At Levi Strauss, organizational members had to go through a major period of relearning before they understood that they did not need to apply the old set of internalized norms. IBM underwent major upheavals to unlearn its old, conservative norms and IT helped it develop new ones that encouraged innovation and responsiveness to customers.

The name given to the process by which organizational members learn the norms of an organization and internalize these unwritten rules of conduct is **socialization**.[28] In general, organizations can encourage the development of *standardized* responses or *innovative* ones. These issues are examined in more detail in Chapter 7.

Socialization
The process by which organizational members learn the norms of an organization and internalize these unwritten rules of conduct.

Standardization versus Mutual Adjustment

The design challenge facing managers is to find a way of using rules and norms to standardize behaviour while at the same time allowing for mutual adjustment to provide employees with the opportunity to discover new and better ways of achieving organizational goals. Managers facing the challenge of balancing the need for standardization against the need for mutual adjustment need to keep in mind that, in general, people at higher levels in the hierarchy and in functions that perform complex, uncertain tasks rely more on mutual adjustment than on standardization to coordinate their actions. For example, an organization wants its accountants to follow standard practices in performing their tasks, but in R&D the organization may want to encourage risk taking that leads to innovation. Many of the integrating mechanisms discussed earlier, such as task forces and teams, can increase mutual adjustment by providing an opportunity for people to meet and work out improved ways of doing things. In addition, an organization can emphasize that rules are not necessarily set in stone but are just convenient guidelines for getting work done. Managers can also promote norms and values that emphasize change rather than stability. For all organizational roles, however, the appropriate balance between these two variables is one that promotes creative and responsible employee behaviour as well as organizational effectiveness, as the experience of Amazon.com suggests (see the Focus on New Information Technology box).

FOCUS ON NEW INFORMATION TECHNOLOGY

Amazon.com, Part 3

How did Jeff Bezos address these design challenges, given his need to create a structure to manage an e-commerce business, which operated through the Internet and never saw its customers, but whose mission was to provide customers great selection at low prices? Since the success of his venture depended upon providing high-quality customer responsiveness, it was vital that customers found Amazon.com's 1-Click (SM) information system Internet software easy and convenient to use and his service reliable. So his design choices were driven by the need to ensure his software linked customers to the organization most effectively.

First, he quickly realized that customer support was the most vital link between customer and organization, so to ensure good customer service he decentralized control and empowered his employees to find a way of meeting customers' needs quickly. Second, realizing that customers wanted the book quickly, he moved quickly to develop an efficient distribution and shipping system. Essentially, his main problem was handling inputs into the system (customer requests) and outputs (delivered books). So, he developed information systems to standardize the work or throughput process to increase efficiency, but also encouraged mutual adjustment at the input or customer end to improve customer responsiveness—employees were able to manage exceptions such as lost orders or confused customers as the need arose. (Note that Amazon's information systems also play the dominant role in integrating across functions in the organization; they provide the backbone for the company's value creation activities.) Third, because Amazon.com employs a relatively small number of people—about 2500 worldwide—Bezos was able to make great use of socialization to coordinate and motivate his employees. All Amazon.com employees are carefully selected and socialized by the other members of their functions so that they quickly learn their organizational roles and—most important—Amazon's important norm of providing excellent customer service. Finally, to ensure Amazon.com's employees are motivated to provide the best possible customer service, Bezos gives all employees stock in the company. Employees currently own 10 percent of their company. Amazon.com's rapid growth suggests that Bezos has designed an effective organizational structure.

MANAGERIAL IMPLICATIONS

The Design Challenges

1. To see whether there is enough integration between your department and the departments that you interact with the most, create a map of the principal integrating mechanisms in use. If there is not enough integration, develop new integrating mechanisms that will provide the extra coordination needed to improve performance.
2. Determine which levels in the managerial hierarchy have responsibility for approving which decisions. Use your findings to decide how centralized or decentralized decision making is in your organization. Discuss your conclusions with your peers, subordinates, and superior to ascertain whether the distribution of authority best suits the needs of your organization.
3. Make a list of your principal tasks and role responsibilities, and then list the rules and SOPs that specify how you are to perform your duties. Using this information, decide how appropriate the rules and SOPs are, and suggest ways of changing them so that you can perform more effectively. If you are a manager, perform this analysis for your department to improve its effectiveness and to make sure the rules are necessary and efficient.
4. Be aware of the informal norms and values that influence the way members of your work group or department behave. Try to account for the origin of these norms and values and the way they affect behaviour. Examine whether they fulfill a useful function in your organization. If they do, try to reinforce them. If they do not, develop a plan for creating new norms and values that will enhance effectiveness.

MECHANISTIC AND ORGANIC ORGANIZATIONAL STRUCTURES

Each design challenge has implications for how an organization as a whole and the people in the organization behave and perform. Useful concepts for addressing the way in which management's responses to the challenges collectively influence how an organizational structure works are the concepts of mechanistic structure and organic structure.[29] The design choices that produce mechanistic and organic structures are contrasted in Figure 4-7 and discussed below.

Mechanistic Structures

Mechanistic structures are designed to induce people to behave in predictable, accountable ways. Decision-making authority is centralized, subordinates are closely supervised, and information flows mainly in a vertical direction down a clearly defined hierarchy. In a mechanistic structure, the tasks associated with a role are also clearly defined. There is usually a one-to-one correspondence between a person and a task. Figure 4-8A depicts this situation. Each person is individually specialized and knows exactly what he or she is responsible for, and behaviour inappropriate to the role is discouraged or prohibited.

Mechanistic structures Structures that are designed to induce people to behave in predictable, accountable ways.

At the functional level, each function is separate, and communication and cooperation among functions are the responsibility of someone at the top of the hierarchy. Thus, in a mechanistic structure, the hierarchy is the principal integrating mechanism both within and between functions. Because tasks are organized to prevent miscom-

Mechanistic structures result when an organization makes these choices.	Organic structures result when an organization makes these choices.
• Individual Specialization Employees work separately and specialize in one clearly defined task.	• Joint Specialization Employees work together and coordinate their actions to find the best way of performing a task.
• Simple Integrating Mechanisms Hierarchy of authority is clearly defined and is the major integrating mechanism.	• Complex Integrating Mechanisms Task forces and teams are the major integrating mechanisms.
• Centralization Authority to control tasks is kept at the top of the organization. Most communication is vertical.	• Decentralization Authority to control tasks is delegated to people at all levels in the organization. Most communication is lateral.
• Standardization Extensive use is made of rules and SOPs to coordinate tasks, and work process is predictable.	• Mutual Adjustment Extensive use is made of face-to-face contact to coordinate tasks, and work process is relatively unpredictable.

FIGURE 4-7
How the Design Challenges Result in Mechanistic or Organic Structures.

munication, the organization does not need to use complex integrating mechanisms. Tasks and roles are coordinated primarily through standardization. Formal written rules and procedures specify role responsibilities, and standardization (together with the hierarchy) is the main means of organizational coordination. Given this emphasis on the vertical command structure, the organization is usually very status conscious, and norms of "protecting one's turf" are common. Promotion is normally steady but slow, usually strongly tied to performance. One's progress in the organization can be charted for years to come. Because of its relative rigidity, a mechanistic structure is best suited to organizations that face stable, unchanging environments.

Organic Structures

Organic structures Structures that promote flexibility, so people initiate change and can adapt quickly to changing conditions.

Organic structures are at the opposite end of the organizational design spectrum from mechanistic structures. **Organic structures** promote flexibility, so people initiate change and can adapt quickly to changing conditions.

Organic structures are decentralized; that is, decision-making authority is distributed throughout the hierarchy, and people assume the authority to make decisions as organizational needs dictate. Roles are loosely defined—people perform various tasks and continually develop skills in new activities. Figure 4-8B depicts this situation. Each person performs all three tasks, and the result is joint specialization and increased productivity. Employees from different functions work together to solve problems and become involved in each other's activities. As a result, a high level of integration is needed so that employees can share information and overcome problems caused by differences in subunit orientation. The integration of functions is achieved by means of complex mechanisms like task forces and teams (see Figure 4-5, p. 117). Coordination is achieved through mutual adjustment as people and functions work out role definitions and responsibilities, and as rules and norms emerge from the ongoing interaction of organizational members.

In an organic structure, informal norms and values develop that emphasize personal competence, expertise, and the ability to act in innovative ways. Status is conferred by the ability to provide creative leadership, not by any formal position in the hierarchy. The Sony Corporation has become the successful giant it is by maintaining an organic structure. (See Organizational Insight 4.4.)

ORGANIZATIONAL INSIGHT 4.4

Sony's Magic Touch

Product engineers at Sony turn out an average of four ideas for new products every day. Despite the fact that Sony is now a huge, diversified organization employing over 115 000 employees worldwide, the company continues to lead the way in innovation in the consumer electronics industry. Why? A large part of the answer lies in the way the company uses its structure to motivate and coordinate employees. First, a policy of "self-promotion" allows Sony engineers, without notifying their supervisors, to seek out projects anywhere in the company where they feel they can make a contribution. If they find a new project to which they can make a contribution, their current boss is expected to let them join the new team. Sony has 23 business groups composed of hundreds of development teams, and this movement of people cross-pollinates ideas throughout the organization.

Sony deliberately emphasizes the lateral movement of people and ideas between design and engineering groups. The "Sony Way" emphasizes communication between groups to foster innovation and change. Sony has a corporate research department full of people in integrating roles who coordinate the efforts of the business groups and product development teams. It is their responsibility to make sure that each team knows what the others are doing, not only to share knowledge but to avoid overlap or duplication of effort. Once a year, the corporate research department organizes an in-house three-day "special event," open only to Sony employees, where each product development team can display its work to its peers.

That Sony's organic structure works is evident from the company's success in the marketplace and from the number of innovative products Sony turns out. Like many other large Japanese companies, Sony has a policy of lifetime employment, which makes it easy for its engineers to take risks with ideas and encourages the development of norms and values that support innovative efforts. Moreover, Sony rewards its engineers with promotion and more control of resources if they are successful.

Sony is hard-headed, however, when it comes to making the best use of its resources. Top management takes pains to distance itself from decision making inside a team or even a business group, so that the magic of decentralized decision making can work. But it does intervene when it sees different groups duplicating one another's efforts. For example, when Sony made a big push into computers, it reorganized the relationship among its audio, video, and computer groups so that they improved the way they coordinated new product developments.[30] Once again, however, Sony takes a lateral view of the way the organization works, and its vertical chain of command is oriented toward finding ways to decentralize authority and still make the best use of resources. This lateral approach to decision making contrasts dramatically with the old IBM's vertical, centralized product development system, in which getting a decision made was, according to one engineer, like wading through a tub of peanut butter.

FIGURE 4-8
Task and Role Relationships.

A. Individual Specialization in a Mechanistic Structure. A person in a role specializes in a specific task or set of tasks.

B. Joint Specialization in an Organic Structure. A person in a role is assigned to a specific task or set of tasks. However, the person is able to learn new tasks and develop new skills and capabilities.

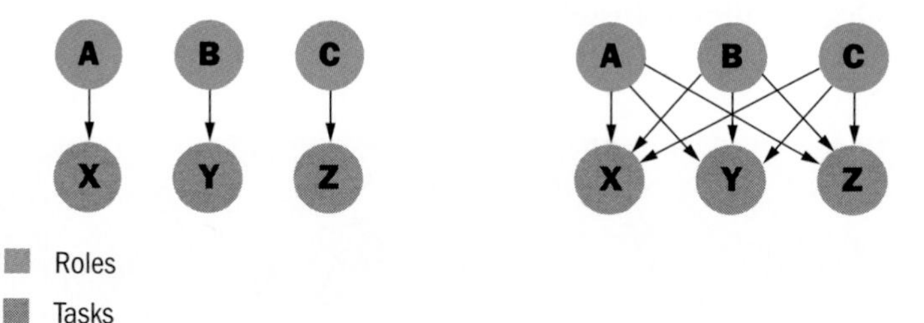

Organic and mechanistic structures have very different implications for the way people behave. Is an organic structure better than a mechanistic structure? It seems to encourage the kinds of innovative behaviours that are in vogue at present: teamwork and self-management to improve quality and reduce the time needed to get new products to market. However, would you want to use an organic structure to coordinate the armed forces? Probably not, because standardization and coordination are vital to success in a complex and dangerous environment. Would you want an organic structure in a nuclear power plant? Probably not, because a creative, novel response to an emergency might produce a catastrophe. Would you even want an organic structure in a restaurant, in which chefs take the roles of waiters and waiters take the roles of chefs and authority and power relationships are worked out on an ongoing basis? Probably not, because the traditional one-to-one correspondence of person and role allows restaurant employees to perform their roles most effectively. Conversely, would you want to use a mechanistic structure in a high-tech company like Apple Computer or Microsoft, where innovation is a function of the skills and abilities of teams of creative programmers working jointly on a project?

The Contingency Approach to Organizational Design

Contingency approach A management approach in which the design of an organization's structure is tailored to the sources of uncertainty facing an organization.

Obviously, the decision about whether to design an organic or a mechanistic structure depends on the particular situation an organization faces: the environment it confronts, its technology and the nature of the tasks it performs, and the type of people it employs. In general, the contingencies or sources of uncertainty facing an organization shape the organization's design. The **contingency approach** to organizational design tailors organizational structure to the sources of uncertainty facing an organization.[31] The structure is designed to respond to various contingencies—things that might happen and therefore must be planned for. One of the most important of these is the nature of the environment in which the organization exists within.

According to contingency theory, in order to manage its environment effectively, an organization should design its structure to fit with the environment in which the organization operates.[32] In other words, an organization must design its internal structure to control the external environment (see Figure 4-9). A poor fit between structure and environment leads to failure; a close fit leads to success. Support for contingency theory comes from two studies of the relationship between structure and the environment. These studies, conducted by Paul Lawrence and Jay Lorsch, and by Tom Burns and G. M. Stalker, are examined next.

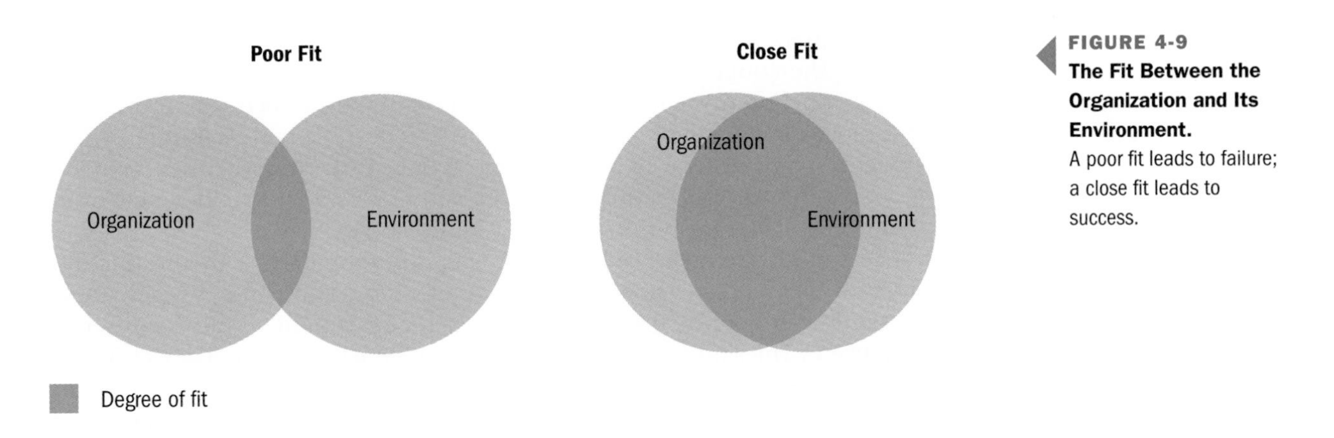

FIGURE 4-9
The Fit Between the Organization and Its Environment.
A poor fit leads to failure; a close fit leads to success.

Lawrence and Lorsch on Differentiation, Integration, and the Environment

The strength and complexity of the forces in the general and specific environments have a direct effect on the extent of differentiation inside an organization.[33] The level of differentiation, the number and size of an organization's functions, mirror the organization's needs to manage exchanges with forces in its environment (see Figure 4-10). Which function handles exchanges with suppliers? Purchasing does. Which function handles exchanges with customers? Sales and marketing. With the government and consumer organizations? Legal and public relations. A functional structure emerges, in part, to deal with the complexity of environmental demands.

Paul Lawrence and Jay Lorsch investigated how companies in different industries differentiate and integrate their structures to fit the characteristics of the industry in which they compete.[34] They selected three industries that, they argued, experienced different levels of uncertainty as measured by variables such as rate of change (dynamism) in the environment. The three industries were (1) the plastics industry,

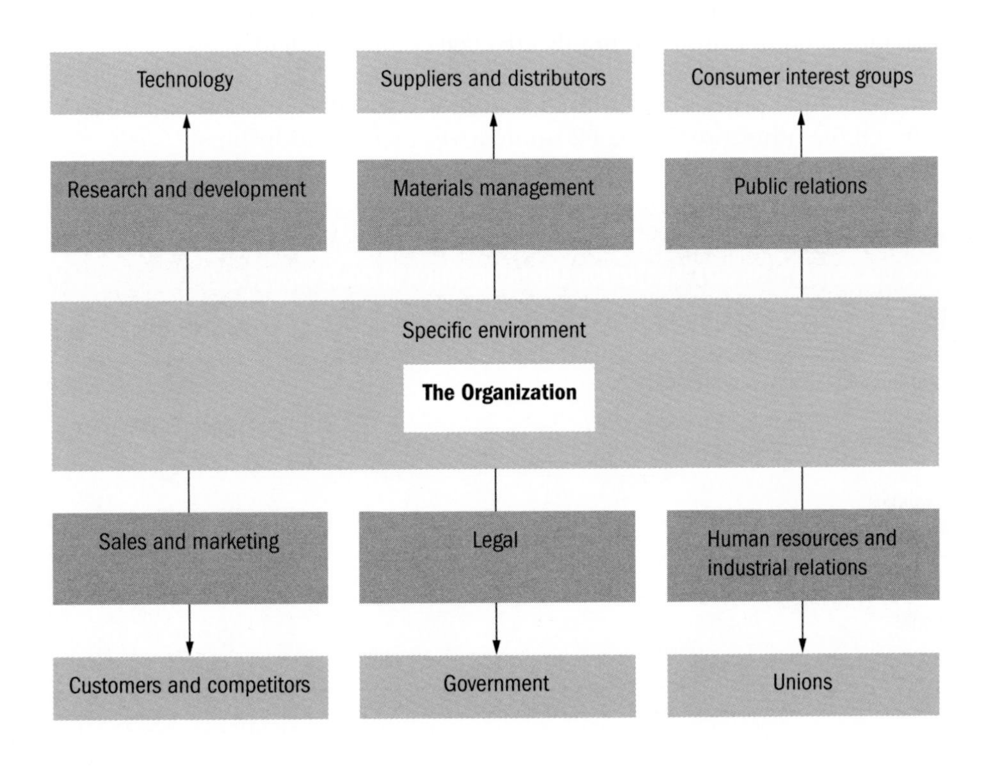

FIGURE 4-10
Functional Differentiation and Environmental Demands.
A functional structure emerges in part to deal with the complexity of demands from the environment.

which they said experienced the greatest level of uncertainty; (2) the food-processing industry; and (3) the container or can-manufacturing industry, which they said experienced the least uncertainty. Uncertainty was highest in plastics because of the rapid pace of technological and product change. It was lowest in containers, where organizations produce a standard array of products that change little from year to year. Food-processing companies were in between because, although they introduce new products frequently, the technology of production is quite stable.

Lawrence and Lorsch measured the degree of differentiation in the production, research and development, and sales departments of a set of companies in each industry. They were interested in the degree to which each department adopted a different internal structure of rules and procedures to coordinate its activities. They also measured differences in subunit or functional orientations (differences in time, goal, and interpersonal orientations). They were interested in the differences between each department's attitude toward the importance of different organizational goals, such as sales or production goals or short- and long-term goals. They also measured how companies in different industries integrated their functional activities. They found that when the environment was perceived by each of the three departments as very complex and unstable, the attitudes and orientation of each department diverged significantly. Each department developed a different set of values, perspectives, and way of doing things that suited the part of the specific environment that it was dealing with. Thus the extent of differentiation between departments was greater in companies that faced an uncertain environment than in companies that were in stable environments.

Lawrence and Lorsch also found that when the environment is perceived as unstable and uncertain, organizations are more effective if they are less formalized, more decentralized, and more reliant on mutual adjustment. When the environment is perceived as relatively stable and certain, organizations are more effective if they have a more centralized, formalized, and standardized structure. Moreover, they found that effective companies in different industries had levels of integration that matched their levels of differentiation. In the uncertain plastics industry, highly effective organizations were highly differentiated but were also highly integrated. In the relatively stable container industry, highly effective companies had a low level of differentiation, which was matched by a low level of integration. Companies in the moderately uncertain food-processing industry had levels of differentiation and integration in between the other two. Table 4-2 summarizes these relationships.

Table 4-2

THE EFFECT OF UNCERTAINTY ON DIFFERENTIATION AND INTEGRATION IN THREE INDUSTRIES

Degree of Uncertainty Variable	Plastics Industry	Food-Processing Industry	Container Industry
Environmental Variable			
Uncertainty (complexity dynamism, richness)	High	Moderate	Low
Structural Variables			
Departmental differentiation	High	Moderate	Low
Cross-functional integration	High	Moderate	Low

As Table 4-2 shows, a complex, uncertain environment (such as the plastics industry) requires that different departments develop different orientations toward their tasks (a high level of differentiation) so that they can deal with the complexity of their specific environment. As a result of this high degree of differentiation, such organizations require more coordination (a high level of integration). They make greater use of integrating roles between departments to transfer information so that the organization as a whole can develop a coordinated response to the environment. In contrast, no complex integrating mechanisms such as integrating roles are found in companies in stable environments because the organization's hierarchy, rules, and SOPs provide sufficient coordination.

The message of Lawrence and Lorsch's study was that organizations must adapt their structures to match the environment in which they operate if they are to be effective. This conclusion reinforced that of a study conducted by Burns and Stalker.

Burns and Stalker on Organic versus Mechanistic Structures and the Environment

Tom Burns and G. M. Stalker also found that organizations need different kinds of structure to control activities when they need to adapt and respond to change in the environment.[35] Specifically, they found that companies with an organic structure were more effective in unstable, changing environments than were companies with a mechanistic structure. The reverse was true in a stable environment: There, the centralized, formalized, and standardized way of coordinating and motivating people that is characteristic of a mechanistic structure worked better than the decentralized, team approach that is characteristic of an organic structure.

What is the reason for those results? When the environment is rapidly changing and on-the-spot decisions have to be made, lower-level employees need to have the authority to make important decisions—in other words, they need to be empowered. Moreover, in complex environments, rapid communication and information sharing are often necessary to respond to customer needs and develop new products.[36] When the environment is stable, in contrast, there is no need for complex decision-making systems. Managing resource transactions is easy, and better performance can be obtained by keeping authority centralized in the top-management team and using top-down decision making. Burns and Stalker's conclusion was that organizations should design their structure to match the dynamism and uncertainty of their environment. Figure 4-11 summarizes the conclusions from Burns and Stalker's and Lawrence and Lorsch's contingency studies.

McDonald's offers an interesting insight into the way a change in an organization's environment can bring about a change in its structure. (See Organizational Insight 4.5.)

Later chapters examine in detail how to choose the appropriate organizational structure to meet different strategic and technological contingencies. For now, it is important to realize that mechanistic and organic structures are ideals: They are useful for examining how organizational structure affects behaviour, but they probably do not exist in a pure form in any real-life organization. Most organizations are a mixture of the two types. Indeed, according to one increasingly influential view of organizational design, the most successful organizations are those that have achieved a balance between the two, so that they are simultaneously mechanistic and organic. An organization may tend more in one direction than in the other, but it needs to be able to act in both ways to be effective. The armed forces, for example, are well known for having a mechanistic structure in which hierarchical reporting relationships are clearly specified. However, in wartime, this mechanistic command structure allows the armed

ORGANIZATIONAL INSIGHT 4.5

McDonald's Changing Environment

McDonald's environment is changing rapidly and becoming increasingly difficult to manage. The company has been experiencing increasing problems in the early 2000s.[37] Consumer tastes are shifting as a health-conscious public is eating less beef and less fat. Environmentalists are attacking the packaging that McDonald's uses. Competitors are becoming more numerous and are seizing McDonald's customers. McDonald's has been searching for ways to increase its control of an environment that is becoming poorer, more complex, and less predictable.

At the centre of its new approach is a dramatic change in McDonald's view of its domain. In the past, at the heart of McDonald's were its standardized production operation and its mechanistic structure based on formalization, which together ensured that burgers and fries served in London and Moscow tasted and looked the same as burgers and fries served in Vancouver, Calgary, Ottawa, or Halifax. The operations manual for the kitchen alone was 600 pages long!

New customers, however, demanded new kinds of food, so McDonald's new approach to production is based on flexibility. It has experimented with over 200 kinds of food—from barbecue to pizza to lobster—and is allowing franchisees to design a menu that appeals to local customers. For example, McDonald's restaurants in Atlantic Canada serve lobster meat sandwiches, and in Mexico, McDonald's has introduced a guacamole burger.[38] McDonald's is also allowing franchisees to design a décor to suit their location: For instance, the McDonald's on Wall Street in New York City has a grand piano.[39] Also, McDonald's has opened many different types of restaurants—for example, Wal-Mart store and air-conditioned playhouse restaurants. In addition, McDonald's is experimenting with owning different kinds of restaurants—it bought a small pizza chain in 1999 and bought Chipotle, a Mexican restaurant, and Boston Market in the late 1990s.[40]

All this flexibility placed a severe strain on McDonald's mechanistic structure. The organization was forced to develop a more organic structure to allow its 8800 restaurants to fashion their own approaches to décor and bill of fare. Moreover, it decentralized authority to managers in the regions to make the important decisions that most affected them. In the new environment, the name of the game is flexibility and quick response to changes in customers' needs and competitors' moves. Nevertheless, McDonald's also needs to maintain the standards of quality and cleanliness that are among its claims to fame; thus it needs the centralized control that has always been the key to the operation of its structure. Managing a more complex environment requires a more complex structure.

forces to become organic and flexible as they respond to the uncertainties of the quickly changing battlefield. Similarly, an organization may design its structure so that some functions (such as manufacturing and accounting) act in a mechanistic way and others (marketing or R&D) develop a more organic approach to their tasks. To achieve the difficult balancing act of being simultaneously mechanistic and organic, organizations need to make appropriate choices (see Figure 4-7, p. 128). Wal-Mart's managers have been better able than McDonald's to achieve this balance. (See Organizational Insight 4.6.)

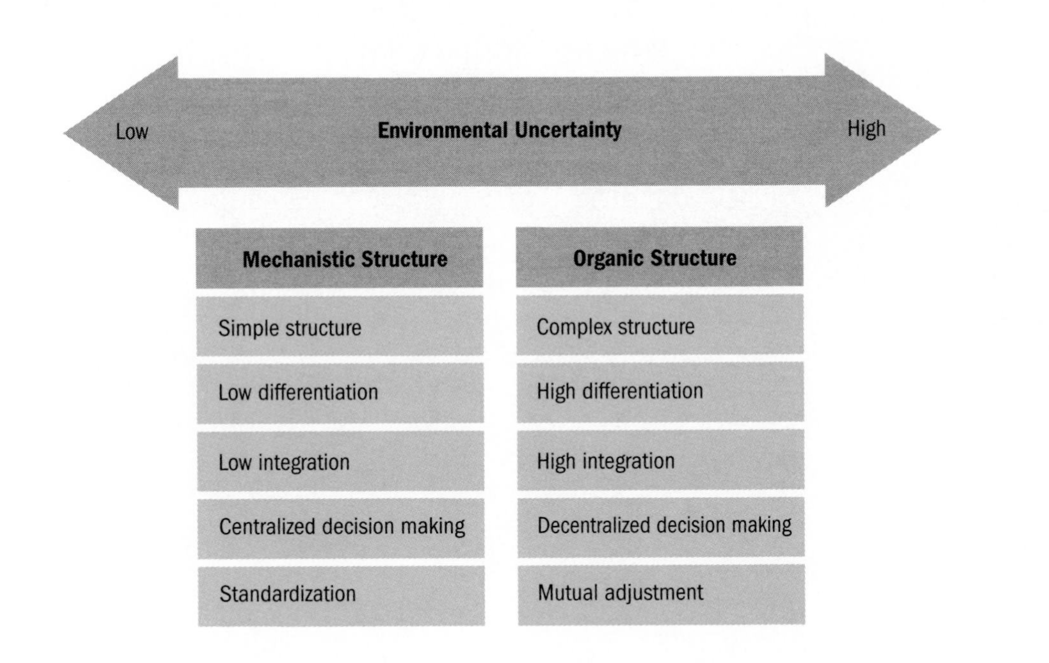

FIGURE 4-11
The Relationship Between Environmental Uncertainty and Organizational Structure.
Studies by Lawrence and Lorsch and by Burns and Stalker indicate that organizations should adapt their structure to reflect the degree of uncertainty in their environment. Companies with a mechanistic structure tend to fare best in a stable environment. Those with an organic structure tend to fare best in an unstable, changing environment.

As this example suggests, Wal-Mart has achieved the difficult balancing act of being mechanistic and organic simultaneously. It is now trying to achieve this same success at a global level. In the next three chapters, we look in more detail at the issues involved in designing organizational structure and culture to improve organizational effectiveness.

ORGANIZATIONAL INSIGHT 4.6

Wal-Mart's Race to the Top

Phenomenal growth has made Wal-Mart the largest and most profitable retailer in the world. While Sears and Kmart have been struggling and failing, Wal-Mart has been earning record profits and opening new kinds of stores at a rapid rate. Analysts attribute the company's success to the way the organization controls and coordinates activities. The efficiency of its store operations impacts very highly on Wal-Mart's effectiveness as a retailer. To control store operations, Wal-Mart has created a vertical operating structure based on a clear and precise definition of authority and responsibility. Each store is run by a manager, three assistant managers, 15 department heads, and the employees under each department head. Inside each store, decision making is highly centralized at the store-manager level. Moreover, store operations are highly standardized, and each store manager uses the same book of rules and procedures and the same accounting standards to operate each store. Thus the performance of all stores can be directly compared.

Each store manager reports to a district manager who is in charge of about a dozen stores. District managers, in turn, report to regional vice presidents, who oversee the work of three or four district managers. Regional vice presidents report to the vice president of operations. District and regional managers frequently visit various Wal-Mart stores to learn what is happening at the store level. They take the information back to top management who sit down regularly to plan a sales campaign for the whole organization. This system allows managers to monitor store operations closely and to intervene and take corrective action if necessary.

Wal-Mart is not just centralized and standardized, however. Mutual adjustment and decentralization of authority are also important parts of its design philosophy. Wal-Mart's approach is based on mutual adjustment as managers scour the country to find innovative products or ideas that they can share with stores to improve their performance. Similarly, although important decisions are made at the top of the organization, Wal-Mart encourages store managers to make quick decisions on their own to improve the success of their stores. Moreover, inside each store, the company encourages its associates to make suggestions, and it listens to what the associates have to say, incorporating their suggestions into its operating system. For example, in one year alone their suggestion program led to the adoption of over 400 suggestions, which resulted in savings of US$38 million.

As Wal-Mart has grown and become more differentiated, it has increased its use of integrating mechanisms. Managers frequently meet in task forces and teams to plan the company's future strategy. Wal-Mart also uses a sophisticated global satellite network to link and coordinate stores and to give the company quick feedback on store needs. Moreover, Wal-Mart has encouraged the development of organizational norms and values that encourage spontaneous behaviour. Its employees participate in a stock option plan (some long-term associates have received stock worth over US$400 000), sing a company song, and participate in other ways that build the Wal-Mart culture.

The continuing emphasis is on creating an organizational structure that not only allows Wal-Mart to coordinate and monitor its operations so that it can reduce costs, but allows it to change and adapt itself to meet changing conditions in the highly competitive global retailing industry.[41] Wal-Mart's core competencies in operating its organization have given the company a competitive advantage over rivals like Sears and Kmart. Although competitors have been copying many aspects of Wal-Mart's organizational design, so far they have not been able to achieve the results that make some of Wal-Mart stakeholders so happy.[42]

SUMMARY

This chapter has analyzed how managers' responses to several organizational design challenges affect the way employees behave and interact and how they respond to the organization. We have analyzed how differentiation occurs and examined three other challenges that managers confront as they try to structure their organization to achieve organizational goals. Chapter 4 has made the following main points:

1. Differentiation is the process by which organizations evolve into complex systems as they allocate people and resources to organizational tasks and assign people different levels of authority.

2. Organizations develop five functions to accomplish their goals and objectives: support, production, maintenance, adaptive, and managerial.
3. An organizational role is a set of task-related behaviours required of an employee. An organization is composed of interlocking roles that are differentiated by task responsibilities and task authority.
4. Differentiation has a vertical and a horizontal dimension. Vertical differentiation refers to the way an organization designs its hierarchy of authority. Horizontal differentiation refers to the way an organization groups roles into subunits (functions and divisions).
5. Managers confront five design challenges as they coordinate organizational activities. The choices they make are interrelated and collectively determine how effectively an organization operates.
6. The first challenge is to choose the right extent of vertical and horizontal differentiation.
7. The second challenge is to strike an appropriate balance between differentiation and integration and use appropriate integrating mechanisms.
8. The third challenge is to strike an appropriate balance between the centralization and decentralization of decision-making authority.
9. The fourth challenge is to strike an appropriate balance between standardization and mutual adjustment by using the right amounts of formalization and socialization.
10. Different organizational structures cause individuals to behave in different ways. Mechanistic structures are designed to cause people to behave in predictable ways. Organic structures promote flexibility and quick responses to changing conditions. Successful organizations strike an appropriate balance between mechanistic and organic structures.
11. Contingency theory argues that in order to manage its environment effectively, an organization should design its structure and control systems to fit with the environment in which the organization operates.

DISCUSSION QUESTIONS

1. Why does differentiation occur in an organization? Distinguish between vertical and horizontal differentiation.
2. Draw an organizational chart of the business school or college that you attend. Outline its major roles and functions. How differentiated is it? Do you think the distribution of authority and division of labour is appropriate?
3. When does an organization need to use complex integrating mechanisms? Why?
4. What factors determine the balance between centralization and decentralization, and between standardization and mutual adjustment?
5. Under what conditions is an organization likely to prefer (a) a mechanistic structure, (b) an organic structure, or (c) elements of both?

ORGANIZATIONAL THEORY IN ACTION

Practising Organizational Theory: Growing Pains

Form groups of three to five people and discuss the following scenario:

You are the founding entrepreneurs of Zylon Corporation, a fast-growing Internet software company that specializes in electronic banking. Customer demand to license your software has boomed so much that in just two years you have added over 50 new software programmers to help develop a new range of software products. The growth of your company has been so swift that you still operate informally with a loose and flexible arrangement of roles, and programmers are encouraged to find solutions to problems as they go along. Although this structure has worked well, there are signs that problems are arising.

There have been increasing complaints from employees that good performance is not being recognized in the organization and that they do not feel equitably treated. Moreover, there have been complaints about getting managers to listen to their new ideas and to act on them. A bad atmosphere seems to be developing in the company, and recently several talented employees left. You are meeting to discuss these problems.

1. Examine your organizational structure to see what might be causing these problems.
2. What kinds of design choices do you need to make to solve them?

Making the Connection #4

Find an example of a company that has been facing one of the design challenges discussed in this chapter. What problem has the company been experiencing? How has it attempted to deal with the problem?

The Ethical Dimension #4

The way an organizational structure is designed affects the way its members behave. Rules can be applied so strictly and punitively that they harm employees by, for example, increasing the stress of the job. Inappropriate norms can develop that might reduce employee incentive to work or cause employees to abuse their peers. Similarly, in some organizations, superiors use their authority to abuse and harangue employees. Think about the ethical implications of the design challenges discussed in this chapter.

1. Using the design challenges, design an organization that you think would result in highly ethical decision making; then design one that would lead to the opposite. Why the difference?
2. Do you think ethical behaviour is more likely in a mechanistic or an organic structure?

Analyzing the Organization: Design Module #4

This module attempts to get at some of the basic operating principles that your organization uses to perform its tasks. From the information you have been able to obtain, describe the aspects of your organization's structure in the assignment follows.

ASSIGNMENT

1. How differentiated is your organization? Is it simple or complex? List the major roles, functions, or departments in your organization. Does your organization have many divisions? If your organization engages in many businesses, list the major divisions in the company.
2. What core competencies make your organization unique or different from other organizations? What are the sources of the core competencies? How difficult do you think it would be for other organizations to imitate these distinctive competencies?
3. How has your organization responded to the design challenges? (a) Is it centralized or decentralized? How do you know? (b) Is it highly differentiated? Can you identify any integrating mechanisms used by your organization? What is the match between the complexity of differentiation and the complexity of the integrating mechanisms that are used? (c) Is behaviour in the organization very standardized, or does mutual adjustment play an important role in coordinating people and activities? What can you tell about the level of formalization by looking at the number and kinds of rules the organization uses? How important is socialization in your organization?
4. Does your analysis in item 3 lead you to think that your organization conforms more to the organic or to the mechanistic model of organizational structure? Briefly explain why you think it is organic or mechanistic.
5. From your analysis so far, what do you think could be done to improve the way your organization operates?

Company Profiles #4*

Choose one or more of the organizations (e.g., companies, government agencies, or nonprofit organizations) that are profiled in this chapter. Do an Internet search to get up-to-date information on each organization you have selected, and answer the following questions:

1. What does the new information tell you about the organization's current ability to create an effective organizational design?
2. How does the information compare with the earlier information provided in the text and what does that tell you about organizations (e.g., does the organization appear to be more or less able to develop effective ways of redesigning its structure than before, and how do you explain this)?

Alternative Perspectives #4

Critical, feminist and, postmodern theories of organization are challenging many of the assumptions that underlie organizational design and the associated challenges and factors. Read one or more of the following readings and list the different ways these challenges are put forward or viewed. In small groups, discuss the differences between the largely normative views in the text with the potential alternative views in the reading(s).

Reading List

Clegg, Stewart R. 1992. Postmodern Management? *Journal of Organizational Change Management.* 5(2): 31–49.

Grant, J., and Tancred-Sheriff, P. 1992. A Feminist Perspective on State Bureaucracy. In A. J. Mills, and P. Tancred-Sheriff, eds., *Gendering Organizational Analysis.* Newbury Park, CA: Sage.

Hawkins, K., and Tolzin, A. 2002. Examining the Team/Leader Interface: Baseball Teams as Exemplars of Postmodern Organizations. *Group & Organization Management,* 27(1): 97–112.

Podolny, J. M., and Page, K. L. 1998. Network Forms of Organization. *Annual Review of Sociology.* 24: 57–76.

Rhodes, C. 2001. D'Oh: The Simpsons, Popular Culture, and the Organizational Carnival. *Journal of Management Inquiry.* 10(4): 374–383.

Sundaram, A. K., and Inkpen, A. C. 2004. The Corporate Objective Revisited. *Organization Science.* 15(3): 350–363.

Webb, J. 2004. Organizations, Self-Identities and the New Economy. *Sociology: The Journal of the British Sociological Association.* 38(4): 719–738.

* The authors would like to receive information from student groups and instructors on any companies where there have been dramatic changes to the information published in this text. We would be happy to publish the best of these changes in a subsequent edition, where we will focus on changing company profiles.

CASE FOR ANALYSIS

The Boston Pizza Way![43]

For over 40 years, owners of Boston Pizza franchises have been dishing up pizza, pasta, and other casual fare to millions of customers across Canada and, more recently, the United States. During that time the parent company, Boston Pizza International, has experienced phenomenal growth—15.6 percent annually for the past 10 years alone—and its sales have topped the $370 million mark. The chain opened its 200th restaurant in 2004 and announced plans to open another 300 stores in the next six years. Headquartered in Richmond, BC, Boston Pizza is now recognized as Canada's "#1 casual dining brand," One key ingredient in the company's success is undoubtedly its approach to organizational design.

CENTRALIZATION

When you examine the structure of Boston Pizza it's clear that co-owners Jim Treliving and George Melville have adopted a highly centralized approach to their business. And they make no secret of the fact that the head office is in charge. As part of its mission statement, Boston Pizza highlights "the need to provide leadership in all areas of operations, marketing and restaurant development" and describes its approach as "hands-on."

Potential franchisees are told right off the top they have to be willing to "adhere to the Boston Pizza system." The company uses what it describes as "a rigorous, systematic approach to franchisee selection" to make sure potential franchisees will be a good fit with the organization. Potential franchise purchasers are carefully screened and then subjected to several interviews with members of the head office team. An interview with the company president and a tour of the head office is the last step in the recruitment process.

Another central group, the research and development team, is responsible for another key aspect of the business—the food. An executive chef in head office works with a team to develop and test new menu items for restaurants. They're also the folks who establish all the prices for the food in the restaurants.

Not surprisingly, the marketing for the chain is also directed centrally with national promotions. Some local store marketing is encouraged, but here again the company has corporate specialists that work with franchisees to develop those promotional plans. And lastly, to help ensure a consistent customer experience, the company also makes use of secret shoppers. That means that once or twice a year, Boston Pizza head office sends out people to eat in the various restaurants and assess them on factors such as quality and cleanliness.

INTEGRATION

A number of elements help ensure good integration of franchises with the parent organization. Special departments like finance and real estate work directly with new franchisees to line up financing for new stores and secure appropriate locations. In many cases, the corporate groups take the lead role and then bring in the franchise owner near the end of the process to finalize the arrangements.

Knowing what's selling and where is key operating information, and Boston Pizza's information technology team helps the company stay on top by providing franchisees with standard IT systems linked to corporate systems. With such integration, head office managers can keep a close watch on individual store sales and dispatch help if a restaurant seems to be going off course. These same IT systems also give franchisees access to an extranet where they can keep up to date with company news and even tap into online manuals and other corporate resources on the company site.

Another way franchises are integrated with the parent company is through their purchasing. Kitchen equipment for new stores and ongoing food purchases represent sizeable expenses and Boston Pizza uses its purchasing power to secure bulk discounts for its franchises.

STANDARDIZATION

For any restaurant chain, ensuring a consistently positive customer experience is key, and that encompasses a lot of elements, from the design and layout of the restaurant to the taste of the food to the service provided by greeters and wait staff. Boston Pizza's solution is to standardize a lot of these elements. For example, when it comes to store construction and design, the company has a project management system that it uses to direct the construction of every new restaurant. The system details everything from the approved blueprints for store designs to how to handle the tendering and awarding of the construction job to how to oversee the building's completion and opening.

To ensure meal consistency, the company uses a standard menu of 100 items and it supplies some key ingredients—like its meat sauces—to all restaurants. New franchise owners and managers have to complete a six-week training course in one of the company's corporate restaurants to learn first-hand how to cook and serve up all these items the Boston Pizza way. They also then take an additional one-week course to learn how to manage the business aspects of the franchise in keeping with Boston Pizza practices.

Does all this centralization, integration, and standardization work? For franchises, one telling statistic is the number of store closures. Boston Pizza's track record is very good with only two restaurant closures in the last six years. And sales within restaurants have been growing steadily at an average rate of 6.6 percent per year, compared with an industry average of 2.2 percent. The company's decision to go public through an income trust fund was also very well received, with one portfolio manager describing Boston Pizza as "probably the most successful of the restaurant income trusts." And to top it off, formal recognition for the company's success has come in other forms. Boston Pizza International Inc. has been named one of "Canada's 50 Best-Managed Private Companies" three years in a row, and was recently recognized with a Canadian Franchise Association Hall of Fame Award.

DISCUSSION QUESTIONS

1. How has Boston Pizza designed its franchise operations? Which functions and processes are centralized, standardized, or integrated? How have these practices contributed to Boston Pizza's success?
2. Identify at least two other restaurant chains with franchisees. What similarities and differences do you see in their approach to organizational design?

REFERENCES

1. T. Parsons, *Structure and Process in Modern Societies* (Glencoe, IL: Free Press, 1960); J. Child, *Organization: A Guide for Managers and Administrators* (New York: Harper and Row, 1977).
2. R. K. Merton, *Social Theory and Social Structure*, 2nd ed. (Glencoe, IL: Free Press, 1957).
3. D. Katz and R. L. Kahn, *The Social Psychology of Organizing* (New York: Wiley, 1966).
4. Ibid., pp. 39–47.
5. P. Selznick, "An Approach to a Theory of Bureaucracy," *American Sociological Review*, 1943, vol. VIII, pp. 47–54.
6. M. E. Porter, *Competitive Strategy* (New York: Free Press, 1980).
7. R. H. Miles, *Macro Organizational Behavior* (Santa Monica, CA: Goodyear, 1980), pp. 19–20.
8. J. Child, *Organization: A Guide for Managers and Administrators* (New York: Harper and Row, 1977).
9. P. R. Lawrence and J. W. Lorsch, *Organization and Environment* (Boston: Graduate School of Business Administration, Harvard University, 1967).
10. J. R. Galbraith, *Designing Complex Organizations* (Reading, MA: Addison Wesley, 1973).
11. B. Dumaine, "The Bureaucracy Busters," *Fortune*, 7 June 1991, p. 42.
12. Organizational Insight by Margaret McKee, based on the following sources: *www.magnaint.com*, 2004; N. E. Boudette, "BMW Steers Magna's Way," *The Globe and Mail Report on Business*, 10 September 2003, p. B10.
13. H. Mintzberg, *The Nature of Managerial Work* (Englewood Cliffs, NJ: Prentice Hall, 1973).
14. *www.whirlpool*, 2002.
15. P. P. Gupta, M. D. Dirsmith, and T. J. Fogarty, "Coordination and Control in a Government Agency: Contingency and Institutional Theory Perspectives on GAO Audits," *Administrative Science Quarterly*, 1994, vol. 39, pp. 264–284.
16. A detailed critique of the workings of bureaucracy in practice is offered in P. M. Blau, *The Dynamics of Bureaucracy* (Chicago: University of Chicago Press, 1955).
17. Dumaine, "The Bureaucracy Busters," pp. 36–50.
18. D. S. Pugh, D. J. Hickson, C. R. Hinings, and C. Turner, "Dimensions of Organizational Structure," *Administrative Science Quarterly*, 1968, vol. 13, pp. 65–91; D. S. Pugh and D. J. Hickson, "The Comparative Study of Organizations," in G. Salaman and K. Thompson, eds., *People and Organizations* (London: Longman, 1973), pp. 50–66.
19. M. Vevrka, "United Way Weighs Pros and Cons of Centralizing," *Wall Street Journal*, Jan 7, 1998, p. 2.
20. J. Flynn, "The Ugly Mess at Waste Management," *Business Week*, 13 April 1992, pp. 76–77.
21. Organizational Insight by Margaret McKee, based on the following sources: K. Brown and M. Heinzl "Nortel Board Finds Accounting Tricks

Behind '03 Profits" *Wall Street Journal* (Eastern ed.), 2 July 2004, p. A.1; Nortel Networks Provides Status Update, *www.nortelnetworks.com*, 19 August 2004.

22. C. L. Loomis, "Can John Akers Save IBM?" *Fortune,* 22 April 1992, pp. 41–56.
23. See H. Mintzberg, *The Structuring of Organizational Structures* (Englewood Cliffs, NJ: Prentice Hall, 1979) for an in-depth treatment of standardization and mutual adjustment.
24. Pugh and Hickson, "The Comparative Study of Organizations."
25. Loomis, "Can John Akers Save IBM?" p. 54.
26. M. Dalton, "The Industrial Ratebuster: A Characterization," *Applied Anthropology,* 1948, vol. 7, pp. 5–18.
27. J. Van Mannen and E. H. Schein, "Towards a Theory of Organizational Socialization," in B. M. Staw, ed., *Research in Organizational Behavior,* vol. 1 (Greenwich, CT: JAI Press, 1979), pp. 209–264.
28. G. R. Jones, "Socialization Tactics, Self-Efficacy, and Newcomers' Adjustments to Organizations," *Academy of Management Journal,* 1986, vol. 29, pp. 262–279; Van Maanen and Schein, "Towards a Theory of Organizational Socialization."
29. T. Burns and G. M. Stalker, *The Management of Innovation* (London: Tavistock, 1966).
30. T. Pruzan, "Sony Testing Campaign to Pump Up Minidiscs," *Advertising Age,* 15 July 1996, p. 6.
31. J. Pfeffer, *Organizations and Organizational Theory* (Boston: Pitman, 1982), pp. 147–162; J. Child, "Organizational Structure, Environment, and Performance: The Role of Strategic Choice," *Sociology,* 1972, vol. 6, pp. 1–22.
32. J. Pfeffer, *Organizations and Organizational Theory* (Boston: Pitman, 1982).
33. P. R. Lawrence and J. W. Lorsch, *Organization and Environment* (Boston: Graduate School of Business Administration, Harvard University, 1967).
34. Ibid.
35. T. Burns and G. M. Stalker, *The Management of Innovation.*
36. J. A. Courtright, G. T. Fairhurst, and L. E. Rogers, "Interaction Patterns in Organic and Mechanistic Systems," *Academy of Management Journal,* 1989, vol. 32, pp. 773–802.
37. J. Forster, "Thinking Outside the Burger Box," *Business Week,* 16 September 2002, pp. 20–22.
38. "McDonald's Goes Local with a Guacamole Burger," *Daily World Wire,* 16 March 1999, p. 1.
39. L. Therrien, "McRisky," *Business Week,* 21 October 1991, pp. 114–122.
40. A. Edgecliffe-Johnson, "McDonald's Buys Pizza Restaurant Chain in Midwest," *Financial Times,* 7 May 1999, p. 19.
41. T. Andreoli, "Wal-Mart Sees Potential Fortune in China Debut," *Discount Store News,* 15 July 1996, p. 1.
42. B. Saporito, "A Week Aboard the Wal-Mart Express," *Fortune,* 24 August 1992, pp. 77–84; B. Saporito, "What Sam Walton Taught America," *Fortune,* 4 May 1992, pp. 104–107.
43. Case by Margaret McKee, based on the following sources: *www.bostonpizza.com,* 2004; *www.bpincome-fund.ca,* 2004; Z. Olijnyk, "What a Slice," *Canadian Business,* 2004, vol. 77, pp. 25–27.

Designing Organizational Structure: Coordination, Communication, and Control

CHAPTER 5

Learning Objectives

The most important characteristic of an organization is its structure. An organizational structure is the way in which the activities of the members of an organization are related to each other to achieve coordination, communication, and control over people and resources. How activities are related to each other will have an important impact on effectiveness, efficiency, and how people feel about the organization. In this chapter we examine the many crucial design choices involving the vertical dimension of organizational structure—the hierarchy of authority that an organization creates to control its members.

After reading this chapter you should be able to:

1. Explain why a hierarchy of authority emerges in an organization, and the process of vertical differentiation.
2. Describe the issues involved in designing a hierarchy to coordinate and motivate organizational behaviour most effectively.
3. Discuss the way in which the design challenges discussed in Chapter 4—such as centralization and standardization—provide methods of control that substitute for the direct, personal control that managers provide and affect the design of the organizational hierarchy.
4. List the principles of bureaucratic structure and explain their implications for the design of effective organizational hierarchies.
5. Explain why organizations are flattening their hierarchies and making more use of empowered teams of employees, both inside and across different functions.

AUTHORITY: HOW AND WHY VERTICAL DIFFERENTIATION OCCURS

A basic design challenge, identified in Chapter 4, is deciding how much authority to centralize at the top of the organizational hierarchy and how much authority to decentralize to middle and lower levels. (Recall from Chapter 2 that *authority* is the power to hold people accountable for their actions and to directly influence what they do and how they do it.) But what determines the shape of an organization's hierarchy—that is, the number of levels of authority within an organization—and the span of control at each level? This question is important because the shape of an organization (evident in its organizational chart) determines how effectively the organization's decision-making and communication systems work. Decisions concerning the shape of the hierarchy and the balance between centralized and decentralized decision making establish the extent of vertical differentiation in an organization.

The Emergence of the Hierarchy

An organization's hierarchy begins to emerge when the organization experiences problems in coordinating and motivating employees.[1] As an organization grows, employees increase in number and begin to specialize, performing widely different kinds of tasks; the level of differentiation increases; and coordinating employees' activities becomes more difficult.[2] The division of labour and specialization produce motivational problems. When each person performs only a small part of a total task, it is often difficult to determine how well an individual performs and how much he or she actually contributes to the task, and it is often difficult to evaluate individual performance. Moreover, if people are cooperating to achieve a goal, it is often impossible to measure individual contributions and to reward individuals for their personal contributions. For example, if two waiters cooperate to serve tables, how does their boss know how much each contributed? If two chefs work together to cook a meal, how is each person's individual impact on food quality to be measured?[3]

An organization does two things to improve its ability to control—that is, coordinate and motivate—its members: (1) It increases the number of managers it uses to monitor, evaluate, and reward employees; and (2) it increases the number of levels in its managerial hierarchy, thereby making the hierarchy of authority taller.[4] Increasing both the number of managers and the levels of management increases vertical differentiation and gives the organization direct, face-to-face control over its members—managers *personally* control their subordinates.

Direct supervision allows managers to shape and influence the behaviour of subordinates in face-to-face interactions in the pursuit of a company's goals. Using direct supervision managers can continually question, probe, and consult with subordinates about problems or new issues they are facing to get a better understanding of the situation. It can also ensure that subordinates are performing their work more effectively by sharing information that could cause problems down the line. Personal control also creates greater opportunity for on-the-job task learning to occur and competencies to develop.

Moreover, when managers personally supervise subordinates, they lead by example and in this way can help subordinates develop and increase their own management skills. The Royal Bank of Canada, for example, places considerable importance on the manager's roles in developing subordinates and improving their chances of being promoted. It is a process directed at both men and women to ensure equity in promotion. The continual improvement of management skills inside the bank is one of its core competencies and is linked to mentoring. Managers are encouraged to learn from their employees while they are working to improve employee skills. Personal authority relationships of this kind can help to bond people into an organization and determine how well they perform.

Size and Height Limitations

Figure 5-1 shows two organizations that have the same number of employees, but one has three levels in its hierarchy and the other has seven. An organization in which the hierarchy has many levels relative to the size of the organization is a **tall organization**. An organization that has few levels in its hierarchy is a **flat organization**. The tall organization in Figure 5-1 has four more levels than the flat organization, and uses many more managers personally to direct and control members' activities. Research evidence suggests that an organization that employs 3000 people is likely to have seven levels in its hierarchy. Thus a 3000-person organization with only four levels in its hierarchy would be flat, and one with nine levels would be tall.

Figure 5-2 illustrates an interesting research finding concerning the relationship between organizational size and the height of the vertical hierarchy. By the time an organization has 1000 members, it is likely to have about four levels in its hierarchy: chief executive officer (CEO), function or department heads, department supervisors, and employees. An organization that has grown to 3000 members is likely to have

Tall organization
An organization in which the hierarchy has many levels relative to the size of the organization.

Flat organization
An organization that has few levels in its hierarchy relative to its size.

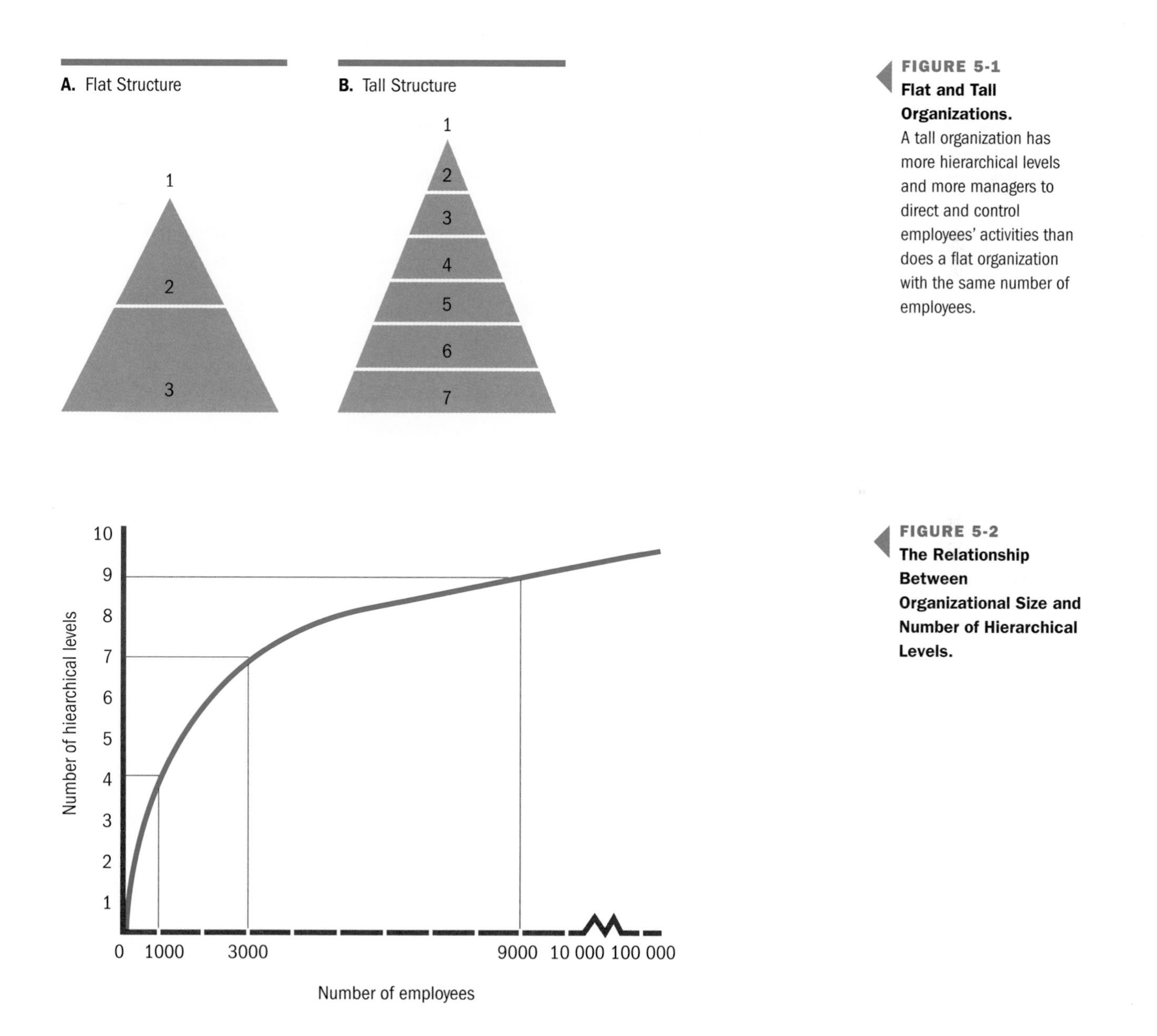

FIGURE 5-1
Flat and Tall Organizations.
A tall organization has more hierarchical levels and more managers to direct and control employees' activities than does a flat organization with the same number of employees.

FIGURE 5-2
The Relationship Between Organizational Size and Number of Hierarchical Levels.

seven levels. After that size is reached, however, something striking happens: Organizations that employ 10 000 or 100 000 employees typically do not have more than nine or ten levels in their hierarchy. Moreover, large organizations do not increase the numbers of managers at each level to compensate for the limited number of hierarchical levels.[5] Thus most organizations have a pyramid-like structure and fewer and fewer managers at each level (see Figure 5-3A), rather than a bloated structure (Figure 5-3B) in which proportionally more managers at all levels control the activities of increasing numbers of members.

In fact, research suggests that the increase in the size of the managerial component in an organization is *less than proportional* to the increase in size of the organization as it grows.[6] This phenomenon is illustrated in Figure 5-4. An increase from 2000 to 3000 employees (a 50 percent increase in organizational size) results in an increase from 300 to 400 managers (a 33 percent increase). However, an increase from 6000 to 10 000 employees (a 66 percent increase) increases the size of the managerial component by only 100 managers (from 700 to 800, a 14 percent increase).

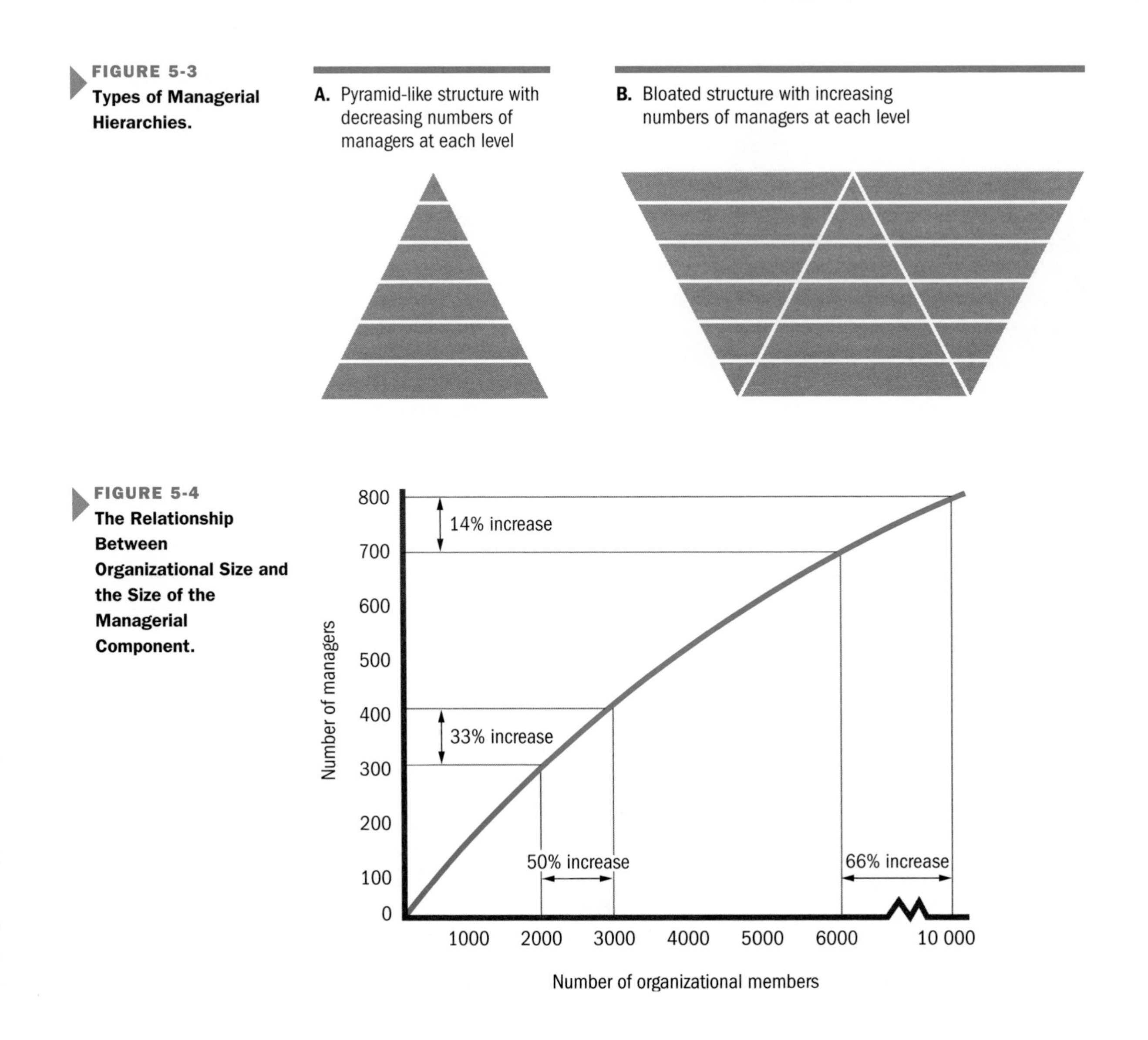

FIGURE 5-3
Types of Managerial Hierarchies.

FIGURE 5-4
The Relationship Between Organizational Size and the Size of the Managerial Component.

Why do organizations seem to actively restrict the number of managers and the number of hierarchical levels as they grow and differentiate? The answer is that many significant problems are associated with the use of tall hierarchies, including issues of morale, discrimination, personality disorders, effectiveness, and efficiency.[7]

Problems with Tall Hierarchies

Choosing the right number of managers and hierarchical levels is important because this decision directly influences organizational effectiveness. The choice affects communication, motivation, and bottom-line profitability.[8]

Communication Problems Having too many hierarchical levels may hinder communication. As the chain of command lengthens, communication between managers at the top and bottom of the hierarchy takes longer. Decision making slows, and the slowdown hurts the performance of organizations that need to respond quickly to customers' needs or the actions of competitors.[9] At RBC Capital Markets, innovative solutions are essential for success, so the company has developed a flat organizational structure; it believes that too many levels of hierarchy would hinder its ability to operate with a diverse workforce in a fast-paced, dynamic, and challenging market.[10] Similarly, when Liz Claiborne was designing the structure of her organization, she was careful to keep the hierarchy flat—four levels for 4000 employees—to maximize the organization's ability to respond to quickly changing fashion trends.

Another significant communication problem is distortion. Information becomes distorted as it flows up and down the hierarchy through many levels of management.[11] Experiments have shown that a message that starts at one end of a chain of people can become something quite different by the time it reaches the other end of the chain.

In addition, managers up and down the hierarchy may manipulate information to serve their own interests. It has been demonstrated that managers can lead others to make certain kinds of decisions by restricting the flow of information or by selectively feeding information to them.[12] When this happens, the top of the hierarchy may lose control over the bottom. Managers at low levels may also selectively transmit up the hierarchy only the information that serves their interests. A rational subordinate, for example, may decide to give to a superior only information that makes him or her or the superior look good. Again, when this happens, the top of the hierarchy may have no idea about or control over what is happening below, and the quality of decision making at all levels suffers.

Studies show that communication problems get progressively worse as the number of hierarchical levels increases. Thus organizations are wise to try to limit the growth of the hierarchy. When the number of levels surpasses seven or eight, communication problems can cause a breakdown in control and slow and unresponsive decision making, as is the case with many tall organizations. In contrast, Eagle Professional Resources has avoided this pitfall by keeping a flat organizational structure. (See Organizational Insight 5.1.)

Motivation Problems As the number of levels in the hierarchy *increases*, the relative difference in the authority possessed by managers at each level *decreases*, as does their area of responsibility. A flat organization (see Figure 5-1, p. 145) has fewer managers and hierarchical levels than a tall organization, so a flat organization's managers possess relatively more authority and responsibility than a tall organization's managers. Many studies have shown that the more authority and responsibility a person has, the more motivating is the person's organizational role, other things being equal. Thus motivation in an organization with a flat structure may be stronger than motivation in a tall organization. Also, when a hierarchy has many levels, it is easy for managers to

ORGANIZATIONAL INSIGHT 5.1

A Flat Organizational Structure at Eagle Builds Trust[13]

Eagle Professional Resources Inc. is a recruitment company contracting with organizations to arrange the employment of professionals primarily for the IT sector. Eagle was only incorporated in 1996, but the company has over 20 years experience in professional recruitment, as it was originally a division of a larger international business integration company. The Eagle of today is an employee-owned business. Home base is in Ottawa, but Eagle also has offices across Canada, from Halifax to Vancouver. Although the company originated from a highly structured organization and is spread across a vast country, one might expect the current company to have a tall organizational structure. Eagle has, in contrast, a fairly flat structure.

Eagle has no regional or branch management and all recruiters and sales staff can report directly to senior management. At the local office level, self-managing recruiting teams and sales teams meet daily to determine priorities and workloads. Team leaders consult with senior staff as may be required. The flat structure works well for Eagle. With bureaucracy at a minimum, there is a maximum sharing of information. This facilitates effective communication that avoids the sort of communication distortion that can happen with multiple layers of management and authority. This structural backdrop helps Eagle to establish and foster a strong sense of trust among organizational members—a foundation to build up a trusting milieu to gain clients' trust. It would appear that this strategy has been working well. Eagle was named one of "Canada's 50 Best-Managed Private Companies" two years in a row and had 18 consecutive profitable quarters and grown from $18 million in first-year revenues to $38 million in 2003. It is currently on track to meet its goal of $50 million in revenues in 2004 and has targeted the $100 million mark as a realistic goal in the next three years.

pass the buck and evade responsibility—actions that worsen the problem of slow decision making and poor communication.

Bureaucratic Costs Managers cost money. The greater the number of managers and hierarchical levels, the greater the bureaucratic costs—that is, the costs associated with running and operating an organization. It has been estimated that in the U. S. the average middle manager costs over US$300 000 per year in salary, bonuses, benefits, and an office. Employing a thousand excess managers, therefore, costs an organization US$300 million a year—an enormous sum that companies often belatedly recognize they do not need to pay. Because of the cost of a tall and bloated hierarchy, it is common, especially during a recession, for a company to announce that it will reduce the number of levels in its hierarchy and lay off excess employees to reduce bureaucratic costs. In 1997, for example, the Katz Group Inc., which owns 11 drugstore chains in Canada and the U.S., purchased Pharma Plus from the Oshawa Group Ltd. and turned around the ailing fortunes of the company by cutting costs and layers of management.[14]

Why do companies suddenly perceive the need to reduce their workforce drastically, thus subjecting employees to the uncertainty and misery of the unemployment line with a minimum of notice? Why do companies not have more foresight and restrict the growth of managers and hierarchical levels to avoid large layoffs? Sometimes layoffs are unavoidable, as when a totally unexpected situation arises in the organization's environment: For example, innovation may render technology obsolete or uncompetitive, or a general economic crisis may abruptly reduce demand for an organization's product. Much of the time, however, dramatic changes in employment and structure are simply the result of bad management.

Managers of an organization that is doing well often do not recognize the need to control, prune, and manage the organization's hierarchy as the organization confronts new or changing situations. Or they may see the need but prefer to do nothing. As organizations grow, managers usually pay little attention to the hierarchy; their most pressing concern is to satisfy customer needs by bringing products or services to the market as quickly as possible. As a result, hierarchical levels multiply as new people are added without much thought about long-term consequences. When an organization matures, its structure is likely to be streamlined as two or more managerial positions are combined into one and levels in the hierarchy are eliminated to improve decision making and reduce costs. The terms *restructuring* and *downsizing* are used to describe the process by which managers streamline hierarchies and lay off managers and workers to reduce bureaucratic costs. This is discussed in detail in Chapter 10, when the issue of organizational change and redesign is the focus of analysis.

The Parkinson's Law Problem

While studying administrative processes in the British Navy, C. Northcote Parkinson, a former British civil servant, came upon some interesting statistics.[15] He discovered that from 1914 to 1928 the number of ships in operation decreased by 68 percent, but the number of dockyard officials responsible for maintaining the fleet had increased by 40 percent and the number of top brass in London responsible for managing the fleet had increased by 79 percent. Why had this situation come about? Parkinson argued that growth in the number of managers and hierarchical levels is controlled by two principles: (1) "An official wants to multiply subordinates, not rivals," and (2) "Officials make work for one another."[16]

Managers in hierarchies value their status in the hierarchy. The fewer managers at their hierarchical level and the greater the number of managers below them, the bigger their "empire" and the higher their status. Not surprisingly, therefore, managers seek to increase the number of their subordinates. In turn, these subordinates realize the status advantages of having subordinates, so they try to increase the number of their subordinates, causing the hierarchy to become taller and taller. As the number of levels increases, managers spend more of their time monitoring and controlling the actions and behaviours of their subordinates and thus create work for themselves. More managers lead to more work—hence the British Navy results. Parkinson further contended that his principles apply to all hierarchies if they are not controlled. Because managers in hierarchies make work for each other, "Work expands so as to fill the time available." That is Parkinson's Law.

The Ideal Number of Hierarchical Levels: The Minimum Chain of Command

Managers should base the decision to employ an extra manager on the difference between the value added by the last manager employed and the cost of the last manager employed. However, as Parkinson noted, a person may have no second thoughts about spending the organization's money to improve his or her own position, status, and power. Well-managed organizations control this problem by simple rules—for example, "Any new recruitment has to be approved by the CEO"—that prompt upper-level managers to evaluate whether another lower-level manager or another hierarchical level is necessary. An even more general principle for designing a hierarchy is the principle of minimum chain of command.

Principle of minimum chain of command
States that an organization should choose the minimum number of hierarchical levels consistent with its goals and the environment in which it operates.

According to the **principle of minimum chain of command**, an organization should choose the minimum number of hierarchical levels consistent with its goals and the environment in which it exists.[17] In other words, the organization should be kept as flat as possible, and managers should be evaluated for their ability to control organizational activities with the smallest number of managers possible.

An organization with a flat structure will experience fewer communication, motivation, and cost problems than will a tall organization. The only reason why an organization should choose a tall structure over a flat structure is that it needs a high level of direct control or personal supervision over subordinates. Nuclear power plants, for example, typically have very tall managerial hierarchies so that managers can maintain effective supervision of operations. Because any error could produce a disaster, upper-level managers constantly oversee and cross-check the work of lower-level managers to ensure that rules and standard operating procedures are followed accurately and consistently.

In Chapter 9 we examine how factors such as technology and task characteristics make tall structures the preferred choice. Here, the issue is that organizations should strive to keep hierarchical levels to the minimum necessary to accomplish their mission. Organizational problems produced by factors such as Parkinson's Law do not satisfy any stakeholder interest, for sooner or later they will be discovered by a new management team, which will purge the hierarchy to reduce excess managers (as has happened at many companies since the 1990s, such as Algoma Steel, IBM, Nortel Networks, AOL–Time Warner, and Lucent, and is currently happening at EMI, profiled in Organizational Insight 5.2.).

Span of Control

Span of control
The number of subordinates a manager manages directly.

Organizations that become too tall inevitably experience problems. Nevertheless, an organization that is growing must control the activities of newly hired personnel; how can an organization avoid becoming too tall? One way is by increasing managers' **span of control**—the number of subordinates a manager directly manages.[18] If the span of control of each manager increases as the number of employees increases, then the number of managers or hierarchical levels does *not* increase in proportion to increases in the number of employees. Instead, each manager coordinates the work of more subordinates, and the organization substitutes an increase in the span of control for an increase in hierarchical levels.

Figure 5-5 depicts two different spans of control. Figure 5-5A shows an organization with a CEO, five managers, and ten employees; each manager supervises two people. Figure 5-5B shows an organization with a CEO, two managers, and ten employees, but Manager A supervises two people, and Manager B supervises eight people. Why does Manager A's span of control extend over only two people and Manager B's extend over eight? Or, more generally, what determines the size of a manager's span of control?

Perhaps the single most important factor limiting a manager's span of control is the manager's inability to supervise increasing numbers of subordinates adequately. It has been demonstrated that an arithmetic increase in the number of subordinates is accompanied by an exponential increase in the number of subordinate relationships that a manager has to manage.[19] Figure 5-6 illustrates this point.

The manager in Figure 5-6A has two subordinates and must manage three relationships: X, Y, and Z. The manager in Figure 5-6B has only one more subordinate

ORGANIZATIONAL INSIGHT 5.2

Using the Hierarchy to Promote Creativity at EMI

EMI is the British record company that launched the careers of the Beatles, Rolling Stones, and Garth Brooks.[20] The 105-year-old company used to be the most profitable in the industry, but during the 1990s its performance collapsed. The reason, believes Alain Levy, its new French-born CEO, is that EMI became managed by a top-heavy team of overpaid executives who lacked the entrepreneurial ability either to recognize and promote new talent or to develop their subordinates so that they would acquire that ability.

So Levy set out to shake up EMI's hierarchy and change the motivation of his top managers. Given the years of problems, he adopted a radical approach. First, he fired almost 2000 entrenched executives and eliminated three levels in the management hierarchy. Then, giving his remaining managers a greater area of responsibility, he abolished the old reward system of guaranteed bonuses based upon signing new talent. Henceforth, EMI managers were put on contracts, their performance bonuses based upon the future performance of the artists they sign up and promote. Executives whose performance seems to be slipping are put on shorter contracts; managers who can demonstrate a track record of success receive longer contracts.[21] No manager has a guaranteed position in EMI's new hierarchy forever, as was true in the old system. A manager's ability to hold a high office is a function of continuing performance. And Levy includes developing subordinates—so they acquire the entrepreneurial skills needed to run a company that depends on recognizing and promoting creative talent—as one of his managers' main responsibilities.

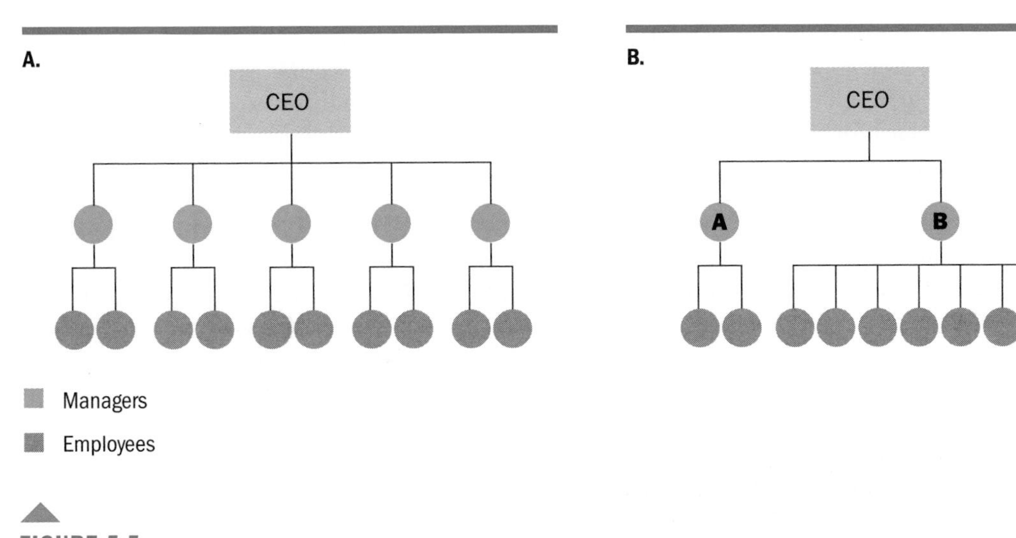

FIGURE 5-5
Spans of Control.

FIGURE 5-6
The Increasing Complexity of a Manager's Job as the Span of Control Increases.

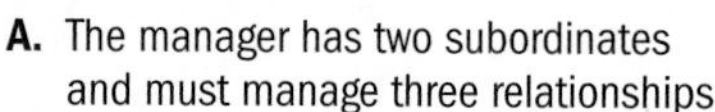

A. The manager has two subordinates and must manage three relationships

B. With the addition of just one more subordinate (for a total of three), the manager has six relationships to handle

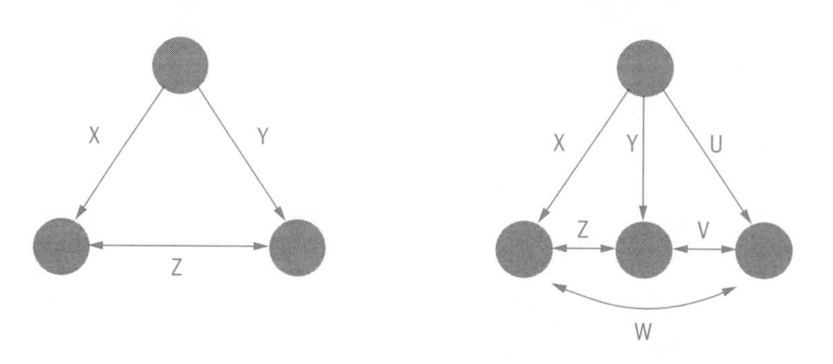

than the manager in Figure 5.6A but must manage six relationships: X, Y, and Z, as well as U, V, and W. (The number of relationships is determined by the formula $n(n-1)/2$. Thus a manager with eight subordinates, as in Figure 5-6B, has 28 relationships to manage.) If managers lose control of their subordinates and the relationships among them, subordinates will have the opportunity to follow their own goals, to coast along on the performance of other group members, or to shirk their responsibilities.

Given these problems, there seems to be a limit to how wide a manager's span of control should be.[22] If the span is too wide, the manager loses control over subordinates and cannot hold them accountable for their actions. In general, a manager's ability to directly supervise and control subordinates' behaviour is limited by two factors: the complexity and the interrelatedness of subordinates' tasks.

When subordinates' tasks are complex and dissimilar, a manager's span of control needs to be small. If tasks are routine and similar so that all subordinates perform the same task, the span of control can be widened. In mass production settings, for example, it is common for a supervisor's span of control to extend over 30 or 40 people. But in the research laboratory of a biotechnology company, supervising employees is more difficult, and the span of control is much narrower. It is sometimes argued that the span of control of a CEO should not exceed six people because of the complexity of the tasks performed by the CEO's subordinates.

When subordinates' tasks are closely interrelated, so that what one person does has a direct effect on what another person does, coordination and control are greater challenges for a manager. In Figure 5-6B, the interrelatedness of tasks means that the manager has to manage relationships V, W, and Z. When subordinates' tasks are not closely interrelated, the horizontal relationships between subordinates become relatively unimportant (in Figure 5-6B, relationships V, W, and Z would be eliminated) and the manager's span of control can be dramatically increased.

Managers supervising subordinates who perform highly complex, interrelated tasks have a much narrower span of control than managers supervising workers who perform separate, relatively routine tasks. Indeed, one of the reasons why organizations are often pictured as a pyramid is that at the upper levels the tasks are complex and interrelated, and the span of control narrows.

In summary: Together, design choices concerning the number of hierarchical levels and the span of control determine the shape of the organizational hierarchy. There are limits to how much an organization can increase the number of levels in the hierarchy, the number of managers, or the span of control. Even though a hierarchy of authority emerges to provide an organization with control over its activities, if the structure becomes too tall or too top-heavy with managers, or if managers become overloaded because they are supervising too many employees, the organization can lose control of its activities. How can an organization maintain adequate control over its activities as it grows but avoid problems associated with a hierarchy that is too tall or a span of control that is too wide?

CONTROL: FACTORS AFFECTING THE SHAPE OF THE HIERARCHY

When there are limits on the usefulness of direct personal supervision by managers, organizations have to find other ways to control their activities. Typically, organizations first increase the level of horizontal differentiation and then decide on their responses to the other design challenges discussed in Chapter 4. Keep in mind that successful organizational design requires managers to meet all of those challenges (see Figure 5-7).

Horizontal Differentiation

Horizontal differentiation leads to the emergence of specialized subunits—functions or divisions. Figure 5-8 shows the horizontal differentiation of an organization into five functions. Each triangle represents a specific function in which people perform the same kind of task.

An organization that is divided into subunits has many different hierarchies, not just one. Each distinct function, department, or division has its own hierarchy. Horizontal differentiation is the principal way in which an organization retains control over employees when it cannot increase the number of levels in the organizational hierarchy without encountering the sorts of problems discussed earlier in the chapter.

In Figure 5-8, the hierarchy of the manufacturing department has seven levels. The production manager, at level 7, reports to the CEO. In contrast, both the research

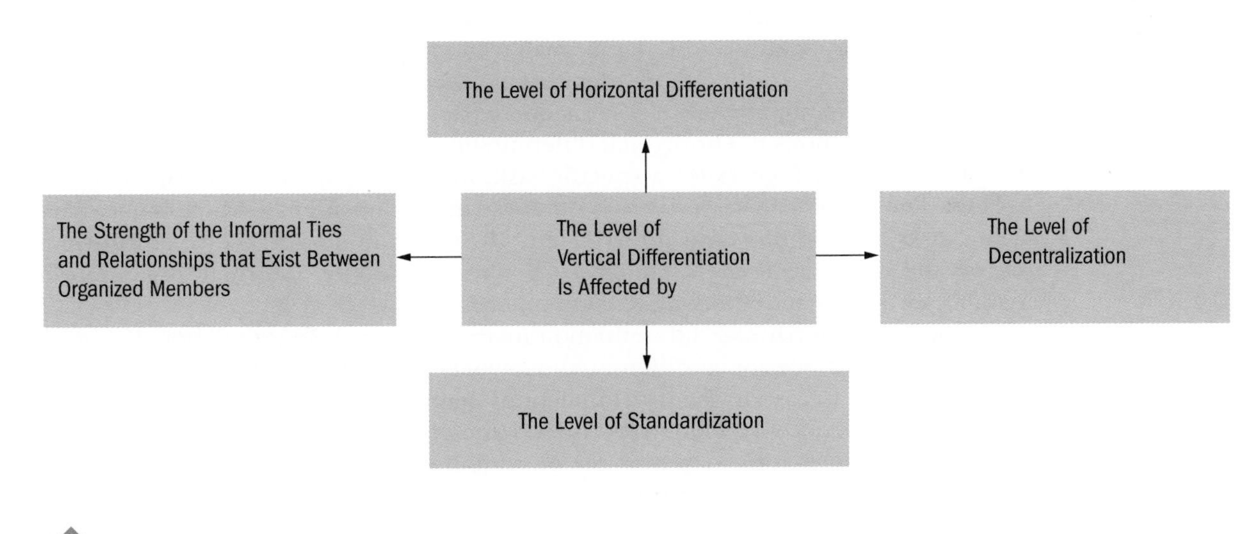

FIGURE 5-7
Factors Affecting the Shape of the Hierarchy.

FIGURE 5-8
Horizontal Differentiation into Functional Hierarchies.
The sales and R&D departments have three levels in their hierarchies; manufacturing has seven.

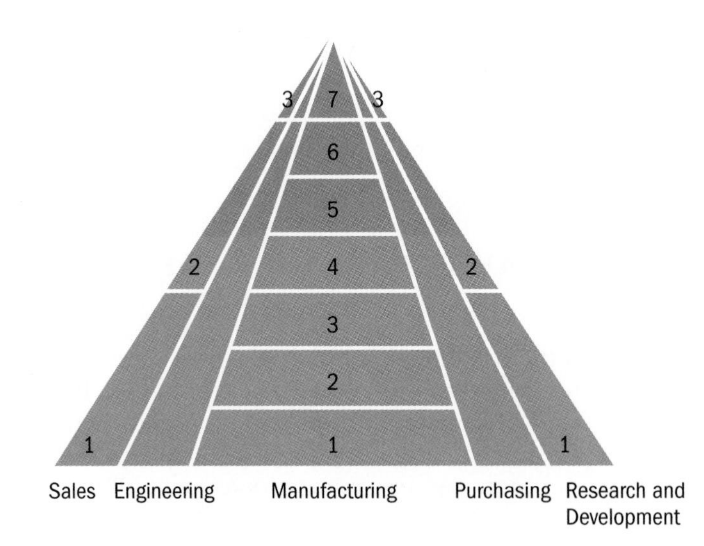

and development and the sales functions have only three levels in their hierarchies. Why? Like the organization as a whole, each function follows the principle of minimum chain of command when designing its hierarchy. Each function chooses the lowest number of hierarchical levels it can live with, given its tasks and goals.[23] The manufacturing function traditionally has many levels because management often feels the need to exert tight and close control over subordinates, and closely monitor and control costs. The sales department has fewer levels because both standardization by means of formalization and output controls are used to monitor and control salespeople; extensive supervision is not needed. The research and development function also usually has few levels, but for a different reason. Personal supervision on a continuing basis is superfluous: R&D tasks are complex, and even if managers monitor researchers, they really cannot evaluate how well the researchers are performing because years may pass before significant research projects come to fruition. In an R&D context, control is generally achieved by scientists working in small teams, where they can monitor and learn from each other. As a result, there can be yet another level of horizontal differentiation within an organization: that within a function or department.

Figure 5-9 shows the horizontal differentiation of the R&D function into project teams. Each team focuses on a specific task, but the teams' tasks are likely to be related. The use of teams is a way to keep the span of control small, which is necessary when tasks are complex and interrelated. Moreover, in an R&D setting, informal norms and values are used to standardize behaviour, and the "informal" organization is an important means of linking R&D to other functions.

Increasing horizontal differentiation increases vertical differentiation within an organization. But horizontal differentiation avoids many of the problems of tall hierarchies because it leads to the development of many subunit hierarchies, which allow the organization to remain flat. Nevertheless, the problems associated with horizontal differentiation such as the development of subunit orientations (see Chapter 4) cause additional coordination and motivation problems. Managers can control these problems by making wise choices concerning centralization, standardization, and the influence of the informal organization. (In Chapter 6 we discuss the coordination of activities between subunits.[24])

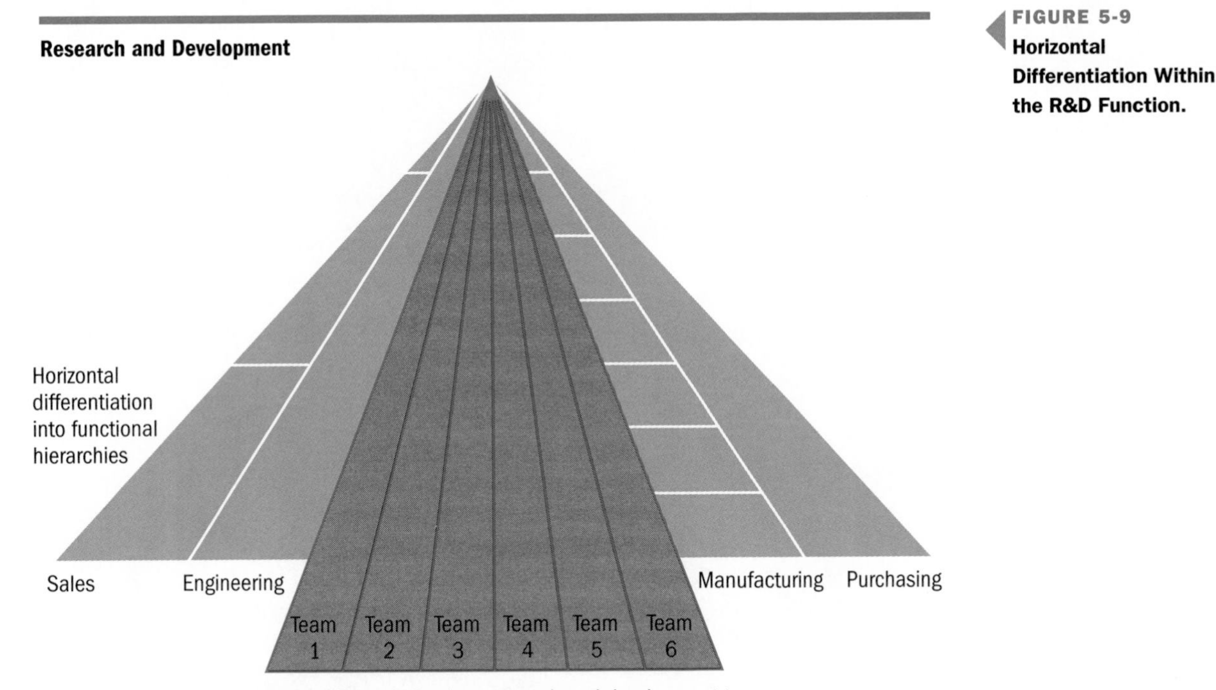

FIGURE 5-9 Horizontal Differentiation Within the R&D Function.

Centralization

As the organizational hierarchy becomes taller and the number of managers increases, communication and coordination problems grow, and soon a manager's principal task is monitoring and supervising other managers' activities. When this happens, the organization loses sight of its goals. A solution to the problem of too many managers and levels is to decentralize authority. With decentralization, less direct managerial supervision is needed. When authority is decentralized, the authority to make significant decisions is delegated to people throughout the hierarchy, not concentrated at the top. The delegation of authority to lower-level managers reduces the monitoring burden on upper-level managers and reduces the need for managers to monitor managers. Organizational Insight 5.3 illustrates how two organizations took steps to decentralize authority so that they could flatten their structures.

Almost all organizations confront similar problems sooner or later. In Canada a number of companies have developed a decentralized approach to deal with different aspects of the global environment. For example, Teknion Furniture Systems, of Downsview, Ontario, adopted a cross-functional team-based approach to deal with international competition. At the General Electric plant in Bromont, Quebec, employees are involved to a greater extent in decision making, including new hires. The traditional work of supervisors has been largely eliminated.[25]

It is perhaps appropriate that Flight Centre is a survivor in the highly competitive travel business. Like the television show *Survivor*, the secret to Flight Centre's success is a structure built around the notion of tribes. The company's 600 retail shops worldwide are managed by small regional groups, or tribes, each controlling its own hiring, training, and marketing. Each shop operates as a profit centre with a profit-sharing

ORGANIZATIONAL INSIGHT 5.3

Union Pacific Decentralizes

Union Pacific, one of the United States' biggest rail freight carriers, was experiencing a crisis. The U.S. economic boom was causing a record increase in the amount of freight that the railroad had to transport but, at the same time, the railroad was experiencing record delays in moving the freight. Union Pacific's customers were irate, complaining bitterly about the problem, and the delays were costing the company millions of dollars in penalty payments—US$150 million![26]

Why was there a problem? Because Union Pacific, in its attempt to cut costs, had developed a very centralized management approach. All the scheduling and route planning was handled centrally at its headquarters office in an attempt to promote operating efficiency. The job of regional managers was largely to ensure the smooth flow of freight through their regions. Now, recognizing that efficiency had to be balanced by the need to be responsive to customers, Union Pacific's CEO Dick Davidson announced a sweeping reorganization to the company's customers. Henceforth, regional managers were to be given the authority to make operational decisions at the level at which it was most important—field operations. Regional managers could now alter scheduling and routing to accommodate customer requests even if this raised costs. The goal of the organization was now to "return to excellent performance by simplifying our processes and becoming easier to deal with."[27] In making this decision, the company was following the lead of its competitors, most of whom had already moved to decentralize their operations, recognizing its many advantages.

arrangement for employees. The tribal system was developed to deal specifically with the dual problem of local markets and a dynamic environment.[28]

Coca-Cola Enterprises, the bottling arm of the soft-drink giant, also faced centralization problems with its organization structure. Its CEO, Summerfield Johnston, noted his company's inability to respond quickly to the changing needs of the different regions in which Coke is bottled. Johnston decided that centralized control (regional operations were controlled from the Atlanta, Georgia, head office) was hurting the bottling operations. Because of the long chain of command, many problems that the regions were experiencing were being dealt with slowly, and managers at the head office were often unaware of the problems faced by people on the front line. Moreover, the hierarchy was very expensive to operate, and Johnston believed that bureaucratic costs could be reduced at the regional level if there was more local control over marketing and production.

Johnston redesigned the management hierarchy. He fired 100 middle and top managers at company headquarters, eliminating several levels in the hierarchy. He then decentralized operations to ten regional units, one for each region, and put a strong vice president in charge of each unit. Each regional vice president was given the responsibility to streamline regional operations and cut costs.[29]

Decentralization alone may not eliminate the need for many hierarchical levels in a large and complex organization that has to control work activities between many subunits. However, it can reduce the amount of direct supervision needed *within* a subunit and can allow even a relatively tall structure to be flexible in its responses to changes in the external environment and other challenges.

Standardization

Managers can gain control over organizational activities by standardizing work activities to make them predictable. Standardization reduces the need for managers and extra levels in the hierarchy because rules and standard operating procedures *substitute* for direct supervision—that is, rules replace face-to-face contact. Organizations standardize activities by creating detailed work rules and by socializing employees to organizational norms and values. As subordinates' tasks are increasingly standardized and controlled by means of rules and norms, and the amount of supervision that is required lessens, a manager's span of control can be increased. Salespeople, for instance, are typically controlled by a combination of sales quotas that they are expected to achieve and written reports that they are required to submit after calling on their clients. Managers do not need to monitor salespeople directly because they can evaluate their performance through those two standardized output controls. Standardization also allows upper-level managers to delegate responsibility more confidently when subordinates have clearly specified procedures to follow.

In summary: We have seen that an organization can control its members and their activities in different ways, ranging from personal control by managers in the hierarchy, to control through formalization and standardization, to informal control by means of norms and values. Structuring an organization to solve control problems requires decisions about all the different methods of control. The structure of every organization reflects the particular contingencies the organization faces, so all organizations' structures are different. Nevertheless, some generalizations can be made about how organizations fashion a structure to control people and resources.

MANAGERIAL IMPLICATIONS

Authority and Control

1. Managers must control the organizational hierarchy and make sure that it matches the current needs of the organization. Periodically, managers should draw a new organizational chart of their organization or department and measure (a) the number of current employees, (b) the number of levels in the hierarchy, and (c) the size of the span of control of managers at different levels.
2. Using that information, managers should consider whether the hierarchy has grown too tall or too centralized. If they find the hierarchy has grown too tall, they should combine managerial positions and eliminate levels in the hierarchy by reassigning the responsibilities of the eliminated positions to managers in the level above or, preferably, by decentralizing the responsibilities to managers or employees in the levels below.
3. If managers find the hierarchy does not provide the control they need to maintain adequate supervision over people and resources, they should consider how to increase organizational control. They may need to add a level to the organizational hierarchy or, preferably, use an alternative means of control, such as increasing standardization or decentralization or making better use of the norms and values of the informal organization.
4. Managers should periodically meet in teams to consider how best to design and redesign the hierarchy so that it allows the organization to create the most value at the lowest operating cost.

First, managers increase the level of vertical differentiation, paying particular attention to keeping the organization as flat as possible and to maintaining an appropriate balance between centralization and decentralization. Second, they increase horizontal differentiation and thereby also increase vertical differentiation. Third, they decide how much they can use rules, SOPs, and norms to control activities. The more they can use them, the less they will need to rely on direct supervision from the managerial hierarchy, and the need for managers and for additional levels in the hierarchy will be reduced.

Organizational design is difficult because all these decisions affect one another and must be made simultaneously. For example, managers very often start out by designing an organic structure (see Chapter 4) with a flat hierarchy and rely on norms and values rather than on rules to control organizational activities. Very quickly, however, as the organization grows, they are forced to add levels to the hierarchy and to develop rules and SOPs to maintain control. Before managers realize it, their organization has a mechanistic structure, and they face a new set of control problems. Organizational structure evolves and has to be managed constantly if an organization is to maintain its competitive advantage.

THE PRINCIPLES OF BUREAUCRACY

Around the turn of the last century, Max Weber (1864–1920), a German sociologist, developed a set of principles that characterized the ideal, typical bureaucracy.[30] He predicted that bureaucracy would come to dominate the organizational world because companies would become more efficient the more closely they came to resemble all of the bureaucratic principles.[31] However, Weber also predicted that the rise of bureaucracy would lead to a soulless existence for its members.[32]

Bureaucracy
A form of organizational structure in which people can be held accountable for their actions because they are required to act in accordance with rules and standard operating procedures.

A **bureaucracy** is a form of organizational structure in which people can be held accountable for their actions because they are required to act in accordance with well-specified and agreed-upon rules and standard operating procedures. Despite Weber's misgivings about the problems of bureaucratic organizing, his principles have been adopted by management theorists as offering a clear prescription for how to create and differentiate organizational structure so that task responsibility and decision-making authority are distributed in a way that maximizes organizational effectiveness. Because his work has been so influential in organizational design, it is useful to examine the six bureaucratic principles that, Weber argued, underlie effective organizational structure. Together these principles define what a bureaucracy or bureaucratic structure is (see Table 5-1).

Principle One: A bureaucracy is founded on the concept of rational-legal authority.

Rational-legal authority
The authority a person possesses because of his or her position in an organization.

Rational-legal authority is the authority a person possesses because of his or her position in an organization. In a bureaucracy, obedience is owed to a person not because of any personal qualities that he or she might possess (such as charisma, wealth, or social status) but because of the level of authority and responsibility that is associated with the organizational position the person occupies. Thus, we obey a police officer not because he or she wears an impressive uniform and carries a gun but because that person holds the position of police officer, which brings with it certain powers, rights, and responsibilities that compel obedience. In theory, a bureaucracy is impersonal. People's attitudes and beliefs play no part in determining the way a bureaucracy oper-

Table 5-1

THE PRINCIPLES OF BUREAUCRATIC STRUCTURE

Principle One: A bureaucracy is founded on the concept of rational-legal authority.
Principle Two: Organizational roles are held on the basis of technical competence.
Principle Three: A role's task responsibility and decision-making authority and its relationship to other roles should be clearly specified.
Principle Four: The organization of roles in a bureaucracy is such that each lower office in the hierarchy is under the control and supervision of a higher office.
Principle Five: Rules, standard operating procedures, and norms should be used to control the behaviour and the relationship between roles in an organization.
Principle Six: Administrative acts, decisions, and rules should be formulated and put in writing.

ates. If people base decisions and orders on their personal preferences instead of on organizational goals, effectiveness may suffer.

Weber's first principle indicates that choices that affect the design of an organization's hierarchy should be based on the needs of the task, not on the needs of the person performing the task.[33] Thus subordinates obey the CEO because of the authority and power vested in the position, not because of the individual currently filling it. For a bureaucracy to be effective, however, the distinction between positions and the people who hold them must be clear: People are appointed to positions; they do not own them.

Principle Two: Organizational roles are held on the basis of technical competence, not because of social status, kinship, or heredity.

In a well-designed hierarchy, roles are occupied by people because they can do the job, not because of who they are or whom they know. Although this principle seems to indicate the only logical way to run an organization, it has often been ignored.

Until 1850, for example, an officer's commission in the British Army could be bought by anybody who could afford the price. The higher the rank, the more the commission cost. As a result, most officers were rich aristocrats who had little or no formal army training. In the Canadian federal public service only men were employed in any of the professional and managerial ranks for much of the 20th century. Women were restricted to lower-level clerical and secretarial ranks. In 1959 women were allowed to apply for the post of clerk but it was the mid-1980s before government intervened to encourage women to be hired at the higher levels.[34] Today, in many organizations and industries, old-boy networks—personal contacts and relations—and not job-related skills influence the decision about who gets a job. The use of such criteria to fill organizational roles can be harmful to an organization because talented people get overlooked, particularly women and minorities, who are rarely included in such networks.

Picking the best person for the job seems an obvious principle to follow. In practice, however, following this principle is a difficult process that requires managers to view all potential candidates objectively. It is important for people always to remember that holding a role in an organization in a legal sense means that their job is to use the organization's resources wisely for the benefit of all stakeholders, not just for personal gain.

Weber's first two principles establish the organizational role (and not the person in that role) as the basic component of bureaucratic structure. The next three principles specify how the process of differentiation should be controlled.

Principle Three: A role's task responsibility and decision-making authority and its relationship to other roles in the organization should be clearly specified.

According to Weber's third principle, a clear and consistent pattern of vertical differentiation (decision-making authority) and horizontal differentiation (task responsibility) is the foundation for organizational effectiveness. When the limits of authority and control are specified for the various roles in an organization, the people in those roles know how much power they have to influence the behaviour of others. Similarly, when the tasks of various roles are clearly specified, people in those roles clearly know what is expected of them. Thus, with those two aspects of a person's role in an organization clearly defined, a stable system emerges in which each person has a clear expectation and understanding of the rights and responsibilities attached to other organizational roles. In such a stable system, all individuals know how much their supervisor can require of them and how much they can require of their subordinates. People also know how to deal with their peers—people who are at the same level in the organization as they are and over whom they have no authority, and vice versa.

Clear specification of roles avoids many problems that can arise when people interact. If, for example, some task responsibilities are assigned to more than one role, the people in those roles may have to fight over the same set of resources or claim responsibility for the same tasks. Is sales or marketing responsible for handling customer requests for information? Is the head of the army or the head of the air force responsible for peacekeeping operations in a particular country? The military is a vast bureaucracy in which the division of labour among the armed services is continually being negotiated to prevent such problems from emerging.

Role conflict
The state of opposition that occurs when two or more people have different views of what another person should do and, as a result, make conflicting demands on that person.

Role ambiguity
The uncertainty that occurs for a person whose tasks or authority are not clearly defined.

A clear pattern of vertical (authority) and horizontal (task) differentiation also cuts down on role conflict and role ambiguity.[35] **Role conflict** occurs when two or more people have different views of what another person should do and, as a result, make conflicting demands on the person. The person may be caught in the crossfire between two supervisors or the needs of two functional groups. **Role ambiguity** occurs when a person's tasks or authority are not clearly defined and the person becomes afraid to act on or take responsibility for anything. Clear descriptions of task and authority relationships solve conflict and ambiguity problems: When people know the dimensions of their position in the organization, they find it easier to take responsibility for their actions and to interact with one another.

Principle Four: The organization of roles in a bureaucracy is such that each lower office in the hierarchy is under the control and supervision of a higher office.

To control vertical authority relationships, the organization should be arranged hierarchically so that people can recognize the chain of command.[36] The organization should delegate to each person holding a role the authority needed to make certain decisions and to use certain organizational resources. The organization can then hold the person in the role accountable for the use of those resources. The hierarchical pattern of vertical differentiation also makes clear that a person at a low level in the hierarchy can go to someone at a higher level to solve conflicts at the low level. In the Canadian legal system, for example, participants in a court case can ask a higher court to review the decision of a lower court if they feel a bad decision was made. The right to appeal to a higher organizational level also needs to be specified in case a subordinate feels that his or her immediate superior has made a bad or unfair decision.

Principle Five: Rules, standard operating procedures, and norms should be used to control the behaviour and the relationships among roles in an organization.

Rules, including standard operating procedures (SOPs), are formal, written instructions that specify a series of actions to be taken to achieve a given end; for example, if A happens, then so does B. Norms are unwritten standards or styles of behaviour that govern how people act and lead people to behave in predictable ways. Rules, SOPs, and norms provide behavioural guidelines that can increase efficiency because they specify the best way to accomplish a task. Over time, all guidelines should change as improved ways of doing things are discovered.

Rules, SOPs, and norms clarify people's expectations about one another and prevent misunderstandings over responsibility or the use of power. Such guidelines can prevent a supervisor from arbitrarily increasing a subordinate's task and can prevent a subordinate from ignoring tasks that are a legitimate part of the job. A simple set of rules established by the supervisor of some custodial workers (Crew G) at a university building clearly established task responsibilities and clarified expectations (see Table 5-2).

Rules and norms enhance the integration and coordination of organizational roles at different levels and of different functions. Vertical differentiation and horizontal differentiation break the organization up into distinct roles that must be coordinated and integrated to accomplish organizational goals.[37] Rules and norms are important aspects of integration. They specify how roles interact, and they provide

Table 5-2

CREW G'S RULES OF CONDUCT

1. All employees must call their supervisor or leader before 5:55 A.M. to notify of absence or tardiness.
2. Disciplinary action will be issued to any employee who abuses sick leave policy.
3. Disciplinary action will be issued to any employee whose assigned area is not up to custodial standards.
4. If a door is locked when you go in to clean an office, it's your responsibility to lock it back up.
5. Name tags and uniforms must be worn daily.
6. Each employee is responsible for buffing hallways and offices. Hallways must be buffed weekly, offices periodically.
7. All equipment must be put in closets during 9:00 A.M. and 11 A.M. breaks.
8. Do not use the elevator to move trash or equipment from 8:50 to 9:05, 9:50 to 10:05, 11:50 to 12:05, or 1:50 to 2:05, to avoid breaks between classes.
9. Try to mop hallways when students are in classrooms, or mop floors as you go down to each office.
10. Closets must be kept clean, and all equipment must be clean and operative.
11. Each employee is expected to greet building occupants with "Good morning."
12. Always knock before entering offices and conference rooms.
13. Loud talking, profanity, and horseplay will not be tolerated inside buildings.
14. All custodial carts must be kept uniform and cleaned daily.
15. You must have excellent "public relations" with occupants at all times.

Your supervisor stands behind workers at all times when the employee is in the right and you are doing what you are supposed to. But when you are wrong, you are wrong. Let's try to work together to better Crew G, because there are many outstanding employees in this crew.

procedures that people should follow to jointly perform a task.[38] For example, a rule could stipulate that "Sales must give production five days' notice of any changes in customer requirements." Or an informal norm could require underutilized waiters to help waiters who have fallen behind in serving their customers. It's important never to underestimate the power of rules, as Organizational Insight 5.4 makes clear.

ORGANIZATIONAL INSIGHT 5.4

Never Underestimate the Power of Rules

General Mills, the cereal maker best known for Cheerios cereal and Yoplait yogurt, created two of the best-known restaurant chains in North America—Red Lobster and the Olive Garden—and has over 1500 restaurants in the United States, Canada, and Japan. Inspired by this success, a few years ago top managers decided that they could use the skills and experience they had gained from operating their current restaurant chains to start a new chain specializing in Chinese food. Called China Coast, a prototype restaurant was opened in Orlando, Florida; customers were favourably impressed by the décor and by the food.

General Mills managers were excited by customers' positive response to the new restaurant and decided that they would rapidly expand the chain. Operating at breakneck speed, managers opened 38 restaurants in nine U.S. states. With the restaurant chain in full swing, however, problems began to arise. Customers were no longer so enthusiastic about the quality of the food or the customer service, and sales volume fell off. What had gone wrong?

Apparently, in the attempt to open so many restaurants so quickly, managers lost control of quality. Chinese food is difficult to prepare properly, and employees require extensive training if they are to keep quality consistently high. Top managers had created a set of companywide food-quality standards for restaurant managers to follow, but the restaurant managers failed to ensure that these output standards were met consistently. Moreover, there were customer complaints about the quality of service that had not been reported to managers at the Orlando prototype. While searching for reasons for the failure of the new restaurants to meet company standards, top managers discovered that the primary problem was that they had not put the right set of bureaucratic rules in place.

Restaurant managers had not received enough restaurant operations training. Top managers had not created enough rules and SOPs for restaurant managers either to follow or to teach to their employees—the cooks who actually prepared the food and the waiters who served it. Top managers thus decided that in the future each restaurant manager would attend a four-month intensive training course during which he or she would be taught the rules to be followed when preparing and serving the food. The rules would be written down and formalized in an operations manual that managers would take back to their restaurants for reference when training employees.

To make sure that restaurant managers did indeed follow the rules to ensure high-quality food and customer service, General Mills's managers created a new layer of managers—regional managers whose responsibility was to supervise restaurant managers. Regional managers also were responsible for giving restaurant managers additional training as new dishes were introduced on the menu and for informing them of any changes in operating procedures that top managers had developed to improve the performance of individual restaurants.

As Organizational Insight 5.4 suggests, these moves came too late to save the chain; nothing kills a restaurant as much as a reputation for poor food quality. Customers tell their friends by word of mouth; the news spread. The China Coast episode illustrates an important lesson in organizational design: Managers must have a structure planned, worked out, and tested before they embark on ambitious attempts at expansion. This is why today, before starting a chain of restaurants or any other kind of business, a prototype is created and tested at some typical location and all the bugs involved in operating the business are worked out, and rules and SOPs developed and codified in operations manuals before the concept is rolled out.

Principle Six: Administrative acts, decisions, and rules should be formulated and put in writing.

When rules and decisions are written down, they become official guides to the way the organization works. Thus, even when someone leaves an organization, an indication of what that person did is part of the organization's written records. A bureaucratic structure provides an organization with memory, and it is the responsibility of members to train successors and ensure that there is continuity in the organizational hierarchy. Written records also ensure that organizational history cannot be altered and that people can be held accountable for their decisions.

The Advantages of Bureaucracy

Almost every organization possesses some features of bureaucracy.[39] The primary advantage of a bureaucracy is that it lays out the ground rules for designing an organizational hierarchy that controls interactions between organizational members and increases the efficiency of those interactions.[40] Bureaucracy's clear specification of vertical authority and horizontal task relationships means that there is no question about each person's role in the organization. Individuals can be held accountable for what they do, and such accountability reduces the transaction costs that arise when people must continually negotiate and define their organizational tasks. Similarly, the specification of roles and the use of rules, SOPs, and norms to regulate how tasks are performed reduce the costs associated with monitoring the work of subordinates and increase integration within the organization. Finally, written rules regarding the reward and punishment of employees, such as rules for promotion and termination, reduce the costs of enforcement and evaluating employee performance.

Another advantage of bureaucracy is that it separates the position from the person. The fairness and equity of bureaucratic selection, evaluation, and reward systems encourage organizational members to advance the interests of all organizational stakeholders and meet organizational expectations.[41] Bureaucracy provides people with the opportunity to develop their skills and pass them on to their successors. In this way, a bureaucracy fosters differentiation, increases the organization's core competencies, and improves its ability to compete in the marketplace against other organizations for scarce resources.[42] Bureaucracies provide the stability necessary for organizational members to take a long-run view of the organization and its relationship to its environment.

If a bureaucracy is based on such clear guidelines for allocating authority and control in an organization, why is bureaucracy considered a dirty word by some people, and why are terms like bureaucrats and bureaucratic red tape meant as insults? Why do bureaucratic structures cause such disgust?

One of the problems that emerges with a bureaucracy is that over time managers fail to properly control the development of the organizational hierarchy. As a result, an organization can become very tall and centralized. Decision making begins to slow down, the organization begins to stagnate, and bureaucratic costs increase because managers start to make work for each other.

Another problem with bureaucracy is that organizational members come to rely too much on rules and SOPs to make decisions, and this overreliance makes them unresponsive to the needs of customers and other stakeholders. Organizational members lose sight of the fact that their job is to provide a service for clients, customers, or the broader social interest (in the case of a government agency), and/or create value for stakeholders. Instead, their chief goal is to follow rules and procedures and obey authority.

Organizations that suffer from those problems are accused of being bureaucratic or of being run by bureaucrats. However, whenever we hear this claim, we must be careful to distinguish between the principles of bureaucracy and the people who manage bureaucratic organizations. When organizations become overly bureaucratic, the fault may lie with the people who run them—with managers who prefer the pursuit of power and status to the pursuit of operating efficiency, who prefer to protect their careers rather than their organizations, and who prefer to use resources to benefit themselves rather than stakeholders. But it may also lie with some of the intrinsic characteristics of the principles of bureaucracy.[43] One technique that can be used to mitigate these problems is management by objectives.

Management by Objectives

Management by objectives
A system of evaluating subordinates on their ability to achieve specific organizational goals or performance standards and to meet operating budgets.

To provide a framework within which to evaluate subordinates' behaviour and, in particular, to allow managers to monitor progress toward achieving goals, many organizations implement some version of management by objectives (MBO). **Management by objectives** is a system of evaluating subordinates for their ability to achieve specific organizational goals or performance standards and to meet operating budgets. Most organizations make some use of MBO because it is pointless to establish goals and then fail to evaluate whether or not they are being achieved. Management by objectives involves three specific steps:

Step 1: Specific goals and objectives are established at each level of the organization.

Management by objectives starts when top managers establish overall organizational objectives, such as specific financial performance targets. Then objective-setting cascades down throughout the organization as managers at the divisional and functional levels set their objectives to achieve corporate objectives. Finally, first-level managers and workers jointly set objectives that will contribute to achieving functional goals.

Step 2: Managers and their subordinates together determine the subordinates' goals.

An important characteristic of management by objectives is its participatory nature. Managers at every level sit down with the subordinate managers who report directly to them and together they determine appropriate and feasible goals for the subordinate, and bargain over the budget that the subordinate will need so as to achieve these goals. The participation of subordinates in the objective-setting process is a way of strengthening their commitment to achieving their goals and meeting their budgets. Another reason why it is so important for subordinates (both individuals and teams) to participate in goal setting is so they can tell managers what they think they can realistically achieve.

Step 3: Managers and their subordinates periodically review the subordinates' progress toward meeting goals.

Once specific objectives have been agreed upon for managers at each level, managers are accountable for meeting those objectives. Periodically, they sit down with their subordinates to evaluate their progress. Normally, salary raises and promotions are linked to the goal-setting process, and managers who achieve their goals receive greater rewards than those who fall short. (The issue of how to design reward systems to motivate managers and other organizational employees is discussed in Chapter 10.)

In the companies that have decentralized responsibility for the production of goods and services to teams, particularly cross-functional teams, MBO works somewhat differently. Managers ask each team to develop a set of goals and performance targets that the team hopes to achieve—goals that are consistent with organizational objectives. Managers then negotiate with each team to establish its final goals and the budget the team will need to achieve them. The reward system is linked to team performance, not to the performance of any one team member.

Investors Group Financial Services has used MBO since 1974 to motivate employees to improve sales performance. Objectives are established through a series of annual meetings of sales representatives and managers where specific goals are agreed for the coming year.[44]

In the U.S., one company that has spent considerable time developing a formal MBO system is Zytec Corporation, a leading manufacturer of power supplies for computers and other electronic equipment. Each of Zytec's managers and workers participates in goal setting. Top managers first establish cross-functional teams to create a five-year plan for the company and to set broad goals for each function. This plan is then reviewed by employees from all areas of the company. They evaluate the plan's feasibility and make suggestions about how to modify or improve it. Each function then uses the broad goals in the plan to set more specific goals for each manager and each team in the organization; these goals are reviewed with top managers. The MBO system at Zytec is organization-wide and fully participatory, and performance is reviewed both from an annual and a five-year time horizon. Zytec's MBO system has been very effective. Not only have organizational costs dropped dramatically, but the company also won the Baldrige Award for quality.

THE INFLUENCE OF THE INFORMAL ORGANIZATION

The hierarchy of authority designed by management that allocates people and resources to organizational tasks and roles is a blueprint for how things are supposed to happen. However, at all levels in the organization, decision making and coordination frequently take place outside the formally designed channels as people interact informally on the job. Moreover, many of the rules and norms that employees use to perform their tasks emerge out of informal interactions between people and not from the formal blueprint and rules established by managers. Thus, while establishing a formal structure of interrelated roles, managers are also creating an informal social structure that affects behaviour in ways that may be unintended. The importance of understanding the way in which the network of personal relationships that develop over time in an organization, the informal organization, affects the way the formal hierarchy works is illustrated in Organizational Insight 5.5.[45]

By reintroducing the plant's formal hierarchy of authority, the new management team totally changed the informal organization that had been governing the way workers thought they should act. The changes destroyed the norms that had made the plant work smoothly (though not very effectively, from top management's perspective). The result of changing the informal organization was lower productivity because of the strikes.

ORGANIZATIONAL INSIGHT 5.5

Wildcat Strikes in the Gypsum Plant

Gypsum is a mineral that is extracted from the ground, crushed, refined, and compacted into wallboard. A gypsum mine and processing plant owned by the General Gypsum Company[46] was located in a rural community, and farmers and labourers frequently supplemented their farm income by working in the plant. The situation in the mine was stable, the management team had been in place for many years, and workers knew exactly what they had to do. Coordination in the plant took place through long-established informal routines that were taken for granted by management and workers alike. Workers did a fair day's work for a fair day's pay. For its part, management was very liberal. It allowed workers to take wallboard for their own personal use and overlooked absences from work, which were especially common during the harvest season.

The situation changed when the corporate office sent a new plant manager to take over the plant's operations and improve its productivity. When the new man arrived, he was amazed by the situation. He could not understand how the previous manager had allowed workers to take wallboard, break work rules (such as those concerning absenteeism), and otherwise take advantage of the company. He decided that these practices had to stop, and he took steps to change the way the company was operated.

He began by reactivating the formal rules and procedures, which, though they had always existed, had never been enforced by the previous management team. He reinstituted rules concerning absenteeism and punished workers who were excessively absent. He stopped the informal practice of allowing employees to take wallboard, and he took formal steps to re-establish management's authority in the plant. In short, he re-established the formal organizational structure—one based on a strict hierarchy of authority and strictly enforced rules that no longer indulged the employees.

The results were immediate. The workforce walked out and, in a series of wildcat strikes, refused to return until the old system was restored. It made no difference to the workers that the formal rules and procedures had always been on the books. They were used to the old, informal routines, and they wanted them back. Eventually, after prolonged negotiation about new work practices, the union and company reached an agreement that defined the relative spheres of authority of management and the union, and established a bureaucratic system for managing future disputes. When the new work routines were in place, the wildcat strikes ended.

This case shows that managers need to consider the effects of the informal organization on individual and group behaviour when they make any organizational changes, because altering the formal structure may disrupt the informal norms that make the organization work. Because an organization is a network of informal social relations, as well as a hierarchy of formal task and authority relations, managers must harness the power of the informal organization in order to achieve organizational goals. People in organizations go to enormous lengths to increase their status and prestige and always want others to know about and recognize their status. Every organization has an established informal organization that does not appear on any formal chart but is familiar to all employees. Much of what gets done in an organization gets done through the informal organization, in ways not revealed by the formal hierarchy. Managers need to consider carefully the implications of the interactions between the formal and informal hierarchies when changing the ways they motivate and coordinate employees.

The informal organization can actually enhance organizational performance. New approaches to organization design argue that managers need to tap into the power of the informal organization to increase motivation and provide informal avenues for employees to use to improve organizational performance. The formal hierarchical structure is the main mechanism of control, but there is no reason not to use the informal structure along with the formal one to allow people to work out solutions to their problems.

MANAGERIAL IMPLICATIONS

Using Bureaucracy to Benefit the Organization

1. If organizational hierarchies are to function effectively and the problems of overly bureaucratized organizations are to be minimized, both managers and employees should develop a critical understanding of bureaucratic principles.
2. Both employees and managers should realize that they do not own their positions in an organization and that it is their primary responsibility to use their authority and control over resources to benefit stakeholders.
3. Managers should strive to make human resource decisions such as hiring, promoting, or rewarding employees as fair and equitable as possible. Managers should not let personal ties or relationships influence their decisions, and employees should complain to managers when they feel that their decisions are inappropriate.
4. Periodically, the members of a work group or function should meet to ensure that reporting relationships are clear and unambiguous and that the rules members are using to make decisions meet current needs.
5. Both managers and employees should adopt a questioning attitude toward the way the organization works in order to uncover the taken-for-granted assumptions and beliefs on which it operates. For example, to make sure that they are not wasting organizational resources by performing unnecessary actions, they should always ask questions such as "Is that rule or SOP really necessary?" and "Who will read the report that I am writing?" An MBO system can also help managers evaluate the working of their hierarchy.

IT, EMPOWERMENT, AND SELF-MANAGED TEAMS

An important trend since the 1990s, often brought about by the use of new information technology, is the increasing use of empowered workers, self-managed teams, cross-functional teams, and contingent or temporary workers. IT is making it much easier for organizations to cost-effectively design a structure and control system that gives managers much more and much better information to monitor subordinates' behaviour and to intervene when necessary. IT, providing as it does a way of standardizing behaviour through the use of a consistent, and often cross-functional, software platform is an important means of controlling behaviour. When all employees or functions use the same software platform to provide up-to-date information on their activities, this codifies and standardizes organizational knowledge and makes it easier to monitor progress toward goals. IT provides people at all levels in the hierarchy with more of the information and knowledge they need to perform their roles effectively. For example, employees are able easily to access information from other employees via cross-functional software systems that keep them all informed about changes in product design, engineering, manufacturing schedules, and marketing plans that will impact their activities. In this sense, IT overlays the structure of tasks and roles that is normally regarded as the "real" organizational structure.

Thus, the increasing use of IT has led to a decentralization of authority in organizations and an increasing use of teams. As discussed earlier, decentralizing authority to lower-level employees and placing them in teams reduces the need for direct, personal supervision by managers, and organizations become flatter. **Empowerment** is the process of giving employees at all levels in an organization's hierarchy the authority to make important decisions and to be responsible for their outcomes. **Self-managed teams** are formal work groups consisting of people who are jointly responsible for ensuring that the team accomplishes its goals and who are empowered to lead themselves. **Cross-functional teams** are formal work groups of employees from across an organization's different functions who are empowered to direct and coordinate the value-creation activities necessary to complete different programs or projects.

Empowerment
The process of giving employees throughout an organization the authority to make important decisions and to be responsible for their outcomes.

Self-managed teams
Work groups consisting of people who are jointly responsible for ensuring that the team accomplishes its goals, and who lead themselves.

Cross-functional teams
Formal work groups of employees from across an organization's different functions who are empowered to direct and coordinate the value-creation activities necessary to complete different programs or projects.

The movement to flatten organizations by empowering workers in this way has been increasing steadily since the 1990s and has met with great success according to many stories in the popular press. However, while some commentators have forecasted the "end of hierarchy" and the emergence of new organizational forms based purely on lateral relations both inside and between functions, other commentators are not so sure. They argue that even a flat, team-based organization composed of empowered workers must have a hierarchy and some minimum set of rules and standard operating procedures if the organization is to have enough control over its activities. Organizations sacrifice the gains from bureaucratic structure only at their peril.[47] The problem for managers is to combine the best aspects of both systems—of bureaucratic structure and empowered work groups. Essentially, what this comes down to is that managers must be sure they have the right blend of mechanistic and organic structure to meet the contingencies they face. Managers should use bureaucratic principles to build a mechanistic structure, and they should enhance the organization's ability to act in an organic way by empowering employees and making teams a principal way of increasing the level of integration in an organization.

Finally, as organizations have flattened their structures, there has been an increasing trend for companies to employ contingent workers to keep costs down. **Contingent workers** are those who are employed for temporary periods by an organization and who receive no indirect benefits such as health insurance or pensions. Contingent workers may work by the day, week, or month performing some functional task, or may contract with the organization for some fee to perform a specific service to the organization. Thus, for example, an organization may employ ten temporary accountants to "do the books" when it is time or it may contract with a software programmer to write some specialized software for a fixed fee.

Contingent workers
Workers who are employed temporarily by an organization and who receive no indirect benefits such as health insurance or pensions.

The advantages an organization obtains from contingent workers are that they cost less to employ since they receive no indirect benefits and they can be let go easily when their services are no longer needed. However, there are also some disadvantages associated with contingent workers. First, there is the ethical problem of creating a disposable workforce of contingent workers. The more that organizations create contingent workforces, the more society in general has to face an increasingly vulnerable set of employees who tend to be among the lowest-paid section of society, and this has implications for pay equity, workplace discrimination, and other social issues.[48] Second, coordination and motivation problems may arise because temporary workers may have less incentive to perform at a high level, given that there is no prospect for promotion or job security. Third, organizations must develop core competencies in their functions to gain a competitive advantage, and it is unlikely that contingent workers will help them develop such competencies, since they do not remain with the organization very long and are, for obvious reasons, not committed to it.

Nevertheless, it has been estimated that up to one-third of the Canadian workforce and approximately 20 percent of the U.S. workforce consist of contingent workers, and these figures are expected to increase as managers spend more time studying their organizational structures to find new ways of reducing bureaucratic costs.[49] Indeed, one method that managers are already employing to keep their structures flat is the use of outsourcing and network structures, which are discussed in detail in the next chapter.

SUMMARY

Stakeholder goals and objectives can be achieved only when organizational skills and capabilities are effectively coordinated and controlled through organizational structure. In bureaucratic organizations the activities of organizational members would be chaotic without a structure that assigns people to roles and directs the activities of people and functions.[50] This chapter has examined how organizations design their hierarchy of authority and choose control systems that create an effective organizational structure. The shape of the hierarchy determines how decision making takes place. It also determines how motivated people will be to pursue organizational goals. In a bureaucratic organization designing the hierarchy should be one of management's major tasks, but, as we have seen, it is a task that many organizations do not do well or fail to consider at all. Chapter 5 has made the following main points:

1. The height of an organization's structure is a function of the number of levels in the hierarchy, the span of control at each level, and the balance between centralization and decentralization of authority.
2. As an organization grows, the increase in the size of the managerial component is less than proportional to the increase in the size of the organization.
3. Problems with tall hierarchies include communication, motivation, and bureaucratic costs.
4. According to the principle of minimum chain of command, an organization should choose the minimum number of hierarchical levels consistent with the contingencies it faces.
5. The span of control is the number of subordinates a manager directly manages. The two main factors that affect the span of control are task complexity and task interrelatedness.
6. The shape of the hierarchy and the way it works are also affected by choices concerning horizontal differentiation, centralization versus decentralization, differentiation versus integration, standardization versus mutual adjustment, and the influence of the informal organization.
7. The six principles of bureaucratic theory specify the most effective way to design the hierarchy of authority in an organization.

8. Bureaucracy has several advantages. It is fair and equitable, and it can promote organizational effectiveness by improving organizational design. However, problems can arise if bureaucratic principles are followed too selectively or too rigidly, and if managers allow the organization to become too tall and centralized.
9. Managers need to recognize how the informal organization affects the way the formal hierarchy of authority works and make sure the two fit to enhance organizational performance.
10. To keep their organizations as flat as possible, managers are increasingly making use of IT and creating self-managed work teams of empowered workers and/or turning to contingent workers.

DISCUSSION QUESTIONS

1. Choose a small organization in your city, such as a restaurant or school, and draw a chart showing its structure. Do you think the number of levels in its hierarchy and the span of control at each level are appropriate? Why or why not?
2. In what ways can the informal organization and the norms and values of its culture affect the shape of an organization?
3. What factors determine the appropriate authority and control structure in (a) a research and development laboratory, (b) a large department store, (c) a small manufacturing company, and (d) a crown corporation or government agency?
4. How can the principles of bureaucracy help managers to design the organizational hierarchy?
5. When does bureaucracy become a problem in an organization? What can managers do to prevent bureaucratic problems from arising?

ORGANIZATIONAL THEORY IN ACTION

Practising Organizational Theory: How to Design a Hierarchy

Form groups of three to five people and discuss the following scenario:

You are the managers charged with reducing high operating costs. You have been instructed by the CEO to eliminate 25 percent of the company's managerial positions and then to reorganize the remaining positions so that the organization still exercises adequate supervision over its employees.

1. How would you go about analyzing the organizational hierarchy to decide which managerial positions should be cut first?
2. How will you be able to ensure adequate supervision with fewer managers?
3. What can you do to help make the downsizing process less painful for those who leave and for those who remain?
4. Do you have a better solution for reducing costs without losing jobs?

Making the Connection #5

Find an example of a company that recently changed its hierarchy of authority or its top-management team. What changes did it make? Why did it make them? What does it hope to accomplish as a result of them? What happened as a result of the changes?

The Ethical Dimension #5

Suppose an organization is purging its top and middle managers. Some managers charged with deciding who to terminate might decide to keep the subordinates they like, and who are obedient to them, rather than the ones who are difficult or the best performers. They might decide to lay off the most highly paid subordinates even if they are high performers. Think of the ethics issues involved in designing a hierarchy and its effect on stakeholders.

1. What ethical rules should managers use when deciding if or whom to terminate when redesigning their hierarchy?
2. Some people argue that employees who have worked for an organization for many years have a claim on the organization at least as strong as its shareholders. What do you think of the ethics of this position: Can employees claim to "own" their jobs if they have contributed significantly to past success?

Analyzing the Organization: Design Module #5

This module focuses on vertical differentiation and understanding the managerial hierarchy in your organization and the way the organization allocates decision-making authority.

ASSIGNMENT

1. How many people does the organization employ?
2. How many levels are there in the organization's hierarchy?
3. Is the organization tall or flat? Does the organization experience any of the problems associated with tall hierarchies? Which ones?
4. What is the span of control of the CEO? Is this span appropriate, or is it too wide or too narrow?
5. How do centralization, standardization, and horizontal differentiation affect the shape of the organization?
6. Do you think your organization does a good or a poor job in managing its hierarchy of authority? Give reasons for your answer.

Company Profiles #5*

Choose one or more of the organizations (e.g., companies, government agencies, or nonprofit organizations) that are profiled in this chapter. Do an Internet search to get up-to-date information on each organization you have selected, and answer the following questions.

1. What does the new information tell you about the organization's current ability to develop successful systems of organizational coordination, communication, and control?
2. How does the information compare with the earlier information provided in the text and what does that tell you about organizations (e.g., does the organization appear to have more or less successful systems of organizational coordination, communication, and control than before, and how do you explain this)?

Alternative Perspectives #5

Feminist research indicates that bureaucracy can have a negative impact on women's employment opportunities. Read one or more of the following readings and list five ways that bureaucracy can have a negative impact and five ways that it can have a positive impact on employment equity. In small groups, discuss how you would deal with the potentially negative aspects of bureaucracy.

Reading List

Ferguson, K. E. 1984. *The Feminist Case Against Bureaucracy*. Philadelphia, PA: Temple University Press.

Grant, J., and Tancred-Sheriff, P. 1992. A Feminist Perspective on State Bureaucracy. In A. J. Mills, and P. Tancred-Sheriff, eds., *Gendering Organizational Analysis*. Newbury Park, CA: Sage.

Kranz, H. 1976. *The Participatory Bureaucracy: Women and Minorities in a More Representative Public Service*. Lexington, MA: Lexington Books.

Morgan, N. 1988. *The Equality Game: Women in the Federal Public Service (1908–1987)*. Ottawa: Canadian Advisory Council on the Status of Women.

Savage, M., and Witz, A., eds. 1992. *Gender and Bureaucracy*. Oxford: Blackwell.

* The authors would like to receive information from student groups and instructors on any companies where there have been dramatic changes to the information published in this text. We would be happy to publish the best of these changes in a subsequent edition, where we will focus on changing company profiles.

CASE FOR ANALYSIS

Reconfiguring the HR Function under the Big Top[51]

Ever think about running away and joining the circus? Well hundreds of people do every year, and for Cirque du Soleil's human resources team, that's presented both an opportunity and a management challenge.

Cirque du Soleil is an undisputed Canadian success story. Formed in 1984 by a small troupe of Quebec street performers, the organization has grown into a US$1.2 billion enterprise running nine different productions on three continents. In 2003, 7 million spectators took in a Cirque show, generating some US$650 million in revenues. The company now has over 2500 employees, with some 1200 working in the Montreal head office, 600 artists performing in shows, and the remainder involved in the staging of the various productions. The average age of these employees is 34, and they represent more than 40 nationalities speaking some 25 languages

Marc Gagnon, the executive vice president of business services and development, is the person who has been managing the people side of the business since 1989. During his tenure, he's witnessed firsthand the phenomenal growth of the company and has had to make changes on the administrative side to facilitate that growth. The move to decentralize the human resource function is just one of those changes.

Historically, the Cirque organization managed its HR function from its Montreal head office. In the early days of Gagnon's tenure during the late 1980s and early 1990s, the company grew from having one touring show with 35 Montreal-based employees to having several touring shows with 200 employees in the head office, a European office, and another 1000 staff on the road. In the early days, it was still relatively easy for Gagnon's team to manage the HR function from one central location. The company's strong hire-from-within policy meant that the company did little external recruiting—despite the fact that they received 30 to 50 résumés a day. As Gagnon himself describes things, "When we started this company, we had our hands in it. We'd be talking to the janitor on a tour 3000 kilometres away." But several events prompted the need for Gagnon to rethink the HR department's structure.

One development that created the need for a more decentralized approach to HR was the creation of permanent shows in cities in the United States and Europe. The first of these was the Las Vegas show, launched in Nevada in 1998. Expansion plans called for three additional permanent shows to be established in 1999, with a second show opening in Las Vegas, and Orlando, Florida, and Berlin, Germany, becoming first-time hosts to other permanent Cirque productions. Now the dynamics were quite different—especially from an employee-recruitment and hiring perspective. Instead of needing a large group of temporary employees to act as ushers, ticket collectors, security, concession stand operators, and the like for a one- or two-week run in a city, Cirque needed dedicated staff for these roles in the locations year-round.

For the travelling tours, the HR needs remained the same as they always had been. Gagnon's team still had to look after the recruiting and hiring of temporary staff, and then take care of everything from housing and meal service for employees on tour to helping them complete their annual tax returns. (And that's no easy feat given that European tour employees can be required to complete up to six returns, each in a different language, while North American tour performers may be required to complete up to nine yearly tax returns.) The challenge though was the sheer number of shows on tour—growing from one to a record level of nine. And the number of different jurisdictions also created complexity. Labour laws, health-care issues, and compensation practices varied—sometimes significantly—across countries and even provinces and states.

Gagnon's solution was to push accountability and responsibility out to the HR officers who were travelling with the tours, and then establish permanent HR functions in the three cities with permanent shows. The resulting operating philosophy favours letting individual HR officers handle their own local issues with little interference from Montreal. That's not to say the ties to head office have been completely cut.

To maintain some measure of control and involvement, Gagnon now focuses his efforts on developing strong relationships with organizational managers, who then in turn are connected with their employees. To do that, Gagnon spends a lot of time in the air, travelling around to visit the various shows and speak one-on-one with managers and employees. He has also ensured that key functions, such as the processes for recruiting and hiring temporary employees, have been standardized. The end result is that temporary employees are thoroughly screened before they are hired, and evaluated in terms of experience, attitude, and professionalism. A central database of potential job candidates is also maintained in Montreal and is accessible by all HR officers. Overall, Gagnon emphasizes good communication. In his words, "Our culture is one of, 'Let's continue communicating together, let's exchange ideas, let's exchange expertise.' I think we do it pretty well."

Others seem to agree. In fact, in 1997, Cirque du Soleil was awarded a *Workforce Magazine* Optimas Award for its HR strategy, a strategy the magazine viewed as helping Cirque succeed in the global marketplace. For Gagnon, letting go of some of the central control almost seemed to be a necessity: "To be a creator, you also have to have a little bit of anarchy," he is reported to have said. "If you over-manage, you get a lousy show."

DISCUSSION QUESTIONS

1. What do you think of Gagnon's decision to decentralize the HR function? What possible weaknesses could such a structure have? Do you think these potential negatives outweigh the positive benefits?
2. What's your reaction to Gagnon's statement about the dangers of overmanaging? Do you think it applies to the HR function equally well as to other areas?

REFERENCES

1. J. R. Galbraith, *Designing Complex Organizations* (Reading, MA: Addison-Wesley, 1973).
2. P. R. Lawrence and J. W. Lorsch, *Organization and Environment* (Boston: Graduate School of Business Administration, Harvard University, 1967).
3. G. R. Jones, "Task Visibility, Free Riding, and Shirking: Explaining the Effect of Organization Structure on Employee Behaviour," *Academy of Management Review*, 1984, vol. 4, pp. 684–695.
4. P. M. Blau, "A Formal Theory of Differentiation in Organizations," *American Sociological Review*, 1970, vol. 35, pp. 201–218.
5. J. Child, *Organization: A Guide for Managers and Administrators* (New York: Harper and Row, 1977), pp. 10–15; P. Blau, "A Formal Theory of Differentiation."
6. P. Blau, "A Formal Theory of Differentiation"; W. R. Scott, *Organizations: Rational, Natural, and Open Systems* (Englewood Cliffs, NJ: Prentice Hall, 1981), pp. 235–240; R.M. Kanter, *Men and Women of the Corporation* (New York: Basic Books, 1977).
7. K. Ferguson, *The Feminist Case Against Bureaucracy* (Philadelphia: Temple University Press, 1984); N. Morgan, *The Equality Game: Women in the Federal Public Service (1909-1987)* (Ottawa: Canadian Advisory Committee on the Status of Women); M. F. R. Kets de Vries, "Alexithymia in Organizational Life: The Organization Man Revisited," *Human Relations*, 1989, vol. 42, pp. 1079–1093; R. K. Merton, "Bureaucratic Structure and Personality," *Social Forces*, 1940, vol. 17, pp. 560–568; D. Baker and J. C. Cullen, "Administrative Reorganization and the Configurational Context: The Contingent Effects of Age, Size, and Changes in Size," *Academy of Management Journal*, 1993, vol. 36, pp. 1251–1277.
8. P. M. Blau and R. A. Schoenherr, *The Structure of Organizations* (New York: Basic Books, 1971).
9. R. Carzo and J. N. Zanousas, "Effects of Flat and Tall Structure," *Administrative Science Quarterly*, 1969, vol.

14, pp. 178–191; A. Gupta and V. Govindarajan, "Business Unit Strategy, Managerial Characteristics, and Business Unit Effectiveness at Strategy Implementation," *Academy of Management Journal*, 1984, vol. 27, pp. 25–41.

10. *www.rbccm.com*, 2004.
11. D. Katz and R. L. Kahn, *The Social Psychology of Organizing* (New York: Wiley, 1966), p. 255.
12. A. M. Pettigrew, *The Politics of Organizational Decision Making* (London: Tavistock, 1973).
13. Organizational Insight by Ellen Rudderham-Gaudet, based on the following sources: British Columbia Technologies Industry Association, "Eagle Professional Resources Inc," *www.bctia.org/members/Eagle_Professional_Resources_Inc.asp*, 2004; David Enders, "Master Managers," *Purple Squirrel*, *www.eagleonline.com/EagleWeb.nsf/0/3760B1168F9D055485256A7700620ABF?OpenDocument*, 2004.
14. Z. Olijnyk, "Chain Reaction: Daryl Katz Has Built a Drugstore Empire by Buying Smaller Retailers and Making Them Part of His Lean Machine," *Canadian Business*, 31 December 2001, p. 52.
15. C. N. Parkinson, *Parkinson's Law* (New York: Ballantine Books, 1964).
16. Ibid., p. 17.
17. See, for example, "Preparing the Company Organization Manual," *Studies in Personnel Policy*, no. 157 (New York: National Industrial Conference Board, 1957), p. 28.
18. V. A. Graicunas, "Relationships in Organizations," in L. Gulick and L. Urwick, eds., *Papers in the Science of Administration* (New York: Institute of Public Administration, 1937), pp. 181–185.
19. Ibid.
20. *www.emi.com*, 2002.
21. C. Goldsmith and J. Ordonez, "Levy Jolts EMI: Can He Reform the Music Industry?" *Wall Street Journal*, 6 September 2002, p. B1, B4.
22. D. D. Van Fleet, "Span of Management Research and Issues," *Academy of Management Journal*, 1983, vol. 4, pp. 546–552.
23. J. W. Lorsch and J. J. Morse, *Organizations and Their Members: A Contingency Approach* (New York: Harper and Row, 1974).
24. Lawrence and Lorsch, *Organization and Environment*.
25. R. W. Griffin, R. J. Ebert, and F. A. Starke, *Business*, 4th Canadian ed. (Toronto: Prentice-Hall, 2002), p. 174.
26. "Union Pacific to Reorganize," *cnnfn.com*, 20 August 1998, p. 20.
27. *www.unionpacific.com*, press release, 1998.
28. S. L. McShane, *Canadian Organizational Behaviour* (Toronto: McGraw-Hill Ryerson, 2004), p. 427.
29. W. Konrad, "The Bottleneck at Coca-Cola Enterprises," *Business Week*, 14 September 1992, pp. 28–30.
30. M. Weber, *From Max Weber: Essays in Sociology*, in H. H. Gerth and C. W. Mills, eds. (New York: Oxford University Press, 1946); M. Weber, *Economy and Society*, in G. Roth and C. Wittich, eds. (Berkeley: University of California Press, 1978).
31. Not all social theorists agree with Weber. Several research studies indicate that bureaucracy can, in fact, be very inefficient when rules become substitutes for goals, when behaviour becomes rigid and rules oriented, where action become strictly impersonal, and/or where bureaucratic values become discriminatory. For a summary of the debate on bureaucracy, see A. J. Mills, T. Simmons, and J. Helms Mills, *Reading Organization Theory* (Toronto: Garamond Press, 2005).
32. Weber referred to this as "the iron cage of bureaucracy"; see Mills et al., *Reading Organization Theory*.
33. C. Perrow, *Complex Organizations*, 2nd ed. (Glenview, IL: Scott, Foresman, 1979).
34. Morgan, *The Equality Game*. Ottawa: Canadian Advisory Council on the Status of Women.
35. R. L. Kahn, D. M. Wolfe, R. P. Quinn, J. D. Snoek, and R. A. Rosenthal, *Organizational Stress: Studies in Role Conflict and Ambiguity* (New York: Wiley, 1964).
36. Weber, *From Max Weber*, p. 331.
37. Lawrence and Lorsch, *Organization and Environment*; J. R. Galbraith, *Organization Design* (Reading, MA: Addison-Wesley, 1977).
38. Lawrence and Lorsch, *Organization and Environment*.
39. Perrow, *Complex Organizations*.
40. G. R. Jones and C. W. L. Hill, "Transaction Cost Analysis of Strategy-Structure Choice," *Strategic Management Journal*, 1989, vol. 9, pp. 159–172.
41. See Perrow, *Complex Organizations*, Ch. 1, for a detailed discussion of these issues.
42. P. S. Adler and B. Borys, "Two Types of Bureaucracy," *Administrative Science Quarterly*, 1996, vol. 41, pp. 61–89.
43. Griffin et al., *Business*, p. 275.
44. Ibid.
45. A. W. Gouldner, *Wildcat Strike: A Study of Worker–Management Relationships* (New York: Harper and Row, 1954).
46. This is a pseudonym used by Gouldner, ibid.

47. L. Donaldson, *Redeeming the Organization* (New York: The Free Press, 1996).

48. *canada.justice.gc.ca/en/payeqsal/2320.html*, 2004; *www.hc-sc.gc.ca/hppb/phdd/overview_implications/01_overview.html*, 2004; *www.fairjobs.org/docs/NC2003-2.pdf*, 2004.

49. *www.iwh.on.ca/products/atwork2002/oct_2002/contin.htm*, 2004.

50. Child, *Organization: A Guide for Managers and Administrators*, pp. 50–72.

51. Case by Margaret McKee, based on the following sources: G. Flynn G. "A Circus Juggles HR Worldwide," *Workforce*, February 1997, vol. 76, p. 50; G. Flynn, "Acrobats, Aerialists and HR: The Big Top Needs Big HR," *Workforce*, August 1997, vol. 76, pp. 38–45; M. Miller, "The Acrobat," *Forbes*, 15 March 2004, vol. 173, p. 100–102; A. Wahl, D. Calleja, K. Libin, and J. Kirby, "The Countdown Begins: The Kickoff of Our Exclusive Ranking of the Top 75 Canadian Companies of all Time," *Canadian Business*, 3 February 2003, vol. 76, pp. 81–86; *www.cirquedusoleil.com*, 2004.

Designing Organizational Structure: Specialization and Coordination

CHAPTER 6

Learning Objectives

In this chapter the second principal issue in organizational design is addressed: how to group and coordinate tasks to create a division of labour that gives an organization a competitive advantage. The design challenge is to create the optimal pattern of vertical and horizontal relationships among roles, functions, teams, and divisions that will enable an organization to best coordinate and motivate people and other resources to achieve its goals.

After studying this chapter you should be able to:

1. Explain why most organizations initially have a functional structure and why, over time, problems arise with this structure that require a change to a more complex structure.
2. Distinguish between three kinds of divisional structures (product, geographic, and market), describe how a divisional structure works, and explain why many organizations use this structure to coordinate organizational activities and increase their effectiveness.
3. Discuss how the matrix and product-team structures differ, and why and when they are chosen to coordinate organizational activities.
4. Identify the unique properties of network structures and the conditions under which they are most likely to be selected as the design of choice.

FUNCTIONAL STRUCTURE

Functional structure
A design that groups people on the basis of their common expertise and experience or because they use the same resources.

In Chapter 4 we noted that the tasks involved in running the B.A.R. and Grille became more numerous and more complex as the number of customers increased and the organization needed to serve more meals. At first, the owners, Bob and Amanda Richards, performed multiple roles, but as the business grew, they became overloaded and were forced to develop specialized roles and institute a division of labour. As we saw in Chapter 4, the assignment of one person to a role is the start of specialization and horizontal differentiation. As this process continues, the result is a **functional structure**, a design that groups people on the basis of their common skills and expertise or because they use the same resources. At the B.A.R. and Grille, waiters and busboys were grouped into the dining-room function, and chefs and kitchen staff were grouped into the kitchen function (see Figure 4-1, p. 109). Similarly, research and development scientists at companies like Amazon.com and Johnson & Johnson are grouped in specialized laboratories because they use the same skills and resources, and accountants are grouped in an accounting function.

Functional structure is the bedrock of horizontal differentiation. An organization groups tasks into functions to increase the effectiveness with which it achieves its principal goal: providing customers with high-quality products at reasonable prices.[1] As functions specialize, skills and abilities improve, and the core competencies that give an organization a competitive advantage emerge. Different functions emerge as an organization responds to increasingly complex task requirements (see Figure 6-1). The owner of a very small business, for example, might hire outside specialists to handle accounting and marketing. As an organization grows in size and complexity, however, it normally develops those functions internally because handling accounting and marketing itself becomes more efficient than hiring outside contractors. This is how organizations become more complex as they grow: They develop not only more functions, but also more specialization within each function. (They also become vertically differentiated and develop a hierarchy of authority, as we saw in Chapter 5.) A good example of the way in which horizontal differentiation leads to the development of a functional structure is provided by Amazon.com, as outlined in the Focus on New Information Technology box.

FIGURE 6-1
Functional Structure.

A. This format shows that each function has its own hierarchy.

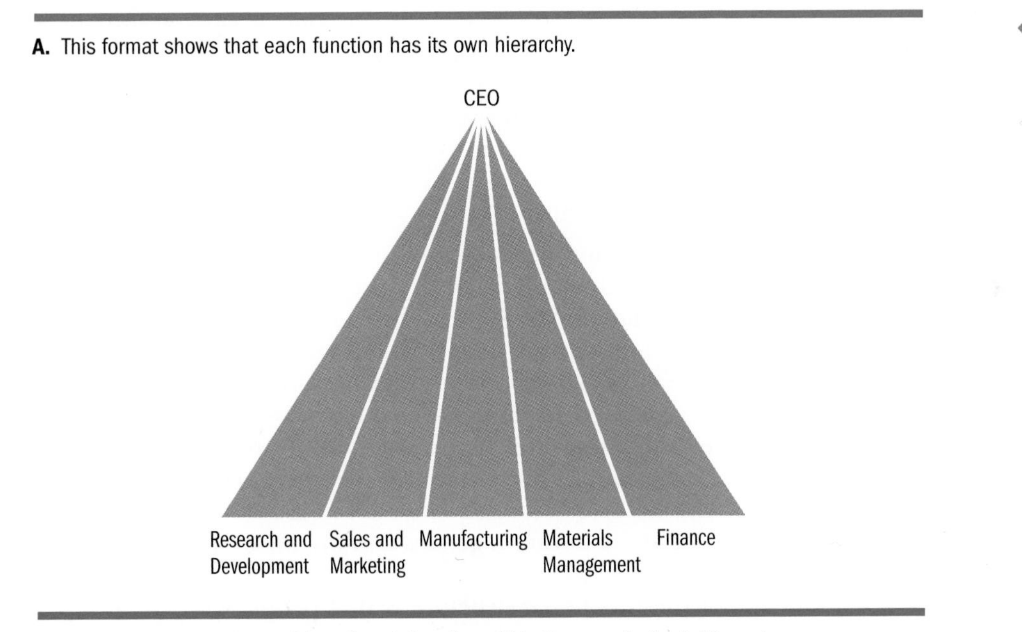

B. This format shows the position of each function within the organization's hierarchy.

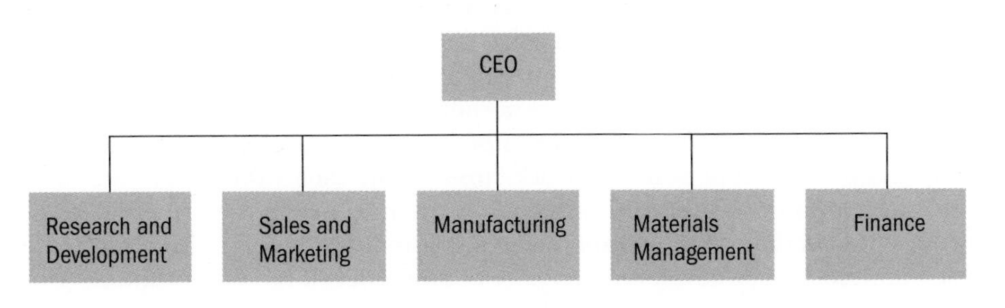

FOCUS ON NEW INFORMATION TECHNOLOGY

Amazon.com, Part 4

As we saw in Chapter 1, Jeff Bezos, the founder of Amazon.com, achieved phenomenal success with his concept for an online bookstore. In large part, his success has been due to the functional structure that he created for his company that has allowed Amazon.com's proprietary Internet software to be used so effectively to link employees to customers.

First, Bezos created the research and development department to continue to develop and improve the in-house software that he had initially developed for Internet-based retailing. Then, he established the information systems department to handle the day-to-day implementation of these systems and to manage the interface between the customer and the organization. Third, he created the materials management/logistics department to devise the most cost-efficient ways to obtain books from book publishers and book distributors and then to ship them quickly to customers. (Currently, the department is trying to develop new information systems to ensure one-day shipping to customers.) Finally, as Amazon.com grew, he created a separate financial department and a strategic planning department to help chart the company's future. As we will see in later chapters, these departments have helped Amazon to expand into providing many other kinds of products for its customers such as music CDs, electronics, and gifts.

By focusing on the best way to divide into functions the total task facing the organization (the creation of value for his customers), and recruiting experienced functional managers from other organizations like Wal-Mart to run them, Bezos created core competencies that allowed his online bookstore to compete effectively with bricks-and-mortar bookstores. Many stores are going out of business because they can't provide customers with the sheer range of books and convenient service as Amazon.com. Amazon.com is able to do this because of the way it has developed a structure to effectively manage its new information technology.

Advantages of a Functional Structure

Functional structure develops first and foremost because it provides people with the opportunity to learn from one another and become more specialized and productive. When people with skills in common are assembled into a functional group, they can learn the best way to solve problems, or the most efficient techniques for performing a task, from one another. The most skilled employees can train new recruits, and the most skilled people can be promoted to supervisors and managers so that they can hire, train, and develop new employees. In this way an organization can increase its store of skills and abilities. For example, Microsoft has revenues of over US$10 billion per year, but only 40 000 employees. Microsoft's value lies in the skills and abilities of its employees and in the way the organization groups and organizes them to promote and develop their skills.

Another advantage of the functional structure is that people who are grouped together by common skills can supervise one another and control each other's behaviour. We discussed in Chapter 5 how a hierarchy develops within each function to help the organization control its activities (see Figure 5-8, p. 154). In addition to functional managers, peers in the same function can monitor and supervise one another and keep work activities on track. Peer supervision is especially important when work is complex and relies on cooperation; in such situations, supervision from above is very difficult.

Finally, people in a function who work closely with each other over extended time periods develop norms and values that allow them to become more effective at what they do. They become team members who are committed to organizational activities. This commitment may develop into a core competency of the organization.

Control Problems in a Functional Structure

All organizations initially are organized by function because the development of separate functions allows organizations to manage an increase in specialization and the division of labour most efficiently. As in Amazon.com, functional structure breeds core competencies and increases an organization's ability to control its people and resources. However, as an organization continues to grow and differentiate, functional structure creates problems. Often the problems arise from the organization's success: As the organization's skills and abilities increase and the organization is able to produce a better or wider variety of goods or services, the organization's ability to service the needs of its growing product line is strained. For example, it becomes increasingly difficult for sales and marketing to provide the in-depth attention that the launch of new products requires, so new products tend not to do well. Similarly, as more customers perceive value in what an organization creates, customer demand goes up. Increasing demand may strain the ability of manufacturing to produce products fast enough or in sufficient quantity. Moreover, costs start to rise as manufacturing is forced to increase production. In turn, the pressure of staying on top and beating the competition puts more pressure on R&D or engineering to further improve the quality or increase the sophistication of products.

The problem facing a successful organization is how to keep control of increasingly complex activities as it grows and differentiates. As it produces more and more products, becomes geographically diverse, or faces increasing competition for customers, control problems impede the organization's ability to coordinate activities.[2]

Communication Problems As more organizational functions develop, each with its own hierarchy, they become increasingly distant from one another. They develop different subunit orientations, which cause communication problems.[3] For example, sales thinks the organization's main problem is the need to satisfy customer demands quickly to increase revenues; manufacturing thinks the main problem is to simplify products to reduce costs; and R&D thinks the biggest problem is to increase a product's technical sophistication. As a result of such differences in perception, communication problems develop that reduce the level of coordination and mutual adjustment among functions and make it more difficult for the organization to respond to customer and market demands. Thus differentiation produces communication problems that companies try to solve by means of integrating mechanisms.

Measurement Problems A key way that organizational managers exercise control over something is to find a way to measure it. Measurement provides a clear basis for evaluation. However, as organizations grow and the number and complexity of their functions, products, and services increase, the information needed to measure the contribution of any one functional group to overall profitability is often difficult to obtain. The reason for the difficulty is that the cost of each group's contribution to product development cannot be isolated. Because of the inability to measure each function's contribution, the organization may not be making the best use of its resources.

Location Problems As a company grows, it may need to set up shop in different geographical regions in order to serve customer needs. Geographical spread can pose a control problem within a functional structure if centralized control at one geographical location does not allow the organization to handle manufacturing and sales and other support activities on a regional basis. An organization with more than one location has to develop an information system that can balance the need to centralize decision-making authority with the need to decentralize authority to regional operations. In fact, as Amazon.com has grown it has established five main U.S. distribution centres, and since 2003 it has established distribution sites in Canada, Japan, China, and the U.K.

Customer Problems As the range and quality of an organization's goods and services increase, the kinds of customers who are attracted to the organization change. Servicing the needs of new kinds of customers and tailoring products to suit them are relatively difficult in a functional structure. Functions like production, marketing, and sales have little opportunity to specialize in the needs of a particular customer group; instead, they are responsible for servicing the complete product range. Thus in an organization with a functional structure, the ability to identify and satisfy customer needs may fall short.

Strategic Problems Top managers may spend so much time trying to find solutions to everyday coordination problems that they have no time to address the longer-term strategic problems facing the company. For example, they are likely to be so involved in solving communication and integration problems that they have no time to plan for future product development. As a result, the organization loses direction.

Solving Control Problems with a Functional Structure

Sometimes managers can solve the control problems associated with a functional structure, such as poor communication between functions, by redesigning the functional structure to increase integration between functions (see Figure 6-2). For example, one ongoing organizational challenge is how to manage the relationship between sales and marketing. Figure 6-2A shows the traditional relationship between them: Each is a separate function with its own hierarchy. Many organizations have recognized the need to alter this design and have combined those activities into one function. Figure 6-2B shows that modification. Such changes to the functional structure increase control by increasing integration between functions.

FROM FUNCTIONAL STRUCTURE TO DIVISIONAL STRUCTURE

If an organization (1) limits itself to producing a small number of similar products, (2) produces those products in one or a few locations, and (3) sells them to only one general type of client or customer, a functional structure will be able to manage most of its control problems. As organizations grow, however, they are likely to produce more and

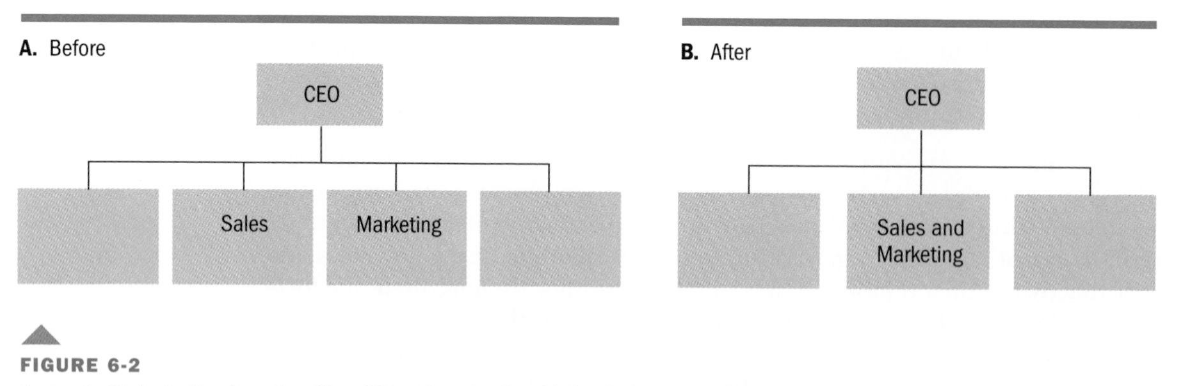

FIGURE 6-2
Improving Integration in a Functional Structure by Combining Sales and Marketing.

more products, which may be very different from one another. For example, General Electric produces hundreds of different models of refrigerators, ranges, and washing machines; its NBC television studio produces hundreds of different kinds of television shows; and its financial services unit is involved in many different kinds of activities, from providing loans to providing insurance. Moreover, when an organization increases its production of goods and services, it usually does so at an increasing number of locations and for many different types of customers.

CHC Helicopter Corp., of St. John's, Newfoundland, is another example of a company that survived and grew by changing function and moving to a number of locations. Until the late 1999s, CHC focused mainly on onshore transportation and repair work. In 1998, under a new CEO, the company sold its repair business and began to focus on offshore, mainly North Sea, oil and gas exploration. In the process it acquired a number of competitors, including British International Helicopters and the Norwegian Helicopter Services Group, giving CHC bases in Canada, the UK, and Norway. Consolidation around a central function contributed to a growth in the company's fortunes since 2000.[4]

MANAGERIAL IMPLICATIONS

Functional Structure

1. For an entrepreneur starting a small business, or for a manager of a work group or department, creating the correct division of labour within a function and between functions is a vital design task.
2. To ensure that the division of labour is correct, list the various functions that currently exist in your organization, and itemize the tasks they perform.
3. Draw a diagram of task relationships both within and between functions, and evaluate to what degree your organization is obtaining the advantages of the functional structure (such as the development of new or improved skills) or experiencing the disadvantages of the functional structure (such as lack of integration between functions).
4. Experiment with different ways of altering the design of the functional structure to increase effectiveness—for example, by transferring task responsibilities from one function to another or by eliminating unnecessary roles.

When organizations grow in these ways, what is needed is a structure that will increase the organization's control of its different subunits so that they can better meet product and customer needs. The move to a more complex structure is based on three design choices:

1. *Increasing vertical differentiation.* To regain control in a vertical direction, the organization needs to increase vertical differentiation. This typically involves (a) increasing the number of levels in the hierarchy; (b) deciding how much decision-making authority to centralize at the top of the organization; and (c) decid-

ing how much to use rules, SOPs, and norms to standardize behaviour and hence exert control over low-level employees.

2. *Increasing horizontal differentiation.* To regain control in a horizontal direction, the organization needs to increase horizontal differentiation. This involves overlaying a functional grouping with some other kind of subunit grouping—most often, self-contained product teams or product divisions that possess all the functional resources they need to meet their goals.
3. *Increasing integration.* To regain control both vertically and horizontally, the organization needs to increase integration between subunits. The higher the level of differentiation, the more complex the integrating mechanisms that an organization needs in order to control its activities. Recall from Chapter 4 that complex integrating mechanisms include task forces, teams, and integrating roles. Organizations need to increase integration between subunits to increase their ability to coordinate activities and motivate employees.

The way those three design choices increase differentiation and integration is shown in Figure 6-3. The organization illustrated in Figure 6-3A has two levels in its hierarchy and three subunits, and the only integrating mechanism that it uses is the hierarchy of authority. Figure 6-3B shows the effects of growth and differentiation. To manage its more complex activities, the organization has developed three levels in its hierarchy and has eight subunits. Because of the increase in differentiation, it needed a greater degree of integration and thus created a series of task forces to control activities among subunits.

FIGURE 6-3
Differentiation and Integration: How Organizations Increase Control over Their Activities.

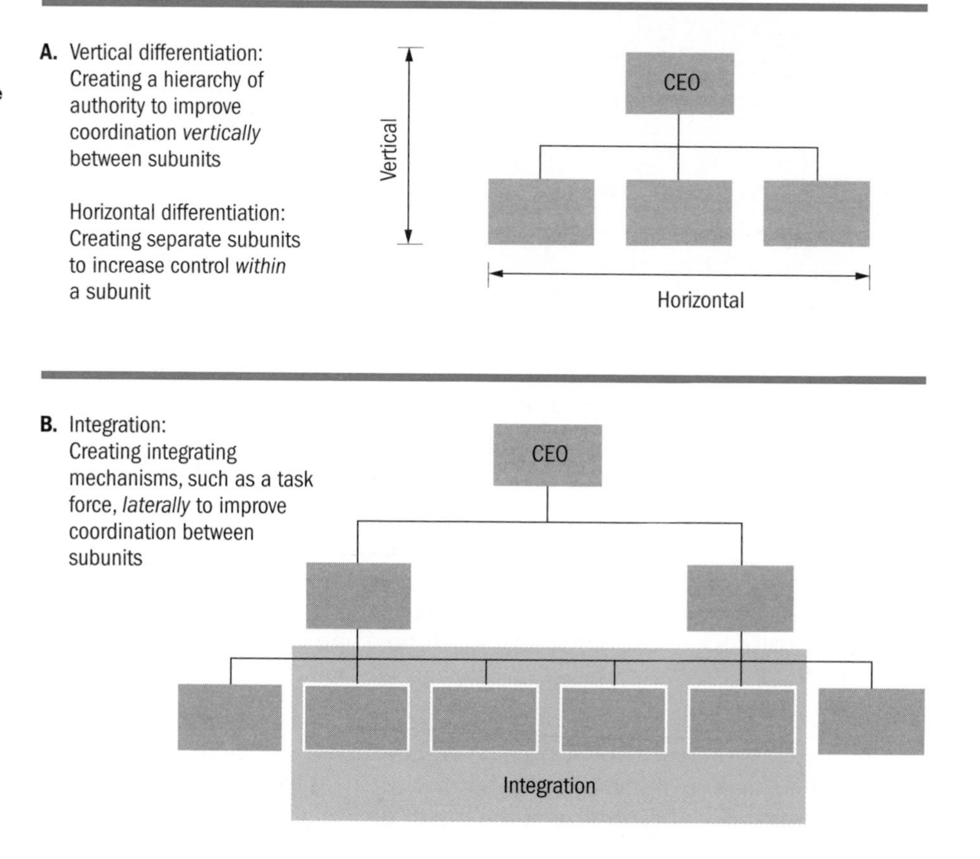

All of the complex organizational structures discussed in the remainder of this chapter come into being as a result of managers' design decisions about vertical differentiation, horizontal differentiation, and integration. The move to a complex structure normally involves changes in all three characteristics.

Moving to a Divisional Structure

The structure that organizations most commonly adopt to solve the control problems that result from producing many different kinds of products in many different locations for many different types of clients is the divisional structure. A **divisional structure** groups functions according to the specific demands of products, markets, or customers. The goal behind the change to a divisional structure is to create smaller, more manageable subunits within an organization. The type of divisional structure managers select depends on the specific control problems to be solved. If the control problem is due to the number and complexity of products, the organization will divide its activities by product and use a *product structure.* If the control problem is due to the number of locations in which the organization produces and sells its products, the organization will divide its activities by region and use a *geographic structure.* If the control problem is due to the need to service a large number of different customer groups, the organization will divide its activities by customer group and use a *market structure.*

Divisional structure
A structure in which functions are grouped according to the specific demands of products, markets, or customers.

Below, we discuss these types of divisional structure, which are designed to solve specific control problems. Each type of divisional structure has greater vertical and horizontal differentiation than a functional structure and employs more complex integrating mechanisms.

DIVISIONAL STRUCTURE I: THREE KINDS OF PRODUCT STRUCTURE

As an organization increases the kinds of goods it manufactures or the services it provides, a functional structure becomes less effective at coordinating task activities. Imagine the coordination problems a furniture maker like Palister would experience if it were to produce 100 styles of sofas, 100 styles of tables, and 50 styles of chairs in the same manufacturing unit. Adequately controlling value-creation activities would be impossible. To maintain effectiveness and simplify control problems as the range of its products increases, an organization is likely to group activities not only by function but also by type of product. To simplify control problems, a furniture maker might create three product groups: one for sofas, one for tables, and one for chairs. A **product structure** is a divisional structure in which products (goods or services) are grouped into separate divisions, according to their similarities or differences, to increase control.

Product structure
A divisional structure in which products (goods or services) are grouped into separate divisions according to their similarities or differences.

An organization that decides to group activities by product must also decide how to coordinate its product divisions with support functions like research and development, marketing and sales, and accounting. In general, there are two choices that the organization can make: (1) Centralize the support functions at the top of the organization so that one set of support functions services all the different product divisions; or (2) create multiple sets of support functions, one for each product division. In general, the decision that an organization makes reflects the degree of complexity of and difference between its products. An organization whose products are broadly similar and aimed at the same market will choose to centralize support services and use a *product division* structure. An organization whose products are very different and that operates in several different markets or industries will choose a *multidivisional structure.* An organization whose products are very complex technologically or whose characteristics change rapidly to suit changes in customer preferences will choose a *product team structure.*

Product Division Structure

Product division structure A divisional structure in which a centralized set of support functions services the needs of a number of different product lines.

A **product division structure** is a structure in which a centralized set of support functions service the needs of a number of different product lines. A product division structure is commonly used by food processors, furniture makers, and companies that make personal care products, paper products, or other products that are broadly similar and use the same set of support functions. Figure 6-4 shows a product division structure for a large food processor such as McCain Foods or the H. J. Heinz Company.

Because controlling the production of different foods within the same manufacturing unit proved to be very difficult and very expensive, Heinz created separate product divisions that produce frozen vegetables, frozen entrees, canned soups, and baked goods. This design decision increased horizontal differentiation within the organization, for each division is a separate manufacturing unit that has its own hierarchy headed by a product division manager. Each product division manager (PDM in Figure 6-4) is responsible for his or her division's manufacturing and service activities. The product division manager is also responsible for coordinating manufacturing and service activities with the activities of central support functions like marketing and materials management. The role of product division manager adds a level to the organizational hierarchy and thus increases vertical differentiation.

Figure 6-4 shows that in a product division structure, support functions such as sales and marketing, research and development, materials management, and finance are centralized at the top of the organization. Each product division uses the services

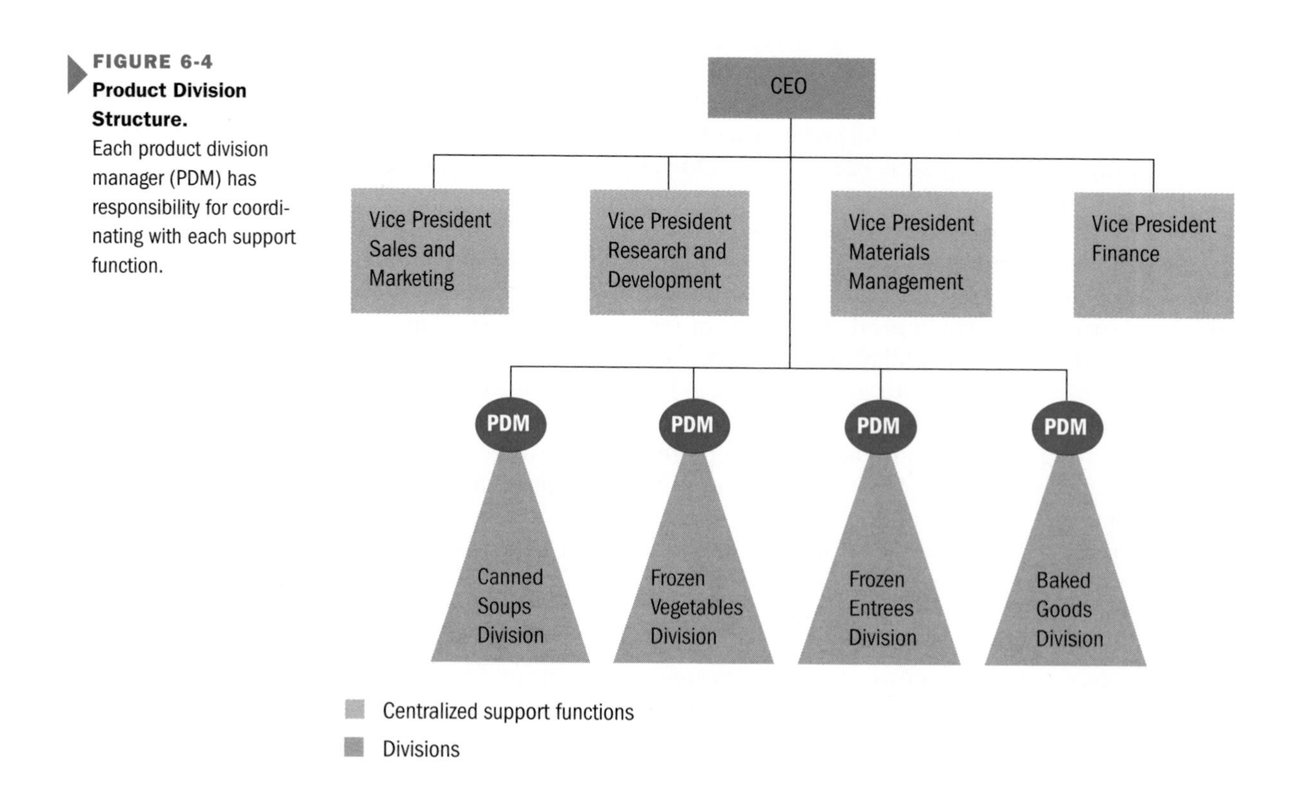

FIGURE 6-4
Product Division Structure.
Each product division manager (PDM) has responsibility for coordinating with each support function.

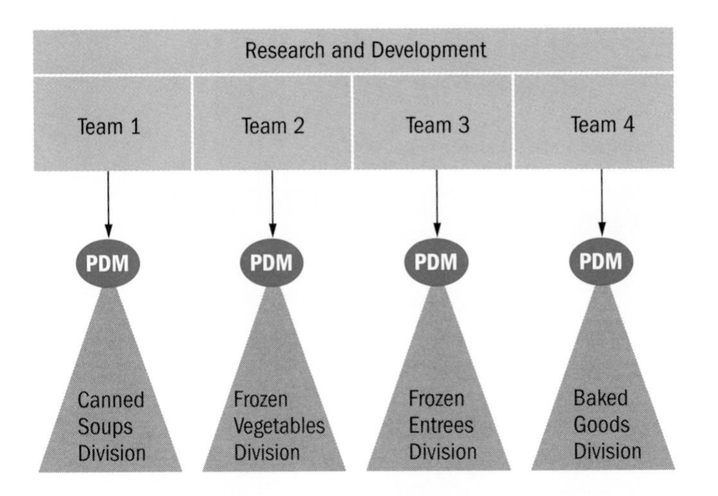

FIGURE 6-5
The Assignment of Product-Oriented Functional Teams to Individual Divisions.

of the central support functions and does not have its own support functions. Creating separate support functions for each product division would be expensive and could be justified only if the needs of the different divisions were so great or so different that different functional specialists were required for each type of product.

Each support function is divided into product-oriented teams of functional specialists who focus on the needs of one particular product division. Figure 6-5 shows the grouping of the research and development function into four teams, each of which focuses on a separate product division. This arrangement allows each team to specialize and become expert in managing the needs of "its" product group. However, because all of the R&D teams belong to the same centralized function, they can share knowledge and information. The R&D team that focuses on frozen vegetables can share discoveries about new methods for quick-freezing vegetables with the R&D team for frozen entrees. Such sharing of skills and resources increases a function's ability to create value across product divisions.

Multidivisional Structure

As an organization begins to produce a wide range of complex products, such as many car or truck models, or to enter new industries and produce completely different products, such as cars and fast food, the product division structure cannot provide the control the organization needs. Managing complex and diverse value-creation activities requires a **multidivisional structure**, a structure in which support functions are placed in self-contained divisions. Figure 6-6 depicts the multidivisional structure used by a large consumer products company. Four divisions are illustrated, although a company such as McCain Foods, GE, Nortel, IBM, Johnson & Johnson, Alcan, or Matsushita might have a large number of different operating divisions.

Multidivisional structure
A structure in which support functions are placed in self-contained divisions.

A comparison of the multidivisional structure shown in Figure 6-6 and the product division structure shown in Figure 6-4 indicates that a multidivisional structure has two innovations that overcome the control problems that a company experiences as it grows and produces a wide range of different products in different industries.[5] The first innovation is the independence of each division. In a multidivisional structure, each division is independent and self-contained (in a product division structure, the divisions share the services of a set of centralized functions). When divisions are **self-contained**, each division has its own set of support functions and controls its own

Self-contained division
A division that has its own set of support functions and controls its own value-creation activities.

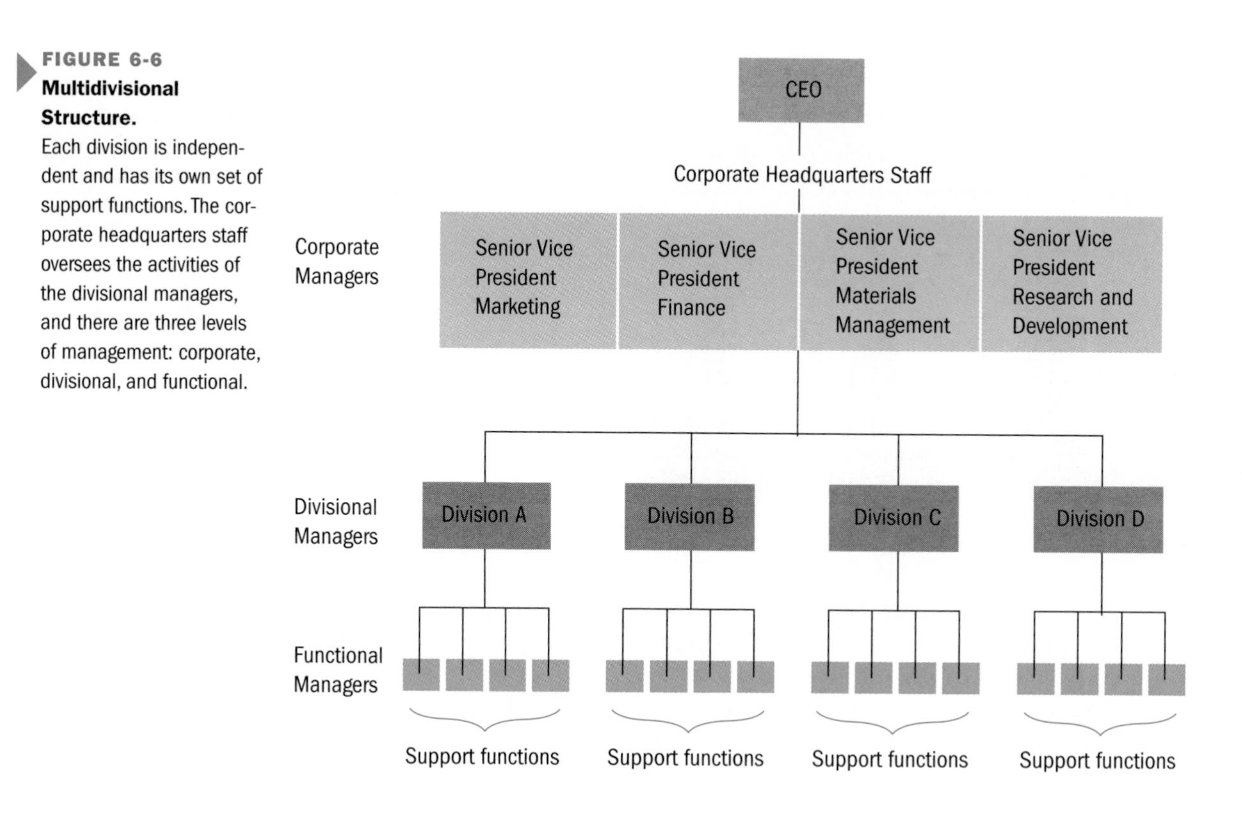

FIGURE 6-6
Multidivisional Structure.
Each division is independent and has its own set of support functions. The corporate headquarters staff oversees the activities of the divisional managers, and there are three levels of management: corporate, divisional, and functional.

value-creation activities. Each division needs its own set of support functions because it is impossible for one centralized set of support functions to service the needs of totally different products—such as automobiles, computers, and consumer electronics. As a result, horizontal differentiation increases.

Corporate headquarters staff
Corporate managers who are responsible for overseeing the activities of the divisional managers heading up the different divisions.

The second innovation in a multidivisional structure is a new level of management, a **corporate headquarters staff**, composed of corporate managers who are responsible for overseeing the activities of the divisional managers heading up the different divisions.[6] The corporate headquarters staff is functionally organized, and one of the tasks of corporate managers is to coordinate the activities of the divisions. For example, managers at corporate headquarters can help the divisions share information and learn from one another so that divisional innovations can be quickly communicated throughout the organization. Recall from Chapter 4 that managers acting in that way are performing an *integrating role.*

One of the ways that McCain Foods (with more than 20 000 employees in 55 production facilities across six continents) achieves coordination is through the use of high-level software designed to pull together product information from across its various divisions. The software provided by Advanced Software Designs is also designed to enhance open communication between departments and speed-to-market benefits.[7]

Because corporate managers constitute another level in the hierarchy, there is an increase in vertical differentiation, which provides more control. The heads of the divisions (divisional managers) link corporate headquarters and the divisions. Compared to a functional or a product division structure, a multidivisional structure provides additional differentiation and integration, which facilitate the control of complex activities.

A corporate staff and self-contained divisions are two factors that distinguish a multidivisional structure from a product division structure. But there are other important differences between them. A product division structure can only be used to control the activities of a company that is operating in one business or industry. In contrast, a multidivisional structure is designed to allow a company to operate in many different businesses. Each division in a multidivisional structure is essentially a different business. Moreover, it is the responsibility of each divisional manager to design the divisional structure that best meets the needs of the products and customers of that division. Thus one or more of the independent divisions within a multidivisional structure could use a product division structure or any other structure to coordinate its activities. This diversity is illustrated in Figure 6-7.

The multidivisional organization depicted in Figure 6-7 has three divisions, each with a different structure. The Automobile Products Division has a functional structure because it produces a small range of simple components. The Personal Computers Division has a product division structure; each of its divisions develops a different kind of computer. The Consumer Electronics Division has a matrix struc-

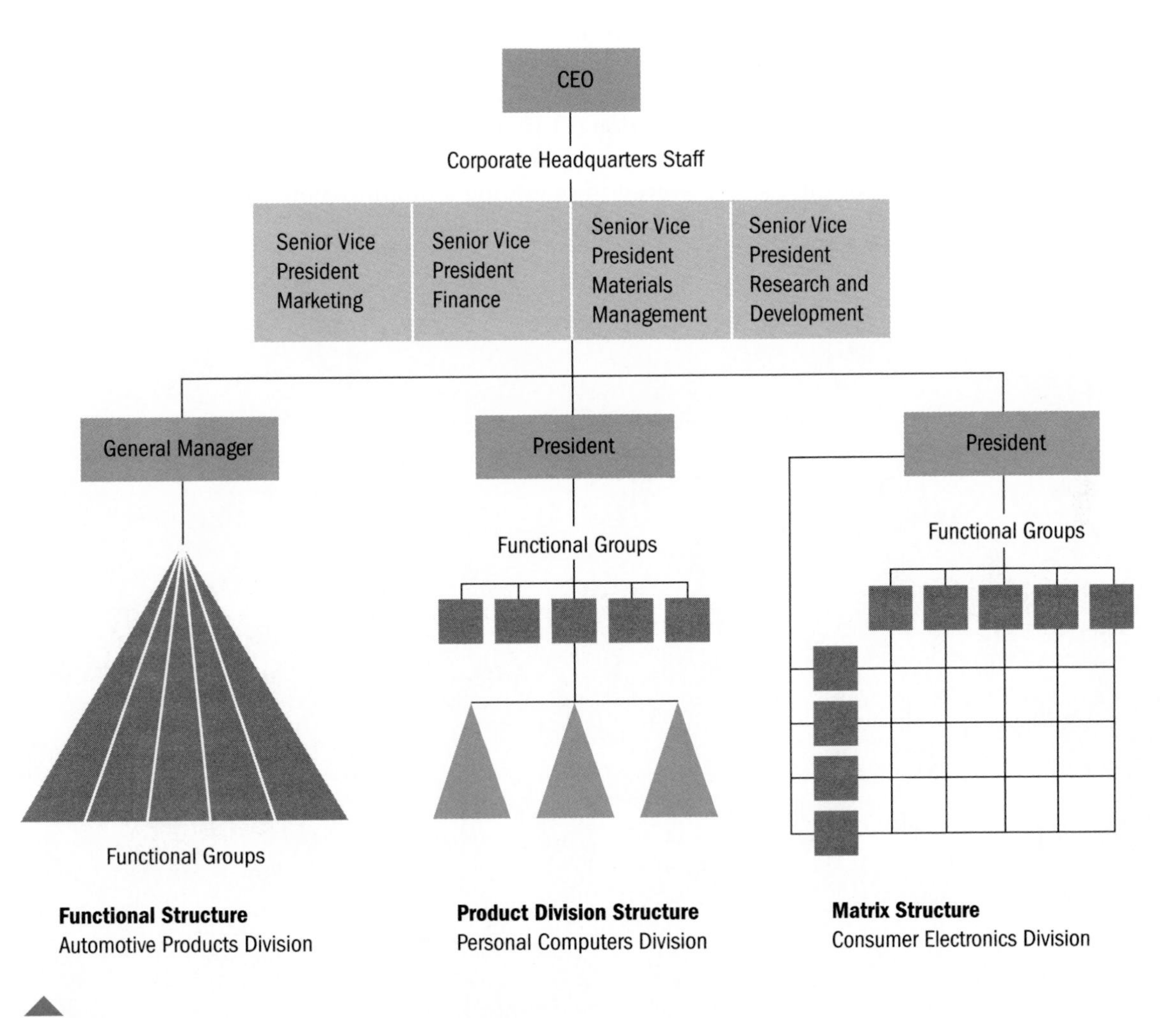

FIGURE 6-7
A Multidivisional Structure in Which Each Division Has a Different Structure.

ture (which we discuss later in the chapter) because it has to respond quickly to customer needs.

Onex Corporation is another example of a multidivisional company. Its different companies include Celestica, an electronics manufacturing provider; Clientlogic, a management services company; J. L. French Automotive, a manufacturer of aluminum die-case components; Performance Logistics Group, an automotive transportation provider and logistics services for light vehicle manufacturers; Commercial Vehicle Group Inc., a supplier of interior systems to the commercial vehicle market; Radian Communication Services, a wireless communications infrastructure and network services company; Oncap, a finance company for acquiring small and mid-sized companies; Cineplex Galaxy, a motion picture exhibitor; Phoenix Pictures, a movie company; Magellen Health Services, a health-care and insurance company; and Res-Care Inc, a provider of residential, therapeutic, educational, and training services.

Most Fortune 500 companies, as well as the top 500 companies in Canada, as listed by the *Financial Post*, use a multidivisional structure because it allows them to grow and expand their operations while maintaining control over their activities. Only when an organization has a multidivisional structure does the management hierarchy expand to include three of the levels of management: corporate managers who oversee the operations of *all* the divisions; divisional managers who run the individual divisions; and functional managers who are responsible for developing the organization's core competencies. The stories of General Motors' decision to move to a multidivisional structure (see Organizational Insight 6.1) and the Bank of Montreal (BMO) Financial Group's move to greater centralization (see Organizational Insight 6.2) illustrate many of the issues involved in operating a multidivisional structure and the difference between it and a product division structure.

ORGANIZATIONAL INSIGHT 6.1

Creating GM's Multidivisional Structure

William C. Durant formed the General Motors Company on September 16, 1908. Into it he brought about 25 different companies. Only four of them—Buick, Olds (now Oldsmobile), Oakland (now Pontiac), and Cadillac—survive as operating divisions today. Originally, each company retained its own operating identity, and the GM organization was simply a holding company, a central office surrounded by 25 satellites. When Alfred P. Sloan took over as president of GM in 1923, he inherited this collection of independently managed car companies, which made their own decisions, did their own research and development, and produced their own range of cars.

GM's principal competitor, Ford, was organized very differently. From the beginning, Henry Ford had emphasized the advantages of economies of scale and mass production and had designed a mechanistic structure to achieve them. He built a highly centralized hierarchy in which he had complete personal control over decision making. To reduce costs, Ford at first produced only one vehicle, the Model T, and gave enormous attention to finding improved ways of producing the car. Because of its organizational design, Ford's company was initially much more profitable than GM. The problem facing Sloan was to compete with Ford, not only in terms of product but in financial performance too.

Confronted with Ford's success, Sloan must have been tempted to close several of GM's small operations and concentrate production in a few locations where the company could enjoy the benefits of fewer models and cost savings from economies of scale. For example, he could have adopted a product division structure, created three product divisions to manufacture three kinds of car, and centralized support functions such as marketing, research and development, and engineering to reduce costs. Sloan, however, recognized the importance of the diverse sets of research, design, and marketing skills and competencies present in the small car companies. He realized that there was a great risk of losing this diversity of talent if he combined all these skills into one centrally located research and design department. Moreover, if the same set of support functions, such as engineering and design, worked for all of GM's divisions, there was a danger that all GM cars would begin to look alike. Nevertheless, Sloan also recognized the advantages of centralized control in achieving economies of scale, controlling costs, and providing for the development of a strategic plan for the company as a whole, rather than for each company separately. So he searched for an organizational structure that would allow him to achieve all these objectives simultaneously, and he found his answer in the multidivisional structure. In 1920, he instituted this change, noting that GM "needs to find a principle for coordination without losing the advantages of decentralization."[8]

Each of GM's different businesses was placed in a self-contained operating division with support services like sales, production, engineering, and finance. Each division became a profit centre and was evaluated on its return on investment. Sloan was quite clear about the main advantage of linking decentralization to return on investment: It raised the visibility of each division's performance. And, Sloan observed, it (1) "increases the morale of the organization by placing each operation on its own foundation, . . . assuming its own responsibility and contributing its share to the final result"; (2) "develops statistics correctly reflecting . . . the true measure of efficiency"; and (3) "enables the corporation to direct the placing of additional capital where it will result in the greatest benefit to the corporation as a whole."[9]

Sloan recommended that transactions between divisions be set by a transfer-pricing scheme based on cost plus some predetermined rate of return. However, to avoid protecting a high-cost internal supplier, he also recommended a number of steps involving analysis of the operations of outside competitors to determine the fair price. Sloan established a strong, professional, centralized headquarters management staff to perform such calculations. Corporate management's primary role was to audit divisional performance and to plan strategy for the total organization. Divisional managers were to be responsible for all product-related decisions.

In the 1980s, after fierce competition from the Japanese, GM took a hard look at its multidivisional structure. The duplication of research and development and engineering, and the purchasing of inputs by each division independently, were costing the company billions of extra dollars. In 1984, GM's five autonomous car divisions were combined into two groups: Chevrolet and Pontiac would concentrate on small cars; Buick, Oldsmobile, and Cadillac would focus on large cars.[10]

GM hoped that the reorganization would reduce costs and speed product development, but it was a disaster. With control of design and engineering more centralized at the group level, the cars of the different divisions started to look the same. Nobody could tell a Buick from a Cadillac or an Oldsmobile. Sales plummeted. Moreover, the reorganization did not speed decision making. It increased the number of levels in the hierarchy by introducing the group level into the organization. As a result, GM had 13 levels in its hierarchy as compared with Toyota, for example, which had just five. Once again the company was in trouble: Before the reorganization, it had been too decentralized; now it was too centralized. What to do?

Realizing its mistake, GM moved to return control over product design to the divisions while continuing to centralize high-cost functions like engineering and purchasing. This restructuring has had some success. Cadillac's management moved quickly to establish a new product identity and design new models. Over the 1990s GM reduced the number of different models it produced and in 2001 it announced that it was closing down its Oldsmobile division. What GM needs are fewer divisions and a flatter structure to compete in the new marketplace. In 2002, GM claimed that by 2005 it would become as efficient as its Japanese counterparts; time will tell.[11]

ORGANIZATIONAL INSIGHT 6.2

Centralizing BMO's IT for Efficiency and Effectiveness[12]

In today's world of telephone and Web-based banking and investing, financial services companies have to have state-of-the-art information technology systems if they are to remain competitive. Customers are demanding convenient, 24/7 access at a low price. Banks have to be able to meet those expectations or risk losing valuable customer business. But information technology solutions tend to be expensive and organizations have limits on what they can afford to invest. So how do big banks manage this key organizational resource? The Bank of Montreal Financial Group, or BMO Financial Group as it is now called, made a strategic decision to centralize its IT resource.

BMO describes itself as "one of the largest financial services providers in North America," and by many measures it is big. At the end of its 2003 fiscal year, the company's assets totalled $256 billion, and it had over 34 000 employees. From an IT perspective, the numbers are equally impressive. BMO's annual IT budget is in the hundreds of millions of dollars.

What the bank found though was that, in the race to be competitive and gain or maintain strategic advantage in the marketplace, it was not consistently subjecting all of its IT investment decisions to a rigorous and disciplined evaluation and management process. With increased use of PCs and open systems, business units and even individual departments were making their own IT investment decisions. This was occurring even though the company's long-established policy was that IT was to be resourced and managed centrally.

With companywide pressure to cut expenses, the IT area was a logical place to look. That's because for BMO Financial, as with most other financial institutions, expenditures on information technology are huge. Banks are said to be the second-largest IT purchasers in Canada, second only to the telecom and communications industry. And within BMO, Chairman and CEO Tony Comper has said IT expenditures rank second, after employee costs. In a cost-cutting environment, the IT area was a logical place to look for savings.

To realize these savings, BMO created a new Technology Solutions (T&S) group with 5600 employees. Creating this centralized resource helped the company eliminate overlap and duplication across lines of business. T&S group leaders were also appointed to act in an advisory capacity to business unit leaders and provide sophisticated advice on IT investment decisions. These same business unit leaders were also charged with the responsibility of demonstrating that any new investments would actually deliver tangible business benefits. IT processes were standardized, with BMO adopting what it calls a "one-organization/one-set-of-processes" mode. The company is said to have standardized its technology, as well as its IT applications, practices, and project management.

As of September 2003, BMO's CEO Tony Comper reported that virtually 100 percent of the company's IT staff and well over 50 percent of its IT assets were controlled by the new centralized function. Savings from the centralization effort were projected in the 15 to 20 percent range. And, the company seemed well on its way of achieving its stated objective of "having an accurate accounting of how each IT investment has paid off."

As the GM and BMO examples suggest, operating a multidivisional structure is no easy task. It is perhaps the biggest challenge that top managers face. Because the multidivisional structure is so widely used, we need to look closely at its advantages and disadvantages.

Advantages of a Multidivisional Structure When the multidivisional structure is managed effectively, it provides a large organization with several advantages.[13]

Increased Organizational Effectiveness. A division of labour generally increases organizational effectiveness. In a multidivisional structure there is a clear division of labour between corporate and divisional managers. Divisional managers are responsible for the day-to-day operations of their respective divisions and for tailoring divisional activities to the needs of customers. Corporate managers are responsible for long-term planning for the corporation as a whole and for tailoring the mission of the divisions to suit the goals of the whole organization.

Increased Control. Corporate managers monitor the performance of divisional managers. The extra control provided by the corporate office can encourage the stronger pursuit of internal organizational efficiency by divisional managers. Knowing that they have to answer to corporate managers, divisional managers may curb their inclination to increase the size of their personal staffs and thus increase their status. They may also think twice before investing in products that increase their status but do little to promote corporate performance.

More generally, as the GM and BMO examples suggest, the creation of self-contained divisions means that corporate managers can develop control systems to compare the performance of one division with the performance of another by measuring profitability or product development time. Consequently, corporate managers are in a good position to intervene and take selective action to correct inefficiencies when they arise.

Profitable Growth. When each division is its own profit centre—that is, when its individual profitability can be clearly evaluated—corporate headquarters can identify the divisions in which an investment of funds is likely to yield the greatest returns.[14] Thus corporate executives can make better capital resource allocation decisions to promote corporate growth. At the same time, their role as monitor rather than as administrator means that they can manage a greater number of different businesses and activities. The multidivisional structure allows a company to grow without suffering from the problems of communication or information overload that can occur when the two roles are mixed, as they are in the functional structure.

Internal Labour Market. The most able divisional managers are promoted to become corporate managers. Thus divisional managers have an incentive to perform well because superior performance could result in promotion to high office. A large divisional company possesses an internal labour market, which increases motivation for people at all levels to increase organizational effectiveness.

Disadvantages of a Multidivisional Structure Like other structures, multidivisional structures are associated with certain problems. Although good management can control most of the problems, it cannot eliminate them.

Managing the Corporate–Divisional Relationship. The central management problem posed by a multidivisional structure is how much authority to centralize at the corporate level and how much authority to decentralize to the operating divisions. On one hand, each division is closest to its particular operating environment and is in the best position to develop plans and objectives to increase its own effectiveness, so decentralization is a logical choice. On the other hand, headquarters' role is to adopt the long-term view and to tailor divisional activities to the needs of the whole organization, so centralization has advantages too. The balance between the two has to be managed all the time. Too much centralization of authority can straitjacket the divisions and let headquarters take responsibility for decision making, and the result can be poor performance. GM's attempt to centralize decision making to reduce costs was a disaster because all GM cars started to look the same. Too much decentralization, however, can result in giving the divisions so much freedom that they slack off and fail to control their costs. This can lead, as it did with BMO, to costly overlaps and duplication across lines of business. The corporate–divisional relationship needs to be managed continually. Over time, as the operating environment changes, the decision about which activities to centralize and which to decentralize will change.

Coordination Problems Between Divisions. When a multidivisional structure is created, measures of effectiveness such as return on investment can be used to compare divisions' performance, and corporate headquarters can allocate capital to the divisions on the basis of their performance. One problem with this approach is that divisions may begin to compete for resources, and the rivalry may prevent them from cooperating with each other. Such a rivalry can harm organizational performance when a company's effectiveness depends on the divisions' sharing of knowledge and information about innovations to enhance the performance of all divisions. It would be counterproductive, for example, if one of GM's divisions invented a new super-efficient engine and refused to share the information with other divisions.

Transfer price
The price at which one division sells a product or information about innovations to another division.

Transfer Pricing. Problems between divisions often revolve around the **transfer price**—the price at which one division sells a product or information about innovations to another division. To maximize its own return on investment, one division will want a high transfer price, but that will penalize the other division, which is, after all, part of the same organization. Thus, as each division pursues its own goals, coordination problems inside the organization can emerge. The role of the corporate centre is to manage such problems, as Sloan of GM noted. It is very important that a multidivisional organization establish integrating mechanisms that enable managers from different divisions to cooperate. Mechanisms like integrating roles and integrating departments are very important in promoting cooperation. The corporate office itself is a type of integrating department.

Bureaucratic Costs. Multidivisional structures are very expensive to operate. Each division has a full complement of support functions, including research and development. Thus there is extensive duplication of activities within the organization.

The cost of operating a multidivisional structure must constantly be evaluated, and if the benefits relative to the costs seem to be falling, the company either should move to reduce the number of divisions or find a way to reduce the costs of its support functions. It might be possible, for example, for an organization to change to a product division structure or to a product team structure (discussion follows) and service the needs of its different products through one set of centralized support functions. When a company is operating in different businesses and producing very different products such as cars and fast food, however, such a restructuring is rarely possible.

Communication Problems. Tall hierarchies tend to have communication problems, particularly the distortion of information. These problems are common in multidivisional structures because they tend to be the tallest of all the structures that organizations use. In them, the gap between the corporate centre and the divisions is especially wide. A divisional manager may deliberately disguise falling performance in his or her division in order to receive larger capital allocations; when a company has 200 divisions, such deception can be hard to detect. In addition, it may take so long for decisions to be made and transmitted to the divisions that responses to competitors are too slow. The more centralized an organization is, the more of a problem communication will be.

Product Team Structure In a product division structure, members of support functions such as marketing and R&D coordinate with the different divisions as their services are needed, but their main loyalty is to their function, not to the division. Increasingly, organizations are finding that the functional orientation of specialists is not in the organization's best interests, because industry competition has become focused on the product and especially on the need to customize the product to suit customer needs. Moreover, increased competition has made it important to reduce the time needed to bring a product to market by speeding product development while reducing product development costs. One solution to this problem might be a multidivisional structure in which each division has its own set of support functions. But, as we just discussed, this structure is very expensive to operate, and communication problems between divisions can slow innovation and product development. Many companies, in their search for a new structure to solve these problems, have re-engineered their divisional structures into a product team structure.

A product team structure is a cross between the product division structure, in which the support functions are centralized, and the multidivisional structure, in which each division has its own support functions. In a **product team structure**, specialists from the support functions are combined into product development teams that specialize in the needs of a particular kind of product (see Figure 6-8). Each team is, in effect, a self-contained division headed by a product team manager (PTM in Figure 6.8), who supervises all the operational activities associated with developing and manufacturing the product. The product teams focus on the needs of one product (or client) or a few related products, and they owe their allegiance not to their functions, but to the product team they join. The vice presidents of the functions, at the top of the organization, retain overall functional control, but decision-making authority for each product is decentralized to the team, and each team becomes responsible for the success of a project. General Dynamics Canada has developed what it calls an "interactive team" concept, whereby staff develop their skills and acquire new ones through participation in integrated product teams.[15]

Product team structure
A divisional structure in which specialists from the support functions are combined into product development teams that specialize in the needs of a particular kind of product.

Hallmark Cards has also found this approach to coordinating functions and products to be an effective way to develop new products quickly. Throughout the 1980s, Hallmark used a functional structure to coordinate activities. A large number of artists, writers, lithographers, and designers working in different functional departments produced a huge array of greeting cards. The problems of coordinating the activities of 700 writers and artists across functional boundaries became so complex and difficult that it was taking Hallmark two years to develop a new card. To solve its product development problems, Hallmark re-engineered to a product team structure. Artists and writers were formed into product teams around particular categories of greeting cards, such as Mother's Day cards, Christmas cards, and so on. With no differences in subunit orientation to impede the flow of information, mutual adjustment became much easier, and work was performed much more quickly. Product development time shrank from years to weeks.

A product team structure is more decentralized than a functional structure or a product division structure, and specialists in the various product teams are permitted to make on-the-spot decisions—something particularly important in service organizations. The grouping into self-contained divisions increases integration because each

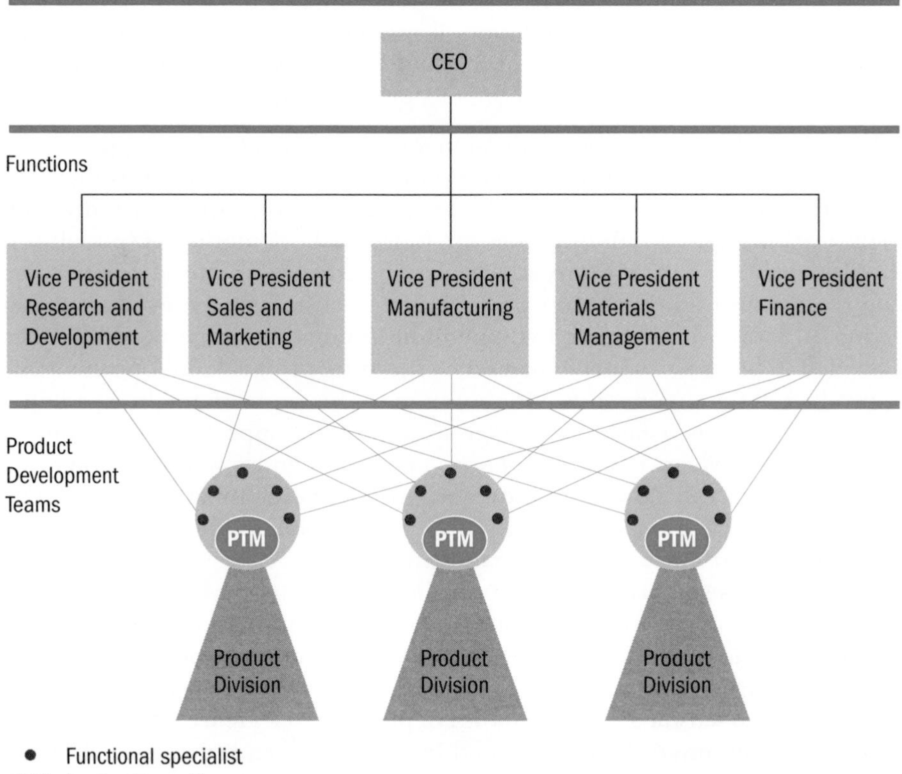

FIGURE 6-8
Product Team Structure.
Each product team manager (PTM) supervises the activities associated with developing and manufacturing a product.

product team becomes responsible for all aspects of its operations. Through close collaboration, team members become intensely involved in all aspects of product development and in tailoring the product to its market. Moreover, the high level of integration produced by teams makes it possible to make decisions quickly to respond to changes in customer requirements. DaimlerChrysler (then just Chrysler) was one of the very first companies to experiment with moving to a product team structure; its choice of this structure saved the company from bankruptcy. (See Organizational Insight 6.3.)

In the mid-1990s, Chrysler's turnaround led to its acquisition by Daimler Benz, which wanted to obtain Chrysler's new competencies in low-cost production and rapid product development and implant them in its own organization. The new DaimlerChrysler has been attempting to combine these competencies with Daimler's engineering and design competencies to produce world-class cars in all price ranges.

The company has run into new problems, however, in combining two very different structures and cultures into a cohesive whole, something that often occurs after a merger. We discuss these issues in Chapter 10, when organizational change and redesign are examined in detail.

In summary: The division of activities by product is the second most common method organizations use to group activities, after grouping them by function. Product structure increases horizontal differentiation and vertical differentiation and leads to the differentiation of managers into corporate-level, division-level, and function-level managers. In recent years, many large companies have moved from one type

ORGANIZATIONAL INSIGHT 6.3

Iacocca Pioneers Chrysler's Team Structure

After Lee Iacocca took over troubled Chrysler in the 1980s, he totally changed its approach to product development. Formerly, the company had come up with an idea for a new model of car, formed a product division to take control of the idea, and made the division managers responsible for obtaining the inputs of the various functions located at the top of the organization. The divisions had made their contributions sequentially; so, for example, design had the idea, engineering designed the prototype, purchasing and supply ordered the inputs, manufacturing made the vehicle, and marketing and sales sold it. Iacocca saw that this approach was very ineffective. Typically, Chrysler took seven or eight years to bring a new car to market, more than twice as long as the three years needed by Toyota or Nissan. Moreover, this system resulted in products with higher costs and lower quality than Japanese products. Why?

According to Iacocca, when a company like Chrysler produces a range of complex and technically sophisticated products, getting the different functional support groups to cooperate and coordinating their activities to arrive at the final product design is a nightmare. One function's activities may conflict with another function's, and no function learns anything from another because of the strength of their respective subunit orientations. The engineering department says, "Our aim is to develop an aerodynamic, lightweight car that gets good mileage, and we are not really interested in how difficult it is to assemble or how costly it is to build." The marketing department says, "You engineers and production folks had better control your costs so that we can price this car competitively."

Iacocca was determined to change this situation. As an experiment, he used what he called a "platform team" to develop the Dodge Viper, a luxury sports car. In a platform team, which is the same as a product development team, the functions are organized around the product. A team consists of product and manufacturing engineers, planners and buyers, designers, financial analysts, and marketing and sales people, and each team has sole responsibility for getting its car to the market. The team concept encourages different specialists to interact and thus speeds communication and allows problems to be solved quickly, creatively, and efficiently. Moreover, as the specialists begin to learn from one another, the quality of the product improves, and the pace of innovation quickens. The concept was wildly successful at Chrysler. "Team Viper" got the product to market in three years—a record time for the organization. Moreover, the car was a hit, and customers lined up to buy it.

With the success of the platform team concept established, Iacocca re-engineered the rest of Chrysler's functionally organized product development operations into product-oriented platform teams. Chrysler had four such teams: large-car, small-car, minivan, and Jeep/truck.[16] Three of these teams operate out of Chrysler's billion-dollar technology centre in Auburn Hills, Michigan, where all the research and engineering resources that the teams need are readily available. Chrysler's new team-based structure resulted in a continuing trend toward lower costs, higher quality, and faster development time.

of product structure to another in an attempt to save money or make better use of their functional resources. It is important for managers continually to evaluate how well their product structure is working because it has a direct impact on the effectiveness of their organization.

DIVISIONAL STRUCTURE II: GEOGRAPHIC STRUCTURE

Geographic divisional structure
A divisional structure in which divisions are organized according to the requirements of the different locations in which an organization operates.

Of the three types of product structure discussed earlier, the multidivisional structure is the one most often used by large organizations. It provides the extra control that is important when a company produces a wide array of complex products or services or enters new industries and needs to deal with different sets of stakeholders and competitive forces. However, when the control problems that companies experience are a function of geography, a **geographic divisional structure**, in which divisions are organized according to the requirements of the different locations in which an organization operates, is available.

As an organization grows, it may develop a national customer base. As it spreads into different regions of a country, it needs to adjust its structure to align its core competencies with the needs of customers in different geographic regions. A geographic structure allows some functions to be centralized at one headquarters location and others to be decentralized to a regional level. For example, the can manufacturer Crown Cork and Seal produces many of the cans used in canning soft drinks, personal hygiene products, vegetables, and fruits. Because cans are bulky objects that are expensive to transport, it makes sense to establish manufacturing plants in the different regions where cans are most used. Also, there is a limit to how many cans the company can efficiently produce at one plant location; when economies of scale become exhausted at one location, it makes sense to establish another plant in a new location. Recognizing these limiting factors, Crown Cork and Seal operates several manufacturing plants throughout the United States and Canada. Each plant has its own purchasing, quality control, and sales departments. Research and development and engineering, however, are centralized at its headquarters location. Similarly, McCain Foods has expanded its market for potato products by acquiring food growing and processing companies throughout the world. This way it gains control over the supply and transportation problems that would otherwise occur if it attempted to ship its product from the New Brunswick base alone.

Neiman-Marcus, the American specialty department store, also has a geographic structure, but for a different reason. When Neiman-Marcus operated only in Texas, it used a functional structure to coordinate activities. But as it opened stores at selected sites across the United States, it confronted a dilemma: how to respond to the customer needs of different regions while achieving the cost advantages of central purchasing. Neiman-Marcus's solution was to establish a geographic structure that groups stores by region (see Figure 6-9). Individual stores are under the direction of a regional office, which is responsible for coordinating the market needs of the stores in its region and for responding to specific product needs—for example, surfboards in Los Angeles and down parkas in Chicago. The regional office feeds information back to headquarters in Dallas, where centralized purchasing functions make decisions for the company as a whole.

When McCain Foods attempted to develop its frozen food line in the South African market, it soon found that it needed to market the products in very different ways. Unlike many other countries in which McCain operates, South Africa has an extremely high unemployment rate, a large segment of the black population that lives in communities without electricity, and a white population that includes many who rely on black maids to cook fresh foods. To overcome the cultural and demographic problems, McCain marketed its products at black funerals (which typically attract 700 people), matching the family's purchase of selected frozen foods and supplying sundry items, such as tents, paper napkins, and cups.[17]

McCain Foods, Crown Cork and Seal, and Neiman-Marcus superimposed a geographic grouping over their basic functional grouping, thereby increasing horizontal differentiation. The creation of a new level in the hierarchy—regional managers—and the decentralization of control to regional hierarchies also increased vertical differentiation. The regional hierarchies provide more control than is possible with one cen-

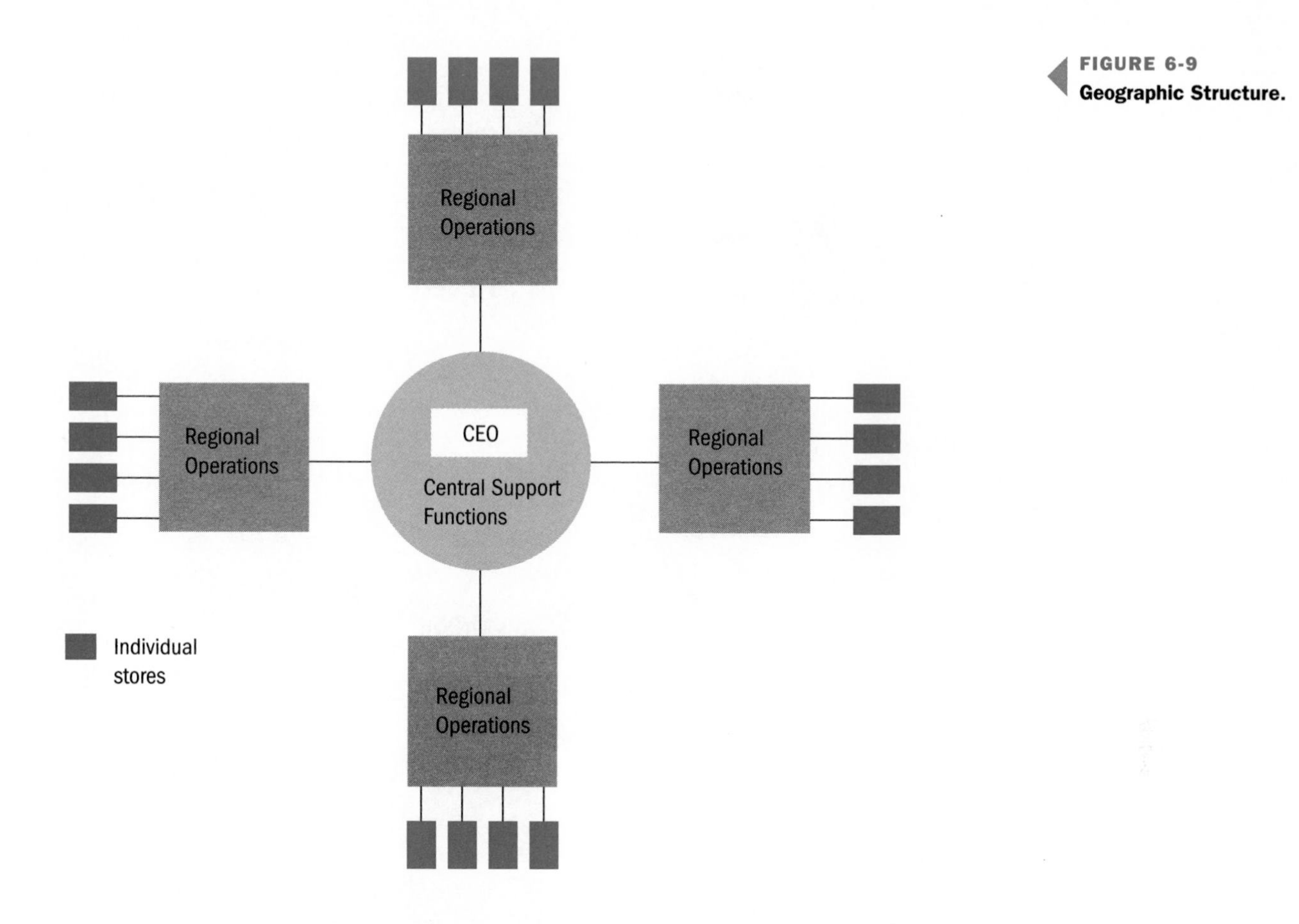

FIGURE 6-9
Geographic Structure.

tralized hierarchy and, in the cases of McCain, Crown Cork and Seal, and Neiman-Marcus, have increased effectiveness. Organizational Insight 6.4 profiles Wal-Mart's geographic structure.

DIVISIONAL STRUCTURE III: MARKET STRUCTURE

The grouping of activities by product or geography makes the product or region the centre of attention. In contrast, a market structure aligns functional skills and activities with the needs of different customer groups. Marketing, not manufacturing, becomes the basis on which the organization establishes divisions. Figure 6-11 shows a market structure designed to meet the needs of commercial, consumer, corporate, and government customers.

Each customer group has a different marketing focus, and the job of each group is to develop products to suit the needs of its specific customers. Each group makes use of centralized support functions. Engineering tailors products to suit the various needs of each group, and manufacturing follows each group's specifications. Because the market structure focuses the activities of the whole organization on the needs of the customer, the organization can quickly sense changes in its market and transfer skills and resources to satisfy the needs of this important stakeholder group. In March 1994 Wal-Mart moved into Canada with the purchase of the Woolco stores of Woolworth Canada. It located its head office in Mississauga, Ontario, and over the next ten years developed over 230 stores and five Sam's Clubs, employing over 60 000 people. Nova Scotia Power achieved more cost effectiveness when it moved from a product structure to a market structure. (See Organizational Insight 6.5)

ORGANIZATIONAL INSIGHT 6.4

Wal-Mart Goes National, Then Global

As we discussed in Chapter 4, Wal-Mart has found the right balance between a mechanistic and organic style of operating and has prospered. Its explosive growth has continued through the 1990s, and in 2001 alone the company opened 150 supercentres, 60 discount stores, and 12 Sam's Clubs, and took over two chains of supermarkets in Europe. Analysts estimate these new openings will add another US$30 billion in sales. The problem facing Wal-Mart has been to choose a structure complex enough to operate its growing empire and yet will allow it to maintain its mechanistic/organic balance. The structure it chose was a geographic structure (see Figure 6-10).

Under the control of CEO David Glass and COO Lee Scott, Wal-Mart centralizes its materials management and sales and marketing activities at corporate headquarters. Then it divides its store operations into regions, including international operations, and gives its regional managers input into what mix of products should be sold in their regions to maximize sales. At the moment, Wal-Mart is working on replicating its materials management and marketing activities in Europe, where it intends to become a major retailer in the decade ahead. As it expands the global scope of its operations, no doubt it will further subdivide its international division to meet customer needs.

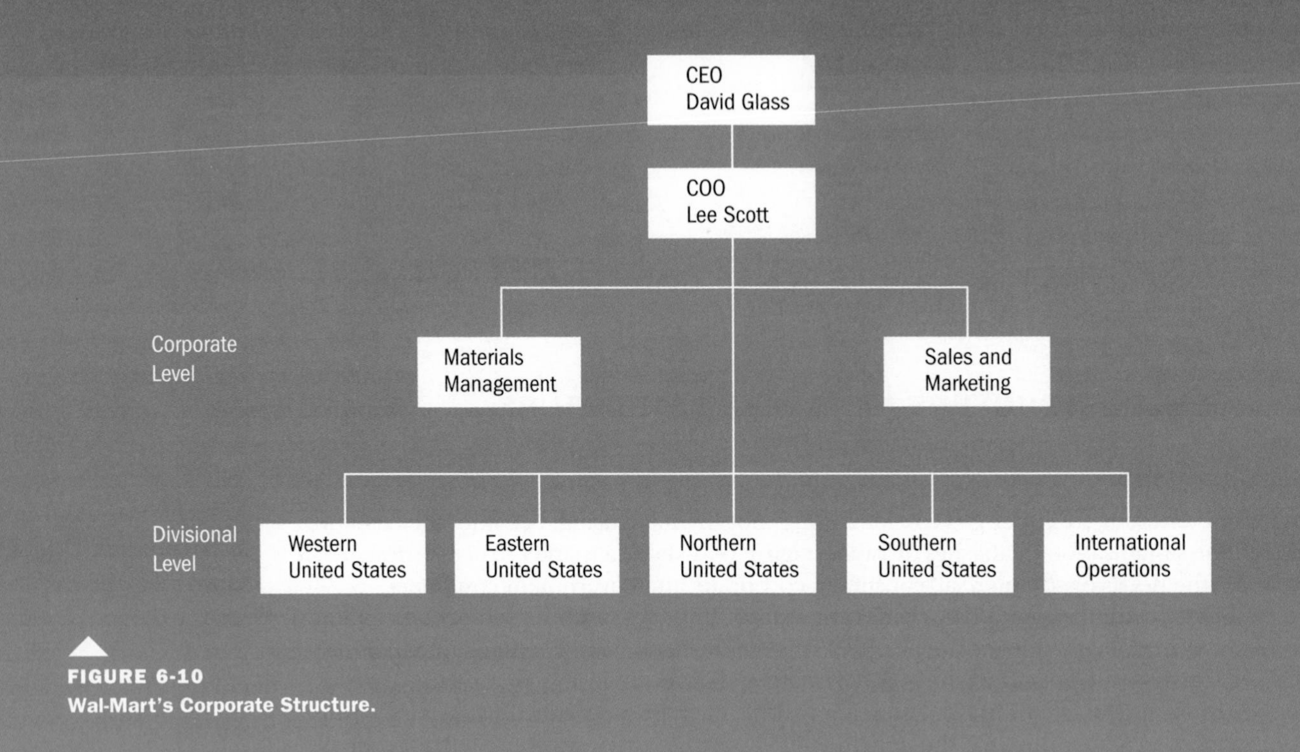

FIGURE 6-10
Wal-Mart's Corporate Structure.

People and Changing Structures

When an organization is structured along functional, product, geographic, or division lines, the lives of those involved are often directly affected. Structures are, after all, arrangements of people to achieve communication, coordination, and control. When a company restructures, some managers may gain through promotion, while others

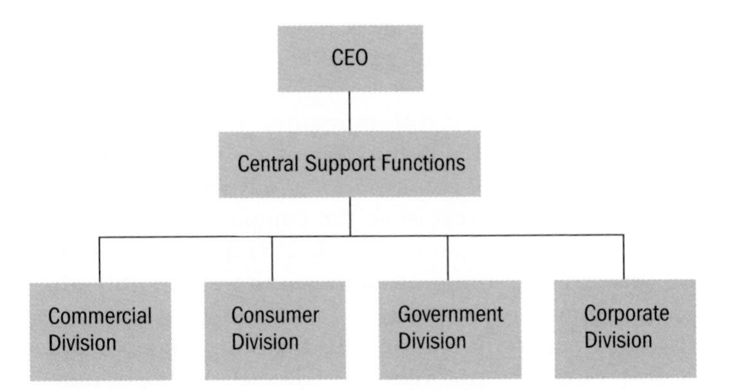

FIGURE 6-11
Market Structure.
Each division focuses on the needs of a distinct customer group.

may suffer demotion or dismissal. The same is true of employees. Often organizational structuring is accompanied by layoffs and the reassignment of jobs. When Wal-Mart moved into Canada, for example, its "no union policy" created a number of problems for unionized employees;[18] when Nova Scotia Power began to re-engineer its workforce, there were not only a series of layoffs, with employee numbers falling from over 2500 to 1900 is less than five years, but also a number of physical and emotional problems associated with the merger of job tasks;[19] and Air Canada's takeover of Canadian

ORGANIZATIONAL INSIGHT 6.5

Re-engineering the Market at Nova Scotia Power

Prior to 1991, Nova Scotia Power (NSP), the largest supplier of electricity in Nova Scotia, had two main divisions, Thermal and Transmission/Distribution. Although each of these divisions was structured around its core activities of the production of electricity and the transmission and distribution of electricity, it seemed as if the two divisions were operating as separate companies and there was little in the way of coordination between them. In terms of structure, NSP's division of labour could best be described as multidivisional, with a focus on the product, not the customer. In fact, the company was more like a construction company than one in the service industry.

All this changed when Nova Scotia Power introduced business process re-engineering. A new focus on process outcomes and customer service literally changed the way NSP did business and it also did away with its traditional organizational structure, as the boundaries between the division of labour became blurred.

In order to enhance customer service, especially in rural areas of the province, the position of the customer service field representative (CSFR) was created. This position was a combination of meter reader, meter installer, and bill collector. While they had previously done only one of those jobs, employees were trained to be able to do all three. This job enlargement enabled Nova Scotia Power to respond more quickly to customer needs and allowed it to be more cost effective by reducing duplication of services and down time. According to Nova Scotia Power, CSFR employees "come from different backgrounds and perform different jobs but they are all focused on the goal of satisfying each and every customer."[20]

Airlines led to a number of problems with seniority rights, as the new employees were allowed to count their previous years of experience at Canadian, leading to considerable bitterness among Air Canada employees.

Restructuring can also lead to unintended discriminatory practices.[21] At Nova Scotia Power, for example, the introduction of a culture change program enhanced the company's decision to introduce a range of employment equity strategies, but the promotion of women eventually took a back seat once the company privatized and introduced re-engineering.[22] A number of companies do pay attention to the human factor when restructuring and this can help the process to run more smoothly while ensuring that employees are not forgotten in the process.

In Canada a number of companies are noted for their focus on "(1) an aligned leadership team; (2) intrinsically motivated employees; (3) flawlessly handled human resources initiatives; (4) effectively executed and communicated employee programs; and (5) employees connected to the business of their employer"[23]—all characteristics used by *The Globe and Mail* to judge the "50 Best Companies to Work For."[24] In 2004 the leading employers were judged to be those "who articulate a clear and consistent vision, starting with the CEO. They're the companies that develop programs to keep staff focused on their goals, while actually listening to them and acting on their suggestions."[25] The winners included BC Biomedical Laboratories Ltd., Flight Centre Ltd., Rothmans, Benson & Hedges Inc., Cintas Canada Ltd., and Hoffman-LaRoche Ltd.

MANAGERIAL IMPLICATIONS

Changing Organizational Structure

1. As an organization grows, be sensitive to the need to change a functional structure to improve the control of organizational activities.
2. When the control problem is to manage the production of a wide range of products, consider using a form of divisional structure.
3. Use a product division structure if the organization's products are generally similar.
4. Move to a multidivisional structure if the organization produces a wide range of different or complex goods and services or operates in more than one business or industry.
5. When the control problem is to reduce product development time by increasing the integration between support functions, consider using a product team structure.
6. When the control problem is to customize products to the needs of customers in different geographic areas, consider using a geographic structure.
7. When the control problem is to coordinate the marketing of all of a company's products to several distinct groups of customers, use a market structure.
8. Always weigh the benefits that will arise from moving to a new structure (that is, the control problems that will be solved) against the costs that will arise from moving to the new structure (that is, the higher operating costs associated with managing a more complex structure) to see whether changing organizational structure will increase organizational effectiveness.
9. Remember to take people into account when considering any structural changes. Keep in mind that any structure refers to an arrangement of people that controls and coordinates their activities.

MATRIX STRUCTURE

The search for better and faster ways to develop products and to respond to customer needs has led companies to adopt a matrix structure, a design that groups people and resources in two ways simultaneously: by function and by product.[26] A matrix structure is both similar to and different from a product team structure.

Before examining those differences, it is necessary to examine how a matrix structure works (see Figure 6-12). In the context of organizational design, a matrix is a rectangular grid that shows a *vertical* flow of *functional* responsibility and a *horizontal* flow of *product* responsibility. In Figure 6-12 the lines pointing down represent the grouping of tasks by function, and the lines pointing from left to right represent the grouping of tasks by product. An organization with a matrix structure is differentiated into whatever functions the organization needs to achieve its goals. The organization itself is very flat, having minimal hierarchical levels within each function and decentralized authority. Functional employees report to the heads of their respective functions (usually, functional vice presidents) but do not work under their direct supervision. Instead, the work of functional personnel is determined primarily by membership in one of several cross-functional product teams under the leadership of a product manager. The members of the team are called **two-boss employees** because they report to two superiors: the product team manager and the functional manager. The defining feature of a matrix structure is the fact that team members have two superiors.

Two-boss employees
Employees who report to two superiors: the product team manager and the functional manager.

The team is both the basic building block of the matrix and the principal mechanism for coordination and integration. Role and authority relationships are deliberately vague because the underlying assumption of matrix structure is that when team members are given responsibility without being given more authority, they are forced to cooperate to get the job done. The matrix thus relies on minimal vertical control from the formal hierarchy and maximal horizontal control from the use of integrating mechanisms—teams—which promote mutual adjustment. Matrix structures are a type of organic structure (see Chapter 4).

Both matrix structure and product team structure make use of teams to coordinate activities, but they differ in two major respects. First, team members in a product team structure have only one boss: the product team manager. Team members in a matrix structure have two bosses—the product manager and the functional manager—and thus divided loyalty. They must juggle the conflicting demands of the function and the product. Second, in the matrix structure, team membership is not fixed. Team members move from team to team, to where their skills are most needed.

In theory, because of those two differences, the matrix structure should be more flexible than the product team structure, in which lines of authority and coordination are more stable. The matrix is deliberately designed to overcome differences in functional orientation and to force integration on its members. Does it work?

Advantages of a Matrix Structure

A matrix structure has four significant advantages over more traditional structures.[27] First, the use of cross-functional teams is designed to reduce functional barriers and overcome the problem of subunit orientation. With differentiation between functions kept to a minimum, integration becomes easier to achieve. In turn, the team structure facilitates adaptation and learning for the whole organization. The matrix's team system is designed to make the organization flexible and able to respond quickly to changing product and customer needs. Not surprisingly, matrix structures were first used in high-tech companies for which the ability to develop technologically advanced

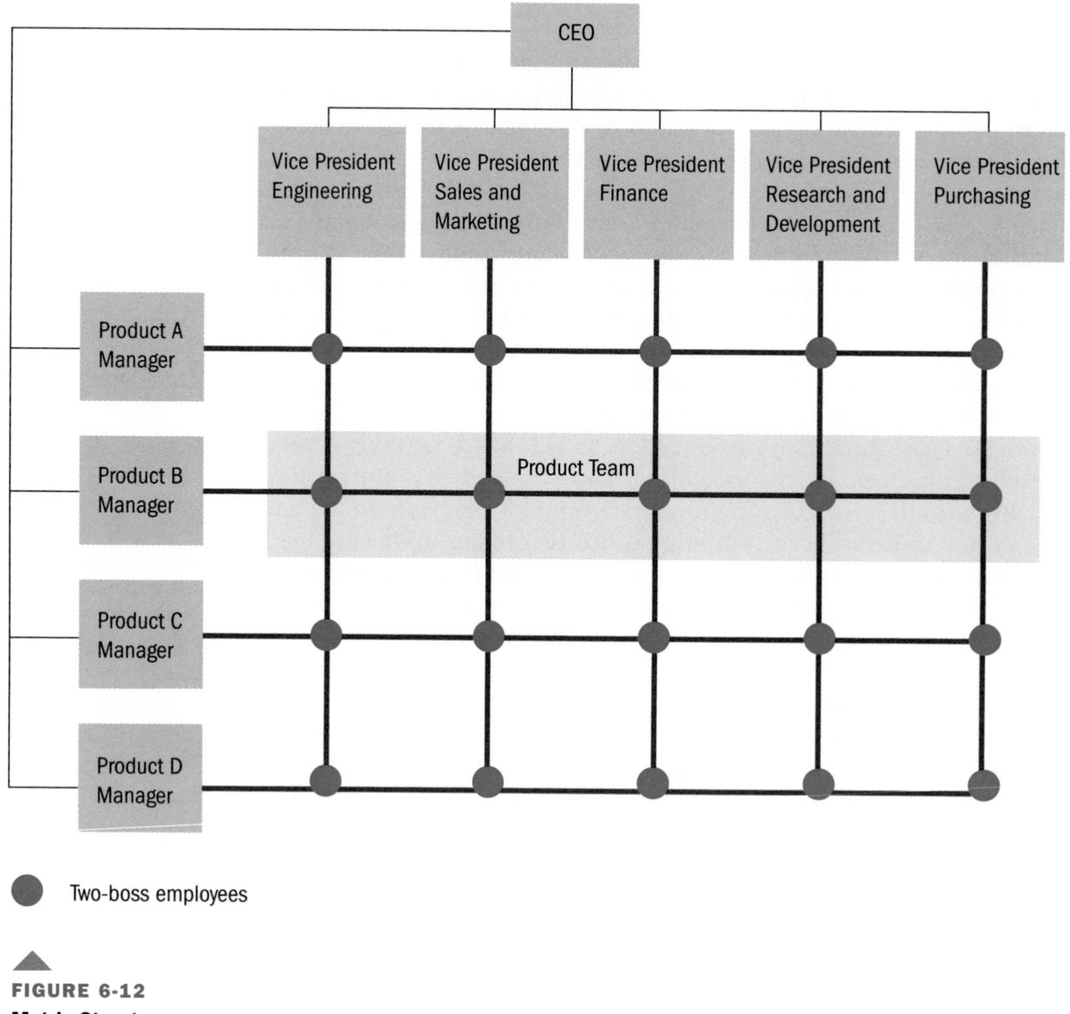

FIGURE 6-12
Matrix Structure.
Team members are two-boss employees because they report to both the product team manager and the functional manager.

products quickly was the key to success. Environment Canada introduced a matrix structure in the early 1990s to deal with the coordination of a very complex structure that spans numerous departments, regions, and stakeholder groups. Prior to 1994 the services that comprise Environment Canada operated separately across designated regions, each with its own identity. In 1994 five regional directors general (RDGs) were appointed, each reporting to the deputy minister. Each RDG is responsible for an integrated service in his or her region with the different regionalized services reporting directly to him or her. This allows RDGs to more effectively respond to regional needs and situations. Concurrently, three services retain a responsibility "for delivering national programs in the fields of meteorology, environmental conservation, and environmental protection."[28] In the private sphere, CAE Inc. has developed a matrix structure to enhance its efficiency in building flight simulators.

A second advantage of the matrix structure is that it opens up communication between functional specialists and provides an opportunity for team members from different functions to learn from one another and develop their skills. Thus matrix structure facilitates technological progress because the interactions of different specialists produce the innovations that give a company its core competencies.

Third, the matrix enables an organization to maximize its use of skilled professionals, who move from product to product as needed. At the beginning of a project, for example, basic skills in R&D are needed, but after early innovation, the skills of engineers are needed to design and make the product. People move around the matrix to wherever they are most needed; team membership is constantly changing to suit the needs of the product.

Fourth, the dual functional and product focus promotes concern for both cost and quality. The primary goal of functional specialists is likely to be technical: producing the highest quality, most innovative product possible (regardless of cost). In contrast, the primary goals of product managers are likely to concern cost and speed of development—doing whatever can be done given the amounts of time and money that are available. This built-in focus on both quality and cost keeps the team on track and keeps technical possibilities in line with commercial realities.

Disadvantages of a Matrix Structure

In theory, the principles underlying matrix structures seem logical. In practice, however, many problems arise.[29] To identify the sources of these problems, consider what is missing in a matrix.

A matrix lacks the advantages of bureaucratic structure (discussed in Chapter 5). With a flat hierarchy and minimal rules and SOPs, the matrix lacks a control structure that leads employees to develop stable expectations of one another. In theory, team members continually negotiate with one another about role responsibilities, and the resulting give-and-take makes the organization flexible. In practice, many people do not like the role ambiguity and role conflict that matrix structures can produce. For example, the functional boss, focused on quality, and the product boss, focused on cost, often have different expectations of the team members. The result is role conflict. Team members become unsure of what to do, and a structure designed to promote flexibility may actually reduce it if team members become afraid to assume responsibility.

The lack of a clearly defined hierarchy of authority can also lead to conflict between functions and product teams over the use of resources. In theory, product managers are supposed to buy the services of the functional specialists on the team (say, for example, the services of ten engineers at $500 per day). In practice, however, cost and resource allocation becomes fuzzy as products exceed their budgets and specialists are unable to overcome technical obstacles. Power struggles emerge between product and functional managers, and politicking takes place to gain the support of top management.

As those examples show, matrix structures have to be carefully managed to retain their flexibility. They do not automatically produce the high level of coordination that is claimed of them, and people who work in a matrix often complain about high levels of stress and uncertainty.

Over time, people in a matrix structure are likely to experience a vacuum of authority and responsibility and move to create their own bureaucracy to provide themselves with some sense of structure and stability. Informal leaders emerge within teams. These people become increasingly recognized as experts or as great "team leaders." A status hierarchy emerges within teams. Team members often resist transfer to other teams in order to remain with their colleagues.

When top managers do not get the results they expect, they sometimes try to increase their control over the matrix and to increase their power over decision making. Slowly but surely, as people jockey for power and authority, a system that started out very flat and decentralized turns into a centralized, less-flexible structure. The matrix becomes bureaucratized, and all the bureaucratic problems noted in Chapter 5 arise because every principle of bureaucracy is being improperly implemented.

Matrix structures need to be managed carefully if their advantages are to outweigh their disadvantages. However, matrix structures are not designed for use in normal, everyday, organizational situations. They are appropriate in situations in which a high level of coordination between functional experts is needed because the organization needs to respond quickly to changing conditions. Given the problems associated with managing a deliberately ambiguous matrix structure, many growing companies have chosen to overlay a functional structure or a product division structure with product teams rather than attempt to manage a full-fledged matrix. The use of IT greatly facilitates this process.

The Multidivisional Matrix Structure

Multidivisional structures allow an organization to coordinate activities effectively but are difficult to manage. Communication and coordination problems arise simply because of the high degree of differentiation within a multidivisional structure. Consequently, a company with several divisions needs to be sure that it has sufficient integration mechanisms in place to handle its control needs. Sometimes the corporate centre becomes very remote from divisional activities and is unable to play this important integrating role. When that happens, organizations sometimes introduce the matrix structure at the top of the organization and create a **multidivisional matrix structure**, a structure that provides for more integration between corporate and divisional managers and between divisional managers. Figure 6-13 depicts this structure.

Multidivisional matrix structure
A structure that provides for more integration between corporate and divisional managers, and between divisional managers.

As the figure shows, this structure allows senior vice presidents at the corporate centre to send corporate-level specialists to each division to perform an in-depth analy-

FIGURE 6-13
Multidivisional Matrix Structure.

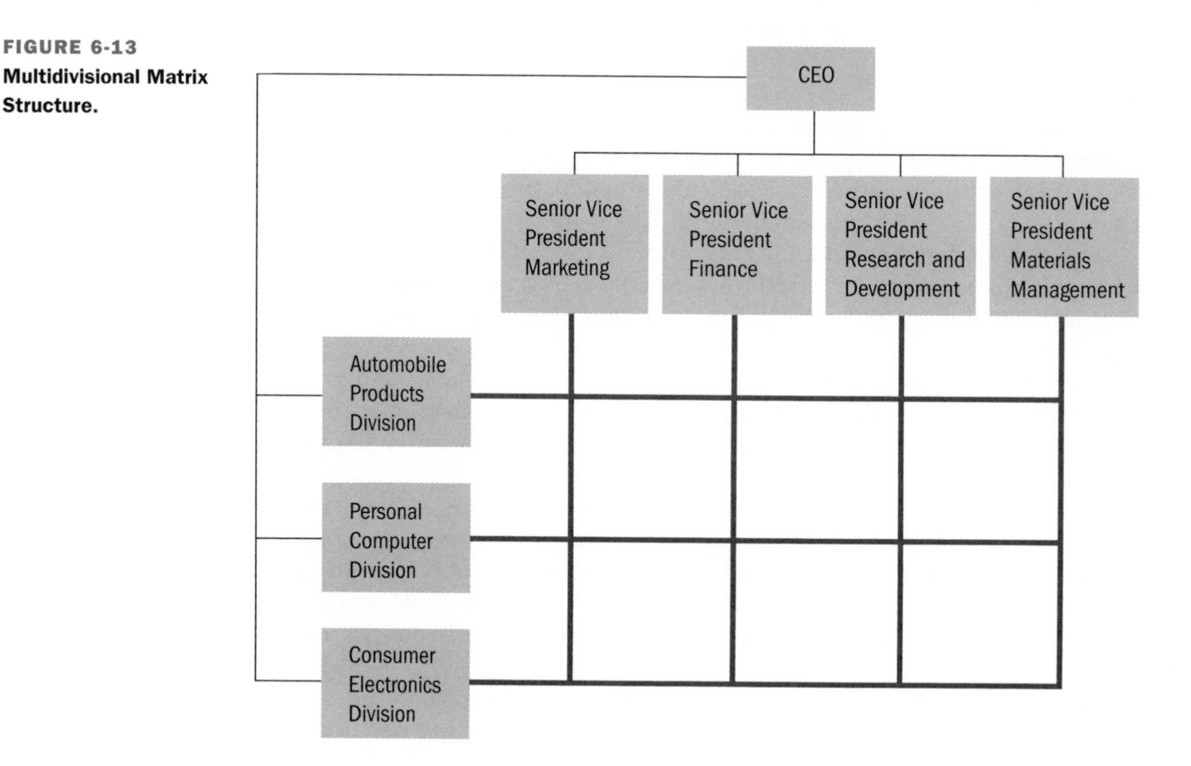

sis of the division's performance and to devise a functional action plan for all divisions. Divisional executives meet with corporate executives to trade knowledge and information and to coordinate divisional activities. The multidivisional matrix structure makes it much easier for top executives from the divisions and from the corporate centre to cooperate and jointly coordinate organizational activities. Many large international companies that operate globally use this structure. However, a discussion of how to design an international organizational structure is left until Chapter 8.

NETWORK STRUCTURE AND THE BOUNDARYLESS ORGANIZATION

Another innovation in organizational design in the use of network structures. Recall from Chapter 3 that a network structure is a cluster of different organizations whose actions are coordinated by contracts and agreements rather than through a formal hierarchy of authority.[30] Very often one organization takes the lead in creating the network as it searches for a way to increase effectiveness; for example, a clothing manufacturer may search for ways to produce and market clothes more cheaply. Rather than manufacturing the clothes in its own factories, the company decides to outsource its manufacturing to a low-cost Asian company; it also forms an agreement with a large domestic advertising agency to design and implement its sales campaign. Recall again how outsourcing is moving a value-creation activity that was done *inside* an organization to the *outside*, where it is done by another company.

Often, network structures become very complex as a company forms agreements with a whole range of suppliers, manufacturers, and distributors to outsource many of the value-creation activities involved in producing and marketing goods and services.[31] Compaq Computers, BMO, Cisco Systems, Celestica Inc., and Nike are companies involved in network structuring. Nike, for example, the largest and most profitable sports shoe manufacturer in the world, has developed a very complex network structure to produce its shoes. At the centre of the network is Nike's product design and research function located in Beaverton, Oregon, where Nike's designers pioneer new innovations in sports shoe design, such as the air pump and "Air Jordans." Almost all the other functional specialisms that Nike needs to produce and market its shoes have been outsourced to companies around the world!

How does Nike manage the relationships between all the companies in its network? Principally though the use of modern information technology (discussed in depth in Chapter 12). Nike's designers use computer-aided design (CAD) to design shoes, and all new product information, including manufacturing instructions, is stored electronically. When the designers have done their work, they relay all the blueprints for the new products electronically to Nike's network of suppliers and manufacturers in Southeast Asia.[32] For example, instructions for the design of a new sole may be sent to a supplier in Taiwan, and instructions for the leather uppers to a supplier in Malaysia. These suppliers then produce the shoe parts, which are then sent for final assembly to a manufacturer in China with whom Nike has established an alliance. From China these shoes are shipped to distributors throughout the world and are marketed in each country by an organization with which Nike has formed a contract.

Advantages of Network Structures

Why does Nike use a network structure to control the value-creation process rather than perform all the functional activities itself? There are several advantages that Nike, and other organizations, can realize by using a network structure.

First, to the degree that an organization can find a network partner that can perform a specific functional activity reliably, and at a lower cost, production costs are reduced.[33] Almost all of Nike's manufacturing is done in Asia, for example, because wages in Southeast Asia are a fraction of what they are in North America. Second, to the degree that an organization contracts with other organizations to perform specific value-creation activities, it avoids the high bureaucratic costs of operating a complex organizational structure. For example, the hierarchy can be kept as flat as possible and fewer managers are needed. Because Nike outsources many functional activities, for example, it is able to stay small and flexible. Control of the design process is decentralized to teams who are assigned to develop each of the new kinds of sports shoes for which Nike is known.

Third, a network structure allows an organization to act in an organic way. If the environment changes, for example, and new opportunities become apparent, an organization can quickly alter its network in response. For example, it can sever the links to companies whose services it no longer needs and develop new ones with companies that have the skills it does need. An organization that performed all of its own functional activities would take a longer time to respond to the changes taking place. Fourth, if any of its network partners fail to perform up to Nike's standards, they can be replaced with new partners. Finally, a very important reason for the development of networks has been that organizations gain access to low-cost foreign sources of inputs and functional expertise, something crucial in today's changing global environment.

Disadvantages of Network Structures

Although network structure has several advantages, it also has some drawbacks in certain situations. To see what these are, imagine a high-tech company racing to bring to market proprietary hardware and software faster than its competitors. How easy would it be to outsource the functional activities necessary to ensure that the hardware and software are compatible and bug-free? Not easy at all. Close interaction is needed between the hardware and software divisions, and between the different groups of hardware and software programmers responsible for designing the different parts of the system. A considerable level of mutual adjustment is needed to allow the groups to interact so that they can learn from one another and constantly improve the final product. Also, managers must be there to integrate the activities of the groups to make sure their activities mesh well. The coordination problems arising from having different companies perform different parts of the work process would be enormous. Moreover, there has to be considerable trust between the different groups so that they can share their ideas, something necessary for successful new product development.

It is unlikely that a network structure would provide an organization with the ability to control such a complex value-creation process because managers would lack the means at their disposal to effectively coordinate and motivate the various network partners. First, it would be difficult to obtain the ongoing learning that builds core competencies over time inside a company because separate companies have less incentive to make such an investment.[34] As a result, many opportunities to cut costs and increase quality would be lost. Second, if one of Nike's suppliers failed to perform well, Nike could easily replace it by forming a contract with another. But how easy is it to find reliable software companies who can both do the job and be trusted not to take proprietary information and give it to a company's competitors?

In general, the more complex the value-creation activities necessary to produce and market goods and services, the more problems there are associated with using a network structure.[35] Like the other structures discussed in this chapter, network structures are appropriate in some situations and not in others.

The Boundaryless Organization

The ability of managers to develop a network structure to produce or provide the goods and services their customers want, rather than create a complex organizational structure to do so, has led many researchers and consultants to popularize the idea of the "boundaryless organization." The boundaryless organization is composed of people who are linked by computers, faxes, computer-aided design systems, and video teleconferencing, and who may rarely or ever see one another face to face.[36] People come and go as their services are needed, much as in a matrix structure, but they are not formal members of an organization, just functional experts who form an alliance with an organization, fulfill their contractual obligations, and then move on to the next project.

The use of outsourcing and the development of network organization are increasing rapidly as organizations recognize the many opportunities they offer to reduce costs and increase flexibility. Clearly, managers have to assess carefully the relative benefits of having their own organization perform a functional activity or make a particular input, versus forming an alliance with another organization to do so to increase organizational effectiveness. Designing organizational structure is becoming an increasingly complex management activity in today's changing world.

SUMMARY

Designing organizational structure is a difficult and challenging task. Managers have to manage the vertical and horizontal dimensions of the structure continually and choose an appropriate allocation of authority and task responsibilities. As an organization grows and becomes more complex, changing its structure to respond to changing needs or contingencies becomes important.

Designing a structure that fits a company's needs is a large challenge. Each structure has advantages and disadvantages, and managers have to be ready and willing to redesign their organization in order to obtain the advantages and anticipate and minimize the problems of whichever structure they choose. An organization that is in control of its structure has an important competitive advantage over one that is not.

Many organizations ignore the coordination problems inherent in the organizing process. Too often, an organization waits until it is already in trouble (in decline) before attempting to deal with coordination and motivation problems. The characteristics of the top-management team are very important in this regard because they determine how decisions get made and how top managers perceive the problems the organization is experiencing. Chapter 6 has made the following main points:

1. A functional structure is a design that groups people because they have similar skills or use the same resources. Functional groups include finance, R&D, marketing, and engineering. All organizations begin as functional structures.
2. An organization needs to adopt a more complex structure when it starts to produce many products or when it confronts special needs, such as the need to produce new products quickly, to deal with different customer groups, or to handle growth into new regions.
3. The move to a more complex structure is based on three design choices: increasing vertical differentiation, increasing horizontal differentiation, and increasing integration.
4. Most organizations move from a functional structure to some kind of divisional structure: a product structure, a geographic structure, or a market structure.
5. There are three kinds of product structure: product division structure, multidivisional structure, and product team structure.

6. Product division structure is used when an organization produces broadly similar products that use the same set of support functions.
7. Multidivisional structures are available to organizations that are growing rapidly and producing a wide variety of products or are entering totally different kinds of industries. In a multidivisional structure, each product division is a self-contained division with the operating structure that best suits its needs. A central headquarters staff is responsible for coordinating the activities of the divisions in the organization. When a lot of coordination between divisions is required, a company can use a multidivisional matrix structure.
8. Product team structures put the focus on the product being produced. Teams of functional specialists are organized around the product to speed product development.
9. Geographic structures are used when organizations expand into new areas or begin to manufacture in many different locations.
10. Market structures are used when organizations wish to group activities to focus on the needs of distinct customer groups.
11. Structures are arrangements of people who are ultimately affected by restructuring decisions.
12. Matrix structures group activities by function and product. They are a special kind of structure that is available when an organization needs to deal with new or technically sophisticated products in rapidly changing markets.
13. Network structures are formed when an organization forms agreements or contracts with other organizations to perform specific functional value creation activities.

DISCUSSION QUESTIONS

1. As organizations grow and differentiate, what problems can arise with a functional structure?
2. How do the product division structure and the multidivisional structure differ?
3. Why might an organization prefer to use a product team structure rather than a matrix structure?
4. What are the principal differences between a functional structure and a multidivisional structure? Why does a company change from a functional to a multidivisional structure?
5. What are the advantages and disadvantages associated with network structures?

ORGANIZATIONAL THEORY IN ACTION

Practising Organizational Theory: Which New Organizational Structure?

Break up into groups of three to five people, and discuss the following scenario:

You are a group of managers of a major soft drink company that is going head to head with Coca-Cola to increase market share. Your strategy is to increase your product range to offer a soft drink bottled water in every segment of the market to attract customers and to begin offering soft drinks and other beverage products tailored to the needs of customers in different regions of the country.

Currently you have a functional structure. What you are trying to work out now is how best to implement your strategy in order to launch your new products. To what kind of structure should you move?

1. Debate the pros and cons of the different possible organizational structures.

2. Which structure will allow you to best achieve your goal at (a) lowest cost; (b) give you most responsiveness to customers; or (c) both?

Making the Connection #6

Find an example of a company that has changed its form of horizontal differentiation in some way. What did the company do? Why did it make the change? What does it hope to accomplish as a result of the change? What structure has it changed to?

The Ethical Dimension #6

When organizations outsource their functional activities, they typically lay off many, if not most, of the employees who used to perform the functional task within the organization's boundary. Levi Strauss, for example, closed down its last two U.S. plants and the remaining three Canadian plants in 2004; Dell Computer outsourced hundreds of its call centre customer service jobs to India; and Air Canada outsourced many of its jobs to small, private contractors.

1. Does it make good business sense to outsource? What are the potential advantages and disadvantages?
2. Given these advantages and disadvantages, when, and under what conditions, is it ethical to outsource organizational activities, lay off workers, and send those jobs abroad?

Analyzing the Organization: Design Module #6

This module focuses on horizontal differentiation in your organization and on the structure the organization uses to coordinate its tasks and roles.

ASSIGNMENT

1. What kind of structure (e.g., functional, product division, multidivisional) does your organization have? Draw a diagram showing its structure, and identify the major subunits or divisions in the organization.
2. Why does the company use this kind of structure? Provide a brief account of the advantages and disadvantages associated with this structure for your organization.
3. Is your organization experiencing any particular problems in managing its activities? Can you suggest a more appropriate structure that your company might adopt to solve these problems?

Company Profiles #6*

Choose one or more of the organizations (e.g., companies, government agencies, or nonprofit organizations) that are profiled in this chapter. Do an Internet search to get up-to-date information on each organization you have selected, and answer the following questions.

1. What does the new information tell you about the organization's current ability to develop successful systems of structure, specialization, and coordination?
2. How does the information compare with the earlier information provided in the text and what does that tell you about organizations (e.g., does the organization appear to have more or less successful systems of structure, specialization, and coordination than before, and how do you explain this)?

Alternative Perspectives #6

Critical and feminist research indicates that specialization can have negative impacts on employees. Read one or more of the following readings and list five ways that specialization can have a negative impact and five ways that it can have a positive impact on employee self-esteem. In small groups, discuss how you would deal with the potentially negative aspects of specialization.

Reading List

Braverman, H. 1974. *Labor and Monopoly Capital.* New York: Monthly Review Press.

Burawoy, M. 1979. *Manufacturing Consent: Changes in the Labor Process Under Monopoly Capitalism.* Chicago, Illinois London: University of Chicago Press.

Davies, S. 1990. Inserting Gender in Burawoy's Theory of the Labour Process. *Work, Employment & Society,* 4(3): 391–406.

Leonard, P. 1984. *Personality and Ideology—Towards a Material Understanding of the Individual.* London: Methuen.

* The authors would like to receive information from student groups and instructors on any companies where there have been dramatic changes to the information published in this text. We would be happy to publish the best of these changes in a subsequent edition, where we will focus on changing company profiles.

Livingstone, D. W., and Luxton, M. 1989. Gender Consciousness at Work: Modifications of the Male Breadwinner Norm Among Steelworkers and Their Spouses. *The Canadian Review of Sociology and Anthropology*, 26(2): 240–275.

Morgan, G., and Knights, D. 1991. Gendering Jobs: Corporate Strategies, Managerial Control and Dynamics of Job Segregation. *Work, Employment & Society*, 5(2): 181–200.

Morgan, N. 1988. *The Equality Game: Women in the Federal Public Service (1908–1987)*. Ottawa: Canadian Advisory Council on the Status of Women.

CASE FOR ANALYSIS

Stantec: A Historic Success Story of Adapting Organizational Structure for Growth[37]

In 2004, Stantec Inc. entered into its 50th year of operations and an impressive 50 years of uninterrupted profitability. The company began as a one-man engineering consulting firm in Edmonton, but has grown into a huge corporation of more than 4000 employees in over 50 offices across North America. Dr. Don Stanley, a Harvard Ph.D. in environmental engineering, began the company in 1954, and into the 1970s built up his company on successful contracts involving mostly municipal water and wastewater projects. In 1962 the company became known as Stanley Associates Engineering, and in 1967 the company took on its first international project. As the company successfully gained more national and international contracts, it began to diversify into other market areas. This diversification and subsequent growth were facilitated significantly by what became an important core competency—the company's ability to make many successful acquisitions.

In the early 1980s, when many companies were grappling with a weak economy, Stanley and Associates confronted the slowdown with a major strategic redirection, including a further diversification of services and more geographic expansion. At the time, Stanley was one of 14 companies to receive the Canada Export Award for its initiative, perseverance, and entrepreneurial endeavours, and it was also the recipient of Alberta's top export honour. In 1983, Ron Triffo became president of the company, and in 1989 he was appointed as CEO of the evolving company, which then became known as the Stanley Technology Group. Triffo was responsible for leading the company onward in growth as it became a well-established affiliation of multiple companies with regional hubs in Phoenix, Arizona, and Kitchener, Ontario. Having the hub-and-spoke structure enabled the company to continue to make acquisitions and add on new competencies without disrupting the whole organizational system.

In 1994, Stanley Technology Group made its initial public offering on the Toronto Stock Exchange, which would further fuel the company's growth potential. In the next few years, the Stanley Group continued to make more acquisitions, including its first into the United States. It also completed major projects that would raise the company profile substantially, such as the Confederation Bridge linking Nova Scotia to Prince Edward Island.

By 1998, under Triffo leadership, the company had evolved into a composite organization of over a dozen consulting firms operating in 30 sites in North America, with close to 2000 employees. The company had become one of few in the industry to provide engineering, architecture, interior design, landscape architecture, surveying, and project management services through one agency. At this time, the rapidly expanding Stanley Group began a new era, under the brand name of Stantec Inc. During the same year of the Stantec corporate launch, Tony Franceschini was appointed president and CEO and Ron Triffo became chairman of the board.

The hub-and-spoke structure of Stantec continued to provide the foundation for further growth with even more acquisitions, but it also enabled the company to provide superior integration and coordination in its multiple competencies. Company clients benefited from the strength and power of a large organization operating through regional offices and delivering services more intimately like a small business.

Subsequently, through the acquisition, development, and advancement of diverse technologies and expertise, the corporate giant's structure has evolved into a more complex matrix scenario. The original matrix idea was introduced in 1997 as a companywide organization structure that combined the practice side of the company with regional service delivery. Franceschini said, "The matrix system enabled us to combine the advantage of the power of our large organization with the service delivery, personality, and entrepreneurism of our people. Now we've evolved that matrix into almost a three-dimensional system. It's complex, but given that we're dealing with very complex individuals who are intelligent, independent, and used to working in a collaborative environment where they are engaged in the decision-making process, we need a complex organization. Part of our success is that we are able to change and evolve with the needs of our staff. Our staff thrives on the challenge of fast-paced change—it reflects the pace of our organization. It's fluid, it's organic, and it can move."

Stantec has set a course of growth to be a top 10 global design firm by 2008, with approximate annual revenues of $1 billion, and to employ at least 10 000 people. The company is expected to accomplish this goal through ongoing expansion and advancing its three-dimensional matrix system. Geographic diversification, practice area specialization, and provision of services are the three main components of the 3D concept that encompasses all phases of the project life cycle. This organizational model minimizes risks throughout operations, whereas there is no dependency on any single geographic region, practice area, or life cycle solution. Just how large and expansive can Stantec become and still maintain a local presence for quality service delivery for complex knowledge management and implementation? Can Stantec maintain its historic pace of aggressive acquisitions and continue to add on and manage new companies, their employees, and their diverse corporate cultures under the one corporate domain of Stantec? Only time will tell.

DISCUSSION QUESTIONS

1. Briefly describe the development of Stantec's current organizational structure.
2. Identify the types of challenges Stantec could have faced or may yet encounter through the evolutionary changes in its corporate structure.

REFERENCES

1. J. Child, *Organization: A Guide for Managers and Administrators* (New York: Harper and Row, 1977); R. Duncan, "What Is the Right Organization Structure?" *Organization Dynamics*, Winter 1979, pp. 59–80; J. R. Galbraith and R. K. Kazanjian, *Strategy Implementation: Structure, System, and Process*, 2nd ed. (St. Paul, MN: West, 1986).
2. O. E. Williamson, *Markets and Hierarchies: Analysis and Antitrust Implications* (New York: Free Press, 1975).
3. P. R. Lawrence and J. W. Lorsch, *Organization and Environment* (Boston: Graduate School of Business Administration, Harvard University, 1967).
4. A. Holloway, "The Sky's the Limit," *Canadian Business*, 2001-08-06. Retrieved from www.canadianbusiness.com/article.jsp?content=32271 on Sept. 12, 2005.

5. A. D. Chandler, *Strategy and Structure* (Cambridge, MA: MIT Press, 1962); Williamson, *Markets and Hierarchies.*
6. Chandler, *Strategy and Structure*; B. R. Scott, *Stages of Development* (Cambridge, MA: Harvard Business School, 1971).
7. *www.asdsoftware.com/news/press_releases/mccain.html*, 2004.
8. A. P. Sloan, *My Years at General Motors* (Garden City, NY: Doubleday, 1946), p. 46.
9. Ibid., p. 50.
10. A. Taylor, III, "Can GM Remodel Itself?," *Fortune*, 13 January 1992, pp. 26–34; W. Hampton and J. Norman, "General Motors: What Went Wrong?" *Business Week*, 16 March 1987, pp. 102–11.
11. "GM will Match Japan Quality in 2–3 years," *www.yahoo.com*, 17 September 2002.
12. Organizational Insight by Margaret McKee, based on the following sources: T. Comper, "Back to the Future: A CEO's Perspective on the IT Post-Revolution," IBM's Global Financial Services Forum, San Francisco, CA, 8 September 2003; D. Carey, "BMO's Five Steps to Delivering IT value," *CIO Canada*, January 2004, vol. 12, pp. 14–19; *www.bmo.com*, 2004.
13. C. W. L. Hill and G. R. Jones, *Strategic Management*, 4th ed. (Boston: Houghton Mifflin, 1998); G. R. Jones and C. W. L. Hill, "Transaction Cost Analysis of Strategy-Structure Choice," *Strategic Management Journal*, 1988, vol. 9, pp. 159–172.
14. Sloan, *My Years at General Motors.*
15. *www.gdcanada.com/employment*, 2004.
16. J. Halliday, "Plymouth Drives Comeback Trail," *Advertising Age*, 15 July 1996, p. 28.
17. S. Nolen, "McCain Learns Tough Cultural Lessons in S. Africa," *Globe and Mail*, 21 October 2004, pp. B17, B19.
18. *sask.cbc.ca/regional/servlet/View?filename=walmart_union040325*, 2004; *www.walmartworkerscanada.com/news.php?articleID=00086*, 2004.
19. J. C. Helms Mills, *Making Sense of Organizational Change* (London: Routledge, 2003).
20. *www.nspower.ca/AboutUs/OurTeam/EmployeeTeam.html*, 2004.
21. G. Morgan and D. Knights, "Gendering Jobs: Corporate Strategies, Managerial Control and Dynamics of Job Segregation," *Work, Employment & Society*, 1991, vol. 5, pp. 181–200.
22. J. Helms Mills, "Organizational Change and Representations of Women in a North American Utility Company," *Gender, Work & Organization*, 2005, vol. 12, pp. 242–269.
23. *www.newswire.ca/en/releases/archive/December2003/29/c6965.html*, 2004.
24. *www.workopolis.com/servlet/Content/printerfriendly/20021227/RO150BEST*, 2004.
25. Ibid.
26. S. M. Davis and P. R. Lawrence, *Matrix* (Reading, MA: Addison-Wesley, 1977); J. R. Galbraith, "Matrix Organization Designs: How to Combine Functional and Project Forms," *Business Horizons*, 1971, vol. 14, pp. 29–40.
27. L. R. Burns, "Matrix Management in Hospitals: Testing Theories of Matrix Structure and Development," *Administrative Science Quarterly*, 1989, vol. 34, pp. 349–368; Duncan, "What Is the Right Organization Structure?"
28. *www.tbs-sct.gc.ca/rma/account/studies/EC-EC_e.asp*, 2004.
29. S. M. Davis and P. R. Lawrence, "Problems of Matrix Organization," *Harvard Business Review*, May–June 1978, pp. 131–142; E. W. Larson and D. H. Gobelli, "Matrix Management: Contradictions and Insight," *California Management Review*, Summer 1987, pp. 126–138.
30. R. E. Miles and C. C. Snow, "Causes of Failure in Network Organizations," *California Management Review*, July 1992, pp. 53–72.
31. W. Baker, "The Network Organization in Theory and Practice," in N. Nohria and R. Eccles, eds., *Networks and Organizations* (Boston: Harvard Business School, 1992), pp. 397–429.
32. G. S. Capowski, "Designing a Corporate Identity," *Management Review*, June 1993, pp. 37–38.
33. J. Marcia, "Just Doing It," *Distribution*, January 1995, pp. 36–40.
34. R. A. Bettis, S. P. Bradley, and G. Hamel, "Outsourcing and Industrial Decline," *Academy of Management Executive*, February 1992, pp. 7–22.
35. C. C. Snow, R. E. Miles, H. J. Coleman, Jr. "Managing 21st Century Network Organizations," *Organizational Dynamics*, Winter 1992, pp. 5–20.
36. J. Fulk and G. Desanctis, "Electronic Communication and Changing Organizational Forms," *Organizational Science*, 1995, vol. 6, pp. 337–349.
37. Case by Ellen Rudderham-Gaudet, based on the following sources: Inside Stantec, "Evolution," *www.stantec.com/inside_stantec/evolution/*, 12 October 2004; L. Herzog, "Embracing Change: Multidisciplinary Stantec Strives to Crack the Top 10," *Award Magazine*, April 2003, vol. 17, pp. 10–13; "Inside Stantec: Celebrating our 50th Anniversary," *www.stantec.com/inside_stantec/evolution/milestones/anniversary/franceschiniera.htm*, 12 October 2004; "Inside Stantec: Growth," *www.stantec.com/inside_stantec/growth/*, 11 October 2004.

Creating and Managing Organizational Culture

CHAPTER 7

Learning Objectives

In this chapter, the hard-to-define concept of organizational culture is examined. Culture is discussed in terms of the values and norms that influence its members' behaviour, determine how its members interpret the environment, bond its members to the organization, and give it a competitive advantage. The global dimension of culture is also examined, and the problems companies encounter when they expand globally addressed.

After studying this chapter you should be able to:

1. Differentiate between values and norms and understand the way culture is shared by an organization's members.
2. Describe how individuals learn culture both formally (i.e., the way an organization intends them to learn it) and informally (i.e., by seeing what goes on in the organization).
3. Identify the four building blocks or foundations of an organization's culture that account for cultural differences among organizations.
4. Understand how an organization's culture, like its structure, can be influenced by management.
5. Discuss an important outcome of an organization's culture: its stance on corporate social responsibility.

WHAT IS ORGANIZATIONAL CULTURE?

Previous chapters have discussed how the most important function of organizational structure is to coordinate, motivate, and control people within an organization. In Chapter 1, we defined **organizational culture** as the set of shared values and norms that guide organizational members' interactions with each other and with suppliers, customers, and other people outside the organization. Just as an organization's structure can be used to achieve competitive advantage and promote stakeholder interests, an organization's culture can be influenced to increase organizational effectiveness.[1] This is because organizational culture guides and controls the way members make decisions, the way they interpret and manage the organization's environment, what they do with information, and how they behave.[2] Culture thus affects an organization's competitive position.

Organizational culture The set of shared values and norms that guides organizational members' interactions with each other and with people outside the organization.

Values
General criteria, standards, or guiding principles that people use to determine which types of behaviours, events, situations, and outcomes are desirable or undesirable.

Terminal value
A desired end state or outcome that people seek to achieve.

Instrumental value
A desired mode or pattern of behaviour.

What are organizational values, and how do they affect behaviour? **Values** are general criteria, standards, or guiding principles that people use to determine which types of behaviours, events, situations, and outcomes are desirable or undesirable. There are two kinds of values: terminal and instrumental (see Figure 7-1).[3] A **terminal value** is a desired end state or outcome that people seek to achieve. Organizations might adopt any of the following as terminal values, that is, as guiding principles: excellence, responsibility, reliability, profitability, innovativeness, economy, morality, quality. Nova Scotia Power, for example, introduced a set of terminal values as part of its culture change in the late 1980s. Those values stressed environmental responsibility, customer satisfaction, employee recognition, and responsiveness to community needs.[4]

An **instrumental value** is a desired mode of behaviour. Modes of behaviour that organizations advocate include working hard, respecting traditions and authority, being conservative and cautious, being frugal, being creative and courageous, being honest, taking risks, and maintaining high standards. In the lead-up to the culture change at Nova Scotia Power, an attitudes survey identified a number of instrumental values that were lacking in its management team, including empathy, effective communication, responsiveness to criticism, feedback, and the ability to emphasize the value of the employee as well as the job.[5] The aim of the culture change, with its emphasis on selected terminal values, was to foster those desired instrumental values.

An organization's culture thus consists of the end states that the organization seeks to achieve (its *terminal values*) and the modes of behaviour the organization encourages (its *instrumental values*). Ideally, as in the case of Nova Scotia Power, instrumental values help the organization to achieve its terminal goals. The way that a company balances its instrumental and terminal values can have a dramatic impact on its overall culture. For example, a computer company whose culture emphasizes the terminal value of innovativeness may attain this outcome through the instrumental values of working hard, being creative, and taking risks. That combination of terminal and instrumental values leads to an entrepreneurial culture. Similarly, a computer company that desires stability and predictability may emphasize caution and obedience to authority. The result will be a conservative culture.

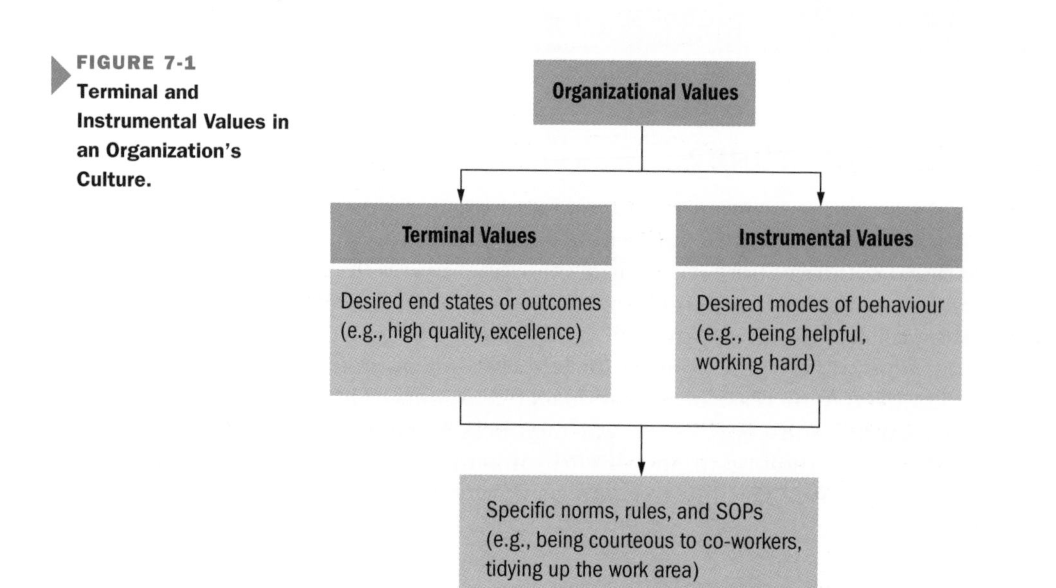

FIGURE 7-1 Terminal and Instrumental Values in an Organization's Culture.

Nova Scotia Power was a Crown corporation in the 1980s when it introduced a culture change. The ownership structure had an impact on the development of the terminal values and led to an emphasis on serving the needs of the provincial government and its voters, employees, and the environment. The outcome was a conservative but socially concerned culture that emphasized good workplace relations and a unified culture. When the company was privatized in the 1990s, it changed its culture through a program of re-engineering, which placed greater value on customer satisfaction, global competitiveness, and serving the needs of the new shareholders. The outcome was more of an entrepreneurial, competitive culture.[6]

Terminal values are reflected in an organization's mission statement and official goals, which tell organization members and other stakeholders that the company values excellence and has high ethical standards. So that members understand instrumental values—that is, the modes of behaviour that they are expected to follow as they pursue desired end states—an organization develops specific norms, rules, and standard operating procedures (SOPs) that embody its instrumental values. In Chapter 4, we defined **norms** as standards or styles of behaviour that are considered acceptable or typical for a group of people. The specific norms of being courteous and keeping the work area clean, for example, will develop in an organization whose instrumental values include being helpful and working hard.

Norms
Standards or styles of behaviour that are considered acceptable or typical for a group of people.

Many of the most powerful and crucial values of an organization are not written down. They exist only in the shared norms, beliefs, assumptions, and ways of thinking and acting that people within an organization use to relate to each other and to outsiders and to analyze and deal with problems facing the organization. Members learn from each other how to interpret and respond to various situations in ways that are consistent with the organization's accepted values. Eventually, members choose and follow appropriate values without even realizing that they are making a choice. Over time, they internalize the organization's values and the specific rules, norms, and SOPs that govern behaviour; that is, organizational values become part of members' mindsets—peoples' own values systems—and affect their interpretation of a situation.[7]

As we saw with McCain Foods expansion into South Africa in Chapter 6, the values and norms of different countries also affect an organization's culture. Indeed, differences between the cultures of different countries because of differences in their national values and norms help reveal the powerful effect organizational culture has on behaviour.[8] To get a feel for the effect of culture on behaviour, consider what happened when a U.S. and a Mexican company attempted to cooperate in a joint venture, in Organizational Insight 7.1.

As Organizational Insight 7.1 suggests, Corning and many other companies that have entered into global agreements have found that doing business in Mexico or in any other country is different from doing business at home. This has also been true for a number of Canadian companies. Molson Inc., for example, faced financial shortfalls after it acquired a majority stake in the Brazilian brewery Cervejarais Kaiser in 2002. Part of the difficulty was due to the differences between Canadian and Brazilian markets. After taking over Cervejarais Kaiser, the company's Brazilian share of the market fell from 18 percent to less than 13 percent. In 2004 Canadian commentators expressed concern about the acquisition of Noranda by China Minmetals. Their concern centred on the different management approach that would be introduced by the Chinese, based on cultural values rooted in bureaucratic, centralized ways of thinking.[9]

Even trade between two countries as apparently similar as the U.S. and Canada can be problematic. For example, despite NAFTA, access to U.S. markets is difficult for Canadian professionals and service providers because, while U.S. qualifications are acceptable across Canada, states vary in qualification requirements. U.S. firms doing

ORGANIZATIONAL INSIGHT 7.1

How Global Culture Affects Organizational Culture

After much negotiation, Pittsburgh-based Corning Glass Works and Vitro, a Mexican glass-making company, formed a joint venture to share technology and market one another's glass products throughout the United States and Mexico. They formed their alliance to take advantage of the opportunities presented by the North American Free Trade Agreement (NAFTA), which opened up the markets of both countries to one another's products. At the signing of the joint venture, both companies were enthusiastic about the prospects for their alliance. Managers in both companies claimed that they had similar organizational cultures. Both companies had a top-management team that was still dominated by members of the founding families; both were global companies with broad product lines; and both had been successful in managing alliances with other companies in the past.

Nevertheless, two years later Corning Glass terminated the joint venture and gave Vitro back the US$150 million it had given Corning for access to Corning's technology.[10] Why had the venture failed? The cultures and values of the two companies were so different that Corning managers and Vitro managers could not work together.

Vitro, the Mexican company, did business the Mexican way, in accordance with values prevailing in Mexican culture. In Mexico, business is conducted at a slower pace than in the United States. Used to a protected market, Mexican companies are inclined to sit back and make their decisions in a "very genteel," consensual kind of way. Managers typically come to work at 9 A.M., spend two or more hours at lunch, often at home with their families, and then work late, often until 9 P.M. Mexican managers and their subordinates are intensely loyal and respectful to their superiors; the corporate culture is based on paternalistic, hierarchical values; and most important decision making is centralized in a small team of top managers. This centralization slows decision making because middle managers may come up with a solution to a problem but will not take action without top-management approval. In Mexico, building relationships with new companies takes time and effort because trust develops slowly. Thus personal contacts that develop slowly between managers in different companies are an important prerequisite for doing business in Mexico.

Corning, the American company, did business the American way, in accordance with values prevailing in American culture. Managers in the United States take short lunch breaks or work through lunch so they can leave early in the evening. In many U.S. companies, decision-making authority is decentralized to lower-level managers, who make important decisions and commit their organization to certain courses of action. U.S. managers like to make decisions quickly and worry about the consequences later.

Aware of the differences in their approaches to doing business, managers from Corning and from Vitro tried to compromise and find a mutually acceptable working style. Managers from both companies agreed to take long working lunches together. Mexican managers agreed to forgo going home at lunchtime, and U.S. managers agreed to work a bit later at night so that they could talk to Vitro's top managers and thus speed decision making. Over time, however, the differences in management style and approach to work became a source of frustration for managers from both companies. The slow pace of decision making was frustrating for Corning's managers. The pressure by Corning's managers to get everything done quickly was frustrating for Vitro's managers. Corning's managers working in Mexico discovered that the organizational cultures of Vitro and Corning were not so similar after all, and they decided to go home. Vitro's managers also realized that it was pointless to prolong the venture when the differences were so great.

business in Canada, on the other hand, are required to label certain goods and services in both French and English. Because values, norms, customs, and etiquette differ from one country to another, managers working abroad must learn to appreciate and respond to those differences.

The terminal and instrumental values in Corning and Vitro, as discussed in Organizational Insight 7.1, produced very different responses in their employees. Although this example is between companies in different countries, the same holds true between different companies in the same countries. Many mergers between companies have failed because of differences in their organizational cultures. The takeover of Canadian Airlines by Air Canada, for example, caused a number of problems because of cultural differences.[11] Operating as rivals for several decades, many long-serving Air Canada employees and former Canadian Airlines employees found it difficult to work together.[12] Recognizing this potential problem, some organizations today who consistently take over companies as they grow, like Microsoft and United Technologies, use seasoned teams of "merger culture" experts who move in after a merger and take the steps necessary to blend the cultures of the merged companies. Other companies have done well from mergers despite culture differences either because they acted quickly and concisely to deal with changes, or because they were actually interested in learning from the acquired company's culture.

Consider the acquisition of Alberta Energy Company by Pancanadian Energy in 2002 to form EnCana. Industry observers expected difficulties because of the very distinct corporate cultures of each company. However, things ran smoothly. The success of the takeover is credited to its speed (operations began within three months of the takeover agreement) and the fact that employees quickly received a personal "high-performance contract," which outlined career objectives and goals. These factors helped to achieve staff integration in the new company within six months.[13] On the other hand, when the Toronto-Dominion Bank (TD) took over Canada Trust in 1999, a big part of the success of the merger was the fact that TD wanted to acquire Canada Trust's customer service model. Eventually, TD grew to look and feel more like the company that it took over.[14] See Organizational Insight 7.2 for a look at some problems that occurred during another merger because of differences in organizational culture.

When Bill Black, the CEO of Maritime Life, contemplated the company's future in early 2004, he was hoping that the company would be able to continue the way it was for the foreseeable future. All that changed when the company merged with Manulife. For Black, any of the other merger deals the company had been considering would have resulted in a better outcome for Maritime Life. In his view, "It was sad, no question about it. It will mean everything that has been here will be dismantled. Organizations have very different styles, and people don't realize how important those style differences are. Manulife's culture is very different" form that of Maritime Life.[15]

Organizational culture is based on relatively enduring values embodied in organizational norms, rules, SOPs, and goals. People in the organization draw on these cultural values in their actions and decisions, and when dealing with ambiguity and uncertainty inside and outside the organization.[16] The values in an organization's culture are important shapers of members' behaviour and responses to situations, and they increase the reliability of members' behaviour.[17] In this context, *reliability* does not necessarily mean consistently obedient or passive behaviour; it may also mean consistently innovative or creative behaviour.[18] It can also mean totally unethical behaviours.[19]

Arthur Andersen, the disgraced accounting firm, was well known for its insistence that its employees abide by its rigid, constraining rules of behaviour and deportment. Its employees had to wear dark blue suits, black shoes, and in some branches the managers insisted those shoes be lace-ups or employees were called to task. It also

ORGANIZATIONAL INSIGHT 7.2

Mergers and Cultures

When BankAmerica merged with Security Pacific, the merger was supposed to be a merger of equals, with the top management of both banks jointly running the new company. Richard Rosenberg, the chairman of BankAmerica, agreed to form an office of the chairman with Security Pacific's chairman Robert Smith; it was also agreed that Smith would succeed Rosenberg as the chairman of the new bank when Rosenberg retired. Similarly, there was supposed to be a 50–50 board split between the directors of both companies, and BankAmerica agreed to name four of Security Pacific's top managers to the new top-management team.

After the merger, however, things did not work out as had been expected. BankAmerica had planned the merger hurriedly, without thoroughly investigating the details of Security Pacific's financial condition. After the merger, BankAmerica's managers began to find major flaws in the way Security Pacific's managers made loans, which had resulted in more than US$300 million of write-offs for the company, with equally large sums to follow. BankAmerica's top-management team came to despise and ridicule the way Security Pacific's managers did business. They blamed a large part of the problem on Security Pacific's culture, which was decentralized, freewheeling, and which allowed top managers to loan large sums of money to clients on the basis of personal ties. Its values had been developed in the savings and loan crisis when unrestrained risk taking, uncurbed by any values of responsibility to stakeholders, had been the norm.

BankAmerica's managers, by contrast, had cultivated a conservative, centralized decision-making style in their organization. Teams of managers made decisions to reduce the possibility of mistakes and fraud, and they curbed the autonomy of lower-level managers to act alone. All loans were made according to companywide criteria scrutinized by top management. Its traditional, moderate values were based on following the rules of the legal system and acting ethically toward its stakeholders. Its norms emphasized conformity to its operating system and caution in decision making.[20]

Believing that their culture was the one that had to be developed in the new, merged organization, BankAmerica's managers began to use their power as the dominant party in the merger (Rosenberg as chairman of the bigger company had more legitimate power than Smith) to strip authority from Security Pacific's managers and to take control of the reins of the new organization. Less than two weeks after the merger, Smith found himself relieved of all important decision-making authority, which was transferred to Rosenberg and his top-management team. Similarly, whenever BankAmerica's top managers were negotiating with Security Pacific's managers over future task and authority relationships, they used their power to cut the authority of Security Pacific's managers and to drive them from the organization. After a few months, almost all of Security Pacific's top managers had left the new organization, followed by thousands of middle-level managers, who, BankAmerica managers felt, could not be trusted to maintain the company's new cultural standards and way of doing business. After all, Security Pacific's managers had not developed the right kind of values to be trusted to work ethically on the part of all the bank's stakeholders.

had in place an extensive and thorough MBO system, and its employees were constantly being evaluated and checked on their performance. Its values were based on obedience to company rules and norms, respect for partners and tradition, and the importance of following rules and SOPs. On the surface, the insistent ways in which the company demanded its employees follow its values and norms would seem sound practice for a company whose business it is to accurately measure and account for the resources used by its clients. Accounting is a relatively precise science; the last thing an accounting company needs is for its employees to practice "creative accounting."

Small wonder then the business world was astounded in 2001 when it became clear that some of Arthur Andersen's most senior partners, its top managers, had apparently been systematically instructing their subordinates, sometimes directly and sometimes indirectly, to overlook or ignore anomalies in its client books in order to obtain large consulting fees and maintain the client business—and to shred documents that revealed its dealings with Enron before government regulators could examine them.

The paradox is that Arthur Andersen's values were so strong that they led subordinates to forget the "real" ethics of what they were doing, and Arthur Andersen's "distorted" ethics became the ones they followed. Apparently, Arthur Andersen's culture was so strong it had an almost cult-like effect on its members, who were afraid to question what was going on because of the enormous status and power the partners wielded, and the threat of sanction if anybody disobeyed or questioned the rules. While the Arthur Andersen case can be said to be atypical of normal business practices, it was not an isolated case in the new millennium. Other major companies involved in unethical practices include Enron Corporation, WorldCom Inc., Tyco International Ltd., Adelphia Communications, Global Crossing, and Imclone Systems.[21] Business ethics were also very much in the news in 2004 when Air Canada and JetsGo Corp., sued WestJet for alleged illegal hacking and theft of internal data and the theft of confidential papers.[22]

A strong organizational culture can be a dangerous thing in the hands of owners or managers who do not behave ethically or legally. On the other hand, a strong organizational culture can be the factor that sends an organization to greatness as its members are inspired to do their utmost to work hard to conceive and make goods and services that improve the welfare of their customers, and thus themselves. There are many ways in which culture can inspire and facilitate the intense kind of personal and team interactions that are necessary to develop organizational competencies and obtain a competitive advantage.

First, cultural values are important facilitators of mutual adjustment in an organization. When shared cultural values provide a common reference point, employees do not need to spend much time establishing rapport and overcoming differences in their perceptions of events. Cultural values can smooth interactions among organizational members. People who share an organization's values may come to identify strongly with the organization, and feelings of self-worth may flow from their membership in it.[23] Employees of companies like WestJet, Southwest Airlines, Creo, and Dell Computer, for example, seem to value greatly their membership in the organization and are committed to it.

Second, organizational culture is a form of informal organization that facilitates the workings of the organizational structure. It is an important determinant of the way employees view their tasks and roles. It tells them, for example, if they should stay within established rules and procedures and simply obey orders or whether they are allowed to make suggestions to their superiors, find better or more creative ways of performing their roles, and feel free to demonstrate their competency without fear of reprisal from their peers or superiors.

This is not trivial. One of the most common complaints of employees and junior managers in organizations is that although they know certain tasks or roles could be accomplished better and should be performed in different ways, their organization's values and norms do not permit them to advise or question their superiors up the organizational hierarchy. They feel trapped, become unhappy, and often leave an organization, causing high turnover. To mitigate this problem, some companies (e.g., WestJet, GE, and Microsoft) have open lines of communication to the CEO, bypassing the superior. They also go out of their way to develop values of equity and fairness, demonstrating their commitment to reward employees who work toward organizational goals, rather than behaving in their own self-interest. GE even has a name for the managers who are out for themselves—"Type 4" managers—and based on feedback from subordinates, these managers are routinely asked to leave to make room for those who can develop empowered, motivated subordinates. The values expressed in GE's practices demonstrate its values to its members.

WestJet CEO Clive Beddoe provides a dramatic example of the open nature of the airline's culture. Returning to work shortly after throwing an expensive barbecue for senior and middle managers, Beddoe was confronted by a maintenance worker who stormed into his office demanding to know why Beddoe was squandering company money. A profit-sharing scheme was in place, and the employee was angry that Beddoe had cut into his potential earnings. Beddoe explained to the employee that he had paid for the barbecue out of his own pocket but he praised the worker for his attitude, viewing actions of this type as an important watchdog role that profit sharing was designed to create. In the words of Beddoe, "That is the spirit of WestJet."[24]

HOW IS AN ORGANIZATION'S CULTURE TRANSMITTED TO ITS MEMBERS?

The ability of an organization's culture to motivate employees and increase organizational effectiveness is directly related to the way in which members learn the organization's values. Organizational members learn pivotal values from an organization's formal socialization practices and from the stories, ceremonies, and organizational language that develop informally as an organization's culture matures.

Socialization and Socialization Tactics

Newcomers to an organization must learn the values and norms that guide existing members' behaviour and decision making.[25] Can they work from 10:00 A.M. to 7:00 P.M. instead of from 8:00 A.M. to 5:00 P.M.? Can they challenge their peers' and superiors' views of a situation or should they simply stand and listen? Newcomers are outsiders, and only when they have learned and internalized the organization's values and act in accordance with its rules and norms will long-time members accept them as insiders.

To learn an organization's culture, newcomers must obtain information about cultural values. They can learn values indirectly, by observing how existing members behave and inferring what behaviours are appropriate and inappropriate. From the organization's perspective, however, the indirect method is risky because newcomers might observe and learn habits that are *not* acceptable to the organization. From the organization's perspective, the most effective way for newcomers to learn appropriate values is through **socialization**, which, as we saw in Chapter 4, is the process by which members learn and internalize the norms of an organization's culture.

Socialization
The process by which members learn and internalize the values and norms of an organization's culture.

Role orientation
The characteristic way in which newcomers respond to a situation.

Van Mannen and Schein developed a model of socialization that suggests how organizations can structure the socialization experience so that newcomers learn the values that the organization wants them to learn. In turn, these values influence the role orientation that the newcomers adopt.[26] **Role orientation** is the characteristic

Table 7-1

HOW SOCIALIZATION TACTICS SHAPE EMPLOYEES' ROLE ORIENTATION

Tactics That Lead to an Institutionalized Orientation	Tactics That Lead to an Individualized Orientation
Collective	Individual
Formal	Informal
Sequential	Random
Fixed	Variable
Serial	Disjunctive
Divestiture	Investiture

way in which newcomers respond to a situation: Do they react passively and obediently to commands and orders? Are they creative and innovative in searching for solutions to problems?

Van Mannen and Schein identified 12 socialization tactics that influence a newcomer's role orientation (see Table 7-1). The use of different sets of these tactics leads to two different role orientations: institutionalized and individualized. An *institutionalized role orientation* results when individuals are taught to respond to a new context in the same way that existing organizational members respond to it. An institutionalized orientation encourages obedience and conformity to rules and norms. An *individualized role orientation* results when individuals are allowed and encouraged to be creative and to experiment with changing norms and values so that an organization can better achieve its values.[27] The following list contrasts the tactics used to socialize newcomers to an institutionalized orientation with those tactics used to develop an individualized orientation:

1. *Collective vs. Individual.* Collective tactics provide newcomers with common learning experiences designed to produce a standardized response to a situation. With individual tactics, each newcomer's learning experiences are unique, and newcomers can learn new, appropriate responses for each situation.
2. *Formal vs. Informal.* Formal tactics segregate newcomers from existing organizational members during the learning process. With informal tactics, newcomers learn on the job, as members of a team.
3. *Sequential vs. Random.* Sequential tactics provide newcomers with explicit information about the sequence in which they will perform new activities or occupy new roles as they advance in an organization. With random tactics, training is based on the interests and needs of individual newcomers because there is no set sequence to the newcomers' progress in the organization.
4. *Fixed vs. Variable.* Fixed tactics give newcomers precise knowledge of the timetable associated with completing each stage in the learning process. Variable tactics provide no information about when newcomers will reach a certain stage in the learning process; once again, training depends on the needs and interests of the individual.
5. *Serial vs. Disjunctive.* When serial tactics are employed, existing organizational members act as role models and mentors for newcomers. Disjunctive processes require newcomers to figure out and develop their own way of behaving; they are not told what to do.

6. *Divestiture vs. Investiture.* With divestiture, newcomers receive negative social support—that is, they are ignored or taunted—and existing organizational members withhold support until newcomers learn the ropes and conform to established norms. With investiture, newcomers immediately receive positive social support from other organizational members and are encouraged to be themselves.

When organizations combine the tactics listed in Table 7-1, there is some evidence that they can influence an individual's role orientation.[28] Military-style socialization, for example, leads to an extremely institutionalized orientation. New soldiers are placed in platoons with other new recruits (*collective*); are segregated from existing organizational members (*formal*); go through pre-established drills and learning experiences (*sequential*); know exactly how long this will take them and what they have to do (*fixed*); have superior officers who are their role models (*serial*); and are treated with zero respect and tolerance until they have learned their duties and "gotten with the program" (*divestiture*). As a result, new recruits develop an institutionalized role orientation in which obedience and conformity to organizational norms and values are the signs of success. New members who cannot or will not perform according to these norms and values leave (or are asked to leave), so that by the end of the socialization process the people who stay are clones of existing organizational members.

No organization controls its members to the extent that the military does, but other organizations do use similar practices to socialize their members. Arthur Andersen, discussed earlier, had a very institutionalized program. Recruits were carefully selected for employment because they seemed to possess the values that Arthur Andersen wants—for example, hard-working, cautious, obedient, thorough. After they were hired, all new recruits attended a six-week course at its training centre, where they are indoctrinated as a group into Arthur Andersen's way of doing business. In formal eight-hour-a-day classes, existing organizational members served as role models and told newcomers what was expected of them. Newcomers also learned informally over meals and during recreation what it meant to be working for Arthur Andersen. By the end of this socialization process, they had learned the values of the organization and the rules and norms that govern the way they are expected to behave when they represented Andersen's clients. This effort to create an institutionalized role orientation worked well until the 1990s when unethical, greedy partners, seeking to maximize their returns at the expense of other stakeholders, took advantage of its strong culture to lead its employees astray. Andersen's training centre was closed down in 2002 after the company's collapse, further hurting its stakeholders.

Should an organization encourage an institutionalized role orientation in which newcomers accept the status quo and perform their jobs in keeping with the commands and orders they are given? Or should an organization encourage an individualized role orientation in which newcomers are allowed to develop creative and innovative responses to the jobs that the organization requires of them? The answer to this question depends on the organization's mission. Arthur Andersen initially developed its strong culture to standardize the way its employees performed auditing activities in order to develop a good reputation for honesty and reliability. A financial institution's credibility and reputation with clients depend on its integrity, so it wants to have control over what its employees do. It needs to adopt a strong socialization program that will reinforce its cultural values, and as in the BankAmerica case earlier, in most cases such an institutionalized orientation is in the best interests of the organization.

One danger of institutionalized socialization lies in the power it gives to those at the top of the organization to manipulate the situation, as in the case of Arthur Andersen, which lost its licence to practise accounting in Texas in 2002. A second danger can lie in the sameness it may produce among members of an organization. If all employees have been socialized to share the same way of looking at the world, how will the organization be able to change and adapt when that world changes? When confronted with changes in the organizational environment (e.g., a new product, a new competitor, or a change in customer demands), employees indoctrinated into old values will be unable to develop new values that might allow them to innovate. As a result, they—and thus the organization—cannot adapt and respond to the new conditions.

An organization whose mission is to provide innovative products for customers should encourage informal, random experiences from which individuals working on the job gain information as they need it. By all accounts, many of the Internet companies such as Yahoo!, Amazon.com, and eBay rely on individualized socialization tactics and allow members to develop skills in areas that capitalize on their abilities and interests.[29] These companies take this approach because their effectiveness depends not on standardizing individual behaviour but on innovation and the ability of members to come up with new and improved solutions to Internet-related problems—such as Amazon.com's push to seek new ways to generate revenues to offset its high operating costs. In 2001, it announced it would start a consultancy arm and sell its IT skills to any interested organizations—something suggested by lower-level employees. Thus an organization's socialization practices not only help members learn the organization's cultural values and the rules and norms that govern behaviour, but also support the organization's mission.

Stories, Ceremonies, and Organizational Language

The cultural values of an organization are often evident in the stories, ceremonies, and language found in the organization.[30] IBM Canada, for example, maintains its cultural values through a formal buddy system. The company sends technical leaders and "buddies" into universities to recruit the next generation of management and technical employees. The buddies are management trainees who have graduated in the past few years. Once students have been recruited to the company, the buddies, who played a part in their recruitment, act as mentors—spending one day a week with the new recruits to smooth their way into the company. IBM Canada claims that as a result of this buddy system, the company has a much higher rate of success in helping new recruits transition into the corporate culture.[31]

Organizations use several types of ceremonial rites to communicate cultural norms and values (see Table 7-2).[32] *Rites of passage* mark an individual's entry to, promotion in, and departure from the organization. The socialization programs used by the army, in colleges, and in companies like IBM Canada, Creo, 3M, the PEAK Financial Group, and Microsoft (which recognize their most creative people with special job titles, plaques, and so on) are rites of passage; so too are the ways in which an

Table 7-2

ORGANIZATIONAL RITES

Type of Rite	Example of Rite	Purpose of Rite
Rite of passage	Induction and basic training	Learn and internalize norms and values
Rite of integration	Office Christmas party	Build common norms and values
Rite of enhancement	Presentation of annual award	Motivate commitment to norms and values

organization grooms people for promotion or retirement. *Rites of integration,* such as shared announcements of organizational success, office parties, and company cookouts, build and reinforce common bonds between organizational members. This kind of approach is the hallmark of the culture of WestJet and Research in Motion (RIM). *Rites of enhancement,* such as awards dinners, newspaper releases, and employee promotions, publicly recognize and reward employees' contributions. Superior Propane developed a motto to encourage employees to work well together. The motto is posted throughout the company to enhance its organizational culture, as Organizational Insight 7.3 describes.

ORGANIZATIONAL INSIGHT 7.3

Creating and Managing Organizational Culture at Superior Propane[33]

Superior Propane Inc. is a wholly owned subsidiary of the Superior Propane Income Fund. The subsidiary is Canada's largest and only national marketer of propane, propane-burning appliances, and related support services. In operation for over 50 years, Superior has grown extensively across Canada through many acquisitions. With over 1800 employees and serving over 300 000 customers, Superior Propane's promotion and ongoing transformations of its organizational culture have been important elements in maintaining a competitive foothold in the energy industry. For example, the company prominently expresses its cultural values through its "RISE" motto to encourage employees to RISE and take the high road. The motto represents basic guidelines about how employees of the company treat each other, work together, and interact with customers and others. RISE stands for *respect, integrity, service,* and *excellence.* By encouraging employees to follow these basic values, the company promotes an organizational culture where employees work well together to meet the needs of customers and to create a positive working environment. Superior displays the RISE values in a company poster.

To establish a more employee-focused culture and to stabilize its market positioning, Superior Propane in 1997 implemented a change in its employee benefits program. The change was part of a larger cultural transformation that was driven by an economic necessity to align both financial and human resource strategies. At the time, the company needed to attract a more diverse workforce and the traditional benefits program in place at the time—a one-size-fits-all concept—did not meet the changing organizational culture. The company therefore began to implement a more flexible benefits program. The culture shift was not readily accepted by all at first, as some had difficulty resigning from the traditional approach. Resistance, however, slowly diminished through ongoing program alterations that recognized employee expectations. Effective communication of changes through face-to-face meetings across the country was also instrumental to the successful culture transition at Superior Propane. The company's vice president has stated that a successful culture change can result by communicating not just the "what" and "how" of the cultural change but also the "why." The progressive employee-focused culture has worked well for the company to attract, recruit, and retain good employees and has positively impacted Superior's bottom-line performance.

Organizational stories and the language of an organization are important media for communicating culture. Stories (whether fact or fiction) about organizational heroes, such as Clive Beddoe of WestJet Airlines, provide important clues about cultural values and norms. Such stories can reveal the kinds of behaviours that the organization values and the kinds of practices that the organization frowns on. Studying stories and language can reveal the values that guide behaviour.[34] Because language is the principal medium of communication in organizations, the characteristic phrases that frame and describe events provide important clues about norms and values. For example, if any manager in IBM's old laptop-computer division used the phrase "I non-concur" to disagree with a proposed plan of action, the plan was abandoned because achieving consensus used to be an important instrumental value at IBM. After divisions were given the authority to control their own activities, however, the language changed. A manager who tried to "non-concur" was told by other managers, "We no longer recognize that phrase," indicating that the division had adopted new terminal values that made old instrumental values obsolete.

The concept of organizational language encompasses not only spoken language but how people dress, the offices they occupy, the company cars they drive, and how they formally address one another. At Maritime Life, before its merge with Manulife in 2004, one of its key cultural artefacts was a splendid cafeteria that had been built for the employees at the company's Halifax headquarters in the late 1980s. More important was the story that went with it. Apparently the original plans for the head office included an executive suite in the space where the employee cafeteria was eventually sited. The head of the company felt that an employee cafeteria would better symbolize Maritime Life's culture, with its commitment to employees and customers.[35]

At Wal-Mart employees are called "associates" to encourage a greater sense of identity with the company. At Microsoft and some other organizations casual dress is the norm, but in investment banks like Goldman Sachs, and luxury department stores like Neiman Marcus and Saks, expensive, well-tailored clothing is the order of the day. When Nova Scotia Power was undergoing culture change in the late 1980s, one of the symbols that it set out to change was the hardhats. Managers traditionally wore white hardhats and employees wore coloured hats according to division and task. Many employees, for example, wore yellow hardhats. In an effort to reduce the hierarchical distance between employees and managers, Nova Scotia Power switched to a one-colour hardhat for employees and managers alike.[36]

Many organizations have technical languages that facilitate mutual adjustment between organizational members.[37] At 3M, inside entrepreneurs have to emphasize the relationship between their product and 3M's terminal values in order to push ideas through the product development committee. Because many 3M products are flat—such as compact discs, Post-it notepads, floppy disks, paper, and transparencies—the quality of flatness embodies 3M's terminal values, and flatness is often a winning theme in 3M's corporate language—it increases a new product's chance of getting funded. At Microsoft, employees have developed a shorthand language of technical software phrases to describe communication problems. Technical languages are used by the military, by sports teams, in hospitals, and in many other specialized work contexts. Like socialization practices, organizational language, ceremonies, stories, and even detailed books of organization-specific rules help people learn the ropes and the organization's cultural values. Take the example of siteRock, profiled in Organizational Insight 7.4.

Finally, organizational symbols often convey an organization's cultural values to its members and to others outside the organization. In some organizations, for exam-

ORGANIZATIONAL INSIGHT 7.4

siteROCK's Military Management Culture

The high tech, dot-com culture is not usually associated with the values and norms that characterize the military. However, managers of the thousands of dot-coms that went belly up in the early 2000s might have benefited from some military-style disciplined values and norms. Indeed, a few dot-coms that survived the shakeout did so because their managers used military-style rules and SOPs to control their employees and ensure high performance. One of these companies is siteROCK, based in Emeryville, California, whose COO, Dave Lilly, is an ex–nuclear submarine commander.

siteROCK is in the business of hosting and managing other companies' Web sites and keeping them up and running and error-free. A customer's site that goes down or runs haywire is the major enemy. To maximize the performance of his employees and to increase their ability to respond to unexpected online events, Lilly decided that he needed to develop an institutionalized role orientation and develop a comprehensive set of rules and standard operating procedures to cover all the major known problems.[38] Lilly insisted that every problem-solving procedure be written down and codified. siteROCK now has over 30 thick binders listing all the processes and checklists that employees need to follow when an unexpected event happens. Their job is to try to solve the problem using these procedures.

Moreover, again drawing from his military experience, Lilly instituted a "two-man" norm: Whenever the unexpected happens, each employee must immediately tell a co-worker and the two should attempt to solve the problem together. The goal is simple: Develop strong norms of cooperation to achieve the quick resolution of a complex issue. If the existing rules don't work, then employees must experiment, and when they find a solution, the solution is turned into a new rule to be included in the procedures book to aid the future decision making of all employees in the organization.

At siteROCK, these written rules and SOPs have resulted in values that lead employees to achieve high levels of customer service. Because the goal is 100 percent reliability, detailed blueprints guide planning and decision making, not seat-of-the-pants problem solving, which might be brilliant 80 percent of the time but result in disaster the rest. Before siteROCK employees are allowed in the control room each day they must read over the most important rules and SOPs. And at the end of a shift, they spend 90 minutes doing paperwork that logs what they have done and states any new or improved rules that they have come up with. Clearly, siteROCK has developed a company-specific testament that symbolizes to employees the need for sustained, cooperative effort.

ple, the size of peoples' offices, their location on the third floor or the thirty-third floor, or the luxury with which they are equipped are symbols that convey images about the values in an organization's culture. Is the organization hierarchical and status conscious, for example, or are informal, participative work relationships encouraged? In GM, the executive suite on the top floor of their Detroit headquarters is isolated from the rest of the building and open only to top GM executives. A private corridor and stairway link top managers' offices, and a private elevator connects to their heated parking garage. This stands in stark contrast to Maritime Life's attempt to signal a less hierarchical culture by establishing its employee cafeteria in a prime location in its head office building. Sometimes, the very design of the building itself is a symbol of an organization's values. For example, Walt Disney hired famed Japanese architect Arata Isozaki to design the Team Disney Building, which houses Disney's "imagineering unit," in Orlando, Florida. This building's contemporary and unusual design featuring unusual shapes and bright colours conveys the importance of imagination and creativity to the Walt Disney Company and to the people who work in it.

MANAGERIAL IMPLICATIONS

Analyzing Organizational Culture

1. Study the culture of your organization, and identify the terminal and instrumental values on which it is based in order to assess how they affect organizational behaviour.
2. Assess whether the goals, norms, and rules of your organization are effectively transmitting the values of the organizational culture to members. Identify areas for improvement.
3. Examine the methods your organization uses to socialize new members. Assess whether these socialization practices are effective in helping newcomers learn the organization's culture. Recommend ways to improve the process.
4. Try to develop organizational ceremonies to help employees learn cultural values, to enhance employee commitment, and to bond employees to the organization.

WHERE DOES ORGANIZATIONAL CULTURE COME FROM?

Now that you have seen what organizational culture is and how members learn and become part of an organization's culture, some difficult questions can be addressed: Where does organizational culture come from? Why do different companies have different cultures? Why might a culture that for many years helped an organization pursue its corporate mission suddenly harm the organization? Can culture be managed?

Organizational culture develops from the interaction of four factors: the personal and professional characteristics of people within the organization, organizational ethics, the property rights that the organization gives to employees, and the structure of the organization (see Figure 7-2). The interaction of these factors produces different cultures in different organizations and causes changes in culture over time. The way in which people's personal characteristics shape culture is discussed first.

Characteristics of People Within the Organization

The ultimate source of organizational culture is the people who make up the organization. If you want to know why cultures differ, look at their members. Organizations A, B, and C develop distinctly different cultures because they attract, select, and retain people who have different values, personalities, and ethics.[39] People may be attracted to an organization whose values match theirs; similarly, an organization selects people

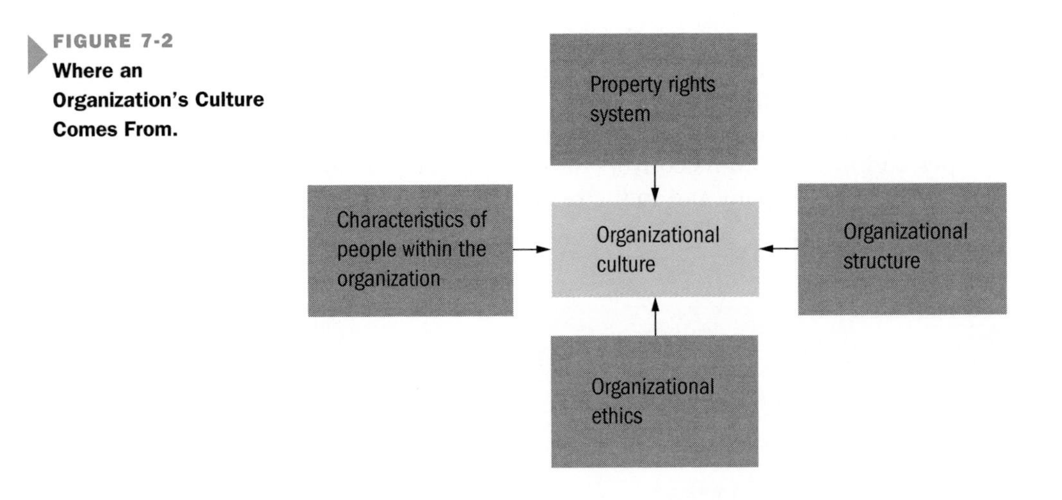

FIGURE 7-2
Where an Organization's Culture Comes From.

who share its values. Over time, people who do not fit in leave. The result is that people inside the organization become more and more similar, the values of the organization become more and more parochial, and the culture becomes more and more distinct from that of similar organizations.

The founder and top manager of an organization has a substantial influence on the organization's initial culture because of his or her personal values and beliefs.[40] Founders set the scene for the later development of a culture because they not only establish the new organization's values, but hire its first members. Presumably, the people selected by the founder have values and interests similar to the founder's.[41] Over time, members buy into the founder's vision and perpetuate the founder's values in the organization.[42] Top managers often play a significant role when they make a decision to completely change the way a company operates.

AOL, Maritime Life, Scandinavian Airways System, British Airways, and Nova Scotia Power provide good illustrations of the important role the founder and top manager play in establishing organizational culture. Steve Chase pioneered an entrepreneurial culture at AOL based on instrumental values of creativity and hard work. At Maritime Life, Bill Black pioneered the notion that an insurance company should be operated in the interests of its policyholders, and the terminal value of customer satisfaction gave rise to a philanthropic, caring culture at Maritime.

In the late 1970s, Jan Carlson had a powerful impact on the airline industry worldwide when he completely revamped Scandinavian Airways System and turned the company's fortunes around.[43] Colin Marshall of British Airways was first to follow Carlson's lead, hiring a consulting company to change British Airways' conservative culture that was based on a hybrid of civil service and military mentalities that focused on the organization and its planes rather than the customers. All employees were put through a culture change program called "Putting People First," where they were encouraged to get into the mindset of their customers to be better able to serve them.[44] Nova Scotia Power's Louis Comeau, faced with the task of overturning a company that was generally viewed as an uncaring, unresponsive construction company, introduced a culture change program focused on employees, customers, local voters, and environmental groups.[45] The type of culture that pervades an organization, however, is not always good for the organization, as the story of the way Procter & Gamble's culture has developed over time, profiled in Organizational Insight 7.5, illustrates.

ORGANIZATIONAL INSIGHT 7.5

Procter & Gamble's Culture Is Hard to Change

Procter & Gamble (P&G), the well-known soap and detergent company, is widely recognized as having one of the most distinct and insular corporate cultures in North America. Although it does try to recruit people from diverse backgrounds, once they join the company, they encounter such a strong and homogeneous set of organizational values and norms that they begin to sound alike, think alike, and even look alike, at least so say the company's critics. Is this a good or a bad thing?

According to former P&G CEO Durk I. Jager, who took control of the company in 1999 but was ousted in 2001, it is a bad thing. As part of his attempt to learn about P&G, Jager took a world tour of the company's facilities. He came to the conclusion that P&G's values and norms that emphasize consensus, obedience to the hierarchy, respect for authority, and participative decision making were causing a bureaucratic nightmare. He believed that P&G's managers were spending over 50 percent of their time working on "non-value-added" work such as memo writing and group meetings rather than in innovating new products and marketing strategies. In Japan, one worker complained to him that all he did was to write and rewrite management charts.[46]

Jager's goal? To break up the stodgy culture that caused slow decision making and disappointing sales growth and to install a new entrepreneurial spirit in the company. He wanted P&G's managers to take risks. In 1999, he started to change the company's culture. He fired 15 000 employees, or 13 percent of P&G's workforce; he transferred thousands more to new jobs; and he linked managers' pay directly to their and to P&G's performance. After shaking up P&G's workforce he announced that in the future, "stretch, innovation, and speed" would be the company's new terminal and instrumental values and that rewards and promotion would come not from conformity but from demonstrating the ability to break out of the mould and increase value.[47]

As you might imagine, the old-guard P&G employees did not like what Jager was up to and did their best to thwart his efforts. Unfortunately for Jager, P&G's performance declined sharply after he took over because of the way his predecessors had mismanaged it, and his critics were able to convince P&G's board to oust him as CEO. One of the old guard once again assumed control of P&G, but the changes Jager made have had lasting effects on the organization and analysts claim they see a distinct change in the way it does business.

As this story illustrates, an important implication of the view that people create the organizational culture is that as organizational members become similar over time, their ability to respond to changes in the environment may lessen.[48] This explains in part why organizations experience inertia in their decision making and why they may be slow to respond to change, as we saw at P&G. This can be the case not only with business decisions but hiring decisions, leading some companies to discriminate against women and people of colour, as was the case at Texaco in the late 1990s.[49] More recently, in 2004, Wal-Mart was ordered to stand trail for companywide sex discrimination, in the largest civil rights class action suit in U.S. history.[50]

In 1984, a Canadian Royal Commission on equality in the workplace found widespread discrimination across Canadian companies. The Abella Commission, as it became known, argued that one of the major causes of workplace discrimination was the culture of organizations or "systemic discrimination."[51]

Some people argue that an organization can guard against inertia and stagnation by deliberately selecting as members people who share different beliefs and values. An organization that does this guards against groupthink and can better adapt to changes in the environment. In Chapter 12, we discuss in depth how factors such as the background or skills of its top- management team, for example, may improve decision making and organizational learning. The "people make the place" view of organizational culture explains how an organization develops the shared cultural values that become such a powerful tool, and it implies that the culture of an organization can be changed by changing the people who control and lead it.[52] This was an important conclusion of the Abella Commission, which argued that cultural changes should begin at the top with clear signals and commitment to change.[53]

Organizational Ethics

Many cultural values derive from the personality and beliefs of the founder and the top-management team and are in a sense out of the control of the organization. These values are what they are because of who the founder and top managers are. Microsoft founder Bill Gates is a workaholic who still often works 18 hours a day. His terminal values for Microsoft are excellence, innovation, and high quality, and the instrumental values he advocates are hard work, creativity, and high standards. Gates expects his employees to put in long workdays because he requires this level of commitment from himself, and he expects them to do everything they can to promote innovation and quality because this is what he does. Employees who do not buy into these values leave Microsoft, and those who remain are pressured by organizational norms to stay on the job after the normal workday is over and to go out of their way to help others and take on new tasks that will help the organization. Cultural values at Microsoft are out of the organization's control because they are based on who Gates is.

An organization can, however, consciously and purposefully develop some cultural values to control members' behaviour. Ethical values fall into this category. As discussed in Chapter 2, organizational ethics are the moral values, beliefs, and rules that establish the appropriate way for organizational members to deal with one another and with the organization's stakeholders (see Figure 7-3).

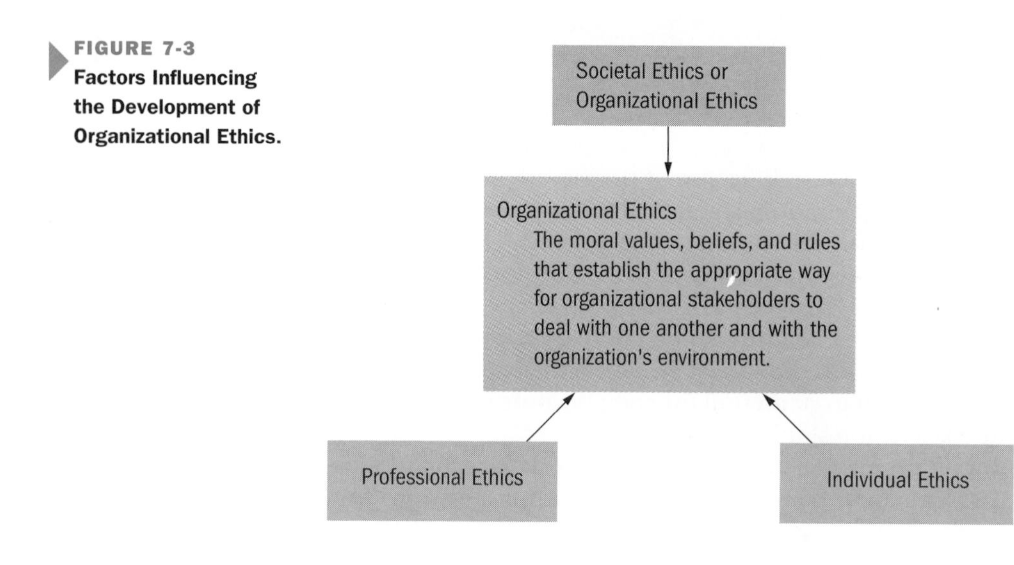

FIGURE 7-3 Factors Influencing the Development of Organizational Ethics.

In developing cultural values, top managers must constantly make choices about the right or appropriate thing to do. IBM or Sears, for example, might wonder whether it should develop procedural guidelines for giving advance notice to employees and middle managers about impending layoffs or store closings. Traditionally, companies have been reluctant to do so because they fear employee hostility and apathy. In 2001 Ford and Firestone had to decide whether to recall Explorers because burst tires were causing many rollovers resulting in serious harm or injury to passengers. In September 2004, Merck faced a similar situation faced with evidence that its arthritis drug Vioxx increased the risk of heart attack and stroke. Despite worldwide annual sales of $US2.55 billion, the company took the ethical decision to pull the drug from the market.[54]

A company must also decide whether to allow its managers to pay bribes to government officials in foreign countries where such payoffs are an illegal yet accepted way of doing business. In such situations, managers deciding on a course of action have to balance the interests of the organization against the interests of other stakeholder groups.[55] To make these decisions, managers rely on ethical instrumental values embodied in the organization's culture.[56] Such values outline the right and wrong ways to behave in a situation in which an action may help one person or stakeholder group, but hurt another.[57] Ethical values, and the rules and norms that they embody, are an inseparable part of an organization's culture because they help shape the values that members use to manage situations and make decisions.

One of top management's main responsibilities is to ensure that organizational members obey the law. Indeed, in certain situations top managers can be held accountable for the conduct of their subordinates. One of the main ways in which top managers can ensure the legality of organizational behaviour is to create an organizational culture that instills ethical instrumental values so that members reflexively deal with stakeholders in an ethical manner. While some companies, such as Johnson & Johnson and Merck, are well known for their ethical cultures, many organizations do act illegally, immorally, and unethically and take few steps to develop ethical values for their employees to follow. Consider the case of Suncor, whose CEO Rick George set out to change a corporate culture that did little to grapple with a bad image as an environmental polluter. (See Organizational Insight 7.6.)

Another interesting case involves Beech-Nut, a maker of baby foods. In the early 1980s, Beech-Nut was in financial trouble as it strived to compete with Gerber Products, the market leader. Threatened with the failure of the company if costs could not be lowered, Beech-Nut entered into an agreement with a low-cost supplier of apple juice concentrate. The agreement was supposed to save the company over US$250 000 annually, at a time when every dollar counted. Soon, one of Beech-Nut's research and development specialists became concerned about the quality of the concentrate. He believed that it was not made from apples alone but contained large quantities of corn syrup, cane sugar, and malic acid. He brought this information to the attention of top managers at Beech-Nut, but they were obsessed with the need to keep costs down and chose to ignore it. The company continued to produce and sell its product as pure apple juice.

Eventually, investigators from the U.S. Food and Drug Administration (FDA), acting on other information, confronted Beech-Nut with evidence that the concentrate was adulterated. The top managers issued denials and quickly shipped the remaining stock of apple juice to the market before their inventory could be seized.

The research and development specialist who had questioned the purity of the apple juice had resigned from Beech-Nut, but he decided to blow the whistle on the

ORGANIZATIONAL INSIGHT 7.6

Suncor's President Instrumental in Creating an Ethical "Green Culture"[58]

Suncor Energy Incorporated is best known for its business of extracting crude from the world's largest petroleum resource in Alberta's oil sands, which it has done since 1967. Today, Suncor is a large integrated energy company that has grown to having four major business divisions with more than 4000 employees.

For many years, operating in what is typically known as a dirty industry, Suncor had a bad reputation for its historical contribution to polluting the environment. It had plenty of bad publicity from toxic fires, dead workers, and big fish kills from toxic spills into the Athabasca River. In 1991, Rick George became president and CEO of Suncor Inc. and faced a serious challenge to improve the troubling financial position of the company as well as the low morale of workers, who carried the weight of the company's negative public image. "But George, ever the optimist," says author Andrew Nikiforuk, "not only met the challenge—he turned one of the continent's messiest industrial char ladies into a something of a social, financial and environmental Cinderella."

Rick George created this turnaround at Suncor by first making sure the company was sustainable from a financial perspective, and then he set out to promote a business culture of sustainable fossil fuel production—which in terms of the oil industry standards was a contradiction of terms. However, it was this new strategy that would kick-start a cultural transition to address the company's biggest challenge of low employee morale and declining public image. Perhaps one of the most important steps in this direction was when Suncor allocated a $100 million investment in wind and other energy alternatives, which was the largest such investment made by any firm in North America.

George also initiated and surpassed Greenpeace initiatives even before the pressure to do so came into play. More recently, many of Suncor's employees have enlisted in the "One-Tonne Challenge" program, a challenge to reduce personal greenhouse emissions by one tonne per year. Suncor now offers employees incentives such as transit tickets and energy-efficient light bulbs to take up this challenge. So, through many such measures, George has determinedly shifted Suncor's image into a positive light. "Suncor is the perfect example of how social and environmental issues go hand in hand with financial success," says Nikiforuk. "And it's so ingrained in the culture, that ethic will survive Rick George."

company. He told the FDA that Beech-Nut's top management had known of the problem with the concentrate and had acted to maximize company profits rather than to inform customers about the additives in the apple juice. In 1987, the company pleaded guilty to charges that it had deliberately sold adulterated juice and was fined over US$2 million. Its top managers were also found guilty and were sentenced to prison terms (which were eventually overturned on a technicality). Consumer trust in Beech-Nut products plummeted, as did the value of Beech-Nut stock. The company was eventually sold to Ralston Purina, which completely revamped it and its management and promoted strict new ethical values to establish a new culture in the organization.[59]

Personal and professional ethics (see Chapter 2) also influence how a person will act in an organization, so an organization's culture is strongly affected by the people who are in a position to establish its ethical values. As we saw earlier, the founder of an organization plays a particularly important role in establishing ethical norms and values.

Property Rights

The values in an organization's culture reflect the ethics of individuals in the organization, of professional groups, and of the society in which the organization exists. The values in an organization's culture also stem from how the organization distributes **property rights**—the rights that an organization gives to its members to receive and use organizational resources.[60] Property rights define the rights and responsibilities of each inside stakeholder group and cause the development of different norms, values, and attitudes toward the organization. Table 7-3 identifies some of the property rights commonly given to managers and the workforce.

Property rights
The rights that an organization gives to its members to receive and use organizational resources.

Shareholders have the strongest property rights of all stakeholder groups because they own the resources of the company and share in its profits. Top managers often have strong property rights because they are given large amounts of organizational resources, such as high salaries, the rights to large stock options, or golden parachutes, which guarantee them large sums of money if they are fired when their company is taken over. Top managers' rights to use organizational resources are reflected in their authority to make decisions and control organizational resources. Managers are usually given strong rights because if they do not share in the value that the organization creates, they are unlikely to be motivated to work hard on behalf of the organization and its other stakeholders.

An organization's workforce may be given strong property rights, such as a guarantee of lifetime employment and involvement in an employee stock-ownership plan (ESOP) or in a profit-sharing plan. Most workers, however, are not given very strong property rights. Few are given lifetime employment or involved in ESOPs, though they may be guaranteed long-term employment or be eligible for bonuses. Often workers' property rights are simply the wages they earn and the health and pension benefits they receive. Workers' rights to use organizational resources are reflected in their responsibilities in the level of control they have over their tasks.

The distribution of property rights has a direct effect on the instrumental values that shape employee behaviour and motivate organizational members.[61] Attempts to limit employees' benefits and reduce their rights to receive and use resources can often result in hostility and high turnover. However, establishing a companywide stock option system and encouraging employees to use organizational resources to find bet-

Table 7-3

COMMON PROPERTY RIGHTS GIVEN TO MANAGERS AND THE WORKFORCE

Managers' Rights	Workforce Rights
Golden parachutes	Notification of layoffs
Stock options	Severance payments
Large salaries	Lifetime employment
Control over organizational resources	Long-term employment
Decision making	Pension and benefits
	Employee stock ownership plans
	Participation in decision making

ter ways of serving customers can foster commitment and loyalty, as at companies like Delta Hotels, Flight Centre Ltd., Edward Jones Canada, and Crystal Decisions Inc.—all of whom made the list of the "50 Best Companies to Work for in Canada." The distribution of property rights to different stakeholders determines (1) how effective an organization is and (2) the culture that emerges in the organization. How different property rights systems promote the development of different cultures is evident in the well-known story of what occurred after GM acquired Electronic Data Systems. (See Organizational Insight 7.7.)

As Organizational Insight 7.7 illustrates, the distribution of property rights influences not only expectations about how people should behave but also the values people use in their dealings with other stakeholders. Managers accustomed to one property rights system will find it hard to function in another. GM managers were used to a conservative, cautious culture that did not reward innovation (in this case, potentially cost-saving behaviour). They found it hard to relate to managers in EDS's more entrepreneurial culture, who were rewarded for performance. In fact, GM and many other companies have since moved to reward their managers with stock options to encourage division managers to become more entrepreneurial.

ORGANIZATIONAL INSIGHT 7.7

A Clash of Two Cultures

When Roger Smith, General Motors CEO at the time, bought Electronic Data Systems (EDS), he bought a company recognized as one of the best computer systems specialists in the world. The deal worked out between Smith and EDS founder Ross Perot was that EDS would take control of GM's computer systems and computer staffs and would manage all of GM's software needs. EDS would make contracts with each GM car division and would price its services as if it were operating in the open market—that is, the price would include a markup for EDS's services even though EDS was part of GM. This practice gave rise to a problem.

The managers of GM's car divisions typically earned a straight salary; they received neither bonuses nor stock options as rewards for performance. Moreover, when they bought inputs from GM's parts divisions, they paid whatever price the parts division asked. There was no incentive for the car division managers to bargain over prices because reducing costs had no effect on their salaries.

At EDS, in contrast, Perot had rewarded his executives with generous stock options on the basis of contract profits. Thus EDS managers were more entrepreneurial than the GM car division managers and had an incentive to strike the best deal they could get (cost plus a markup for profit) with the car divisions.

The difference in the way property rights were awarded to employees in EDS and GM led to a culture clash. GM's car division managers did not want to sign contracts with managers from GM's new EDS division because the EDS managers would personally gain from the markup charged to the car divisions. GM's 57 car division managers refused to sign contracts with EDS because they did not want to enrich other GM employees.[62] Thus the potential gains to the corporation as a whole from EDS management of GM's 100 different computer networks were only slowly realized. GM, realizing that EDS would be better off on its own, decided to spin off EDS and allow it to become an independent company once again, free to pursue its own interests.

The power of property rights over people's expectations is also apparent in a situation that occurred at Apple Computer. For its first ten years in operation, Apple had never had a layoff, and employees had come to take job security for granted. Although no written document promised job security, employees believed they were appreciated and possessed an implicit property right to their jobs. Imagine, then, what happened in 1991 when Apple announced the layoff of several thousand middle and lower-level personnel to reduce costs. Employees were dumbfounded: This was not how Apple treated its employees. They demonstrated outside Apple headquarters for several weeks. What effect did the layoff have on Apple's culture? It destroyed the belief that Apple valued its employees, and it destroyed an organizational culture in which employees had been motivated to put forth effort above and beyond their formal job descriptions. At Apple, employee loyalty turned into hostility.

Similar attitudes surfaced at Nova Scotia Power in the mid-1990s. As a Crown corporation, its employees were used to thinking that a job with Nova Scotia Power was a job for life. As a government employer, with a strong union environment, employees were rarely laid off. When Louis Comeau took over as CEO in 1983, the company had about 2300 employees. During the culture change phase from 1988 to 1991, employment soared to nearly 2600 employees. Following privatization and the introduction of re-engineering in 1992–93 a number of job cuts were made, and employment in the company began to fall steadily, from 2200 in 1994 to roughly 1600 in 1998. Despite the fact that a number of employees were offered early-retirement packages, many employees lost the trust they had in the company during the earlier culture change program.[63]

Apple, Air Canada, Nortel, Bombardier, and other large companies that have recently laid off large numbers of employees are in the peculiar position of needing increased commitment from those who remain in order to turn their businesses around. Can they reasonably expect this? How can they encourage it? Perhaps they can give remaining employees property rights that will engender commitment to the organization. That task is the responsibility of top managers.

Top Management and Property Rights Top managers are in a strong position to establish the terms of their own employment, their salary and benefits packages, and their termination and pension benefits. Top managers also determine the property rights received by others and thus determine what kind of culture will develop in an organization. The core competencies of Apple Computer and Microsoft, for example, depend on the skills and capabilities of their personnel. To gain employee commitment, these organizations reward their top programmers and functional experts highly and give them very strong property rights. Apple has a position called "Apple Fellow," which gives top programmers the right to work on any project in the corporation or start any new project that they find promising. Both corporations reward important employees with large stock options. Over 1500 people who joined Microsoft in the 1970s and 1980s, for example, are now multimillionaires as a result of stock options that they received in the past and continue to receive. It is not difficult to imagine how committed they are to the organization. Microsoft founder Bill Gates does not hand out stock options because he is generous, however; he does so because he wants to encourage terminal values of excellence and innovation and instrumental values of creativity and hard work. He also wants to prevent his best people from leaving to found their own firms (which would most likely compete with Microsoft) or going to work for Microsoft's competitors.

Does giving stronger property rights to production line or staff workers produce a culture in which they are committed to the organization and motivated to perform highly? The introduction of an employee stock option plan at Bimba Manufacturing had dramatic effects on employee behaviour and the culture of the organization. (See Organizational Insight 7.8.)

As the Bimba story illustrates, changing the property rights system changes the corporate culture by changing the instrumental values that motivate and coordinate employees. At Bimba, gone is the need for close supervision and the use of rigid rules and procedures to control behaviour. Instead, coordination is achieved by teams of employees who value cooperation and are motivated by the prospect of sharing in the value created by the new work system. Other companies that offer profit sharing and stock option schemes include Edward Jones Canada, Crystal Decisions Inc., PLC Construction Group Inc., QLT Inc., Canadian Tire Corp. Ltd., McDonald's Restaurants of Canada Ltd., Nexen Inc., Dofasco Inc., RBC Financial Group, Envision Financial, and Dun and Bradstreet Canada.

Can Property Rights Be Too Strong? As the Bimba story suggests, the worth of a person's behaviour and the level of his or her performance are, in part, consequences of the rights the person has in the job. Sometimes those rights have been developed as a

ORGANIZATIONAL INSIGHT 7.8

Bimba Changes Its Property Rights System

The Bimba Manufacturing Company, based in Monee, Illinois, manufactures aluminum cylinders. Its owner, Charles Bimba, decided to sell the company to its employees by establishing an employee stock ownership plan. He kept 10 percent of the shares; the other 90 percent was sold to employees. Some of the employees' money came from an already existing profit-sharing plan; the rest was borrowed from a bank.

Changes in the company since the ESOP was introduced have been dramatic, and the orientation of the workforce to the organization has totally changed. Previously, the company had two groups of employees: managers who made the rules and workers who carried them out. Workers rarely made suggestions and generally just obeyed orders. Now, cross-functional teams composed of managers and workers meet regularly to discuss problems and find new ways to improve quality. These teams also meet regularly with customers to better meet their needs.

Because of the incentives provided by the new ESOP, management and workers have developed new working relationships based on teamwork to achieve excellence and high quality. Each team hires its own members and spends considerable time socializing new employees in the new culture of the organization. The new cooperative spirit in the plant has forced managers to relearn their roles. They now listen to workers and act as advisers rather than superiors.

So far, changing the company's property rights system has paid off. Sales have increased by 70 percent and the workforce has grown by 59 percent. Bimba has expanded to a new, large facility and has opened a facility in England. Furthermore, workers have repaid over 60 percent of the loan they took out to finance the employee stock purchase. The ESOP has totally changed Bimba's corporate culture and altered the commitment of its work force. In the words of one worker, it has led to "an intense change in the way we look at our jobs."[64]

result of decisions made by those in charge of the organization. Sometimes those rights are the result of years of labour-relations bargaining between employer and unions. At Creo, for example, CEO Amos Michelson sees himself as the protector of the company's culture. New hires meet not only with senior managers but also with as many as ten employees. Those ten employees have an equal say in the hiring decision. The idea is to ensure that new applicants are a good fit with the company. However, it also strengthens employee notions of property rights by encouraging them to feel that they are sharing their workplace with others. At Air Canada it took years of trade union development, negotiation, and industrial unrest to establish certain levels of job security.[65] Thus, whether employees' property rights are considered too be to strong will depend in large part on where that opinion is coming from.

For example, over the years IBM developed a very conservative culture in which employees had strong rights, such as the implicit promise of lifetime employment. As a result, according to Lou Gerstner, one of its CEOs, IBM employees had become cautious and noninnovative. Gerstner claimed that the organization protected IBM employees so well that they had no motivation to perform, to take risks, or to rock the boat. He suggested that the property rights of IBM employees were too strong.

At Nova Scotia Power in the late 1980s, employees were asked to devote considerable time and energy to developing a new culture. As part of the process, they were rewarded with a promise of a new culture that would value them as employees and encourage managers to communicate more effectively with those under them. Despite the fact that the culture change actually strengthened employee property rights in their jobs, the culture became far more dynamic and led to greater efficiencies.

At Air Canada, property rights were a vital issue in the merger with Canadian Airlines. In order to ensure an effective takeover of the ailing Canadian Airlines, Air Canada CEO Robert Milton negotiated a deal that saw the absorption of former Canadian Airlines employees that guaranteed them no layoffs for at least two years and the maintenance of seniority rights. In the process, existing Air Canada employees found that their job seniority was severely affected, with some losing their jobs. The result has been a period of bitterness and low morale across the company as it struggled to stay in business.

It is easy to understand how senior managers can view employee property rights as too strong. But it is also easy to see why employees resist attempts to change those rights because changes can lead to decreased job security and job status, reduced seniority and even unemployment. As the culture change process at Nova Scotia Power suggests, a strong sense of employee property rights can actually contribute to the development of a dynamic culture and more efficient business. When senior managers step in to change existing property rights, they need to take care in how the issue is handled. Handled incorrectly and it can encourage employees to take steps to protect their rights and resist attempts by others to wrest their rights away. The result is conflict, internal power struggles, and a loss of flexibility and innovation as the organization loses sight of its mission because its members are preoccupied with their own—not the organization's—interests. Managers must continually evaluate and address this difficult challenge.

IBM's Gerstner took steps to change the company's property rights system and create an entrepreneurial culture by distributing more rewards based on performance and by eliminating employees' expectations of lifetime employment. To create a certain kind of culture, an organization needs to create a certain kind of property rights system. In part, organizational culture reflects the values that emerge as a result of an organization's property rights system.

Organizational Structure

We have seen how the values that coordinate and motivate employees result from the organization's people, its ethics, and the distribution of property rights among various stakeholders. The fourth source of cultural values is organizational structure. Recall from Chapter 1 that *organizational structure* is the formal system of task and authority relationships that an organization establishes to coordinate and control its activities. Because different structures give rise to different cultures, managers need to design a certain kind of organizational structure to create a certain kind of organizational culture. Mechanistic structures and organic structures, for example, give rise to totally different sets of cultural values. The values, rules, and norms in a mechanistic structure are different from those in an organic structure.

Recall from Chapter 4 that *mechanistic structures* are tall, highly centralized, and standardized, and *organic structures* are flat and decentralized and rely on mutual adjustment. In a tall, centralized organization, people have relatively little personal autonomy, and desirable behaviours include being cautious, obeying superior authority, and respecting traditions. Thus mechanistic structure is likely to give rise to a culture in which predictability and stability are desired end states. In a flat, decentralized structure, people have more freedom to choose and control their own activities, and desirable behaviours include being creative or courageous and taking risks. Thus an organic structure is likely to give rise to a culture in which innovation and flexibility are desired end states.

An organization's structure can promote cultural values that foster integration and coordination. Out of stable task and role relationships, for example, emerge shared norms and rules that help reduce communications problems, prevent the distortion of information, and speed the flow of information. Moreover, norms, values, and a common organizational language can improve the performance of teams and taskforces. It is relatively easy for different functions to share information and trust one another when they share similar cultural values. One reason why product development time is short and the organization is flexible in product team structures and matrix structures is that the reliance on face-to-face contact between functional specialists in teams forces those teams quickly to develop shared values and common responses to problems.

Whether a company is centralized or decentralized also leads to the development of different kinds of cultural values. By decentralizing authority, an organization can establish values that encourage and reward creativity or innovation. The founders of Hewlett-Packard established the "Hewlett-Packard Way," an organizational philosophy that gives employees access to equipment and resources so that they can be creative and conduct their own research informally, outside of their normal job responsibilities. At Flight Centre a number of small regional groups oversee the company's stores and are responsible for their own hiring, training and marketing. In both these companies, the organizational structure produces cultural values that tell members that it is all right to be innovative and to do things in their own way, as long as their actions are consistent with the good of the organization.

Conversely, in some organizations, it is important that employees do not make decisions on their own and that their actions be open to the scrutiny of superiors. In such cases, centralization can be used to create cultural values that reinforce obedience and accountability. For example, in nuclear power plants, values that promote stability, predictability, and obedience to superior authority are deliberately fostered to prevent disasters.[66] Through norms and rules, employees are taught the importance of behaving consistently and honestly, and they learn that sharing information with supervisors, especially information about mistakes or errors, is the only acceptable form of behaviour.[67]

In sum, organizational structure affects the cultural values that guide organizational members as they perform their activities. In turn, culture improves the way structure coordinates and motivates organizational resources to help an organization achieve its goals. One source of a company's competitive advantage is its ability to design its structure and manage its culture so that there is a good fit between the two. This gives rise to a core competency that is hard for other organizations to imitate. However, when companies fail to achieve a good fit, or when structural changes produce changes in cultural values, problems start to occur.

CAN ORGANIZATIONAL CULTURE BE MANAGED?

Managers interested in understanding the interplay between an organization's culture and the organization's effectiveness at creating value for stakeholders must take a hard look at all four of the factors that produce culture: the characteristics of organizational members (particularly the founder and top managers), organizational ethics, the property rights system, and organizational structure. To change a culture can be very difficult because those factors interact and because major alterations are often needed to change an organization's values.[68] To change its culture, an organization might need to redesign its structure and revise the property rights it uses to motivate and reward employees. The organization might also need to change its people, especially its top-management team. Keeping in mind the difficulty of managing organizational culture, let's look at how Microsoft's culture evolved as a result of the interaction of the four factors.

As we discussed above, Bill Gates's personal values and beliefs and his vision of what Microsoft could achieve form the core of Microsoft's culture, with its terminal values of excellence and innovation. With its initial success established by its MS-DOS and Microsoft Word systems, Microsoft began to attract the best software engineers in the world. Gates was therefore in a position to select those people who bought into his values and who could perform at the level that he and his managers required. Over time, norms based on the need for individual initiative (to enhance the instrumental values of creativity and risk taking) and for teamwork (to enhance cooperation) emerged, and Microsoft built a campus-like headquarters complex to promote the development of an informal atmosphere in which people could develop strong working bonds.

Gates designed an organic structure for Microsoft and kept it as flat and decentralized as possible by using small teams to coordinate work activities. This design encourages risk taking and creativity. He also used a product team structure to reinforce the team atmosphere and norms of "team spirit." Gates also established a culture for innovation by rewarding successful risk taking and creativity with strong property rights. Many key employees receive stock options based on company performance, and all employees are eligible to receive bonuses. Furthermore, Microsoft offers high-quality pensions and benefits and has never had to lay off any employees. Finally, the company has a history of behaving ethically toward its employees and customers. Microsoft's people, its structure, its property rights, and its ethics interact and fit together to make up Microsoft's culture.

Compare Microsoft's culture to the one Louis Gerstner, IBM's former CEO, had to change to turn around the failing company: IBM had a conservative, stable culture produced by (1) property rights tied not to performance but to employee longevity in the organization and (2) a tall, centralized structure that promoted obedience and conformity. The people attracted to and retained by this IBM culture were those who liked working in a stable environment where they knew their place, who accepted the status quo, and who did not mind that the culture limited their opportunities to innovate or be creative. Although there was a match among the factors producing IBM's culture, the culture did not serve the company well. Because its cultural values emphasized stability, IBM was unable to adapt to changes in the environment, such as changes in technology and customer needs.

Can a company maintain a creative, entrepreneurial culture as it grows? Analysts have asked whether Gates will be able to maintain Microsoft's dynamic and freewheeling culture as the company grows. He has said that his policy of using small product development teams and spinning off into a separate product team any unit that reaches 200 people will help Microsoft preserve its entrepreneurial values and prevent the development of inertia and complacency.

To prevent an organization's culture from changing in ways that reduce effectiveness as the organization grows, top managers must design its structure to offset the control problems that occur with large size and complexity.[69] IBM, for example, was reorganized into 13 autonomous business units in an attempt to break IBM's old conservative culture and give each unit the opportunity to develop a new culture supportive of values such as customer responsiveness and excellence. IBM also made changes in its property rights system to try to change the cultural values guiding employee behaviour; now performance, not seniority, determines the distribution of property rights. Furthermore, Gerstner decided to build IBM a new campus-style headquarters building to encourage its members to adopt a more flexible, team-based cross-divisional perspective.

Will changing the structure, property rights, and top people be enough to change cultural values? Many studies have demonstrated that norms and values are stable and resistant to change.[70] Under Gerstner's leadership, IBM's culture did change, although on several occasions he complained about how difficult it was to get people to change. Gerstner changed the foundations on which the old culture was built and a new, more entrepreneurial culture emerged as values and norms changed and IBM's performance soared. The new IBM is a totally different company.

MANAGERIAL IMPLICATIONS

Designing Organizational Culture

1. Try to identify the source of the values and norms of your organization's culture and analyze the relative effects of people, ethics, property rights, and structure on influencing organizational culture.
2. Use this analysis to produce an action plan for redesigning the culture of the organization to improve effectiveness.
3. Be sure that the action plan takes all four factors into consideration, for each one affects the others. Changing one factor alone may not be sufficient to change organizational culture.
4. Make the development of ethical organizational values one of your major priorities.

SOCIAL RESPONSIBILITY

One very important consequence of the values and norms of its culture is an organization's stance with regard to social responsibility. The term social responsibility refers to a manager's duty or obligation to make decisions that nurture, protect, enhance, and promote the welfare and well-being of stakeholders and society as a whole. Many kinds of decisions signal an organization's interest in being socially responsible (see Table 7-4).

Approaches to Social Responsibility

The strength of an organization's commitment to social responsibility ranges from low to high (see Figure 7-4).[71] At the low end of the range is an **obstructionist approach**. Obstructionist managers choose not to behave in a socially responsible way. Instead, they behave unethically and illegally and do all they can to prevent knowledge of their behaviour from reaching other organizational stakeholders and society at large. Managers at the Mansville Corporation adopted this approach when evidence that asbestos causes lung damage was uncovered. Managers at Beech-Nut who sought to hide evidence about the use of corn syrup in their apple juice also adopted this approach. The managers of these organizations chose an obstructionist approach. The result was not only a loss of reputation but devastation for their organizations and for all stakeholders involved.

Obstructionist approach The low end of the organization's commitment to social responsibility.

A **defensive approach** indicates at least a commitment to ethical behaviour. Defensive managers stay within the law and abide strictly within legal requirements, but make no attempt to exercise social responsibility beyond what the law dictates. Managers adopting this approach do all they can to ensure that their employees behave legally and do not harm others. But when making ethical choices, these managers put the claims and interests of their shareholders first, at the expense of other stakeholders.

Defensive approach An approach indicating a commitment to ethical behaviour.

The very nature of a capitalist society—in which managers' primary responsibility is to the owners of the corporation, its shareholders—probably encourages the

Table 7-4

FORMS OF SOCIALLY RESPONSIBLE BEHAVIOUR

Managers are being socially responsible and showing their support for their stakeholders when they:

- Provide severance payments to help laid-off workers make ends meet until they can find another job.
- Provide workers with opportunities to enhance their skills and acquire additional education so they can remain productive and do not become obsolete because of changes in technology.
- Allow employees to take time off when they need to and provide health care and pension benefits for employees.
- Contribute to charities or support various civic-minded activities in the cities or towns in which they are located. (Target and Levi Strauss both contribute 5 percent of their profits to support schools, charities, the arts, and other good works.)
- Decide to keep open a factory whose closure would devastate the local community.
- Decide to keep a company's operations in the home country to protect the jobs of domestic workers rather than move abroad.
- Decide to spend money to improve a new factory so that it will not pollute the environment.
- Decline to invest in countries that have poor human rights records.
- Choose to help poor countries develop an economic base to improve living standards.

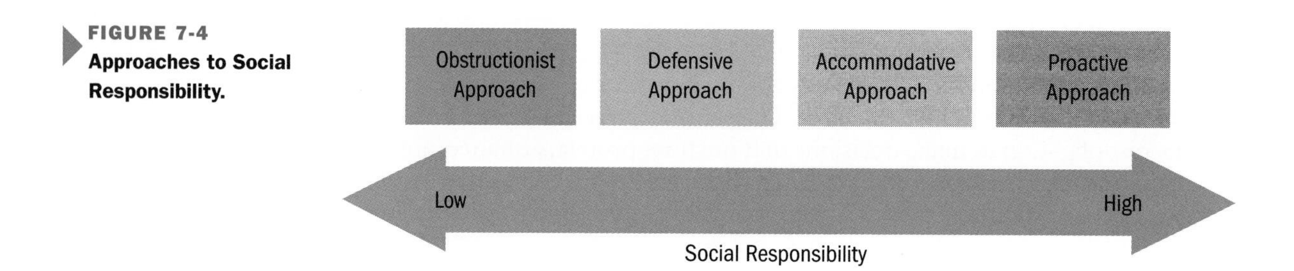

FIGURE 7-4
Approaches to Social Responsibility.

defensive response. Some economists believe that managers in a capitalistic society should always put shareholders' claims first, and that if these choices are not acceptable to other members of society and are considered unethical, then society must pass laws and create rules and regulations to govern the choices managers make.[72] From a defensive perspective, it is not managers' responsibility to make socially responsible choices; their job is to abide by the rules that have been legally established. Thus, defensive managers have little active interest in social responsibility.

Accommodative approach The acknowledgment of the need to support social responsibility.

An **accommodative approach** is an acknowledgment of the need to support social responsibility. Accommodative managers agree that organizational members ought to behave legally and ethically, and they try to balance the interests of different stakeholders against one another so that the claims of shareholders are seen in relation to the claims of other stakeholders. Managers adopting this approach want to make choices that are reasonable in the eyes of society and want to do the right thing when called on to do so.

Proactive approach An approach in which managers actively embrace the need to behave in socially responsible ways, go out of their way to learn about the needs of different stakeholder groups, and are willing to utilize organizational resources to promote the interests not only of shareholders, but of the other stakeholders.

Managers taking a **proactive approach** actively embrace the need to behave in socially responsible ways, go out of their way to learn about the needs of different stakeholder groups, and are willing to utilize organizational resources to promote the interests not only of shareholders, but of the other stakeholders. Such companies—including The Body Shop, Lush, Shell Canada, Zenon Environmental Inc., Ben & Jerry's Homemade, Husky Injection Molding Systems, Suncor Energy Inc., Petro-Canada, RBC, and the Bank of Nova Scotia—are at the forefront of campaigns for causes such as a pollution-free environment, recycling and conservation of resources, minimizing or avoiding the use of animals in drug and cosmetic testing, and reducing crime, illiteracy, and poverty.[73] Senior management at Husky Injection Molding Systems, for example, has a very clear idea about the company's moral priorities. (See Organizational Insight 7.9.)

Why Be Socially Responsible?

Several advantages are argued to result when managers and organizations behave in a socially responsible manner. First, workers and society benefit directly, because organizations (rather than governments) bear some of the costs of helping workers. Second, it has been said that if all organizations in a society were socially responsible, the quality of life as a whole would be higher. Indeed, several management experts have argued that the way organizations behave toward their employees determines many of a society's values and norms and the ethics of its citizens. It has been suggested that if all organizations adopted a caring approach and agreed that their responsibility is to promote the interests of their employees, a climate of caring would pervade the wider society.[74] Experts point to Japan, Sweden, Germany, the Netherlands, Switzerland, and Canada as countries where organizations are very socially responsible and where, as a result, crime and unemployment rates are relatively low, the literacy rate is relatively

ORGANIZATIONAL INSIGHT 7.9

Social Responsibility Evident at Husky Injection Molding Systems Ltd.[75]

Husky Injection Molding Systems is a leading supplier of injection moulding equipment and services to the plastics industry; its customers are primarily manufacturers of plastic goods for resale. The company's headquarters is in Ontario, but Husky has a worldwide presence with an estimated 2800 employees working in more than 40 sales and service offices for customers in over 100 different countries. In 2004, Husky was on the list of the "50 Best Employers in Canada" for its third time. Employees are important to the company, and corporate responsibility, in general, is an integral part of the company's success. Husky prominently expresses its core values of having "a passion for excellence, bold goals, proactive environmental responsibility, making a contribution and uncompromising honesty" as the foundation of its business practices worldwide.

The strong social responsibility backbone of Husky stems from its founding owner, Robert Schad, who had a mission and corporate goals to do business respecting people and the environment, well before such standards became fashionable in the 1980s. Unlike many other corporations who have espoused social concerns superficially, Husky has indeed followed through with its founder's social philosophy in many ways. For example, Husky has spent a great deal on ensuring employee and community health, and the employee cafeteria promotes healthy living. Husky also has top-notch child-care facilities for its employees' dependents. The corporate hallways are decorated in Canadian art, mainly wildlife scenes and the surrounding naturalistic setting at headquarters, which is a testament to how Husky strongly supports environmental causes. Many believe that Husky's socially responsible core values have been key to its success, and this is particularly notable when one considers that during a depressed market for injection moulding, Husky boosted its sales by 40 percent and returned to profitability.

high, and sociocultural values promote harmony between different groups of people. Other reasons for being socially responsible are that it is the right thing to do and that companies that act responsibly toward their stakeholders benefit from increasing business and see their profits rise.[76]

Given these advantages, why would anyone quarrel over the pursuit of social responsibility by organizations and their managers? One issue that comes up is that although some stakeholders benefit from managers' commitment to social responsibility, other stakeholders, particularly shareholders, may think they are being harmed when organizational resources are used for socially responsible courses of action. Some people argue that business has only one kind of responsibility: to use its resources for activities that increase its profits and thus reward its shareholders.[77]

How should managers decide which social issues they will respond to and to what extent their organizations should trade profits for social gain? Obviously, illegal behaviour should not be tolerated; all managers and workers should be alert to its occurrence and report it promptly. The term **whistle-blower** is used to refer to a person who reports illegal or unethical behaviour and takes a stand against unscrupulous managers or other stakeholders who are pursuing their own ends.[78] Laws now exist to pro-

Whistle-blowing Informing (by an employee) an outside person or agency, such as a government agency or a newspaper or television reporter, about an organization's (its managers') illegal or immoral behaviour.

tect the interests of whistle-blowers, who risk their jobs and careers to reveal unethical behaviour. In the U.S., these laws were, in part, enacted because of the experiences of two engineers at Morton Thiokol who warned that the Challenger space shuttle's O-ring gaskets would be adversely affected by cold weather at launch.[79] Their warnings were ignored by everyone involved in the headlong rush to launch the shuttle. As a result, seven astronauts died when the Challenger exploded shortly after launch in January 1986. Although the actions of the engineers were applauded by the committee of inquiry, their subsequent careers suffered because managers at Morton Thiokol blamed them for damaging the company's reputation and harming its interests.

Another way in which managers can ascertain whether they are acting socially responsibly is to apply ethical standards and values. Managers' own ethics influence their behaviour, and their own values strongly influence whether they will take a proactive approach to social responsibility. An organization's code of ethics, usually printed in its annual reports and mission statements, also influences how conscientiously managers seek to support the interests of all their stakeholders. Some organizations, like Johnson & Johnson, view the company's code of ethics as the only policy to follow when an ethical dilemma is evident, and they allow this code to govern their choices. Other organizations pay lip service to the organization's ethical code and, as a result, managers facing a moral dilemma seek to protect their own interests first and worry later about how other stakeholders will be affected. When such managers talk about protecting the organization, what they are really talking about is protecting their own interests: their jobs, bonuses, careers, and abilities to use organizational resources for their own ends.

Evidence suggests that managers who behave socially responsibly will, in the long run, most benefit all organizational stakeholders (including shareholders). It appears that socially responsible companies, in comparison with less responsible competitors, are less risky investments, tend to be somewhat more profitable, have a more loyal and committed workforce, and have better reputations, which encourage stakeholders (including customers and suppliers) to establish long-term business relationships with them.[80] Socially responsible companies are also sought out by communities, which encourage such organizations to locate in their cities and offer them incentives such as property-tax reductions and the construction of new roads and free utilities for their plants. Thus, there are many reasons to believe that, over time, strong support of social responsibility confers the most benefits on organizational stakeholders (including shareholders) and on society at large.

SUMMARY

Organizational culture powerfully guides the interactions of organizational members with each other and with outsiders. By supplying people with a toolbox of values, norms, and rules that tell them how to behave, organizational culture is instrumental in determining how they interpret and react to a situation. Thus an organization's culture can be a source of competitive advantage. Chapter 7 has made the following main points:

1. Organizational culture is a set of shared values that provide organizational members with a common understanding of how they should act in a situation.
2. There are two kinds of organizational values: terminal (a desired end state or outcome) and instrumental (a desired mode of behaviour). Ideally, instrumental values help the organization to achieve its terminal goals.

3. Organizational culture affects organizational effectiveness because it can (a) provide an organization with a competitive advantage, (b) improve the way an organizational structure works, and (c) increase the motivation of employees to pursue organizational interests.
4. Culture is transmitted to an organization's members by means of (a) socialization and training programs and (b) stories, ceremonies, and language used by members of the organization.
5. Organizational culture develops from the interaction of (a) the characteristics of organization members, (b) organizational ethics, (c) the property rights distributed among the people in the organization, and (d) organizational structure.
6. Different organizational structures give rise to different patterns of interaction among people. These different patterns lead to the formation of different organizational cultures.
7. Social responsibility is an organization's moral responsibility to stakeholder groups affected by the organization's actions. There are four stances on social responsibility and they have very different implications for organizational behaviour.

DISCUSSION QUESTIONS

1. What is the origin of organizational culture? Why do different organizations have different cultures?
2. How do newcomers learn the culture of an organization? How can an organization encourage newcomers to develop (a) an institutionalized role orientation and (b) an individualized role orientation?
3. In what ways can organizational culture increase organizational effectiveness? Why is it important to obtain the right fit between organizational structure and culture?
4. "An organization should always adopt a broad stance on social responsibility." Explain why you agree or disagree with this statement.

ORGANIZATIONAL THEORY IN ACTION

Practising Organizational Theory: Developing a Service Culture

Form groups of three to five people and discuss the following scenario:

You are the owner/managers of a new five-star resort hotel opening up in the beautiful mountain city of Banff in Alberta. For your venture to succeed, you need to make sure that hotel employees focus on providing customers with the highest-quality customer service possible. You are meeting to discuss how to create a culture that will promote such high-quality service, that will encourage employees to be committed to the hotel, and that will reduce the level of employee turnover and absenteeism, which are typically high in the hotel business.

1. What kinds of organizational values and norms encourage employees to behave in ways that lead to high-quality customer service?
2. Using the concepts discussed in this chapter (e.g., people, property rights, socialization), discuss how you will create a culture that promotes the learning of these customer service values and norms.
3. Which factor is the most important determinant of the kind of culture you expect to find in a high-quality hotel?

Making the Connection #7

Identify an organization that has been trying to change its culture. Describe the culture that it is trying to alter. Why is this culture no longer effective? How has the organization tried to bring about change? How successful has it been?

The Ethical Dimension #7

The chapter discussed how Arthur Andersen's organizational culture had become so strong that some of its partners and their subordinates began to act unethically and pursue their own short-run interests at the expense of other stakeholders. Many employees knew they were doing wrong, but were afraid to refuse to follow orders.

1. Why is it that an organization's values and norms can become too strong and lead to unethical behaviour?
2. What steps can a company take to prevent this problem, to stop its values and norms from becoming so inwardly focused that managers and employees lose sight of their obligations to their stakeholders?

Analyzing the Organization: Design Module #7

In this module you will analyze the culture of your organization, discuss the characteristic ways in which members act, and its stance on social responsibility.

ASSIGNMENT

1. Do managers and employees use certain words and phrases to describe the behaviour of people in the organization? Are any stories about events or people typically used to describe the way the organization works? (*Hint*: Look at the company's Web page.)
2. How does the organization socialize employees? Does it put them through formal training programs? What kind of programs are used, and what is their goal?
3. What beliefs and values seem to characterize the way people behave in the organization? How do they affect people's behaviour?
4. Given the answers to the first three questions, how would you characterize the organization's culture and the way it benefits or harms the organization? How could the culture be improved?
5. Can you find a written statement of the organization's stance on social responsibility? Are there stories in the press about the company? If there are, what do they say?

Company Profiles #7*

Choose one or more of the organizations (e.g., companies, government agencies, or nonprofit organizations) that are profiled in this chapter. Do an Internet search to get up-to-date information on each organization you have selected, and answer the following questions.

1. What does the new information tell you about the organization's current ability to develop a successful organizational culture?
2. How does the information compare with the earlier information provided in the text and what does that tell you about organizations (e.g., does the organization appear to be more or less successful in developing a successful organizational culture than before, and how do you explain this)?

Alternative Perspectives #7

Critical and feminist research indicates that organizational culture can have negative impacts on employees. Read one or more of the following readings and list five ways that the culture of an organization can have a negative impact and five ways that it can have a positive impact on employees. In small groups, discuss how you would deal with the potentially negative aspects of organizational culture.

Reading List

Aaltio, I., and Mills, A. J. (Eds.). 2002a. *Gender, Identity and the Culture of Organizations.* London: Routledge.

Aaltio, I., and Mills, A. J. 2002b. Organizational Culture and Gendered Identities in Context. In I. Aaltio, and A. J. Mills (Eds.), *Gender, Identity and the Culture of Organizations*, pp. 3–18. London: Routledge.

* The authors would like to receive information from student groups and instructors on any companies where there have been dramatic changes to the information published in this text. We would be happy to publish the best of these changes in a subsequent edition, where we will focus on changing company profiles.

Aaltio, I., Mills, A. J., and Helms Mills, J. 2002a. Exploring Gendered Organizational Cultures. *Culture and Organization,* 8(2): 77–79.

Aaltio, I., Mills, A. J., and Helms Mills, J. C. (Eds.). 2002b. *Exploring Gendered Organizational Cultures* (Special Edition).

Aaltio-Marjosola, I. 1994. Gender Stereotypes as Cultural Products of the Organization. *Scandinavian Journal of Management,* 10(2): 147–162.

Martin, J., and Frost, P. 1996. The Organizational Culture War Games: a Struggle for Intellectual Dominance. In S. R. Clegg, C. Hardy, and W. R. Nord (Eds.), *Handbook of Organization Studies,* pp. 599–621. London: Sage.

Mills, A. J. 1992. Organization, Gender and Culture. In A. J. Mills, and P. Tancred (Eds.), *Gendering Organizational Analysis,* pp. 93–111. Newbury Park, CA.: Sage.

Mills, A. J. 1994. *The Gendering of Organizational Culture: Social and Organizational Discourses in the Making of British Airways.* Proceedings of the Women in Management Division of the Administrative Sciences Association of Canada, Halifax, Nova Scotia.

Smircich, L. 1985. Is the Concept of Culture a Paradigm for Understanding Organizations and Ourselves? In P. J. Frost, L. F. Moore, M. R. Louis, C. C. Lundberg, & J. Martin (Eds.), *Organizational Culture,* pp. 55–72. Beverley Hills, CA: Sage.

CASE FOR ANALYSIS

Gildan Activewear's Approach to Social Responsibility[81]

Gildan Activewear, Inc., is a public, vertically integrated manufacturer of premium-quality branded active wear. It markets primarily to the wholesale imprinted active wear segments in Canada, the U.S., and Europe. The corporation sells its products as blanks to other businesses, which subsequently print designs and logos on the clothing to sell to consumers.

Margins are typically slight in this type of clothing industry. Gildan's approach is to pay very close attention to cost control. By focusing on a few high-quality items and religiously controlling expenses throughout the process, the company has had the economies of scale needed to compete with competitors like Fruit of the Loom and Hanes. Part of the success in offering high-quality products at low prices has been established by having the labour-intensive sewing process for the products done in Central America. Gildan keeps at home in Canada the business of knitting, dyeing, and finishing—the main steps before sewing—which requires relatively little direct labour.

Gildan has had some bad publicity over its strategic use of a cheap labour supply. Maquila Solidarity Network (MSN), a Canadian network promoting solidarity with groups in Mexico, Central America, and Asia to improve conditions for employees, has criticized Gildan in regards to anti-union activities, its labour practices and working conditions, and various other faults in its managing of the out-of-country labour supply. Gildan unequivocally and categorically denied MSN's allegations.

Gildan is now taking a more proactive approach to position itself as a socially responsible corporation by both refuting negative propositions such as those from MSN and by promoting its socially responsible accomplishments. Here are some of the accomplishments as cited from Gildan's corporate Web site:

- Gildan was recognized in February 2003 by the Canadian International Development Agency when it won the Award for Excellence in Corporate Social and Ethical Responsibility.

- Gildan has been certified under the Worldwide Responsible Apparel Production code (WRAP). WRAP is composed of an independent board of directors with a professional staff that evaluates and verifies that manufacturing facilities conform to its standards.
- Gildan is preparing to obtain additional ethical and social certification on behalf of its workers granted by the Fair Labour Association (FLA). The FLA is an independent monitoring system that holds its participating companies accountable for the conditions under which their products are produced. To advance fair, decent, and humane working conditions, the FLA enforces an industry-wide workplace code of conduct, which is based on the core labour standards of the International Labour Organization (ILO).

On April 7, 2004, Gildan announced that it had become the first manufacturer catering to the wholesale imprinted active-wear industry to obtain the Oeko-tex Standard 100 certification, the most internationally recognized eco-label designation in the textile supply chain. The Oeko-tex Standard 100 represents the first standard of its type in the textile industry that ensures the production processes and the textiles themselves are of no risk to human health. Gildan purports that this certification further solidifies the company's position as a leader in environmental sustainability and corporate social responsibility.

DISCUSSION QUESTIONS

1. Defend a position on whether you think Gildan's approach to social responsibility is more defensive, accommodating, or proactive in nature.
2. What impact can Gildan's socially responsible initiatives have on its organizational culture?

REFERENCES

1. E. Schein, *Organizational Culture and Leadership* (San Francisco: Jossey-Bass, 1992).
2. S. D. N. Cook and D. Yanow, "Culture and Organizational Learning," *Journal of Management Inquiry,* 1993, vol. 2, pp. 373–390; J. Helms Mills, *Making Sense of Change* (London: Routledge, 2003).
3. M. Rokeach, *The Nature of Human Values* (New York: The Free Press, 1973).
4. Helms Mills, *Making Sense of Organizational Change.*
5. Schein, *Organizational Culture and Leadership.*
6. Helms Mills, *Making Sense of Organizational Change.*
7. P. L. Berger and T. Luckman, *The Social Construction of Reality* (Garden City, NY: Anchor Books, 1967); K. E. Weick, "The Significance of Corporate Culture," in P. Frost, L. Moore, M. Louis, C. Lundberg, and J. Martin, eds., *Organizational Culture,* (London: Sage, 1985), pp. 381–398.
8. E. H. Schein, "Culture: The Missing Concept in Organization Studies," *Administrative Science Quarterly,* 1996, vol. 41, pp. 229–240; G. Hofstede, B. Neuijen, D. D. Ohavy, and G. Sanders, "Measuring Organizational Culture: A Qualitative and Quantitative Study across Twenty Cases," *Administrative Science Quarterly,* 1990, vol. 35, pp. 286–316; G. Hofstede, *Culture's Consequences* (London: Sage, 1980).
9. E. Reguly, "Outcry over Noranda Buyer Rings Hollow," *Globe and Mail,* 2 October 2004, p. B2.
10. *www.corning.com,* 2002.
11. A. J. Mills and J. C. H. Hatfield, "Air Canada vs. Canadian: Competition and Merger in the Framing of Airline Culture," *Studies in Cultures, Organizations and Societies,* 1998, vol. 4, pp. 93–124.
12. Interviews with Air Canada employees, 2003.
13. "You Win Some. Inside Three Megadeals that Paid Off—Big Time," *Canadian Business,* 16 February 2004, *www.canadianbusiness.com/article.jsp?content=20040216_58463_58463.*
14. Ibid.
15. J. DeMont, "Live and Learn: Bill Black," *Canadian Business,* July 19, 2004.
16. J. P. Walsh and G. R. Ungson, "Organizational Memory," *Academy of Management Review,* 1991, vol. 1, pp. 57–91.

17. K. E. Weick, "Organizational Culture as a Source of High Reliability," *California Management Review,* 1984, vol. 9, pp. 653–669.

18. J. A. Chatman and S. G. Barsade, "Personality, Organizational Culture, and Cooperation: Evidence from a Business Simulation," *Administrative Science Theory,* 1995, vol. 40, pp. 423–443.

19. R. Jackall, *Moral Mazes* (Oxford: Oxford University Press, 1988).

20. *www.bankofamerica.com,* 2002.

21. *www.ctv.ca/servlet/ArticleNews/story/CTVNews/20021231/business_scandals_confidence_021231/,* 2004.

22. B. Jang, "JetsGo Files Lawsuit against WestJet," *Globe and Mail,* 16 October 2004, p. B5.

23. A. Etzioni, *A Comparative Analysis of Organizations* (New York: The Free Press, 1975).

24. P. Verburg, "Prepare for Takeoff," *Canadian Business,* 2000-12-25. Retrieved from www.canadianbusiness.com/article.jsp?content=37832 on Sept. 12, 2005

25. G. R. Jones, "Psychological Orientation and the Process of Organizational Socialization: An Interactionist Perspective," *Academy of Management Review,* 1983, vol. 8, pp. 464–474.

26. J. Van Mannen and E. H. Schein, "Towards a Theory of Organizational Socialization," in B. M. Staw, ed., *Research in Organizational Behavior,* vol. 1 (Greenwich, Conn.: JAI Press, 1979), pp. 209–264.

27. G. R. Jones, "Socialization Tactics, Self-Efficacy, and Newcomers' Adjustments to Organizations," *Academy of Management Review,* 1986, vol. 29, pp. 262–279.

28. Ibid.

29. M. A. Cusumano and R. W. Selby, *Microsoft's Secrets* (New York: The Free Press, 1995).

30. H. M. Trice and J. M. Beyer, "Studying Organizational Culture Through Rites and Ceremonials," *Academy of Management Review,* 1984, vol. 9, pp. 653–669.

31. A. Holloway, "It's Who You Know," *Canadian Business,* 2001-04-30. Retrieved from www.canadianbusiness.com/article.jsp?content=1307 on Sept. 12, 2005.

32. H. M. Trice and J. M. Beyer, *The Cultures of Work Organizations* (Englewood Cliffs, NJ: Prentice Hall, 1993).

33. Organizational Insight by Ellen Rudderham-Gaudet, based on the following sources: Superior Propane, "About Superior," *www.superiorpropane.com/external/bins/content_page.asp?cid=1-90&lang=1,* 6 July 2004; Superior Propane, "RISE Values," *www.superiorpropane.com/external/bins/content_page.asp?cid=1-13-93&lang=1,* 7 July 2004; C. O'Bright, "Flex Benefits Drive Culture Change, Contain Costs at Superior Propane," *Canadian HR Reporter,* 2003, vol. 16, p. 16.

34. Trice and Beyer, "Studying Organizational Culture Through Rites and Ceremonials."

35. J. H. Sheridan, "Lessons from the Best," *Industry Week,* 20 February 1995, pp. 13–22.

36. J. C.Helms Mills, *Making Sense of Organizational Change* (London: Routledge, 2003).

37. A. M. Pettigrew, "On Studying Organizational Cultures," *Administrative Science Quarterly,* 1979, vol. 24, pp. 570–582.

38. B. Elgin, "Running the Tightest Ships on the Net," *Business Week,* 29 January 2001, pp. 125–126.

39. B. Schneider, "The People Make the Place," *Personnel Psychology,* 1987, vol. 40, pp. 437–453.

40. E. H. Schein, "The Role of the Founder in Creating Organizational Culture," *Organizational Dynamics,* 1983, vol. 12, pp. 13–28.

41. J. M. George, "Personality, Affect, and Behavior in Groups," *Journal of Applied Psychology,* 1990, vol. 75, pp. 107–116.

42. E. Schein, *Organizational Culture and Leadership,* 2nd ed. (San Francisco: Jossey-Bass, 1992).

43. J. Carlson, *Moments of Truth* (Cambridge, MA: Ballinger, 1987); A. Sampson, *Empires of the Sky. The Politics, Contests and Cartels of World Airlines* (New York: Random House, 1984).

44. T. Jick, *Managing Change: Cases and Concepts* (Boston: Irwin McGraw-Hill, 1993); K. Labich, "The Big Comeback at British Airways," *Fortune International,* 5 December 1988, p. 104; B. R. Lewis, "Customer Care in Service Organizations," *Management Decision,* 1991, vol. 29, pp. 31–34; R. Poulet and Moult, "Putting Values Into Evaluation," *Training and Development Journal,* July 1987, pp. 62–66; A. Reed, *Airline: The Inside Story of British Airways* (London: BBC Books, 1990); D. Young, *British Airways: Putting the Customer First* (Ashridge: Strategic Management Centre, 1989).

45. Helms Mills, *Making Sense of Organizational Change.*

46. T. Parker-Pope, "New CEO Preaches Rebellion for P&G's 'Cult'." *Wall Street Journal,* 11 December 1998, p. B1.

47. G. Fairclough, "P&G to Slash 15,000 Jobs, Shut 10 Plants." *Wall Street Journal,* 10 June 1999, p. A3.

48. M. Hannan and J. Freeman, "Structural Inertia and Organizational Change," *American Sociological Review,* 1984, vol. 49, pp. 149–164.

49. *www.courttv.com/archive/legaldocs/business/texaco,* 2004.

50. *www.fastcompany.com/magazine/77/walmart.html*, 2004; *www.cmht.com/casewatch/civil/walmart.html*, 2004.

51. R. S. Abella, *Equity in Employment: A Royal Commission Report* (Ottawa: Ministry of Supply and Services Canada, 1984).

52. George, "Personality, Affect, and Behavior in Groups"; D. Miller and J. M. Toulouse, "Chief Executive Personality and Corporate Strategy and Structure in Small Firms," *Management Science,* 1986, vol. 32, pp. 1389–1409.

53. Abella, *Equity in Employment: A Royal Commission Report.*

54. *edition.cnn.com/2004/HEALTH/09/30/vioxx.withdrawn.reut/index.html*, 2004.

55. R. E. Goodin, "How to Determine Who Should Get What," *Ethics,* July 1975, pp. 310–321.

56. T. M. Jones, "Ethical Decision Making by Individuals in Organizations: An Issue Contingent Model," *Academy of Management Review,* 1991, vol. 2, pp. 366–395.

57. T. L. Beauchamp and N. E. Bowie, eds., *Ethical Theory and Business* (Englewood Cliffs, NJ: Prentice Hall, 1979); A. MacIntyre, *After Virtue* (South Bend, IN: University of Notre Dame Press, 1981).

58. Organizational Insight by Ellen Rudderham-Gaudet, based on the following sources: Suncor Energy, "About Suncor," *www.suncor.com/default.aspx?ID=1*, 18 September 2004; A. Nikiforuk, "Saint or Sinner? Rick George Has Engineered A Dramatic Turnaround at Suncor, While Making Peace with Greens," *Canadian Business,* 2002, vol. 75, pp. 55–59.

59. "What Led Beech-Nut Down the Road to Disgrace," *Business Week,* 22 February 1988, pp. 124–128; "Bad Apples in the Executive Suite," *Consumer Reports,* May 1989, p. 296; R. Johnson, "Ralston to Buy Beech-Nut, Gambling It Can Overcome Apple Juice Scandal," *Wall Street Journal,* 18 September 1989, p. B11.

60. H. Demsetz, "Towards a Theory of Property Rights," *American Economic Review,* 1967, vol. 57, pp. 347–359.

61. G. R. Jones, "Transaction Costs, Property Rights, and Organizational Culture: An Exchange Perspective," *Administrative Science Quarterly,* 1983, vol. 28, pp. 454–467.

62. T. Moore, "Make or Break Time for General Motors," *Fortune,* 15 February 1988, pp. 32–42.

63. Helms Mills, *Making Sense of Organizational Change.*

64. "ESOP Binges Change in Corporate Culture," *Employee Benefit Plan Review,* July 1992, pp. 25–26.

65. C. A. Ashley, *A Study of Trans-Canada Air Lines: The First Twenty-Five Years* (Toronto: Macmillan, 1963); G. Lothian, *Flight Deck: Memoirs of an Airline Pilot* (Toronto: McGraw-Hill Ryerson, 1979); A. J. Mills and J. C. Helms-Hatfield, J.C. "Air Canada vs. Canadian: Competition and Merger in the Framing of Airline Cultures," Metaphors in Organizational Theory and Behaviour Conference, Kings University, London, 28–30 July 1994; N. J. Newby, *The Sky's The Limit* (Vancouver: Mitchell Press Ltd., 1986); P. Smith, *It Seems Like Only Yesterday* (Toronto: McClelland & Stewart, 1986).

66. C. Perrow, *Normal Accidents* (New York: Basic Books, 1984).

67. H. Mintzberg, *The Structuring of Organizational Structures* (Englewood Cliffs, NJ: Prentice Hall, 1979).

68. G. Kunda, *Engineering Culture* (Philadelphia: Temple University Press, 1992).

69. J. P. Kotter and J. L. Heskett, *Corporate Culture and Performance* (New York: The Free Press, 1992).

70. K. L. Bettenhausen and J. K. Murnighan, "The Emergence of Norms in Competitive Decision Making Groups," *Administrative Science Quarterly,* 1985, vol. 30, pp. 350–372.

71. E. Gatewood and A. B. Carroll, "The Anatomy of Corporate Social Response," *Business Horizons,* September–October 1981, pp. 9–16.

72. M. Friedman, "A Friedman Doctrine: The Social Responsibility of Business Is to Increase Its Profits," *New York Times Magazine,* 13 September 1970, p. 33.

73. *www.corporateknights.ca/resources/media/globe1.asp*, 2004.

74. W. G. Ouchi, *Theory Z: How American Business Can Meet the Japanese Challenge* (Reading, MA: Addison-Wesley, 1981).

75. Organizational Insight by Ellen Rudderham-Gaudet, based on the following sources: "Best Employers in Canada—The List," *was4.hewitt.com/bestemployers/canada/best_companies/the_list/the_list_2004.htm*, 12 July 2004; Husky, "Corporate Information," *www.husky.ca/corpcult/culturehome.html*, 12 July 2004; D. Mills, "Core Values Make Good Business Sense," *Canadian Plastics,* 2003, vol. 61, pp. 22–23.

76. J. B. McGuire, A. Sundgren, and T. Schneewis, "Corporate Social Responsibility and Firm Financial Performance," *Academy of Management Review,* 1988, vol. 31, pp. 854–872.

77. Friedman, "A Friedman Doctrine," pp. 32, 33, 122, 124, 126.

78. J. B. Dozier and M. P. Miceli, "Potential Predictors of Whistleblowing: A Prosocial Perspective," *Academy of Management Review,* 1985, vol. 10, pp. 823–836; J. P. Near and M. P. Miceli, "Retaliation Against

Whistleblowers: Predictors and Effects," *Journal of Applied Psychology*, 1986, vol. 71, pp. 137–145.

79. "The Uncommon Good," *The Economist*, 19 August 1995, p. 55.
80. E. D. Bowman, "Corporate Social Responsibility and the Investor," *Journal of Contemporary Business*, Winter 1973, pp. 49–58.
81. Case by Ellen Rudderham-Guadet, based on the following sources: "Gildan Activewear Obtains Prestigious International Environmental Certification," *Canada NewsWire*, 7 April 2004, p. 1; Scott McCormack, "Stick to Your Knitting," *Forbes* 28 December 1998, vol. 162, pp. 82–83; "Memorandum to Gildan Activewear Shareholders Re: Status Report on Gildan's Labour Practices," 3 February 2004, *www.maquilasolidarity.org/campaigns/gildan/shareholdermemo.htm*, 10 April 2004; "Response to Allegations; Official Statement," *gildan.com/en/company/allegation.cfm*, 10 April 2004.

Organizational Design and Strategy in a Changing Global Environment

CHAPTER 8

Learning Objectives

Finding the right strategy to respond to changes taking place in the environment (such as changes in the needs of customers or actions of competitors overseas) is a complex issue facing managers. In a changing global environment it is easy to make mistakes, and managers must constantly monitor their strategies and structures to make sure that they are working effectively both at home and abroad.

After reading this chapter you should be able to:

1. Identify the ways managers can use functional-level strategy to develop core competencies that allow an organization to create value and give it a competitive advantage.
2. Explain how the way managers combine their organization's distinctive competencies can create a successful business-level strategy that allows them to compete for scarce resources.
3. Differentiate among the corporate-level strategies companies can use to enter new domains where they can continue to grow and create value.
4. Appreciate the importance of linking strategy to structure and culture at each level—functional, business, and corporate—to increase the ability to create value.
5. Understand how global expansion strategies allow an organization to seek new opportunities to exploit its core competencies to create value for stakeholders.

STRATEGY AND THE ENVIRONMENT

Strategy
The specific pattern of decisions and actions that managers take to use core competencies to achieve a competitive advantage and outperform competitors.

As discussed in Chapter 1, an organization's **strategy** is a specific pattern of decisions and actions that managers take to use core competencies to achieve a competitive advantage and outperform competitors.[1] An organization develops a strategy to increase the value it can create for its stakeholders. In this context, value is anything that satisfies the needs and desires of organizational stakeholders. Shareholders want a company to set goals and develop an action plan that maximizes the long-run profitability of the company and the value of their stock. Customers are likely to respond to a strategy that is based on the goal of offering high-quality products and services at competitive prices.

Through its strategy, an organization seeks to use and develop core competencies to gain a competitive advantage so that it can increase its share of scarce resources in its environment. Recall that **core competencies** are skills and abilities in value-creation activities, such as manufacturing, marketing, or R&D, that allow a company to achieve superior efficiency, quality, innovation, or customer responsiveness. An organization that possesses superior core competencies can outperform its rivals. Organizational strategy allows an organization to shape and manage its domain to exploit its existing core competencies and develop new competencies that make it a better competitor for resources.

Core competencies
The skills and abilities in value-creation activities that allow a company to achieve superior efficiency, quality, innovation, or customer responsiveness.

McDonald's, for example, used its existing core competencies in the production of fast food such as burgers and fries to provide fast food for the breakfast segment of the fast-food domain. By investing in food-testing facilities, McDonald's developed R&D competencies that led to the development of breakfast items (such as the Egg McMuffin) that could be produced quickly. By using its existing core competencies in new ways, and by developing new competencies, McDonald's created a new line of breakfast food, which contributes 35 percent to its revenues. Similarly, Gillette applied its skills in marketing razor blades to selling men's toiletries and expanded its domain into toiletries.

The more resources an organization can obtain from the environment, the better able it is to set ambitious long-term goals and then develop a strategy and invest resources to create core competencies to allow it to achieve those goals. In turn, improved competencies give an organization a competitive advantage, which allows the organization to attract new resources—for example, new customers, highly qualified employees, or new sources of financial support. Figure 8-1 shows this cyclical value-creation process.

Sources of Core Competencies

The ability to develop a strategy that allows an organization to create value and outperform competitors is a function of the organization's core competencies. The

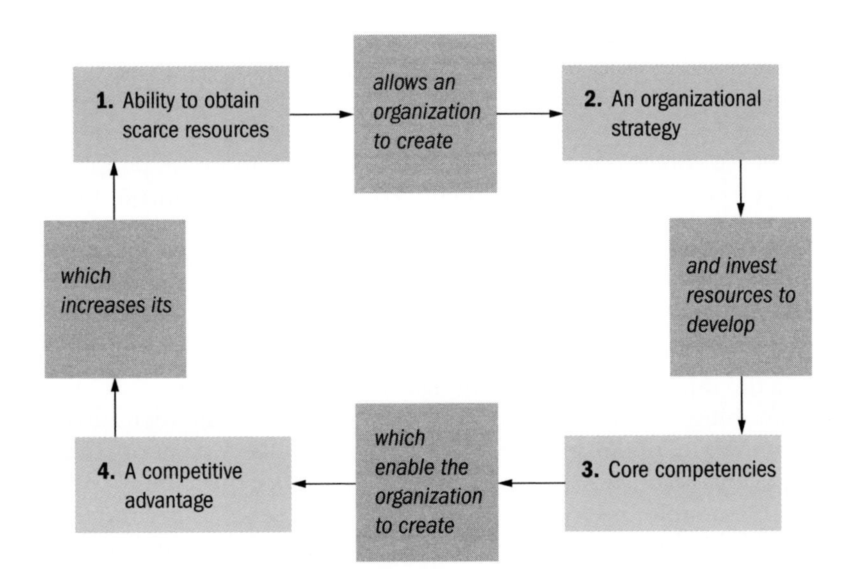

FIGURE 8-1
The Value-Creation Cycle.
Ample resources, a well-thought-out strategy, and distinctive competencies give an organization a competitive advantage, which facilitates the acquisition of still more resources.

strength of its core competencies is a product of the specialized resources and coordination abilities that it possesses and other organizations lack.[2]

Functional resources
The skills possessed by an organization's functional personnel.

Specialized Resources Two kinds of resources give an organization a competitive advantage: functional resources and organizational resources. **Functional resources** are the skills, talents, and personal attributes possessed by an organization's functional personnel. The skills of Microsoft's software design groups constitute Microsoft's single biggest functional resource. The quality of 3M's R&D department is the source of 3M's continued growth. Procter & Gamble's skill in new product development is P&G's greatest functional resource. High-quality functional resources, however, are not enough to give an organization a competitive advantage. To be a source of competitive advantage, a function's core competency must be unique or special and difficult to imitate.[3] Microsoft's claim to uniqueness rests in the breadth and depth of the software talent that it possesses. In theory, a rich competitor like IBM could come along and buy up Microsoft's best people, or Du Pont could lure away 3M's scientists. If that were to happen, those companies' claims to uniqueness would disappear. To maintain its long-term competitive advantage, an organization needs to protect the source of its functional competencies. That is why Microsoft gives its best people strong property rights, including making them owners in the company, and why 3M is well known for its long-term employment policies—important mechanisms designed to protect these competencies.

Organizational resources
The attributes that give an organization a competitive advantage such as the skills of the top-management team or possession of valuable and scarce resources.

Organizational resources are the attributes that give an organization a competitive advantage. They include the skills of a company's top-management team, the vision of its founder or CEO, and the possession of valuable and scarce resources such as land, capital reserves, and plant equipment. They also include intangibles such as a company's brand name and its corporate reputation.[4] Like functional resources, to provide a competitive advantage, organizational resources must be unique or difficult to imitate. When organizations can hire away one another's managers, or when any organization can buy the most advanced computer-controlled manufacturing technology from Hitachi or Bombardier, organizational resources are not unique and do not give an organization a competitive advantage. However, brand names like Coca-Cola, Tim Hortons, and Levi Strauss and reputations such as Toyota's and Microsoft's are organizational resources that are unique and difficult to imitate. Obtaining those resources would entail buying the whole company, not just hiring away individual managers.

Coordination ability
An organization's ability to coordinate its functional and organizational resources to create maximal value.

Coordination Abilities Another source of core competencies is **coordination ability**, an organization's ability to coordinate its functional and organizational resources to create maximal value. Effective coordination of resources (achieved through the control provided by organizational structure and culture) leads to a competitive advantage.[5] The control systems that an organization uses to coordinate and motivate people at the functional and organizational levels can be a core competency that contributes to the organization's overall competitive advantage. Similarly, the way an organization decides to centralize or decentralize authority or the way it develops and promotes shared cultural values increases its effectiveness and allows the organization to manage and protect its domain better than its competitors can protect theirs. Microsoft designs its structure and culture around small teams in order to coordinate activities in a way that facilitates the rapid development and launch of new products.

An organization's ability to use its structure and culture to coordinate its activities is also important at the functional and organizational levels.[6] The way an organization coordinates people and resources within functions determines the strength of its core competencies. For example, several organizations have access to fast-food production technology (a functional resource) similar to the technology that McDonald's uses, but none has been able to imitate the rules, standard operating procedures, and norms that make McDonald's production operations so efficient. Competitors have been unable to duplicate the coordination of people and resources that enables McDonald's to produce hamburgers so efficiently and reliably.

Similarly, at the organizational level, the ability to use structure and culture to coordinate and integrate activities between departments or divisions gives some organizations a core competency and thus a competitive advantage. For example, the success of 3M and Procter & Gamble can be explained in part by their ability to develop integrating mechanisms that allow their marketing, product development, and manufacturing departments to combine their skills to develop innovative products. Similarly, PepsiCo's success stems in part from its sharing of resources among its different divisions (Pepsi-Cola, Frito-Lay, and so on).

Although many functional and organizational resources are not unique and can be imitated, an organization's ability to coordinate and motivate its functions and departments is difficult to imitate. It might be possible to buy the functional expertise or technical knowledge of 3M or Microsoft, but the purchase would not include access to the practices and methods that either organization uses to coordinate its resources. These intangible practices are embedded in the way people interact in an organization—in the way organizational structure focuses organizational behaviour—and they make these companies successful competitors.

Global Expansion and Core Competencies

Expanding globally into overseas markets can be an important facilitator of the development of an organization's core competencies, which in turn contribute to increased competitiveness and value creation. Figure 8-2 summarizes four ways in which global expansion allows an organization to create value for its stakeholders.

Transferring Core Competencies Abroad Value creation at the global level begins when an organization transfers a core competency in one or more of its functions to an overseas market to produce cheaper or improved products that will give the organization a low-cost or differentiation advantage over its competitors in that market. For example, Microsoft, with its competency in the production of technologically advanced software, takes this differentiation advantage and produces software tailored to the needs of consumers in different countries. As a result of the transfer of its core competencies abroad, over 50 percent of Microsoft's revenue comes from overseas sales.

Establishing a Global Network Generally, when an organization decides to transfer its competencies abroad, it locates its value-creation activities in countries where eco-

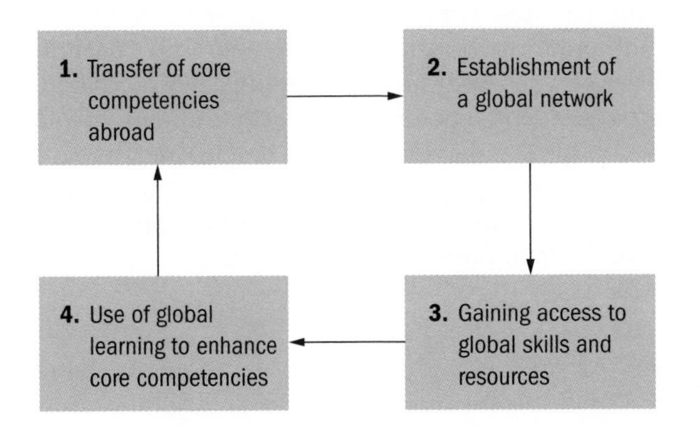

FIGURE 8-2
The Creation of Value Through Global Expansion.

nomic, political, and cultural conditions are likely to enhance its low-cost or differentiation advantage. It then establishes a global network—sets of task and reporting relationships among managers, functions, and divisions that link an organization's value creation activities around the world. To lower costs, an organization may locate its value-creation functions in the countries in which factor costs—the costs of raw materials, unskilled or skilled labour, land, and taxes—are lowest. To lower costs, a video game company like Nintendo may perform its assembly operations in one country and its design operations in another, have its headquarters in a third country, and buy its inputs and raw materials from still other countries. To link these far-flung activities, the organization creates a global network.

Gaining Access to Global Resources and Skills An organization with a global network has access to resources and skills throughout the world. Because each country has unique economic, political, and cultural conditions, different countries have different resources and skills that give them a competitive advantage. Organizations can, therefore, establish themselves in these other countries seeking these competitive advantages. So, for example, a Canadian organization is likely to benefit from establishing itself in countries with low-cost or differentiation core competencies so that it can then gain access to and learn how to develop these competencies. If organizations in one country have an R&D competency, it would benefit a Canadian company to establish operations in that country to gain access to the competencies. Japan, for example, has skills in "lean" production and total quality manufacturing, and many companies such as Kodak, IBM, Ford established divisions in Japan to learn these skills.

Toys "R" Us, the world's largest toy retailer, has benefited from having created a global network. The company established a network of stores throughout Europe to take advantage of its core competency in the distribution and retailing of toys. While establishing a network of suppliers in Europe, Toys "R" Us found many new, high-quality toys, produced by German and Swiss companies, that it believed would appeal to North American consumers; arranged to sell these toys in its North American stores; and thus enhanced its differentiation advantage, creating more value. Similarly, Bombardier established European production facilities for railway engines and cars in order to capitalize on the domestic knowledge and skills of the workforce there.

Using Global Learning to Enhance Core Competencies Organizations set up their global activities to gain access to knowledge that will allow them to improve their core competencies. The access to global resources and skills that a global network provides exposes an organization to new ways of improving itself. After an organization masters these new skills, it can transfer them to its domestic base to enhance its core competencies and then transfer its enhanced competencies back to its overseas operations to increase its competitive advantage abroad. For example, after World War II, the founders of Toyota, Panasonic, and other Japanese companies went to the United States to learn American production and marketing methods, which they then took back to Japan. They were not content just to learn the new techniques, however: They spent considerable time and effort trying to improve them. The engineers who founded Toyota studied GM's and Ford's production techniques and took what they had learned back to Japan, where they improved upon it and adapted it to the Japanese environment. As a result, Japanese companies obtained a competitive advantage over American companies, which made no attempt to improve the techniques they were using.

Four Levels of Strategy

An organization should match its strategy and structure so that it can create value from both its functional and organizational resources. But where is an organization's strategy created, and by whom? Strategy is formulated at four organizational levels: the functional, business, corporate, and global levels. An organization's ability to create value at one level is an indication of its ability to manage the value-creation process at the other levels.

Functional-level strategy is a plan of action to strengthen an organization's functional and organizational resources, as well as its coordination abilities, in order to create core competencies.[7] DaimlerChrysler, for example, invests heavily to improve its skills in R&D and product design, and Coca-Cola invests heavily to devise innovative approaches to marketing. To strengthen their technical and human resources, functional managers train and develop subordinates to ensure that the organization has skills that match or exceed the skills of its competitors. Another part of the functional manager's job is to scan and manage the functional environment to ensure that the organization knows what is going on both inside and outside its domain.

Functional-level strategy A plan of action to strengthen an organization's functional and organizational resources, as well as its coordination abilities, in order to create core competencies.

R&D functional managers, for example, need to understand the techniques and products of their competitive rivals. R&D functional managers at car companies routinely buy competitors' cars and strip them down to their component parts to study the technology and design that went into their manufacture. Taking this information, they can then learn how to imitate the best aspects of competitors' products. It is also the job of R&D experts to scan other industries to find innovations that may help their company. Innovations in the computer software and microchip industries, for example, are important in product development in the car industry. If all of the functional managers in an organization monitor their respective functional environments and develop their functional resources and abilities, the organization will be better able to manage the uncertainty of its environment.[8]

Business-level strategy is a plan to combine functional core competencies in order to position the organization so that it has a competitive advantage in its domain.[9] Mercedes-Benz takes its skills in R&D and positions itself in the luxury segment of the car market. Coca-Cola uses its marketing skills to defend its niche against Pepsi-Cola.

Business-level strategy A plan to combine functional core competencies in order to position the organization so that it has a competitive advantage in its chosen domain.

Business-level strategy is the responsibility of the top-management team (the CEO and vice presidents in charge of various functions). Their job is to decide how to position the organization to compete for resources in its environment. CBC, City TV, CTV, and Global, for example, compete with each other and with American networks such as CBS, Fox, CNN, and Turner Broadcasting to attract viewers (customers). Programming is the key variable that these companies can manipulate. They rely on functional experts in their news, documentary, comedy, and drama departments (among others) to scan the environment and identify future viewing trends so that they can commission programs that will give them a competitive advantage. Because all of the networks are doing this and are trying to outguess their rivals, programming is a complex and uncertain process.

Corporate-level strategy is a plan to use and develop core competencies so that the organization not only can protect and enlarge its existing domain but can also expand into new domains.[10] Mercedes-Benz used its competencies in R&D and product development to enter the household products and aerospace industries. Coca-Cola took its marketing skills and applied them globally in the soft-drink industry.

Corporate-level strategy A plan to use and develop core competencies so that the organization can not only protect and enlarge its existing domain but can also expand into new domains.

Corporate-level strategy is the responsibility of corporate-level managers—the top-management team of a multi-business organization. Their responsibility is to take the value-creation skills present in the divisions and in corporate headquarters and combine them to improve the competitive position of each division and of the organization as a whole. Corporate strategists use the combined resources of the organization to create more value than could be obtained if each division operated alone and

Global expansion strategy A plan that involves choosing the best strategy to expand into overseas markets to obtain scarce resources and develop core competencies.

independently. For example, Honda takes its strengths in engine production and uses them to produce many different kinds of products such as cars, motorbikes, jet skis, and lawnmowers, creating value in many different markets.

Finally, **global expansion strategy** involves choosing the best strategy to expand into overseas markets to obtain scarce resources and develop core competencies as discussed above. How does strategy at each level advance the goal of creating value?

FUNCTIONAL-LEVEL STRATEGY

The strategic goal of each function is to create a core competency that gives the organization a competitive advantage. As we have seen, McDonald's production and marketing functions have given the organization important core competencies. No competitor can match the efficiency of McDonald's production process, and no competitor has developed the brand-name reputation that McDonald's enjoys.

An organization creates value by applying its functional skills and knowledge to inputs and transforming them into outputs of finished goods and services. To gain a competitive advantage, an organization must be able to do at least one of the following: (1) perform functional activities at a cost lower than that of its rivals or (2) perform functional activities in a way that clearly differentiates its goods and services from those of its rivals—by giving its products unique qualities that customers greatly desire.[11]

Strategies to Lower Costs or Differentiate Products

Any function that can lower the cost at which a product is produced or that can differentiate a product adds value to the product and to the organization. Table 8-1 summarizes the ways in which different organizational functions can advance the goal of value creation.

The manufacturing function can lower the costs of production by pioneering the adoption of the most efficient production methods, such as computer-controlled flex-

Table 8-1

LOW-COST AND DIFFERENTIATION ADVANTAGES RESULTING FROM FUNCTIONAL-LEVEL STRATEGY

Value-Creating Function	Source of Low-Cost Advantage	Source of Differentiation Advantage
Manufacturing	• Development of skills in flexible manufacturing technology	• Increase in product quality and reliability
Human resource management	• Reduction of turnover and absenteeism	• Hiring of highly skilled personnel • Development of innovative training programs
Materials management	• Use of just-in-time inventory system/computerized warehousing • Development of long-term relationships with suppliers and customers	• Use of company reputation and long-term relationships with suppliers and customers to provide high-quality inputs and efficient distribution and disposal of outputs
Sales and marketing	• Increased demand and lower production costs	• Targeting of customer groups • Tailoring products to customers • Promoting brand names
Research and development	• Improved efficiency of manufacturing technology	• Creation of new products • Improvement of existing products

ible manufacturing systems. Because manufacturing skills and competencies can improve product quality and reliability, manufacturing can also contribute to product differentiation.[12] Sony and Toyota, for example, lead the world in lean manufacturing techniques, which both reduce production costs and increase quality by lowering the number of defects. Manufacturing thus gives Sony and Toyota products a low-cost advantage and a differentiation advantage.

On the input side, the human resource management (HRM) function can lower costs by designing appropriate control and reward systems to increase employee motivation and reduce absenteeism and turnover.[13] HRM can contribute to differentiation by selecting and hiring high-quality employees and managers and by running innovative training programs. The use of employee stock ownership plans, the linking of pay to performance for different job categories, and the development of flexible work hours to allow employees to dovetail work activities with nonwork obligations are all ways in which the HRM function can advance the cause of value creation. EnCana, Bombardier, Xerox, and other companies have developed sophisticated HRM systems for selecting and training their employees.

The role of materials management on both the input and the output sides is also crucial. Just-in-time inventory systems and computerized warehousing reduce the costs of carrying and shipping inventory. Purchasing managers' skills in developing long-term links with suppliers and distributors and in fostering an organization's reputation can lead to a low-cost or differentiation advantage.[14] Suppliers who trust an organization may offer more favourable payment terms or be more responsive to the organization when it needs more or different types of inputs in a hurry. The quality of a company–supplier relationship can also affect the quality of inputs. A supplier has more incentive to invest in specialized equipment to produce higher-quality inputs if it trusts the organization.[15] Highly skilled purchasing negotiators may be able to strike good contract terms with suppliers, too.

VF Company, the clothes manufacturer that makes Lee and Wrangler jeans, has developed a low-cost core competency on the output side of the value-creation process. VF Company has a state-of-the-art inventory control system. A computer network links its manufacturing and distribution plants directly to its retail customers. When a customer buys a pair of VF jeans, for example, a record of the sale is transmitted electronically from the retailer to a VF warehouse, which restocks the retailer within five days. When a specified number of garments have been shipped from the VF warehouse, a reorder is automatically placed with the manufacturing plant. This system allows the VF organization to maintain a 97 percent in-stock rate (the industry average is 70 percent) and reduce lost sales for both the retailer and the manufacturer.

At the output end of the value-creation process, the skills and expertise of sales and marketing can contribute directly to a low-cost or differentiation advantage. A core competency in marketing can lower the cost of value-creation activities. Suppose a marketing department devises a campaign that significantly increases the sales of a product and, as a result, the organization's market share steadily rises. As the organization expands its output to satisfy the increased demand, it is likely to obtain manufacturing economies of scale, and its costs are likely to fall. Sony and Panasonic have a low-cost advantage because their marketing and sales efforts have developed global markets whose enormous size enables the companies to produce huge volumes of a product at lower and lower unit costs.

Marketing and sales help differentiate products because they tell customers about why one company's products are better than another's. They target customer groups and discover, analyze, and transmit to the product development and R&D departments the needs of customers so that those functions can design new products to attract more customers.[16] A core competency in marketing can allow an organization to discover and respond to customer needs quickly. This speed gives the organization's products a differentiated appeal. Coca-Cola, Philip Morris, and Campbell's Soup are all known for innovative marketing that constantly promotes their brand names and protects their domains from competitors.

Research and development can also contribute significantly to an organization's value-creation activities.[17] R&D can reduce costs by developing cheaper ways of making a product or through the development of new products. Skills in R&D have allowed Japanese companies to develop low-cost, flexible manufacturing techniques that are being copied by Xerox, H-P, DaimlerChrysler, and other North American manufacturers. A core competency in R&D that results in the improvement of existing products or the creation of new products gives an organization a strong competitive advantage through lowering costs or through differentiation. For example, Newfoundland-based Fishery Products International has an extensive R&D facility that does both. It develops ways to prepare its products more efficiently, thus contributing to lower costs, and develops new products and product lines using underutilized fish species, thus contributing to its differentiation within the seafood products market. Similarly, Intel's creation of faster and improved microchips is an example of incremental product improvement. DVD/CD-ROM technology developed by Microsoft and other companies has led to the birth of a new generation of computer products. All makers of personal computers rush to modify their products to use a new chip; otherwise, they fear, their products are likely to lose their differentiated appeal.

Functional-Level Strategy and Structure

Every function in an organization can develop a core competency that allows the organization to perform value-creation activities at a cost lower than its rivals' costs or that allows the organization to create clearly differentiated products. One goal of the organization is to provide its functions with the resources and the setting they need to develop superior skills and competitive expertise. Thus organizational structure and culture are very important to the development of functional-level strategy. We first consider structure.

The strength of a function's core competency depends not only on the function's resources, but on its ability to coordinate the use of its resources. An organization's coordination abilities are, in turn, a product of its structure.[18] In Chapter 4, we discussed Lawrence and Lorsch's findings about how the degree of functional differentiation in the production, sales, and research and development departments within an organization and the extent of integration among those functions directly affect organizational performance. In the most effective organizations, each of the three departments develops an orientation specific to its functional tasks and develops its own ways of responding to its particular functional environment.

According to contingency theory, an organization's design should permit each function to develop a structure that suits its human and technical resources. We will continue to follow the contingency theory approach as we examine how to design a structure that allows the R&D, manufacturing, and sales functions to develop core competencies.[19] Figure 8-3 summarizes the characteristics of structures that support the development of core competencies by those three functions.

Successful research and development reflects the ability of R&D experts to apply their skills and knowledge in innovative ways and to combine their activities with technical resources to produce new products. The structure most conducive to the development of functional abilities in R&D is a flat, decentralized structure in which mutual adjustment among teams is the main means of coordinating human and technical

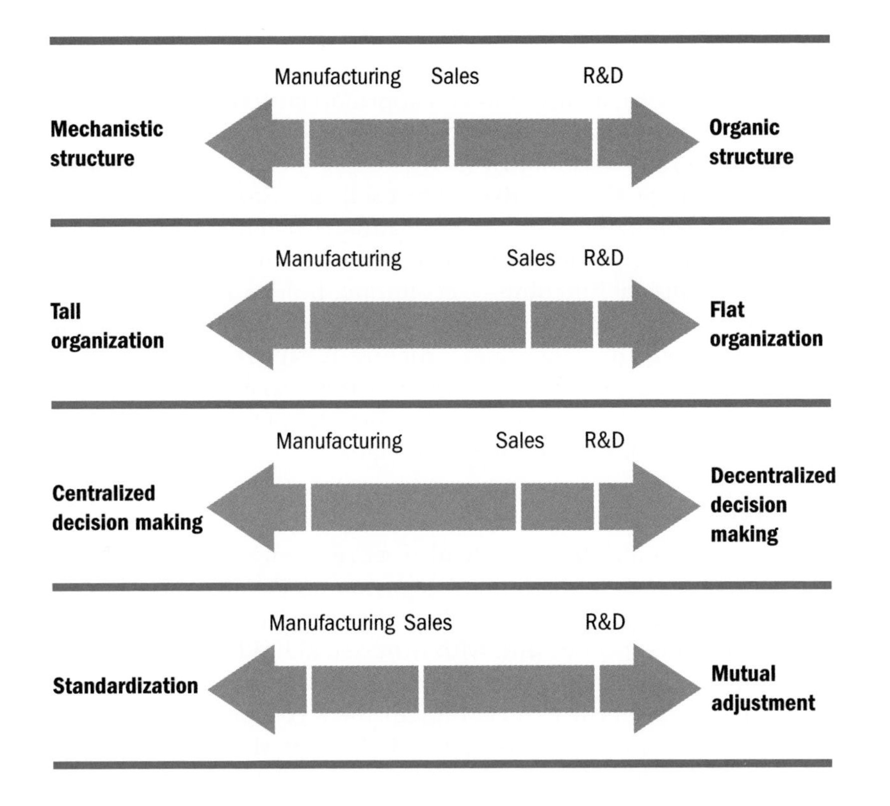

FIGURE 8-3
Structural Characteristics Associated with the Development of Core Competencies in Production, Sales, and Research and Development.

resources. In such an organic structure, functional norms and values based on self-control and team control are likely to emerge, and a core competency in R&D is likely to be developed.

What sort of structure supports the development of a core competency in production? Traditionally, the manufacturing function has used a tall hierarchy in which decision making is centralized and the speed of the production line controls the pace of work.[20] Standardization is achieved through the use of extensive rules and procedures, and the result of these design choices is a mechanistic structure. Has such a structure led to a core competency in manufacturing for North American companies? If we compare North American manufacturing companies with Japanese manufacturing companies, we see that North American companies today do not have a core competency in manufacturing. What do the Japanese do differently? The manufacturing function in Japanese companies has a more organic structure than the manufacturing function in Canadian and U.S. companies: It is flatter, more decentralized, and relies more on mutual adjustment.

A core competency based on coordination abilities in sales is another important source of competitive advantage that should be planned for in an organization's strategy. Typically, the sales function uses a flat, decentralized structure to coordinate its activities, because incentive pay systems, rather than direct supervision by managers, are the primary control mechanism in sales settings.[21] Salespeople are generally paid on the basis of how much they sell, and information about customer needs and changing customer requirements is relayed to the salespeople's superiors through a standardized reporting system. Because salespeople often work alone, mutual adjustment is relatively unimportant. Thus the structure of the sales function is likely to be relatively mechanistic, compared to that used by the R&D function, but not as mechanistic as that used by manufacturing.

In some sales settings, however, a differentiated appeal to customers is necessary. Luxury stores such as Holt Renfrew in Canada or Nordstrom and Neiman-Marcus in the U.S. do not use incentive compensation. In such settings, the last thing the organization wants to do is encourage a standardized hard sell to customers. Instead, it wants salespeople to develop competency in a sales technique based on a courteous, personalized, customer-oriented approach. The same strategic considerations shape the structure of other organizational functions—accounting, human resources, materials management, and so on. The coordination abilities of each function reflect the skill with which managers design the functional structure to suit the resources the function uses in its value creation activities. The greater the organization's skills at coordinating functional resources, the stronger are the core competencies the organization develops and the greater is its competitive advantage.

Functional-Level Strategy and Culture

The development of functional abilities that lead to core competencies is also a result of the culture that emerges in a function or department. Recall from Chapter 7 that organizational culture is a set of shared values that organizational members use when they interact with one another and with other stakeholders. What is the importance of culture for functional-level strategy? A competitor can easily imitate another organization's structure, but it is very difficult for a competitor to imitate another organization's culture, for culture is embedded in the day-to-day interactions of functional personnel. Culture is very difficult to control and manage, let alone imitate or copy, so a company that has an effective culture has an important source of competitive advantage.[22]

Many organizations imitated GM and Du Pont and moved to a multidivisional structure to improve their ability to control their operations. Organizations can also imitate one another's incentive pay systems. GM has moved to give its managers stock options like those offered by its competitors, and retail stores have copied Wal-Mart's policy of establishing an employee stock ownership plan. Kmart, however, despite changes to its structure, found it impossible to imitate Wal-Mart's cultural values of thrift and economy, and GM (except for its Saturn plant) does not operate like Toyota, even though it has imitated many of Toyota's operating systems. The reason for such differences (despite structural similarities) is that the coordination abilities that stem from an organization's culture emerge gradually and are a product of many factors: an organization's property rights system, its structure, its ethics, and the characteristics of its top-management team. Because these factors can be combined in many different ways, reproducing another organization's culture is difficult.

To develop functional abilities and produce a core competency, it is necessary to choose the property rights, functional structure, and functional managers that seem most likely to enhance a function's coordination ability. We just saw that R&D uses a flat, decentralized structure and small teams to create norms and values that emphasize teamwork and cooperation. There are other ways in which an organization can build a culture to reinforce those norms and values. Employees can be given strong property rights, including job tenure and a share in the organizational profits; and an organization can recruit people who share its terminal values and socialize them to its functional instrumental values.[23] Microsoft deliberately creates an entrepreneurial culture by using small teams to socialize its programmers to its instrumental values of hard work and cooperation. The same is true in biotech companies like Amgen and Genentech and consumer products companies like Sony.

The coordination abilities of the manufacturing function are also affected by its culture. In some manufacturing cultures (as in North America traditionally), the focus is on reducing the level of skill required to perform a task, transferring control to managers, and creating a mechanistic hierarchy in which workers have minimal control over tasks. In such settings, management develops a culture based on values of economy, in order to reduce production costs. As we saw earlier, however, empowering workers and developing cultural values and norms that encourage participation, cooperation, and commitment may be the source of the increased product quality traditionally enjoyed by Japanese automakers. Honda claims that its overseas manufacturing plants can produce cars more cheaply than its Japanese plants. Honda empowers its workers, involves them in decision making, and uses a pay system based on performance. In 1993, when demand for the Accord dropped because Honda was introducing a new model, Honda showed its commitment to its North American workforce by using the downtime in production to train the workers to repair broken machinery rather than laying them off until demand for the new model increased. Similarly, at GM's Saturn plant, values and norms based on employee involvement have dramatically increased product quality. The range and types of abilities that a function develops are a product of both organizational design decisions and organizational culture.

In sum, to create value at the functional level, the organizational strategy must allow and encourage each function to develop a core competency in lowering costs or differentiating its products from those of competitors. Ultimately, the sources of core competencies lie in the resources that the organization assigns to each function and in the abilities of functional experts to coordinate those resources. To gain a competitive advantage, an organization needs to design its functional structure and culture to provide a setting in which core competencies develop. The more a function's core competency is based on coordination abilities embedded in the way people in the organization interact, the more difficult it is for competing organizations to duplicate the core competency and the greater is the organization's competitive advantage.

MANAGERIAL IMPLICATIONS

Functional-Level Strategy

1. As a member or manager of a function, identify the functional resources or coordination abilities that give your function a core competency. Having identified the sources of your function's core competency, establish a plan to improve or strengthen them, and create a set of goals to measure your progress.
2. Study your competitors and the methods and practices they use to control their functional activities. Compare and contrast these to those you have already identified. Pick your most effective competitor, study its methods, and use them as a benchmark for what you wish to achieve in your function.
3. Analyze the way your functional structure and culture affect functional resources and abilities. Experiment to see whether changing a component of structure or culture can enhance your function's core competency.

BUSINESS-LEVEL STRATEGY

At the business level the task facing the organization is to take the core competencies created by the functions and combine them to exploit opportunities in the organizational environment. Strategists at the business level select and manage the domain in which the organization uses its value-creation resources and coordination abilities to obtain a competitive advantage.[24] For example, core competencies in three functions—manufacturing, marketing, and materials management—jointly give McDonald's a competitive advantage over rivals such as Burger King and Wendy's. Obtaining a competitive advantage is important because, as we noted in Chapter 3, organizations in the same environment (e.g., fast food) are in competition for scarce resources. Any organization that fails to devise a business-level strategy to attract resources is at a disadvantage vis-à-vis its rivals and in the long run is likely to fail. Thus the organization needs a business-level strategy that does both of the following: (1) selects the domain the organization will compete in and (2) positions the organization so that it can use its resources and abilities to manage its specific and general environments in order to protect and enlarge that domain.

Strategies to Lower Costs or Differentiate Products

We have seen that the two basic ways in which an organization can create value are by reducing the cost of its value-creation activities and by performing those activities in a way that gives its products a differentiated appeal. Business-level strategy focuses on selecting the domain in which an organization can exploit its functional-level core competencies.

Recall from Chapter 3 that the organizational domain is the range of goods and services that the organization produces to attract customers and other stakeholders. Once an organization has chosen its domain, it has two bases on which it can position itself to compete with its rivals. First, it can use its skills in low-cost value-creation activities to produce for a customer group that wants low-priced goods and services. This plan is called a **low-cost business-level strategy**. Or, second, it can use its skills at differentiation to produce for a customer group that wants and can afford differentiated products that command a high or premium price. This plan is called a **differentiation business-level strategy**.[25] Wal-Mart and Zellers, for example, specialize in selling low-priced clothing to customers who want or can afford to pay only a modest amount for their attire, Mark's Work Wearhouse targets customers who want good-quality mid-cost clothes, and Holt Renfrew specializes in selling high-priced clothing made by exclusive designers to wealthy customers.

Low-cost business-level strategy
A plan whereby an organization produces low-priced goods and services for all customer groups.

Differentiation business-level strategy
A plan whereby an organization produces high-priced, quality products aimed at particular market segments.

Both Wal-Mart and the Bay are in the retail clothing industry but have chosen different domains in which to compete. They have decided to sell different products to different groups of customers. In essence, the Bay and other higher-end retailers have chosen a business-level strategy based on core competencies in differentiation in order to charge a premium price, and Wal-Mart and Zellers have chosen a business-level strategy based on core competencies in low-cost value-creation activities in order to charge a low price.

To compete successfully, an organization must develop a low-cost or differentiation strategy to protect and enlarge its domain. An organization can also attempt to pursue both strategies simultaneously and produce differentiated products at low cost.[26] Doing so is extremely difficult and requires an exceptionally strong set of core competencies as these two strategies essentially compete with one another. Differentiated products generally cost more to create than mass-produced products. On the other hand, mass-produced products do not necessarily have the same differentiated appeal to certain customer segments. McDonald's and Tim Hortons are organizations that have successfully pursued both low-cost and differentiation strategies simultaneously. Both of these organizations have developed a unique brand-name reputation by means of sophisticated advertising and marketing programs. Each has also developed low-cost skills in its manufacturing and distribution functions. Moreover, both Tim Hortons and McDonald's have used many of the interorganizational strategies discussed in Chapter 3 to pursue both strategies simultaneously. They have formed strategic alliances with their suppliers and they obtain everything from their soda fountain drinks, their bread, doughnuts and rolls, coffee, and even their restaurant fittings (tables, chairs, lights, and so on) from companies with which they have long-term contracts, or have developed long-term relationships, or in which they have a minority ownership interest. Tim Hortons and McDonald's both use franchising to maintain the reliability and efficiency of their retail outlets and they own many of the sources of their inputs. MacDonald's even owns herds of cattle in Brazil, so it can ensure itself of a large supply of good quality beef, and Tim Hortons owns the company that provides its coffee.

Over time, an organization has to change its business-level strategy to match changes in its environment. New technological developments, foreign competitors, and changes in customer needs and tastes may all affect the way an organization tries to compete for resources. Amazon.com offers an interesting example of the way changes in information technology affect a company's choice of business-level strategy. (See the Focus on New Information Technology box.)

As Amazon.com's strategy suggests, organizations have to defend, protect, and sometimes alter the sources of their competitive advantage if they are to successfully control their environment in the long run. Industry leaders, such as Amazon.com, Toyota, and McDonald's, are able to sustain their competitive advantage by maintaining and developing their functional-level resources and abilities. These organizations constantly scan their functional and organizational domains in order to maintain or improve their competencies. Amazon.com, for example, is constantly updating its information systems to take advantage of any new technological developments that will allow Amazon to maintain its advantage over its competitors, such as the use of streaming audio and video at its Web site.

Focus Strategy

Another business-level strategy is the focus strategy—or the specialization in one segment of a market, and focusing all of the organization's resources on that segment.[27] Subway specializes in the sandwich segment of the fast-food market; Tiffany specializes in the high-price, luxury segment of the jewellery market; Rolls Royce focuses on the highest-price segment of the car market—a Rolls Royce Silver Sprite costs US$265 000.

Business-Level Strategy and Structure

The value that an organization creates at the business level depends on its ability to use its core competencies to gain a competitive advantage. This ability is a product of the way the organization designs its structure.[28] An organization pursuing a differentiation business-level strategy generally confronts design choices different from those faced by organizations pursuing a low-cost strategy. Figure 8-4 summarizes the differences.

The competitive strengths of an organization with a differentiation strategy come from functional skills that give the organization's products unique or state-of-the-art features that distinguish them from the products of competitors. An organization pursuing a differentiation strategy has to be able to develop products quickly,

FIGURE 8-4
Types of Business-Level Strategy.

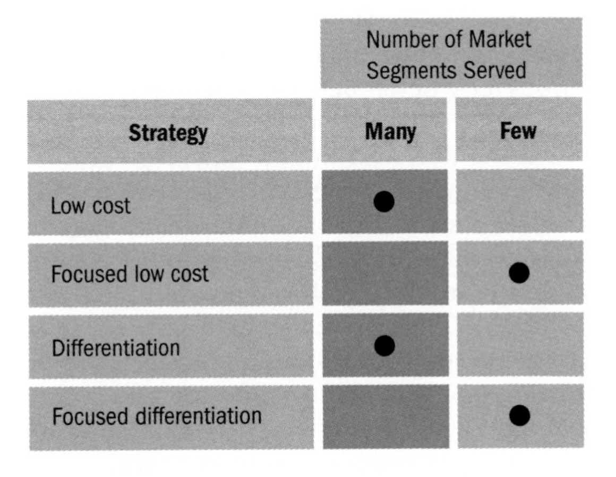

	Number of Market Segments Served	
Strategy	**Many**	**Few**
Low cost	●	
Focused low cost		●
Differentiation	●	
Focused differentiation		●

FOCUS ON NEW INFORMATION TECHNOLOGY

Amazon.com, Part 5

Before the advent of online bookstores, competition among bookstores was limited at best. The market was essentially divided between two kinds of competitors: (1) large bookstore chains such as Indigo, Chapters, Barnes & Noble, or Borders whose stores were often located in malls and which offered customers the latest lines of best-selling books and (2), independent bookstores that in large cities could be very large and offer a huge selection of books, or could be the small, specialized bookstores found in most cities in Canada and the United States. The large bookstore chains used their huge purchasing power to negotiate low prices with book publishers and they pursued a low-cost strategy, often offering price discounts. Bookstores that offered a large selection of books (compared to the chains) or which specialized in some way pursued a differentiation strategy. Thus, the different kinds of bookstores were not in competition and all of them were able to make comfortable profits.

Amazon founder Jeff Bezos's idea of using new Internet information technology to sell books online made it possible to develop a simultaneous low-cost and differentiation strategy and thus outperform existing bookstore competitors. First, on the differentiation side, the ability of a computerized online catalogue to both describe and make available to customers every book in the English language offered customers a selection that could not be rivalled. Second, on the low-cost side, his use of information technology to interface inexpensively with book publishers, distributors, and customers allowed Amazon to offer these customers books at discounted prices, and to deliver them directly to customers at a low cost as well.

Small wonder then that this new low-cost/differentiation strategy has given Amazon.com a competitive advantage over its rivals. Many small and large stand-alone bookstores have exited the market; the large chains have responded by opening up book superstores and by going online themselves. However, they have yet to repeat Amazon.com's success story; Amazon.com has over 18 million customers in its database and claims that over 45 percent of its business is from repeat customers. Its share price has soared, as investors believe it possesses the business-level strategy that will dominate in the years ahead.

because it is only when it gets its products to customers ahead of its competitors that it can exploit its differentiation advantage. Close cooperation between functions is likely to be required to bring new products to market quickly. For example, R&D, marketing, manufacturing, and product development must be able to communicate easily and adjust their activities to one another smoothly in order to speed the development process. All these factors make it likely that an organization pursuing a differentiation strategy has a more organic structure. An organic structure is needed for the development of a decentralized, cross-functional team approach to decision making, which is one of the keys to speedy new product development.

A low-cost strategy is associated with the need for close control of functional activities to monitor and lower the costs of product development.[29] Manufacturing and materials management become the central functions for an organization pursuing a low-cost strategy. The other functions (R&D, marketing, and so on) tailor their skills to achieve the goal of producing a low-cost product. A speedy response to market changes is not as vital to the competitive success of a low-cost organization as it is for one with a differentiation strategy. Often, because product development is so expensive, such an organization waits to develop a new or improved product until customers clearly demand it. The low-cost organization generally imitates the differentiator's product and always remains one step behind in order to capitalize on the efforts of the differentiator (market presence, development, and demand) in order to keep costs as low as possible. Consequently, a more mechanistic structure is often the most appropriate choice for an organization pursuing a low-cost strategy (see Figure 8-5). Centralized decision making allows the organization to maintain close control over functional activities and thus over costs. Also, because there is less of a need to respond quickly or innovatively, a mechanistic structure provides sufficient coordination to meet the demands of the competitive domain.

Further evidence for the match between differentiation strategy and organic structure, and the match between low-cost strategy and mechanistic structure, comes from contingency theory. Recall from Chapter 4 that contingency theory suggests that organizations in uncertain, rapidly changing environments require a greater degree of

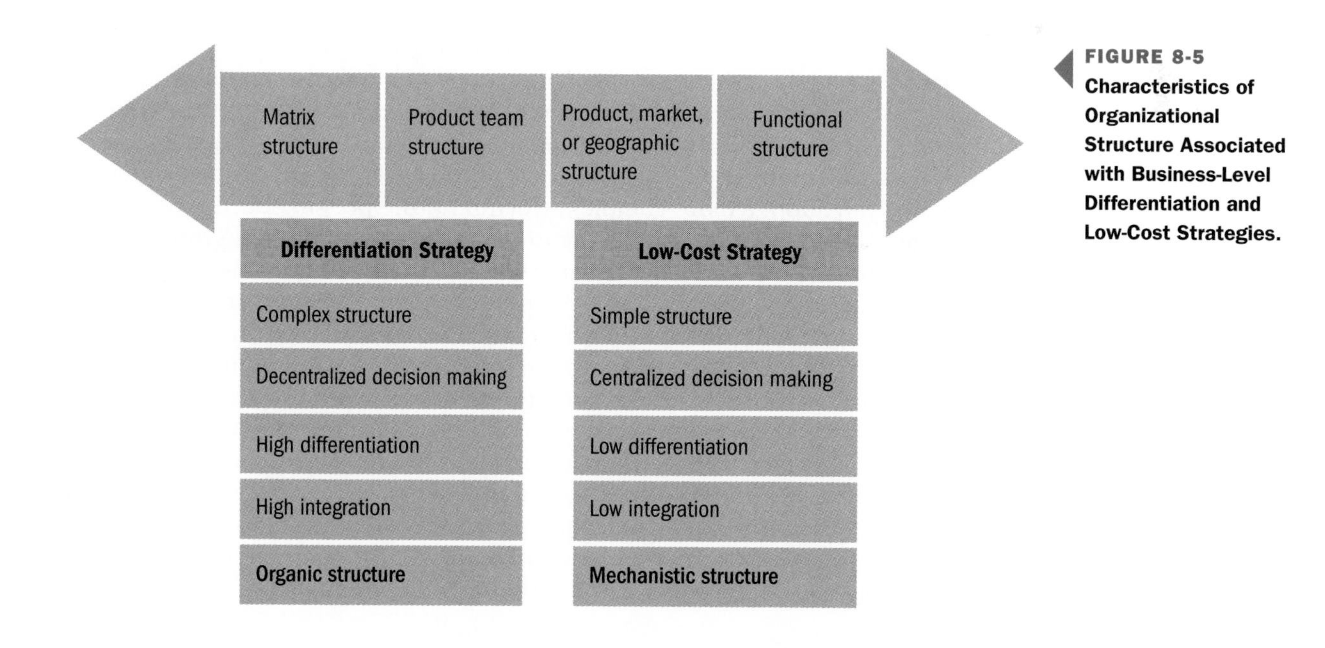

FIGURE 8-5 Characteristics of Organizational Structure Associated with Business-Level Differentiation and Low-Cost Strategies.

differentiation and integration than do organizations in more stable environments.[30] Because differentiators generally compete in a complex, uncertain environment where they need to react quickly to rivals' actions, and because low-cost companies usually compete in slow-moving environments, contingency theory suggests that effective differentiators will structurally have greater differentiation and integration than low-cost companies have. Given that organizational structures with extensive differentiation and integration are costly to operate; contingency theory implies that low-cost companies should use the simplest structure possible (i.e., a more mechanistic structure) because it will help to keep down the cost of value creation.[31]

In addition to examining the relationship between business-level strategy and organic and mechanistic structures, we can also look at the relationship between strategy and the types of organizational structure that we discussed in Chapter 6: functional, divisional, and matrix structures. From a strategy perspective, three factors affect an organization's choice of a structure to create a competitive advantage for itself:

1. As an organization produces a wider range of products, it will need greater control over the development, marketing, and production of these products.
2. As an organization seeks to find new customer groups for its products, it will need a structure that allows it to serve the needs of its customers.
3. As the pace of new product development in an industry increases, an organization will need a structure that increases coordination among its functions.

Organizations following a low-cost strategy typically focus on producing only one product, or a few products, in order to reduce production costs. BIC Corporation, for example, produces one disposable razor for both men and women. A low-cost company does not face the challenges and coordination problems of dealing with a wide range of products or with many customer groups. Moreover, low-cost companies are usually not leaders in product development. Because they are imitators, they do not have the challenges and problems of coordinating the activities of many different functional groups. For all these reasons, low-cost companies generally adopt the simplest structure possible that is consistent with their strategy. Normally, a functional structure (one in which people are grouped by common skills or use of similar resources) is sufficient to coordinate the core competencies of a low-cost organization.

By contrast, differentiators typically produce a wide range of products to suit the needs of different groups of customers. Also, to the degree that competition between differentiators is based on the development of new and innovative products (a situation found in the car and personal computer industries), differentiators need a structure that allows functional experts to cooperate and coordinate so that they can quickly develop and continually introduce new products. For these reasons, differentiators are likely to adopt a more complex structure. If the pressing need is to handle a wide range of products, a product structure (in which products are grouped into separate divisions that are served by the same set of support functions) is an appropriate choice. If handling different groups of customers is the key to success, a market structure or a geographic structure (in which functional activities are grouped to best meet the needs of different types of customers) will best fit the differentiator's needs. A product team structure or a matrix structure (in which product development is coordinated by teams of cross-functional specialists) can be adopted when rapid product development and speedy response to competitors are the keys to maintaining the organization's competitive advantage.

All of those structures can provide an organization with the ability to coordinate functional and organizational resources to create a core competency. Intel, the microchip manufacturer, has decided that the only way to maintain its lead in the industry is to produce several generations of microchips at the same time. So it has established a product team structure in which teams of research and development specialists work side by side to plan the chips of the future.[32]

To summarize, an organization must match its business-level strategy to the organizational structure that allows the organization to use its functional and organizational resources to create a competitive advantage. A top-quality R&D department is useless unless an organization has a structure that coordinates R&D activities with a marketing department that can correctly forecast changes in customer needs and a product development department that can translate research and marketing findings into commercial products. Choosing the right structure has major payoffs by permitting an organization a low-cost or differentiation advantage at the business level. Conversely, having a structure that does not permit effective response to the environment in which the organization competes can result in deteriorating performance, as Organizational Insight 8.1 demonstrates.

Business-Level Strategy and Culture

Organizational culture is another major determinant of the ability to use functional and organizational resources effectively. The challenge at the business level is to develop organization-wide values, and specific norms and rules, all of which allow the organization to combine and use its functional resources to the best advantage. Over time, different functions usually develop different subunit orientations, which can impede communication and coordination. But if the various functions share common values and norms of behaviour, then communication and coordination problems can be minimized. If managers in different functions can develop common ways of dealing with problems, an organization's competitive advantage will often be enhanced.

How does the culture of a low-cost organization differ from that of a differentiator? Organizations pursuing a low-cost strategy must develop values of economy and frugality.[33] Frequently, specific norms and rules develop that reflect the organization's terminal and instrumental values. For example, when Ken Iverson was CEO of Nucor, a leading low-cost steel manufacturer, he operated the company in a frugal, careful way. Top managers at Nucor worked in small, unpretentious corporate offices with few of the trappings of luxury. They drove their own cars to work, flew economy class, and on business trips shared rooms in hotels to reduce costs.

The functions within a low-cost organization are likely to develop goals that reflect the organization's values of economy. Marketing views its job as finding the most efficient ways of attracting customers. R&D sees its role as developing new products that offer the greatest potential return for the smallest investment of organizational resources.

In low-cost organizations, a common "language" and a code of behaviour based on low-cost values develop. In a differentiator, by contrast, the need to be different from competitors and to develop innovative products puts product development or marketing at centre stage. Values that promote innovation and responsiveness to customers, stories of products that became winners or of winning products that were not developed, and boosting the status of employees who create new products all make organizational members aware of the need to be the first or the best.[34] Cultural values of innovation, quality, excellence, and uniqueness help a differentiator implement its chosen strategy, and they become a source of competitive strength. Organizational Insight 8.2 offers a glimpse at the way culture can influence a company's business-level strategy.

An organizational culture that promotes norms and rules that increase effectiveness can be a major source of competitive advantage. In Chapter 7, we saw how

ORGANIZATIONAL INSIGHT 8.1

Bombardier Restructures[35]

Bombardier, originally known as L'Auto-Neige Bombardier Limitée, was founded in 1942 by J.-Armand Bombardier to produce vehicles that could travel on snow—the ubiquitous icon of Canadian winters, the snowmobile. The company's name was changed to Bombardier Limited in 1967, and in 1969 Bombardier was listed on the Montreal and Toronto stock exchanges. Bombardier made an initial public offering of two million shares. In the early 1970s, it acquired the Austrian company Lohnerwerke GmbH and its subsidiary Rotax-Werk AG, the supplier of the Rotax engine used in snowmobiles.

Bombardier is now a leading manufacturer of planes, trains, and recreational vehicles and is currently traded on the Toronto, Brussels, and Frankfurt stock exchanges. However, in response to increasing competition and poor financial performance in the 1990s, Bombardier had been forced to restructure, and the company was reorganized into five groups: Bombardier Aerospace, Bombardier Transportation, Bombardier Recreational Products, Bombardier Services, and Bombardier Capital. Since that time it has had two different chief executive officers, Robert Brown (appointed in February 1999) and Paul Tellier (appointed in January 2003). Since Tellier's appointment, the pressure has been on him to again restructure the company and turn it around financially.

Bombardier's restructuring plan then involved refocusing the company on aerospace and transportation, divesting itself of its many subsidiaries, and selling off a number of assets to improve the corporate balance sheet. In 2003, Bombardier sold off the recreational division, the Belfast City Airport, and its Military Aviation Services unit. Additionally, cost reductions were sought through layoffs, and thousands of jobs were eliminated that same year.

The ongoing restructuring effort has seen a positive effect on the finances of the company. In 2002 Bombardier had revenues of $21.189 billion and a loss of $615 million. In 2003 revenues increased to $21.321 billion, with a significantly lower loss of just $89 million. However, early in 2004, Tellier once more had to cut back, focusing on cost reductions again, and he announced that the company would be restructuring its train division. This resulted in the closing of seven European plants, resulting in 6600 additional layoffs.

Despite experiencing some success and a much better year, the restructuring of Bombardier has been a difficult challenge, and Tellier again came under attack from shareholders who were impatient for an end to the company's losses and a return to financial health. The promised shareholder returns had not happened and executives of the company, including Tellier, have been criticized as being overpaid and overconfident in their attempts to turn the corporation around.

The restructuring of Bombardier is expected to continue as Paul Tellier himself was replaced as CEO in December of 2004 by Laurent Beaudoin, the son-in-law of the company founder. While the end of the Bombardier story still remains to be written, it may be that the cultures of the various divisions remaining in Bombardier are sufficiently different to still hamper the restructuring efforts of any single CEO.

ORGANIZATIONAL INSIGHT 8.2

How Culture Derailed the Merger Between AHP and Monsanto

After considerable negotiations, American Home Products (AHP), the giant pharmaceutical maker, announced that it would buy Monsanto, another large pharmaceutical and chemical company, for US$33 billion. Analysts applauded the merger, believing that it would provide important differentiation and low-cost advantages for the combined firm. Specifically, the merged companies would have a much broader product range and the merger would eliminate expensive duplication of production facilities leading to major cost savings.

Analysts were therefore shocked when the two companies later announced that the merger was off because it was not in the best interests of shareholders. Why were the companies forced to give up these potential sources of competitive advantage? AHP has a culture characterized by a short-term focus on bottom-line profits. Its managers are cost-conscious and only want to invest in products that have a short-term payoff. Monsanto, on the other hand, has a long-term orientation. It is driven by a desire to produce innovative new products, many of which may not pay off except in the long run. Thus it has strong values of innovation and excellence.

Managers at these companies came to realize that it was impossible to harmonize these different cultures and driving values. They foresaw that the potential low cost and differentiation gains might be wiped out by politics and infighting between managers of these two companies and it was just not worth the risk to go ahead with the merger.

organizations deliberately shape their culture to achieve their goals. Sony and Microsoft, for example, promote innovation by establishing norms and rules that enable employees to move to positions where their talents are most valuable to the organization.

Recall, too, that organizational structures are chosen because of their effect on culture. Organic structures foster the development of cultural values of innovation and quality. In contrast, mechanistic structures foster economical values that focus attention on improving existing rules and SOPs, not finding new ones. Low-cost companies that seek to develop Japanese-style lean production systems will find a mechanistic structure useful because it focuses all efforts on improving existing work procedures.

In sum, organizational culture is another important factor shaping an organization's business-level strategy for improving its value-creation skills. As technology changes, as new products and markets come into being, and as the environment changes, an organization's culture likewise will change. Like organizational structure, the way in which organizational culture supports an organization's strategy for value creation can also be a source of competitive advantage. That is one reason why there has been continuing interest in culture as an explanation for differences in organizational effectiveness.

MANAGERIAL IMPLICATIONS

Business-Level Strategy

1. Managers in each function should understand their function's contribution to the organization's low-cost advantage or differentiated appeal. Members of a function should examine their interactions with members of other functions to see if they can devise new ways of reducing costs or to develop a differentiated appeal.
2. Managers should act like entrepreneurs and always be on the lookout for new opportunities to protect and enlarge the domain of their organization. They must continually experiment to see whether they can enlarge the existing organizational domain, find new uses for existing products, or develop new products to satisfy customer needs.
3. Managers must always evaluate whether the current organizational structure and culture are congruent with the organization's business-level strategy. If they are not, managers should move quickly to make changes that align themselves with the organizations' chosen strategy so they can help improve their competitive position.

CORPORATE-LEVEL STRATEGY

Often, an organization that cannot create more value in its current domain tries to find a new domain in which to compete for resources. Corporate-level strategy involves a search for new domains in which to exploit and defend an organization's ability to create value from the use of its low-cost or differentiation core competencies.[36] Corporate-level strategy is a continuation of business-level strategy because the organization takes its existing core competencies and then looks to apply them in new domains. If an organization takes marketing skills developed in one domain and applies them in a new domain, for example, it can create value in that new domain. When Philip Morris took marketing skills developed in the tobacco industry, applied them to Miller Brewing, and made Miller Light the market leader, it created value for Miller's customers and for Philip Morris's shareholders. Now we look in detail at how vertical integration and diversification, two important corporate-level strategies, can help an organization increase the value of its activities or create new value activities.

Vertical Integration

Vertical integration
A strategy in which an organization takes over and owns its suppliers (backward vertical integration) or its distributors (forward vertical integration).

An organization pursuing a strategy of **vertical integration** establishes—or takes over and buys—its suppliers (backward vertical integration) or its distributors (forward vertical integration).[37] In this way, it increases the control over the production of its inputs or the disposal of its outputs (see Figure 8-6). As an illustration, Figure 8-7 shows a soft-drink company that enters new domains that overlap its core domain so that it can use, enhance, or protect its low-cost or differentiation value-creation skills.

How does vertical integration allow an organization to use or enhance its core competency in value creation? An organization that supplies its own inputs or disposes of its own outputs may be able to keep for itself the profits that would have been previously earned and retained by its suppliers or distributors. Moreover, production cost savings can sometimes be obtained when an organization owns its input suppliers. Inputs can be designed so that they can be assembled at a lower cost, and control of

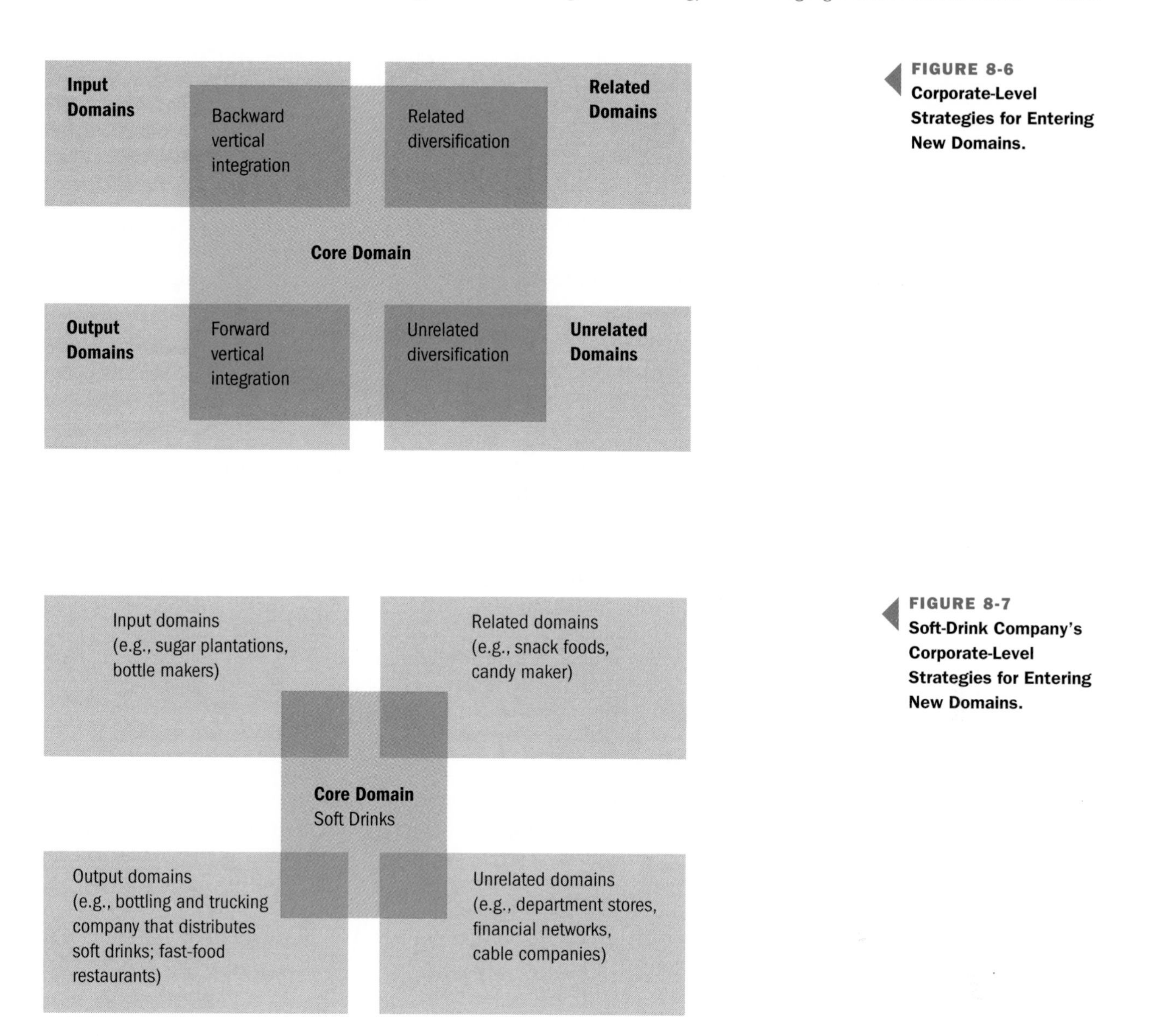

FIGURE 8-6 Corporate-Level Strategies for Entering New Domains.

FIGURE 8-7 Soft-Drink Company's Corporate-Level Strategies for Entering New Domains.

the reliability and quality of inputs can save an organization a great deal of money if products eventually have to be repaired under guarantee.

An organization can call attention to its uniqueness by making its products different from its rivals'. One way to do this is by controlling the inputs that make a product unique. Coca-Cola, for example, has sole control over the Coke formula, so Coca-Cola tastes like no other cola drink. Controlling inputs also helps the organization control quality, which confers uniqueness on a product. Rolls Royce carefully tends the flocks of sheep from which it obtains the leather for its car upholstery: The sheep are kept in enclosures without barbed wire and are protected so that the leather has no flaws and blemishes. Finally, taking over a supplier by vertical integration avoids the problem that results when there are only a few suppliers in an industry. When suppliers are small in number they have greater influence or control in the market. They can inflate the costs of their products (other organizations' inputs) and they have control over the quality of those inputs (they may reduce quality in order to lower costs and increase profits for themselves). These actions increase uncertainty for those organizations that depend on these inputs for their own processes.

Controlling the way a product is distributed can also result in a low-cost or differentiation advantage. Tandy Corporation, for example, owns Radio Shack, so Tandy obtains all the profit from sales of Radio Shack consumer electronic products and accessories, profit that otherwise would have been made by other retail stores. Tandy can also control the quality of the sales and repair service that Radio Shack customers receive and thus build customer loyalty—a differentiation advantage.

Control of overlapping input and output domains enhances an organization's competitive advantage in its core domain and creates new opportunities for value creation. But an organization also needs to look at the bureaucratic costs associated with full ownership of suppliers and distributors.[38] The organization needs to evaluate whether minority ownership, strategic alliances, and other interorganizational strategies are viable alternatives to vertical integration.[39] The value-creation advantages of vertical integration can sometimes be obtained at much lower bureaucratic costs by means of strategic alliances with already existing businesses, because an organization avoids the costs associated with having to operate the business. The more an organization pursues vertical integration, the larger the organization becomes, and the bureaucratic costs associated with managing the strategy are likely to rise sharply because of communication and coordination problems and the simple fact that managers are expensive to employ. Too much vertical integration can be a strategic mistake. Thus managers must be careful to make design choices about organizational structure and culture that will enhance and support such a strategy.

Related Diversification

Related diversification The entry into a new domain that is related in some way to an organization's domain.

Related diversification occurs when an organization enters a new domain in which it can exploit one or more of its existing core competencies to create a low-cost or differentiated competitive advantage in that new domain. When Honda entered the small-car and lawn mower markets, for example, it entered a domain in which it could exploit functional skills in engine design and manufacture that it had developed in its core domain, motorbikes, to achieve a low-cost advantage. Whenever an organization enters a new domain to exploit an opportunity to use any of its core competencies in a way that can lower costs or create uniqueness, it creates value through related diversification.

Unrelated Diversification

Unrelated diversification The entry into a new domain that is not related in any way to an organization's core domain.

The value created by related diversification comes from exploiting any of an organization's core competencies in a new domain; when a company pursues unrelated diversification, it enters new domains that have nothing in common with its core domain. The value created by **unrelated diversification** comes from exploiting one particular core competency: a top-management team's ability to control a set of organizations better than the organizations' existing top-management teams.[40]

Suppose a retail organization's top-management team has developed unique skills in economizing on bureaucratic costs by designing and managing organizational structure. If the team sees an organization in some new domain—for example, fast food—that is being managed inefficiently and is not making the best use of its resources, team members may see an opportunity for their organization to expand into this new domain and create value there. If the top-management team takes over the inefficient organization, restructures its operations, reduces bureaucratic costs, and increases its profitability, it has created value that did not previously exist in the fast-food organization.

An organization that takes over inefficient companies and restructures them to create value is pursuing a strategy of unrelated diversification. If it continues to manage these organizations from a pure profitability standpoint and buys and sells them on the basis of their return on investment, it is also pursuing a strategy of unrelated diversification. For example, Hanson Trust, an organization that is a collection of unrelated British and American divisions, seeks out underperforming organizations, sells off the divisions it does not want, and keeps the divisions it feels it can restructure and operate profitably. Designing an efficient organizational structure is an important part of the strategy of unrelated diversification because companies that perform poorly often do so because they have high bureaucratic costs, or their structures are otherwise inefficient, or not aligned with their chosen corporate or business strategies.

Corporate-Level Strategy and Structure

The appropriate organizational structure must be chosen at the corporate level in order to realize the value associated with vertical integration and related and unrelated diversification. In general, as we discussed in Chapter 6, for organizations that are operating in more than one domain, a multidivisional structure is the appropriate choice (see Figure 6.6, p. 186). The use of self-contained operating divisions supported by a corporate headquarters staff provides the control the organization needs to coordinate resource transfers between divisions so that core competencies can be shared across the organization. There are a few variants of the multidivisional structure. Each is suited to realizing the benefits associated with either unrelated or related diversification.

Conglomerate Structure and Unrelated Diversification Organizations pursuing a strategy of unrelated diversification attempt to create value by purchasing underperforming businesses, restructuring them, and then managing them more efficiently. This strategy frees the managers of the parent organization from involvement in the day-to-day running of the various companies that the organization owns. After the restructuring, corporate management's only role is to monitor each company's performance and intervene to take selective action when necessary. Organizations with a strategy of unrelated diversification are likely to use a conglomerate structure.

As Figure 8-8 shows, in a **conglomerate structure**, each unrelated business is a self-contained division. Because there is no need to coordinate activities between divisions, only a small corporate headquarters staff is needed. Communication is from the top down and occurs most often on issues that concern bureaucratic costs, such as decisions about the level of financial expenditure necessary to pursue new value-creation opportunities. The conglomerate Hanson Trust, for example, operated with a corporate staff of only 120 people to oversee more than 50 companies; it operated primarily through rules that controlled bureaucratic costs. Hanson Trust had a rule that required a corporate executive to approve any expenditure over US$3000.[41] Beyond this, it made little attempt to intervene in the affairs of the operating divisions.

Conglomerate structure A structure in which each business is placed in a self-contained division and there is no contact between divisions.

Structures for Related Diversification An organization pursuing a strategy of related diversification tries to obtain value by sharing resources or by transferring functional skills from one division to another—processes that require a great amount of coordination and integration. Related diversification requires lateral communication between divisions as well as vertical communication between divisions and corporate headquarters. As a result, integrating roles and teams of functional experts are needed

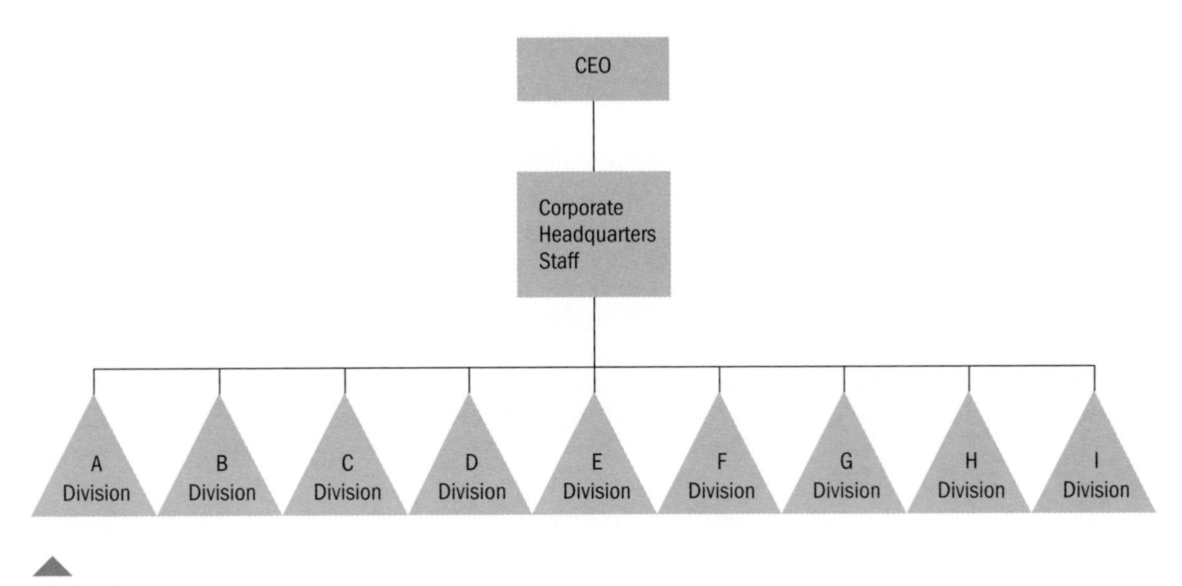

FIGURE 8-8

Conglomerate Structure.

A structure in which each business is placed in a self-contained division and there is no contact between divisions.

to coordinate skill and resource transfers. Coordination is complicated because divisions may fight for resources and may not wish to share information and knowledge unless they are equitably rewarded for doing so. To obtain from related diversification a set of gains comparable to those obtained from unrelated diversification, a much larger corporate headquarters staff is required to coordinate interdivisional activities, and much more managerial time and effort is needed. Hitachi's corporate structure offers an interesting insight into the management of a strategy of related diversification. (See Organizational Insight 8.3.)

Because Hitachi has 28 operating divisions, its coordination problem is intense. Imagine the coordination problem that arises when an organization has over 150 divisions, as do GE and Textron. Often, the coordination problem becomes so severe that a multidivisional matrix structure is used to increase integration (see Figure 6.13, p. 204). As we saw in Chapter 6, this structure provides the coordination between the divisions and corporate headquarters that allows for the transfer of skills and the sharing of resources around the organization. It gives top-level functional, divisional, and corporate managers the opportunity to meet in teams to plan the organization's future strategy.

The bureaucratic costs associated with managing related diversification (whether in a multidivisional structure or a matrix multidivisional structure) are much greater than those associated with vertical integration or unrelated diversification.[42] Considerably more communication and coordination are needed to create value from related diversification than from the other corporate-level strategies. Bureaucratic costs increase as the size of the corporate staff and the amount of time that both divisional and corporate managers spend in coordinating with other divisions increase. In contrast, the bureaucratic costs associated with unrelated diversification are likely to be low, because there is less or almost no need to coordinate resource transfers between divisions—the divisions do not exchange anything.

ORGANIZATIONAL INSIGHT 8.3

Hitachi Ltd.

Hitachi Ltd. is one of Japan's biggest and most innovative companies.[43] Every year the US$62 billion giant accounts for 6 percent of Japan's expenditures on R&D and over 2 percent of Japan's gross domestic product. Like its biggest competitors, IBM and Fujitsu, Hitachi is a major computer organization. Unlike them, however, it is also engaged in non–computer-based businesses that rely heavily on computer technology: consumer electronics, power plants, transportation, medical equipment, and telecommunications.[44] It is pursuing a strategy of related diversification on a grand scale, and research and development forms the bedrock of the organization and its value-creation activities.

Hitachi has 28 divisions. Each has its own R&D laboratory and is responsible for product development from the initial conception to design and final marketing. Control is decentralized to each division, and each division has the ultimate responsibility for choosing its domain. This decentralized approach puts a heavy burden on Hitachi to find ways to integrate and coordinate its divisions so that they can share skills and resources and increase their level of innovation. Hitachi has responded to the need for interdivisional coordination by adopting various integrating mechanisms:

1. Hitachi employs a large number of corporate executives in integrating roles to oversee each division's activities and control information flows from one division to another.
2. Hitachi has a corporate R&D laboratory that has the responsibility for coordinating the flow of new knowledge among the divisions' R&D laboratories and for disseminating the knowledge it creates to the divisions.
3. Hitachi uses a sophisticated telecommunications and teleconferencing network to link its laboratories, so that scientists and engineers in different labs can effectively work face-to-face to trade knowledge and cooperate on joint research.
4. Hitachi has developed a strong corporate culture based on values of cooperation and teamwork between scientists, and norms that support innovation flourish.

Through all those means, Hitachi has enhanced its ability to transfer its R&D skills around the organization and secure the gains from its strategy of related diversification.

In Hitachi, there are enormous opportunities for finding new ways to create value because the divisions are related to one another through their reliance on computer and electronic technology. The bureaucratic costs of pursuing this strategy, however, are very high because so much time and money is spent on integrating the 28 R&D laboratories in order to keep them aware of each other's activities. The enormous costs of operating so many R&D units also eat into profits. Hitachi has chosen to bear these costs in order to obtain the benefits of its strategy of related diversification. Because it has a time horizon for product development that extends for many years, it is not concerned with the bottom-line results of any single division in the short run. What matters to Hitachi is maintaining its long-term ability to create value.

Corporate-Level Strategy and Culture

Just as a move to a more appropriate organizational structure can reduce bureaucratic costs, so can a move to a more appropriate organizational culture. Cultural values and the common norms, rules, and goals that reflect those values can greatly facilitate the management of a corporate strategy. For example, Hanson Trust, which pursued a strategy of unrelated diversification, put most value on economy, cost cutting, and the efficient use of organizational resources. Divisional managers at Hanson Trust could not spend large amounts of money without the approval of corporate executives. Knowing that their performance was scrutinized closely, their actions were shaped by corporate values tied to bottom-line results.

By contrast, suppose an organization is pursuing a strategy of related diversification. What kinds of values, norms, and rules are most useful in managing the strategy? Because the creation of value from related diversification requires a large amount of coordination and integration, norms and values that emphasize cooperation between divisions are important. This type of culture lowers the costs of exchanging resources and is likely to feature a common corporate language that the various divisions can use in their dealings with one another. Each division will have its own culture, but the corporate culture can overcome differences in divisional orientation, just as at the business level an organization's culture can overcome differences in functional orientation.

At Sony, for example, corporate values of innovation and entrepreneurship are passed on in the stories that organizational members use to frame significant corporate events. New employees are socialized into the innovative culture and learn the corporate language from their interactions with other people. In its promotions to the corporate headquarters staff, Sony also sends a message about the kinds of values and behaviours that are associated with success in the organization—actions that lead to innovative new products. Similarly, an organization that rewards managers who successfully manage interdivisional attempts to share skills and trade resources has a culture that supports a strategy of related diversification.

Thus different cultures help support an organization's different corporate-level strategies. An organization needs to create a culture that reinforces and builds on the strategy it pursues and the structure it adopts. In an organization that has a conglomerate structure, in which there is no connection between divisions, it would be pointless to develop a common corporate culture across divisions because the managers in the different divisions would not know one another. In fact, because they do not know one another, or have only limited contact with one another, it is unlikely that any common set of shared values or norms would develop in the first instance. A multidivisional matrix structure, in contrast, does support the development of a cohesive corporate culture because it permits the rapid interchange of ideas and the transfer of norms and values around the organization. In sum, as we saw in Chapter 7, corporate culture is an important tool that organizations can use to coordinate and motivate employees.

As at the business level, the interorganizational strategies discussed in Chapter 3 are an important means of increasing the value an organization can create through its corporate strategy. Interorganizational strategies increase value by allowing the organization to avoid the bureaucratic costs often associated with managing a new organization in a new domain. As the number of an organization's divisions increases, for example, the bureaucratic costs associated with managing interdivisional activities increase. Interorganizational strategies such as strategic alliances may allow an organization to obtain the gains from cooperation between divisions without experiencing the costs. Suppose two organizations establish a joint venture to produce a range of products in a domain that is new to both of them. Each organization contributes a different skill or resource to the venture. One provides low-cost manufacturing skills; the other, differentiated R&D and marketing skills. By establishing the joint venture, they have avoided the bureaucratic costs that would be incurred if one organization took over the other or if either organization had to internally coordinate the new resource transfers necessary to make the new venture work. Similarly, the gains from vertical integration can often be realized through minority ownership or long-term contracts, which avoid the need to own the supplier or distributor. An organization that can use an interorganizational strategy to enter and compete in a new domain can often secure the benefits of the diversification and integration strategies without incurring these bureaucratic costs.

MANAGERIAL IMPLICATIONS

Corporate-Level Strategy

1. To protect the organization's existing domains and to exploit the organization's core competencies to create value for stakeholders, managers should carefully analyze the environment.
2. To distinguish between a value-creation opportunity and a value-losing opportunity, managers should carefully evaluate the benefits and costs associated with entering a new domain.
3. As part of this analysis, managers should weigh the benefits and costs of various strategies for entering the domain—for example, takeover of an existing company, versus establishing a new organization, versus using a strategic alliance such as a joint venture.
4. No matter which corporate strategy managers pursue, as the organization grows, managers must be careful to match their organization's structure and culture to the strategy they are pursuing.

IMPLEMENTING STRATEGY ACROSS COUNTRIES

Global strategy can play a crucial role in strengthening a company's control over its environment. There are four principal strategies that companies can use as they begin to market their products and establish production facilities abroad: (1) a *multidomestic strategy*, oriented toward local responsiveness—a company decentralizes control to subsidiaries and divisions in each country in which it operates to produce and customize products to local markets or to meet the needs of local customers; (2) an *international strategy*, based on R&D and marketing being centralized at home and all the other value-creation functions being decentralized to national units; (3) a *global strategy*, oriented toward cost reduction, with all the principal value-creation functions centralized at the lowest-cost global location; and (4) a *transnational strategy*, focused so that it can achieve both local responsiveness *and* cost reduction—some functions are centralized, while others are decentralized at the global location best suited to achieving these objectives.

The need to coordinate and integrate global activities increases as a company moves from a multidomestic to an international to a global and then to a transnational strategy. For example, to obtain the benefits of pursuing a transnational strategy, a company must transfer its distinctive competencies to the global location where they can create the most value and establish a global network to coordinate its divisions both at home and abroad. The objective of such coordination is to obtain the benefits from transferring or leveraging competencies across a company's global divisions. Thus the bureaucratic costs associated with solving communications and measurement problems that arise in managing transfers across countries to pursue a transnational strategy are much higher than those of pursuing the other strategies. The multidomestic strategy does not require coordination of activities on a global level because value-creation activities are handled locally, by country or geographic region. The international and global strategies fit between these other two strategies: Although products have to be sold and marketed globally, and hence global product transfers must be managed, there is less need to coordinate skill and resource transfers than for a transnational strategy.

The implication is that as companies change from a multidomestic to an international, global, or transnational strategy, they will require a more complex structure, control system, and culture to coordinate the value-creation activities associated with implementing that strategy. In general, the choice of structure and control systems for managing a global business is a function of three factors:

1. The decision on how to distribute and allocate responsibility and authority between managers at home and abroad so that effective control over a company's global operations is maintained
2. The selection of the organizational structure that groups divisions both at home and abroad in a way that allows the best use of resources and serves the needs of different customers most effectively
3. The selection of the right kinds of integration and control mechanisms and organizational culture to make the overall global structure function effectively

Table 8-2 summarizes the appropriate design choices for companies pursuing each of these strategies.

Implementing a Multidomestic Strategy

When a company pursues a multidomestic strategy, it generally operates with a global geographic structure (see Figure 8-9). When using this structure, a company duplicates all value-creation activities and establishes an overseas division in every country or world area in which it operates. Authority is then decentralized to managers in each individual country or region and they are responsible to devise the appropriate strategy for responding to the needs of their local or regional environment. Managers at global headquarters use market and output controls, such as ROI, growth in market share, and operation costs, to evaluate the performance of their overseas divisions. On the basis of such global comparisons, they can make decisions about capital or other resource allocations and they can orchestrate the transfer of new knowledge among divisions to improve performance overall.

A company that makes and sells the same products in many different countries often groups its overseas divisions into geographic regions to simplify the coordination of products across countries. Europe might be one region, the Pacific Rim another, and the Middle East a third. Such grouping allows the same set of output and behaviour controls to be applied across all divisions inside a given region. Thus, global companies can reduce communications and transfer problems because information can be transmitted more easily across countries with broadly similar cultures. For example, consumers' preferences regarding product design and marketing are likely to be more similar among countries in one world region than among countries in different world regions.

Table 8-2

STRATEGY–STRUCTURE RELATIONSHIPS IN THE INTERNATIONAL ENVIRONMENT

	Multidomestic Strategy	International Strategy	Global Strategy	Transnational Strategy
	Low ←	Need for Coordination	→	High
Vertical Differentiation Choices				
Levels in the hierarchy	Relatively flat	Relatively tall	Relatively tall	Relatively flat
Centralization of authority	Decentralized	Core Competencies centralized, others decentralized	Centralized	Simultaneously centralized and decentralized
Horizontal Differentiation	Global geographic structure	Global product group structure	Global product group structure	Global matrix or "matrix in the mind"
Integration				
Need for integrating mechanisms such as task forces and integrating roles	Low	Medium	Medium	High
Need for electronic integration and management networks	Medium	High	High	Very high
Need for integration by international organizational culture	Low	Medium	High	Very high
	Low ←	Bureaucratic Costs	→	High

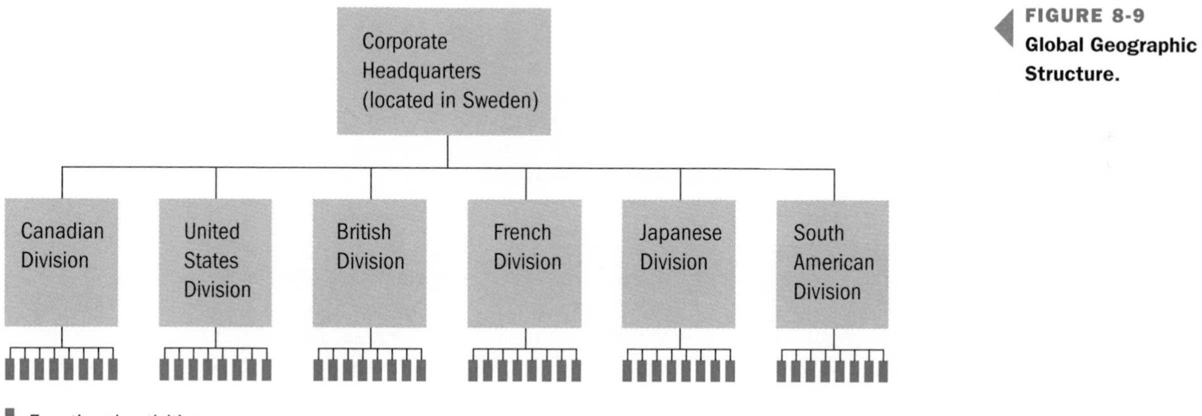

FIGURE 8-9
Global Geographic Structure.

Because the overseas divisions themselves may have little or no contact with those in different regions, few if any integrating mechanisms are needed. Nor does a global organizational culture develop because there are no transfers of skills or resources or transfer of personnel among managers from across the various world regions. Historically, car companies such as DaimlerChrysler, GM, and Ford used global-area structures to manage their overseas operations. Ford of Europe, for example, had little or no contact with its U.S. parent, and capital was the only principal resource exchanged.

One problem with a global geographic structure and a multidomestic strategy is that the duplication of specialist activities across countries raises a company's overall cost structure. Moreover, the company is not taking advantage of opportunities to transfer, share, or leverage its competencies and capabilities on a global basis: For example, it cannot apply the low-cost manufacturing expertise that may have developed in one world region to another. Thus, multidomestic companies lose the many benefits of operating globally.

Implementing International Strategy

A company pursuing an international strategy adopts a different route to global expansion. A company with many different products or businesses has the challenging problem of coordinating the flow of different products across different countries. To manage these transfers, many companies use a global product group structure and create product group headquarters to coordinate the activities of domestic and foreign divisions within each product group. Product managers are responsible for organizing all aspects of value creation on a global level (see Figure 8-10).

This arrangement of tasks and roles reduces the transaction costs involved in managing handoffs across countries and geographic or world regions. However, geographic or regional managers are essentially under the control of managers in the international division and if these domestic and overseas managers compete for control of strategy making, conflict and lack of cooperation may result. Many companies such as IBM, Citibank, and DaimlerChrysler have experienced this problem. Very often, significant strategic control has been decentralized to overseas divisions. When cost pressures force corporate managers to reassess their strategy, and they decide to intervene, this frequently provokes resistance, much of it due to differences in culture—not just corporate culture, but national cultural differences.

FIGURE 8-10
Global Product Group Structure.

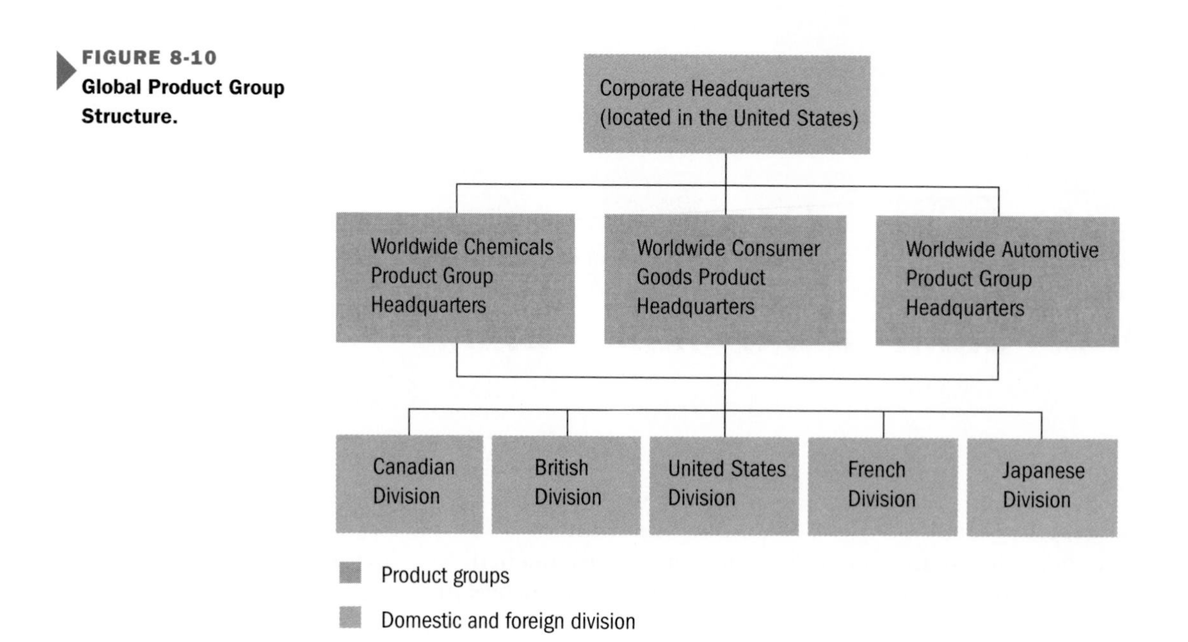

Implementing Global Strategy

When a company embarks on a global strategy today, it usually locates its manufacturing and other value chain activities at the global location that will allow it to increase efficiency and quality. In so doing, it then has to solve the problems of coordinating and integrating its global activities. It ideally has to find a structure that lowers the bureaucratic costs associated with resource transfers between corporate headquarters and its global divisions and yet which provides the centralized control that a global strategy requires. The answer for many companies is also a global product group structure (see Figure 8-10).

Once again, the product groups coordinate the activities of domestic and overseas operations. Then, within each division, headquarters managers decide where to locate the different functions at the optimal global location for performing that activity. For example, Philips has one division responsible for global R&D, manufacturing, marketing and sales of its light bulbs, another for medical equipment, and so on. The headquarters of the medical division and its R&D is located in Bothell, Washington; manufacturing, on the other hand, is done in Taiwan; and the products are sold by sales subsidiaries in each local market.

The product-group structure allows managers to decide how best to pursue a global strategy—for example, to decide which value-chain activities, such as manufacturing or product design, should be performed in which country to increase efficiency. Increasingly, organizations from leading developed economies, such as Canada and Japan, are moving manufacturing to low-cost countries such as China, but they are also establishing product-design centres in Europe or the United States to take advantage of foreign skills and capabilities so as to obtain the maximum benefits from this strategy.

Implementing Transnational Strategy

The main failing of the global product-group structure is that while it allows a company to achieve superior efficiency and quality, it is weak when it comes to responsiveness to customers because the focus is still on centralized control. Moreover, this structure makes it difficult for the different product groups to trade information and knowledge and to obtain the benefits from transferring, sharing, and leveraging their competencies. Sometimes the potential gains from sharing product, marketing, or R&D knowledge between product groups are very high, but so too are the bureaucratic costs associated with achieving these gains. Is there a structure that can simultaneously economize on these costs and provide the coordination necessary to obtain these benefits?

In the 1990s many companies implemented a global matrix structure to simultaneously lower their global cost structures and differentiate their activities through superior innovation and responsiveness to customers globally. See Figure 8-11: On the vertical axis are the company's overseas divisions in the various countries or world regions in which it operates. Managers at the regional or country level control local operations. On the horizontal axis are the company's corporate product groups, which provide specialist services such as R&D, product design, and marketing information to its overseas divisions, which are grouped by world region. These might be the chemicals, consumer goods, and automobile product groups. Through a system of output and behaviour controls they then report to corporate product group personnel back in the home country and ultimately to the CEO or president. The heads of the world regions or country managers are also responsible for working with domestic product group managers to develop the control and reward sys-

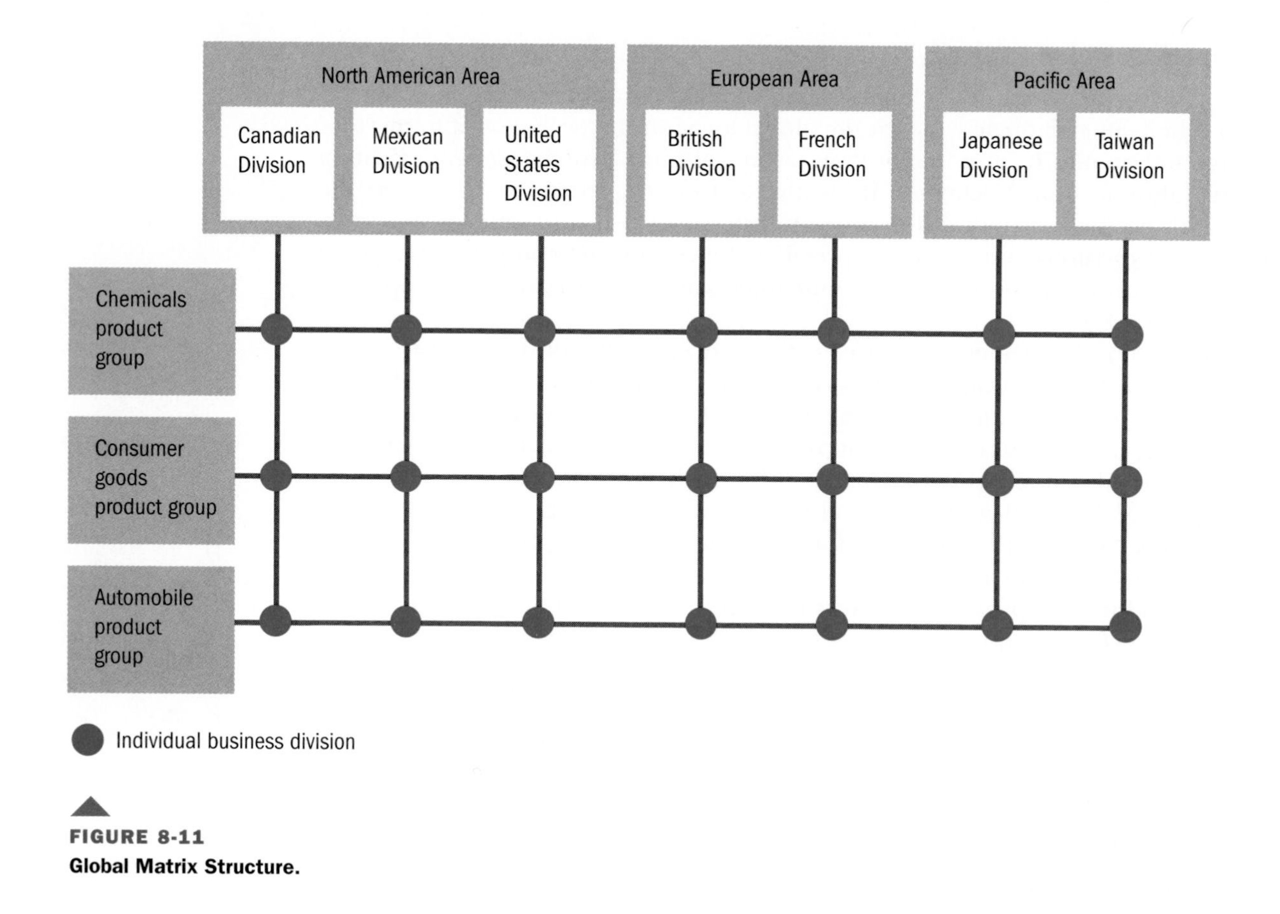

FIGURE 8-11
Global Matrix Structure.

tems that will promote the transfer, sharing, or leveraging of competencies that will result in superior performance.

Implementing a matrix structure thus decentralizes control to overseas managers and provides them with considerable flexibility for managing local issues, but can still give product and corporate managers in the home country the centralized control they need to coordinate company activities on a global level. The matrix structure can allow knowledge and experience to be transferred among geographic regions, among product groups, and among product groups and regions. Since it offers many opportunities for face-to-face contact between managers at home and abroad, the matrix facilitates the transmission of a company's norms and values and, hence, the development of a global corporate culture. This is especially important for a company with far-flung global operations for which lines of communication are longer. Club Med, for instance, uses a matrix to standardize high-quality customer service across its global vacation villages.

SUMMARY

Organizational strategy is a plan of action that an organization undertakes to create value. Organizations that do not constantly set ambitious new goals and try to find effective means of reaching those goals are likely to be threatened by younger, more agile competitors in search of ways to seize resources for themselves. Consequently, organizational members at all levels in the organization—functional, business, corporate, and global—must develop their value-creation skills and abilities. Managers must manage the interrelationship of strategy (at all levels), structure, and culture to maximize the organization's ability to manage, enhance, and protect its domain(s) so that it can create value to satisfy stakeholders. Chapter 8 has made the following main points:

1. The value that an organization creates by means of its strategy is a function of how the organization positions itself in its environment so that it can use its core competencies to compete for resources.
2. An organization's core competencies are products of its functional and organizational resources and its coordination ability.
3. An organization must formulate strategy at four levels: functional, business, corporate, and global.
4. The goal of functional-level strategy is to create in each function a low-cost or differentiation competency that gives the organization a competitive advantage.
5. Functional structure and culture produce functional abilities that support the development of functional resources.
6. The goal of business-level strategy is to combine functional low-cost and differentiation competencies in order to exploit opportunities in the organizational environment. Business-level strategy selects and manages the domain in which an organization uses its value-creation resources and coordination abilities.
7. The two main business-level strategies are low-cost business-level strategy and differentiation business-level strategy.
8. An organization chooses a structure and culture to develop coordination abilities that support its business-level strategy.
9. The goal of corporate-level strategy is to use and develop low-cost and differentiation competencies so that the organization can protect and enlarge its existing domain and expand into new ones.
10. Three main types of corporate-level strategy are vertical integration, related diversification, and unrelated diversification.
11. An appropriate corporate-level structure and culture can help reduce the bureaucratic costs of managing a strategy.
12. The four strategies that companies use to manage global expansion are a multidomestic strategy, an international strategy, a global strategy, and a transnational strategy. Each is associated with a different approach to value creation and a different set of organizational design problems.

DISCUSSION QUESTIONS

1. How should an organization design its structure and culture to obtain a core competency in manufacturing research and development?
2. Pick an organization such as a restaurant or a department store, and analyze how it might pursue a low-cost or a differentiation strategy. How would structural choices support either of these strategies?
3. What is the difference between a low-cost strategy and a differentiation strategy for structure?

How should a differentiated biotechnology organization and a low-cost fast-food organization design their structures and cultures to promote their respective competitive advantages?

4. Compare the competitive advantages enjoyed by a large restaurant chain, and the sources of competitive advantages enjoyed by a small, local restaurant. How closely are these tied to the culture of the organization?
5. Why would an organization choose a corporate-level strategy to expand its value-creation activities beyond its core domain? Discuss how an organization's structure and culture might change as the organization begins to enter new domains.
6. How and why do bureaucratic costs increase as a company goes from a multidomestic to an international to a global to a transnational strategy?

ORGANIZATIONAL THEORY IN ACTION

Practising Organizational Theory: What Kind of Supermarket?

Form groups of three to five people and discuss the following scenario:

You are a group of investors who are contemplating opening a new supermarket in your city. You are trying to decide what business-level strategy would provide your supermarket with a competitive advantage that would allow you to attract customers and outperform your prospective rivals.

1. List the supermarket chains in your city and identify their business-level strategies (e.g., low-cost, differentiation, or focus). Also, list any particular kinds of functional strengths or weaknesses that they might have (such as a great bakery or a terrible fish counter).
2. On the basis of this analysis, what type of business-level strategy do you think will best succeed in the local market? What will the specific elements of this strategy be? (For example: What kind of supermarket will it be? What kind of functional strengths will you try to develop? What kinds of customers will you aim for? What will you do to attract them?)

Making the Connection #8

Find an example of an organization pursuing a business, corporate, or global expansion strategy. What kind of strategy is it pursuing? Why did it choose this strategy? How does the strategy create value? How does the strategy affect the organization's structure or culture?

The Ethical Dimension #8

Bribery and corruption are common in some countries and for people in those countries, they are a normal part of doing business. Canadian law bans any Canadian company from paying bribes to foreign officials, or taking any steps to use illegal means to secure valuable foreign contracts or resources.

1. Why does Canada adopt this ethical and legal stance if people in the country accept bribery as the norm?
2. What could Canadian companies do to help reduce the incidence of bribery in these countries and promote ethical business practices?

Analyzing the Organization: Design Module #8

This module focuses on the kinds of goods and services that your organization produces, the markets that it competes in, and the kinds of strategies that it uses to create value for its stakeholders.

ASSIGNMENT

This assignment asks you to explore how your company creates value through its strategy and structure for managing the environment.

1. Briefly describe your organization's domain—that is, the goods and services that it produces and the customer groups that it serves.
2. What core competencies give the organization a competitive advantage? What are the organization's functional-level strategies?

3. What is your organization's principal business-level strategy: low cost or differentiation? How successfully is the organization pursuing this strategy? In what ways does it need to improve its core competencies to improve its competitive position?
4. In what ways do your organization's structure and culture match its strategy? Is there a good match? In what ways could the match be improved? Is the organization experiencing any problems with its structure?
5. Is your organization operating in more than one domain? If it is, what corporate-level strategies is it pursuing? How is it creating value from these strategies? Is it successful?
6. What kind of strategy is your organization pursuing in the international environment? What kind of structure does your organization use to manage this strategy?

Company Profiles #8*

Choose one or more of the organizations (e.g., companies, government agencies, or nonprofit organizations) that are profiled in this chapter. Do an Internet search to get up-to-date information on each organization you have selected, and answer the following questions.

1. What does the new information tell you about the organization's current ability to develop a successful global strategy?
2. How does the information compare with the earlier information provided in the text and what does that tell you about organizations (e.g., does the organization appear to have a more or less successful global strategy than before, and how do you explain this)?

Alternative Perspectives #8

Critical, feminist, and postmodern theories of organization are challenging many of the assumptions that underlie organizations and the strategies they use to capitalize on the globalization of the world's markets. Read one or more of the following readings and then compare this perspective with that of the largely normative views in the text. In small groups, discuss similarity or difference.

Reading List

Allen, D. and Raynor, M. E. 2004. Preparing for a New Global Business Environment: Divided and Disorderly or Integrated and Harmonious? *The Journal of Business Strategy.* 25(5): 16–25.

Andreotti, A. 2004. Globalisation and Corporation Internalisation: A Critical Viewpoint. *International Journal of Entrepreneurship and Innovation Management.* 4(4): 360–372.

Ciscel, D. H, Smith, B. E., and Mendoza, M. 2003. Ghosts in the Global Machine: New Immigrants and the Redefinition of Work. *Journal of Economic Issues.* 37(2): 333–342.

Clegg, S., Clarke, T. and Ibarra, E. 2001. Millennium Management, Changing Paradigms and Organizational Studies. *Human Relations.* 54(1): 31–36.

Kobrin, S. J. 1998. Neomedievalism and the Postmodern Digital World Economy. *Journal of International Affairs.* 51(2): 361–387.

Munck, R. 2004. Globalization, Labour and the "Polanyi Problem." *Labour History.* 45(3): 251–269.

Ricart, J., Enric, E., Michael, J., Ghemawat, P., Hart, S. L., and Khanna, T. 2004. New Frontiers in International Strategy. *Journal of International Business Studies.* 35(3): 175–212.

Therborn, G. 2000. Globalizations: Dimensions, Historical Waves, Regional Effects, Normative Governance. *International Sociology.* 15(2): 151–179.

*The authors would like to receive information from student groups and instructors on any companies where there have been dramatic changes to the information published in this text. We would be happy to publish the best of these changes in a subsequent edition, where we will focus on changing company profiles.

CASE FOR ANALYSIS

Air Canada Restructures for Survival in a Changed Global Industry[45]

Air Canada, based in Montreal, began operations in 1937 under the name of Trans-Canada Airlines, with $5 million and three airplanes. It grew steadily over the years and in 1964 it was renamed Air Canada and became Canada's national airline. It was later privatized in 1989, and in 2000 Air Canada merged with its main Canadian rival Canadian Airlines. The merger resulted in the organization becoming the tenth largest airline in the world.

Since that time, it has grown to comprise a fleet of over 200 aircraft, which fly to over a 150 different destinations, its services offering vacation packages to almost 100 destinations. At its operational peak it maintained over 600 flights daily, serving over 20 million customers annually, to approximately 100 international destinations globally. As a member of the Star Alliance, Air Canada was networked with other allied air carriers globally, allowing its customers to travel to over 700 international airports in over 100 countries. In addition to its national and international passenger flight operations, Air Canada operates a large cargo service and provides maintenance, airport handling services, and training to other airlines. Air Canada was internationally renowned as a world leader in flight operations, customer service, and safety for over a decade.

However, also over the past decade, Air Canada, like many other major air carriers around the world, has struggled for profitability if not just for simple survival. Globally the airline industry and related businesses have been seriously impacted by the terrorist attacks in September 2001, the outbreak of SARS, and the increasing cost of fuel. All of these pressures have resulted in a significant downturn in both domestic and international air travel, increasing costs for service and production, and reducing revenue generation capability. To compound the already turbulent industry, the Canadian market saw increased price competition from a growing number of new domestic and international discount airlines, as the industry as a whole went into a downturn. Competition from these new and aggressive airlines, such as WestJet, JetsGo, and CanJet, saw Air Canada attempting to hold on to an ever-decreasing share of the domestic market. In 2003, Air Canada had revenue in excess of $8 billion, but it sustained a loss of almost $2 billion. These types of losses continued, with Air Canada accumulating a debt in excess of $12 billion. As a consequence, Air Canada has been under legal protection from its creditors since April 1, 2003.

Air Canada has responded to these challenges by attempting to significantly restructure the organization through cost reduction and organizational streamlining—all while it seeks a major investor to rescue its financially imperilled existence. To date, cost-reduction strategies have been more successful than differentiation and restructure strategies. Air Canada has negotiated with its seven unions to reduce labour costs, and it is actively restructuring supplier contracts and aircraft leases. These actions have reduced operating costs by approximately $2 billion.

Air Canada has undertaken to streamline its entire structure and all of its operations. It is attempting to copy the model of its fastest-growing competitor, WestJet Airlines. WestJet is modelled after Southwest Air, a highly successful American carrier and an industry leader. WestJet focuses on low operating flight costs, extremely low prices offered to customers, and operations focused on high-volume traffic and quick flight operations turnaround, enabling it to use its planes very efficiently (e.g., maximizing flights within the limitations of flight crew rest and airframe maintenance). Air Canada intends to copy these elements of the WestJet model. Additionally, it plans to downsize its main fleet, shifting its smaller, less expensive aircraft to the smaller regional markets in order to lower flight costs and thus offer competitive ticket prices that reflect the actual cost of operations. (In the past, industry analysts have criticized Air Canada for selling flight seats below the actual cost in an effort to artificially prop up its market share.) These actions are intended to reduce the number of unsold and below-cost seats, to become more competitive, and to meet the market concerns with the actual cost of operations. Air Canada also plans to reduce its overall major aircraft fleet to fewer than 200 planes by the end of 2006, again to reduce costs and increase maintenance efficiency and turn-around times. It is also redirecting resources and operational effort to Air Canada Jazz, its subsidiary discount airline, which has proven a financially successful element of the company. Air Canada is also attempting to give its functional units (aircraft maintenance, terminal operations, baggage handling, etc.) greater ability to offer and deliver services to other airlines and other customers.

Air Canada had grown into a leading international airline, but due to changes in the industry, the security environment, and increased competition, it has now found itself in jeopardy. Its restructuring efforts are an ongoing attempt to rescue itself and ensure its survival. It has chosen a very broad approach to both strategy implementation and change in its restructuring efforts. It is trying to take a low-cost leadership approach while trying to differentiate itself through its customer offerings, all while moving to a leaner structure. As with most airlines around the world, Air Canada continues to face challenges to its continued profitability. Recently, chances for Air Canada's success improved as one of its competitors, JetsGo, ceased operations. In early 2005, the overall downturn in the industry in combination with the aggressive moves from other airlines, including Air Canada, forced JetsGo to collapse into bankruptcy. Whether Air Canada or any of its competitors follows remains to be seen, as the airline industry around the globe struggles to survive and change.

DISCUSSION QUESTIONS

1. Consider the strategic orientation of Air Canada's change efforts in light of the challenges it faces. Can Air Canada reposition itself to beat WestJet at its own game? Can Air Canada adopt similar structure and operations and yet still differentiate itself from the competition?
2. In many ways, the Canadian airline industry is a microcosm reflecting the global situation facing most other airlines. Will the strategic efforts used in the domestic market help Air Canada internationally? Why or why not?

REFERENCES

1. A. D. Chandler, *Strategy and Structure: Chapters in the History of the Industrial Enterprise* (Cambridge, MA: MIT Press, 1962).
2. C. W. L. Hill and G. R. Jones, *Strategic Management: An Integrated Approach*, 4th ed. (Boston: Houghton Mifflin, 1998).
3. M. E. Porter, *Competitive Strategy* (New York: The Free Press, 1980).
4. K. Weigelt and C. Camerer, "Reputation and Corporate Strategy." *Strategic Management Journal*, 1988, vol. 9, pp. 443–454.
5. Hill and Jones, *Strategic Management*, Ch. 10.
6. R. R. Nelson and S. Winter, *An Evolutionary Theory of Economic Change* (Cambridge, MA: Harvard University Press, 1982).
7. M. E. Porter, *Competitive Advantage: Creating and Sustaining Superior Performance* (New York: The Free Press, 1985).
8. R. W. Ruekert and O. C. Walker, "Interactions Between Marketing and R&D Departments in Implementing Different Business Strategies," *Strategic Management Journal*, 1987, vol. 8, pp. 233–248.
9. Porter, *Competitive Strategy*.
10. K. N. M. Dundas and P. R. Richardson, "Corporate Strategy and the Concept of Market Failure," *Strategic Management Journal*, 1980, vol. 1, pp. 177–188.
11. Porter, *Competitive Advantage*.
12. S. C. Wheelright, "Manufacturing Strategy: Defining the Missing Link," *Strategic Management Journal*, 1984, vol. 5, pp. 77–91.
13. D. Ulrich, "Linking Strategic Planning and Human Resource Planning," in L. Fahey, ed., *The Strategic Planning Management Reader* (Englewood Cliffs, NJ: Prentice Hall, 1989), pp. 421–426.
14. E. S. Buffa, "Positioning the Production System—A Key Element in Manufacturing Strategy," in Fahey, *The Strategic Planning Management Reader*, pp. 387–395.

15. O. E. Williamson, *Markets and Hierarchies* (New York: The Free Press, 1975).
16. R. M. Johnson, "Market Segmentation: A Strategic Management Tool," *Journal of Marketing Research,* 1971, vol. 8, pp. 15–23.
17. V. Scarpello, W. R. Boulton, and C. W. Hofer, "Reintegrating R&D into Business Strategy," *Journal of Business Strategy,* 1986, vol. 6, pp. 49–56.
18. D. Miller, "Strategy Making and Structure: Analysis and Implications for Performance," *Academy of Management Journal,* 1987, vol. 30, pp. 7–32.
19. P. R. Lawrence and J. W. Lorsch, *Organization and Environment* (Boston: Graduate School of Business Administration, Harvard University, 1967).
20. J. Woodward, *Industrial Organization: Theory and Practice* (London: Oxford University Press, 1965).
21. K. M. Eisenhardt, "Control: Organizational and Economic Approaches," *Management Science,* 1985, vol. 16, pp. 134–138.
22. J. B. Barney, "Organization Culture: Can It Be a Source of Sustained Competitive Advantage?" *Academy of Management Review,* 1986, vol. 11, pp. 791–800.
23. S. M. Oster, *Modern Competitive Analysis* (New York: Oxford University Press, 1990).
24. Porter, *Competitive Strategy,* Ch. 2.
25. Ibid.
26. R. E. White, "Generic Business Strategies, Organizational Context and Performance: An Empirical Investigation," *Strategic Management Journal,* 1986, vol. 7, pp. 217–231; G. R. Jones and J. E. Butler, "Costs, Revenue, and Business-Level Strategy," *Academy of Management Review,* 1988, vol. 13, pp. 202–213.
27. Porter, *Competitive Strategy.*
28. White, "Generic Business Strategies, Organizational Context and Performance"; D. Miller, "Configurations of Strategy and Structure," *Strategic Management Journal,* 1986, vol. 7, pp. 223–249.
29. S. Kotha and D. Orne, "Generic Manufacturing Strategies: A Conceptual Synthesis," *Strategic Management Journal,* 1989, vol. 10, pp. 211–231.
30. P. R. Lawrence and J. W. Lorsch, *Organization and Environment* (Cambridge, MA: Harvard University Press, 1967).
31. D. Miller, "Strategy Making and Structure: Analysis and Implications for Performance," *Academy of Management Journal,* 1987, vol. 30, pp. 7–32.
32. A. Deutschman, "If They're Gaining on You, Innovate," *Fortune,* 2 November 1992, p. 86.
33. T. J. Peters and R. H. Waterman, Jr., *In Search of Excellence* (New York: Harper and Row, 1982).
34. E. Deal and A. A. Kennedy, *Corporate Cultures* (Reading, MA: Addison-Wesley, 1985).
35. Organizational Insight by Scott MacMillan, based upon the following sources: Bombardier, *2004 Annual Report, www.bombardier.com,* 2004; CBC Archives, "Bombardier: The Snowmobile Legacy," *archives.cbc.ca/IDD-1-73-362/politics_economy/bombardier,* 6 June 2004. J. Kirby, "Best Turnarounds," *Canadian Business,* 2004, vol. 77, pp. 62–72; B. Marotte, "Bombardier Recreational Profit Plunges," *Globe and Mail,* 29 May 2004, p. B5; B. Marotte, "Bombardier Shareholders Vent Anger," *Globe and Mail,* 2 June 2004, p. B22; T. Weber, "Tellier Asks for Patience," *Globe and Mail,* 1 June 2004, p. B2.
36. M. E. Porter, "From Competitive Advantage to Competitive Strategy," *Harvard Business Review,* May–June 1987, pp. 43–59.
37. Based on Chandler, *Strategy and Structure.*
38. Chandler, *Strategy and Structure;* J. Pfeffer and G. R. Salancik, *The External Control of Organizations* (New York: Harper and Row, 1978).
39. Williamson, *Markets and Hierarchies;* K. R. Harrigan, *Strategic Flexibility* (Lexington, MA: Lexington Books, 1985).
40. Porter, "From Competitive Advantage to Competitive Strategy."
41. C. W. L. Hill, "Hanson PLC," in C. W. L. Hill and G. R. Jones, *Strategic Management: An Integrated Approach,* 4th ed. (Boston: Houghton Mifflin, 1998), pp. 764–783.
42. G. R. Jones and C. W. L. Hill, "Transaction Cost Analysis of Strategy–Structure Choice," *Strategic Management Journal,* 1988, vol. 9, pp. 159–172.
43. *www.hitachi.com,* 2002.
44. "New In-Flight Adapter Adds to Hitachi's Mobilized Computing Vision and Extends Flexibility and Mobility," *Business Wire,* 20 October 1997.
45. Case by Scott MacMillan, based upon the following sources: Air Canada, *Annual Report 2003, www.aircanada.ca,* 2004; "Air Canada Reaches Tentative Agreement with CAW and Achieves Overall Cost Realignment Target: Deutsche Bank and GECAS Conditions Satisfied," *micro.newswire.ca,* 7 June 2004; CBC News, "Indepth: Air Canada," *www.cbc.ca,* 6 June 2004; CBC News, "Indepth: A History of Air Canada," *archives.cbc.ca,* 6 June 2004; CTV News, "PM Tells Union and Air Canada to Keep Talking," *www.ctv.ca,* 8 June 2004; F. Fiorino, "Rocky Road to Recovery; Air Canada's Restructuring Progresses, But It's Too Early to Declare the Airline out of the Woods," *Aviation Week & Space Technology,* 2004, vol. 160, 55; J. Patridge, "Deadline Looms for Air Canada Equity Bids," *Globe and Mail,* 18 June 2004, p. B4.

Organizational Design, Competencies, and Technology

CHAPTER 9

Learning Objectives

This chapter focuses on technology and examines how organizations use it to build competencies and create value. Then, it discusses why certain kinds of organizational structures are likely to be used with certain kinds of technology (just as earlier chapters used a similar contingency approach to examine why certain environments or strategies typically require the use of certain kinds of structure).

After studying this chapter you should be able to:

1. Identify what technology is and how it relates to organizational effectiveness.
2. Differentiate between three different kinds of technology that create different competencies.
3. Understand how each type of technology needs to be matched to a certain kind of organizational structure if an organization is to be effective.
4. Understand how technology affects organizational culture.
5. Appreciate how advances in technology, and new techniques for managing technology, are helping to increase organizational effectiveness.

WHAT IS TECHNOLOGY?

When we think of an organization, we are likely to think of it in terms of what it does. We think of manufacturing organizations like Whirlpool or Ford as places where people use their skills in combination with machinery and equipment to assemble inputs into appliances, cars, and other finished products. We view service organizations like hospitals and banks as places where people apply their skills, a form of intangible raw material, in combination with machinery or equipment to make sick people well or to facilitate customers' financial transactions. In all manufacturing and service organizations, actions are taken to create value—that is, inputs are converted into goods and services that satisfy people's needs.

Technology
The combination of skills, knowledge, abilities, techniques, materials, machines, computers, tools, and other equipment that people use to convert or change raw materials, both tangible and intangible, into valuable goods and services.

Mass production
The organizational technology that uses a system of progressive assembly processes to manufacture standardized goods in mass quantities.

Craftswork
The technology that involves groups of skilled workers who interact closely to produce usually limited numbers of custom-designed products.

Technology is the combination of skills, knowledge, abilities, techniques, materials, machines, computers, tools, and other equipment that people use to convert or change raw materials, both tangible and intangible, into valuable goods and services. When people at the GM plant, staff at the Toronto Hospital for Sick Children, and tax consultants at H&R Block use their skills, knowledge, materials, machines, and so forth to produce a finished car, a cured patient, or a completed tax return, they are using different technologies to bring about change to something—to add value to it.

Inside an organization, technology exists at three levels: individual, functional or departmental, and organizational. At the *individual* level, technology is the personal skills, knowledge, and competencies that individual women and men possess. At the *functional* or *departmental* level, the procedures and techniques that groups use to perform their work create competencies that constitute technology. The interactions of the members of a surgical operating team, the cooperative efforts of scientists in a research and development laboratory, and techniques developed by assembly-line workers are all examples of competencies and technology at the functional or departmental level.

The way an organization converts inputs into outputs is often used to characterize technology at the *organizational* level. **Mass production** is the organizational technology based on competencies in using a standardized, progressive assembly process to manufacture goods. **Craftswork** is the technology that involves groups of skilled workers, interacting closely and blending their competencies to produce custom-designed products. The difference between these two forms of technology is clearly illustrated by the way Henry Ford revolutionized car production. (See Organizational Insight 9.1.)

ORGANIZATIONAL INSIGHT 9.1

Progressive Manufacture at Ford

In 1913, Henry Ford opened the Highland Park plant to produce the Model T car. In doing so, he changed forever the way complex products like cars are made, and the new technology of "progressive manufacture" (Ford's term), or mass production, was born. Before Ford introduced mass production, most cars were manufactured by craftswork. A team of workers—a skilled mechanic and a few helpers—performed all the operations necessary to make the product. Individual craftsworkers in the automobile and other industries have the skills to deal with unexpected situations as they arise during the manufacturing process. They can modify misaligned parts so that they fit together snugly, and they can follow specifications and create small batches of a range of products. Because craftswork relies on workers' skills and expertise, it is a costly and slow method of manufacturing. In searching for new ways to improve the efficiency of manufacturing, Ford developed the process of progressive manufacture.

Ford outlined three principles of progressive manufacture:

1. Work should be delivered to the worker; the worker should not have to find the work.[1] At the Highland Park plant, a mechanized, moving conveyor belt brought cars to the workers.

Workers did not move past a stationary line of cars under assembly.

2. Work should proceed in an orderly and specific sequence so that each task builds on the task that precedes it. At Highland Park, the implementation of this idea fell to managers, who worked out the most efficient sequence of tasks and coordinated them with the speed of the conveyor belt.
3. Individual tasks should be broken down into their simplest components in order to increase specialization and create an efficient division of labour. The assembly of a taillight, for example, might be broken into two separate tasks to be performed all day long by two different workers. One person puts light bulbs into a reflective panel; the other person screws a red lens onto the reflective panel.

By following those three principles, Ford made the conversion of inputs (component parts) into outputs (finished cars) much more controllable and predictable than it had been with craftswork. The speed of the conveyor belt relieved supervisors of the need to monitor and direct each employee. In the new work system, a supervisor's job was to evaluate performance and discipline workers for poor performance. Ford's three principles reduced the level of skill and competence needed by production workers: A new worker needed only two days to learn the skills necessary to perform a typical assembly-line job.

As a result of this new work system, by 1914 Ford plants employed 15 000 workers, but only 255 supervisors (not including top management) to oversee them. The ratio of workers to supervisors was 58 to 1. This very wide span of control was possible because the sequence and pacing of the work were not directed by the supervisors but were controlled by work programming and the speed of the production line.[2] The mass-production system helped Ford control many workers with a relatively small number of supervisors, but it also created a tall hierarchy. The hierarchy at a typical Ford plant had six levels, reflecting the fact that management's major preoccupation was the vertical communication of information to top management, which controlled decision making for the whole plant.

The introduction of mass-production technology to auto making was only one of Henry Ford's technological manufacturing innovations. Another was the use of interchangeable parts. When parts are interchangeable, the components from various suppliers fit together; they do not need to be altered to fit during the assembly process. With the old craftswork method of production, a high level of worker competence was needed to fit together the components provided by different manufacturers, which often differed in size or quality. Ford insisted that component manufacturers follow detailed specifications so that parts needed no remachining, and his relatively unskilled workforce would be able to assemble them easily. Eventually, the desire to control the quality of inputs led Ford to embark on a massive program of vertical integration. Ford mined iron ore in its mines in Upper Michigan and transported the ore in a fleet of Ford-owned barges to Ford's steel plants in Detroit, where it was smelted, rolled, and stamped into standard body parts.

As a result of these technological innovations in manufacturing, by the early 1920s Henry Ford's organization was making over 2 million cars a year. Because of his efficient manufacturing methods, Ford reduced the price of a car by two-thirds. This low-price advantage, in turn, created a mass market for his product.[3] Clearly, as measured by standards of technical efficiency and the ability to satisfy external stakeholders such as customers, Ford Motor Company was a very effective organization. Inside the factories, however, the picture was not so rosy.

Workers hated their work. Ford managers responded to their discontent with repressive supervision. Workers were watched constantly. They were not allowed to talk on the production line, and their behaviour both in the plant and outside was closely monitored (e.g., they were not allowed to drink alcohol, even when they were not working). Supervisors could instantly fire workers who disobeyed any rules. So repressive were conditions that by 1914 so many workers had been fired or had quit that 500 new workers had to be hired each day to keep the workforce at 15 000.[4] Clearly, the new technology of mass production was imposing severe demands on individual workers.

TECHNOLOGY AND ORGANIZATIONAL EFFECTIVENESS

Recall from Chapter 1 that organizations take inputs from the environment and create value from the inputs by transforming them into outputs through conversion processes (see Figure 9-1). Although we usually think of technology only at the conversion stage, technology is present in all organizational activities: input, conversion, and output.[5]

At the *input* stage, technology—skills, procedures, techniques, and competencies—allows each organizational function to handle relationships with outside stakeholders so that the organization can effectively manage its specific environment. The human resource function, for example, has techniques such as interviewing procedures and psychological testing that it uses to recruit and select qualified employees. The materials management function has developed competencies in dealing with input suppliers, for negotiating favourable contract terms, and for obtaining low-cost, high-quality component parts. The finance department has techniques for obtaining capital at a cost favourable to the company.

At the *conversion* stage, technology—a combination of machines, techniques, and work procedures—transforms inputs into outputs. The best technology allows an organization to add the most value to its inputs at the least cost of organizational resources. Organizations often try to improve the efficiency of their conversion processes, and they can improve it by training employees in new time-management techniques and by allowing employees to devise better ways of performing their jobs.

At the *output* stage, technology allows an organization to effectively dispose of finished goods and services to external stakeholders. To be effective, an organization must possess competencies in testing the quality of the finished product, in selling and marketing the product, and in managing after-sales service to customers.

The technology of an organization's input, conversion, and output processes is an important source of a company's competitive advantage. Why is Microsoft the most successful software company? Why is Toyota the most efficient car manufacturer? Why is McDonald's the most efficient fast-food company? Why does Wal-Mart consistently outperform Zellers and Sears? Each of these organizations excels in the development, management, and use of technology to create competencies that lead to higher value for stakeholders.

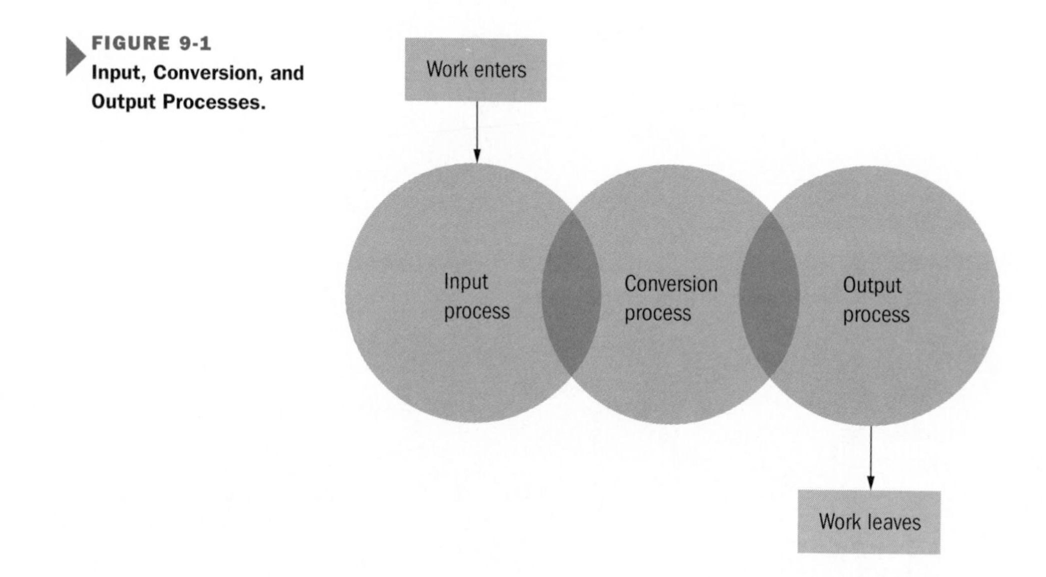

FIGURE 9-1
Input, Conversion, and Output Processes.

Recall from Chapter 1 the three principal approaches to measuring and increasing organizational effectiveness (see Table 1-1, p. 19). An organization taking the *external resource approach* uses technology to increase its ability to manage and control external stakeholders. Any new technological developments that allow an organization to improve its service to customers, such as the ability to customize products or to increase products' quality and reliability, increases the organization's effectiveness.

An organization taking the *internal systems approach* uses technology to increase the success of its attempts to innovate, to develop new products, services, and processes, and to reduce the time needed to bring new products to market. As we saw earlier, the introduction of mass production at the Highland Park plant allowed Henry Ford to make a new kind of product—a car for the mass market.

An organization taking the *technical approach* uses technology to improve efficiency and reduce costs while simultaneously enhancing the quality and reliability of its products. Ford increased his organization's effectiveness by organizing its functional resources to create better-quality cars at lower costs to both manufacturer and consumer.

Organizations use technology to become more efficient, more innovative, and better able to meet the needs and desires of stakeholders. Each department or function in an organization is responsible for building competencies and developing technology that allow it to make a positive contribution to organizational performance. When an organization has technology that enables it to create value, it needs a structure that maximizes the effectiveness of the technology. Just as environmental characteristics require organizations to make certain organizational design choices, so do the characteristics of different technologies affect an organization's choice of structure. EllisDon Construction of London, Ontario, is an organization that has not only used various technologies to competitive advantage, but has now reached the point where the very technologies that it has used to its advantage are causing the company to transform itself. (See Organizational Insight 9.2.)

In the next three sections we examine three theories of technology that are attempts to capture the way different departmental and organizational technologies work and affect organizational design. Note that these three theories are *complementary* in that each illuminates some aspects of technology that the others don't. All three theories are needed to understand the characteristics of different kinds of technologies. Managers and employees, at all levels and in all functions, can use these theories to (1) choose the technology that will most effectively transform inputs into outputs and (2) design a structure that allows the organization to operate the technology effectively. Thus it is important for both employees and managers to understand the concept of technical complexity, the underlying differences between routine and complex tasks, and the concept of task interdependence.

TECHNICAL COMPLEXITY: THE THEORY OF JOAN WOODWARD

Programmed technology
A technology in which the procedures for converting inputs into outputs can be specified in advance so that tasks can be standardized and the work process can be made more predictable.

Some kinds of technology are more complex and difficult to control than others because some are more difficult to program than others. Technology is said to be **programmed** when procedures for converting inputs into outputs can be specified in advance so that tasks can be standardized and the work process be made predictable. McDonald's uses a highly programmed technology to produce hamburgers, and automakers use a highly programmed technology to produce cars. They do so to control the quality of their outputs—hamburgers or cars. The more difficult it is to specify

ORGANIZATIONAL INSIGHT 9.2

Evolving with Technology at EllisDon Construction[6]

EllisDon Construction has been in business for over 50 years. Two brothers started the construction company, and their first job was to build a minor addition to a house. At that time, the company operated out of a small office in London, Ontario, and the families of the brothers helped out with the company administration and bookkeeping. From this somewhat humble beginning the company expanded quickly and soon was involved in larger projects, including the construction of schools and hospitals, first in Ontario, and later in other parts of Canada.

Since the 1980s, EllisDon has taken on other large and diverse international projects. The company was involved in the construction of the Olympic Village in Atlanta, the Canary Wharf Development in London, England, a $150 million institute in Malaysia, and the Basketball and Athlete's Medical Clinic for the Athens Olympics. The company has also completed other projects around the world, including in Latvia, Lithuania, Mexico, and the Caribbean. In 1988, EllisDon completed the $500 million Cami Automotive Plant, the largest of its kind in North America, which was completed under a design and build, with a guaranteed price contract. The company's remarkable success and reputable market positioning has had a lot to do with its ability to guarantee prices, completion dates, and quality performance as a designer/builder. At the heart of this performance has been the company's ability to use technology more effectively and efficiently than its competitors.

The technologically induced changes to EllisDon's operations and structure began in 1968 when EllisDon became the first Canadian construction company to fully computerize its accounting and cost-control systems. This early use of information technology to gain a competitive advantage was a milestone event for the company, and the company structure would continually evolve with the technology it used. At first the technology simply permitted efficiencies in operations, by accelerating the pace of communications within the firm and increasing the efficiency of the administration of its workflow. As the firm it increased its technological competence, the firm was able to compete more aggressively in the market. As EllisDon grew and took on larger and more complex projects, it also increasingly came to rely on the technology capability of its systems for communication, coordination, administration, and management. Eventually, EllisDon adapted its structure to take full advantage of the benefits of technology within its market.

In 2000, EllisDon and Bell Canada announced the launch of Bell e-Construction Site, an innovative Web-based solution for design and construction project management. EllisDon's major competency is now its ability to accurately forecast costs and other performance variables, which allows the company to guarantee the prices of its services through its innovative technological platform. At the heart of this service is EdgeBuilder, EllisDon's state-of-the-art project management system used to manage all aspects of any construction project. The system enables project staff, developers, architects, consultants, and subcontractors to work collaboratively via the Internet. It is a comprehensive working medium for documentation, knowledge and workflow management, administration, and cost control.

With EdgeBuilder as the leading project management software in the construction industry, EllisDon Construction received the highest award in the Canadian Information Productivity Awards (CIPA) for 2003. The recognition for the innovative design and application of the EdgeBuilder represents more than just the success and prosperity. The development and advancement of this technology also signifies how EllisDon is changing the way it does business. The company is no longer just a construction business; it's becoming just as much about research and development, construction engineering, information technology, and client services as it is about constructing buildings. The use and evolution of the technology adopted and designed by EllisDon has completely transformed its structure and operations.

the process for converting inputs into outputs, the more difficult it is to control the production process and make it more predictable.

According to one researcher, Joan Woodward, the **technical complexity** of a production process—that is, the extent to which it can be programmed so that it can be controlled and made predictable—is the important dimension that differentiates technologies.[7] *High technical complexity* exists when conversion processes can be programmed in advance and fully automated. With full automation, work activities and the outputs that result from them are standardized and can be predicted more accurately. *Low technical complexity* exists when conversion processes depend primarily on people and their skills and knowledge and not on machines. With increased human involvement and less reliance on machines, work activities cannot be as programmed in advance, and most results depend on the skills of the people involved.

Technical complexity
A measure of the extent to which a production process can be programmed so that it can be controlled and made more predictable.

The production of services, for example, typically relies much more on the knowledge and experience of employees who interact directly with customers to produce the final output than it relies on machines and other equipment. The labour-intensive nature of the production of services makes standardizing and programming service activities and controlling their work process especially difficult. When conversion processes depend primarily on the performance of people, rather than on machines, technical complexity is low, and the difficulty of maintaining high quality and consistency of production is greater.

Joan Woodward identified ten levels of technical complexity, which she associated with three types of production technology: (1) small-batch and unit technology, (2) large-batch and mass-production technology, and (3) continuous-process technology (see Figure 9-2).[8]

Small-Batch and Unit Technology

Organizations that employ small-batch and unit technology make one-of-a-kind, customized products or small quantities (batches) of products. Examples of such organizations include a furniture maker that constructs furniture designed to suit the tastes of only a few individuals; or a printer that supplies custom engraved wedding invitations for specific couples; and teams of surgeons and hospitals, which provide a great variety of services that are customized to the needs of individual patients. Small-batch and unit technology scores lowest on the dimension of technical complexity (see Figure 9-2) because any machines used during the conversion process are less important than skills and knowledge of the persons using them. People decide how and when machines will be used, and the production process reflects their decisions about when and how to apply their knowledge. A custom furniture maker, for example, uses an array of tools—including lathes, hammers, planes, and saws—to transform boards into a cabinet. However, which tools are used and the order in which they are used depends on how the furniture maker chooses to build the cabinet. With small-batch and unit technology, the conversion process is flexible because the worker adapts techniques to suit the orders of individual customers.

The flexibility of small-batch technology gives an organization the capacity to produce a wide range of products that can be customized for individual customers. For example, high-fashion designers and makers of products like fine perfume, custom-built cars, and specialized furniture use small-batch technology. Small-batch technology allows a custom furniture maker, for example, to satisfy the customer's request for a certain style of table made from a certain kind of wood.

Small-batch technology is relatively expensive to operate because the work process is unpredictable and the production of customized, made-to-order products makes advance programming of work activities difficult. Additionally, because the

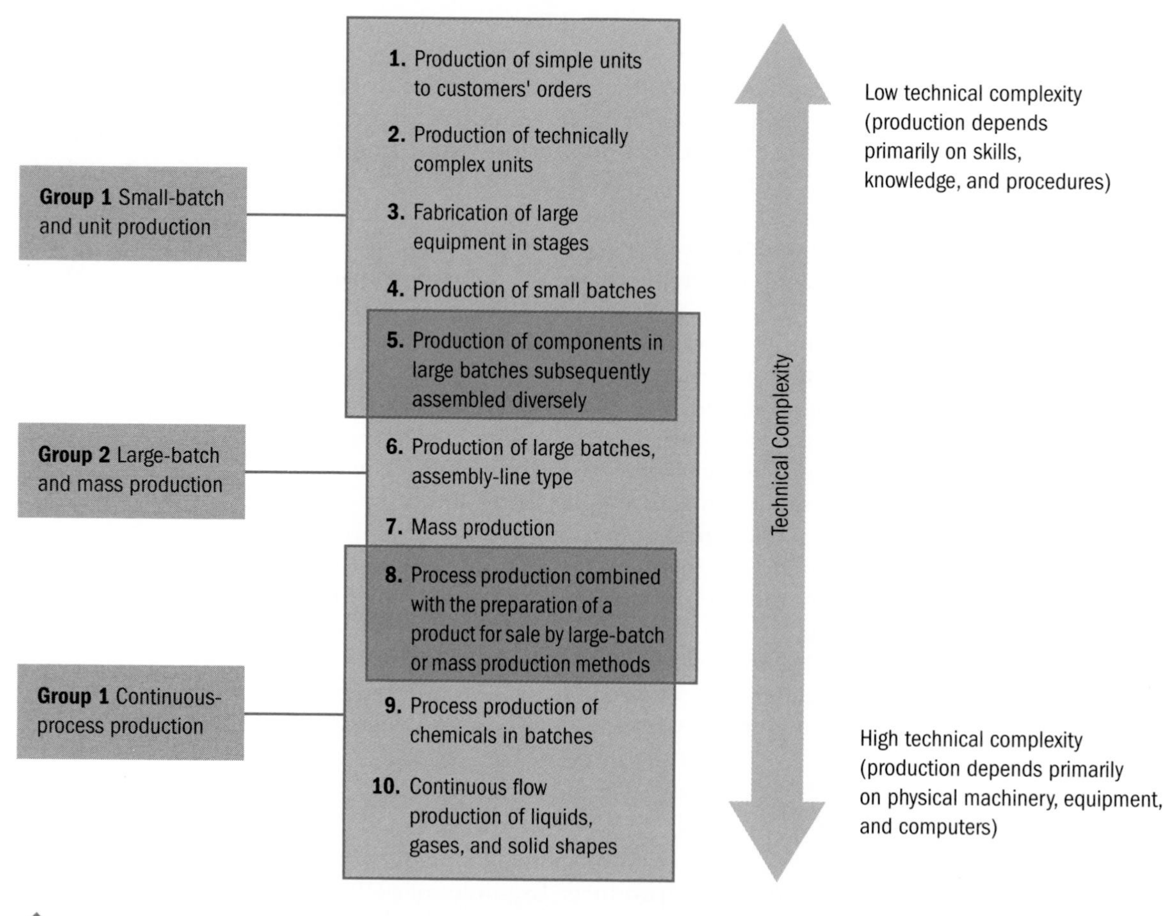

FIGURE 9-2

Technical Complexity and Three Types of Technology.

Joan Woodward identified ten levels of technical complexity, which she associated with three types of production.

Source: Adapted from Joan Woodward, "*Management and Technology,*" London: Her Majesty's Stationery Office, 1958, p. 11. Reproduced with permission of the Controller of Her Britannic Majesty's Stationery Office.

tools are really an extension of the skills and knowledge of the persons using them, the processes are usually labour intensive, which adds to the cost of production. However, flexibility and the ability to respond to a wide range of customer needs make this technology ideally suited to producing new or complex products. For example, Microsoft uses small-batch technology when it assigns a team of programmers to work together to develop new software applications.

Large-Batch and Mass-Production Technology

To increase control over the work process and make it more predictable, organizations try to increase their use of machines and equipment—that is, they try to increase the level of technical complexity with a view to increasing their efficiency. Organizations that employ large-batch or mass-production technology produce large volumes of standardized products such as cars, razor blades, aluminum cans, and soft drinks. Examples of such organizations include Ford, Gillette, Alcan, and Coca-Cola. With large-batch and mass-production technology, machines themselves usually control the work process. Their use allows tasks to be specified and programmed in advance. As a result, work activities are standardized, and the production process is highly controllable.[9] Instead of a team of craftsworkers making custom furniture piece by piece, for example, high-speed saws and lathes cut and shape boards into standardized components that are assembled into thousands of identical tables or chairs by workers on a production line. Since the machines themselves control most of the process, the skills and knowledge needed by those working with mass-production technology is usually less than those working in a small-batch environment.

The control provided by large-batch and mass-production technology allows an organization to save money on production and charge a lower price for its products. As we saw in Organizational Insight 9.1 (p. 292), Henry Ford changed manufacturing history when he replaced small-batch production (the assembly of cars one by one by skilled craftsmen) with mass production to manufacture the Model T. The use of a conveyor belt, standardized and interchangeable parts, and specialized, progressive tasks made conversion processes at the Highland Park plant more efficient and productive. Production costs plummeted, and Ford was able to lower the cost of a Model T and create a mass market for his product.

Continuous-Process Technology

With continuous-process technology, technical complexity reaches its height (see Figure 9-2, p. 298). Organizations that employ continuous-process technology include companies that make oil-based products and chemicals, such as Husky Energy, Petro-Canada and Du Pont, and brewing companies such as Molson and Big Rock Brewing Company. In continuous-process production, the conversion process is almost entirely automated and mechanized; employees generally are not directly involved. Their role in this form of production is to monitor the plant and its machinery and ensure its efficient operation.[10] The task of employees engaged in continuous-process production is primarily to manage exceptions in these work processes, such as a machine breakdown or other malfunctioning equipment.

The hallmark of continuous-process technology is the continuity and smoothness of its operation. Production continues with little variation in output rates and it rarely stops. In an oil refinery, for example, crude oil brought continuously to the refinery by tankers flows through pipes to cracking towers, where its individual component chemicals are extracted and sent to other parts of the refinery for further refinement. Final products such as gasoline, fuel oil, benzene, and tar leave the plant in outgoing tankers to be shipped to customers. Workers in a refinery or in a chemical plant rarely see what they are producing. Production takes place through pipes and machines. Employees in a centralized control room usually simply monitor gauges and dials to ensure that the process functions smoothly, safely, and efficiently.

Continuous-process production tends to be more technically efficient than mass production because it is more extensively mechanized and automated and thus is more predictable and easier to control. It is more cost efficient than both unit and mass production because labour expenses are such a small proportion of overall cost. When operated at full capacity, continuous-process technology has the lowest production costs of any form of technology.

Woodward noted that an organization usually seeks to increase its use of machines (if it is practical to do so) and move from small-batch to mass-production to continuous-process production in order to reduce costs associated with production. There are, however, exceptions to this progression. For many organizational activities, the move to automate production is not possible or practical. Prototype development activities for new products, basic research into new drugs, or technology such as computer chips, and the service operations of hospitals and schools, for example, are intrinsically unpredictable and thus would be difficult to program in advance with an automated machine. A pharmaceutical company cannot say, "Our research department will invent three new drugs—one for diabetes and two for high blood pressure—every six months." Such inventions depend on the skills and knowledge of the researchers and are usually the result of experimentation and trial and error. Moreover, many customers are willing to pay high prices for custom-designed products that suit their individual tastes, such as custom-made suits, jewellery, or even cars. Thus there is a market for the products of small-batch companies even though the production costs associated with this technology form are often quite high.

Technical Complexity and Organizational Structure

One of Woodward's goals in classifying technologies according to their technical complexity was to discover whether an organization's technology affected the design of its structure. Specifically, Woodward wanted to see whether effective organizations had structures that matched the needs of their technologies. When she compared the structural characteristics of organizations pursuing each of the three types of technology, she found systematic differences in the technology–structure relationship. Figure 9-3 shows some of her findings together with a simplified model of the organizational structure associated with each type of technology.

On the basis of her findings, Woodward argued that each technology is associated with a different structure because each technology presents different control and coordination problems. Organizations with small-batch technology typically have three levels in their hierarchy; organizations with mass-production technology, four levels; and organizations with continuous-process technology, six levels. As technical complexity increases, organizations become taller, and the span of control of the CEO widens. The span of control of first-line supervisors first expands and then narrows. It is relatively small with small-batch technology, widens greatly with mass-production technology, and contracts dramatically with continuous-process technology. These findings result in the very differently shaped structures shown at the bottom of Figure 9-3. Why does the nature of an organization's technology produce these results?

The main coordination problem associated with *small-batch technology* is the great challenge of programming conversion activities in advance because production depends on the skills and experience of people working together. An organization that uses small-batch technology has to give people the freedom to make their own decisions so that they can respond quickly and flexibly to the customer's requests and produce the exact product the customer wants. For this reason, such an organization has a relatively flat structure (three levels in the hierarchy), and decision making is decentralized to small teams where first-line supervisors have a relatively small span of control (23 employees). With small-batch technology, each supervisor and work group decides how to manage each decision as it occurs at each step of the input-conversion-output process. This type of decision making requires mutual adjustment — face-to-face communication with co-workers and quite often with the customers themselves. The most appropriate structure for unit and small-batch technology is a more organic structure in which managers and employees work closely to coordinate their activities to meet changing work demands—hence the relatively flat structure shown in Figure 9-3.[11]

In an organization that uses *mass-production technology*, the ability to program tasks in advance allows the organization to standardize the manufacturing process and make it much more predictable. The first-line supervisor's span of control increases to

Structural Characteristics	Small-Batch Technology	Mass Production Technology	Continuous-Process Technology
	Low	Technical Complexity	High
Level in the hierarchy	3	4	6
Span of control of CEO	4	7	10
Span of control of first-line supervisor	23	48	15
Ratio of managers to nonmanagers	1 to 23	1 to 16	1 to 8
Approximate shape of organization	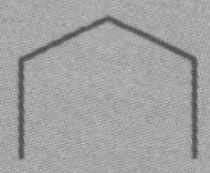 *Relatively flat, with narrow span of control*	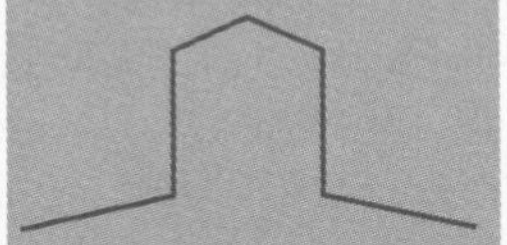 *Relatively tall, with wide span of control*	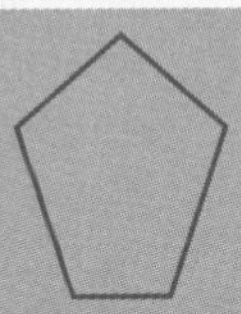 *Very tall, with very narrow span of control*
Type of structure	Organic	Mechanistic	Organic
Cost of operation	High	Medium	Low

FIGURE 9-3

Technical Complexity and Organizational Structure.

Woodward's research indicated that each technology presents different control and coordination problems and is, thus, associated with a different organizational structure.

Source: Adapted from J. Woodward, "*Industrial Organization: Theory and Practice,*" London: Oxford University Press, 1965. Reprinted by permission of Oxford University Press.

48 because formalization through rules and procedures becomes the principal method of coordination. Decision making becomes centralized, and the hierarchy of authority becomes taller (four levels) as managers rely on vertical communication to control the work process. A more *mechanistic design* becomes the appropriate structure to control work activities in a mass-production setting, and the organizational structure becomes taller and wider, as shown in Figure 9-3.

In an organization that uses *continuous-process technology,* tasks can be programmed far in advance, and the work process is highly predictable and controllable in a technical sense, but there is still the potential for a major systems breakdown. The principal control problem facing the organization is monitoring the production process to control and correct unforeseen events before they can lead to disaster. The consequences of a faulty pipeline in an oil refinery or chemical plant, for example, are potentially disastrous. Accidents at a nuclear power plant, another user of continuous-process technology, can also have catastrophic effects, as shown by accidents at Chernobyl and Three Mile Island. In each of these cases, technology-based safeguards failed, the reactor core was damaged, and harmful radiation from nuclear material was released into the environment.

The need to constantly monitor the operating system, and to make sure that each employee conforms to the accepted operating procedures, is the reason why continuous-process technology is associated with the tallest hierarchy of authority (six levels). Managers at all levels must closely monitor their subordinates' actions. The diamond-shaped hierarchy shown in Figure 9-3 reflects the fact that first-line supervisors have a narrow span of control. Many supervisors are needed to supervise lower-level employees and to monitor and control sophisticated equipment. Because employees also work together as a team and jointly work out procedures for managing and reacting to unexpected situations, mutual adjustment becomes the primary means of coordination. Thus a more *organic structure* is the appropriate structure for managing continuous-process technology, because the potential for unpredictable events requires the capability to provide quick, flexible responses.

One researcher, Charles Perrow, argues that complex continuous-process technology such as the technology used in nuclear power plants is so complicated that it is uncontrollable.[12] Perrow acknowledges that control systems are designed with backup systems to handle problems as they arise and that backup systems exist to compensate for failed backup systems. He believes nevertheless that the number of unexpected events that can occur when technical complexity is very high (as it is in nuclear power plants) is so great that managers cannot react quickly enough to solve all the problems that might arise. Perrow argues that some continuous-process technology is so complex that no organizational structure can allow managers to safely operate it, no standard operating procedures can be devised to manage problems in advance, and no use of mutual adjustments will be able to solve problems as they arise. One implication of Perrow's view is that nuclear power stations should be closed because they are too complex to operate safely. Other researchers, however, disagree, arguing that when the right balance of centralized and decentralized control is achieved, even highly complex technology can be operated safely.

The Technological Imperative

Woodward's results, which have been replicated by several researchers, strongly suggest that technology is a main factor in determining the design of organizational structures.[13] Her results imply that if a company operates with a certain type of technology, then it needs to adopt a certain kind of structure to be effective. If a company uses mass-production technology, for example, then it should have a mechanistic structure with six levels in the hierarchy, a span of control of one to 48, and so forth, to be effective. The argument that technology determines structure is known as the **technological imperative**.

Technological imperative
The argument that technology determines structure.

Other researchers also interested in the technology–structure relationship became concerned that Woodward's results may have been a consequence of the sample of companies she studied and that this limitation may have overstated the importance of technology in her results.[14] They pointed out that most of the companies that Woodward studied were relatively small (82 percent had fewer than 500 employees) and suggested that her sample may have biased her results. They acknowledged that technology may have a major impact on structure in a small manufacturing company, because improving the efficiency of manufacturing may be management's major priority. But they suggested that the structure of an organization that has 5000 or 500 000 employees (such as Irving, GM, or IBM) is less likely to be determined primarily by the technology used to manufacture its various products.

In a series of studies known as the Aston Studies, researchers agreed that technology has some effect on organizational structure: The more an organization's technology is mechanized and automated, the more likely the organization is to have a highly centralized and standardized mechanistic structure. But, the Aston Studies concluded, organizational size is more important than technology in determining an organization's choice of structure.[15] We have seen in earlier chapters that as an organization grows and differentiates, control and coordination problems emerge that must be addressed by changes in the organization's structure. The Aston researchers argued that although technology may strongly affect the structure of small organizations, the structure adopted by large organizations may be a product of other factors that cause an organization to grow and differentiate.

We saw in Chapter 8 that organizational strategy and the decision to produce a wider range of products and enter new markets can cause an organization to grow and adopt a more complex structure. Thus the strategic choices that an organization—especially a large organization—makes about what outputs to produce for which markets are at least as important to the design of the organization's structure as the technology the organization uses to produce those outputs. For small organizations or for the functions or departments within large organizations, the importance of technology as a predictor of structure may be more important than it is for large organizations themselves.[16]

ROUTINE TASKS AND COMPLEX TASKS: THE THEORY OF CHARLES PERROW

To understand why some technologies are more complex (more unpredictable and difficult to control) than others, it is necessary to understand why the tasks associated with some technologies are more complex than the tasks associated with other technologies. What causes one task to be more difficult than another? Why, for example, do we normally think that the task of serving hamburgers in a fast-food restaurant is more routine—that is, more predictable and controllable—than the task of programming a computer or performing brain surgery? If we think of the range of tasks that people perform, what characteristics of these tasks cause us to believe that some are more complex than others? According to Charles Perrow, two dimensions underlie the difference between routine and nonroutine or complex tasks and technologies: task variability and task analyzability.[17]

Task Variability and Task Analyzability

Task variability is the number of exceptions—new or unexpected situations—that a person encounters while performing a given task. Exceptions may occur at the input, conversion, or output stages. Task variability is high when a person can expect to encounter many new situations or problems when performing his or her task. In a hospital operating room during the course of surgery, for example, there is much opportunity for unexpected problems to develop. The patient's condition may be more serious than the doctors thought it was, or the surgeon may make a mistake. No matter what happens, the surgeon and the operating team must have the capacity to adjust quickly to new situations as they occur. Similarly, great variability in the quality of the

Task variability
The number of exceptions—new or unexpected situations—that a person encounters while performing a task.

raw materials makes it especially difficult to manage and maintain consistent quality during the conversion stage. The surgeons, for example, may discover an additional unexpected complication during surgery, which requires an additional procedure, perhaps involving a different specialist surgeon or staff.

Task variability is low when a task is highly standardized or repetitious so that a worker encounters the same situation time and time again.[18] In a fast-food restaurant, for example, the number of exceptions to a given task is limited. Each customer places a different order, but all customers must choose from the same limited menu, so employees rarely confront unexpected situations. In fact, the menu in a fast-food restaurant is specifically designed for low task variability, to maximize standardization, which keeps costs down and efficiency up.

Task analyzability The degree to which search activity is needed to solve a problem.

Task analyzability is the degree to which search activity is needed to solve a problem. The more analyzable a task is the more routine it is because the procedures for completing it have been worked out or programmed in advance. For example, although a customer may select thousands of combinations of food from a menu at a fast-food restaurant, the order taker's task of fulfilling each customer's order is relatively easy. The problem of combining the customer's order in a take-out bag is easily analyzable: The order taker picks up the drink and puts it in the bag, then adds the fries, burger, and so on, folds down the top of the bag, and hands the bag to the customer. Little analysis or judgment is needed to complete an order.

Tasks are hard to analyze when they cannot be programmed—that is, when procedures for carrying them out and dealing with exceptions cannot be worked out in advance. If a person encounters an exception, procedures for dealing with it must be sought. For example, a scientist trying to develop a new cancer-preventing drug that has no side effects, or a software programmer working on a program to enable computers to understand the spoken word, has to spend considerable time and effort working out the procedures for solving problems, and may fail because he or she cannot find a solution. People working on tasks with low analyzability have to draw on their knowledge and judgment to search for new procedures to solve problems. When a great deal of search activity is needed to find a solution to a problem and procedures cannot be programmed in advance, tasks are complex and nonroutine.

Together, task analyzability and task variability explain why some tasks are more routine than others. The greater the number of exceptions that workers encounter in the work process and the greater the amount of search behaviour that is required to find a solution to each exception, the more complex and less routine tasks are. For tasks that are routine, there are, in Perrow's words, "well-established techniques which are sure to work and these are applied to essentially similar raw materials. That is, there is little uncertainty about methods and little variety or change in the task that must be performed."[19] For tasks that are complex, "there are few established techniques; there is little certainty about methods, or whether or not they will work. But it also means that there may be a great variety of different tasks to perform."[20]

Four Types of Technology

Perrow used task variability and task analyzability to differentiate among four types of technology: routine manufacturing, craftswork, engineering production, and nonroutine research (see Figure 9-4).[21] Perrow's model can be used to categorize the technology of an organization and the technology of departments and functions inside an organization.

Routine Manufacturing Routine manufacturing is characterized by low task variability and high task analyzability. Few exceptions are encountered in the work process, and

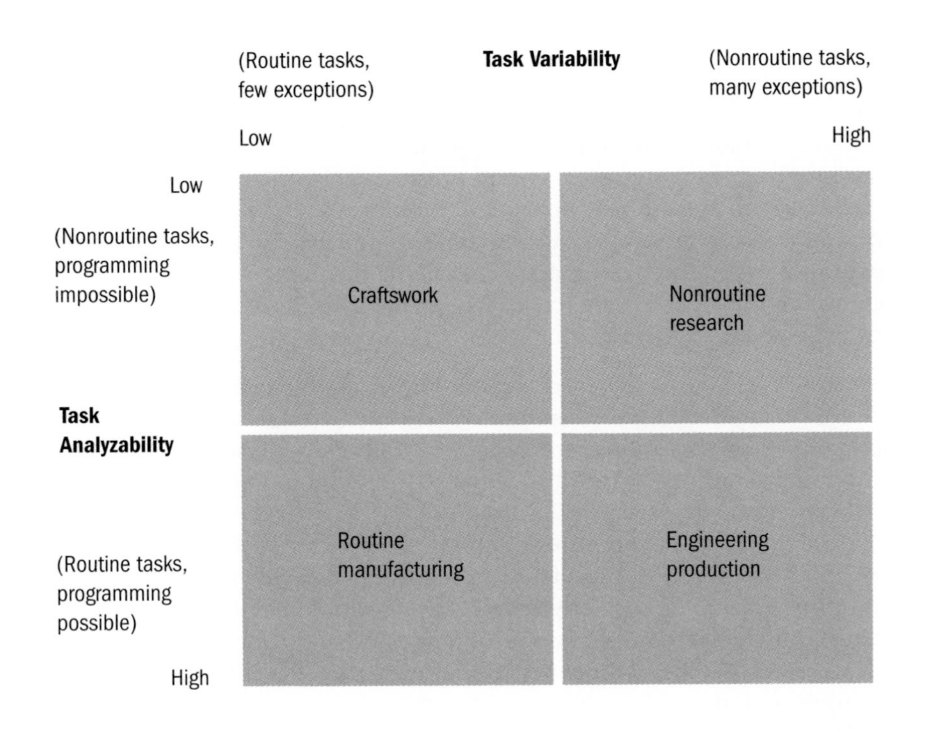

FIGURE 9-4
Task Variability, Task Analyzability, and Four Types of Technology. Charles Perrow defined two factors—task variability and task analyzability—that account for differences between tasks and technologies.
Source: Adapted from Charles Perrow, *Organizational Analysis: A Sociological View* (Belmont, CA: Wadsworth, 1970), p. 78.

when an exception does occur, little search behaviour is required to deal with it. Mass production is representative of routine manufacturing technology.

In mass-production settings, tasks are broken down into a series of simple steps that minimize the possibility that exceptions will occur, and inputs are standardized to minimize disruptions to the production process. There are standard procedures to follow if an exception or a problem presents itself. The low-cost advantages of mass production are obtained by making tasks low in variability and high in analyzability. One reason why McDonald's costs are lower than its competitors' costs is that McDonald's constantly streamlines its menu choices and standardizes the associated work activities to reduce task variability and increase task analyzability.

Craftswork With craft technology, task variability is low (only a narrow range of exceptions is encountered), and task analyzability is also low (a high level of search activity is needed to find a solution to problems). Employees in an organization using this kind of technology need to adapt existing procedures to new situations and find new techniques to handle existing problems more effectively. This technology was used to build early automobiles, as we saw in Organizational Insight 9.1 (p. 292). Other examples of craftswork are the manufacture of specialized or customized products like furniture, clothing, and machinery, and trades such as carpentry and plumbing. The tasks that a plumber, for example, is called on to perform centre on installing or repairing bathroom or kitchen plumbing. But because every house is different, and each customer may want something different for that house, a plumber needs to adapt the techniques of the plumbing craft to each situation to find a unique solution for each house.

Engineering Production With engineering production technology, task variability is high and task analyzability is high. The number or variety of exceptions that workers may encounter in the task is high, but finding a solution is relatively easy because well-understood standard procedures have been established to handle the exceptions.

Because these procedures are often codified in technical formulas, tables, or manuals, solving a problem is often a matter of identifying and applying the right technique. Thus, in organizations that use engineering production technology, existing procedures are used to make many kinds of products. A manufacturing company may specialize in custom building machines such as drill presses or electric motors. A firm of architects may specialize in customizing apartment buildings to the needs of different builders. A civil engineering group may use its skills in constructing airports, dams, and hydroelectric projects to service the needs of clients throughout the world. Like craftswork, engineering production is a form of small-batch technology because people are primarily responsible for developing techniques to solve particular problems.

Nonroutine Research Nonroutine research technology is characterized by high task variability and low task analyzability and is the most complex and least routine of the four technologies in Perrow's classification. Tasks are complex because not only is the number of unexpected situations large, but search activity is high. Each new situation creates a need to expend resources to deal with it.

High-tech research and development activities are examples of nonroutine research. For people working at the forefront of technical knowledge, there are no prepackaged solutions to problems. There may be a thousand well-defined steps to follow when building the perfect bridge (engineering production technology), but there are few well-defined steps to take to discover a cure for cancer or AIDS, or to develop a new type of computer chip.

An organization's top-management team is another example of a group that uses research technology. The team's job is to chart the future path of the organization and make resource decisions that are likely to ensure its success. They make these decisions in an uncertain context, however, not knowing how successful they will be. Planning and forecasting by top management, and other nonroutine research activities, are inherently risky and uncertain because the nature of the technology is difficult to manage.

Routine Technology and Organizational Structure

Just as the types of technology identified by Woodward have implications for an organization's structure, so do the types of technology in Perrow's model. Perrow and others have suggested that an organization should move from a mechanistic to an organic structure as tasks become more complex and less routine.[22] Table 9-1 summarizes this finding.

When technology is routine, employees perform clearly defined tasks according to well-established rules and procedures. The work process is programmed in advance and as standardized as possible. Because the work process is standardized in routine technology, employees need only learn the procedures for performing the task effectively. For example, McDonald's uses written rules and procedures to train new personnel so that the behaviour of all McDonald's employees is consistent and predictable. Each new employee learns the right way to greet customers, the appropriate way to fulfill customer orders, and the correct way to make Big Macs. Before McDonald's introduces new menu choices, all of its personnel are trained on the standard way to operate the equipment needed to prepare the item.

Because employee tasks can be standardized with routine technology, the organizational hierarchy is relatively tall and decision making is centralized. Management's responsibility is to supervise employees and to manage the few exceptions that may occur, such as a breakdown of the production line. Because tasks are routine, all important production decisions are made at the top of the production hierarchy and

Table 9-1

ROUTINE AND NONROUTINE TASKS AND ORGANIZATIONAL DESIGN

Structural Characteristic	Nature of Technology	
	Routine Tasks	**Nonroutine Tasks**
Standardization	High	Low
Mutual adjustment	Low	High
Specialization	Individual	Joint
Formalization	High	Low
Hierarchy of authority	Tall	Flat
Decision-making authority	Centralized	Decentralized
Overall structure	Mechanistic	Organic

are transmitted down the chain of command as orders to lower-level managers and workers. It has been suggested that organizations with routine technology, such as that found in mass-production settings, deliberately "de-skill" tasks, meaning that they simplify jobs by using machines to perform complex tasks and by designing the work process to minimize the degree to which workers' initiative or judgment is required.[23]

The result of all these design choices is a more mechanistic structure for organizations operating a routine technology. However, as we will see in the next chapter, this choice may no longer be appropriate for an organization seeking to maintain a competitive advantage in the global environment.

Nonroutine Technology and Organizational Structure

Organizations operating a nonroutine technology face a different set of factors that affect the design of the organization.[24] As tasks become less routine and more complex, an organization has to develop a structure that allows employees to respond quickly to and manage an increase in the number and variety of exceptions and to develop new procedures to handle new problems.[25] As we saw in Chapter 4, an organic structure allows an organization to adapt rapidly to changing conditions. Organic structures are based on mutual adjustment between employees who work together, face to face, to develop procedures to find solutions to problems. Mutual adjustment through task forces and teams becomes especially important in facilitating communication and increasing integration between team members. Employees often perform closely related activities in which it is difficult to separate out each individual's contribution.[26]

The more complex an organization's work processes are, the more likely the organization is to have a relatively flat and decentralized structure that allows employees the authority and autonomy to cooperate to make decisions quickly and effectively.[27] The use of work groups and product teams to facilitate rapid adjustment and feedback among employees performing complex tasks is a key feature of such an organization.

The same design considerations are applicable at the departmental or functional level: To be effective, departments employing different technologies need different structures.[28] In general, departments performing nonroutine tasks are likely to have more organic structures, and those performing routine tasks are likely to have more mechanistic structures. An R&D department, for example, is typically very organic, and decision making in it is usually highly decentralized; but the manufacturing and sales functions are usually quite mechanistic, and decision making within them tends to be more centralized. The kind of technology employed at the departmental level determines the choice of structure.[29]

TASK INTERDEPENDENCE: THE THEORY OF JAMES D. THOMPSON

Task interdependence The manner in which different organizational tasks are related to one another.

Woodward focused on how an organization's technology affects its choice of structure, and Perrow's model of technology focuses on the way in which the complexity of tasks affects organizational structure. Another view of technology, developed by James D. Thompson, focuses on the way in which **task interdependence**, the manner in which different organizational tasks are related to one another, affects an organization's technology and structure.[30] When task interdependence is low, people and departments are individually specialized—that is, they work separately and independently to achieve organizational goals. When task interdependence is high, people and departments are jointly specialized—that is, they depend on one another for supplying the inputs and resources they need to get the work done. Thompson identified three types of technology: mediating, long-linked, and intensive (see Figure 9-5). Each of them is associated with a different form of task interdependence.

FIGURE 9-5
Task Interdependence and Three Types of Technology.
James D. Thompson's model of technology focuses on how the relationship among different organizational tasks affects an organization's technology and structure.

Type of technology	Form of task interdependence	Main type of coordination	Strategy for reducing uncertainty	Cost of coordination
Mediating	Pooled 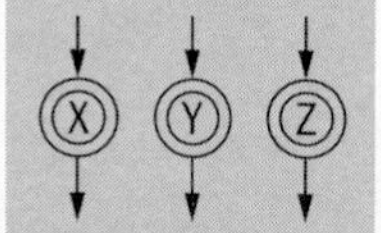 X Y Z *(e.g., piecework or franchise)*	Standardization	Increase in the number of customers served	Low
Long-linked	Sequential 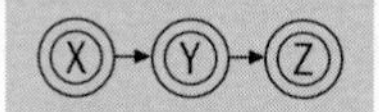 X → Y → Z *(e.g., assembly-line or continuous-process plant)*	Planning and scheduling	Slack resources Vertical integration	Medium
Intensive	Reciprocal 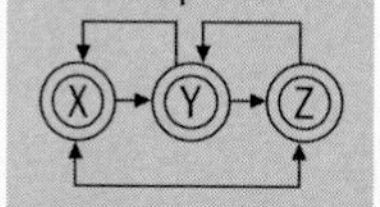 X ↔ Y ↔ Z *(e.g., general hospital or research and development laboratory)*	Mutual adjustment	Specialism of task activities	High

Mediating Technology and Pooled Interdependence

Mediating technology is characterized by a work process where input, conversion, and output activities can be performed independently of one another. Mediating technology is based on *pooled task interdependence*, which means that each part of the organization—whether a person, team, or department—contributes separately to the performance of the whole organization. With mediating technology, task interdependence is low because people do not directly rely on others to help them perform their tasks. As illustrated in Figure 9-5, each person or department—X, Y, and Z—performs a separate task. In a management consulting firm or hair salon, each consultant or hairdresser works independently to solve a client's problems. The success of the organization as a whole, however, depends on the collective efforts of everyone employed. The activities of a gymnastic team also illustrate pooled task interdependence. Each team member performs independently and can win or lose a particular event, but the collective score of the team members determines which team wins. The implications of mediating technology for organizational structure can be examined at both the departmental and the organizational level.

Mediating technology A technology characterized by a work process in which input, conversion, and output activities can be performed independently of one another.

At the departmental level, piecework systems best characterize the way this technology operates. In a piecework system, each employee performs a task independently from other employees. In a machine shop, each employee might operate a lathe to produce bolts, and each is evaluated and rewarded on the basis of how many bolts he or she produces. The performance of the manufacturing department as a whole depends on how well each employee individually performs, but employees themselves are not interdependent because one employee's actions have no effect on the actions of others. Similarly, the performance of the sales department depends on the performance of each salesperson, but the performance of one salesperson is not affected by the performance of others in the department.

The use of a mediating technology to accomplish departmental or organizational activities makes it easy to monitor, control, and evaluate the performance of each individual because the output of each person is observable and the same standards can be used to evaluate each employee.[31]

At the organizational level, mediating technology is found in organizations where the activities of different departments are performed separately and there is little need for integration between departments to accomplish organizational goals. In a bank, for example, the activities of the loan department and the chequing account department are essentially independent. The routines involved in lending money have no relation to the routines involved in receiving money, but the performance of the bank as a whole depends on how well each department does its job.[32]

Mediating technology at the organizational level is also found in organizations that use franchise arrangements to organize their businesses or that operate a chain of stores. For example, each Tim Hortons franchise or Wal-Mart store operates essentially independently. The performance of one store does not affect another store, but together all stores determine the performance of the whole organization. Indeed, one strategy for improving organizational performance for an organization operating a mediating technology is to try to attract new sets of customers by increasing the number of operating units or the number of products it offers. A fast-food chain can open a new restaurant. A retail organization can open a new store. A bank can increase the number of financial services it offers customers to attract new business. Indeed, one major goal of banks is to be given the right to sell stocks or mutual funds to increase their population of potential customers.

Over the past decades the use of mediating technology has been increasing because it is relatively inexpensive to operate and manage. Costs are low because organizational activities can be controlled by standardization. Bureaucratic rules and procedures can be used to specify how the activities of different departments are to be coordinated and to outline the procedures that a department needs to follow to ensure that its activities are compatible with those of other departments. Standard operating procedures and electronic media such as e-mail provide the coordination necessary to manage the businesses. Wal-Mart, for example, coordinates its stores through a satellite system that informs managers about new product introductions or changes in rules and procedures.

As computers become more important in coordinating the activities of independent employees or departments, it becomes possible to use a mediating technology to coordinate more types of production activities. Network organizations, discussed in Chapter 6, are developing as computer technologies allow the different departments of an organization to operate separately and at different locations. Similarly, the growth of outsourcing—companies' contracting with other companies to perform their value-creation activities (like production or marketing) for them—shows the increasing use of mediating technology as a way of doing business.

Recall from Chapter 3 how Nike contracts with manufacturers throughout the world to produce and distribute products to its customers on a global basis. Nike designs a shoe but then contracts manufacturing, marketing, and other functional activities out to other organizations. Coordination is achieved by standardization of the product range. Nike has rules and procedures specifying the required quality of input materials, the nature of the manufacturing process, and the required quality of the finished product. Nike constantly monitors production and sales information from its network by means of a sophisticated global computer system.

Long-Linked Technology and Sequential Interdependence

Long-linked technology
A technology characterized by a work process in which input, conversion, and output activities must be performed in series.

Long-linked technology, the second type of technology that Thompson identified, is based on a work process where input, conversion, and output activities must be performed in series. Long-linked technology is based on *sequential task interdependence,* which means that the actions of one person or department directly affect the actions of another, so work cannot be successfully completed by allowing each person or department to operate independently. Figure 9-5 illustrates the dynamics of sequential interdependence. X's activities directly affect Y's ability to perform her task, and in turn the activities of Y directly affect Z's ability to perform.

Mass-production technology is based on sequential task interdependence. The actions of the employee at the beginning of the production line determine how successfully the next employee can perform his or her task, and so forth on down the line. Because sequential interactions have to be carefully coordinated, long-linked technology requires more coordination than mediating technology. One result of sequential interdependence is that any error that occurs at the beginning of the production process becomes magnified at later stages. Sports activities like relay races or football, in which the performance of one person or group determines how well the next can perform, are based on sequential interdependence. In football, for example, the performance of the defensive line determines how well the offence can perform. If the defence is unable to secure the ball, the offence cannot perform its task: scoring touchdowns.

An organization with long-linked technology can respond in a variety of ways to the need to coordinate sequentially interdependent activities. The organization can program the conversion process to standardize the procedures used to transform inputs into outputs. The organization can also use planning and scheduling to manage linkages among input, conversion, and output processes. To reduce the need to coordinate these stages of production, an organization often creates **slack resources**—extra or surplus resources that enhance its ability to deal with unexpected situations. For example, a mass-production organization stockpiles inputs and holds inventories of component parts so that the conversion process is not disrupted if there is a problem with suppliers. Similarly, an organization may stockpile finished products so that it can respond quickly to an increase in customer demand without changing its established conversion processes. Another strategy to control the supply of inputs or distribution of outputs is *vertical integration,* which, as we saw in Chapter 8, involves a company taking over its suppliers or distributors.

Slack resources
Extra or surplus resources that enhance an organization's ability to deal with unexpected situations.

The need to manage the increased level of interdependence increases the coordination costs associated with long-linked technology. However, this type of technology also provides the organization with enormous benefits, stemming primarily from specialization and the division of labour associated with sequential interdependence. Changing the method of production in a pin factory from a system where each worker produces a whole pin to a system where each worker is responsible for only one aspect of pin production, such as sharpening the pin, for example, can result in a major gain in productivity. Essentially, the factory moves from using a *mediating* technology, in which each worker performs all production tasks, to a *long-linked* technology, in which tasks become sequentially interdependent.

Tasks are routine in long-linked technology because sequential interdependence allows managers to simplify tasks so that the variability of each worker's task is reduced and the analyzability of each task is increased. On mass-production assembly lines, for example, the coordination of tasks is achieved principally by the speed of the line and the way tasks are ordered. Programming and the constant repetition of simple tasks increase production efficiency. As we saw in Organizational Insight 9.1 (p. 292), Henry Ford was the innovator of long-linked technology. Capitalizing on the gains from specialization and the division of labour, he recognized the cost savings that could result from organizing tasks sequentially and controlling the pace of work by the speed of the production line. This system, however, has two major disadvantages. Employees may not become highly skilled (they learn only a narrow range of simple tasks), and they may not develop the ability to improve their skills because they must follow specified procedures.

At the organizational level, sequential interdependence means that the outputs of one department become the inputs for another and one department's performance determines how well another department performs. The performance of the manufacturing department depends on the ability of the materials management department to obtain adequate amounts of high-quality inputs in a timely manner. The ability of the sales function to sell finished products depends on the quality of the products coming out of the manufacturing department. Failure or poor performance at one stage has serious consequences for performance at the next stage and for the organization as a whole. In the 1970s, for example, U.S. car manufacturers' ability to sell their products was seriously hampered by the poor quality of the cars they were making in their outdated factories, and their inefficient manufacturing was in part the result of outdated materials management practices.

The pressures of competition in today's global markets are increasing the need for interdependence between departments and thus are increasing organizations' need to coordinate departmental activities. As we saw in Chapter 6, many organizations are moving toward the product team structure to increase interdepartmental coordination. This type of coordination encourages different departments to develop procedures that lead to greater production innovation and efficiency. Managing interdependence in complex organizations is a massive task. Increasingly, technology is being used to manage these linkages—particularly in those organizations where the scheduling of linked resources is critical and cost-sensitive, such as airlines. (See Organizational Insight 9.3.)

Intensive Technology and Reciprocal Interdependence

Intensive technology
A technology characterized by a work process in which input, conversion, and output activities are inseparable.

Intensive technology, the third type of technology identified by Thompson, is characterized by a work process where input, conversion, and output activities are inseparable. Intensive technology is based on *reciprocal task interdependence,* which means that the activities of all people and all departments are fully dependent on one another. Not only do X's actions affect what Y and Z can do, but the actions of Z also affect Y's and X's performance. The task relationships of X, Y, and Z are reciprocally interdependent (see Figure 9-5, p. 308). Reciprocal interdependence makes it impossible to program in advance a sequence of tasks or procedures to solve a problem because, in Thompson's words, "the selection, combination, and order of [the tasks'] application

ORGANIZATIONAL INSIGHT 9.3

Scheduling Effectiveness with AD OPT Technology[33]

AD OPT Technologies Inc. was founded in 1987 by five university mathematicians from McGill and the Université de Montreal who were members of the internationally renowned research group GERAD. Using technologies developed and advanced by GERAD, AD OPT has now become a leading provider of specialized software for workforce planning, scheduling, and management solutions. The company is headquartered in Montreal and has offices in British Columbia and Australia.

The firm now collectively provides industry-specific planning solutions for more than 400 facilities worldwide. In particular, the company offers three main industry product lines: *Shiftlogic*, for workforce management; *TotalCare*, for health-care services; and *Altitude*, for airline operation scheduling. Large modern firms competing in the global market face complex logistical circumstances connecting employees to numerous labour variables, challenges to effective management, and heavy reliance on coordination and scheduling of a vast array of discrete elements. AD OPT, while a relatively small corporation with just over 100 employees, offers technology solutions that potentially have a huge positive impact on the profitability of much larger companies facing costly and complex scheduling issues.

For example, AD OPT's streamlined software programming, based on complicated mathematical logarithms, sorts out optimal work scheduling for large airlines. Its product capabilities go far beyond simply time scheduling, and the company's comprehensive software organizes and optimizes schedules for over 3000 of Air Canada's pilots, taking into consideration collective agreements, seniority of personnel, their entitlement for vacations, all of the related direct and indirect budget costs, productivity projections, and any changes made to planes and destinations. Similarly, AD OPT has designed software for hospital staff and the complex related processes that take place in health-care settings each day. The organizing and planning processes within large and complex organizations are obviously essential for effectiveness, efficiency, and subsequently profitability.

are determined by *feedback from the object [problem] itself.*"[34] Thus the move to reciprocal interdependence and intensive technology has two effects: Technical complexity declines as the ability of managers to control and predict the work process lessens, and tasks become more complex and nonroutine.

Hospitals are organizations that operate an intensive technology. A hospital's greatest source of uncertainty is the impossibility of predicting the types of problems for which patients (clients) will seek treatment. At any time, a general hospital has to have on hand the knowledge, machines, and services of specialist departments capable of solving a huge number and great variety of medical problems. The hospital requires, for example, an emergency room, X-ray facilities, a testing laboratory, an operating room and staff, skilled nursing staff, doctors, and hospital wards. What is wrong with each patient determines the selection and combination of activities and technology to convert a hospital's inputs (sick people) into outputs (well people). The uncertainty of the input (patient) means that tasks cannot be programmed in advance, as they can be when interdependence is sequential.

Hockey, soccer, and rugby are other activities that depend on reciprocal interdependence. The current state of play determines the sequence of moves from one player to the next. The fast-moving action of these sports requires players to make judgments quickly and obtain feedback from the state of play before deciding what moves to make.

On a departmental level, research and development departments operate with an intensive technology. The sequence and content of an R&D department's activities are determined by the problems the department is trying to solve—for example, a cure for cancer. R&D is so expensive because the unpredictability of the input-conversion-output process makes it impossible to specify in advance the skills and resources that will be needed to solve the problem at hand. A pharmaceutical company like Merck, for example, creates many different research and development teams. Every team is equipped with whatever functional resources it needs in the hope that at least one team will stumble onto a wonder drug that will justify the immense resource expenditures (each new drug costs about US$400 million to develop).

The difficulty of specifying the sequencing of tasks that is characteristic of intensive technology makes necessary a high degree of coordination and makes intensive technology more expensive to manage than either mediating or long-linked technology. Mutual adjustment replaces programming and standardization as the principal method of coordination. Product team and matrix structures are suited to operating intensive technologies because they provide the coordination and the decentralized control that allow departments to cooperate to solve problems. At Microsoft, for example, the whole company is organized into product teams so that it can quickly shift resources to the projects that seem most promising. Also, mutual adjustment and a flat structure allow an organization to quickly exploit new developments and areas for research that arise during the research process itself. Hewlett-Packard designed a new organizational structure to operate its new intensive approach to product development. (See Organizational Insight 9.4.)

Organizations do not voluntarily use an intensive technology to achieve their goals because it is so expensive to operate. They are forced to use it by the nature of the output they choose to produce. Whenever possible, organizations attempt to reduce the task interdependence necessary to coordinate their activities and revert to a long-linked technology, which is more controllable and predictable. In recent years, for example, hospitals have attempted to control escalating management costs by using forecasting techniques to determine how many resources they need to have on hand to meet customer (patient) demands. If, over a specified period, a hospital

ORGANIZATIONAL INSIGHT 9.4

A New Approach at Hewlett-Packard

In 1989, Hewlett-Packard (H-P), based in the high-tech Silicon Valley of California, was under siege by competitors who were bringing out competing products such as computer workstations and minicomputers at a rate that H-P could not match. Then CEO John A. Young traced the source of the problem to H-P's product development process. Product development at H-P was a sequential process. New projects went from one department to another, and 23 committees oversaw every decision in every department before moving a project to the next stage—for example, from product R&D to engineering to manufacturing to marketing. The result was slow decision making and late-to-market products.

Young decided to reorganize the technology of the conversion process and the form of task interdependence among departments. His goal was to cut the time needed to bring out H-P's next generation of workstations or laser printers. He reorganized several functions into small product development teams in which people from each function worked together from the beginning to the end of a project.

To manage the complexity of this reciprocal task interdependence, Young redesigned the company's structure. He flattened the organizational hierarchy by cutting two layers of management; he decentralized control of the product development process to the team; and he assigned each team its own sales staff to speed the introduction of the product to the market. He also dissolved much of the committee structure that had slowed decision making.[35] With this new, streamlined, organic structure, H-P dramatically cut the time it took to bring new products to market. What used to take months or years now took only weeks, and the company once again became a dominant force in the computer industry.

However, by the late 1990s, H-P was once again in trouble because of the speed at which developments in the Internet software industry had changed the nature of the competitive game. In 1999 H-P appointed a new CEO, Carly Fiorino, to try to speed up the company's product development program; she instituted changes to help H-P employees act more entrepreneurially and to loosen up the company's famous culture, which was unable to respond fast enough to the changes currently taking place.[36]

knows on average how many broken bones or cardiac arrests it can expect, it knows how many operating theatres it will need to have in readiness and how many doctors, nurses, and technicians to have on call to meet patient demand. This knowledge allows the hospital to control costs. Similarly, in R&D, an organization needs to develop decision-making rules that allow it to decide when to stop investing in a line of research that is showing little promise of success and how to allocate resources among projects to try to maximize potential returns from the investment.

Specialism
Producing only a narrow range of outputs.

Another strategy that organizations can pursue to reduce the costs associated with intensive technology is **specialism**—producing only a narrow range of outputs. A hospital that specializes in the treatment of cancer or heart disease narrows the range of problems to which it is exposed and can target all its resources to solving those problems. It is the general hospital that faces the most uncertainty. Similarly, a pharmaceutical company typically restricts the areas in which it does research. A company may decide to focus on drugs that combat high blood pressure or diabetes or depression. This specialist strategy allows the organization to use its resources efficiently and reduces problems of coordination.[37]

MANAGERIAL IMPLICATIONS

Analyzing Technology

1. Analyze an organization's or a department's input-conversion-output processes to identify the skills, knowledge, tools, and machinery that are central to the production of goods and services.
2. Analyze the level of technical complexity associated with the production of goods and services. Evaluate whether technical complexity can be increased to improve efficiency and reduce costs. For example, is an advanced computer system available? Are employees using up-to-date techniques and procedures?
3. Analyze the level of task variety and task analyzability associated with organizational and departmental tasks. Are there ways to reduce task variability or increase task analyzability to increase effectiveness? For example, can procedures be developed to make the work process more predictable and controllable?
4. Analyze the form of task interdependence inside a department and between departments. Evaluate whether the task interdependence being used results in the most effective way of producing goods or servicing the needs of customers. For example, would raising the level of coordination between departments improve efficiency?
5. After analyzing an organization's or a department's technology, analyze its structure, and evaluate the fit between technology and structure. Can the fit be improved? What costs and benefits are associated with changing the technology–structure relationship?

FROM MASS PRODUCTION TO ADVANCED MANUFACTURING TECHNOLOGY

As discussed earlier, one of the most influential advances in technology in the last century was the introduction of mass-production technology by Henry Ford. To reduce costs, a mass-production company must maximize the gains from economies of scale and from the division of labour associated with large-scale production. There are two ways to do this. One is by using dedicated machines and standardized work procedures. The other is by protecting the conversion process against production slowdowns or stoppages.

Traditional mass production is based on the use of **dedicated machines**—machines that can perform only one operation at a time, such as repeatedly cutting or drilling or stamping out a car body part.[38] To maximize volume and efficiency, a dedicated machine produces a narrow range of products but does so cheaply. Thus this method of production has traditionally resulted in low production costs.

Dedicated machines Machines that can perform only one operation at a time, such as repeatedly cutting, drilling, or stamping out a car body part.

When the component being manufactured needs to be changed, a dedicated machine must be retooled—that is, fitted with new dies or jigs—before it can handle the change. When Ford retooled one of his plants to switch from the Model T to the Model A, he had to close the plant for over six months. Because retooling a dedicated machine can take days, during which no production is possible, long production runs are required for maximum efficiency and lowest costs. Thus, for example, Ford might make 50 000 right-side door panels in a single production run and stockpile them until they are needed, because the money saved by using dedicated machines outweighs the combined costs of lost production and carrying the doors in inventory. In a similar way, both the use of a production line to assemble the final product and the employment of **fixed workers**—workers who perform standardized work procedures—increase an organization's control over the conversion process.

Fixed workers
Workers who perform standardized work procedures, increasing an organization's control over the conversion process.

A mass production organization also attempts to reduce costs by protecting its conversion processes from the uncertainty that results from disruptions in the external environment.[39] Threats to the conversion process come from both the input and the output stages, but an organization can stockpile inputs and outputs to reduce these threats (see Figure 9-6A).

At the input stage, an organization tries to control its access to inputs by keeping raw materials and semi-finished components on hand to prevent shortages that would lead to a slowdown or break in production. The role of purchasing, for example, is to negotiate with suppliers contracts that guarantee the organization an adequate supply of inputs. At the output stage, an organization tries to control its ability to dispose of its outputs. It does so by stockpiling finished products so that it can respond quickly to customer demands. An organization can also advertise heavily to maintain customer demand. In that case, the role of the sales department is to maintain demand for an organization's products so that production does not need to slow down or stop because no one wants the organization's outputs. Another method to achieve this objective is to match production of output and marketing efforts to create levels of customer demand on a seasonal or cyclical basis. This permits forward planning, production, and stockpiling in anticipation of customer demand. This seasonal approach can be seen in the winter holiday season, or when new car models are introduced on an annual basis. The computer industry uses the "new" model introduction mechanism extensively.

The high technical complexity, the routine nature of production tasks, and the sequential task interdependence characteristic of mass production all make an organization very inflexible. The term *fixed automation* is sometimes used to describe the traditional way of organizing production. The combination of dedicated machines (which perform only a narrow range of operations), fixed workers (who perform a narrow range of fixed tasks), and large stocks of inventory (which can be used to produce only one product or a few related products) makes it very expensive and difficult for an organization to begin to manufacture different kinds of products when customer preferences change.

Suppose an organization had a new technology that allowed it to make a wide range of products—products that could be customized to the needs of individual customers. This ability would increase demand for its products. If the new technology also allowed the organization to rapidly introduce new products that incorporated new features or the latest design trends, demand would increase even more. Finally, suppose the cost of producing this wide range of new, customized products with the new technology was the same as, or only slightly more than, the cost of producing a narrow, standardized product line. Clearly, the new technology would greatly increase organizational effectiveness and allow the organization to pursue both a low-cost and a differentiation strategy, to attract customers by giving them advanced, high-quality, reliable products at low prices.[40]

Input Stage

Inputs come from suppliers in advance and are stockpiled until they are needed.

Conversion Stage

Inputs are assembled into subassemblies and are put in inventory for use by the next workstation.

Output Stage

Finished products are stockpiled until they are needed. They eventually are shipped to customers.

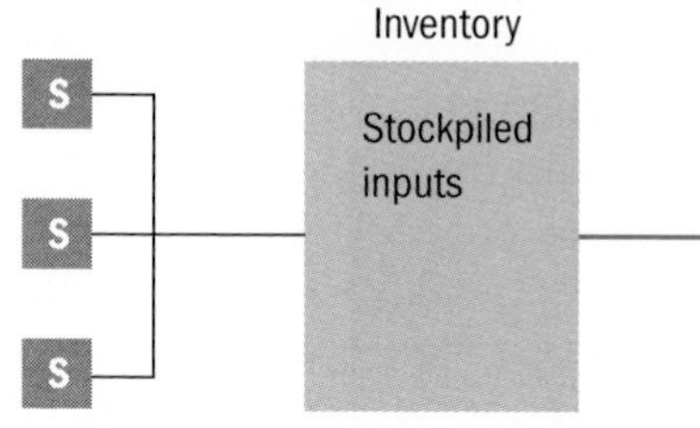

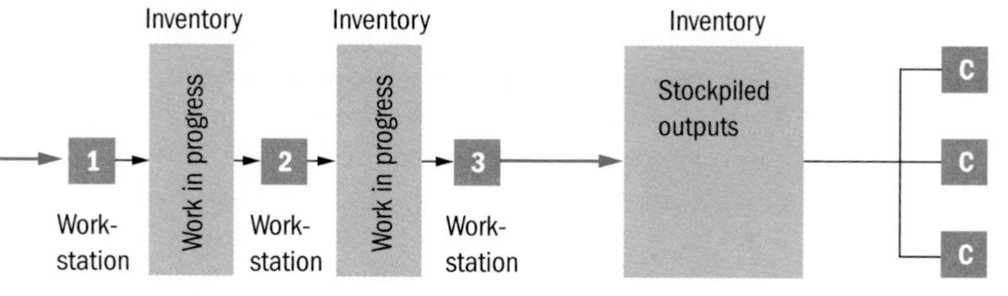

Suppliers

Customers

A. The Work Flow in Mass Production. Inventory is used to protect the conversion process and to prevent slowdowns or stoppages in production.

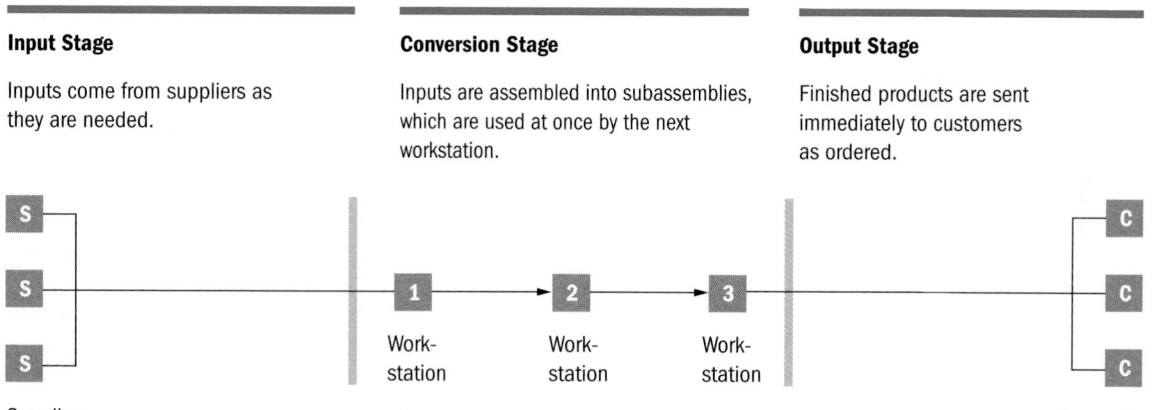

B. The Work Flow with Advanced Manufacturing Technology. No inventory buffers are used between workstations.

FIGURE 9-6

A. The Work Flow in Mass Production.

Inventory is used to protect the conversion process and to prevent slowdowns or stoppages in production.

B. The Work Flow with Advanced Manufacturing Technology.

No inventory buffers are used between workstations.

What changes would an organization need to make to its technology to make it flexible enough to respond to customers while controlling costs? In the last 20 years, many new technological developments have allowed organizations to achieve these two goals. The new developments are sometimes called *flexible production, lean production, or computer-aided production.* This type of production is a form of *mass customization* and here we will consider them all to be components of advanced manufacturing technology.[41] **Advanced manufacturing technology** (AMT) consists of innovations in *materials technology* and in *knowledge technology* that change the work process of traditional mass-production organizations.

Advanced manufacturing technology
Technology that consists of innovations in materials and in knowledge that change the work process of traditional mass-production organizations.

ADVANCED MANUFACTURING TECHNOLOGY: INNOVATIONS IN MATERIALS TECHNOLOGY

Materials technology
Technology comprising machinery, other equipment, and computers.

Materials technology comprises machinery, other equipment, and computers. Innovations in materials technology are based on a new view of the linkages between input, conversion, and output activities.[42] Traditional mass production tries to protect the conversion process from disruptions at the input and output stages by using stockpiles of inventory as buffers to increase control and reduce uncertainty. With AMT, however, the organization actively seeks ways to increase its ability to integrate or coordinate the flow of resources between input, conversion, and output activities. AMT allows an organization to reduce uncertainty not by using inventory stockpiles but by developing the capacity to adjust and control its procedures quickly to eliminate the need for inventory at both the input and the output stages (see Figure 9-6B).[43] Several innovations in materials technology allow organizations to reduce the costs and speed the process of producing goods and services. Computer-aided design, computer-aided materials management, just-in-time inventory systems, modularity, and computer-integrated manufacturing affect one another and jointly improve organizational effectiveness. The first three are techniques for coordinating the input and conversion stages of production. The last two increase the technical complexity of the conversion stage.

Computer-Aided Design

Mass-production systems are set up to produce a large quantity of a few products. To some degree, this arrangement reflects the fact that a large part of the cost associated with mass production is incurred at the design stage.[44] In general, the more complex a product, the higher the design costs. The costs of designing a new car, for example, are enormous. Ford's new world car, the Mondeo, cost over US$6 billion to develop.

Traditionally, the design of new parts involved the laborious construction of prototypes and scale models, a process akin to unit or small-batch production. **Computer-aided design (CAD)** is an advanced manufacturing technique that greatly simplifies the design process. CAD makes it possible to design a new component or microcircuit on a computer screen and then have the prototype specifications stored in some form of digital memory file. Computer-aided manufacturing (CAM) may then be used to build the prototype. Using a CAM prototyping system, the computer can send the digital information to a special "printer." This printer then "prints" the prototype object. These printers can, for example, squirt a stream of liquid metal or plastic droplets to create a three-dimensional representation of the prototype object. Detailed prototypes can then be further sculpted according to the computer specifications. This process speeds up the design and prototyping as the digital prototype can be redesigned quickly if necessary. Thus, for example, an engineer at Ford who wants to see how a new gear will work in a transmission assembly can experiment quickly and cheaply to fine-tune the design of these inputs.[45]

Computer-aided design (CAD)
An advanced manufacturing technique that greatly simplifies the design process.

Cutting the costs of product design by using CAD/CAM can contribute to both a low-cost and a differentiation advantage. Design advances that CAD/CAM makes possible can improve the efficiency of manufacturing. Well-designed components are easily fitted together into a subassembly, and well-designed subassemblies are easily fitted to other subassemblies. Improvements at the input design stage also make selling and servicing products easier at the output stage. The risk of later failure or of breakdown is reduced if potential problems have been eliminated at the design stage. Designing quality into a product up front improves competitive advantage and reduces costs. Toyota's core competency in product design, for example, evidenced by its relatively low recall rates, gives its cars a competitive advantage. Finally, CAD/CAM enhances flexibility because it reduces the difficulty and lowers the cost of customizing a product to satisfy particular customers. In essence, computer-aided design and manufacture bring to large-scale manufacturing one of the benefits of small-batch production—customized product design—but at far less cost. They also enhance an organization's ability to respond quickly to changes in its environment.[46]

Computer-Aided Materials Management

Materials management, the management of the flow of resources into and out of the conversion process, is one of the most complex functional areas of an organization.[47] Computers are now the principal tool for processing the information that materials managers use for sound decision making, and computer-aided materials management is crucial to organizational effectiveness. **Computer-aided materials management (CAMM)** is an advanced manufacturing technique that is used to manage the flow of raw materials and component parts into the conversion process, to develop master production schedules for manufacturing, and to control inventory.[48] The difference between traditional materials management and the new computer-aided techniques is the difference between the so-called push and pull approaches to materials management.[49]

Computer-aided materials management (CAMM) An advanced manufacturing technique that is used to manage the flow of raw materials and component parts into the conversion process, to develop master production schedules for manufacturing, and to control inventory.

Traditional mass production uses the *push* approach. Materials are released from the input to the conversion stage when the production control system indicates that the conversion stage is ready to receive them. The inputs are pushed into the conversion process in accordance with a previously determined plan.

Computer-aided materials management makes possible the *pull* approach. The flow of input materials is governed by customer requests for supplies of the finished products, so the inputs are pulled into the conversion process in response to a pull from the output stage rather than a push from the input stage. Consider how VF Corporation, the manufacturer of Lee jeans, meets customer demand. As jeans sell out in stores, the stores issue requests by computer to Lee to manufacture different styles or sizes. Lee's manufacturing department then pulls in raw materials, such as cloth and thread, from suppliers as it needs them. If Lee were using the push approach, Lee would have a master plan that might say, "Make 30 000 pairs of style XYZ in May," and at the end of the summer 25 000 pairs might remain unsold in the warehouse because of lack of demand.

CAMM technology allows an organization to increase integration of its input, conversion, and output activities. The use of input and output inventories (see Figure 9-6, p. 317) allows the activities of each stage of the mass-production process to go on relatively independently. CAMM, however, tightly couples these activities. CAMM increases *task interdependence* because each stage must be ready to react quickly to demands from the other stages. CAMM increases technical complexity because it makes input, conversion, and output activities a continuous process, in effect creating a pipeline connecting raw materials to the customer. Because the high levels of task interdependence and technical complexity associated with CAMM require greater coordination, an organization may need to move toward an organic structure, which will provide the extra integration that is needed.

CAMM also helps an organization pursue a low-cost or differentiation strategy. The ability to control the flow of materials in the production process allows an organization to avoid the costs of carrying excess inventory and to be flexible enough to adjust to product or demand changes quickly and easily.

Just-in-Time Inventory Systems

Another advanced manufacturing technique for managing the flow of inputs into the organization is the just-in-time inventory system. Developed from the Japanese kanban

Just-in-time inventory (JIT) system
A system that requires inputs and components needed for production to be delivered to the conversion process just as they are needed, neither earlier nor later, so that input inventories can be kept to a minimum.

system (a *kanban* is a card), a **just-in-time inventory (JIT) system** requires inputs and components needed for production to be delivered to the conversion process just as they are needed, neither earlier nor later, so that input inventories can be kept to a minimum.[50] Components are kept in bins, and as they are used up, the empty bins are sent back to the supplier with a request on the bin's card (kanban) for more components. Computer-aided materials management is necessary for a JIT system to work effectively because CAMM provides computerized linkages with suppliers—linkages that facilitate the rapid transfer of information and coordination between an organization and its suppliers.

In theory, a JIT system can extend beyond components to raw materials. A company may supply Ford or Toyota with taillight assemblies. The supplier itself, however, may assemble the taillights from individual parts (screws, plastic lenses, bulbs) provided by other manufacturers. Thus the supplier of the taillight assembly could also operate a JIT system with its suppliers, who in turn could operate JIT systems with their suppliers. Figure 9-7 illustrates a just-in-time inventory system that goes from the customer, to the store, and then back through the manufacturer to the original suppliers.

A JIT system increases task interdependence between stages in the production chain. Traditional mass production draws a boundary between the conversion stage and the input and output stages and sequences conversion activities only. JIT systems break down these barriers and make the whole value-creation process a single chain of sequential activities. Because organizational activities become a continuous process, technical complexity increases, in turn increasing the efficiency of the system.

At the same time, JIT systems bring flexibility to manufacturing. The ability to order components as they are needed allows an organization to widen the range of products it makes and to customize products, because it is not tied to one product by large inventories.[51] JIT systems thus allow a modern mass-production organization to obtain the benefits of small-batch technology (flexibility and customization) with little loss of technical efficiency.

Like CAMM, JIT systems require an extra measure of coordination, and an organization may need to adopt new methods to manage this new technology. One of these, as we saw in Chapter 3, is to implement new strategies for managing relations with suppliers. Toyota, which owns a minority stake in its suppliers, periodically meets with its suppliers to keep them informed about new product developments. Toyota also works closely with its suppliers to reduce the costs and raise the quality of input components, and it shares the cost savings with them.[52] Because owning a supplier can

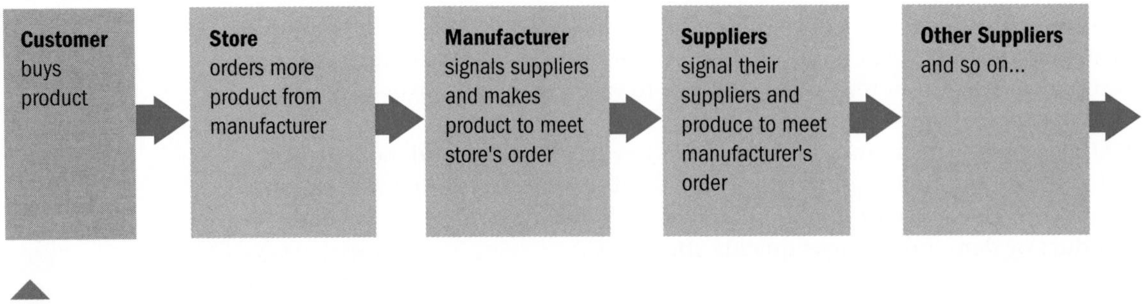

Customer buys product → **Store** orders more product from manufacturer → **Manufacturer** signals suppliers and makes product to meet store's order → **Suppliers** signal their suppliers and produce to meet manufacturer's order → **Other Suppliers** and so on... →

FIGURE 9-7
Just-in-Time Inventory System.
The system is activated by customers making purchases.

increase costs, many organizations try to avoid the need to integrate vertically. Long-term contracts with suppliers can create cooperative working relationships that have long-term benefits for both parties.

In sum, just-in-time inventory systems, computer-aided materials management, and computer-aided design and manufacture increase technical complexity and task interdependence and thus increase the degree to which a traditional mass-production system operates like a continuous-process technology; they also increase efficiency and reduce production costs. The three advanced manufacturing techniques also give modern mass production the benefits of small-batch production: heightened flexibility and the ability to respond to customer needs and increased product quality. Together these techniques confer a low-cost and a differentiation advantage on an organization.

Now that we have looked at advanced techniques for coordinating the input and conversion stages, we can look at new developments inside the conversion stage. At the centre of AMT's innovations of conversion processes is the creation of a system based on flexible workers and flexible machines.

Flexible Manufacturing Technology and Computer-Integrated Manufacturing

Traditional mass-manufacturing technology utilizes dedicated machines, which perform only one operation at a time. **Flexible manufacturing technology**, by contrast, allows the production of many kinds of components at little or no extra cost on the same machine. Each machine in a flexible manufacturing system is able to perform a range of different operations, and the machines in sequence are able to vary their operations so that a wide variety of different components can be produced. Flexible manufacturing technology combines the variety advantages of small-batch production with the low-cost advantages of continuous-process production. How is this achieved?

Flexible manufacturing technology
Technology that allows the production of many kinds of components at little or no extra cost on the same machine.

In flexible manufacturing systems, the key factor that prevents the cost increases associated with changing operations is the use of a computer-controlled system to manage operations. **Computer-integrated manufacturing (CIM)** is an advanced manufacturing technique that controls the changeover from one operation to another by means of the commands given to the machines through computer software. A CIM system eliminates the need to retool machines physically. Within the system are a number of computer-controlled machines, each capable of automatically producing a range of components. They are controlled by a master computer, which schedules the movement of parts between machines in order to assemble different products from the various components that each machine makes.[53] Computer-integrated manufacturing depends on computers programmed to (1) feed the machines with components, (2) assemble the product from components and move it from one machine to another, and (3) unload the final product from the machine to the shipping area.

Computer-integrated manufacturing (CIM)
An advanced manufacturing technique that controls the changeover from one operation to another by means of commands given to the machines through computer software.

The use of robots is integral to CIM. A group of robots working in sequence is the AMT equivalent of a dedicated transfer machine. Each robot can be quickly programmed by software to perform different operations, and the costs of reprogramming robots are much lower than the costs associated with retooling dedicated transfer machines. Motorola's cellular phone factory illustrates many of the advantages of robots and advanced manufacturing technology. (See Organizational Insight 9.5.)

Sequential task interdependence is the basis for manufacturing any kind of product. However, the combination of flexible machines and computerization allows any given set of machines to perform many different sequences. In effect, a CIM system has the potential to act reciprocally and to produce a wide range of customized prod-

ORGANIZATIONAL INSIGHT 9.5

Motorola's Factory of the Future

Motorola, one of the U.S.'s oldest consumer electronics organizations, developed the world's first car radio in 1930 and quickly entered the home audio and television market. In the 1970s, however, under pressure from the Japanese, it abandoned the home electronics market and entered the high-tech electronics sector. Today, it is a world leader in communications technology, and the organization generates over US$8 billion in revenue from the sales of cellular telephones, pagers, information networking systems, and automotive and industrial electronics.

Once again, however, Motorola is experiencing intense competitive pressure from both domestic and foreign competitors for control of the rapidly growing information technology sector. Hitachi, Panasonic, and Samsung already operate state-of-the art factories based on advanced manufacturing technology, and their low production costs make them fierce competitors. Motorola has had to figure out how to use AMT to its advantage.

Motorola decided to use AMT not only to increase technical efficiency, but to better meet the needs of customers. Using advanced manufacturing technology, Motorola has focused both product design and manufacturing on the customer. At Motorola, salespeople, not engineers, are empowered to direct the company's activities. The sales function is at the top of the organizational hierarchy; the other functions serve its needs. What does this mean for the way the organization utilizes AMT?

Motorola created a "factory of the future" that is able to customize products to individual customer needs within hours. At this futuristic factory at Boynton Beach, Florida, Motorola can respond to a customer order for even one unit of a custom-designed pager within two hours. A salesperson in the field takes the customer's order for a pager that will operate on a specific frequency, be of a certain size, and contain one of a number of customized features. The salesperson electronically relays this information as a bar code to the factory. A computer scans the specifications and through software creates the circuit board design for the pager. The conversion process is handled by a series of computer-controlled robots. As the pager passes down the production line, each robot reads the bar code and performs the necessary operations. Each pager in the line can be different, because CIM adapts the conversion process to the specific needs of each item. Finished products are electronically scanned and tested and are shipped to the customer.

Using AMT in this way is expensive. However, the ability to produce hundreds of different models customized to individual customers gave Motorola a strong competitive advantage and allowed the company to charge a premium price for its products. Unfortunately for Motorola, its competitors began creating such factories of their own and locating them globally where costs were low. As a result, they have been able to outperform Motorola, which has seen its share of the pager market plunge.

ucts.[54] It increases technical complexity. It allows an organization's resources to be used more efficiently because it quickens the pace of work and the speed of production. With computer-integrated manufacturing, the conversion of inputs becomes more like a continuous process instead of a mass-production process.

In sum, computer-integrated manufacturing, just-in-time inventory systems, computer-aided materials management, and computer-aided design and manufacture give organizations the flexibility to make a variety of products, as well as different models of the same product, rapidly and cost-effectively. They break down the traditional barriers separating the input, conversion, and output stages of production; as a result, input, conversion, and output activities merge into one another. These four innovations in materials technology decrease the need for costly inventory buffers to protect conversion processes from disruptions in the environment. In addition, they increase product reliability because they increase automation and technical complexity.

SUMMARY

Technical complexity, the differences between routine and nonroutine tasks, and task interdependence jointly explain why some technologies are more complex and difficult to control than others and why organizations adopt different structures to operate their technology. In general, input, conversion, and output processes that depend primarily on people and departments cooperating and trading knowledge that is difficult to program into standard operating routines require the most coordination. An organization that needs extensive coordination and control to operate its technology also needs an organic structure to organize its tasks. Chapter 9 has made the following main points:

1. Technology is the combination of skills, knowledge, abilities, techniques, materials, machines, computers, tools, and other equipment that people use to convert raw materials into valuable goods and services.
2. Technology is involved in an organization's input, conversion, and output processes. An effective organization manages its technology to meet the needs of stakeholders, foster innovation, and increase operating efficiency.
3. Technical complexity is the extent to which a production process is controllable and predictable. According to Joan Woodward, technical complexity differentiates small-batch and unit production, large-batch and mass production, and continuous-process production.
4. Woodward argued that each technology is associated with a different organizational structure because each technology presents different control and coordination problems. In general, small-batch and continuous-process technologies are associated with an organic structure, and mass production is associated with a mechanistic structure.
5. The argument that technology determines structure is known as the technological imperative. According to the Aston Studies, however, organizational size is more important than technology in determining an organization's choice of structure.
6. According to Charles Perrow, two dimensions underlie the difference between routine and nonroutine tasks and technologies: task variability and task analyzability. The higher the level of task variability and the lower the level of task analyzability, the more complex and nonroutine organizational tasks are.
7. Using task variability and analyzability, Perrow described four types of technology: craftswork, nonroutine research, engineering production, and routine manufacturing.
8. The more routine tasks are, the more likely an organization is to use a mechanistic structure. The more complex tasks are, the more likely an organization is to use an organic structure.
9. James D. Thompson focused on the way in which task interdependence affects an organization's technology and structure. Task interdependence is the manner in which different organizational tasks are related to one another and the degree to which the performance of one person or department depends on and affects the performance of another.
10. Thompson identified three types of technology, which he associated with three forms of task interdependence: mediating technology and pooled interdependence; long-linked technology and sequential interdependence;

and intensive technology and reciprocal interdependence.

11. The higher the level of task interdependence, the more likely an organization is to use mutual adjustment rather than standardization to coordinate work activities.
12. Advanced manufacturing technology consists of innovations in materials technology that change the work process of traditional mass production organizations. Innovations in materials technology include computer-aided design, computer-aided materials management, just-in-time inventory systems, flexible manufacturing technology, and computer-integrated manufacturing.

DISCUSSION QUESTIONS

1. How can technology increase organizational effectiveness?
2. How does small-batch technology differ from mass-production technology?
3. Why is technical complexity greatest with continuous-process technology? How does technical complexity affect organizational structure?
4. What makes some tasks more complex than others? Give an example of an organization that uses each of the four types of technology identified by Perrow.
5. What level of task interdependence is associated with the activities of (a) a large accounting firm, (b) a fast-food restaurant, and (c) a biotechnology company? What different kinds of structure are you likely to find in these organizations? Why?
6. Find an organization in your area, and analyze how its technology works. Use the concepts discussed in this chapter: technical complexity, nonroutine tasks, and task interdependence.
7. Discuss how AMT and innovations in materials technology and in knowledge technology have increased task interdependence and the technical complexity of the work process. How have these innovations changed the structure of organizations operating a mass-production technology?

ORGANIZATIONAL THEORY IN ACTION

Practising Organizational Theory: Choosing a Technology

Form groups of three to five people and discuss the following scenario:

You are investors who are planning to open a large computer store in a major city. You plan to offer a complete range of computer hardware, ranging from UNIX-based workstations, to powerful PCs and laptop computers, to a full range of printers and scanners. In addition, you propose to offer a full range of software products, from office management systems to personal financial software and children's computer games. Your strategy is to be a one-stop shopping place where all kind of customers—from large companies to private individuals—can get everything they want from salespeople who can design a complete system to meet each customer's unique needs.

You are meeting to decide which kind of technology—which combination of skills, knowledge, techniques, and task relationships—will best allow you to achieve your goal.

1. Analyze the level of (a) technical complexity and (b) task variability and task analyzability associated with the kinds of tasks needed to achieve your strategy.
2. Given your answer to item 1, what kind of task interdependence between employees/

departments will best allow you to pursue your strategy?

3. Based on this analysis, what kind of technology will you choose in your store, and what kind of structure and culture will you create to manage your technology most effectively?

Making the Connection #9

Find an example of a company operating with one of the technologies identified in this chapter. Which technology is the company using? Why is the company using it? How does this technology affect the organization's structure?

The Ethical Dimension #9

The chapter discussed some of Henry Ford's strict labour practices that cause such high turnover. Workers were not allowed to talk on the production line, for example, and he employed detectives to spy on them when they were at home.

1. What limits should be placed on a company's right to monitor and control its employees from an ethical perspective? For example, think about monitoring e-mail use at work, or perhaps the use of computer keyboard monitoring or surveillance cameras.
2. What moral rules would you create to help managers decide when, and which actions and behaviours, they have a right to influence and control? How do you separate work from non-work behaviours?

Analyzing the Organization: Design Module #9

This module focuses on the technology your company uses to produce goods and services and the problems and issues associated with the use of this technology.

ASSIGNMENT

Using the information at your disposal, and drawing inferences about your company's technology from the activities that your organization engages in, answer the following questions.

1. What kinds of goods or services does your organization produce? Are inputs, conversion, or output activities the source of greatest uncertainty for your organization?
2. What role does technology in the form of knowledge play in the production of the organization's goods or services?
3. What role does materials technology play in the production of the organization's goods and services?
4. What is the organization's level of technical complexity? Does the organization use a small-batch, mass-production, or continuous-process technology?
5. Use the concepts of task variability and task analyzability to describe the complexity of your organization's activities. Which of the four types of technology identified by Perrow does your organization use?
6. What forms of task interdependence between people and between departments characterize your organization's work process? Which of the three types of technology identified by Thompson does your organization use?
7. The analysis you have done so far might lead you to expect your company to operate with a particular kind of structure. What kind? To what extent does your organization's structure seem to fit with the characteristics of the organization's technology? For example, is the structure organic or mechanistic?
8. Do you think that your organization is operating its technology effectively? Do you see any ways in which it could improve its technical efficiency, innovativeness, or ability to respond to customers?

Company Profiles #9*

Choose one or more of the organizations (e.g., companies, government agencies, or nonprofit organizations) that are profiled in this chapter. Do an Internet search to get up-to-date information on each organization you have selected, and answer the following questions.

1. What does the new information tell you about the organization's current ability to develop organizational competencies and technology?

* The authors would like to receive information from student groups and instructors on any companies where there have been dramatic changes to the information published in this text. We would be happy to publish the best of these changes in a subsequent edition, where we will focus on changing company profiles.

2. How does the information compare with the earlier information provided in the text and what does that tell you about organizations (e.g., does the organization appear to be more or less successful in developing organizational competencies and technology than before, and how do you explain this)?

Alternative Perspectives #9

Critical, feminist, and postmodernist researchers contend that strategies of organizational use of technology often adversely impact employees as the organization pursues increased profit or returns on investment. Technology is affecting organizations in many ways and one of the fundamental changes is to the nature of work and the place of the worker in the firm. Ever-increasing technological use leads to the de-skilling of employees' work; a more impersonal management environment; increased and more pervasive control of employees and their work; or the outright exploitation of employees' creativity, knowledge, or circumstances. Read one or more of the following readings and then compare and contrast the advantages and disadvantages of technology in organizations. In small groups, discuss ways of gaining from the benefits of technology without the adverse effects.

Reading List

Bell, S. A. 2001. Are Employment Relations Undergoing a Fundamental Change That Threatens the Future of Capitalism? A Critique of Hodgson's View of the Labour Contract, *Journal of Economic Issues,* 35(2), 335–343.

Davies, S. 1990. Inserting Gender in Burawoy's Theory of the Labour Process. *Work, Employment & Society.* 4(3): 391–406.

Diamond, W. J., and Freeman, R. B. 2002. Will Unionism Prosper in Cyberspace? The Promise of the Internet for Employee Organization, *British Journal of Industrial Relations,* 40(3): 569–596.

Felstead, A., Jewson, N., and Walters, S. 2003. Managerial Control of Employees Working at Home. *British Journal of Industrial Relations,* 41(2): 241–264.

Grant, J., and Tancred-Sheriff, P. 1992. A Feminist Perspective on State Bureaucracy. In A. J. Mills and P. Tancred-Sheriff, eds., *Gendering Organizational Analysis.* Newbury Park, CA: Sage.

Leonard, P. 1984. *Personality and Ideology—Towards a Material Understanding of the Individual.* London: Methuen.

Mann, S., and Holdsworth, L. 2003. The Psychological Impact of Teleworking: Stress, Emotions and Health, *New Technology, Work, and Employment,* 18(3): 196–211.

Ratliff, J. M. 2004. The Persistence of National Differences in a Globalizing World: The Japanese Struggle for Competitiveness in Advanced Information Technologies. *Journal of Socio-Economics,* 33(1), 71–78.

Russ-Eft, D. 1995. Defining Competencies: A Critique. *Human Resource Development Quarterly,* 6(4): 329–335.

Scarbrough, H. 1998. Path(ological) Dependency? Core Competencies from an Organizational Perspective. *British Journal of Management,* 9(3): 219–232.

Tietze, S. 2002. When "Work" Comes "Home": Coping Strategies of Teleworkers and Their Families, *Journal of Business Ethics,* 41(4): 385–396.

CASE FOR ANALYSIS

The Shape of Things to Come

Intense global competition in the 1990s caused many companies to take another look at the way they manufactured products. In Japan, in particular, the soaring price of the yen in the 1990s put particular pressure on large car and electronics manufacturers to look at ways to cut production costs. To find ways to cut costs, Japanese companies scrutinized the technology they were using, and the mass-production system was the subject of most of this attention.

Traditionally, Japanese companies have used the conveyor-belt system pioneered by Ford to mass-produce large volumes of identical products. In this system, workers are positioned along a straight or linear production line that can be 100 or more metres long. In examining how this system works, Japanese production managers have come to realize that a considerable amount of handling time is wasted as the product being assembled is passed from worker to worker, and that a line can only move as fast as the least capable worker. Moreover, this system is only efficient when large quantities of the same product are being produced. If customized products are needed, the production line is typically down while it is being retooled for the next product.

Recognizing these problems, production engineers began to search for assembly-line layouts that could alleviate these problems, and experimented with layouts of various shapes, such as spirals, Ys, 6s, or even insects. At a Sony camcorder plant in Kohda, Japan, for example, Sony dismantled its previous mass-production system in which 50 workers worked sequentially to build a camcorder, and replaced it with a spiral arrangement only 12 metres long in which four workers perform all the operations necessary to assemble the camcorder. Sony says this new arrangement is 10 percent more efficient than the old system. Why? Because it allows the most efficient assemblers to perform at a higher level: It reduces handling time and work is not being passed from one worker to another.[55]

In North America and Europe, these new production layouts, normally referred to as cell layouts, are becoming increasingly common. It has been estimated that 40 percent of small companies and 70 percent of large companies have experimented with these new designs. Bayside Controls Inc., for example, a small gearhead manufacturer in Queens, New York, converted its 35-person assembly line into a four-cell design where seven to nine workers form a cell. The members of each cell perform all the operations involved in making the gearheads, such as measuring, cutting, and assembling the new gearheads. Bayside's managers say that the average production time it takes to make a gear has dropped to two days from six weeks, and it now makes 75 gearheads a day (up from 50 before the change) so costs have also gone down.[56] Once again, there has been a large saving in handling costs, inventory costs are lower because production is faster, and employees are more motivated to produce high-quality products with the new system. An additional advantage is that cell designs allow companies to be very responsive to the needs of individual customers, as this system permits the quick manufacture of small quantities of customized products.

DISCUSSION QUESTIONS

1. How do the new "cell" designs change the level of technical complexity, task variability and task analyzability, and task interdependence?
2. Based on this analysis, of what type of technology discussed in the chapter does the new system remind you?
3. What are the advantages associated with the use of the new technology?

REFERENCES

1. H. Ford, "Progressive Manufacture," *Encyclopedia Britannica,* 13th ed. (New York: The Encyclopedia Co., 1926).
2. R. Edwards, *Contested Terrain: The Transformation of the Workplace in the Twentieth Century* (New York: Basic Books, 1979).
3. "Survey: The Endless Road," *The Economist,* 17 October 1992, p. 4.
4. Edwards, *Contested Terrain,* p. 119.
5. D. M. Rousseau, "Assessment of Technology in Organizations: Closed versus Open Systems Approaches," *Academy of Management Review,* 1979, vol. 4, pp. 531–542; W. R. Scott, *Organizations: Rational, Natural, and Open Systems* (Englewood Cliffs, NJ: Prentice Hall, 1981).
6. Organizational Insight by Ellen Rudderham-Gaudet, based upon the following sources: EllisDon Corporate History, *www.Ellisdon.com,* 2004; J. Parks, "EllisDon Takes Top Honours: Canadian Information Productivity Awards," *CIO Canada,* 2004, vol. 11, p. 9.
7. J. Woodward, *Management and Technology* (London: Her Majesty's Stationery Office, 1958), p. 12.
8. Woodward, *Management and Technology,* p. 11.
9. J. Woodward, *Industrial Organization: Theory and Practice* (London: Oxford University Press, 1965).
10. Woodward, *Industrial Organization.*
11. Woodward, *Management and Technology.*
12. C. Perrow, *Normal Accidents: Living with High Risk Technologies* (New York: Basic Books, 1984).
13. E. Harvey, "Technology and the Structure of Organizations," *American Sociological Review,* 1968, vol. 33, pp. 241–259; W. L. Zwerman, *New Perspectives on Organizational Effectiveness* (Westport, CT: Greenwood, 1970).
14. D. J. Hickson, D. S. Pugh, and D. C. Pheysey, "Operations Technology and Organizational Structure: An Empirical Reappraisal," *Administrative Science Quarterly,* 1969, vol. 14, pp. 378–397; D. S. Pugh, "The Aston Program of Research: Retrospect and Prospect," in A. H. Van de Ven and W. F. Joyce, eds., *Perspectives on Organizational Design and Behavior* (New York: Wiley, 1981), pp. 135–166; H. E. Aldrich, "Technology and Organizational Structure: A Reexamination of the Findings of the Aston Group," *Administrative Science Quarterly,* 1972, vol. 17, pp. 26–43.
15. J. Child and R. Mansfield, "Technology, Size, and Organization Structure," *Sociology,* 1972, vol. 6, pp. 369–393.
16. Hickson, Pugh, and Pheysey, "Operations Technology and Organizational Structure."
17. C. Perrow, *Organizational Analysis: A Sociological View* (Belmont, CA: Wadsworth, 1970).
18. Ibid.
19. Ibid., p. 21.
20. Ibid.
21. This section draws heavily on C. Perrow, "A Framework for the Comparative Analysis of Organizations," *American Sociological Review,* 1967, vol. 32, pp. 194–208.
22. Perrow, *Organizational Analysis*; C. Gresov, "Exploring Fit and Misfit with Multiple Contingencies," *Administrative Science Quarterly,* 1989, vol. 34, pp. 431–453.
23. Edwards, *Contested Terrain.*
24. J. Beyer and H. Trice, "A Re-Examination of the Relations Between Size and Various Components of Organizational Complexity," *Administrative Science Quarterly,* 1985, vol. 30, pp. 462–481.
25. L. Argote, "Input Uncertainty and Organizational Coordination of Subunits," *Administrative Science Quarterly,* 1982, vol. 27, pp. 420–434.
26. G. R. Jones, "Task Visibility, Free Riding, and Shirking: Explaining the Effect of Structure and Technology on Employee Behavior," *Academy of Management Review,* 1984, vol. 9, pp. 684–696.
27. R. T. Keller, "Technology-Information Processing Fit and the Performance of R&D Project Groups: A Test of Contingency Theory," *Academy of Management Review,* 1994, vol. 37, pp. 167–179.
28. C. Perrow, "Hospitals: Technology, Structure, and Goals," in J. March, ed., *The Handbook of Organizations* (Chicago: Rand McNally, 1965), pp. 910–971.
29. D. E. Comstock and W. R. Scott, "Technology and the Structure of Subunits," *Administrative Science Quarterly,* 1977, vol. 22, pp. 177–202; A. H. Van de Ven and A. L. Delbecq, "A Task Contingent Model of Work Unit Structure," *Administrative Science Quarterly,* 1974, vol. 19, pp. 183–197.
30. J. D. Thompson, *Organizations in Action* (New York: McGraw-Hill, 1967).
31. W. G. Ouchi, "The Relationship Between Organizational Structure and Organizational Control," *Administrative Science Quarterly,* 1977, vol. 22, pp. 95–113.
32. Thompson, *Organizations in Action,* p. 15.

33. Organizational Insight by Ellen Rudderham-Gaudet, based upon the following sources: About AD OPT, *www.ad-opt.com,* 2004; Industrial Newsroom, "Workforce Planning Software Determines Shift Deployments," *www.industrialnewsroom.com,* 9 August 2002; N. Van Praet, "Scheduling Company Thrives As Times Become More Complex," *CanWest News,* 25 July 2003.
34. Thompson, *Organizations in Action,* p. 17.
35. R. D. Hof, "From Dinosaur to Gazelle," *Business Week,* 12 August 1992, p. 7.
36. "Hewlett-Packard Sees Pressure on Sales," *Investor's Business Daily,* 4 October 1999, p. A7.
37. Thompson, *Organizations in Action*; G. R. Jones, "Organization–Client Transactions and Organizational Governance Structures," *Academy of Management Journal,* 1987, vol. 30, pp. 197–218.
38. C. Edquist and S. Jacobsson, *Flexible Automation: The Global Diffusion of New Technology in the Engineering Industry* (London: Basil Blackwell, 1988).
39. Ibid.
40. M. Jelinek and J. D. Goldhar, "The Strategic Implications of the Factory of the Future," *Sloan Management Review,* 1984, vol. 25, pp. 29–37; G. I. Susman and J. W. Dean, "Strategic Use of Computer Integrated Manufacturing in the Emerging Competitive Environment," *Computer Integrated Manufacturing Systems,* 1989, vol. 2, pp. 133–138.
41. C. A. Voss, *Managing Advanced Manufacturing Technology* (Bedford, England: IFS [Publications] Ltd., 1986).
42. J. F. Krafcik, "Triumph of the Lean Production System," *Sloan Management Review,* 1988, 30(1): 41–52.
43. Ibid.; M. T. Sweeney, "Flexible Manufacturing Systems—Managing Their Integration," in Voss, *Managing Advanced Manufacturing Technology,* pp. 69–81.
44. D. E. Whitney, "Manufacturing by Design," *Harvard Business Review,* July–August 1988, pp. 210–216.
45. "Microtechnology, Dropping Out," *The Economist,* 9 January 1993, p. 75.
46. F. M. Hull and P. D. Collins, "High Technology Batch Production Systems: Woodward's Missing Types," *Academy of Management Journal,* 1987, vol. 30, pp. 786–797.
47. R. H. Hayes and S. C. Wheelright, *Restoring Our Competitive Edge: Competing Through Manufacturing* (New York: Wiley, 1984).
48. C. A. Voss, "Managing Manufacturing Technology," in R. Wild, ed., *International Handbook of Production and Operations Management* (London: Cassel, 1989), pp. 112–121.
49. C. C. New and G. R. Clark, "Just-in-Time Manufacturing," ibid., pp. 402–417.
50. S. M. Young, "A Framework for the Successful Adoption and Performance of Japanese Manufacturing Practices in the United States," *Academy of Management Review,* 1992, vol. 17, pp. 677–700.
51. A. Ansari and B. Modarress, *Just-in-Time Purchasing* (New York: The Free Press, 1990).
52. J. P. Womack, D. T. Jones, D. Roos, and D. Sammons, *The Machine That Changed the World* (New York: Macmillan, 1990).
53. H.-J. Warnecke and R. Steinhilper, "CIM, FMS, and Robots," in Wild, *International Handbook of Production and Operations Management,* pp. 146–173.
54. P. L. Nemetz and L. W. Fry, "Flexible Manufacturing Organizations: Implications for Strategy Formulation and Organizational Design," *Academy of Management Review,* 1988, vol. 13, pp. 627–638.
55. M. Williams, "Back to the Past," *Wall Street Journal,* 24 October 1994, p. A1.
56. S. N. Mehta, "Cell Manufacturing Gains Acceptance at Smaller Plants," *Wall Street Journal,* 15 September 1994, p. B2.

Types and Forms of Organizational Change

CHAPTER 10

Learning Objectives

Today, as never before, organizations are facing an environment that is changing rapidly, and the task facing managers is to help organizations identify, respond, and adjust to the changes taking place. This chapter discusses the various types of change that organizations can face, and how organizations can manage the process of change to stay ahead in today's competitive environments.

After reading this chapter you should be able to:

1. Understand the relationship among organizational change, redesign, and organizational effectiveness.
2. Distinguish among the major forms or types of evolutionary and revolutionary change organizations may need to manage.
3. Recognize the problems inherent in managing change and the obstacles that must be overcome.
4. Describe the change process and understand the techniques that can be used to help an organization achieve its desired future state.

WHAT IS ORGANIZATIONAL CHANGE?

Organizational change The process by which organizations move from their present state to some desired future state to increase their effectiveness.

Organizational change is the process by which organizations move from their present state to some desired future state to increase their effectiveness. The goal of planned organizational change is to find new or improved ways of using resources and capabilities in order to increase an organization's ability to create value and improve returns to its stakeholders.[1] An organization in decline may need to restructure its resources to improve its fit with the environment. Nortel, Air Canada, AT&T Canada, and Creo Inc., for example, experienced falling demand for their products in the new millennium and have been searching for new ways to use their resources to improve their performance and attract customers back. On the other hand, even a thriving organization may need to change the way it uses its resources so that it can develop new products or find new markets for its existing products. Wal-Mart, Blockbuster Video, and Toys "R" Us, for example, have been moving aggressively to expand their scale of operations and open new stores to take advantage of the popularity of their products. This has included major expansion into Canada in the past few years. In the last decade, over half of all Fortune 500 and Financial Post 500 companies have undergone major organizational changes to allow them to increase their ability to create value.

Targets of Change

Planned organizational change is normally targeted at improving effectiveness at one or more of four different levels: human resources, functional resources, technological capabilities, and organizational capabilities.

Human Resources Human resources consist of the people of an organization—its employees and managers. They are an organization's most important asset. Ultimately, an organization's distinctive competencies lie in the skills and abilities of its employees. Because these skills and abilities give an organization a competitive advantage, organizations must continually monitor their structures to find the most effective way of motivating and organizing its people to fully utilize and develop their skills. Typical kinds of change efforts directed at human resources include: (1) new investment in training and development activities so that employees acquire new skills and abilities; (2) socializing employees into the organizational culture so that they learn the new routines on which organizational performance depends; (3) changing organizational norms and values to motivate a multicultural and diverse workforce; (4) ongoing examination of the way in which promotion and reward systems operate in a diverse workforce; and (5) changing the composition of the top-management team to improve organizational learning and decision making.

Functional Resources As discussed in previous chapters, each organizational function needs to develop procedures that allow it to manage the particular environment it faces. As the environment changes, organizations often transfer resources to the functions where the most value can be created. Crucial functions grow in importance, while those whose usefulness is declining shrink.

An organization can improve the value that its functions create by changing its structure, culture, and technology. The change from a functional to a product team structure, for example, may speed the new product development process. Alterations in functional structure can help provide a setting in which people are motivated to perform. The change from traditional mass production to a manufacturing operation based on self-managed work teams often allows companies to increase product quality and productivity if employees can share in the gains from the new work system.

Technological Capabilities Technological capabilities give an organization an enormous capacity to change itself in order to exploit market opportunities. The ability to develop a constant stream of new products or to modify existing products so that they continue to attract customers is one of an organization's core competencies. Similarly, the ability to improve the way goods and services are produced in order to increase their quality and reliability is a crucial organizational capability. At the organizational level, an organization has to provide the context that allows it to translate its technological competencies into value for its stakeholders. This task often involves the redesign of organizational activities. IBM, for example, has recently moved to change its organizational structure to better capitalize on its strengths in providing IT consulting. Previously, it had been unable to translate its technical capabilities into commercial opportunities because its structure was not focused on consulting, but on making and selling computer hardware and software rather than providing advice. As we shall see in Chapter 13, technological change is often linked to innovation.

Organizational Capabilities Through the design of organizational structure and culture, an organization can harness its human and functional resources to take advantage of technological opportunities. Organizational change often involves changing the relationships between people and functions to increase their ability to create value. Changes in structure and culture take place at all levels of the organization and include changing the routines an individual uses to greet customers, changing work group relationships, improving integration between divisions, and changing corporate culture by changing the top-management team.

These four levels at which change can take place are obviously interdependent; it is often impossible to change one without changing another. Suppose an organization invests resources and recruits a team of scientists who are experts in a new technology—for example, biotechnology. If successful, this human resource change will lead to the emergence of a new functional resource and a new technological capability. Top management will be forced to re-evaluate its organizational structure and the way it integrates and coordinates its other functions, to ensure that they support its new functional resources. Effectively utilizing the new resources may require a move to a product team structure. It may even require downsizing and the elimination of functions that are no longer central to the organization's mission.

FORCES FOR AND RESISTANCE TO ORGANIZATIONAL CHANGE

The organizational environment is constantly changing, and an organization may need to adapt to these changes in order to survive.[2] Figure 10-1 lists the most important forces for and impediments to change that confront an organization and its managers.

FIGURE 10-1
Forces for and Resistances to Change.

Forces for Change	Resistances to Change
Competitive Forces Economic Forces Political Forces Global Forces Demographic Forces Social Forces Ethical Forces	Organizational Level • Structure • Culture • Strategy Functional Level • Differences in Subunit Orientation • Power and Conflict Group Level • Norms • Cohesiveness • Groupthink Individual Level • Cognitive Biases • Uncertainty and Insecurity • Selective Perception and Retention • Habit

Forces for Change

Recall from Chapter 3 that many forces in the environment have an impact on an organization and that recognizing the nature of these forces is one of a manager's most important tasks.[3] If managers are slow to respond to competitive, economic, political, global, and other forces, the organization will lag behind its competitors and its effectiveness will be compromised (see Figure 10-1).

Competitive Forces Organizations are constantly striving to achieve a competitive advantage.[4] Competition is a force for change because unless an organization matches or surpasses its competitors in efficiency, quality, or its capability to innovate new or improved goods or services it will not survive.[5]

To lead on the dimensions of efficiency or quality, an organization must constantly adopt the latest technology as it becomes available. The adoption of new technology usually brings a change to task relationships as workers learn new skills or techniques to operate the new technology.[6] Later in this chapter we discuss total quality management and re-engineering, two change strategies that have been widely adopted by organizations across North America to achieve efficiency or quality.[7]

To lead on the dimension of innovation and obtain a technological advantage over competitors, a company must possess skills in managing the process of innovation, another source of change that we discuss later. This point is further developed in Chapter 13.

Economic, Political, and Global Forces Economic, political, and global forces continually affect organizations and compel them to change how and where they produce goods and services. Economic and political unions among countries are becoming an increasingly important force for change.[8] The North American Free Trade Agreement (NAFTA) paved the way for cooperation among Canada, the United States, and Mexico. The European Union (EU) includes 25 members eager to exploit the advantages of a large, protected market. Japan and other fast-growing Asian countries such as Malaysia, Thailand, and China, recognizing that economic unions protect member nations and create barriers against foreign competitors, have moved to increase their presence in foreign countries. Many Japanese companies, for example, have opened new manufacturing plants in Canada, the United States, and Mexico, and in European countries such as Spain and the U.K., so that they can share in the advantages offered by NAFTA and the European Union. Toyota, Honda, and Nissan have all opened large car plants in England to supply cars to EU member countries. No organization can afford to ignore the effects of global economic and political forces on its activities.[9]

Other global challenges facing organizations include the need to change an organizational structure to allow expansion into foreign markets, the need to adapt to a variety of national cultures, and the need to help expatriate managers adapt to the economic, political, and cultural values of the countries in which they are located.[10] DaimlerChrysler's German parent, for example, sent 30 managers already experienced in both North American and Japanese-style manufacturing methods to head its new operations in the United States. This has also been the case with Japanese and Korean vehicle manufacturers operating in Canada.

Demographic and Social Forces Managing a diverse workforce is one of the biggest challenges to confront organizations in the new millennium.[11] Changes in the composition of the workforce and the increasing diversity of employees have presented organizations with many challenges and opportunities.[12] Increasingly, changes in the demographic characteristics of the workforce have led managers to change their styles of managing all employees and to learn how to understand, supervise, and motivate diverse members effectively. Managers have had to abandon the stereotypes they unwittingly may have used in making promotion decisions, and they have had to accept the importance of equity in the recruitment and promotion of new hires, and acknowledge employees' desire for a lifestyle that strikes an acceptable balance between work and leisure. Many companies have helped their workers keep up with changing technology by providing support for advanced education and training. Increasingly, organizations are coming to realize that the ultimate source of competitive advantage and organizational effectiveness lies in fully utilizing the skills of their members, by, for example, empowering employees to make important and significant decisions.[13]

Ethical Forces Just as it is important for an organization to take steps to change in response to changing demographic and social forces, it is also important for an organization to take steps to promote ethical behaviour in the face of increasing government, political, and social demands for more responsible and honest corporate behaviour.[14] Many companies have created the position of ethics officer, a person to whom employees can report ethical lapses by an organization's managers or workers and can turn for advice on difficult ethical questions. Organizations are also trying to promote ethical behaviour by giving employees more direct access to important decision makers and by protecting whistle-blowers who turn the organization in when they perceive ethical problems with the way certain managers behave.

Many organizations need to make changes to allow managers and workers at all levels to report unethical behaviour so that an organization can move quickly to eliminate such behaviour and protect the general interests of its members and customers.[15] Similarly, if organizations operate in countries that pay little attention to human rights or to the well-being of organizational members, they have to learn how to change these standards and to protect their foreign employees. The story of sports shoemakers battling with accusations that their shoes are produced in sweatshops in third-world countries illustrates this issue. (See Organizational Insight 10.1.)

From customer design preferences, to the issue of where clothes should be produced, to the question of whether economic or political unrest will affect the availability of raw materials, the forces of change bombard organizations from all sides. Effective organizations are agile enough to adjust to these forces. But many forces internal to an organization make the organization resistant to change and thus threaten its effectiveness and survival.

Resistances to Change

In the last decade many of Canada's best-known (and formerly strongest and most successful) companies—Corel, Air Canada, Eaton's, JDS, and Stelco—have seen their fortunes decline. Some, such as Eaton's and Stelco, have gone bankrupt; others, such as Nortel, Bombardier, and Air Canada, are still in trouble; and some, such as GM Canada, have reversed their decline and recovered. How did such former powerhouses lose their effectiveness? The main explanation for such decline is almost always an organization's inability to change in response to changes (such as an increase in competition) in its environment. Research suggests that one of the main reasons for some organizations' inability to change is organizational inertia, the tendency of an organization to maintain the status quo. Resistance to change lowers an organization's effectiveness and reduces its chances of survival.[16] Resistances or impediments to change that cause inertia are found at the organization, group, and individual levels[17] (see Figure 10-1, p. 332).

ORGANIZATIONAL INSIGHT 10.1

Nike, Reebok, Adidas, and the Sweatshops

As all kinds of products increasingly are being manufactured in poor third-world countries, the behaviour of companies that outsource production to subcontractors in these countries has come under increasing scrutiny. Nike, the giant sports shoemaker with sales of over US$9 billion a year, was one of the first to experience a backlash when it became known how workers in these countries were being treated. Indonesian workers were stitching together shoes in hot, noisy factories for only 80 cents a day, or about US$18 a month.[18] Workers in Vietnam and China fared better; they could earn US$1.60 a day. In all cases, however, critics charged that at least US$3 a day was needed to maintain an adequate living standard.

These facts generated an outcry in the United States, where Nike was roundly attacked for its labour practices; there was a backlash against sales of Nike products, and Phil Knight, Nike's billionaire owner, was asked to defend how, when his net worth was over US$3 billion, he could defend paying a worker 80 cents a day. As criticism mounted he was forced to re-evaluate Nike's labour practices. Nike announced that henceforth all the factories producing its shoes and clothes would be independently monitored and inspected. Then, after Reebok, a competitor criticized for similar labour practices, announced that it was raising wages in Indonesia by 20 percent, Nike raised them by 25 percent, to US$23 a month.[19] Nonetheless, controversy continues to rage around the extent to which Nike is a socially responsible company.[20]

In Europe, Adidas, another sportswear company, had largely escaped such criticism. But in 1999 it was reported that in El Salvador, a Taiwan-based Adidas subcontractor was employing girls as young as 14 in its factories and making them work over 70 hours a week. They were only allowed to go to the washroom twice a day and if they stayed longer than three minutes they lost a day's wages.[21] Adidas moved swiftly to avoid the public relations nightmare that Nike had experienced. Adidas announced that, henceforth, its subcontractors would also be required to abide by more strict labour standards. Thus, throughout the industry companies were forced to re-evaluate the ethics of their labour practices, and promise to keep a constant watch on subcontractors in the future. This will become increasingly critical as numbers of Canadian companies, such as Air Canada, move their operations to underdeveloped countries.

Organization-Level Resistance to Change

Many forces inside an organization make it difficult for the organization to change in response to changing conditions in its environment.[22] The most powerful organization-level impediments to change include power and conflict, differences in functional orientation, mechanistic structure, and organizational culture.

Power and Conflict Change usually benefits some people, functions, or divisions at the expense of others. When change causes power struggles and organizational conflict, an organization is likely to resist it.[23] Suppose that a change in purchasing practices will help materials management to achieve its goal of reducing input costs but will harm manufacturing's ability to reduce manufacturing costs. Materials management will push for the change, but manufacturing will resist it. The conflict between the two functions will slow the process of change and perhaps prevent change from occurring at all. If powerful functions can prevent change, an organization will not change. At IBM, for example, managers in the mainframe computer division were the most powerful in the corporation. To preserve their established prestige and power in the organization, they fought off attempts to redirect IBM's resources to produce the personal computers or minicomputers that customers wanted. This failure to change in response to customer demands severely reduced IBM's speed of response to its competitors. Chapter 14 is devoted to discussing this important obstacle to change.

Differences in Functional Orientation Differences in functional orientation are another major impediment to change and a source of organizational inertia. Different functions and divisions often see the source of a problem differently because they see an issue or problem primarily from their own viewpoint. This "tunnel vision" increases organizational inertia because the organization must spend time and effort to secure agreement about the source of a problem before it can even consider how the organization needs to change to respond to the problem.

Mechanistic Structure Recall from Chapter 4 that a mechanistic structure is characterized by a tall hierarchy, centralized decision making, and the standardization of behaviour through rules and procedures. By contrast, organic structures are flat and decentralized and rely on mutual adjustment between people to get the job done.[24] Which structure is likely to be more resistant to change?

Mechanistic structures are more resistant to change. People who work within a mechanistic structure are expected to act in certain ways and do not develop the capacity to adjust their behaviour to changing conditions. The extensive use of mutual adjustment and decentralized authority in an organic structure fosters the development of skills that allow workers to be creative, responsive, and able to find solutions for new problems. A mechanistic structure typically develops as an organization grows and is a principal source of inertia, especially in large organizations.

Organizational Culture The values and norms in an organization's culture can be another source of resistance to change. Just as role relationships result in a series of stable expectations between people, so values and norms cause people to behave in predictable ways. If organizational change disrupts taken-for-granted values and norms and forces people to change what they do and how they do it, an organization's culture will cause resistance to change. For example, many organizations develop conservative values that support the status quo and make managers reluctant to search for new ways to compete. As a result, if the environment changes and a company's products become obsolete, the company has nothing to fall back on, and failure is likely.[25] Sometimes, values and norms are so strong that even when the environment is changing and it is clear that a new strategy needs to be adopted, managers cannot change because they are committed to the way they presently do business. Organizational Insight 10.2 illustrates how the organizational culture of the United Nations failed to avert genocide in Rwanda.

Group-Level Resistance to Change

Much of an organization's work is performed by groups, and several group characteristics can produce resistance to change. First, many groups develop strong informal norms that specify appropriate and inappropriate behaviours and govern the interactions between group members.[26] Often, change alters task and role relationships in a group; when it does, it disrupts group norms and the informal expectations that group members have of one another. As a result, members of a group may resist change because a whole new set of norms may have to be developed to meet the needs of the new situation.

ORGANIZATIONAL INSIGHT 10.2

Genocide in Rwanda: A Monumental Failure of Organization

The most dramatic demonstration that power, conflict, structure, and organizational culture can prevent adequate responses to change can be viewed in the failure of the United Nations (UN) to prevent genocide in Rwanda in the early 1990s. In 1993 the UN appointed Lieutenant-General Romeó Dallaire to lead a small peacekeeping force in Rwanda to prevent conflict between rival forces in the country. The leading belligerents had signed a peace agreement that was to come into effect later that year. The UN force under Dallaire was to monitor the situation and attempt to prevent further bloodshed. However, when Dallaire began to identify that Rwandan government-sponsored forces were encouraging genocide along ethnic lines, he came up against both international and organizational politics that prevented him from taking firm action or from receiving adequate support. Ultimately, the UN moved incredibly slowly while 800 000 Rwandans—mostly from the minority Tutsi tribe—were openly murdered. According to Dallaire, the UN did not have the ability to provide any political will without an elaborate series of international meetings, bargaining, and negotiation, and it seemed equally unable to provide material support—when even possible—in periods less than six months.[27] Following his tour of duty, Dallaire concluded: "The UN must undergo a renaissance if it is to be involved in conflict resolution. This is not limited to the Secretariat, its administration and bureaucrats, but must encompass the member nations, who need to rethink their roles and recommit to a renewal of purpose. Otherwise the hope that we will ever truly enter an age of humanity will die as the UN continues to decline into irrelevance."[28]

Group cohesiveness, the attractiveness of a group to its members, also affects group performance. Although some level of cohesiveness promotes group performance, too much cohesiveness may actually reduce performance because it stifles opportunities for the group to change and adapt. A highly cohesive group may resist attempts by management to change what it does or even who is a member of the group. Group members may unite to preserve the status quo and to protect their interests at the expense of other groups.

Groupthink is a pattern of faulty decision making that occurs in cohesive groups when members discount negative information in order to arrive at a unanimous agreement. Escalation of commitment worsens this situation because even when group members realize that their decision is wrong, they continue to pursue it because they are committed to it. These group processes make changing a group's behaviour very difficult. And the more important the group's activities are to the organization, the greater the impact of these processes on organizational performance.

Individual-Level Resistance to Change

There are also several reasons why individuals within an organization may be inclined to resist change.[29] First, people tend to resist change because they feel uncertain and insecure about what its outcome will be.[30] Workers might be given new tasks. Role relationships may be reorganized. Some workers might lose their jobs. Some people might benefit at the expense of others. Workers' resistance to the uncertainty and insecurity surrounding change can cause organizational inertia. Absenteeism and turnover may increase as change takes place, and workers may become uncooperative, attempt to delay or slow the change process, and otherwise passively resist the change in an attempt to quash it.

Moreover, there is a general tendency for people to selectively perceive information that is consistent with their existing views of their organizations. Thus, when change takes place, workers tend to focus only on how it will affect them or their function or division personally. If they perceive few benefits, they may reject the purpose behind the change. Not surprisingly, it can be difficult for an organization to develop a common platform to promote change across an organization and get people to see the need for change in the same way.

Habit, people's preference for familiar actions and events, is a further impediment to change. The difficulty of breaking bad habits and adopting new styles of behaviour indicates how resistant habits are to change. Why are habits hard to break? Some researchers have suggested that people have a built-in tendency to return to their original behaviours, a tendency that stymies change.

Lewin's Force-Field Theory of Change

Force-field theory
A theory of organizational change that argues that two sets of opposing forces within an organization determine how change will take place.

A wide variety of forces make organizations resistant to change, and a wide variety of forces push organizations toward change. Researcher Kurt Lewin developed a theory about organizational change, much of which was concerned with reducing conflict and overcoming prejudice.[31] According to his **force-field theory**, these two sets of forces are always in opposition in an organization.[32] When the forces are evenly balanced, the organization is in a state of inertia and does not change. To get an organization to change, managers must find a way to *increase* the forces for change, *reduce* resistance to change, or do *both* simultaneously. Any of these strategies will overcome inertia and cause an organization to change.

Figure 10-2 illustrates Lewin's theory. An organization at performance level P1 is in balance: Forces for change and resistance to change are equal. Management, how-

FIGURE 10-2
Lewin's Force-Field Theory of Change.

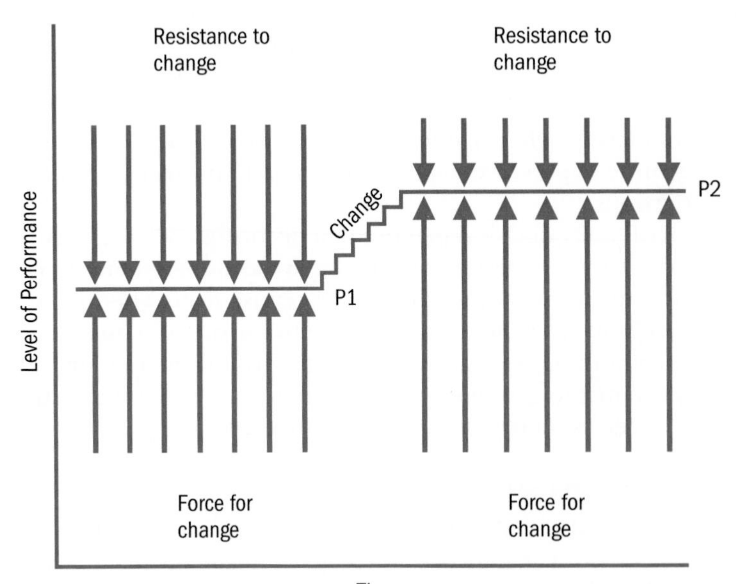

ever, decides that the organization should strive to achieve performance level P2. To get to level P2, managers must increase the forces for change (the increase is represented by the lengthening of the up arrows), reduce resistance to change (the reduction is represented by the shortening of the down arrows), or do both. If they pursue any of the three strategies successfully, the organization will change and reach performance level P2.

Before we look in more detail at the techniques that managers can use to overcome resistance and facilitate change, we need to look at the types of change they can implement to increase organizational effectiveness.

MANAGERIAL IMPLICATIONS

Forces for and Resistances to Change

1. Periodically analyze the organizational environment and identify potential forces for change.
2. Analyze how the change in response to these forces will affect people, functions, and divisions inside the organization.
3. Using this analysis, decide what, if any, type of change to pursue, and develop a plan to overcome possible resistance to change and to increase the forces for change.

EVOLUTIONARY AND REVOLUTIONARY CHANGE IN ORGANIZATIONS

Managers continually face choices about how best to respond to the forces for change. There are several types of change that managers can adopt to help their organizations achieve desired future states. In general, types of change fall into two broad categories: evolutionary change and revolutionary change.[33]

Evolutionary change is gradual, incremental, and narrowly focused. Evolutionary change involves not a drastic or sudden altering of the basic nature of an organization's strategy and structure but a constant attempt to improve, adapt, and adjust strategy and structure incrementally to accommodate to changes taking place in the environment.[34] Sociotechnical systems theory, total quality management, and the creation of empowered, flexible work groups are three instruments of evolutionary change that organizations use in their attempt to make incremental improvements in the way work gets done. Such improvements might be a better way to operate a technology or to organize the work process.

Evolutionary change
Change that is gradual, incremental, and specifically focused.

Evolutionary change is accomplished gradually, incrementally. Some organizations, however, need to make major changes quickly. They do not want to take the time to set up and implement programs that foster evolutionary change or wait for the performance results that such programs can bring about. Faced with drastic, unexpected changes in the environment (e.g., a new technological breakthrough) or with impending disaster resulting from years of inaction and neglect, an organization needs to act quickly and decisively. Revolutionary change is called for.

Revolutionary change
Change that is sudden, drastic, and organization-wide.

Revolutionary change is rapid, dramatic, and broadly focused. Revolutionary change involves a bold attempt to quickly find new ways to be effective. It is likely to result in a radical shift in ways of doing things, new goals, and a new structure. It has repercussions at all levels in the organization—corporate, divisional, functional, group, and individual. Re-engineering, restructuring, and innovation are three important instruments of revolutionary change.

DEVELOPMENTS IN EVOLUTIONARY CHANGE

Sociotechnical Systems Theory

Sociotechnical systems theory
A theory that proposes the importance of changing role and task or technical relationships to increase organizational effectiveness.

Sociotechnical systems theory was one of the first theories that proposed the importance of changing role and task or technical relationships to increase organizational effectiveness.[35] It emerged from a study of changing work practices in the British coal-mining industry.[36]

After World War II, new technology that changed work relationships between miners was introduced into the British mining industry. Before the war, coal mining was a small-batch or craft process. Teams of skilled miners dug coal from the coalface underground and performed all the other activities necessary to transport the coal to the surface. Work took place in a confined space where productivity depended on close cooperation between team members. Workers developed their own routines and norms to get the job done and provided each other with social support to help combat the stress of their dangerous and confining working conditions.

This method of coal mining, called the "hand got method," approximated small-batch technology (see Chapter 9). To increase efficiency, managers decided to replace it with the "long wall method." This method utilized a mechanized, mass-production technology. Coal was now cut by miners using powered drills, and it was transported to the surface on conveyor belts. Tasks became more routine as the work process was programmed and standardized. On paper, the new technology promised impressive increases in mining efficiency. But after its introduction at the mines, however, efficiency rose only slowly, and absenteeism among miners, which had always been high, increased dramatically. Consultants were called to the mines to figure out why the expected gains in efficiency had not occurred.

The researchers pointed out that, to operate the new technology efficiently, management had changed the task and role relationships among the miners. The new task and role relationships had destroyed informal norms and social support, disrupted long-established informal working relationships, and reduced group cohesiveness. To solve the problem, the researchers recommended linking the new technology with the old social system by recreating the old system of tasks and roles and decentralizing authority to work groups. When management redesigned the production process, productivity improved and absenteeism fell.

This study led to the development of sociotechnical systems theory, which argues that managers need to fit or "jointly optimize" the workings of an organization's technical and social systems—or, in terms of the present discussion, culture—to promote effectiveness.[37] A poor fit between an organization's technology and social system leads to failure, but a close fit leads to success. The lesson to take from sociotechnical systems theory is that when managers change task and role relationships, they must recognize the need to adjust the technical and social systems gradually so that group norms and cohesiveness are not disrupted. By taking this gradual approach, an organization can avoid the group-level resistance to change that we discussed earlier in this chapter.

This pioneering study has been followed by many other studies that show the importance of the link between type of technology and cultural values and norms.[38] Managers need to be sensitive to the fact that the way they structure the work process affects the way people and groups behave. Compare the following two mass-production settings, for example. In the first, managers routinize the technology, standardize the work process, and require workers to perform repetitive tasks as quickly as possible; workers are assigned to a place on the production line and are not allowed to move or switch jobs; and managers monitor workers closely and make all the decisions involving control of the work process. In the second, managers standardize the work process but encourage workers to find better ways to perform tasks; workers are allowed to switch jobs; and workers are formed into teams that are empowered to monitor and control important aspects of their own performance.

What differences in values and norms will emerge between these two types of sociotechnical systems? And what will be their effect on performance? Many researchers have argued that the more team-based system will promote the development of values and norms that will boost efficiency and product quality. Indeed, the goal of total quality management, the continuous improvement in product quality, draws heavily on the principles embedded in sociotechnical systems theory; so does the development of flexible workers and workgroups, both discussed next.

Total Quality Management

Total quality management (TQM) is an ongoing and constant effort by all of an organization's functions to find new ways to improve the quality of the organization's goods and services.[39] In many companies, the initial decision to adopt a TQM approach signals a radical change in the way their activities are organized. Once TQM is adopted by an organization, however, it leads to continuous, incremental change, and all functions are expected to cooperate with each other to improve quality.

Total quality management (TQM)
A technique developed by W. Edwards Deming to continuously improve the effectiveness of flexible work teams.

First developed by a number of American business consultants such as W. Edwards Deming and Joseph Juran, total quality management was eagerly embraced by Japanese companies after World War II. For Japanese companies, with their tradition of long-term working relationships and cooperation between functions, the implementation of the new TQM system was an incremental step. Shop-floor workers in Japan, for example, had long been organized into **quality circles**, groups of workers who met regularly to discuss the way work is performed in order to find new ways to increase performance.[40] Changes frequently inspired by TQM include altering the design or type of machines used to assemble products and reorganizing the sequence of activities—within or between functions—necessary to provide a service to a customer. As in sociotechnical systems theory, the emphasis in TQM is on the fit between technical and social systems.

Quality circles
Groups of workers who meet regularly to discuss the way work is performed in order to find new ways to increase performance.

Changing cross-functional relationships to help improve quality is very important in TQM. Poor quality often originates at crossover points or after handoffs, when people turn over the work they are doing to people in different functions. The job of intermediate manufacturing, for example, is to assemble inputs that are assembled into a final product. Coordinating the design of the various inputs so that they fit together smoothly and operate effectively together is one area of TQM focus. Members of the different functions work together to find new ways to reduce the number of inputs needed or to suggest design improvements that will enable inputs to be assembled more easily and reliably. Such changes increase quality and lower costs. Note that the changes associated with TQM (as with sociotechnical systems theory) are changes in task, role, and group relationships. The results of TQM activities can be dramatic, as illustrated in Organizational Insight 10.3.

More and more companies are embracing the continuous, incremental type of change that results from the implementation of TQM programs. In Canada, a vast range of organizations have introduced TQM, including New York University, Air Canada, the Bank of Montreal, and Dofasco.[41] Many companies have found, however, that implementing a TQM program is not always easy, because it requires workers and managers to adopt new ways of viewing their roles in an organization. In some cases, TQM may not be the appropriate mode of change initiative for the organization. This was arguably the case when senior administrators attempted to introduce TQM into the Ontario hospital system in the 1990s. The attempt to implement a business strategy into the public health-care system revealed some of the underlying problems of the universal application of a method of change. For example, a number of staff were trained and assigned to different "teams," but in the process well-established groups

ORGANIZATIONAL INSIGHT 10.3

Citibank Uses TQM to Increase Customer Loyalty

Citibank is a leading global financial institution and has established the goal to become *the* premier institution in the 21st century. To achieve this lofty goal it has started to use TQM to increase its responsiveness to customers, recognizing that, ultimately, its customer base and customer loyalty determine the bank's future success.

As the first step in its TQM effort, Citibank focused upon identifying the factors that dissatisfy its customers. When it analyzed the complaints it found that most of them concerned the time it took to complete a customer's request, such as responding to an account problem or getting a loan. So Citibank's managers began to examine how they handled each kind of customer request. For each distinct kind of request, they formed a cross-functional team of people whose job was to break down a specific request into the steps between people and departments that were needed to complete the request and analyze them. These teams found that often many steps in the process were unnecessary and could be done away with by the use of the right information systems. They also found that very often delays occurred because employees simply did not know how to handle the request. They were not being given the right kind of training and when they couldn't handle a request, they simply put it aside until a supervisor could deal with it.

So Citibank decided to implement an organization-wide TQM program. Managers and supervisors were charged with reducing the complexity of the work process and finding the most effective way to process a particular request, such as for a loan. They were also charged with training employees on how to answer each specific request. The results were remarkable. For example, in the loan department the TQM program reduced the number of handoffs necessary to process a request by 75 percent; average time taken to respond to a customer dropped from several hours to 30 minutes. Within one year, over 92 000 employees had been trained worldwide in the new TQM processes and Citibank could easily measure TQM's effectiveness by the increased speed with which it was handling an increased volume of customer requests. By 2002, it had over 100 million customers in over 100 countries.

were disrupted because their existing ways of working were not viewed as consistent with the TQM notion of teams. (See Organizational Insight 10.4.)

ORGANIZATIONAL INSIGHT 10.4

The Total Quality Management of Ontario Hospitals[42]

Over time the application of TQM had become associated with success in a large number of manufacturing organizations throughout North America, and other, not-for-profit organizations were beginning to take note. In particular, health-care organizations found the principles of TQM attractive to their way of operating. For example, in 1991 the Ontario Premier's Council on Health Strategy was to declare that the "health sector can learn a great deal from modern management science—and particularly from the Japanese and American experiences in the total quality management of individuals and organizations." The council believed that the methods used to reorganize Japanese car plants were "equally applicable to manufacturing or service operations," and its view was shared by many senior health-care administrators throughout Ontario.

Within a short time, TQM was adopted within a number of Ontario hospitals. Consultants were hired, training programs were put into effect, and major reorganization of work practices and processes was implemented. In the mid-1990s a group of researchers examined the impact of TQM on the Ontario health-care service and produced a preliminary report suggesting that the philosophy and implementation of TQM was inappropriate as a system for managing hospitals. The report, titled "Medical Alert"—found that employees were often not involved in decision making about the introduction and implementation of TQM; the selection of people for TQM training and serving on TQM committees remained firmly under management control; TQM training was often seen as trivial and a waste of resources by employees; many middle managers, whose jobs were threatened by TQM, resisted the implementation of TQM; cost-reduction and cost-cutting took precedence over empowerment and innovation; a focus on the elimination of waste was centrally concerned with employing fewer people and getting the remaining employees to work harder; and instead of developing multiskilled personnel, hospitals were developing multitasked employees who were often paid less and were untrained for the extra tasks. In particular, the researchers found that aspects of the TQM philosophy seemed unsuited to health-care organizations. For instance, the use of the term "customer" (rather than "patient") was refocusing health-care relationships on profit outcomes rather than health-care concerns and, likewise, the standardization of services did not gel with a system that has to cope with people who need varying forms of care and treatment. The team concept of TQM is fundamentally different from past practices within health care and, ironically, was seen as making teamwork less desirable and effective. While the previous system *encouraged* groups of people to develop and to help one another, under TQM people were formally *required* to form teams, and those teams were given greater formal responsibility, a requirement to take over certain administrative functions, more formal reporting, and at no extra pay.

The researchers conclude that "many of the problems result from the failure to recognize that hospitals are not factories and patients are not customers," but they note that, against a background of sharp cost-cutting within the health-care system, TQM is being abandoned and the newest form of management technique—re-engineering—is taking its place.

Managers must be willing to decentralize control of decision making, empower workers, and assume the role of facilitator rather than supervisor. The "command and control" model gives way to an "advise and support" model. It is important that workers, as well as managers, share in the increased profits that successful TQM programs can provide. In Japan, for example, performance bonuses frequently account for 30 percent or more of workers' and managers' salaries, and salaries can fluctuate widely from year to year as a result of changes in organizational performance.

Resistance to the changes a TQM program requires can be serious unless management explicitly recognizes the many ways that TQM affects relationships between functions and even divisions. We discuss ways to deal with resistance to change at length later in this chapter.

Despite the success that many organizations have had with TQM, many other organizations have not obtained the increases in quality and reductions in cost that are often associated with TQM and have abandoned their TQM programs. Three reasons for a lack of success with TQM are (1) underestimates of the degree of commitment from people at all levels in the organization that is necessary to implement a TQM program, (2) the long time frame that is necessary for TQM efforts to succeed and show results, and (3) a rush to adopt the latest change program without giving adequate consideration to whether it is appropriate for the company involved.[43] TQM is not a quick fix that can turn an organization around overnight. It is an evolutionary process that bears fruit only when it becomes a way of life in an organization.[44]

Flexible Workers and Flexible Work Teams

In many modern manufacturing settings, attention to the goals behind sociotechnical systems theory and TQM has led many organizations to embrace the concept of flexible workers and work teams as a way of changing employee attitudes and behaviours. First, employees need to acquire and develop the skills to perform any of the tasks necessary for assembling a range of finished products.[45] A worker first develops the skills needed to accomplish one work task and over time is trained to perform other tasks. Compensation is frequently tied to the number of different tasks that a person can perform. Each worker can substitute for any other worker. As the demand for components or finished products rises or falls, flexible workers can be transferred to the task most needed by the organization. As a result, the organization is able to respond quickly to changes in its environment. Performing more than one task also cuts down on repetition, boredom, and fatigue and raises workers' incentives to improve product quality. When workers learn one another's tasks, they also learn how the different tasks relate to each other. This understanding often leads to new ways of combining tasks or to the redesign of a product to make its manufacture more efficient and less costly.

Flexible work team
A group of workers who assume responsibility for performing all the operations necessary for completing a specified stage in the manufacturing process.

To further speed the development of functional capabilities, flexible workers are then grouped into flexible work teams.[46] A **flexible work team** is a group of workers who assume responsibility for performing all the operations necessary for completing a specified stage in the manufacturing process. Production line workers who were previously responsible for only their own tasks are placed in groups and are jointly assigned responsibility for one stage of the manufacturing process. At Ford plants, for example, one work team is responsible for assembling the car transmission and sending it to the body assembly area, where the body assembly team is responsible for fitting it to the car body. A flexible work team is self-managed: The team members jointly assign tasks and transfer workers from one task to another as necessary.

Figure 10-3 illustrates the way in which flexible work teams perform their activities. Separate teams assemble different components and turn those components over

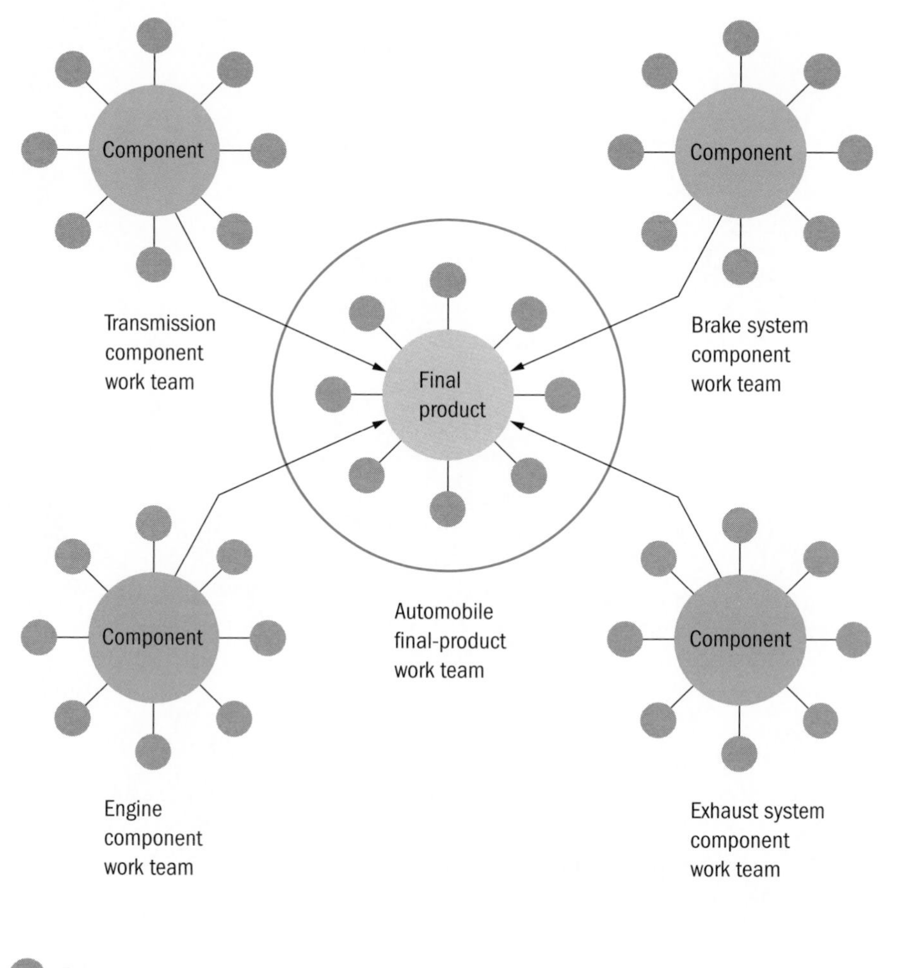

FIGURE 10-3
The Use of Flexible Work Teams to Assemble Cars.
Self-managed teams assemble brake systems, exhaust systems, and other components in accordance with the demands of the final-product team. Driven by customers' demands, the final-product team assembles components to produce a car.

to the final-product work team, which assembles the final product. Each team's activities are driven by demands that have their origins in customer demands for the final product. Thus each team has to adjust its activities to the pull coming from the output side of the production process. The experience of Globe Metallurgical, Inc., illustrates many of the factors associated with the use of flexible work teams. (See Organizational Insight 10.5.)

Flexible work teams are involved in more than just conversion or assembly activities: They also assume responsibility for controlling TQM efforts. Because a large, separate quality control function is no longer needed at the end of the production line, the use of work teams reduces costs. Flexible work teams are also responsible for devising ways to improve the efficiency of the manufacturing process. New ideas often originate in quality control circles, team meetings that bring members together specifically to discuss ways of improving productivity. Moreover, the most experienced members of a team assume responsibility for training new members. All team members are often responsible for selecting new recruits who they think will fit in with the team. In this way, a work-team culture emerges.

ORGANIZATIONAL INSIGHT 10.5

Flexible Work Teams at Globe

Globe Metallurgical, Inc. of Beverly, Ohio, and Selma, Alabama, was the first small company to win the Malcolm Baldrige National Quality Award. Globe makes specialty steel products and is one of the most successful U.S. organizations in its industry, surpassing its competitors in product quality, sales, and profit growth.

Globe's emergence as a leader in quality and particularly in its use of self-managed work teams came in an unusual way. In 1986, Globe wanted to introduce new, flexible work systems in order to raise profitability. When the unions refused to relax rigid work rules so that the new technology could be introduced, the company experienced a year-long strike. To continue operation, ten managers and 35 salaried workers took control of two of Globe's furnaces (they closed three others). Lack of manpower forced these 45 people to find new, more efficient ways to produce Globe's output.

With both managers and workers directly involved in production, many possibilities for improving the way the work was performed emerged. In the absence of work rules and job classifications specifying how the furnaces were to be operated, managers experimented with new ways to run them and within two weeks increased productivity by 20 percent. Every day brought new suggestions. It soon became obvious that productivity could be increased if welders, crane operators, furnace operators, forklift operators, stokers, furnace tappers, and tapper assistants worked cooperatively in teams. By trial and error, management discovered that a flexible work team of seven employees (one from each function), each of whom could do the others' jobs, could efficiently operate one furnace. Each team was put under the supervision of a team leader, who took responsibility for coordinating that team's work and schedules with those of other teams and with top management.

After the strike was over, Globe found that by using self-managed work teams it could operate all five furnaces with 120 employees (down from the 350 needed before the strike). The unions' fears about the shift to the new technology were justified: Flexible workers and flexible work teams resulted in a loss of jobs. For the employees who remained, however, Globe instituted a profit-sharing plan that allows workers to reap some of the benefits created by the new work system. Today, Globe is the largest supplier of specialty metals in the United States.

The managers' role in this system is not to monitor and supervise the work teams' activities but to facilitate team activities and do all they can to allow the teams to develop improved procedures. Since 1983, GM and Toyota have been cooperating in a joint venture that uses flexible work teams. The story of this venture is instructive. (See Organizational Insight 10.6.)

DEVELOPMENTS IN REVOLUTIONARY CHANGE

Re-engineering

The term re-engineering has been used to refer to the process by which managers redesign how tasks are bundled into roles and functions to improve organizational effectiveness. In the words of Michael Hammer and J. Champy, who popularized the term, re-engineering involves the "fundamental rethinking and radical redesign of

ORGANIZATIONAL INSIGHT 10.6

GM and Toyota Give Plant a New Lease on Life

In 1963, General Motors opened a car plant in Fremont, California, 55 kilometres east of San Francisco. From the outset, the plant was a loser. Productivity and quality were poor. Drug and alcohol abuse were widespread. Absenteeism was so high that hundreds of extra workers were employed to ensure that enough workers were on hand to operate the plant. Managers at the Fremont plant, as at all GM plants, constantly analyzed the worker–task relationship in order to design jobs to raise productivity. Workers strongly resisted these moves, and finally, seeing no chance of improvement, GM closed the plant in 1981.

In 1983, GM and Toyota announced a joint venture: They would cooperate to reopen the Fremont plant. GM wanted to learn how Toyota operated its production system, and Toyota wanted to see whether it could achieve its customary high level of productivity by using Japanese techniques with American workers. In 1984, the new organization, New United Motors Manufacturing Inc. (NUMMI), opened under the control of Japanese management. By 1986, productivity at NUMMI was higher than productivity at any other GM factory, and the plant was operating at twice the level it had operated at under GM management. Moreover, alcohol and drug abuse had virtually disappeared, and absenteeism had almost stopped. How had this miracle been achieved?

At the NUMMI factory, Toyota divided the workforce into 350 flexible work teams consisting of from five to seven people plus a team leader. Each worker could do the jobs of the other workers, and the workers regularly rotated jobs. In addition, all workers were taught procedures for analyzing jobs to improve the employee–task relationship. Team members designed each team's jobs, timed each other with stopwatches, and continually attempted to find better ways of performing the tasks. In the past, GM had employed 80 managers to perform this analysis. Now, flexible work teams not only perform the analysis but also monitor product quality. What is the role of managers in the NUMMI factory? The manager's job is defined explicitly as providing shop-floor workers with support, not monitoring or supervising their activities.

Why do employees buy into this new system? NUMMI has a no-layoff policy; workers are given extensive training; and the use of flexible work teams gives workers, not managers, control over the production line. Apparently, most workers still consider assembly-line work a "lousy job"—but the best job they can expect to get. And in the new work system they at least have some control over what they do.[47]

business processes to achieve dramatic improvements in critical, contemporary measures of performance such as cost, quality, service, and speed."[48] Change resulting from re-engineering requires managers to go back to the basics and pull apart each step in the work process to identify a better way to coordinate and integrate the activities necessary to provide customers with goods and services. Instead of focusing on an organization's *functions*, the managers of a re-engineered organization focus on business *processes*. Processes, not organizations, are the object of re-engineering. Companies don't re-engineer their sales or manufacturing departments; they re-engineer the work the people in those departments do.

As this definition suggests, an organization that undertakes re-engineering must completely rethink how it goes about its business. Instead of focusing on an organiza-

Business process
An activity that cuts across functional boundaries and is vital to the quick delivery of goods and services, or that promotes high quality or low costs.

tion's functions in isolation from one another, managers make business processes the focus of attention. A **business process** is any activity (such as order processing, inventory control, or product design) that cuts across functional boundaries; it is the ability of people and groups to act in a cross-functional way that is the vital factor in determining how quickly goods and services are delivered to customers or that promotes high quality or low costs. Business processes involve activities across functions. Because re-engineering focuses on business processes and not functions, an organization must rethink the way it approaches organizing its activities.

Organizations that take up re-engineering deliberately ignore the existing arrangement of tasks, roles, and work activities. They start the re-engineering process with the customer (not the product or service) and ask the question "How can I reorganize the way we do our work, our business processes, to provide the best-quality, lowest-cost goods and services to the customer?" Frequently, when companies ask this question, they realize that there are more effective ways of organizing their activities. For example, a business process that currently involves members of ten different functions working sequentially to provide goods and services might be performed by one or a few people at a fraction of the original cost, after re-engineering.

A good example of how to use re-engineering to increase functional integration to increase control of activities comes from attempts to redesign the materials management function to improve its effectiveness (see Figure 10-4). In the past, the three main components of materials management—purchasing (which is responsible for obtaining inputs), production control (responsible for using inputs most efficiently), and distribution (responsible for disposing of the finished product)—were typically in separate functions and had little to do with one another. Figure 10-4A shows the traditional functional design. The problem with the traditional design is that when all aspects of materials management are separate functions, coordinating their activities is difficult. Each function has its own hierarchy, and there are problems in both vertical and horizontal communication. The structure shown in Figure 10-4A makes it difficult to process information quickly in order to secure cost savings. Computerized production and warehousing, for example, require the careful coordination of activities, but the traditional design of materials management activities does not provide enough control for this to be achieved.

Realizing that this separation of activities has often slowed down production and raised costs, many organizations have moved to re-engineer the materials management process. Today, most organizations put all three of the functional activities involved in the materials management process inside one function, as shown in Figure 10-4B. Now, one hierarchy of managers is responsible for all three aspects of materials management and communication among those managers is easy because they are within the same function. According to Michael Hammer, the three guidelines for performing re-engineering successfully are:[49]

1. Organize around outcomes, not tasks. Where possible, organize work so that one person or one function can perform all the activities necessary to complete the process, thus avoiding the need for transfers (and integration) between functions.
2. Have those who use the output of the process perform the process. Since the people who use the output of the process know best what they want, establish a system of rules and SOPs that will allow them to take control over it.
3. Decentralize decision making to the point where the decision is made. Allow the people on the spot to decide how best to respond to specific problems that arise.

Take the case of Hallmark Cards, profiled in Organizational Insight 10.7.

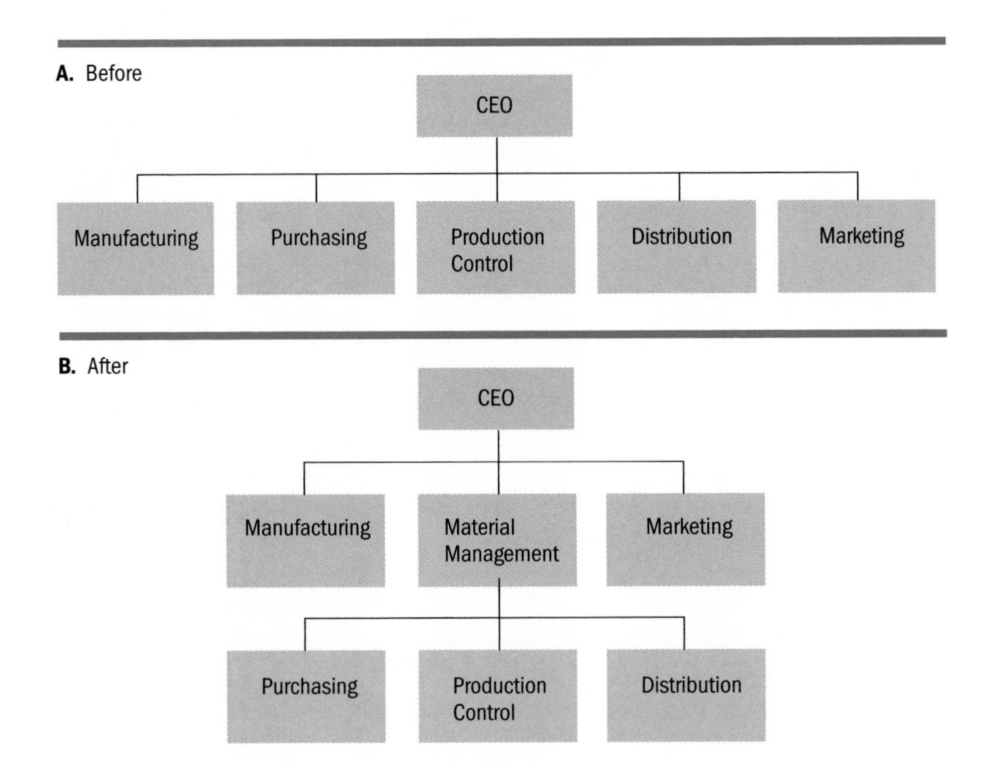

FIGURE 10-4
Improving Integration in Functional Structure in Creating a Materials Management Function.

As Organizational Insight 10.7 suggests, re-engineering and TQM are highly interrelated and complementary. After revolutionary re-engineering has taken place and the question "What is the best way to provide customers with the goods or service they require?" has been answered, evolutionary TQM takes over with its focus on "How can we now continue to improve and refine the new process and find better ways of managing task and role relationships?" Successful organizations examine both questions simultaneously, and they continuously attempt to identify new and better processes for meeting the goals of increased efficiency, quality, and responsiveness to customers. However, there is some evidence that a focus on role relationships may not be enough. One study of the culture of the greeting card industry suggests that employees are "culturally overtrained not only to think in terms of certain consensually validated unwritten rules of the game but also to withhold information that will in any way threaten the current social order."[50]

E-Engineering The term e-engineering refers to companies' attempts to use all kinds of information systems to improve their performance. In previous chapters there have been many examples of how the use of Internet-based software systems can change the way a company's strategy and structure operates. New information systems can be employed in all aspects of an organization's business and for all kinds of reasons. For example, Cypress Semiconductor's CEO, T. J. Rodgers, uses the company's online management information system to monitor his managers' activities continually and help him to keep the organizational hierarchy flat. Rodgers claims that he can review the goals of all his 1500 managers in about four hours, and he does so each week. The importance of e-engineering is increasing as it changes the way a company organizes

ORGANIZATIONAL INSIGHT 10.7

How to Stay on Top in the Greeting Card Business

Hallmark Cards, based in Kansas City, Missouri, sells 55 percent of the 8 billion birthday, Christmas, and other kinds of cards sold each year in the United States.[51] However, in the 1990s, it came under increasing attack from smaller and more agile competitors who pioneered new kinds of specialty greeting cards and sold them, often at discount prices, in supermarkets and discount stores. So, to keep Hallmark on top of its market, it was decided to examine how things were currently being done at Hallmark, in order to determine what changes needed to be made.

Top management began this evaluation by placing 100 managers into teams to analyze Hallmark's competitors, the changing nature of customer needs, the organizational structure the company was using to coordinate its activities, and the ways the company was developing, distributing, and marketing its cards—its basic business processes. What the teams found startled managers from the top down and showed that there was a need for change.

Managers discovered that although Hallmark had the world's largest creative staff—over 700 artists and writers who design over 24 000 new cards each year—it was taking over three years to get a new card to market. Once an artist designed a new card and a writer came up with an appropriate rhyme or message, it took an average of three years for the card to be produced, packaged, and shipped to retailers. Information on changing customer needs, a vital input into decisions about what cards should be designed, took many months to reach artists. That delay made it difficult for Hallmark to respond quickly to its competitors.

Armed with this information, the 100 team managers presented top management with 100 recommendations for changes that would allow the company to do its work more quickly and effectively. The recommendations called for a complete change in the way the company organized its basic business processes. Hallmark began by completely restructuring its activities. The organization had been using a functional structure. Artists worked separately from writers, and both artists and writers worked separately from materials management, printing, and manufacturing personnel. From the time a card went from the creative staff to the printing department, 25 hand-offs (work exchanges between functions) were needed to produce the final product, and 90 percent of the time work was simply sitting in somebody's in- or out-basket. Taking the advice of the teams, Hallmark changed to a cross-functional team structure. People from different functions—artists, writers, editors, and so on—were grouped into teams responsible for producing a specific kind of card, such as Christmas cards, get-well cards, or new lines of specialty cards.

To eliminate the need for hand-offs between departments, each team is responsible for all aspects of the design process. To reduce the need for handoffs within a team, all team members work together from the beginning to plan the steps in the design process, and all are responsible for reviewing the success of their efforts. To help each team evaluate its efforts and to give each team the information it needs about customer desires, Hallmark introduced a computerized point-of-sales merchandising system in each of its Hallmark Card stores, so each team has instant feedback on what and how many kinds of cards are selling. Each team can now continuously experiment with new card designs to attract more customers.

The effects of these changes have been dramatic. Not only are cards introduced in less than one year, but some reach the market in a matter of months. Quality has increased as each team focuses on improving its cards, and costs have fallen because the new work system is so efficient. Increased competition from the Internet, in particular the increasing use of free online greetings from Yahoo and other companies, is putting pressure on Hallmark in the 2000s, however. Its managers are currently seeking to increase its online presence in order to fight back, and are once again re-engineering its processes to make the company a leader in the e-card business.

its value-creation functions and links them to improve its performance. We discuss this important issue at length in Chapters 12 and 13.

Restructuring

Restructuring and re-engineering are also closely linked, for in practice the move to a more efficient organizational structure generally results in the layoff of employees, unless the organization is growing so rapidly employees can be transferred or absorbed elsewhere in the organization. It is for this reason that re-engineering efforts are unpopular both among workers (who fear they will be re-engineered out of a job) and among managers (who fear the loss of their authority and empires as new and more efficient ways of structuring task and role relationships are found).

Nevertheless, **restructuring** refers to the process by which managers change task and authority relationships and redesign organizational structure and culture to improve organizational effectiveness. The move from a functional to some form of divisional structure, and the move from one divisional structure to another, represents one of the most common kinds of restructuring effort. As the environment changes, and as the organization's strategy changes, managers must analyze how well their structure now fits them. Frequently, they find that there is a better way of grouping the products they now make to serve customer needs and move, for example, from one kind of product structure to another for reasons outlined in Chapter 6.

Restructuring The process by which managers change task and authority relationships and redesign organizational structure and culture to improve organizational effectiveness.

Another type of organizational restructuring that has become very common in recent years is **downsizing**, the process by which managers streamline the organizational hierarchy and lay off managers and workers to reduce bureaucratic costs. The size and scope of these recent restructuring and downsizing efforts has been enormous. It is estimated that in the last ten years Fortune 500 companies have downsized so much that they now employ about 10 percent fewer managers than they used to. Moreover, even when the economy is booming, some companies lay off large numbers of employees as they restructure to reduce costs and improve efficiency.

Downsizing The process by which managers streamline the organizational hierarchy and lay off managers and workers to reduce bureaucratic costs.

The drive to reduce bureaucratic costs is often a response to increasing competitive pressures in the environment as companies fight to increase their performance and introduce new information technology.[52] For example, the wave of mergers and acquisitions that occurred in the 1990s in many industries such as telecommunications, banking, and defence has also resulted in downsizing because merged companies typically require fewer managers. For example, the merger of Time Warner with Turner Broadcasting System in 1996 resulted in the layoff of over 8000 managers as the merged company combined many of its operating functions, such as finance and accounting. The merger between AOL and Time Warner in 2002 resulted in the layoff of 15 000 more employees.

Often, after one industry company downsizes, other industry companies are forced to examine their own structures to search out inefficiencies; thus downsizing waves take place across companies in an industry.

While there is no doubt that companies have realized considerable cost savings by downsizing and streamlining their hierarchies, some analysts are now wondering whether this process has gone far enough, or even too far.[53] There are increasing reports that the remaining managers in downsized organizations are working under severe stress, both because they fear they might be the next employees to be let go and because they are forced to do the work that was previously performed by the lost employees—work that often they cannot cope with.

Moreover, there are concerns that in pushing their downsizing efforts too far, organizations may be trading off short-term gains from cost savings for long-term losses because of lost opportunities. The argument is that organizations always need some level of "surplus" managers who have the time and energy to improve current operating methods and search the environment to find new opportunities for growth and expansion.[54] Downsized organizations lack the middle managers who perform this vital task, and this may hurt them in the future. Hence, the terms anorexic or hollow have been used to refer to organizations that have downsized too much and have too few managers.

While clearly there are disadvantages associated with excessive downsizing, it remains true that many organizations became too tall and bloated because their past top-management teams failed to control the growth of their hierarchies and design their organizational structures appropriately. In such cases, managers are forced to restructure their organizations to remain competitive and even to survive. Organizations experiencing a rapid deterioration in performance frequently resort to eliminating divisions, departments, or levels in the hierarchy to lower operating costs. Change in the relationships between divisions or functions is a common outcome of restructuring. For example, in August of 2004 Nortel cut 3500 jobs and undertook a major realignment of its operating structure.

Why does restructuring become necessary, and why may an organization need to downsize its operations? Sometimes, an unforeseen change in the environment occurs: Perhaps a shift in technology makes the company's products obsolete, or a worldwide recession reduces demand for its products. Sometimes an organization has excess capacity because customers no longer want the goods and services it provides if they are outdated or offer poor value for money (see Organizational Insight 10.8). Sometimes organizations downsize because they have grown too tall and bureaucratic and their operating costs have become much too high.

All too often, companies are forced to downsize and lay off employees because they have not continually monitored the way they operate—their basic business processes—and have not made the incremental changes to their strategies and structures that would have allowed them to contain costs and adjust to changing conditions. Paradoxically, because they have not paid attention to the need to re-engineer themselves, they are forced into a position where restructuring becomes the only way they can survive and compete in an increasingly competitive environment.

Restructuring, like re-engineering, TQM, and other change strategies, generates resistance to change. Often, the decision to downsize will require the establishment of new task and role relationships. Because this change may threaten the jobs of some workers, they resist the changes taking place. Many plans to introduce change, including restructuring, take a long time to implement and fail because of the high level of resistance that they encounter at all levels of the organization.

Innovation

Restructuring is often necessary because changes in technology make the technology an organization uses to produce goods and services, or the goods and services themselves, obsolete. For example, changes in technology have made computers much cheaper to manufacture and more powerful and have changed the type of computers customers want. If organizations are to avoid being left behind in the competitive race to produce new goods and services, they must take steps to introduce new products or develop new technologies to produce those products reliably and at low cost.

Innovation
The process by which organizations use their skills and resources to develop new goods and services or to develop new production and operating systems so that they can better respond to the needs of their customers.

Innovation is the successful use of skills and resources to create new technologies or new goods and services so that an organization can change and better respond to the needs of customers.[55] Innovation is one of the most difficult instruments of change to manage. Chapter 13 describes issues involved in managing innovation and in increasing the level of creativity and entrepreneurship inside an organization.

ORGANIZATIONAL INSIGHT 10.8

Organizational Changes at Stelco[56]

Stelco Inc., headquartered in Hamilton, Ontario, is a group of businesses consisting of both wholly and partially owned companies that collectively operate in all major segments of the steel industry. The corporation produces through its integrated steel business, minimills, and manufactured products businesses. With yearly production around 5 million tonnes of steel, Stelco Inc. is Canada's largest steel manufacturer. Although production can be high, Stelco's viability and long-term survival is a going concern. The company has been under pressure to change with industry fluctuations or face serious consequences.

After experiencing serious losses in 2003, in January of 2004 Stelco Inc. sought creditor protection from the courts. The company had not been able to react quickly enough to various changes in the industry, such as unprecedented price swings, excess industry production, restricted capital investment, and adversarial labour relations. There are many issues that Stelco must consider, but the company believes it can make a turn around if stakeholders cooperate.

Under the court's supervision, Stelco has initiated changes to orchestrate the turnaround. Its most important step to change critical circumstances was to restructure, and in July 2004, Stelco announced its intentions to close one of its steel rod mills. This decision reflected the beginning of Stelco's strategic plan to reorganize the corporation so that it could focus on its core business of profitable product lines and divest itself of those operations that Stelco could not make profitable.

With threats of striking workers and a major customer hesitating with product orders, Stelco is pressed daily to consider its alternatives. Even with a sudden increase of steel prices and profits on the horizon, Stelco's long-term sustainability is of grave concern. Restructuring plans remain a strong element in the story but appeasing labour is also critical if Stelco is to get out of trouble. It would appear that Stelco must develop strategies to manage constant change in the steel industry or risk failure.

MANAGING CHANGE: ACTION RESEARCH

No matter what type of evolutionary or revolutionary change an organization adopts, managers face the problem of getting the organization to change. Kurt Lewin, whose force-field theory argues that organizations are balanced between forces for change and resistance to change, has a related perspective on how managers can bring change to their organization (see Figure 10-5).

In Lewin's view, implementing change is a three-step process: (1) unfreezing the organization from its present state, (2) making the change, and (3) refreezing the organization in the new, desired state so that its members do not revert to their previous work attitudes and role behaviours.[57] Lewin warns that resistance to change will quickly cause an organization and its members to revert to their old ways of doing things unless the organization actively takes steps to refreeze the organization with the changes in place. It is not enough to make some changes in task and role relationships and expect the changes to be successful and to endure. To get an organization to remain in its new state, managers must actively manage the change process.

Action research A strategy for generating and acquiring knowledge that managers can use to define an organization's desired future state and to plan a change program that allows the organization to reach that state.

Action research is a strategy for generating and acquiring knowledge that managers can use to define an organization's desired future state and to plan a change pro-

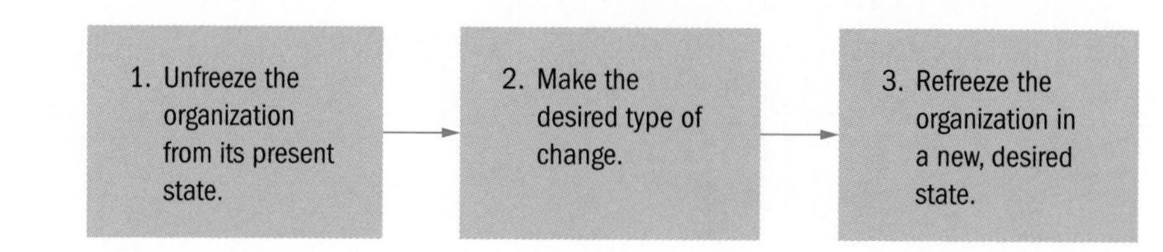

FIGURE 10-5
Lewin's Three-Step Change Process.

gram that allows the organization to reach that state.[58] The techniques and practices of action research, developed by experts, help managers to unfreeze an organization, move it to its new, desired position, and refreeze it so that the benefits of the change are retained. Figure 10-6 identifies the main steps in action research.

Diagnosing the Organization

The first step in action research requires managers to recognize the existence of a problem that needs to be solved and acknowledge that some type of change is needed to solve it. In general, recognition of the need for change arises because somebody in

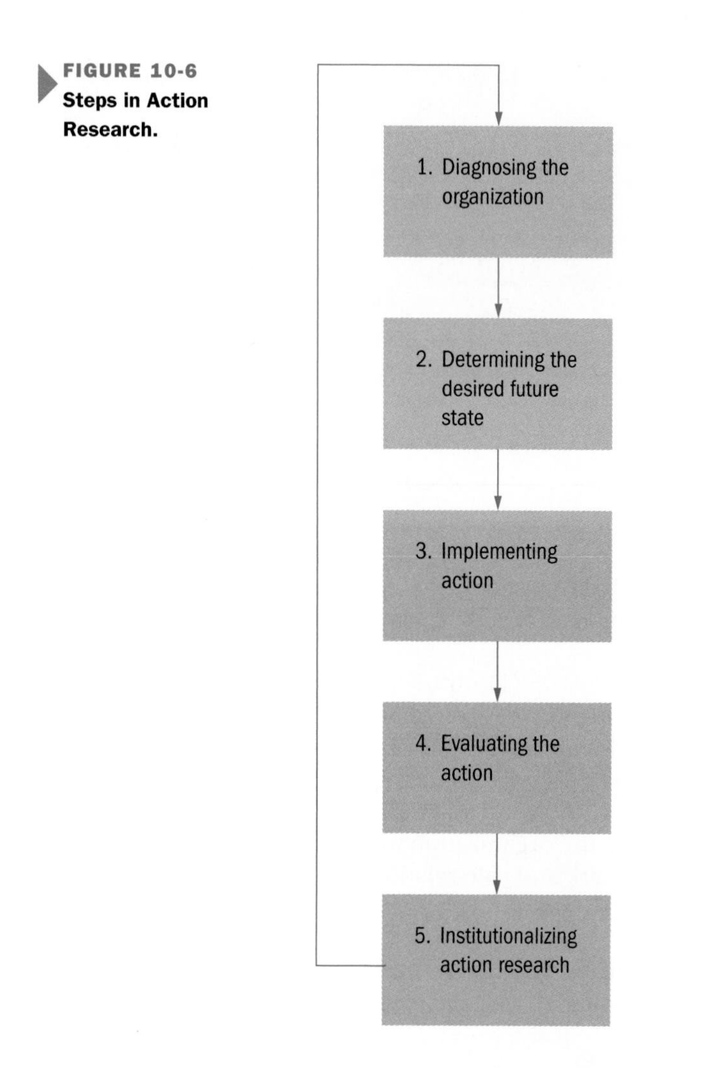

FIGURE 10-6
Steps in Action Research.

the organization perceives a gap between desired performance and actual performance. Perhaps customer complaints about the quality of goods or services have increased. Perhaps profits have recently fallen, or operating costs have been escalating. Perhaps turnover among managers or workers has been excessive. In the first stage of action research, managers need to analyze what is going on and why problems are occurring.

Diagnosing the organization can be a complex process. Like a doctor, managers have to distinguish between symptoms and causes. For example, there is little point in introducing new technology to reduce production costs if the problem is that demand is falling because customers do not like the design of the product. Managers have to carefully collect information about the organization to diagnose the problem correctly and get employees committed to the change process. At this early stage of action research, it is important for managers to collect information from people at all levels in the organization and from outsiders such as customers and suppliers. Questionnaire surveys given to employees, customers, and suppliers, and interviews with workers and managers at all levels, can provide information that is essential to a correct diagnosis of the organization's present state.

Determining the Desired Future State

After identification of the present state, the next step is to identify where the organization needs to be—its desired future state. This step also involves a difficult planning process, as managers work out various alternative courses of action that could move the organization to where they would like it to be and determine what type of change to implement. Identifying the desired future state involves deciding what the organization's strategy and structure should be. Should the organization focus on reducing costs and increasing efficiency? Or are raising quality and responsiveness to customers the keys to future success? What is the best kind of organizational structure to adopt to realize organizational goals—a product structure or perhaps a cross-functional team structure?

Implementing Action

Implementing action is the third step of action research.[59] It is a three-step process. First, managers need to identify possible impediments to change that they will encounter as they go about making changes—impediments at the organization, group, and individual levels.[60] When the senior management of Nova Scotia Power introduced a culture change in the late 1980s, they provided a four-day training program for all managers, who then went on to give one-day training sessions for all employees. What the managers did not anticipate was that the unionized employees in their Cape Breton divisions would react against the training program itself. Workers walked out of sessions claiming that while managers received four-day sessions, workers were only receiving one-day sessions, and many saw this as a sign that management was not serious about a culture change that supposedly valued the employees.[61]

Suppose managers choose to re-engineer the company from a functional to a cross-functional team structure to speed product development and reduce costs. They must anticipate the obstacles they will encounter when they unfreeze the organization and make the changes. Functional managers, for example, are likely to strongly resist efforts to change the company because the change will reduce their power and prestige in the organization. Similarly, members of each function who have grown accustomed to working with the same people and to stable task and role relationships will resist being assigned to a new team where tasks and roles have to be worked out again and new interpersonal relationships have to be learned.

The more revolutionary the change that is adopted, the greater the problem of implementing it. Managers need to find ways to minimize, control, and co-opt resistance to change. They also need to devise strategies to bring organizational members on board and foster their commitment to the change process. Managers must also look to the future and seek ways to refreeze the changes that they have made so that people cannot slide back into old behaviours. In an attempt to stave off resistance, senior management at Nova Scotia Power in the early 1990s established a series of process task groups consisting of the "best" employees. These groups were charged with identifying ways of improving the various processes that provided a service to customers. In this way, the company hoped to engage the energy and enthusiasm of a large number of employees.[62]

The second step in implementing action is deciding who will be responsible for actually making the changes and controlling the change process. The choices are to employ **external change agents**, outside consultants who are experts in managing change; **internal change agents**, managers from within the organization who are knowledgeable about the situation; or some combination of both.[63]

External change agents People who are outside consultants that are experts in managing change.

Internal change agents Managers from within the organization who are knowledgeable about the situation to be changed.

The principal problem with using internal change agents is that other members of the organization may perceive them as being politically involved in the changes and biased toward certain groups. External change agents, in contrast, are likely to be perceived as less influenced by internal politics. Another reason for employing external change agents is that as outsiders they have a detached view of the organization's problems and can distinguish between the "forest and the trees." Insiders can be so involved in what is going on that they cannot see the true source of the problems. Management consultants from Ernst & Young are frequently brought in by large organizations to help the top-management team diagnose an organization's problems and suggest solutions. Many consultants specialize in certain types of organizational change, such as restructuring, re-engineering, or implementing total quality management. Nova Scotia Power, for example, hired local consultants for its culture change program, and it brought in Ernst & Young to implement its business process re-engineering program.[64]

The third step in implementing action is deciding which specific change strategy will most effectively unfreeze, change, and refreeze the organization. Specific techniques for implementing change are discussed later in this chapter. The types of change that these techniques give rise to fall into two categories: top-down and bottom-up.[65]

Top-down change Change that is implemented by managers at a high level in the organization.

Top-down change is change that is implemented by managers at a high level in the organization. The result of radical organizational restructuring and re-engineering is top-down change. Managers high up in the organization decide to make a change, realizing full well that it will reverberate at all organizational levels. The managers choose to manage and solve problems as they arise at the divisional, functional, or individual levels.

Bottom-up change Change that is implemented by employees at low levels in the organization and gradually rises until it is felt throughout the organization.

Bottom-up change is change that is implemented by employees at low levels in the organization and gradually rises until it is felt throughout the organization. When an organization wants to engage in bottom-up change, the first step in the action research process—diagnosing the organization—becomes pivotal in determining the success of the change. Managers involve employees at all levels in the change process, to obtain their input and to lessen their resistance. By reducing the uncertainty employees experience, bottom-up change facilitates unfreezing and increases the likelihood that employees will retain the new behaviours that they learn during the change process. Top-down change proceeds rapidly and forces employees to keep up with the pace of change, troubleshooting to solve problems as they arise.

In general, bottom-up change is easier to implement than top-down change because it provokes less resistance. Organizations that have the time to engage in bottom-up change are generally well-run organizations that pay attention to change, are used to change, and change often. Poorly run organizations, those that rarely change or postpone change until it is too late, are forced to engage in top-down restructuring simply to survive. For example, Compaq Computer did not have the luxury of being able to use bottom-up change when its performance declined precipitously in 1999. Compaq CEO Michael Capellas had to take immediate action to reduce costs and develop new products. In fact, his efforts were not enough, and Compaq merged with H-P in 2002 in the effort to restructure and combine both companies' operations to turn around the performance of both.

Organizations that change the most are able to exploit the advantages of evolutionary bottom-up change because their managers are always open to the need for change and constantly use action research to find new and better ways to operate and increase effectiveness. Organizations in which change happens rarely are likely candidates for revolutionary top-down change. Because their managers do not use action research on a continuing basis, they attempt change so late that their only option is some massive restructuring or downsizing to turn their organization around.

Evaluating the Action

The fourth step in action research is evaluating the action that has been taken and assessing the degree to which the changes have accomplished the desired objectives. Armed with this evaluation, management decides whether more change is needed to reach the organization's desired future state or whether more effort is needed to refreeze the organization in its new state.[66]

The best way to evaluate the change process is to develop measures or criteria that allow managers to assess whether the organization has reached its desired objectives. When criteria developed at the beginning of action research are used consistently over time to evaluate the effects of the change process, managers have ample information to assess the impact of the changes they have made. They can compare costs before and after the change to see whether efficiency has increased. They can survey workers to see whether they are more satisfied with their jobs. They can survey customers to see whether they are more satisfied with the quality of the organization's products. As part of its TQM effort, managers at Citibank carefully surveyed their customers to make sure that service had improved, for example. That information helped them to evaluate the success of their change effort.

Assessing the impact of change is especially difficult because the effects of change may emerge slowly. The action research process that we have been describing may take several years to complete. Typically, re-engineering and restructuring take months or years, and total quality management, once underway, never stops. Consequently, managers need valid and reliable measures that they can use to evaluate performance. All too often poorly performing organizations fail to develop and consistently apply criteria that allow them to evaluate their performance. For those organizations, the pressure for change often comes from the outside, as shareholders complain about poor profits, parents complain about their children's poor grades, or inspectors find high rates of post-surgery infection in hospitals.

Institutionalizing Action Research

The need to manage change is so vital in today's quickly changing environment that organizations must institutionalize action research—that is, make it a required habit or a norm adopted by every member of an organization. The institutionalization of action research is as necessary at the top of the organization (where the top-management team plans the organization's future strategy) as it is on the shop floor (where workers meet in quality circles to find new ways to increase efficiency and quality). Because change is so difficult and requires so much thought and effort to implement, members at all levels of the organization must be rewarded for being part of successful change efforts. Top managers can be rewarded with stock options and bonus plans linked to organizational performance. Lower-level members can be rewarded through an employee stock-ownership plan and by performance bonuses and pay linked to individual or group performance. Indeed, tangible, performance-related rewards help refreeze an organization in its new state because they help people learn and sustain desired behaviours.

MANAGERIAL IMPLICATIONS

Designing a Plan for Change

1. Develop criteria to evaluate whether change is necessary, and use these criteria systematically throughout the change process to assess progress toward the ideal future state.
2. After analyzing resistances to change, carefully design a plan that both reduces resistance to and facilitates change.
3. Recognize that change is easiest to manage when an organization and its members are used to change, and consider developing a process of workplace learning as a way of keeping the organization attuned to the need for change.
4. Be sure to take into account the ethical implication of change that results in job losses and/or negatively impacts the local economy.

ORGANIZATIONAL DEVELOPMENT

Organizational development (OD) A series of techniques and methods that managers can use in their action research program to increase the adaptability of their organization.

Organizational development (OD) is a series of techniques and methods that managers can use in their action research program to increase the adaptability of their organization.[67] In the words of organizational theorist Warren Bennis, OD refers to a "complex educational strategy intended to change beliefs, attitudes, values, and structure of organizations so that they can better adapt to new technologies, markets, and challenges and the dizzying rate of change itself."[68] The goal of OD is to improve organizational effectiveness and to help people in organizations reach their potential and realize their goals and objectives. As action research proceeds, managers need to continually unfreeze, change, and refreeze managers' and workers' attitudes and behaviours. Many OD techniques have been developed to help managers do this. We first look at OD techniques to help managers unfreeze an organization and overcome resistances to change. We then look at OD techniques to help managers change and refreeze an organization in its new, desired state.

OD Techniques to Deal with Resistance to Change

Resistance to change occurs at all levels of an organization. It manifests itself as organizational politics and power struggles between individuals and groups, differing perceptions of the need for change, and so on. Tactics that managers can use to reduce resistance to change include education and communication, participation and empowerment, facilitation, bargaining and negotiation, manipulation, and coercion.[69]

Education and Communication One of the most important impediments to change is uncertainty about what is going to happen. Through education and communication, internal and external agents of change can provide organizational members with information about the change and how it will affect them. Change agents can communicate this information in formal group meetings, by memo, in one-on-one meetings, and, increasingly, through electronic means such as e-mail and videoconferencing. Wal-Mart, for example, has a state-of-the-art videoconferencing system. Managers at corporate headquarters put on presentations that are beamed to all Wal-Mart stores so that both managers and workers are aware of the changes that will be taking place.

Even when plant closures or massive layoffs are planned, it is still best—from both an ethical and a change standpoint—to inform employees about what will happen to them as downsizing occurs. Many organizations fear that disgruntled employees may try to hurt the organization as it closes or sabotage the closing process. Most often, however, employees are cooperative until the end. As organizations become more and more aware of the benefits offered by incremental change, they are increasing communication with the workforce to gain workers' cooperation and to overcome their resistance to change.

Participation and Empowerment Inviting workers to participate in the change process is becoming a popular method of reducing resistance to change. Participation complements empowerment, increases workers' involvement in decision making, and gives them greater autonomy to change work procedures to improve organizational performance. In addition, to encourage workers to share their skills and talents, organizations are opening up their books to inform workers about the organization's financial condition. Some organizations use employee stock-ownership plans (ESOPs) to motivate and reward employees and to harness their commitment to change. Participation and empowerment are two key elements of most TQM programs. (See Organizational Insight 10.9)

Facilitation Both managers and workers find change stressful because established task and role relationships alter as it takes place. There are several ways in which organizations can help their members to manage stress: providing them with training to help them learn how to perform new tasks, providing them with time off from work to recuperate from the stressful effects of change, or even giving senior members sabbaticals to allow them to recuperate and plan their future work activities. Companies such as Microsoft and Apple Computer, for example, give their most talented programmers time off from ordinary job assignments to think about ways to create new kinds of products.

Many companies employ psychologists and consultants who specialize in helping employees to handle the stress associated with change. During organizational restructuring, when large layoffs are common, many organizations employ consultants to help laid-off workers deal with the stress and uncertainty of being laid off and having to find new jobs. Some companies pay consultants to help their CEOs manage the responsibilities associated with their own jobs, including the act of laying off workers, which CEOs find particularly stressful, for they understand the impact that layoffs have on employees and their families.

ORGANIZATIONAL INSIGHT 10.9

Competitive Advantage: Achieving Change Through Empowering Work Groups

When work-group members are empowered, workers often make many of the decisions and have a lot of the responsibility that used to be part of middle managers' jobs. As a result, one major change that has taken place in many organizations is the reduction in the number of middle managers. What do the remaining middle managers do when empowered work groups take on many of their former responsibilities? Essentially they serve as coaches, facilitators, teachers, and sponsors of the empowered groups. They are, in a sense, what some people call the "new nonmanager managers."[70]

One of these new nonmanager managers is 37-year-old Cindy Ransom, a middle manager in charge of a Clorox manufacturing plant in Fairfield, California, that employs around 100 workers. In the attempt to improve plant performance, Ransom decided to empower her subordinates by asking them to reorganize the entire plant. Teams of workers earning hourly wages were suddenly setting up training programs, drafting rules governing absenteeism, and redesigning the plant into five customer-focused business groups. Ransom intentionally did little to interfere with what the workers were doing; her input consisted mainly of answering questions. Middle managers traditionally may have told workers what to do and how and when to do it, but managers of empowered work groups see it as their responsibility to ask the right questions and allow their work groups to decide on the answers.

Two years later, Ransom's plant showed the most improvement in performance in its division. What did Ransom do as workers started taking over many of the responsibilities and tasks she used to perform? She focused on identifying and satisfying the needs of Clorox's customers and suppliers, activities on which she had not spent much time in the past. All in all, empowerment has changed the nature of middle managers' jobs. They have lost some of their old responsibilities, but have gained new ones.

Bargaining and Negotiation Bargaining and negotiation are important tools that help managers manage conflict. Because change causes conflict, bargaining is an important tool in overcoming resistance to change. By using action research, managers can anticipate the effects of change on interpersonal and intergroup relationships. Managers can use this knowledge to help different people and groups negotiate their future tasks and roles and reach compromises that will lead them to accept change. Negotiation also helps individuals and groups understand how change will affect others so that the organization as a whole can develop a common perspective on why change is taking place and why it is important.

Manipulation When it is clear that change will help some individuals and groups at the expense of others, senior managers need to intervene in the bargaining process and deal with the situation to secure the agreement, or at least the acceptance, of various people or groups to the results of the change process. As we discuss in Chapter 14, powerful managers have considerable ability to resist change, and in large organizations infighting among divisions can slow or halt the change process unless it is carefully managed. Politics and political tactics like co-optation and building alliances become important as ways of overcoming the opposition of powerful functions and divisions that feel threatened by the changes taking place.

Coercion The ultimate way to eliminate resistance to change is to coerce the key players into accepting change and threaten dire consequences if they choose to resist. Workers and managers at all levels can be threatened with reassignment, demotion, or even termination if they resist or threaten the change process. Top managers attempt to use the legitimate power at their disposal to quash resistance to change and to eliminate it. The advantage of coercion can be the speed at which change takes place. The disadvantage is that it can leave people angry and disenchanted and can make the refreezing process difficult.

Managers should not underestimate the level of resistance to change. Organizations work because they reduce uncertainty by means of predictable rules and routines that people can use to accomplish their tasks. Change wipes out the predictability of rules and routines and perhaps spells the end of the status and prestige that accompany some positions. It is not surprising that people resist change and that organizations themselves, as collections of people, are so difficult to change.

OD Techniques to Promote Change

Many OD techniques are designed to make changes and to refreeze them. These techniques can be used at the individual, group, and organization levels. The choice of techniques is determined by the type of change. In general, the more revolutionary a change is, the more likely an organization is to use OD techniques at all three levels. Counselling, sensitivity training, and process consultation are OD techniques directed at changing the attitudes and behaviour of individuals. Different techniques are effective at the group and organization levels.

Counselling, Sensitivity Training, and Process Consultation The personalities of individuals differ and these differences lead individuals to interpret and react to other people and events in a variety of ways. Even though personality cannot be changed significantly in the short run, people can be helped to understand that their own perceptions of a situation are not necessarily the correct or the only possible ones. People can also be helped to understand that they should learn to tolerate differences in perception and to embrace and accept human diversity. Counselling and sensitivity training are techniques that organizations can use to help individuals to understand the nature of their own and other people's personalities and to use that knowledge to improve their interactions with others.[71] The highly motivated, driven boss, for example, must learn that his or her subordinates are not disloyal, lazy, or afflicted with personality problems because they are content to go home at 5 o'clock and want unchallenging job assignments. Instead, they have their own set of work values, and they value their leisure time. Traditionally, one of OD's main efforts has been to improve the quality of the work life of organizational members and increase their well-being and satisfaction with the organization.

Organizational members who are perceived by their superiors or peers to have certain problems in appreciating the viewpoints of others or in dealing with certain types of organizational members are counselled by trained professionals such as psychologists. Through counselling they learn how to more effectively manage their interactions with other people in the organization.

Sensitivity training is an intense type of counselling.[72] Organizational members who are perceived as having problems in dealing with others meet in a group with a trained facilitator to learn more about how they and the other group members view the world. Group members are encouraged to be forthright about how they view

Sensitivity training
An OD technique that consists of intense counselling in which group members, aided by a facilitator, learn how others perceive them and may learn how to deal more sensitively with others.

themselves and other group members, and through discussion they learn the degree to which others perceive them in similar or different ways. Through examining the source of differences in perception, members of the group may reach a better understanding of the way others perceive them and may learn how to deal more sensitively with others.

Participation in sensitivity training is a very intense experience because a person's innermost thoughts and feelings are brought to light and dissected in public. This process makes many people very uncomfortable, so certain ethical issues may be raised by an organization's decision to send "difficult" members for sensitivity training in the hope that they will learn more about themselves.

Is a manager too directive, too demanding, or too suspicious of subordinates? Does a manager deliberately deprive subordinates of information in order to keep them dependent? **Process consultation** provides answers to such questions. Process consultation bears a resemblance to both counselling and sensitivity training.[73] A trained process consultant, or facilitator, works closely with a manager on the job to help the manager improve his or her interaction with other group members. The outside consultant acts as a sounding board so that the manager can gain a better idea about what is going on in the group setting and can discover the interpersonal dynamics that are determining the quality of work relationships within the group.

Process consultation
An OD technique in which a facilitator works closely with a manager on the job to help the manager improve his or her interactions with other group members.

Process consultation, sensitivity training, and counselling are just three of the many OD techniques that have been developed to help individuals learn to change their attitudes and behaviour so that they can function effectively both as individuals and as organizational members. It is common for many large organizations to provide their higher-level managers with a yearly budget to be spent on individual development efforts such as these, or on more conventional knowledge-gaining events such as executive education programs.

Team Building and Intergroup Training To manage change within a group or between groups, change agents can employ three different kinds of OD techniques. **Team building**, a common method of improving relationships within a group, is similar to process consultation except that all the members of a group participate together to try to improve their work interactions.[74] For example, group members discuss with a change agent who is a trained group facilitator the quality of the interpersonal relationships between team members and between the members and their supervisor. The goal of team building is to improve the way group members work together—to improve group processes to achieve process gains and reduce process losses that are occurring because of shirking and free-riding. Team building does *not* focus on what the group is trying to achieve.

Team building
An OD technique in which a facilitator first observes the interactions of group members and then helps them become aware of ways to improve their work interactions.

Team building is important when re-engineering reorganizes the way people from different functions work together. When new groups are formed, team building can help group members quickly establish task and role relationships so that they can work together effectively. Team building facilitates the development of functional group norms and values and helps members develop a common approach to solving problems.

The change agent begins the team-building process by watching group members interact and identifying the way the group currently works. Then the change agent talks with some or all of the group members one on one to get a sense of the problems that the group is experiencing or just to identify where the group process could be improved. In a subsequent team-building session that normally takes place at a location away from the normal work context, the change agent discusses with group members the observations he or she has made and asks for their views on the issues brought to their attention. Ideally, through this discussion team members develop a new appreciation about the forces that have been affecting their behaviour. Group members may form small task forces to suggest ways of improving group process or to discuss specific ways of handling the problems that have been arising. The goal is to establish a platform from which group members themselves, with no input from the change agent, can make continuous improvements in the way the group functions.

Intergroup training takes team building one step further and uses it to improve the ways different functions or divisions work together. Its goal is to improve organizational performance by focusing on a function's or division's joint activities and output. Given that cross-functional coordination is especially important in re-engineering and total quality management, intergroup training is an important OD technique that organizations can exploit to implement change.

Intergroup training
An OD technique that uses team building to improve the work interactions of different functions or divisions.

A popular form of intergroup training is called **organizational mirroring**, an OD technique designed to improve the effectiveness of interdependent groups.[75] Suppose that two groups are in conflict or simply need to learn more about each other and one of the groups calls in a consultant to improve intergroup cooperation. The consultant begins by interviewing members of both groups to understand how each group views the other and to uncover possible problems the groups are having with each other. The groups are then brought together in a training session, and the consultant tells them that the goal of the session is to explore perceptions and relations in order to improve work relationships. Then, with the consultant leading the discussion, one group describes its perceptions of what is happening and its problems with the other group, while the other group sits and listens. Then the consultant reverses the situation—hence the term *organizational mirroring*—and the group that was listening takes its turn discussing its perceptions of what is happening and its problems, while the other group listens.

Organizational mirroring
An OD technique in which a facilitator helps two interdependent groups explore their perceptions and relations in order to improve their work interactions.

As a result of that initial discussion, each group appreciates the other's perspective. The next step is for members of both groups to form task forces to discuss ways of dealing with the issues or problems that have surfaced. The goal is to develop action plans that can be used to guide future intergroup relations and provide a basis for follow-up. The change agent guiding this training session needs to be skilled in intergroup relations because both groups are discussing sensitive issues. If the process is not managed well, intergroup relations can be further weakened by this OD technique.

Total Organizational Interventions A variety of OD techniques can be used at the organization level to promote organization-wide change. One is the **organizational confrontation meeting**.[76] At this meeting, all of the managers of an organization meet to confront the issue of whether the organization is effectively meeting its goals. At the first stage of the process, again with facilitation by a change agent, top management invites free and open discussion of the organization's situation. Then the consultant divides the managers into groups of seven or eight, ensuring that the groups are as heterogeneous as possible and that no bosses and subordinates are members of the same group (so as to encourage free and frank discussion). The small groups report their findings to the total group, and the sorts of problems confronting the organization are categorized. Top management uses this statement of the issues to set organizational priorities and plan group action. Task forces are formed from the small groups to take responsibility for working on the problems identified, and each group reports back to top management on progress that has been made. The result of this process is likely to be changes in the organization's structure and operating procedures. Restructuring, re-engineering, and total quality management often originate in

Organizational confrontation meeting
An OD technique that brings together all of the managers of an organization to meet to confront the issue of whether the organization is effectively meeting its goals.

organization-wide OD interventions that reveal the kinds of problems that an organization needs to solve.

MAKING SENSE OF ORGANIZATIONAL CHANGE

Recent studies of organizational change suggest that in many cases senior managers readily adopt change programs because it is the latest fad or fashion rather than because there is an identifiable need to change.[77] Companies can spend tens of millions of dollars hiring consultants to introduce change programs that may be unnecessary, or inappropriate.[78] This finding may explain in part why a number of TQM, culture change, and re-engineering programs are badly implemented and end in failure.[79] In addition to wasted money, some change programs, such as re-engineering and restructuring, can lead to layoffs. Some research indicates that certain changes, if not adequately thought out, can exacerbate workplace discrimination where female-dominated work is downgraded.[80] This research suggests that senior managers first need to decide whether a major change initiative is necessary, whether a particular program of change (e.g., TQM, re-engineering) is required or necessary, and what the ethical considerations are and how can they be balanced with the economic considerations.

SUMMARY

Organizational change is an ongoing process that has important implications for organizational effectiveness. An organization and its members must be constantly on the alert for changes from within the organization and from the outside environment, and they must learn how to adjust to change quickly and effectively. But they must also step back and assess whether or to what extent a major change initiative is warranted. Often, the revolutionary types of change that result from restructuring and re-engineering are necessary only because an organization and its managers ignored or were unaware of changes in the environment and did not make incremental changes as needed. The more an organization changes, the easier and more effective the change process becomes. Developing and managing a plan for change are vital to an organization's success. Chapter 10 has made the following major points:

1. Organizational change is the movement of an organization away from its present state and toward some future state to increase its effectiveness. Forces for organizational change include competitive forces, economic, political, and global forces, demographic and social forces, and ethical forces. Organizations are often reluctant to change because resistance to change at the organization, group, and individual levels has given rise to organizational inertia.
2. Sources of organization-level resistance to change include power and conflict, differences in functional orientation, mechanistic structure, and organizational culture. Sources of group-level resistance to change include group norms, group cohesiveness, and groupthink and escalation of commitment. Sources of individual-level resistance to change include uncertainty and insecurity, selective perception and retention, and habit.
3. According to Lewin's force-field theory of change, organizations are balanced between forces pushing for change and forces resistant to change. To get an organization to change, managers must find a way to increase the forces for change, reduce resistance to change, or do both simultaneously.
4. Types of change fall into two broad categories: evolutionary and revolutionary. The main instruments of evolutionary change are

sociotechnical systems theory, total quality management, and the development of flexible workers and work teams. The main instruments of revolutionary change are re-engineering, restructuring, and innovation.

5. Action research is a strategy that managers can use to plan the change process. The main steps in action research are (1) diagnosis and analysis of the organization, (2) determining the desired future state, (3) implementing action, (4) evaluating the action, and (5) institutionalizing action research.
6. Organizational development (OD) is a series of techniques and methods to increase the adaptability of organizations. OD techniques can be used to overcome resistance to change and to help the organization to change itself.
7. OD techniques for dealing with resistance to change include education and communication, participation and empowerment, facilitation, bargaining and negotiation, manipulation, and coercion.
8. OD techniques for promoting change include, at the individual level, counselling, sensitivity training, and process consultation; at the group level, team building and intergroup training; and at the organizational level, organizational confrontation meetings.
9. Managers need to make sense of organizational change by assessing the extent to which they are responding to an actual need or a perceived need influenced by the widespread adoption of certain change programs.
10. Change initiatives carry enormous ethical considerations that need to be weighed in the process.

DISCUSSION QUESTIONS

1. How do evolutionary change and revolutionary change differ?
2. What is a business process, and why is re-engineering a popular instrument of change today?
3. Why is restructuring sometimes necessary for re-engineering to take place?
4. What are the main steps in action research?
5. What is organizational development, and what is its goal?

ORGANIZATIONAL THEORY IN ACTION

Practising Organizational Theory: Managing Change

Break up into groups of three to five people and discuss the following scenario:

You are a group of top managers of one of the Big Three carmakers. Your company has been experiencing increased competition from other carmakers whose innovations in car design and manufacturing methods have allowed them to produce cars that are higher in quality and lower in cost than yours. You have been charged with preparing a plan to change the company's structure to allow you to compete better, and you have decided on two main changes. First, you plan to re-engineer the company and move from a multidivisional structure (in which each division produces its own range of cars) to one in which cross-functional product teams become responsible for developing new car models that will be sold by all the divisions. Second, you have decided to implement a total quality management program to raise quality and decentralize decision-making authority to the teams and make them responsible for achieving higher quality and lower costs. Thus the changes will disrupt role relationships at both the divisional and functional levels.

1. Discuss the nature of the obstacles at the divisional, functional, and individual level that you will encounter in implementing this new structure. Which do you think will be the most important obstacles to overcome?
2. Discuss some ways you can overcome obstacles to change to help your organization move to its desired future state.

Making the Connection #10

Find an example of a company that has recently gone through a major change. What type of change was it? Why did the organization make the change, and what does it hope to achieve from it?

The Ethical Dimension #10

Imagine that you are managers responsible for reengineering an organization into cross-functional teams that will result in the layoff of over 30 percent of employees.

1. Discuss the resistance to change at the organization and individual levels that you will likely encounter.
2. Discuss alternative plans for retaining the existing workforce and cutting 30 percent of the workforce. In the first case, explain how you would balance economic stability with employment considerations. In the second case, explain how you would manage the change process to behave ethically to those employees who will be terminated, and to those who will be reassigned to new jobs and face a new organizational culture.

Analyzing the Organization: Design Module #10

This module focuses on the extent to which your organization has been involved in major change efforts recently and on its approach to promoting innovation.

1. Does *revolutionary* or *evolutionary* best describe the changes that have been taking place in your organization?
2. In what types of change (such as restructuring) has your organization been most involved? How successful have these change efforts been?
3. With the information that you have at your disposal, discuss (a) the forces for change, (b) obstacles to change, and (c) the strategy for change your organization has adopted.

Company Profiles #10*

Choose one or more of the organizations (e.g., companies, government agencies, or nonprofit organizations) that are profiled in this chapter. Do an Internet search to get up-to-date information on each organization you have selected, and answer the following questions.

1. What does the new information tell you about the organization's current ability to develop a successful change strategy?
2. How does the information compare with the earlier information provided in the text and what does that tell you about organizations (e.g., does the organization appear to be more or less successful at change strategy than before, and how do you explain this)?

Alternative Perspectives #10

Critical and feminist research indicates that organizational change programs can have negative impacts on employees. Read one or more of the following readings and list five ways that organizational change programs can have a negative impact and five ways that it can have a positive impact on employees. In small groups, discuss how you would deal with the potentially negative aspects of organizational change.

Reading List

Abrahamson, E. 1996. Management Fashion. *Academy of Management Review*, 21(1): 254–285.

Fondas, N. 1997. Feminization Unveiled: Management Qualities in Contemporary Writings. *The Academy of Management Review*, 22(1): 257–282.

Helms Mills, J. 2003. *Making Sense of Organizational Change*. London: Routledge.

Jackson, B. 2001. *Management Gurus and Management Fashions*. London: Routledge.

* The authors would like to receive information from student groups and instructors on any companies where there have been dramatic changes to the information published in this text. We would be happy to publish the best of these changes in a subsequent edition, where we will focus on changing company profiles.

Kieser, A. 1997. Rhetoric and Myth in Management Fashion. *Organization,* 4(1): 49–74.

Morgan, G., and Knights, D. 1991. Gendering Jobs: Corporate Strategies, Managerial Control and Dynamics of Job Segregation. *Work, Employment & Society,* 5(2): 181–200.

Rinehart, J. 1986. Improving the Quality of Working Life Through Job Redesign: Work Humanization or Work Rationalization. *The Canadian Review of Sociology and Anthropology,* 23(4): 507–530.

Thomas, R., Mills, A. J., and Helms Mills, J., eds. 2004. *Identity Politics at Work: Gendering Resistance, Resisting Gender.* London: Routledge.

CASE FOR ANALYSIS

Organizational Change at Coast Mountain Bus[81]

Coast Mountain Bus Company (CMBC) is a transit bus and ferry company operating in Vancouver, with its head office in Surrey, British Columbia. The company is a relatively young transit company, established in April 1999. The company was formerly know as BC Transit and is a part of a larger group of subsidiaries of the parent company Translink that have evolved from a long history of transit service in the Vancouver area that dates back to 1890. Over 3800 employees at CMBC provide service to what is the largest single transit service area in Canada.[82]

When CMBC employees went on strike in 2001, it was no surprise that the crippling effect on transit service in the Vancouver area had a significant impact on the company's public position. The strike lasted four months and it ended when employees were legislated back to work. At the time, CMBC was voted the least respected company in British Columbia. Obviously, major change was needed for the company to get back respect from the public and its employees.

Drastic changes did come quickly in various forms. Restructuring was the immediate change. Several of the top company executives left the company and were replaced by an executive team whose top priorities were to establish better relations with the three employee unions involved and to establish a more employee-focused organization. The company does not own its vehicles or its facilities. CMBC is a business that relies highly on its employees, so restructuring to focus more on human resources was an imperative.

When employees did come back to work, workplace relations were difficult enough to address, but CMBC was also facing a $14.5 million budget cut problem. CMBC could have saved money through vacation time cost deductions due to the strike, but this would have been an antagonistic move. In contrast, the company opted for a restructuring approach that emphasized an appreciation for the return of their employees to a company that would change and become more supportive. The company has since worked more closely with employees and the unions on various fronts. In particular, their work together in improving productivity contributed to reversing the budget-cut problem to having a $3.1 million surplus budget.[83]

Coast Mountain Bus Company's current mission, core values, and goal statements reflect the new and improved positioning that has positively moved the company beyond the crisis brought on by the strike. How the changes have been communicated and promoted are also reflected in the following excerpts from CMBC's message from the president:

> Over the past two years, Coast Mountain Bus Company employees have worked hard to put our "house" in order and 2004 is the time to enjoy the dividends. We've begun to think differently at the Company, with a spirit of innovation, cooperation, efficiency and service. Feedback on quality of service and performance continues to rate us very high. In 2004, I want CMBC employees to make decisions and take action as if they

owned the company and wrote our core values and goals. Let's use this stability and positive momentum to build a company that commands the respect and admiration you deserve.[84]

DISCUSSION QUESTIONS

1. What brought on significant change at Coast Mountain Bus Company?
2. Write a short summary of the evolutionary changes that have occurred in CMBC's long history in transit service and compare it to this more recent revolutionary change that has taken place in the company.
3. Discuss the underlying themes in the president's message.

REFERENCES

1. M. Beer, *Organizational Change and Development* (Santa Monica, CA: Goodyear, 1980); J. I. Porras and R. C. Silvers, "Organization Development and Transformation," *Annual Review of Psychology*, 1991, vol. 42, pp. 51–78.
2. C. Argyris, R. Putman, and D. M. Smith, *Action Science* (San Francisco: Jossey-Bass, 1985).
3. R. M. Kanter, *The Change Masters: Innovation for Productivity in the American Corporation* (New York: Simon and Schuster, 1984).
4. C. W. L. Hill and G. R. Jones, *Strategic Management: An Integrated Approach*, 3rd ed. (Boston: Houghton Mifflin, 1995).
5. Ibid.
6. G. R. Jones, *Organizational Theory: Text and Cases* (Reading, MA: Addison-Wesley, 1995).
7. J. Helms Mills, *Making Sense of Organizational Change* (London: Routledge, 2003).
8. C. W. L. Hill, *International Business* (Chicago, IL: Irwin, 1994).
9. C. A. Bartlett and S. Ghoshal, *Managing Across Borders* (Boston: Harvard Business School Press, 1989).
10. C. K. Prahalad and Y. L. Doz, *The Multinational Mission: Balancing Local Demands and Global Vision* (New York: Free Press, 1987).
11. D. Jamieson and J. O'Mara, *Managing Workforce 2000: Gaining a Diversity Advantage* (San Francisco: Jossey-Bass, 1991); C. Agocs *Employment Equity: Cooperative Strategies for Organizational Change* (New York: Klewer Law International, 1992); C. Agocs, *Workplace Equality: International Perspectives on Legislation, Policy and Practice* (New York: Klewer Law International, 2002).
12. P. Prasad, A. J. Mills, M. Elmes and A. Prasad, *Managing the Organizational Melting Pot* (Thousand Oaks, CA: Sage, 1997).
13. S. E. Jackson and Associates, *Diversity in the Workplace: Human Resource Initiatives* (New York: Guilford Press, 1992); S. H. Appelbaum, D. Herbert, and S. Leroux "Empowerment: Power, Culture and Leadership—A Strategy or Fad for the Millennium? *Journal of Workplace Learning*, 1999, vol. 11, pp. 233–254; D. Boje and G. A. Rosile "Where's the Power in Empowerment, Answers from Follett and Clegg," *Journal of Applied Behavioral Science*, 2001, vol. 37, pp. 90–117.
14. W. H. Shaw and V. Barry, *Moral Issues in Business*, 6th ed. (Belmont, CA: Wadsworth, 1995); R. Jackall, *Moral Mazes* (Oxford: Oxford University Press, 1988); M. Drohan, *Making a Killing: How and Why Corporations Use Armed Force to Do Business* (Toronto: Random House Canada, 2003).
15. T. Donaldson, *Corporations and Morality* (Englewood Cliffs, NJ: Prentice Hall, 1982); N. B. Rapoport and B. G. Dharan, *Enron: Corporate Fiascos and Their Implications* (New York: Foundation Press, 2004); I. Stuart and B. Stuart, *Ethics in the Post-Enron Age* (Mason, OH: SouthWestern/Thomson, 2004).
16. M. Hannan and J. Freeman, "Structural Inertia and Organizational Change," *American Sociological Review*, 1989, vol. 49, pp. 149–164.
17. L. E. Greiner, "Evolution and Revolution as Organizations Grow," *Harvard Business Review*, July–August 1972, pp. 37–46.

18. "Nike Battles Backlash from Overseas Sweatshops," *Marketing News*, 9 November 1998, p. 14.

19. J. Laabs, "Nike Gives Indonesian Workers a Raise," *Workforce*, December 1998, pp. 15–16.

20. See, for example, *cbae.nmsu.edu/mgt/handout/boje/bnike/index.html.*

21. W. Echikson, "It's Europe's Turn to Sweat About Sweatshops," *Business Week*, 19 July 1999, p. 96.

22. R. M. Kanter, *When Giants Learn to Dance: Mastering the Challenges of Strategy* (New York: Simon and Schuster, 1989).

23. J. P. Kotter and L. A. Schlesinger, "Choosing Strategies for Change," *Harvard Business Review*, March–April 1979, pp. 106–114.

24. T. Burns and G. M. Stalker, *The Management of Innovation* (London: Tavistock, 1961).

25. P. R. Lawrence and J. W. Lorsch, *Organization and Environment* (Boston: Harvard Business School Press, 1972).

26. R. Dallaire, *Shake Hands with the Devil* (Toronto: Vintage Canada, 2004).

27. Ibid, p. 520.

28. F. J. Roethlisberger and W. J. Dickson, *Management and the Worker* (Cambridge, MA: Harvard University Press, 1939).

29. R. Likert, *The Human Organization* (New York: McGraw-Hill, 1967); S. Dubb, *Logics of Resistance: Globalization and Telephone Unionism in Mexico and British Columbia* (New York: Garland, 1999); J. Jermier, D. Knights and W. R. Nord, *Resistance and Power in Organizations* (London: Routledge, 1994); R. Thomas, A. J. Mills, and J. Helms Mills, *Identity Politics at Work: Gendering Resistance, Resisting Gender* (London: Routledge, 2004).

30. C. Argyris, *Personality and Organization* (New York: Harper and Row, 1957).

31. B. Cook, "Writing the Left out of Management Theory: The Historiography of the Management of Change," *Organization*, 1999, vol. 6, pp. 81–105; A. F. Marrow, *The Practical Theorist: The Life and Work of Kurt Lewin* (New York: Basic Books, 1969).

32. This section draws heavily on K. Lewin, *Field-Theory in Social Science* (New York: Harper and Row, 1951).

33. D. Miller, "Evolution and Revolution: A Quantum View of Structural Change in Organizations," *Journal of Management Studies*, 1982, vol. 19, pp. 11–151; D. Miller, "Momentum and Revolution in Organizational Adaptation," *Academy of Management Journal*, 1980, vol. 2, pp. 591–614.

34. C. E. Lindblom, "The Science of Muddling Through," *Public Administration Review*, 1959, vol. 19, pp. 79–88; P. C. Nystrom and W. H. Starbuck, "To Avoid Organizational Crises, Unlearn," *Organizational Dynamics*, 1984, vol. 12, pp. 53–65.

35. E. L. Trist, G. Higgins, H. Murray, and A. G. Pollock, *Organizational Choice* (London: Tavistock, 1965); J. C. Taylor, "The Human Side of Work: The Socio-Technical Approach to Work Design," *Personnel Review*, 1975, vol. 4, pp. 17–22.

36. E. L. Trist and K. W. Bamforth, "Some Social and Psychological Consequences of the Long Wall Method of Coal Mining," *Human Relations*, 1951, vol. 4, pp. 3–38; F. E. Emery and E. L. Trist, "Socio-Technical Systems" (London: Proceedings of the 6th Annual International Meeting of the Institute of Management Sciences, 1965), pp. 92–93.

37. E. L. Trist, G. Higgins, H. Murray, and A. G. Pollock, *Organizational Choice* (London: Tavistock, 1965); J. C. Taylor, "The Human Side of Work: The Socio-Technical Approach to Work Design," *Personnel Review*, 1975, vol. 4, pp. 17–22.

38. For a review, see D. R. Denison, "What Is the Difference Between Organizational Culture and Organizational Climate? A Native's Point of View on a Decade of Paradigm Wars," *Academy of Management Review*, 1996, vol. 21, pp. 619–654.

39. W. Edwards Deming, *Out of the Crisis* (Cambridge, MA: MIT Press, 1989); M. Walton, *The Deming Management Method* (New York: Perigee Books, 1990).

40. J. McHugh and B. Dale, "Quality Circles," in R. Wild, ed., *International Handbook of Production and Operations Research* (London: Cassel, 1989).

41. Helms Mills, *Making Sense of Organizational Change.*

42. Adapted from A. J. Mills, J. Helms Mills, J. Bratton and C. Foreshaw, *Organizational Behaviour in Context* (Toronto: Garamond Press, 2006).

43. Helms Mills, *Making Sense of Organizational Change*; B. Jackson, *Management Gurus and Management Fashions* (London: Routledge, 2001); A. Kieser "Rhetoric and Myth in Management Fashion," *Organization*, 1997, vol. 4, pp. 49–74.

44. S. M. Young, "A Framework for the Successful Adoption and Performance of Japanese Manufacturing Techniques in the U.S.," *Academy of Management Review*, 1992, vol. 17, pp. 677–700.

45. Young, "A Framework for the Successful Adoption and Performance of Japanese Manufacturing Practices in the U.S."

46. R. Parthasarthy and S. P. Sethi, "The Impact of Flexible Automation on Business Strategy and Organizational Structure," *Academy of Management Review*, 1992, vol. 17, pp. 86–111.

47. "Return of the Stopwatch," *The Economist*, 23 January 1993, p. 69.
48. M. Hammer and J. Champy, *Reengineering the Corporation* (New York: HarperCollins, 1993).
49. M. Hammer, "Reengineering Work: Don't Automate, Obliterate," *Harvard Business Review*, July–August 1990, pp. 104–112.
50. "Facts About Hallmark," *www.hallmark.com*, 2000.
51. A. C. Lampe, "The Silencing of Voices: The Corporate 'Darkness' Nobody Hears," *Culture and Organization*, 2002, vol. 8, pp. 129–144, at p. 129.
52. S. J. Freeman and K. S. Cameron, "Organizational Downsizing: A Convergence and Reorientation Framework," *Organizational Science*, 1993, vol. 4, pp. 10–29.
53. R.-L. DeWitt, "The Structural Consequences of Downsizing," *Organizational Science*, 1993, vol. 4, pp. 30–40.
54. "The Salaryman Rides Again," *The Economist*, 4 December 1995, p. 64.
55. Jones, *Organizational Theory*; R. A. Burgelman and M. A. Maidique, *Strategic Management of Technology and Innovation* (Homewood, IL: Irwin, 1988).
56. Organizational Insight compiled by Ellen Rudderham-Gaudet using the following sources: Stelco, "Corporate Profile," *www.stelco.ca/corporate/*, 16 October 2004; Stelco "Situation Overview," *www.stelco.com/restructuring/pdf/situation_overview.pdf*, 16 October 2004; "Stelco to Close Rod Mill in September," *Platt's Metals Week*, 26 July 2004, vol. 75, p. 14; Greg Keenan, "Major Stelco Client Warns on Contract," *Globe and Mail*, 9 October 2004, p. B5.
57. Lewin, *Field-Theory in Social Science*, pp. 172–174.
58. This section draws heavily on P. A. Clark, *Action Research and Organizational Change* (New York: Harper and Row, 1972); L. Brown, "Research Action: Organizational Feedback, Understanding and Change," *Journal of Applied Behavioral Research*, 1972, vol. 8, pp. 697–711; N. Margulies and A. P Raia, eds., *Conceptual Foundations of Organizational Development* (New York: McGraw-Hill, 1978).
59. W. L. French and C. H. Bell, *Organizational Development* (Englewood Cliffs, NJ: Prentice Hall, 1990).
60. L. Coch and J. R. P. French, "Overcoming Resistance to Change," *Human Relations*, 1948, vol. 1, pp. 512–532.
61. Helms Mills, *Making Sense of Organizational Change.*
62. Ibid.
63. French and Bell, *Organizational Development.*
64. Helms Mills, *Making Sense of Organizational Change.*
65. Coch and French, "Overcoming Resistance to Change."
66. W. L. French, "A Checklist for Organizing and Implementing an OD Effort," in W. L. French, C. H. Bell, and R. A. Zawacki, *Organizational Development and Transformation* (Homewood, IL: Irwin, 1994), pp. 484–495.
67. J. Kotter, L. Schlesinger, and V. Sathe, *Organization* (Homewood, IL: Irwin, 1986), p. 487.
68. W. G. Bennis, *Organizational Development: Its Nature, Origins, and Perspectives* (Reading, MA: Addison-Wesley, 1969).
69. Kotter and Schlesinger, "Choosing Strategies for Change."
70. B. Dumaine, "The New Non-Manager Managers," *Fortune*, 22 February 1993, pp. 80–84.
71. E. H. Schein, *Organizational Psychology* (Englewood Cliffs, NJ: Prentice Hall, 1980).
72. R. T. Golembiewski, "The Laboratory Approach to Organization Change: Schema of a Method," in Margulies and Raia, eds., *Conceptual Foundations of Organizational Development*, pp. 198–212; J. Kelley "Organizational Development Through Structured Sensitivity Training," ibid., pp. 213–228.
73. E. H. Schein, *Process Consultation* (Reading, MA: Addison-Wesley, 1969).
74. M. Sashkin and W. Warner Burke, "Organization Development in the 1980s," *Journal of Management*, 1987, vol. 13, pp. 393–417; D. Eden, "Team Development: Quasi-Experimental Confirmation Among Combat Companies," *Group and Organization Studies*, 1986, vol. 5, pp. 133–146; K. P. DeMeuse and S. J. Liebowitz, "An Empirical Analysis of Team Building Research," *Group and Organization Studies*, 1981, vol. 6, pp. 357–378.
75. French and Bell, *Organization Development.*
76. R. Beckhard, "The Confrontation Meeting," *Harvard Business Review*, March–April 1967, pp. 159–165.
77. Helms Mills, *Making Sense of Organizational Change*; Jackson, *Management Gurus and Management Fashions*; Kieser, "Rhetoric and Myth in Management Fashion."
78. P. Armstrong, H. Armstrong, J. Choiniere, E. Mykhalovskiy, and J. White, *Medical Alert: New Work Organizations in Health Care* (Toronto: Garamond Press, 1997); Helms Mills, *Making Sense of Organizational Change*; Jackson, *Management Gurus and Management Fashions*; Kieser, "Rhetoric and Myth in Management Fashion."
79. C. Bak "Lessons from the Veterans of TQM," *Canadian Business Review*, Winter 1992, pp. 17–19; S.

Becker, "TQM Does Work: Ten Reasons Why Misguided Efforts Fail," *Management Review*, 1993, vol. 82, pp. 30–34; D. A. Buchanan "The Limitations and Opportunities of Business Process Re-engineering in a Politicized Organizational Climate," *Human Relations*, 1997, vol. 50, pp. 51–72; "TQM Backlash Prompts Questions," *Hospitals*, 5 June 1992, p. 30.

80. G. Morgan and D. Knights "Gendering Jobs: Corporate Strategies, Managerial Control and Dynamics of Job Segregation," *Work, Employment & Society*, 1991, vol. 5, pp. 181–200; A. J. Mills "Strategy, Sexuality and the Stratosphere: Airlines and the Gendering of Organization," in E. S. Lyon and L. Morris, eds., *Gender Relations in Public and Private: New Research Perspectives* (London: MacMillan, 1996), pp. 77–94.

81. Case developed by Ellen Rudderham-Gaudet.

82. "About Coast Mountain Bus Company," *www.coastmountainbus.com/Welcomefiles/About.html*, 10 July 2004.

83. Uyen Vu, "Long Strike Sparks Change at B.C. Bus Firm," *Canadian HR Reporter*, 1 December 2003, p. 1.

84. "Coast Mountain Bus Company Changing to Meet the Future" (President's Message), *www.coastmountainbus.com/Welcomefiles/Pres_message.html*, 10 July 2004.

Organizational Transformations: Birth, Growth, Decline, and Death

CHAPTER 11

Learning Objectives

Organizations that successfully carve out a niche in their environments so that they can attract resources (such as customers) face a series of problems in their struggle for growth and survival. This chapter examines the organizational change and transformation problems that occur over the life cycle of an organization. Managers who understand the factors that lead to organizational birth and growth, that influence maturity, and that cause decline and death will be able to change their organization's strategy and structure to increase its effectiveness and chances of survival.

After reading this chapter you should be able to:

1. Appreciate the problems involved in surviving the perils of organizational birth and what founders can do to help their new organizations to survive.
2. Describe the typical problems that arise as an organization grows and matures, and how an organization must change if it is to survive and prosper.
3. Discuss why organizational decline occurs, identify the stages of decline, and assess how managers can change their organizations to prevent failure and eventual death or dissolution.

THE ORGANIZATIONAL LIFE CYCLE

Organizational life cycle A sequence of stages of growth and development through which organizations may pass.

Why do some organizations survive and prosper while others fail and die? Why do some organizations have the ability to manage their strategies, structures, and cultures to gain access to environmental resources while others fail at this task? To answer these questions, researchers have suggested that we need to understand the dynamics that affect organizations as they seek a satisfactory fit with their environment.[1] It has been suggested that organizations experience a predictable sequence of stages of growth and change: the **organizational life cycle**.

The four principal stages of the organizational life cycle are birth, growth, decline, and death (see Figure 11-1).[2] Organizations pass through these stages at different rates, and some do not experience every stage. Moreover, some companies go directly from birth to death without enjoying any growth if they do not attract customers or resources. Some organizations spend a long time in the growth stage, and many researchers have identified various substages of growth through which an organization must navigate. There are also substages of decline. Some organizations in decline take corrective action, change quickly, and turn themselves around.

The way an organization can change in response to the problems it confronts determines whether and when it will go on to the next stage in the life cycle and survive and prosper or fail and die. Each stage is examined in detail next.

ORGANIZATIONAL BIRTH

Organizations are born when individuals recognize and take advantage of opportunities to use their skills and competencies to generate support or create value.[3] These individuals, known as **entrepreneurs**, can be leaders who take the initiative to found a new organization (such as a trade union, a political party, or a charity) or they can be businesspeople who start up a new business. In the United States, Harry Bridges founded the International Longshoremen's and Warehousemen's Union in 1934 to fight for the rights of dockworkers. At around the same time in Canada, Tommy Douglas was founding the Co-operative Commonwealth Federation (CCF) in Saskatchewan (the CCF was later renamed the New Democratic Party). In 1980 Terry Fox began his "Marathon of Hope," running across Canada to raise funds for cancer research; as a result of Fox's run, Isadore Sharp, chairman and CEO of Four Seasons Hotels and Resorts, pledged to organize a fundraising run that would be held every year in Terry's name. In the mid-1990s Mike Lazaridis developed the world's first complete, wireless e-mail solution for accessing corporate e-mail from a single handheld device—the BlackBerry, which is produced by his company Research in Motion (RIM).

Entrepreneurs
People who recognize and take advantage of opportunities to use their skills and competencies to create value.

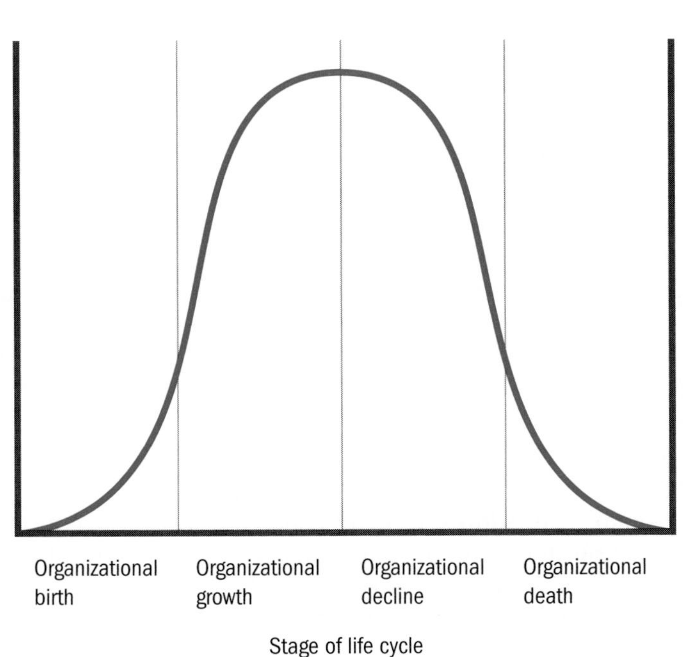

FIGURE 11-1
A Model of the Organizational Life Cycle.
Organizations pass through these four stages at different rates, and some do not experience every stage.

Organizational birth
The founding of an organization—a dangerous life cycle stage associated with the greatest chance of failure.

Liability of newness
The dangers associated with being the first in a new environment.

Organizational birth, the founding of an organization, is a dangerous stage of the life cycle and is associated with the greatest chance of failure. The failure rate is high because new business organizations experience the **liability of newness**—the dangers associated with being the first in a new environment.[4] This liability is great for several reasons.

Entrepreneurship is an inherently risky process. Because entrepreneurs undertake *new* ventures, there is no way to predict or guarantee success.[5] Entrepreneurs bear this uncertainty because they stand to earn potentially huge returns if their businesses take off. Much of the time, however, entrepreneurs make mistakes in judgment or planning, and the result is organizational death.[6]

A new organization is fragile because it lacks a formal structure to give its value-creation processes and actions stability and certainty. At first everything is done by trial and error. An organizational structure emerges gradually, as decisions about procedures and technology are made. Eventually, for example, it may become clear that one manager should manage money coming in from customers (accounts receivable), another should manage money being paid out to suppliers (accounts payable), and another should obtain new accounts. But at first, in a new organization, the structure is in the mind of the founder; it is not formalized in a chart or a set of rules. The structure is flexible and responsive, allowing the organization to adapt and perfect its routines to meet the needs of its environment.

A flexible structure can be an advantage when it allows the organization to change and take advantage of new opportunities, but it can also be a disadvantage. A formal structure provides stability and certainty by serving as the organization's memory. Structure specifies an organization's activities and the procedures for getting them done. If such procedures are not written down, a new organization can literally forget the skills and procedures that made it successful. A formal structure provides an organization with a firm foundation from which to improve on existing procedures and develop new ones.[7]

Another reason why organizational birth is a dangerous stage is that conditions in the environment may be hostile to a new organization. Resources, for example, may be scarce or difficult to obtain because many established organizations are competing for them. This can affect a charity that has to compete with a multitude of other charities. In the 1990s, for example, due to the dangerous nature of the illness, extensive publicity, celebrity endorsement, and government support, AIDS research became one of the best-supported charities in North America. As a result, many other charities experienced a decline in support. Throughout much of the 20th century, developing trade unions and left-wing political parties faced severe hostility from governments and employees and often did not survive as a result. Today new political parties may have to fold or reinvent themselves if they are unable to attract enough members and voter support. This was the case with the Reform Party that was formed in Alberta in the late 1980s. When the party failed to win popular support across the country in the late 1990s, it reformed itself and became the Alliance Party. As its fortunes continued to falter, the party merged with the Progressive Conservative Party in 2003 to form the Conservative Party of Canada.

Developing a Plan for a New Business

One way in which entrepreneurs can address difficult issues is through the crafting of a business plan that outlines how they plan to compete in the environment. The steps in the development of a business plan are listed in Table 11-1.

Planning for a new business begins when an entrepreneur notices an opportunity to develop a new or improved good or service for the whole market or for a spe-

Table 11-1

DEVELOPING A BUSINESS PLAN

1. Notice a product opportunity, and develop a basic business idea
   - Goods/services
   - Customers/markets
2. Conduct a strategic (SWOT) analysis
   - Identify opportunities
   - Identify threats
   - Identify strengths
   - Identify weaknesses
3. Decide whether the business opportunity is feasible
4. Prepare a detailed business plan
   - Statement of mission, goals, and financial objectives
   - Statement of strategic objectives
   - List of necessary resources
   - Organizational timeline of events

cific market niche. For example, an entrepreneur might notice an opportunity in the fast-food market to specialize in a particular style of meal or product. In 1984 Jay and Hal Gould, two brothers from Brantford, Ontario, were living in New York when they were given a tip about a vender selling "the best fries in New York." They investigated, liked what they saw, and bought the company, calling it New York Fries. Ten years later, they had opened stores in Canada, Korea, Australia, and the United Arab Emirates. Similarly, in 1987, Cora Mussely Tsouflidou identified a need for old-fashioned Quebec-style family breakfasts and set up shop in a defunct snack bar in the Ville Saint-Laurent district of Montreal. In 1994 Tsouflidou began to franchise the company, and now there are 65 Cora's restaurants across Canada.

The next step is to test the feasibility of the new product idea. The entrepreneur conducts as thorough a strategic planning exercise as possible, using SWOT analysis, the analysis of organizational *strengths* and *weaknesses* and environmental *opportunities* and *threats*. Potential threats might be that large fast-food chains may try to imitate the idea and offer its customers different types of fries or a range of breakfast products. The entrepreneur should conduct a thorough analysis of the external environment (see Chapter 3) to test the potential of a new product idea and must be willing to abandon the idea if it seems likely that the threats and risks will overwhelm the opportunities and returns. Entrepreneurship is always a very risky process, and many entrepreneurs become so committed to their new ideas that they ignore or discount the potential threats and forge ahead—only to lose their shirts or their skirts.

If the environmental analysis suggests that the product idea is feasible, the next step is to examine the strengths and weaknesses of the idea. At this stage the main strength is the resources possessed by the entrepreneur. Does the entrepreneur have access to an adequate source of funds? Does the entrepreneur have any experience in the fast-food industry, such as managing a restaurant? Cora Tsouflidou, for example, spent many years in the fast-food and restaurant business before she opened her own restaurant. To identify weaknesses, the entrepreneur needs to assess how many and what kinds of resources will be necessary to establish a viable new venture—such as a chain of chicken restaurants. Analysis might reveal that the new product idea will not generate an adequate return on investment. Or it might reveal that the entrepreneur needs to find partners to help provide the resources needed to open a chain on a sufficient scale to generate a high enough return on investment.

After conducting a thorough SWOT analysis, if the entrepreneur decides that the new product idea is feasible, the hard work begins: developing the actual business plan that will be used to attract investors or funds from banks. Included in the business plan should be the same basic elements as in the product development plan: (1) a statement of the organization's mission, goals, and financial objectives; (2) a statement of the organization's strategic objectives, including an analysis of the product's market potential, based on the SWOT analysis that has already been conducted; (3) a list of all the functional and organizational resources that will be required to implement the new product idea successfully, including a list of technological, financial, and human resource requirements; and (4) a timeline that contains specific milestones for the entrepreneur and others to use to measure the progress of the venture, such as target dates for the final design and the opening of the first restaurant.

Many entrepreneurs do not have the luxury of having a team of cross-functional managers to help develop a detailed business plan. This obviously is true for solo ventures. One reason why franchising has become so popular in Canada and the United States is that an entrepreneur can purchase and draw on the business plan and experience of an already-existing company, thereby reducing the risks associated with opening a new business. Cora's Restaurants' Web site, for example, lists the following strengths of franchising: "A concept with success factors that can be easily identified and measured: (a) original concept, (b) premium quality food and service, (c) targeted locations, (d) proven operating system, (e) proven profitability, (f) customer satisfaction with recipes and products.[8]

In sum, entrepreneurs have a number of significant challenges to confront and conquer if they are to be successful. It is not uncommon for an entrepreneur to fail repeatedly before he or she finds a venture that proves successful. It also is not uncommon for an entrepreneur who establishes a successful new company to sell it in order to move on to new ventures that promise new risks and returns. An example of such entrepreneurs involves brothers Michael and Paul Donovan, who made a success in television and film production through their company Salter Street Films. (See Organizational Insight 11.1.)

A POPULATION ECOLOGY MODEL OF ORGANIZATIONAL BIRTH

Population ecology theory seeks to explain the factors that affect the rate at which new organizations are born (and die) in a population of existing organizations.[9] A **population of organizations** comprises the organizations that are competing for the same set of resources in the environment. All the fast-food restaurants in Moncton, New Brunswick, constitute a population of restaurants that compete to obtain environmental resources in the form of dollars that busy employees are willing to spend on food. IBM, Compaq, Dell, AST, Gateway, and the other personal computer companies constitute a population of organizations that are seeking to attract environmental resources in the form of dollars that consumers are willing to spend on personal computing. Different organizations within a population may choose to focus on different **environmental niches**, or particular sets of resources. Dell Computer chose to focus on the mail-order niche of the personal computer environment; IBM and Compaq originally focused on the business niche; and Apple focused on the higher education niche.

Population ecology theory
A theory that seeks to explain the factors that affect the rate at which new organizations are born (and die) in a population of existing organizations.

Population of organizations
The organizations that are competing for the same set of resources in the environment.

Environmental niches
Particular sets of resources.

ORGANIZATIONAL INSIGHT 11.1

The Rise and Fall of Salter Street Films[10]

Salter Street Films Limited, a Halifax-based company, was founded by brothers Michael and Paul Donovan in 1981. Its mandate was to be an "integrated entertainment company," and create and produce original film and television programming for worldwide distribution. The company became a Nova Scotia success story, growing steadily over the next 17 years, and in May 1998 made an initial public offering that raised $16 million. In July of the same year, Salter Street acquired another successful Halifax film company, Charles Bishop Productions. Salter Street met its mandate and produced successful shows such as the comedy hit *This Hour Has 22 Minutes*, *The Awful Truth with Michael Moore*, and the science-fiction series *LEXX*.

Salter Street gradually expanded its operations to include a sound stage facility, an interactive multimedia division, a post-production operation, and a distribution organization providing programming to over 30 countries. Revenues and profits increased over the years. In 2000 Salter Street had revenues of $54 million and a net income of $4.65 million, up from the previous year's revenues of $49 million and net income of $4.3 million.

In November 2000, Salter Street was awarded the rights to the digital television licence for the Independent Film Channel, a tier-one channel that must be available on basic cable. This was considered a major coup in the television industry. However, in February 2001, Salter Street changed direction. It was sold for a reported $58.4 million to Toronto-based Alliance Atlantis Communications Inc. Alliance said that the reason for the purchase was Salter's television show list and its impressive record of producing comedy television shows. At the time of the acquisition, industry analysts felt that part of the motivation behind the purchase was to acquire the Independent Film Channel, which Salter had the rights to.

Michael Donovan, in support of the transaction, said, "We have been making films and television programs in Canada and distributing them internationally for over 22 years. There have been many significant milestones and developments, but this transaction is without a doubt the most significant and positive to date. We believe that this partnership with Alliance Atlantis is the best way going forward to continue to grow and develop Canadian films and television in Atlantic Canada. We also believe it is in the best interest of our shareholders."

Alliance Atlantis's mandate is to be a "leading vertically integrated broadcaster, creator and distributor of filmed entertainment." The company, which is traded on the Toronto Stock Exchange, has three operating groups including the Broadcast Group, the Motion Picture Distribution Group, and the Entertainment Group. In addition to its Toronto headquarters, it has offices in Los Angeles, London, Montreal, Dublin, Edmonton, Shannon, and Sydney, and, until the closing of Salter Street, it maintained an office in Halifax. Unfortunately, in recent years Alliance has been experiencing financial difficulties. In 2003, Alliance had revenues of $889.6 million and an operating loss of $18.8 million.

After becoming a subsidiary of Alliance, Salter Street Films continued to flourish under the direction of chairman and CEO Michael Donovan, a native Haligonian and a respected leader in the Canadian entertainment industry. In 2002 Salter Street produced the Michael Moore–directed documentary *Bowling for Columbine*, which went on to win the Academy Award for best documentary feature of the year, bringing international acclaim to Salter Street.

However, despite its success, Salter Street was gradually downsized after being acquired, and in 2003 Alliance closed Salter Street as part of a major restructuring plan. Due to the financial straits it was in, the parent company had decided to change its strategy to focus on higher-margin Canadian broadcasting operations.

Number of Births

Population density
The number of organizations that can compete for the same resources in a particular environment.

According to population ecology theory, the availability of resources determines the number of organizations in a population. The amount of resources in an environment limits **population density**—the number of organizations that can compete for the same resources in a particular environment.[11] Population ecology theorists assume that growth in the number of organizational births in a new environment is rapid at first as new organizations are founded to take advantage of new environmental resources, such as dollars that people are willing to spend on personal computing (see Figure 11-2).[12]

Two factors account for the rapid birth rate. The first is that as new organizations are founded, there is an increase in the knowledge and skills available to generate similar new organizations. Many new organizations are founded by entrepreneurs who leave existing companies to set up their own companies. Many new computer companies were founded by people who left pioneering organizations such as Hewlett-Packard and IBM.

The second factor accounting for the rapid birth rate in a new environment is that when a new kind of organization is founded and survives, it provides a role model. The success of a new organization makes it relatively easy for entrepreneurs to found similar new organizations, because success confers legitimacy, which will attract stakeholders. Fast-food restaurants, for example, were a relatively untested kind of organization until McDonald's proved their ability to attract resources in the form of customers. Entrepreneurs watched McDonald's create and succeed in the U.S. fast-food market and then imitated McDonald's by founding similar companies, such as Burger King and Wendy's. McDonald's became a U.S. institution, gave the population of fast-food organizations legitimacy, and allowed them to attract stakeholders such as customers, employees, and investors. Now fast food is taken for granted in many countries around the world.

In Canada, former hockey player and entrepreneur Tim Horton began his business venture with a string of hamburger restaurants. The venture was not very successful, so Horton turned to the idea of selling just coffee and doughnuts, opening his first coffee shop in Hamilton, Ontario, in 1964. More than four decades later, there are close to 2000 Tim Hortons across Canada and in parts of the United States.

FIGURE 11-2
Organizational Birth Rates over Time.
According to population ecology theory, the rate of birth in a new environment increases rapidly at first and then tapers off as resources become less plentiful and competition increases.

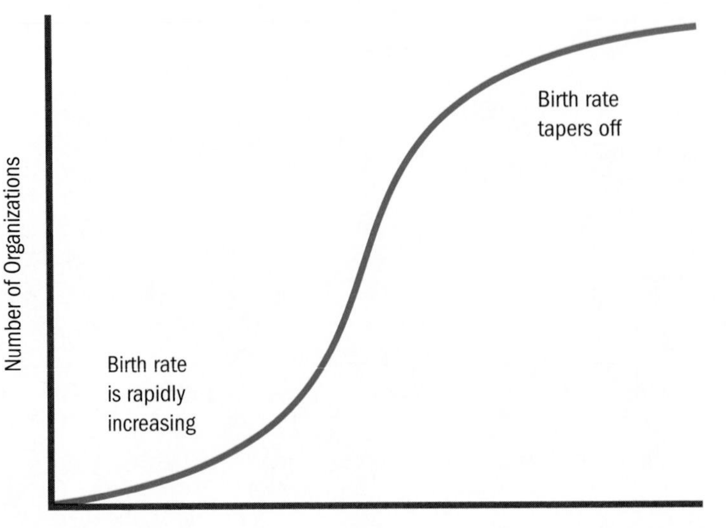

Once an environment is populated with a number of successful organizations, the organizational birth rate tapers off (see the S-shaped curve in Figure 11-2).[13] Two factors work to decrease the rate at which organizations are founded. First, births taper off as the availability of resources in the environment for late entrants diminishes.[14] Companies that start first, like McDonald's, Tim Hortons, or Microsoft, have a competitive edge over later entrants because of first-mover advantages. **First-mover advantages** are the benefits an organization derives from being an early entrant into a new environment. They include customer support, a recognized brand name, and the best locations for new businesses like restaurants. Latecomers enter an environment that is partially depleted of the resources that they need to grow. Investors, for example, are reluctant to lend money to new firms because their chances of survival in an established competitive environment are poor unless they can somehow discover and keep control of a new niche, as Dell Computer did. Similarly, the best managers and workers prefer to work in organizations that have established reputations and offer secure employment opportunities.

First-mover advantages
The benefits an organization derives from being an early entrant into a new environment.

The second factor that decreases the birth rate is the difficulty of competing with existing organizations for resources.[15] Potential entrepreneurs are discouraged from entering an industry or market because they understand that the larger the number of companies already competing for resources, the more difficult and expensive the resources will be to obtain. To obtain new customers, new companies may need to overspend on advertising or innovation, or they may need to reduce their prices too much. Moreover, existing companies may band together and make it very hard for new companies to enter the market. Companies such as Wal-Mart are so powerful that they can control supplier production and pricing that make it difficult for competitors to enter the market. Less powerful companies may engage in collusion, agreeing (illegally) to set their prices at artificially low levels to drive new rivals out of an industry, or they may erect barriers to entry by investing heavily in advertising so that it is very expensive for new companies to enter the market.

Survival Strategies

Population ecologists have identified two sets of strategies that organizations can use to gain access to resources and enhance their chances of survival in the environment: (1) r-strategy versus K-strategy and (2) specialist strategy versus generalist strategy.

r-Strategy versus K-Strategy Organizations that follow an **r-strategy** are founded early in a new environment—they are early entrants. The YMCA (see Organizational Insight 11.2, p. 383) is an example of an early entrant. Organizations that follow a **K-strategy** are founded late—they are late entrants.[16] The advantage of an r-strategy is that an organization obtains first-mover advantages and has first pick of the resources in the environment. As a result, the organization is usually able to grow rapidly and develop skills and procedures that increase its chance of surviving and prospering. Organizations that follow a K-strategy are usually established in other environments and wait to enter a new environment until the uncertainty in that environment is reduced and the correct way to compete is apparent. These organizations then take the skills they have established in other environments and use them to develop effective procedures that allow them to compete with and often dominate organizations following the r-strategy.

r-strategy
A strategy of entering a new environment early.

K-strategy
A strategy of entering an environment late, after other organizations have tested the water.

The difference between r-strategy and K-strategy is evident in the situation that emerged in the personal computer industry. In 1977, Apple Computer founded the personal computer market by developing the Apple I. Other small companies quickly followed Apple's lead. Each of them pursued an r-strategy and developed its own personal computer. Many of these companies were successful in attracting resources, and the population of personal computer companies grew quickly. IBM, the dominant player in the mainframe computer market, realized the potential in the personal computer market. It adopted a K-strategy and moved to develop its own personal computer (based on Microsoft's MS-DOS operating system), which it introduced in 1981. The ability to put its massive resources to work in the new environment and to exploit its brand name gave IBM a competitive advantage. As the MS-DOS operating system became the industry standard, IBM drove many of the smaller r-strategists out of the market. IBM even threatened Apple Computer for a while, but Apple was able to hang on to its loyal customers and weather the storm of competition.

K-strategists can often outperform r-strategists when they are competing for the same environmental niche. Apple Computer, for example, focused its activities very heavily on the school and university markets for computers. IBM competed heavily in the business market. Thus IBM primarily hurt competitors that were trying to occupy the business niche.

Specialist Strategy versus Generalist Strategy The difference between a specialist and a generalist strategy is defined by the breadth of the environmental niche—the set of resources—for which an organization competes. Specialist organizations (or **specialists**) concentrate their skills to pursue a narrow range of resources in a single niche. Generalist organizations (or **generalists**) spread their skills thinly to compete for a broad range of resources in many niches.[17] By focusing their activities in one niche, specialists develop core competencies that allow them to outperform generalists in that niche. Specialists are likely to offer customers much better service than the service offered by generalists, or they may be able to develop superior products because they invest all their resources in a narrow range of products. Intel, for example, invests all its resources in producing state-of-the-art microprocessors and does not bother with other kinds of electronic or computer components.

Specialists
Organizations that concentrate their skills to pursue a narrow range of resources in a single niche.

Generalists
Organizations that spread their skills thinly to compete for a broad range of resources in many niches.

Generalists can often outcompete specialists when there is considerable uncertainty in the environment and when resources are changing so that niches emerge and disappear continually. Generalists can survive in an uncertain environment because they have spread their resources thinly. If one niche disappears they still have others in which to operate. If a specialist's niche disappears, however, there is a much higher chance of organizational failure and death.

Specialists and generalists often coexist in many environments. The reason for their coexistence is that successful generalists create the conditions that allow specialists to operate successfully.[18] Large department stores, for example, create a demand for different kinds of fashionable clothes. To meet that demand, boutiques set up and specialize in one kind of clothing, such as evening wear or sportswear. This is the opportunity for the entrepreneur.

The Process of Natural Selection

The two sets of strategies—specialist versus generalist and r versus K—give rise to four strategies that organizations can pursue: r-specialist, r-generalist, K-specialist, and K-generalist (see Figure 11-3).[19]

Early in an environment, as a niche develops and new resources become available, new organizations are likely to be r-specialists—organizations that move quickly to focus on serving the needs of particular customer groups. Many new organizations grow and prosper, as did Apple Computer. As they grow, they often become generalists and compete in new niches. While this is happening, however, K-generalists (usually the divisions or subsidiaries of large companies like IBM or General Electric) move

	Specialist Strategy (operates in one niche)	Generalist Strategy (operates in several niches)
r-Strategy (early entry into environment)	r-Specialist	r-Generalist
K-Strategy (late entry into environment)	K-Specialist	K-Generalist

FIGURE 11-3
Strategies for Competing in the Resource Environment.

into the market and threaten the weakest r-specialist organizations. Eventually, the strongest r-specialists, r-generalists, and K-generalists dominate the environment by serving multiple market segments and by pursuing a low-cost or differentiation strategy. Large companies, having chosen the K-generalist strategy, often create niches for new firms to enter the market, so K-specialists are founded to exploit the new market segments. In this way, generalists and specialists can coexist in an environment because they are competing for different sets of resources.

The early beginnings of the car industry provide a good example of this organizational birth process. The first car companies (such as Packard and Dusenberg) were small crafts operations that produced high-priced cars for small market segments. These companies were the original r-specialists. Then Henry Ford realized the potential for establishing a mass market via mass production, and he decided to pursue a K-generalist strategy by producing a low-priced, standardized car for the mass market. Similarly, at GM, Alfred Sloan was rapidly pursuing a K-generalist strategy based on differentiation. He positioned GM's different car divisions to serve the whole range of market segments, from low-priced Chevrolets to high-priced Cadillacs. The low price and variety of car models available eventually drove many of the small r-specialists out of business. GM and Ford, together with Chrysler, proceeded to dominate the environment. Many new small companies pursuing K-specialist strategies then emerged to serve specialist segments that these companies had left open. Luxury-car manufacturers like Cord and Packard produced high-priced vehicles and prospered for a while, and European car manufacturers such as Rolls Royce, Mercedes, and Bugatti were popular. In the 1970s, Japanese companies like Toyota and Honda entered the North American market with a K-specialist strategy, producing cars much smaller than the vehicles that the Big Three were making. The huge popularity of these new cars gave the Japanese companies access to resources and allowed them to switch to a K-generalist strategy, directly threatening the Big Three. Thus, over time, new generations of organizations are born to take advantage of changes in the distribution of resources and the appearance of new niches.

Natural selection
The process that ensures the survival of organizations that have the skills and abilities that best fit with the environment.

New organizations are always emerging to take advantage of new opportunities. The driving force behind the population ecology model of organizational birth is **natural selection**, the process that ensures the survival of the organizations that have the skills and abilities that best fit with the environment.[20] Over time, weaker organizations, such as those with old-fashioned or outdated skills and competencies or those that cannot adapt their procedures to fit with changes in the environment, are selected out of the environment and die. New kinds of organizations emerge and survive if they can stake a claim to an environmental niche. In the car industry, Ford was a more efficient competitor than the craft shops, which declined and died because they lost their niche to Ford. In turn, Japanese companies, which continued to innovate and develop new skills, entered the North American car market. When customers selected Japanese cars because they wanted smaller, better quality vehicles, North American carmakers were forced to imitate their Japanese competitors in order to survive.

The Young Men's Christian Association (YMCA) is an example of an organization whose early entrant status in its field (health and physical development) turned into a weakness over time as it came to be seen as outmoded and old-fashioned in the face of for-profit fitness clubs. The YMCA was forced to rapidly adapt to meet the challenge. (See Organizational Insight 11.2.)

Natural selection is a competitive process. New organizations survive if they can develop skills that allow them to fit with and exploit their environment. Entrepreneurship is the process of developing new capabilities that allow organizations to exploit new niches or find new ways of serving existing niches more efficiently. Over time, entrepreneurship leads to a continuous cycle of organizational birth as new organizations are founded to exploit new opportunities in the environment. Amazon.com offers a good illustration of this process (see the Focus on New Information Technology box).

THE INSTITUTIONAL THEORY OF ORGANIZATIONAL GROWTH

If an organization survives the birth stage of the organizational life cycle, what factors affect its search for a fit with the environment? Organizations seek to change themselves to obtain control over scarce resources and reduce uncertainty. They can increase their control over resources by growing and becoming larger.

Organizational growth
The life-cycle stage in which organizations develop value-creation skills and competencies that allow them to acquire additional resources.

Organizational growth is the life-cycle stage in which organizations develop value-creation skills and competencies that allow them to acquire additional resources. Growth allows an organization to increase its division of labour and specialization and thus develop a competitive advantage. An organization that is able to acquire resources is likely to generate surplus resources that allow it to grow further. Over time, organizations thus transform themselves: They become something very different than they were when they started. Microsoft took the resources that it obtained from its popular MS-DOS system, for example, and used them to employ more computer programmers, who developed new software applications to bring in additional resources. In this way, Microsoft grew from strength to strength and transformed itself into a software company that competes in almost all segments of the market: It is trying to become the dominant player in the wireless and online entertainment and videogame industry, for example.

Although largeness can increase an organization's chances of survival and stability, Microsoft and other companies do not usually pursue growth as an end in itself. Growth is a by-product of their ability to develop core competencies that satisfy the needs of their stakeholders and so give them access to scarce resources.[21] **Institutional theory** studies how organizations can increase their ability to grow and survive in a competitive environment by becoming legitimate in the eyes of their stakeholders.

Institutional theory
Studies how organizations can increase their ability to grow and survive in a competitive environment by satisfying their stakeholders.

New organizations suffer from the liability of newness, and many die because they do not develop the competencies they need to attract customers and obtain scarce

ORGANIZATIONAL INSIGHT 11.2

The YMCA's Response to Global Changes[22]

The Young Men's Christian Association (YMCA) is a registered charitable organization located in over 120 countries. It was started in London, England, in 1841 and the first North American YMCA opened in Montreal in 1851. Today the YMCA serves 61 communities across Canada.

Individual YMCAs are independent organizations providing charitable programs to their local community and linked with other YMCAs in Canada in a national federation. Each YMCA has its own unique mission; however, they tend to mirror each other closely. The mission statement of the YMCA of Greater Toronto reads, "The YMCA is a charity offering opportunities for personal growth through participation and service to the community," and its vision is that "the YMCA will be a leader in enhancing civil society, where people are respectful and supportive of one another, within Canada's most diverse community." The YMCA provides health and fitness programs, child-care, camping services, leadership training, and literacy training, job-creation, and new immigrant services.

Originally, the YMCA was a unique organization and the only one offering child-care and health and fitness programs in the community. When parents wanted their children to learn to swim or when people wanted to exercise, they joined the YMCA. There were no other options available.

However, in the 1980s, the YMCA's environment was forever changed, forcing it evolve in response to a changing world. Physical activity trends changed, more and more people started to exercise on a regular basis, and women who previously stayed home entered the workforce. As a result, municipal recreation centres and for-profit health clubs and child-care centres emerged. The YMCA was no longer the only game in town and was now facing a very strong competitor. The for-profit clubs offered state-of-the-art equipment and facilities, which the YMCA did not possess, and they marketed themselves heavily to the public. They were businesses and governed themselves accordingly.

The YMCA had no choice but to redo its operations. It decided to overhaul its operations to compete with its new competitors. Changing the way the YMCA operated meant embracing two strategies: (1) developing "businesslike" organizations, and (2) developing new facilities. Embarking on this strategy was risky as it posed a threat to remaining true to the YMCA's charitable mission. The change would prove to be a delicate balancing act.

The YMCA raised large sums of money in the community and developed new state-of the-art-health and fitness facilities. As a result of changes, the YMCA became a financially successful organization, while still maintaining its charitable mission. It had responded to the new environment successfully.

However, the success brought a new challenge to the YMCA. The private health clubs challenged the YMCA's tax status as a charity, which allows it to raise charitable money for capital projects and subsidize its annual operations, and provides tax breaks, which for-profit businesses are not entitled to. In the U.S., YMCAs have both won and lost cases that have been brought against them in court. To date, no Canadian YMCA has gone to court although there have been rumblings in some Canadian cities such as Calgary.

"It's frustrating when tax-paying operations compete with tax-consuming ones," says Lynn White, head of the National Child Care Association, which represents many for-profit daycare centres. "But taking on the Y is like taking on God, country and apple pie."

FOCUS ON NEW INFORMATION TECHNOLOGY

Amazon.com, Part 6

Jeff Bezos was the first entrepreneur both to realize that the Internet could be used to effectively sell books and to act on the opportunity by establishing Amazon.com. As such he gave his company a first-mover advantage over rivals, which has been an important component of its strong position in the marketplace. Being early, Amazon.com was able to capture customer attention, and keep their loyalty—45 percent of its business is repeat business. Moreover, Amazon.com's very success has made it difficult for new competitors to enter the market and the birth rate into the industry has tapered off substantially.

First, new "unknown" competitors face the major hurdle of attracting customers to their Web sites rather than to Amazon.com's. Second, even "known" competitors such as Barnes & Noble and Borders, which have imitated Amazon's strategy and developed their own online bookstores, have faced the problem of luring away Amazon's customer base and securing their position. Being late entrants, these organizations essentially followed a K-strategy, while Amazon.com followed an r-strategy. This delay in going online has cost them dearly in the current highly competitive environment.

Indeed, the process of natural selection has been operating in the book-selling industry. As we have seen in earlier chapters, many small, specialized bookstores have closed their doors. Even large bricks-and-mortar bookstores that may carry hundreds of thousands of books have been unable to compete with an online bookstore that can offer customers all 1.5 million books in print at a 10 percent price discount.

In the spring of 1999 a new round of competition took place in the book-selling industry when Amazon.com and its competitors announced a 50 percent discount off the price of new best-selling books in the attempt to keep and grow their market share. Amazon.com and its largest competitors, Barnes & Noble and Borders, were locked in a fierce battle to see who would dominate the book-selling industry in the new millennium.

Amazon.com won the online book-selling war when Barnes & Noble gave up the struggle and withdrew from the market. However, this did not provide Amazon with enough additional resources to survive and become profitable. Amazon.com was forced to change its strategy and to try to find more market niches in which to compete. It expanded its offerings, and as we saw in an earlier chapter, it started to sell every kind of product and moved from being a specialist online bookstore to a generalist online retailer. The changes to its strategy and structure have allowed it to survive.

resources. To increase their survival chances as they grow, organizations must gain acceptability and legitimacy from their stakeholders by satisfying the latter's needs. Institutional theory argues that it is as important to study how organizations develop skills that increase their legitimacy in stakeholders' eyes as it is to study how they develop skills that increase their technical efficiency. Institutional theory also argues that to increase their chances of survival, new organizations adopt many of the rules and codes of conduct found in the institutional environment surrounding them.[23]

Institutional environment The set of values and norms in an environment that governs the behaviour of a population of organizations.

The **institutional environment** is the set of values and norms that govern the behaviour of a population of organizations. For example, the institutional environment of the banking industry comprises strict rules and procedures about what banks can and cannot do and penalties and actions to be taken against banks that break those rules. Banks that follow rules and codes of conduct are considered trustworthy and legitimate by stakeholders, such as customers, employees, and any group that controls the supply of scarce resources.[24] Banks that are considered legitimate are able to attract resources and improve their chances of survival. A new organization can strengthen its legitimacy by imitating the goals, structure, and culture of successful organizations in its population.[25]

Organizational Isomorphism

As organizations grow, they may copy one another's strategies, structures, and cultures and try to adopt certain behaviours because they believe doing so will increase their chances of survival. As a result, **organizational isomorphism**—the similarity among organizations in a population—increases. Three processes that explain why organizations become similar have been identified: coercive, mimetic, and normative isomorphism.[26]

Organizational isomorphism The similarity among organizations in a population.

Coercive Isomorphism Isomorphism is said to be *coercive* when an organization adopts certain norms because of pressures exerted by other organizations and by society in general. As the dependence of one organization on another increases, the dependent organization is likely to become increasingly similar to the more powerful organization. For example, the general public has put pressure on Wal-Mart and other organizations to boycott goods made by children in third-world countries and these companies have responded by creating codes of supplier conduct. Coercive isomorphism also results when organizations are forced to adopt nondiscriminatory, equitable hiring practices because they are mandated by law. The Employment Equity Act (1995) is a prime example of legislation designed to ensure that companies conform to equitable hiring practices.

Mimetic Isomorphism Isomorphism is *mimetic* when organizations intentionally imitate and copy one another to increase their legitimacy. A new organization is especially likely to imitate the structure and processes of successful organizations when the environment is very uncertain and the new organization is trying to find the structure, strategy, culture, and technology that will allow it to survive.[27] Because of mimetic isomorphism, the similarity of a population of similar organizations, such as fast-food restaurants, increases along the lines suggested by the S-shaped curve in Figure 11-2 (p. 378).

McDonald's was the first organization to operate a national chain of fast-food restaurants. Ray Kroc, the man who orchestrated its growth, developed rules and procedures that were easy to replicate in every McDonald's restaurant. Standardization allowed the individual restaurants within the McDonald's organization to imitate one another, so that each part could reach the same high standards of performance. Entrepreneurs who later entered the fast-food industry saw how successful McDonald's was and imitated many of the techniques and procedures that McDonald's had developed. Thus customers expect to see the same kinds of food on the menus of all fast-food restaurants, they expect certain standards of speed and cleanliness, and they expect to clear their own tables. Retail stores also imitated one another in devising their codes of ethical conduct so that no particular retailer could be singled out as being unresponsive.

Although imitating the most successful organizations in a population increases efficiency and chances for success, there is a limit to how much a new organization should imitate an existing one. The first organization in the industry gains a first-mover advantage. If late arrivals model themselves too closely on the leader, customers might see no reason to try the newer restaurant. Each new organization needs to develop some unique competencies to differentiate itself and define the niche where it has access to most resources. Wendy's principal claim to fame is that it can provide customers with a customized burger, unlike the McDonald's burger, which is totally standardized; and Burger King, unlike McDonald's, offers charbroiled instead of fried burgers.

Normative Isomorphism Isomorphism is *normative* when organizations come to resemble each other because over time they indirectly adopt the norms and values of other organizations in the environment. Organizations acquire norms and values in several ways. Managers and employees often move from one organization to another and bring with them the norms and values of their former employers. Many new telecommunications companies, for example, recruit managers from large companies such as AT&T and Verizon. Similarly, Dell Computer recruits managers who know how to run a growing computer company because they have worked in one. Organizations also indirectly acquire norms and values through industry, trade, and professional associations. Through meetings and publications, these associations promote specific ideas to their members. Because of this indirect influence, organizations within an industry come to develop a similar view of the world.

Disadvantages of Isomorphism

Although organizational isomorphism can help new and growing organizations develop stability and legitimacy, it has some disadvantages.[28] Organizations may learn ways to behave that have become outdated and no longer lead to organizational effectiveness. The pressure to imitate may reduce the level of innovation in the environment. For many years, for example, the Big Three North American carmakers were happy to imitate one another and produce big, fuel-inefficient cars. Innovations to reduce the costs of making a car or to significantly improve design, efficiency, and quality were few and slow in coming because no company took the lead. The entry of new companies from abroad was needed to show North American automakers that new manufacturing procedures could be developed.

Isomorphism has also been associated with discriminatory practices. In the early days of commercial flight, airlines mimicked first-class class rail and ocean-going transportation by employing white-coated stewards to serve passengers in flight. Not only did they mimic the name ("steward"), the uniform (white coats), and the service but also the practice of only hiring men. United Air Lines broke the pattern in 1930, on an "experimental" basis, hiring attractive young women with nursing qualifications to serve as flight attendants. In the following decade, most airlines, including Pan American Airlines and Imperial Airways (the predecessor of British Airways) refused to hire female flight attendants until the mid-1940s. Those airlines that did hire women mimicked United by insisting that the women be young, attractive, and hold nursing qualifications. These major forms of isomorphic mimicry had a major impact on the airline industry through to the end of the 20th century and led to a various charges of discriminatory practice.[29]

GREINER'S MODEL OF ORGANIZATIONAL GROWTH

Institutional theory is one way to look at how the need to achieve legitimacy leads a growing organization to change its structure, strategy, and culture and imitate those of successful organizations. If organizations do model themselves on one another in this way, it follows that both the imitators and the imitated encounter similar kinds of strategic and structural problems as they grow. Many organizational life-cycle theorists believe that organizations encounter a predictable series of problems that must be managed if organizations are to grow and survive in a competitive environment. One of the best known of these life-cycle models of organizational growth is Greiner's model (see Figure 11-4), which proposes that an organization passes through five sequential growth stages during the course of organizational evolution and that each stage ends in a crisis due to a major problem that the organization encounters.[30] To advance from one stage to the next, an organization must successfully change itself and solve the organizational problem associated with each crisis.

Stage 1: Growth Through Creativity

Greiner calls the first stage in the cycle the *growth through creativity* stage. In this stage (which includes the birth of the organization), entrepreneurs develop the skills and abilities to create and introduce new products for new market niches. As entrepreneurs create completely new procedures and adjust existing procedures, a great deal of organizational learning occurs. The organization learns which products and procedures work and continually adjusts its activities so that it can continue to expand. In this stage, innovation and entrepreneurship go hand in hand, as an organization's founders work long hours to develop and sell their new products with the hope of being rewarded by future profits. Compaq, for example, was started by some former Texas Instruments managers who designed a new computer from scratch and brought the first model to market in 18 months on a shoestring budget. In the creativity stage, the norms and values of the organization's culture, rather than the hierarchy and organizational structure, control people's behaviour.

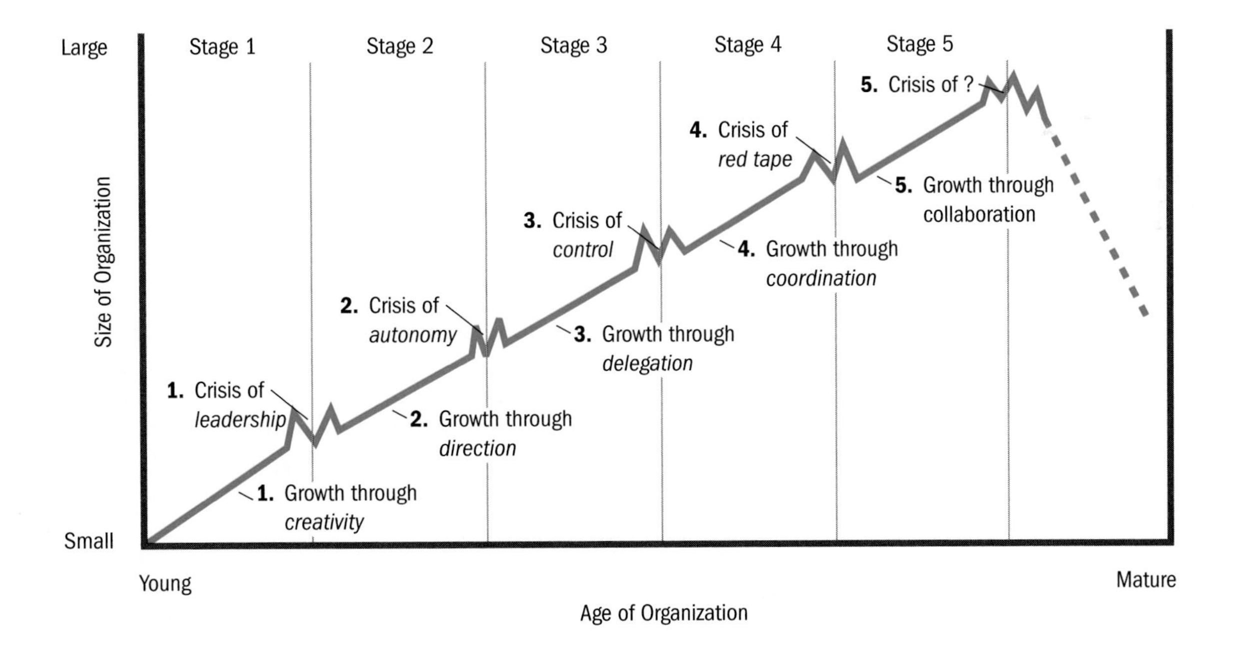

FIGURE 11-4

Greiner's Model of Organizational Growth.

Each stage that Greiner identified ends with a crisis that must be resolved before the organization can advance to the next stage.

Source: Reprinted by permission of *Harvard Business Review*. An excerpt from "Evolution and Revolution as Organizations Grow," by L. E. Greiner, July–August 1972, by the President and Fellows of Harvard College; all rights reserved.

One of the best-known examples of entrepreneurial creativity is the development of the BlackBerry by Mike Lazaridis. The idea came to him in the middle of the night when he was up taking care of his newborn son. He thought to himself that it would be great thing if people could check their work e-mail wherever they were—at home, on the road, at work, or while on vacation. Over the next three years, he set to work on the idea that eventually became the BlackBerry.

Once a new organization is up and running, a series of internal forces begin to change the entrepreneurial process. As the organization grows, the founding entrepreneurs confront the task of having to manage the organization, and they discover that management is a very different process from entrepreneurship. Management involves utilizing organizational resources to effectively achieve organizational goals. Thus, for example, in its manufacturing operations, management is confronted with the problem of making the production process more efficient. Early in the life of a new company, however, management is not likely to pay much attention to efficiency goals. Entrepreneurs are so involved in getting the organization off the ground that they forget the need to manage organizational resources efficiently. Similarly, they are so involved in providing customers with high-quality products that they ignore the costs involved. Thus, after securing a niche, the founding entrepreneurs are faced with the task of managing their organization, a task to which they are often not really suited and for which they lack the skills.

Crisis of Leadership Frequently, when an entrepreneur takes control of the management of the organization, significant problems arise that eventually lead to a *crisis of leadership*. CEO and founder Rod Canion, for example, had made Compaq a dominant force in the computer market. But when the price of computers tumbled in 1992, Compaq, a high-priced computer maker, lost its market niche. The firm's stock price plunged, and shareholders realized that the founding entrepreneur was not the best person to manage the company as it searched for a way to turn itself around. The board of directors replaced Canion with a professional manager, Ekhard Pfeiffer, who implemented a low-cost strategy that was very successful. However, in 1999 Pfeiffer was replaced by Michael Capellas, his deputy at Compaq, because of his failure to successfully integrate Digital Equipment into Compaq after Compaq merged with this company.

Stage 2: Growth Through Direction

The crisis of leadership ends with the recruitment of a strong top-management team to lead the organization through the next stage of organizational growth: *growth through direction*. The new top-management team takes responsibility for directing the company's strategy, and lower-level managers assume key functional responsibilities. In this stage, a new CEO such as Michael Capellas chooses an organizational strategy and designs a structure and culture that allow the organization to meet its effectiveness goals as it grows. As we saw in Chapter 6, a functional or divisional structure is established to allow the organization to regain control of its activities, and decision making becomes more centralized. Then the adoption of formal, standardized rules and procedures allows each organizational function to better monitor and control its activities. Managers in production, for example, develop procedures to track cost and quality information, and the materials management function develops efficient purchasing and inventory control systems.

Often, growth through direction turns around an organization's fortunes and propels the organization up the growth curve to new levels of effectiveness, as happened at Compaq in the early 1990s. As an organization continues to grow rapidly, however, the move to centralize authority and formalize decision making often leads to a new crisis.

When Chief Terrance Paul took over the Membertou Band Council in the Cape Breton region of Nova Scotia, it led to dramatic changes, including the development of a business model of operation and the recruitment of external corporate leadership. The results were wide reaching and successful (see Organizational Insight 11.3).

Crisis of Autonomy With professional managers now running the show, many organizations experience a *crisis of autonomy,* which arises because the organization's creative people in departments such as R&D, product engineering, and marketing become frustrated by their lack of control over new product development and innovation. The structure designed by top managers and imposed on the organization centralizes decision making and limits the freedom to experiment, take risks, and be internal entrepreneurs. Thus the increased level of bureaucracy that comes in the growth-through-direction stage lowers entrepreneurial motivation. For instance, top-management approval may be needed to start new projects, and successful performance at low levels of the hierarchy may go unnoticed or at least unrewarded as the organization searches for ways to reduce costs. Entrepreneurs and managers in functional areas such as R&D begin to feel frustrated when their performance goes unrecognized and when top managers fail to act on their recommendations to innovate. Employees and managers feel lost in the growing organizational bureaucracy and become more and more frustrated with their lack of autonomy. This situation occurred in Compaq toward the end of the 1990s, when its rapid growth but deteriorating performance because of competition from Dell Computer led its top managers to more tightly control costs and expenses. The level of innovation fell and Compaq was slow to respond to the need to move online, both to sell its computers and to obtain low-cost inputs. Things started to go from bad to worse and the company was plunged into crisis.

What happens if the crisis of autonomy is not resolved? Internal entrepreneurs are likely to leave the organization. In high-tech industries, entrepreneurs often cite frustration with bureaucracy as one of the main reasons they leave one company to start their own.[31] In the 1980s, for example, Kodak bought many small entrepreneurial companies to help increase its sales and profitability. Top Kodak managers then intervened in these companies and imposed centralized control over many of them. As a result, many of their managers left because they resented their loss of control and decision making.

The departure of an organization's entrepreneurs not only reduces its ability to innovate but also creates new competitors in the industry. By not resolving the crisis of autonomy, an organization creates a major problem for itself and limits its ability to grow and prosper.[32]

Stage 3: Growth Through Delegation

To solve the crisis of autonomy, organizations must delegate authority to lower-level managers in all functions and divisions and link their increased control over organizational activities to a reward structure that recognizes their contributions. Thus, for example, managers and employees may receive bonuses and stock options that are directly linked to their performance. In essence, *growth through delegation* allows the organization to strike a balance between the need for professional management to improve technical efficiency and the need to provide room for entrepreneurship so that the organization can innovate and find new ways of reducing costs or improving its products. We have already seen how Bill Gates at Microsoft delegates authority to small teams and creates a setting in which members can act entrepreneurially and con-

ORGANIZATIONAL INSIGHT 11.3

The Membertou First Nation: Regenerating a Community through Corporatization[33]

When we think of organizations pursuing ISO 9001 registration—the prestigious international designation for assurance of quality management—we're likely to think of companies from such sectors as agriculture, construction, manufacturing, medical science, and information technology. But in 2001, Nova Scotia's Membertou First Nation made history by becoming the first Native group in North America to receive an ISO 9001 certificate. Attainment of the designation has proven to be one of several key steps that have helped this urban Aboriginal community to reinvent itself, and prosper both economically and socially.

In the mid-1990s, Cape Breton was hit by market downturns in the coal, steel, and mining industries, which were the economic lifeblood of the region, and the Membertou First Nation was especially hard hit. The unemployment level among the 1000 Mi'kmaq reserve members topped 95 percent, suicide rates were climbing among young men, and the band was facing a $1 million deficit on a $4.5 million operating budget. Band leaders recognized they had to make some drastic changes in order to turn the situation around.

The Membertou Band Council, under the direction of Chief Terrance Paul, looked to the corporate sector and decided to reorganize the band's operations to emulate more of a business model. Their first priority was to recruit new managerial talent with the skill and experience necessary to help them map out a plan and execute it. They went to the heart of corporate Canada—Toronto's Bay Street—and hired a lawyer from a high-profile commercial law firm. The new recruit was Bernd Christmas, the first Mi'kmaq Aboriginal to receive a law degree. Christmas was also a member of the Membertou community, although he had grown up in a military family and had never actually lived there.

In 2000, the Band Council created the Membertou Development Corporation to oversee its business interests in commercial fishing and gaming, and established strategic alliances with government and corporate partners. The council appointed Christmas as the Corporation's CEO, and in 2002 established a business presence in downtown Halifax. By opening a corporate office in the province's capital, the band signalled to the corporate community that it was "open for business," and it immediately drew the attention of business and government. In short order, Membertou formed business alliances with some high-profile companies, including Clearwater Fine Foods, SNC Lavalin, Sodexho Canada, and Lockheed Martin.

At the same time, Chief Paul and CEO Christmas decided to pursue ISO 9001 accreditation, a good example of mimetic isomorphism. In commenting on the move, Christmas said, "ISO compliance was the next logical step towards ensuring accountability, transparency and openness" in Membertou's operations and noted it would allow the band to position itself as "a very credible player in the global market economy." The investment of time and effort required to attain ISO 9001 certification does seem to have paid off for Membertou. It has won national recognition for the move, and new partnerships have since been announced with Grant Thornton LLP, Fujitsu Canada, and gaming company Techlink Entertainment. And, the corporation boasts an operating budget of $44.5 million with no deficit, and 250 full-time employees.

The signs of success are visible within the Membertou community. Employment is now at the 90 percent mark. The reserve has a new school and health centre, and just opened a new $7 million convention centre that is expected to bring even more economic opportunities. According to band representatives, all this success has fostered pride and confidence among the Membertou reserve members. As Christmas notes, "It's a very strong community of 1000 people who are cognizant of not only their rights but the opportunities that they have."

trol their own activities. Gates also rewards team members with stock options, and the most successful team members become highly visible stars of the organization. At the same time, however, Gates and his top-management team control the meshing of the activities of different teams to execute the company's long-term strategy. Gates designed Microsoft's structure to avoid the crisis of autonomy, and the organization has profited hugely from his forethought.

Thus, in the growth-through-delegation stage, more autonomy and responsibility are given to managers at all levels and functions. Moving to a product team structure or a multidivisional structure, for example, is one way in which an organization can respond to the need to delegate authority. These structures can reduce the time needed to get new products to market, improve strategic decision making, and motivate product or divisional managers to penetrate markets and respond faster to customer needs. At this stage in organizational growth, top managers intervene in decision making only when necessary. Growth through delegation allows each department or division to expand to meet its own needs and goals, and organizational growth often proceeds at a rapid pace. Once again, however, the organization's very success brings on another crisis: Explosive growth can cause top managers to feel that they have lost control of the company as a whole.

Crisis of Control When top managers compete with functional managers or corporate-level managers compete with divisional managers for control of organizational resources, the result is a *crisis of control.* The need to resolve the crisis of autonomy by delegating authority to lower-level managers increases their power and control of organizational resources. Lower-level managers like this extra power because it is associated with prestige and access to valued rewards. If managers use this power over resources to pursue their own goals at the expense of organizational goals, the organization becomes less effective. Thus power struggles over resources can emerge between top and lower-level managers. Sometimes during this power struggle top management tries to recentralize decision making and take back control over organizational activities. However, this action is doomed to failure because it brings back the crisis of autonomy. How does the organization solve the crisis of control so that it can continue to grow?

Stage 4: Growth Through Coordination

To resolve the crisis of control, as we saw in Chapter 4, an organization must find the right balance between centralized control from the top of the organization and decentralized control at the functional or divisional level. Top management takes on the role of coordinating different divisions and motivating divisional managers to take a companywide perspective. In many organizations, for example, divisions can cooperate and share resources in order to create new products and processes that benefit the organization as a whole. In Chapter 8, we saw how this kind of coordination is very important for companies pursuing a strategy of related diversification. If companies are growing internationally, coordination is even more important. Top functional managers and corporate headquarters staff must create the "matrix in the mind" that facilitates international cooperation between divisions and countries.

At the same time, corporate management must use its expertise to monitor and oversee divisional activities to ensure that divisions efficiently use their resources, and must initiate companywide programs to review the performance of the various divisions. To motivate managers and align their goals with those of the organization, organizations often create an internal labour market in which the best divisional managers are rewarded with promotion to the top ranks of the organization, while the most successful functional-level managers gain control over the divisions. If not managed correctly, all this coordination and the complex structures to handle it will bring about yet another crisis.

Crisis of Red Tape Achieving growth through coordination is a complex process that has to be managed continuously if organizations are to be successful. When organizations fail to manage this process, they are plunged into a *crisis of red tape.* The number of rules and procedures increases, but this increased bureaucracy does little to increase organizational effectiveness and is likely to reduce it by stifling entrepreneurship and other productive activity. The organization becomes overly bureaucratic and relies too much on the formal organization and not enough on the informal organization to coordinate its activities. How can an organization cut itself free of all the confining red tape so that it can once again function effectively?

Stage 5: Growth Through Collaboration

In Greiner's model, *growth through collaboration* becomes the way to solve the crisis of red tape and push the organization up the growth curve. Growth through collaboration emphasizes "greater spontaneity in management action through teams and the skillful confrontation of interpersonal differences. Social control and self-discipline take over from formal control."[34] For organizations at this stage of the growth cycle, Greiner advocates the use of the product team and matrix structures, which, as we discussed in Chapter 6, many large companies use to improve their ability to respond to customer needs and introduce new products quickly. Developing the interpersonal linkages that underlie the "matrix in the mind" for managing global linkages is also a part of the collaborative strategy. Collaboration makes an organization more organic by making greater use of mutual adjustment and less use of standardization.

Changing from a mechanistic to an organic structure as an organization grows is a difficult task fraught with problems. Although both Chrysler and Xerox moved to a product team structure to streamline their decision making, this change was not made until *after* both companies had experienced huge problems with their structures—problems that increased costs, reduced product quality, and severely reduced their effectiveness. Indeed, both companies came close to bankruptcy.

MANAGERIAL IMPLICATIONS

Organizational Birth and Growth

1. Analyze the resources available in an environment to determine whether a niche to be exploited exists.
2. If a niche is discovered, analyze how the population of organizations currently in the environment will compete with you for the resources in the niche.
3. Develop the competencies necessary to pursue a specialist strategy in order to attract resources in the niche.
4. Carefully analyze the institutional environment to learn the values and norms that govern the behaviour of organizations in the environment. Imitate the qualities and actions of successful organizations,

but be careful to differentiate your product from theirs to increase the returns from your specialist strategy.

5. If your organization survives the birth stage, recognize that it will encounter a series of problems as it grows and differentiates.
6. Recognize the importance of creating an effective top-management team and of delegating authority to professional managers in order to build a stable platform for future growth.
7. Then, following principles outlined in earlier chapters, manage the process of organizational design to meet each growth crisis as it emerges. Establish an appropriate balance between centralizing and decentralizing authority, for example, and between standardization and mutual adjustment.

ORGANIZATIONAL DECLINE AND DEATH

Greiner's growth model shows organizations continuing to grow through collaboration until they encounter some new, unnamed crisis, but it is possible that an organization's growth path leads down, as shown by the direction of the dashed line in Figure 11-4 (p. 387). For many organizations, the next stage in the life cycle is not continued growth but organizational decline.

Greiner's model suggests that organizations at all stages of growth encounter problems—crises that will lead to organizational decline if an organization does not change its strategy or structure. **Organizational decline** is the life-cycle stage that an organization enters when it fails to "anticipate, recognize, avoid, neutralize, or adapt to external or internal pressures that threaten [its] long-term survival."[35] The liability of newness, for example, threatens young organizations, and the failure to develop a stable structure can cause early decline and failure. Similarly, in Greiner's model, the failure to adapt strategy and structure to suit changing conditions can result in crisis and failure. Regardless of whether decline sets in at the birth or the growth stage, it results in the decrease of an organization's ability to obtain resources from its stakeholders.[36] A declining company may be unable to attract financial resources from banks, customers, or human resources, because the best managers or employees prefer to work for the most successful organizations.

Organizational decline
The life-cycle stage that an organization enters when it fails to anticipate, recognize, avoid, neutralize, or adapt to external or internal pressures that threaten its long-term survival.

Decline sometimes occurs because organizations grow too much.[37] The experience of Compaq, IBM, and Chrysler suggests that there is a tendency for organizations to grow past the point that maximizes their effectiveness. Figure 11-5 illustrates the relationship between organizational size and organizational effectiveness. The figure shows that organizational effectiveness is highest at point A, where effectiveness E_1 is associated with organizational size S_1. If an organization grows past this point—for example, to point S_2—effectiveness falls to E_2, and the organization ends up at point B.

Greiner's model assumes that managers have the ability to identify and solve organizational crises so that they can maintain the organization at point A. But suppose that managers cannot do this and that external and internal forces outside their control prevent the organization from growing. Suppose they lack the ability, motivation, and desire to manage the relationship between growth and effectiveness. Two factors that cause an organization to grow too much or to grow in ways that lead to organizational decline are organizational inertia and environmental changes.

Organizational Inertia

An organization may not easily adapt to meet changes in the environment because of **organizational inertia**—the forces inside an organization that make it resistant to

Organizational inertia
Forces inside an organization that make it resistant to change.

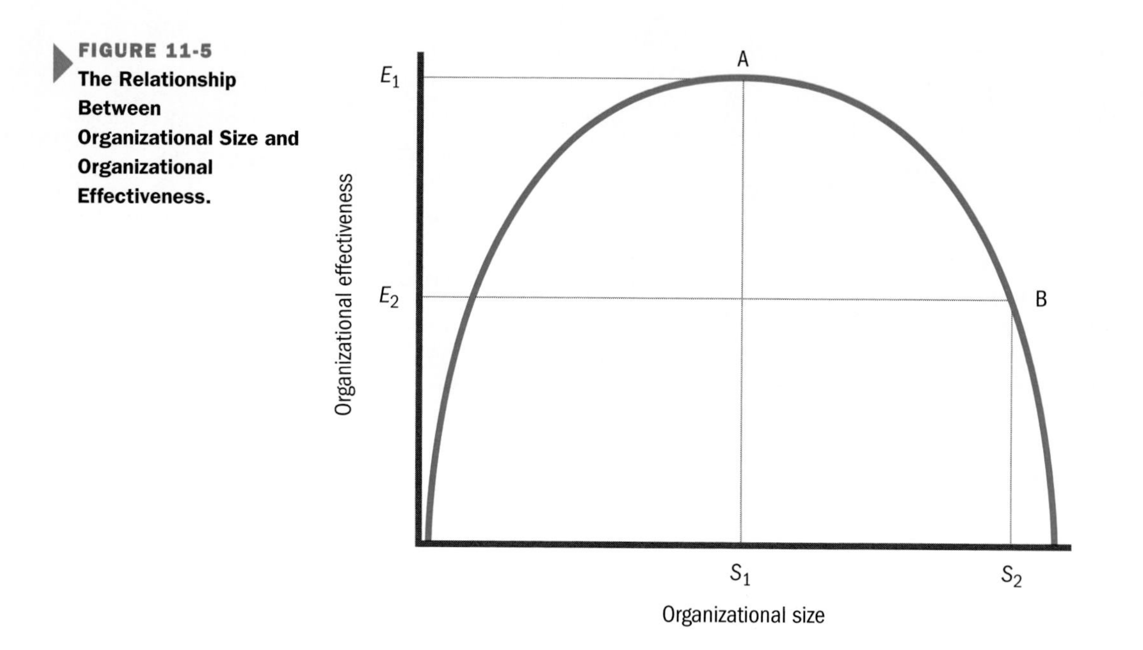

FIGURE 11-5 The Relationship Between Organizational Size and Organizational Effectiveness.

change. Greiner and other adaptation theorists focus on organizations' ability to change and adapt to new conditions in their environments. Population ecology theorists are more pessimistic, believing that organizations do not have the ability to quickly or easily change their strategy or structure to avoid decline. Instead, they believe that organizations are subject to considerable inertia, which prevents them from changing. Some factors that cause inertia were discussed in the last chapter; three more are risk aversion, the desire to maximize rewards, and an overly bureaucratic culture. When these factors operate together, the problems facing managers are greatly compounded.

Risk Aversion As organizations grow, managers often become risk averse—that is, they become unwilling to bear the uncertainty associated with entrepreneurial activities.[38] As a result, the organization becomes increasingly difficult to change. Risk aversion may set in for several reasons. Managers' overriding concern may be to protect their positions; thus they undertake relatively safe or inexpensive projects, so that if the projects fail, their burden of blame will be light. Managers might try to maximize the chance of success by pursuing projects that have already brought the organization success. Managers might institute bureaucratic rules and procedures that give close control over new ventures, but also stifle innovation and entrepreneurship.

The Desire to Maximize Rewards Research suggests that managers' desire for prestige, job security, power, and the strong property rights that bring large rewards is associated more with organizational size than with profitability.[39] Thus managers may increase the size of the company to maximize their own rewards even when this growth reduces organizational effectiveness. The management teams of many large companies such as Goodyear, Kodak, and Polaroid have been accused of pursuing their own goals at the expense of shareholders, customers, and other stakeholders. Those management teams lacked any incentive to improve organizational effectiveness because they would not gain personally from doing so, and until recently there were no powerful stakeholders to discipline them and force them to streamline operations. The changes made at both Chrysler and Xerox, for example, came when new management teams took over. Of course in companies such as Tyco, Enron, and Arthur Andersen, the pursuit of personal interest led to many unethical and illegal acts that led to the downfall of these companies.

Overly Bureaucratic Culture As discussed in Chapter 7, in large organizations, property rights (such as salaries and stock options) can become so strong that managers spend all their time protecting their specific property rights instead of working to advance the organization's interests. Top managers, for example, resist attempts by subordinate managers to take the initiative and act entrepreneurially because subordinates who demonstrate superior skills and abilities may threaten the position of their managers and their managers' property rights.[40] Another bureaucracy-related problem is that, as C. Northcote Parkinson pointed out, in a bureaucracy, managers want to multiply subordinates, not rivals. To this end, managers limit the freedom of subordinates to protect their own positions. One way of limiting freedom is to establish a tall organizational hierarchy so that subordinates can be closely controlled and scrutinized. Another way is to develop a bureaucratic culture that emphasizes the status quo and the need for conformity to organizational procedures. Such a culture might be desirable in the military, but it is not beneficial to a large company fighting for survival in an uncertain environment.

Although the behaviour of managers is sometimes a major cause of organizational inertia and decline, it is important to realize that managers may not be deliberately trying to hurt the organization. Bureaucratization and risk aversion may creep up on organizations unexpectedly.

Changes in the Environment

Environmental changes that affect an organization's ability to obtain scarce resources may lead to organizational decline. The major sources of uncertainty in the environment are complexity, the number of different forces that an organization has to manage; dynamism, the degree to which the environment is changing; and richness, the amount of resources available in the environment (see Figure 3-2, p. 74). The greater the uncertainty in the environment, the more likely that some organizations in a population, especially organizations affected by inertia, will go into decline.

Sometimes the niche that an organization occupies erodes, and managers no longer have the incentive or ability to change strategy to improve the organization's access to resources. That is what happened to IBM when the demand for mainframe computers fell.[41] Sometimes the environment becomes poorer, and increased competition for resources threatens existing organizations that have not been managing their growth very effectively. Sometimes an "environmental jolt" changes the forces in the environment and precipitates an immediate crisis.[42] When the Cold War ended, for example, the huge reduction in the size of government defence spending caused serious problems for large defence contractors such as General Dynamics and TRW. Both of them responded with downsizing that involved the layoff of thousands of employees.

The combination of an uncertain, changing environment and organizational inertia makes it difficult for top management to anticipate the need for change and to manage the way organizations change and adapt to the environment. In Chapter 12, we examine how organizations can promote organizational learning, a process that facilitates changes and overcomes inertia. Here we discuss a model that charts the main stages of the decline process, just as Greiner's model charted the main stages of the growth process.

Weitzel and Jonsson's Model of Organizational Decline

Organizational decline occurs by degrees; Weitzel and Jonsson have identified five stages of decline (see Figure 11-6).[43] At each stage except the dissolution stage, management action (shown by the dashed line) can reverse the decline.

Stage 1: Blinded In the blinded stage, the first decline stage identified by Weitzel and Jonsson, organizations are unable to recognize the internal or external problems that threaten their long-term survival. The most common reason for this blindness is that organizations do not have in place the monitoring and information systems that they need to measure organizational effectiveness and identify sources of organizational inertia. Internal signals that indicate potential problems are excessive numbers of personnel, a slowdown in decision making, a rise in conflict between functions or divisions, and a fall in profits. At this stage, access to good information and an effective top-management team can prevent the onset of decline and allow the organization to maintain its pattern of growth. To avoid decline, managers need to monitor internal and external factors continuously so that they have the information to take timely corrective action. Taking action to correct problems at this stage and to reverse the decline process, however, does not necessarily mean that the organization will continue to grow. As General Dynamics' response to the slowdown in the defence industry suggests, a company may reorganize itself to use its existing resources more effectively. (See Organizational Insight 11.4.)

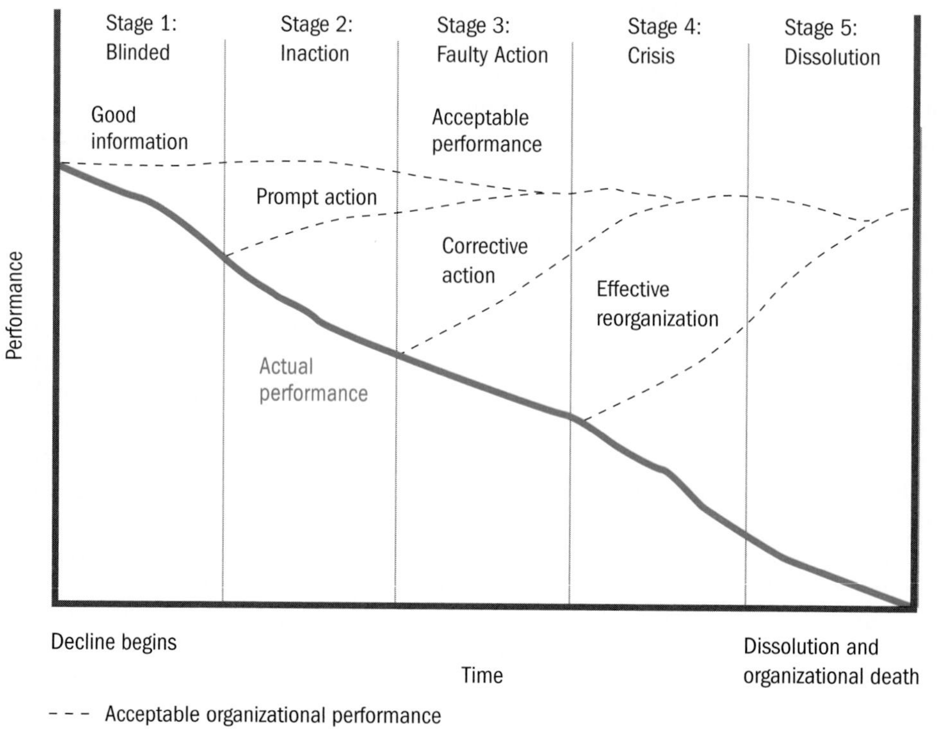

FIGURE 11-6 Weitzel and Jonsson's Model of Organizational Decline. At each stage, action by management can halt the decline.

Source: Adapted from "Decline in Organizations: A Literature Integration and Extension," by W. Weitzel and E. Jonsson, published in *Administrative Science Quarterly,* © Cornell University, 1989, vol. 34, no. 1. Reprinted by permission.

ORGANIZATIONAL INSIGHT 11.4

General Dynamics Goes from Weakness to Strength

In 1990, General Dynamics lost US$578 million. In 1991, it made a profit of US$305 million and its stock price tripled in 18 months. How has this major defence contractor (which specializes in making tactical aircraft, nuclear submarines, and armoured vehicles) been able to avoid the problems brought on by the loss of resources in the environment as a result of the end of the Cold War and drastic cuts in defence spending? The answer lies in the way the General Dynamics top-management team, led by William A. Anders, has been managing the decline process.

Faced with a lack of demand for its major products, General Dynamics has been selling off many of its US$8.7 billion in assets and shrinking its operations to allow it to focus on four key areas: aircraft, submarines, armoured vehicles, and space launch systems. The company downsized by laying off more than 25 percent of its workforce across its businesses. It then sold many of its assets to other companies. Those sales brought in over US$1.2 billion to be distributed to shareholders or reinvested in core businesses. For example, General Dynamics sold its information technology unit for US$184 million; it sold the Cessna aircraft unit to Textron for US$600 million; and by the late 1990s it had sold its commercial aircraft components, materials service, electronics, ship management, and financial units, and its missile systems business.

Top managers realized that General Dynamics could not support all of its traditional activities in an environment where resources were declining so rapidly. They responded quickly to the need to shrink and downsize, and they reorganized to focus more intently on the organization's core competencies. Although the company has shrunk, shareholders, who have seen the value of their investments rise rapidly, view it as very effective. Clearly, this top-management team was not blinded by the first stages of organizational decline and has moved rapidly to adjust the organization to its new environment. It has positioned itself as a strong player in the global defence industry, and its performance has increased steadily.[44]

Stage 2: Inaction If an organization does not realize that it is in trouble in the blinded stage, its decline advances to the inaction stage. In this stage, despite clear signs of deteriorating performance such as decreased sales or profits, top management takes little action to correct problems. This inaction may reflect managers' misinterpretation of information and belief that the situation reflects a short-term environmental change that the organization will weather. Inaction may also occur because managers are pursuing goals that benefit them at the expense of other stakeholders. Organizational inertia, too, may delay managers' response to the situation. Management may follow tried-and-true approaches to solve the organization's problems—approaches that may be inappropriate in the present situation.[45]

As the inaction stage progresses, as Figure 11-6 shows, the gap between acceptable performance and actual performance increases, and prompt action by managers is vital to reverse the decline. Managers may take steps to downsize by reducing the number of personnel, or they may scale back the scope of their operations. They may also change the organization's structure to overcome any organizational inertia that has set in as a result of the organization's large size or complex operations.

Stage 3: Faulty Action When managers fail to halt decline at the inaction stage, the organization moves into the faulty action stage. Problems continue to multiply despite corrective action. Managers may have made the wrong decisions because of conflict in the top-management team, or they may have changed too little too late because they feared that a major reorganization might do more harm than good. Often managers fear that radical change may threaten the way the organization operates and put the organization at risk.[46] For example, Rod Canion, Compaq's founder, could not bring himself to make the radical structural and strategy changes that were needed to turn the company around. After Ekhard Pfeiffer, the new CEO, took over, Compaq moved to a low-cost strategy and slashed its workforce by 35 percent, but by then Compaq was in stage 4, the crisis stage. Very often, an organization reaches the faulty-action stage because managers become overly committed to their present strategy and structure and fear changing them even though they are clearly not working to halt the decline.

Stage 4: Crisis By the time the crisis stage has arrived, only radical changes to an organization's strategy and structure can stop the decline and allow the organization to survive. An organization experiencing a crisis has reached a critical point in its history, and the only chance of recovery is a major reorganization. If managers wait until the organization reaches stage 4 before taking action, change is very difficult to achieve and must be drastic because organizational stakeholders are starting to dissolve or restrict their relationships with the organization.[47] The best managers may already have left because of fighting in the top-management team. Investors may be unwilling to risk lending their money to the organization. Suppliers may be reluctant to send the inputs the organization needs because they are worried about getting paid.

Very often by the crisis stage only a new top-management team can turn a company around. To overcome inertia, an organization needs new ideas so that it can adapt and change in response to new conditions in the environment.[48] Often the new organization that emerges from an effective reorganization resembles the old organization in name only.

Stage 5: Dissolution When an organization reaches the dissolution stage, it cannot recover, and decline is irreversible. At this point, the organization has lost the support of its stakeholders, and its access to resources shrivels as its reputation and markets disappear. If new leaders have been selected, they are likely to lack the organizational resources to institute a successful turnaround and develop new routines. The organization probably has no choice but to divest its remaining resources or liquidate its assets and enter bankruptcy proceedings. In either case, it moves into dissolution, and organizational death is the outcome.

As organizational death occurs, people's attachment to the organization changes. They realize that the end is coming and that their attachment to the organization is only temporary.[49] The announcement of organizational death signals to people that efforts to prevent decline have failed and that further actions by participants are futile. As the disbanding process begins, the organization severs its links to its stakeholders and transfers its resources to other organizations. Inside the organization, formal closing or parting ceremonies serve as a way of severing members' ties to the organization and focusing members on their new roles outside the organization.

The need to manage organizational decline is as great as the need to manage organizational growth. In fact, the processes of growth and decline are closely related to one another: The symptoms of decline often signal that a new path must be taken to allow the organization to grow successfully. As many large organizations have found, the solution to their problem may be to shrink and downsize and focus their resources on a narrower range of products and markets. If an organization cannot adapt to a changing environment, it generally faces organizational death.

MANAGERIAL IMPLICATIONS

Organizational Decline

1. To prevent the onset of organizational decline, continually analyze the organization's structure to pinpoint any sources of inertia that may have emerged as your organization has grown and differentiated.
2. Continually analyze the environment, and the niche or niches that your organization occupies, to identify changes in the amount or distribution of resources.
3. Recognize that because you are a part of the organization it may be difficult for you to identify internal or external problems. Call on other managers, members of the board of directors, and outside consultants to analyze the organization's current situation or stage of decline.
4. If you are the founder of the business, always keep in mind that you have a duty to your stakeholders to maximize the chances of your organization's survival and success. Be prepared to step aside and relinquish control if new leadership is required.

SUMMARY

Organizations have a life cycle consisting of four stages: birth, growth, decline, and death. They pass through these stages at different rates, and some do not experience every stage. To survive and prosper, organizations have to change in response to various internal and external forces. An organization must make changes to its structure and culture at critical points in its life cycle. If successfully managed, an organization continues to grow and differentiate. An organization must adapt to an uncertain and changing environment and overcome the organizational inertia that constantly threatens its ability to adapt to environmental changes. The fate of organizations that fail to meet these challenges is death. Their place is taken by new organizations, and a new cycle of birth and death begins. Chapter 11 has made the following main points:

1. Organizations pass through a series of stages as they grow and evolve. The four stages of the organizational life cycle are birth, growth, decline, and death.
2. Organizations are born when leaders and entrepreneurs use their skills and competencies to create value. Organizational birth is associated with the liability of newness.

Organizational birth is a dangerous stage because entrepreneurship is a risky process, organizational procedures are new and undeveloped, and the environment may be hostile.

3. Population ecology theory states that organizational birth rates in a new environment are very high at first but taper off as the number of successful organizations in a population increases.
4. The number of organizations in a population is determined by the amount of resources available in the environment.
5. Population ecologists have identified two sets of strategies that organizations can use to gain access to resources and to enhance their chances of survival: r-strategy versus K-strategy (r = early entry; K = late entry) and specialist strategy versus generalist strategy.
6. The driving force behind the population ecology model is natural selection, the process that ensures the survival of the organizations that have the skills and abilities that best fit with the environment.
7. As organizations grow, they increase their division of labour and specialization and develop the skills that give them a competitive advantage, which allows them to gain access to scarce resources.
8. Institutional theory argues that organizations adopt many of their routines from the institutional environment surrounding them in order to increase their legitimacy and chances of survival. Stakeholders tend to favour organizations that they consider trustworthy and legitimate.
9. A new organization can enhance its legitimacy by choosing the goals, structure, and culture that are used by other successful organizations in its populations. Similarity among organizations is the result of coercive, mimetic, and normative isomorphism.
10. According to Greiner's five-stage model of organizational growth, organizations experience growth through (a) creativity, (b) direction, (c) delegation, (d) coordination, and (e) collaboration. Each growth stage ends in a crisis that must be solved by making the appropriate changes if the organization is to advance successfully to the next stage and continue to grow.
11. If organizations fail to manage the growth process effectively, the result is organizational decline, the stage an organization enters when it fails to anticipate, recognize, or adapt to external or internal pressures that threaten its survival.
12. Factors that can precipitate organizational decline include organizational inertia and changes in the environment.
13. Organizational decline occurs by degrees. Weitzel and Jonsson have identified five stages of decline: (a) blinded, (b) inaction, (c) faulty action, (d) crisis, and (e) dissolution. Managers can turn the organization around at every stage except the dissolution stage.
14. Organizational death occurs when an organization divests its remaining resources or liquidates its assets. As the disbanding process begins, the organization severs its links to its stakeholders and transfers its resources to other organizations.

DISCUSSION QUESTIONS

1. What factors influence the number of organizations that are founded in a population? How can pursuing a specialist strategy increase a company's chances of survival?
2. How does r-strategy differ from K-strategy? How does a specialist strategy differ from a generalist strategy? Use companies in the fast-food industry to provide an example of each strategy.
3. Why do organizations grow? What major crisis is an organization likely to encounter as it grows?
4. Why do organizations decline? What steps can top management take to halt decline and restore organizational growth?
5. What is organizational inertia? List some sources of inertia in a company like Nortel or Air Canada.

6. Choose an organization or business in your city that has recently closed, and analyze why it failed. Could the organization have been turned around? Why or why not?

ORGANIZATIONAL THEORY IN ACTION

Practising Organizational Theory: Growing Pains

Form groups of three to five people and discuss the following scenario:

You are the top managers of a rapidly growing company that has been having great success in developing Web sites for major companies. Currently, you employ over 150 highly skilled and qualified programmers, and to date you have operated with a loose, organic operating structure that has given them considerable autonomy. While this has worked, you are now experiencing problems. Performance is dropping because your company is fragmenting into different self-contained teams that are not cooperating and not learning from one another. You have decided that somehow you need to become more bureaucratic or mechanistic, but you recognize and wish to keep all the advantages of your organic operating approach. You are meeting to discuss how to make this transition.

1. What kind of crisis are you experiencing according to Greiner's model?
2. What kind of changes will you make to your operating structure to solve this crisis, and what will be the problems associated with implementing these changes?

Making the Connection #11

Find an example of an organization that is experiencing a crisis of growth or an organization that is trying to manage decline. What stage of the life cycle is the organization in? What factors contributed to its growth crisis? What factors led to its decline? What problems is the organization experiencing? How is top management trying to solve the problems?

The Ethical Dimension #11

Managers have many opportunities to pursue their own interests, and as discussed above can use their power to take advantage of their subordinates, limit their freedom, and even steal their ideas. At the same time, managers may have a natural tendency to become risk averse.

1. What kind of ethical code should an organization create to try to prevent the selfish managerial behaviours that can contribute to inertia?
2. How can an organization use ethics to encourage managers to maintain a risk-taking attitude that benefits all stakeholders?

Analyzing the Organization: Design Module #11

This module focuses on the way your organization is managing (a) the dynamics associated with the life-cycle stage that it is in and (b) the problems it has experienced as it evolved.

ASSIGNMENT

Using the information at your disposal, answer the following questions.

1. When was your organization founded? Who founded it? What opportunity was it founded to exploit?
2. How rapid was the growth of your organization, and what problems did it experience as it grew? Describe its passage through the growth stages outlined in Greiner's model. How did managers deal with the crisis that it encountered as it grew?
3. What stage of the organizational life cycle is your organization in now? What internal and external problems is it currently encountering? How are managers trying to solve these problems?
4. Has your organization ever shown any symptoms of decline? How quickly were managers in the organization able to respond to the problem of decline? What changes did they make? Did they turn the organization around?

Company Profiles #11*

Choose one or more of the organizations (e.g., companies, government agencies, or nonprofit organizations) that are profiled in this chapter. Do an Internet search to get up-to-date information on each organization you have selected, and answer the following questions.

1. What does the new information tell you about the organization's current ability to survive?
2. How does the information compare with the earlier information provided in the text and what does that tell you about organizations (e.g., does the organization appear to be more or less able to survive than before, and how do you explain this)?

Alternative Perspectives #11

Critical theorists contend that the death of capitalist organizations, resulting in job losses for employees and potential devastation for local communities, is the outcome of the pursuit of profit in a market economy. Read one or more of the following readings and identify different ways of organizing. In small groups, compare and contrast the different organizational types and their potential for growth and survival.

Reading List

Baldersheim, H., and Ståhlberg, K. 1994. *Towards the Self-Regulating Municipality: Free Communes and Administrative Modernization in Scandinavia.* Aldershot, England: Dartmouth Publishing Co.

Clegg, S., and Dunkerley, D. 1980. *Organization, Class and Control.* London: Routledge and Kegan Paul.

Clegg, S. R. 1990. *Modern Organizations.* Newbury Park, CA.: Sage.

Coates, K. 1981. *Work-ins, Sit-ins and Industrial Democracy.* Nottingham: Spokesman.

Hacker, S. 1989. *Pleasure, Power and Technology.* Boston, MA: Unwin.

Kropotkin, P. 1914. *Mutual Aid.* London: Heinemann.

Martin, P. Y. 1990. Rethinking Feminist Organizations. *Gender & Society,* 4(2): 182–206.

Marx, K., and Engels, F. 1967. *The Communist Manifesto* (With an introduction by A. J.P. Taylor, ed.). Harmondsworth: Penguin.

Oakshott, R. 1978. *The Case for Workers' Co-ops.* London: Routledge and Kegan Paul.

Sirianni, C. 1987. *Worker Participation and the Politics of Reform.* Philadelphia: Temple University Press.

Woodcock, G. 1962. *Anarchism.* Harmondsworth: Penguin.

* The authors would like to receive information from student groups and instructors on any companies where there have been dramatic changes to the information published in this text. We would be happy to publish the best of these changes in a subsequent edition, where we will focus on changing company profiles.

CASE FOR ANALYSIS

Cell-Loc's Organizational Transformation, Rebirth, and . . . ?[50]

Cell-Loc Inc. was incorporated in 1995 in Calgary. The company was created to commercialize years of research on wireless location technology. Its patented technology is known as Cellocate™, a family of network-based wireless location products that enable location-based services. The outlook for such a company was very positive with burgeoning demand for 911 emergency services using wireless technology. However, the financial burden of research and development to advance the technology has not been easy, and Cell-Loc and its competitors have had to find ways to survive until technology meets with federal communication standards. Through the years, Cell-Loc has remained afloat with worldwide marketing of various diversified products and services using the Cellocate technology. It has marketed related products and services for locating people and pets, tracking inventory and fleets, and for protecting assets. In order to survive, Cell-Loc has also gone through interesting reorganization phases that resulted in a rebirth of the company.

Cell-Loc's future looked the brightest when its stock peaked at near $80 per share in March 2000 during the dot-com bubble. But in September 2003, its 52-week range was between 35 cents and $1.20. It was at this time the company's managers were planning to transform Cell-Loc into an energy company, Capitol Energy Resources Ltd., and a subsidiary company. This was a strategic multistage manoeuvre to manage an accumulated debt load and to acquire capital. As of December 2003, Capitol Energy Resources Ltd., noted as the former Cell-Loc Inc., began to sell shares on the Toronto Stock Exchange, and Cell-Loc Inc. shares were delisted. But, at the same time, the subsidiary company of Cell-Loc Location Technologies Inc., also noted as the former Cell-Loc Inc., began selling shares on the exchange as well. Thus, as a survival strategy, Cell-Loc was reorganized, transformed, and reborn.

Reports on performance since the rebirth of Cell-Loc have been bleak. Operation losses and accumulation of debt have been countered by the hope for breakthroughs in a fast-paced, ever-changing industry. The new Cell-Loc has said its chances for success will depend on being able to develop the rapidly changing market for location-based cellular services. The company has speculated that the required research and testing on products could continue to impact negatively on the company's resources. Shares in Cell-Loc closed at 31 cents, up 2.5 cents, in February 2004.

According a company statement, "To remain competitive the company must be able to keep pace with technological developments and change its product lines to meet new demands. The company will depend on designing and developing products that have not been commercially tested to achieve much of its future growth."

DISCUSSION QUESTIONS

1. What were the catalytic circumstances that led up to a rebirth of Cell-Loc?
2. How is Cell-Loc doing now? Using what you've learned in this chapter and checking Internet resources, describe and analyze Cell-Loc's birth, growth, decline, and rebirth phases. In your analysis, include an updated synopsis of the company's circumstances.

REFERENCES

1. R. E. Quinn and K. Cameron, "Organizational Life Cycles and Shifting Criteria of Effectiveness: Some Preliminary Evidence," *Management Science,* 1983, vol. 29, pp. 33–51.
2. I. Adizes, "Organizational Passages: Diagnosing and Treating Life Cycle Problems of Organizations," *Organizational Dynamics,* 1979, vol. 8, pp. 3–25; D. Miller and P. Freisen, "Archetypes of Organizational Transitions," *Administrative Science Quarterly,* 1980, vol. 25, pp. 268–299.
3. F. H. Knight, *Risk, Uncertainty, and Profit* (Boston: Houghton Mifflin, 1921); I. M. Kirzner, *Competition and Entrepreneurship* (Chicago: University of Chicago Press, 1973).
4. A. Stinchcombe, "Social Structure and Organizations," in J. G. March, ed., *Handbook of Organizations* (Chicago: Rand McNally, 1965), pp. 142–193.
5. J. A. Schumpeter, *The Theory of Economic Development* (Cambridge, MA: Harvard University Press, 1934).
6. H. Aldrich, *Organizations and Environments* (Englewood Cliffs, NJ: Prentice Hall, 1979).
7. R. R. Nelson and S. Winter, *An Evolutionary Theory of Economic Change* (Cambridge, MA: Harvard University Press, 1982).

8. *www.chezcora.com/Main-en/Historique-en.htm*, 2004.

9. M. T. Hannan and J. H. Freeman, *Organizational Ecology* (Cambridge, MA: Harvard University Press, 1989).

10. Organizational Insight compiled by Scott MacMillan from the following sources: Alliance Atlantis, "Corporate Profile," *www.allianceatlantis.com/corporate/profile/*, 7 July 2004; CBC News Online, "Award-Winning Salter Street Films Closes," (16 December 2003), *www.cbc.ca/arts/stories/salterstclose161203*, 2 June 2004; Alliance Atlantis News Release (24 April 2002), "Salter Street Films, *Bowling For Columbine*, a Michael Moore Film invited to Cannes in Competition," *www.allianceatlantis.com/corporate/press_media/2002/AA C02_54.html*, 3 June 2004; Nova Scotia Economic Development, Ministerial Statement (1 April 2003), *www.gov.ns.ca/econ/speeches/20030401_film.asp*, 3 June 2004; "Alliance Atlantis to Buy Salter," *Wall Street Journal*, 13 February 2001, p. 1; P. Lee, "Merger Mania Hits Salter Street Films," *Halifax Herald*, 7 July 1998, *jam.canoe.ca/TelevisionShowsS/salterstreetfilms.html*; Salter Street News Release (20 May1998), "Salter Street Closes Initial Public and Secondary Offering," *http://www2.cdn-news.com/scripts/ccn-release.pl?/1998/05/20/ssf052098.html?cp=ssf*, 7 July 2004; Salter Street News Release (December 18, 2000), "Salter Street Films Limited Reports Financial Results for the Fourth Quarter and Fiscal Year 2000," *www2.cdn-news.com/scripts/ccn-release.pl?/2000/12/18/1218067n. html?cp=ssf*, 7 July 2004; Salter Street News Release (12 February 2001), "Alliance Atlantis Reaches Agreement to Acquire Salter Street Films," *www2.cdn-news.com/scripts/ccn-release.pl?/2001/02/12/0212006n.html?cp=ssf*, 7 July 2004.

11. G. R. Carroll, "Organizational Ecology," *Annual Review of Sociology*, 1984, vol. 10, pp. 71–93; G. R. Carroll and M. Hannan, "On Using Institutional Theory in Studying Organizational Populations," *American Sociological Review*, 1989, vol. 54, pp. 545–548.

12. Aldrich, *Organizations and Environments*.

13. J. Delacroix and G. R. Carroll, "Organizational Foundings: An Ecological Study of the Newspaper Industries of Argentina and Ireland," *Administrative Science Quarterly*, 1983, vol. 28, pp. 274–291; Carroll and Hannan, "On Using Institutional Theory in Studying Organizational Populations."

14. Ibid.

15. M. T. Hannan and J. H. Freeman, "The Ecology of Organizational Foundings: American Labor Unions, 1836–1975," *American Journal of Sociology*, 1987, vol. 92, pp. 910–943.

16. J. Brittain and J. Freeman, "Organizational Proliferation and Density Dependent Selection," in J. Kimberly and R. Miles, eds., *Organizational Life Cycles* (San Francisco: Jossey-Bass, 1980), pp. 291–338; Hannan and Freeman, *Organizational Ecology*.

17. G. R. Carroll, "The Specialist Strategy," *California Management Review*, vol. 3, pp.126–137; G. R. Carroll, "Concentration and Specialization: Dynamics of Niche Width in Populations of Organizations," *American Journal of Sociology*, 1985, vol. 90, pp. 1262–1283.

18. Carroll, "Concentration and Specialization."

19. M. Lambkin and G. Day, "Evolutionary Processes in Competitive Markets," *Journal of Marketing*, 1989, vol. 53, pp. 4–20; W. Boeker, "Organizational Origins: Entrepreneurial and Environmental Imprinting at the Time of Founding," in G. R. Carroll, *Ecological Models of Organization* (Cambridge, MA: Ballinger, 1987), pp. 33–51.

20. Aldrich, *Organizations and Environments*, p. 27.

21. J. Pfeffer and G. R. Salancik, *The External Control of Organizations* (New York: Harper and Row, 1978).

22. Organizational Insight compiled by Scott MacMillan from the following sources: M. Berss, "Taxation by Other Means," *Forbes*, 11 April 1994, pp. 64–65; YMCA Canada, *www.ymca.ca*, 16 June 2004; Toronto YMCA, *www.ymcatoronto.org/home.asp*, 16 June 2004.

23. J. Meyer and B. Rowan, "Institutionalized Organizations: Formal Structure as Myth and Ceremony," *American Journal of Sociology*, 1977, vol. 83, pp. 340–363; B. E. Ashforth and B. W. Gibbs, "The Double Edge of Organizational Legitimation," *Organization Science*, 1990, vol. 1, pp. 177–194.

24. L. G. Zucker, "Institutional Theories of Organization," *Annual Review of Sociology*, 1987, vol. 13, pp. 443–464.

25. B. Rowan, "Organizational Structure and the Institutional Environment: The Case of Public Schools," *Administrative Science Quarterly*, 1982, vol. 27, pp. 259–279; P. S. Tolbert and L. G. Zucker, "Institutional Sources of Change in the Formal Structure of Organizations: The Diffusion of Civil Service Reform, 1880–1935," *Administrative Science Quarterly*, 1983, vol. 28, pp. 22–38.

26. P. DiMaggio and W. Powell, "The Iron Cage Revisited: Institutional Isomorphism and Collective Rationality in Organizational Fields," *American Sociological Review*, 1983, vol. 48, pp. 147–160.

27. J. Galaskiewicz and S. Wasserman, "Mimetic Processes Within an Interorganizational Field: An Empirical Test," *American Sociological Review*, 1983, vol. 48, pp. 454–479.

28. Ashforth and Gibbs, "The Double Edge of Organizational Legitimation."

29. A. J. Mills, "The Gendering of Organizational Culture: Social and Organizational Discourses in the Making of British Airways," in M. DesRosiers, ed., *Proceedings of the Administrative Sciences Association of Canada, Women in Management Division*, vol. 15 (Halifax: Administrative Sciences Association of Canada, 1994), pp. 11–20; A. J. Mills, "Managing Subjectivity, Silencing Diversity: Organizational Imagery in the Airline Industry: The Case of British Airways," *Organization*, 1995, vol. 2, pp. 243–269; A. J. Mills, "Corporate Image, Gendered Subjects and the Company Newsletter—The Changing Faces of British Airways," in G. Palmer and S. Clegg, eds., *Constituting Management: Markets, Meanings and Identities* (Berlin: de Gruyter, 1996), pp. 191–211; A. J. Mills, "Cockpits, Hangars, Boys and Galleys: Corporate Masculinities and the Development of British Airways," *Gender, Work & Organization*, 1998, vol. 5, pp. 172–188; G. P. Nielsen, *From Sky Girl to Flight Attendant: Women and the Making of a Union* (New York: ILR Press, 1982).

30. This section draws heavily on L. E. Greiner, "Evolution and Revolution as Organizations Grow," *Harvard Business Review*, July–August 1972, pp. 37–46.

31. A. C. Cooper, "Entrepreneurship and High Technology," in D. L. Sexton and R. W. Smilor, eds., *The Art and Science of Entrepreneurship* (Cambridge, MA: Ballinger, 1986), pp. 153–168; J. R. Thorne and J. G. Ball, "Entrepreneurs and Their Companies," in K. H. Vesper, ed., *Frontiers of Entrepreneurial Research* (Wellesley, MA: Center for Entrepreneurial Studies, Babson College, 1981), pp. 65–83.

32. G. R. Jones and J. E. Butler, "Managing Internal Corporate Entrepreneurship: An Agency Theory Perspective," *Journal of Management*, 1992, vol. 18, pp. 733–749.

33. Insight written by Margaret McKee from the following sources: "About ISO," *www.iso.ch/iso/en/aboutiso/introduction/index.html#eleven*, 9 December 2004; A. Holloway, "Band on a Run," *Canadian Business*, 2004, vol. 77, p. 10; "Innovation in Canada: Bernd Christmas, Chief Executive Officer, Membertou Development Corporation," *www.innovation.gc.ca/gol/innovation/stories.nsf/veng/ss01040e.htm*, 8 December 2004; "Corporate Office," *www.membertou.ca/corporate.html*, 8 December 2004; *www.ainc-inac.gc.ca*, 2002; "Membertou Becomes the First Indigenous Government to Become ISO 90012000 Registered," *www.ainc-inac.gc.ca/nr/prs/j-a2002/iso_e.html*, 8 December 2004 from; *www.ainc-inac.gc.ca*, 2001; "Membertou First Nation Applauded for Fiscal Accountability and Good Management," *www.ainc-inac.gc.ca/nr/prs/m-a2001/2-01170_e.html*, 8 December 2004; *www.grantthornton.ca*, 2003; "New Alliance Provides Solutions for First Nations Indebtedness," *www.grantthornton.ca/media/mr_template.asp?MRID=53*, 9 December 2004; *www.fujitsu.com*, 2003; "Fujitsu Consulting and Membertou Create New Company to Pursue IT Services Opportunities," *www.fujitsu.com/ca/en/news/pr/fc_20031017-01.html*, 9 December 2004; *www.membertou.ca*, 2003; "Membertou and Techlink Entertainment Agree to Partner in Long-Term Strategic Plan," *www.membertou.ca/news/press2003april28.html*, 9 December 2004; C. Petten, "Membertou's Star Shines," *Windspeaker*, December 2003, vol. 21, p. 30.

34. Greiner, "Evolution and Revolution as Organizations Grow," p. 43.

35. W. Weitzel and E. Jonsson, "Decline in Organizations: A Literature Integration and Extension," *Administrative Science Quarterly*, 1989, vol. 34, pp. 91–109.

36. K. S. Cameron, M. U. Kim, and D. A. Whetten, "Organizational Effects of Decline and Turbulence," *Administrative Science Quarterly*, 1987, vol. 32, pp. 222–240; K. S. Cameron, D. A. Whetten, and M. U. Kim, "Organizational Dysfunctions of Decline," *Academy of Management Journal*, 1987, vol. 30, pp. 126–138.

37. G. R. Jones, R. Kosnik, and J. M. George, "Internationalization and the Firm's Growth Path: On the Psychology of Organizational Contracting," in R. W. Woodman and W. A. Pasemore, *Research in Organizational Change and Development* (Greenwich, CT: JAI Press, 1993).

38. A. D. Chandler, *The Visible Hand* (Cambridge, MA: Belknap Press, 1977); H. Mintzberg and J. A. Waters, "Tracking Strategy in an Entrepreneurial Firm," *Academy of Management Journal*, 1982, vol. 25, pp. 465–499; J. Stopford and L. T. Wells, *Managing the Multinational Enterprise* (London: Longman, 1972).

39. A. A. Berle and C. Means, *The Modern Corporation and Private Property* (New York: Macmillan, 1932); K. Williamson, "Profit, Growth, and Sales Maximization," *Economica*, 1966, vol. 34, pp. 1–16.

40. R. M. Kanter, *When Giants Learn to Dance: Mastering the Challenges of Strategy* (New York: Simon and Schuster, 1989).

41. L. Greenhalgh, "Organizational Decline," in S. B. Bacharach, Ed., *Research in the Sociology of Organizations* (Greenwich, CT: JAI Press, 1983), pp. 231–276.

42. A. Meyer, "Adapting to Environmental Jolts," *Administrative Science Quarterly*, 1982, vol. 27, pp. 515–537.

43. Weitzel and Jonsson, "Decline in Organizations."

44. "Defense Contractor Reports Earnings Up 14.5 percent." *Business News*, 29 October 1999, p. 3.

45. W. H. Starbuck, A. Greve, and B. L. T. Hedberg, "Responding to Crisis," in C. F. Smart and W. T. Stansbury, eds., *Studies in Crisis Management* (Toronto: Butterworth, 1978), pp. 111–136.

46. M. Hannan and J. Freeman, "Structural Inertia and Organizational Change," *American Sociological Review*, 1984, vol. 49, pp. 149–164; D. Miller, "Evolution and Revolution: A Quantum View of Structural Change in Organizations," *Journal of Management Studies*, 1982, vol. 19, pp. 131–151.

47. Weitzel and Jonsson, "Decline in Organizations," p. 105.

48. B. L. T. Hedburg, P. C. Nystrom, and W. H. Starbuck, "Camping on Seesaws, Prescriptions for a Self-Designing Organization," *Administrative Science Quarterly*, 1976, vol. 21, pp. 31–65; M. L. Tushman, W. H. Newman, and E. Romanelli, "Convergence and Upheaval: Managing the Steady Pace of Organizational Evolution," *California Management Review*, 1986, vol. 29, pp. 29–44.

49. R. I. Sutton, "The Process of Organizational Death," *Administrative Science Quarterly*, 1987, vol. 32, pp. 542–569.

50. Case developed by Ellen Rudderham-Gaudet using the following sources: Cell-Loc, "Who We Are," *www.cell-loc.com/who_company.html*, 13 July 2004; B. Harter, "Location Services Stood Up," *M-Business*, 1 November 2001, pp. 53–54; Canadian Press, "Cell-Loc to Spin off Technology, Become Energy Company in $4.9M Restructuring," *NewsWire*, 23 September 2003; Cell-Loc, "News Archive" (4 December 2003), *www.cell-loc.com/news_archive.html*, 13 July 2004; Canoe Money, "Cell-Loc Location Technologies loses $373G in First Month as Restructured Firm" (1 March 2004), *money.canoe.ca/News/Sectors/Telecommunication/2004/03/01/366829-cp.html*, 13 July 2004.

Decision Making, Learning, Knowledge Management, and Information Technology

CHAPTER 12

Learning Objectives

Decision making results in choices that determine the way an organization operates and how it changes or transforms itself over time. Organizations have to continually improve the way decisions are made so that managers and employees can learn new, more effective ways to act inside the organization and respond to a changing environment.

By the end of this chapter you should be able to:

1. Differentiate between several models of decision making that describe how managers make decisions.
2. Describe the nature of organizational learning and the different levels at which learning occurs.
3. Explain how organizations can use knowledge management and information technology to promote organizational learning to improve the quality of their decision making.
4. Identify the factors, such as the operation of cognitive biases, that reduce the level of organizational learning and result in poor decision making.
5. Discuss some techniques that managers can use to overcome these cognitive biases and thus open the organization up to new learning.

ORGANIZATIONAL DECISION MAKING

In previous chapters, we have discussed how an organization and its managers design a structure and a culture that match the organization's environment; choose a technology to convert inputs into outputs; and choose a strategy to guide the use of organizational skills and resources to create value. In making these choices, managers are making decisions. Indeed, everything that goes on in an organization involves a decision of some kind. Clearly, an organization is not only a value-creation system but a decision-making system as well. At every level and in every subunit, people continuously make decisions, and how well they make them determines how much value their organization creates.

Organizational decision making
The process of responding to a problem by searching for and selecting a solution or course of action that will create value for organizational stakeholders.

Organizational decision making is the process of responding to a problem by searching for and selecting a solution or course of action that will create value for organizational stakeholders. Here we must carefully define what a "problem" is. A problem may either be a positive, a neutral, or a negative set of circumstances. For example, if an organization's introduction of a new product failed in the market, then this is a negative state of affairs. The organization would rather have a successful introduction. On the other hand, if an organization introduces a new product or service that is extremely successful, to the point that the organization cannot meet the demand, then this is also a problem. When organizations make decisions, it is helpful to think of an organizational problem as the difference between a given state of affairs and a desired state of affairs. Hence, whether the problem is to find the best inputs, to decide on the right way to provide a service to customers, or to figure out how to deal with an aggressive competitor, managers and employees must decide what to do. In general, organizational members are called upon to make two kinds of decisions: programmed and nonprogrammed.

Programmed decisions
Decisions that are repetitive and routine.

Programmed decisions are repetitive and routine. Rules, routines, and standard operating procedures can be developed in advance to handle them.[1] Many of the routines and procedures for selecting appropriate solutions are formalized in an organization's rules and standard operating procedures and in the values and norms of its culture. Managers and employees are given certain responsibilities and authorities to make decisions on behalf of the organization.

Nonprogrammed decisions
Decisions that are novel and unstructured.

Nonprogrammed decisions are novel and unstructured. No rules, routines, or standard operating procedures can be developed to handle them. Solutions must be worked out as problems arise.[2] Nonprogrammed decision making requires much more search activity and mutual adjustment by managers and employees to find a solution than does programmed decision making. For example, nonroutine research and development is based on nonprogrammed decision making by researchers who continually experiment to find solutions to problems. Similarly, the creation of an organization's strategy involves nonprogrammed decision making by managers who experiment to find the best way to use an organization's skills and resources to create competencies and value, and who never know in advance whether they are making the right decision.

Nonprogrammed decision making forces organizational decision makers to rely on judgment, intuition, and creativity to solve organizational problems; they cannot rely on rules and standard operating procedures to provide nonprogrammed solutions. *Nonprogrammed decisions* may often lead to the creation of a new set of rules and procedures that would allow organizational members to make appropriate *programmed* decisions.

All organizations have to develop the capacity to make both programmed and nonprogrammed decisions. Programmed decision making allows an organization to increase its efficiency and reduce the costs of making goods and services. Nonprogrammed decision making allows the organization to change and adapt to its environment and to generate new ways of behaving so that it can effectively take advantage of its environment. Programmed decision making provides stability and increases predictability. Nonprogrammed decision making allows the organization to change and adapt itself so that it can deal with unpredictable events. In the next section, we examine several models of organizational decision making.

MODELS OF ORGANIZATIONAL DECISION MAKING

Early models of decision making portrayed decision making as a rational process in which "all-knowing" managers made decisions that allowed organizations to adjust perfectly to the environment in which they operated.[3] Newer models recognize that decision making is an inherently uncertain process in which managers and employees grope for solutions that may or may not lead to outcomes favourable to organizational stakeholders.

The Rational Model

According to the *rational model,* decision making is a straightforward, three-stage process (see Figure 12-1).[4] In stage 1, decision makers identify problems that need to be solved. The managers of an effective organization, for example, spend a great deal of time analyzing all aspects of their organization's specific and general environments to identify conditions or problems that call for new action. To achieve a good fit between an organization and its environment, they must analyze the environment and recognize the opportunities or threats it presents. In stage 2, decision makers individually or collectively seek to design and develop a list of alternative solutions and courses of action to the problems they have identified. They study ways to take advantage of the organization's skills and resources to respond to opportunities and threats. In stage 3, decision makers compare the likely consequences of each alternative and decide which course of action offers the best solution to the problem they identified in stage 1.

Under what "ideal" circumstances can organizational decision makers be sure that they have made a decision that will maximize stakeholders' satisfaction? The ideal situation is one in which there is no uncertainty: that is, the decision makers know all the courses of action open to them. They know the exact effects of all alternatives on stakeholders' interests. They are able to use the same set of objective criteria to evaluate each alternative. And they use the same decision rules to rank each alternative and thus can make the one best or right decision—the decision that will maximize the return to organizational stakeholders.[5] Do such conditions exist? If they did, organizational decision makers could always make decisions that would perfectly position their organizations in the environment to acquire new resources and make the best use of existing resources.

This ideal state is the situation assumed by the rational model of organizational decision making. The rational model ignores the ambiguity, uncertainty, and chaos that typically plague decision making. Researchers have criticized as unrealistic or simplistic the three assumptions underlying the rational model: (1) the assumption that decision makers have all the information they need; (2) the assumption that decision makers are smart; and (3) the assumption that decision makers agree about what needs to be done.

Information and Uncertainty The assumption that decision makers are aware of all alternative courses of action and their consequences is unrealistic. In order for this assumption to be valid, those persons making the decision would need access to all the information necessary to make a decision, would need to collect information about every possible situation the organization might encounter, and would need complete and accurate knowledge about the likelihood of each situation's occurring.[6] Clearly, collecting all this information would be very expensive, and the *information costs,* a form of transaction costs, associated with this model would be exorbitant.[7]

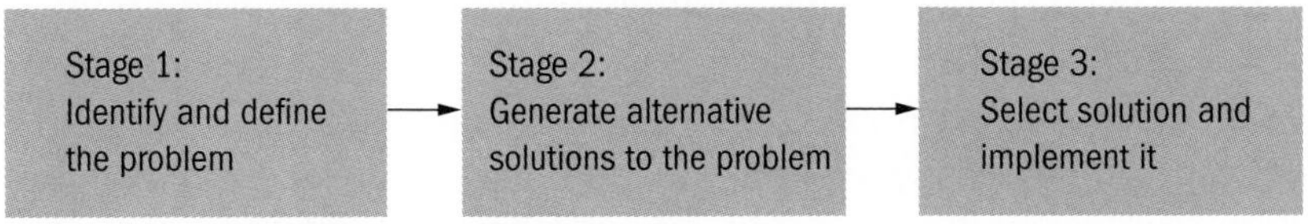

Stage 1: Identify and define the problem → Stage 2: Generate alternative solutions to the problem → Stage 3: Select solution and implement it

FIGURE 12-1
The Rational Model of Decision Making.
This model ignores the uncertainty that typically plagues decision making.

The assumption that it is possible to collect all the information needed to make the best decision is also unrealistic.[8] Because the environment is inherently uncertain, every alternative course of action and its consequences cannot be known. Furthermore, even if it were possible to collect information to eliminate all uncertainty, the costs of doing so would be as great as, or greater than, any potential profit the organization could make from selecting the best alternative. Thus nothing would be gained from the information.

Suppose a fast-food company thinks that some new kind of sandwich has the potential to attract large numbers of new customers. According to the rational model, to identify the right kind of sandwich, the company would do extensive market research, test different kinds of sandwiches with different groups of customers, and evaluate all alternatives. The cost of adequately testing *every* alternative for *all* possible different groups of customers, however, would be so high that it would swallow up any profit the new sandwich might generate from increased sales. The rational model ignores the fact that organizational decision making always takes place in the midst of uncertainty, which poses both an opportunity (a positive state of affairs) and a threat (a negative state of affairs) for an organization.

Managerial Abilities The rational model assumes that decision makers possess the intellectual capability not only to evaluate all the possible alternative choices but to select the best solution. In reality, they have only a limited ability to process the information required to make decisions, and most do not have the time to act as the rational model demands.[9] The intelligence required to make a decision according to the rational model would exceed any one individual's mental abilities and necessitate the employment of an enormous number of organizational decision makers. The rational model ignores the high level of *decision maker costs.*

Preferences and Values The rational model assumes that different individual decision makers have the same preferences and values and that they will use the same rules to decide on the best alternative. The model also assumes that they agree about what are the most important organizational goals. These "agreement assumptions" are unrealistic.[10] In Chapter 4, we discussed how managers and employees in different functions are likely to have different subunit orientations that lead them to make decisions that favour their own interests over those of other functions, other stakeholders, or the organization as a whole.

To sum up, the rational model of decision making is unrealistic because it rests on assumptions that ignore the information and managerial problems associated with decision making. The Carnegie model and other newer models take these factors into consideration and provide a more accurate picture of how organizational decision making actually takes place.

The Carnegie Model

In an attempt to describe the realities of the decision-making process more accurately, researchers introduced into decision-making theory a new set of assumptions that have come to be called the *Carnegie model.*[11] Table 12-1 summarizes the differences between the Carnegie and the rational models of decision making. The Carnegie model recognizes the effects of "satisficing," bounded rationality, and organizational coalitions.

Satisficing
Limited information searches to identify problems and alternative solutions.

Satisficing In an attempt to explain how organizations avoid the costs of obtaining information, the Carnegie model suggests that decision makers engage in **satisficing**, limited information searches to identify problems and alternative solutions.[12] Instead

Table 12-1

DIFFERENCES BETWEEN THE RATIONAL AND THE CARNEGIE MODELS OF DECISION MAKING

Rational Model	Carnegie Model
Information is available	Limited information is available
Decision making is costless	Decision making is costly (e.g., managerial costs, information costs)
Decision making is "value free"	Decision making is affected by the preferences and values of decision makers
The full range of possible alternatives is generated	A limited range of alternatives is generated
Solution is chosen by unanimous agreement	Solution is chosen by compromise, bargaining, and accommodation between organizational coalitions
Solution chosen is best for the organization	Solution chosen is satisfactory for the organization

of searching for all possible solutions to a problem, as the rational model suggests, individuals resort to satisficing behaviour—that is, they decide on certain criteria that they will use to evaluate possible acceptable solutions.[13] The criteria automatically limit the set of possible alternatives that may be investigated. The decision makers then select one alternative from the range of alternatives that they have generated. Thus satisficing involves a much less costly information search and puts far less of a burden on managers or other decision makers than does the rational model.

Bounded Rationality The rational model assumes that decision makers possess the intellectual capacity to evaluate all possible alternatives. The Carnegie model assumes that individuals are limited by **bounded rationality**—a limited capacity to identify appropriate information or to effectively process information. The fact that they have limited information-processing capacity, however, does not mean that decision makers will take only the first acceptable solution they are offered.[14] People may improve their decision making by learning to sharpen and enhance their analytical skills. Decision makers can also use facilitating technology, such as computers, to more effectively collect and analyze large quantities of information in order to improve their decision-making skills.[15] Thus the concept of bounded rationality does not necessarily imply a lack of ability or motivation on the part of decision makers, but much of the decision-making process itself is very subjective and is reliant on an individual's prior experience, beliefs, and intuition. This limitation may lead to decisions that emphasize the status quo, and "out-of-the-box" solutions may never be recognized or considered. As decision making may be bounded by the experience and shared views of the decision makers themselves if they are a homogenous group (say, all men or all whites), then their decisions or decision choices may be more limited than if they were a heterogeneous group. Diverse groups are less likely to suffer from the limitations of bounded rationality.

Bounded rationality A limited capacity to process information.

Organizational Coalitions The rational model ignores the variation in decision maker preferences and values and the impossibility of developing decision rules that allow them to evaluate different alternatives in the same way. The Carnegie model, in contrast, explicitly recognizes that the preferences and values of decision makers differ and that conflict between managers, employees, and different stakeholder groups is inevitable.[16] However, this does not mean that the organization has to bear the costs of forcing all decision makers to agree to use the same criteria to make decisions.

The Carnegie model views an organization as a coalition of different interests, in which decision making takes place by compromise, bargaining, and negotiation between managers or employees from different functions and areas of the organization. Any solution chosen meets the approval of the dominant coalition, the collection of managers or stakeholders who have the power to select a solution and commit resources to implement it.[17] Over time, as interests change, the makeup of the dominant coalition changes and so does decision making. The Carnegie model recognizes that decision making is not a neutral process with objective decision rules but a process during which organizational decision makers formulate decision rules as they pursue their goals and interests.

To sum up, the Carnegie model recognizes that decision making takes place in an uncertain environment where information is often incomplete and ambiguous. It also recognizes that decisions are made by people who are limited by bounded rationality, who satisfice, and who form coalitions to pursue their own interests. The Carnegie model offers a more accurate description of how decision making takes place in an organization than does the rational model. Yet Carnegie-style decision making is rational because organizational decision makers act intentionally to find the best solution to reach their desired goal, despite uncertainty and disagreement over goals. The response of General Electric to the question of whether GE should continue to make its own washing machines or buy machines made by other companies illustrates decision making in accordance with the Carnegie model. (See Organizational Insight 12.1.)

The Incrementalist Model

In the Carnegie model, satisficing and bounded rationality drastically reduce the number and complexity of alternatives that need to be analyzed. According to the *incrementalist model* of organizational decision making, decision makers select alternative courses of action that are only slightly, or incrementally, different from those used in the past, thus lessening their chances of making a mistake.[18] Often called the science of "muddling through," the incrementalist model implies that organizational decision makers rarely make major decisions that are radically different from decisions they have made before.[19] Instead, they correct or avoid mistakes through a succession of incremental changes, which eventually may lead to a completely new course of action. During the muddling-through process, organizational goals and the courses of action for achieving them may change, but they change very slowly so that corrective action can be taken if things start to go wrong.

The incrementalist model is very different from the rational model. According to the rational model, an all-knowing decision maker weighs every possible alternative course of action and chooses the best solution. According to the incrementalist model, those who are making the decisions, limited by lack of information and lack of foresight, move cautiously one step at a time to limit their chances of being wrong.

The Unstructured Model

The incrementalist approach works best in a relatively stable environment where decision makers can accurately predict movements and trends. In an environment that changes suddenly or abruptly, the incrementalist approach might prevent them from changing quickly enough to meet new conditions, thus causing the organization to go into decline. The *unstructured model* of organizational decision making, developed by Henry Mintzberg and his colleagues, describes how decision making takes place when uncertainty is high.[20]

The unstructured model recognizes the incremental nature of decision making and how decision making takes place in a series of small steps that collectively add up to a major decision over time. Incremental decisions are made within an overall deci-

ORGANIZATIONAL INSIGHT 12.1

Should GE Make or Buy Washing Machines?

In the 1990s GE faced a major decision. GE's appliance division, maker of well-known products such as dishwashers, ranges, refrigerators, and washing machines, was fighting declining profitability; and Appliance Park, GE's complex of factories near Louisville, Kentucky, which employed 10 000 of the company's 22 000 workers, was losing a substantial amount of money. The washing machine operations, technologically outdated, were contributing significantly to this loss, and GE had to evaluate two alternative courses of action: Should GE spend US$70 million and make a major investment in new technology to bring the washing machine operations up to date so that GE could compete into the next century, or should GE close down its washing machine operations and buy from another manufacturer washing machines that it would sell under its own brand name?

To evaluate each alternative, GE's managers tried to decide which one would lead to the best long-term outcome for the organization. They used criteria such as manufacturing costs, quality, profitability, and product development costs to evaluate each alternative. One of the factors that GE was most concerned about was whether the unions in its Appliance Park operations would agree to flexible work arrangements that would reduce labour costs. There had already been significant job losses, and GE managers had been sitting down with the unions to hammer out a new work agreement that would allow the corporation to evaluate its future labour costs. Using information on future labour costs and internal forecasts of future product development and manufacturing costs, managers tried to assess whether the investment would lead to a profit. At the same time, managers talked to companies like Maytag and Whirlpool to determine what it would cost GE to have them make a washing machine according to GE specifications.[21]

If GE could buy another manufacturer's washing machine for less than it would pay to make its own, then it seemed to make sense to choose the less costly alternative. However, GE's managers had to evaluate the effects of other factors. For example, if GE stopped making washing machines, it would lose a core competency in washing machine production that it would be unable to recover. Suppose the company that GE chose as its supplier failed to live up to its agreement and put only its old technology into the machines it supplied GE, or suppose it produced for GE machines that were much lower in quality than the machines it produced for itself. GE would be at the mercy of its suppliers. On the other hand, suppose the unions reneged on the contract and refused to cooperate after GE had made the investment in modernizing the washing machine plant.

The situation was further complicated by appliance division managers who were lobbying for the investment because it would protect their jobs and the jobs of 1500 workers. The division managers championed the advantages of the investment for improving the competitive advantage of the division. Corporate managers, however, had to evaluate the potential return of the investment to the entire organization.

GE's managers had a very difficult time evaluating the pros and cons of each alternative. Because of uncertainty, they could not accurately predict the consequences of any decision they made and had to rely on their knowledge of and experience in the appliance market. However, they decided that GE would make the investment and continue to produce its own washing machines. New lines of modern washing machines were introduced throughout the 1990s. In 1999, GE opened a US$5 million reliability Growth Test Center and it tripled the amount it spends on research and development in 1999 to produce appliances that never break down and which "delight" its customers.[22] Nevertheless in the early 2000s, GE, like Maytag, was still losing money from its appliance division, while main rival Whirlpool was experiencing record sales and profits and GE's managers were still trying to figure out what to do.[23]

sion-making framework consisting of three stages—identification, development, and selection—that are similar to the stages shown in Figure 12-1 (p. 409). In the *identification* stage, individuals develop routines to recognize problems and to understand what is happening to the organization. In the *development* stage, they search for and design alternatives to solve the problems they have defined. Solutions may be new plans or modifications of old plans, as in the muddling-through approach. Finally, in the *selection* stage, organizational decision makers use an incremental selection process—judgment and intuition, bargaining, and to a lesser extent formal analysis (typical of the rational model)—to reach a final decision.[24]

In the unstructured model (unlike the incrementalist model), whenever organizations encounter roadblocks, they rethink their alternatives and go back to the drawing board. Thus decision making is not a linear, sequential process but a process that may evolve unpredictably in an unstructured way. For example, decision making may be constantly interrupted because uncertainty in the environment alters the interpretations of a problem and thus casts doubt on the alternatives that have been generated or the solutions that have been chosen. The decision makers must then generate new solutions and find new strategies that help the organization adapt to and modify its environment.

Mintzberg's approach emphasizes the unstructured nature of incremental decision making: Managers and employees often make decisions in a haphazard, intuitive way, and uncertainty forces them to constantly adjust to find new ways to behave in the constantly changing situation. The organization tries to make the best decisions it can, but uncertainty forces it to adopt an unstructured way of making decisions. Thus the unstructured model tries to explain how organizations make nonprogrammed decisions, and the incrementalist model tries to explain how organizations improve their programmed decisions over time.

The Garbage Can Model

The view of decision making as an unstructured process is taken to its extreme in the *garbage can model* of organizational decision making.[25] This model turns the decision-making process around and argues that organizations are as likely to start making decisions from the *solution side* as from the *problem side*. In other words, decision makers may propose solutions to problems that do not exist; they create a problem that they can solve with solutions that are already available.

Garbage can decision making arises in the following way: An organization has a set of solutions, or skills, with which it can solve certain problems—for example, how to generate new customers, how to lower production costs, or how to innovate products. Possessing these skills, the organization seeks ways to use them, so organizational decision makers create problems (remember that a problem may be represented as either a positive or negative set of circumstances, and usually involves the difference between a current state and a desired state), or decision-making opportunities, for themselves. Suppose a company has skills in making custom-designed furniture. The head of the marketing department persuades the company president that the organization should take advantage of these skills by expanding internationally. Thus a new problem—how to manage international expansion—is created because of the existence of a solution—the ability to make superior custom-designed furniture.

While an organization is encountering new problems of its own making, it is also trying to find solutions to problems it has identified in its environment or in its internal operations. To further complicate the decision-making process, different coalitions of decision makers may champion different alternatives and compete for resources to implement their own chosen solutions. Thus decision making becomes like a "garbage can" in which problems, solutions, and the preferences of different individuals and coalitions all mix and contend with one another for organizational attention and action. In this situation, an organization becomes an organized anarchy in which the selection of alternatives depends on which coalition's or senior manager's definition of the situation holds sway at the moment.[26] Chance, luck, and timing are important determinants of what the organization decides to do; because the problem that is currently the major source of uncertainty facing the organization has the best chance of being dealt with. Outcomes for the organization become more uncertain than usual, and decision making becomes fluid, unpredictable, and even contradictory.

The reality of decision making in organizations is clearly a far cry from the process described by the rational model. Instead of benefiting from the wisdom of all-knowing managers generating all possible solutions and agreeing on the best one so that decisions can be programmed over time, real organizations are forced to make unprogrammed decisions in an unstructured, garbage-can-like way in order to deal with the uncertainty of the environment that surrounds them. The way in which Microsoft dealt with the Netscape challenge is instructive in this respect, as discussed in Organizational Insight 12.2.

In summary, decision making drives the operation of an organization. At the core of every organization is a set of decision-making rules and routines that bring stability and allow the organization to reproduce its structure, activities, and core competencies over time. These routines provide the organization with a memory and provide managers with programmed solutions to problems, which in turn increase organizational effectiveness.[27] However, as we saw in Chapter 11, routines also can give rise to inertia. If an organization gets in a rut and cannot make decisions that allow it to change and adapt to and modify its environment, it may fail and die. To prevent this from happening, managers need to encourage organizational learning.

THE NATURE OF ORGANIZATIONAL LEARNING

Because decision making takes place in an uncertain environment, it is not surprising that many of the decisions that managers and employees in organizations make are mistakes and end in failure. Others, of course, allow the organization to adapt to the environment and to succeed beyond the decision makers' wildest dreams. Organizations survive and prosper when correct decisions are made—sometimes through skill and sound judgment, sometimes through chance and good luck. For decision making to be successful over time, organizations must improve their ability to learn new behaviours and unlearn inefficient old ones. One of the most important processes that helps decision makers to make better nonprogrammed decisions—decisions that allow them to adapt to, modify, and change the environment to increase an organization's chances of survival—is organizational learning.[28] **Organizational learning** is the process through which the organization seeks to improve organizational members' desire and ability to understand and manage the organization and its environment so that they make decisions that continuously raise organizational effectiveness.[29]

Organizational learning The process through which organizations seek to improve organizational members' capacity to understand and manage the organization and its environment so that they can make decisions that continuously raise organizational effectiveness.

Today, organizational learning is a vital process for organizations to manage because of the rapid pace of change affecting every organization. As previous chapters have discussed, organizations are racing to develop new and improved core competencies that can give them a competitive advantage. They are fighting to respond to the low-cost competitive challenges from foreign organizations. They are searching for every opportunity to use advanced materials technology and information systems to more effectively pursue their strategies and manage their structures. Indeed, the

ORGANIZATIONAL INSIGHT 12.2

Microsoft Is Not All-Seeing After All

The success of Microsoft might lead to a belief that Bill Gates and his managers possess some superhuman ability to predict the future and thus make the choices that will lead it to dominate in most segments of the computer market in which it competes. While there is no doubt that Microsoft has many talented managers, indeed it employs several "futurists" whose only job is to try to predict how the future of the software industry will evolve, it has nevertheless found itself caught unaware by changes in the environment at several points in its history. The way in which it confronted the challenge from Netscape in the Internet browser market is one of these.

Microsoft, like most other large computer companies, was aware of developments in the Internet and the importance of the growing World Wide Web in the 1990s. Indeed, it began its MSN Internet service to provide consumers access to the Web and to provide information and entertainment content for customers. However, Microsoft's managers had a vision of the Internet as a thing that they could control through the MSN network. They believed the typical customer would be happy to come to Microsoft for service and thus they could actually control the way the Web developed over time. This belief proved totally erroneous because of the speed at which the Web was growing and developing and the many avenues customers could use to gain access to the Web and to its content.

What shocked Microsoft most was the introduction, by Netscape, of its first Web browser at the end of 1994, which made it easy for people to surf the Web and to explore its potential. The Netscape browser was hugely popular and by the summer of 1995 it enjoyed an 80 percent market share. Microsoft had no such product under development, although it had been warned by two low-level programmers of the threat that Microsoft faced because of its arrogant stance with regard to developing its proprietary MSN service.

In a classic example of garbage-can thinking, in the fall of 1994 Bill Gates decided that the fate of Microsoft hung on the development of its own Web browser—this was the solution to its survival. He mobilized over half of the company's software resources to counter this threat. Hundreds of teams of programmers were created and were instructed to take apart the Netscape browser; each was to focus on developing one part of the new browser software. Their task was to produce a Microsoft browser clone that would be compatible with its new Windows 95 operating system, due for release in 1995.

At record-breaking speed these teams worked to develop the new browser software; cost was no object—survival was the goal. In August 1995, less than one year after the Netscape revolution, Microsoft had its own browser, Internet Explorer, and thereafter Microsoft used its enormous market power to promote its browser and to crush Netscape. Microsoft's decision to give its browser away free, something made possible because of its control of the operating and applications market, effectively made it impossible for Netscape to become profitable. Internet Explorer's market share increased rapidly and Netscape was bought and integrated into AOL in November 1998.

The power of Microsoft is its ability to marshal its enormous resources to address and solve potential problems and threats once it knows what the solution is. Faced with this juggernaut, many small companies that lead in different segments of the software market are happy to be bought by Microsoft and absorbed into its operations rather than to suffer the fate of Netscape.

increasing tendency of organizations to experiment with restructuring and re-engineering that occurred in the 1990s was motivated by the realization that organizations must learn new ways to operate more efficiently if they are to survive. Consequently, managers and employees must understand how organizational learning occurs and those factors that can promote or impede it.

Types of Organizational Learning

In studying organizational learning, James March has proposed that two principal types of organizational learning strategies can be pursued: exploration and exploitation.[30] **Exploration** involves organizational members searching for and experimenting with new kinds or forms of organizational activities and procedures to increase effectiveness. Exploration usually involves unprogrammed activities. Learning through exploration might involve finding new ways of managing the environment—such as experimenting with the use of strategic alliances and network organizations—or inventing new kinds of organizational structures for managing organizational resources—such as product team structures and cross-functional teams.

Exploration
Organizational members' search for and experimentation with new kinds or forms of organizational activities and procedures.

Exploitation involves organizational members learning ways to refine and improve existing organizational activities and procedures in order to increase effectiveness. Exploitation usually starts with the programmed or routine activities in an organization. Learning through exploitation might involve implementing a total quality management program to promote the continuous refinement of existing operating procedures, or developing an improved set of rules to perform specific kinds of functional activities more effectively. Exploration is therefore a more radical learning process than exploitation, although both are important in increasing organizational effectiveness.[31]

Exploitation
Organizational members' learning of ways to refine and improve existing organizational procedures.

A **learning organization** is an organization that purposefully designs and constructs its structure, culture, and strategy so as to enhance and maximize the potential for organizational learning (explorative and exploitative) to take place.[32] How do organizations create and foster a learning organization, one capable of allowing its members to appreciate and respond quickly to changes taking place around it? By increasing the ability of employees, at every level in the organization, to question and analyze the way an organization currently performs its activities and especially to experiment with new ways to change it to increase effectiveness.

Learning organization
An organization that purposefully designs and constructs its structure, culture, and strategy so as to enhance and maximize the potential for organizational learning to take place.

Levels of Organizational Learning

In order to create a successful learning organization, managers and employees need to encourage and engage in learning at four levels: individual, group, organizational, and interorganizational[33] (see Figure 12-2). Some principles for creating a learning organization at each level have been developed by Peter Senge and are discussed below.[34]

Individual At the individual level, organizational members need to do all they can to facilitate the learning of new skills, norms, and values so that individuals can increase their own personal skills and abilities and thereby help build the organization's core competencies. Senge has argued that for organizational learning to occur, each person in an organization needs to develop a sense of *personal mastery,* by which he means that organizations should empower individuals and allow them to experiment and create and explore what they want. The goal is to give employees the opportunity to develop an intense appreciation for their work that translates into a distinctive competency for the organization. As part of attaining personal mastery, and to give employees a deeper understanding of what is involved in a particular activity, organi-

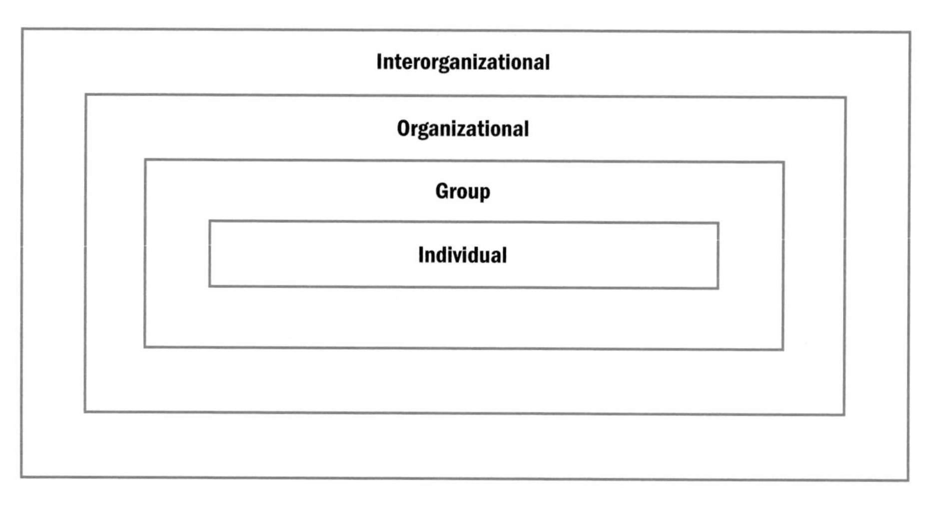

FIGURE 12-2
Levels of Organizational Learning.
To create a learning organization, managers must use systems thinking and recognize the effects of one level of learning on another.

zations need to encourage employees to develop and use complex *mental models* that challenge them to find new or better ways of performing a task. To give an analogy, a person might mow the lawn once a week and treat this as a chore that has to be done. However, suppose the person decides to study how the grass grows and to experiment with cutting the grass to different heights and using different fertilizers and watering patterns. Through this study, he or she notices that cutting the grass to a certain height and using specific combinations of fertilizer and water promote thicker growth and fewer weeds, resulting in a better-looking lawn that needs less mowing. What had originally been a chore was transformed through learning and new knowledge into a hobby and the personal mastery achieved from the new way of looking at the task may become a source of deep personal satisfaction. This is the message behind Senge's first principle for developing a learning organization—namely, organizations must encourage each of their individual members to develop a similar commitment and attachment to their jobs so that they will develop a taste for experimenting and risk taking.[35]

A learning organization can encourage employees to form complex mental models and develop a sense of personal mastery by providing them with the opportunity to assume more responsibility for their decisions. This can be done in a variety of different ways. Employees might be cross-trained so that they can perform many different tasks, and the knowledge that they gain may give them new insight into how to improve work procedures. On the other hand, perhaps a specific task that was performed by several different workers can be redesigned or reengineered so that one worker, aided by an advanced information system, can perform the complete task. Again, the result may be an increase in the level of organizational learning as the employee finds new ways to get the job done. Recall that one of the aims of re-engineering is to fundamentally rethink basic business processes. Re-engineering is mostly concerned with promoting organizational learning.

Group At the group level, organizations need to encourage learning by promoting the use of various kinds of groups—such as self-managed groups, cross-functional teams, or (as we saw in Chapter 9) production cells—so that individuals can share or pool their skills and abilities to solve problems. Groups allow for the creation of synergism—the idea that the whole is much more than the sum of its parts—which can enhance performance. In terms of Thompson's model of task interdependence discussed in Chapter 9, for example, the move from a pooled, to a sequential, to a reciprocal form of task interdependence will increase the potential for synergism and group-level learning because group members have more opportunity to interact and learn from one another over time. "Group routines" and "shared pools of collective meaning" that enhance group effectiveness may develop from such group interactions.[36] Senge refers to this kind of learning as *team learning* and he argues that team learning is more important than individual-level learning in promoting organizational learning because most important decisions are made in subunits such as groups, functions, and divisions.

The ability of teams to bring about organizational learning was unmistakable when Toyota revolutionized the work process in the former GM factory discussed in Organizational Insight 10.6 (p. 347). Large performance gains were achieved in the factory when Toyota's managers created work teams and empowered team members to take over the responsibility for measuring, monitoring, and controlling their own behaviour to find ways continuously to increase performance. The power of teams to bring about organizational learning is also revealed in another of Toyota's attempts to increase effectiveness.

Experimenting with ways to increase technical efficiency, Toyota decided to produce cars in fully roboticized factories embodying the latest, most advanced manufacturing technology. As a result, when it built a new manufacturing plant in Kyoto, Toyota's engineers focused on perfecting the plant's materials technology, and the consideration of factory employees was secondary to the requirements for automation. Within a few years, however, it had become clear to Toyota's managers that the new technology had not produced the large performance gains that they had expected. Why? According to Toyota, the new factories had eliminated the opportunity for team learning; factory employees were neither asked nor expected to contribute their ideas for improving efficiency. Computers are only as good as the people who program them, and programmers were not the ones working on the production line. Toyota has since junked its fully roboticized factories, and in its new factories it has made sure that people in teams can contribute their knowledge and skills to increase effectiveness.

Organization At the organizational level, managers can promote organizational learning through the way they create an organization's structure and culture. An organization's structure can be designed to inhibit or facilitate intergroup communication and problem solving, and this affects team members' approach to learning. Mechanistic and organic structures, for example, encourage different approaches to learning. The design of a mechanistic structure seems likely to facilitate exploitative learning, while the design of an organic structure seems more likely to facilitate explorative learning. Indeed, organizations need to strike a balance between a mechanistic and an organic structure in order to take advantage of both types of learning.

Culture, too, is likely to be an important influence on learning at the organizational level. Another of Senge's principles for designing a learning organization emphasizes the importance of *building shared vision,* by which he means building the ongoing frame of reference or mental model that all organizational members use to frame problems or opportunities and that binds them to an organization. At the heart of this vision is likely to be the set of terminal and instrumental values and norms that guide behaviour in a particular setting and that affect the way people interact with individuals and groups outside an organization, that is, organizational culture. Thus yet another important aspect of organizational culture is its ability to promote or inhibit organizational learning and change.

Indeed, in a study of 207 companies, John Kotter and James Heskett distinguished between adaptive cultures and inert cultures in terms of their ability to facili-

Adaptive cultures
Cultures that value innovation and encourage and reward experimentation and risk-taking by middle and lower-level managers.

Inert cultures
Cultures that are cautious and conservative, and do not encourage risk-taking by middle and lower-level managers.

tate organizational learning.[37] **Adaptive cultures** are those that value innovation and encourage and reward experimenting and risk taking by middle and lower-level managers. **Inert cultures** are those that are cautious and conservative, do not value middle and lower-level managers taking such action, and, indeed, may actively discourage such behaviour. According to Kotter and Heskett, organizational learning is higher in organizations with adaptive cultures because managers can quickly introduce changes in the way the organization operates that allow the organization to adapt to changes occurring in the environment. This does not occur in organizations with inert cultures. As a result, organizations with adaptive cultures are more likely to survive in a changing environment and, indeed, should have higher performance than organizations with inert cultures—exactly what Kotter and Heskett found.

Interorganizational Organizational structure and culture not only establish the shared vision or framework of common assumptions that guide learning inside an organization, but also determine how learning takes place at the interorganizational level. For example, organizations with organic, adaptive cultures are more likely to actively seek out new ways to manage interorganizational linkages with other organizations while mechanistic, inert cultures are slower to recognize or to take advantage of new kinds of linkage mechanisms.

In general, interorganizational learning is important because organizations can improve their effectiveness by copying and imitating each other's distinctive competencies. The last chapter discussed how mimetic, coercive, and normative processes encourage organizations to learn from each other in order to increase their legitimacy, but this can also increase their effectiveness. In the automobile industry, for example, Japanese car manufacturers came to the United States after World War II to learn U.S. manufacturing methods and took this knowledge back to Japan where they improved upon it. This process was then reversed in the 1980s when struggling U.S. carmakers went to Japan to learn about the advances that Japanese carmakers had pioneered, took this knowledge back to the U.S., and improved upon it.

Similarly, organizations can encourage explorative and exploitative learning by cooperating with their suppliers and distributors to find new and improved ways of handling inputs and outputs. Enterprise-wide IT systems, business-to-business networks, strategic alliances, and network organizations are important vehicles for increasing the speed at which new learning takes place because they open up the organization to the environment and give organizational members new opportunities to experiment, learn, and find new ways to increase effectiveness.

In fact, Senge's fifth principle of organizational learning, *systems thinking*, emphasizes that in order to create a learning organization, managers must recognize the effects of one level of learning on another. Thus, for example, there is little point in creating teams to facilitate team learning if an organization does not also take steps to give its employees the freedom to develop a sense of personal mastery. Similarly, the nature of interorganizational learning is likely to be affected by the kind of learning going on inside an organization.

By encouraging and promoting organizational learning at each of these four levels—that is, by looking at organizational learning as a system—managers can create a learning organization that facilitates an organization's quick response to the changes in the environment that are constantly taking place around it. To enhance an organization's ability to create value, managers and employees need to promote both explorative and exploitative learning and then use this learning in ways that will promote organizational effectiveness. Managers need to recognize, however, that empowering employees, allowing teams to take control of their own activities, and creating an organic, adaptive organization all expose an organization to risk. Risk increases because the explorative learning that takes place may disrupt taken-for-granted routines and assumptions so that managers have to carefully manage the changes taking place (an issue discussed in Chapter 13). On the other hand, very often the problem is not too *much* learning taking place but too *little*. Several factors may impede organizational learning, and when this happens the quality of decision making falls and organizational effectiveness suffers. In the next section an important technique for promoting organizational learning, knowledge management, is discussed. Then the many factors that may impede learning are examined.

KNOWLEDGE MANAGEMENT AND INFORMATION TECHNOLOGY

As we have seen in previous chapters, new information technologies are having profound effects on the way an organization operates. IT-enabled organizational structures allow for new kinds of tasks and job reporting relationships among electronically connected people that promote superior communication and coordination. One type of IT-enabled organizational relationship that has important implications for both organizational learning and decision making is **knowledge management**, the sharing and integrating of expertise within and between functions and divisions through real-time, interconnected IT.[38] To understand the importance of knowledge management, consider how Telus, profiled in Organizational Insight 12.3, has a developing knowledge management system that evolved from a communication need, in order to make internal improvements, to a systematic way to manage the firm's operations and to better serve its clientele.

Knowledge management
A type of IT-enabled organizational relationship that has important implications for both organizational learning and decision making.

As the example of Telus suggests, one important benefit from developing and utilizing a knowledge management system is the potential of synergies it can afford to people and groups. The increase of synergies across groups within an organization, or between an organization and outside stakeholders such as customers, maximizes the potential for the application of organizational knowledge. This may result in competitive advantage in the form of product or service differentiation. Unlike more rigid bureaucratic organizing methods, IT-enabled organizations can respond more quickly to changing environmental conditions such as increased global competition.

What kind of knowledge management system should managers design for their organizations? Is the same kind of system suitable for all kinds of organizations? Or would we expect organizations with a more mechanistic or organic orientation to develop and adopt different kinds of systems?

Knowledge Management: Codification versus Personalization One solution to this question has been proposed by Hansen, Nohria, and Tierney, who argue that organizations should choose between a codification or personalization approach to creating an IT-based knowledge management system.[39] With a *codification approach,* knowledge is carefully collected, analyzed, and stored in databases where it can be retrieved easily by users who input organization-specific commands and keywords. Essentially, a codification approach results in collection of standardized organization best practices, rules, and SOPs that can be drawn upon by anyone who needs them. It is a form of bureaucratic control than can result in major gains in technical efficiency and allow an organization better to manage its environment. For example, Dell Computer uses an advanced in-house codification approach to manage its transactions with its global suppliers. All suppliers have access to Dell's knowledge management system, which

ORGANIZATIONAL INSIGHT 12.3

Developing Knowledge Management Capability at Telus[40]

Telus, one of the largest telecommunications companies in Canada, has annual revenues of roughly $7 billion, almost 5 million network access lines, and 4 million wireless subscribers. The company employs approximately 24 000 people and has offices in all major centres across Canada. While the company utilizes advanced network technologies and offers a full range of telecommunications products and services to its customers, the company itself has been using these technologies to improve its own internal communications.

As Telus began to grow and make acquisitions, it needed to contend with the task of melding together a more cohesive organizational culture. To do so, the firm had to strategically align the efforts of all its employees. Past communications audits showed that even when the company became fully Web-enabled, many of its employees were still not regularly communicating. This meant that knowledge, solutions, and the practical know-how of employees were not being adequately shared. In order to get employees communicating, the CEO began to write weekly e-mails to all staff, and a virtual CEO mailbox was set up to demonstrate the CEO's interest in receiving feedback from employees at all levels. After a few years of development, the CEO mailbox evolved into a comprehensive internal communication management process. It has become a reliable process for tracking, analyzing, and compiling information from employees' online correspondence. The CEO mailbox process is now managed daily and programming has been set up to identify and classify e-mail correspondence as negative, positive, neutral, constructive, or critical. The reporting, management, and display processes of the system itself have been developed so that yearly changes can be detected. There also is a password-protected Web site for the summary analysis report, graphic representations, and hot-linked letters from employees. The e-mail address for the CEO mailbox was also passed on to customers, so there is a comprehensive collection of information that was developing into knowledge management processes. Not only did this system have a profound transforming effect on the organizational culture, but the information generated by employees and customers is allowing Telus to increase internal effectiveness and efficiency of operations and to provide better service to its customers. As Telus knowledge is aggregated, analyzed, and moved around within the firm, to as many employees as possible regardless of level or location, Telus is reaping the advantages of knowing more about itself, its operations, and its clientele.

gives them real-time access to its changing input demands, and allows them to forecast demand for their products months in advance and to redesign their products so they will fit better with Dell's future needs. The cost savings that have resulted from this system have been tremendous and have made Dell and its suppliers the low-cost leaders in the PC industry.

A codification approach, however, is only suitable when the product or service being provided is itself quite standardized so that best practices can continually be discovered and entered into the knowledge management system to be used by others in the organization. It works best when the different functions in the organization are able to provide standardized information—about changing customer demands or product specifications, for example—that provides vital input to other functions so that the level of mutual adjustment and learning between functions increases, resulting in major gains in effectiveness. In this sense, a knowledge management system allows an organization with a more mechanistic structure to react in a more "organic" fashion, albeit the flexibility is provided by new, sophisticated IT protocols based on the codification of standardized organizational knowledge.

By contrast, a *personalization approach* to knowledge management is pursued when an organization needs to provide customized products or solutions to clients, when technology is changing rapidly, and when employees rely much more on know-how, insight, and judgment to make decisions. In these cases, it is very difficult (often impossible) to write down or even verbalize a course of action that leads to a solution. Often, the solution results from mutual adjustments between people, such as occurs in the intensive technology described in Chapter 9.

In a personalization approach, information systems are designed to show employees who in the organization might possess the knowledge they might need or who might have confronted a similar problem in the past. In a consulting company such as Accenture, for example, individual consultants will write up synopses of the ways they have solved client problems, and the nature of these problems, so that others in the organization can gain a sense of what they are doing. Working in teams, consultants can also spread their knowledge across the organization, often globally, and IT is used to facilitate direct interactions between people and the exchange of know-how by informing employees about upcoming seminars and visiting internal experts, for example.

Over time, as an organization like Accenture confronts more examples of a similar type of problem, consultants can increasingly codify this informal know-how into best practices that can be shared more widely throughout the organization. An organization's information system plays an especially crucial role, for competitive success depends on the speed with which it can provide clients with a state-of-the-art solution to their problems. And given that software is advancing all the time, such solutions change continually. An organization's ability to provide a quick, customized solution, and to translate this rapidly into best practices, will often depend on the degree to which it is *specialized*—for example, by industry or product or service—and therefore deals with a narrower and deeper range of problems. That is why so many small specialized software and consulting computer companies exist.

Knowledge management is therefore an important tool for increasing the level of integration inside an organization, among people, functions, and even divisions. Since the 1990s many companies have moved to develop electronic knowledge management systems to speed learning and decision making, and for many of them it has resulted in success. It is important to remember, however, that knowledge management is expensive; people must be employed to help digitize knowledge and disseminate it throughout the organization. Today, so much information is available to managers through IT systems that an organization can be literally swamped in it, and the process of discovering the best practices and solutions requires a lot of search activity and personal judgment in its own right. While organizations engaging in knowledge management practices have saved hundreds of millions of dollars by implementing knowledge management systems, they also are spending hundreds of millions to maintain these systems. Organizations must always compare the benefits and costs of using IT and knowledge management to facilitate learning, and over time modify them to suit changing conditions.

FACTORS AFFECTING ORGANIZATIONAL LEARNING

While knowledge management can enhance organizational learning, a model that illustrates several factors that may actually *reduce* the level of learning over time has been developed by Paul C. Nystrom and William H. Starbuck. This model illustrates how problems may arise that prevent an organization from learning and adapting to its environment and that therefore cause an organizational crisis to emerge.[41] Nystrom and Starbuck define a crisis as any situation that seriously threatens an organization's survival.

According to Nystrom and Starbuck, as organizations learn to make decisions, they develop rules and standard operating procedures that facilitate programmed decision making. If an organization achieves success by using its standard procedures, this success may lead to complacency and deter managers from searching for and learning from new experiences.[42] Thus past (successful) learning can inhibit new learning and lead to organizational inertia. If programmed decision making drives out nonprogrammed decision making, the level of organizational learning drops. Blindness and rigidity in organizational decision making may then set in and lead to a full-blown crisis.

Managers often discount warnings that problems are impending and do not perceive that crises are developing. Even if they notice, they may attribute the source of the problems to temporary disturbances in the environment and implement what Nystrom and Starbuck call "weathering-the-storm strategies," such as postponing investments, downsizing the workforce, or centralizing decision making and reducing the autonomy of people at low levels in the organization. Managers adopt this incrementalist approach to decision making because sticking to what they know (exploitive learning) is much safer than setting off in new directions (explorative learning) where consequences are unknown. Managers continue to rely on the information obtained from their existing operating routines to solve problems—information that does not reveal the real nature of the problems they are experiencing.

Another reason why past learning inhibits new organizational learning is that managers' mindsets or cognitive structures shape their perception and interpretation of problems and solutions. A **cognitive structure** is the system of interrelated beliefs, preferences, expectations, and values that a person uses to define problems and events.[43] In an organization, cognitive structures reveal themselves in plans, goals, stories, myths, and jargon. Cognitive structures shape the way a CEO or members of the top-management team make decisions, they predetermine what managers perceive as opportunities and threats in the environment, and they determine the perceived roles and expectations of employees at all levels. Any two managers (or two top-management teams) or group of employees, for example, might perceive the same "objective" environment very differently because of differences in their cognitive structures.

Cognitive structure
The system of interrelated beliefs, preferences, expectations, and values that a person uses to define problems and events.

A classic example of how cognitive structure influences decision making occurred in the United States after World War II, when the then-dominant retailer stores Sears Roebuck and Montgomery Ward were planning their postwar strategies. The top-management team at Sears believed that there would be a boom in consumer spending after the war and that the environment was very favourable for large-scale investment and expansion. Managers at Sears set out to establish a nationwide store system to take advantage of the anticipated surge in demand. Managers at Montgomery Ward interpreted the environment differently. They believed that consumers would save their money. Consequently, Montgomery Ward's postwar expansion program was much smaller and less ambitious than Sears's. After the war, consumer spending boomed, and the environment became richer and richer. Sears could take advantage of this change in the environment, but Montgomery Ward could not. As a result, Sears grew to become the dominant retailer of the 1960s.

Just as top managers' cognitive structures can produce successful learning, they can also cause a crisis. During the early 1990s, for example, Sears was unable to respond to the challenges posed by the new retailing environment because it relied on past learning to make new business decisions (an incrementalist approach to decision making). Sears's decisions have been shown to be inferior to those made by Wal-Mart, for example, whose top-management team has made the best predictions about customer demands for low-cost retailing since the 1980s. Why do top managers often cling to outdated ideas and use inappropriate cognitive structures to interpret events and problems—something that leads to faulty learning? It is useful to look at some factors that distort managers' perceptions and hinder organizational learning and decision making.

Organizational Learning and Cognitive Structures

As noted above, cognitive structures are the systems of beliefs, preferences, expectations, and values that develop over time and predetermine a person's responses to and interpretations of situations. When a decision maker confronts a problem, his or her cognitive structure shapes the interpretation of the information at hand; that is, the decision maker's view of a situation is shaped by prior experience and customary ways of thinking—by the decision maker's mindset.[44] That view, however, might be distorted.

Over many years, for example, the cognitive structures of IBM's top managers reinforced the idea that organizations needed mainframe computers to handle their information-processing needs. IBM, therefore, sought to develop core competencies in the design, manufacture, and servicing of mainframe computers. When desktop PCs became increasingly popular in the early 1980s, IBM viewed them as machines suitable only for managers' personal information-processing needs or as a way of linking managers to a mainframe. IBM did not regard personal computers as a serious alternative to the mainframe style of computer because its managers were fixated on the idea that mainframes, and only mainframes, could satisfy an organization's information-processing needs. When major advances in software and microchip technology allowed PCs to handle and store increasing volumes of information, IBM managers discounted these developments. The company searched for better ways to tie PCs into mainframes through networking, and it worked to improve the network capabilities of mainframe computers by developing new operating languages such as UNIX.

The cognitive structures of IBM managers led to a misinterpretation or undervaluing of new information. IBM's managers never recognized or discounted the threat that PCs posed and continued to operate as if mainframe computers would dominate the market forever. When events proved their view of the environment to be distorted, it was too late to take corrective action. IBM was in crisis. A new CEO, Lou Gerstner, was brought in to change the programmed routines and cognitive structures that were dominating and skewing decision making. His solution was to move IBM into the computer consulting business, and by 2002 IBM was making over 40 percent of its revenues from this new business. This new IBM approach only worked because it had changed the mindsets of its managers and employees.

Types of Cognitive Biases

Researchers have also identified several factors that lead managers to develop a cognitive structure that causes them to misperceive and misinterpret information. These factors are called **cognitive biases** because they systematically bias cognitive structures

Cognitive biases
Factors that systematically bias cognitive structures and affect organizational learning and decision making.

and affect organizational learning and decision making. As Figure 12-3 shows, cognitive biases affect the way individuals process information. Cognitive dissonance, illusion of control, and several other cognitive biases that influence organizational learning and decision making are discussed next and are illustrated by an examination of IBM's problems in changing its strategy and structure in the 1990s.[45]

Cognitive Dissonance

Cognitive dissonance The state of discomfort or anxiety that a person feels when there is an inconsistency between his or her beliefs and actions.

Cognitive dissonance is the state of discomfort or anxiety that a person feels when there is an inconsistency between his or her beliefs and actions. According to cognitive dissonance theory, decision makers try to maintain consistency between their images of themselves, their attitudes, and their decisions.[46] Managers seek or interpret information that confirms and reinforces their beliefs, and they ignore information that does not. Managers also tend to seek information that is only incrementally different from the information they already possess, and that therefore supports their established position.

Cognitive dissonance theory explains why managers tend to misinterpret the real threats facing an organization and attempt to muddle through even when it is clear to many observers that the organization is in crisis. The operation of this cognitive bias might help account for the faulty learning and decisions of IBM's top managers during the 1980s. Whenever they received outside information suggesting that PC research was threatening the viability of mainframes, they discounted it and relied on information that they had generated to support their own view of mainframes. The desire to reduce cognitive dissonance pushes organizational decision makers to adopt flawed incremental solutions. This approach is incrementalist, as decision makers rely on their received view of the situation, and consequently organizational learning potential is reduced as explorative learning has no opportunity to take place.

Illusion of Control

Some people, like entrepreneurs, seem able to bear high levels of uncertainty; others prefer the security associated with working in established organizations. Regardless of

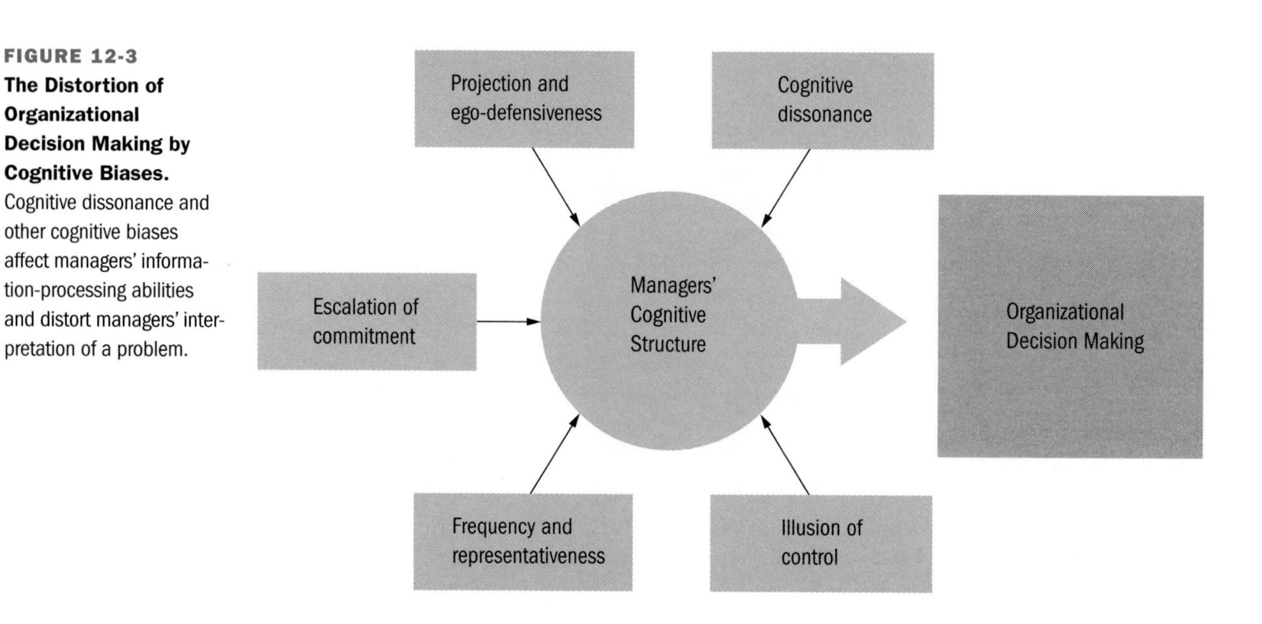

FIGURE 12-3 The Distortion of Organizational Decision Making by Cognitive Biases. Cognitive dissonance and other cognitive biases affect managers' information-processing abilities and distort managers' interpretation of a problem.

one's tolerance for ambiguity, however, uncertainty is very stressful. When an organization's environment or future is uncertain, decision makers do not know whether they have made the right choices, and considerable organizational resources are often at stake. Research has shown that managers can reduce their level of stress about uncertainty by strengthening their perception that they are in control of a situation.[47] Belief in one's personal ability to control uncertainty can reduce the level of stress one feels. However, as a manager's perception of control increases, the cognitive bias known as illusion of control alters his or her perceptions.

Illusion of control is a cognitive bias that causes managers to overestimate the extent to which the outcomes of an action are under their personal control and the extent to which they possess the skills and abilities needed to manage uncertainty and complexity.[48] In uncertain situations in which their ability and competence are really being tested, managers may develop irrational beliefs about their personal ability to manage uncertainty. They may, for example, overestimate their ability to use their skills in new ventures and embark on a huge acquisition program. Soon, however, they encounter problems and realize that they lack the ability to manage the more complex organization effectively.

Illusion of control
A cognitive bias that causes managers to overestimate the extent to which the outcomes of an action are under their personal control.

Very frequently, when top managers lose control, they try to centralize authority, in the mistaken belief that centralization will increase their control and allow them to turn the situation around. Because their perception of control is an illusion, the organizational crisis deepens. IBM, for example, finally established a PC division to produce and market personal computers. But the division never got the autonomy it needed to devise a strategy that would have allowed it to compete successfully with the various PC clone makers and respond to the frequent price cutting and discounting characteristic of the personal computer industry. Managers in the PC division were constantly overseen by IBM's top managers, who believed that they alone had the ability to control the division's strategy. Because they were blinded by the illusion of control, no organizational learning was taking place; the PC division's managers were unable to respond quickly to the moves of its competitors and were unable to develop a long-term strategy to give the division a strong competitive advantage.

It is not uncommon for a strong CEO or the members of an entrenched top-management team to develop the illusion that only they have the ability to manage the uncertainty facing the organization and to lead the organization to success, even when it is in crisis. When a CEO or top-management team suffers from this illusion and when they retain sole control for decision making in the organization, then organizational learning is not occurring across all levels; organizational learning literally stops, and the consequences are usually severe as the organization can no longer respond well to the changing environment.

Frequency and Representativeness

Frequency and representativeness are tendencies that often lead people to misinterpret information.[49] **Frequency** is a cognitive bias that deceives people into assuming that extreme instances of a phenomenon are more prevalent than they really are. Suppose purchasing managers have had a particularly bad experience with a supplier that has been shipping them large quantities of defective goods. Because of severe manufacturing problems caused by the defective parts, the managers decide to sever relations with that supplier. The frequency bias may cause them to become very fearful of relying on other suppliers for their inputs. They may instead decide to vertically integrate their operations so that they control their inputs, even though vertical integration will increase costs. Although there is no rational reason to believe that a new

Frequency
A cognitive bias that deceives people into assuming that extreme instances of a phenomenon are more prevalent than they really are.

supplier will be as bad as, or worse than, the rejected supplier, the managers jump to an expensive solution to avoid the risk, as faulty organizational learning has occurred.

Representativeness
A cognitive bias that leads managers to form judgments based on small and unrepresentative samples.

Representativeness is a cognitive bias that leads managers to form judgments based on small and unrepresentative samples. Exposure to a couple of unreliable suppliers, for example, prompts managers to generalize and believe that all suppliers are untrustworthy and unreliable, again leading to faulty organizational learning.

Frequency and representative biases can also work in the opposite direction. A company that has great success with a new product may come to believe that this product is the wave of the future and devote all its resources to developing a new product line for which there actually is little demand. FedEx, for example, believed that the demand for international express delivery would increase dramatically as companies became increasingly global. It came to this conclusion because it had been receiving more and more requests for international delivery. Federal Express thus decided to invest a huge amount of resources to buy and operate a fleet of planes and overseas facilities to handle global express delivery. The decision was a disaster. The volume of express packages shipped to Europe turned out to be only half of that shipped domestically, and the cost of operating the new global structure was enormous. After major losses, Federal Express decided to form strategic alliances with foreign delivery companies to deliver the mail (rather than go it alone), and this new strategy has been successful. As this example shows, a bad decision can be made because a CEO and top-management team overgeneralize from a limited range of knowledge and experience. The operation of many of these cognitive biases can be seen in the story of e-grocers like Webvan, some of the thousands of dot-com companies that failed because of their managers' mistaken beliefs about the ease of operating virtual companies and developing viable business models that were heavily technologically based. (See Organizational Insight 12.4.)

Projection and Ego-Defensiveness

Projection
A cognitive bias that allows managers to justify and reinforce their own preferences and values by attributing them to others.

Projection is a cognitive bias that allows managers to justify and reinforce their own preferences and values by attributing them to others.[50] Suppose a top-management team is dominated by managers who are threatened by a deteriorating economic situation and doubt their ability to manage it. Feeling threatened and powerless, the team may accuse other lower-level managers of being unable to control the situation or of lacking the ability or desire to do so. Thus top managers project their own feelings of helplessness onto others and blame them. Obviously, when projection starts to operate, it can become self-reinforcing: Everybody blames everybody else, and the culture of the organization deteriorates into one of blame shifting and organizational learning stops.

Ego-defensiveness
A cognitive bias that leads managers to interpret events in such a way that their actions appear in the most favourable light.

Ego-defensiveness also affects the way managers interpret what is happening in the organization. **Ego-defensiveness** is a cognitive bias that leads managers to interpret events in such a way that their actions appear in the most favourable light. If an organization is employing more and more managers but profitability is not increasing, managers may emphasize that they are positioning the organization for future growth by putting in place the infrastructure to support future development, such as happened at Webvan and the other e-grocers. Ego-defensiveness results in little organizational learning, and this type of faulty decision making ultimately may lead to a manager's replacement or to an organization's failure.

Escalation of Commitment

The bias toward escalation of commitment is another powerful cause of flawed learning and faulty decision making.[51] According to the Carnegie model of decision mak-

ORGANIZATIONAL INSIGHT 12.4

Mistakes and More Mistakes at the E-grocers

The potential uses of information technology and the Internet for improving responsiveness to customers became clear to companies in many industries in the late 1990s. One of these industries was the food-delivery or supermarket industry. Entrepreneurs decided that developing an online ordering system that allowed customers to use the Internet to order their food online and creating a production system to deliver the food to their homes had enormous potential. For example, virtual grocer Webvan raised more than US$1 billion to develop both the information system and physical infrastructure of warehouses and hot-and-cold delivery trucks that it needed to deliver food to customers. Other competitors like GroceryWorks.com and Homegrocer.com made similar kinds of investments. These online stores did attract customers, and by 2000 they had more than US$1 billion in sales.

Bricks-and-mortar (B&M) supermarkets watched with some trepidation as their online rivals developed and managed their operations. By 2001, the question of which operating model was going to be the most successful was settled when many of the online grocers like Webvan announced that they were going out of business because of mounting losses. Why?

First, the new e-grocers did not possess the experience and ability to master the complex inventory management, sourcing, transportation, distribution, warehousing, and logistics necessary to operate successfully in this market, unlike their well-established B&M rivals. Second, e-grocers had totally underestimated the problems and costs of operating the production and physical delivery service necessary to get products to customers. The average cost of home delivery for Webvan and other grocers was around US$30, a cost they could not pass on to the customers they were trying to attract.

Managers at the e-grocers had totally overestimated their ability to manage the value-chain activities necessary to get products to customers. In other words, they suffered from the illusion of control bias in believing they had the skills to manage what is a very complex organization. E-grocers had also totally underestimated the complexity of their operating environment because of their misplaced confidence in the power of the Internet. In retrospect it is clear that dot-com entrepreneurs had watched other new startups and had suffered from the frequency and representativeness biases in overestimating how many of these startups were successes and how easy a virtual business model is to operate. It is also interesting that dot-com companies also rarely gave up the battle until their resources were completely exhausted and their shareholders would lend no new money, since the value of their stock was plunging. This situation might be explained by the operation of the cognitive biases discussed here.

ing, managers generate a limited number of alternative courses of action, from which they choose one that they hope will lead to a satisfactory (if not optimum) outcome. But what happens if they choose the wrong course of action and experience a negative outcome, such as when FedEx found itself losing enormous amounts of money as a result of its international express delivery venture? A logical response to a negative outcome would be a re-evaluation of the course of action. Research, however, indicates

Escalation of commitment A cognitive bias that leads managers to remain committed to a losing course of action and refuse to admit that they have made a mistake.

that managers who have made an investment in a mistake tend to persist in the same behaviour and increase their commitment to it, even though it is leading to poor returns and organizational ineffectiveness. **Escalation of commitment** is a cognitive bias that leads managers to remain committed to a losing course of action, and to refuse to admit that they have made a mistake, perhaps because of ego-defensiveness or because they are gripped by the illusion of control. In later decision making, they try to correct and improve on their prior (bad) decision rather than acknowledge that they have made a mistake and turn to a different course of action. Fortunately at FedEx, for example, the CEO realized the error and quickly moved to redeploy resources to make the international express delivery venture viable, and he succeeded.

At IBM, by contrast, managers' commitment to their conceptualization of the viability of mainframe computers escalated even though the market for mainframes was shrinking. Top managers at IBM refused to redeploy significant organizational resources to develop skills in servers and PCs. They continued to invest resources to improve mainframes and continued to try to position them as the technology of the future. IBM spent billions of dollars to improve the storage and information processing capacity of mainframe computers instead of finding new ways to take advantage of IBM's skills and resources.

The bias toward escalation of commitment is clearly reinforced by an incrementalist approach to decision making. Managers prefer to modify existing decisions to make them fit better with new conditions rather than to work out new solutions. Although this method of decision making may work in stable environments, it is disastrous when technology or competition is rapidly changing. This is why organizations need to find a balance between levels of effort associated with explorative and exploitative learning strategies. They must be matched to the environment within which the organization must operate, and they must be changed when the environment changes.

The net effect of all of the cognitive biases is that organizations may lose their ability to see new problems or situations clearly and to devise new responses to new challenges—and the level of learning falls. The flawed decision making that results from these biases hampers an organization's ability to adapt and modify its environment. By hampering organizational learning, biased decision making threatens an organization's ability to grow and survive. What can an organization do to develop a less incremental and more unstructured approach to decision making? How can it make managers receptive to learning new solutions and to challenging the assumptions they use to make decisions? Nystrom and Starbuck argue that when organizational learning and decision making are seriously affected by out-of-date or wrong cognitive structures, only radical actions can correct the situation and bring the organization back on the path to success.[52] Research has suggested several steps that managers and organizations can take to raise the level of organizational learning and promote organizational change.

IMPROVING DECISION MAKING AND LEARNING

Organizational inertia and cognitive biases make it difficult to promote organizational learning and maintain the quality of organizational decision making over time. How can managers avoid using inappropriate routines, beliefs, and values to interpret and solve problems? There are several ways in which an organization can overcome the effect of cognitive biases in order to promote organizational learning and change. It can implement strategies for organizational learning, increase the breadth and diversity of the top-management team, use devil's advocacy and dialectical inquiry to evaluate proposed solutions, utilize game theory, and develop a collateral organizational structure.

Strategies for Organizational Learning

Managers have to continuously unlearn old ideas and constantly test their decision-making skills by confronting errors in their beliefs and perceptions. Three ways in which they can stimulate the unlearning of old ideas (and the learning of new ones) are by listening to dissenters, by converting events into learning opportunities, and by experimenting.[53]

Listening to Dissenters To improve the quality of decision making, top managers can make it their policy to surround themselves with people who hold different and often opposing points of view. They can try to collect new information to evaluate the new interpretations and alternatives generated by these dissenters.

Unfortunately, research has shown that top managers often do not listen carefully to their subordinates and they also tend to surround themselves with "yes-men" who distort the information they provide, enhancing good news and suppressing bad news.[54] Moreover, because of the tendency to engage in bounded rationality, managers may be reluctant to encourage dissent because dissent will increase the amount of information they have to process and the amount of uncertainty they will have to deal with.

Converting Events into Learning Opportunities Nystrom and Starbuck discuss one unidentified company that appointed a "Vice President for Revolutions," whose job was to step in every four years and shake up the organization by transferring managers and reassigning responsibilities so that old, taken-for-granted routines were re-examined and people could bring new points of view to various situations. It did not make much difference what specific changes were made. The objective was to make them large enough so that people were forced to make new interpretations of situations. After each shake-up, productivity increased for two years and then declined for the next two, until the organization was shaken up again.[55]

More generally, an organization needs to design and manage its structure and culture—in ways that were discussed earlier—so that managers are motivated to find new or improved responses to a situation. Total quality management, for example, is based on the idea of making people responsible for continuously re-examining their jobs to see whether improvements that result in increased quality and productivity can be made. Similarly, as noted earlier, different kinds of organizational structure (e.g., mechanistic or organic) can encourage or discourage organizational learning.

An interesting study conducted in the U.S. when hospitals were jolted by a doctors' strike shows the influence of organizational culture in decision making. The study found that responses by hospitals to this crisis were strongly influenced by the way in which each hospital typically made decisions in uncertain situations.[56] Hospitals that had organic structures characterized by decentralized decision making and that frequently redesigned their structures were accustomed to both learning and unlearning. As a result, these hospitals dealt with the strike much better than did hospitals with centralized, mechanistic structures and a formalized, programmed approach to decision making.

Experimenting To encourage explorative learning, organizations must encourage experimenting, the process of generating new alternatives and testing the validity of old ones. Experimenting can be used to improve both incremental and garbage-can decision-making processes. To test new ways of behaving, such as new ways to serve customers or to manufacture a product, managers can run experiments that deviate only slightly from what the organization is currently doing. Or, taking a garbage-can approach, managers can brainstorm and come up with new solutions that surprise even themselves. Managers who are willing to experiment avoid overcommitment to previously worked-out solutions, reduce the likelihood of misinterpreting a situation, and can learn from their failures.

Utilizing Game Theory

As we have already discussed, organizations are in a constant competitive struggle with rivals in their industry to secure scarce resources. In understanding the dynamics of decision making between competitors in the environment, a useful tool that can help managers improve decision making and enhance learning is *game theory,* in which interactions between organizations are viewed as a competitive game. If companies understand the nature of the competitive game they are playing, they can often make better decisions that increase the likelihood of their obtaining scarce resources.[57]

From a game theory perspective, companies in an industry can be viewed as players that are all simultaneously making choices about which decisions to make that will maximize their effectiveness. The problem managers face is that the potential effectiveness of each decision they make—for example, of which competitive strategy they select—is not some "fixed or stable amount." What value they will get from making a certain choice—the payoff—will vary depending on the strategies that rivals also select. There are two basic types of game—sequential move games and simultaneous move games. In a *sequential move game,* such as chess, players move in turn, and one player can select a strategy to pursue after considering the rival's choice of strategies. In a *simultaneous move game,* the players act at the same time, in ignorance of their rival's current actions.

In the environment both sequential and simultaneous move games are commonplace, as managers compete for scarce resources. Indeed, game theory is particularly useful in analyzing situations where a company is competing against a limited number of rivals in its domain and they are highly interdependent—something very common in most environments. In such a setting, the value that can be created by making a certain choice—for example, to pursue a low cost or differentiation strategy—depends critically on the strategies pursued by rivals. The basic principles that underlie game theory can be useful in determining which choices to make and strategies to select to manage the environment.

A fundamental premise of game theory is that when making decisions managers need to think in two related ways. First, they need to look forward—think ahead and anticipate how rivals will respond to whatever might be their competitive moves. Second, managers need to reason backward to determine which moves their company should pursue today given their assessment of how their rivals will respond to various future moves. If managers do both these things, they should be able to make the decision that will lead to the best choice—to make the move that will lead to the greatest potential returns. This cardinal principle of game theory is known as *look forward and reason back:* to understand its importance, consider the following scenario.

UPS and FedEx, which specialize in the next-day delivery of packages, dominate the air express industry. They have very high costs because they need to invest in a capital-intensive network of aircraft, trucks, and package-sorting facilities. For these companies, the key to increasing their effectiveness is to attract more customers, growing volume so that they can reduce the average cost of transporting each package. Suppose a manager at UPS calculates that if UPS cuts prices for their next-day delivery service by 10 percent, the volume of packages they ship will grow by over 25 percent, and so will UPS's total revenues and profits. Is this a smart choice? The answer depends upon whether the manager has remembered to look forward and reason back and think through how FedEx would respond to UPS's price cuts.

Because UPS and FedEx are competing directly against each other, their choices are interdependent. If UPS cuts prices, FedEx will lose market share, its volume of shipments will decline, and its profits will suffer. FedEx is unlikely to accept this. Rather, if UPS cuts prices by 10 percent, FedEx is likely to follow, make the same choice and cut its prices by 10 percent to hold onto its customers. The net result is that the average level of prices in the industry will fall by 10 percent, as will revenues, and both players will see their profits decline and the environment will become poorer. To avoid this situation, and make better decisions, managers need always to look forward and reason back—an important principle of learning.

Decision trees can be used to help in the process of looking forward and reasoning back. Figure 12-4 maps out the decision tree for the simple game analyzed above from the perspective of UPS. (Note that this is a sequential move game.) UPS moves first, and then FedEx must decide how to respond. Here you see that UPS has to choose between two strategies, cutting prices by 10 percent or leaving them unchanged. If it leaves prices unchanged, it will continue to earn its current level of profitability, which is $100 million. If it cuts prices by 10 percent, one of two things can happen—FedEx matches the price cut, or FedEx leaves its prices unchanged. If FedEx matches UPS's price cut (FedEx decides to fight a price war), profits are competed away and UPS's profit will be $0. If FedEx does not respond, however, and leaves its prices unaltered, UPS will gain market share and its profits will rise to $300 million. So the best pricing strategy for UPS to pursue depends upon its assessment of FedEx's likely response.

You will note that Figure 12-4 assigns probabilities to the different responses from FedEx; specifically there is a 75 percent chance that FedEx will match UPS's price cut and a 25 percent chance that it will do nothing. These probabilities come from each company's assessment of the other's likely decision based on their past history of making decisions in the environment—from looking at the history of FedEx's responses to UPS's price moves and vice versa. Although both sets of managers cannot calculate exactly what the profit impact and probabilities would be, they make an

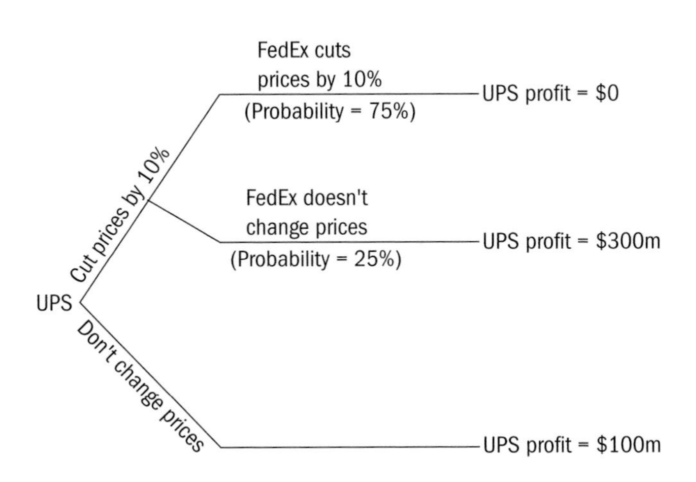

FIGURE 12-4
A Decision Tree for UPS's Pricing Strategy.

informed decision by collecting information and devoting resources to learning about their rivals and about the environment. This illustrates a second basic principle of game theory: Know thy rivals! To improve learning, managers must put themselves in the position of a rival to answer the question of how that rival is likely to act in a particular situation. If a company's managers are to be effective at looking forward and reasoning back, they must have a good understanding of what their rival is likely to do under different scenarios, and they need to be able to extrapolate their rival's future behaviour based on this understanding.

Nature of the Top-Management Team

The way the top-management team is constructed and the type of people who are on it affect the level of organizational learning.[58] There are various ways to construct a top-management team, and each has different implications for the processing of information, organizational learning, and the quality of decision making.[59] Figure 12-5 shows two top-management configurations, each of which has different implications for the level of learning taking place. In the wheel configuration, organizational learning is decreased because managers from the different functions report separately to the CEO. Rather than coordinate their own actions as a team, they send all information to the CEO, who processes this information, arrives at a decision, and communicates the decision back to the top managers. Research suggests that the wheel works best when problems are simple and require minimal coordination among top team members.[60] When problems are complex and nonprogrammed decision making is required, the wheel configuration slows organizational learning because all coordination takes place through the CEO. Additionally, the CEO's decisions may be restricted or limited by any one or more of the cognitive biases we have discussed. If this is the case, organizational learning may also be limited or faulty as a result.

In the circle configuration, top managers from different functions interact with each other and with the CEO. That is, they function as a team—something that promotes team and organizational learning. Research has suggested that the circle works best for complex problems requiring coordination among group members to arrive at a solution. The circle design solves complex problems much more quickly than the wheel arrangement: Communication around the circle takes less time because there is more opportunity for team and organization learning between all top managers.[61]

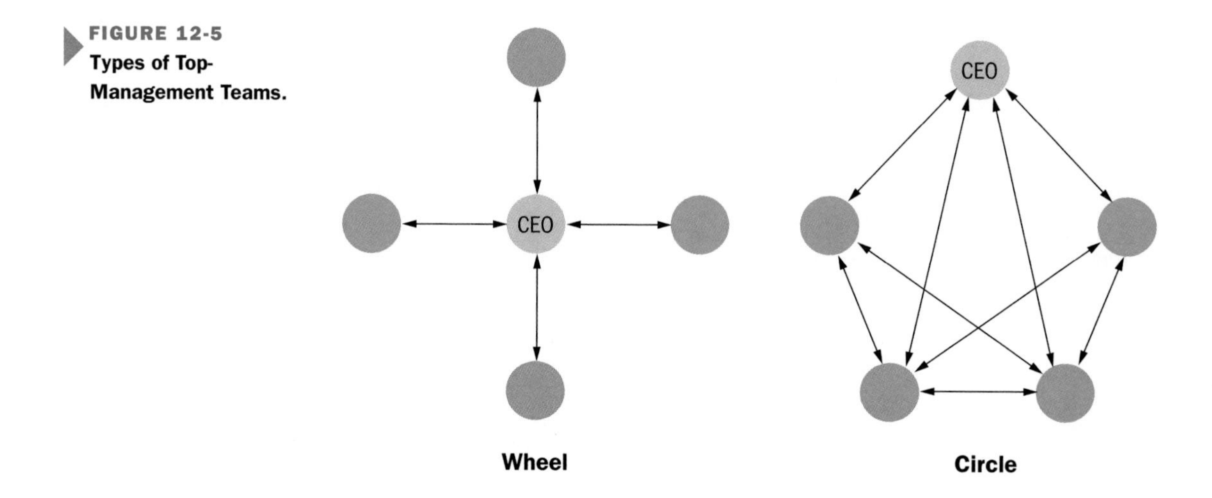

FIGURE 12-5
Types of Top-Management Teams.

The level and quality of organizational learning and decision making by the top-management team is also a function of the personal characteristics and backgrounds of team members.[62] An organization that draws its top-management team from many different industries and different functional backgrounds can more easily promote organizational learning and decision making. Diversity in the top-management team also exposes managers to the implications and consequences of many alternative courses of action. Such exposure may cause managers to examine their own expectations and assumptions more closely.

At IBM, for example, members of the top-management team had been promoted from within the organization. There were no outsiders to propose credible alternative courses of action and thus force IBM's top managers to examine their assumptions. By contrast, Coca-Cola was concerned that its top managers' lack of international experience could hurt the organization's emerging global strategy. To provide new direction, many overseas-born managers were appointed to its top-management team; one of them, Roberto Goizueta, was once its CEO.

It has been found that the most learning takes place when there is considerable heterogeneity, or various differences, among team members and when managers from different functions have an opportunity to express their views. When managers bring different information and viewpoints to bear on a problem, the organization can avoid **groupthink**, the conformity that emerges when like-minded people reinforce one another's tendencies to interpret events and information in similar ways.[63] It has also been found that top-management teams function most effectively when their membership is stable and there is not too much entry into or departure from the team.[64] When team membership is stable, group cohesiveness increases and promotes communication among members and improved decision making.[65]

Groupthink
The conformity that emerges when like-minded people reinforce one another's tendencies to interpret events and information in similar ways.

Designing and managing the top-management team to promote organizational learning is a vital task for a CEO.[66] Often, an organization picks as CEO the person who has the functional and managerial background needed to deal with the most pressing issues facing the organization. Caterpillar, GM, and Ford all picked as CEOs managers who had extensive experience in international business because the organizations' major problems all centred on the challenge of meeting global competition.[67]

Sometimes the only way to promote organizational learning is to change the CEO or the top-management team. Although an organization might retain the rare top manager who has dissented from prevailing beliefs and perceptions, removing top managers can be the quickest way to erase organizational memory and programmed decision making, so that the organization can develop new routines. Thus, for example, IBM's board of directors ousted John Akers and installed Louis Gerstner, who had no previous experience in the computer industry, as CEO. The board's rationale seemed to be that IBM needed a new person with new views and new solutions to turn the organization around and lead it out of crisis.

Devil's Advocacy and Dialectical Inquiry

Devil's advocacy and dialectical inquiry are also ways of overcoming cognitive biases and promoting organizational learning.[68] Figure 12-6 shows how these strategies differ from one another and from the rational approach to decision making. The goal of both is to improve decision making.

An organization that uses devil's advocacy institutionalizes dissent by assigning a manager or management team the role of devil's advocate. The **devil's advocate** is responsible for critiquing ongoing organizational learning and for questioning the assumptions the top-management team uses in the decision-making process.

Devil's advocate
A person who is responsible for critiquing ongoing organizational learning.

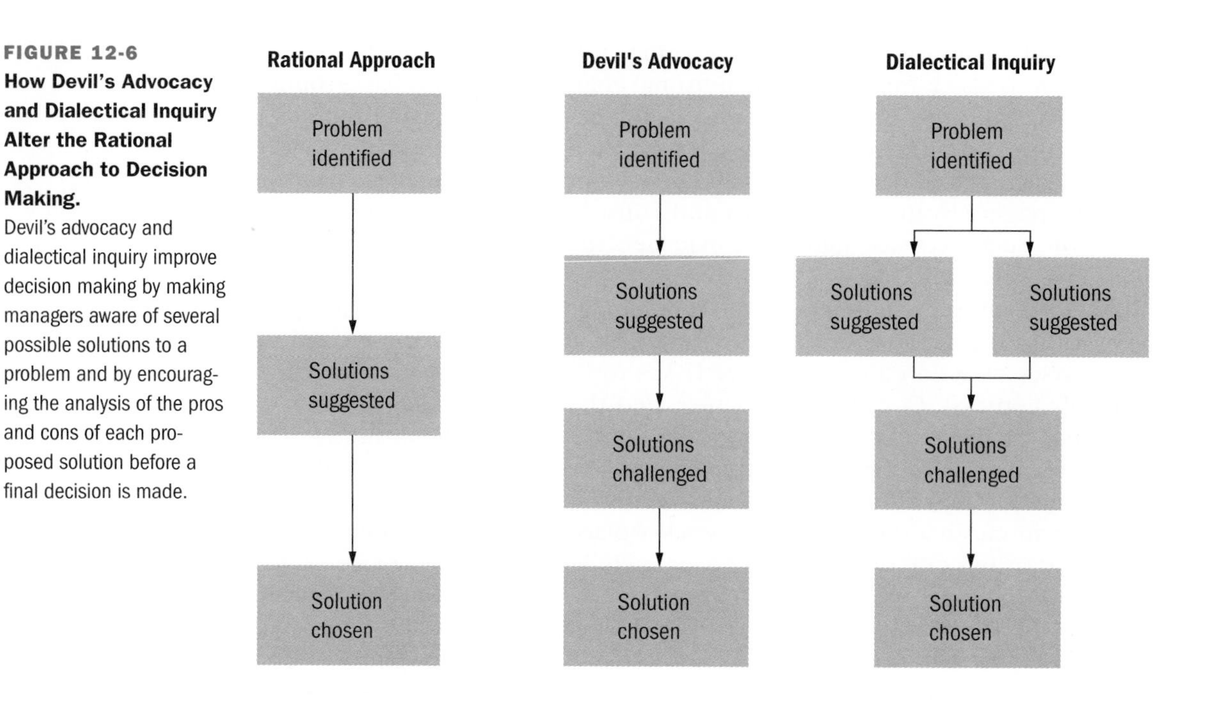

FIGURE 12-6
How Devil's Advocacy and Dialectical Inquiry Alter the Rational Approach to Decision Making.
Devil's advocacy and dialectical inquiry improve decision making by making managers aware of several possible solutions to a problem and by encouraging the analysis of the pros and cons of each proposed solution before a final decision is made.

3M makes excellent use of devil's advocacy. At 3M, product managers submit proposals for a new product to a product development committee composed of top managers. The committee acts as devil's advocate. It critiques the proposal and challenges assumptions (such as the estimated size of the market for the product or its cost of manufacturing) in order to improve the plan and verify its commercial viability. 3M directly attributes its product development successes to the use of devil's advocacy.

An organization that uses dialectical inquiry creates teams of decision makers. Each team is instructed to generate and evaluate alternative scenarios and courses of action and then recommend the best one. After hearing each team's alternatives, all of the teams and the organization's top managers sit down together to cull the best parts of each plan and synthesize a final plan that offers the best chance of success.

Collateral Organizational Structure

Finally, an organization can attempt to improve learning and decision making by establishing a *collateral organizational structure*—that is, an informal organization of managers that is set up parallel to the formal organizational structure to "shadow" the decision making and actions of managers in the formal organization.[69] Managers in the formal structure know that their decisions are being evaluated by others and become used to examining the assumptions that they use to test alternatives and arrive at a solution. An organization establishes a collateral structure to improve the organization's ability to learn and adjust to new situations, and to enhance its ability to make decisions in an unstructured way. A collateral organizational structure allows an organization to maintain its capacity for change at the same time that it maintains its stability.

MANAGERIAL IMPLICATIONS

Decision Making and Learning

1. Try to guard against blindness and rigidity in decision making, be on the lookout for new problems, and be open to new solutions.
2. Develop a questioning attitude, and never discount warnings that problems are impending.
3. Analyze the cognitive structures through which you and your subunit define problems. Question whether these beliefs or values reflect the realities of the situation.
4. Examine your decision making to determine whether cognitive biases are affecting the quality of your decisions.
5. To protect the quality of your decision making, develop strategies to enhance organizational learning. For example, listen to your opponents, experiment with new solutions, encourage diversity, and use dialectical inquiry.

SUMMARY

The problems that many established companies encounter are a warning about the need to encourage organizational learning so that organizations have the ability to continuously adapt to and modify their environments. Strategy and structure are the tools that an organization uses to fashion its future; the decisions about strategy and structure that an organization makes now will determine its fate years from now. Too often, managers view strategy and structure as given and unchangeable and not as things to be experimented with and altered to move the organization forward. When strategy and structure are seen as something to be protected or hidden behind, they become a source of organizational inertia that eventually may bring an organization to its knees. Managers need to understand the way in which an organization's current strategy and structure can constrain organizational learning, and they need to understand how cognitive biases can affect learning and distort the decision-making process. Chapter 12 has made the following main points:

1. Organizational decision making is the process of responding to a problem by searching for and selecting a solution or course of action that will create value for organizational stakeholders.
2. Managers make two basic types of decisions: programmed and nonprogrammed. Programmed decisions provide an organization with stability and increase efficiency. Nonprogrammed decisions allow an organization to adapt to changes in its environment and find solutions to new problems.
3. The rational model of decision making outlines how decision making takes place when there is no uncertainty. It ignores the effects of information costs and managerial costs.
4. Newer models of decision making recognize the effects of uncertainty, information, bounded rationality, satisficing, and bargaining by coalitions on the decision-making process. The Carnegie, incrementalist, unstructured, and garbage-can models provide a more realistic picture of how organizational decision making takes place.
5. Organizational learning is the process through which managers seek to improve organization

members' desire and ability to understand and manage the organization and its environment so that they can make decisions that continuously raise organizational effectiveness. There are two main kinds of learning—explorative and exploitative—and both are necessary to raise the quality of decision making.

6. The routines and procedures that an organization uses to make programmed decisions can cause organizational inertia. When programmed decision making drives out nonprogrammed decision making, the level of organizational learning drops. To encourage organizational learning, managers must act at the individual, group, organizational, and interorganizational levels.
7. Information technology and knowledge management systems can be developed to improve decision making and enhance organizational learning. The two main approaches to knowledge management are codification and personalization.
8. Cognitive structures (sets of interrelated beliefs, preferences, expectations, and values) affect the way managers interpret the problems facing an organization and shape the way they make decisions.
9. Cognitive biases may distort the way managers process information and make decisions. Common cognitive biases include cognitive dissonance, the illusion of control, frequency and representativeness, projection and ego-defensiveness, and escalation of commitment.
10. There are several ways in which an organization can counter the effect of cognitive biases and raise the level of learning and decision making. It can implement strategies for organizational learning, use game theory, increase the breadth and diversity of the top-management team, use devil's advocacy and dialectical inquiry to evaluate proposed solutions, and develop a collateral organizational structure.

DISCUSSION QUESTIONS

1. What are the critical differences between the rational and the Carnegie approaches to decision making? What are the critical differences between the incrementalist and the garbage-can models? Which models best describe how decision making takes place in (a) a fast-food restaurant and (b) the research and development laboratory of a major drug company?
2. What is organizational learning? In what ways can managers promote the development of organizational learning by acting at various levels in the organization? By using knowledge management?
3. How can knowledge management promote organizational learning? What determines which kind of knowledge management system a company should adopt?
4. How do cognitive biases affect organizational learning and the quality of decision making? What can be done to reduce their negative impact?

ORGANIZATIONAL THEORY IN ACTION

Practising Organizational Theory: Store Learning

Form groups of three to five people and discuss the following scenario:

You are a group of top managers of a major clothing store who are facing a crisis. Your establishment has been the leading clothing store in your city for the last 15 years. In the last three years, however, two other major clothing store chains have opened up in your city and they have steadily been luring away your customers—your sales are down 30 percent. To find out why, you have been surveying some of your former customers and have learned that they perceive, for whatever reason, that your store is just not keeping up with changing fashion trends and new forms of customer service. In examining the way your store operates, you have come to realize that over time the ten buyers who purchase the clothing and accessories for your store have been buying increasingly from the same set of clothing suppliers, and have become reluctant to try new ones. Moreover, your salespeople rarely, if ever, make suggestions for changing the way your store operates. Your goal is to shake up store employees and turn around store performance.

1. Devise a program to increase the level of organizational learning.
2. In what specific ways can you promote the level of learning at all levels?

Making the Connection #12

Find an example of an organization that has been using information technology to change the way it makes decisions or increases its level of learning. Why is the organization making these changes? What is it doing to stimulate new learning?

The Ethical Dimension #12

Managers' desire or willingness to act ethically and make ethical decisions can be affected by any cognitive biases that are operating in a particular context.

1. Discuss how the various cognitive biases can lead managers to behave unethically. Do you see any theme or pattern in how these biases operate on ethics?
2. Which kinds of techniques or tools discussed in this chapter — for example, a knowledge management system — can be best used to combat the problem of cognitive biases?

Analyzing the Organization: Design Module #12

This module focuses on organizational decision making and learning and on the way your company has changed its strategy and structure over time.

ASSIGNMENT

1. Given the pattern of changes your organization has made to its strategy and structure over time, which of the decision-making models best characterizes the way it makes decisions?
2. At what hierarchical level does responsibility for nonprogrammed decision making seem to lie in your organization? What problems do you see with the way your company makes decisions?
3. Characterize your organization's ability to learn over time. Evaluate its capacity to adapt itself to and modify the environment.
4. Can you pinpoint any cognitive biases that may have affected the way managers made decisions or influenced their choice of strategy or structure? What was the effect of these cognitive biases?

Company Profiles #12*

Choose one or more of the organizations (e.g., companies, government agencies, or nonprofit organizations) that are profiled in this chapter. Do an Internet search to get up-to-date information on each organization you have selected, and answer the following questions.

1. What does the new information tell you about the organization's current ability to learn?
2. How does the information compare with the earlier information provided in the text and what does that tell you about organizations (e.g., does the organization appear to be more or less able to learn than before, and how do you explain this)?

* The authors would like to receive information from student groups and instructors on any companies where there have been dramatic changes to the information published in this text. We would be happy to publish the best of these changes in a subsequent edition, where we will focus on changing company profiles.

Alternative Perspectives #12

Decision Making

Decision making in organizations has been studied primarily from a rational perspective. That is, decisions in organizations are made intentionally, are based upon explicit information, and are arrived at in a relatively logical fashion, by those who have been formally assigned responsibility for making decisions. While research has shown that the assumptions of total rationality, perfect information, perfect logic, and formal authority are not necessarily as strong as first thought, there still remains a major rational assumptive bias. Read one or more of the following readings and compare and contrast them with the views in the text. In small groups, discuss the implications for decision making in organizations.

Reading List

Bartlett, D. 2003. Management and Business Ethics: A Critique and Integration of Ethical Decision-Making Models. *British Journal of Management.* 14(3): 223–235.

Bromiley, P. 1999. Debating Rationality: Nonrational Aspects of Organizational Decision Making/Rational Choice Theory and Organizational Theory: A Critique. *The Academy of Management Review.* 24(1): 157–160.

Nutt, P. C. 1999. Surprising But True: Half the Decisions in Organizations Fail. *Academy of Management Executive.* 13(4): 75–90.

Perlow, L. A., Okhuysen, G. A., and Repenning, N. P. 2002. The Speed Trap: Exploring the Relationship Between Decision Making and Temporal Context. *The Academy of Management Journal.* 45(5): 931–955.

Sadler-Smith, E. and Shefy, E. 2004. The Intuitive Executive: Understanding and Applying "Gut Feel" in Decision Making. *Academy of Management Executive.* 18(4): 76–91.

Tsang, E. W. K. 2004. Superstition and Decision-Making: Contradiction or Complement? *Academy of Management Executive.* 18(4): 92–104.

KNOWLEDGE MANAGEMENT

Organizational learning and knowledge management have received a great deal of research and practitioner attention over the last decade, as they are expected to be needed for organizations to compete successfully in the future. Read one or more of the following readings and compare and contrast these views with those of the text. In small groups, discuss the implications for managers, employees, and learning and knowledge in organizations.

Reading List

Blackler, F., Reed, M., and Whitaker, A. 1993. Editorial Introduction: Knowledge Workers and Contemporary Organizations. *Journal of Management Studies.* 30(6): 1017–1020.

Bratton, J., Helms Mills, J., Pyrch, T., and Sawchuck, P. 2004. *Workplace Learning: A Critical Introduction.* Toronto: Garamond Press.

Gherardi, S., and Nicolini, D. 2000. To Transfer Is to Transform: The Circulation of Safety Knowledge. *Organization.* 7(2): 329–348.

Jacques, R. 1996. *Manufacturing the Employee: Management Knowledge from the 19th to 21st Centuries.* London: Sage.

McAdam, R., and McCreedy, S. 2000. A Critique of Knowledge Management: Using a Social Constructionist Model. *New Technology, Work, and Employment,* 15(2): 155–168.

Newell, S. 2002. *Managing Knowledge Work.* New York: Palgrave.

Styhre, A. 2003. *Understanding Knowledge Management: Critical and Postmodern Perspectives.* Malmö: Copenhagen Business School Press.

TECHNOLOGY

In many ways organizations may be considered technical entities where technology in its various forms permits an organization to manufacture and produce, create and provide a service, coordinate, control, and manage resources. Technology in the modern organization is usually portrayed in a positive, advantageous light. Read one or more of the following readings and compile a list of the potential negative implications of technology. Produce a comparative list of positive implications drawn from the text and compare and contrast the two lists. In small groups, discuss the implications for managers, employees, and organizations.

Reading List

Ball, K. and Wilson, D. C. 2000. Power, Control and Computer-Based Performance Monitoring: Repertoires, Resistance and Subjectivities. *Organization Studies.* 21(3): 539–565.

Blauner, R. 1964. *Alienation and Freedom: The Factory Worker and His Industry.* Chicago: University of Chicago.

Braverman, H. 1974. *Labour and Monopoly Capital: The Degradation of Work in the Twentieth Century*. New York and London: Monthly Review Press.

Clegg, S. R. 1999. Globalizing the Intelligent Organization: Learning Organizations, Smart Workers, (Not So) Clever Countries and the Sociological Imagination, *Management Learning*. 30(3): 259–280.

Friedmann, G. 1961/1964. *The Anatomy of Work: Labour, Leisure and the Implications of Automation*. London: Heinemann Educational, 1961 (and Free Press, 1964).

Ritzer, G. 2000. *The McDonaldization of Society*. Pine Forge: Sage Publications.

Rosenthal, P. 2004. Management Control as an Employee Resource: The Case of the Front-line Service Workers. *Journal of Management Studies*. 41(4): 601–622.

Shalla, V. 1997. Technology and the Deskilling of Work: The Case of Passenger Agents at Air Canada. In A. Duffy, D. Glenday and N. Pupo, eds., *Good Jobs, Bad Jobs, No Jobs*, pp. 76–96. Toronto: Harcourt Brace.

CASE FOR ANALYSIS

Encouraging Learning in the Canadian Public Service[70]

In the 2002–2003 fiscal year, the Canadian Centre for Management Development (CCMD) had a training and development budget of some $32.5 million. With the help of its 207 employees, the CCMD offered training to some 11 000 federal government employees, representing a 40 percent increase over the previous year. In commenting on the CCMD's work, then–prime minister Jean Chrétien said, "The government has made a commitment to Canadians to help create a skills and learning foundation to promote and sustain workplace learning. The Public Service is inextricably linked to this goal. Developing the Public Service as a learning organization will have a profound impact on determining Canada's success."

For the CCMD, the group charged with supporting the learning, training, and development needs of Canada's public service managers, this has meant grappling with some very big questions: What are the current and future training needs of public service managers, and can information technology play a role in helping address those knowledge gaps in an effective and efficient manner? Then there is the issue of how to assess the learning of participants and collect that information in a central location so that future training investment decisions about whether to continue with existing programs or explore new alternatives, can be made with greater confidence. To develop the best possible solution to these challenges, CCMD executives decided to pilot various delivery approaches.

In April 2003, the CCMD launched Campus*direct*, an e-learning training initiative with $10 million in funding over a three-year term. Designed as a Web portal, Campus*direct* integrates over 150 course offerings—including universities, colleges, private training companies, and federal government trainers—that meet the specific training and career development needs of government employees. Employees interested in promotion and advancement within the public service can complete courses to develop their knowledge and skills in areas such as leadership and management, personal and interpersonal effectiveness, technology, financial management, project management, and strategic management and planning. A Core Learning Series has also been established for all public service managers. It consists of four components that address the key government stewardship issues of financial management, access to information and privacy, contracting for services, and human resources management.

By centralizing all the course offerings in one location, CCMD is providing federal government employees with one comprehensive, current source of possible learning options. Now instead of looking at dozens of Web sites and course calendars, employees can use the portal for one-stop shopping. For those approving training expenditures, Campus*direct* offers equally important benefits. If the courses are part of the Core Learning Series, then senior managers know their employees will be acquiring knowledge and skills that will enable them to be more effective in their roles. They also have the added benefit of knowing all courses in the e-library, as well as the learning providers, have been pre-approved by the federal government's training and development experts.

With only a three-year timeframe to prove itself, the managers of Campus*direct* are working hard to promote the e-learning portal to potential users as a means of effectively delivering training and development at a reasonable cost. To attract potential users, the CCMD is marketing Campus*direct* both to government departments and agencies, and to individual end users.

So far the CCMD has six federal government departments who have signed up for corporate licences, thereby entitling all their employees to take Campus*direct* courses. Another six federal departments and three provincial departments are piloting the program with a limited number of user licences· Employees of these government departments qualify for free unlimited access to the course library. Employees from departments without a corporate licence can simply pay a $250 annual subscription fee to access all the courses, or a $150 fee to complete the Core Learning Series. Both groups of subscribers are also entitled to user support from a central resource, and can receive a regular newsletter and participate in online discussion forums about training initiatives. To help them assess their progress and incorporate their learning on the job, course participants can use self-assessment tools such as online quizzes and printable job aids.

With effective knowledge transfer being a priority of the federal government, course evaluation is also important. So, at the end of each session, users are asked to complete a detailed assessment of their course. The ratings from these evaluations are collected in a central location where they are tabulated and analyzed by Campus*direct* staff. That way Campus*direct* maintains up-to-date assessments of all its courses and can put this valuable knowledge to effective use. If a course isn't being well received, Campus*direct* staff can spot the problem early and take steps to address the issues before other employees sign up as new registrants.

Another step that's been taken to help ensure the success of the pilot is to build support for e-based learning. Campus*direct* staff recognized the need to help foster organizational cultures that are supportive of learning, and specifically of e-learning. To accomplish this objective, Campus*direct* staff will hold e-learning orientation sessions for departmental HR and training staff, as well as departmental employee groups. They will even consult with departmental staff to help develop internal Campus*direct* marketing programs.

To date, all the efforts seem to paying off. As of March 2004, Campus*direct* had over 5600 subscribers. The results of their over 11 000 course evaluations were very positive, with 92 percent of learners recommending their courses to future participants. Its success is attracting attention from outside Canada as well. In fact, CCMD staff recently helped the government of Mexico develop its own e-learning initiative, modelled after Campus*direct*, for its more than 300 000 public service workers. With two more years left for the pilot program, the Campus*direct* e-learning model seems well on its way to demonstrating its value.

DISCUSSION QUESTIONS

1. What are the advantages of online learning systems from the employee's perspective? Can you think of possible disadvantages from the employee's or the employer's perspective?
2. How is the CCMD evaluating the success of its program? Do you think the measures are appropriate ones? Why or why not?
3. Review the cognitive biases outlined in the chapter. How do think these biases will affect the CCMD's decision on whether or not to turn the e-learning pilot into a permanent program? Can you identify ways it might improve the organization's learning and decision making and avoid bias?

REFERENCES

1. H. A. Simon, *The New Science of Management Decision* (New York: Harper and Row, 1960), p. 206.
2. Ibid.
3. S. Keiser and L. Sproull, "Managerial Response to Changing Environments: Perspectives on Sensing from Social Cognition," *Administrative Science Quarterly,* 1982, vol. 27, pp. 548–570; G. T. Allison, *The Essence of Decision* (Boston: Little, Brown, 1971).
4. Simon, *The New Science of Management Decision.*
5. H. A. Simon, *Administrative Behavior* (New York: Macmillan, 1945).
6. Ibid.; J. G. March and H. A. Simon, *Organizations* (New York: Wiley, 1958).
7. J. G. March, "Bounded Rationality, Ambiguity, and the Engineering of Choice," *Bell Journal of Economics,* 1978, vol. 9, pp. 587–608.
8. J. G. March, "Decision Making Perspective," in A. Van De Ven and W. Joyce, eds., *Perspectives on Organizational Design and Behavior* (New York: Wiley, 1981), pp. 205–252.
9. Simon, *Administrative Behavior.*
10. R. M. Cyert and J. G. March, *A Behavioral Theory of the Firm* (Englewood Cliffs, NJ: Prentice Hall, 1963).
11. P. D. Larkey and L. S. Sproull, *Advances in Information Processing in Organizations,* vol. 1 (Greenwich, CT: JAI Press, 1984), pp. 1–8.
12. March and Simon, *Organizations.*
13. H. A. Simon, *Models of Man* (New York: Wiley, 1957); A. Grandori, "A Prescriptive Contingency View of Organizational Decision Making," *Administrative Science Quarterly,* 1984, vol. 29, pp. 192–209.
14. Simon, *The New Science of Management Decision.*
15. H. A. Simon, "Making Management Decisions: The Role of Intuition and Emotion," *Academy of Management Executives,* 1987, vol. 1, pp. 57–64.
16. Cyert and March, *A Behavioral Theory of the Firm.*
17. Ibid.
18. C. E. Lindblom, "The Science of Muddling Through," *Public Administration Review,* 1959, vol. 19, pp. 79–88.
19. Ibid., p. 83.
20. H. Mintzberg, D. Raisinghani, and A. Theoret, "The Structure of Unstructured Decision Making," *Administrative Science Quarterly,* 1976, vol. 21, pp. 246–275.
21. Z. Schiller, "GE's Appliance Park: Rewire, or Pull the Plug?" *Business Week,* 8 February 1993, p. 30.
22. J. Ward, "GE Center Makes Things Fail So It Can Make Them Better," *The Courier Journal,* 12 September 1999, p. 1.
23. *www.ge.com,* 2002.
24. Ibid., p. 257.
25. M. D. Cohen, J. G. March, and J. P. Olsen, "A Garbage Can Model of Organizational Choice," *Administrative Science Quarterly,* 1972, vol. 17, pp. 1–25.
26. Ibid.
27. G. P. Huber, "Organizational Learning: The Contributing Processes and the Literature," *Organizational Science,* 1991, vol. 2, pp. 88–115.
28. B. Hedberg, "How Organizations Learn and Unlearn," in W. H. Starbuck and P. C. Nystrom, eds., *Handbook of Organizational Design,* vol. 1 (New York: Oxford University Press, 1981), pp. 1–27.
29. P. M. Senge, *The Fifth Discipline: The Art and Practice of the Learning Organization* (New York: Doubleday, 1990).
30. J. G. March, "Exploration and Exploitation in Organizational Learning," *Organizational Science,* 1991, vol. 2, pp. 71–87.
31. T. K. Lant and S. J. Mezias, "An Organizational Learning Model of Convergence and Reorientation," *Organizational Science,* 1992, vol. 5, pp. 47–71.
32. M. Dodgson, "Organizational Learning: A Review of Some Literatures," *Organizational Studies,* 1993, vol. 14, pp. 375–394.
33. A. S. Miner and S. J. Mezias, "Ugly Duckling No More: Pasts and Futures of Organizational Learning Research," *Organizational Science,* 1990, vol. 7, pp. 88–99.
34. P. Senge, *The Fifth Discipline: The Art and Practice of the Learning Organization* (New York: Doubleday, 1990).
35. P. Senge, "The Leader's New Work: Building Learning Organizations," *Sloan Management Review,* Fall 1990, pp. 7–23.
36. Miner and Mezias, "Ugly Ducking No More."
37. J. P. Kotter and J. L. Heskett, *Corporate Culture and Performance* (New York: The Free Press, 1992).
38. N. Venkatraman, "Information Technology: The Challenge of Strategic Transformation," in E. Collins and M. Devanna, eds., *The New Portable MBA* (New York: John Wiley, 1994), pp. 160–183.

39. M.T. Hansen, N. Nohria, and T. Tierney, "What's Your Strategy for Managing Knowledge?" *Harvard Business Review,* March–April 1999, pp. 3–19.
40. Organizational Insight by Ellen Rudderham-Gaudet, based upon the following sources: "Q2 2004 Investor Fact Sheet," *about.telus.com,* 2004; M. Barry, "Canadian Telephone Company Enhances Corporate Dialogue with CEO Mailbox," *Communication World,* 2004, vol. 21, pp. 50–51.
41. P. C. Nystrom and W. H. Starbuck, "To Avoid Organizational Crises, Unlearn," *Organizational Dynamics,* 1984, vol. 12, pp. 53–65.
42. Y. Dror, "Muddling Through—Science or Inertia?" *Public Administration Review,* 1964, vol. 24, pp. 103–117.
43. Nystrom and Starbuck, "To Avoid Organizational Crises, Unlearn."
44. S. T. Fiske and S. E. Taylor, *Social Cognition* (Reading, MA: Addison-Wesley, 1984).
45. See G. R. Jones, R. Kosnik, and J. M. George, "Internalization and the Firm's Growth Path: On the Psychology of Organizational Contracting," in R. W. Woodman and W. A. Pasemore, eds., *Research in Organizational Change and Development,* vol. 7 (Greenwich, CI: JAI Press, 1993), pp. 105–135, for an account of the biases as they operate during organizational growth and decline.
46. L. Festinger, *A Theory of Cognitive Dissonance* (Stanford, CA: Stanford University Press, 1957); E. Aaronson, "The Theory of Cognitive Dissonance: A Current Perspective," in L. Berkowitz, ed., *Advances in Experimental Social Psychology,* 1969, vol. 4, pp. 1–34.
47. J. R. Averill, "Personal Control over Aversive Stimuli and Its Relationship to Stress," *Psychological Bulletin,* 1973, vol. 80, pp. 286–303.
48. E. J. Langer, "The Illusion of Control," *Journal of Personality and Social Psychology,* 1975, vol. 32, pp. 311–328.
49. A. Tversky and D. Kahneman, "Judgment Under Uncertainty: Heuristics and Biases," *Science,* 1974, vol. 185, pp. 1124–1131.
50. R. De Board, *The Psychoanalysis of Organizations* (London: Tavistock, 1978).
51. B. M. Staw, "The Escalation of Commitment to a Course of Action," *Academy of Management Review,* 1978, vol. 6, pp. 577–587; B. M. Staw and J. Ross, "Commitment to a Policy Decision: A Multi-Theoretical Perspective," *Administrative Science Quarterly,* 1978, vol. 23, pp. 40–64.
52. Nystrom and Starbuck, "To Avoid Organizational Crises, Unlearn."
53. Ibid.
54. L. Porter and K. Roberts, "Communication in Organizations," in M. Dunnette, ed., *Handbook of Industrial and Organizational Psychology* (Chicago: Rand McNally, 1976).
55. Nystrom and Starbuck, "To Avoid Organizational Crises, Unlearn."
56. A. D. Meyer, "Adapting to Environmental Jolts," *Administrative Science Quarterly,* 1982, vol. 27, pp. 515–537; A. D. Meyer, "How Ideologies Supplant Formal Structures and Shape Responses to Environments," *Journal of Management Studies,* 1982, vol. 7, pp. 31–53.
57. For a basic introduction to game theory, see A. K. Dixit and B. J. Nalebuff, *Thinking Strategically* (London: WW Norton, 1991). Also see A. M. Brandenburger and B. J. Nalebuff, "The Right Game: Using Game Theory to Shape Strategy," *Harvard Business Review,* July–August 1995, pp. 59–71; and D. M. Kreps, *Game Theory and Economic Modeling* (Oxford: Oxford University Press, 1990).
58. D. C. Hambrick, *The Executive Effect: Concepts and Methods for Studying Top Managers* (Greenwich, CI: JAI Press, 1988).
59. D. G. Ancona, "Top-Management Teams: Preparing for the Revolution," in J. S. Carroll, ed., *Applied Social Psychology and Organizational Settings* (Hillsdale, NJ: Lawrence Erlbaum Associates, 1990).
60. M. Shaw, "Communications Networks," in L. Berkowitz, ed., *Advances in Experimental Social Psychology,* vol. 1 (New York: Academic Press, 1964).
61. Ibid.
62. S. Finkelstein and D. C. Hambrick, "Top-Management Team Tenure and Organizational Outcomes: The Moderating Role of Managerial Discretion," *Administrative Science Quarterly,* 1990, vol. 35, pp. 484–503.
63. I. L. Janis, *Victims of Groupthink,* 2nd ed. (Boston: Houghton Mifflin, 1982).
64. K. M. Eisenhardt and C. B. Schoonhoven, "Organizational Growth: Linking Founding Team, Strategy, Environment, and Growth Among U.S. Semiconductor Ventures, 1978–1988," *Administrative Science Quarterly,* 1990, vol. 35, pp. 504–529; L. Keck and M. L. Tushman, "Environmental and Organizational Context and Executive Team Structure," *Academy of Management Journal,* 1993, vol. 36, pp. 1314–1344.
65. A. J. Lott and B. E. Lott, "Group Cohesiveness and Interpersonal Attraction: A Review of Relationships with Antecedent and Consequent Variables," *Psychological Bulletin,* 1965, vol. 14, pp. 259–309.

66. D. L. Helmich and W. B. Brown, "Successor Type and Organizational Change in the Corporate Enterprise," *Administrative Science Quarterly,* 1972, vol. 17, pp. 371–381; D. C. Hambrick and P. A. Mason, "Upper Echelons: The Organization as a Reflection of Its Top Managers," *Academy of Management Journal,* 1984, vol. 9, pp. 193–206.

67. R. F. Vancil, *Passing the Baton* (Boston: Harvard Business School Press, 1987).

68. C. Schwenk, "Cognitive Simplification Processes in Strategic Decision Making," *Strategic Management Journal,* 1984, vol. 5, pp. 111–128.

69. D. Rubenstein and R. W. Woodman, "Spiderman and the Burma Raiders: Collateral Organization Theory in Practice," *Journal of Applied Behavioral Science,* 1984, vol. 20, pp. 1–21; G. R. Bushe and A. B. Shani, *Parallel Learning Structures: Increasing Innovations in Bureaucracies* (Reading, MA: Addison-Wesley, 1991).

70. Case by Margaret McKee, based upon the following sources: "CCMD Performance Report, for the Period Ending March 31, 2003," *www.tbs-sct.gc.ca,* 2004; *www.campusdirect.gc.ca,* 2004; Canadian Centre for Management Development, "Departmental Performance Report, for the period ending March 31, 2004."

Innovation, Intrapreneurship, and Creativity

CHAPTER 13

Learning Objectives

As discussed in Chapter 10, innovation is one of the most important types of organizational change because it results in a continuing stream of new and improved goods and services that create value for customers and profit for a company. Indeed, one important way of assessing organizational effectiveness is the rate or speed at which a company can bring new products to market; this is a function of the level of intrapreneurship and creativity inside an organization.

After studying this chapter you should be able to:

1. Describe how innovation and technological change affect each other.
2. Discuss the relationship among innovation, intrapreneurship, and creativity.
3. Understand the many steps involved in creating an organizational setting that fosters innovation and creativity.
4. Identify the ways in which information technology can be used to foster creativity, and speed innovation and new product development.

INNOVATION AND TECHNOLOGICAL CHANGE

Innovation
The process by which organizations use their skills and resources to develop new goods and services or to develop new production and operating systems so that they can better respond to the needs of their customers.

Innovation is the process by which organizations use their resources and competencies to develop new or improved goods and services or to develop new production and operating systems so that they can better respond to the needs of their customers.[1] Innovation can result in spectacular success for an organization. Research In Motion revolutionized the mobile communications world with the introduction of the BlackBerry; Apple Computer changed the face of the computer industry when it introduced its personal computer; Honda changed the face of the small motor-bike market when it introduced small 50 cc motorcycles; Mary Kay cosmetics changed the nature of the way cosmetics are sold when it introduced its at-home cosmetics parties and personalized style of selling; Toyota revolutionized the car production system to increase product quality; and Chrysler's adoption of a new operating system, the product-team structure, was an innovation that many other companies have copied.

Although innovation brings about change, it is also associated with a high level of risk because the outcomes of research and development activities are often uncertain.[2] It has been estimated that only 12 to 20 percent of R&D projects result in products that get to market.[3] Thus, while innovation can lead to change of the sort that organizations want—the introduction of profitable new technologies and products—it can also lead to the kind of change that they want to avoid—technologies that are inefficient and products that customers don't want. (The way in which organizations can manage the innovation process to increase the chance of successful learning taking place is discussed in detail later in the chapter.)

In Chapter 9, technology is defined as the skills, knowledge, experience, body of scientific knowledge, tools, machines, and equipment that are used in the design, production, and distribution of goods and services. Technology is central to the operations and products of most organizations. Changes in technology are at the heart of the innovation process, and at present the world is characterized by a rapid rate of technological change.[4]

Generally speaking, there are two types of technological change: quantum change and incremental change. **Quantum technological change** refers to a fundamental shift in technology that revolutionizes products or the way in which they are produced. Recent examples of quantum changes in technology include the development of the first personal computers, which revolutionized the computer industry, and the development of genetic engineering techniques (biotechnology), which are promising to revolutionize the treatment of illness by replacing conventional pharmaceutical compounds with genetically engineered medicines. New products or operating systems that incorporate a quantum technological improvement are referred to as **quantum innovations**. The introduction in 1971 of Intel's 4004 microprocessor, the first "computer on a chip" ever produced, is an example of a quantum product innovation. Quantum innovations are likely to cause major changes in an environment and to increase uncertainty because they force organizations to change the way they operate.

Quantum technological change
A fundamental shift in technology that revolutionizes products or the way they are produced.

Quantum innovations
New products or operating systems that incorporate quantum technological improvements.

Incremental technological change refers to technological change that represents a refinement of some base technology, and **incremental innovations** refer to products or operating systems that incorporate those refinements. For example, since 1971, Intel has produced a series of improvements of its original 4004 microprocessor. These subsequent improvements include the 8088, 8086, 286, 386, 486, and Pentium chips. Similarly, flexible manufacturing, robots, and TQM are examples of incremental innovations. They improved the quality of cars and forced North American carmakers to make major organizational changes in response to conditions in the new competitive environment.[5]

Incremental technological change
Technological change that represents a refinement of some base technology.

Incremental innovations
Products or operating systems that incorporate refinements of some base technology.

As one might expect, quantum innovations are relatively uncommon. As Philip Anderson and Michael Tushman note, "At rare and irregular intervals in every industry, innovations appear that command a decisive cost or quality advantage and that strike not at the margins of the profits and the outputs of existing firms, but at their foundations and their very lives."[6] Anderson and Tushman call these kinds of quantum innovations "technological discontinuities," and in their model of innovation, a technological discontinuity sets off an era of ferment (see Figure 13-1) where there is intense competition between companies in an industry to develop the design that will become the dominant model for others to copy—just as Intel's chips are the dominant design in the microprocessor industry.

After the dominant design emerges, the next period of the technology cycle involves an era of incremental change and innovation where companies compete to elaborate on the base technology. Most companies spend most of their time engaged in incremental product innovation. For example, every time a car company redesigns a basic model, it is engaged in incremental product innovation, but this is nevertheless a very competitive process. In 2001, for example, five models of hatchback car were competing in the market. By 2002, all the major carmakers had sensed the growing

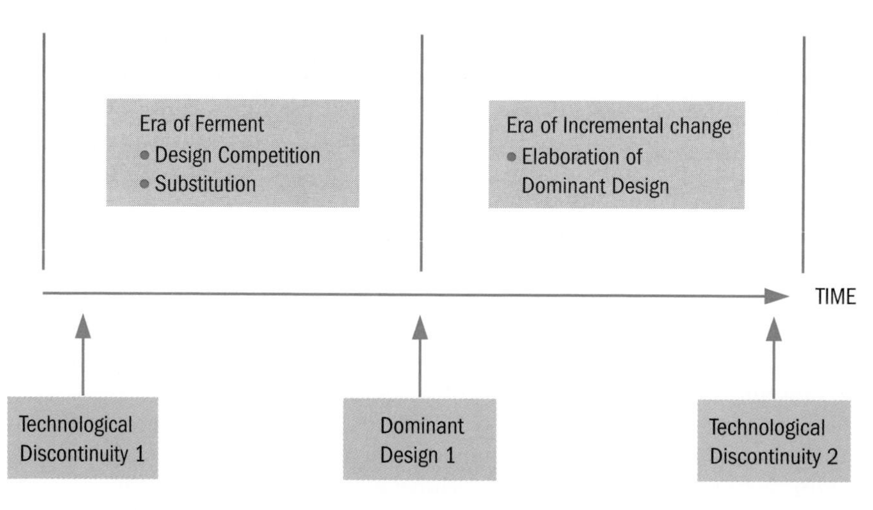

FIGURE 13-1
The Technology Cycle.
Source: "Technological Discontinuities and Dominant Designs: A Cyclical Model of Technological Change," by P. Anderson and M. L. Tushman, published in *Administrative Science Quarterly,* 1990, 35. Reprinted by permission of *Administrative Science Quarterly,* © 1990, Cornell University.

popularity of the hatchback car and 25 hatchback models were competing for the same customers.

Sometimes, a second technological discontinuity may occur, which starts the whole process again. For example, in 2002 Toyota announced the introduction of an emission-free new SUV powered by fuel cell technology that threatened to revolutionize the car industry. The only waste product the car produces is water.

The innovations that result from quantum and incremental technological change are all around us. Microprocessors, PCs, wireless phones and personal digital assistants (PDAs), word-processing software, online information services, computer networks, camcorders, compact disc players, videocassette players, and the genetically engineered medicines produced by biotechnology either did not exist a generation ago or were considered to be exotic and expensive products. Now these products are commonplace, and they are being continually improved. Organizations whose managers helped develop and exploit these new technologies have often reaped enormous gains. They include many of the most successful and rapidly growing organizations today: Research in Motion, Dell Computer, Microsoft, Intel, AOL, Cisco Systems, Motorola, Sony, Matsushita, and Amgen.

However, while some organizations have benefited from technological change, others have seen their markets threatened. The decline of mainframe and midrange computer companies such as IBM, and the failure of others such as DEC, Unisys, and Wang, is a direct reflection of the rise of the PC. Traditional telephone companies the world over have seen their market dominance threatened by companies offering wireless service. And the decline of once-dominant consumer electronics companies such as RCA can be directly linked to their failure to develop innovative products such as VCRs and compact disc players.

Technological change is thus both an opportunity and a threat—it is both creative and destructive.[7] It helps create new product innovations that managers and their organizations can exploit, but at the same time these new innovations can harm or even destroy demand for older, established products. Thus, for example, the development of the microprocessor by Intel has helped create a host of new product opportunities, including PCs, but at the same time it has destroyed demand for older products. Conventional typewriters, for instance, have been replaced by the combination of PCs and word-processing software—putting typewriter companies out of business in the process.

The Product Life Cycle

When technology is changing, organizational survival requires that managers quickly adopt and apply new technologies to innovate. Managers who do not do so soon find that they have no market for their products—and destroy their organizations. The rate of technological change in an industry—and particularly the length of the product life cycle—determines how important it is for managers to innovate.

Product life cycle The changes in demand for a product that occur over time.

The **product life cycle** reflects the changes in demand for a product that occur over time.[8] Demand for most successful products passes through four stages: the embryonic stage, growth, maturity, and decline. In the *embryonic stage* a product has yet to gain widespread acceptance; customers are unsure what the product has to offer, and demand for it is minimal. If a product does become accepted by customers (and many do not), demand takes off, and the product enters its growth stage. In the *growth* stage many consumers are entering the market and buying the product for the first time; demand increases rapidly. This is the stage that PDAs, such as Palm Pilots, are currently in. The growth stage ends and the *mature stage* begins when market demand peaks because most customers have already bought the product (there are relatively few first-time buyers left). At this stage demand is typically replacement demand. In the car market, for example, most cars are bought by people who already have a car and are either trading up or replacing an old model. Products such as wireless telephones, PCs for home use, and online information services are also currently in this stage. The *decline stage* follows the mature stage if and when demand for a product falls. Falling demand often occurs because a product has become technologically obsolescent and superseded by a more advanced product. For example, demand for every generation of VCR, CD, or DVD falls as they are superseded by newer, technically advanced models with more features. Dixons, the major UK electronics retailer, for example, announced at the end of 2004 that it would no longer be selling VCRs. Noting a rapid downturn in VCR sales and an even more dramatic upswing in the purchase of DVD technology, a spokesperson for Dixons announced that VCRs would be out of their shops before Christmas. DVD players were outstripping VCR sales at Dixons by 40 to one.[9]

Rate of Technological Change One of the main determinants of the length of a product's life cycle is the rate of technological change.[10] Figure 13-2 illustrates the relationship between the rate of technological change and the length of product life cycles. In some industries—such as PCs, semiconductors, and disk drives—technological change is rapid and product life cycles are very short. For example, technological change is so rapid in the computer disk drive industry that a disk drive model becomes technologically obsolete about 12 months after introduction. The same is true in the PC industry, where product life cycles have shrunk from three years during the late 1980s to a few months today.

In other industries the product life cycle is somewhat longer. In the car industry, for example, the average product life cycle is about five years. The life cycle of a car is so short because fairly rapid technological change is producing a continual stream of incremental innovations in car design, such as the introduction of door airbags, advanced electronic microcontrollers, plastic body parts, and more fuel-efficient engines. In contrast, in many basic industries where the pace of technological change is slower, product life cycles tend to be much longer. In steel or electricity, for example, change in product technology is very limited, and products such as steel girders and electrical cable can remain in the mature stage indefinitely.

Role of Fads and Fashion Fads and fashion are important determinants of the length of product life cycles.[11] A five-year-old car design is likely to be technologically out-

FIGURE 13-2
Technological Change and Length of the Product Life Cycle.

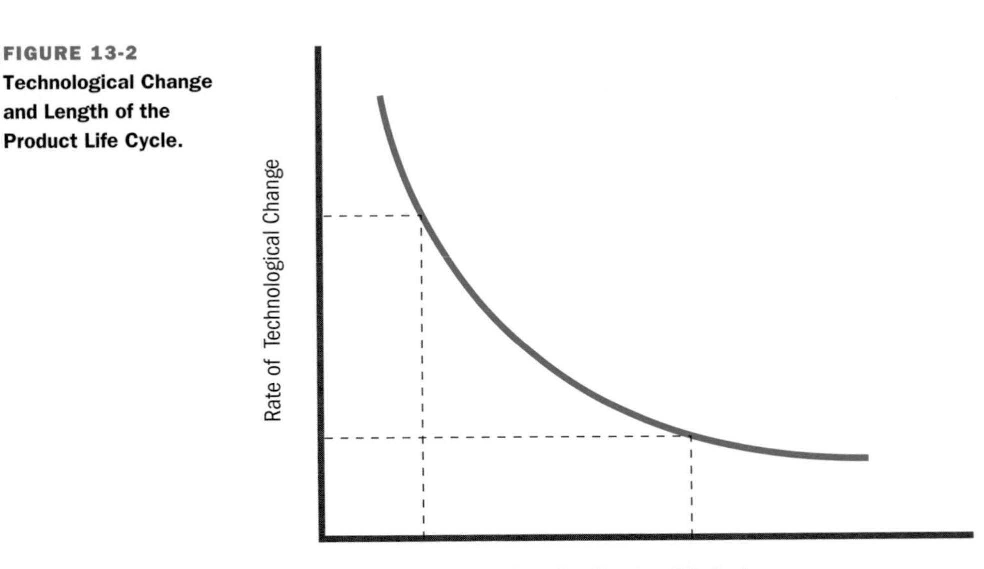

moded and to look out of date and thus lose its attractiveness to customers. Similarly, in the restaurant business, the demand for certain kinds of food changes rapidly. The Cajun cuisine popular one year may be history the next as Caribbean fare becomes the food of choice. Fashion considerations are even more important in the highfashion end of the clothing industry, where last season's clothing line is usually out of date by the next season, and product life cycles may last no more than three months. Thus, fads and fashions are another reason why product life cycles may be short and why operating in such an industry can be risky, as the experience of The Gap suggests. (See Organizational Insight 13.1.)

Whether short product life cycles are caused by rapid technological change, changing fads and fashions, or some combination of the two, the message for managers is clear: The shorter the length of your product's life cycle, the more important it is to innovate products quickly and on a continuing basis. In industries where product life cycles are very short, managers must continually develop new products; otherwise, their organizations may go out of business. The PC company that cannot develop a new and improved product line every six months will soon find itself in trouble. The fashion house that fails to develop a new line of clothing for every season cannot succeed, nor can the small restaurant, club, or bar that is not alert to current fads and fashions. Even in the car industry it is vital that managers continually develop new and improved models every five years or so.

Increasingly, there is evidence that in a wide range of industries product life cycles are becoming more compressed as managers focus their organizations' resources on innovation to increase responsiveness to customers. To attract new customers, managers are trying to outdo each other by being the first to market with a product that incorporates a new technology or that plays to a new fashion trend.[12] In the car industry, a typical five-year product life cycle is being reduced to three years as managers are increasingly competing with one another to attract new customers and encourage existing customers to upgrade and buy the newest product.[13] The airline industry is also subject to dramatic changes in customer needs and new technology and, as senior management at WestJet well understand, it can take a lot of creativity and a well-thought-out strategy to stay in business (see Organizational Insight 13.2).

ORGANIZATIONAL INSIGHT 13.1

Innovation at The Gap

The environment of the clothing industry is highly uncertain, meaning it is very difficult to predict customers' changing tastes and thus stock the clothing that will most appeal to them. The CEO of The Gap, Millard "Mickey" Drexler, brought his chain of stores to prominence in the 1990s because of his uncanny ability to predict customer tastes and design clothing to suit them—the form that innovation takes in the clothing industry. The Gap brand became a fashion statement of the 1990s and by 2000, sales revenue at Gap Inc., the well-known clothes store chain, rose above US$10 billion for the first time ever. However, its stock price, which had hit a peak in 1999, had declined sharply. Why?

To build sales, Millard's strategy had been to open new kinds of stores that offered a different mix of clothing to customers. So, for example, in its Gap division the company had opened Kids Gap stores and Baby Gap. It also started the Banana Republic store chain, and, very important, the Old Navy store chain that grew rapidly and had been responsible for much of Gap's increase in sales.[14]

By the late 1990s, however, Drexler found that he could not manage the innovation process—manage the design process for all the clothes sold by each of his three main divisions. He decided to delegate full responsibility for innovating to the presidents of each store chain. Jenny Ming, for example, was the president of Old Navy, and she and her team of managers were charged with finding the best selection of clothing to appeal to customers. One result of their actions was to champion a line of purple clothing for the spring season.

Drexler's decision to decentralize authority over innovation to the store level caused major problems.[15] The presidents of his chains did not have his ability to predict future clothing trends, fads, and fashions and made mistakes in the kinds of clothing they stocked; the decision to carry purple was a disaster, for example, and the clothes were left on the shelves. Chain managers also began to stock similar kinds of clothes so customers became confused about why the chains were different and this also hurt sales and revenues. The Gap was doing a much poorer job of meeting the needs of its customers.

By the summer of 2000, Drexler decided that while he was right to give divisional managers major responsibility to manage the design process, it was also necessary to have centralized control at the top. Such control would provide the coordination necessary between store chains to ensure that they all worked together to stock a unique mix of clothing, and that it would be one to appeal to customer tastes. He took back more control, installed a new IT system to speed the design process, and The Gap's performance improved in the 2000s.[16] However, Drexler could not regain his early momentum and in 2002 he turned over the helm to Paul Dressler, a former Disney manager who once ran the Magic Kingdom. CEO Dressler hopes to use his skills in brand marketing to turn around The Gap's performance. However, analysts are wondering if a person with no prior experience in the fashion business can help it emerge as a leader in the world of changing fads and fashions.[17]

Innovation, Intrapreneurship, and Creativity

The leaders of innovation and new product development in established organizations are **intrapreneurs**, employees who notice opportunities for either quantum or incremental product improvements and are responsible for managing the product development process to obtain them. Many managers, scientists, or researchers employed by existing

Intrapreneurs
Entrepreneurs inside an organization who are responsible for the success or failure of a project.

ORGANIZATIONAL INSIGHT 13.2

The WestJet Experience[18]

WestJet airlines was founded in 1996 by Clive Beddoe, Mark Hill, Tim Morgan, and Donald Bell. The four Calgary entrepreneurs felt that there was a market for a Canadian discount airline service patterned partially after the successful U.S. airlines Southwest Air and Morris Air. WestJet is headquartered in Calgary and Clive Beddoe is president and CEO.

WestJet has been a phenomenal Canadian success story based on innovation. It took the best of Southwest and Morris Air's model as a starting point and then implemented an evolving strategy that has led to remarkable growth. WestJet started with 220 employees and three aircraft in February 1996, and by the end of 2003 had 3396 full-time equivalents and 44 aircraft. In 1999, WestJet had revenues of $203 million and a profit of $15.8 million. In 2003, revenues had increased to $859 million with a profit of $60.5 million, a remarkable improvement. In 1999 WestJet also completed an initial public offering of 2.5 million common shares, which raised the funds needed for major capital expansion over the coming years, and in 2003 it completed a $150 million equity issue.

In 2003, the annual survey of "Canada's Most Respected Corporations" conducted by Ipsos-Reid surveyed 255 of the leading CEOs in Canada. In the results, WestJet was ranked second overall (up from seventh the previous year), first in high-quality service/product, first in customer service, second in human resources management, fifth in innovation and product/service development, and sixth in financial performance. WestJet also had the second-best on-time performance of all airlines in North America in 2003.

WestJet's success is due to a number of key strategies including quick turnaround of aircraft, a standardized fleet, minimal operating costs, friendly service, profit-sharing programs for employees, and treating passengers as guests.

WestJet operates on ten core management principles:

1. Find a model and copy it.
2. Treat employees as number one.
3. Share the wealth.
4. Hire for attitude and train for skills.
5. Empower the front lines.
6. Embrace technology.
7. First you get the business plan; then you get the money.
8. Find new uses for existing assets.
9. Fly union-free.
10. Celebrate success.

These principles have been extremely successful. WestJet continues to expand and is now venturing into the United States. In 2004 it began providing service to Los Angeles, Fort Lauderdale, and Orlando, and seasonal service to Phoenix and Palm Springs.

WestJet is continuing its strategy of innovation. It is planning to make flying a more enjoyable and personal experience by installing satellite TV in the backs of the chairs on all planes. Passengers will be able to view whatever they wish to from the satellite TV menu.

companies engage in intrapreneurial activity. On the other hand, people like Jeff Bezos, Mike Lazaridis, Debby Fields, or John Stanton (see Organizational Insight 13.3) who start new business ventures and found organizations are entrepreneurs. They assume the risk and receive many of the returns associated with the new business venture.[19]

ORGANIZATIONAL INSIGHT 13.3

Running Room[20]

Running Room was founded in 1984 by John Stanton. Stanton was a vice-president in grocery retailing when he became interested in physical fitness and running after his wife entered him and his son in a three-kilometre walk. This led to a keen interest in competitive running and he opened his first store in a house in Edmonton.

Over the past two decades, Running Room has grown from that one initial store to over 60 locations, and it has more than 600 employees throughout Canada and the United States. Revenue has grown an average of 27 percent per year, and annual sales are now in excess of $50 million. By 2003, the company had a store in every province. Running Room sells a "lifestyle of wellness" and its product line includes running shoes, clothing, books, and accessories, and it provides running clinics for all levels.

The Running Room's success has been attributed to two strengths: (1) the personal magnetism and hustle of John Stanton, and (2) an innovative company strategy. Rather than attempting to penetrate and capture a percentage of the existing running-products market, it develops and continually expands its own market and at the same time creates strong customer loyalty. It has done so by developing running programs designed to get nonrunners involved in running. It offers running clinics for beginners to marathoners. Running Room's programs are designed to expand the running market and make people feel part of the club. This strategy has been remarkably successful.

According to Adrienne Goddard, a retail advisor from Kubas Consultants, Running Room's most impressive quality is its ability to foster a sense of community around running. "They make you feel part of something bigger than just going out for a run—you're part of a group, you're accepted, you're part of this 1% of the population that can run more than a mile," notes Goddard. "It's that community they create amongst their followers that serves them so well."

The goal of Running Room has been to become the number one specialty fitness retailer in Canada, a goal it is well on is way to achieving through its innovative approach. Running Room is now venturing out of Canada and expanding into the U.S. It has already opened three stores in St. Paul, Minnesota, and is planning to open an additional ten to twelve U.S. stores in the next couple of years.

There is an interesting relationship between entrepreneurs and intrapreneurs. Many intrapreneurs become dissatisfied when their superiors decide neither to support their creative new product ideas nor to fund development efforts that the intrapreneurs think will succeed. What do intrapreneurs who feel that they are getting nowhere do? Very often they decide to leave an organization and start their own organization to take advantage of their new product ideas. In other words, intrapreneurs become entrepreneurs and found companies that may compete with the companies they left.

Many of the world's most successful organizations have been started by frustrated intrapreneurs who became entrepreneurs. William Hewlett and David Packard left Fairchild Semiconductor, an early industry leader, when managers of that company would not support their ideas; their company, H-P, soon outperformed Fairchild. Compaq Computer was founded by Rod Canion and some of his colleagues, who left

Texas Instruments (TI) when managers there would not support Canion's idea that TI should develop its own personal computer. To prevent the departure of talented people, organizations need to take steps to promote internal entrepreneurship. In the next section, we consider issues involved in promoting successful entrepreneurship in both new and existing organizations. First, however, it is useful to discuss the origin of these new product ideas—creativity.

All innovation begins with creative ideas. It is important to realize, however, that creative ideas are not just those that lead to major new inventions or achievements: Creative ideas are any that take existing practices a step farther than the norm. **Creativity** is nothing more than going beyond the current boundaries, whether those boundaries are technology, knowledge, social norms, or beliefs.[21] Deciding that PCs don't have to be beige and could be black or blue or even made of clear plastic is a creative idea, just as putting together the first PC was a creative idea. While the latter may be more memorable, and made Steve Jobs and Stephen Wozniak, the founders of Apple Computer famous, the millions of small creative ideas and actions that have gone into improving PCs are nevertheless highly significant and valuable. And Michael Dell's creative idea of selling PCs over the phone, while not in the same league as making the first PC, has nevertheless made him as famous as Jobs and Wozniak, and a good deal richer.

Creativity
Ideas going beyond the current boundaries, whether those boundaries are based on technology, knowledge, social norms, or beliefs.

From this perspective, most people have been and will be creative in their normal endeavours. Thus, it is important in an organization that employees grasp the fact that their input, suggestions, and ideas are valuable. An organization should take steps to acknowledge their importance. Organizations can do this through the values and norms of their organizational culture, as discussed later, or they can do so by providing financial rewards for good suggestions, as many organizations do. It is important to realize that creativity is everywhere, not just confined to some far-away research laboratory.

Creativity is not just making new things; it is also combining and synthesizing two or more previously unrelated facts or ideas and making something new or different out of them. It is also modifying something to give it a new use or to make it perform better. Synthesis and modification are much more common than creation, and this is why incremental innovation is more common than radical innovation. As Anderson puts it, "We forget that moving a desk so that work flows smoother is also creativity. It's modification. And creativity also blooms when we redesign a job description so that related tasks are given to the same person. That's synthesis. It's even creativity when we cut our losses on a worthless industrial adhesive by slapping it on the back of our secretary's note pad . . . that bit of creation is the 3M 'Post-it' notes . . . but nothing is going to make your firm creative unless you first help individuals to unlock their willingness to try.[22]

As Nonaka puts it, the process of innovation and creating new knowledge depends on the ability of managers to tap into the tacit or hidden and highly subjective insights, intuitions, and hunches of people everywhere in an organization.[23] The source can be a brilliant researcher's insight, a middle manager's intuition about changing market trends, or a shop-floor worker's tacit knowledge built up by intense involvement in the work process over a number of years. The issue is to transform personal knowledge into organizational knowledge that results in new products. This can be very complicated because such tacit knowledge is very difficult to verbalize; it is know-how accumulated by experience and often hard to articulate in rules, formulas, or principles.

To obtain such tacit knowledge it is often necessary to learn through observation, imitation, or modeling. Also, over time, through team interactions, team members learn how to share their knowledge and often team routines and "recipes" develop that are specific to a group and to an organization that lead to innovative kinds of behaviours. Some of these can be written down, though many are present only in the interactions between team members—in their knowledge of each other. Note too that from such interactions additional tacit knowledge may be created so that organizational knowledge builds up and spills over.[24]

A **knowledge-creating organization** is one where such innovation is going on at all levels and in all areas. Often, different teams will meet to pool their information. In this way knowledge is shared throughout the organization and new heights can be reached. Team leaders, as middle managers, have to confront the hard task of translating creative new ideas into the stream of products that customers will buy. It is at this point that the question of how to create and design an organizational setting to promote creativity and innovation becomes the crucial issue. Note that the process of creating such a setting is equally a form of innovation as the development of the actual products that can result from it.

Knowledge-creating organization
An organization where innovation is going on at all levels and in all areas.

MANAGING THE INNOVATION PROCESS

How should managers control the innovation process in high-tech companies, software and dot-com companies like Amazon.com, or in supermarkets and restaurants in order to raise the level of both quantum and incremental innovation? There are several related methods that managers can use. These same methods also serve to overcome the resistances to change discussed in Chapter 10, which will reduce the level of innovation if left unattended. For example, different functions may be differently affected by the kinds of technological change taking place and thus resist change, and managers may fail to recognize new product opportunities because of the existence of cognitive biases.

PROJECT MANAGEMENT

One technique that has proved useful at promoting radical, but especially incremental, innovation is **project management**, the process of leading and controlling a project so that it results in the effective creation of new or improved products. A **project** is a subunit whose goal centres on developing the products or service on time, within budget, and in conformance with predetermined performance specifications—the criteria for assessing effectiveness. In the race to produce advanced technological products quickly, the issues of managing a project both to reduce the time it takes to bring a new product to market and to reduce the costs of innovation are becoming increasingly important. It is useful to examine the role of project managers and analyze what they do.

Project management
The process of leading and controlling a project so that it results in the creation of effective new or improved products.

Project
A subunit whose goal centres on developing the products or service on time, within budget, and in conformance with predetermined performance specifications.

Effective project management begins with a clearly articulated plan that takes a product from its concept phase, to its initial test phase, to the modification phase, and to the final manufacturing or—in the case of services—setup phase. Of all these phases the concept phase typically involves the most work and cost, since the task facing the product development team is to take the latest research findings or thinking and to use them to create goods and services that people and organizations will want to use.

How does a project manager's job differ from that of a typical manager in a organization? First, a project manager (PM) is managing a higher proportion of highly skilled and educated professionals. Typically, there will be many scientists and engineers of all kinds working on a project. The most immediate issues to face are how to balance the centralization and decentralization of authority and how to hold these professional employees accountable for their actions so that their creative efforts can be harmonized with a project's time frame. However, it is the uncertainty surrounding a project—the fact that unexpected problems, delays, and breakthroughs may be encountered—that creates the sense of urgency, risk, and suspense surrounding its completion. Harmonizing creative effort with cost and time considerations is a very difficult thing to do.

Often, PMs' past experience and intuition will allow them to judge how well or how poorly progress is being made toward a goal. Balancing the conflicting demands of performance, budget, and time schedule, and resolving the conflicts among them is a difficult process, especially as projects often are ongoing for one to three years or longer. One of the hardest tasks of a PM is to maintain the momentum of the project, as team members such as engineers or designers fail repeatedly to come up with solutions to problems, and the project threatens to flounder. Overcoming inertia, suggesting possible solutions, brainstorming, and providing encouragement and positive feedback are an essential part of the PM's job. On the other hand, scientists and engineers can be perfectionists whose only goal is to increase the product's performance and it is important that the PM keep the goals of time and cost in mind, convincing engineers that the search for a perfect product will turn out to be a disaster if it results in one that is so expensive customers will not wish to buy it.

It is the ability to think ahead and perform effective advance planning, which is often key to a PM's success. Based on past experience, effective PMs know what typical problems arise, and they know how to organize and control employees to address them. Thus when a crisis occurs, as it usually does, resources will be ready to confront it.

Another important aspect of PMs' advanced planning involves a plan to deal with top corporate executives, who will be watching anxiously and evaluating the performance of the project, looking for signs of success or failure. Selling their ideas and their project is the never-ending job of PMs. Later, we discuss how PMs must be product champions, the people who have to believe in the project; if they are not committed to its success, others in the organization are likely to have little enthusiasm for it. The ability to present new product ideas effectively and to crystallize the meaning and importance of a project are major determinants of a PM's ability to obtain continuing funding for a slow-moving project—even to ensure the survival of the project, for it is common for many projects to be terminated mid-course.

To help with advanced planning, to uncover bottlenecks and prevent crises where possible, and to help speed progress toward the goal, a tool commonly employed by project managers is *quantitative modelling.* Modelling allows PMs to develop "What if?" scenarios and to experiment with finding new and better ways of performing the sequential, and parallel, steps involved in reaching the final product.

One common modelling approach is to develop a *PERT/CAM network* or *GANTT chart,* which are essentially flowcharts of a project that can be built with many proprietary software packages (such as Microsoft's Project 2000).[25] These software packages focus on (1) modelling the sequence of actions necessary to reach a project's goal and (2) relating these actions to cost and time criteria, such as the per-week cost of the scientists and engineers employed in the project, to (3) sort out and define the optimal path for reaching the goal. Once the PM has chosen a particular path to follow, these programs provide ongoing feedback on project performance that can be used to assess project performance.

One of the first, and simplest, of these modelling techniques, the *critical path method (CPM),* captures the essence of what these models try to achieve. The goal of CPM is to determine (1) which particular tasks or activities of the many that have to be performed are critical in their effect on project time and cost and thus (2) to determine how to sequence or schedule critical tasks so that a project can meet a target date at a minimum cost. Finding the critical path thus provides an optimal solution to the needs of a particular project. The flow chart in Figure 13-3 illustrates the critical tasks involved in building a house.

The optimal sequencing of tasks that have to be performed to reach the completed product is often worked out by a team that experiments with different possible sequences. In this simple example of building a house, the most efficient sequencing of steps can be easily discovered. For many more complex projects, however, the analysis of these steps constitutes an important learning tool; many unforeseen interactions between these steps can be uncovered by a careful analysis. Attention is then paid to how to shorten the path—how to reorganize, combine, or resequence tasks to cut time and cost and improve performance. Frequently, a team will experiment by building prototypes of a new facilities layout or task structure if how to make a product or provide a service is the key issue.

Note the link to re-engineering an organization, discussed in Chapter 10, where the move to combine the activities of different specialists or functions and focus on business processes, not activities, is also a way of shortening the critical path. PERT/CRM software packages permit the user to examine and compare many differ-

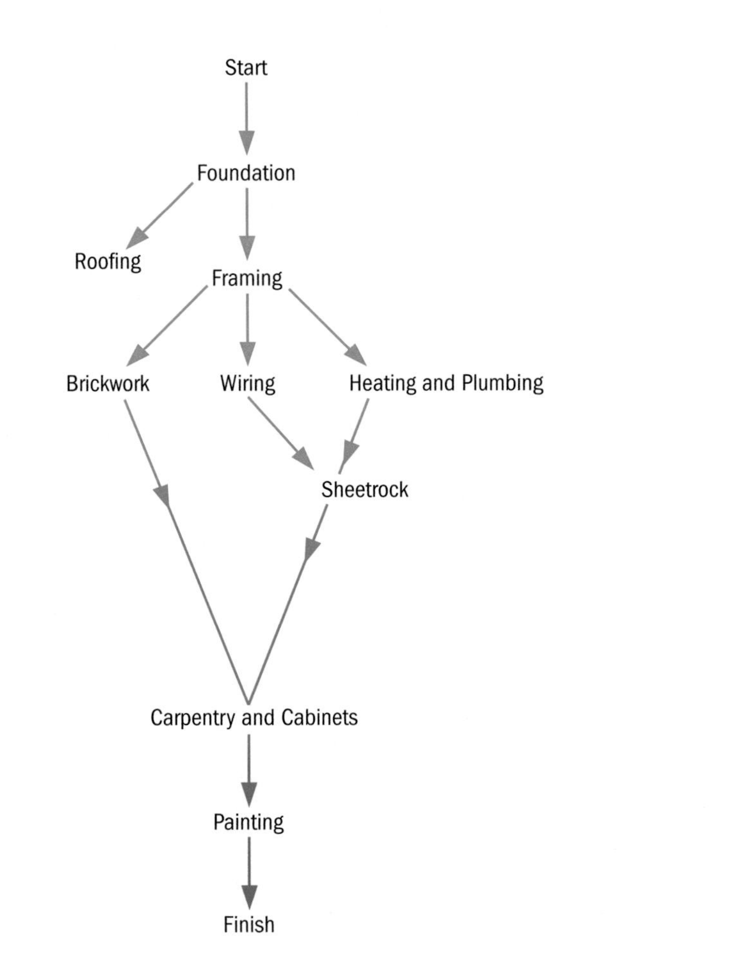

FIGURE 13-3
CPM Project Design.

ent kinds of configurations to find the best path to job completion. Modern IT systems, such as computer-aided design (CAD) (discussed in Chapter 9), can completely change task sequencing, especially when organizational developments such as flexible work teams, product teams, and network structures are factored into the equation.

Indeed, such developments have made the job of the project manager increasingly prominent in many organizations. Successful PMs are often those who rise to more general management positions because of their demonstrated competency in understanding how to design organizational structure and IT systems to facilitate the flow of innovative new goods and services. Project management is often a prerequisite for promotion to top management positions today.

Stage-Gate Development Funnel

One of the mistakes that top managers often make in managing the innovation process is trying to fund too many development projects at any one point in time. The result is that limited financial, functional, and human resources are spread thinly over too many different projects. As a consequence, no single project or PM is given the resources that are required to make a project succeed and the level of successful innovation falls.

Given the nature of this problem, it is necessary for managers to develop a structured process for evaluating different new product development proposals and deciding which to support. A common solution to this problem is to implement a stage-gate development funnel[26] (Figure 13-4). The purpose of a *stage-gate funnel* is to establish a structured and coherent innovation process that both improves control over the product development effort and forces managers to make choices among competing new product development projects so that resources are not spread thinly over too many projects.

The funnel has a wide mouth (stage 1) in order initially to promote innovation by encouraging as many new product ideas as possible from both new and established

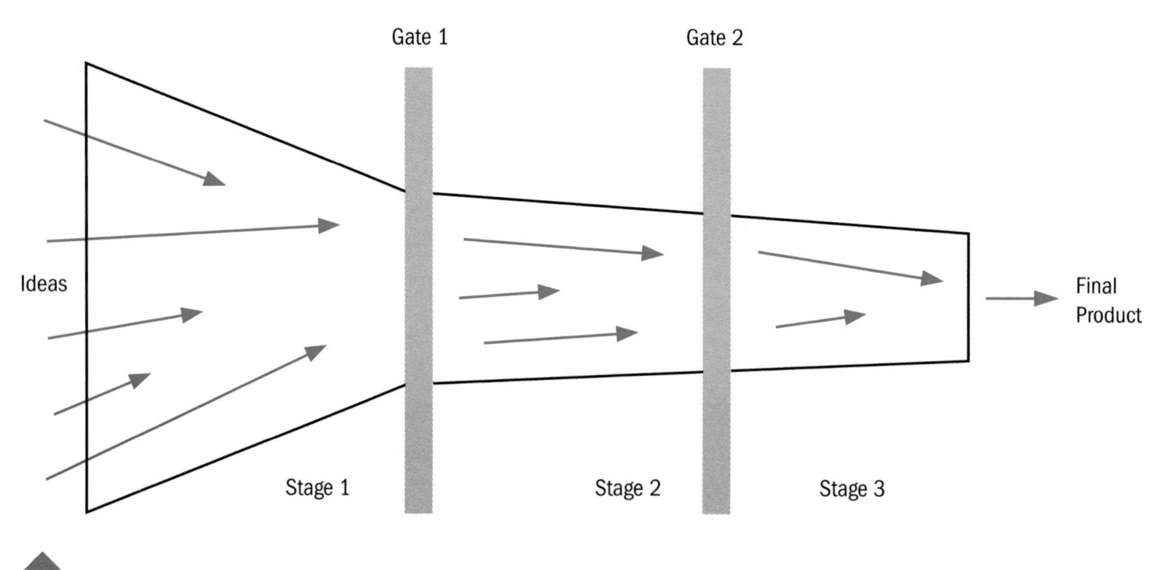

FIGURE 13-4
A Stage-Gate Development Funnel.

project managers. Companies establish a wide mouth by creating incentives for employees to come up with new product ideas. Some organizations run "bright ideas" programs, which reward prospective project managers for submitting new product ideas that eventually make it through the development process. Others allow research scientists to devote a certain amount of work time to their own projects. For example, Hewlett-Packard and 3M have a 15 percent rule: 15 percent of a research scientist's work week can be devoted to working on a project of his or her own choosing. Ideas may be submitted by individuals who may assume the role of project manager if a project is approved.

These new product ideas are then written up in the form of a brief new product development proposal and submitted to a cross-functional team of managers who evaluate the proposal at gate 1. At gate 1, the proposal is reviewed in terms of its fit with the strategy of the organization and its technical feasibility. Proposals that are consistent with the strategy of the organization and judged technically feasible will be passed on to stage 2; the rest will be turned down (although the door is often left open for reconsidering the proposal at a later date).

The primary goal in stage 2 is for the prospective project manager to draft a detailed new product development plan that specifies all of the information required to make a decision about whether to go ahead with a full-blown product development effort. Included in the new product development plan should be factors such as strategic and financial objectives, an analysis of market potential, a list of desired product features, a list of technological requirements, a list of financial and human resource requirements, a detailed development budget, and a timeline that contains specific milestones (e.g., dates for prototype completion and final launch). The project manager is often aided in drafting the plan by a cross-functional team that spends considerable time in the field with customers trying to understand how to tailor the product to their needs.

Once completed, the plan is reviewed by a senior management committee (at gate 2). Here the review focuses on a detailed look at the new product development plan and considers whether the proposal is attractive given its market potential, and viable given the technological, financial, and human requirements of actually developing the product. This review is made in light of all other product development efforts being undertaken by the organization. One goal at this point is to ensure that limited technical, financial, and human resources are used to their maximum effect.

At gate 2, projects are either rejected, sent back for revision, or allowed to proceed to the development phase (stage 3). The stage 3 development effort can last anywhere from six months to ten years, depending upon the industry and product type. For example, some electronics products have development cycles of six months; it takes three to five years to develop a new car; about five years to develop a new jet aircraft; and as much as ten years to develop a new medical drug.

Using Cross-Functional Teams and a Product Team Structure

As just noted, establishing cross-functional teams is a critical element in any structured new product development effort.[27] Although successful innovation begins in the R&D function, the way the activities of the R&D department are coordinated with the activities of other functions is crucial.[28] Figure 13-5 identifies the many functions necessary for successful innovation. In addition to R&D, they include product engineering, process engineering, materials management, manufacturing, and marketing.

Because those different groups usually have different orientations and attitudes, coordinating their activities is difficult. The link between R&D and the product and process engineering groups, for example, is vital to the conversion of research results

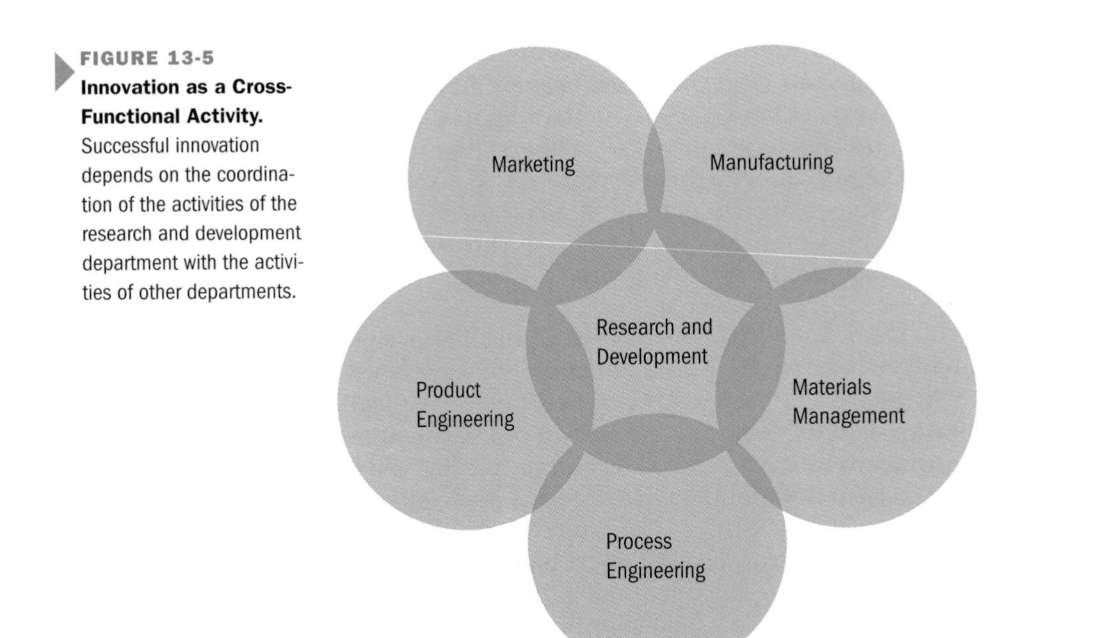

FIGURE 13-5
Innovation as a Cross-Functional Activity. Successful innovation depends on the coordination of the activities of the research and development department with the activities of other departments.

into a product that is designed efficiently and can be produced cheaply. R&D scientists, however, may complain that the potential of "their" new product is being sacrificed if the engineers tinker with its design to make production either easy or cheap. In turn, engineering may feel that R&D is too emotionally committed to the product and has lost sight of the market in its pursuit of technical excellence.

Both R&D and engineering also need to coordinate with manufacturing to ensure that the new product can be made cost-effectively and reliably. A link with marketing will ensure that the product possesses the features and qualities that customers need and want and that R&D resources are not being spent to create or improve a product that customers do not want. Marketing may discover, for example, that customers are not willing to pay the price that the organization will be forced to charge for the product. This marketing information may conflict with R&D's and engineering's views about producing a high-quality product, even at a high price.

Marketing, engineering, and manufacturing personnel need to be core members of successful new product development teams. The term *core members* refers to a nucleus of three to six people who bear primary responsibility for the product development effort. In addition to core members, others typically work on the project as the need arises, but it is the core members who stay with the project from inception to completion of the development effort. To ensure that core members are not distracted by other development projects, they are usually assigned to only one development project at a time. In addition, for particularly important new product development projects, core members may be taken out of their regular functional role for the duration of the project and assigned to work on the project full-time.

Many organizations have been unable to manage the functional linkages necessary for successful product innovation, and the results have often been disastrous. A list of innovative products for which there was little demand includes the RCA laser disc player, the Kodak photo CD player, and the cost-ineffective supersonic Concorde airliner. In Chapter 6, we discussed various structures that organizations can use to manage activities in conditions of great uncertainty. Two of them, product team structure and matrix structure, are especially suitable for managing innovation in high-tech organizations. Both of these structures focus on creating cross-functional teams to pursue new product development from the concept and design stage, through manufacturing, to the marketing and sales stage. These structures allow each function to develop an understanding of the problems and interests of the other functions, and they reduce communication problems. Decentralizing authority to the team also forces team members to cooperate and develop a shared understanding of the project.

Even though a product team structure facilitates innovation and the new product development process, it is often not sufficient to solve the coordination problem. Many organizations use additional integrating mechanisms to facilitate innovation: team leaders and project champions, "skunk works," new venture divisions, and joint ventures.

Team Leadership

While establishment of a cross-functional product development team may be a necessary condition for successful innovation, it is not a sufficient condition. If a cross-functional team is to succeed, it must have the right kind of leadership, and it must be managed in an effective manner.[29]

One important consideration is to have a team leader who can rise above his or her functional background and take a cross-functional view. Another issue is how much power and authority should be given to the team leader. Here a distinction can be made between lightweight and heavyweight team leaders.[30] A *lightweight team leader* is a mid-level functional manager who has lower status than the head of a functional department. The lightweight team leader is not given control over human, financial, and functional resources. Not a true project manager, this leader remains under the control of a functional department head. If the lightweight leader wants access to resources, he or she must pursue the heads of functional departments to allocate them for a period of time. This arrangement weakens the power and authority of the team leader, who is subservient to the heads of functional departments. The result can be limited cross-functional coordination. Still, this arrangement might be appropriate in those cases where minor modifications of an existing product are all that is required.

A *heavyweight team leader* is a true project manager who has higher status within the organization. The heavyweight team leader is given primary control over key human, financial, and technical resources for the duration of the project. This allows the heavyweight leader to lay first claim to key resources and, if necessary, to override the wishes of the heads of the functions. For example, the heavyweight leader may be able to insist that a certain marketing and engineering manager be assigned full-time to the project, even if the heads of the engineering and marketing departments are not in favour of this assignment. This power gives the heavyweight team leader a much greater chance of assembling a cross-functional team capable of successfully developing a new product. Researchers who study this issue argue that heavyweight team leaders make most sense in the case of important new product development efforts.[31]

Heavyweight team leaders often function as product champions—the people who take ownership of the project, solve problems as they occur, smooth over disputes between team members, and provide leadership to the team. Sometimes the product champion is not formally appointed and emerges informally during the innovation process. The way in which Don Frey, a product champion at Ford, worked with Lee Iacocca to develop the Ford Mustang in the early 1960s illustrates the importance of the product champion role. (See Organizational Insight 13.4.)

ORGANIZATIONAL INSIGHT 13.4

Championing the Mustang

Don Frey, an R&D engineer, was a product champion at Ford Motor Company. At Ford's R&D laboratories, Frey was assigned to projects that seemed new and interesting, but he never got to talk to customers and never got involved in operational decision making about what to offer the customer and how much new developments would cost. As a result, for many years, he and other R&D engineers worked on products that never got to market. Frustrated by the lack of payoff from his work, Frey began to question the utility of a corporate R&D laboratory that was so far removed from operations and the market. In 1957, he moved from R&D to head the passenger car design department, where he would be closer to market operations. In this new position, Frey was much closer to the customer and directed the energies of his department to producing innovations that customers wanted and were willing to pay for.

Frey soon concluded that in the automobile business the best R&D was incremental: Year by year a car was improved to meet customer demands. He also saw how important it was to use customer complaints as a guide for investing R&D resources to get the most benefit. Equipped with this new perspective on innovation, he was made a member of Ford's top planning committee in 1961, and he became interested in developing a new car for the emerging "sporty car segment."

Frey and his staff saw the possibility of designing a car for this segment, and began championing the development of a product. Ford, however, had just lost a fortune on the Edsel and was reluctant to start a new car. Because there was no corporate support for Frey's ideas, all of the early engineering and styling of what became the Mustang were carried out with bootleg funds—funds earmarked for something else. By 1962, Frey and his team had produced the first working prototype of the Mustang and believed they had a winner. Top management in general and Henry Ford II in particular were not impressed and offered no support, still fearing the new car might turn out to be another Edsel.

Luckily for the Mustang team, Lee Iacocca became vice president and general manager of Ford in 1962, and he bought into the Mustang concept. Believing that the Mustang would be a huge success, Iacocca risked his reputation to convince top management to back the idea. In the fall of 1962, after much pressure, funds to produce the car were allocated. With Frey as product champion, the Mustang was completed from approval to market in only 18 months. When the Mustang was introduced in 1964, it was an instant success, and over 400 000 Mustangs were sold.

Frey went on to champion other innovations in Ford vehicles, such as disc brakes and radial tires. Reflecting on his experiences as a product champion, he offered some coaching tips for future product champions: Innovation can start anywhere and from small beginnings, and product champions must be prepared to use all the skill they have to pull people and resources together and to resist top managers and financial experts who use numbers to kill new ideas.[32] As Frey's experience suggests, innovation is a risky business, and product champions have to go out on a limb to take on the disbelievers.

Skunk Works and New Venture Divisions

A *skunk works* is a task force, a temporary team, that is created to expedite new product design and to promote innovation by coordinating the activities of functional groups.[33] The task force consists of members of the engineering and research departments and other support functions such as marketing and is assigned to other facilities, often at a location away from the rest of the organization. This setting provides the opportunity for the intensive face-to-face interactions necessary to generate successful innovation. Together, the members of the task force "own the problem" and become internal entrepreneurs, or *intrapreneurs,* people inside an organization who are responsible for the success or failure of the project. Thus a skunk works is an island of innovation and provides a large organization with a small-organization-type setting in which team members have the opportunity and motivation to bring a new product to market quickly. Ford created a skunk works to develop the new Mustang that was introduced in 1993.

Hewlett-Packard, 3M, and other organizations have also recognized the advantages of a small-organization atmosphere for fostering entrepreneurship in their employees. Thus, as viable new product developments occur in corporate R&D laboratories, these organizations create a *new venture division,* a new division that is allocated a complete set of value-creating functions to manage a project from beginning to end.[34] Unlike a skunk works, which is dissolved when the product is brought to market, a new venture division assumes full responsibility for the commercialization of the product and is normally an independent division. Project members become the heads of the division's functions and are responsible for managing the functional structure created to bring the new product to market.

Establishing the balance of control between the division and the corporate centre can become a problem in a new venture division. As the new division absorbs more and more resources to fulfill its mission, the corporate centre may become concerned about the commercial success of the project. If corporate managers begin to intervene in the division's activities, divisional managers begin to lose their autonomy, and the division's entrepreneurial attitude may start to decline. On the other hand, major problems can arise if an organization sets up many independent new venture divisions to spur innovation, as the example of Lucent suggests. (See Organizational Insight 13.5.)

Managing new venture divisions is a difficult process that requires considerable organizational skill. Managers must create the right kind of organizational structure if they are to be successful; utilizing the right kinds of IT systems is also vital; this important issue is discussed later in the chapter.

Joint Ventures

Joint ventures between two or more organizations, discussed in Chapter 3, are another important means of managing high-tech innovation. A joint venture allows organizations to combine their skills and technologies and pool their resources to embark on risky R&D projects. A joint venture is similar to a new venture division in that a new organization is created in which people can work out new procedures that lead to success. This was the case with Tembec Inc., whose successful collaboration with Dofasco Inc. and McMaster University led to the Synergy Award of Innovation in 2003 (see Organizational Insight 13.6).

When two or more companies share revenues, risks, and costs, this often can result in the development of a stream of profitable new products. Joint ventures can also cause problems, however, if the venture partners begin to come into conflict over future development plans. This often happens when, over time, the venture begins to favour one partner over another. Given this possibility, many joint venture agreements have clauses allowing one partner to buy the other out, or giving one partner 51 percent ownership of the venture, to ensure that the gains from future innovation can be achieved.

ORGANIZATIONAL INSIGHT 13.5

Too Much Innovation at Lucent

In the early 2000s, increasing competition made it imperative for many high-tech companies to find a way to innovate and differentiate their products to sustain or increase their competitive advantage. Take Lucent Technologies, which makes Internet routers and other communications equipment. Lucent was one of the high-flying high-tech companies of the 1990s. To promote the speedy development of new products, former CEO Richard McGinn had decided that Lucent should be set up as 11 independent business divisions, each of which would focus on a particular product and market.[35] His goal was to drive innovation and develop a steady stream of new products to compete with market leader Sysco Systems.

In creating venture divisions, however, McGinn set in motion a whole set of problems that ultimately led to the company's downfall. First, enormous communications and coordination problems arose because managers in one division did not know what managers in the others were doing. Incompatible kinds of products were being developed, new technology was not being shared across divisions, and it was a nightmare trying to sell Lucent's range of products globally because the 11 business units were each handling their own global sales. For example, because of poor decision making and communication, managers had backed the development of the wrong kind of router, one based on capacity rather than speed; speed turned out to be what customers wanted. By contrast, Nortel Networks, one of Lucent's major competitors, had developed fast optical or light-based routers and its market share was surging. Second, the cost of managing all these new venture divisions was enormous since they each had their own set of functions, including R&D, which is a major expense for a high-tech organization. Thus not only were revenues falling, but costs were increasing.

The failed new venture strategy forced McGinn to leave the company. His successor, Henry Schacht, decided effectiveness would increase if Lucent reorganized the 11 different units into just five business units. This would make managers more accountable for their actions and they would be better able to communicate and avoid mistaken innovation and failed product development. Schacht and his managers spent hundreds of millions of dollars to restructure the company and laid off over 15 000 employees.

By 2001, however, it was clear that Lucent could no longer afford the luxury of having even five divisions because of mounting losses and the need to reduce costs. In July and October, Schacht announced that Lucent would reorganize again, both to reduce costs and allow it to better focus its resources to speed the new product development process. Another 20 000 employees were to be laid off (a total of almost one-half of Lucent's employees were laid off as a result of the restructuring). And Lucent announced that it was combining the five units into only two business divisions:[36] An Integrated Network Solutions division would handle all its landline products such as routers, switching, and data software; and a Mobility Solutions division would handle the company's wireless products.

Managers hoped this new structure would perform more flexibly and organically and allow it to respond faster and more effectively to the rapidly changing information technology environment. They also knew it would save billions of dollars and would be a much more efficient method of organizing. However, these changes may have come too late to turn around its fortunes. In September 2002 it announced another huge loss, its stock plunged, and it seemed doubtful that it would survive in its battle with Nortel and Cisco.[37]

ORGANIZATIONAL INSIGHT 13.6

Tembec's "Company of People" Joining with Others in Successful Ventures[38]

Tembec Inc. is a large forest/wood products company with over 10 000 employees. It has more than 50 manufacturing plants in six provinces, as well as international operations in the United States, France, and Chile. With annual sales near $4 billion, the company has become quite a success story. The company first started in 1973 in Temiscaming, Quebec. It was there that a multinational company closed the town's mill plant, which represented the primary economic foothold of the community. With determination, the people of the small community worked hard to save the mill. The mill reopened as Tembec through the joint efforts of the community, local entrepreneurs, government, the workers, and their union. This dramatic rebirth through a well-spirited joint venture created not only a thriving wood products company, but also a steadfast vision whereby Tembec became a "company of the people building their own future."

The "company of people" theme has translated into ongoing success stories of people working together at Tembec to advance the company as a leader in innovation, technology, and unique labour management relations. The ethic of working together within the company has also extended to positive relations and partnerships with other organizations, as well as successful outcomes in the acquisitions of other forestry companies. A joint effort with McMaster University and Dofasco Inc., for example, proved to be a beneficial venture of innovation for all three parties. This successful venture won the prestigious Synergy Award of Innovation in 2003.

The Natural Sciences and Engineering Research Council and the Conference Board of Canada sponsor the Synergy Award to recognize the best Canadian industry–university partnerships in developing innovative solutions. McMaster, Dofasco, and Tembec won the award for collaboratively advancing the application of Multivariate Statistics (MVS) methods to extract valuable information from manufacturing processes data flows. Tembec has benefited from this venture in terms of greater efficiencies and has also used the MVS methods to improve its environmental performance at the Temiscaming wastewater treatment plant. In the company of its own people and with others, Tembec has done and continues to do well in joint ventures.

Creating a Culture for Innovation

Organizational culture also plays an important role in shaping and promoting innovation. Values and norms can reinforce the entrepreneurial spirit and allow an organization to respond quickly and creatively to a changing environment. As we saw in Chapter 7, three factors that shape organizational culture are organizational structure, people, and property rights (see Figure 7-2, p. 228).

Organizational Structure Because organizational structure influences the way people behave, creating the right setting is important to fostering an intrapreneurial culture. Several factors can stunt innovation and reduce the ability of an organization to introduce new products as it grows.

Increasing organizational size may slow innovation. As organizations grow, decision making slows down. Decisions have to be made through established channels in a sizable hierarchy, and a thriving bureaucracy may stifle the entrepreneurial spirit. As an organization becomes more bureaucratic, people may become more conservative and unwilling to take risks, and those most willing and able to innovate may become discouraged and leave the organization.

As organizations age, they tend to become less flexible and less innovative.[39] Relatively old, inflexible organizations may fail to notice new opportunities for new products because of what one writer has described as "the inability of many traditional mature firms to anticipate the need for productive change and their resistance to ideas advanced by creative people."[40] In addition, it is difficult for people to remain entrepreneurial throughout their careers. Thus, as organizations and their personnel age, there may be an inherent tendency for both to become more conservative.

With organizational growth comes complexity, and an increase in vertical and horizontal differentiation may hurt innovation. An increase in hierarchical levels makes it hard for employee entrepreneurs to exercise meaningful authority over projects. They may be under the constant scrutiny of upper-level managers who insist on signing off on projects. Similarly, when the skills and knowledge needed for innovation are spread across many subunits and functions, it is difficult for a product manager or product champion to coordinate the innovation process and secure the resources needed to bring a project to fruition.[41]

To promote innovation, organizations need to adopt a structure that can overcome those problems. Organic structures based on norms and values that emphasize lateral communication and cross-functional cooperation tend to promote innovation. Matrix and product team structures possess these organic characteristics and provide the autonomy for people to make their own decisions. In addition, many organizations use the informal organization to overcome obstacles presented by the formal structure. Such organizations give their employees wide latitude to act outside formal task definitions and to work on projects where they think they can make a contribution. Hewlett-Packard and 3M informally grant employees the right to use organizational resources to work on projects of their own choosing. Sony allows its scientists to move from project to project and to select a team to work on where they feel they can make the best contribution. Apple and Microsoft confer on their top R&D scientists the title research fellow and give them the autonomy and resources to decide how to put their skills to best use. When a research fellow's research leads to a promising new product development, a project team is established.

People The culture of innovation in high-tech organizations is fostered by the characteristics of employees themselves. In many research settings, people cooperate so closely on product development that they become increasingly similar to one another. They buy into the same set of organizational norms and values and thus are able to communicate well with each other. In turn, organizational members select new members who buy into the same set of values, so that over time a recognizable culture that promotes communication and the flow of new ideas emerges. However, an organization needs to guard against too much similarity in its scientists, lest they lose sight of new or emerging trends in the industry. IBM scientists, for example, fixated on improving mainframe computers and ignored signs that customers wanted better personal computers, not more sophisticated mainframes. To maintain a capacity to innovate successfully, a high-tech organization must strive to maintain diversity in its scientists and to allow them to follow divergent paths. The uncertainty associated with innovation makes it important for people to be adaptable and open to new ideas. One way to encourage flexibility and open-mindedness is to recruit people who are committed to innovation but who travel along different pathways to achieve it.

Property Rights The uncertainty associated with innovation makes it difficult for managers to evaluate the performance of highly skilled R&D scientists. Managers cannot watch scientists to see how well they are performing. Often their performance can be evaluated only over a long time—perhaps years. Moreover, innovation is a complex, intensive process that demands skills and abilities inherent in the scientist, not in the organization. When scientists come up with a new idea, it is relatively easy for them to take it and establish their own organizations to exploit the benefits from it. Indeed, much technological innovation occurs in new organizations founded by scientists who have left large organizations to branch out on their own. Given these issues, strong property rights are needed to align the interests of R&D scientists with the interests of the organization.[42] One company that challenged conventional thinking on property rights is Mountain Equipment Co-operative. Its strategy of cooperative ownership has been highly successful, much to the chagrin of some privately owned competitors. (See Organizational Insight 13.7.)

ORGANIZATIONAL INSIGHT 13.7

Innovation at Mountain Equipment Co-operative[43]

Mountain Equipment Co-operative (MEC) was founded in Vancouver in 1971. The idea for the company came from a group of six University of British Columbia Students who were stormbound on a mountain in 1970. The main company to buy outdoor equipment back then was REI in Seattle. However, many Canadians did not want to pay additional money at customs when they came back across the border, so some chose not to declare their purchases. This strategy became known to Canada Customs officials who began recording B.C. licence plate numbers from REI's parking lot. The students decided that the best solution would be to create a nonprofit Canadian company that would sell products to outdoor enthusiasts throughout Canada. The key company strategy would be to offer a range of high-quality products at reasonable prices.

From its one Vancouver store in 1971, MEC has grown to include stores in Calgary, Edmonton, Toronto, Halifax, Ottawa, Winnipeg, and Montreal. It is now the largest supplier of outdoor equipment in Canada with over two million members. In 2003, sales were over $160 million, a $7 million increase over the previous year. The company operates under the core values of ethical conduct, respect for others, and respect for the environment.

MEC is collectively owned by its members who purchase a lifetime membership. A share in MEC costs $5, represents ownership in the company, and entitles the bearer to participate in annual profits (if there are any). The share value has not changed since 1971. MEC offers two types of shares—subscription shares, which are purchased to shop at MEC stores, and patronage shares, which are allocated based on how much a person spends at the stores each year. MEC has worked hard to expand its product line through an in-house design department, and now almost 60 percent of sales are from the company's own designed products. The products, such as sleeping bags, tents, backpacks, and clothing, are made at contracted factories both in Canada and abroad and must meet stringent standards for the treatment of employees and the environment. The employees consider trying out new products as one of the perks of working for MEC. Additionally, MEC offers outdoor adventure programs and an urban adventure challenge race to encourage more people to get involved in outdoor pursuits.

MEC does not pay corporate income tax on profits and any surplus benefits members through lower prices, expanded services, and rebates. Its products are priced below recommended markups, giving the company a strategic advantage over its competitors in the marketplace. Another part of MEC's strategy is to minimize operating costs and use profits to finance strategically planned growth.

Since MEC doesn't pay income tax on profits, it has been accused of unfair business practices by competing firms. MEC has dismissed these charges, and CEO Peter Robinson has noted that "any company could reap a tax benefit by surrendering ownership, becoming a co-op, and dispensing with profits."

MEC plans to continue what has proven to be a very successful strategy. The current goal of the company, as noted in its catalogue is to "work more mindfully towards making positive changes in the world."

An organization can create career paths for its R&D employees and project managers and demonstrate that success is closely linked to future promotion and rewards. Career paths can be established not only inside the R&D function but among R&D, project management, and general management functions. Inside the R&D function, successful scientists can be groomed to manage future R&D projects. After some years in R&D, however, many scientists move to take control of manufacturing operations or to assume other management responsibilities. Because of the experience they gained in various functions, these managers are in a position to ensure that future R&D activities are aligned with customer needs and to serve as project managers.

Strong property rights can also be created if an organization ties individual and group performance to large monetary premiums. Innovative employees should receive bonuses and stock options that are proportional to the increase in profitability that can be attributed to their efforts. Making employees owners in the organization will discourage them from leaving and will provide them with a strong incentive to perform well. Many successful high-tech organizations, such as Merck and Apple, do this; and one in five of Microsoft's employees is a millionaire as a result of the organization's policy of giving stock options to employees. Remember, the last thing that Bill Gates wants is for his best employees to leave and found their own organizations that then compete with Microsoft.

By focusing on property rights, people, and structure, an organization can create a culture in which norms and values foster innovation and the search for excellence in new product development.

MANAGERIAL IMPLICATIONS

Innovation

1. Research and development activities must be integrated with the activities of the other functions if the innovation process is to be successful.
2. Employees must be given autonomy and encouraged to use organizational resources to facilitate the continuous development of new products and processes.
3. Project managers, a stage-gate product development funnel, cross-functional teams, appropriate team leadership, a skunk works, and new venture divisions should be created to provide a setting that encourages entrepreneurship.
4. Top management must create a culture that supports innovation and that recognizes and rewards the contributions of organizational members—for example, by linking rewards directly to performance.

INNOVATION AND INFORMATION TECHNOLOGY

Previous chapters have discussed how IT can raise organizational effectiveness, particularly by reducing operating costs. Why? Because of **information efficiencies**, the cost and time savings that occur when IT allows individual employees to perform their current tasks at a higher level, assume additional tasks, and expand their roles in the organization due to advances in the ability to gather and analyze data.[44] The ability of IT to enhance a person's task knowledge and technical skills is also an important input into the innovation process, however. In fact, IT facilitates the innovation process because it promotes creativity in many ways and affects many aspects of the process of bringing new problem-solving ideas into use.

Information efficiencies The cost and time savings that occur when IT allows individual employees to perform their current tasks at a higher level, assume additional tasks, and expand their roles in the organization due to advances in the ability to gather and analyze data.

First, IT facilitates creativity by improving the initial base of knowledge to draw from when employees engage in problem solving and decision making. To the degree that IT creates a larger and richer pool of codified knowledge for any given employee to draw from, and allows these employees to work together, innovative potential is increased. Examples of knowledge codification from utilizing knowledge management were discussed in Chapter 12. For example, at large consultancy firms like Accenture and McKinsey & Co., groups of experienced consultants assemble knowledge online from every level of the firm, and then use in-house IT to disseminate information to consultants throughout the organization—information that would otherwise not have been available to them.

Knowledge or information availability alone will not lead to innovation; it is the ability to *creatively use* knowledge that is the key to promoting innovation and creating competitive advantage.[45] Prahalad and Hamel, for example, suggest that it is not the level of knowledge a firm possesses that leads to innovation and competitive advantage, but the velocity with which it is circulated in the firm.[46] Organizations must take steps to ensure that they use knowledge to develop distinctive competencies at both the individual and functional levels, and particularly between functions.

Similarly, it is very likely that a reshuffling of tasks will occur as new IT systems increase the ability of people or subunits to acquire and process information. This leads to many more opportunities for creatively combining, modifying, and synthesizing information, leading to the incremental innovations discussed earlier. For example, what before might have been a task that requires the inputs of three different people or subunits becomes a task that one individual or function can perform more creatively and effectively because IT helps to increase both the amount and quality of information that can be adequately processed. IT also facilitates cross-functional and divisional communication and coordination that can promote the sharing of tacit knowledge between people and groups, leading to increased organizational knowledge.

Innovation and Information Synergies

In fact, one of the most important performance gains that result from IT occurs when two or more individuals or subunits pool their resources and cooperate and collaborate across role or subunit boundaries, creating **information synergies**. Information synergies occur when IT allows individuals or subunits to adjust their actions or behaviours to the needs of the other individuals or subunits on an ongoing basis and achieve gains from team-based cooperation.

Information synergies The knowledge-building created when two or more individuals or subunits pool their resources and cooperate and collaborate across role or subunit boundaries.

IT changes organizational forms and promotes creativity and innovation inside both network and virtual organizational forms. IT-enabled virtual forms composed of electronically connected people or firms facilitate knowledge sharing and innovation. Compared to face-to-face communication, for example, the use of electronic communication increases the amount of communication within the organization. IT's ability to link and enable employees within and between functions and divisions—whether through database repositories, teleconferencing, or e-mail—helps lead to information synergies. The application of IT has been shown to promote cross-functional workflows, makes critical information more accessible and transparent to employees, and increases the incidence of problem-solving leading to innovation.[47]

The downside to linking employees must be noted as well. It is possible that not only the amount of good advice information-seekers receive will increase—bad advice may increase as well. However, many firms work to ensure the reliability of information received via electronically weak ties by forming online communities where collections of experienced employees within a given area can be located (e.g., a software developers' forum, a sales force intranet, a manufacturing discussion group). Developing a knowledge management system also helps to ensure high-quality information and advice, given when requested.

Boundary-spanning activity The interactions of people and groups across the organizational boundary to obtain valuable information and knowledge from the environment to help promote innovation.

IT also allows for an increase in **boundary-spanning activity**—interacting with individuals and groups outside the organization to obtain valuable information and knowledge from the environment—that helps promote innovation. IT allows an employee to search for and absorb new knowledge that is relevant to a problem at hand.[48] For example, in complex organizations employees working on one task or project may wish to obtain useful knowledge residing in other operating units, but the employees may not know whether or not this knowledge exists and where it might reside. IT, through knowledge management systems, allows employees to search their network for information.

IT has many other useful properties that can promote incremental and quantum technological change. IT allows researchers and planners to communicate more easily and less expensively across time and geographic location; to communicate more rapidly and with greater precision to targeted groups; to more selectively control access and participation in a communication event or network; to more rapidly and selectively access information created outside the organization; to more rapidly and accurately combine and reconfigure information; and to more concisely store and quickly use experts' judgments and decision models. All these qualities can enhance creativity and make project management more effective. Amazon.com is a company using IT to make creative decisions and broaden its product line, becoming a consultant itself and selling its own creative ideas. (See the Focus on New Information Technology box.)

IT and Organizational Structure and Culture

IT also affects the innovation process through its many effects on organizational structure. Specialization typically leads to the development of subunit orientations that reduce the ability of employees to understand the wider context within which they are contributing their skills and expertise. IT can mitigate this tendency by providing greater information access to specialists through such technologies as e-mail, corporate intranets, access to the Internet, and so on.

To speed innovation, many organizations have begun to move decision making lower in the organization to take advantage of specialized workers who possess more

FOCUS ON NEW INFORMATION TECHNOLOGY

Amazon.com, Part 7

Jeff Bezos's use of the Internet to sell books can probably be regarded as a quantum innovation in this industry. However, innovation at Amazon.com has not stopped there. Bezos and his top-management team have engaged in a series of incremental innovations to grow and expand Amazon.com's core competencies as an online retailer.[49]

While Bezos initially chose to focus on selling books, he soon realized that Amazon.com's information technology could be used to sell other kinds of products. He began to search for products that could be sold profitably over the Internet. First, he realized CDs were a natural product extension to offer customers, and Amazon.com announced its intention of becoming the "earth's biggest book and music store." Then Amazon opened a holiday gift store to entice customers to send gifts as well as books and CDs as presents, and offered a gift-wrapping service and launched a free electronic greeting card service to announce the arrival of the Amazon gift. Finally, realizing the popularity of online auctions, Bezos moved to enter this market by purchasing Livebid.com, the Internet's only provider of live on-line auctions, and then in 1999 entered into an agreement with Sotheby's, the famous auction house.

Since 2000, Bezos has moved aggressively to use Amazon.com's developing expertise in the virtual storefront to forge alliances with companies like Toys "R" Us, Office Depot, Circuit City, Target, and many others to allow their customers to buy at Amazon.com but to pick up purchases from their stores. It has also offered a consulting service to organizations that wish to develop the customer-friendly storefront that Amazon.com is famous for. As discussed in previous chapters, it has also used its IT competencies to widen its product line, and to keep its line up to date with regard to the ongoing changes in electronics and digital technology that are constantly altering the mix of products it offers in its virtual store.

As a result of these incremental innovations to Amazon.com's business, Bezos has transformed his company from "online bookseller" to "leading Internet product provider." The company's share price rose by 40 percent in 2002, after plunging during the dot-com bust, as investors believed that Amazon.com was poised to become profitable in the online retail business.

accurate and timely local information. IT helps this process in two ways. First, IT gives lower-level employees more detailed and current knowledge of consumer and market trends and opportunities. For example, IT in customer-support centres directed at solving customer problems via the Internet has become a widespread means of increasing effectiveness.

Second, IT can produce information synergies because it facilitates increased communication and coordination between decentralized decision makers and top managers. Now, as decision-making authority moves lower in the hierarchy, it may become better aligned.[50] The Gap, discussed earlier, would have greatly benefited from a sophisticated online computer-aided design system (CAD) that allows designers throughout the organization to see what the others are doing.

Third, IT means that fewer levels of managers are needed to handle problem solving and decision making, which results in a flatter organization. In addition, since IT provides lower-level employees with more freedom to coordinate their actions, information synergies may emerge, as employees experiment and find better ways of performing their tasks.

IT can also promote innovation through its effects on organizational culture. IT facilitates the sharing of beliefs, values, and norms because it allows for the quick transmission of rich, detailed information between people and subunits. IT thus can enhance the motivational effects of cultural values supportive of innovation. Using IT, an organization can make available to employees a slew of supportive messages and statements, often contained in an organization's mission statement, corporate goals, operating procedures, and so on. E-mail, voice mail, and intranets, for example, provide mechanisms for transferring and disseminating information about the organization to employees and can help promote the cultural shared norms, values, and expectations that can facilitate innovation.

SUMMARY

Managing the process of innovation and change to enhance organizational effectiveness is a central challenge facing managers and organizations today. An increasing rate of technological change and an increase in global competition are two forces that are putting enormous pressure on organizations to find new and better ways of organizing their activities to increase their ability to innovate and create value. Chapter 13 has made the following major points:

1. Innovation is the development of new products or new production and operating systems (including new forms of organizational structures).
2. There are two types of innovation: quantum innovations, which are the result of quantum shifts in technology, and incremental innovations, which result from the refinements to an existing technology. Technological change that results in quantum innovations can create opportunities for an organization to introduce new products, but it can also be a threat, since it can increase the level of competition.
3. Innovation, intrapreneurship, and creativity are closely related concepts and each is vital to build a knowledge-creating organization.
4. There are a number of techniques that managers can use to help promote innovation. These include project management, using a stage-gate development funnel, using cross-functional teams and a product team structure, establishing strong team leadership, making use of skunk works and new venture divisions, and creating a culture for innovation.

5. IT creates information efficiencies and information synergies and thus is an important tool for promoting creativity and innovation, especially through its effects on organizational design, structure, and culture.

DISCUSSION QUESTIONS

1. What is the relationship between quantum and incremental technological change?
2. What is the relationship among creativity, intrapreneurship, and innovation?
3. What is project management? How should managers decide which projects to pursue?
4. What steps would you take to create (a) a structure and (b) a culture congenial to innovation in a high-tech organization?
5. What are information synergies and in what ways can they enhance innovation?

ORGANIZATIONAL THEORY IN ACTION

Practising Organizational Theory: Managing Innovation

Break up into groups of three to five people and discuss the following scenario:

You are the top managers in charge of a chain of stores selling high-quality, high-priced men's and women's clothing. Store sales are flat, and you are increasingly concerned that the clothing your stores offer to customers is failing to satisfy changing customer needs. You think that the purchasing managers are failing to spot changing fads and fashions in time, and you believe that store management is not doing enough to communicate to purchasing managers what customers are demanding. You want to revitalize your organization's product development process, which, in the case of your stores, means designing, selecting, and stocking the products that customers want.

1. Using the chapter material, outline the way you will create a program to increase creativity and intrapreneurship at the store and corporate level. For example, how will you encourage input from employees and customers, and who will be responsible for managing the program?
2. How will you make use of IT and organizational structure to facilitate the innovation process?

Making the Connection #13

Find an example of an organization that has been trying to promote its level of innovation. What kind of innovation is it principally trying to promote? How is it attempting to do so? What has been its success so far?

The Ethical Dimension #13

Some intrapreneurs make discoveries that earn millions or even billions of dollars of product sales for the companies they work for, but because this was not provided for in their employment contracts they do not share in these profits. Other intrapreneurs make discoveries in the course of their work but do not share this information with their companies. They leave their organizations and found their own to exploit this knowledge.

1. Think about the ethical issues involved in each of these scenarios. Is it ethical either for the organization or the individual to act in this way?

2. Is there a way of solving the ethical dilemma posed in each of these cases?

Analyzing the Organization: Design Module #13

This module focuses on the extent to which your organization has been involved in efforts to promote innovation.

1. With the information that you have at your disposal, discuss (a) the forces for change, and (b) obstacles to change in your company.
2. With what kind of innovation (quantum or incremental) has your organization been most involved?
3. In what ways, if any, has your organization sought to manage the innovation process and alter its structure or culture to increase its capacity to develop new products or services?

Company Profiles #13*

Choose one or more of the organizations (e.g., companies, government agencies, or nonprofit organizations) that are profiled in this chapter. Do an Internet search to get up-to-date information on each organization you have selected, and answer the following questions.

1. What does the new information tell you about the organization's current ability to innovate?
2. How does the information compare with the earlier information provided in the text and what does that tell you about organizations (e.g., does the organization appear to be more or less able to innovate than before, and how do you explain this)?

Alternative Perspectives #13

Critical, feminist, and postmodernist researchers contend that strategies of innovation in capitalist organizations are often pursued without regard for their impact on employees and local communities. Read one or more of the following readings and list five ways that strategies of innovation can have a negative impact and five ways that they can have a positive impact on employees. In small groups, discuss how you would deal with the potentially negative aspects of innovation strategies.

Reading List

Helms Mills, J. 2003. *Making Sense of Organizational Change.* London: Routledge.

Laxer, G. 1995. Social Solidarity, Democracy and Global Capitalism. *The Canadian Review of Sociology and Anthropology*, 32(3): 287–313.

Mills, A. J., Simmons, T., and Helms Mills, J. 2005. *Reading Organization Theory: A Critical Approach to the Study of Organizational Behaviour and Structure*, 3rd ed. Toronto: Garamond Press.

Morgan, G., and Knights, D. 1991. Gendering Jobs: Corporate Strategies, Managerial Control and Dynamics of Job Segregation. *Work, Employment & Society*, 5(2): 181–200.

Rinehart, J. 1986. Improving the Quality of Working Life Through Job Redesign: Work Humanization or Work Rationalization. *The Canadian Review of Sociology and Anthropology*, 23(4): 507–530.

* The authors would like to receive information from student groups and instructors on any companies where there have been dramatic changes to the information published in this text. We would be happy to publish the best of these changes in a subsequent edition, where we will focus on changing company profiles.

CASE FOR ANALYSIS

Big Changes at Boeing

In October 1990, the Boeing Corporation committed itself to developing an all-new wide-bodied 400-seat commercial jet aircraft, the Boeing 777. Competition is fierce in the passenger jet aircraft business. Boeing's managers recognized that they had to come up with a new way to operate in order to simultaneously reduce costs, increase quality, and design a new aircraft that its customers would want.

Boeing began the innovation process when it moved to a product team structure and created cross-functional design teams to develop its new aircraft. Engineering and production employees were put together in scores of teams, each of which was given the responsibility of developing a specific portion of the new plane and making it easy to manufacture. Boeing also brought 18 major suppliers into the 777 program to consult with project engineers in order to rectify any problems that might arise in production ahead of time, thereby reducing the need for costly design changes late in the development cycle. The suppliers became informal members of the team that became most committed to raising quality and finding innovative ways to keep costs low.

To build a plane that was designed with customer requirements in mind, Boeing also invited eight airlines to help them design the aircraft. The group included United, which launched the program with orders for 32 planes, American, Delta, British Airways, and Japan Air Lines. For almost a year, technical representatives from these airlines took up residence in Boeing's Seattle facility and met with the engineering staff assigned to the 777 project. Making customers an integral part of the innovation process was a dramatic change for Boeing, which hitherto had always been very secretive about its design work.

The input from the eight carriers had a major effect on the design of the new 777. The eight airlines demanded a fuselage that was wider than rival McDonnell Douglas and Airbus models so that they could pack another 30 or so seats onto the aircraft. The result was an aircraft 13 cm wider than the McDonnell Douglas MD-11 and 64 cm wider than the Airbus's A-330. The airlines also wanted a plane in which the galleys and lavatories could be quickly relocated almost anywhere within the plane, so Boeing designed a plane whose interior can be completely reconfigured in three to four hours, with one, two, or three classes, depending on a carrier's market of the moment. American Airlines, in particular, wanted the 777 to have an option for folding wing tips so that the plane could utilize the same airport space as American's DC-10s and 767s. Boeing devised a way of folding 6.5 m of each wing, leaving a parked 777 with roughly the same wingspan as a DC-10 or 767.

In another major change for Boeing, the 777 was the first airliner to be designed entirely by computer. Boeing's engineers innovated a state-of-the-art, 3D computer-aided design technology to engineer and test parts in virtual space. The new system dramatically cut back on the need for expensive mock-ups and design changes and cut down on development time. Indeed, the 777 was the first commercial jet aircraft ever built without a full-sized mock-up. Pre-assemblies were first created and put together in "virtual space" on a computer screen to make sure that every component fit. When components didn't fit, they were redesigned on the computer until they did, and only then were real parts and subassemblies manufactured.

The success of its new innovation process was demonstrated when the first 777 took off only four years later from Boeing's Everett, Washington, production facility. The four-year development time for the 777 represented a triumph for Boeing; the typical development time for jet aircraft is at least six years. Moreover, by the time the 777 took off, Boeing already had 150 firm orders for the plane, and airlines had taken out options on another 150 planes. This kind of advanced ordering is a sure sign that Boeing had developed an aircraft that customers wanted. By changing its technology and operating system, Boeing had succeeded in raising the speed of new product innovation and developing a new product that its customers would want.

DISCUSSION QUESTIONS

1. Chart the major steps that Boeing took to encourage innovation and new product development.
2. How easy would it be for other organizations to follow its lead?

REFERENCES

1. R. A. Burgelman and M. A. Maidique, *Strategic Management of Technology and Innovation* (Homewood, IL: Irwin, 1988).
2. G. R. Jones and J. E. Butler, "Managing Internal Corporate Entrepreneurship: An Agency Theory Perspective," *Journal of Management,* 1992, vol. 18, pp. 733–749.
3. E. Mansfield, J. Rapaport, J. Schnee, S. Wagner, and M. Hamburger, *Research and Innovation in the Modern Corporation* (New York: Norton, 1971).
4. R. D'Aveni, *Hyper-Competition* (New York: The Free Press, 1994).
5. P. Engardio and N. Gross, "Asia's High Tech Quest: Can the Tigers Compete Worldwide?" *Business Week,* 7 December 1992, pp. 126–130.
6. P. Anderson and Michael L. Tushman, "Technological Discontinuities and Dominant Designs: A Cyclical Model of Technological Change," *Administrative Science Quarterly,* 1990, vol. 35, pp. 604–633; quoting J. Schumpeter, *Capitalism, Socialism, and Democracy* (New York: Harper Brothers, 1942).
7. The concept of creative destruction goes back to the classic work of J. A. Schumpeter, ibid.
8. V. P. Buell, *Marketing Management* (New York: McGraw-Hill, 1985).
9. *www.theregister.co.uk/2004/11/22/dixons_vcr/,* 2004.
10. See M. M. J. Berry and J. H. Taggart, "Managing Technology and Innovation: A Review," *R&D Management,* 1994, vol. 24, pp. 341–53; and K. B. Clark and S. C. Wheelwright, *Managing New Product and Process Development* (New York: The Free Press, 1993).
11. E. Abrahamson, "Managerial Fads and Fashions: The Diffusion and Rejection of Innovations," *Academy of Management Review,* 1991, vol. 16, pp. 586–612.
12. See Berry and Taggart, "Managing Technology and Innovation"; M. Gort and J. Klepper, "Time Paths in the Diffusion of Product Innovations," *Economic Journal,* September 1982, pp. 630–653. Looking at the history of 46 products, Gort and Klepper found that the length of time before other companies entered the markets created by a few inventive companies declined from an average of 14 years for products introduced before 1930 to 4.9 years for those introduced after 1949—implying that product life cycles were being compressed. See also A. Griffin, "Metrics for Measuring Product Development Cycle Time," *Journal of Production and Innovation Management,* 1993, vol. 10, pp. 112–125.
13. Clark and Wheelwright, *Managing New Product and Process Development.* See also G. Stalk and T. M. Hout, *Competing Against Time* (New York: The Free Press, 1990).
14. *www.gapinc.com,* 2000.
15. L. Clifford, "A Gap Mishap—But It Still Deserves a Look," *Fortune,* 18 September 2000, pp. 45–47.
16. *www.gap.com,* 2002.
17. B. Stone, "Filling in The Gap," *Newsweek,* 7 October 2002, p. 48.
18. Organizational Insight compiled by Scott MacMillan from the following sources: A. A. Davis, "Sky High," *Profit,* 2004, vol. 23, pp. 20–23; WestJet Airlines Ltd., 2003 Annual Report; *www.westjet.com,* 12 July 2004.
19. T. Lonier, "Some Insights and Statistics on Working Solo," *www.workingsolo.com.*
20. Organizational Insight prepared by Scott MacMillan from the following sources: C. Cornell, "Marathon Man," *Profit,* 2004, vol. 23, pp. 36–40; R. Rabinovitch, "Training and Development," *Canadian HR Reporter,* 2004, vol. 17, pp. 7–10; *www.runningroom.com,* 2 June 2004.
21. J. V. Anderson, "Weirder than Fiction: The Reality and Myth of Creativity," *Academy of Management Executive,* 1992, vol. 6, pp. 40–46.
22. Ibid., p. 43.

23. I. Nonaka, "The Knowledge Creating Company," *Harvard Business Review,* 1991, November–December, pp. 1–9.

24. Ibid.

25. *www.microsoft.com/mspress/books/sampchap/4652a.asp?*, 2002.

26. Clark and Wheelwright, *Managing New Product and Process Development.*

27. A. Griffin and J. R. Hauser, "Patterns of Communication among Marketing, Engineering, and Manufacturing," *Management Science,* 1992, vol. 38, pp. 360–373; and R. K. Moenaert, W. E. Sounder, A. D. Meyer, and D. Deschoolmeester, "R&D-Marketing Integration Mechanisms, Communication Flows, and Innovation Success," *Journal of Production and Innovation Management,* 1994, vol. 11, pp. 31–45.

28. Burgelman and Maidique, *Strategic Management of Technology and Innovation.*

29. G. Barczak and D. Wileman, "Leadership Differences in New Product Development Teams," *Journal of Product Innovation Management,* 1989, vol. 6, pp. 259–267; E. F. McDonough and G. Barczak, "Speeding Up New Product Development: The Effects of Leadership Style and Source of Technology," *Journal of Product Innovation Management,* 1991, vol. 8, pp. 203–211; and K. B. Clark and T. Fujimoto, "The Power of Product Integrity," *Harvard Business Review,* November–December 1990, pp. 107–119.

30. K. B. Clark and S. C. Wheelwright, *Managing New Product and Process Development* (New York: The Free Press, 1993).

31. Ibid.

32. D. Frey, "Learning the Ropes: My Life as a Product Champion," *Harvard Business Review,* September–October 1991, pp. 46–56.

33. M. A. Maidique and R. H. Hayes, "The Art of High Technology Management," *Sloan Management Review,* Winter 1984, pp. 18–31.

34. R. A. Burgelman, "Designs for Corporate Entrepreneurship in Established Firms," *California Management Review,* 1984, vol. 26, pp. 154–166.

35. C. Arnst, R. O. Crockett, A. Reinhardt, and J. Shinai, "Lucent: Clean Break, Clean Slate," *Business Week,* 6 November 2000, pp. 172–180.

36. *www.lucent.com,* 2001.

37. *www.lucent.com,* 2002.

38. Organizational Insight compiled by Ellen Rudderham-Gaudet using the following sources: Tembec, "Our History," *www.tembec.com/DynamicPortal?key=web&lng=en-US&crit=about_ourhistory&page=tpl_about,* 14 October 2004 from; "Tembec, McMaster University and Dofasco Win the Prestigious 2003 Synergy Award for Innovation," *Canada NewsWire,* 28 October 2003.

39. H. Mintzberg and J. A. Waters, "Tracking Strategy in an Entrepreneurial Firm," *Academy of Management Journal,* 1982, vol. 25, pp. 465–499; P. Strebel, "Organizing for Innovation over an Industry Life Cycle," *Strategic Management Journal,* 1987, vol. 8, 117–124.

40. R. M. Kanter, *The Change Masters* (New York: Simon and Schuster, 1983).

41. G. R. Jones and J. E. Butler, "Managing Internal Corporate Entrepreneurship: An Agency Theory Perspective," *Journal of Management,* 1992, vol. 18, pp. 733–749.

42. Ibid.

43. Organizational Insight developed by Scott MacMillan from the following sources: *www.mec.ca,* 8 June 2004; K. MacQueen, "The Anti-Retailer: Vancouver's Mountain Equipment Co-op Succeeds in Spite of Itself," *Maclean's,* 29 April 2002, p. 30.

44. T. Dewett and G. R. Jones, "The Role of Information Technology in the Organization: Review, Model, and Assessment," *Journal of Management,* 2001, vol. 27, pp. 313–346.

45. B. Leavy, "The Concept of Learning in the Strategy Field: Review and Outlook," *Management Learning,* 1998, vol. 29, pp. 447–466.

46. C. K. Prahalad and G. Hamel, "The Core Competency of the Corporation," *Harvard Business Review,* May–June 1990, pp. 43–59.

47. J. F. Rockart and D. DeLong, *Executive Support Systems: The Emergence of Top Management Computer Use* (Burr Ridge, IL: Dow-Jones Irwin, 1988); J. F. Rockart and J. E. Short, "IT and the 1990s: Managing Organizational Interdependencies," *Sloan Management Review,* 1989, vol. 30, pp. 17–33.

48. M. T. Hanson, "The Search Transfer Problem: The Role of Weak Ties in Sharing Knowledge Across Organizational Subunits," *Administrative Science Quarterly,* 1999, vol. 44, pp. 82–111.

49. *www.amazon.com,* 2002.

50. Dewett and Jones, "The Role of Information Technology in the Organization: Review, Model, and Assessment."

Managing Conflict, Power, and Politics

CHAPTER 14

Learning Objectives

This chapter focuses on the social and interpersonal processes that affect the way managers make decisions and the way organizations change and adapt to their environments. Specifically, it examines the causes, nature, and consequences of organizational conflict, power, and politics.

After studying this chapter you should be able to:

1. Describe the nature of organizational conflict, its sources, and the way it arises between stakeholders and subunits.
2. Identify the mechanisms by which managers and stakeholders can obtain power and use that power to influence decision making and resolve conflict in their favour.
3. Explain how and why individuals and subunits engage in organizational politics to enhance their control over decision making and obtain the power that allows them to influence the change process in their favour.
4. Appreciate the importance of managing an organization's power structure to overcome organizational inertia, and to bring about the type of change that promotes performance.

WHAT IS ORGANIZATIONAL CONFLICT?

As noted in Chapter 2, an organization consists of different groups of stakeholders, each of which contributes to the organization in return for rewards. Stakeholders cooperate with one another to contribute jointly the resources an organization needs to produce goods and services. At the same time, however, stakeholders compete with one another for the resources the organization generates from these joint activities.[1] To produce goods and services, an organization needs the skills and abilities of managers and employees, the capital provided by shareholders, and the inputs provided by suppliers. Inside and outside stakeholders, such as employees, management, and shareholders, however, compete over their share of the rewards and resources that the organization generates.

To grow, change, and survive, an organization must manage both cooperation and competition among stakeholders. As Figure 14-1 suggests, each stakeholder group has its own goals and interests, which overlap somewhat with those of other groups because all stakeholders have a common interest in the survival of the organization. But stakeholders' goals and interests are not identical, and conflict arises when one group pursues its own interests at the expense of other groups. **Organizational conflict** is the clash that occurs when the goal-directed behaviour of one group blocks or thwarts the goals of another.

Organizational conflict
The clash that occurs when the goal-directed behaviour of one group blocks or thwarts the goals of another.

Because the goals, preferences, and interests of stakeholder groups differ, conflict is inevitable in organizations.[2] Although conflict is often perceived as something negative, research suggests that some conflict is good for an organization and can improve organizational effectiveness. Beyond some point (point A in Figure 14-2), however, extreme conflict between stakeholders can hurt organizational performance.[3]

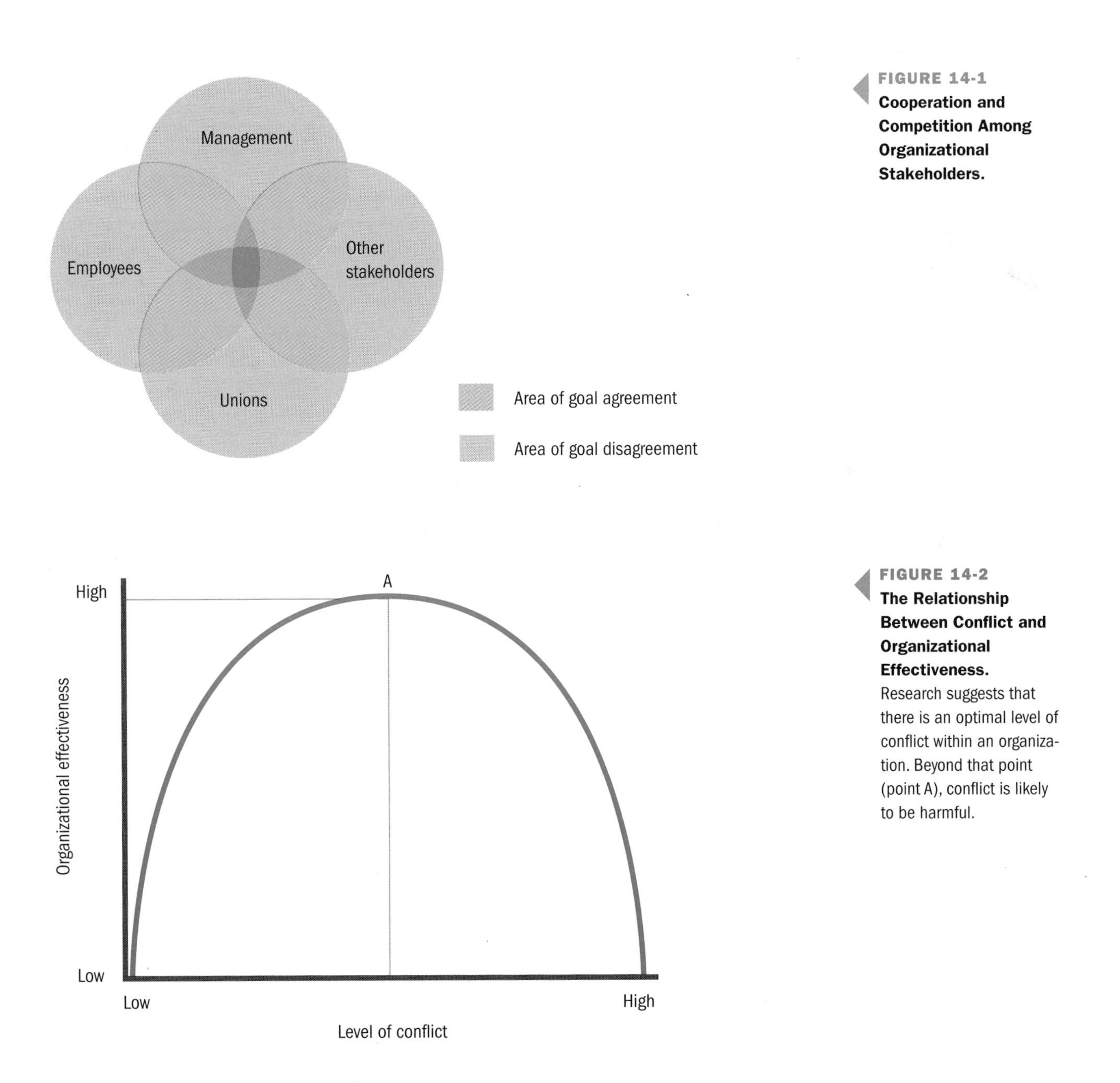

FIGURE 14-1
Cooperation and Competition Among Organizational Stakeholders.

FIGURE 14-2
The Relationship Between Conflict and Organizational Effectiveness.
Research suggests that there is an optimal level of conflict within an organization. Beyond that point (point A), conflict is likely to be harmful.

Why is some conflict good for an organization? Conflict can be beneficial because it can overcome organizational inertia and lead to organizational learning and change. When conflict within an organization or conflict between an organization and elements in its environment arises, the organization and its managers must re-evaluate their view of the world. As we saw in Chapter 12, conflict between different managers or between different stakeholder groups can improve decision making and organizational learning by revealing new ways of looking at a problem or the false or erroneous assumptions that distort decision making. For example, conflict at AT&T between the board of directors and top managers about the slow pace at which top managers were restructuring the company caused a radical change in managerial attitudes. A new top-management team was appointed to increase the pace of change and to overcome AT&T's conservative approach. Similarly, conflict between divisional managers at IBM resulted in a major change in organizational focus, from a purely mainframe focus to a more consulting-oriented focus.

The conflict that arises when different groups perceive the organization's problems in different ways and are willing to act on their beliefs is a built-in defence against the organizational inertia produced by a top-management team whose members have the same vision of the world. In short, conflict can improve decision making and allow an organization better to change and adapt to its environment.[4]

Beyond a certain point, however, conflict stops being a force for good and can become a major source of disruption and can cause organizational decline. For example, conflict over the direction of Bombardier made headlines in December 2004 when Laurent Beaudoin, son-in-law of the company's founder, announced that he was returning to the position of chairman, replacing existing chairman Paul Tellier. Tellier had not expected to retire until 2006. Two other board members resigned following the decision, including Michael McCain. McCain was no stranger to family feuds and organizational conflict—having resigned from McCain Foods in 1994 when it was in the midst of one of the country's most prominent family conflicts over the future of McCain Foods.[5] Also in 2004, the owners and players of the National Hockey League were locked in a major conflict that led to the cancellation of the hockey season for that year (see the Case for Analysis, p. 508).

In some cases, conflict between managers (or between other stakeholders) becomes chronic, so that managers cannot agree about organizational priorities or about how best to allocate resources to meet organizational needs. In this situation, managers spend all their time bargaining and fighting, and the organization gets so bogged down in the process of decision making that organizational change is slow in coming. Innovation is, of course, more or less impossible in such a setting. In a somewhat vicious cycle, the slow and ponderous decision making characteristic of organizations in decline leads to even greater conflict because the consequences of failure are so great. An organization in trouble spends a lot of time making decisions—time that it cannot afford because it needs to adapt quickly to turn itself around. Thus, although some conflict can jolt an organization out of inertia, too much conflict can cause organizational inertia: As different groups fight for their own positions and interests, they fail to arrive at consensus, and the organization drifts along; failure to change makes the organization go from bad to worse.[6]

Many analysts claim that both AT&T and IBM faced this difficult situation. Top managers knew they had to make radical changes to their organization's strategy and structure, but they could not do so because different groups of managers lobbied for their own interests and for cutbacks to fall on other divisions. Conflict between divisions and the constant fight to protect each division's interests resulted in a slow rate of change and worsened the situation. In both companies, the boards of directors removed the CEO and brought in newcomers—Michael Armstrong and Louis Gerstner—who they hoped would overcome opposition to change and develop a strategy that would promote organizational interests, not just the interests of a particular group.

On balance, then, organizations need to be open to conflict, to recognize its value both in helping to identify problems and in contributing to the generation of alternative solutions that improve decision making. Conflict can promote organizational learning. However, in order to exploit the functional aspects of conflict and avoid the dysfunctional effects, managers must learn how to control it. Louis R. Pondy developed a useful model of organizational conflict. Pondy first identifies the sources of conflict and then examines the stages of a typical conflict episode.[7] His model provides many clues about how to control and manage conflict in an organization.

PONDY'S MODEL OF ORGANIZATIONAL CONFLICT

Pondy views conflict as a process that consists of five sequential episodes or stages, summarized in Figure 14-3. No matter how or why conflict arises, managers can use Pondy's model to interpret and analyze a conflict situation and take action to resolve it—for example, by redesigning the organization's structure.

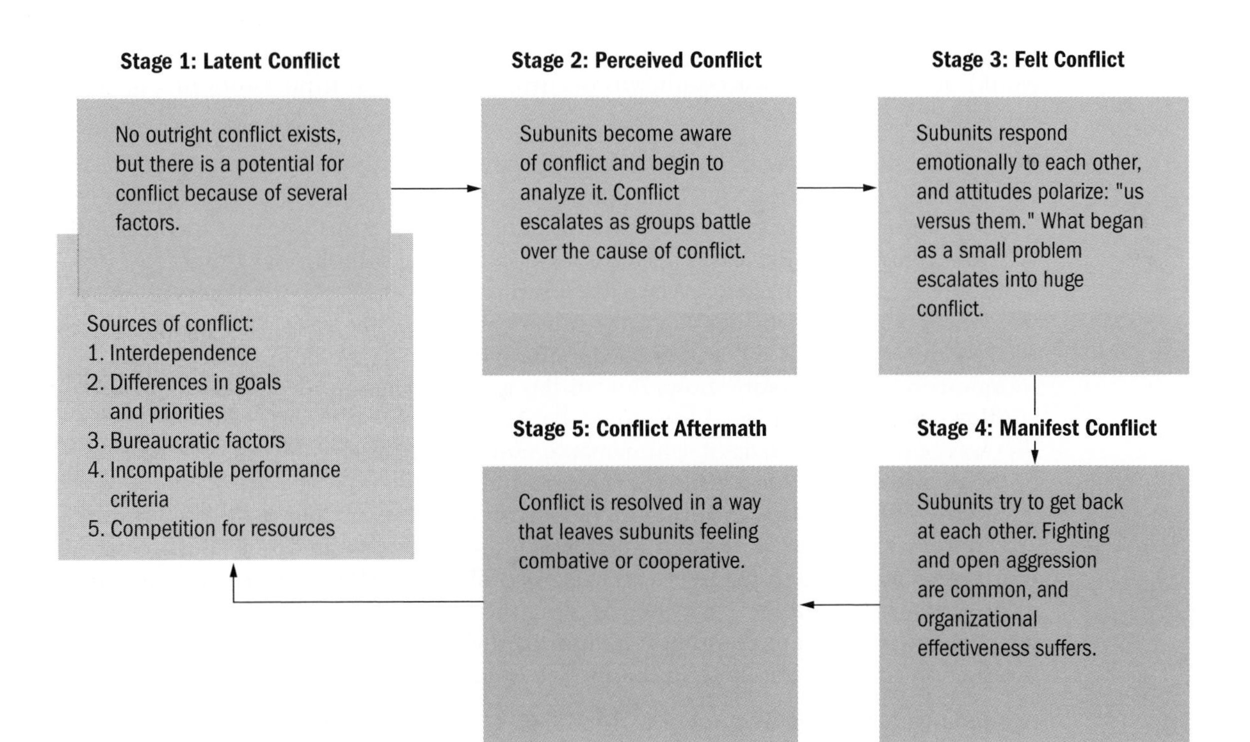

FIGURE 14-3
Pondy's Model of Organizational Conflict.

Stage 1: Latent Conflict

In the first stage of Pondy's model, *latent conflict,* no outright conflict exists; however, the potential for conflict to arise is present, though latent, because of the way an organization operates. According to Pondy, all organizational conflict arises because vertical and horizontal differentiation lead to the establishment of different organizational subunits with different goals and often different perceptions of how best to realize those goals. In business enterprises, for example, managers in different functions or divisions can generally agree about the organization's central goal, which is to maximize the organization's ability to create value in the long run. But they may have different ideas about how to achieve this goal: Should the organization invest resources in manufacturing to lower costs or in research to develop new products? Five potential sources of conflict between subunits have been identified: subunits' interdependence, subunits' differing goals, bureaucratic factors, incompatible performance criteria, and competition for resources.[8]

Interdependence As organizations differentiate, each subunit develops a desire for autonomy and begins to pursue goals and interests that it values over the goals of other subunits or of the organization as a whole. Because the activities of different subunits are interdependent, subunits' desire for autonomy leads to conflict between groups. Eventually, each subunit's desire for autonomy comes into conflict with the organization's desire for coordination.

In terms of Thompson's model of technology, discussed in Chapter 9, the move from pooled to sequential to reciprocal task interdependence between people or subunits increases the degree to which the actions of one subunit directly affect the actions of others.[9] When task interdependence is high, conflict is likely to occur at the individual, functional, and divisional levels. If it were not for interdependence, there would be no potential for conflict to occur among organizational subunits or stakeholders.[10]

Differences in Goals and Priorities Differences in subunit orientation affect the way each function or division views the world and cause each subunit to pursue different goals that are often inconsistent or incompatible. Once goals become incompatible, the potential for conflict arises because the goals of one subunit may thwart the ability of another to achieve its goals. As we discussed in Chapter 12, top managers often have different goals and priorities that may cause conflict in the decision-making process. The way in which the CEO and chief operating officer of Kodak fought over plans for reorganizing the company shows how differences in goals can lead to organizational conflict. (See Organizational Insight 14.1.) At Shermag, on the other hand, the conflict was between the goals of senior management and the employees over the future of the company. (See Organizational Insight 14.2.)

One company that recently gained from conflict within another company is Vancouver's Lions Gate Entertainment, which took over production of Kevin Spacey's film *Beyond the Sea* when the previous backers pulled out. MDP World Wide pulled out of the project just before Spacey began filing the biopic about singer Bobby Darin, citing that Spacey's aim to complete the film by the end of 2003 conflicted with its own production schedule. In the end, Lions Gate stepped in to finance the project.[11]

Bureaucratic Factors The way in which task relationships develop in organizations can also be a potential source of conflict. Over time, conflict can occur because of status inconsistencies between different groups in the organization's bureaucracy. A classic type of bureaucratic conflict occurs between staff and line functions.[12] A *line function* is directly involved in the production of the organization's outputs. In a

ORGANIZATIONAL INSIGHT 14.1

Conflict Causes Slow Change at Kodak

Eastman Kodak has been experiencing declining performance for years. As with IBM and General Motors, Kodak was slow to react to the threat of competition in its central business, and a ponderous decision-making style has stifled its attempts to restructure its activities. In the early 1990s, CEO Kay Whitmore, a Kodak veteran, was reluctant to make the drastic changes that Kodak needed to regain its competitiveness. Although Kodak's management had repeatedly tried to turn the company's fortunes around, nothing had really worked, and the company's share price had been declining steadily for years.

Thus, in 1993, investors were delighted to hear about the appointment of Christopher Steffen as Kodak's new chief operating officer. Steffen has a reputation as a "turnaround artist" who performed miracles at Chrysler and Honeywell, and news of his appointment sent Kodak's stock price up by 17 percent. Investors thought that an outsider would finally bring a breath of fresh air and fresh ideas to Kodak's inbred top-management team. Investors were therefore shocked when Steffen announced his resignation from the company less than a week after his appointment, citing "differences with the company's approach to problem solving."[13]

Apparently he and CEO Whitmore had very different ideas about how to restructure the company and the speed at which restructuring should be done. Steffen reportedly wanted to institute a massive cost-cutting regime, including large layoffs. He proposed a revolutionary change strategy and wanted to implement it right away. Whitmore, pursuing Kodak's traditional consensus approach to decision making, wanted much slower, evolutionary change, even though this approach had failed in the past. In short, Steffen and Whitmore came into conflict over the company's priorities. As in the past, Kodak's entrenched management team had the power to carry the day and resist attempts by Steffen and shareholders to change the way the company operated. Shareholders reacted to Steffen's departure by sending the company's share price down by over 10 percent, but within months the price shot back up when Whitmore was ousted by a concerned board of directors and replaced by the chairman of Motorola, George Fisher. Fisher made several changes that Kodak needed, but he was unable to turn its performance around.

In January 2000, Kodak's board decided on a new CEO, Dan Carp, and Fisher was out. Karp, a Kodak veteran, got the job because he had great support from other Kodak executives to expand its push into electronic imaging.[14] They backed his candidacy in some part to protect their own jobs. By the fall of 2002, Karp had been able to do little and Kodak's performance continued to decline. So far, no one has made the really radical changes Kodak needs to reduce its high costs.

manufacturing company, manufacturing is the line function; in a hospital, doctors are the line function; and in a university, professors are the line function. *Staff functions* advise and support the line function and include functions such as personnel, accounting, and purchasing. In many organizations, people in line functions come to view themselves as the critical organizational resource and people in staff functions as secondary players. Acting on this belief, the line function constantly uses its suppos-

ORGANIZATIONAL INSIGHT 14.2

Conflict Closes up Shop at Shermag Plant but Resolution Brings New Hope[15]

On September 25, 2004, furniture manufacturer Shermag officially announced that it would close its plant in Disraeli, and would be laying off 245 workers. Since April of the same year, three of Shermag's Quebec plants have had a strike. The union workers of the other two plants had accepted agreements with Shermag, but Disraeli had not. It looked like this was the end of the line for the dispute but also for the plant. The strike started at the Quebec plants in rebellion to the company's demands for a more flexible work schedule with interchangeable duties and an end to summertime holiday shutdown. Shermag needed these concessions in order to compete against low-cost Chinese imports and the impact of a strong Canadian dollar. The strength of the dollar is an important factor for Shermag's profitability because the company exports 75 percent of its goods to the United States to big department stores like Macy's and Marshall Field's.

Shermag Inc., with its head office in Sherbrooke, Quebec, has been manufacturing and distributing residential furniture for over 25 years. The company employs almost 2400 people in a network of sawmills, a veneer facility, and manufacturing plants. From the forests to the manufacturing plants and then to the distribution channels of the North American marketplace, Shermag has become a leading company, competing against international producers. However, it is an ongoing struggle and balancing act for Shermag to maintain positive returns on shareholders' investments and to offer fair working conditions to its employees.

On October 7, 2004, the employees' fight and plight at the recently closed Disraeli plant met with a more positive turnaround. On just the Sunday before, the plant's unionized workers met for a special general assembly and finally agreed to meet Shermag's demands. A government mediator was involved and negotiations resulted in Shermag reversing its decision to close the plant. It would reopen but, unfortunately, rehire only half the employees. The company was planning new product development and other projects, so it was hopeful that most employees would eventually be rehired.

Although it would appear that the company "won" this conflict, Shermag undoubtedly needs to be more attentive to the balancing act; that is, the company now needs to address a serious situation of low employee morale following such dramatic events of the employee–company conflict.

edly lofty status as the producer of goods and services to justify putting its interests ahead of the other functions' interests. The result is conflict.[16]

Incompatible Performance Criteria Sometimes conflict arises between subunits not because their goals are incompatible but because the organization's way of monitoring, evaluating, and rewarding different subunits brings them into conflict. Production and sales can come into conflict when, to achieve the goal of increased sales, the sales department asks manufacturing to respond quickly to customer orders—an action that raises manufacturing costs. If the organization's reward system benefits sales personnel (who get higher bonuses because of increased sales) but penalizes manufacturing (which gets no bonus because of higher costs), conflict will arise.

The way an organization designs its structure to coordinate subunits can affect the potential for conflict. The constant conflict between divisions at CS First Boston shows how incompatible reward systems can produce conflict. (See Organizational Insight 14.3.)

When Stephen Jarislowsky, an institutional investment manager with Velan Inc., the Montreal valve producer, quit the company in 2002, he publicly cited differences with the CEO. Jarislowskly claimed that the CEO was no longer capable of running the company, warned investors that the company lacked a CEO succession plan, and claimed that board meetings were unproductive.[17]

Competition for Scarce Resources Conflict would never be a problem if there was always an abundance of resources for subunits to use. When resources are scarce, as

ORGANIZATIONAL INSIGHT 14.3

How Rewards Produced Conflict at CS First Boston

CS First Boston, a large American investment bank, was formed by the merger of two smaller banks: First Boston (based in New York) and Crédit Suisse (based in London). From the beginning, the two divisions of the new bank were at odds. Although the merger was formed to take advantage of synergies in the growing transatlantic investment banking business, the divisions could never cooperate with one another, and managers in both were fond of openly criticizing the banking practices of their peers to anybody who would listen.

As long as the performance of one unit of the bank did not affect the other, the lack of cooperation between them was tolerated, although analysts pointed out that the loss in synergy from the arrangement kept CS First Boston out of the top league of investment banks. In the 1990s, however, the performance of the European unit began to affect the American unit, and conflict started to build. First Boston made record profits from issuing and trading fixed-income debt securities, and its managers were expecting hefty bonuses. However, those bonuses were not paid. Why? The London arm of the organization had incurred huge losses, and although the losses were not the fault of the Boston-based bank, the corporation's top managers decided not to pay bonuses to their U.S. employees because of the losses from Europe.

This inequitable decision, punishing U.S. employees for an outcome that they could not control, led to considerable conflict within the organization. Relations between the U.S. and European arms of the bank became even more strained; the divisions began fighting with top management; and when employees decided that the situation would not change in the near term, they began to leave CS First Boston in droves. Many senior managers left for competitors, such as Merrill Lynch and Goldman Sachs. With the organization in disarray, top managers faced the job of trying to restore cooperative relations.[18] Clearly, redesigning the reward system so that it does not promote conflict between divisions should be one of their major priorities.[19]

they always are, choices about resource allocation have to be made, and subunits have to compete for their share.[20] Divisions fight to increase their share of funding because the more funds they can obtain and invest, the faster they can grow. Similarly, at the functional level there can be conflict over the amount of funds to allocate to sales, or to manufacturing, or to R&D to meet organizational objectives. Thus, to increase access to resources, functions promote their interests and importance often at one another's expense.

Together, these five factors have the potential to cause a significant level of conflict in an organization. At stage 1, however, the conflict is latent. The potential for conflict exists, but conflict has not yet surfaced. In complex organizations with high levels of differentiation and integration, the potential for conflict is especially great. The subunits are highly interdependent and have different goals and complicated reward systems, and the competition among them for organizational resources is intense. Managing organizational conflict to allocate resources to where they can produce the most value in the long run is very difficult.

Stage 2: Perceived Conflict

The second stage of Pondy's model, *perceived conflict,* begins when a subunit or stakeholder group perceives that its goals are being thwarted by the actions of another group. In this stage, each subunit begins to define why the conflict is emerging and to analyze the events that have led up to it. Each group searches for the origin of the conflict and constructs a scenario that accounts for the problems that it is experiencing with other subunits. The manufacturing function, for example, may suddenly realize that the cause of many of its production problems is defective inputs. When production managers investigate, they discover that materials management always buys inputs from the lowest-cost sources of supply and makes no attempt to develop the kind of long-term relationships with suppliers that can raise the quality and reliability of inputs. Materials management reduces input costs and improves this function's bottom line, but it raises manufacturing costs and worsens that function's bottom line. Not surprisingly, manufacturing perceives materials management as thwarting its goals and interests.

Normally at this point the conflict escalates as the different subunits or stakeholders start to battle over the cause of the problem. To get materials management to change its purchasing practices, manufacturing complains about materials management to the CEO and whomever else will listen. Materials management is likely to dispute the charge that its purchase of low-cost inputs leads to inferior quality. Instead, it attributes the problem to manufacturing's failure to provide employees with sufficient training to operate new technology and dumps responsibility for the quality problems back in manufacturing's lap. Even though both functions share the goal of superior product quality, they attribute the poor quality to very different causes.

Stage 3: Felt Conflict

At the *felt conflict* stage, subunits in conflict quickly develop an emotional response toward each other. Typically, each subunit closes ranks and develops a polarized us-versus-them mentality that puts the blame for the conflict squarely on the other subunit. As conflict escalates, cooperation between subunits falls, and so does organizational effectiveness. It is difficult to speed new product development, for example, if research and development, materials management, and manufacturing are fighting over quality and final product specifications.

As the different subunits in conflict battle and argue their point of view, the conflict escalates. The original problem may be relatively minor, but if nothing is done to solve it, the small problem will escalate into a huge conflict that becomes increasingly difficult to manage. If the conflict is not resolved now, it quickly reaches the next stage.

Stage 4: Manifest Conflict

In the *manifest conflict* stage of Pondy's model, one subunit gets back at another subunit by attempting to thwart its goals. Manifest conflict can take many forms. Open aggression between people and groups is common. There are many stories and myths in organizations about boardroom fights in which managers actually come to blows as they seek to promote their interests. Infighting in the top-management team is very common as managers seek to promote their own careers at the expense of others. When Lee Iacocca was at Ford Motor Company, for example, and Henry Ford II decided to bring in the head of General Motors as the new Ford CEO, Iacocca engineered the downfall of the new CEO within one year in order to promote his own rise to the top. Eventually, Iacocca lost the battle: Henry Ford forced Iacocca out because he feared that Iacocca would usurp his power. In 2003 the shareholders of Holliger International were warned of a potential conflict between the interests of Lord Conrad Black and those of other shareholders. (See Organizational Insight 14.4.)

A very effective form of manifest conflict is passive aggression—frustrating the goals of the opposition by doing nothing. Suppose there is a history of conflict between sales and production. One day, sales desperately needs a rush order for an important client. What might the manager of production do? One strategy is to agree informally to the sales department's request but do nothing. When the head of sales comes banging on the door, the production manager says innocently, "Oh, you meant last Friday. I thought you meant *this* Friday."

In general, once conflict is manifest, organizational effectiveness suffers because coordination and integration between managers and subunits break down. Managers need to do all they can to prevent conflict from reaching the manifest stage, for two reasons: because of the breakdown in communication that is likely to occur and because of the aftermath of conflict.

Stage 5: Conflict Aftermath

Sooner or later, organizational conflict is resolved in some way, often by the decision of some senior manager. And sooner or later, if the sources of the conflict have not been resolved, the disputes and problems that caused the conflict arise again in another context. What happens when the conflict reappears depends on how it was resolved the first time. Suppose that sales comes to production with a new request. How are sales and production likely to behave? They probably will be combative and suspicious of each other and will find it hard to agree on anything. But suppose that sales and marketing had been able to solve their earlier dispute amicably and were able to agree on the need to respond flexibly to the needs of an important customer. The next time sales comes along with a special request, how is production likely to react? The production manager will probably have a cooperative attitude, and both parties will be able to sit down and work out a joint plan that suits the needs of both functions.

Every episode of conflict leaves a *conflict aftermath* that affects the way both parties perceive and react to future episodes. If a conflict is resolved before it gets to the manifest-conflict stage, then the aftermath will promote good future working relationships. If conflict is not resolved until late in the process, or is not resolved at all, the aftermath will sour future working relationships, and the organizational culture will be poisoned by permanently uncooperative relationships. Managers at First

ORGANIZATIONAL INSIGHT 14.4

The Trouble with Hollinger International

Until November 2003, Lord Conrad Black was the CEO, chairman of the board, and a major shareholder of Hollinger International. But things became to unravel for Black and Hollinger when, among other things, Black attempted to sell control of his newspaper empire to a U.K. interest, run by the Barclay brothers. In the process, the legality of Black's business practices were also questioned.

Part of the problem appears to lie with the structure of the company and Black's holdings which, according to one commentator, "operated so closely together that they resemble a set of dominoes."[21] In addition to Black's role as CEO and chairman of Chicago-based Hollinger International, he was also CEO and chairman of Hollinger Inc. (a Toronto-based holding company), Ravelston Corp. (another of Black's holding companies), Ravelston Management Inc. (his management services firm), and Argos Corp. It has been argued that this "'unusual structure' made it made it nearly impossible for Black to avoid serious conflicts of interest, even if he felt inclined to do so."[22] Nonetheless, other leading members of the board of Hollinger International saw the problem.

Things came to a head towards the end of 2003 when Black set out to sell off his newspaper empire to a U.K. interest—the powerful Barclay brothers—but the manner in which he did so raised serious concerns with other board members and ended up before a court in Delaware in February of 2004. Among the charges levelled at Black was that he attempted to conceal negotiations with the Barclay brothers from the Hollinger International board and in the process threatened various board members. The judge agreed with Hollinger International and handed down a ruling that criticized Black for "repudiating his obligations to Hollinger International's shareholders."[23] The judge went on to state, "Black had misled his former colleagues at Hollinger International, violated his fiduciary duties to its shareholders on numerous occasions and acted in bad faith on others, and may have committed a 'fraud on the Board' in the manner of his dealings with Hollinger International."[24] The judge also agreed with Hollinger International in upholding the claim that Black had attempted to negotiate a secret deal with the Barclay brothers, and that he'd used "confidential company information for his own purposes."[25]

Boston, for example, made it a point of honour to denigrate their colleagues in the other divisions of the organization. They went out of their way to be uncooperative, and they are still doing so.

MANAGING CONFLICT: CONFLICT RESOLUTION STRATEGIES

Because organizational conflict can rapidly escalate and sour an organization's culture, managing organizational conflict is an important priority.[26] An organization must balance the need to have some "good" conflict (which overcomes inertia and allows new organizational learning) with the need to prevent "good" conflict from escalating into "bad conflict" (which causes a breakdown in coordination and integration between functions and divisions). In this section, we look at a few conflict resolution strategies designed to help organizations manage organizational conflict. Later in the chapter, we look at organizational politics as another way of managing organizational conflict when the stakes are high and when divisions and functions can obtain power to influence organizational outcomes, such as decisions about how to change or restructure an organization, in their favour.

The method an organization chooses to manage conflict depends on the source of the problem. At CS First Boston, the problem was an inequitable reward system that penalized one subunit for the poor performance of another. To solve this problem, CS First Boston's management needs to remove the source of the conflict by changing the way its reward systems operate—that is, by devising an equitable reward system. At Kodak, the source of the conflict was top managers' fight to protect their positions and property rights, and the conflict was resolved only by changing the top-management team. These examples suggest the two strategies that managers are likely to use to resolve conflict: changing an organization's structure to reduce or eliminate the cause of the conflict or trying to change the attitudes of individuals or replacing the individuals themselves.[27]

Acting at the Level of Structure

Because task interdependence and differences in goals are two major sources of conflict, altering the level of differentiation and integration to change task relationships is one way to resolve conflict. An organization might change from a functional structure to a product division structure in order to remove a source of conflict between manufacturing managers who are unable to control the overhead costs associated with different kinds of products. Moving to a product structure makes it much easier to assign overhead costs to different product lines. Similarly, if product managers are finding it difficult to convince departments to cooperate to speed product development, the move to a product team structure, in which different functional managers are assigned permanently to a product line, will remove the source of the problem.

If divisions are battling over resources, corporate managers can increase the number of integrating roles in the organization and assign top managers the responsibility for solving conflicts between divisions and for improving the structure of working relationships.[28] In general, increasing the level of integration is one major way in which organizations can manage the problem of differences in subunit goals. To resolve potential conflict situations, organizations can increase their use of liaison roles, task forces, teams, and integrating mechanisms (see Figure 4-5, p. 117).

Another way to manage conflict is to make sure that the design of an organization's hierarchy of authority is in line with its current needs. As an organization grows and differentiates, the chain of command lengthens, and the organization is likely to lose control of its hierarchy. This loss of control can be a major source of conflict because people are given the responsibility for making decisions but lack the authority to do so because a manager above them must sign off on every move they make. Flattening the hierarchy, so that authority relationships are clearly defined, and decentralizing authority can remove a major source of organizational conflict. One source of such conflict occurs when two or more people, departments, or divisions compete for the same set of resources. This situation is likely to be disastrous because decision making is impossible when different people claim the right to control the same resources. For this reason, the military and some other organizations have established very clear lines of authority; there is no ambiguity about who reports to whom and who has control of what resources.

Good organizational design should result in the creation of an organizational structure that minimizes the potential for organizational conflict. However, because of inertia, many organizations fail to manage their structures and change them to suit the needs of a changing environment. As a result, conflict increases and organizational effectiveness falls.

Acting at the Level of Attitudes and Individuals

Differences in goals and in beliefs about the best way to achieve organizational goals are inevitable because of differences between functions and divisions. One way to harness conflict between subunits and prevent the polarization of attitudes that results during the stage of felt conflict in Pondy's model is to set up a procedural system that allows parties in conflict to air their grievances and hear other groups' points of view. Committees or teams, for example, can provide a forum in which subunits in dispute can meet face to face and negotiate directly with one another. In this way, subunits can clarify the assumptions they are using to frame the problem, and they can develop an understanding of one another's motives. Very often the use of a procedural system reveals that the issue in dispute is much smaller than was previously thought and that the positions of the parties are more similar than anyone had realized.

A procedural system is especially important in managing industrial conflicts between managers and unions. When a union exists, formal procedures govern the resolution of disputes to ensure that the issue receives a fair hearing. Indeed, an important component of bargaining in labour disputes is attitudinal structuring—a process designed to influence the attitudes of the opposing party and to encourage the perception that both parties are on the same side and want to solve a dispute amicably.[29] Thus strikes become the last resort in a long process of negotiation.

Often, an organization engages a *third-party negotiator* to moderate a dispute between subunits or stakeholders.[30] The third-party negotiator can be a senior manager who occupies an integrating role or an outside consultant employed because of expertise in solving organizational disputes. The negotiator's role is to prevent the polarization of attitudes that occurs during the felt-conflict stage and thus prevent the escalation to manifest conflict. Negotiators are skilled in managing organizational conflict so as to allow new learning to take place. Often, the negotiator supports the weaker party in the dispute to make sure that both sides of the argument get heard.

Another way of managing conflict through attitude change is by the exchange and rotation of people between subunits to encourage groups to learn each other's points of view. This practice is widespread in Japan. Japanese organizations continually rotate people from function to function so that they can understand the problems and issues facing the organization as a whole.[31]

When attitudes are difficult to change because they have developed over a long period of time, the only way to resolve a conflict may be to change the people involved. This can be done by permanently transferring employees to other parts of the organization, promoting them, or firing them. We have already seen that top-management teams are often replaced to overcome inertia and change organizational attitudes. Analysts attribute a large part of the conflict at CS First Boston to the attitudes of a few key top managers who had to be removed.

An organization's CEO is an important influence on attitudes in a conflict. The CEO personifies the values and culture of the organization, and the way the CEO acts affects the attitudes of other managers directly. As head of the organization, the CEO also has the ultimate power to resolve conflict between subunits. A strong CEO actively manages organizational conflict and opens up a debate, allowing each group to express its views. The strong CEO can then use his or her power to build a consensus for a resolution and decision and can motivate subunits to cooperate to achieve organizational goals. In contrast, a weak CEO can actually increase organizational conflict. When a CEO fails to manage the bargaining and negotiation process between subunits, the strongest subunits (those with the most power) are encouraged or allowed to fight for their goals at the expense of other subunits. A weak CEO produces a power vacuum at the top of the organization, enabling the strongest members of the organization to compete for control. As we saw from Organizational Insight 14.4 (p. 488), sometimes it can be the CEO who generates destructive conflict situations. As consensus is lost and infighting becomes the order of the day, conflict becomes destructive.

MANAGERIAL IMPLICATIONS

Conflict

1. Analyze the organizational structure to identify potential sources of conflict.
2. Change or redesign the organizational structure to eliminate the potential for conflict whenever possible.
3. If conflict cannot be eliminated, be prepared to intervene quickly and early in the conflict to find a solution.
4. Choose a way of managing the conflict that matches the source of the conflict.
5. Always try to achieve a good conflict aftermath so that cooperative attitudes can be maintained in the organization over time.

WHAT IS ORGANIZATIONAL POWER?

The presence of a strong CEO is important in managing organizational conflict. Indeed, the relative power of the CEO, the board of directors, and other top managers is important in understanding how and why organizations change and restructure themselves and why this benefits some people and subunits more than others. To understand how and why organizational conflict is resolved in favour of different subunits and stakeholders, we need to look closely at the issue of power.

What is power, and what is its role in organizational conflict? According to many management researchers, **organizational power** is the mechanism through which conflict gets resolved. It can be defined as the ability of one person or group to overcome resistance by others to achieve a desired objective or result.[32] More specifically, organizational power is the ability of A to cause B to do something that B would not otherwise have done.[33] Thus, when power is used to resolve conflict, the element of coercion exists. Actors with power can bring about outcomes they desire over the opposition of other actors.

Organizational power
The ability of one person or group to overcome resistance by others to resolve conflict and achieve a desired objective or result.

The possession of power is an important determinant of the kind of decisions that resolve a conflict—for example, decisions concerning the allocation of resources or the assignment of responsibility between managers and subunits.[34] When decisions are made through bargaining between organizational coalitions, the relative power of the various coalitions to influence decision making is what determines how conflicts get resolved and which subunits benefit from the decision-making process.

Thus conflict and power are intimately related. Conflict is caused by the existence of different individuals or groups that need to cooperate to achieve organizational objectives but must compete for organizational resources and have different individual or group goals and priorities. When a situation arises that causes these groups to compete for resources, conflict emerges. When the issue is sufficiently important, individuals and groups use their power to influence decision making and obtain outcomes that favour them.

Power can also be about how a person or group of people influence how people think about the organization and themselves.[35] In Robert Jackall's classic study of corporate business ethics, it was found that the moral attitudes of the people at the top of the organization could influence the morality of employees as a whole. In Jackall's study of selected U.S. companies, he found that the corrupt behaviours of those at the top became ingrained in the organization's culture and way of thinking.[36] Organizational cultures can also influence employment equity through a constant association of lower-level jobs with women and higher-level jobs with men.[37] In these cases, power stems not only from position in the hierarchy and ownership but also from the legitimation of ways of thinking and ideas. For example, if skill is only associated with men (e.g., engineering skill) and caring only associated with women (e.g., nursing attributes), this may have a powerful influence on the way we associate certain characteristics with masculinity and femininity.[38]

SOURCES OF ORGANIZATIONAL POWER

If people, groups, and divisions engage in activities to gain power within an organization, where do they get it from? What gives one person or group the power to influence, shape, or control the behaviour of others? To answer these questions, we must recognize the sources of power in an organization. Figure 14-4 identifies seven of them; they are examined below.

Authority

Authority, power that is legitimized by the legal and cultural foundations on which an organization is based, is the ultimate source of power in an organization.[39] The authority in a business organization derives from the organization's legal charter, which allows shareholders, through the board of directors, to grant a CEO the formal power, or authority, to use organizational resources to create value for shareholders. In turn, the CEO has the right to grant authority to other top managers in the organization, and they have the right to confer it on their subordinates.

People who join an organization accept the legal right of the organization to coordinate and control their behaviour, within the limits of broad socio-legal expectations and constraints. In exercising authority, a manager exercises a legal right to control resources, including human resources. The way in which authority is distributed depends on the organizational setting. As discussed in Chapter 5, in organizations that are centralized, authority is retained by top managers. In organizations that are decentralized, authority is delegated to those lower in the hierarchy, who are then held

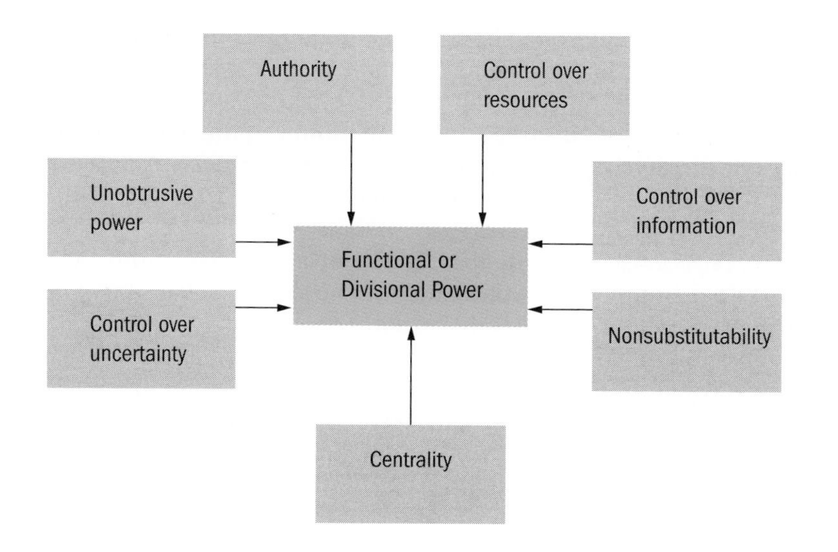

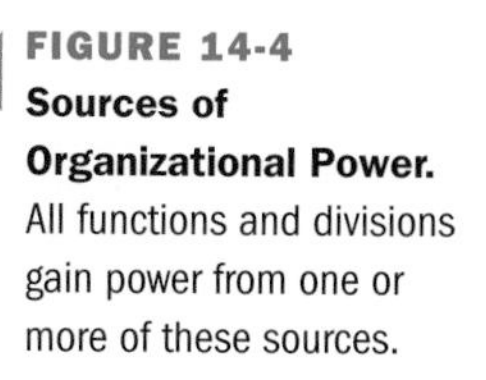
FIGURE 14-4
Sources of Organizational Power.
All functions and divisions gain power from one or more of these sources.

responsible for the way they use organizational resources. When authority is centralized, there is generally less scope for people to engage in behaviours aimed at gaining power. Because top managers keep power among themselves, it is difficult for coalitions to form. In such centralized organizations, however, a culture often develops in which people become afraid to take responsibility for decisions or to initiate new action for fear they will overstep their authority and be censured by top management. Instead, subordinates ingratiate themselves to top management in the hope of receiving favour, and they compete to curry favour with their superiors. Thus the effectiveness of decision making in a centralized organization can be reduced as managers surround themselves with yes-men and yes-women and few important decisions get made.

Frequently, managers negotiate the limits of their authority among themselves, and more senior managers give authority to subordinates by making a conscious decision to decentralize. Sometimes, however, a subordinate who is active or competitive can indirectly take away a superior's authority by gradually assuming more and more of the supervisor's duties and responsibilities. The result, over time, is that even though the superior has legitimate authority, the subordinate has the real power. Superiors who are aware that this indirect seizure of authority can happen may take steps to prevent it. They may make a point of exercising their authority to show subordinates that they possess it, or they may insist on the display of certain rituals or symbols of their power—such as a big office and a personal secretary. Behaviour of this type can have profound implications for leadership[40] and equitable relations[41] in an organization.

One of the classic ways in which superiors hold onto power is by restricting the information they give to subordinates to make a decision. If a manager gives out too much information, the subordinate will know as much as the manager does, and power over the subordinate will be lost. As a result of this fear, managers hoard information and do not share it with subordinates. However, if managers withhold too much and subordinates cannot make decisions, managers are likely to become overburdened, and the quality of decision making in the organization declines.

Managers have to realize that there is a difference between the decentralization of authority and the loss of authority: Decentralizing authority to a subordinate does not necessarily reduce a manager's authority, because the manager continues to bear the responsibility for whatever decisions the subordinate makes. Thus, when subordinates make decisions that have important consequences, the responsibility and authority of the superior also increase. If subordinates fail, however, the manager also bears the consequences. If the failure is big enough, the decision to decentralize can result in the loss of power—that is, the loss of the official position that carries the authority in the organization.

As noted elsewhere, *empowerment* is the deliberate decentralization of authority to encourage subordinates to assume responsibility for organizational activities.[42] The goal of empowerment is to give subordinates wide latitude to make decisions and thus motivate them to make best use of their skills to create value. In an organization that decentralizes authority and empowers employees, all organizational members can gain authority as the organization prospers and attracts more resources. Employees who assume more authority and responsibility often demand more rights from the organization, such as higher salaries, increased job security, or bonuses tied to organizational performance.

Empowerment is also important at the corporate divisional level. As we have seen, in some organizations the corporate centre is reluctant to delegate authority to the divisional level and prefers to centralize decision making. The problem with this choice is that divisional managers become afraid to experiment and to initiate new action even though they are close to a problem and have more information and knowledge about it than corporate managers have. Thus divisions become unable to devise strategies that allow them to capitalize on opportunities in the environment, and both divisional and organizational performance suffer. For this reason, Bill Gates, chairman of Microsoft, and many other CEOs deliberately empower divisional managers and make them responsible for their divisions' ultimate success in the marketplace. Gates believes that it is impossible to manage a company as large and diverse as Microsoft unless managers at the divisional level and below have the authority and responsibility to innovate and make decisions. At Microsoft, the corporate centre's primary role is to make resource allocation decisions for the whole organization, and to ensure the different divisions produce software that can be seamlessly integrated with the software written by other divisions so that Microsoft can offer its standardized software platform to all kinds of customers.

Control over Resources

Power is not a fixed quantity. Managers who make decisions and perform actions that benefit the organization, such as making changes that raise performance, can increase their power. Just as an organization's power grows as the organization controls more and more resources in its environment, power within an organization comes from the control of resources.[43] To survive, organizations require resources such as capital, human skills, raw materials, and customers. If a resource is particularly critical for an organization, the individual or subunit that has control over that resource has a good deal of power. At a company like Merck, for example, the R&D skills and knowledge necessary to develop new drugs are a critical resource. Given this fact, who has the most power at Merck? The answer is senior scientists, because they possess the knowledge on which the success of the organization depends. Similarly, at companies that rely heavily on the success of their marketing efforts, like Coca-Cola or McDonald's, the marketing department has considerable power because it is the department that can attract customers—the critical scarce resource.

Money or capital is, in a way, the ultimate organizational resource because money buys other resources. This explains the ultimate power of top managers.

Legally, they control the allocation of money in the organization and thus control its future. The ability to allocate financial resources, however, is not the only source of a manager's or subunit's power. The ability to generate financial resources is also an important source of power.[44] The power of top managers at Merck rests in their ability to allocate R&D funds to various projects. The scientists, however, are the ones who invent the drugs that generate future revenues for the company, and their ability to generate resources gives them supreme power in the organization. In a multidivisional company, the divisions that generate revenues from customers have considerable power. In a university setting, the most powerful departments are ones like engineering, chemistry, and agriculture, which generate the most revenues because they attract millions of dollars for sponsored research. At many schools, athletics programs and alumni groups have considerable power because of their ability to generate revenues.

Control over Information

Information can be a very important and scarce organizational resource. Access to strategic information and the control of the information flow to, from, and between subunits are sources of considerable power in the decision-making and change process.[45] It is possible to shape the views of others by carefully tailoring the information they receive. Andrew Pettigrew, in a study of the decision to buy a certain kind of computer system at a department store, showed how Jim Kenny, the head of management services, was able to influence the behaviour of other senior managers by controlling the flow of information to them. Kenny was able to act as a "gatekeeper." Pettigrew observed, "By sitting at the junction of the communications channels between his subordinates, the manufacturers, and the board, Kenny was able to exert biases in favour of his own demands and at the same time feed the board negative information about the demands of his opponents."[46] Even in the face of strong opposition by other managers, Kenny was able to bring about change that resolved the conflict in his favour by controlling the information used to evaluate alternatives. In conflicts, senior managers have been known to deliberately manipulate other managers by supplying them with information that causes them to make bad decisions, so that in the contest for power in the organization they lose out to managers with better performance records.[47] At Hollinger International, Conrad Black attempted to control the sale of his newspaper empire by keeping negotiations secret from his board. His aim was to present the sale as a "fait accompli" to his directors.[48]

The control of information is the source of the power of many people or subunits in specialized roles.[49] The power of doctors in a hospital or mechanics in a garage stems from their ability to control specific knowledge and information. People who consult an expert have to take that person's word on trust or else get a second opinion. Similarly, functions may have power because they control the information and knowledge that are necessary to solve organizational problems. Researcher Michael Crozier found that maintenance engineers in the French tobacco-processing plants he was investigating enjoyed an inordinate amount of power despite their low status in the organizational hierarchy.[50] The reason for their power was that the principal problem in the company's routine mass production technology was machine breakdown. The maintenance engineers were the only people who knew how to repair the machines, and they had systematically used this knowledge to develop a considerable power base in the organization. Moreover, they jealously guarded their knowledge, refusing to write down repair procedures or share them with others, realizing that if they did so they would undermine their own power.

All subunits possess some expert information and knowledge, but the functions or divisions that control critical information have the most. They are the ones most able to bring about change, especially change that favours their interests, although this is no guarantee that such change will benefit the whole organization. This is the danger that accompanies the use of power in the organizational change process: how to ensure change will increase, rather than reduce organizational performance.

Nonsubstitutability

If no one else can perform the tasks that a person or subunit performs, that person or subunit is nonsubstitutable. Only it can provide resources that another subunit or the organization wants. The maintenance engineers at the French tobacco plant had made themselves nonsubstitutable: Only they could reduce one of the major uncertainties facing the plant—machine breakdown. As a result of their nonsubstitutability, they exerted considerable power.[51]

Centrality

As we saw above, Jim Kenny had power because he could control information flows and was central to the decision-making process. In his role as manager of information services, he could provide others with information that reduced the uncertainty they were experiencing about orders or accounts. Similarly, the subunits that are most central to resource flows have the ability to reduce the uncertainty facing other subunits.[52] Often, an organization's strategy is a crucial determinant of which subunit is central in an organization. In a company like Coca-Cola that is driven by marketing, other subunits—product development, manufacturing, sales—depend on the information collected by the marketing department. The marketing department is central because it supplies a resource that all the other functions need: knowledge about customers and their future needs. R&D is not central at Coca-Cola because it responds to the needs of other functions—for example, to the marketing function's decision that the company should develop "vanilla" Coke. In a biotechnology company like Amgen, whose differentiation strategy depends on R&D, R&D becomes the central function, and marketing shapes its behaviour to suit the needs of R&D.

Control over Uncertainty

A subunit that can actually control the principal sources of uncertainty or the contingencies facing the organization has significant power.[53] The R&D function in a biotechnology organization is powerful because the major source of uncertainty is whether the organization can discover safe, new drugs. In a hospital, doctors have power because only they have the ability to diagnose and treat patient problems, the main source of uncertainty for a hospital.

Over time, as the contingencies facing an organization change, some subunits rise in power, while the power of others whose services are no longer so valuable falls.[54] In business organizations after World War II, for example, the main source of uncertainty was the need to manufacture products fast enough to meet the demand for consumer goods that had built up during the war years. Manufacturing became the most important subunit during the postwar period, and many CEOs came from the manufacturing department. Then, during the 1960s, with manufacturers producing at full capacity, companies' main contingency became the need to sell their products, and marketing rose in prominence. With the 1970s came recession. Companies diversified to compete in new industries, and accounting and finance became the powerful organizational function. Thus the power of subunits rises and falls as their ability to cope with organizational uncertainties changes.

Unobtrusive Power: Controlling the Premises of Decision Making

Another important source of power is the power of the dominant coalition—that is, the coalition that has the most power—to control the decision-making process so that the decisions made in a conflict situation favour the interests of the coalition. When different subunits share similar interests, they often join in a coalition to increase their power to pursue their common goals. The enhanced power of the coalition is then brought to bear on the decision-making process against coalitions that are pursuing different goals. The power flowing from the ability to control the premises behind decision making is called *unobtrusive power* because others are generally not aware that the coalition is shaping their perceptions or interpretations of a situation.[55]

The power of a coalition lies in its ability to control the assumptions, goals, norms, or values that managers use to judge alternative solutions to a problem. As a result of unobtrusive power, many alternatives that some parties in a conflict might like to evaluate are ruled out because they do not fit with the ruling coalition's view of the situation. Thus, even before decision making starts, the coalition in power has ensured that the decision that is eventually made will support its interests.

An example will clarify how unobtrusive power can work. Profits can be increased in two basic ways: by expanding sales revenues or by decreasing costs. If sales and marketing form the dominant coalition in an organization, then the option of cutting costs receives little attention, and decision making focuses on how the organization should invest its resources to increase sales. Conversely, when production is in the power seat, the goal of investing resources in new advanced machinery to reduce costs is likely to be an important factor influencing the selection of a course of action.

A specific coalition's ability to resolve conflict in its favour depends on which coalition has the balance of power in the organization. Organizational power is a dynamic concept, and organizational strategy can change quickly as the balance of power shifts from one coalition to another.[56]

Knowledge and Discourse

What senior managers choose to value in the operation of an organization can have a powerful influence on which activities are privileged and important, and which type of person is privileged and important. In Rosabeth Moss Kanter's study of a major corporation, she found that the way some jobs were structured restricted some men and a large number of women from achieving promotion above a certain point. She refers to these people as "the stuck."[57] As a result "the stuck" are not only *in* lower-level jobs but come to view themselves as having lesser skills and abilities. Studies of the airline industry indicate that by valuing the association between military experience and piloting, companies such as British Airways and Air Canada were privileging masculinity over femininity and men over women.[58] Similarly, by associating attributes of caring, nurturing, and certain forms of female sexuality with flight attending, those airlines also helped to restrict female employment to a limited number of jobs.[59] In other words, the power to influence how we come to view ourselves and others is embedded in important organizational ideas about skill, goals, processes, and so on.

USING POWER: ORGANIZATIONAL POLITICS

Organizational politics Activities taken within organizations to acquire, develop, and use power and other resources to obtain one's preferred outcomes in a situation in which there is uncertainty or disagreement about choices.

Given the size of the benefits that can be gained by managers who use organizational power to bring about change that resolves conflicts in their favour, it is not surprising that managers want to acquire as much power as they can and then use it to get what they want. **Organizational politics** comprises, in the words of Jeffrey Pfeffer, "activities taken within organizations to acquire, develop, and use power and other resources to obtain one's preferred outcomes in a situation in which there is uncertainty or disagreement about choices."[60] To manage the change process to get conflicts resolved in their favour, individuals, subunits, and coalitions often engage in political activity and behaviour to enhance the power and influence they have. Even if organizational members or subunits have no personal desire to play politics, they still must understand how politics operates because sooner or later they will come up against a master player of the political game. In such situations, apolitical managers (those who do not engage in politics) get all the tedious assignments or the responsibility for projects that do little to enhance their career prospects. Astute political managers get the visible and important projects that bring them into contact with powerful managers and allow them to build up their own power base, which they can use to enhance their chances of promotion.

Tactics for Playing Politics

To understand the political component of organizational life, we need to examine the political tactics and strategies that individuals and subunits use to increase their chances of winning the political game. The reward for success is change that gives them a greater share of organizational resources—authority, money, status, and so on. Individuals and subunits can use many political tactics to obtain the power to achieve their goals and objectives.

Increasing Indispensability One prime political tactic that an individual or subunit can use to increase power is to become indispensable to the organization. Indispensability can be achieved by an increase in nonsubstitutability or an increase in centrality.

Increasing Nonsubstitutability Wily managers deliberately engage in behaviours and actions that make them nonsubstitutable.[61] They may develop specialized organizational skills, such as knowledge of computers, that allow them to solve problems for other managers. They may specialize in an area of increasing concern to the organization—such as international trade regulations, pollution control, or health and safety—so that they eventually are in a position to control a crucial contingency facing the organization. Individuals and subunits that use these tactics are often called in to solve problems as they arise, and the ability to come up with solutions increases their status and prestige.

Increasing Centrality Managers can increase their indispensability by making themselves more central to an organization. They can deliberately accept responsibilities that bring them into contact with many functions or with many managers so that they can enhance their personal reputation and that of their function. By being central, they may also enhance their ability to obtain information that they can use to make themselves and their functions nonsubstitutable. By being able to reduce the uncertainty experienced by others—for example, by obtaining and supplying information or by helping out on rush projects—they make others dependent on them. Then, in return for their help, they can request favours (such as access to privileged information) from other people and groups and feed this information to other managers, who in turn become obligated to them and who share even more information. Following this process, politically astute managers cultivate both people and information and are able to build within the organization a personal network of contacts that they can use to pursue personal goals such as promotion, and functional goals such as increasing the supply of scarce resources.

Associating with Powerful Managers Another way to obtain power is by attaching oneself to powerful managers who are clearly on their way to the top. By supporting a powerful manager and making oneself indispensable to that person, it is possible to rise up the organizational ladder with that person. Top managers often become mentors to aspiring lower-level managers because planning for the managerial succession is an important organizational task of top managers.[62] CEOs typically promote their friends, not their enemies. Managers who have taken the initiative to develop skills that make them stand out from the crowd and who are central and nonsubstitutable have the best chance of being selected as protégés by powerful managers who are seeking people to groom as their successors.

To identify the powerful people in an organization, it is necessary to develop skills in sensing who has power. A politically savvy manager figures out the key people to cultivate and the best ways to get their attention. Indicators of power include an individual's personal reputation and ability to (1) influence organizational decision-making outcomes, (2) control significant organizational resources, and (3) display symbols of prestige and status such as access to the corporate jet or limousine.[63]

A secondary way to form an attachment with powerful people is to take advantage of common ties such as graduation from the same school or university or similarity in socioeconomic background. Recall from Chapter 7 on organizational culture that top managers typically select as associates or successors other managers who are like themselves. They do so because they believe that shared norms and values are evidence of reliability or trustworthiness. Not surprisingly, then, it is not uncommon for managers to go to considerable lengths to look and behave like their superiors and to imitate or copy the habits or preferences of a senior person. Imitation has been called the sincerest form of flattery, and flattery is never wasted on those in power. The more powerful the person, the more he or she is likely to appreciate it. Nowhere is this clearer than in the behaviour of top managers and the board of directors at the corrupt telecommunications company, WorldCom. (See Organizational Insight 14.5.) As the recent Nortel scandals have indicated, Canadian companies have not been exempt from these kinds of problems. (See Organizational Insight 14.6.)

Building and Managing Coalitions Forming a coalition of different interests, stakeholders, individuals, and subunits around some common issue is a political tactic that a manager can use to obtain the power to resolve a conflict in her or his favour. Coalitions are often built around a trade-off: A supports B on an issue of interest to B in return for B supporting A on an issue of interest to A. Coalitions can be built through many levels in an organization, between various functions or divisions, and between important external or internal stakeholders. It is very important, for example, for top-level managers to build personal relationships with powerful shareholders or with members of the board of directors. Many of the most intense political contests occur at this level because the stakes are so high. The CEO needs the support of the board in any contest with members of the top-management team. Without it, the CEO's days are numbered. At Hollinger International, Conrad Black lost the support of his board once it was felt that they were being kept in the dark about key negotiations.

Building alliances with important customers is another valuable tactic, as is developing long-term relationships with the officers of the banks and other financial institutions from which a company obtains its capital. The more external linkages top managers can develop, the more chips they have to put on the table when the political game gets rough. Similarly, the ability to forge inside alliances with the managers of the most important subunits provides aspiring top managers with a power base that

ORGANIZATIONAL INSIGHT 14.5

Power Struggles and Corporate Greed at WorldCom

In 2002 WorldCom, the giant telecommunications company, started bankruptcy proceedings after it was revealed that its top executives had deliberately overinflated revenues by US$7.68 billion. Not only its top executives (such as former CEO Bernie Ebbers) were implicated—so were eight of WorldCom's 11-member board of directors who were at the helm when the company booked these billions of dollars and provided US$408 million in personal loans and lucrative pensions benefits to Ebbers. How could WorldCom's board of directors have failed in their oversight role?

Four of these eight board members had long-term personal and business ties to Ebbers and had been appointed to the board at his urging. Two of these four directors sat on WorldCom's compensation and stock option committee, which granted Ebbers these huge personal loans. At least one of these two directors reportedly also struck a deal with Ebbers whereby Ebbers gave him access to company aircraft for US$1 a month plus a US$400-an-hour usage fee, when the real cost of using such aircraft is hundreds of thousands of dollars a year. In return, this director agreed to Ebbers's huge severance package, which also ran into the hundreds of millions after he resigned.[64]

Small wonder then that in the fall of 2002 with these directors still collecting large fees and receiving huge perks from WorldCom, critics were calling for their removal from the board. They had not resigned voluntarily and legally the company could not unilaterally replace them until WorldCom's next general meeting. However, WorldCom was able to fill three other vacancies with new directors, such as former U.S. Attorney General Nicholas Katzenbach and Dennis Beresford, a former chairman of the Financial Accounting Standards Board, who can ensure that these unethical directors can do no more harm to a company that has cost its shareholders billions of dollars and whose future is still in doubt.

they can use to promote their personal agendas. In the game of organizational politics, having a lot of friends greatly enhances one's claim to power in the organization.

Skills in coalition building are important to success in organizational politics because the interests of parties to a coalition change frequently, as the environment changes. To maintain the coalition's consensus, the coalition has to be actively managed. Co-optation is a particularly important tool in coalition management. Recall from Chapter 3 that co-optation is a strategy that allows one subunit to overcome the opposition of a second subunit by involving it in decision making. Giving an opponent a place on an important committee or an important managerial role in solving organizational problems makes the opponent part of the coalition, with rights to share in the rewards from the outcome of the political decision-making process.

Influencing Decision Making Perhaps the most important political tactic a manager, group, division, or coalition can pursue to acquire, increase, and use power is to influence the politics of decision making. Possessing and using power (as a result of

ORGANIZATIONAL INSIGHT 14.6

Those in Power at Nortel Bring on Serious Troubles for Powerless Employees[65]

The Enron and WorldCom scandals have been joined by the Canadian version, that of Nortel Networks. Nortel has experienced not just one incident, but a second one where power holders again abused their executive positions of trust and control in misrepresenting company performance. For the second episode of suspect financial reporting, the president, chief executive officer, chief financial officer, and controller of Nortel were all fired "for cause." However, the damages extend well beyond the big guys, with the inevitable consequences of layoffs of innocent employees—the collateral damage from negative publicity and scorned investors. For the more recent scandal, Nortel projected layoffs of 3500, close to 10 percent of its workforce.

Nortel Networks has a corporate history of over 100 years, providing communication products and service since the time when the telephone was first invented. It grew from a small telephone product manufacturer into a dominant global player for the supply of communication and network capabilities. In 2001, Nortel was in the number one position in global telecommunications equipment, with year-to-year growth of 41.6 percent. Nortel's financial outlook looked too good to be true, but that was in fact the essence of Nortel's corporate scandals.

One perspective on Nortel's first corporate scandal was that John Roth, then the CEO, in his leadership role did what came naturally and created a picture and told a story in a compelling fashion. "John Roth's capacity to create a story about Nortel that so few questioned or doubted is an example of both the power of charismatic leadership and the risks of being believed too much." In the second, more recent scandal, it is believed that irresistible bonuses for high performance may have been an influential factor for Nortel executives to report inaccurate quarterly financials. The CEO this time was Frank Dunn and it is believed that "Mr. Dunn and his colleagues scrambled to achieve a financial turnaround of the troubled venture, not because it was part of the job description, but because attaining that fundamental objective had a $14 million bonus attached." Whatever the truth of the scandals may be, it begs the question as to how such scandalous events can be prevented to protect the innocent employees, customers, and investors.

increasing indispensability, associating with powerful people, and knowing how to build and manage coalitions) is not the only skill needed to play politics. Knowing how and when to use power is equally important. As we saw earlier, the use of power to influence decision making is most effective when the power is unobtrusive. If other managers and coalitions become aware that they are being manipulated, they are likely to oppose the interests of the coalition doing the manipulating—or at least to insist that any decisions that are made also favour their interests. This is the thought behind the notion that a person who uses power loses it: Once the opposition realizes that a manager is using power to influence a decision in his or her favour, opponents will start to lobby for their interests and try to protect their claims to the resource at stake.

Two tactics for controlling the decision-making process so that the use of power seems to be legitimate—that is, in the organization's interests and not in the pursuit of self-interest or self-promotion—are controlling the agenda and bringing in an outside expert.[66]

Controlling the Agenda Managers and coalitions like to be on, and particularly in control of, committees so that they can control the agenda or business of the committee. By controlling the agenda, they are able to control the issues and problems to be considered by important decision makers—such as how and when to change an organization's strategy and structure. Thus a coalition of powerful managers can prevent consideration of any issue that they do not support by not putting it on the agenda. In this way conflict remains either latent or in the felt stage because the opposition does not get the chance to air its view on problems or solutions. The ability to control the agenda is similar to the ability to control the premises of decision making. Both tactics limit the alternatives considered in the decision-making process.

Bringing in an Outside Expert

When a major conflict exists, such as when top managers are deciding how to change or restructure the organization, all managers and coalitions know that individuals and groups are fighting for their interests and perhaps for their political survival. Every subunit manager wants the axe to fall on other subunits and wants to try to benefit from whatever change takes place. Self-interested managers and coalitions, knowing that the solution they want will be perceived by other subunits as politically motivated, are eager to legitimize their position, and so they often bring in an outside expert who is considered to be neutral. The supposedly objective views of the expert are then used to support the position of the coalition in power.

In some cases, however, the experts are not neutral at all but have been coached by the coalition in power and know exactly what the coalition's view is so that they can develop a favourable scenario. When this scenario is presented to the groups in conflict, the "objectivity" of the expert's plan is used to sway decision making in favour of the coalition in power. The opposition is outgunned and accepts the inevitable.

In sum, there are many tactics that individuals, managers, subunits, and coalitions can use to obtain power and play organizational politics. The success of attempts to influence and control decision making to resolve conflicts in a certain way depends on individuals' ability to learn the political ropes and hone their political skills.

The Costs and Benefits of Organizational Politics

Organizational politics is an integral part of decision making in an organization. Coalitions form to control the premises behind decision making, to lobby for their interests, to control the path of organizational change, and to resolve organizational conflict in their own favour. Because the stakes are high—the control of scarce resources like promotions and budgets—politics is a very active force in most organizations. When we look to see what changes an organization makes to its strategy or structure, we need to recognize the role that politics plays in these choices. It can improve the choices and decisions that an organization makes, but it can also produce problems and promote conflict if it is not managed skillfully. If, for example, different coalitions continually fight about resource allocation decisions, more time is likely to be spent in making decisions than in implementing the decisions that are made. As a result, organizational effectiveness suffers.

To manage organizational politics and gain its benefits, an organization must establish a balance of power in which alternative views and solutions can be offered and considered by all parties and dissenting views can be heard (see Figure 14-5). It is also important for the balance of power to shift over time, toward the party that can best manage the uncertainty and contingencies facing the organization. An organization that confers power on those who can promote the changes that will help it the most can take advantage of the political process to improve the quality of organizational decision making. By allowing managers to use their power to advance their future objectives, and to form coalitions that compete for support for their agendas, an organization can improve the quality of decision making by encouraging useful and productive debate about alternatives. Thus politics can improve organizational effectiveness if it results in change that allocates resources to where they can produce more value.

An organization's ability to obtain the benefits of politics depends on the assumption that power flows to those who can be of most help to the organization. This assumption means that unsuccessful managers lose power to successful managers and that there is a constant movement of power in the organization as an individual's or a group's power ebbs and flows. Suppose, however, that the top-management team in power becomes entrenched and is able to defend its power and property rights against its opponents even though the performance of the organization is faltering. Suppose a top-management team has institutionalized its power by occupying all important roles on organizational committees and by carefully selecting supporters for top organizational roles. Suppose the CEO occupies the role of board chair so that he or she can dominate the board of directors. In this situation, top management can use its power to fend off shareholders' attempts to restructure the organization to make better use of organizational resources. Similarly, top management, far from encouraging dissent among promising middle managers, might deny them promotion or decision-making power. By doing this, top management encourages the departure of those who threaten top management's dominant position. In this situation, the power that the top-management team has obtained as a result of its ability to control the distribution of property rights threatens organizational performance and survival.[67] Power holders are notoriously reluctant to give up the positions that give them the right to allocate resources and enrich themselves. CEOs in particular rarely give up their positions voluntarily.

FIGURE 14-5
Maintaining a Balance of Power.

A. Power Balance. Decisions result from bargaining between subunits, which improves the quality of organizational decision making.

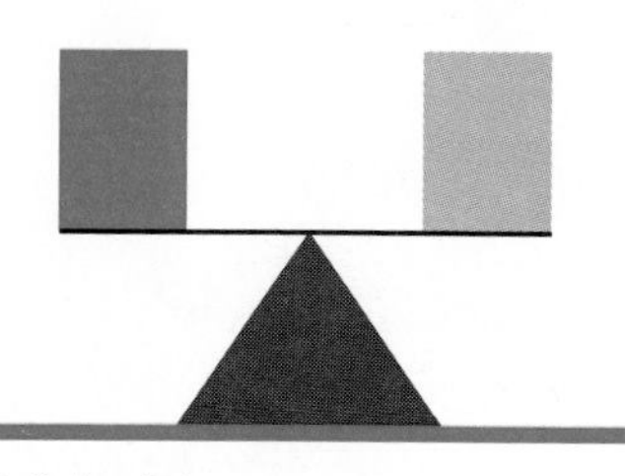

B. Power Imbalance. Decisions are made in the interests of one subunit. As a result, the quality of decision making may decline.

■ Subunit A
■ Subunit B

When the balance of power between stakeholders or subunits does not force the allocation of resources to where they can best create value, organizational effectiveness suffers. When powerful managers can suppress the views of those who oppose their interests, debate becomes restricted, checks and balances fade, bad conflict increases, and organizational inertia increases. Today, after the recent scandals in organizations such as Enron, WorldCom, and so on, there is increasing support for measures that would increase the power of stakeholders to remove inefficient top-management teams and CEOs who pay themselves exorbitant salaries that often are not tied to organizational performance. Thus, ultimately, whether power and politics benefit or harm an organization is a function of the balance of power among organizational stakeholders.

MANAGERIAL IMPLICATIONS

Power and Politics

1. Recognize that politics is a fact of organizational life, and develop the skills to understand how politics shapes organizational decision making.
2. Develop a personal power base to influence decision making, and use it to prevent political managers or groups from pursuing their interests at the expense of organizational interests.
3. To obtain power, try to associate with powerful managers and find a powerful mentor, make yourself central and nonsubstitutable, develop personal skills so that you can reduce uncertainty for other subunits or for the organization, seek membership on committees that will give you access to information, and obtain control of organizational resources.
4. Seek to maintain a power balance between individuals or subunits in an organization in order to preserve the quality of organizational decision making.
5. Identify the key organizational discourses and how they bestow power of different people.

SUMMARY

Managing conflict, power, and politics is one of an organization's major priorities because these factors determine which decisions the organization makes and therefore, ultimately, its survival. Chapter 14 has made the following main points:

1. Organizational conflict is the clash that arises when the goal-directed behaviour of one group blocks or thwarts the goals of another.
2. Conflict can be functional if it overcomes organizational inertia and brings about change.

However, too high a level of conflict can reduce the level of coordination and integration between people and subunits and reduce organizational effectiveness.

3. The five stages of Pondy's model of organizational conflict are latent conflict, perceived conflict, felt conflict, manifest conflict, and conflict aftermath.
4. There are five sources of conflict between subunits: interdependence, differences in goals and priorities, bureaucratic factors, incompatible performance criteria, and competition for scarce resources.
5. Conflict resolution strategies are used to manage organizational conflict and to prevent it from becoming destructive. Two important strategies are acting at the level of structure to change task relationships and acting at the level of attitudes and individuals to change the attitudes of the parties or the parties themselves.
6. Organizational power is the ability of one actor or stakeholder to overcome resistance by other actors and achieve a desired objective or result.
7. The main sources of power available to managers and subunits are authority, control over resources, control over information, nonsubstitutability, centrality, control over uncertainty or contingencies, unobtrusive power, and knowledge/discourse.
8. Organizational politics comprises activities carried out within organizations to acquire, develop, and use power and other resources to obtain one's preferred outcomes.
9. Tactics that individuals and subunits can use to play politics include increasing indispensability, associating with powerful managers, building and managing coalitions, controlling the agenda, and bringing in an outside expert.
10. Using power to play organizational politics can improve the quality of decision making if the people who have the power are those who can best serve the needs of the organization. However, if top managers have the ability to control and hoard power and entrench themselves in the organization, the interests of other organizational stakeholders may be jeopardized as decisions are made to serve top management's personal interests. Thus there needs to be a balance of power between organizational stakeholders.

DISCUSSION QUESTIONS

1. Why and under what conditions can conflict be good or bad for an organization? Would you expect a higher level of conflict in a mechanistic or an organic structure? Why?
2. You have been appointed to manage a large R&D laboratory. You find a high level of conflict between scientists in the unit. Why might this conflict be arising? How will you try to resolve it?
3. Why is it important to maintain a balance of power between different groups of organizational stakeholders?
4. What is unobtrusive power? Why is it so important?
5. How can the design of the organization's structure and culture give some subunits more power than others?
6. Discuss how you, as manager of the R&D function in a cosmetic products company, might try to increase your power and the power of your subunit to control more resources in a battle with marketing and manufacturing.

ORGANIZATIONAL THEORY IN ACTION

Practising Organizational Theory: Managing Conflict

Form groups of three to five people and discuss the following scenario:

You are a group of top managers of a large, well-established pharmaceutical company that has made its name by pioneering innovative new drugs. Intense competition from other companies in the pharmaceutical industry, plus increasing government pressure to reduce the price of drugs, has put pressure on you to find ways to reduce costs and speed product development. In addition, other large buyers of drugs have made marketing drugs much more difficult, and marketing managers are demanding an increased say in which drugs should be developed and when. To respond to these pressures, you have decided to create cross-functional teams composed of people from R&D, marketing, finance, and top management to evaluate the potential of new drug products and to decide if they should be pursued.

1. How will the change in structure affect the relative power of the different functions?
2. How likely is conflict to occur because of these changes, and what will be the source of the conflict?
3. What can you do to help manage the conflict process to make the new operating system work as you hope it will?

Making the Connection #14

Find an example of a conflict occurring between the managers, or between the managers and other stakeholders, of a company. What is the source of the conflict? How are managers using their power to influence the decision-making process?

The Ethical Dimension #14

The behaviour of WorldCom's top managers and members of its board of directors is said to be quite common in many companies today. CEOs have considerable power to appoint board members, and the members of a company's compensation and stock option committee have wide latitude to reward the CEO and other top managers as they see fit.

1. Is it ethical for CEOs to be able to appoint the directors who will be evaluating their performance and determining their compensation?
2. What kinds of ethical rules should be developed to ensure that abuses of power and political plays such as those that occurred at WorldCom can be prevented in the future?
3. What can an organizational leader do to ensure that organizational discourses do not result in inequitable outcomes based on race or gender?

Analyzing the Organization: Design Module #14

This module focuses on conflict, power, and politics in your organization.

ASSIGNMENT

1. What do you think are the likely sources of conflict that may arise in your organization? Is there a history of conflict between managers or between stakeholders?
2. Analyze the sources of power of the principal subunits, functions, or divisions in the organization. Which is the most central subunit? Which is the most nonsubstitutable subunit? Which one controls the most resources? Which one handles the main contingencies facing the organization?
3. Which subunit is the most powerful? Identify any ways in which the subunit has been able to influence decision making in its favour.
4. To what degree are the organization's strategic and operational decisions affected by conflict and politics?

Company Profiles #14*

Choose one or more of the organizations (e.g., companies, government agencies, or nonprofit organizations) that are profiled in this chapter. Do

* The authors would like to receive information from student groups and instructors on any companies where there have been dramatic changes to the information published in this text. We would be happy to publish the best of these changes in a subsequent edition, where we will focus on changing company profiles.

an Internet search to get up-to-date information on each organization you have selected, and answer the following questions.

1. What does the new information tell you about the organization's current ability to manage organizational power, politics, and conflict?
2. How does the information compare with the earlier information provided in the text and what does that tell you about organizations (e.g., does the organization appear to be more or less successful in managing organizational power, politics, and conflict than before, and how do you explain this)?

Alternative Perspectives #14

Critical, postmodern, and feminist researchers contend that organizational power and politics are rooted in discourses that privilege company interests over employees interests, managers over workers, men over women, and whites over people of colour.

Read one or more of the following readings and identity five ways that organizational discourses can have a negative impact and five ways that they can have a positive impact on employees. In small groups, discuss how you would deal with the potentially negative aspects of dominant organizational discourses.

Reading List

Mills, A. J. 1993. Organizational Discourse and the Gendering of Identity. In M. Parker, and J. Hassard, ed., *Postmodernity and Organizations*, pp. 132–147. London: Sage.

Mills, A. J. 1997a. Business Education as Gendered Discourse. *Proceedings of the Women in Management Division of the Administrative Sciences Association of Canada*, 18(11): 22–32.

Mills, A. J. 1997b. Duelling Discourses—Desexualization versus Eroticism in the Corporate Framing of Female Sexuality in the British Airline Industry, 1945–60. In P. Prasad, A. J. Mills, M. Elmes, and A. Prasad, ed., *Managing the Organizational Melting Pot: Dilemmas of Workplace Diversity*, pp. 171–198. Newbury Park, CA: Sage.

Morgan, G., and Knights, D. 1991. Gendering Jobs: Corporate Strategies, Managerial Control and Dynamics of Job Segregation. *Work, Employment & Society*, 5(2): 181–200.

Prasad, A. 1997a. The Colonizing Consciousness and Representations of the Other: A Postcolonial Critique of the Discourse of Oil. In P. Prasad, A. J. Mills, M. Elmes, and A. Prasad, eds., *Managing the Organizational Melting Pot: Dilemmas of Workplace Diversity*, pp. 285–311. Thousand Oaks, CA: Sage.

Prasad, A., and Prasad, P. 2002. Otherness at Large: Identity and Difference in the New Globalized Organizational Landscape. In I. Aaltio, and A. J. Mills, eds., *Gender, Identity and the Culture of Organizations*, pp. 57–71. London: Routledge.

Prasad, P. 1997b. The Protestant Ethic and the Myths of the Frontier: Cultural Imprints, Organizational Structuring, and Workplace Diversity. In P. Pradas, A. J. Mills, M. Elmes, and A. Prasad, eds., *Managing the Organizational Melting Pot*, pp. 129–147. Thousand Oaks. CA: Sage.

Prasad, P., and Mills, A. J. 1997. From Showcase to Shadow: Understanding the Dilemmas of Managing Workplace Diversity. In P. Prasad, A. J. Mills, M. Elmes, and A. Prasad, eds., *Managing the Organizational Melting Pot: Dilemmas of Workplace Diversity*, pp. 3–27. Thousand Oaks, CA: Sage.

Thomas, R., and Davies, A. 2002. Gender and the New Public Management. *Gender, Work & Organization*, 9(4): 372–396.

CASE FOR ANALYSIS

The Future of the National Hockey League[68]

The National Hockey League (NHL) has talked of organizational restructuring for many years. It may now have a new opportunity. The current collective bargaining agreement, which has been in place for ten years, expired on September 15, 2004. Immediately following this date, the owners of the NHL "locked out" the players. In other words, the owners cancelled all games and kept players away from home ice until they were willing to renegotiate the contract according to terms established by the owners. The league (i.e., the team owners) is at major odds with the professional players it employs over the future of the organization. The players are represented by the National Hockey League Players Association (NHLPA), led by Bob Goodenow, the executive director.

The main source of contention is the division of league revenue. The owners want to implement a salary cap system whereby each team would be limited in how much they could spend in total on player salaries. The players, as have all professional sports players, have historically resisted any sort of restriction on their salaries. According to the NHL, over the past nine years, league revenues have grown 173 percent but player salaries have increased at a faster rate, 261 percent. During this time the league also reports that it has lost a total of US$1.5 billion and that currently 75 percent of revenues are paid out in player salaries.

The current contract (the 1994–95 agreement) was originally supposed to be for six years but it is has been extended twice. In the 94–95 negotiations, the league attempted to implement mechanisms that would act as a control on escalating salaries. These included a rookie salary cap and restrictions on free agency. However, the owners were not successful in negotiating for an overall salary cap and eventually capitulated in negotiations.

The NHLPA argues that the owners are their own worst enemy and that they are the ones who control salaries and yet continue to sign players at increasingly higher salaries. In negotiations in 2003, the NHLPA suggested a luxury-tax and revenue-sharing system, which they estimate would provide $200 million to the financially less well-off teams, and also offered to roll back average salaries by around 24 percent.

The value of NHL teams has dropped to an average of US$161 million. In contrast, National Basketball Association (NBA) team values have increased to an average of $275 million. In 1999, the New Jersey Nets were only worth $150 million. The NHL's recently negotiated contract with U.S. television broadcasters is much lower than the previous one. It will lower annual league revenue by 50 percent to $60 million, while the new NBA deal is worth $766 million annually. In the U.S. television market, the NHL ranks in popularity behind arena football and NASCAR racing.

Currently two of the four major professional sports leagues, the NBA and the National Football League (NFL) have team salary caps, while the Major Baseball League Association (MBLA) and the NHL do not. Compounding the problem is the wide discrepancy between team revenues. Some large-market teams such as the New York Rangers, Detroit Red Wings, and Toronto Maple Leafs generate large profits and have huge financial resources. Most of the other league teams, however, generate far less revenue due to being located in much smaller markets.

Additionally, as the lockout progresses, a new professional hockey league is in the process of being formed. Analysts believe that the new league is hoping to capitalize on the shutdown of the NHL. If the NHL shuts down for a prolonged period, the new league will be able to attract NHL players and have a much greater chance of success.

DISCUSSION QUESTIONS

1. What does the owners' lockout tell you about conflict resolution in the NHL?
2. Were the owners right to lock the players out to force an agreement? Explain.

REFERENCES

1. T. Burns, "Micropolitics: Mechanism of Institutional Change," *Administrative Science Quarterly*, 1961, vol. 6, pp. 257–281.
2. J. G. March, "The Business Firm as a Coalition," *Journal of Politics*, 1962, vol. 24, pp. 662–678.
3. L. Coser, *The Functions of Social Conflict* (New York: The Free Press, 1956); S. P. Robbins, *Managing Organizational Conflict: A Non-Traditional Approach* (Englewood Cliffs, NJ: Prentice Hall, 1974).
4. J. McCann and J. R. Galbraith, "Interdepartmental Relationships," in P. C. Nystrom and W. H. Starbuck, eds., *Handbook of Organizational Design*, vol. 2 (New York: Oxford University Press, 1981), pp. 60–84.
5. P. Waldie, "As Tellier and 2 Directors Leave, a Family Firm Comes Full Circle," *Globe and Mail*, 14 December 2004, p. B7; B. Jang, "Next Stop: Make-or-Break Decision on Jets," 14 December 2004, p. B7; Bertrand Marotte, "Bombardier Thrown into Turmoil over Tellier's Sudden Departure," *Globe and Mail*, 14 December 2004, p. B1; Simon Tuck, "Ottawa Eyes National Aerospace Plan," *Globe and Mail*, 15 December 2004, pp. B1, B18.
6. A. C. Amason, "Distinguishing the Effects of Functional and Dysfunctional Conflict and Strategic Decision Making: Resolving a Paradox for Top Management Teams," *Academy of Management Review*, 1996, vol. 39, pp. 12–148.
7. The following discussion draws heavily on these sources: L. R. Pondy, "Organizational Conflict: Concepts and Models," *Administrative Science Quarterly*, 1967, vol. 2, pp. 296–320; and R. E. Walton and J. M. Dutton, "The Management of Interdepartmental Conflict: A Model and Review," *Administrative Science Quarterly*, 1969, vol. 14, pp. 62–73.
8. J. D. Thompson, "Organizational Management of Conflict," *Administrative Science Quarterly*, 1960, vol. 4, pp. 389–409; and K. Thomas, "Conflict and Conflict Management," in M. D. Dunnette, ed., *The Handbook of Industrial and Organizational Psychology* (Chicago: Rand McNally, 1976).
9. J. D. Thompson, *Organizations in Action* (New York: McGraw-Hill, 1967).
10. J. A. Litterer, "Conflict in Organizations: A Reexamination," *Academy of Management Journal*, 1966, vol. 9, pp. 178–186.
11. Z. Olijnyk, "In Like a Lion," *Canadian Business*, 13 September 2004, *www.canadianbusiness.com/article.jsp?content=20040913_61794_61794.*
12. M. Dalton, "Conflicts Between Staff and Line Managerial Officers," *American Sociological Review*, 1950, vol. 15, pp. 342–351.
13. A. Miller, S. Nayyar, and S. Sevante, "Picture This Executive Battle," *Newsweek*, 10 May 1993, p. 54.
14. "Kodak Forms 15-member Senior Management Team," *Business Wire*, 14 October 1999.
15. Organizational Insight compiled by Ellen Rudderham-Gaudet using the following sources: Shirley Won, "Shermag Permanently Closing Plant in Disraeli, Que.," *Globe and Mail*, 25 September 2004; *www.shermag.com/eng/shermag.html*, 15 October 2004; "Shermag Issues Statement Concerning Disraeli Facility," *Canada NewsWire*, 7 October 2004, p. 1.
16. P. R. Lawrence and J. R. Lorsch, *Organization and Environment* (Homewood, IL: Irwin, 1967).
17. M. McClearn, "Code of Silence," *Canadian Business*, 13 September 2004, *www.canadianbusiness.com/article.jsp?content=20040913_61913_61913.*
18. "CS First Boston: All Together Now?" *The Economist*, 10 April 1993, p. 90.
19. M. Siconolfi, "CS First Boston's Hennessy to Relinquish Top Posts," *Wall Street Journal*, 3 July 1996, p. C1.
20. Coser, *The Functions of Social Conflict.*
21. Matthew McClearn, "The Verdict. On the Field of Battle in Delaware, Press Baron Conrad Black Did Not Carry the Day," *Canadian Business*, 1 March 2004, *www.canadianbusiness.com/article.jsp?content=20040301_58878_58878.*
22. Ibid.
23. Ibid.
24. Ibid.
25. Matthew McClearn, "Did Anybody Even Read This? Hollinger International Has a Very Thorough Code of Ethics. Too Bad It Was Ignored," *Canadian Business*, 24 May 2004, *www.canadianbusiness.com/article.jsp?content=20040524_60226_60226.*
26. R. H. Miles, *Macro Organizational Behavior* (Santa Monica, CA: Goodyear, 1980).
27. This discussion draws heavily on E. H. Nielsen, "Understanding and Managing Intergroup Conflict," in P. R. Lawrence, L. B. Barnes, and J. W.

Lorsch, *Organizational Behavior and Administration* (Homewood, IL: Irwin, 1976).

28. Lawrence and Lorsch, *Organization and Environment.*
29. R. E. Walton and R. B. McKersie, *A Behavioral Theory of Labor Negotiations: An Analysis of a Social Interaction System* (New York: McGraw-Hill, 1965).
30. R. E. Walton, "Third-Party Roles in Interdepartmental Conflict," *Industrial Relations,* 1967, vol. 7, pp. 29–43.
31. W. G. Ouchi, *Theory Z: How American Business Can Meet the Japanese Challenge* (Reading, MA: Addison-Wesley, 1981).
32. R. M. Emerson, "Power–Dependence Relations," *American Sociological Review,* 1962, vol. 27, pp. 31–41; and J. Pfeffer, *Power in Organizations* (Boston: Pitman, 1981).
33. R. A. Dahl, "The Concept of Power," *Behavioral Science,* 1957, vol. 2, pp. 210–215.
34. M. Gargiulo, "Two-Step Leverage: Managing Constraint in Organizational Politics," *Administrative Science Quarterly,* 1993, vol. 38, pp. 1–19.
35. M. Foucault, *Madness and Civilization: A History of Insanity in the Age Of Reason* (New York: Pantheon Books, 1965); M. Foucault, *The Archaeology of Knowledge* (London: Routledge, 1972); M. Foucault, *The Birth of the Clinic* (New York: Vintage, 1975).
36. R. Jackall, *Moral Mazes* (Oxford: Oxford University Press, 1988).
37. R. M. Kanter, *Men and Women of the Corporation* (New York: Basic Books, 1977); R. M. Kanter, "Power Failure in Management Circuits," *Harvard Business Review,* 1979, vol. 57, 65–75; I. Aaltio and A. J. Mills, *Gender, Identity and the Culture of Organizations* (London: Routledge, 2002).
38. O. C. Brenner, J. Tomkiewicz, and V. E. Schein, "The Relationship Between Sex Role Stereotypes and Requisite Management Characteristics Revisited," *The Academy of Management Journal,* 1989, vol. 32, pp. 662–669; V. E. Schein, "The Relationship Between Sex Role Stereotypes and Requisite Management Characteristics Among Female Managers," *Journal of Applied Psychology,* 1973, vol. 57, pp. 89–105. V. E. Schein, "Relationships Between Sex Role Stereotypes and Requisite Management Characteristics Among Female Managers," *Journal of Applied Psychology,* 1975, vol. 60, pp. 340–344.
39. M. Weber, *The Theory of Social and Economic Organization* (New York: The Free Press, 1947).
40. M. F. R. Kets de Vries, *Organizations on the Couch: Clinical Perspectives on Organizational Behavior and Change* (San Francisco, Jossey-Bass, 1991); M. F. R. Kets de Vries, "The Leader as Mirror: Clinical Reflections," *Human Relations,* 1989, vol. 42, pp. 607–623; M. F. R. Kets de Vries and D. Miller, *The Neurotic Organization* (San Francisco, Jossey-Bass, 1984); C. Lasch, *The Culture of Narcissism* (New York: Warner Books, 1979).
41. L. Lowe, A. J. Mills and J. Mullen, "Gendering the Silences: Psychoanalysis, Gender and Organization Studies," *Journal of Managerial Psychology,* 2002, vol. 17, pp. 422–434; A. J. Mills, "Organizational Discourse and the Gendering of Identity," in M. Parker and J. Hassard, eds., *Postmodernity and Organizations* (London: Sage, 1993), pp. 132–147; G. A. Walter, "Psyche and Symbol," in L. R. Pondy, P. Frost, G. Morgan, and T.C. Dandridge, eds., *Organizational Symbolism* (Greenwich, CT: JAI Press, 1983), pp. 257–271.
42. J. A. Conger and R. N. Kanungo, "The Empowerment Process: Integrating Theory and Practice," *Academy of Management Review,* 1988, vol. 13, pp. 471–481.
43. G. R. Salancik and J. Pfeffer, "The Bases and Uses of Power in Organizational Decision Making," *Administrative Science Quarterly,* 1974, vol. 19, pp. 453–473; J. Pfeffer and G. R. Salancik, *The External Control of Organizations: A Resource Dependence View* (New York: Harper and Row, 1978).
44. Salancik and Pfeffer, "The Bases and Uses of Power in Organizational Decision Making."
45. A. M. Pettigrew, "Information Control as a Power Resource," *Sociology,* 1972, vol. 6, pp. 187–204.
46. A. M. Pettigrew, *The Politics of Organizational Decision Making* (London: Tavistock, 1973), p. 191.
47. C. Perrow, *Organizational Analysis: A Sociological View* (Belmont, CA: Wadsworth, 1970).
48. McClearn, "The Verdict on the Field of Battle in Delaware, Press Baron Conrad Black Did Not Carry the Day."
49. D. Mechanic, "Sources of Power of Lower-Level Participants in Complex Organizations," *Administrative Science Quarterly,* 1962, vol. 7, pp. 349–364.
50. M. Crozier, *The Bureaucratic Phenomenon* (Chicago: University of Chicago Press, 1964).
51. D. J. Hickson, C. R. Hinings, C. A. Lee, R. E. Schneck, and J. M. Pennings, "A Strategic Contingencies Theory of Intraorganizational Power," *Administrative Science Quarterly,* 1971, vol. 16, pp. 216–227.
52. Ibid.
53. Ibid.
54. Pfeffer, *Power in Organizations,* Ch. 3.

55. S. Lukes, *Power: A Radical View* (London: MacMillan, 1974).

56. Pfeffer, *Power in Organizations,* pp. 115–121.

57. Kanter, *Men and Women of the Corporation.*

58. A. J. Mills, "The Gendering of Organizational Culture: Social and Organizational Discourses in the Making of British Airways," in M. DesRosiers, ed., *Proceedings of the Women in Management Division of the Administrative Sciences Association of Canada,* 1994, vol. 15 (11), pp. 11–20; A. J. Mills, "Managing Subjectivity, Silencing Diversity: Organizational Imagery in the Airline Industry—The Case of British Airways," *Organization,* 1995, vol. 2, pp. 243–269; J. Helms Mills, "Employment Practices and the Gendering of Air Canada's Culture During Its Trans Canada Airlines Days," *Culture & Organization,* 2002, vol. 8, pp. 117–128; N. J. Newby, *The Sky's the Limit* (Vancouver: Mitchell Press Ltd., 1986).

59. Newby, *The Sky's the Limit.*

60. Pfeffer, *Power in Organizations,* p. 7.

61. Hickson, Hinings, Lee, Schneck, and Pennings, "A Strategic Contingencies Theory of Intraorganizational Power."

62. E. E. Jennings, *The Mobile Manager* (New York: McGraw-Hill, 1967).

63. J. R. P. French, Jr., and B. Raven, "The Bases of Social Power," in D. Cartwright and A. F. Zander, eds., *Group Dynamics* (Evanston, IL: Row Peterson, 1960), pp. 607–623.

64. J. Hall, "WorldCom Board Expected to Be Wiped Clean," *www.Reuters.com,* 8 October 2002.

65. Organizational Insight by Ellen Rudderham-Gaudet, based on the following sources: "Nortel to Eliminate 3500 Jobs," *Money,* 19 August 2004, *money.cnn.com/2004/08/19/technology/nortel/*; Nortel Networks, "History of Being First," *www.nortelnetworks.com/corporate/corptime/index.html,* 15 October 2004; P. Bradshaw and P. Jackson, "Loyal Opposition," *CA Magazine,* 2001, vol. 134, pp. 35–36; Dierdre McMurdy, "Nortel in Trouble: So Here We Go Again," *finance.sympatico.msn.ca/content/investing/markets/deirdremcmurdy/P27201.asp,* 15 October 2004.

66. This discussion draws heavily on J. Pfeffer, *Power in Organizations,* Ch. 5.

67. O. E. Williamson and W. G. Ouchi, "The Markets and Hierarchies Program of Research: Origins, Implications, Prospects," in A. E. Van De Ven and W. F. Joyce, eds., *New Perspectives on Organizational Design and Behavior* (New York: Wiley, 1981), pp. 347–406.

68. Case prepared by Scott MacMillan from the following sources: *CBA News, www.nhlcbanews.com/current.html,* 9 June 2004; E. Duhatschek, "The Feeling Is That the NHL Will Be Shutting Down Operations," *Globe and Mail,* 9 June 2004, p. S1; K. Rook, "To Strike or Not to Strike," *www.journalism.ryerson.ca/online/downlo/macabre/krook.htm,* 9 June 2004; T. Wharnsby, "Union Trumpets Plan to Cut Salaries," *Globe and Mail,* 12 June 2004, p. S3; P. Wilde, "NHL Teams Worth Less, Report Says," *Globe and Mail,* 26 June 2004, p. S3; S. Brunt, "Options Exist for Hockey Sides to Avoid Clobbering Each Other," *Globe and Mail,* 12 June 2004, p. S3.

CASE 1

The Problem and "I": Some Reflections on Problems, Perception, Action, and Wisdom

Shripad G. Pendse

ABSTRACT

Two orientations to problem solving are compared: the "objective," where the problem is seen as an object distinct from ourselves, and the "introspective," where we view the problem as an interaction between ourselves and the situation. Managers attempting to solve problems typically adopt the objective orientation, which often backfires.

Two classic cases are used to illustrate how managers gravitate to the objective approach, and how it can worsen the situation. The paper concludes that combining the two orientations leads to wisdom, which in turn makes effective problem solving possible in case analysis as well as real life.

There is a story about eight young children who were out playing. Their teacher had told them to do a count every so often to ensure that they all stayed together. After playing for a while, one of them did the count. He counted only seven heads. Feeling scared, he asked another child to repeat the count, but the result did not change. Now all the children took turns counting, but could not find the eighth child. In a panic they ran to the teacher. The teacher found that all the eight children were there after all. With a smile she said to them: "You know what the problem was? Each of you forgot to include yourself in the count!"

CASE ANALYSIS IN MANAGEMENT: DEFINING THE PROBLEM

When teaching by the case method in a business school, the instructor frequently initiates the discussion by asking: "What is the problem in this case"? This question echoes a view expressed in most organizational behaviour and management texts. For example, Greenberg, Baron, Sales, and Owen (2000, p. 306) state, "To decide how to solve a problem, one must first recognize and identify the problem." Identifying the problem is considered the first step in the "rational decision-making model," leading to later steps such as developing alternative solutions to the problem, choosing the best one, and implementing and evaluating that solution (McShane, 2004, p. 278). As another example, Cravens and Lamb (1986) stress the importance of problem identification this way: "Identification of the main problem, opportunity, or issue in a case is crucial.... A major pitfall in defining problems/decisions is confusing symptoms with *problems*. . . . " Nor is the importance of problem identification limited to management textbooks. For example, Einstein argued that "the formulation of a problem is often more essential than its solution" (Einstein and Infeld, 1942, p. 95, cited in Zikmund, 1997, p. 45).

Given this evident importance of identifying or defining a "problem," it is important to think carefully about the meaning conveyed by the word "problem" and the nature of that concept. Management text authors do not usually offer a rigorous analysis of the concept of a problem. Some texts give a definition of the word while others do not. Thus the only explicit definition to be found in Zikmund's (1997, p. 43) book on business research methods is that "The word *problem,* in general usage, suggests something has gone wrong." Similarly, Greenberg et al. (2000, p. 306) do not define what a problem is but do give an example to illustrate the difficulty in identifying a problem: "For example, an executive may identify as a problem the fact that the company cannot meet its payroll obligations. . . . "

Two Orientations on the Nature of a Problem

Among the authors who define the word "problem," there are two quite different orientations or perspectives on how to view a problem.

According to one perspective, the problem has an "objective" (i.e., "object-like") status—it exists in the world in its own right, somewhat like a stone. There are various properties one associates with an object such as a stone. For example, objects can be counted; they can be ordered in terms of some characteristic such as their magnitude or difficulty; and some operations can be carried out on them such as splitting them. Thus Cravens and Lamb (1986) view a problem as an object, although they caution, as mentioned above, that it may be hard to identify since it may be hidden behind surface appearances of something different, namely symptoms. It takes hard work and persistence to see behind the symptom to home in on the "real" problem. As they put it, "Keep asking the question WHY until you are satisfied that you have identified the problem . . . and not just another symptom . . . ." Zikmund (1997, p. 85) also sees a problem as an object and makes a similar distinction between problems and symptoms. "Certain occurrences that appear to be 'the problem' may be only symptoms of a deeper problem."

According to the second orientation, a problem is not an object that exists in its own right, but rather it is a process, an interaction or a transaction taking place between a person and a situation. Thus this second perspective sees a problem as having an introspective or psychological dimension rather than being solely an object. Seen from the introspective view, a problem (like beauty) lies partly in the eye of the beholder, and not just in the external situation. As a result, as Robbins and Langton (2001, p. 460) put it, "one person's *problem* is another person's *acceptable status quo*" [Emphasis in the original]. A "problem" in this perspective is person-specific.

What is the nature of the interaction between the situation and the person from the introspective approach to a problem? Robbins and Langton (2001, p. 460) define a problem as an interaction between "some *current* state of affairs and some *desired* state" [Emphasis in the original]. Similarly Gause and Weinberg (1990, p. 15) define a problem as "the difference between things as desired and things as perceived." Similar definitions are given by McShane (2004, p. 278) and Johns and Saks (2001, p. 345). For convenience and brevity of expression, I will refer to the desired state as DS and the current or actual state as CS. It can be noticed that the DS is a function of the person while the CS is a function of the external reality or "facts" of the situation.

Thus in the introspective approach a problem exists only to the extent that a person desires certain things, and believes that the actual or current state, CS, is different from that desired state, DS. Within a given situation, therefore, a problem may exist for one person and not for another depending on the desired states of the two persons.

Similarly, this perspective suggests that a problem may change or even disappear entirely if the person (a) changes what they desire (DS), or (b) changes their perception of the current state of affairs, CS.

(The distinction between objective and introspective perspectives here is similar to one made by Roethlisberger, 1977, between the "rational" and "social system" conceptions of organizations. I will return to this similarity in a later section.)

To paraphrase the popular television show *The X-Files*, in the objective perspective the problem, like truth, is "out there." It can be located and hunted down as long as one is willing to put some effort into doing so. In the introspective perspective, the quarry is much more elusive, may change its appearance from time to time, and may not even exist at all. If a "hunt" for the problem as an object is one that requires a gun, the "hunt" for a problem from an introspective view requires a mirror, that is self-understanding, as the first tool. According to the introspective perspective, if one assumes that the problem exists and fires the gun, it is likely that one would shoot oneself in the foot instead.

PROBLEM IDENTIFICATION IN MANAGEMENT

The discussion of the two contrasting approaches above may seem to be purely philosophical and not of any practical value. In reality our tendency to see the problem from an objective perspective has tremendous influence on our day-to-day behaviour. This tendency occurs to a great extent because of the nature of the (English) language in which the word "problem" is a noun and we use nouns for objects. (It is said that in some languages, especially tribal ones, reality is seen as a happening or a process rather than as having an "objective" state, and it may be that people using those languages hold a different type of orientation to a problem).

Thus when a group of managers start a discussion with the question "What is the problem in this situation here?" the very question is likely to invoke a tacit understanding in the group that the problem should be seen from the objective perspective. Similarly, if an instructor asks this question of his students during a case analysis, students are all the more likely to see the problem as having an object-like status since the message comes from the authority figure in the classroom. This is likely to happen regardless of whether one finds an objective or an introspective definition of a problem in the text. In particular, the objective orientation suggests that the problem exists outside the problem solver and therefore he or she can act on it in somewhat the same way as a person can deal with a stone by breaking it into pieces.

This in turn has important practical implications for students as well as managers when they attempt to identify problems and take actions to solve them. As a result, while attempting to "solve a problem," managers may sometimes shoot themselves in the foot, as illustrated in the cases discussed below.

Shooting Oneself in the Foot: Two Case Examples

Unfortunately there are far too many situations in which managers can be seen to create bigger problems in the process of seeking to solve smaller problems. For convenience and specificity, I will consider two illustrative "classic" cases that many of us are familiar with: "Mr. Yarkoni's Worries" and "The Road to Hell." One or both are printed in various case collections, such as Glover, Hower, and Tagiuri (1973, pp. 429–432, and 365–370), and Hodgetts and Luthans (2003); and various authors have written commentaries on them (e.g., Bartolome, 1986). I have attempted to provide sufficient original information about the cases, within the space constraints of this paper, for the reader to learn the full flavour of each situation and make their own judgment. As is common in management cases, the names and situations are somewhat disguised by their original authors.

CASE 1: MR. YARKONI'S WORRIES The case begins with the following two paragraphs:

> Mr. David Yarkoni, a veteran industrialist in Israel and the owner of a number of factories, had been worried of late by unexpected organizational and other problems which followed his decision to introduce an improved system of cost accounting in one of his plants.
>
> In July—Mr. Yarkoni engaged the services of a consulting firm with country-wide reputation to devise a plan for improving the cost accounting system at Yarkon Metal Works. Mr. Yarkoni believed that the cost accounting system at Yarkon urgently needed revising in order to gain a better knowledge of production costs for the local management and to give guidance in setting the price policy for the market. He also wanted to facilitate his own control over the activities in the works since he is a busy man who cannot visit the factory regularly.

The consultant studied the factory operations and then made several technical recommendations, including clearer job descriptions for various managers and a different method for the allocation of overhead costs. The consultant also reported that the two senior managers, Mr. Jaffet and Mr. Simon (Mr. Yarkoni's brother-in-law) were resisting his recommendations.

The consultant concluded with this final recommendation: "It is our suggestion that Mr. Jaffet and Mr. Simon be forced to agree through suitable action on your part." The title of the case, "Mr. Yarkoni's Worries," implies that Mr. Yarkoni is worrying about how to implement the consultant's recommendations.

As is common with case discussion pedagogy, class discussion usually starts with the question "What is the problem in this case?" Students almost never ask: "What do you mean by a 'problem'?" or "Whose problem are we talking about?" Instead they assume that they know what the word "problem" means, and that "the" problem exists. They then proceed invariably to take what I have called the objective perspective to defining the problem. They are inclined to believe in the consultant's expertise, and are impressed that most of the suggestions seem to use technical terms from cost accounting. So they assume that his diagnosis of the problem must be correct: that the problem lies with the senior managers—and their behaviour must be changed through better motivation, training, or some other means.

What would be an introspective approach to this case situation? This perspective does not assume that there is a problem. Instead it asks: How can someone like Mr. Yarkoni establish that there is indeed a problem? What is his desired state (DS), and why? What does he see as the current state (CS) and what evidence does he have that he perceives the CS accurately?

As for the first (DS) question, there is no indication in the case as to why Mr. Yarkoni had wanted to change the cost accounting system. It simply mentions his "decision to introduce an improved system of cost accounting" since he "believed that the cost accounting system . . . urgently needed revising." The case adds that he wanted to "facilitate his own control" over the activities. The introspective perspective would, therefore, suggest that Mr. Yarkoni should start by carefully questioning his "desired state." At least on the surface it seems strange that Mr. Yarkoni, in spite of his being a "busy man," wants to "facilitate his own control over the activities" in the factory. Is it the right thing for him to want to "facilitate his own control"? Are there better ways available to achieve his desired state than by revising the cost accounting system? Might he, a busy man, be better off delegating the control to his top managers instead, and requiring them to produce the results he wants?

The second question is about the "current state" (CS) of his business that he wants to change. Does he have an adequate basis on which to evaluate the current state of his business? For example, does he have any measurable indicators regarding his business? Are his sales or profits decreasing? Are customers complaining about quality? Are employees threatening a strike? If he could identify some measurable indicators of the current state such as these, then a solution to change that state could be considered. It may or may not involve changing the cost accounting system. All in all, one wonders whether Mr. Yarkoni has brought his worries on himself because he has not evaluated what he wants (DS), and why; whether the current state (CS) is indeed poor as he seems to believe; and whether changing the cost accounting system would really deliver the DS he seems to want.

Many students find these questions rather surprising. They comment, rightly, that the case does not give any "data" to analyze or answer such questions. But we note that students are often encouraged to play the role of the manager in the case since the purpose of case analysis is to learn how to become an effective manager. So if they were to assume the role of Mr. Yarkoni, would they as Mr. Yarkoni have the necessary data? They presumably would. Should they not ask themselves these questions before taking any action about the consultant's recommendations?

Students respond by asserting that Mr. Yarkoni must have had good reason to hire the consultant and the consultant appears to be knowledgeable. But we note that the case begins with Mr. Yarkoni being worried "of late by unexpected . . . problems which followed his decision." Why unexpected? Does it not suggest that perhaps Mr. Yarkoni had not paid enough attention to the introspective aspect of the problem, if any?

And what options does he have now anyway? What might be the consequences for the factory if he forces his senior managers to agree to the consultant's recommendations? (Not to mention consequences to Mr. Yarkoni's family harmony, given that one manager is his brother-in-law!) And leaving aside consequences on the human side, is there any evidence that the consultant's recommendations have merit, and would produce any improvements?

The introspective perspective on Mr. Yarkoni's "problem" thus suggests some new approaches and questions. It is possible that taking such a perspective would have kept Mr. Yarkoni from taking the actions that are now causing him to worry.

(One could make a related comment here about the role of consultants. It is common for managers, such as Mr. Yarkoni, to hire consultants when faced with a problem, but it is ultimately the manager's responsibility to decide whether or not to implement the consultant's recommendations. So students, as managers-in-training, need to develop skills in assessing the merits of a consultant's suggestions. In the Yarkoni case it is difficult to judge the technical merits of the consultant's recommendations about cost accounting without firsthand data. But one can certainly question the consultant's ability to understand people and thus to influence their behaviour. After all, his proposal for implementing the change is that the two senior managers should be forced to follow his recommendations, a potentially unwise approach to achieving results.)

CASE 2: THE ROAD TO HELL The second illustrative case, "The Road to Hell," was written by Gareth Evans for Shell-BP Petroleum Development Company of

Nigeria. (A very insightful analysis of this case is presented in Bartolome, 1986, in which he discusses the difficulties inherent in giving negative feedback.)

The case describes a meeting between John Baker, an expatriate Englishman who is the chief engineer of Caribbean Bauxite Company, and Matthew Rennalls, his subordinate, who is a native "Barracanian."

It is John's last afternoon on the job before he leaves for his transfer to a Canadian posting. Matthew is to take over John's position the next day. It has been John's responsibility to groom Matthew to take over as the chief engineer. John is pleased with Matthew's technical competence on the job, but is uneasy that Matthew has had trouble getting along with various expatriates. "It was, Baker knew, Rennalls's well-repressed sense of race consciousness" which had caused the trouble. John had tried to talk to Matthew about this in his performance appraisal interview a year earlier, but without much effect. John reflects to himself that the problem seemed to be ongoing. "Jackson, the senior draughtsman, had complained only yesterday about the rudeness of Rennalls."

I give students this first part of the case, up to the point where Matthew is about to come in for his interview with John, and ask: "What should John say to Matthew in this last meeting before he departs for Canada?" The students almost invariably say that John ought to advise Matthew that he must change his racial attitude and make a better attempt at getting along with the expatriates. They feel strongly that it is John's duty as the superior officer to talk to Matthew along these lines, both in the company's interest as well as in Matthew's own interest (Bartolome, 1986). Again, their answers reflect an objective perspective in assuming that a problem exists. They believe that John must do something—the only analysis required is in deciding what that should be.

The introspective perspective again asks: "What is the basis on which we can come to the conclusion that a problem exists"? Regarding the current state (CS), the case states that John "knew" that Matthew had a "well-repressed sense of race consciousness." How does he know this? The only direct evidence cited in the case is that Jackson has only yesterday complained about Matthew's behaviour. Is there some other evidence? Has John asked Matthew about how he feels about expatriates in general and Jackson in particular? Might Jackson have given some cause for Matthew's alleged rudeness?

Again, students find these questions surprising and unsettling. They consider it an obvious fact that Matthew had difficulty dealing with expatriates, and that John must try to change Matthew's attitude before he leaves. This is what John seems to believe, and so it must be true. They complain, again correctly, that there are no data in the case from which to answer the questions above. But would John have those data? Should he be asking these questions of himself before he acts? The introspective perspective says that he should. According to this perspective, John should ask himself what it is that he considers his "desired state" (and why), and what evidence he has to establish that the current state is as he perceives it.

Unlike in the Yarkoni case, we know what happens next in this case. The case goes on to tell us what John actually said to Matthew in their final interview, and what the consequences were. The name of the case, "The Road to Hell," hints at the consequences. As with the students, John too takes the objective view of the problem and tries to get Matthew to change his behaviour, presumably with "good intentions." The conversation goes horribly wrong, however. Matthew resigns since he believes that John has insulted him and informs the top management of the company of his reasons.

So just as John is about to leave for his new post, the person he was supposed to have trained as his successor has suddenly resigned, leaving behind a much bigger problem than the one that John was trying to solve. Perhaps an introspective view might have prevented John from going down the road he has paved and from reaching the "hot" destination.

Reflecting Before Acting

The introspective component of problem solving thus suggests the following kind of reflection on a problem before acting. First, one asks "How do I know that my perception of the current state, CS, is accurate, and not just an untested assumption on my part?" This requires that one do some data gathering regarding one's perception before concluding that it is indeed reality. The classical story of *Don Quixote*, who was inclined to see enemies where others saw only windmills, serves as a good illustration and caution.

Second, this approach suggests that one should question one's own "desired" state, DS. "Do I really know what my goals or motives are in this situation?" And also: "Does it make sense for me to have this goal or desired state?" It is not unknown for a person to have only a very fuzzy conception of their goal, or to have one motive on the conscious level and another at the subconscious level. The example of King Midas, who wanted everything he touched to turn into gold, illustrates how a desire based on ignorance rather than wisdom can cause us distress on achieving it. As a famous proverb warns, one should be careful what one asks for—one may get it and live to regret it.

SOME PEDAGOGICAL IMPLICATIONS

While I have discussed only two illustrative cases, there are a number of other cases that could be reviewed from the perspectives given above. Student responses in all cases typically follow the same general pattern. Students generally start with the assumption that there is a problem, which needs some action to resolve. Why should this be so? I can think of two main issues involved here.

First, as mentioned earlier, the students' responses are in part an artifact of our pedagogy. We often start the case discussion with a question in the form of: "What is the problem in this case?" This question presumes that there is a certain problem to be identified. If we asked: "Who in this case seems to be experiencing a problem, and what causes him or her to see that as a problem?" the students may well see the problem from an introspective point of view.

This leads to the second issue. It is not easy for us to ask this kind of question because cases are generally written to emphasize the "objective" or factual aspects of a situation, and students are expected to evaluate the behaviour of one or more persons in the case. The classroom norms often value the student's willingness to evaluate and act, rather than to understand and reflect. ("Don't just stand there, do something.") This context of case discussion discourages them (and us) from asking questions regarding matters that involve introspective experiences of characters in a case. (See a similar conclusion by Pfeffer and Veiga, 1999, p. 9, on the tendency of managers to value explicit analysis over tacit understanding based on years of experience.)

I have found that one way to deal with these two issues is to have students write at least one case from their own experience. When they then analyze this case using both the introspective and objective perspectives, they are in a better position to begin to understand the conditions under which they, as an individual, are likely to experience a situation introspectively as a "problem." This self-understanding in turn may prevent them from acting in an ill-considered way, as Yarkoni and Baker seem to have done.

Asking students to write their own case has another perhaps more important advantage. Writing their own case puts the students into a decision-making and managerial role much more realistically than having them analyze a case based on someone else's situation. Any lessons they learn from their own case are likely to have a real impact on their future behaviour both on and off the job. This is because the habit of looking at problems both introspectively and objectively is something that is useful not just as a teaching device but also for "managing" real-life issues.

IMPLICATIONS FOR MANAGERIAL ACTION

The import of this discussion about a problem being seen from the two perspectives goes beyond the classroom. Cases such as "Mr. Yarkoni's Worries" and "The Road to Hell" illustrate that managers sometimes take actions that are detrimental because they do not pay sufficient attention to their own role in perceiving a problem. These managers tend to operate from the objective perspective, or what Roethlisberger (1977) has called "The rational conception of organization." As Roethlisberger puts it, "The rational conception tends to see things from an external frame of reference. It puts the manager outside the system he is administering" (p. 184).

The introspective perspective encourages what Roethlisberger (1977, p. 186) calls "The social system conception of organization." As he remarks: "In the social system conception, the administrator is an involved member of the system he is administering. He is both affecting and being affected by it; he cannot escape from it." Thus to understand the "problem" one must look both outward and inward, both at the situation "out there," and at oneself as the person who is experiencing and labelling the situation "in here."

Mr. Yarkoni wants to "facilitate his own control," and John Baker wants to change Matthew's behaviour. Why? Reading the cases with this question in mind leads to some new "in-sights." It seems, for example, that what Baker desires is not so much to help Matthew (which is his surface or conscious motivation) but to prove to himself that he has a real "innate knack... of knowing just how to get on with regional staff" in third world countries. Rennalls's resistance to be influenced by Baker, even in this last meeting, appears to Baker as something of a challenge to his self-image as a person with an innate knack. So Baker feels "disappointed once again at not being able to 'break through' to Rennalls" (Bartolome, 1986). This disappointment in turn causes him to say some things to Rennalls that Rennalls considers insulting and so Rennalls decides to resign instead. "The road to hell" is paved not just with good intentions, but also with a lack of self-understanding.

BALANCING THE TWO PERSPECTIVES

While I have discussed primarily the introspective approach in this paper, it is not my intention to suggest that the objective approach does not have its uses. The objective and introspective perspectives are both useful in problem solving. The objective perspective may be usually appropriate and sufficient when dealing with cases in subjects such as finance (e.g., when a company is in trouble because it is using a high debt/equity ratio and the interest rates have gone up sharply), or in marketing (e.g., where a company is experiencing rapidly falling sales). In such situations the nature of the problem is (fairly) clear. The dominant focus of analysis can then turn to determining the best action to solve the problem.

But in situations that deal primarily with behaviour between two or more people, the problem is usually more obscure, and here it may be best to start with an introspective approach when attempting to solve it. This might lead to the conclusion that one does have the right information about the actual situation, and that one's desired goals are indeed clear and appropriate. If this is the conclusion after an introspective analysis, then at this point the objective perspective will come into its own. Here is also where the "rational decision making model" mentioned earlier can come in to play an important role (McShane, 2004, p. 278). How to search for the best solution to narrow the gap between the (previously tested and confirmed) desired and actual states is the domain of the rational decision making model, and appropriately so. Since the use of the rational decision making model is extensively discussed in the literature, however, I have not expanded on it here. I have chosen, instead, to discuss in detail the introspective perspective because it has received relatively less attention.

Thus in behavioural situations the two perspectives are needed to balance each other. This need for balancing both approaches is also underlined in many important works of literature, such as *Oedipus Rex* and two of Shakespeare's greatest tragedies—*Hamlet* and *Othello.* Hamlet illustrates an extreme example of the use of the introspective approach alone, and how it leads to paralysis of action. Hamlet spends a great deal of effort trying to learn the truth behind his father's murder, and ponders what he should do about it. He hesitates to take any action and acts only when it is clear that he is about to die.

Othello shows the other extreme, where he uses the objective approach without the benefit of introspection. Othello is an action-oriented general, rather like the managers in the cases discussed earlier. He kills his wife, Desdemona, in an attempt to solve a perceived problem: in reality a problem that did not exist.

The two perspectives in balance with each other, on the other hand, lead to wisdom. A combination of the qualities of Hamlet and Othello, the thinker and actor in one, will enable wise action rather than the tragedies resulting from either no action at all or a hasty and ill-considered action.

Unfortunately, knowing about the two perspectives is not, by itself, sufficient to ensure that one always looks introspectively as well as externally when determining the nature of a problem. One also needs ongoing awareness and patience. For example, a while ago I was undergoing a short course of medication for an eye condition. Soon after leaving the doctor's office I stopped at a restaurant and ordered my favourite cola drink. It was served from a fountain and tasted odd. I complained to the server and was given another glass, which also tasted odd.

Based on the objective perspective of the problem as being "out there," I concluded that the fountain mechanism must be defective. So I purchased a *can* of the drink next time. Much to my surprise, it too had the odd taste. When I mentioned my experience to the eye specialist, he laughed and apologized for not telling me that the medication would have an effect on my taste perception. Reflecting now, it seems ironic that it took an ophthalmologist to help me "see" the tunnel vision involved in the objective orientation. As in the case of the children in the story at the beginning of this paper, I had forgotten to include myself when accounting for the problem.

EPILOGUE

Near the end of his life, Fritz Roethlisberger looked back on his forty years' experience in researching and teaching about organizations and managers. In his younger years he had played a major role in the classic Hawthorne studies leading to the awareness in management about the "Hawthorne Effect"—about how perception can affect behaviour. In his posthumously published wonderful autobiography *The Elusive Phenomena,* he reflects on the relationship between understanding and action in problem solving:

> At this time... taking action was an important ingredient of the case method of teaching at the Harvard Business School. After the analysis or diagnosis of a case was made, the students, as budding executives, were supposed to take action....
>
> At one level of abstraction I agreed with [this]. We could not have students training to be executives just trying to understand problems without doing anything about them, could we now? Yet I thought that for practitioners, understanding preceded action.... Moreover, wasn't trying to understand something taking a certain kind of action?... In the process, for example, a problem sometimes changed its character, although it did not usually disappear. It was not solved in a mathematical sense; it was resolved.... Understanding was just a first step along the way. (Roethlisberger, 1977, pp 171–172)

REFERENCES

Bartolome, Fernando. 1986. Teaching about Whether to Give Negative Feedback. *Journal of Management Education,* vol. 11, no 2.

Cravens, D., and Lamb, C. W. 1986. *Strategic Marketing: Cases and Applications,* 2nd ed. Homewood, IL: Irwin. (Later edition published as David W. Cravens, Charles W. Lamb, and Victoria Lynn Crittenden, 2001, *Strategic Marketing Management Cases,* New York: McGraw-Hill.)

Einstein, A. and Infeld, L. 1942. *The Evolution of Physics.* New York: Simon and Schuster.

Gause, D. C., and Weinberg, G. M. 1990. *Are Your Lights On? How to Figure Out What the Problem Really Is.* New York: Dorset.

Glover, J. D., Hower, R. M., and Tagiuri, R., eds. 1973. *The Administrator: Cases on Human Aspects of Management,* 5th ed. Homewood, IL: Irwin.

Greenberg, J., Baron, R. A., Sales, C., and Owen, F. 2000. *Behaviour in Organizations: Understanding and Managing the Human Side of Work,* 2nd Canadian ed. Toronto: Prentice-Hall Canada.

Hodgetts, Richard M., and Luthans, Fred. 2003. *International Management,* 5th ed. New York: McGraw-Hill.

Johns, Gary, and Sacks, Alan M. 2001. *Organizational Behaviour,* 5th ed. Toronto: Addison Wesley Longman.

McShane, S. L. 2004. *Canadian Organizational Behaviour,* 5th ed. Toronto: McGraw-Hill Ryerson.

McShane, S. L., and Von Glinow, M. A. 2000. *Organizational Behavior.* Boston: Irwin McGraw-Hill.

Pfeffer, J., and Veiga, J. F. 1999. Putting People First for Organizational Success. *The Academy of Management Executive,* vol. 13, no. 2.

Robbins, S. P., and Langton, N. 2001. *Organizational Behaviour: Concepts, Controversies, and Applications,* 2nd Canadian ed. Toronto: Prentice-Hall Canada.

Roethlisberger, F. J. 1977. *The Elusive Phenomena.* Boston: Harvard University Press.

Zikmund, W. G. 1997. *Business Research Methods,* 5th ed. Fort Worth, TX: Dryden Press.

CASE 2

Groupe Noel

Hari Das

Jean Noel is worried—and with good reason. His accomplishments of the past four decades could disappear if he makes a wrong decision now. What he does today could not only risk his entire organization but also the future of his children.

As chairman and CEO of Groupe Noel, his decision is still critical. In the last two years, he has delegated most important decisions to his two sons, and has also informally indicated that his eldest son, François, 40, who currently works as VP (Operations), will be his likely successor. However, everyone still looks to Jean to approve all important corporate decisions. To complicate matters, his second son, Michel, who is trained in law and currently works as VP (Marketing), has not agreed with some of François's decisions. This has meant that Jean has to make a final decision that is acceptable to everyone in his family, as well as to the management.

THE HISTORY OF GROUP NOEL

Jean Noel's father was a popular general practitioner in east-end Montreal. With his freshly inked pharmacist's degree in 1953, Jean became a salesman with Bennis Pharmaceuticals Ltd. and so greatly exceeded his first year sales quota that Bennis hiked it dramatically the next year. Seeing too much whip and too little carrot, Noel quit to become a partner in his older cousin's pharmacy, and by 1959 had gone solo with his own drugstore on the south side of rue Ste-Cathérine. Noel was soon running four drugstores in an industry that hadn't changed much since the 1920s and 1930s, with individual pharmacists still preparing their own cough mixtures, ointments and the like.

However, the scene changed dramatically in the 1960s and '70s. Over-the-counter drugs flourished and drugstores found themselves reduced to price competition. Alarmed, Noel teamed up with another pharmacist, André Cotré, in 1967 and opened a discount health-product store that they figured was the right type of operation for the new era. They were wrong. Without a regular, in-store pharmacist to handle prescriptions, customers simply were not interested in coming in for the more expensive (and profitable) medicines. Two years later, Noel and Cotré offered a mixture of the old and the new: a slightly larger store with a full-time pharmacist's counter. They also displayed a broad array of goods at discount prices, everything from chocolates to cod-liver oil.

Since they were still called a "pharmacy," they could remain open for extended hours and on the weekends when all other stores were closed. The duo named the store Pharmacie François. Jean Noel, who was a fan of the French film director François Truffaut, kept a large picture of the actor in his store and played theme music from his films. Some of the customers assumed a relationship between the pharmacist and the artist. "François visits us on Sunday afternoons," Noel would whisper when they asked. Little did the customers realize that he was talking about his own son.

FRANCHISING AND AFTER

In the mid-1970s, Jean Noel decided to franchise his store. By 1981, this had resulted in the establishment of 17 stores, and by 1989 the group had expanded into 31 stores, generating annual sales of approximately $70 million. The founders, however, were growing apart.

Cotré, a one-time provincial tennis champion, harboured business dreams beyond mere pharmacies, such as building "sportsplexes" and tennis clubs. Jean, on the other hand, wasn't keen on straying too far away from his main business. In 1989, Jean bought out the interests of André and renamed the chain "Groupe Noel." The change in ownership caused a precarious financial position for the firm, and the Noel family, that lasted until 1994.

At the same time, challenges emerged from other large chain drugstores such as Shoppers' Drug Mart and Pharmasave. The picture worsened when Wal-Mart Canada Inc. installed prescription counters in all 122 former Woolco outlets. Other chain stores (such as Big V pharmacies in Ontario and Groupe Coutu in Quebec) were also competing in the relatively stagnant market. "We've had some golden years in pharmacy," Jean Noel lamented, "but now they are bronze years." Some long-established Groupe Noel franchisees who were used to over $300 000 in annual profits now felt lucky to get $180 000. Traditionally, new franchisees didn't break even until at least their third year of operation; recently, most didn't come close to achieving this goal. Twenty of them fell so far behind in their payments that Groupe Noel had to assign $7 million for *the* contingency.

In this context, the opportunity to purchase the Sybil Group in the U.S. appeared very attractive. The Sybil chain of 13 drugstores in New England was up for sale because the owners were diversifying into an unrelated sector. True, the average sales of a Sybil store were only about 70 percent of those in a Noel store, but that was primarily due to the smaller sizes of the stores (which also generated operational economies in areas such as site lease cost). Extensive financial evaluation of the company showed that Sybil's purchase price was "very reasonable," if not profitable.

Even more attractive was the growth potential of Sybil. It was true that the top six chains in the U.S. controlled nearly 40 percent of the drug industry sales in the country. A mammoth consolidation had seen 14 chains with a total of 2500 outlets gobbled up in 1994 alone, widening the huge gulf that already separated big operators from small chains. Walgreen, for instance, posted nearly US$10 billion in annual sales in 1995 and was building nearly 200 new stores annually, hoping to reach 3000 by the millennium. The new "managed health care" systems meant that third parties who administer employee pharmaceutical benefit plans dispensed drugs through sanctioned drugstores and chains. Noel was hopeful of getting Sybil hooked up to a few major health-care providers. It also hoped to follow the lead of the biggest pharmacy chains and get into managed care itself in the long term. Prescriptions now accounted for a little over 40 percent of a U.S. store's sales.

In recent years operating a pharmacy in the U.S. has become more like a grocery-style business in which sheer volume makes up for narrow profit margins. Compared to Noel's net margin of 4 percent (or 52 cents on the average $13 purchase), the margin of the best operators in the U.S. was only 3 percent; but even a small store had a high volume of business. The U.S. pharmacies sell food, impulse and promotional merchandise, natural foods, homeopathic medicines, and even flowers. (One store in New England is reported to have sold $10 000 worth of flowers on Valentine's Day in 1994). Some of the larger chains have also begun to include electronic products, computer accessories, and photographic supplies (beyond the films and batteries that almost everyone carries).

Part of the reason for the high volume is the sheer size of the U.S. population in relation to that of Canada. Demographic changes in the U.S. have also helped the drugstores: Between 1990 and 1994, the U.S. population aged 65 or more grew by 2 million to 33 million people, 37 percent of whom visit a drugstore at least five times a month. So far, no single chain covers (let alone dominates) the entire U.S. The six New England states, with a combined population of 13.5 million, represent a manageably small market by U.S. standards.

The investment needed to buy the chain and operate it for the first few years (before reselling to franchisees) will amount to a considerable proportion of Groupe Noel's assets. A liberal estimate shows that it could be as high as 57 percent, but a more conservative estimate shows it in the 37–40 percent range. To complicate the decision, Jean Noel's sons François and Michel have differing views on the project. François, like his father, is a risk taker and supports the expansion; Michel, the more conservative brother, considers it a gamble. He believes that internal changes in Groupe Noel and a strategic reorientation should help the group recover its previous financial and market position. His three daughters, Louise, Anne, and Hélène, have so far not been actively involved in the family business (though they are on the board).

To Jean Noel, this decision also highlights the risk of a possible sibling war in the future when he is no longer in the CEO's chair:

> The last thing I want is a repetition of the Steinberg or McCain's fights in my family. But I realize that François and Michel are temperamentally different. And while I am healthy at the moment, I have to recognize the fact that I am 71. What will happen after I leave this world? I often wake up in the middle of the night with that question.

CASE 3

Norton's Department Stores

Hari Das

Mark Norton, chairman of the board of the 85-store Norton's chain of department stores, looked down at the dark streets through his office window. Thirty-five floors below, he could see a few shoppers braving the cold, mid-March winds of Toronto to walk toward Norton's. He noted that there were not too many of them. What a contrast to the past years when Norton's biggest sale event, "Maple Leaf Days," brought in thousands to Norton's.

The hands of the distant clock tower showed it was half past eight. "My God!" Norton whispered to himself. "Is it already 8:30? And I haven't had dinner!" For that matter, Norton had had no lunch either. It had been a very difficult week, and the next few weeks didn't look any easier.

Norton looked at the other person in the room. Poor John! He looked tired. Probably he had not been eating much either. He read the quotation on the wall behind John Craig's chair, attributed to John Norton, his grandfather: "Only those who risk going too far can possibly find out how far one can go." Next to it was his own favourite quotation: "All work is God's work. Honour your creator and fulfill yourself. Be the best you can be."

Well, Norton thought, pulling Norton's through the present crisis will challenge my best. "Don't lose hope, don't lose hope," he muttered to himself.

He sipped water from a handcrafted glass engraved in gold with the initials "M.N." Then he told John in a low tone: "The creditors and suppliers are getting impatient. I'm going to announce my decision tomorrow afternoon. I'll think over the options and talk to you tomorrow morning. 6:30 for breakfast?"

John Craig, the chief operating officer of the Norton's chain, nodded at his boss. His eyes showed understanding. Behind that, Mark could also see traces of tears.

THE HISTORY OF NORTON'S

In the early 1950s, the Norton's empire—12 main stores and mail order offices in more than 175 locations—accounted for over 50 percent of all department store sales in Canada. In the late 1940s, the main store in Toronto boasted the biggest telephone switchboard in the world, which gave prompt service to thousands of customers. There were Norton's factories in five locations, making everything from clothing to stoves. As a newspaper wrote about the Norton's in the 1940s, "You can have a meal or send a message to your mother by telegram; you can buy your shoes, pay for your stamps and get parts of a sewing machine. You can have your suit dry-cleaned and get materials for a dental clean-up. You can buy a cake, or get all the ingredients needed (including a stove) to make one, or ask Norton's to make a special one for your sister's wedding."

Founded by Thomas Norton in 1869, the firm had been expanded by four generations of the Norton family across the country and through mail order offices into every hamlet. They coined a sales pitch—"The customer is number one at Norton's"—that was copied by other Canadian merchandisers.

And, until 25 years ago, the family's department store chain ruled Canadian retailing. Norton's set Canadian retailing style; the family lived like kings, occupying private castles and even erecting their own church. Norton's was one of the largest employers in the country; the company's 60 stores moved goods worth over $25 million a week; Norton's catalogue adorned coffee tables in over 17 million residences and offices. Although the family idea of staging elaborate Easter parades in downtowns was copied by other retailers, the kids knew which rabbit to trust. "Norton's bunny was the real one," recalled a Newfoundlander who had once been among the thousands of children who lined the parade route. "You can't fool kids about something as important as that."

Everyone at Norton's remembers the company's humble beginnings and is guided by the dictum established by Thomas Norton 130 years ago: "Always do the right thing for the customer." From its unremarkable beginning on 19th-century Toronto's soot-stained and manure-dotted lower Yonge Street, Thomas Norton's dry goods store flourished with the country to become a dependable and customer-friendly merchandising empire. Thomas, who was born in Ireland to a family of nine children, began working at 13 as a low-paid assistant at a general store ten miles away from his home. Each day he walked to the store and—after working 14 hours—back home. After seven years, he had had enough. In 1850, he emigrated to Canada, then touted as the "faraway land of opportunity." Thomas, who settled in a suburb of Toronto, started a bakery two years later. However, it folded after a few months. Undaunted by the failure, Thomas simply rented another store and notified his customers that he was switching from bread to dry goods, boots, and patent medicines, which would be "sold cheap." He did little except work, not closing the store until late at night when the street was totally empty.

Eight years later, Thomas Norton moved his store, an expanded version of his earlier shop, to downtown Toronto. Despite the presence of six other dry goods shops on the street, Norton's store flourished. From the very beginning, its long hours, high quality, and friendly staff separated it from its rivals. And Thomas was quick to innovate. In 1884, he expanded operations in a big way by introducing the first mail order catalogue—30 pages of descriptions of goods that would be "sold at one price to rich and poor alike." The catalogue contained, among other things, lace curtains in 300 patterns, 51 types of women's gloves, and stout boots starting at 90 cents a pair. By 1899, gold-seekers heading for the Yukon could order a year's supply of food along with all the necessary camping and gold-panning equipment from the Norton stores. Thomas staged Grand Promenade Concerts to attract trade from far and wide. His store offered the novelty of electric lights and a sprinkler system, whose value was demonstrated when one of the major competing stores nearby burned to the ground.

SUCCESS AND GROWTH

Opening stores in other cities and towns was the logical extension of Norton's success in Toronto. Less than 15 years after it began, Norton's opened its five-storey store in Winnipeg. Stores in other centres such as Montreal and Quebec City soon followed. When Thomas Norton died in 1905, he left behind the blueprint for what was later to become the Norton empire. Norton's by now had a workforce of over 8000 employees and a presence in major cities across the country.

Jack Norton, who took over as the CEO of the group, was a different man from his father. While Thomas was austere, private, and religious, the 30-year-old Jack was an extroverted playboy who indulged himself in horseracing, fancy cars, and yachts. He spent huge sums of money on foreign trips and built a 60-room mansion for the family.

When one section of Norton's workforce went on strike, Jack first fired them and then simply offered to reinstate the workers—provided they apologized. The strike collapsed three months later. Jack also introduced changes that benefited his employees, although he took no credit for them ("I am just carrying out my father's wishes"). He introduced the five-and-a-half-day workweek at Norton's in 1919 and gave the 18 000 employees entire Saturdays off in July and August.

When he died at the age of 46, his widow, Margaret Norton, took over the leadership and continued until her son, Michael Norton, became president in 1942. Midway through the Second World War, Norton's prosperity reached an all-time high, and its workforce reached a whopping 30 000.

THE COMPETITION

In the 1960s, increasing competition from other department stores, including Sears and Simpsons, began to hurt the firm. Firms such as the Hudson's Bay Company were fast making inroads into Norton's traditional markets. Despite this, when Michael retired in 1969 due to poor health, the Norton empire was worth over $400 million. His son, Ken, who was named as the president of the firm, lasted only about five years, and when Ken left the country "in search of new pastures," his brother, Mark Norton, took over the presidency.

Norton's, under Mark's regime, faced perhaps the toughest competitive environment in the company's history. The rugged retail terrain of the 1990s offered few comforts to any retailer—big or small, established or novice in the market. A major share of the department store market, estimated to be worth approximately $14.4 billion, was shared by a few large firms such as Wal-Mart, Sears, and Hudson's Bay. Wal-Mart, a U.S. discount chain that had entered the Canadian market, acquired 24 percent of the market share in just a few years. In contrast, Norton's market share had shrunk to a mere 12 per cent by the same year. (Exhibit 1 shows the market shares held by the top four retailers in the country).

Norton's reputation for quality merchandise and customer satisfaction was simply not enough to compete in a turbulent market that yearned for value. The catalogue was discontinued in 1976, after 92 years, and the Easter parade was taken over by other sponsors in the 1980s. Several retailers, including such household names as Simpson's, Henry Birks & Sons, Peoples Jewellers, Woodward's, and Consumer's Distributing either disappeared or stumbled into insolvency or receivership. Bargain Harold's Discount Ltd., supposedly recession-proof because of its focus on everyday necessities and low-value items, declared bankruptcy. On the top of this, "category killers" such as Office Depot and Price Club posed a threat to specific departments within department store operations. At least five major Canadian retailers (including Woolco and K-Mart) were forced out of business or into the arms of larger chains in the years following 1992.

Canada's overcapacity problem is more acute than that of the U.S. and is often fatal for department stores. As one industry spokesperson noted, "It is a wickedly competitive market. Sellers are falling over themselves trying to get business." Newly arrived discounters like Wal-Mart "do such high volume that they suck business out of the entire retail channel." Wal-Mart has been a consistent beneficiary of the downfall of several of the chains.

To respond to the new retailing realities, stores such as the Bay and Sears had to significantly alter their strategies. For instance, from 1994, the Bay began to de-emphasize hardware and highlight clothing and fashion. The company also spent over $10 million to renovate the menswear and cosmetics sections in some of its stores, and spent heavily on promotion, hoping to get results by having more excitement, more discounts, and more sales events. Sears, in a similar vein, began pushing fashion goods, although the clothes it focused on were more casual and aimed at a slightly lower-income group than the Bay's clientele. To meet the competition from "category killers" like Leon's Furniture and the Brick, Sears moved some of its furniture departments into separate, freestanding stores. Both the Bay and Sears also introduced more high-margin private label products. The Bay aimed at becoming "Canada's Fashion Store" by devoting more space to high-profile labels such as Tommy Hilfiger, as well as its own brands. Departments such as carpets and hardware were dropped and others including furniture were reduced in size. The Bay also increased its advertising, using supermodels such as Claudia Schiffer, while Sears revved up an old standby—its catalogue—to gain an edge. The 1997 Sears Catalogue reached 4 million households, or almost 39 percent of Canadians, and resulted in over 3 million orders a year. Sears is aiming for even more catalogue sales of everything from sweaters to stoves, and it is targeting urban dwellers in particular. Sears also introduced a 24-hour toll-free order number to attract dual-career families who cannot shop during regular office hours. In the early months of the system, Sears' catalogue operation was receiving 5000 calls a day during the off-hours of 9 P.M. to 8 A.M.

Other retailers had faced the increasing competition by making it easy to shop—looking at everything from store layout to speed of service, as well as thinking about parking and convenience of location. "Not every one is looking for the cheapest price," says a marketing executive, "People don't mind spending $2 for a coffee at Starbucks if it helps them relax. The key is that they should believe they are receiving value."

While Norton's did not stand still in its marketing, it was somewhat slow to initiate similar changes. It lagged behind its competitors in store makeovers. Historically, Norton's had followed the classic department store strategy of "high-low pricing." (As an industry marketing expert explained, "You have high prices in the store, and every week you bang out flyers with stuff on special to bring the shoppers into the store"). Then came the era of "everyday low pricing," which was intended to

Exhibit 1

MARKET SHARES OF TOP RETAILERS

Department Store	Market Share (%)
Wal-Mart	24
Zellers	23
Sears Canada	18
Hudson's Bay	15

improve customers' sense of value, a strategy made famous by retailing powerhouse Wal-Mart and big-box stores such as Home Depot and Price Club. In the early 1990s, Norton's switched to everyday low pricing, permanently cutting prices on a number of fast-moving items to reduce advertising costs and bring back customers who had gone to the discount chains. "And then," continued the industry expert, "they slowly migrated back to high-low with some everyday low pricing. The result was confusion in the minds of the customers, who were not sure what additional value Norton's offered them." Often, it led to a perception of Norton stores as dowdy. Even when the company decided to resurrect its Canada-wide "Maple Leaf Sale Days," it did not have the intended impact. "Norton's was not perceived as being much better than its competitors," notes an ex-employee who left the firm to join a competing company. The company's idea of everyday low pricing was fine for socks or kitchenware, but not for the mainstay fashion apparel. The result was a continuous decline in profits. In just two years in the mid-1990s, Norton's lost 15 to 20 percent of its total sales revenue. More than 250 employees were purged from the Toronto area alone in a year. Some analysts note that Norton's annual sales are currently around the $ 1.5 billion mark (down from over $2 billion three years ago). Exhibit 2 shows the declining profitability of the chain (the loss of over $75 million is before taxes and real estate transactions).

Mark Norton and John Craig shared a belief in the crucial importance of technology in contemporary retailing. They attempted to modernize the company's logistics operation and to update the firm's antiquated computer system. But neither has ever been regarded as an inspirational manager or sold a pair of socks.

In 1994, the company also launched the Norton School of Retailing, which was intended "to raise the level of professionalism not only within the organization but within the entire retailing sector in Canada. The program was expected to impart "soft" skills such as leadership and communication as well as extensive training in retailing.

Norton's altered its relationship with suppliers, expecting them to comply with rules on packaging, labelling, and shipment accuracy, or face penalties. While some suppliers felt oppressed, others willingly complied. Norton's also reduced the number of suppliers: for specific items, the number of suppliers came down from as many as 21 to four. Norton's insisted that all its suppliers be able to communicate electronically, deal with just-in-time ordering, and meet the demands of its highly automated warehouse procedures. However, despite this, analysts believe that Norton's was well behind other Canadian and U.S. retailers on the technology curve, generally rating the firm's technology as "average" or only slightly above.

A market leader in urban mega-malls 25 years ago, Norton made decisions to expand in the late 1980s that proved "disastrous," says Kim Wipro, a Toronto market analyst. The firm bet heavily on small-market downtown locations just as many shoppers were moving to the suburbs. It invested in single-store anchored malls where Norton's name was expected to draw customers by itself.

Historically, Norton's had been less obsessed with profits and growth than a public company could afford to be. During the Depression, the family earned a reputation for keeping its employees while everyone else was laying off theirs. Michael Norton in the 1970s is said to have discouraged his executives from trying to make the firm *too* profitable. He considered a return of 3 percent on sales to be perfectly adequate, and saw no point in squeezing large margins out of the operation.

Indeed, many industry observers and strategists believe that department stores have become the dinosaurs of the industry. "Department stores are founded on the premise of serving a mass mar-

Exhibit 2

NORTON'S DECLINING PROFITABILITY (MILLIONS OF DOLLARS)

	This Year	Last Year	Two Years Ago	Three Years Ago
Total Revenues	1500	1600	1800	2000
Net income	-75.4	-19.5	-6.0	+5.2

ket," a marketing specialist commented, "but there is no longer a traditional mass market. For the price-conscious middle market, category killers and warehouse stores are offering a cheaper and more effective alternative."

THE MANAGEMENT

Norton, being a privately held organization, does not make any of its financial statements public. Consequently, very little information about its operations is currently available to the public. Privacy and control remain central to the family that denied entry to public shareholders and beat back all attempted incursions by organized labour. Not much is known about the extent of the family holdings and even many top company managers are not privy to the information.

Generations of corporate executives at Norton's have learned that their autonomy extends only so far. All major financial decisions are made by the family, aided by professional analysts whose power within the firm is only advisory. Mark Norton, 60, as chairman of Norton of Canada Ltd., the family holding company, is personally involved in making all major decisions affecting the group. The other family members are consulted in major decisions affecting the fortunes of the company. In the words of a senior manager who departed from Norton's a few years ago, "The big decisions are made by the brothers around a dinner table." Many managers cite the example of Karl Wanderson, who was the president and CEO of Norton's for two years in the past. Wanderson resisted the sort of interference that Norton family members have always regarded as one of the prerogatives of sole ownership. His show of independence earned him a one-way ticket out the front door. Under Wanderson, the company attracted a number of bright young men and women, but not many of them are still with the company. Worse, a number of them have joined Norton's competitors, often quickly rising to the top levels of management.

Norton's strengths and weaknesses both stem from family management. Norton's is now in its fourth generation of family ownership, and some of the fifth generation members are already active in the company (see Exhibit 3). John Norton, Mark's eldest son, is the company spokesperson for retail operations. It is expected that Aaron Norton, Ken's son, will also be more active in the management of the business in the future.

Everyone who knows Mark Norton testifies to his hands-on management style' He is usually at his desk by 7 A.M. and seldom leaves the office before 8 P.M. He is known to be a careful and patient listener and a glutton for information. "He came in knowing nothing about retail business," said a former colleague, "but the guy is really quite a sponge. He soaks up a lot of information very rapidly." Mark is also well known for his obstinacy, never changing his view once it is formed. He has been known to wander into the advertising department and casually mention that he doesn't like a slogan that is the centrepiece of a marketing campaign.

Ken Norton, during his brief reign as president, was known as a "coach." "He was motivational in his approach and had a style about him that was inspirational," one former employee commented, "but Mark is more like a cop." Mark is also very keen on translating the latest management jargon and practices into corporate reality. Total quality management, total customer service, focused marketing, employee empowerment are all used.

Exhibit 3

WHO THE NORTONS ARE

Mark Norton, 60: Chairman of Norton's of Canada Limited, the family holding company.

Ken Norton, 59: Brother of Mark; former president of T. Norton Co., left Canada to become a senior member of the country's permanent trade missions in the Americas and Europe. Now Chairman of Norton's of Canada Executive Committee.

Rick Norton, 54: Brother of Mark; concentrates on his own investments including breeding and racing horses.

Andrew Norton, 51: Brother of Mark; stepped in for a very short period as president of T. Norton Co. when Ken left the country and before Mark took over the position. Interested in racecar driving.

Aaron Norton, 31: Son of Ken; moving through the ranks in retail operations.

John Norton, 35: Mark's eldest son; company spokesperson for retail operations.

Once, after generations of having shunned outside advice, the company finally hired an outside consultant to design the marketing strategy. However, the consultant did not last two years. "He came in and got everyone upset except Mark," one manager recalled. "He was so controlling. He tried to get the merchants to pay minute attention to what they sold. He thought they should be selecting buttons for the shirts." Worse, at a time when many retailers recognize that people skills are the key ingredient of retail management, Norton's still pays its executives by about 20 percent below the industry norms and subjects its senior people to the whims and caprices of family-type management.

John Craig was brought in to the top management with the mandate to do whatever was necessary to return the chain to profitability. Craig, who worked his way up from the store's credit department in Vancouver, was perceived as a man who could make necessary but unpopular decisions. "John's reputation is that he can make the tougher calls on cost cutting—calls that someone else will not make," said a senior manager. Another manager commented, "Craig is there because he is a numbers guy. The bankers wanted it, in view of the company's losses, but I think that's the biggest mistake they could have made. What we need now is a visionary."

Mark and John worked well as a smooth team. Both had limited formal education. Both were also feisty and aggressive in their style. "John manages the team by threat," one manager whispered as if the walls could hear his comment. "At his first meeting after he became the Chief Operating Officer, he told his executive committee, 'For now, your titles all stay the same. In six months, I'll let you know whether I still want you around.'" Although he had never personally sold so much as a pair of socks, Craig was considered an innovative manager who understood the crucial role of technology in running a department store. Some managers also ascribed the success of the Norton Credit Card to his visionary leadership when he managing the operations in Vancouver.

One of the main constraints on the firm's growth, according to some ex-employees who now work for competitors, is not financial, but personal. Mark and John, for all their considerable skills, are not regarded by some pessimistic analysts as being particularly proficient at employee relations. And while Norton's main opportunities lie in skillful merchandising and strengthening customer relations, such strategies require the enthusiastic backing of thousands of employees. Optimists, on the other hand, believe that Norton's is already doing exactly the right things: strengthening its position as the everything-for-everybody store—something not practised by any major retailer.

Tradition weighs heavily on the Nortons. While they seek new opportunities, they have stated their commitment to slog it out in the department store wars their family once dominated. To do this, Norton's updated its technology and rejuvenated its outmoded logistics. It also invested $300 million in a facelift of its stores. It embarked on the ambitious effort to embody the trendiest of the decade's buzzwords—a learning organization. In one of its newly renovated stores, customers can wander through a designer's paradise of tiled walkways between carpeted boutique areas filled with stylish wooden display cases and friendly salespersons. However, just a few kilometres away, another—unrenovated—Norton's store still remains as a symbol of retailing in all its prehistoric ugliness. Deserted sales desks punctuate a messy disorganized store where remnants of food eaten by the employees and customers litter the in-store deli.

In many locations, understaffing is common because of pressing financial concerns. As sales slipped, Norton's had to lay off staff. In many cases, experienced managers were replaced by younger staff brought in from other retailers. "They have energy and they're cheaper than the people they replace," noted an ex-Norton employee. "But they don't have any experience in merchandising on the scale that Norton's needs." Also, the staff who remain are under pressure. "The workload is unbelievable," says an ex-Nortonian. "Managers are putting in incredible, unreasonable hours. It is not a fun place to work anymore."

In recent years, Canadian customers have been increasingly focused on getting value for their money. The new brand of customer is tight-fisted and does not like to shop. Further, they will buy only what they really want. In general, Norton's competitors like the Bay and Sears have positioned themselves below Norton's in pricing, which appeals to value-conscious customers. Further, many shoppers today consider shopping for day-to-day items such as clothing and food very frustrating and time consuming. Consequently, home shopping has been increasing dramatically. It is estimated that over $2 billion worth of goods and services are purchased each year through TV and the Internet, and the industry is growing at about 20 percent each year. As cable systems upgrade to offer hundreds of channels, and eventually digital, interactive and other technologies, home shopping promises to proliferate in ever more elaborate forms. The ultimate scenario is a sort of video mall, where shoppers will browse through channels as through individual stores, ask for information and advice, order and pay—all without leaving the comfort of home.

A strategy adopted by Norton's to meet the turbulent times was to diversify its interests. Many of the family's diverse business investments are woven through its holding company, Norton's of Canada Limited. This firm is owned equally by the four brothers, Mark, Ken, Rick, and Andrew. While the family's main holding is the 85 Norton's department stores, its retail operations also include ten related businesses ranging from real estate management to a delivery service, a travel agency, and a drug company. The family began Norton Financial Services in 1970 to sell products in Norton's stores, and the company grew to hold assets of over $1 billion by the mid-1980s. It was sold to the Maxim Group for $101 million in 1986. Norton's holds a 10 percent share in the Maxim Group, which, besides Norton Financial Services, now also owns a large number of other ventures including a bank.

Broadcasting is another long-time family interest. The Nortons control Carton Communication Inc. of Toronto, which has controlling interests in a few national and regional broadcasters. Norton's helped the Cartino family to buy a major newspaper group and later on purchased a 42 percent share of the new Carton Communication Group, which now owns newspapers and broadcasting stations. In fact, the name Carton is a combination of the names Cartinto and Norton. An approximate chart of Norton corporate empire is shown in Exhibit 4.

THE DECISION

It was 10:45 A.M. on a grey morning, reflecting the sombre mood of the senior managers gathered in Mark's office. For over 30 minutes, Mark Norton had gone through the key financial and operating figures of the department store chain. Much of

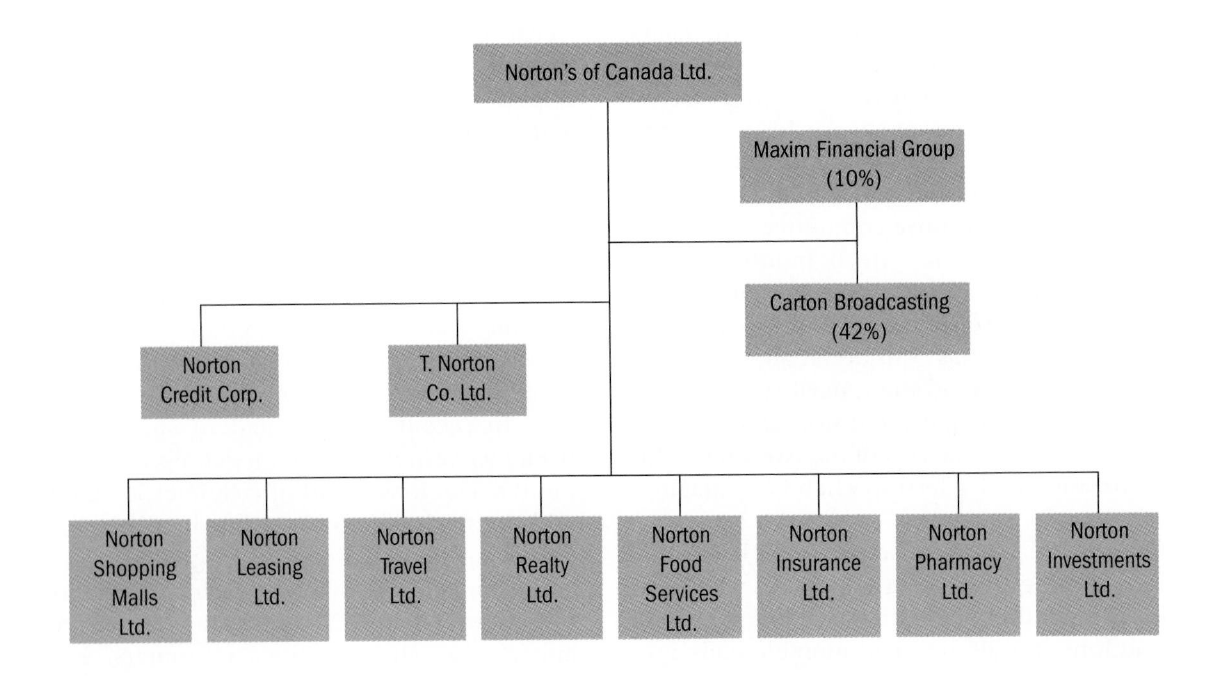

EXHIBIT 4
The Norton Corporate Empire

what he said was a repetition of the conclusion that he and John Craig had formed earlier that day at the breakfast meeting.

In a slightly trembling voice, Mark continued, "We obviously thought that retail was in much better shape than it was." Saving the company now, he pointed out, would require sacrifices by employees, suppliers, landlords, and banks. The financial problems were compounded, he added, by the fact that the two major lending banks were reluctant to continue with operating lines of credit. The banks had previously extended a $200 million operating facility with no security, but the facility had now matured and was payable on demand. Norton's also owed another $150 million to suppliers.

"Given the grim financial picture, we have no alternative but to file for bankruptcy protection under the Companies' Creditors Arrangement Act," Mark continued. "This will give the firm some breathing space in which to restructure its operations, if it can, without having to worry about our creditors. It will also mean that we have the next 60 days to come up with a restructuring plan. None of our accumulated debts will be paid until the rescue plan is finalized and voted on by creditors. The other options available to our firm at this time are even less attractive....

"I am pleased to tell you that we have already begun work on the restructure of Norton's. We have identified two dozen or so Norton stores with sagging sales which will be the first candidates for review and appropriate action. We may have to close or sell off stores, lay off employees, or terminate leases to help us move forward.

"About 1800 employees currently work in these stores targeted for closure, downsizing and/or restructuring. We would like to give the employees affected by the closings such options as termination benefits, continuation of various benefits, and help in finding new jobs. Nonetheless, there is no alternative but to reduce the size of our workforce right now.

"Painful as these steps are. I am optimistic that at the end we will emerge stronger and more viable in today's competitive environment."

REFERENCES

1. "Wal-Mart's Golden Opportunity," *Globe and Mail*, 28 November 1996, p. B15.
2. *Globe and Mail*, 27 March 1991, p. B14.

CASE 4

Southam Newspaper Group: Equalizing Employment Equity

Alexander Mikalachki, Dorothy R. Mikalachki, and Ronald J. Burke

Russ Mills, president of Southam Newspaper Group (SNG), had a difficult problem to deal with: How could he persuade the 17 publishers at SNG to commit themselves and their managers to the ten recommendations of the task force on Women's Opportunities? At least two of the publishers had already indicated their disagreement with one of the key recommendations.

His problem was exacerbated by the fact that SNG functions from its divisions upwards, and the publishers have a great deal of autonomy. Normally, directives from

headquarters to the publishing units are sent out as suggestions to be adapted by the different publishers depending on how the strategy fits into their own environments. While they cannot ignore the directives completely, the publishers exercise a great deal of discretion in deciding how and when to implement them. The publishers report to Mills and meet as a group quarterly. They work to a series of objectives which they work out with Mills, and he adjusts their remuneration according to the achievement of these objectives.

SOUTHAM NEWS GROUP

SNG is one of four subsidiaries of Southam Inc. The other three are Graphics, Book Retailing, and Business Information and Communications. John Fisher is president and CEO of Southam Inc. Russ Mills reports to him. (See Appendix 1 for a partial organization chart.) SNG produces half of the parent company's revenue and more than half of its profits. Of SNG's 7300 employees, approximately 25 work at headquarters in Toronto. The rest are scattered from Montreal to Vancouver, working in the different newspaper publishing units. SNG is Canada's largest daily newspaper group in terms of circulation, with an average daily circulation of 1 573 000. Examples of newspapers it owns are *The Montreal Gazette, The Hamilton Spectator, The Edmonton Journal,* and *The Vancouver Sun.*

TASK FORCE ON WOMEN'S OPPORTUNITIES

In 1988, when Paddy Sherman was president of SNG, he became concerned with the lack of women at the senior management level. (In 1989, Sherman returned to the west coast to become chairman of Pacific Press, publisher of *The Vancouver Sun* and *The Province.*) This absence of women was brought to his attention by the women themselves, who were troubled by their lack of progress. Sherman was also concerned with the succession from senior manager to publisher. With no women at the senior management level, he was aware of the one-sided, and therefore smaller, pool of talent from which to draw new publishers.

At Sherman's initiative, a Task Force on Women's Opportunities was formed which eventually consisted of 18 members. They represented every unit in the organization. The majority of task force members were women, including the co-chairs. The original mandate of the group was to identify the barriers to the advancement of women within SNG, particularly senior women. However, as the work progressed, the mandate broadened. As the authors of the task force report stated, "Practically speaking, to integrate women into the senior levels of the company, it makes sense that SNG recruit, hire, develop, promote, and retain women at all levels."

The task force held six meetings over one-and-one-half years. Meetings were difficult to arrange because of the geographical problems and the financial cost. However, between meetings, members were busy gathering research to help them with their mandate. The information they compiled was collected in the following ways:

- Gathering company-wide data at SNG relating to the numbers and ranks of women.
- Using inside and outside consultants to examine systemic bias and the corporate culture at SNG.
- Consulting with other organizations with experience in employment equity.
- Using attitudinal surveys within various divisions, in the form of either written surveys or informal discussion groups.

RESEARCH RESULTS

1. As of October 1, 1989, SNG had 126 senior managers. (Senior managers are publishers, those reporting to publishers, and senior staff at SNG headquarters.) Of these, 120, or 95 percent were male.
2. In 1989 there were 33 appointments to senior management positions. All those appointed were male. Eight were appointed to publisher and above. Twenty-nine were promoted from within SNG.
3. Women represent approximately 36 percent of SNG's employees. (There are 2636 females and 4711 males.) They are found most widely in the clerical departments. Their numbers indicate that more of them are in these pink ghetto jobs than in the workplace at large.
4. Women are underrepresented at SNG in the following job categories: sales, supervisors, professional/semi-professional, senior or middle management, general managers/executives. (See Appendix 2 for figures.)
5. In 1989 in the seven divisions polled, women represented 53 percent of new hires. However, in the

same year, the proportion of women hired in all of the above-mentioned categories, except sales, was lower than the status quo. In these categories, things got worse, not better.

6. Forty-five percent of those receiving promotion in 1989 were women. The majority came from the clerical group, and 19 percent of them were promoted to supervisory positions. In the same year, two men were promoted to executive and 17 to senior manager. No women were promoted to these positions.
7. The attitudinal surveys indicated that women believe SNG is a good company; however, they believe, as the report stated, that "... the deck is strongly stacked against them in terms of advancement and of juggling home and career."

TASK FORCE RECOMMENDATIONS

In April of 1990, two years after its formation, the Task Force on Women's Opportunities issued its report to Russ Mills. No quotas were mentioned, as the task force members did not think they would be accepted, and in any event, would probably cause a backlash from the men. The following is a summary of the ten recommendations with some additional explanations.

1. The president of SNG should circulate to all divisions a policy statement indicating that SNG is committed to full equity for women, including the recruitment and promotion of women to redress a serious imbalance within the organization and at its divisions.

   The report indicated that employers cannot rely on able-bodied white males to fill key positions in the future, since this group represents a shrinking component of the workforce. It emphasized that an employment equity program, like other important company initiatives, should be supported from the top of the organization if it were to succeed.
2. The annual performance assessments and compensation of all publishers and senior managers should be influenced by the degree to which they have recruited, developed, and promoted women.

   The goal for all divisions should be to achieve an equitable representation of women in all key occupations, including senior management and feeder positions for these jobs, and in other non-traditional jobs. Each division and each manager should establish his or her own objectives in the light of their own circumstances. Head office could act in an advisory capacity by providing overall SNG objectives and acting as a resource for the divisions without eroding the autonomy of individual divisions. All divisions should report progress on an annual basis.
3. Each short list for promotion or recruitment to a senior position should include the name of at least one women. If necessary, managers should search for potential women candidates outside the division or outside SNG. SNG generally promotes from within, which can perpetuate existing patterns. Thus, all divisions should adopt a formal, proactive recruitment and hiring policy aimed at women. The report emphasized that equal employment opportunity is a business issue, which ensures that employers have access to the larger talent pool, which includes women: "Companies with effective programs will enjoy a competitive advantage. It is as simple as that."
4. Publishers should encourage their senior managers to be open to the concept of part-time work flextime, four-day weeks, and job sharing. All requests for such alternative working arrangements should be reported to the publisher. The report underlined the importance of flexible working arrangements for employees with young children or those with elderly family members. It deplored the loss to the company if valuable employees leave SNG because their schedules are too rigid to allow them to address both their work and family responsibilities. It mentioned some flexible working arrangements already established at SNG, such as job sharing between two editorial writers at *The Ottawa Citizen* and a UIC maternity leave supplementary plan at *The Montreal Gazette*.
5. Where possible, SNG division should establish or support the provision of child-care centres on or near the grounds, and where economically feasible, the division should assume or share capital costs for a child-care facility. The report mentioned U.S. research that indicated that on-site child-care centres improve staff morale, help recruitment, and reduce absenteeism and turnover. It reported on the daycare centre at *The Calgary Herald*, begun in 1988, which was the first on-site child-care centre at a North American newspaper. In addition, *The Edmonton Journal*, which already has an equal opportunity committee, is building a daycare cen-

tre in its new building. The costs to the divisions of supporting the centres are tax deductible.

6. SNG and all divisions should adopt supportive policies on maternity, paternity, adoption, and dependent sick leave. In many divisions, women believe that if or when they take maternity leave, their male supervisors mentally consign them to the dead-end jobs for unambitious people. But the discussions and surveys done by the committee indicated clearly that most women who are mothers continue to take their jobs very seriously. Regarding dependent sick leave, the writers stated "... surely it is no part of decent corporate policy to make employees feel they must lie about a basic human responsibility.... Allowing a few days a year for dependent sick leave would pay enormous benefits in employee morale and loyalty."
7. Information on training and development programs should be made widely available at all divisions. Senior managers should be required by publishers to recruit women for such programs and to encourage women employees in planning career paths. There was a strong desire in many divisions for more and better training. Most respondents indicated that they had rarely, if ever, participated in formal job training. Women are not yet part of the informal network at SNG, where male managers advise each other and form alliances and friendships. Thus, women particularly need formal training, and need to know what is available.
8. SNG should develop a policy on harassment at work to serve as a model for all divisions. All SNG employees should be made aware that the company will not tolerate harassment of any kind in the workplace. In one division, 20 percent of the women responding said they personally had been the target of sexist behaviour and 5 percent said they had personally suffered sexual harassment. Moreover, the climate seems to be one in which the abusers suffer at most a minor interruption in their careers. SNG has already drafted a proposed sexual harassment policy. The challenge now is to send an unambiguous message: under no circumstances will harassment be tolerated anywhere.
9. To assist in implementing and monitoring the recommendations, SNG should appoint a full-time equal opportunity coordinator reporting to the president. Although each division will be expected to handle these problems according to its own objectives, a highly placed, full-time person would provide impetus, assistance, and coordination.
10. SNG and all divisions should review and revise all application forms, the job interview process, the wording of job descriptions, performance appraisals, job postings, and evaluations to remove any gender bias. Collective agreements should be reviewed as well.

NEXT STEPS

The task force suggested several initiatives to be taken in the following year:

- A concerted effort to appoint women to senior, nontraditional, and middle-management positions.
- A study of salary, bonuses, and perquisites for men and women that would highlight any existing imbalances in pay and other rewards.
- The development of a Human Resources Information System to be used in employee development and equal opportunity assessment, implementation, monitoring, and reporting.
- A study of perquisites and corporate habits to discover any practices that might discriminate against women (e.g., sponsorship of senior managers to all-male clubs).
- An inventory of high-potential women for senior and approach positions.

After receiving the report from the task force, Mills set up an implementation group at headquarters in Toronto. Its members are Mills; Tim Peters, vice-president, human resources; David Perks, publisher of *The Montreal Gazette*; and two women from the task force. This group receives feedback from the publishers regarding their progress with the ten recommendations.

A publishers' meeting was held on April 26, 1990, at which time the task force report was discussed. The publishers agreed that all their employees would have access to the report, and that each of them would appoint an employee equity coordinator who would act as a contact person for the implementation committee.

Following the meeting, Mills sent a memo to all employees supporting the task force report. In part, he wrote, "My objective and that of the publishers is to ensure that complete fairness without discrimination exists in the workplace for all employees at all levels. Not only must our policies and procedures be fair; they must be seen to be fair and fairly applied." He said that each recommendation would be given serious consideration by the implementation group and the conclusions reviewed with the publishers.

Two publishers decided to begin redressing the imbalance immediately. David Perks, publisher of *The Montreal Gazette*, and Clark Davey, *The Ottawa Citizen* publisher, publicly indicated that they would tie salaries and advancement of their senior managers partly to the efforts they made to recruit, develop, and promote women (but without quotas).

At that time, John Fisher, president and CEO of Southam Inc., was interviewed regarding this step. He indicated he was "somewhat lukewarm" regarding this particular recommendation of the task force "from a practical point of view." As reported in *The Globe and Mail*, he said, "I'm somewhat reluctant to accept something that is a force-feeding, to work for any sort of ratios... I think we want to level the playing field, not tip it the other way for the catch-up." He added that this was only his personal view and that all the recommendations would receive thorough discussion.

The issue was discussed at a publishers' meeting in June, but no decision was reached. A newspaper article in *The Windsor Star* on July 16, 1990, indicated that not all publishers agreed with Perks and Davey (see Appendix 3). Several publishers indicated their disapproval of linking compensation to the hiring and promoting of women.

On July 23, Mills wrote to all publishers saying that SNG would link compensation of publishers and other divisional heads to their performance in removing barriers to the recruitment, development, and promotion of women. (The discretionary part of the bonus compensation can be up to 5 percent of salary.) In effect, head office would tie the compensation of the publishers to their efforts on behalf of women, but it would be up to the publishers to decide whether they would do the same thing with their own senior managers.

In the same memo, Mills asked the publishers to send him one or two important objectives to improve opportunities for women at each newspaper: "Performance in meeting these objectives will be one of the factors considered in determining the discretionary part of bonuses for 1990."

IMPLEMENTATION GROUP

The implementation group has studied the objectives of the publishers regarding women and has found some of them to be a disappointment in that they are very soft. The group is considering a variety of actions to achieve employment equity, including the following:

- Using outside as well as inside resources to advise them.
- Providing a variety of training programs (e.g., management programs for women, sensitivity programs for male managers, and training for employment equity coordinators in the divisions).
- Providing more help to those units too small to have their own human resource departments.

At the end of each year, Southam Inc. gives president's awards for outstanding accomplishments of employees and groups. In addition to the recognition conveyed, these awards are accompanied by shares in the company. In 1990, the Task Force on Women's Opportunities won a President's Award.

OTHER FACTORS FOR CONSIDERATION

Until recently, SNG has not had a strong human resources presence. It is only in the last five years that its importance has grown. However, it is gaining credibility in the boardroom, where human resources is one of five committees of the board. The other four are executive, audit, pension, and nominating.

The task force, in supporting flexible work arrangements, emphasized that women are entering the workforce in increasing numbers, and by the year 2000 will move beyond the 45 percent of the labour force they now represent to 50 percent. The group also noted that the percentage of women in journalism schools across the country is consistently greater than the enrolment of men. In the well-known Journalism School at Carleton University, approximately 80 percent of the students are women.

An American study presented at a Columbia School of Journalism seminar showed that American newspapers lost 25 percent of their female readers from 1983 to 1987. One reason given for this loss is the male domination of senior positions in newspapers, and the lack of a feminist perspective in the writing and editing of some papers.

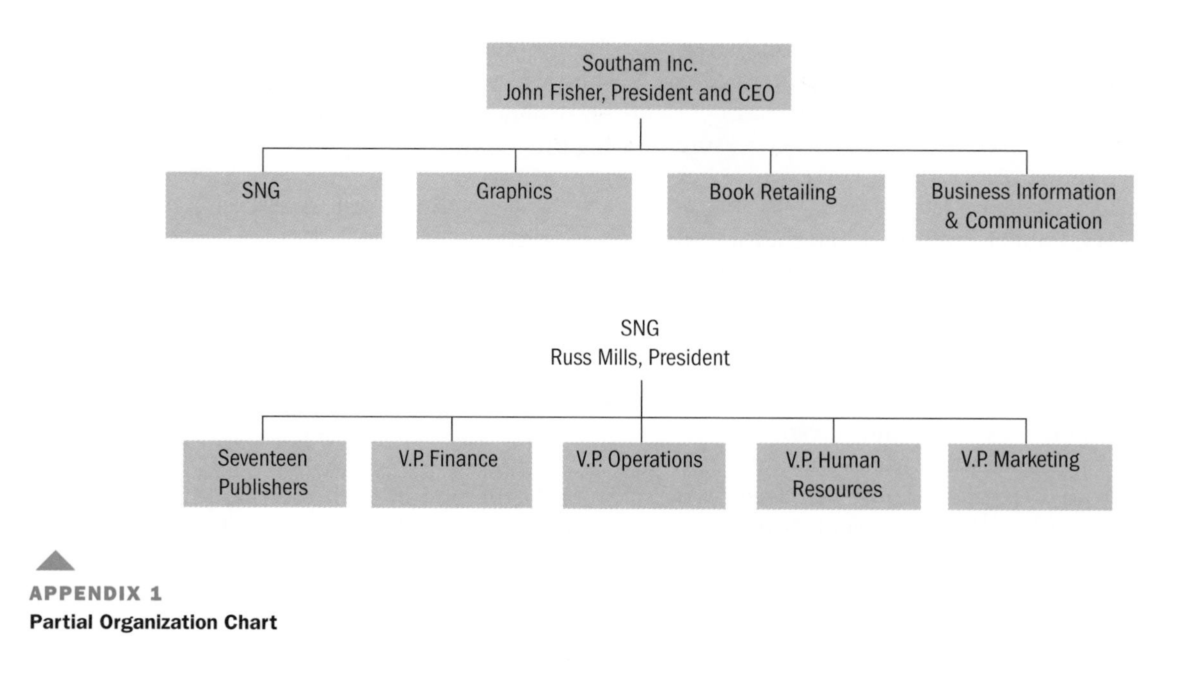

APPENDIX 1
Partial Organization Chart

MILLS'S DILEMMA

Russ Mills realizes that he and the implementation group will be hampered in carrying out the ten recommendations because employment equity does not visibly affect the bottom line of a newspaper. This issue is particularly important in 1990, as SNG will be short of its budget. Return on revenues is down from 15 percent in 1989 to 12 percent in 1990. The last quarter in 1990, usually the company's best, was very weak; advertising lineage dropped in the last two quarters. The prospects for 1991 look about the same: Mills does not expect to see an improvement until the last quarter of 1991. These economic factors have resulted in a near hiring freeze, and not as many positions have opened up as was expected a year ago. Consequently, it will be more difficult to encourage the publishers to make any changes that involve extra money being spent.

Mills rates employment equity quite highly on his list of priorities. His two main concerns now are the recession and how to preserve SNG's profitability, and the longer-term issue of readership: many younger people do not read newspapers. He ranks employment equity after these two, and is highly committed to enacting the recommendations. He is concerned with how he can keep the publishers on track regarding the recommendations so that SNG retains the goodwill of its employees and meets their expectations. An additional concern involves the kinds of goals he should expect from the publishers and how to measure their success in terms of the results they achieve.

Generally, when Mills and the publishers have disagreements, they talk them out at the quarterly meetings. If there are still problems following the meeting, Mills talks to the publishers one-on-one, counting on persuasion and logical argument to win them over. In this case, he wonders how he can get commitment from all of the publishers to support employment equity as embodied in the ten recommendations.

Appendix 2

PERCENTAGE OF VARIOUS SNG JOBS HELD BY WOMEN

Clerical	85%
Sales	38%
Supervisors	31%
Professional/semi-professional	30%
Senior and middle managers	18%
Skilled/semi-skilled trade workers	17%
Forepersons	10%
General managers/executives	6%

Southam Grapples with Job Equity*

Readers of *The Windsor Star* may notice it, but their newspaper is struggling over how to become a better place for women to work.

At issue is a task-force report from *The Star*'s parent company, Southam Newspaper Group, that recommends 10 steps be taken to raise Southam's meagre record for promoting women, and one of the proposals has already caused a split among publishers.

The key recommendation aims "to give force to the commitment to equal opportunity" by recommending "that the annual performance assessments of all publishers and senior managers be influenced by the degree to which they have recruited, promoted and developed women. This should be part of each manager's yearly objectives, and a factor in determining compensation."

The recommendation would apply to senior managers at *The Star* and 15 other Southam newspapers.

Windsor Star publisher James Thomson wants no part of that recommendation, saying it smacks of quotas and tokenism. Gordon Bullock, publisher of *The Spectator* in Hamilton and former *Windsor Star* publisher, is also opposed, but their counterparts at the *Ottawa Citizen* and *Montreal Gazette* have already implemented the policy at their papers.

Other Southam newspapers contacted by *The Star* reported their publishers either support the recommendation or are awaiting further study.

The proposal is also supported by Southam Newspaper Group president Russell Mills but he said it probably won't be forced on individual newspapers by head office. Southam is the largest-circulation newspaper group in Canada.

Southam publishers met June 26 and discussed the report but took no action on the controversial aspects of the report.

Instead, they ordered that a statement in support of employment equity be drafted and that information be exchanged between newspapers on how each newspaper responds to the report.

A spokesman for Southam said no action was taken on the recommendation that would tie the publishers' own bonuses to their records on advancing women.

Mills' boss, Southam Inc. president John Fisher, declined to be interviewed by *The Star* but in an earlier interview with the *Globe and Mail* he said he is personally lukewarm about the proposal. "I'm somewhat reluctant to accept something that is a force-feeding, to work for any sort of ratios . . . I think we want to level the playing field, not tip it the other way for the catch-up."

Staff at *The Star* are split over the issue, but their publisher has no doubts. He praised some of the other recommendations but called the adoption of the compensation policy by *The Gazette* and *Citizen* "grandstanding" and premature.

"I can tell you right here that I am not going to operate by that policy at *The Windsor Star*," Thomson said. He said he would only go along if forced by head office but would "object strenuously."

"I've always felt the person should get the job who earns it," he said. "You have to be very careful. . . . You don't want to forget that an applicant for a job is a person, whether they're male or female, and you judge them on their abilities to handle the job."

Editorial page writer Karen Hall said she sees both sides of the issue but feels that the monetary motivation is needed to reverse a historical imbalance at *The Star*. Without it, the status quo will remain, she said.

Everyone agrees the numbers look bad.

The Star has never promoted a woman to a senior management position. Its record is even worse than average for the Southam group, which has women in only five per cent of its senior jobs, compared to 17 per cent for the average Canadian corporation.

APPENDIX 3

*Brian Bannon, "Southam Grapples with Job Equity," *The Windsor Star*, 16 July 16 1990.

The situation is not getting better, according to the Southam task force that made the recommendations. In 1989, all 33 appointments to senior management jobs at Southam went to men.

The task force made 10 recommendations, including:

- Circulating policy statements about the need to correct a "serious imbalance" within the company in promoting women;
- Trying to include at least one woman on each short list for promotion to senior positions;
- Considering new policies on maternity leave, part-time work, day-care centres in or near the workplace, sexual harassment and training women for senior jobs;
- Appointing an equal-opportunity coordinator to implement and monitor the task force recommendations;
- Removing any gender bias from the processes used at Southam papers to hire or promote.

But the recommendation to tie managers' compensation to the advancement of women is the only one that uses money as a motivator. It has become the focal point of the report.

Joan Fraser, editorial page editor at *The Gazette* and co-chair of the task force, said the monetary recommendation was made to give force to the commitment to equal opportunity, but it is also intended to be fair and workable.

The task force rejected quotas and tokenism, she said, despite studies that show policy statements without quotas don't work. Fraser said the proposal is not aimed at promoting women over more-qualified men.

It would use the female issue as only one of several criteria for setting bonuses. The Gannett newspaper chain in the U.S. has taken similar steps in the past and now has a far better balance of men and women than Southam, she said.

Linda Balga, community relations manager at *The Windsor Star*, was on Fraser's committee and signed the report, but she now says she has "difficulties" with the monetary recommendation.

"What scares me about that," she said, "is that there may be some managers who will promote women on a dollars-and-cents basis rather than on merit.

"Men look at hookers with dollars and cents in their eyes. I don't want them to look at me with dollars and cents in their eyes."

Balga said the proposal may result in a "flash-in-the-pan" effect where many women are suddenly promoted but then fail, hurting both themselves and the newspaper.

She said it would be better to concentrate on training and developing women for future promotions. "I don't think you can be successful through intimidation."

Balga has been appointed by Thomson to head a *Star* committee to suggest ways to implement the task force recommendations but Thomson said he would overrule the committee if it recommends adopting the monetary proposal.

Southam Newspaper Group president Mills said the reaction from other papers has been positive.

He said it would be foolish for a manager to promote a woman solely to get a higher bonus. He doubts anyone would do it.

Edmonton Journal editor Linda Hughes, who sat on the task force, said Thomson's view is a misinterpretation of the recommendation. She said it does not mean a manager's income will be at risk if he or she doesn't promote women. It just means that efforts to train, develop, recruit and promote women should be one of many factors in assessments, and will depend on the situation in each department. A manager who makes every effort to find a qualified woman candidate but fails will not be penalized for hiring or promoting a man, she said.

The bottom line, Mills said, is that the merit system at Southam papers has not been working and something must be done to correct it. Managers should still promote the best person for each job, he said, and this recommendation just means they will be encouraged to look harder and perhaps further afield to find a woman who qualifies.

The Spectator's Bullock said he found the report "very moderate. It's not a radical document." But he said tying bonuses to the advancement of women "is very, very hard to measure and invites an awful lot of hypocrisy and game playing."

He says a certain amount of prejudice probably exists but he expects it will be eliminated because the report is making everyone more sensitive.

Ottawa Citizen publisher Clark Davey said there is no conflict between the merit system and the policy tying the advancement of women to managers' compensation, which he has implemented at his newspaper. "It's obvious that the merit system has not been working" and that an "old boys' network" has been keeping talented women from being promoted, he said.

Davey said the policy does not mean women will be promoted over men. If a manager has made an honest attempt to be fair he or she will not be penalized, he said.

Star editor Carl Morgan said he doesn't know what to think about the monetary proposal but there "will be some practical changes at *The Star*. There has to be!"

Morgan said he has been bothered for years that the newsroom, largest department at *The Star*, has a reputation as a bastion of male dominance. Women have complained to him that they feel they can't get ahead, he said.

"I don't see it," he said. "I really don't see it but I'll take their word for it."

Morgan said attempts have been made to attract and promote more women but the numbers still don't show it. *The Star*'s reputation for being run by a male clique may be to blame for its difficulty in attracting women to even entry-level jobs.

Once here, not all women want to move up, he said, and the number of openings for senior newsroom jobs is limited.

He said some men at *The Star* will feel they are victims of discrimination under an affirmative action program "but I don't know any way around that."

It takes time to train a manager, Morgan said, so a major change won't happen overnight.

One employee who said he would be upset if passed over for promotion in favour of a less-qualified woman is Tony Weir, who is comptroller in *The Star*'s business office.

He said he recognizes there is a problem with few women in management but is unsure whether they haven't been given the opportunity or they haven't sought the jobs.

Extra education is needed to be a supervisor, he said, and some women in his department are currently taking night classes.

However, he said, tying bonuses and annual reviews to advancing women could be abused.

"I still think that you've got to pick the best person for the job."

Weir said that if he thought *The Star* had a policy of "reverse discrimination" he might go to another company where he could get ahead on merit.

Circulation manager Bill Bealor said he opposes tying bonuses to advancing women because his current hiring and promotion practice is working well. Of three supervisors in his department one was a woman and she recently retired. No women from *The Star* showed an interest in the job, Bealor said, so he advertised and last week named a man to the position.

"Its a cliché to talk about the glass ceiling but I hit it," said former *Star* staffer Sandra Precop, who took several post-graduate courses to upgrade her journalism skills while at *The Star*.

After 20 years, she worked her way up to be assignment editor but said it became clear to her that she would advance no further.

"All the reports and policies in the world won't fix it," she said. "It takes commitment."

Precop is now an assignment editor with CBC television in Windsor. One thing she appreciates, she said, is that at the CBC there are several women occupying senior positions.

All the non-management *Star* employees interviewed for this story supported the monetary recommendation.

Doug Millar in the circulation department and Marty Beneteau in the newsroom said they could accept that there might be a bias toward promoting women in order to correct past discrimination against them.

"It's just something we've got to accept," Millar said. "I think the movement is on now."

Beneteau said men will suffer because when applicants for a job have equal abilities, managers will be under pressure to choose women, but he feels the men in the newsroom are progressive and will be understanding about it.

An added problem at *The Star*, he said, is that there have been very few openings for senior positions in the last few years.

The Star's Saturday features editor, Lisa Monforton, sits on a committee of newsroom staff set up to study the Southam report. She said she personally has advanced quickly but few other women have done so and she is unsure if she will go higher.

The atmosphere in the *Star*'s newsroom is definitely male-dominated and traditional, she said.

The Southam report's recommendations are not radical or unreasonable, Monforton said. If managers' bonuses are tied to advancing women, she hopes there will still be fairness.

"The important thing is that beliefs change, that there is an education process."

Kevin Peterson, publisher at Southam's *Calgary Herald*, said he fully supports all 10 recommendations in the report, and boasts that his paper's sexual harassment policy was used as an example in the task force report. *The Herald* also has one of the first day-care centres in any North American newspaper, another task force recommendation.

While *The Herald* may have a better record than most Southam papers, more needs to be done, Peterson said. He has made it mandatory that every manager read the report and committees are being set up within departments to implement it.

Since the report came out, *The Herald* has made public all the figures regarding promotions of women at the paper, where they work and how promotions are decided.

Managing editor Crosbie Cotton believes the issue goes far beyond employee relations. "Studies I've read indicate women readers are abandoning newspapers at a much quicker rate than male readers.

"I consider it a top priority to make our paper appropriate and compelling to the interests of women as much as men."

Montreal Gazette publisher David Perks endorsed all the task force proposals but said flexible working hours might be inhibited by union contracts. He said a *Gazette* policy to give preference to internal promotions would continue, unless it would indefinitely postpone redressing the gender imbalance at *The Gazette*.

Chief executives at the *Vancouver Sun* and *Province* and at the *Edmonton Journal* have told their staffs they generally support the recommendations and have set up committees to recommend ways to implement them.

The Journal formed a task force on the issue of advancing women a year ago and it has been recalled to study the new report.

Most people interviewed for this story agreed that the attention the report is receiving at all Southam newspapers should spur managers to try harder to advance women, and it should give a signal to women that opportunities for them exist at Southam papers.

CASE 5

Lightco: The Case of the Serial Changers

Jean Helms Mills

THE CULTURE CHANGE

It was a beautiful late summer day and David White was seated at his desk, enjoying the view from his 18th floor office, as he contemplated what to do next. White had just received the results of an employee attitude survey, which confirmed what he already suspected. His company, Lightco, was facing a serious morale problem among its employees and White knew he had to do something about it quickly.

Since being appointed as president of the publicly owned utility, White had travelled extensively throughout the region in order to meet all of the 2600 employees. It was during these visits that he started to notice the employee discontent. As the largest employer of engineers in the province, it was true that Lightco was often referred to as a construction company, rather than an electric utility. White could see that the employees, in addition to those who were located in head office's 18-storey office tower, were spread over six thermal plants, a couple of hydro plants, and four zone (regional) offices. As such, the divisions seemed to operate as a number of separate companies, with little interaction among them. White was also aware that traditionally the management positions were held mainly by engineers, whose style of management was autocratic at worst and paternalistic at best. It seemed to White, who had only been in the position a short time, that task accomplishment was Lightco's primary goal and that inanimate resources were being given more consideration than human resources. For White, who had been both a politician and college president prior to this current appointment, morale problems were disturbing because, in addition to affecting the efficiency of the Crown corporation, they also contradicted his basic values and beliefs. White asked his human resources director to conduct an employee attitude survey to see if he could get to the bottom of this problem so he could look for some solutions.

Eight months later, the results were in and they confirmed what White already knew. Employees were dissatisfied with the way they were being treated and managers were unhappy with the lack of communication and support from head office. It was time to take action.

From J. Helms Mills, *Making Sense of Organizational Change.* London: Routledge, 2003.

IMPLEMENTING THE CULTURE CHANGE

A few days later, White called a meeting of the executive and presented them with an idea that he had been thinking about for a while. Recently he had read of another utility, which had faced similar problems and had turned to culture change as a way of both increasing efficiency and boosting morale. Also, he knew that the local telephone company was introducing corporate values in an effort to change its culture. He suggested to the executive that maybe a planned culture change would work for Lightco. Within short order, tenders were sent out and a local consulting firm was hired to help Lightco establish its values and lead them into the change process.

The Human Resource Department, working closely with the consultants, began the day-to-day process of operationalizing the change. It was decided, after a series of meetings with the executive, to focus on four values: the province, the environment, the customer, and the employee.

The human resource manager and the consultants then decided to invite all the senior managers to a four-day session that would educate them about the culture change and give them the skills they would need to become facilitators for the one-day sessions that would be offered to the remaining employees to explain the values and the change. In the meantime, in order to reinforce the importance of the program, employees were given coffee mugs printed with "we value the environment," pens, and fridge magnets that highlighted the four values, and "values" posters were prominently on display in all locations. Although employees certainly could identify the values, few knew how to recognize them in action, and fewer still were able to understand how and when the culture change would become obvious. Most employees were focused on the value of "employee" and waited to see how their contribution to Lightco would be rewarded.

Six Months Later . . .

Phil Roberts, an engineer in the thermal division, who was a ten-year veteran of the company, had seen the company introduce a number of different changes, but he hadn't paid much attention to them. The various techniques that the company had tried had little direct effect on him or how he carried out his day-to-day activities. But recently he had attended a mandatory four-day training session for managers on changing the culture through the four values. This seemed very different from the change techniques that Lightco normally used because instead of focusing on how to get the job done, the company finally seemed to want to recognize the input of its employees and the importance of its customers. Maybe this new president was going to be okay after all. If anyone or anything could turn around the morale in this company, this could only benefit the company.

At the end of the four-day session, when volunteers were being solicited to act as facilitators for the one-day sessions for nonmanagerial employees, Phil decided to sign up. He was convinced that incorporating the values into everyday work activities would help to bring the different company divisions together and improve morale throughout.

It was late Friday afternoon and Carol Isenor was anxious to get home. It had been a rough week. As a customer service clerk in the district office, Isenor had borne the brunt of disgruntled customers' anger and frustration because of the latest hike in electricity rates. The last thing she had wanted to do was to end her week by attending this one-day "facilitation" meeting about the culture change program Lightco had recently embarked upon. Like many of the others in the room, Carol felt that if Lightco really did value her as an employee, they would have given her a four-day training session, led by a consultant, like all the managers had received, not this one-day meeting with some engineer from the thermal division acting as a facilitator. What did he know about her job and why was this program any different from the others that Lightco had tried? Since starting with the company eight years earlier, Carol had seen the company introduce a variety of changes. While this latest "flavour of the month" seemed to be talking about corporate values as a way to build employee commitment, Carol found it difficult to see how this could have any direct affect on her. And it already seemed that the abbreviated training session contradicted the value of "employee" that the facilitator was talking about. Carol looked at her watch again. Only 15 more minutes and she could catch the 5 P.M. bus home.

One Year Later . . .

Carol was in the lunchroom waiting for the kettle to boil. Looking around the room, she was reminded how much a part of their lives the Lightco values had become in such a short period of time. Not only were there tangible reminders of the values, but people were starting to act differently too. Early on, the values had been reinforced through a number of symbols, slogans, and practices. For example, four posters, depicting the four values, were on the wall behind Carol, and the styrofoam coffee cups on the shelf had been replaced by ceramic mugs that said "At Lightco, we value the environment." Now employees throughout the company had made values an issue. At one extreme were those who viewed them in a negative way—saying that everything had become a values issue—while others embraced them in an evangelical way and used values as a template for day-to-day behaviour.

Most, like Carol, saw the culture change as a positive step in the direction of making Lightco a better place to work. Although she and others had initially been skeptical about how long the company's commitment to the culture change would last, she had to admit that they certainly seemed to be trying to make it work. In fact, in the most recent annual report, the president's report promised a commitment to employment equity and stated that "visible minorities and more women in management" would be a bigger part of the company. An Equity Advisory Committee had just been set up and women were being encouraged to go into previously male-dominated trades. But it was the recently announced job-sharing program that was of greatest interest to Carol. For the first time since joining the company, she could apply to a program that would allow her to share her work duties with another co-worker, in order to give her more time and flexibility to spend with her family.

Phil was in his office studying the results of the latest employee attitude survey. Since becoming a facilitator, Phil had done a number of the one-day training sessions throughout the province. Initially, there had been a great deal of suspicion about the company's motives for change. But over time, and with the help of some of the union members who had also become facilitators, even the most skeptical employees had begun to believe that the company was serious about changing its ways and living the values. For example, the recent decision to do away with the different coloured hardhats, which distinguished management from nonmanagement employees, had done a lot to blur the boundaries between management and staff in the Transmission and Distribution Division. Now, instead of management wearing a white hat and the trade employees wearing yellow, everyone would wear yellow. As well, in Phil's plant, the manager had decided to let employees finish their shift 15 minutes early so that they could shower and leave the plant on time and clean. Although these were only little things, together they were changing the perception of Lightco as large, bureaucratic, and uncaring. Despite the usual complainers, most employees seemed to regard the changes that had been made in the past year as positive. The only real problem that Phil could identify was that people were probably far too happy with the values and saw them as a way to justify reasons for getting what they wanted. Still things could be worse and it certainly was good to see that morale had improved and employees were less suspicious of management's motives. Phil had to give a lot of credit to David White—as a president, he certainly was one of the people and employees liked and trusted him.

PRIVATIZATION

Since taking over the reins of Lightco in 1983, David White had known that the Crown corporation would one day have to stand on its own two feet. By 1991, several key developments were beginning to impact decision making within the company and causing a major change in thinking. Canada had entered into a North American Free Trade Agreement (NAFTA) with the U.S. that promised (or threatened) to open up a number of areas new to competition, including telecommunications and electricity supply. In order to meet the demands of remaining effective in a highly competitive environment, White knew that the company needed to take action and needed a strategy to achieve this. It came as no surprise to White when the premier of the province announced that Lightco would be privatized in June 1992. Although he was still committed to the culture change, White now had other issues to think about, the most important being to find ways to make the company more efficient and competitive. These factors dominated his thinking, as White looked for ways to achieve these new challenges while still remaining committed to the culture change.

RE-ENGINEERING

David White had just met with Lightco's auditors in order to finalize their statement for the 1992 annual report. Following privatization, he had been trying to reconcile various methods that would allow for the increase of the efficiency and effectiveness of the company, while still maintaining the integrity of the corporate culture and its values. When Lightco's auditors mentioned that their firm had a consulting arm with an established reputation for developing and implementing business process improvement (BPI), he was interested. And when he found out that their consultants had successfully re-engineered a number of major electrical companies in Canada, White began to think that maybe they could do the same for Lightco. After discussing it a bit further, a meeting was arranged between the consulting division and White for later in the week.

After laying out a proposal, the consultants had little trouble convincing White and Lightco's senior executives that their re-engineering strategy would provide them with the key to creating an effective organization to meet the demands of competition and globalization now facing the newly privatized company. Quickly, an agreement was signed and several consultants were assigned to work full-time with Lightco's internal change agent, the director of internal auditing. Early on, a series of "effectiveness" bulletins were circulated among employees to explain the latest strategy. Employees who had previously worked as facilitators were encouraged to "volunteer" to be members of the re-engineering project assessment teams. Although the commitment to the values and the "new" corporate culture was not forgotten, it became the consultants' job to take Lightco into the second stage of the culture change, called "organizational effectiveness." Soon it became clear that this change program was going to be quite different from the culture change program and its concern for the employee. For one thing, the director of employee development was not directly involved with the planning and implementation of the re-engineering initiatives, and for another, the focus was on the value of the job, rather than the value of the employee.

In conjunction with the newly created "corporate effectiveness" department, composed of a project manager, an external consultant, a human resources specialist, and six communications support staff, the consultants formed the initial assessment team. Early on, it had become evident to the re-engineering leadership that Lightco was overstaffed and had a great deal of duplication of services. So these "business process improvement teams" interviewed and observed employees in the units being re-engineered, in order to decide how to streamline jobs and cut down on unnecessary costs. This process, which had taken 16 weeks, and included an analysis of the current method of carrying out the task, "creating a vision and detailed concept of the future state of the process," and developing an implementation plan, was now concluding. With advice from the consultants, the process teams had identified jobs that didn't offer "value" to the accomplishment of organizational goals and had offered employees in these positions the chance to take early retirement or to apply for jobs that were considered as having "added value." In this way, over 300 positions had already been eliminated, mostly through attrition, before the two pilot projects were initiated.

When Carol first heard that customer service was one of the departments that had been selected to be part of the re-engineering pilot projects, she was excited. This restructuring, combined with the earlier mandate of the culture change to promote women into positions of management through the value of employee, meant that she might finally have a chance at promotion. Although Carol had been with the company long enough to be considered for promotion and everyone said she knew the job better than anyone else, she had been overlooked the last few times a supervisory position had opened up in favour of her male colleagues. This time might be different. The company had certainly changed since this emphasis on values and culture had started and it really did seem to value its employees and to be committed to making the workplace more equitable.

SIX MONTHS LATER . . .

Following the announcement that the company was going to implement two pilot projects, employees in the Customer Service Division had been advised that one of the projects was going to involve the centralization and consolidation of all customer service–related activities to one large call centre. This meant that employees would be trained to carry out a number of different tasks that would not only serve the customer better but give customer service representatives, like Carol, more autonomy and variety in doing their jobs.

It was only when Lightco called a meeting and announced that the closure of the satellite offices meant that 150 dislocated employees would now have to compete for about 70 new positions that would be created in the new call centre that the enormity of the project set in. As well, in addition to the competition from employees in the soon-to-be-closed locations, "linesmen" from the recently cancelled apprenticeship program would also be competing for the same 70 positions. Rumour had it that those who weren't successful would be let go with a severance package.

Suddenly, Carol wasn't worried about promotion, as job security became a primary focus. While the latest annual report had described re-engineering as "revolutionizing the way we work," nothing had prepared her for this. Not only was she overworked because the company had drastically underestimated the staff it would need for this new centre, but it was a joke to hear her manager describe the external consultant as a "visionary." But then he had been on the team that had thought up this whole scheme. Yesterday she had heard one co-worker refer to the consultant as "undertakers" and "hatchet men." Even her supervisor called them "gunslingers" when he thought no one was listening. What had happened to valuing the employee, Carol wondered. Things were certainly a mess. Many of her co-workers, fed up and stressed by the constant understaffing, were calling in sick. Others were resentful that their former co-workers had lost their jobs and many like Carol were wondering what would happen next. Although the company had just announced that it had retained the services of a psychological counselling firm to deal with employees' problems, the rumour that more layoffs were about to occur was even more urgent.

Following the announcement that volunteers were being sought to serve on the business process team, Phil Roberts was encouraged to volunteer. Since his experience as a facilitator of the culture change had been so positive, Phil looked forward to again meeting with employees in other divisions and serving as an ambassador for Lightco. He was assigned to the team that was assessing the feasibility of consolidating the regional call centres. Initially, the team met two to three times a week for a few hours and Phil was able to return to the project he was completing in his own division. As the project got well underway, Phil was assigned full-time to the team and was seconded to the Internal Audit Division.

It was late Tuesday and Phil had just returned from another meeting that had gone on far longer than he anticipated. If he had known that employees were going to blame him personally for the problems created by the re-engineering processes, he would never have agreed to take on this task. Today had been particularly upsetting. An employee who had just been given two weeks notice had come to him crying and begging him to do something to help her get her job back. After all this, Phil was anxious to get home but first he had to return a call to his boss that was marked urgent. When he hung up, Phil was speechless. It seemed that the company had decided to outsource the work that Phil's department had been doing. Phil was waiting for security to arrive and escort him off the premises. After all the work he had done for Lightco, he was being given 20 minutes to clear out his desk.

At the same time, David White had just come from a meeting with the senior managers. Things were not good. Following the latest round of layoffs, morale among the remaining employees was at an all-time low. The managers were reporting that employees were angry, unhappy, and stressed by the amount of work they were having to do and did not feel that their efforts were being acknowledged. White was hearing reports that employees felt that the changes that were occurring were not being explained in a timely manner, and rumours surrounding the changes were causing panic at all levels. More importantly, employees felt that Lightco was not holding true to the values and that the culture change was a thing of the past.

While re-engineering had seemed the ideal solution, White now wondered how he had failed to recognize that re-engineering would be a fairly rigid process that focused on getting tasks done in the most efficient and cost-effective manner, while de-emphasizing the importance of creating a happy workforce and employee well-being. It seemed that his plans for creating a humanistic workplace and promoting employment equity had been derailed by factors that were out of his control. The culture had changed, but not in the way that he had hoped. Had he made a mistake? Should he have stuck with the original plan and not been talked into changing the company's strategy? Was it too late to gain back the trust of his employees?

CASE 6

The Westray Mine Explosion

Caroline O'Connell and Albert J. Mills

INTRODUCTION

It was the sixth of February 1996. Carl Guptill sat at his kitchen table nursing a cup of coffee. He was a beefy man with long hair, often tucked through the back of a baseball cap. The next day he would testify at the Commission of Inquiry into the Westray Mine Explosion and friends had been phoning to offer their support. One caller, a geologist from nearby Antigonish, hadn't been in touch since working with Guptill at a mine in Guysborough County more than five years ago, but he wanted Carl to know he was thinking of him.

Carl Guptill's thoughts drifted back to another kitchen table—Roy Feltmate's. Roy, a long-time friend, had worked on B crew at the Westray Mine. In April of 1992, three months after he had left his job at Westray, Guptill met up with Roy and four other members of B crew, at Feltmate's home. Talk quickly turned to safety at the mine. Conditions had continued to deteriorate and the men believed that an explosion or a cave-in was inevitable. They calculated their odds of being the crew underground when it happened at 25 percent. The men made Guptill promise that if they died in the mine, he would "go public" and tell the world what he knew. Mike MacKay implored him to "do it for our widows."

On May 9, 1992, a few short weeks after that kitchen meeting, the odds caught up with Roy Feltmate, Mike MacKay, Randy House, Robbie Fraser, and 22 other members of B crew. At 5:20 A.M. an explosion ripped through the Westray Mine. All 26 miners underground died. Fifteen bodies were recovered but 11 bodies, including Roy Feltmate's and Mike MacKay's, remained in the mine. Guptill would keep his promise to them.

ONE MINER'S TALE

Carl Guptill had worked in hard-rock mines in Nova Scotia prior being hired at Westray. At the Gay's River Mine, he had chaired the health and safety committee, and at the Forest Hill Mine he'd been a shift supervisor to a crew of 35 or more men. He had completed an advanced management course at Henson College, the continuing education arm of Halifax's Dalhousie University. He was mine rescue certified and had been captain of a mine rescue team. As both a miner and a supervisor, he'd enjoyed a good working relationship with Albert McLean, the provincial mine inspector. Guptill had ended up working at Westray more by happenstance than by design. He had offered to drive his buddy to the mine site to fill out an application and had ended up hired on himself. Guptill put safety first and believed he'd made that clear to Roger Parry, underground manager at Westray, when Parry interviewed him for a job. He demonstrated that commitment by joining the safety committee.

After only a few shifts, Guptill began to question safety practices at Westray. On his very first day, Bill MacCullogh, the mine's training officer, wasn't able to answer some of his questions. He noticed that farm tractors, which shouldn't even be used underground, were loaded beyond their capacity. Combustible coal dust was allowed to build up underground, the rock dust that should be spread to neutralize it wasn't anywhere to be found, levels of explosive methane gas were too high, and the methanometers that detected the gas were rigged to circumvent their intended purpose of warning miners when gas levels were dangerous. In addition, miners worked 12-hour shifts, often without breaks. The batteries for miners' headlamps could not sustain their charge and were often dim or out by the end of a shift. There were no underground toilets and miners relieved themselves in unused corners of the mine.

Complaints fell on deaf ears. One supervisor answered Guptill's concerns with the comment that "they got a few thousand applications up on top, men willing to come down here and take your place." On only his 13th shift, Guptill's supervisor ordered him to continue working after his lamp had dimmed. In the dark, Guptill stumbled and a steel beam he was attempting to move landed on him and injured him. After three days in hospital, he called Roger Parry. The conversation quickly turned into a shouting match. Guptill then contacted Claude White, the provincial director of mine safety. White, in turn, sent him to mine inspector Albert McLean. Shortly thereafter, Guptill met with McLean, John Smith, the man responsible for inspection of electrical and mechanical equipment in mines, and Fred Doucette, in charge of mine rescue. In this meeting Carl Guptill spoke of his accident and of the many safety violations he had observed in his short time working at Westray. Guptill expected that his report would result in a shutdown of the mine and a complete investigation. Weeks later, having heard nothing, he again called inspector Albert McLean. The two met once more, this time in a local motel room, instead of the labour department's offices. McLean kept the television on high volume throughout the meeting. Puzzled, Guptill later concluded that McLean was fearful he would tape the meeting. McLean told Guptill that the other men had not backed up his complaints and he could do little. He did offer to "put in a good word" for Guptill with management if he wanted to return to work. This was the story Carl Guptill told the Commission of Inquiry.

A SNAPSHOT OF MINING IN PICTOU COUNTY

The four communities of Trenton, New Glasgow, Westville, and Stellarton run into each other to make up Pictou County, Nova Scotia. All told, 25 000 people live there, descendants of Scots that landed with the ship *Hector* and immigrants from the other British Isles and Europe that followed Britain's General Mining Association oversees in the early 19th century. Hardy stock, they had mined the county's 25 seams of coal for generations. One historian estimated that nearly 600 residents lost their lives in coal mines, as many as had been killed in both world wars. Although full of coal, the seams were considered among the most dangerous in the world: the beds were uneven and the ash content was high. The mines were subject to rock falls and flooding. Most significant were the high levels of explosive methane gas.

At its peak in 1875, Pictou coal mines produced 250 000 tons of coal a year and employed over 1600 men and boys. The last mine operating in Pictou was the small, privately operated Drummond Mine that closed in 1984. By the mid-1980s, the only coal mines left in Nova Scotia were operating under heavy federal subsidy in Cape Breton, an economically depressed area in the northernmost part of the province. Cape Breton mines might have met the same fate as those in Pictou had they not been in the territory of a powerful federal member of parliament as the oil crisis in the Middle East dominated headlines and economies in the 1970s. Under OPEC, oil from the Middle East was subject both to price hikes and embargoes. This rejuvenated the dying Cape Breton coal industry and coal rebounded as a source of energy in Nova Scotia. In the late 1980s and early 1990s, a similar opportunity presented itself to the industry in Pictou. An evolving environmental agenda was driving power generation. The provincial electrical utility, Nova Scotia Power Corporation, was seeking to lower its sulphur dioxide emissions. It needed an alternative to high-sulphur Cape Breton coal. Enter Clifford Frame.

POLITICS AND BIG GUNS

Clifford Frame, a big man, who drove big cars, raised cattle, and smoked expensive cigars, was a self-made tycoon in the style of a previous era. In his youth he turned down a chance to play for the New York Rangers' farm team. Instead he got a degree in mine engineering and worked his way from the pit to the corner office. After rising to the post of president of Denison Mines, he'd been fired in 1985 after a very public project failure in British Columbia. He formed Curragh Resources in 1985 and had early success reviving a lead-zinc mine in the Yukon. In 1987, the industry publication the *Northern Miner* named him "Mining Man of the Year." That same year he incorporated Westray Coal, and in 1988, he bought out Suncor's coal rights in Pictou County. In his time at Denison, Frame had come to know key political players in Ottawa. Through these connections he was introduced to Elmer MacKay, then federal representative for Pictou, and minister of public works. Frame aggressively sought federal and political support for his operation. Pictou County was burdened by a 20 percent unemployment rate and Frame promised that his mine would employ at least 250 people in jobs paying $35 000–$60 000 for 15 years. Economic spin-off in neighbouring communities would total in the millions of dollars.

Politicians, including then-premier John Buchanan, supported Frame. Perhaps the project's greatest advocate was local provincial MLA (member of the legislative assembly) Donald Cameron who became minister of economic development as the project evolved, and ultimately was elected premier, his position at the time of the explosion. Frame successfully negotiated a $12 million equity loan with the provincial government as well as an $8 million interim loan when federal negotiations lagged. He also struck a so-called "take or pay" agreement that guaranteed a market for Westray coal. Under this contract, the Nova Scotia government would buy 275 000 tons of coal if other buyers did not materialize. Westray would pay back any revenues from this agreement without interest at the end of 15 years.

The federal government proved a tougher sell and discussions dragged out over three years. Ultimately the federal government came through with a loan guarantee of $85 million and an interest buy-down of nearly $27 million. This was much less than the amount originally sought by Frame and much more than the government's policies usually allowed for such projects. Harry Rogers, a federal deputy minister, was involved in the negotiations and would later describe Clifford Frame as "... personally abrasive and abusive .... Probably the most offensive persona I have met in business or in government."

However a deal was struck and in September of 1991, at Westray's official opening, politicians at both levels lined up to congratulate each other. Nor did they hesitate to parlay their support into jobs for constituents. One phone call from a politician's assistant could result in the hiring of an inexperienced young man with the right family connections. Indeed, Bill MacCullogh had been able to jump from the development agency where his job included lobbying government to support the mine's development directly onto Westray's payroll. In August of 1991 he became the company's training officer.

RULES OF THE GAME

Mining is dangerous work. The first regulations to protect the safety of miners date back to 1873 and provided for the inspection of mines. In 1881 legislation allowed for the certification of miners and mine officials. The new rules also called for gas testing and banned smoking underground. This legislation followed a disaster in which 60 miners died and made Nova Scotia mines the safest in the world, according to one mining historian. In 1923 the age limit for working underground was raised from 12 to 16. (It would not be raised to age 18 until 1951.) By 1927, the maximum allowable level of methane in a mine was 2.5 percent. At the time of the Westray explosion, a methane reading of 2.5 percent required the removal of all workers from the site, while a reading of 1.25 percent mandated the shutdown of electricity that could spark an explosion.

At the time the Westray Mine exploded, the regulation of coal mining in Nova Scotia fell primarily under the Coal Mines Regulation Act, a 160-page piece of legislation considered 30 years out of date. An example of its anachronisms could be found in section 94 that outlined the duties of stablemen who tended the horses underground. The section provided for care of the horses and cleanliness of the stables. A further indication of just how out of date the legislation was, and how limited was its power to deter unsafe behaviours, was the fine schedule. The maximum fine that could be levied under the act was $200. It also regulated the qualifications required for various levels of mining competency, including miners, managers, owners, and inspectors. Most significantly, for Westray, the legislation regulated maximum allowable levels of methane. It also stipulated the removal of highly combustible coal dust and the spreading of limestone dust to neutralize its effects. The act included provisions for roof supports and the prohibition of tobacco products and matches underground; it permitted worker inspections of the mines and limited shift duration to eight hours. All would become issues for public scrutiny after the explosion.

Operating in parallel was the provincial Occupational Health and Safety Act enacted in 1986. It imposed on employers the obligation to ensure workplace safety and to provide appropriate training, equipment, facilities, and supervision.

This legislation also required employees to take safety precautions, to wear appropriate clothing or equipment, and to cooperate with employers, regulators, and other employees in these goals. The act also mandated joint occupational health and safety committees for workplaces with designated numbers of employees. These committees made up of both employer and worker representatives were charged with educating on safety issues, maintaining records, inspecting the workplace, and responding to complaints. A key element of this legislation was a worker's right to refuse unsafe work and not to be discriminated against, or punished for doing so. The act also provided that the legislation itself must be available for inspection by workers so that they might be aware of their rights. It also required employers to report to the regulators any accident resulting in an injury.

When the occupational health and safety legislation was passed, responsibility for enforcement was transferred from the provincial Department of Mines and Energy to the Department of Labour. Inspectors also retained jurisdiction over the Coal Mines Regulation Act. Both acts authorized inspectors to order a work stoppage, and the Coal Mines Regulation Act, under section 64, specifically empowered an inspector to order a dangerous mine closed.

TRAINING AT WESTRAY

William (Bill) MacCulloch began his job as the training officer at Westray on August 1, 1991, just over a month before the official opening of the mine. He had been on the job nine months when the mine blew up. Previously, he had worked as an economic development officer with the local municipality, providing information and support to the business community. In particular, he helped companies from outside the area that were considering investing in Pictou County. In this capacity he had brokered relations between Curragh executives and local contacts; he had lobbied government for funding and had promoted the project prior to the mine's opening. His connections in the community were extensive. Earlier in his career he'd worked both as a bank teller and radio personality. He had a high school diploma and a certificate in economic development acquired through part-time studies at the University of Waterloo, along with some accounting courses. He had no mining experience.

In his time at Westray, MacCulloch attempted to create a comprehensive training package that included certification in underground skills and equipment operation, mine rescue, health and safety, first aid, and the handling of hazardous materials. Much of the training protocol was already enshrined in legislation. This was reflected, for example, in the employee manual that included, among other provisions, the following:

> **Health & Safety Philosophy**:
>
> It's the personal responsibility of each member of the management team to ensure that the necessary education and training to equip all employees, to encourage a zero accident rate while reducing possible threats to good health and safety is provided . . .
>
> . . . It's the personal responsibility of each supervisor to ensure that employees receive adequate training in work procedures so maximum productivity can be achieved within a safe work environment.

MacCulloch understood his job to be that of administrator of the program, ensuring schedules and facilities as well as sourcing materials and expertise.

Of particular importance at Westray was the training of inexperienced miners. Legislation stipulated a 12-month progression, under a "black tag" (certified) miner. In this time, a miner would begin with basic labour and would gradually be introduced to and trained in the safe operation of the bolter, the continuous miner, and other equipment. This period could be shortened to six months if systematic training took place at a work face in the mine designated as a training area.

MacCulloch developed a three-day orientation program, building on a handbook already in existence when he began the job. He envisioned classroom modules on gas levels and safe ventilation, and practical demonstrations with equipment like the self-rescuer. His plan was forwarded to the provincial labour department as required.

THE UNION DRIVE

Bob Burchell had been a miner and mine inspector for almost a decade. In his current role with the United Mine Workers of America, he organized union drives, lobbied for political and social reform, negotiated on behalf of miners, and advocated for safe mining practices. He had trained at the Mine Safety and Health Administration (MSHA) Academy and returned annually to maintain and upgrade his credentials. He was unabashedly zealous in his work and could, on occasion, be loud, aggressive, and profane.

Burchell had been on what he termed a "scouting" mission at Westray over the summer months of 1991. Some of his contacts had passed on the word that conditions underground were not optimal. Burchell positioned himself near the mine's entrance, hoping to catch miners coming or going. Early response was less than encouraging. He had to jump out of the way of the miners' cars as they raced on or off the property. "They knew who I was," he said. It wasn't long before management also delivered a message. Having refused Burchell access to the men at shift change, they sent a police officer to remove him. When Burchell persisted, management drove down the access road, parked nearby and either watched him silently or engaged him directly in conversation. One day, Gerald Phillips even sent his wife down to chat. To the miners, management presence at the entrance was a clear message.

Undaunted, and continuing to hear rumours of unsafe practices, Burchell established a base in nearby New Glasgow. A few emboldened miners stopped one day and talked to him. They told him about the use of farm equipment underground. They expressed concern for their safety but were pessimistic about the union's potential for a successful certification drive. They told Burchell that many miners had moved to take jobs at Westray and would have to repay their relocation expenses if they stayed less than a year. Despite the miners' fears of repercussions, the union drive progressed slowly and under a cloak of secrecy. The men asked Burchell not to take notes at their meetings. A local woman, who owned the restaurant where Burchell often met the men, told him that she'd received a call from Bill MacCulloch at Westray. He had asked her, "as a long-time friend," to "keep tabs" on who was coming and going at the restaurant and to report back to him. Offended, she refused.

Burchell received permission from his Washington superiors to send union cards out in the mail instead of delivering them in person. Miners could sign them in the privacy of their homes and return them by mail. Meanwhile, information continued to accumulate painting a picture of ill-trained miners working without adequate safety knowledge. In one meeting, Burchell listened as one young man, a new miner, described his high-quality, stainless-steel first-aid kit, issued to him with the words "Here, this is in case of an emergency." Burchell realized the young man was unwittingly referring to his self-rescuer—the only thing between the miner and death in the event of a cave-in. "It blew my mind," said Burchell.

Ultimately, the union lost the certification drive by 20 votes.

A DAY IN THE LIFE*

The continuous miner roared, cutting coal from the face of the mine and loading it into shuttle cars for transport to a conveyor belt. A huge machine, it allowed previously unheard-of quantities of coal to be mined in a day. Pictou miners knew it was a far cry from the pick and shovels of their grandfathers' mines and the explosives of their fathers' mines. The men at work that day were the usual mixed bag of experienced miners and untried "greenhorns." Like most days at Westray, even those with underground experience had gained it in hard-rock mines, not coal mines. There were simply not enough certified coal miners in the area to fill the jobs. Claude White had granted the company an exemption under the Coal Mines Regulation Act to use hard-rock miners in their place.

Lenny Bonner and Shaun Comish were old friends and veterans of hard-rock mining. They had been hired together and their pit talk this morning centred on a recent accident in the mine. A young kid, Matthew Sears, had his leg crushed when he tried to replace a roller on the conveyor belt. As he stood on the belt, it started up without the usual warning and his leg was jammed in a large roller. The men in the mine at the time had reported that Ralph Melanson kept pulling the safety cable to stop the belt, but it kept restarting. Sears had been through five surgeries since the

*All events described in this section are based on the sworn testimony of miners and other witnesses to the Commission of Inquiry. They are told here as if they happened on one workday. Except for this change in chronology, they are an accurate depiction of work underground at Westray as described by the parties.

accident and would be months off work. "Poor kid," said one to the other, "he told me that his first day on the job he didn't even know how to turn his lamp on." Roger Parry had sent him down alone to meet his crew and he'd stood there, shocked by how dark it was. Both Bonner and Comish recalled their first day at Westray. Without any orientation, they'd been issued their self-rescuers and sent underground. At the time they had laughed because neither of them understood most of what Roger Parry said to them. Between his British accent and his wad of chewing tobacco, they were lucky to catch half of what he said. Both men had progressed quickly underground from installing arches on the roadway and roof supports in the rooms being mined to operating equipment—drills, the bolter, the shuttle car. Neither had received any specific instruction. As Comish put it, "I got on it and [he] showed me what levers to move and what was your brake and what was your throttle and away you go." He recalled with some nostalgia the mine in Ontario where he had learned to drive a scoop tram in a designated training area, away from production. Both men knew that at Westray, the more equipment a miner could operate, the higher his pay would be.

The continuous miner had come to a stop. This meant the methanometer or "sniffer" had detected too much gas. Comish pressed the reset button a few times to no effect. Bonner was running the shuttle car and waited. Comish overpowered the trip switch and kept filling the shuttle car. He disliked overriding a safety measure that was really for his own protection but he'd been shown how to do it and he understood what was expected. The mine's bonus system was simple: more coal meant more money. As he did every four days when he was back underground, Comish thought about quitting; he thought again about the roof over his family's heads and the food on their plates, sighed, and got back to work. Some days, there was no need to override the sniffer. Comish recalled working in the southwest section of the mine one shift when the methanometer wasn't working. Comish had turned to Donnie Dooley and joked, "If we get killed, I'll never speak to you again." Despite the jokes and the camaraderie, Comish couldn't escape the feeling that things weren't quite right. He decided that this day he just didn't want to be in the mine. He planned to tell his supervisor that he had to leave at five to get his car fixed—a harmless white lie.

Some of the men underground that day wondered when Eugene Johnson would be back from Montreal. His name had been selected from a draw to go to a ceremony where the industry association would give out the John T. Ryan award honouring Westray as the safest coal mine in Canada. The award was based on reported accident statistics. The men had laughed off the award since they knew management had "jigged" the accident stats to ensure a good record. Nonetheless, they didn't begrudge their co-worker and friend a trip to the big city. Johnson and his wife were scheduled to see the Toronto Maple Leafs play. They were having a big night out with Clifford Frame and his wife. The men were sure Eugene would have some good stories from his trip.

Bonner asked Comish if Wayne Cheverie was underground that day. Neither could recall seeing him at the beginning of the shift. With no tag system in the deployment area, at any given time there was no way of knowing who or how many people were underground. Lenny Bonner thought back to his time at the Gay's River Mine. The tag system there had been stringently enforced. One day, he'd forgotten to tag out, meaning that his tag was on the board and therefore, he was officially still underground. Although his shift boss had watched him leave the property, he could not remove a miner's tag from the board. Instead, Bonner had driven back, tagged out, and his shift boss had been required to wait since he could not leave until all men under his charge were accounted for.

The men were interested in Wayne Cheverie because he was making a lot of noise about safety lately. Even back in September at the official opening of the mine, he had buttonholed Albert McLean after the ceremonies. Cheverie reported that he had told McLean many of his concerns about roof conditions and the lack of stone dust and asked him point-blank if he had the power to shut the mine down. McLean told him no. Cheverie knew the outcome for other miners who had complained—harassment and intimidation. However, it was well known among the men that Cheverie was coming to the end of his rope. He was not only talking about complaining to the Department of Labour, but he was also threatening to go to the media. Recently, after refusing work,

Cheverie had been told by Arnie Smith, his direct supervisor, that if he left the mine, he'd be fired. His response, "fired or dead, Arnie, that's not much of a choice, is it?" Bonner understood how Cheverie felt. A chunk of the mine's roof had fallen on his head one day. Bonner had gone home with a sore leg and back and an egg on his head. He'd had to fight with management to get paid for the day. Roger Parry had said, "We don't pay people for going home sick." Bonner had replied, "If you call the roof coming in and chunks of coal hitting you on the head and the back and almost killing you, you call that 'going home sick'!" Eventually he had been paid for the shift. He reflected that at least he was better off than that poor kid Todd MacDonald. On MacDonald's first day of work, there'd been a roof fall and the kid had been buried up to his waist. He was flat on his back, facing the roof, as if he'd watched it fall instead of running the hell out of there.

Bonner and Comish and a few of the other men stopped work for a quick and belated break. They often didn't get to their lunches until after their shifts. Bonner sat down with his lunch pail but jumped up again quickly. He had picked a spot too close to a pile of human waste but in the dark had not noticed it until the stink hit him. Back when he'd first started work at the mine, Bonner had spoken to mine manager Gerald Phillips about installing underground toilets. Phillips had told him that he was considering a number of different models. In the meantime, Bonner felt demeaned, like an animal forced to crouch on the ground like a dog. As it turned out, their lunch break was short-lived anyway. Shaun Comish had warned the others that he saw a light approaching and the men had scattered like rats, fearing that Roger Parry was on his way down. With his usual profanities he would send them back to work. End of shift couldn't come soon enough.

DISASTER AND AFTER

Within minutes of the explosion, neighbours and family members began to gather at the mine site. Within hours, local, national, and international media had set up equipment and reporters in the community centre that served as their hub. Family members, in an arena directly across from the centre, where they awaited news of their loved ones, resented the prying cameras and intrusive questions. For six days they waited, they cried, they drank coffee, they smoked cigarettes, and comforted their children and each other with hopes for a triumphant rescue. Each silently held close the tale of the Springhill mine disaster of 1958. After eight days, the last men there were taken alive out of the mine after the explosion or "bump." Their story remains that of the longest that men underground have ever survived in a mine disaster, and the lore of their dramatic rescue resonated with fearful families.

Family and community, producers and reporters, along with viewers everywhere, grew to know Colin Benner as the "face of Westray." He had been appointed to the position of president of operations in April and had been responsible for the Westray Mine less than one month when it blew up. He had just barely begun the processes that he hoped would help dig Westray out of its financial hole. Production was short, with the mine failing to provide the 60 000 tons a month to Nova Scotia Power for which it had contracted. Sales in the previous six months had reached $7.3 million, but costs had exceeded $13 million. Benner had also heard rumblings about safety, about discontent among the miners, and about the heavy-handed techniques of Gerald Phillips and Roger Parry.

All this, however, was put aside as he dealt with the crisis. He served as media liaison, updating on the progress of the rescue efforts. By the sixth day he was showing the strain—his tie off, his sleeves rolled, his shirt wrinkled with sweat and with wear as his hands raked through his hair. It was with obvious sorrow on May 14 that he announced the search was being called off as there was no hope that anyone could have survived the blast. It was simply too dangerous for the rescue crews to continue.

THE SEARCH FOR TRUTH

On May 15, the day after Colin Benner had announced that the search for the miners had been suspended, Premier Donald Cameron appointed Justice Peter Richard to a Commission of Inquiry into the explosion. His terms of reference were broad and mandated him to look into all aspects of the establishment, management, and regulation of the Westray Mine. They specifically empowered the Inquiry to determine if any "neglect had caused or contributed to the occurrence" and if the events could have been prevented. A tangled web of legal proceedings held up the Inquiry for more than three years. In that time both provincial health and safety charges and federal criminal charges were laid, and then withdrawn against the company and its managers.

The Inquiry heard its first testimony on November 6, 1995. Justice Richard also undertook substantial study on coal mining and mine safety to prepare for the task. He visited mines in Canada and the United States and consulted with experts in South Africa, Great Britain, and Australia. He commissioned technical reports from six experts in subjects that included mining ventilation and geotechnology. He commissioned academic studies in history, economics, psychology, and political science. These reports provided him with insight into the history of mining in Pictou, the multiplier effect of large-scale employment on the communities, the impact of production bonuses on miners' behaviour and the role of ministerial responsibility in the public sector. The Inquiry heard 71 witnesses in 76 days of testimony and produced 16 815 pages of transcripts; it entered 1579 exhibits into evidence after examining 800 boxes of documents. The total cost of the Inquiry was nearly $5 million.

More than 20 miners testified before the Inquiry. All told similar tales of life underground with little training and less respect. They told of accidents never documented and management promises never kept. They told of conversations with Inspector Albert McLean that he testified never happened. The Inquiry questioned McLean about his response to Carl Guptill's complaints. McLean authenticated a memorandum to his director in which he stated, "in conclusion, I find no flagrant violation of regulation in this case." In a dramatic moment of testimony, shown repeatedly on television news, McLean admitted that he did not know what the word "flagrant" meant. Bill Burchell of the United Mine Workers testified that prior to Westray he had felt great respect for Albert McLean, calling him responsible and efficient—"one of the best inspectors I've ever worked with." He said that his response to McLean's inaction was similar to the betrayal felt by a cuckolded spouse. Another pivotal moment in the Inquiry was the examination of former premier Donald Cameron, who blamed the accident on miners who smoked underground. Bill MacCulloch, Westray's training officer, acknowledged that he could produce no records of completed training and that he had assumed that the required supervised progression underground had occurred. He also testified that he had misrepresented to the board of mine examiners the hours of classroom training miners had received.

The Inquiry also felt the presence of a group that came to be known as the Westray Families Group. Legal counsel represented the group and had standing to question all Inquiry witnesses. The group exerted its influence to ensure that the testimony of the miners would be heard "at home" in Pictou County but lost an application to have the entire Inquiry take place there rather than Halifax, the provincial capital and seat of government. Media coverage of the proceedings often focused on their taut faces and passionate pleas.

Justice Richard's findings are contained in a three-volume, 750-page report entitled *The Westray Story: A Predictable Path to Disaster.* He released his report on December 1, 1997. His key conclusion was that the explosion was both predictable and preventable. He acknowledged the 20/20 vision that accompanies hindsight, but in specific, detailed, and readable prose he isolated the many factors that contributed to an explosion that cost 26 men their lives, left over 20 women widows, and over 40 children fatherless. He set the tone of his report by quoting the French sociologist and inspector general of mines Frederic Le Play (1806–1882), who said, "The most important thing to come out of a mine is the miner." In dedicating the report to the memory of the lost miners, Justice Richard, in the preface, stated, "the *Westray Story* is a complex mosaic of actions, omissions, mistakes, incompetence, apathy, cynicism, stupidity, and neglect." He noted with some dismay the overzealous political sponsorship of Westray's start-up but he clearly implicated management as the entity most responsible through its arrogance, its lack of training, its tacit and overt support of unsafe practices, and its production bonus system. Only Colin Benner and Graham Clow, an engineering consultant to Westray, were singled out for praise. Each had attended the Inquiry without subpoena and at his own expense. They were the only Curragh executives to testify after numerous attempts to subpoena Clifford Frame, Gerald Phillips, and Roger Parry failed. Benner, in particular, offered key testimony on his plans for the mine. He had struck a Mine Planning Task Force to address the safety and production problems in the mine. His goal had been to design a safe and achievable mine plan that incorporated human relations and mutual respect among workers and managers. His plans had been cut short by the explosion. Justice Richard also noted the many failures of the provincial inspectorate, describing it as "markedly derelict." He singled out inspector Albert McLean for his incompetence and lack of diligence, but did not spare his supervisors to whom McLean's failings should have been obvious. Finally, he vindicated Carl Guptill. He concluded that McLean's treatment of him was a "disservice to a miner with legitimate complaints."

EPILOGUE

In 1993 a review by Coopers and Lybrand of Nova Scotia's Labour Department's management and practices recommended sweeping changes that included staff training, development, and performance reviews. In 1997, a revised Occupational Health and Safety Act became law. In 1995, all criminal charges against Westray and mine officials were stayed for procedural reasons. In 1998, in embarrassed response to the findings of the Commission of Inquiry, the Canadian Institute of Mining, Metallurgy and Petroleum (CIM) rescinded the John T. Ryan award for safety, presented to the late Eugene Johnson on behalf of Westray on the eve of the explosion. In 1999, Alexa MacDonough, the federal leader of the New Democratic Party, introduced a private member's bill in the House of Commons to amend the Criminal Code to hold corporations, executives, and directors liable for workplace deaths. The bill died on the order paper after an election call. In 2001, the Nova Scotia Court of Appeal denied the Westray Families Group the right to sue the provincial government, concluding that such a lawsuit contravened provincial workers' compensation legislation. The Supreme Court of Canada upheld this ruling in 2002. In May of 2002, ten years after the explosion and despite all lobbying and legislative efforts, the federal government was still considering the issue of corporate criminal liability.

Albert McLean and others were fired from their positions in the Department of Labour. Donald Cameron won a provincial election in 1993 but was defeated in 1998. Shortly thereafter, he accepted a posting in Boston as Consul General to the United States. It was reported that Gerald Phillips had been charged with attempted homicide in Honduras as a result of an injury to a young man caught up in a protest to prevent a mine operation that threatened his village. A Vancouver-based mining company subsequently hired Phillips in 1998. Although Curragh Resources dissolved into bankruptcy as a result of the explosion, Clifford Frame continued to attract investors and at last report was still developing mines. Roger Parry was last known to be driving a bus in Alberta. Many miners left Pictou County and looked for work in western and northern Canada. Carl Guptill operates an aquaculture business on Nova Scotia's Eastern Shore. Some of the "Westray widows" have moved, remarried, and rebuilt their lives, while others remain frozen in loss. The bodies of 11 miners remain underground.

CASE 7

Three Roads to Innovation

Ronald A. Mitsch

Innovation is important to most companies, but it is our lifeblood at 3M. We like to keep innovation coming from all directions: by developing new technologies and new applications for them, by assessing customer needs, and by anticipating market trends in all areas in which we operate.

That presents a considerable management challenge. How do you develop all those channels for innovation and keep them open? How do you turn innovation into product successes? How do you ensure that those processes are going on, day in and day out, year in and year out?

One thing 3M discovered is that innovation does not just happen unless you make sure people know it is a top priority—and then provide them with enough freedom and resources to make it work. It certainly is not going to happen without top management's commitment to innovation as a key ingredient in the company's overall business strategy and planning.

Finally, it will not happen without a continuing reassessment of the barriers to innovation that tend to develop over time, despite management's best efforts. To keep abreast of the pace of technological change in the global marketplace, this company needs to continually enhance the prospects for successful innovation. Ultimately, the goal of innovation must be continued quality growth.

One of 3M's best-known examples of quality growth is also a classic case of how the company nurtures one channel of innovation: the development of new technologies and new applications for existing technologies.

3M scientist Arthur Fry had the freedom and found the resources in the company to develop Post-it brand Notes. At the time, he was working on a bookshelf-arranger tape. While doing research for this project, he came up with the idea for a removable, sticky-backed bookmarker as he was singing in a church choir.

Journal of Business Strategy. Sept/Oct 1990, pp. 18–21.
Reprinted with permission of Faulkner & Gray. Inc., II Penn Plaza. New York, NY 10001. 800-535-8403.

Fry began devoting more of his time to the sticky-backed pieces of paper and less and less time to the bookshelf tape, especially when he realized that the former promised to open up a whole new channel of communication. No one complained, because 3M has a company policy that encourages researchers to use 15 percent of their time on projects of their own choosing.

The adhesive Fry used was developed by another scientist, Spencer Silver, in 3M's corporate research laboratories. It was a technology available to Fry and to any other researcher in the company.

At one point, Post-it Notes faced the possibility of an early demise when an initial market test failed. But management sponsors gave it a second life. They personally took the product into the field to see how customers responded.

Freedom, sharing of technologies, and management sponsorship are all essential ingredients of the lab-to-market channel of innovation. These elements have been institutionalized in the 3M culture.

In the company's formative years, 3M's president, William L. McKnight, established policies and philosophies that have withstood the test of more than six decades. He was convinced that new product development and diversification were important to the company's continued growth. McKnight established a practice of promotion from within, encouraged individual initiative, and gave people room to grow on the job.

He also believed that failure is not fatal. Freedom to make honest mistakes is a good general policy, but it is particularly applicable to innovation. No person likes to fail, but it does happen occasionally when a company wants to grow by sponsoring new products and taking risks. The important thing is, one mistake is not a ticket to oblivion.

Out of McKnight's philosophies have developed policies like the 15 percent option, management sponsorship, and a dual-ladder system of promotion. Laboratory employees can advance up a technical ladder, as well as a management ladder, and continue with their first love—research and development.

McKnight's philosophies have been passed on from one management level to another, from one generation to another. But more recent managements have also set strategies to reinforce the innovation philosophy.

NURTURING NEW PRODUCTS

To ensure that the company's early pattern of growth through innovative new products continues, a quantifiable new products target has become part of 3M's financial goals. *The company aims to achieve at least 25 percent of its growth each year through new products developed within the last five years.* Every operating unit and its people are evaluated on their ability to reach this goal. To encourage innovation, 3M, in the past decade, has increased the ratio of spending on R&D from 4.6 percent of sales to 6.5 percent.

3M continues to expand and build on two dozen core technologies, which provide a rich source of new products. From the company's nonwoven technology have come oil sorbents; from adhesives, a new class of foam-backed tapes that can replace mechanical fasteners; from fluorochemicals, a new line of carpet stain release treatments; and from the company's oldest technology, abrasives, a line of microabrasives for finishing and polishing high-tech components.

3M does research and development on three levels. Division laboratories develop products and technologies for specific markets, doing shorter-term research for the most part. Sector laboratories work on technologies and applications the divisions will need three to ten years from now. Corporate laboratories conduct basic research that may not lead to products for ten to twenty years.

Sharing technologies and these laboratory resources across the company is of prime importance. Whereas products belong to individual operating units, technologies belong to anyone in the company who needs them. Both formal and informal forums allow technical people from all of the company's divisions and corporate and sector laboratories to share information.

Innovation is recognized in many ways. Two examples: The Golden Step program honors cross-functional teams that introduce successful new products. The Carleton Society, a hall of fame for 3M scientists, honors those who have made long-range contributions to 3M's product and technological leadership. All of these steps nurture the lab-to-market channel.

Yet, the lab-to-market channel is only one route to innovation from which the company derives its growth. Equally important are assessing customer needs and anticipating market trends. All three are increasingly intertwined and essential to innovation.

From 3M's standpoint, one of the critical issues facing the company is to continually focus activities throughout the corporation to produce quality growth. Each of our operating units is encouraged to spend more time in planning and setting priorities for product development based on customer needs and expectations.

The question is, How do we balance priority setting with a climate of freedom? Prioritizing and providing freedom to innovate cannot be trade-offs; both are needed.

Contrary to what one might think, we have found that prioritizing not only enhances productivity and the flow of the products but also affords individual researchers more time for projects of their own choosing.

Once the priorities are in place, the second critical challenge is to develop the products and bring them to market as quickly as possible. The idea is to overcome time-consuming delays and roadblocks built into traditional new product development schedules. Product development often has moved from laboratory to market in sequential order. Process development, marketing, manufacturing, packaging, and other functions become involved step-by-step. But by having all functions involved from the start, development time can be compressed dramatically.

After priorities are established, cross-functional teams are empowered by management to design and develop a product that will meet customer expectations. Several 3M divisions have set up cross-functional action teams to address their most important new product challenges.

The Occupational Health and Environmental Safety Division cut its product development time in half through this process. It substantially increased the number of major new products introduced through action teams consisting of laboratory, marketing, manufacturing, engineering, quality, packaging, and financial people.

Each team is led by a product champion, someone who believes strongly in the value of the project and is committed to making it successful. Each team also has a management sponsor who serves as a cheerleader, helps get access to needed resources, and helps teams stay on track.

A third critical issue for the 1990s is the need to satisfy customer expectations. Staying close to customers is a 3M tradition that dates back to McKnight. He believed in going into the back shops of factories to see how the company's products were being used and to get ideas for new products. The vertical organizational structure he set up has made it easy to keep 3M operating units small enough so that people, from top management on down, get to know their customers.

In the 1990s, 3M is adding some new twists to this practice. The company's divisions are doing more involved market research to pinpoint present and future customer needs. The goal is to reemphasize a longstanding tradition of regularly sending lab people into the field to help keep research focused on high-priority projects that meet customer expectations.

Cross-functional teams work closely with customers. For example, many of 3M's carpet treatments and many of its tape closures for disposable diapers were developed either in joint efforts or in close consultation with carpet-fiber makers and diaper makers.

A recent addition to 3M's line of data cartridges for off-line storage of computer data illustrates how innovation occurs in response to changing customer needs and expectations.

The company's Data Storage Products Division found that with equipment and usage changing, one computer maker needed a cartridge that operated in environmental temperature extremes, another wanted to reduce friction in tape handling, and a third needed better acoustic noise properties.

A multifunctional team developed a new line of cartridges that not only met those challenges but also operated at higher speeds. Other data cartridge users, as well as the three customers seeking special features, are benefiting from this new product line.

Another major channel of innovation—anticipating market trends—also requires the organization to stay close to the customer.

Studying industry trends and talking to customers of our X-ray films made it clear that electronic diagnostic equipment was the wave of the future. That knowledge prompted the development of one of the company's most recent new products—the 3M Laser Imager for electronic medical imaging.

The Laser Imager "writes" digital signals from CAT scanners and other electronic diagnostic equipment onto a proprietary 3M film. It gives doctors a high-quality, hard-copy image of the scanner information that they had never had before.

Development of the Laser Imager drew on existing 3M imaging, materials, and hardware technologies. The high-priority effort eventually brought together a team from five different laboratories from the United States and abroad, as well as outside optical suppliers.

The project was initiated by management, but it was the persistence and diligence of the team that proved to be the driving force once the project began.

FAILURE IS NOT FATAL

If we gain a lot from each successful program at 3M, we also learn as much or more from every failure. For example, we tried to market a line of suntan lotions that adhered to the skin without being sticky; it protected the skin even after a 30-minute swim. There was nothing wrong with the product's performance: however, we were not successful in the marketplace. The suntan lotions were competing against the products of well-established competitors who offered broad lines of well-known skin care products.

CASE 8

Southwest Airlines

For more than three years, seemingly endless rounds of litigation had thwarted the plan to launch a new Texas airline, to be known as Southwest Airlines. The Texas Aeronautics Commission approved the application in 1968, but legal challenges by incumbent airlines facing new competition for the first time in decades stretched the proceedings all the way to the Texas Supreme Court, which unanimously ruled in Southwest's favor on May 13, 1970.

When the U.S. Supreme Court upheld the Texas court ruling in December, Southwest's founders believed the courtroom battles lay behind them. However, the delays and litigation nearly wrecked Southwest's finances. The company had long since exhausted its original $543,000 in capital, but was able to continue the litigation only because its attorney, determined not to lose, agreed to absorb the legal costs himself.

The lawyer was Herb Kelleher, a transplanted New Jersey native who came to San Antonio to practice law. Kelleher had first been introduced to the idea of creating a new airline by his client. Rollin King, who had an idea that a commercial airline serving Texas's three largest markets might be able to make money. To illustrate his idea, King drew a triangle on a cocktail napkin, with the corners representing the Texas cities of Dallas, Houston, and San Antonio. Initially, Kelleher was skeptical, but as the discussion progressed, so did his interest. By one account, Kelleher's ultimate resolve was cemented with the words, "Rollin, you're crazy. Let's do it." Kelleher agreed to do the initial legal work for a 25 percent discount, but he wound up doing much of the work for free.

In exploring the feasibility of the project, Kelleher's research turned up some intriguing aspects of King's seemingly outlandish idea. Kelleher knew that the Civil Aeronautics Board, the federal regulatory body that had jurisdiction over the airlines, had not authorized the creation of a new major airline since before World War II. Indeed, the major function of the CAB was to prevent competition. But the CAB's jurisdiction extended only to interstate airlines—those with routes extending across state lines. By flying only within the state of Texas, Southwest might be able to avoid CAB jurisdiction.

In fact, a precedent existed. In California, Pacific Southwest Airlines (PSA) had flown for years as an intrastate airline. By avoiding the suffocating regulation of the CAB, PSA was able to offer low fares and frequent flights and had achieved great popularity with its customers. With the stimulus of competition, the California airline market had become the most highly developed in the world. Why couldn't Texas support the same kind of service?

On the competitive front, King and Kelleher were familiar with the sorry state of air service in Texas. Fares were high, flights were often late, and schedules frequently were dictated by the availability of aircraft after flying more lucrative, longer-haul flights where the CAB-regulated airlines made their real money. Short-haul, intrastate service was merely an afterthought, existing primarily as a tail-end segment of a longer flight coming in from New York or Minneapolis, for example.

Kelleher concluded that Texas was ripe for an airline that would focus on the intrastate passenger, offering good, reliable service at a reduced fare and on a schedule designed to meet the needs of local travelers rather than passengers coming in from far-off points.

After three years of litigation, Southwest still had no airplanes, no management team, no employees, and no money. But when the U.S. Supreme Court ruled in its favor, the founders quickly went to work and hired M. Lamar Muse as Southwest's president in January 1971. Muse was a wily veteran of the airline business, trained as an accountant, but possessed the brash and daring temperament of an entrepreneur.

With the certificate from the Texas Aeronautics Commission as Southwest's only valuable asset and its bank account down to $142, Muse somehow managed to raise $1.25 million through the sale of promissory notes. For his management

Southwest Airlines. *Spirit*, June, 1996. Reprinted courtesy of Southwest Airlines *Spirit*.

team, Muse put together a group of industry veterans, most of whom had either retired from or been cut loose by old-line airlines. Muse is reported to have claimed that all the top people he hired had been fired by other airlines. "I figured the other airlines were doing such a lousy job that anybody they fired had to be pretty good."

As luck would have it, a slow market caused Boeing to have three new 737–200 aircraft sitting on the tarmac. Southwest recognized the 737 as the perfect aircraft for the mission it had in mind. The 737's modern, fuel-efficient, twin-engine configuration would allow highly reliable, efficient, and economical operation in Texas' short-haul intrastate markets. Boeing executives accommodated the cash-strapped Texans by agreeing to finance 90 percent of the cost of the new planes—unheard-of terms for such desirable aircraft.

With airplanes secured and crews hired, Southwest's long-awaited inaugural flight finally seemed at hand. But the entrenched airlines hadn't quit. First, they asked the CAB to exercise its jurisdiction to block the new competition in Texas. The CAB declined to interfere, throwing out the complaints by Braniff and Texas International on June 16, 1971—just two days before Southwest's first scheduled flight. Within hours, lawyers for Braniff and Texas International won a restraining order from a friendly district judge in Austin, banning Southwest from beginning service.

Southwest's leaders were simultaneously outraged and crestfallen. For more than three years, they had fought and won the legal battles. Now, on the eve of seeing their dream come to fruition, they faced the prospect of starting all over.

Kelleher, having left his San Antonio law office without a toothbrush or change of clothes, was in Dallas when he heard of the Austin judge's restraining order. An already rumpled-looking Kelleher headed to Austin, hitching a ride on a proving flight of one of Southwest's new and brightly painted red, orange, and desert-gold 737s. In Austin, Kelleher located Texas Supreme Court Justice Tom Reavely, the man who had written the court's unanimous 1970 opinion authorizing Southwest to fly. Kelleher persuaded Reavely to convene an extraordinary session of the Supreme Court the next day.

Kelleher worked through the night to prepare his papers and arguments for the court. The next day, June 17, 1971, sleepless and wearing the same well-worn suit, he appeared before the full Supreme Court, asking again that Southwest be allowed to take flight.

Finally, the phone in Muse's office rang. It was Kelleher. The Supreme Court not only had heard the arguments, it already had ruled. The district court's restraining order was thrown out. Southwest was free to start service the next day.

"What do I do if the sheriff shows up tomorrow with another restraining order?" Muse asked.

"Leave tire tracks on his back," Kelleher replied.

As 1973 began, Southwest had operated for a year and a half without approaching profitability. Start-up capital, including proceeds of a 1971 stock offering, was almost depleted. A fourth aircraft had been acquired, but it had to be sold to raise cash. Almost miraculously, the schedule had been maintained when Southwest employees, under the leadership of vice president Bill Franklin, invented the "10-minute turnaround," enabling a plane to be fully unloaded and reloaded in 10 minutes at the gate. With the increased productivity from the 10-minute turnaround, Southwest's management found that three planes could do the work of four. Thus was borne one of the precepts of Southwest's success—a plane doesn't make money sitting on the ground.

Still, cash was dwindling, and profitability remained a mere dream. The Dallas–Houston run was doing okay, but loads on the Dallas–San Antonio route were poor, draining the airline of its remaining cash. Muse decided to try a bold move. On January 22, 1973, he cut fares in half, to $13, on the Dallas–San Antonio route—every seat, every flight, no restrictions. What followed was one of the most widely reported and publicly watched conflicts in the history of the airline industry.

Braniff struck back, running full-page ads announcing a "Get Acquainted" fare of $13 between Dallas and Houston. Braniff's plan meant that Southwest would surely go broke if it matched the $13 fare between Dallas and Houston, Southwest's only profitable route.

Southwest's leaders frantically searched for a response. Even if they had known at the time that Braniff and Texas International ultimately would be convicted of federal criminal antitrust violations for their tactics, it would have provided little solace.

The judicial system's ultimate judgment was years away. Insolvency was only days away.

The spark of inspiration that saved Southwest from certain liquidation finally came. The airline would give anybody who paid the full $26 fare a bottle of premium liquor—Chivas Regal, Crown Royal, or Smirnoff. But passengers could pay the $13 fare if they preferred.

Southwest vice president Franklin was dispatched to get a truckload of liquor delivered to the airport. To accommodate nondrinkers, Southwest vice president Jess Coker located a stash of leather ice buckets that hadn't sold well at Christmas and bought thousands of them. Somebody asked if it would be legal. Muse said to let Kelleher take care of that.

Muse then decided to write his company's reply to Braniff, which would be carried in Southwest's own full-page ads. After Kelleher removed the profanities and polished up Muse's initial draft, the ad ran under the headline "Nobody's going to shoot Southwest out of the sky for a lousy $13."

Suddenly, public attention was riveted on the air war over Texas. It became front-page news, the lead story on television and radio. For two months, Southwest was the largest liquor distributor in Texas. It was a defining moment, one in which people decided their allegiances for a lifetime.

The overwhelming response to Southwest's underdog crusade produced the first quarterly profit in the company's history and made 1973 Southwest's first profitable year.

"Tell the mayor that Southwest Airlines will be the best partner the city of Chicago ever had," Kelleher is saying into the telephone. It is November 1991, and Kelleher's face betrays a hint of tension and excitement as he makes his pitch to one of the mayor's closest advisers. For years, Southwest's efforts to expand in Chicago were stymied because of the unavailability of gate facilities at Midway Airport.

Southwest had grown beyond its Texas roots. With the passage of the federal Airline Deregulation Act of 1978, the end of the CAB's stranglehold on competition in interstate markets was assured. Southwest promptly became an interstate airline, flying first from Houston to New Orleans in January 1979. Although expansion out of Dallas's Love Field was limited by a 1979 congressional enactment known as the Wright Amendment, named for then-Congressman Jim Wright, who represented Fort Worth and sought to protect the growth of Dallas–Fort Worth International Airport, Southwest nonetheless found abundant opportunities for expansion outside Texas.

Kelleher had moved from the role of lawyer to executive, first becoming acting president in 1978 when Muse resigned after a disagreement with the board of directors, and then becoming full-time president and chief executive officer in September 1981 when Howard Putman resigned to become president of Braniff. Expansion in the West had proved highly successful, although not free of competitive challenges. Using Phoenix as the major base for its westward push, Southwest penetrated most of the major markets in California and the southwestern United States during the eighties and early nineties.

But Chicago had been a particularly frustrating situation. Although Southwest offered 43 flights out of its four overcrowded gates, the demand existed for many more flights, to more destinations. Southwest could not expand to meet the demand because all remaining gates were leased—mostly to hometown favorite Midway Airlines. However, rumors now were swirling that Midway Airlines was about to shut down. Southwest had attempted to obtain leases on some of the gates in return for a cash payment and/or loan that might allow Midway Airlines to remain open. But Midway had transferred leases on all the gates to Northwest Airlines, in anticipation of an acquisition of the entire airline by Northwest. When Northwest announced on November 13, 1991, that it was abandoning plans to acquire the airline, Midway barely had enough cash to finish out the day.

Kelleher desperately wanted access to the Midway gates, which would now sit empty if Midway Airlines shut down. Although the lease belonged to Northwest, Jim Parker, Southwest's creative General Counsel, knew of a loophole—the city retained the right to permit another airline to use the gates any time they were not being used by the primary tenant. If Midway shut down that night, as seemed likely, Parker reasoned there was no way Northwest could occupy all of Midway's gates by the next day. Kelleher arranged a 9 o'clock meeting the next morning in Chicago between Southwest's representatives and top advisers to Mayor Richard M. Daley.

When Southwest's delegation arrived at their Chicago hotel at 1:00 A.M., live TV reports from Midway Airport were confirming the shutdown of Midway Airlines. While Southwest's lawyers planned their strategy that night, the airline's Facilities and Technical Services departments swung into action, diverting deliveries and pulling computer equipment, backwall signage, podium inserts, and hold-room chairs from other cities throughout the system, and shipped them to Chicago. Everyone knew that time was of the essence.

The entire city of Chicago was concerned about the shutdown of Midway Airlines. Not only were 4,300 employees thrown out of work, but serious concern existed about the future of Midway Airport itself, a longtime economic engine of the south side of Chicago. When Southwest's representatives met with the city's leaders at 9:00 A.M., they told the mayor's aides that Southwest Airlines was prepared to spend at least $20 million for the development and promotion of the airport and commit to a program of substantial expansion at Midway Airport if the city would exercise its authority to assure Southwest access to the facilities necessary to effect its growth plan. Negotiations continued throughout the day, as Southwest lawyers pointed to the airline's financial stability, record of developing underutilized airports, outstanding record of customer satisfaction, excellent employee relations, and commitment to community involvement as reasons why the city should choose Southwest over any competitor as its partner for the redevelopment of Midway Airport.

The people of Chicago didn't know much about Southwest Airlines, but apparently they were impressed. At mid-afternoon, the mayor's press aide entered the negotiating room and asked, "You guys have a deal yet? The mayor is having a press conference at 3:30." A letter of agreement and press release were quickly hammered out, and the deal was done.

Taking a side trip on his way into the press conference, Parker called Calvin Phillips, his contact from the Facilities Department, who had arrived in Chicago along with a dedicated band of volunteers from the Technical Services Department.

"Where's the equipment?" Parker hurriedly inquired.

"It's in Chicago, in a warehouse near the airport."

"We have a letter of agreement. Let's go."

"What if somebody from the department of aviation or Northwest tries to stop us?"

"Tell them to talk to the mayor," Parker replied.

When Mayor Daley announced Southwest Airlines as Chicago's new partner for the redevelopment of Midway Airport, a reporter inquired when he could expect to see some sign of Southwest's growth at the airport. A Southwest spokesman stepped forward, "If you go to the airport, you can see it right now." Daley beamed as reporters scurried for the door to head to the airport. News reports that night were filled with pictures of Midway Airport in transition, with Southwest workers toiling through the night to install Southwest signage and equipment at gate after gate.

A meeting was arranged the next day between representatives of Southwest and Northwest, the titular leaseholder.

"How far have your troops advanced?" the Northwest representative asked.

"I think they stopped at the edge of the A Concourse," Parker replied.

A deal ultimately was negotiated, whereby Northwest relinquished its claim to the former Midway Airlines gates and the city of Chicago entered into a direct lease with Southwest, assuring Southwest's ability to expand in Chicago and the Midwest.

Kelleher sits in his windowless office, contemplating his company's upcoming expansion into Florida. It is January 1996, and Southwest Airlines is approaching the twenty-fifth anniversary of that day in 1971 when Kelleher told Muse to leave tire tracks on the sheriff's back, if necessary.

Southwest's fleet has grown from three 737–200s to more than 220 modern Boeing 737 aircraft. So strong is Southwest's loyalty to the 737 that it is the only major U.S. airline with an all-Boeing fleet. The little airline that had to ask for 90 percent financing from Boeing in 1971 has served as the launch customer for three new models of the 737: the 737–300, now the workhorse of the fleet, the 737–500, and the upcoming 737–700, which will be delivered in 1997.

Since recording its first profit in 1973, Southwest is about to report its 23rd consecutive year of profitability. The halls and walls of Southwest's headquarters are filled with mementos of employee celebrations and accomplishments. The "Triple Crown" trophy sits proudly in the lobby, commemorating Southwest's unparalleled record of having the best on-time performance record, fewest mishandled bags, and fewest customer complaints, according to U.S. Department of Transportation consumer reports for four consecutive years. Southwest has become so successful that a 1993 U.S. Department of Transportation study described Southwest Airlines as "the principal driving force behind dramatic fundamental changes" in the U.S. airline industry.

The walls also include mementos of other innumerable achievements—the 1993 book by Robert Levering and Milton Moskowitz naming Southwest Airlines one of the 10 best companies to work for in America; the Air Transport World designation of Southwest as "Airline of the Year" for 1991; the *Condé Nast Traveler* magazine recognition of Southwest as the safest airline in the world for its accident-free history; the 1994 *Fortune* magazine cover with a zany picture of Kelleher and the caption, "Is Herb Kelleher America's Best CEO?"

But Kelleher is intense, uncharacteristically humorless, as he contemplates his company's upcoming expansion into Florida, a market he has coveted for more than a decade. He knows the competition will be intense, and his mind flashes back to past battles. Florida in 1996 bears striking similarities to California in 1989. Air fares are high, intrastate service poor, and the geography of the state lends itself to a need for high-frequency, low-fare, reliable air service between major metropolitan areas. In California, Southwest's one-time role model, PSA, and its in-state competitor, Air Cal, long ago lost their way and were swallowed up by megacarriers who cared little for short-haul intrastate markets, leaving a vacuum that Southwest gladly filled. Southwest's friendly low-fare service was quickly embraced by Californians with such enthusiasm that Southwest soon carried a majority of California's intrastate passengers.

The West Coast had become intensely competitive, however, United, the largest airline in the world, targeted Southwest as an unwanted intruder, and articulated a goal of eliminating, or at least slowing, Southwest's expansion. To this end, United created its own "airline within an airline," designed to offer low fares and fly largely in markets served by Southwest. In anticipation of the massive resources that could be thrown into the battle by United, an airline many times Southwest's size, Southwest had acquired Salt Lake City–based Morris Air, and launched a major expansion of its own into the Northwest.

After 15 months of competition, though, Southwest seemed to be at least holding its own. Despite a huge influx of new competitive service, Southwest's California traffic was actually up. United officials were no longer maintaining even a pretense that the effort to erode Southwest's base of loyal customers had been successful. To the contrary, Southwest was about to report its most profitable year ever.

Suddenly, a Southwest executive interrupts Kelleher's concentration. "Herb, you're not going to believe what one of our customers just told us."

"What?"

"Guess what happens if you pick up your phone and call 1-800-SOUTHWEST?"

"You mean 1-800-1 FLY SWA. That's our reservations number."

"I know, But guess what happens if you call 1-800-SOUTHWEST?"

Kelleher walks over to his telephone and dutifully dials the number. The answer comes after four rings.

"Shuttle by United reservations. This is Todd."

"What?" Kelleher exclaims in dismay.

"May I help you?"

"Uh. No, thanks."

After a moment of stunned silence, Kelleher explodes in laughter. The world's largest airline has been reduced to impersonating Southwest in an attempt to hold onto its West Coast passengers. An exquisite look of satisfaction settles over Kelleher's face as the laughter subsides.

A moment later, the look of intensity is back.

"Let's talk about Florida."

CASE 9
Philips NV

Charles W. L. Hill

Established in 1891, the Dutch company Philips NV is one of the world's largest electronics enterprises. Its business is grouped into four main divisions: lighting, consumer electronics, professional products (computers, telecommunications, and medical equipment), and components (including chips). In each of these areas it ranks alongside the likes of Matsushita, General Electric, Sony, and Siemens as a global competitor. In the late 1980s, the company had several hundred subsidiaries in 60 countries, it operated manufacturing plants in more than 40 countries, it employed approximately 300,000 people, and it manufactured thousands of different products. However, despite its global reach by 1990, Philips was a company in deep trouble. After a decade of deteriorating performance, in 1990 Philips lost $2.2 billion on revenues of $28 billion. A major reason seems to have been the inability of Philips to adapt to the changing competitive conditions in the global electronics industry during the 1970s and 1980s.

PHILIPS' TRADITIONAL ORGANIZATION

To trace the roots of Philips' current troubles, one has to go back to World War II. Until then, the foreign activities of Philips had been run out of its head office in Eindhoven. However, during World War II the Netherlands was occupied by Germany. Cut off from their home base, Philips' various national organizations began to operate independently. In essence, each major national organization developed into a self-contained company with its own manufacturing, marketing, and R&D functions.

Following the war, top management felt that the company could be most successfully rebuilt through its national organizations. There were several reasons for this belief. First, high trade barriers made it logical that self-contained national organizations be established in each major national market. Second, it was felt that strong national organizations would allow Philips to be responsive to local demands in each country in which it competed. And third, given the substantial autonomy that the various national organizations had gained during the war, top management felt that reestablishing centralized control might prove difficult and yield few benefits.

At the same time, top management felt the need for some centralized control over product policy and R&D in order to achieve some coordination between national organizations. Its response was to create a number of worldwide product divisions (of which there were fourteen by the mid-1980s). In theory, basic R&D and product development policy were the responsibilities of the product divisions, whereas the national organizations were responsible for day-to-day operations in a particular country. Product strategy in a given country was meant to be determined jointly by consultation between the responsible national organization and the product divisions. It was the national organizations that implemented strategy.

Another major feature of Philips' organization was the duumvirate form of management. In most national organizations, top-management responsibilities and authority were shared by two managers—one responsible for "commercial affairs" and another responsible for "technical activities." This form of management had its origins in the company's founders—Anton and Gerard Philips. Anton was a salesman and Gerard an engineer. Throughout the company there seemed to be a vigorous, informal competition between technical and sales managers, with each attempting to outperform the other. Anton once noted:

> The technical management and the sales management competed to outperform each other. Production tried to produce so much that sales would not be able to get rid of it; sales tried to sell so much that the factory would not be able to keep up. [Aguilar and Yoshino, 1987]

The top decision-making and policy-making body in the company was a 10-person board of management. While board members all shared general management responsibility, they typically

Charles W. L. Hill, University of Washington. Reprinted with permission.

maintained a special interest in one of the functional areas of the company (for example, R&D, manufacturing, marketing). Traditionally, most of the members of the management board were Dutch and had come up through the Eindhoven bureaucracy, although most had extensive foreign postings, often as a top manager in one of the company's national organizations.

ENVIRONMENTAL CHANGE

From the 1960s onward, a number of significant changes took place in Philips' competitive environment that were to profoundly affect the company. First, due to the efforts of the General Agreement on Tariffs and Trade (GATT), trade barriers fell worldwide. In addition in Philips' home base, Europe, the emergence of the European Economic Community, of which the Netherlands was an early member, led to a further reduction in trade barriers between the countries of Western Europe.

Second, during the 1960s and 1970s a number of new competitors emerged in Japan. Taking advantage of the success of GATT in lowering trade barriers, the Japanese companies produced most of their output at home and then exported to the rest of the world. The resulting economies of scale allowed them to drive down unit costs below those achieved by Western competitors such as Philips that manufactured in multiple locations. This significantly increased competitive pressures in most of the business areas where Philips competed.

Third, due to technological changes, the cost of R&D and manufacturing increased rapidly. The introduction of transistors and then integrated circuits called for significant capital expenditures in production facilities—often running into hundreds of millions of dollars. To realize scale economies, substantial levels of output had to be achieved. Moreover, the pace of technological change was declining and product life cycles were shortening. This gave companies in the electronics industry less time to recoup their capital investments before new-generation products came along.

Finally, as the world moved from a series of fragmented national markets toward a single global market, uniform global standards for electronic equipment were beginning to emerge. This standardization showed itself most clearly in the videocassette recorder business, where three standards initially battled for dominance—the Betamax standard produced by Sony, the VHS standard produced by Matsushita, and the V2000 standard produced by Philips. The VHS standard was the one most widely accepted by consumers, and the others were eventually abandoned. For Philips and Sony, both of which had invested substantially in their own standard, this was a significant defeat. Philips's attempt to establish its V2000 format as an industry standard was effectively killed off by the decision of its own North American national organization, over the objections of Eindhoven, to manufacture according to the VHS standard.

ORGANIZATIONAL AND STRATEGIC CHANGE

By the early 1980s Philips realized that, if it was to survive, it would have to restructure its business radically. Its cost structure was high due to the amount of duplication across national organizations, particularly in the area of manufacturing. Moreover, as the V2000 incident demonstrated, the company's attempts to compete effectively were being hindered by the strength and autonomy of its national organizations.

The first attempt at change came in 1982 when Wisse Dekker was appointed CEO. Dekker quickly pushed for manufacturing rationalization, creating international production centers that served a number of national organizations and closing many small inefficient plants. He also pushed Philips to enter into more collaborative arrangements with other electronics firms in order to share the costs and risks of developing new products. In addition, Dekker accelerated a trend that had already begun within the company to move away from the dual leadership arrangement within national organizations (commercial and technical), replacing this arrangement with a single general manager. Furthermore, Dekker tried to "tilt" Philips' matrix away from national organizations by creating a corporate council where the heads of product divisions would join the heads of the national organizations to discuss issues of importance to both. At the same time, he gave the product divisions more responsibility to determine companywide research and manufacturing activities.

In 1986, Dekker was succeeded by Cor van de Klugt. One of van de Klugt's first actions was to specify that profitability was to be the central criterion for evaluating performance within Philips. The product divisions were given primary responsibility for achieving profits. This was followed in late 1986 by his termination of the U.S. Philips trust, which had been given control of Philips's North American operations during World War II and which still maintained control as of 1986. By terminating the trust, van de Klugt in theory reestablished Eindhoven's control over the North American subsidiary. Then, in May 1987, van de Klugt announced a major restructuring of Philips. He designated four product divisions—lighting, consumer electronics, components, and telecommunications and data systems—as "core divisions," the implication being that other activities would be sold off. At the same time he reduced the size of the management board. Its policy-making responsibility was devolved to a new group management committee, comprising the remaining board members plus the heads of the core product divisions. No heads of national organizations were appointed to this body, thereby further tilting power within Philips away from the national organizations toward the product divisions.

Despite these changes, Philips' competitive position continued to deteriorate. Many outside observers attributed this slide to the dead hand of the huge head office bureaucracy at Eindhoven (which comprised more than 3,000 people in 1989). They argued that while van de Klugt had changed the organizational chart, much of this change was superficial. Real power, they argued, still lay with the Eindhoven bureaucracy and their allies in the national organizations. In support of this view, they pointed out that since 1986 Philips' work force had declined by less than 10 percent, instead of the 30 percent reduction that many analysts were calling for.

Alarmed by a 1989 loss of $1.06 billion, the board forced van de Klugt to resign in May 1990. He was replaced by Jan Timmer. Timmer quickly announced that he would cut Philips's worldwide work force by 10,000, to 283,000, and launch a $1.4 billion restructuring. Investors were unimpressed—most of them thought that the company needed to lose 40,000–50,000 jobs—and reacted by knocking the share price down by 7 percent. Since then, however, Timmer had made some progress. In mid-1991, he sold off Philips's minicomputer division—which at the time was losing $1 million per day—to Digital Equipment. He also announced plans to reduce costs by $1.2 billion by cutting the work force by 55,000. In addition, he entered into a strategic alliance with Matsushita, the Japanese electronic giant, to manufacture and market the Digital Compact Cassette (DCC). Developed by Philips and due to be introduced in late 1992, the DCC reproduces the sound of a compact disc on a tape. The DCC's great selling point is that buyers will be able to play their old analog tape cassettes on the new system. The DCC's chief rival is a portable compact disc system from Sony called Mini-Disk. Many observers see a replay of the classic battle between the VHS and Betamax video recorder standards in the coming battle between the DCC and the Mini-Disk. If the DCC wins it could be the remaking of Philips.

REFERENCES

Aguilar, F. J., and M. Y. Yoshino. "The Philips Group: 1987." Harvard Business School, Case #388–050.

Anonymous. "Philips Fights the Flab." *The Economist,* April 7, 1992, pp. 73–74.

Bartlett, C. A., and S. Ghoshal. *Managing Across Borders: The Transnational Solution.* Boston, Mass.: Harvard Business School Press, 1989.

Kapstein, J., and J. Levine. "A Would-Be World Beater Takes a Beating." *Business Week,* July 16, 1990, pp. 41–42.

Levine, J. "Philips's Big Gamble." *Business Week,* August 5, 1991, pp. 34–36.

CASE 10

"Ramrod" Stockwell

Charles Perrow

The Benson Metal Company employs about 1,500 people, is listed on the stock exchange, and has been in existence for many decades. It makes a variety of metals that are purchased by manufacturers or specialized metal firms. It is one of the five or six leading firms in the specialty steel industry. This industry produces steels in fairly small quantities with a variety of characteristics. Orders tend to be in terms of pounds rather than tons, although a 1,000-pound order is not unusual. For some of the steels, 100 pounds is an average order.

The technology for producing specialty steels in the firm is fairly well established, but there is still a good deal of guesswork, skill, and even some "black magic" involved. Small changes are made in the ingredients going into the melting process, often amounting to the addition of a tiny bit of expensive alloying material in order to produce varieties of specialty steels. Competitors can analyze one another's products and generally produce the same product without too much difficulty, although there are some secrets. There are also important variations stemming from the type of equipment used to melt, cog, roll, and finish the steel.

In the period that we are considering, the Benson Company and some of its competitors were steadily moving into more sophisticated and technically more difficult steels, largely for the aerospace industry. The aerospace products were far more difficult to make, required more research skills and metallurgical analysis, and required more "delicate" handling in all stages of production, even though the same basic equipment was involved. Furthermore, they were marketed in a different fashion. They were produced to the specifications of government subcontractors, and government inspectors were often in the plant to watch all stages of production. One firm might be able to produce a particular kind of steel that another firm could not produce even though it had tried. These steels were considerably more expensive than the specialty steels, and failures to meet specifications resulted in more substantial losses for the company. At the time of the study about 20 percent of the cash value output was in aerospace metals.

The chairman, Fred Benson, had been president (managing director) of the company for two decades before moving up to this position. He is an elderly man but has a strong will and is much revered in the company for having built it up to its present size and influence. The president, Tom Hollis, has been in office for about four years; he was formerly the sales director and has worked closely with Fred Benson over many years. Hollis has three or four years to go before expected retirement. His assistant, Joe Craig, had been a sales manager in one of the smaller offices. It is the custom of this firm to pick promising people from middle management and put them in the "assistant-to" position for perhaps a year to groom them for higher offices in their division. For some time these people had come from sales, and they generally went back as managers of large districts, from whence they might be promoted to a sales manager position in the main office.

Dick Benson, the executive vice president (roughly, general manager), is the son of Fred Benson. He is generally regarded as being willing, fairly competent, and decent, but weak and still much under his father's thumb. Traditionally, the executive vice president became president. Dick is not thought to be up to that job, but it is believed that he will get it anyway.

Ramsey Stockwell, vice president of production, had come into the organization as an experienced engineer about six years before. He rose rather rapidly to his present position. Rob Bronson, vice president of sales, succeeded Dick Benson after Benson had a rather short term as vice president of sales. Alan Carswell, the vice president of research, has a doctorate in metallurgy and some patents in his name, but he is not considered an aggressive researcher or an aggressive in-fighter in the company.

THE PROBLEM

When the research team studied Benson Metal, there were the usual problems of competition and price-cutting, the difficulties with the new aerospace metals, and inadequate plant facilities for a growing industry and company. However, the problem that particularly interests us here concerned the vice president of production, Ramsey Stockwell. He was regarded as a very competent production man. His loyalty to the company was unquestioned. He managed to keep outdated facilities operating and still had been able to push through the construction of quite modern facilities in the finishing phases of the production process. But he was in trouble with his own staff and with other divisions of the company, principally sales.

It was widely noted that Stockwell failed to delegate authority to his subordinates. A steady stream of people came into his office asking for permission for this and that or bringing questions to him. People who took some action on their own could be bawled out unmercifully at times. At other times they were left on their own because of the heavy demands on Stockwell's time, given his frequent attention to details in some matters, particularly those concerning schedules and priorities. He "contracted" the lines of authority by giving orders directly to a manager or even to a head foreman rather than by working through the intermediate levels. This violated the chain of command, left managers uninformed, and reduced their authority. It was sometimes noted that he had good men under him but did not always let them do their jobs.

The key group of production men rarely met in a group unless it was to be bawled out by Stockwell. Coordinating committees and the like existed mainly on paper.

More serious perhaps than this was the relationship to sales. Rob Bronson was widely regarded as an extremely bright, capable, likable, and up-and-coming manager. The sales division performed like a well-oiled machine but also had the enthusiasm and flashes of brilliance that indicated considerable adaptability. Morale was high, and identification with the company was complete. However, sales personnel found it quite difficult to get reliable information from production as to delivery dates or even what stage in the process a product was in.

Through long tradition, they were able to get special orders thrust into the work flow when they wanted to, but they often could not find out what this was going to do to normal orders, or even how disruptive this might be. The reason was that Stockwell would not allow production people to give any but the most routine information to sales personnel. In fact, because of the high centralization of authority and information in production, production personnel often did not know themselves. "Ramrod" Stockwell knew, and the only way to get information out of him was to go up the sales line to Rob Bronson. The vice president of sales could get the information from the vice president of production.

But Bronson had more troubles than just not wanting to waste his time by calling Stockwell about status reports. At the weekly top-management meeting, which involved all personnel from the vice presidential level and above, and frequently a few from below that level, Bronson would continually ask Stockwell whether something or other could be done. Stockwell always said that he thought it could be. He could not be pressed for any better estimations, and he rarely admitted that a job was, in fact, not possible. Even queries from President Tom Hollis could not evoke accurate forecasts from Stockwell. Consequently, planning on the part of sales and other divisions was difficult, and failures on the part of production were many because it always vaguely promised so much. Stockwell was willing to try anything, and worked his head off at it, but the rest of the group knew that many of these attempts would fail.

While the men under Stockwell resented the way he took over their jobs at times and the lack of information available to them about other aspects of production, they were loyal to him. They admired his ability and they knew that he fought off the continual pressure of sales to slip in special orders, change schedules, or blame production for rejects. "Sales gets all the glory here," said one. "At the semiannual company meeting last week, the chairman of the board and the managing director of the company couldn't compliment sales enough for their good work, but there was only the stock 'well done' for production; 'well done given the trying circumstances.' Hell, Sales is what is trying us." The annual reports over the years credited sales for the good years and referred to equipment failures, crowded or poor production facilities, and the like in bad years. But it was also true that problems still remained even after Stockwell finally managed to pry some new production facilities out of the board of directors.

Stockwell was also isolated socially from the right group of top personnel: He tended to work later than most, had rougher manners, was less concerned with cultural activities, and rarely played golf. He occasionally relaxed with the manager of aerospace sales, who, incidentally, was the only high-level sales person who tended to defend Stockwell. "Ramrod's a rough diamond; I don't know that we ought to try to polish him," he sometimes said.

But polishing was in the minds of many. "Great production man—amazing when he gets out of that mill. But he doesn't know how to handle people. He won't delegate; he won't tell us when he is in trouble with something; he builds a fence around his men, preventing easy exchange," said the president. "Bullheaded as hell—he was good a few years ago, but I would never give him the job again," said the chairman of the board. He disagreed with the president that Stockwell could change. "You can't change people's personalities, least of all production men." "He's in a tough position," said the vice president of sales, "and he has to be able to get his men to work with him, not against him, and we all have to work together in today's market. I just wish he would not be so uptight."

A year or so before, the president had approached Stockwell about taking a couple of weeks off and joining a leadership training session. Stockwell would have nothing to do with it and was offended. The president waited a few months, then announced that he had arranged for the personnel manager and each of the directors to attend successive four-day T-group sessions run by a well-known organization. This had been agreed on at one of the directors' meetings, though no one had taken it very seriously. One by one, the directors came back with marked enthusiasm for the program. "It's almost as if they had our company in mind when they designed it," said one. Some started having evening and weekend sessions with their staff, occasionally using the personnel manager, who had had more experience with this than the others. Stockwell was scheduled to be the last one to attend the four-day session, but he canceled at the last minute—there were too many crises in the plant, he said, to go off that time. In fact, several had developed over the previous few weeks.

That did it, as far as the other vice presidents were concerned. They got together themselves, then with the president and executive vice president, and said that they had to get to the bottom of the problem. A top-level group session should be held to discuss the tensions that were accumulating. The friction between production and sales was spilling over into other areas as well, and the morale of management in general was suffering. They acknowledged that they put a lot of pressure on production, and were probably at fault in this or that matter, and thus a session would do all the directors good, not just Stockwell. The president hesitated. Stockwell, he felt, would just ride it out. Besides, he added, the "Old Man" (chairman of the board) was skeptical of such techniques. The executive vice president was quite unenthusiastic. It was remarked later that Stockwell had never recognized his official authority, and thus young Dick feared any open confrontation.

But events overtook the plan of the vice president. A first-class crisis had developed involving a major order for their oldest and best customer, and an emergency top-management meeting was called, which included several of their subordinates. Three in particular were involved: Joe Craig, assistant to the president, who knows well the problems at the plant in his role as troubleshooter for the managing director; Sandy Falk, vice president of personnel, who is sophisticated about leadership training programs and in a position to watch a good bit of the bickering at the middle and lower levels between sales and production; Bill Bletchford, manager of finishing, who is loyal to Stockwell and who has the most modern-equipped phase of the production process and the most to do with sales. It was in his department that the jam had occurred, due to some massive scheduling changes at the rolling phase and to the failure of key equipment.

In the meeting, the ground is gone over thoroughly. With their backs to the wall, the two production men, behaving somewhat uncharacteristically in an open meeting, charge sales with devious tactics for introducing special orders and for acting on partial and misinterpreted information from a foreman. Joe Craig knows, and admits, that the specialty A sales manager made promises to the customer without checking with the vice president of sales, who could have checked with Stockwell. "He was right," says vice president Bronson, "I can't spend all my time calling Ramsey about status reports; if Harrison can't find out from production on an official basis, he has to do the best he can." Ramsey Stockwell, after his forceful outburst about misleading information through devious tactics, falls into a hardened silence, answering only direct questions, and then briefly. The manager of finishing and the specialty A sales manager start working on each other. Sandy Falk, of personnel, knows they have been enemies for years, so he intervenes as best he can. The vice president of research, Carswell, a reflective man, often worried about elusive dimensions of company problems, then calls a halt with the following speech:

> You're all wrong and you're all right. I have heard bits and pieces of this fracas a hundred times over the last two or three years, and it gets worse each year. The facts of this damn case don't matter unless all you want is to score points with your opponents. What is wrong is something with the whole team here. I don't know what it is, but I know that we have to radically rethink our relations with one another. Three years ago this kind of thing rarely happened; now it is starting to happen all the time. And it is a time when we can't afford it. There is no more growth in our bread-and-butter line, specialty steels. The money, and the growth, is in aerospace; we all know that. Without aerospace we will just stand still. Maybe that's part of it. But maybe Ramsey's part of it too; this crisis is over specialty steel, and more of them seem to concern that than aerospace, so it can't be the product shift or that only. Some part of it has to be people, and you're on the hot seat, Ramsey.

Carswell let that sink in, then went on.

> Or maybe it's something more than even these . . . . It is not being pulled together at the top, or maybe, the old way of pulling it together won't work anymore. I'm talking about you, Tom [Hollis], as well as Fred [Benson, the chairman of the board, who did not attend these meetings] and Dick [the executive vice president, and heir apparent]. I don't know what it is, here are Ramsey and Rob at loggerheads; neither of them are fools, and both of them are working their heads off. Maybe the problem is above their level.

There is a long silence. Assume you break the silence with your own analysis. What would that be?

CASE 11

Rondell Data Corporation

John A. Seeger

"God damn it, he's done it again?" Frank Forbus threw the stack of prints and specifications down on his desk in disgust. The Model 802 wide-band modulator, released for production the previous Thursday, had just come back to Frank's Engineering Services Department with a caustic note that began, "This one can't be produced either. . . . " It was the fourth time production had kicked the design back.

Frank Forbus, director of engineering for Rondell Data Corporation, was normally a quiet man. But the Model 802 was stretching his patience; it was beginning to look just like other new products that had hit delays and problems in the transition from design to production during the eight months Frank had worked for Rondell. These problems were nothing new at the sprawling old Rondell factory; Frank's predecessor in the engineering job had run afoul of them, too, and had finally been fired for protesting too vehemently about the other departments. But the Model 802 should have been different. Frank had met two months before (July 3, 1978) with the firm's president, Bill Hunt, and with factory superintendent Dave Schwab to smooth the way for the new modulator design. He thought back to the meeting . . . .

"Now we all know there's a tight deadline on the 802," Bill Hunt said, "and Frank's done well to ask us to talk about its introduction. I'm counting

John A. Seeger, Professor of Management, Bentley College.
Reprinted with permission.

on both of you to find any snags in the system and to work together to get that first production run out by October 2nd. Can you do it?"

"We can do it in production if we get a clean design two weeks from now, as scheduled," answered Dave Schwab, the grizzled factory superintendent. "Frank and I have already talked about that, of course. I'm setting aside time in the card room and the machine shop, and we'll be ready. If the design goes over schedule, though, I'll have to fill in with other runs, and it will cost us a bundle to break in for the 802. How does it look in engineering, Frank?"

"I've just reviewed the design for the second time," Frank replied. "If Ron Porter can keep the salesmen out of our hair and avoid any more last-minute changes, we've got a shot. I've pulled the draftsmen off three other overdue jobs to get this one out. But, Dave, that means we can't spring engineers loose to confer with your production people on manufacturing problems."

"Well, Frank, most of those problems are caused by the engineers, and we need them to resolve the difficulties. We've all agreed that production bugs come from both of us bowing to sales pressure, and putting equipment into production before the designs are really ready. That's just what we're trying to avoid on the 802. But I can't have 500 people sitting on their hands waiting for an answer from your people. We'll have to have some engineering support.

Bill Hunt broke in. "So long as you two can talk calmly about the problem I'm confident you can resolve it. What a relief it is, Frank, to hear the way you're approaching this. With Kilmann (the previous director of engineering) this conversation would have been a shouting match. Right, Dave?" Dave nodded and smiled.

"Now there's one other thing you should both be aware of," Hunt continued. "Doc Reeves and I talked last night about a new filtering technique, one that might improve the signal-to-noise ratio of the 802 by a factor of two. There's a chance Doc can come up with it before the 802 reaches production, and if it's possible, I'd like to use the new filters. That would give us a real jump on the competition."

Four days after that meeting, Frank found that two of his key people on the 802 design had been called to production for emergency consultation on a bug found in final assembly: two halves of a new data transmission interface wouldn't fit together because recent changes in the front end required a different chassis design for the back end.

Another week later, Doc Reeves walked into Frank's office, proud as a new parent, with the new filter design. "This won't affect the other modules of the 802 much," Doc had said. "Look, it takes three new cards, a few connectors, some changes in the wiring harness, and some new shielding, and that's all."

Frank had tried to resist the last-minute design changes, but Bill Hunt had stood firm. With a lot of overtime by the engineers and draftsmen, engineering services should still be able to finish the prints in time.

Two engineers and three draftsmen went onto 12-hour days to get the 802 ready, but the prints were still five days late reaching Dave Schwab. Two days later, the prints came back to Frank, heavily annotated in red. Schwab had worked all day Saturday to review the job and had found more than a dozen discrepancies in the prints—most of them caused by the new filter design and insufficient checking time before release. Correction of those design faults had brought on a new generation of discrepancies; Schwab's cover note on the second return of the prints indicated he'd had to release the machine capacity he'd been holding for the 802. On the third iteration, Schwab committed his photo and plating capacity to another rush job. The 802 would be at least one month late getting into production. Ron Porter, vice president for sales, was furious. His customer needed 100 units NOW, he said. Rondell was the customer's only late supplier.

"Here we go again," thought Frank Forbus.

COMPANY HISTORY

Rondell Data Corporation traced its lineage through several generations of electronics technology. Its original founder, Bob Rondell, had set the firm up in 1920 as "Rondell Equipment Company" to manufacture several electrical testing devices he had invented as an engineering faculty member at a large university. The firm branched into radio broadcasting equipment in 1947 and into data transmission equipment in the early 1960s. A well-established corps of direct salespeople, mostly engineers, called on industrial, scientific, and government accounts, but concentrated heavily on original equipment manufacturers. In this market,

Rondell had a long-standing reputation as a source of high-quality, innovative designs. The firm's salespeople fed a continual stream of challenging problems into the Engineering Department, where the creative genius of Ed "Doc" Reeves and several dozen other engineers "converted problems to solutions" (as the sales brochure bragged). Product design formed the spearhead of Rondell's growth.

By 1978, Rondell offered a wide range of products in its two major lines. Broadcast equipment sales had benefited from the growth of UHFTV and FM radio; it now accounted for 35 percent of company sales. Data transmission had blossomed, and in this field an increasing number of orders called for unique specifications, ranging from specialized display panels to entirely untried designs.

The company had grown from 100 employees in 1947 to over 800 in 1978. (Exhibit 1 shows the 1978 organization chart of key employees.) Bill Hunt, who had been a student of the company's founder, had presided over most of that growth and took great pride in preserving the "family spirit" of the old organization. Informal relationships between Rondell's veteran employees formed the backbone of the firm's day-to-day operations; all the managers relied on personal contact, and Hunt often insisted that the absence of bureaucratic red tape was a key factor in recruiting outstanding engineering talent. The personal management approach extended throughout the factory. All exempt employees were paid on a straight salary plus a share of the profits. Rondell boasted an extremely loyal group of senior employees and very low turnover in nearly all areas of the company.

The highest turnover job in the firm was Frank Forbus's. Frank had joined Rondell in January 1978, replacing Jim Kilmann, who had been director of engineering for only 10 months. Kilmann, in turn, had replaced Tom MacLeod, a talented engineer who had made a promising start but had taken to drink after a year in the job. MacLeod's predecessor had been a genial old-timer who retired at 70 after 30 years in charge of engineering. (Doc Reeves had refused the directorship in each of the recent changes, saying, "Hell, that's no promotion for a bench man like me. I'm no administrator.")

For several years, the firm had experienced a steadily increasing number of disputes between research, engineering, sales, and production people—disputes generally centered on the problem of new product introduction. Quarrels between departments became more numerous under MacLeod, Kilmann, and Forbus. Some managers associated those disputes with the company's recent decline in profitability—a decline that, in spite of higher sales and gross revenues, was beginning to bother people in 1977. President Bill Hunt commented:

> Better cooperation, I'm sure, could increase our output by 5–10 percent. I'd hoped Kilmann could solve the problems, but pretty obviously he was too young, too arrogant. People like him—conflict type of personality—bother me. I don't like strife, and with him it seemed I spent all my time smoothing out arguments. Kilmann tried to tell everyone else how to run their departments, without having his own house in order. That approach just wouldn't work here at Rondell. Frank Forbus, now, seems much more in tune with our style of organization. I'm really hopeful now.
>
> Still, we have just as many problems now as we did last year. Maybe even more. I hope Frank can get a handle on engineering services soon . . . .

THE ENGINEERING DEPARTMENT: RESEARCH

According to the organization chart (see Exhibit 1), Frank Forbus was in charge of both research (really the product development function) and engineering services (which provided engineering support). To Forbus, however, the relationship with research was not so clear-cut:

> Doc Reeves is one of the world's unique people, and none of us would have it any other way. He's a creative genius. Sure, the chart says he works for me, but we all know Doc does his own thing. He's not the least bit interested in management routines, and I can't count on him to take any responsibility in scheduling projects, or checking budgets, or what-have-you. But as long as Doc is director of research, you can bet this company will keep on leading the field. He has more ideas per hour than most people have per year, and he keeps the whole engineering staff fired up. Everybody loves Doc—and you can count me in on that, too. In a way, he works for me, sure. But that's not what's important.

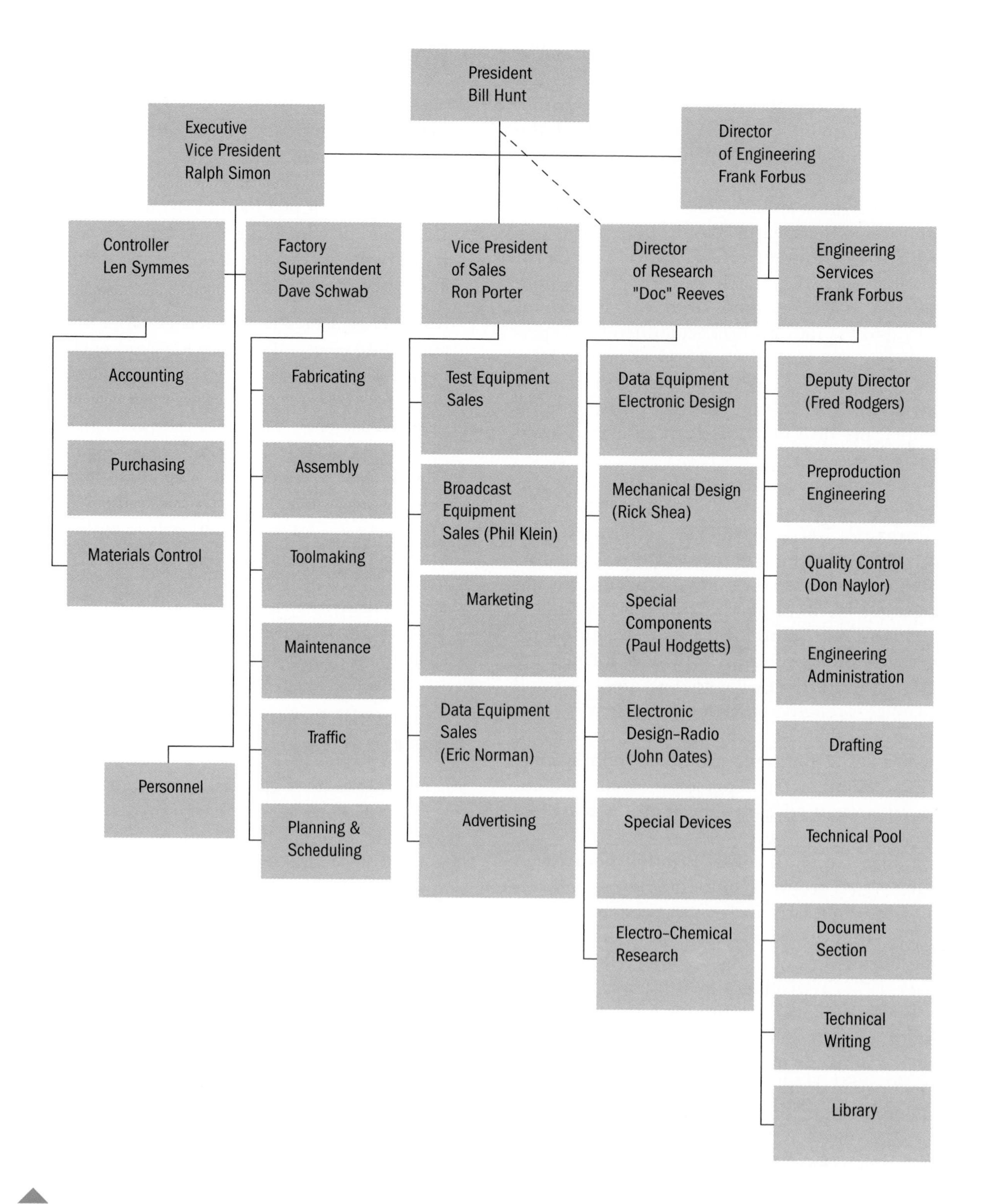

EXHIBIT 1
Rondell Data Corporation 1978 Organization Chart.

"Doc" Reeves—unhurried, contemplative, casual, and candid—tipped his stool back against the wall of his research cubicle and talked about what was important:

> Development engineering. That's where the company's future rests. Either we have it there, or we don't have it.
>
> There's no kidding ourselves that we're anything but a bunch of Rube Goldbergs here. But that's where the biggest kicks come from—from solving development problems, and dreaming up new ways of doing things. That's why I so look forward to the special contracts we get involved in. We accept them not for the revenue they represent, but because they subsidize the basic development work which goes into all our basic products.
>
> This is a fantastic place to work. I have a great crew and they can really deliver when the chips are down. Why, Bill Hunt and I (he gestured toward the neighboring cubicle, where the president's name hung over the door) are likely to find as many people here at work at 10:00 P.M. as at 3:00 in the afternoon. The important thing here is the relationships between people; they're based on mutual respect, not on policies and procedures. Administrative red tape is a pain. It takes away from development time.
>
> Problems? Sure, there are problems now and then. There are power interests in production, where they sometimes resist change. But I'm not a fighting man, you know. I suppose if I were, I might go in there and push my weight around a little. But I'm an engineer and can do more for Rondell sitting right here or working with my own people. That's what brings results.

Other members of the Research Department echoed Doc's views and added some additional sources of satisfaction with their work. They were proud of the personal contacts they built up with customers' technical staffs—contacts that increasingly involved travel to the customers' factories to serve as expert advisers in the preparation of overall system design specifications. The engineers were also delighted with the department's encouragement of their personal development, continuing education, and independence on the job.

But there were problems, too. Rick Shea, of the mechanical design section, noted:

> In the old days I really enjoyed the work—and the people I worked with. But now there's a lot of irritation. I don't like someone breathing down my neck. You can be hurried into jeopardizing the design.

John Oates, head of the radio electronic design section, was another designer with definite views:

> Production engineering is almost nonexistent in this company. Very little is done by the preproduction section in engineering services. Frank Forbus has been trying to get preproduction into the picture, but he won't succeed because you can't start from such an ambiguous position. There have been three directors of engineering in three years. Frank can't hold his own against the others in the company, Kilmann was too aggressive. Perhaps no amount of tact would have succeeded.

Paul Hodgetts was head of special components in the R&D department. Like the rest of the department, he valued bench work. But he complained of engineering services:

> The services don't do things we want them to do. Instead, they tell us what they're going to do. I should probably go to Frank, but I don't get any decisions there. I know I should go through Frank, but this holds things up, so I often go direct.

THE ENGINEERING DEPARTMENT: ENGINEERING SERVICES

The Engineering Services Department provided ancillary services to R&D and served as liaison between engineering and the other Rondell departments. Among its main functions were drafting; management of the central technicians' pool; scheduling and expediting engineering products; documentation and publication of parts lists and engineering orders; preproduction engineering (consisting of the final integration of individual design components into mechanically compatible packages); and quality control (which included inspection of incoming parts and materials, and final inspection of subassemblies and finished equipment). Top management's description of the department included the line, "ESD is responsible for maintaining cooperation with other departments, providing services to the development engineers, and freeing more valuable people in R&D from essential activities that are diversions from and beneath their main competence."

Many of Frank Forbus's 75 employees were located in other departments. Quality control people were scattered through the manufacturing and receiving areas, and technicians worked primarily in the research area or the prototype fabrication room. The remaining ESD personnel were assigned to leftover nooks and crannies near production or engineering sections. Frank Forbus described his position:

> My biggest problem is getting acceptance from the people I work with. I've moved slowly rather than risk antagonism. I saw what happened to Kilmann, and I want to avoid that. But although his precipitate action had won over a few of the younger R&D people, he certainly didn't have the department's backing. Of course, it was the resentment of other departments that eventually caused his discharge. People have been slow accepting me here. There's nothing really overt, but I get a negative reaction to my ideas.
>
> My role in the company has never been well defined really. It's complicated by Doc's unique position, of course, and also by the fact that ESD sort of grew by itself over the years, as the design engineers concentrated more and more on the creative parts of product development. I wish I could be more involved in the technical side. That's been my training, and it's a lot of fun. But in our setup, the technical side is the least necessary for me to be involved in.
>
> Schwab (production head) is hard to get along with. Before I came and after Kilmann left, there were six months intervening when no one was really doing any scheduling. No work loads were figured, and unrealistic promises were made about releases. This puts us in an awkward position. We've been scheduling way beyond our capacity to manufacture or engineer.
>
> Certain people within R&D—for instance. John Oates, head of the radio electronic design section—understand scheduling well and meet project deadlines, but this is not generally true of the rest of the R&D department, especially the mechanical engineers who won't commit themselves. Most of the complaints come from sales and production department heads because items—like the 802—are going to production before they are fully developed, under pressure from sales to get out the unit, and this snags the whole process. Somehow, engineering services should be able to intervene and resolve these complaints, but I haven't made much headway so far. I should be able to go to Hunt for help, but he's too busy most of the time, and his major interest is the design side of engineering, where he got his own start. Sometimes he talks as though he's the engineering director as well as president. I have to put my foot down; there are problems here that the front office just doesn't understand.

Salespeople were often observed taking their problems directly to designers, while production frequently threw designs back at R&D, claiming they could not be produced and demanding the prompt attention of particular design engineers. The latter were frequently observed in conference with production supervisors on the assembly floor. Frank went on:

> The designers seem to feel they're losing something when one of us tries to help. They feel it's a reflection on them to have someone take over what they've been doing. They seem to want to carry a project right through to the final stages, particularly the mechanical people. Consequently, engineering services people are used below their capacity to contribute and our department is denied functions it should be performing. There's not as much use made of engineering services as there should be.

Frank Forbus's technician supervisor added his comments:

> Production picks out the engineer who'll be the "bum of the month." They pick on every little detail instead of using their heads and making the minor changes that have to be made. The 15-to-20-year people shouldn't have to prove their ability any more, but they spend four hours defending themselves and four hours getting the job done. I have no one to go to when I need help. Frank Forbus is afraid. I'm trying to help him but he can't help me at this time. I'm responsible for fifty people and I've got to support them.

Fred Rodgers, whom Frank had brought with him to the company as an assistant, gave another view of the situation:

> I try to get our people in preproduction to take responsibility, but they're not used to it and people in other departments don't usually see them as best qualified to solve the problem. There's a real barrier for a newcomer here. Gaining people's confidence is hard. More and more, I'm wondering whether there really is a job for me here.

(Rodgers left Rondell a month later.) Another of Forbus's subordinates gave his view:

If Doc gets a new product idea, you can't argue. But he's too optimistic. He judges that others can do what he does—But there's only one Doc Reeves. We've had 900 production change orders this year—they changed 2,500 drawings. If I were in Frank's shoes I'd put my foot down on all this new development. I'd look at the reworking we're doing and get production set up the way I wanted it. Kilmann was fired when he was doing a good job. He was getting some system in the company's operations. Of course, it hurt some people. There is no denying that Doc is the most important person in the company. What gets overlooked is that Hunt is a close second, not just politically but in terms of what he contributes technically and in customer relations.

This subordinate explained that he sometimes went out into the production department but that Schwab, the production head, resented this. Personnel in production said that Kilmann had failed to show respect for old-timers and was always meddling in other departments' business. This was why he had been fired, they contended.

Don Taylor was in charge of quality control. He commented:

I am now much more concerned with administration and less with work. It is one of the evils you get into. There is tremendous detail in this job. I listen to everyone's opinion. Everybody is important. There shouldn't be distinctions—distinctions between people. I'm not sure whether Frank has to be a fireball like Kilmann. I think the real question is whether Frank is getting the job done. I know my job is essential. I want to supply service to the more talented people and give them information so they can do their jobs better.

THE SALES DEPARTMENT

Ron Porter was angry. His job was supposed to be selling, he said, but instead it had turned into settling disputes inside the plant and making excuses to waiting customers. He jabbed a finger toward his desk:

You see that telephone? I'm actually afraid nowadays to hear it ring. Three times out of five, it will be a customer who's hurting because we've failed to deliver on schedule. The other two calls will be from production or ESD, telling me some schedule has slipped again.

The Model 802 is typical. Absolutely typical. We padded the delivery date by six weeks, to allow for contingencies. Within two months, the slack had evaporated. Now it looks like we'll be lucky to ship it before Christmas. (It was now November 28.) We're ruining our reputation in the market. Why, just last week one of our best customers—people we've worked with for 15 years—tried to hang a penalty clause on their latest order.

We shouldn't have to be after the engineers all the time. They should be able to see what problems they create without our telling them.

Phil Klein, head of broadcast sales under Porter, noted that many sales decisions were made by top management. Sales was understaffed, he thought, and had never really been able to get on top of the job.

We have grown further and further away from engineering. The director of engineering does not pass on the information that we give him. We need better relationships there. It is very difficult for us to talk to customers about development problems without technical help. We need each other. The whole of engineering is now too isolated from the outside world. The morale of ESD is very low. They're in a bad spot—they're not well organized.

People don't take much to outsiders here. Much of this is because the expectation is built up by top management that jobs will be filled from the bottom. So it's really tough when an outsider like Frank comes in.

Eric Norman, order and pricing coordinator for data equipment, talked about his own relationships with the Production Department:

Actually, I get along with them fairly well. Oh, things could be better of course, if they were more cooperative generally. They always seem to say, "It's my bat and ball, and we're playing by my rules." People are afraid to make production mad; there's a lot of power in there. But you've got to understand that production has its own set of problems. And nobody in Rondell is working any harder than Dave Schwab to try to straighten things out.

THE PRODUCTION DEPARTMENT

Dave Schwab had joined Rondell just after the Korean War, in which he had seen combat duty (at the Yalu River) and intelligence duty at Pyong

Yang. Both experiences had been useful in his first year of civilian employment at Rondell: The wartime factory superintendent and several middle managers had been, apparently, indulging in highly questionable side deals with Rondell's suppliers. Dave Schwab had gathered evidence, revealed the situation to Bill Hunt, and stood by the president in the ensuing unsavory situation. Seven months after joining the company, Dave was named factory superintendent.

His first move had been to replace the fallen managers with a new team from outside. This group did not share the traditional Rondell emphasis on informality and friendly personal relationships and had worked long and hard to install systematic manufacturing methods and procedures. Before the reorganization, production had controlled purchasing, stock control, and final quality control (where final assembly of products in cabinets was accomplished). Because of the wartime events, management decided on a checks-and-balance system of organization and removed these three departments from production jurisdiction. The new production managers felt they had been unjustly penalized by this organization, particularly since they had uncovered the behavior that was detrimental to the company in the first place.

By 1978, the production department had grown to 500 employees, 60 percent of whom worked in the assembly area—an unusually pleasant environment that had been commended by *Factory* magazine for its colorful decoration, cleanliness, and low noise level. An additional 30 percent of the work force, mostly skilled machinists, staffed the finishing and fabrication department. About 60 others performed scheduling, supervisory, and maintenance duties. Production workers were nonunion, hourly-paid, and participated in both the liberal profit-sharing program and the stock purchase plan. Morale in production was traditionally high, and turnover was extremely low.

Dave Schwab commented:

> To be efficient, production has to be a self-contained department. We have to control what comes into the department and what goes out. That's why purchasing, inventory control, and quality ought to run out of this office. We'd eliminate a lot of problems with better control there. Why, even Don Taylor in QC would rather work for me than for ESD; he's said so himself. We understand his problems better.
>
> The other departments should be self-contained too. That's why I always avoid the underlings and go straight to the department heads with any questions. I always go down the line.
>
> I have to protect my people from outside disturbances. Look what would happen if I let unfinished, half-baked designs in here—there'd be chaos. The bugs have to be found before the drawings go into the shop, and it seems I'm the one who has to find them. Look at the 802, for example. (Dave had spent most of Thanksgiving Day [it was now November 28] red-penciling the latest set of prints.) ESD should have found every one of those discrepancies. They just don't check drawings properly. They change most of the things I flag, but then they fail to trace through the impact of those changes on the rest of the design. I shouldn't have to do that. And those engineers are tolerance crazy. They want everything to a millionth of an inch. I'm the only one in the company who's had any experience with actually machining things to a millionth of an inch. We make sure that the things that engineers say on their drawings actually have to be that way and whether they're obtainable from the kind of raw material we buy.
>
> That shouldn't be production's responsibility, but I have to do it. Accepting bad prints wouldn't let us ship the order any quicker. We'd only make a lot of junk that had to be reworked. And that would take even longer.
>
> This way, I get to be known as the bad guy, but I guess that's just part of the job. (He paused with a wry smile.) Of course, what really gets them is that I don't even have a degree.

Dave had fewer bones to pick with the Sales Department because, he said, they trusted him.

> When we give Ron Porter a shipping date, he knows the equipment will be shipped then.
>
> You've got to recognize, though, that all of our new-product problems stem from sales making absurd commitments on equipment that hasn't been fully developed. That always means trouble.
>
> Unfortunately, Hunt always backs sales up, even when they're wrong. He always favors them over us.

Ralph Simon, age 65, executive vice president of the company, had direct responsibility for Rondell's production department. He said:

> There shouldn't really be a dividing of departments among top management in the company. The president should be czar over all. The production people

> ask me to do something for them, and I really can't do it. It creates bad feelings between engineering and production, this special attention that they [R&D] get from Bill. But then Hunt likes to dabble in design. Schwab feels that production is treated like a poor relation.

THE EXECUTIVE COMMITTEE

At the executive committee meeting on December 6, it was duly recorded that Dave Schwab had accepted the prints and specifications for the Model 802 modulator, and had set Friday, December 29, as the shipping date for the first 10 pieces. Bill Hunt, in the chairperson's role, shook his head and changed the subject quickly when Frank tried to open the agenda to a discussion of interdepartmental coordination.

The executive committee itself was a brainchild of Rondell's controller, Len Symmes, who was well aware of the disputes that plagued the company. Symmes had convinced Bill Hunt and Ralph Simon to meet every two weeks with their department heads, and the meetings were formalized with Hunt, Simon, Ron Porter, Dave Schwab, Frank Forbus, Doc Reeves, Symmes, and the personnel director attending. Symmes explained his intent and the results:

> Doing things collectively and informally just doesn't work as well as it used to. Things have been gradually getting worse for at least two years now. We had to start thinking in terms of formal organization relationships. I did the first organization chart, and the executive committee was my idea too—but neither idea is contributing much help, I'm afraid. It takes top management to make an organization click. The rest of us can't act much differently until the top people see the need for us to change.
>
> I had hoped the committee especially would help get the department managers into a constructive planning process. It hasn't worked out that way because Mr. Hunt really doesn't see the need for it. He uses the meetings as a place to pass on routine information.

MERRY CHRISTMAS

"Frank, I didn't know whether to tell you now, or after the holiday." It was Friday, December 22, and Frank Forbus was standing awkwardly in front of Bill Hunt's desk.

"But, I figured you'd work right through Christmas Day if we didn't have this talk, and that just wouldn't have been fair to you. I can't understand why we have such poor luck in the engineering director's job lately. And I don't think it's entirely your fault. But . . . "

Frank only heard half of Hunt's words, and said nothing in response. He'd be paid through February 28 . . . . He should use the time for searching . . . . Hunt would help all he could . . . . Jim Kilmann was supposed to be doing well at his own new job, and might need more help . . . .

Frank cleaned out his desk and numbly started home. The electronic carillon near his house was playing a Christmas carol. Frank thought again of Hunt's rationale: Conflict still plagued Rondell—and Frank had not made it go away. Maybe somebody else could do it.

"And what did Santa Claus bring you, Frankie?" he asked himself.

"The sack. Only the empty sack."

CASE 12

Oliver Davis's Entrepreneurial Success Story: No Lost Clients, No Employee Terminations, No Debt

Rosemary McGowan

Oliver Davis, founder and owner of Green Meadows Lawn Services in Ottawa, was wrapping up his eighth season in the outdoor lawn-maintenance business. Through those eight seasons, Oliver sustained his enviable record of no lost clients, no employee terminations, and no debt. His revenues had continued to grow and, as a university student, he was pleased that the gross revenue for his summer job was six figures. The previous year marked another accomplishment for the young entrepreneur. Oliver was awarded the 2003 CIBC Student Entrepreneur of the Year for his company, Green Meadows. It had been a great summer but now the lawn-care season was coming to an end and Oliver was becoming increasingly preoccupied with the future. The challenge of sustaining his personal commitment to growing the company while not losing touch with his employees, his clients, and his values weighed on his mind. As he headed to the coffee shop to meet his crew at the end of the day, he knew that the changing seasons signalled a need to focus on a plan for the future.

THE COMPANY

In the summer of 1996, Oliver Davis had just finished Grade 8 and, like a lot of his friends, was at loose ends. He was not old enough to have a "real" paying job but he wanted to earn some money. His father suggested that Oliver offer to cut their neighbour's lawn—the idea appealed to Oliver. So, with a $300 loan from his father, Oliver purchased his first lawn mower and started Green Meadows. Through word of mouth, Oliver found that his work snowballed. Within a few weeks, Oliver was cutting his neighbour's lawn, the lawn of a friend of the neighbour's, and then a friend of that friend. Too young to drive, Oliver's father drove Oliver and his lawn mower to the various homes. The summers through high school found Oliver's little grass-cutting business growing steadily. His reputation for courteous, reliable, and thorough service spread. By the end of high school, Oliver had a crew of three employees working for him.

In the spring of 2001 Oliver doubled his number of lawn-care clients. John Simpson,[1] the owner of a local lawn-care company was selling his business. Oliver bought out all the contracts (40 to 50 contracts in total) from Simpson, who Oliver describes as a "born entrepreneur." Oliver first met Simpson at a McDonald's and, as Oliver says, "we just got chatting." Over the months, their paths crossed on a fairly regular basis at a variety of coffee and fast food shops favoured by the lawn-care crews working in the area. Crews on break were easy to spot—pick-up trucks with trailers loaded with lawn mowers, rakes, and assorted garden equipment. Oliver's baby blue trucks were especially noticeable. Oliver's signature baby blue trucks became Green Meadows primary form of promotion. On occasion, Simpson would ask Oliver if he would take a job that his crews were too busy to service and vice versa. After some months, Oliver learned that Simpson was interested in selling out his contracts but only to someone who would look after his customers the way he had done over the years. Oliver felt that the two companies were very similar. They both strove for excellence in customer service, and treated their crews fairly and equitably. What started as a casual coffee shop conversation developed into a win–win situation for both men: for Simpson, who was looking to sell to someone who would look after his clients with the same care and

[1] The owner's name has been disguised.

attention to detail that his customers had come to expect, and for Oliver, who valued the growth opportunity. Oliver's chance encounter led to his successful buyout of his competition, with a doubling of his lawn-care contracts.

Oliver prides himself on his company's reputation for customer service. He would often "go the extra mile for clients." Oliver credits his father with instilling the "do what it takes" attitude. Oliver found that "doing the job until the customer is satisfied" paid off in spades. In one instance, a customer was removing patio stones in order to install interlocking brick. A friend of the customer wanted the stones for his own property. Green Meadows removed the stones and delivered them to the customer's friend—free of charge. Green Meadows had also developed a reputation for community service. A local seniors' complex was in need of lawn-care service and Green Meadows provided that service free of charge for the complex.

Much of Oliver's day sees him at job sites and talking with his customers. He found that an increasing number of his customers were either installing or inquiring about interlocking patios, walkways, and driveways. Sensing a growth opportunity for Green Meadows, Oliver was determined to expand his services to include the design and installation of interlocking bricks. He knew that with some training he could provide as good, if not better, interlock design and installation for his valued clients. To Oliver each lost interlocking opportunity was simply lost revenue for his company. Green Meadows expanded into the interlock market in 2001. Within two summers, the interlock side of his business (listed as "other services" under revenues) exceeded the lawn-care side of his operations. Green Meadows' 2003 gross revenues also showed an impressive increase from 2002 (see Exhibit A for the 2002 and 2003 Income Statements).

Oliver takes customer service very seriously. At the end of every season, Oliver distributes a "Customer Report Card" for his clients to evaluate his company's performance (see Exhibit 2). Oliver firmly believes that his strong customer focus is central to Green Meadows' continued revenue growth. After a little research, Oliver found that between 2000 and 2002 Green Meadows' growth consistently outpaced that of the landscape industry (see Exhibit 3). The company's mission states that:

Exhibit 1

Green Meadows 2002 and 2003 Income Statements (January 1 to December 31)

	2002	2003
Revenue		
Revenue–Lawn Mowing	50 262.41	55 155.55
Revenue–Dethatch & Fertilizer	3 223.30	2 035.00
Revenue–Other Services	41 768.55	80 173.33
Revenue–GST Quick Method	1 905.09	2 706.57
Total Revenue	97 159.35	140 070.15
Expense		
Payroll Expenses		
Wages & Salaries	18 859.61	22 665.32
EI Expense	601.34	642.04
CPP Expense	708.50	885.27
WCB Expense	1 477.67	1 149.13
Total Payroll Expense	21 647.12	25 341.76
Operating Expenses		
Liability Insurance	1 296.00	1 834.62
Advertising & Promotions	463.46	1 429.93
Bad Debts	0	190.91
Supplies	10 338.25	18 721.07
License Fees	222.00	328.00
Credit Card Charges	11.25	149.09
Amortization	2 707.00	1 896.00
Interest & Bank Charges	130.90	81.45
Office Supplies	1 170.08	939.00
Equipment–Fuel & Oil	912.09	48.74
Equipment–Repairs & Maintenance	701.55	1 733.35
Small Equipment Purchases	1 591.07	4 888.76
Rent	286.40	278.20
Miscellaneous	167.41	284.44
Cellular Telephone	1 340.95	1 810.58
Travel & Entertainment	221.78	257.60
Vehicle–Fuel & Oil	2 351.00	3 021.44
Vehicle–Repairs & Maintenance	647.24	2 205.48
Vehicle–Insurance	1 621.01	1 457.49
Total Operating Expenses	26 179.44	41 556.15
Total Expense	47 826.56	66 897.91
Net Income	49 332.79	73 172.24

Green Meadows provides customers with a sense of pride and satisfaction in their home landscape. Green Meadows provides employees with the opportunity to be creative and achieve personal growth. Green Meadows has a strong focus when it comes to the community, customers, work quality, and employees.

Oliver's financial strategy has been to "grow the business from existing cash flow, with the intent of growing the business for long-term stability rather than growing the business quickly at all costs" (Davis, Company Report, 2003). Oliver prides himself on keeping costs down whenever possible. Both of the company's trademark blue trucks were bought used . . . well used. In the off-season, Oliver has them serviced in the high school auto shop program where his father teaches. New, $60 000 trucks are just not a luxury that Oliver feels he could afford. He would rather offer his employees a higher wage rate than spend his company's money on depreciating assets. In comparison with

Exhibit 2

CUSTOMER SATISFACTION REPORT CARD—2002 SEASON

	Question (1 = Poor, 10 = Excellent)	Score
1.	Was your property cut often enough?	8.8
2.	Was your grass cut at an appropriate length?	8.7
3.	Were you satisfied with the trimming around gardens and flower beds?	8.2
4.	Were you satisfied with the cleanup of grass clippings—lawn, walkways, and driveways?	8.3
5.	Would you recommend us to a neighbour?	8.6
6.	Was your lawn furniture, etc., left in order?	8.6
7.	Were you happy with our courteous service?	8.7
Total		8.5

Source: Oliver Davis, Company Report Prepared for CIBC Student Entrepreneurship Presentation (2003).

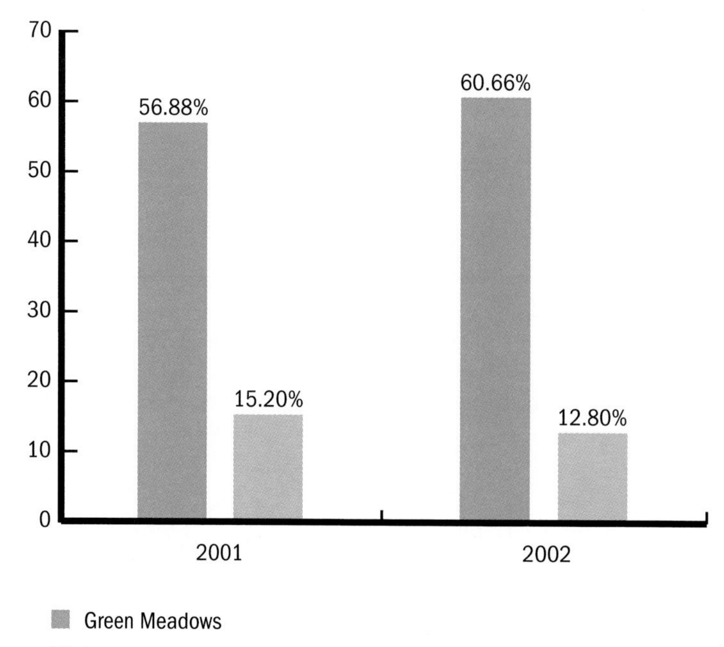

EXHIBIT 3
Comparative Growth Rates

other local lawn-care companies, Green Meadows' pay scales are above average. Oliver does insist, however, on the purchase of top-of-the-line lawn-care and interlock equipment. To Oliver, downtime from unreliable and inferior equipment was an unnecessary cost.

Oliver cites a mentor relationship with Thomas Wright,[2] a local corporate executive, as invaluable in helping him develop his business skills. Like his relationship with Simpson, this connection started from an impromptu conversation in a local restaurant. While dining out one evening, Wright overheard Oliver talking about his business and he became intrigued by the young man who was running his own business. Oliver soon learned that Wright was an accountant and chief financial officer in a large corporation. Wright offered to manage the books for Oliver's company. According to Oliver, Wright "is excellent for just sitting around and chatting. He shares lots of life's lessons with me." Recently, however, Wright's schedule was involving an increasing amount of out-of-country travel and was generally taking up almost all his time. Oliver sensed that the day would soon come that the CFO would simply not be available for Green Meadows.

Oliver's typical 15-hour days see him working from 7:30 A.M. to 10:30 P.M., and according to Oliver, it has been that way for at least the past three seasons. It was only recently that Oliver took the occasional weekend off work, just to bring some respite to his demanding schedule: "I could probably step out of working but I enjoy it. I often wake up in the middle of the night thinking about business. I find myself thinking about other projects . . . what else I could do? How else I could expand the business? The opportunities and possibilities are just so exciting that I can't sleep; it keeps me up at night."

Oliver incurred a frightening injury on a job site a couple of summers ago. While he was operating a gas-powered hedge trimmer, he had a momentary lapse of attention and nearly completely severed one of his fingers. Unable to get back to the jobsites for several days, his Dad helped manage the crews. For Oliver, "That type of thing, which could take me away from my company, scares me, scares me, really, really scares me. I know my Dad and Bob could step in, but. . . . "

[2] Name has been disguised.

THE CREWS

In the two years since the buyout, Oliver's company had grown to include two crews: a lawn-maintenance crew and a garden/patio (interlock) design crew. The lawn-maintenance crew looks after routine lawn maintenance of over 120 properties across four towns. The activities of this crew include grass cutting, dethatching, aerating, organic fertilizing, and top dressing. The second, four-man crew looks after garden design and maintenance, the design of interlocking brick driveways and patios, garden walls, and retaining walls. Although crew members work primarily on one type of job, there was frequent rotation between crews. Lawn-cutting jobs could take anywhere from 30 minutes to a couple of hours depending on the size of the property. Interlocking jobs were much more time consuming. Installation often involves up to three or four days of work. That time is in addition to the consultation time with clients, and the time needed to develop the design and place orders with suppliers.

In the four years since he started hiring for the crews, Oliver had never had an employee leave, nor had he terminated anyone—a unique and remarkable staffing record in the lawn-care business. Lawn-care companies are usually staffed with temporary, seasonal staff and marked by significant employee turnover. Oliver was cautious in his employee selection—always hiring someone for an initial probationary period. If they didn't have the attention to detail, the desire to do an excellent job, or a willingness to work as part of the team, they did not get to stay past week one. Most potential employees, however, made the initial screening and continued on with Green Meadows. Oliver's selection process disregarded the old axiom of "not hiring friends." In fact, so far he has only hired people that he knew or who were recommended by friends. He looked for employees with a work ethic and customer service orientation similar to his own.

Among Oliver's staff, six of his seven employees were connections from high school. Like Oliver, they attended university or college and wanted to work outdoors in the summertime. Oliver's seventh employee, Bob, is a 40-something expert in the design and installation of interlocking brick. Like most of Oliver's other business relationships, Oliver's association with Bob started with a chance meeting at one of his job sites. As Oliver recalled, Bob stopped by one of Oliver's job sites and asked Oliver if he needed some help. Oliver quickly realized that Bob had skills in the design and installation of interlocking bricks—skills that could help Oliver grow the interlocking side of the business. Bob's easy-going style, twinned with his strong work ethic and customer-service focus, was an ideal match for Green Meadows. Oliver invited Bob to join the company. Two summers later, Bob was still employed full-time during the outdoor maintenance season (typically April to November). As Oliver notes, "Bob knows a lot of the tricks of the trade. He knows how to talk to the customers." On the job site, Bob and the crews started referring to Oliver as "boss," something that makes Oliver both chuckle and wince. The owner–employee relationship between Oliver and Bob has gradually evolved into one where Bob frequently joins Oliver for a beer after work and has became a sort of confidant, advisor, and sounding board for business ideas.

As with many of his other relationships, his connection with Bob, his most senior employee, started informally. As Bob recalls:

> I had just finished with a company and I was out walking in my neighbourhood and I saw some young lads working on interlock and I said something like, "Gee, you probably need some help. Where's your boss? Who's your boss?" Then we saw him coming down the road. I said to him, "I think you need some more help." He agreed and I asked him, "When do I start?" It was a quick handshake, nothing formal. It's been as easy at that ever since . . . very easy.

To Bob, an employee with 20-plus years of industry experience:

> Ollie treats us all pretty damned good. If someone didn't have a lunch, Ollie brings him a sandwich and a drink. I'm 49 years old and the rest are 22. Ollie's the boss but I can show him ways to do interlock jobs more efficiently because of my years of experience. That's good for the job, that's good for the company and good for all of us. I do his layout, start to finish and make sure it's done right . . . . I execute it. Ollie does all the legwork, the hard work. He's often out visiting clients until 10:30 at night, getting the clients and dealing with people is something that's very stressful.
>
> This kid's a pleasure to work for. He's very easy going. He's not cocky or pushy or anything. He never gets mad, he never gets rattled. Sometimes I say to him, "JC, Ollie why don't you scream a little once in a while?

Oliver's days usually start and end with a coffee shop meeting with his crews. Over coffee, the day is plotted out or reviewed. During the day, Oliver is always available on his cell phone and spends most of his time split between the two job sites. In managing his teams, Oliver says that:

> I want an empowered workforce. They're important, the employees are important for sure. I'm not into yelling at the guys or getting on their backs and I don't have to with my crews. How would I feel if someone was yelling at me? I don't yell. There's no point. Some of the work is pretty tedious, so you don't need someone yelling at you. When we go to a job site, we're laughing when we hear all the yelling that goes on with some of the crews. You'd be surprised how many people in this business rant and rave at their employees. It's just treating people the same as you would want to be treated. Bob told me that he had worked for 23 years for another employer and then took one day off when his wife had a baby. He was back at work the next day. Bob's former boss actually phoned the homeowner to see if was working the day after the birth—Bob quit two days later.
>
> I want all my guys doing everything. I'll talk to them about the jobs. Like, if I'm unsure about the best course of action, I'll say, "I don't like the look of this, come over here, what do you think?" I think that four heads are always better than one. I always try to get their input, definitely . . . but obviously my decision stands. They've starting calling me "Boss" now. That's the joke now.
>
> I like to keep my guys happy. We all do all the work. Some of it is grunt work and we all do it. How can someone be happy if they are the one who does all the grunt work, all the time? That's not a team. I have built a team over the years. I'm into constant team building. Brett came over last year; he is a friend of one of the other employees, Paul. Brett's a great guy and we just hang out. As I said, we're into constant team building. We get together after work and we go out at the end of the year.

Oliver has also been able to offer his seasonal employees Christmas bonuses and, during the off-season, has taken his crews to Ottawa Senators' hockey games. During busy periods, Oliver's crew will expand to include his father who helps out with the grass cutting side of the business. Oliver credits his father with providing the foundation for his belief system. In talking about his father, a retired police officer and currently a teacher, Oliver says, "Oh yeah, my Dad's super. We do things the same way."

CLIENT RELATIONS

The customer is at the centre of Green Meadows Lawn Care. In describing his clients and the way he manages them, Oliver says:

> I don't screw anyone around. If I say I'm going to do something, I do it. We do a good job. Doing good and being nice and kind are the foundations of what we do . . . . Just being kind to clients, just helping people out if they're in a jam. One of our clients fractured her ankle last winter. She phoned when I was home on Christmas break so I went with one of the guys to shovel her walk. That's just the kind of relationship I have with the clients. It's the little things, if clients want something done, it usually only takes one hour, I ask them just pay me for cost or don't even worry about it. That's probably how your name gets passed on.

Oliver's client focus has resulted in the extraordinary record of never having lost a client—a unique record in his industry. Getting clients is tough in the industry—retaining them is key to his success. Oliver estimates that for every 20 quotes, he secures two contracts. Typically working Monday to Friday from 7 A.M. to 3:30 P.M. with the crews, evenings and weekends are spent visiting potential clients and preparing quotes. As Oliver says, "I can't get to the cottage as much as I'd like." As mentioned earlier, in 2003, for the first time in a long time, Oliver started taking the occasional weekend off.

To build his business, Oliver has also actively built a network of relationships with contractors and suppliers in the area. One local contractor had some extra gravel aggregate (GA) building compound left over from a job. He had no need for it, but Oliver knew that he could use it for one of his sites. The contractor, who knew Oliver, told him to take as much as he wanted. Oliver's willingness to haul the GA away from the construction site saved the contractor the cost of removal.

Comments from two of Oliver's clients describe Oliver as his clients see him. Anna Smith, a Green Meadows client for the past five years, says that Oliver:

> . . . has a really friendly attitude. It's not so much that he develops a business relationship with his clients but it's the relationship you develop with him as a person. You can call the company at any time. There is a strong service orientation. He's not too big but I hope he doesn't get too big. I think his father's a big component. It's a family thing. Costing too, it's a good service at a reasonable price.
>
> I would absolutely recommend him. He's such a nice kid. You have to appreciate that he was a kid when he started. So, we've sort of watched Oliver grow up. He had a vision, which is crucial. He has defined his business and anything else that he has expanded into has been a natural fit that has allowed him to keep control and the quality. He's such an amiable person. He's got charm and charisma. He's come so far for someone so young. He's got a lot of emotional intelligence.

Diane Miller, whose family has been a client of Oliver's for over five years, says:

> He has the perfect personality for business. He's so professional, yet in a way, he's laid back; therefore, he just puts you at ease. Our family has gotten quite close to Oliver. He will just pop in for a coffee. He's just a real, nice young man. We couldn't be happier. He presents himself always as very clean despite the business he's in. He has the whole package. You just like him when you meet him. My Dad has referred him to others. We would never change. As long as he's here and we're here, we would never change!

LOOKING AHEAD

On his way back to the coffee shop, Oliver drove his baby blue truck to a newly built, upscale neighbourhood where his interlocking crew was just finishing up for the day. Getting out of his truck to talk to the crew, he was pleased to see the crew doing the routine end-of-the-day job-site clean-up. Bob was hosing down the white garage door to remove the reddish stone dust residue that was kicked up while cutting the interlocking stones. The other three crew members were reloading the truck, sweeping the driveway, and washing down the front door of the house. Leaving the job site clean and organized for the client's return at the end of the workday was one of the trademarks of a Green Meadows job. Leaving the job site in immaculate condition was not only for the benefit of the client but for the company as well. As Oliver reminds his crews, "the neighbours are watching!"

Getting back in the truck to meet the other crew at the coffee shop, Oliver found himself thinking about the next stage in Green Meadows' evolution. For Oliver, entrepreneurship and sole proprietorship had been financially and personally rewarding and now with his university studies half finished (as was the case for many of his crew), the goal was to plan for the future. As Oliver says, "For me, five years is the short term." I plan to just keep going as hard as I can. In the long term, I think there are endless opportunities. I can integrate things vertically so that I could supply my business. I want to grow, keep it profitable, but I want to still be able to control it. I just need another me."

Company Index

A

ABC Bücherdienst/Telebuch.de, 78
Accenture, 423, 469
AD OPT Technologies Inc., 312
Adelphia Communications, 24, 36, 219
Adidas, 335
Adobe Systems, 80
Advanced Software Designs, 186
Air Cal, 560
Air Canada, 2, 5, 7, 15, 17, 29, 77, 199–200, 217, 219, 235, 237, 288–289, 312, 330, 334, 335, 342, 497
Airbus, 475
Alberta Energy Company, 217
Alcan, 10, 185, 299
Algoma Steel, 150
Aliant, 40
Alliance Atlantis Communications Inc., 377
Alliance Party, 374
Amazon.com, 3, 4, 5, 15, 23*t*, 78, 126, 177, 178, 179, 223, 265, 266, 382, 384, 455, 471
Amazon.co.uk, 78
Amazon.de, 78
America Online (AOL), 17, 18, 228, 351, 416, 448
American Airlines, 77, 89, 475
American Home Products (AHP), 271
Amgen, 262, 448, 496
Anchor Food Products, 102
AOL. *See* America Online (AOL)
AOL-Time Warner, 18, 150
Apple Computer, 13–14, 16, 29, 46, 79, 90, 119, 130, 235, 359, 380, 446, 454, 466, 468
Argos Corp., 488
Arthur Andersen, 24, 57, 59, 217–219, 222, 223, 395
AST, 376
AT&T, 85, 386, 480
AT&T Canada, 330
Atlantic Canada Opportunities Agency (ACOA), 2, 39

B

Baby Gap, 451
Ballard Power Systems, 83, 84
Banana Republic, 451
Bang & Olufsen, 90
Bank of Montreal (BMO), 2, 205, 342
see also BMO Financial Group
Bank of Nova Scotia, 242
BankAmerica, 218
B.A.R. and Grille, 107, 108, 110, 111-, 120, 176
Barnes & Noble, 78, 266, 384
the Bay, 264
Bayside Controls Inc., 327
BC Biomedical Laboratories Ltd., 200
BC Transit, 367
Bechtel Corporation, 83
Becton Dikinson, 115
Beech-Nut, 231–232, 241
Belfast City Airport, 270
Bell Canada, 7, 122, 296
Ben & Jerry's Homemade, 242
Benson & Hedges Inc., 200
BIC Corporation, 268
Big Rock Brewing Company, 299
Bimba Manufacturing Company, 236
Blockbuster Video, 330
BMO Financial Group, 188, 190, 191, 192
see also Bank of Montreal (BMO)
BMW, 70, 95
The Body Shop, 53, 242
Boehringer Ingelheim Company, 58
Boeing Corporation, 475, 557
Bombardier Aerospace, 270, 334
Bombardier Capital, 270
Bombardier Inc., 7, 15, 17, 49, 111, 235, 254, 256, 259, 270, 480
Bombardier Limited, 270
Bombardier Recreational Products, 270
Bombardier Services, 270
Bombardier Transportation, 270
Bookpages, 78
Borders, 78, 266, 384
Boston Market, 134
Boston Pizza International Inc., 139–141
Braniff, 557
Bristol-Myers-Squibb, 77
British Airways, 228, 386, 475, 497
British Army, 159
British International Helicopters, 181
Bugatti, 381
Buick, 188–189
Burger King, 96, 264, 378, 386
Burntsand, 21, 22
Business Development Bank of Canada, 39
Business Week, 29

C

Cadillac, 188–189
The Calgary Herald, 531, 538
Cami Automotive, 296
Campbell's Soup, 260
Campus*direct*, 441–442
Canada Economic Development for Quebec Regions, 39
Canada Trust, 217
Canadian Airlines, 2, 200, 217, 237, 288
Canadian Apparel Manufacturers, 54
Canadian Auto Workers, 2
Canadian Broadcasting Corporation (CBC), 37, 38, 40, 257
Canadian Centre for Management Development (CCMD), 441–442
Canadian Coalition for Good Governance (CCGG), 36
Canadian Franchise Association, 141
Canadian Imperial Bank of Commerce. *See* CIBC
Canadian Institute of Mining, Metallurgy and Petroleum (CIM), 552
Canadian International Development Agency, 247
Canadian Radio-television and Telecommunications Commission (CRTC), 38
Canadian Retailers Advancing Responsible Trade (CRART), 54
Canadian Royal Commission, 229
Canadian Shoe Manufacturers, 54
Canadian Tire Corp. Ltd., 236
CanadianBusiness, 29
CanJet, 288
Canon, 86
CanWest, 48
Capitol Energy Resources Ltd., 403
Carleton University, 533
Caterpillar, 435
CBC. *See* Canadian Broadcasting Corporation (CBC)
CBS, 257
Celestica Inc., 188, 205
Cell-Loc Inc., 402–403
Cell-Loc Location Technologies Inc., 403
Cervejarais Kaiser, 215
Chapters, 78, 266
Charles Bishop Productions, 377
CHC Helicopter Corp., 181
Chevrolet, 189
China Coast, 162, 163
China Minmetals, 215
Chipotle, 134
Chrysler, 118, 194, 195, 381, 392, 393, 395, 446, 483
see also DaimlerChrysler AG
CIBC, 23, 64–65
Cineplex Galaxy, 188
Cintas Canada Ltd., 200
Circuit City, 471
Cirque du Soleil, 172–173
Cisco Systems, 205, 448, 464
Citibank, 282, 342
City TV, 257
Civil Aeronautics Board, 556–557

Clearwater Fine Foods, 390
Clientlogic, 188
Clorox, 360
CNN, 257
Co-operative Commonwealth Federation (CCF), 373
Coast Mountain Bus Company (CmBC), 367
Coca-Cola Enterprises, 10, 156, 254, 257, 260, 273, 299, 435, 494, 496
Columbia School of Journalism, 533
Commercial Vehicle Group Inc., 188
Compaq Computers, 20, 79, 80, 119, 205, 357, 376, 387, 388, 389, 393, 398, 453
Concorde, 460
Condé Nast Traveler, 560
Conference Board of Canada, 465
Conservative Party of Canada, 2, 374
Continental Airlines, 77
Coopers and Lybrand, 552
Coors, 91
Cora's Restaurants, 375, 376
Cord, 381
Corel Corporation, 10, 334
Corning Glass Works, 215, 216, 217
Council on Health Strategy (Ontario), 343
Covisint, 95
Crédit Suisse, 485
Creo Inc., 219, 223–224, 236–330
Crown Cork and Seal, 196–197
Crystal Decisions Inc., 234, 236
CS First Boston, 485, 489
CTV, 257
Curragh Resources, 545, 552
Cymat Corp., 31
Cypress Semiconductor, 349

D

Daimler Benz, 194
DaimlerChrysler AG, 6, 84, 95, 194, 257, 260, 282, 333
  see also Chrysler
DEC, 448
Dell Computer Corp., 13–14, 16, 79–80, 83, 219, 376, 379, 386, 421–422, 448
Delta Airlines, 77, 475
Delta Hotels, 234
Denison Mines, 545
Detroit Red Wings, 508
Digital Equipment, 388, 563
Dixons, 449
Dofasco Inc., 236, 342, 463, 465
Du Pont, 119, 254, 262, 299
Dun and Bradstreet Canada, 236
Dusenberg, 381
Dylex, 2
Dynatec, 31

E

Eagle Professional Resources Inc., 148
Eastman Kodak. *See* Kodak
Eaton's, 2, 334
eBay, 223
The Economist, 54
The Edmonton Journal, 531, 538
Edmonton Oilers, 2
Edward Jones Canada, 234, 236
Electronic Data Systems, 234
EllisDon Construction, 295–296
EMI, 150, 151
EnCana, 217, 259
Enron Corporation, 24, 36, 42, 57, 59, 64, 219, 395, 501, 504
Environment Canada, 202
Envision Financial, 236
Ernst & Young, 356

F

Fair Labour Association (FLA), 248
Fairchild Semiconductor, 453
Federal Express, 82, 124, 428, 432–434
FedEx. *See* Federal Express
Fiat, 70
Financial Accounting Standards Board, 500
Financial Post, 29, 188, 331
Firestone, 231
Fishery Products International, 260
Flight Centre Ltd., 200, 234, 238
Forbes, 29
Ford Motor Company, 7, 46, 75, 76, 84, 88, 89, 90, 95, 111, 118, 188, 231, 256, 282, 292–293, 299, 320, 344, 381, 382, 435, 461, 462, 487
Ford of Europe, 282
Fortune, 29, 188, 331, 351, 560
Four Seasons Hotels and Resorts, 373
Fox Network, 257
Frito-Lay, 255
Fruit of the Loom, 247
Fuji Bank, 86, 87*f*
Fujitsu, 277
Fujitsu Canada, 390

G

Gannett newspaper chain, 536
The Gap, 451, 472
Gateway Computers, 79, 376
Geac Computer, 10
Genentech, 262
General Dynamics, 395, 396, 397
General Dynamics Canada, 193
General Electric, 46, 74, 75, 111, 155, 181, 185, 220, 276, 380, 412, 413, 561
General Gypsum Company, 166
General Mills, 70, 89, 162
General Motors Canada, 334
General Motors Company, 5, 6, 49, 91, 95, 96, 118, 188, 189, 191, 192, 225–227, 234, 256, 262, 263, 282, 292, 346, 347, 381, 419, 435, 483
GERAD, 312
Gerber Products, 70, 71, 231
Gildan Activewear, Inc., 247–248
Gillette, 53, 253, 299
Global Crossing, 36, 219
Global Television, 257
Globe and Mail, 29, 200, 533
Globe Metallurgical, Inc., 345, 346
Goldman Sachs, 225, 485
Goodyear, 394
Google, 29
Grant Thornton LLP, 390
Green Meadows Lawn Services, 576–582
Greenpeace, 2, 232

H

Hallmark Cards, 193, 350
H&R Block, 292
Hanes, 247
Hanson Trust, 275, 278
Heinz. *See* H.J. Heinz Company
Hertz Rent-a-Car, 88
Hewlett-Packard, 20, 238, 260, 314, 357, 378, 453, 463, 466
Hitachi Ltd., 86, 254, 276, 277
H.J. Heinz Company, 184
Hoffman-LaRoche Ltd., 200
Hollinger Inc., 488
Hollinger International, 487, 488, 495, 499
Holt Renfrew, 262, 264
Honda Motor Co., 6, 70, 73, 84, 263, 274, 381, 446
Honeywell, 483
Hudson's Bay Company, 54
Husky Energy, 299
Husky Injection Molding Systems, 242–243

I

IBM, 5, 29, 49, 79, 90, 91, 93, 97, 124, 125, 150, 185, 225, 231, 237, 239–240
IBM Canada, 23, 223
IfiniBand, 83
Imclone Systems, 219
Imperial Airways, 386
Inco, 10
Independent Film Channel, 377
Indigo, 78, 266
Indigo-Chapters, 78
Intel Corporation, 7, 79–80, 81, 90, 125, 260, 268, 447, 448
International Labour Organization (ILO), 248
International Longshoremen's and Warehousemen's Union, 373
Investors Group Financial Services, 165
Ipsos-Reid, 452
Irving Oil, 88

J

Japan Air Lines, 475
J.B. Hunt Transport, 83
JDS, 334
JetsGo Corp., 219, 288, 289
J.L. French Automotive, 188
Johnson & Johnson, 177, 185, 231, 244
Journalism School at Carleton University, 533

K

Katz Group Inc., 148
Kellogg Company, 70, 85
Kids Gap, 451
Kinko's, 2
Kmart, 135, 136, 262
Kodak, 17, 97, 256, 389, 394, 460, 483, 489
Kubas Consultants, 453

L

Laker Airlines, 89
L'Auto-Neige Bombardier Limitée, 270
Les Ailes de la Mode, 24
Les Boutiques San Francisco Inc., 24
Levi Strauss, 72, 120, 123, 125, 254
Li & Fung, 98
Liberal Party of Canada, 2
Lions Gate Entertainment, 482
Livebid.com, 471
Liz Claiborne, 147
Lockheed Martin, 390
Logitech Inc., 80
Lohnerwerke GmbH, 270
Lucent Technologies, 150, 464
Lush, 242

M

Magellen Health Services, 188
Magna International Inc., 2, 5, 23, 95, 117, 118, 118*f*
Major Baseball League Association (MBLA), 508
Mansville Corporation, 241
Maple Leaf Foods Inc., 23, 48
Maquila Solidarity Network (MSN), 247
Maritime Life, 217, 225, 226, 228
Mark's Work Wearhouse, 54, 264
Mary Kay Cosmetics, 446
Matsushita, 185, 448, 561, 562, 563
Mazda, 90
McCain Foods Limited, 15, 102, 184, 185, 186, 196, 215, 480
McDonald's, 2, 5, 5*f*, 75, 88, 96–97, 133, 134, 253, 254, 258, 264–265, 294, 295, 306, 378, 379, 385–386, 494
McDonald's Restaurants of Canada Ltd., 236
McDonnell Douglas, 475
McGill University, 312
MCI, 122
McKinsey & Co., 469
McMaster University, 463, 465
MDP World Wide, 482
Membertou Band Council, 389, 390
Membertou Development Corporation, 390
Mercedes-Benz, 257, 381
Merck, 77, 231, 313, 468, 494, 495
Merrill Lynch, 485
Microelectronics and Computer Corporation, 90
Microsoft Corp., 8–20, 79, 80, 83, 130, 217, 219–220, 223, 225, 230, 235, 239, 240, 254, 255, 262, 271, 294, 298, 313, 359, 379, 380, 382, 389–391, 415, 416, 448, 456, 466, 468, 494
Miller Brewing, 272
Mine Safety and Health Administration (MSHA) Academy, 548
Ministry of International Trade and Industry (Japan), 90
Mitsubishi Motor Co., 84
Molson Inc., 48, 91, 215, 299
Monsanto, 271
Montgomery Ward, 424–425
The Montreal Gazette, 531, 532, 533, 535, 538
Morris Air, 452, 560
Morton Thiokol, 244
Motorola, 90, 321, 322, 448, 483
Mountain Equipment Co-operative, 467, 468
MSN, 416

N

National Basketball Association (NBA), 508
National Child Care Association, 383
National Football League (NFL), 508
National Hockey League (NHL), 40, 480, 508
National Hockey League Players Association (NHLPA), 508
National Post, 29
Natural Sciences and Engineering Research Council, 465
NBC, 181
Neiman-Marcus, 196–197, 225, 262
Netscape, 415, 416
New Democratic Party, 2, 373
New Jersey Nets, 508
New United Motors Manufacturing Inc. (NUMMI), 347
New York Fries, 375
New York Rangers, 508
New York Stock Exchange, 64, 73
Newsweek, 29
Nexen Inc., 236
NEXT, 14
NHL. *See* National Hockey League (NHL)
Nike, 85, 97, 205, 206, 310, 335
Nissan Motor Co., 84, 86
NKK, 86
Noranda, 215
Nordstrom, 262
Norsk Hydro, 31
Nortel Networks Corp., 15, 17, 36, 48, 49, 121, 122, 150, 185, 235, 330, 334, 464, 499, 501
Northern Miner, 545
Norwegian Helicopter Services Group, 181
Nova Scotia Power Corporation, 3, 7, 9, 10, 11, 15, 23*t*, 197, 199–200, 214, 215, 225, 228, 235, 237, 355, 356, 545
Nucor, 269

O

Oakland, 188–189
Office Depot, 471
Old Navy, 451
Oldsmobile, 188–189
Olive Garden, 162
OMERS, 36
Oncap, 188
Onex Corporation, 188
Ontario Hydro, 12
Ontario Power Generation, 3, 10, 12, 15
Ontario Teachers Pension Plan, 36
Ore-Ida, 102
Organisation for Economic Co-operation and Development (OECD), 8
Oshawa Group Ltd., 148
The Ottawa Citizen, 531, 533, 535, 537

P

Pacific Southwest Airlines, 556, 560
Packard, 381
Palister, 183
Pan American Airlines, 386
Panasonic, 90, 256, 259
Pancanadian Energy, 217
PEAK Financial Group, 223
PepsiCo, 10, 255, 257
Performance Logistics Group, 188
Petro-Canada, 242, 299
Peugeot. *See* PSA Peugeot Citroën
Pharma Plus, 148
Philip Morris, 260, 272
Philips NV, 90, 283, 561–563
Phoenix Pictures, 188
Pixar, 14
PLC Construction Group Inc., 236
Polaroid, 394
Pontiac, 188–189
PriceWaterhouse Coopers, 73
Procter & Gamble, 111, 228, 229, 254, 255
Progressive Conservative Party, 374
PSA Peugeot Citroën, 31, 70
Public Works and Government Services Canada, 22

Q

QLT Inc., 236

R

Radian Communication Services, 188
Radio Shack, 274
Ralston Purina, 232
Ravelston Corp., 488
Ravelston Management Inc., 488
RBC. *See* Royal Bank of Canada (RBC)
RBC Capital Markets, 147
RBC Financial Group, 236
RCA, 448, 460
Red Lobster, 162
Reform Party, 374
REI, 467
Renault, 70
Res-Care Inc., 188

Research in Motion (RIM), 224, 373, 388, 446, 448
Retail Council of Canada, 54
Rogers Wireless Communications Inc., 29
Rolls Royce, 265, 273, 381
Roots Company, 20
Rotary Club, 2
Rotax-Werk AG, 270
Rothmans, 200
Royal Bank of Canada (RBC), 73, 144, 242
Running Room, 453

S

Saks, 225
Salter Street Films, 376, 377
Salvation Army, 5
Sam's Clubs, 197, 198
Santa Fe Pacific Corporation, 83
Saskatchewan Rough Riders, 2
Saturn, 263
Scandinavian Airways System, 228
Scotiabank. *See* Bank of Nova Scotia
Sears Roebuck, 17, 54, 135, 136, 231, 294, 424, 425
Second Cup, 2
Security Pacific, 218
Shell Canada, 242
Shermag Inc., 484
Siemens, 111, 561
siteROCK, 226
SNC Lavalin, 390
Sodexho Canada, 390
Sony Corporation, 90, 129, 259, 271, 278, 327, 448, 466, 561, 562, 563
Sotheby's, 471
Southam Inc., 530
Southam Newspaper Group, 529–538
Southwest Airlines, 219, 288, 452, 556–560
The Spectator, 535
Stanley Associates Engineering, 210
Stanley Technology Group, 210
Stantec Inc., 210–211
Star Alliance, 288
Starbucks, 3
Stelco Inc., 334, 353
Suncor Energy Incorporated, 231, 232, 242
Suncor Inc., 232
Superior Propane Inc., 224
Superior Propane Income Fund, 224
Swiss Chalet, 2
Sydney Steel, 2
Sympatico, 2

T

Tandy Corporation, 274
Target, 471
Techlink Entertainment, 390
Teknion Furniture Systems, 155
Telus, 421, 422
Tembec Inc., 463, 465
Tex Instruments, 454
Texaco, 229
Texas Aeronautics Commission, 556
Texas Instruments, 387
Texas International, 557–558
Textron, 276, 397
3M, 223, 225, 254, 255, 427–436, 463, 553–555
Tiffany, 265
Tim Hortons, 254, 265–309, 378, 379
Time, 18, 29
Time Warner, 17, 18, 351
Toronto -Dominion Bank (TD), 217
Toronto Blue Jays, 2
Toronto Hospital for Sick Children, 292
Toronto Maple Leafs, 508
Toronto Stock Exchange, 31, 64, 73, 210, 377, 403
Toronto Sun, 38
Toyota Motor Co., 6–7, 70, 73, 89, 96, 118, 189, 254, 256, 259, 262, 265, 294, 318, 320, 346, 347, 381, 419, 446, 448
Toys "R" Us, 256, 330–471
Trans-Canada, 48
Trans-Canada Air Lines, 7
Translink, 367
TRW, 395
Tungsram, 74, 75
Turner Broadcasting System, 257, 351
Tyco International Ltd., 219, 395

U

Union Pacific, 156
Unisys, 448
United Air Lines, 386
United Mine Workers of America, 547, 551
United Nations, 336, 337
United Technologies, 217
United Way, 121
Université de Montreal, 312
University of British Columbia, 467
Upjohn, 77
UPS, 432–434, 433*f*
U.S. Food and Drug Administration, 231
U.S. Securities Exchange Commission, 39

V

The Vancouver Province, 538
The Vancouver Sun, 530, 538
Velan Inc., 485
Verizon, 122, 386
VF Company, 259, 319
Vitro, 216, 217
Vivendi, 49
Volkswagen, 70, 84, 95, 118
Volvo, 70

W

Wal-Mart, 54, 134, 135–136, 178, 197, 198, 198*f*, 198–199, 225, 229, 262, 264, 294, 309, 310, 330, 359, 379, 385, 425
Wall Street Journal, 29
Walt Disney Company, 227
Wang, 448
Webvan, 428, 429
Wendy's Restaurants, 264, 378, 385
Western Economic Diversification Canada, 39
WestJet Airlines Ltd., 2, 219, 220, 224, 225, 288–289, 450, 452
Westray Coal, 544–552
Whirlpool Corporation, 119
Willbros Group Inc., 83
The Windsor Star, 533, 535–538
Woolco, 197
Woolworth Canada, 197
Workforce Magazine, 173
WorldCom Inc., 24, 36, 42, 59, 219, 499, 500, 501, 504
Worldwide REsponsible Apparel Production (WRAP), 248

X

Xerox Corporation, 91, 259, 260, 392, 395

Y

Yahoo!, 29, 223, 350
YMCA, 379, 382, 383
Young Men's Christian Association. *See* YMCA

Z

Zellers, 264, 294
Zenon Environmental Inc., 242
Zytec Corporation, 165

Name Index

A
Akers, John, 435
Anders, William A., 397
Anderson, J.V., 454
Anderson, Philip, 447, 448*n*
Armstrong, Michael, 480–481

B
Balga, Linda, 536
Bannon, Brian, 535
the Barclay brothers, 488
Bealor, Bill, 537
the Beatles, 151
Beaudoin, Laurent, 270, 480
Beddoe, Clive, 220, 225, 452
Bell, Donald, 452
Beneteau, Marty, 537–538
Benner, Colin, 550–551
Bennis, Warren, 358
Beresford, Dennis, 500
Bezos, Jeffrey, 3, 4, 7, 78, 126, 178, 266, 452, 471
Bimba, Charles, 236
Black, Bill, 217, 228
Black, Conrad, 487, 488, 499
Bombardier, J.-Armand, 270
Bonner, Lenny, 548–550
Bridges, Harry, 373
Brioux, Bill, 38
Brooks, Garth, 151
Brown, Robert, 270
Buchanan, John, 546
Bullock, Gordon, 535, 536
Burchell, Bob, 548–551
Burke, Ronald J., 529
Burns, Tom, 130, 133, 134, 135*f*
Bush, George W., 36

C
Cameron, Donald, 546, 550, 551, 552
Canion, Rod, 388, 398, 453
Capellas, Michael, 357, 388
Carlson, Jan, 228
Carp, Dan, 483
Champy, J., 346
Chase, Steve, 228
Cheverie, Wayne, 549
Chrétien, Jean, 441
Christmas, Bernd, 390
Claiborne, Liza, 147
Clow, Graham, 551
Comeau, Louis, 7, 9, 10, 11, 23*t*, 228, 235
Comish, Shaun, 548–550
Comper, Tony, 190
Cotton, Crosbie, 538
Crozier, Michael, 495

D
Das, Hari, 520, 522
Davey, Clark, 533, 537
Davidson, Dick, 156
Davis, Oliver, 576–582
Dekker, Wisse, 562
Dell, Michael, 13, 14, 454
Deming, W. Edwards, 341
Donovan, Michael, 376, 377
Donovan, Paul, 376, 377
Dooley, Donnie, 549
Doucette, Fred, 545
Douglas, Tommy, 373
Dressler, Paul, 451
Drexler, Millard ("mickey"), 451
Dunn, Frank, 501
Durant, William C., 188

E
Ebbers, Bernie, 500

F
Feltmate, Roy, 544
Fields, Debby, 452
Fiorino, Carly, 314
Fisher, George, 483
Fisher, John, 530, 535
Ford, Henry, 188, 292, 293, 295, 315, 381
Ford, Henry II, 462, 487
Ford, Henry III, 46
Fox, Terry, 373
Fox, Wayne, 65
Frame, Clifford, 545–546, 552
Franklin, Bill, 557, 558
Fraser, Joan, 536
Fraser, Robbie, 544
Frey, Don, 461, 462
Fry, Arthur, 553
Fung, Victor, 98
Fung, William, 98

G
Gagnon, Marc, 172–173
Gates, Bill, 8–9, 20, 230, 235, 239, 240, 389, 468, 494
George, Rick, 231, 232
Gerstner, Lou, 237, 240, 425, 435, 480–481
Glass, David, 198
Goddard, Adrienne, 453
Goizueta, Roberto, 435
Goodenow, Bob, 508
Gould, Hal, 375
Gould, Jay, 375
Greiner, L.E., 386–392, 387*n*
Guptill, Carl, 544, 545, 551, 552

H
Hall, Karen, 535
Hamel, G., 469
Hammer, Michael, 346
Hansen, M.T., 421
Heskett, James, 419–420
Hewlett, William, 453
Hill, Charles W.L., 561
Hill, Mark, 452
Horton, Tim, 378
House, Randy, 544
Hughes, Linda, 536
Hunkin, John, 65

I
Iacocca, Lee, 195, 461, 462, 487
Isozaki, Arata, 227
Iverson, Ken, 269

J
Jackall, Robert, 492
Jager, Durk I., 229
Jarislowsky, Stephen, 485
Jobs, Steve, 13, 14, 46, 454
Johnson, Eugene, 549, 552
Johnston, Summerfield, 156
Jonsson, E., 396–398, 396*n*
Juran, Joseph, 341

K
Kanter, Rosabeth Moss, 497
Katzenbach, Nicholas, 500
Kelleher, Herb, 556–560
Kenny, Jim, 495, 496
King, Robin, 556
Kotter, John, 419–420
Kroc, Ray, 385

L
Lawrence, Paul, 130, 131–133, 135*f*, 260
Lazaridis, Mike, 373, 388, 452
Le Play, Frederic, 551
Levering, Robert, 560
Levy, Alain, 151
Lewin, Kurt, 338–339, 338*f*, 353, 354*f*
Liik, Michael, 31
Lilly, Dave, 226
Lorsch, Jay, 130, 131–133, 135*f*, 260

M
MacCullogh, Bill, 544, 546, 547, 548, 551
MacDonald, Todd, 550
MacDonough, Alexa, 552
MacKay, Elmer, 545

MacKay, Mike, 544
March, James, 417
Marshall, Colin, 228
McCain, Andrew, 102
McCain, Harrison, 102
McCain, Michael, 480
McCain, Robert, 102
McCain, Wallace, 102
McGinn, Richard, 464
McGowan, Rosemary, 576
McKnight, William L., 553–554, 555
McLean, Albert, 544, 545, 549, 551, 552
Melanson, Ralph, 548
Melville, George, 140
Michelson, Amos, 237
Mikalachki, Alexander, 529
Mikalachki, Dorothy R., 529
Millar, Doug, 537
Miller, Diane, 581
Mills, Albert J., 544
Mills, Jean Helms, 539
Mills, Russ, 529–530, 531, 532, 533, 534, 535, 536
Milton, Robert, 237
Ming, Jenny, 451
Mintzberg, Henry, 412, 414
Mitsch, Ronald A., 553
Monforton, Lisa, 538
Moore, Michael, 377
Morgan, Carl, 537
Morgan, Tim, 452
Morrison, Dale, 102
Moskowitz, Milton, 560
Muse, M. Lamar, 556–557, 558

N

Nasser, Jacques, 46
Nikiforuk, Andrew, 232
Nohria, M., 421
Nonaka, I., 454
Nystrom, Paul C., 424, 430, 431

O

O'Connell, Caroline, 544
Owens, Bill, 122

P

Packard, David, 453
Parker, Jim, 558, 559
Parkinson, C. Northcote, 149, 395
Parry, Roger, 544–545, 549, 550, 552
Paul, Terrance, 389, 390
Pendse, Shripad, 512
Perks, David, 532, 533, 538
Perot, Ross, 234
Perrow, Charles, 302, 303–308, 305*n*, 564
Peters, Tim, 532
Peterson, Kevin, 538
Pettigrew, Andrew, 495
Pfeffer, Jeffrey, 497
Pfeiffer, Ekhard, 388, 398
Philips, Anton, 561
Philips, Gerard, 561
Phillips, Calvin, 559
Phillips, Gerald, 548, 550, 552
Pittman, Bob, 17, 18
Pondy, Louis R., 481, 487
Prahalad, C.K., 469
Precop, Sandra, 537

R

Rabinovitch, Robert, 38
Ramson, Cindy, 360
Reavely, Tom, 557
Reich, Robert, 54
Richard, Peter, 550–552
Richards, Amanda, 107–108, 111, 176
Richards, Bob, 107–108, 111, 176
Robinson, Peter, 468
Rodgers, T.J., 349
Rogers, Harry, 546
Rolling Stones, 151
Rosenberg, Richard, 218
Roth, John, 501

S

Sant, Roger, 120
Schacht, Henry, 464
Schad, Robert, 243
Schein, E.H., 220–221
Scott, Lee, 198
Sculley, John, 13
Sears, Matthew, 548
Seeger, John A., 567
Senge, Peter, 417, 418, 419, 420
Sharp, Isadore, 373
Sherman, Paddy, 530
Silver, Spencer, 553
Simpson, John, 576
Sloan, Alfred P., 188, 189, 192, 381
Smith, John, 545
Smith, Robert, 218
Smith, Roger, 234
Spacey, Kevin, 482
Stalker, G.M., 130, 133, 134, 135*f*
Stanley, Don, 210
Stanton, John, 452, 453
Starbuck, William H., 424, 430, 431
Steffen, Christopher, 483
Stronach, Frank, 118

T

Tellier, Paul, 270, 480
Thompson, James D., 308, 308*f*, 312, 482
Thomson, James, 535
Tierney, T., 421
Timmer, Jan, 563
Treliving, Jim, 140
Triffo, Ron, 210
Tsouflidou, Cora Mussely, 375
Tushman, Michael, 447, 448*n*

V

van de Klugt, Cor, 562–563
Van Mennen, J., 220–221

W

Weber, Max, 158, 159, 160
Weir, Tony, 537
Weitzel, W., 396–398, 396*n*
White, Claude, 545–548
Whitman, David, 119
Whitmore, Kay, 483
Woodward, Joan, 295–303, 301*n*
Wozniak, Steven, 13, 454
Wright, Jim, 558

Y

Young, John A., 314

Subject Index

A

Abella Commission, 16, 229–230
absenteeism, 338, 347
accommodative approach, 242
action research
  bottom-up change, 356–357
  defined, 353
  desired future state, 355
  diagnosing the organization, 354–355
  evaluating the action, 357
  external change agents, 356
  implementing action, 355–357
  institutionalizing, 357–358
  internal change agents, 356
  steps in, 354*f*
  top-down change, 356
adaptive cultures, 419–420
adaptive functions, 111
advanced manufacturing technology (AMT)
  computer-aided design (CAD), 318
  computer-aided materials management (CAMM), 319
  computer-integrated manufacturing (CIM), 321–323
  flexible manufacturing technology, 321–323
  just-in-time inventory (JIT) systems, 319–321, 320*f*
  materials technology innovations, 318–323
  movement towards, 315–317
  work flow in, 317*f*
advise and support model, 344
agency problem, 48, 49–50
agency theory perspective
  agency problem, 48, 49–50
  career paths, 49–50
  incentives, 49–50
  moral hazard problem, 48–49
  promotion tournaments, 49–50
  solving the agency problem, 49–50
  stock-based compensation schemes, 49
agenda, control of, 502
airline industry, 77
allocation of rewards, 43–44
and specific assets, 93
animal testing, 53
anticompetitive practices, 88–89, 91
Aston studies, 303
attitude changes, 490–491
authority, 492–494
  defined, 44
  and differentiation, 110
  flat organization, 145, 145*f*, 148
  height limitations, 144–146
  hierarchical levels, ideal number of, 149–150
  hierarchy, emergence of, 144
  hierarchy of authority, 115
  Parkinson's law problem, 149
  principle of minimum chain of command, 149–150
  rational-legal authority, 158–159
  and senior management, 44–48
  size limitations, 145–146
  span of control, 150–153, 151*f*, 152*f*
  tall organizations, 145, 147–149
  vertical differentiation, 143–153

B

banking industry, 384
bargaining, 360
birth stage. *See* organizational birth
blinded stage, 396
board of directors
  agency theory perspective, 48–50
  function of, 44
  principal role of, 49
bottom-up change, 356–357
boundary-spanning activity, 470–471
boundaryless organization, 207
bounded rationality, 92–93, 411
bribery, 74, 82
British mining industry, 340
bureaucracy
  advantages of, 163–164
  bureaucratic principles, 158–163, 159*t*
  defined, 158
bureaucratic costs
  multidivisional structure, 192
  tall organization, 148–149
  transaction cost theory, 94
bureaucratic culture, 395
bureaucratic principles, 159*t*
  clarity of roles, 160
  rational-legal authority, 158–159
  roles, organization of, 160
  rules, SOPs and norms, 161–163
  technical competence, 159–160
business-level strategy
  and culture, 269–271
  defined, 257
  described, 257, 264
  differentiation strategy, 264–265
  focus strategy, 265
  low-cost strategy, 264–265
  and structure, 265–269, 267*f*
  types of, 266*f*
business plan, 374–376, 375*t*
business process, 347–348

C

Canadian Charter of Rights and Freedoms, 52
Canadian Information Productivity Awards, 296
capital keiretsu, 85–86
career paths, 49–50
Carnegie model, 410–412, 411*t*, 428
cartel, 88–89
cases
  "Air Canada restructures for survival in a changed global industry," 288–289
  "Banking on a culture of ethics: restoring the reputation of the CIBC," 64–65
  "Big changes at Boeing," 475
  "The Boston Pizza way!", 139–141
  "Cell-Loc's organizational transformation and rebirth," 402–403
  "Change for McCain Foods Limited," 102
  "Encouraging learning in the Canadian public service," 441–442
  "The future of the National Hockey League," 508
  Gildan Activewear's approach to social responsibility", 247–248
  "Groupe Noel," 520–521
  "Lightco: the case of the serial changers," 539–543
  "Norton's Department Stores," 522–529
  "Oliver Davis's entrepreneurial success story: no lost clients, no employee terminations, no debt," 576–582
  "Organizational change at Coast Mountain Bus," 367–368
  "Organizational structure transformations at Cymat Corp.", 31
  "Philips NV," 561–563
  "The problem and 'I': Some reflections on problems, perception, action and wisdom," 512–519
  "'Ramrod' Stockwell," 564–567
  "Reconfiguring the HR function under the Big Top," 172–173
  "Rondell Data Corporation," 567–575
  "The shape of things to come," 327
  "Southam Newspaper Group: Equalizing employment equity," 529–538
  "Southwest Airlines," 556–560
  "Stantec: a historic success story of adapting organizational structure for growth," 210–211
  "Three roads to innovation," 553–555
  "The Westray Mine explosion," 544–552
centrality, 496, 498
centralization, 120–123, 155–156

ceremonies, 223–227
chain of command, 46, 149–150
Challenger space shuttle, 244
change
  organizational change. *See* organizational change
  political change and organizational functions, 11
  technological change. *See* technological change
change management, 353–358
  see also action research
chief executive officer (CEO)
  function of, 46–47
  salaries, 43
chief operating officers (COOs), 17, 47
child labour, 54
chiseller, 125
co-optation, 82
coalition-building, 499–500
codification approach, 421–423
coercion, 361
coercive isomorphism, 385
cognitive biases
  cognitive dissonance, 426
  devil's advocate, 435–436
  ego-defensiveness, 428
  escalation of commitment, 428–430
  frequency, 427
  illusion of control, 426–427
  projection, 428
  representativeness, 428
  types of, 425–426
cognitive dissonance, 426
cognitive structure, 424–425
collaboration, 392
collateral organizational structure, 436
collective socialization tactics, 221
collusion, 88–89
command and control model, 344
common ties, 499
communication, 359
communication problems
  functional structure, 179
  multidivisional structure, 192–193
  tall organizations, 147
community dependency, 40–41
compensation
  CEO salaries, 43
  stock-based compensation schemes, 49
competing goals, 42–43
competitive advantage
  defined, 16
  empowerment of work groups, 360
  functions and, 112
  gaining, 16
  technology, international transfer of, 72
competitive forces, 333
competitive interdependencies
  cartel, 88–89
  collusion, 88–89
  defined, 79–80
  management strategies, 88–91
  merger, 90–91
  strategic alliances, 90
  takeover, 90–91
  third-party linkage mechanisms, 89–90
complex tasks, 303–307
computer-aided design (CAD), 318
computer-aided manufacturing (CAM), 318
computer-aided materials management (CAMM), 319
computer-aided production, 317
computer-integrated manufacturing (CIM), 321–323
conflict
  see also organizational conflict
  resistances to change, 335–336
  role conflict, 160
conflict aftermath, 487
conflict resolution strategies
  attitude changes, 490–491
  choice of method, 489
  individual changes, 490–491
  structural changes, 489–490
conglomerate structure, 275, 276*f*
contingency, 15, 26
contingency approach, 130
contingent workers, 168
continuous-process technology, 299–300, 302
contributions, 34, 35*t*
control
  of agenda, 502
  centralization, 155–156
  crisis of control, 391
  decentralization, 156
  and differentiation, 110
  and effectiveness, 19, 20
  functional structure problems, 179–180
  horizontal differentiation, 153–154, 154*f*, 155*f*
  illusion of control, 426–427
  and multidivisional structure, 191
  and organizational structure, 153–158
  organizations and, 7–8
  over decision making premises, 497
  over information, 495
  over resources, 494–495
  over uncertainty, 496
  production control, 111
  quality control, 111
  span of control, 150–153, 151*f*, 152*f*
  standardization, 157–158
control systems, 254
conversion stage, 4, 294, 294*f*
coordination, 391–392
coordination ability, 254–255
core competencies
  coordination ability, 254–255
  defined, 16, 112, 253
  and global expansion, 255–256
  and global learning, 256
  global network, 255–256
  global resources and skills, access to, 256
  sources of, 253–255
  specialized resources, 254
  structural characteristics, 261*f*
  transfer abroad, 255
corporate governance, 39
corporate headquarters staff, 186–187
corporate-level strategy
  conglomerate structure, 275, 276*f*
  and culture, 277–279
  defined, 257
  described, 257–258, 272
  for entering new domains, 273*f*
  related diversification, 274, 275–276
  and structure, 275–276
  unrelated diversification, 274–275
  vertical integration, 272–274
corporate managers, 47
corporate scandals, 39
corruption, 74
cosmetics testing, 53
costs
  bureaucratic costs, 94, 148–149, 192
  decision maker costs, 410
  information costs, 409
  transaction costs, 7, 56, 92
counselling, 361
craftswork, 292, 305
creativity
  defined, 454
  growth through creativity stage, 387–388
  and innovation, 454–455
crisis of autonomy, 389
crisis of control, 391
crisis of leadership, 388
crisis of red tape, 392
crisis stage, 398
critical path method (CPM), 457
cross-functional teams, 168, 459–461, 460*f*
Crown corporations, 15, 235
cultural forces, 73–74
culture. *See* global culture; organizational culture
customer-centric approach, 122
customer loyalty, 342
customer problems, 180
customers, 37
customers, alliances with, 499

D

decentralization, 120–123, 156
decision maker costs, 410
decision making. *See* organizational decision making
decision trees, 433, 433*f*
decline. *See* organizational decline
decline stage, 449
dedicated machines, 315
defensive approach, 241–242
delegation, 389–391
demographic forces, 73–74, 333–334
design. *See* organizational design
desired future state, 355
devil's advocate, 435–436, 436*f*
diagnosing the organization, 354–355
dialectical inquiry, 435–436, 436*f*
differentiation
  authority, 110
  at B.A.R. and Grille, 111–112
  building blocks, 110*f*
  in complex organization, 107
  control, 110
  defined, 106–107
  design challenge, 109*f*, 113
  division of labour, 107, 108
  divisions, 110–111
  and the environment, 131–133

functions, 110–111, 131*f*
horizontal differentiation. *See* horizontal differentiation
increasing, and divisional structure, 181–182, 182*f*
vs. integration, 119–120
integration, balancing with, 114–120
organizational role, 108–110
in simple organization, 107
subunits, 110–111
uncertainty, effect of, 132*t*
vertical differentiation. *See* vertical differentiation
differentiation business-level strategy, 264–265
differentiation functional-level strategy, 258–260, 258*t*
direct contact, 115
directors, 44–45
discourse, 497
disjunctive socialization tactics, 221
dissolution stage, 398
diversification, 274–275, 276
diversity management, 16
divestiture, 222
division
defined, 110–111
self-contained division, 112
subunit orientation, 114
division of labour, 6, 107, 108, 311
divisional managers, 48
divisional structure
defined, 183
geographic structure, 183, 196
market structure, 183, 197–200, 199*f*
movement to, 181–182, 183–184
multidivisional structure, 185–193
product division structure, 184–185, 184*f*, 185*f*
product structure, 183, 194–195
product team structure, 193–195, 194*f*
self-contained division, 185
downsizing, 149, 351–352
dynamic environment, 76

E

e-engineering, 349–351
e-grocers, 429
economic forces, 72, 333
economies of scale, 6
economies of scope, 6
education, 359
effectiveness
allocation of rewards, 43–44
competing goals, 42–43
control, 19, 20
in different areas, 24
efficiency, 19, 21–22
external resource approach, 20
innovation, 19, 20
internal systems approach, 20
measurement of, 18–19, 19*t*
and multidivisional structure, 191
and organizational conflict, 479*f*
organizational goals, 22–24
and organizational size, 394*f*
stakeholders' goals and interests, 41–44
technical approach, 21
and technology, 294–295
efficiency, 16–17, 19, 21–22
ego-defensiveness, 428
embryonic stage, 449
employee stock-ownership plan (ESOP), 233
employees
contingent workers, 168
empowerment, 168–169, 359
fixed workers, 316
informal norms, 125
and innovation, 466–467
intrapreneurs, 451–454
and organizational ethics, 50–57
participation, 359
as stakeholders, 37
two-boss employees, 201
unionized employees, 40
values, trapped by, 220
whistle-blowing, 60
Employment Equity Act, 385
empowerment, 168–169, 359, 494
engineering, 111
engineering production, 305–306
enterprise-wide information technology systems, 420
entrepreneurs, 373
entrepreneurship, 2, 374
environment, 69*f*
changes in, and decline, 395
defined, 68
and differentiation, 131–133
dynamic environment, 76
fit with organization, 131–135, 131*f*
general environment, 72–74
institutional environment, 384
and integration, 131–133
and mechanistic structures, 133–135
and organic structures, 133–135
resource-poor environments, 76
specific environment, 70–72
stable environment, 76
and strategy, 252–258
uncertainty, 74–77, 74*f*, 92–93
unstable environment, 76
environmental complexity, 75–76
environmental dynamism, 76
environmental forces, 72–73
environmental niches, 376
environmental richness, 76–77
escalation of commitment, 428–430
ethical culture, 60–61
ethical forces, 334
ethical organizations, 59–61
ethics
corporate scandals, 39
defined, 50
development of ethical rules, 55–57
factors influencing development of, 230*f*
individual ethics, 55
justice model of decision making, 51, 51*t*
moral rights model of decision making, 51, 51*t*
and organizational culture, 219, 230–233
and outside pressure, 59
personal ethics, 58–59
professional ethics, 55
reputation effect, 56–57
self-interest, 59
societal ethics, 52–53
sources of organizational ethics, 52–55
support for stakeholder interests, 61
tragedy of the commons problem, 55
and transaction costs, 56
unethical behaviour, occurrence of, 57–59
utilitarian model of decision making, 51, 51*t*
whistle-blowing, 60, 231–232, 243
European Community (EC), 71
European Union (EU), 333
evaluation of action, 357
evolutionary change
defined, 339
developments in, 340–346
flexible workers and work teams, 344–346, 345*f*
sociotechnical systems theory, 340–341
total quality management (TQM), 341–344, 349
experimentation, 431–432
exploitation, 417
exploration, 417
external change agents, 356
external environment, management of, 7
external resource approach, 20, 295

F

Fabry's disease, 58
fads, 449–450
fashion, 449–450
faulty action stage, 398
felt conflict, 486
financial keiretsu, 85, 86
first-mover advantages, 379
fixed automation, 316
fixed socialization tactics, 221
fixed workers, 316
flat organization, 145, 145*f*, 148, 168
flexible manufacturing technology, 321–323
flexible production, 317
flexible work teams, 344–346, 345*f*
flexible workers, 344
focus strategy, 265
force-field theory of change, 338–339, 338*f*
forces for change
competitive forces, 333
demographic forces, 333–334
economic forces, 333
ethical forces, 334
global forces, 333
political forces, 333
social forces, 333–334
formal socialization tactics, 221
formalization, 124
franchising, 96–97
frequency, 427
function
adaptive functions, 111
defined, 110

human resource management (HRM) function, 259
line function, 483
maintenance functions, 111
managerial functions, 111
mechanistic structure, 127
production functions, 111
staff function, 483
subunit orientation, 114
support functions, 111
functional differentiation, 131*f*
functional hierarchies, 154*f*
functional-level strategy
and culture, 262–263
defined, 257
described, 257
goal, 258
low-cost strategy, 258–260, 258*t*
product differentiation strategies, 258–260, 258*t*
and structure, 260–262, 261*f*
functional managers, 48
functional orientation differences, 336
functional resources, 254, 331
functional structure
advantages of, 178
communication problems, 179
control problems, 179–180
customer problems, 180
defined, 176–177
horizontal differentiation and, 177
integration, improvement of, 180*f*
location problems, 179
measurement problems, 179
solving control problems, 180
strategic problems, 180
Fuyo keiretsu, 86, 87*f*

G

game theory, 432–434
GANTT chart, 456
garbage can model of decision making, 414–415
general environment
cultural forces, 73–74
defined, 72
demographic forces, 73–74
economic forces, 72
environmental forces, 72–73
political forces, 72–73
social forces, 73–74
technological forces, 72
general public, 41
generalists, 380
geographic divisional structure, 183, 196–197*f*, 281*f*
geographical spread, 179
global culture, 216
global expansion strategy, 258
global forces, 333
global geographic structure, 281*f*
global learning, 256
global matrix structure, 284*f*
global network, 255–256
global product group structure, 282*f*
global resources and skills, 256
global strategy
implementation of, 279–284
international strategy, 282
multidomestic strategy, 280–282
strategy-structure relationships, 281*t*
transnational strategy, 283–284
global trade
Canada's history in, 68
North American Free Trade Agreement (NAFTA), 216, 215, 333
protectionism, 71–72
globalization, and core competencies, 255–256
goals
differences in, 482
official goals, 22
operative goals, 23–24
organizational goals, 22–24
resource dependence theory, 79
stakeholders' goals, 41–44
governance mechanisms, 49
government, 39
"green culture," 232
Greiner's model of organizational growth
crisis of autonomy, 389
crisis of control, 391
crisis of leadership, 388
crisis of red tape, 392
described, 386–387, 387*f*
growth through collaboration, 392
growth through coordination, 391–392
growth through creativity stage, 387–388
growth through delegation stage, 389–391
growth through direction stage, 388–389
group cohesiveness, 337
group level of organizational learning, 418–419
group-level resistance to change, 337–337
groupthink, 337, 435
growth. *See* organizational growth
growth stage, 449
growth through collaboration, 392
growth through coordination, 391–392
growth through creativity stage, 387–388
growth through delegation stage, 389–391
growth through direction stage, 388–389

H

habit, 338
health care, 57–58, 92, 343
heavyweight team leader, 461
height limitations, 144–146
hierarchy
and creativity, 151
defined, 45–46, 112
emergence of, 144
factors affecting shape of, 153*f*
ideal number of levels, 149–150
managerial hierarchies, 146*f*
principle of minimum chain of command, 149–150
tall hierarchies, problems with, 147–149
hierarchy of authority, 115
high technical complexity, 297
horizontal differentiation
and control, 153–154, 154*f*, 155*f*
defined, 113
effect of, 161–162
and effectiveness, 160
functional structure, 177
increasing, and divisional structure, 182
and self-contained division, 185
human resource management (HRM) function, 259
human resources, 331

I

implementing action, 355–357
inaction stage, 397
incremental innovations, 447
incremental technological change, 447
incrementalist model of decision making, 412–430
indispensability, 498
individual changes, 490–491
individual ethics, 55
individual level of organizational learning, 417–418
individual-level resistance to change, 337–338
individual socialization tactics, 221
individualized role orientation, 221, 222
inducements, 34, 35*t*
inert cultures, 419–420
informal organization, influence of, 165–167
informal socialization tactics, 221
information, 409–410, 495
information costs, 409
information efficiencies, 469
information synergies, 470–471
information technology
boundary-spanning activity, 470–471
and empowerment, 167–169
enterprise-wide systems, 420
information efficiencies, 469
information synergies, 470–471
and innovation, 469–472
knowledge management, 421–423
and organizational culture, 471–472
and organizational structure, 471–472
and self-managed teams, 167–169
innovation
and creativity, 454–455
defined, 352, 446
and employees, 466
incremental innovations, 447
and information technology, 469–472
and intrapreneurs, 451–454
knowledge-creating organization, 455
and organizational change, 16–17
and organizational culture, 465–468
organizational effectiveness, 19, 20
and organizational structure, 465–466
and property rights, 467–468
quantum innovations, 447
as revolutionary change, 352
and risk, 446–447
innovation process management
cross-functional teams, 459–461, 460*f*
joint venture, 463
new venture divisions, 463
product team structure, 459–461, 460*f*

project management, 455–458
skunk works, 462–463
stage-gate development funnel, 458–459, 458*f*
team leadership, 461
innovative responses, 125
input stage, 294, 294*f*
inputs, 69
inside directors, 44–45
inside stakeholders, 35, 37
institutional environment, 384
institutional investors, 36
institutional theory
defined, 382
organizational isomorphism, 385–386
institutionalized role orientation, 221, 222
institutionalizing action research, 357–358
instrumental values, 214, 214*f*, 217
integrating mechanisms, 115–119, 116*t*, 117*f*
integrating role, 119
integration
defined, 115
vs. differentiation, 119–120
differentiation, balancing with, 114–120
direct contact, 115
and the environment, 131–133
in functional structure, 180*f*
hierarchy of authority, 115
increasing, and divisional structure, 182, 182*f*
integrating mechanisms, 115–119, 116*t*, 117*f*
integrating role, 119
and knowledge management, 423
liaison roles, 116
materials management function, 349*f*
task force, 117
teams, 117–119
uncertainty, effect of, 132*t*
intensive technology, 312–314
interdependence. *See* task interdependence
intergroup training, 363
interlocking directorate, 82
internal change agents, 356
internal labour market, 191
internal systems approach, 20, 295
international strategy, 282
interorganizational level of organizational learning, 420–421
interorganizational strategies
competitive interdependency management, 79, 88–91
franchising, 96–97
keiretsu, 85–86, 96
outsourcing, 97–98
symbiotic interdependency management, 79, 81–88
transaction cost theory, 95–98
intrapreneurs, 451–454
investiture, 222
ISO 9001 certification, 390
isomorphism, 385–386

J

janitorial services, 111
Japan, 256, 327, 341
joint venture, 86, 87*f*, 463
just-in-time inventory (JIT) systems, 259, 319–321, 320*f*
justice model of decision making, 51, 51*t*

K

K-strategy, 379–380
kanban system, 320
keiretsu
capital keiretsu, 85–86
defined, 85
financial keiretsu, 85, 86
Fuyo keiretsu, 86, 87*f*
and transaction cost theory, 96
knowledge, and power, 497
knowledge-creating organization, 455
knowledge management
codification approach, 421–423
defined, 421
and integration, 423
personalization approach, 423
knowledge technology, 317

L

large-batch technology, 298–299
large-scale technology, 6
latecomers, 379
latent conflict
bureaucratic factors, 482–484
described, 482
goals, differences in, 482
interdependence, 482
performance criteria, incompatible, 484–485
priorities, differences in, 482
scarce resources, 485–486
leading employers, 200
lean production, 317
learning. *See* organizational learning
learning organization, 417
see also organizational learning
legal affairs, 111
Lewin's force-field theory of change, 338–339, 338*f*
Lewin's three-step change process, 353, 354*f*
liability of newness, 374
liaison roles, 116
lightweight team leader, 461
line function, 483
line role, 47
linkage mechanisms
third-party linkage mechanisms, 89–90
and transaction cost theory, 93–94, 95
local communities, 40–41
location problems, 179
long-linked technology, 310–311
long-range planning, 111
long-term contracts, 83–85
look forward and reason back, 432
low-cost business-level strategy, 264–265
low-cost functional-level strategy, 258–260, 258*t*
low technical complexity, 297

M

maintenance functions, 111
Malcolm Baldrige National Quality Award, 165, 346
management by objectives (MBO), 164–165
managerial abilities, 410
managerial functions, 111
managerial hierarchies, 146*f*
managers
corporate managers, 47
divisional managers, 48
functional managers, 48
line role, 47
and organizational ethics, 50–57
powerful managers, association with, 499
risk aversion, 394
senior management, 44–48
see also senior management
span of control, 150–153, 151*f*, 152*f*
staff role, 47
as stakeholders, 35–37
top-management hierarchy, 45*f*
and total quality management (TQM), 344
manifest conflict, 487
manipulation, 360
market research, 111
market structure, 183, 197–200, 199*f*
marketing, 111, 259
mass customization, 317
mass production, 292, 293, 298–299, 300–315–317, 317*f*
materials management, 259
materials technology
computer-aided design (CAD), 318
computer-aided materials management (CAMM), 319
computer-integrated manufacturing (CIM), 321–323
defined, 318
flexible manufacturing technology, 321–323
innovations in, 317, 318–323
just-in-time inventory (JIT) systems, 319–321, 320*f*
matrix structure
advantages of, 201–203
described, 201
disadvantages of, 203–204
multidivisional matrix structure, 204–205, 204*f*
vs. product team structure, 201
two-boss employees, 201
mature stage, 449
measurement problems, 179
mechanistic structures, 127–128, 130, 133–135, 238, 301, 336
mediating technology, 309–310
medical care in Canada, 57–58
mental models, 418
mergers
competitive interdependencies, 90–91
"merger culture," 217
and organizational culture, 218, 271
symbiotic interdependences, 88
mimetic isomorphism, 385

minimum chain of command, 149–150
minority ownership, 85–86
mission, 22
modelling approaches, 456–458
moral hazard problem, 48–49
moral rights model of decision making, 51, 51*t*
motivation problems, 147
multidivisional matrix structure, 204–205, 204*f*
multidivisional structure, 186*f*, 187*f*
  advantages of, 191
  bureaucratic costs, 192
  communication problems, 192–193
  control, 191
  corporate-divisional relationship, management of, 191–192
  corporate headquarters staff, 186–187
  defined, 185
  disadvantages, 191–193
  internal labour market, 191
  organizational effectiveness, 191
  problem coordination between divisions, 192
  profitable growth, 191
  and self-contained division, 185
  transfer pricing, 192
  use of, 188–191
multidomestic strategy, 280–282
mutual adjustment
  defined, 124
  intensive technology and, 313
  norms, 124–125
  and organizational culture, 219
  vs. standardization, 125–126
  standardization, balancing with, 123–126

N

natural selection, 380–382
negotiation, 360
network structures, 205–206
networks, 85
new venture divisions, 463
nonprogrammed decisions, 408
nonroutine research technology, 306
nonroutine tasks, 307*t*
nonroutine technology, 307
nonsubstitutability, 496, 498
normative isomorphism, 386
norms, 124–125, 161–163, 215
North American Free Trade Agreement (NAFTA), 216, 215, 333
nuclear power plant accidents, 302

O

obstructionist approach, 241
Oeko-tex Standard 100 certification, 248
official goals, 22
operative goals, 23–24
opportunism, 93
organic structures, 128–130, 133–135, 238, 302
organization-level resistance to change, 335–336
organizational analysis, 29–30
organizational birth
  business plan, 374–376, 375*t*
  defined, 374
  failure rate, 374
  first-mover advantages, 379
  flexible structure, 374
  fragility of new organizations, 374
  generalist strategy, 380
  K-strategy, 379–380
  liability of newness, 374
  natural selection, 380–382
  number of births, 378–379
  population ecology model, 376–382
  r-strategy, 379–380
  rates over time, 378*f*
  resource environment, competition strategies, 381*f*
  specialist strategy, 380
  survival strategies, 379–380
  SWOT analysis, 375
organizational capabilities, 332
organizational change
  action research, 353–358
  bottom-up change, 356–357
  change management, 353–358
  competitive advantage, 16
  components of, 25*f*, 26–27
  contingency, 15
  defined, 11, 330
  described, 330
  diversity management, 16
  efficiency, speed and innovation, 16–17
  evolutionary change, 339–346
  forces for change, 333–334
  importance of, 15–17
  Lewin's three-step change process, 353, 354*f*
  making sense of, 364
  organizational development (OD) techniques. *See* organizational development (OD)
  and organizational theory, 9*f*, 11–14
  promoting change, 361–363
  resistances to change. *See* resistances to change
  revolutionary change, 340, 346–352
  targets of change, 331–332
  top-down change, 356
organizational charge, 112, 113*f*
organizational coalitions, 411–412
organizational conflict
  benefits of, 480
  bureaucratic factors, 482–484
  chronic conflict, 480
  conflict aftermath, 487
  conflict resolution strategies, 488–491
  and decision making, 480
  defined, 478–479
  and effectiveness, 479*f*
  felt conflict, 486
  goals, differences in, 482
  latent conflict, 482–486
  manifest conflict, 487
  perceived conflict, 486
  performance criteria, incompatible, 484–485
  Pondy's model, 481–487
  and power, 492
  priorities, differences in, 482
  scarce resources, 485–486
organizational confrontation meeting, 363
organizational culture
  adaptive cultures, 419–420
  bureaucratic culture, overly, 395
  and business-level strategy, 269–271
  ceremonies, 223–227
  characteristics of people within organization, 227–230
  and corporate-level strategy, 277–278
  culture clash, 234
  defined, 10, 213
  described, 213–220
  differences in, 10
  ethical culture, 60–61
  and ethics, 219, 230–233
  and functional-level strategy, 262–263
  and global culture, 216
  "green culture," 232
  inert cultures, 419–420
  as informal organization, 219
  and information technology, 471–472
  and innovation, 465–468
  instrumental values, 214, 214*f*, 217
  management of, 239–240
  "merger culture," 217
  and mergers, 218, 271
  military management culture, 226
  and mutual adjustment, 219
  norms, 215
  organizational language, 223–227
  organizational rites, 223*t*, 223–224
  and organizational structure, 238–239
  and organizational theory, 9*f*
  property rights, 233–237
  and resistance to change, 336
  role orientation, 221–222, 221*t*, 222
  and social responsibility, 241–244
  socialization, 220–223, 221*t*
  sources of, 227–239
  stories, 223–227
  terminal values, 214, 214*f*, 217
  transmission of, 220–227
  values and decision making, 217–219
organizational decision making
  see also organizational learning
  capacity for, 408
  collateral organizational structure, 436
  control over decision making premises, 497
  defined, 408
  game theory, 432–434
  improved decision making, 430–436
  influencing, and politics, 500–502
  nonprogrammed decisions, 408
  programmed decisions, 408
  top-management team, 434–435, 434*f*
organizational decision making models
  Carnegie model, 410–412, 428
  garbage can model, 414–415
  incrementalist model, 412
  incrementalist model of decision making, 430
  rational model, 409–410
  unstructured model, 412–414
organizational decline
  defined, 393

organizational inertia, 393–395
reasons for, 393
Weitzel and Jonsson's model, 396–398
organizational design
centralization-decentralization balance, 120–123
competitive advantage, 16
components of, 25*f*, 26
contingency, 15
contingency approach, 130
customer-centric approach, 122
defined, 10
differentiation, challenges of, 106–113, 109*f*, 131–133
diversity management, 16
efficiency, speed and innovation, 16–17
and environment, 131–135, 131*f*
importance of, 15–17
integration, challenges of, 114–120, 131–133
mechanistic structures. *See* mechanistic structures
mutual adjustment, 123–126
organic structures. *See* organic structures
and organizational theory, 9*f*, 10
poor design, consequences of, 17
standardization, 123–126
strategy. *See* strategy
structure. *See* organizational structure
technology. *See* technology
organizational development (OD)
bargaining, 360
coercion, 361
communication, 359
counselling, 361
defined, 358
education, 359
empowerment, 359
intergroup training, 363
manipulation, 360
negotiation, 360
organizational mirroring, 363
participation, 359
process consultation, 362
promoting change, 361–363
resistance to change, dealing with, 359–361
sensitivity training, 361–362
team building, 362
total organizational interventions, 363
organizational domain, 69
organizational effectiveness. *See* effectiveness
organizational ethics. *See* ethics
organizational goals, 22–24
organizational growth
defined, 382
Greiner's model, 386–392
institutional theory, 382–386
organizational isomorphism, 385–386
organizational inertia, 393–395
organizational isomorphism
coercive isomorphism, 385
defined, 385
disadvantages of, 386
mimetic isomorphism, 385
normative isomorphism, 386
organizational language, 223–227
organizational learning
see also organizational decision making
cognitive biases, 425–430
cognitive structure, 424–425
collateral organizational structure, 436
conversion of events to learning opportunities, 431
defined, 415
devil's advocate, 435–436
dialectical inquiry, 435–436
experimentation, 431–432
exploitation, 417
exploration, 417
factors affecting, 424–430
group level, 418–419
improved learning, 430–436
individual level, 417–418
interorganizational level, 420–421
and knowledge management, 421–423
learning organization, 417
levels of, 417–421, 418*f*
listening to dissenters, 431
organizational level, 419–420
types of, 417
organizational level of organizational learning, 419–420
organizational life cycle
defined, 372
four principal stages of, 373
organizational birth, 373–376, 382
organizational decline and death, 393–399
organizational growth, 382–392
organizational mirroring, 363
organizational politics
association with powerful managers, 499
centrality, 498
coalition-building, 499–500
control of agenda, 502
costs and benefits, 502–504
decision making, influencing, 500–502
defined, 497–498
indispensability, 498
maintenance of power balance, 503*f*
nonsubstitutability, 498
outside experts, 502
tactics, 498–502
organizational power
authority, 492–494
centrality, 496
and conflict, 492
decision making premises, control over, 497
defined, 491
discourse, 497
information, control over, 495
knowledge, 497
maintenance of power balance, 503*f*
nonsubstitutability, 496
organizational politics, 497–504
resources, control over, 494–495
sources of, 492–497, 493*f*
uncertainty, control over, 496
unobtrusive power, 497
use of, 497–504
organizational resources, 254
organizational rites, 223*t*, 223–224
organizational role, 108–110
organizational structure, 9*f*
see also organizational design
authority, 143–153
boundaryless organization, 207
bureaucracy, advantages of, 163–164
bureaucratic principles, 158–163, 159*t*
and business-level strategy, 265–269, 267*f*
centralization, 155–156
collateral organizational structure, 436
and conflict resolution, 489–490
conglomerate structure, 275, 276*f*
contingent workers, 168
control, 153–158
and corporate-level strategy, 275–276
cross-functional teams, 168
decentralization, 156
defined, 8–9
described, 8–9
divisional structure. *See* divisional structure
empowerment, 168–169
flat organization, 145, 145*f*, 148, 168
and functional-level strategy, 260–262, 261*f*
functional structure, 176–180
global geographic structure, 281*f*
global matrix structure, 284*f*
global product group structure, 282*f*
height limitations, 144–146
hierarchical levels, ideal number of, 149–150
horizontal differentiation, 153–154, 154*f*, 155*f*
ideals, 133
informal organization, influence of, 165–167
and information technology, 167–169, 471–472
and innovation, 465–466
management by objectives (MBO), 164–165
matrix structure, 201–205
mechanistic structures, 127–128, 130, 133–135, 238
network structures, 205–206
nonroutine technology, 307
organic structures, 128–130, 133–135, 238
and organizational culture, 238–239
Parkinson's law problem, 149
people, and changing structures, 198–200
principle of minimum chain of command, 149–150
related diversification, 275–276
routine technology, 306–307
self-managed teams, 168–169
size limitations, 145–146
span of control, 150–153, 151*f*, 152*f*
standardization, 157–158
strategy-structure relationships, in international environment, 281*t*
tall hierarchies, problems with, 147–149
tall organizations, 145, 145*f*, 147–149
and technical complexity, 300–302

unrelated diversification, 275
vertical differentiation, 143–153
organizational theory
and change, 9*f*, 11–14
components of, 25*f*
and culture, 9–10, 9*f*
defined, 8
and design, 9*f*, 10
and organizational structure, 8–9, 9*f*
organizations
boundaryless organization, 207
control, 7–8
defined, 2
described, 1–3
division of labour, 6
ethical organizations, 59–61
external environment, management of, 7
flat organization, 145, 145*f*, 148, 168
knowledge-creating organization, 455
large-scale technology, 6
learning organization, 417
power, 7–8
purpose of, 6–8
specialization, 6
tall organizations, 145, 145*f*, 147–149
transaction costs, 7
value, creation of, 3–5, 4*f*
output stage, 294, 294*f*
outside directors, 44–45
outside experts, 502
outside stakeholders, 35, 37–41
outsourcing, 97–98

P

Parkinson's law problem, 149
participation, 359
perceived conflict, 486
performance criteria, 484–485
Perrow's theory, 303–308
personal computer industry, 79
personal ethics, 58–59
personalization approach, 423
personnel, 111
PERT/CAM network, 456
pharmaceutical industry, 77
political change, 11
political forces, 72–73, 333
politics. *See* organizational politics
Pondy's model of organizational conflict
conflict aftermath, 487
felt conflict, 486
latent conflict, 482–486
manifest conflict, 487
perceived conflict, 486
pooled task interdependence, 309–310
poor organizational design, 17
population density, 378
population ecology theory
defined, 376
environmental niches, 376
generalist strategy, 380
K-strategy, 379–380
natural selection, 380–382
number of births, 378–379
population density, 378
population of organizations, 376
r-strategy, 379–380
specialist strategy, 380
survival strategies, 379–380
population of organizations, 376
power, 7–8, 335–336
see also organizational power
powerful managers, 499
preferences of decision makers, 410
price fixing, 89
price leadership, 89
principle of minimum chain of command, 149–150
proactive approach, 242
process consultation, 362
processes, 347
product division structure, 184–185, 184*f*, 185*f*
product life cycle
decline stage, 449
defined, 449
embryonic stage, 449
fads, 449–450
fashion, 449–450
growth stage, 449
mature stage, 449
rate of technological change, 449, 450*f*
product structure
defined, 183
global product group structure, 282*f*
multidivisional structure, 185–193
product division structure, 184–185, 184*f*, 185*f*
product team structure, 193–195, 194*f*, 201
self-contained division, 185
types of, 183
use of, 183
product team structure, 193–195, 194*f*, 201, 459–461, 460*f*
production control, 111
production functions, 111
production operations, 111
productivity measures, 21
professional ethics, 55
profit-sharing plans, 233
programmed decisions, 408
programmed technology, 295
project, 455
project management, 455–458
projection, 428
promoting change, 361–363
promotion tournaments, 49–50
property rights
common rights given to employees, 233*t*
defined, 233
distribution of, 233
employee stock-ownership plan (ESOP), 233
and expectations, 234–235
and innovation, 467–468
and organizational culture, 233–237
profit-sharing plans, 233
strong property rights, 236–237
and top management, 235–236
protectionism, 71–72
the public, 41
public relations, 111
pull approach, 319
purchasing, 111
purpose of organizations, 6–8
push approach, 319

Q

quality circles, 341
quality control, 111
quantitative modelling, 456
quantum innovations, 447
quantum technological change, 447

R

r-strategy, 379–380
random socialization tactics, 221
ratebuster, 125
rational-legal authority, 158–159
rational model of decision making, 409–410, 409*f*, 411*t*
re-engineering, 199, 200, 346–349–351
reciprocal task interdependence, 312–314
red tape, 392
regulations, 39
related diversification, 274, 275–276
reliability, 217
Report on Equality in Employment (Abella Commission), 16
representativeness, 428
reputation effect, 56–57, 81–82
research and development, 111, 154, 155*f*, 260
resistances to change
bargaining, 360
coercion, 361
communication, 359
conflict, 335–336
education, 359
empowerment, 359
force-field theory of change, 338–339, 338*f*
functional orientation differences, 336
group-level resistance to change, 337–337
individual-level resistance to change, 337–338
Lewin's force-field theory of change, 338–339, 338*f*
manipulation, 360
mechanistic structures, 336
negotiation, 360
organization-level resistance to change, 335–336
and organizational culture, 336
organizational development (OD) strategies, 359–361
participation, 359
power, 335–336
total quality management program, 344
resource dependence theory, 78–79
see also resource interdependencies
resource environment, competition strategies, 381*f*
resource interdependencies
competitive interdependencies, 79–80, 88–91
interorganizational management strategies, 79–81
resource dependence theory, 78–79

symbiotic interdependencies, 79–80, 81–88
resource-poor environments, 76
resources
acquisition and control of, 111
control over, 494–495
functional resources, 254, 331
global resources and skills, 256
organizational resources, 254
scarce resources, 485–486
slack resources, 311
specialized resources, 254
restructuring, 149, 200, 270, 351–352
revolutionary change
defined, 340
innovation, 352
re-engineering, 346–349–351
restructuring, 351–352
rewards
allocation of, 43–44
blending reward mechanisms, 50
maximization of, 394–395
risk, and specific assets, 93
risk aversion, 394
rites of enhancement, 224
rites of integration, 223–224
rites of passage, 223
robots, 321
role ambiguity, 160
role conflict, 160
role orientation, 221–222, 221*t*, 222
role relationships, 130*f*
roles
clarity of, 160
organization of, 160
routine manufacturing, 304–305
routine tasks, 303–307, 307*t*
routine technology, 306–307
rules, 124–125, 161–163, 162
Rwanda, 336, 337

S

sales, 111, 259
Sarbanes Oxley Act, 36, 73
satisficing, 410–411
scarce resources, 485–486
self-contained division, 112, 185
self-interest, 55, 59
self-managed teams, 168–169
senior management
agency theory perspective, 48–50
career paths, 49–50
chief executive officer (CEO), 46–47
divisional managers, 48
promotion tournaments, 49–50
and property rights, 235–236
stock-based compensation schemes, 49
top-management hierarchy, 45*f*
top-management team, 47, 434–435, 434*f*
sensitivity training, 361–362
sequential interdependence, 310–311, 321
sequential move game, 435
sequential socialization tactics, 221
serial socialization tactics, 221
shareholders, 35, 233
simultaneous move game, 435
size
and effectiveness, 394*f*
limitations, 144–146
skunk works, 462–463
slack resources, 311
small-batch technology, 297–298, 300
small numbers, 93
social forces, 73–333–334
social responsibility
accommodative approach, 242
advantages of, 242–244
approaches, 241–242, 242*f*
defensive approach, 241–242
obstructionist approach, 241
and organizational culture, 241–244
proactive approach, 242
socialization, 124–125, 220–223, 221*t*
socialization tactics, 220–223
societal ethics, 52–53
sociotechnical systems theory, 340–341
span of control, 150–153, 151*f*, 152*f*
special interest groups, 41
specialism, 314
specialists, 380
specialization, 6, 110–311
specialized resources, 254
specific environment, 70–72
speed, 16–17
stable environment, 76
staff function, 483
staff role, 47
stage-gate development funnel, 458–459, 458*f*
stakeholders
allocation of rewards, 43–44
competition, 479*f*
contributions, 34, 35*t*
cooperation, 479*f*
customers, 37
defined, 34
ethics, and support for stakeholder interests, 61
general public, 41
goals and interests, 41–44
government, 39
inducements, 34, 35*t*
inside stakeholders, 35, 37
local communities, 40–41
managerial employees, 35–37
nonmanagerial employees, 37
outside stakeholders, 35, 37–41
property rights, 233
shareholders, 35
special interest groups, 41
suppliers, 37–39
transactions, structure of, 69–70
unionized employees, 40
standard operating procedures (SOPs), 123–124, 161–163
standardization
and control, 157–158
defined, 124
formalization, 124
vs. mutual adjustment, 125–126
mutual adjustment, balancing with, 123–126
standardized responses, 125
stock-based compensation schemes, 49
stock markets, 90
stories, 223–227
strategic alliances, 83, 83*f*, 90
strategic problems, 180
strategy
business-level strategy, 257, 264–271
core competencies, sources of, 253–255
corporate-level strategy, 257–278
defined, 16, 252
and the environment, 252–258
four levels of, 256–258
functional-level strategy, 257, 258–263
and global expansion, 255–256
global expansion strategy, 258
global strategy, implementation of, 279–284
international strategy, 282
interorganizational strategies. *See* interorganizational strategies
multidomestic strategy, 280–282
resource environment, competition strategies, 381*f*
strategy-structure relationships, in international environment, 281*t*
transnational strategy, 283–284
strikes, 40
structure. *See* organizational structure
subunit orientation, 114
subunits, 110–111
suppliers, 37–39
support functions, 111
sweatshops, 335
SWOT analysis, 375
symbiotic interdependencies
co-optation, 82
defined, 79–80
joint venture, 86, 87*f*
keiretsu, 85–86
long-term contracts, 83–85
management strategies, 81–88
merger, 88
minority ownership, 85–86
networks, 85
reputation effect, 81–82
strategic alliances, 83, 83*f*
takeover, 88
trust, 82
Synergy Award of Innovation, 463, 465
systems thinking, 420

T

takeover, 88, 90–91
tall organization, 145*f*
bureaucratic costs, 148–149
communication problems, 147
defined, 144–145
motivation problems, 147
targets of change
functional resources, 331
human resources, 331
organizational capabilities, 332
technological capabilities, 331
task analyzability
craftswork, 305
defined, 304
described, 304
engineering production, 305–306

and four types of technology, 304–306, 305*f*
nonroutine research technology, 306
nonroutine technology, 307
routine manufacturing, 304–305
routine technology, 306–307
task force, 117
task forces, 363
task interdependence
and computer-aided materials management, 319
defined, 308
intensive technology, 312–314
long-linked technology, 310–311
mediating technology, 309–310
pooled task interdependence, 309–310
reciprocal interdependence, 312–314
sequential interdependence, 310–311, 321
task relationships, 130*f*
task variability
craftswork, 305
defined, 303
described, 303–304
engineering production, 305–306
and four types of technology, 304–306, 305*f*
nonroutine research technology, 306
nonroutine technology, 307
routine manufacturing, 304–305
routine technology, 306–307
team building, 362
team leadership, 461
team learning, 419
teams
cross-functional teams, 168, 459–461, 460*f*
defined, 117
empowerment of work groups, 360
flexible work teams, 344–346, 345*f*
groupthink, 337, 435
informal norms, 125
as integrating mechanism, 117–119
product team structure, 193–195, 194*f*, 459–461, 460*f*
self-managed teams, 168–169
structuring with, 118
two-boss employees, 201
technical approach, 21–295
technical competence, 159–160
technical complexity
continuous-process technology, 299–300, 302
defined, 297
high technical complexity, 297
large-batch technology, 298–299
low technical complexity, 297
mass production, 298–299, 300–301
and organizational structure, 300–302
small-batch technology, 297–298, 300
technological imperative, 302–303
unit technology, 297–298
technological capabilities, 331
technological change
effect of, 448
incremental technological change, 447
quantum technological change, 447
rate of, and product life cycle, 449, 450*f*
technological forces, 72
technological imperative, 302–303
technology
advanced manufacturing technology, 315–317
advantages of use of, 295
continuous-process technology, 299–300, 302
conversion stage, 294, 294*f*
craftswork, 292, 305
defined, 292
at departmental level, 292
engineering production, 305–306
external resource approach, 295
at functional level, 292
at individual level, 292
input stage, 294, 294*f*
intensive technology, 312–314
internal systems approach, 295
international transfer of, 72
knowledge technology, 317
large-batch technology, 298–299
long-linked technology, 310–311
mass production, 292, 298–299, 300–315–317
materials technology, 317, 318–323
mediating technology, 309–310
nonroutine research technology, 306
nonroutine technology, 307
and organizational effectiveness, 294–295
at organizational level, 292
output stage, 294, 294*f*
Perrow's theory, 303–308
programmed technology, 295
routine manufacturing, 304–305
routine technology, 306–307
small-batch technology, 297–298, 300
task analyzability, 303–308
task interdependence, 308–315
task variability, 303–308
technical approach, 295
technical complexity, 295–303
Thompson's theory, 308–314
types of, 304–306, 305*f*
unit technology, 297–298
Woodward's theory, 295–303
technology circle, 448*f*
terminal values, 214, 214*f*, 217
third-party linkage mechanisms, 89–90
Thompson's theory, 308–314
top-down change, 356
top management. *See* senior management
top-management hierarchy, 45*f*
top-management team, 47, 434–435, 434*f*
total quality management (TQM), 341–344, 349
trade association, 89–90
tragedy of the commons problem, 55
transaction cost theory
bounded rationality, 92–93
bureaucratic costs, 94
defined, 92
environmental uncertainty, 92–93
interorganizational strategy, choice of, 95–97
linkage mechanisms, 93–94
opportunism, 93
risk and specific assets, 93
small numbers, 93
sources of transaction costs, 92–93
transaction costs, 7, 56, 92
transfer price, 192
transnational strategy, 283–284
trucking industry, 89
trust, 82
turnover, 338
two-boss employees, 201

U

uncertainty
control over, 496
and differentiation, 132*t*
environmental complexity, 75–76
environmental dynamism, 76
environmental richness, 76–77
and integration, 132*t*
rational model of decision making, 409–410
sources of, 74–77, 74*f*
and structure, 133–135, 135*f*
and transaction costs, 92–93
unethical behaviour, 57–59
unionized employees, 40
unit technology, 297–298
unobtrusive power, 497
unrelated diversification, 274–275
unstable environment, 76
unstructured model of decision making, 412–414
unwritten values and norms, 123
utilitarian model of decision making, 51, 51*t*

V

value-creation cycle, 253*f*, 259
see also strategy
value creation model, 5
values
and decision making, 217–219
ethical values. *See* ethics
instrumental values, 214, 214*f*, 217
and rational model of decision making, 410
terminal values, 214, 214*f*, 217
trapped by, 220
variable socialization tactics, 221
vertical differentiation
authority and, 143–153
defined, 112
effect of, 161–162
and effectiveness, 160
increasing, and divisional structure, 181
vertical integration, 272–274

W

Weitzel and Jonsson's model of organizational decline, 396–399
whistle-blowing, 60, 231–232, 243
women
and restructuring, 200
as "the stuck," 497
Woodward's theory, 295–303
written rules, 124